Handbook of Multi-Commodity Markets and Products

For other titles in the Wiley Finance series
please see www.wiley.com/finance

Handbook of Multi-Commodity Markets and Products

Structuring, Trading and Risk Management

Edited by

ANDREA RONCORONI
GIANLUCA FUSAI
MARK CUMMINS

WILEY

This edition first published 2015

Registered office
John Wiley & Sons Ltd, The Atrium, Southern Gate, Chichester, West Sussex, PO19 8SQ, United Kingdom

For details of our global editorial offices, for customer services and for information about how to apply for permission to reuse the copyright material in this book please see our website at www.wiley.com.

A catalogue record for this book is available at the Library of Congress.

A catalogue record for this book is available from the British Library.

ISBN 978-0-470-74524-3 (hardback)
ISBN 978-0-470-66183-3 (ebk)
ISBN 978-0-470-66250-2 (ebk)
ISBN 978-1-119-01159-0 (obk)

Cover design: Wiley
Cover image: TK

Set in 10/12pt Times by Aptara Inc., New Delhi, India
Printed in Great Britain by TJ International Ltd, Padstow, Cornwall, UK

Andrea Roncoroni
To Yanelis, for always being there with love and patience, and to our wonderful daughters Isabella and Beatrice

Gianluca Fusai
For Lucia, Stefano, Martino and Raffaele

Mark Cummins
To my wife Edel and son Aidan, thanks for all your love and support

Contents

Preface

Commodity markets have traditionally developed along paths leaving them structurally independent from each other. In the last thirty years, several markets have undergone a process of deregulation and liberalisation, turning the corresponding goods into tradable commodities. This is the case, for instance, with energy markets, such as oil, gas and, more recently, electricity. As a result, both the amount of traded products and the degree of heterogeneity among products in the market has grown.

According to major market players, the next ongoing step in market evolution is underway. It is a process of integration across markets of different types, such as energy, agricultural, metals, and standardised services. This shift raises important questions which merit attention by financial literature; questions about the identification and analysis of actual opportunities carried over by financial deals involving several commodities. To cite but a few:

- How, in terms of profit-making or risk management, can we exploit pay-off profiles and trading strategies by betting on the evolution of a diversified set of commodity prices?
- How should we price energy products and other commodities belonging to markets segmented across specific structural features (e.g., storable vs. non-storable, material vs. immaterial)?
- Which methods and models should we develop or select to make appropriate estimations of the future evolution of prices, specifically in terms of trend and market risk?
- What measures of risk should we adopt for the purpose of correctly assessing the exposure from multi-commodity portfolios?
- What financial opportunities are there at major energy and commodity markets such as Singapore, London and New York?

The nature of multi-commodity deals makes it necessary for the professional to:

- Become acquainted with the structure, functioning, rules and practices across a wide spectrum of commodity markets;
- Master a large set of different skills and bodies of knowledge. In particular, the convergence of topics such as arbitrage valuation, econometric modelling, market structure analysis, contract engineering, risk assessment and management. Scenario simulation is also necessary to structure and manage both simple and more sophisticated multi-commodity deals.

Two facts provide the impetus to undertake our systematic study of multi-commodity markets and contracts. First, an increasing number of complex contracts are negotiated within each of the commodity markets analysed in our study. Operators thus tend to borrow existing methods from non-commodity markets for the purpose of trading, structuring and risk managing multi-commodity deals. In addition, this in turn tends to implicitly establish a common structure upon which one may ground valuation and hedging methods for multi-commodity deals. Second, the high-level profits generated across all commodity markets worldwide drives an increasing number of investors to enter into deals, which involve a wide spectrum of commodity prices. Hence it comes as no surprise that accurate, scientifically-conducted studies of multi-commodity contracts are rapidly becoming a topic of great importance for any institution involved in energy and/or commodity trading.

The aim of this book is to offer the reader an up-to-date *reference handbook* on multi-commodity markets and products. The book boasts a wide coverage of energy and commodity, and related, markets.

Presentations are developed at an introductory-intermediate level. We address those who wish to rapidly acquire a sound body of knowledge on one or several commodity markets, independently of their previous exposure to any commodity market. The distinctiveness of this book lies in the contributions from both industry participants and academic experts at the forefront of energy and commodity markets practice and research.

On this basis, the target market for the book includes:

- Marketers, Traders, Structurers and Risk Managers wishing to broaden their knowledge of multi-commodity markets;
- Academics professionals, including masters students and doctoral candidates;
- Professionals enrolled in programs for continuing education in finance and economics.

The content of the book is organised into two parts. Part I contains chapters devoted to a wide variety of commodity markets. including the core energy markets of oil, coal, gas and electricity, along with the key commodity markets of industrial metals and agriculturals. Shipping markets as the fundamental link in the globalisation of commodities are presented, in addition to other important related markets such as emissions, weather and foreign exchange. Presentations are self-contained and can be read independently of one another or, in line with the focus of the book, jointly in any desired sequence. Market features and main functioning rules of the market in question are introduced at the outset of each chapter. Then, basic financial products and standardised deals are described using case examples, where appropriate, underlying the contract structure and the corresponding financial use for the client. Quantitative models for pricing and hedging commodity derivatives are presented and illustrated using practical examples. Issues in structuring, pricing, selling, and hedging are examined from a problem-solving viewpoint.

Part II contains chapters of a technical and methodological nature. Our practical approach allows us to deliver a comprehensive reference manual that the user may consult when tackling daily valuation, hedging and econometric problems. Excessively technical details are left to further reading. Our primary focus is on the concrete implementation of the proposed methodologies. The chapters are presented in a self-contained manner and introduce the reader to topics such as: stochastic modelling;modelling and estimation, using filtering and non-parametric techniques, of commodity price and volatility dynamics; construction of forward curves in commodity markets, with a special emphasis on electricity; GARCH models and variance modelling with applications to risk analysis; pricing and hedging of strategically important derivative structures, such as spread options and asian options; measurement of counterparty credit risk arising in OTC non-collateralized derivative transactions; modelling of natural gas storage capacity; and techniques for the quantitative trading of commodities, with applications to the optimization and assessment of commodity portfolios and spread trading.

Our vision for this book is that it becomes the standard *reference handbook* for the multi-commodity industry, with future editions likewise providing the latest in market developments and technical innovations.

Acknowledgements

We would like to express our utmost thanks to all of the industry and academic contributors to this book. The quality of the book overall reflects the time and effort dedicated by them to structuring and writing their individual contributions, along with their willingness to impart their valuable knowledge and expertise. We look forward to future collaborations.

We would like to thank all of the dedicated staff at Wiley who supported us throughout the publication process. Your guidance to us and your work in producing the book to the highest of professional standards is much appreciated.

We would also like to thank Thomson Reuters, and in particular Alessandro Sanos, Carlo Mondani and Amrit Singh, who generously gave their time to sourcing and providing us with a range of professional figures and charts for Part I of the book. We would also like to thank Bloomberg, and in particular Ian McFarlane, for the screenshot permissions provided for the natural gas chapter.

About the Editors

Andrea Roncoroni

Andrea Roncoroni is Professor of Finance at ESSEC Business School (Paris-Singapore) and Fellow at Bocconi University (Milan). He holds PhD's in Applied Mathematics and in Finance. His research interests primarily cover energy and commodity finance, financial risk management, quantitative modelling, security structuring and pricing. Andrea put forward the Threshold Model for price simulation in spiky electricity markets, and devised FloRisk Metrics^{TM}, an effective approach to monitor and manage corporate risk exposure. He publishes in academic journals, professional reviews, financial book series, and acts as Associate Editor for the Journal of Energy Markets and Co-Editor for Argo Review. As a professional advisor, he consulted for private companies and public institutions, including Dong Energy, Edison, Enel, GDF, Natixis, and TEI Enery. He is founder and CEO of Energisk SAS, an ICT service provider for companies dealing with energy and commodity markets.

Gianluca Fusai

Gianluca Fusai is Full Professor in Financial Mathematics at the University of Eastern Piedmont, Italy, and a PT Reader in Mathematical Finance at Cass Business School, City University of London, UK. He holds a PhD in Finance from Warwick Business School, an MSc in Statistics and Operational Research from the University of Essex and a BSc in Economics from Bocconi University. His research interests focus on Energy Markets, Financial Engineering, Numerical Methods for Finance, Quantitative Risk Management. He has published extensively on these topics in top-tier international reviews. Gianluca has also co-authored the best-selling textbook *Implementing Models in Quantitative Finance* (Springer Finance). Gianluca has cooperated to several projects in energy markets including a multi-energy risk assessment tool developed in conjunction with a pool of energy and industrial companies and a forward curve builder for the power and gas markets nowadays used for trading and marking to market. He has also been a consultant for private and public sector on building pricing tools of derivative products. Gianluca has been an expert witness in several derivative disputes.

Mark Cummins

Mark Cummins is Senior Lecturer in Finance at the Dublin City University Business School and holds a PhD in Quantitative Finance. Mark's research interests include a broad range of energy and commodity modelling, derivatives, risk management and trading topics. Mark has published in international journals such as Energy Economics, Applied Energy and the Journal of Energy Markets, as well as mainstream finance journals such as the Journal of

Financial Markets, International Review of Financial Analysis and Quantitative Finance.Mark has previous industry experience working as a Quantitative Analyst within the Global Risk function for BP Oil International Ltd. As part of the Risk Quantitative Analysis team, primary responsibilities included derivatives and price curve model validation and development, with a global remit across BP's energy and commodity activities. Mark is engaged in ongoing industry training and consultancy activities, focused on the energy sector primarily.

List of Contributors

Laura Ballotta, *Cass Business School, City University of London*

Fred Espen Benth, *University of Oslo*

Ruggero Caldana, *Accenture and Università degli Studi del Piemonte Orientale*

Cristiano Campi, *ENI Trading & Shipping SpA*

Álvaro Cartea, *University College London*

Antonio Castagna, *Iason Ltd*

James Cheeseman, *BP*

Marc Chesney, *University of Zurich*

Francis Declerck, *ESSEC Business School*

Dimitris N. Dimitrakopoulos, *Athens University of Economics and Business*

Viviana Fanelli, *Università degli Studi di Bari*

Gianna Figà-Talamanca, *Università degli Studi di Perugia*

Stefano Fiorenzani, *EcoWay Srl*

Francesco Galdenzi, *ENI Trading & Shipping SpA*

Jonathan Gheyssens, *University of Zurich*

Rachid Id Brik, *ESSEC Business School*

Sebastian Jaimungal, *University of Toronto*

Manolis G. Kavussanos, *Athens University of Economics and Business*

Giovanni Longo, *Università degli Studi del Piemonte Orientale*

Marina Marena, *Università degli Studi di Torino*

Alessandro Mauro, *Energy Risk Professional*

Bernard Murphy, *University of Limerick*

Alessandro Porru, *Banca IMI*

Chiara Quaglini, *ENOI SpA*

Eduardo Rossi, *Università degli Studi di Pavia*

Lars Schernikau, *HMS Bergbau AG*

Filippo Spazzini, *Edison Trading SpA*

Luca Taschini, *London School of Economics*

Ilias D. Visvikis, *World Maritime University*

Hanna Zdanowicz, *University of Oslo*

Part One

Commodity Markets and Products

CHAPTER 1

Oil Markets and Products

Cristiano Campi and Francesco Galdenzi

1.1 INTRODUCTION

The price of crude oil and oil products, once discussed solely in industry and government circles, has taken centre stage in the past 15 years among the lead indicators of the state of the economy and is now always quoted when forecasting economic trends. This phenomenon has occurred in conjunction with the growing acceptance of commodities as a mainstream financial and investment asset class, with the resulting growth in the volume and variety of financial instruments linked to them and the widespread use of these financial instruments in hedging, risk management and investments products.

This chapter focuses on two important offshoots of this 'coming of age' of the energy markets: the implementation of financially settled risk management policies by corporations exposed to fluctuating oil and oil product prices and the growth of hedging activities for companies active in physical oil trading. Before going further, it is worth looking at some key elements that determine the economics in the oil and oil products value chain. The oil industry is based on two main types of processes:

1. *Upstream.* This part of the oil cycle is associated with the exploration and production of crude oil.
2. *Downstream.* This part encompasses the transportation, refining and marketing of refined oil products (gasoline, diesel, jet fuel, naphtha, etc.).

The production of crude represents the starting point of the oil cycle. A producer is a company dedicated to extracting crude oil, which is supplied to the refinery system for the production of products needed to satisfy the demand of its energy consumers. The oil cycle is composed of the following elements.

1. The production of crude oil by several kinds of players, including:
   (a) Integrated oil companies, such as Royal Dutch Shell in the UK, Eni in Italy, China National Petroleum Corporation in China and Exxon in the United States.

Handbook of Multi-Commodity Markets and Products: Structuring, Trading and Risk Management. Edited by Andrea Roncoroni, Gianluca Fusai and Mark Cummins.

  - **(b)** Independent oil companies, such as Cairn Energy in the UK and Perenco in France.
  - **(c)** National oil companies (NOCs), such as Petrobras in Brazil, Saudi Aramco in Saudi Arabia or Petronas in Malaysia.
2. The demand for crude oil by the refinery system to produce oil products from:
  - **(a)** Refineries owned and managed by integrated oil companies or NOCs sourcing crude oil from their own production as well as buying it from international oil markets.
  - **(b)** Independent refineries, such as Saras in Italy and Valero in the United States, sourcing crude oil from the international oil markets.
3. The demand for oil products by final consumers, such as utilities, airlines, shipping companies, energy-intensive manufacturers, petrochemical companies, gasoline and diesel retailers.

The cycle described above is complemented by the transportation system, a vast and complex network of pipelines, crude oil and product carriers (by sea, rail and road) and storage facilities dedicated to the logistics behind the delivery of crude oil to refineries and of products to the final consumers.

The price of crude oil and oil products is driven by many factors, from macroeconomics to environmental legislation, from geopolitics to the weather and from production levels to taxation. The list in Table 1.1 proposes a scheme of the key factors observed by market operators when trying to assess price trends for oil and oil products.

1.2 RISK MANAGEMENT FOR CORPORATIONS: HEDGING USING DERIVATIVE INSTRUMENTS

1.2.1 Crude Oil and Oil Products Risk Management for Corporations

1.2.1.1 Corporate Risk Management Overview Companies with exposure to the price volatility of oil and oil products are taking an active role in managing this risk. They do so by entering into financially settled derivatives transactions, with the goal of achieving one of the following objectives:

1. Budget and/or profit margin protection.
2. Stabilization of cash flow and control of supply chain prices.
3. Gaining competitive advantage through swift reactions to changes in market prices.

Effective energy price risk management requires expertise in both financial instruments and oil markets: one must find financial instruments that mimic the prices from the suppliers (or to the customers) and constantly analyse oil price movements in the commodity markets. Because so few organizations have the in-house resources to support such specialization, energy price risk management expertise is often externally sourced from consultants or performed with the support of the sales and trading desks of investment banks, brokers and trading companies.

TABLE 1.1 Key factors impacting price trends of oil and oil products

Macroeconomics	Gross domestic product (GDP) growth is generally linked to the increased consumption of energy and is positively correlated with spot and forward prices for crude and refined products.
Technology developments	Technological breakthroughs in the exploration sector (such as horizontal drilling, hydraulic fracturing or 'fracking', oil sand extraction, deep sea drilling) often force a re-evaluation of available oil reserves and can impact spot and forward prices.
Level of proven reserves	Technological developments such as those listed above plus improved seismic surveys often lead to new discoveries or to upgrading the amount of recoverable oil in existing oil reservoirs, with a potential impact on the level of forward prices.
Commercial and strategic storage	Additions to the worldwide network of commercially operated storage facilities or to state-controlled strategic storage can impact the behaviour of spot versus forward prices.
Weather	Hurricanes and typhoons can severely disrupt the logistics around oil and oil product markets, often impacting spot prices. Unusually cold or hot weather patterns can affect the consumption of gas and electricity, with an indirect impact on the spot and forward prices of oil products.
Arbitrage among energy commodities	The relative value of oil products versus that of other energy commodities can push prices up or down. For example, if the price of natural gas goes up, some industrial consumers using natural gas for heat and steam production may decide to switch to fuel oil if this proves to be cheaper on a per unit of heat basis. This would increase the demand for fuel oil and up its price, reducing the demand and price for natural gas.
Geopolitics	Trouble in important oil-producing countries (wars, terrorism, resource nationalism, etc.) will most likely lead to spikes in spot and forward prices, especially when spare production capacity is limited.
Financial markets	Crude oil is now an established asset class for financial investors (via index products or exchange-traded funds or directly on the futures markets). Changes in investment allocations by large players such as pension funds and asset managers can lead to material changes in oil future prices.
Exchange rates	Oil markets are denominated in US dollars, so US currency movements have a direct impact on the cost of consuming oil and oil products when expressed in the local currency, thus causing increases or reductions in demand.
Refining capacity	The construction of an oil refinery is a long and capital-intensive process; thus, when a global refinery system's spare capacity is limited, sudden increases in demand for oil products will likely lead to increases in oil product prices.
Shipping	Shipping rates for the transportation of crude and oil products, among the various production and consumption points, are a traded commodity per se. Changes in shipping rate levels have a direct impact on oil and oil product prices.
Taxation policy	Taxation policy can affect oil price economics at the upstream level (royalties policy, petroleum revenue taxes, etc.) by impacting the profitability of the extraction of crude oil and at the downstream level by taxing certain kinds of oil products differently (e.g., diesel cars receive more favourable tax treatment than gasoline cars in certain countries).
Environmental policy	Environmental policies generally lead to an improvement in efficiency of the consumption of oil products (e.g., mandatory minimum fuel efficiency ratings for cars), resulting in a reduction in the demand for oil products and a progressive elimination of pollutants (e.g., reduction in the sulphur content of diesel and fuel oil), resulting in an increased demand for higher-quality crude oil (e.g., with a lower sulphur content).

Many factors affect the decision as to what is the appropriate risk management instrument, including the following:

1. *Payoff structure.* The hedging tools used need to create a cash flow consistent with the stated requirements of the hedging policy.
2. *Credit exposure.* The choice of hedging strategy can be influenced by its impact on the credit exposure versus the hedging counterpart. For example:
   - (a) Swaps are generally more credit intensive (i.e., they generate a higher credit exposure) than options structures.
   - (b) A strategy based on a combination of options and/or swaps plus options can help reduce the consumption of credit lines.
   - (c) Long-term maturities are more credit intensive than short-term ones.
3. *Documentation.* Hedging counterparts with master agreements – such as with the International Swap Dealers Association (ISDA) – in place with a credit support annex (CSA) generally generate less credit exposure compared with their hedging counterparts without such documentation.
4. *Accounting rules.* Hedging instruments compliant with accounting rules (such as International Accounting Standards (IAS) 39, *Financial Instruments: Recognition and Measurement*) tend to be preferred to limit their impact on financial reporting activity. Regulation IAS 39 requires that all derivatives are marked to market, with changes in the mark to market being taken to the profit and loss account. For many entities this would result in a significant amount of profit and loss volatility arising from the use of derivatives spilling over into the financial reports. Customers can mitigate the profit and loss effect arising from derivatives used for hedging by using hedging instruments that comply with certain tests of hedging effectiveness defined in the IAS regulations.
5. *Financial legislation.* New legislation on financial markets introduced after the financial crisis of 2008 (e.g., Dodd–Frank in the UNITED STATES or MIFID and EMIR in the EU) is having a deep impact on the hedging strategies and behaviour of the market participants.
6. *Suitability.* Not all hedging instruments and strategies are suitable for all customers. Local and international financial regulations require banks, trading companies and other providers of risk management services to assess the suitability of the product or strategy offered against several factors, such as the customer's actual risk management needs and ability to understand the implications of the products offered and whether the customer is authorized to enter into such a transaction.
7. *Basis risk.* Most hedging strategies will not match the exact price behaviour of the underlying physical commodity price exposure, since physical contracts can be pricing off indexes that are similar but not equal to the indexes traded on the financial markets. An important part of the risk manager's job is to find the most effective instrument (or the right combination of instruments) to minimize this residual risk.
8. *Liquidity of the instruments.* The choice of the most effective risk management strategy is also driven by market liquidity factors. Hedging large volumes and long tenors generally restricts the strategy to the most liquid indexes and instruments available.
9. *Internal hedging policy.* Most corporations active in the energy risk management space have risk management policies – approved at board level or issued by the chief financial officer (CFO) – defining the hedging volume profile, maximum tenors and derivatives strategies that can be used.

10. *Market risk measurability.* The correct evaluation (fair value) of the risk of the hedging structure at any time during the life of the transaction depends on the availability of reliable market data points across the maturities and volatility of the traded commodities. The availability of these data varies greatly across commodities. Many companies are barred from entering into transactions where the fair value cannot be properly calculated.
11. *'Bookability' and the back office.* A hedging strategy is often defined by the limits of the counterparts booking and documenting the trade, with only transactions that are bookable eventually being executed.

1.2.1.2 Oil and Oil Products Overview The oil we find underground is called crude oil, and it is a mixture of hydrocarbons – from almost solid to gaseous – produced when plants and animals decayed under layers of sand and mud millions of years ago. Many grades of crude oil are produced today, each grade identified by many characteristics (listed in a document called an 'assay'), such as viscosity, flash point and aniline point. For the purposes of this chapter, only two of the main characteristics are considered: the American Petroleum Institute (API) gravity and the sulphur content.

1. *API gravity.* This is a measure of the crude oil density relative to the density of water, an index developed by the API and expressed in the range from 0° to 100°, with 0° being the heaviest and 100° the lightest. Water has an API gravity of 10° and the majority of crude oils have an API gravity in the range of 30° to 40° (also called intermediate or medium crude oils) – most refineries are configured to process crude oil within this range. Crude oils with an API gravity above 40° are called light and those with an API gravity below 30° are called heavy. The higher the API gravity, the higher the proportion of high-added-value products (such as gasoline, kerosene and naphtha) that can be obtained from a specific crude oil during the refining process. Light crude oil trades at a premium compared with intermediate crude oils, and intermediate crude oils trade at a premium to heavy crude oils.
2. *Sulphur content.* The higher a crude oil's sulphur content, the lower its value, since a higher number of sulphur molecules displace hydrocarbon molecules. High sulphur content also has other negative side effects, such as increasing the speed of corrosion in pipelines and refinery equipment, and is an atmospheric pollutant when the oil or oil product is burned. Sulphur content is expressed as a percentage of weight, with three main categories: sour (>1.5%), medium sour (0.5–1.5%) and sweet (<0.5%). Sweet crude oil trades at a premium to medium sour and sour crudes.

The API grade and sulphur content are the main elements defining the value of crude oil. Figure 1.1 presents the main crude oil benchmarks traded in the international markets.

Before crude oil can be used for anything it must be processed in an oil refinery. Crude oil is a mix of different chemical compounds, a combination of hydrogen and carbon atoms called hydrocarbons. Each of these chemical compounds has its own boiling temperature. Hence if one progressively raises the temperature of crude oil in a container, one obtains progressive separation by evaporating the various chemical compounds; once separated, the compounds are cooled and turned back into liquid. The temperatures at which the different chemical compounds reach their boiling points define what is called a distillation curve, and different types of crudes have different distillation curves. The main refinery techniques are discussed later, when we examine the refinery sector's hedging strategies.

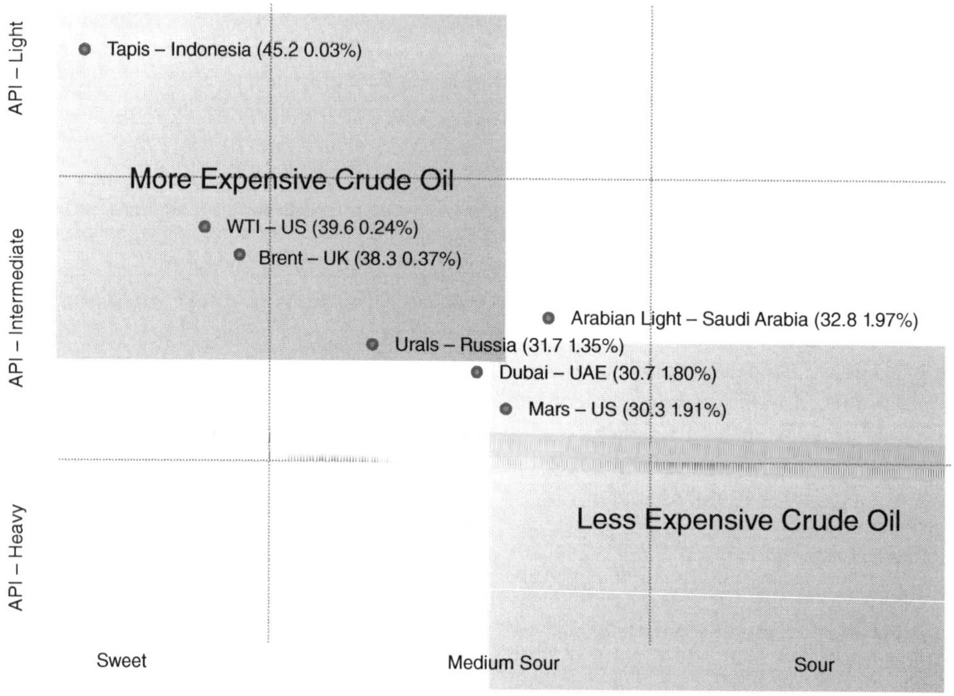

FIGURE 1.1 Main crude oil benchmarks (API and sulphur content)

A single crude oil or mix of crude oils (called a 'crude slate') can be used as feedstock and processed in a refinery, with the resulting mix of oil products called a 'product slate' (see Figure 1.2). Refinery operators always try to optimize production by purchasing a crude slate that maximizes the desired product slate. The percentage of each oil product produced per unit of feedstock is called the 'yield' (see Table 1.2). Local market requirements, product demand seasonality and the complexity of the refinery all affect the yield values for refineries around the world.

1.2.1.3 Oil Price Risk Management Overview The implementation of hedging strategies to protect against the movement of oil and oil product prices affects many different industrial sectors, from those (such as crude oil exploration and production and oil refinery) where the value of oil or oil products is the main driver of business strategy and business economics to those (such as transportation and power generation) where the value of oil and oil products is a key component of the cost line, although not necessarily the main one (but it is often the most volatile).

Corporate hedging strategies are not homogeneous across different industrial sectors and, even within the same industry sector, substantially different hedging strategies are used by the various market participants. The general principle is that smaller/newer corporations tend to have no hedging policy in place or will be active in the hedging market on a 'one-off' basis; the more such companies increase in size and knowledge and/or confidence (in terms of the hedging process, oil markets and tools), the more likely they will be to develop a proper risk management policy. A larger company will also have a better credit risk profile, and will

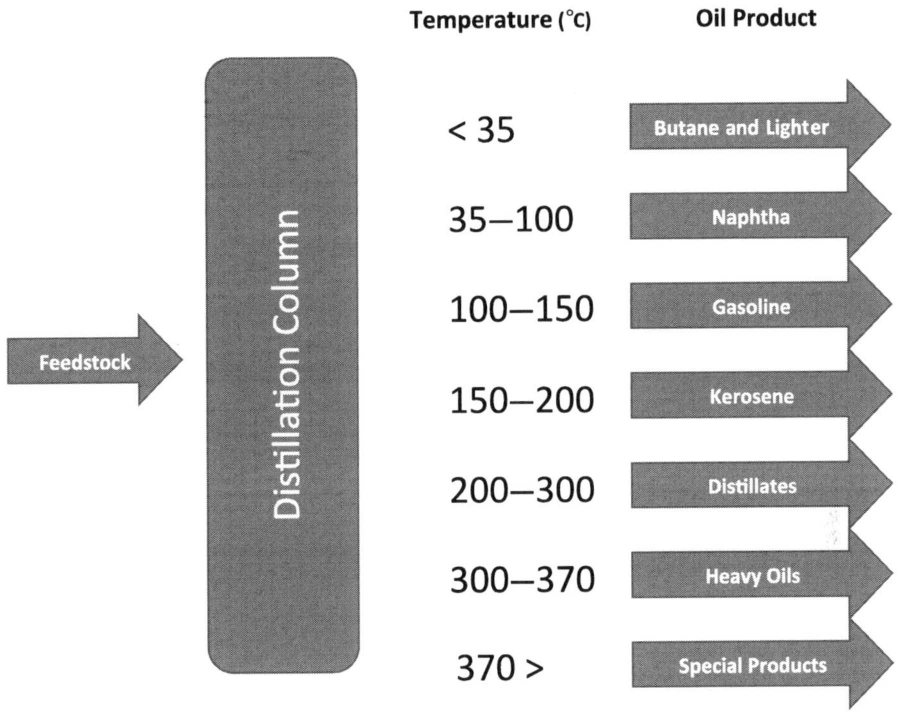

FIGURE 1.2 Distillation column

therefore have access to a wider group of risk management service providers (e.g., futures and over-the-counter (OTC) clearing platforms), thus improving the quality and price of the hedging structures they can transact. Medium to large companies often have a dedicated risk management team that manages oil price exposure and is involved with the preparation and execution of risk management strategy.

A company's risk management strategy is often approved at the board level (or at least at the CFO level) and defines the size and scope of the risk management activity. The following elements are generally included:

1. Derivative instruments that can be used, such as swaps, options and exotics.
2. Underlyings that can be used for risk management purposes, such as ICE Brent, fuel oil and gasoil cracks.
3. The volumes of the product that need to be hedged.
4. Maximum maturities for the above-mentioned instruments, such as ICE Brent up to five years but fuel oil up to two years only.
5. A hedging matrix (or hedging envelope), which defines the combination of instruments, underlyings and maturities that can be used when implementing a hedging strategy.
6. A credit envelope, which defines the criteria the hedging counterparts of a corporation need to meet to qualify as a counterpart (e.g., credit ratings, legal documentation).
7. A list of the people authorized to trade on behalf of the company.
8. Set-up and credit limits with futures exchanges and OTC clearing houses.

TABLE 1.2 Average yield structure

Product category	Subproducts	Typical use	Average yield (EIA data: Global Refineries)
Butane and lighter	Methane	Home heating, fertilizers, petrochemicals	9%
	Ethane	Petrochemicals	
	Propane	Petrochemicals	
	Butanes	Blended with gasoline	
Naphtha	Light naphtha	Petrochemicals	6%
	Heavy naphtha	Blended with gasoline, fertilizers	
Gasoline	Motor gasoline	Automotive petrol engines	26%
Kerosene	Jet fuel	Jet propulsion aircraft fuel	8%
	Gas turbine fuel	Power generation turbine	
	Kerosene	Heating and lighting	
Distillate	Diesel (auto and marine)	Auto and marine diesel engines	27%
	Heating oil	Heating and power generation	
Heavy oil	Marine fuel oil (bunker)	Marine engines	14%
	Heavy industrial fuel oil	Power generation	
Speciality products	Base oil	Lubricants	10%
	Waxes	Candles, packaging, food industry	
	Bitumen	Asphalt and construction	
	Petroleum coke	Fuel used in steel and cement industries	
	Carbon black	Rubber tyres	

A typical risk management strategy comprises two components:

1. A non-discretionary component defining transactions that the risk management team executes automatically, either at specific dates during the hedging year or whenever the market reaches certain levels.
2. A discretionary component where the risk management team is authorized to have a more opportunistic approach and transact whenever they see fit.

Before analysing in depth the risk management strategies of different energy-intensive customers, it is worth examining the way oil and oil product prices are created and reported. Some of the most traded oil products – such as Brent and West Texas intermediate (WTI) crude oil, European gasoil and heating oil in the United States – have their prices reported on the major oil futures exchanges (such as the Intercontinental Exchange (ICE) for Brent and European gasoil and the New York Mercantile Exchange (NYMEX) for WTI and heating oil).

Together with the energy futures exchanges, the major providers of energy price assessments are Platts and Argus. These companies publish news, research, commentary, market data and analysis and several hundred price assessments daily that are widely used as benchmarks in the physical futures markets and for OTC financial hedging. Their products and services include real-time news and price information, end-of-day market data, newsletters and reports.

A market-appropriate methodology is used to assess prices in the various markets covered. This methodology is generally produced in consultation with a range of market participants. To assess the price of a certain oil product, it first needs to be properly identified. Without going too much into the specifics of the methodologies used by the price providers, three elements are generally used in oil product classification:

1. *Product type.* For example, fuel oil, diesel, gasoil and jet fuel.
2. *Sulphur content.* For example, fuel oil 3.5%, diesel 10 parts per million (ppm), gasoil 0.1%.
3. *Delivery information.* That is, the geographic point at which the title to goods transfers from the seller to the buyer. This is generally either free on board (FOB), where the buyer assumes the risk of loss and any further freight and handling charges at the crude oil loading facility or refinery terminal or cost insurance and freight (CIF), where the quoted price includes the cost of the goods, insurance and freight charges for a crude or oil product terminal in a specific region. For example, Fuel Oil 3.5% FOB Mediterranean (MED), Diesel 10 ppm CIF North West Europe (NWE) and Jet Fuel Singapore (Sing).

As a final note, while at the time of printing the product references are deemed to be correct and a good reflection of the various products used in risk management in the various trading regions, it is important to remember that this is a slow but constantly changing market. Occasionally regulations on chemical additives for some of the oil products may change, thus forcing the creation of a new specification. In addition, there is constant pressure to phase out polluting products (like sulphur) in favour of products with a lower impact on the environment.

Please also note that the swap, forward and option premium levels in the hedging strategy examples presented in the next paragraphs are for illustration purpose only and do not reflect actual market trading levels.

1.2.2 Aviation: Risk Profile and Hedging Strategies

1.2.2.1 Introduction: The Aviation Industry The term *aviation industry* encompasses both civil and military aviation. Civil aviation is further divided into general aviation (i.e., everything that is not a military flight, such as scheduled civil and cargo flights) and scheduled air transport. To analyse risk management activity, we focus on scheduled air transport companies, namely:

1. Large regional airlines.
2. Medium and large international airlines.

It is worth noting that one occasionally encounters hedging activity from cargo airlines and national military air forces.

The aviation industry is a major consumer of oil products in the form of jet fuel (or aviation fuel), a product of the family of middle distillates. According to the International Air Transport Association (IATA, *Economic Briefing*, December 2012), following the increase in energy prices of 2007, jet fuel is now the largest expense for airlines, accounting for roughly a third of the industry's total variable cost base (up from 28% in 2007 and 14% in 2003), followed by labour costs (including pensions).

While fuel makes up a significant portion of an airline's total costs, efficiency among different carriers can vary widely:

1. Short-haul airlines typically get lower fuel efficiency because takeoffs and landings consume high amounts of jet fuel.
2. Low-cost airlines generally have more modern and hence more fuel-efficient fleets.
3. Low-cost airlines tend to have a lower cost base compared with national carriers; hence, fuel costs often represent a higher percentage of the overall cost.

Large airlines are among the most sophisticated players in corporate oil risk management, with dedicated teams actively trading the swap and option markets for crude oil, gasoil and jet fuel for maturities from six months to five years forward.

1.2.2.2 Jet Fuel and the Jet Engine Aviation fuel is a specialized type of petroleum-based fuel used to power aircraft. It is generally of higher quality than fuels used in less critical applications, such as heating and road transport, and often contains additives to reduce the risk of icing and explosion due to high temperatures, among other properties. The most commonly used jet fuel types are Jet A and Jet A-1, but other kinds of jet fuels are available (JP-8, JP-5, etc.) for military use, with higher specifications (such as a lower freezing point or higher flash point).

Another type of fuel, aviation gasoline (avgas), is generally used in the high-compression sparkplug ignition piston engines of small private propeller airplanes and helicopters. It is sold in much lower volumes but to many more individual aircraft, whereas jet fuel is sold in high volumes to large aircraft operated typically by airlines, the military and large corporations. For the purposes of this chapter, the focus of the analysis is on references that are useful for scheduled air transport only: jet fuel, gasoil and crude oil.

Although modern aircraft engines contain some of the most sophisticated engineering technology in everyday use, their basic principles are quite simple and have changed little since jet engines came into use at the end of World War II. In its simplest form, the jet engine is a tube into which air is sucked before being compressed, mixed with fuel and burnt. Combustion causes the fuel–air mixture to expand and accelerate towards the rear of the engine. This high-speed exhaust generates the thrust to push the engine forward.

1.2.2.3 Product Specifications

Europe, Middle East and Africa Regions The jet fuel references generally used by European-based airlines for risk management purposes are published by Platts, as follows:

1. Jet Kero CIF NWE Cargoes (in US$ per metric tonne (USD/MT)). Platts considers the prices of cargoes delivered into Amsterdam, Rotterdam and Antwerp (ARA), the UK and northern France for the assessment.
2. Jet Cargoes FOB NWE (USD/MT). Platts considers transactions from ARA, Ghent and Flushing. Any transactions at other loading ports in NWE are typically normalized on a freight differential basis back to Rotterdam.

3. Jet Barges FOB ARA (USD/MT). Platts considers as transactions basis FOB Rotterdam. Any transactions occurring at other loading ports in NWE are typically normalized on a freight differential basis back to Rotterdam. Platts considers bids and offers from Rotterdam, Antwerp, Amsterdam, Ghent and Flushing.
4. Jet Fuel FOB MED (USD/MT). Platts derives this quote from the Jet Kero CIF NWE Cargoes quote adjusted for the cost of transportation from NWE into the Mediterranean region (Augusta, Italy).

Jet fuel is not the only price reference used by European airlines when hedging price risk. The market for financial OTC products for jet fuel has limited liquidity in terms of maximum volume and maximum tenor executable. Hence, airlines often use crude oil and oil product references whenever the volume to be hedged is too large or the tenor is too long to be accommodated within the liquidity of jet fuel references. The main alternative references used by European airlines are as follows:

1. ICE Brent (in US$ per barrel (USD/bbl)), based on the daily settlement price of the ICE Brent futures contract.
2. ICE gasoil (USD/MT), based on the daily settlement price of the ICE gasoil futures contract.
3. NYMEX WTI (USD/bbl), based on the daily settlement price of the NYMEX WTI futures contract.
4. Jet differential (USD/MT) = jet fuel – ICE gasoil.
5. Jet crack (USD/bbl) = jet fuel/7.45 (conversion factor MT to bbl) – ICE Brent.
6. ICE gasoil crack (USD/bbl) = ICE gasoil/7.45 (conversion factor MT to bbl) – ICE Brent.

Asian Region The references generally used by Asian airlines for risk management purposes are published by Platts:

Jet Kerosene FOB Cargoes Singapore ($/bbl). The Singapore physical assessment reflects transactions, bids and offers of a minimum of 100,000 bbl and a maximum of 250,000 bbl, and loading within 15–30 days from the date of publication.

Asian airlines also use other crude oil and oil product references whenever the volume is too large or the tenor is too long to be accommodated within the liquidity of jet fuel references. The main alternative references used by Asian-based airlines are as follows:

1. NYMEX WTI (USD/bbl), based on the daily settlement price of the NYMEX WTI futures contract.
2. ICE Brent (USD/bbl), based on the daily settlement price of the ICE Brent futures contract.
3. Singapore Gasoil Reg 0.5% Sulphur (USD/bbl).

Americas Region The references generally used by airlines in the Americas region for risk management purposes are published by Platts and include:

US Gulf Coast Jet Kerosene 54 Waterborne (in USD cents per gallon (USDc/gal)).

Airlines also use other crude oil and oil product references whenever the volume is too large or the tenor is too long to be accommodated within the liquidity of jet fuel references. The main alternative references used by Americas-based airlines are as follows:

1. NYMEX Heating Oil (HO) (USD/bbl), also known as #2 contract, based on the daily settlement price of the NYMEX heating oil futures contract.
2. NYMEX WTI (USD/bbl), based on the daily settlement price of the NYMEX WTI futures contract.

1.2.2.4 Risk Management Strategies for the Aviation Industry The airlines sector has no such thing as a generic hedging strategy: the approach to what and when to cover exposure to jet fuel prices varies widely across the various players and is based on many factors, including local accounting regulations, the size of the airline, the presence of an approved hedging programme, tolerance and understanding of basis risk at the CFO and board levels, oil market dynamics, what the competition is doing and fuel surcharge policies.

Important elements affecting an airline's risk management behaviour are its credit standing and the contractual arrangements put in place with hedging counterparts:

1. *Credit considerations.* Large international airlines generally obtain larger and longer credit lines from banking counterparts. Hence, they are able to execute more refined hedging strategies compared with those that can be executed by smaller airlines with access to smaller and shorter credit lines. Some large airlines are also actively using futures and OTC cleared platforms.
2. *Contractual considerations.* Large international airlines have the resources to negotiate master ISDA agreements (and an occasional CSA, although this is not very common in the airline industry). Smaller airlines do not have the internal legal resources and are, in general, more resistant to enter into ISDAs and tend to rely on single trade (long-form) confirmations. The presence of an ISDA master agreement generally leads to obtaining better credit terms with trading counterparts.

Based on observations of the behaviour of market participants, some generic conclusions on risk management behaviour can be drawn.

1. Small to medium airlines (e.g., with a total consumption of less than 500,000 MT of jet fuel per year) tend to implement and execute risk management strategies with the following characteristics:
   (a) Involving short to medium maturities (e.g., less than three years), generally covering no more than three seasons ahead (winter season is from October to March and summer season is from April to September).
   (b) Mainly using swaps or plain vanilla options.
   (c) Limited exposure to basis risk between jet fuel and gasoil or jet fuel and crude oil.
2. Medium to large airlines (with jet fuel consumption of 500,000 MT per year and above) generally have a dedicated team for the structuring, implementation and execution of hedging programmes and their strategies have the following characteristics:
   (a) Involving short to long maturities (up to seven years), depending on what product is used (e.g., short maturities for jet fuel quotes, long maturities for crude oil quotes).

   (b) A hedging schedule, approved at the board level and an integral part of the financial strategy communicated to shareholders, with typical hedging ratios of
      (i) up to 75% of forecasted consumed volumes one year ahead
      (ii) up to 50% of forecasted consumed volumes two years ahead
      (iii) up to 35% of forecasted consumed volumes three years ahead
      (iv) up to 25% of forecasted consumed volumes four years ahead and beyond.
   (c) Using a combination of swaps, plain vanilla options and exotic structures.
   (d) Exposure and active management of basis risk.
3. On a regional basis, European and American airlines tend to use exotic structures less than Asian airlines.

Common risk management structures used by airlines are discussed next.

Jet Fuel Swaps: Simple and Straightforward *Situation.* An airline, let it be called DreamAir, has a strategic hedging programme in place with a provision that at any time at least 55% of the forecasted jet fuel consumption over the next 12 months needs to be at a fixed price. DreamAir's forecasted consumption over the next 12 months is 350,000 MT.

Strategy. DreamAir will enter over time into several swap transactions, for a total volume of $350{,}000 \times 55\% = 192{,}500$ MT for a tenor of 12 months. Every month (or as often as stated by the hedging policy), DreamAir will adjust the hedged volumes to take into consideration expired periods and changes in fuel consumption forecasts.

Pros. Swap transactions are the basic building block of any risk management structure. They are generally the simplest and most liquid tools available for hedging purposes. Hence, they are well understood and accepted by customer boards and auditors. Pricing is easy and relatively transparent (depending on the location of the Platts quote).

Cons. The beauty of the swap is also its main limitation. The customer is locked into a fixed price level. Hence, if the jet fuel price moves in favour of the customer (e.g., the jet fuel price goes down in the future for an airline), DreamAir will eventually be paying for jet fuel at a fixed level higher than the price paid by its competitors that did not hedge (or hedged less) with swaps. Volumes are also fixed and so if the forecasted consumption changes (e.g., as a result of expected reduced demand for air travel due to economic recession), then DreamAir can find itself with a hedging ratio higher than that which would have been desired.

Example. Figure 1.3 represents a situation where DreamAir has entered into a swap on jet fuel for 12 months forward at 525\$/MT (straight line). If we assume that no other hedges are put in place until the expiry of this hedge, the net result of this hedging strategy is as follows.

1. DreamAir is effectively paying its jet fuel consumption at 525\$/MT during the 12-month period, since (assuming the price of jet fuel moves as described by the dashed line):
   (a) In months 1 to 3 and 10 to 12 DreamAir pays its physical supplier of jet fuel a price below 525\$/MT but also pays to the hedging bank the difference between 525\$/MT and the market price.
   (b) In months 4 to 9 DreamAir pays its physical supplier of jet fuel a price above 525\$/MT but also receives from the hedging bank the difference between the market price and 525\$/MT.

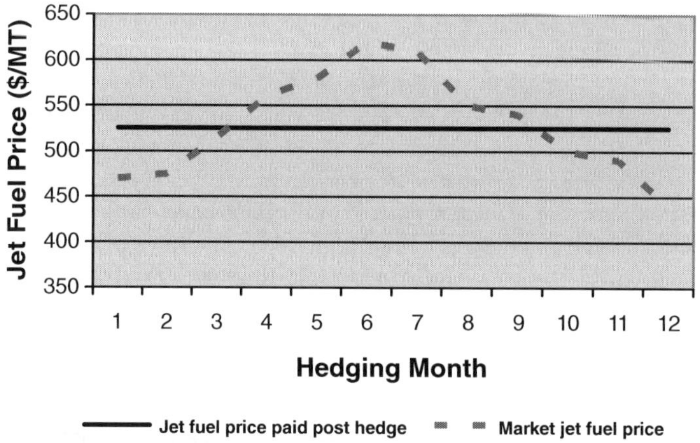

FIGURE 1.3 Jet fuel swap

Gasoil and Jet Fuel Differential: Optimizing Relative Value *Situation.* DreamAir now wants to protect additional volumes of jet fuel but, while the CFO is concerned about the price trend for oil products, there are worries about changes in the relative value of jet fuel against that of other oil products due to the increased refinery capacity from the opening of new refineries in India and China. The CFO wants to protect DreamAir against a general increase in the oil complex but also has a view that jet fuel may be weaker in the future compared with other oil products.

Strategy. DreamAir initially enters into a swap transaction on ICE gasoil for a tenor of 12 months. After this initial transaction (which leaves DreamAir exposed to the ICE gasoil differential with Jet), DreamAir continues to monitor the differential between jet fuel and gasoil for that hedged period. If the CFO is correct and this forward differential is reducing over time (as a result of the increased volumes of jet fuel coming onto the physical markets from the new refineries in India and China), DreamAir will enter, at a later stage, into a second transaction buying the swap differential (jet swap differential = jet fuel swap – ICE gasoil swap) between jet fuel and ICE gasoil, effectively transforming the initial ICE gasoil hedge into a jet fuel hedge for the same period:

$$\text{ICE gasoil swap} + (\text{jet fuel swap} - \text{ICE gasoil swap}) = \text{jet fuel swap}$$

Pros. DreamAir can take advantage of expected developments on the jet fuel physical markets (e.g., expected increases in jet fuel production from new or upgraded refineries) or from reductions in demand (e.g., reductions in air traffic linked to events such as the economic crisis, the severe acute respiratory syndrome (SARS) epidemic of 2003 and volcanic ash closing airspaces in 2010). As a result of this two-stage strategy, DreamAir may be able to lock in the price of jet fuel at a cheaper relative price compared with buying jet fuel directly in stage one.

Cons. If the expected market events do not materialize and jet fuel does not become cheaper than gasoil, DreamAir will end up locking the price of jet fuel at a level that is relatively more expensive than what would have been obtained by buying a jet fuel swap directly in stage one.

Payoff analysis Swap market situation on 1 June 2014:

Gasoil	Jet fuel
Swap Jan15–Dec15	
650	750

For the period January 2015 to December 2015 DreamAir buys gasoil swaps at 650$/MT, taking the view that the jet fuel differential (currently at 750 – 650 = 100$/MT) will come down in the next three months.

Swap market situation on 15 September 2014:

Gasoil	Jet fuel
Swap Jan15–Dec15	
750	800

The jet fuel market differential has moved as expected, the energy complex has moved up, but jet fuel is now relatively cheaper compared with gasoil. DreamAir can now complete its hedging transaction as follows:

1. DreamAir sells the January 2015 to December 2015 gasoil swap at 750$/MT, realizing a gain of 100$/MT.
2. DreamAir buys the January 2015 to December 2015 jet fuel swap at 800$/MT, realizing an overall gain of 50$/MT (100$/MT of gain on the gasoil transaction – 50$/MT loss on the increased cost of jet fuel).

ICE Brent and Gasoil Crack: Optimizing Relative Value *Situation.* DreamAir needs to put in place a hedging programme for a large volume of jet fuel, but in order to minimize liquidity costs, it decides to initially put a hedging position using either ICE Brent or ICE gasoil. The ICE gasoil positions can then be rolled into jet fuel by using the jet differential strategy described in the previous section.

Strategy. DreamAir's CFO believes that ICE gasoil is relatively too expensive compared with ICE Brent. DreamAir initially enters into a swap transaction on ICE Brent for a tenor of 18 months. After this initial transaction, it continues to monitor the relative value between ICE Brent and ICE gasoil, called the 'crack' and expressed as the differential between gasoil (quoted in $/MT but converted to $/bbl using a fixed volume conversion factor of 7.45) and Brent (quoted in $/bbl):

$$\text{ICE gasoil crack swap }(\$/\text{bbl}) = \text{ICE gasoil swap}/7.45 - \text{ICE Brent swap}$$

If the CFO's view of the oil markets is correct and this crack reduces over time, DreamAir will enter into further transactions, buying the ICE gasoil crack and effectively transforming the initial ICE Brent hedge into an ICE gasoil hedge for the same hedging period.

Pros. DreamAir can take advantage of expected positive developments in the crude and middle distillate markets. As a result of this strategy, DreamAir has built up a position in ICE gasoil at a better level than they would have obtained if they had locked an ICE gasoil swap at the beginning of the hedging programme.

Cons. If the ICE gasoil crack increases over time, DreamAir will end up locking the price of the ICE gasoil swap at a more expensive level than they would have obtained by buying a ICE gasoil swap directly in stage one.

Payoff analysis Swap market situation on 1 June 2014:

ICE Brent ($/bbl)	ICE gasoil ($/MT)
Swap Jan15–Jun16	
80	710

DreamAir buys the January 2015 to June 2016 ICE Brent swap at $80/bbl and takes the view that ICE gasoil crack (currently at 710/7.45 – 80 = $15.3/bbl) will come down in the coming months.

Swap market situation on 15 November 2014:

ICE Brent ($/bbl)	ICE gasoil ($/MT)
Swap Jan15–Jun16	
93	792

The gasoil and Brent markets have moved as expected and the energy complex has moved up, but gasoil is now relatively cheaper than Brent. DreamAir can now complete its hedging transaction as follows:

1. DreamAir buys the January 2015 to June 2016 ICE gasoil crack swap at 13.30$/bbl.
2. The gasoil crack swap added to the existing ICE Brent swap creates an actual position on ICE gasoil at a level of 80$/bbl (original ICE Brent swap) + 13.3$/bbl (new ICE gasoil crack swap) = 93.3$/bbl. Using a conversion factor of 7.45, this is equivalent to an ICE gasoil swap at 695$/MT – hence, 15$/MT better than if DreamAir had closed the ICE gasoil swap at the original level on 1/6/2014.

ICE Brent Three Ways – When There are Credit Line Constraints *Situation.* DreamAir wants to put in place a two-year hedge to protect against an increase in oil prices (see Figure 1.4). To minimize liquidity and transaction costs, DreamAir chooses to execute the trade using ICE Brent and, in selecting the structure, needs to keep in mind two constraints:

1. Limited budget for paying premiums for options.
2. Limited credit lines available from counterparty banks.

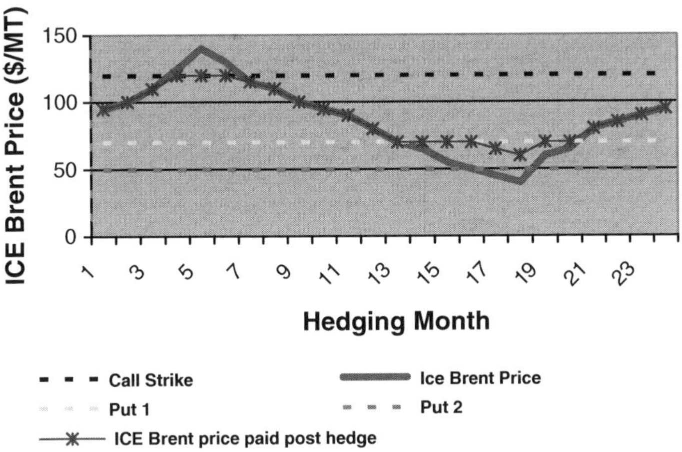

FIGURE 1.4 ICE Brent three ways

Strategy. To successfully put in place the required protection against the potential increase of ICE Brent prices and to satisfy the constraints above, DreamAir will have to do the following:

1. Buy a call option on ICE Brent (e.g., at a strike of 120$/bbl for a premium of 3.5$/bbl).
   - The call option provides protection for price increases above $120/bbl.
2. Sell a put option on ICE Brent (e.g., at a strike of 70$/bbl for a premium of 1.5$/bbl).
   - The put option partially finances the cost of the call option.
3. Buy a put option on ICE Brent (e.g., at a strike of 50$/bbl for a premium of 0.5$/bbl).
   - The second put option locks the maximum amount DreamAir will ever have to pay in case the first put option is exercised. This reduces DreamAir's credit risk since the maximum exposure (e.g., the maximum amount DreamAir can be asked to pay to the hedge provider under this strategy) is now capped at 70 – 50 = 20$/bbl × number of hedged barrels.

Pros. The overall cost of the structure is 3.5 – 1.5 + 0.5 = $2.5/bbl, cheaper than just buying the call option at 120$/bbl, and provides the same upside oil price protection. In case of an extreme drop in oil prices, DreamAir is locked by the first put option only up to the strike of the second put option (partial downside price reparticipation). The credit line consumption from this structure is lower than that which would have originated from a simple collar (e.g., call at 120$ with put at 70$) since the maximum payout of the 70$ put is capped at 20$/bbl.

Cons. The structure is more expensive than a simple collar equivalent, which would have cost 3.5 – 1.5 = 2$/bbl.

ICE Brent Knock-Out Swaps: Cheaper (and Riskier) *Situation.* DreamAir wants to enter into a 24-month swap on ICE Brent but the current swap market is deemed too high (see Figure 1.5).

Strategy. DreamAir needs to sell some of the price upside to finance a better swap level. This can be done by entering into a knock-out swap and whenever the monthly settlement is

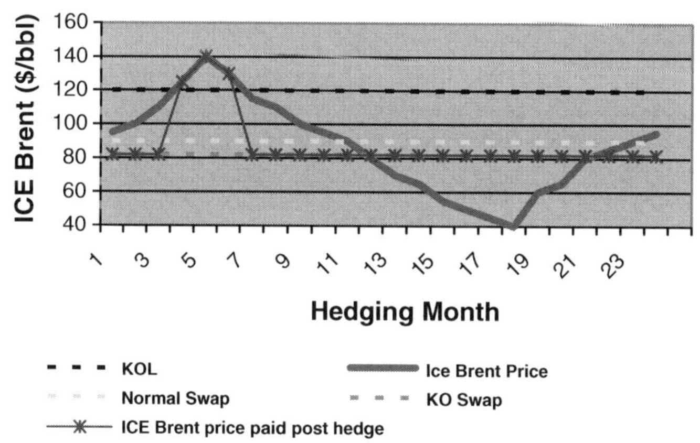

FIGURE 1.5 ICE Brent knock-out swap

above a certain strike level, the knock-out level (KOL), the swap settlement will be suspended for that specific month.

Pros. In exchange for giving up price protection above the KOL, DreamAir is able to enter into a swap level better than the one that would have been obtained using a normal swap structure.

Cons. DreamAir loses the whole swap protection whenever the monthly ICE Brent settles above the KOL.

1.2.3 Shipping: Risk Profile and Hedging Strategies

1.2.3.1 Introduction: The Shipping Industry The shipping industry encompasses a vast universe that can broadly be classified as follows:

1. Transport of people – ferries, cruise ships.
2. International transport of goods – bulk carriers, tankers and container ships.
3. Service ships – dredgers and tugboats.
4. Local transport of goods – barges and coasters.
5. Military ships.

The use of risk management tools is not confined to particular areas of the shipping industry, although the majority of activity comes from shipping companies active in the international transportation of goods. The cost of the ship's fuel (commonly referred to as *bunker fuel* in the industry) is anywhere between 25% and 50% of an average ocean-going vessel's operating costs (e.g., not including chartering costs).

The costs of operating a vessel incurred during a charter primarily consist of the following:

1. Fuel.
2. Crew's wages and associated costs.
3. Insurance premiums.
4. Lubricants, spare parts, repair and maintenance costs.
5. Port charges.

To provide risk management services to the shipping sector, it is important to understand that the ship owner is not necessarily the one paying the fuel bill. There are four basic contractual agreements used in the shipping industry:

1. A *voyage charter* is the hiring of a vessel and crew for a voyage between a load port and a discharge port. The charterer pays the vessel owner on a per ton or lump sum basis. The owner pays the port costs (excluding stevedoring), fuel costs and crew costs.
2. A *time charter* is the hiring of a vessel for a specific period of time. The owner still manages the vessel but the charterer selects the ports and directs where the vessel goes. The charterer pays for all the fuel that the vessel consumes, in addition to port charges and a daily hire to the vessel owner.
3. A *bareboat charter* is an arrangement for the generally long-term hiring of a vessel whereby no administration or technical maintenance is included as part of the agreement. The charterer pays for all operating expenses, voyage expenses, port expenses and hull insurance.
4. A *demise charter* shifts the control and possession of the vessel. The charterer takes full control of the vessel along with any of its legal and financial responsibilities.

A ship's engine room typically contains several engines for different purposes. The main engines, or propulsion engines, are used to turn the ship's propeller and move the ship through the water. They typically burn heavy fuel oil or diesel and can sometimes switch between the two. There are many propulsion arrangements for motor vessels, some including multiple engines, propellers and gearboxes.

The propulsion technology most used on modern ships is based on the 'diesel cycle reciprocating' engine. The rotating crankshaft can power the propeller directly for slow-speed engines (<450 rpm), via a gearbox for medium- and high-speed engines or via an alternator and electric motor in diesel–electric vessels. The reciprocating marine diesel engine first came into use in 1903, quickly displacing the less efficient steam turbine technology.

The majority of modern ships use oil distillate products to power ship engines. The greater part of the world's commercial fleet (wet and dry cargoes, container ships, some cruise ships and ferries) uses fuel oil as fuel, while the rest uses gasoil as the main fuel (mostly high-speed ferries), natural gas (liquefied natural gas (LNG) tankers) or nuclear-powered steam engines (mostly military ships). Bunker consumption represents a little more than 50% of the world's total fuel oil production, roughly equivalent to 4 million barrels per day of the roughly 7 million barrels of fuel oil produced daily (as of 2010). Because bunker fuel contains a large percentage of sulphur (between 1% and 5%) it is, for environmental legislation reasons, typically used only in ocean-going ships' primary or main engines once in international waters.

Bunker fuel is technically any type of fuel oil used aboard ships. It gets its name from the containers on ships and in ports in which it is stored, which used to be coal bunkers in the days of steam engines but are now bunker fuel tanks. Bunker fuel in the shipping industry can also be referred to by other names:

1. Heavy oil.
2. #6 oil.
3. Resid (as in residual oil product).
4. Bunker C.

5. Blended fuel oil.
6. Furnace oil and other locally used names.

The International Standards Organization (ISO) has issued marine fuels standards (ISO 8217) and introduced some uniformity to the international marine fuel markets. Bunker fuel has the following characteristics:

1. Its colour is always black, dark brown or at least very dark. This colour arises from the asphaltenes in the crude oil.
2. Bunker is generally viscous, especially when first produced at the refinery. Certain residuals are actually solid at ambient temperatures.

The following are the two main factors identifying fuel oil.

1. *Sulphur content.* The most commonly traded marine fuels have a sulphur content of 1% (low-sulphur fuel oil, or LSFO) and 3.5% (high-sulphur fuel oil, or HSFO). The higher the sulphur content, the cheaper the fuel oil. The introduction of more stringent environmental regulations by the International Maritime Organization (IMO) has been progressively reducing the sulphur content in the bunker by issuing Marine Pollution (MARPOL) regulations, with the following limits being phased in:
   (a) Reduction of the maximum sulphur content in the bunker used by members of the IMO to 3.5% by 2012 and to 0.5% by 2015.
   (b) Creation of sulphur emission control areas (SECAs) where the maximum sulphur content in the bunker cannot be higher than 1% (March 2010), dropping to 0.1% by 2015. Vessels entering a SECA will have to switch to a bunker of lower sulphur quality (e.g., have a separate bunker for LSFO) or blend the bunker fuel sulphur levels down to under the SECA sulphur limits before entering the area. As of June 2010, the SECAs are the Baltic Sea, the UNITED KINGDOM North Sea and the California coast.
2. *Viscosity* (measured in centistokes, or cst). Fuel oils of 180 cst and 380 cst are the most commonly traded. The higher the value in centistokes, the higher the viscosity. A higher viscosity means cheaper fuel oil, because it makes the fuel more difficult for engines to burn.

The most commonly used marine fuels are colloquially referred to as intermediate fuel oils (IFOs). The reason they are called intermediate is that they can contain up to 7% middle distillates, used as 'cutter stock' to lower the viscosity of heavy fuel oil. Generally, IFOs are named after their viscosity at 50°C (viscosity is temperature dependent, such that the higher the temperature, the lower the viscosity), which is the normal handling temperature for marine fuels to reduce viscosity and allow for the pumping of the fuel into fuel tanks and engine rooms. The most commonly used IFOs are called IFO 180 cst and IFO 380 cst.

The pricing of fuel oil can be referenced to three different prices:

1. According to Bunkerwire, which refers to pricing in specific ports where fuel oil of different grades and qualities are mixed together. The Bunkerwire price is the equivalent of a retail price, paid by the shipping companies for filling up.
2. Cargo prices are a wholesale price for deliveries of 200,000 barrels or more.

3. Barge prices are a wholesale price for deliveries of up to 50,000 barrels. Barges generally go for a premium compared with cargoes, since they involve smaller volumes and can deliver to more destinations.

Fuel oil is also used for power generation. Hence, in certain locations, it is important to consider the effect of the activity of utilities over the price of a bunker. For example:

1. Whenever the price of natural gas becomes too expensive compared with the price of fuel oil, then utilities may consider increasing the use of fuel oil to generate electricity. The increased fuel oil demand results in increased bunker prices for shippers.
2. If the prices of emission certificates in Europe drop, then utilities have an incentive to use more fuel oil for power generation (fuel oil is more polluting than natural gas), hence affecting the cost of bunkers for shippers.

The shipping industry is also a consumer of diesel (marine diesel), used in the auxiliary engines of large ships. It is used when a vessel is close to shore (diesel is less polluting than fuel oil) or for manoeuvring in a harbour. Auxiliary engines also generate electricity for a ship while in port.

1.2.3.2 Product Specifications

Europe, Middle East and Africa Regions The main fuel oil references generally used by shipping companies for risk management purposes are published by Platts:

1. Fuel Oil 3.5% Barges (Platts considers parcels of 2000 to 5000 MT FOB in Rotterdam), in USD/MT.
2. Fuel Oil 3.5% Cargoes CIF NWE (Platts considers parcels of 25,000 MT delivered CIF NWE basis Rotterdam), in USD/MT.
3. Fuel Oil 3.5% Cargoes FOB MED (Platts considers parcels of 25,000–30,000 MT delivered FOB basis Italy), in USD/MT.

Quality. Platts generally considers fuel oil with a 3–4% sulphur content and a viscosity of around 380 cst.

For risk management transactions, shipping companies also use crude oil whenever the volume is too large or the tenor is too long to be accommodated within the liquidity of fuel oil references. The main alternative references used by European-based shipping companies are as follows:

1. ICE Brent (USD/bbl), based on the daily settlement price of the ICE Brent futures contract.
2. Fuel oil crack (USD/bbl) = fuel oil × conversion factor (MT to bbl) – ICE Brent, generally a negative number since fuel oil trades at a discount to crude.

Asian Region The main references generally used by shipping companies for risk management purposes are published by Platts:

1. Singapore 180 cst, in USD/MT.
2. Singapore 380 cst, in USD/MT.

Quality. Platts generally considers fuel oil with a sulphur content of up to 5%.

Shipping companies also use other crude oil and oil product references whenever the volume is too large or the tenor is too long to be accommodated within the liquidity of fuel oil references. The main alternative reference used by Asian-based shipping companies is:

- ICE Brent in USD/bbl, based on the daily settlement price of the ICE Brent futures contract.

Americas Region The main references generally used by shipping companies for risk management purposes are published by Platts:

- Fuel Oil 1% US New York Harbour Cargoes (NYHC), in USD/bbl.

Shipping companies also use other crude oil and oil product references whenever the volume is too large or the tenor is too long to be accommodated within the liquidity of the fuel oil references. The main alternative reference used by shipping companies based in the Americas is:

- NYMEX WTI (USD/bbl), based on the daily settlement price of the NYMEX WTI futures contract.

1.2.3.3 Risk Management Strategies for the Shipping Industry European and American shipping companies generally adopt less complex hedging tactics compared with the aviation industry and their structures tend to be mostly plain vanilla and for short to medium tenors. As seen for the aviation industry, there are many variables affecting the implementation of a risk management programme. There are also some shipping-industry-specific elements that should be considered.

1. Many shipping companies are privately owned and managed by the founder or the founder's successors. This often makes the decision process cumbersome and sub-optimal when implementing risk management decisions.
2. Shipping customers can be divided broadly into owners and charterers, where owners buy ships and rent them on short- or long-term leases to charterers. The fuel costs are borne by the company operating the ship. Hence, owners generally have no exposure to oil prices since this is paid by the charterers operating the ships. Sometimes shipping companies are structured into two divisions, one operating as an owner and the other as a charterer.
3. For insurance, tax and liabilities management reasons, shipping companies are often divided into management and operational subsidiaries. This may make the process of opening a credit line for trading purposes difficult due to the perceived weakness of the counterpart from the credit point of view.
4. Based on observations of the behaviour of market participants, some generic conclusions on risk management behaviour can be drawn.
5. Small to medium shipping companies (e.g., with a yearly consumption of up to 250,000 MT of fuel oil) tend to implement and execute risk management strategies with the following characteristics:
   (a) Short to medium maturities (e.g., less than two years).
   (b) Mainly based on the use of swaps.
   (c) Limited exposure to basis risk.

6. Medium to large shipping companies (with a consumption of 250,000 MT and above) generally have a dedicated team for the structuring, implementation and execution of a hedging programme, and their strategies have the following characteristics:
   (a) Short to long maturities (up to five years), depending on the product they use (e.g., short maturities for fuel oil quotes and long maturities for crude oil quotes).
   (b) Use of a combination of swaps, plain vanilla options and exotic structures.
   (c) Active management of basis risk.
7. On a regional basis, European and American shipping companies tend to use exotic structures less compared with Asian-based shipping companies.

Fuel Oil Capped Swaps: A Cheaper Swap *Situation.* A containers shipping company, call it SeaHorse, has a strategic hedging programme in place where one of the provisions is that at any time at least 75% of the forecasted bunker consumption over the next 12 months needs to be at a fixed price at a level not higher than 10% of the budgeted bunker price for the calendar year (see Figure 1.6). SeaHorse's forecasted consumption over the next 12 months is 500,000 MT. The budgeted bunker price for the next calendar year is 325$/MT, and the swap price for bunker (using a 3.5% Fuel Oil FOB Barges reference) for the next calendar year is 375$/MT.

Strategy. SeaHorse buys a swap for the next calendar year on a Fuel Oil 3.5% FOB Barges reference for 500,000 × 75%/12 = 31,250 MT per month at $375/MT and at the same time sells a call option for the next calendar year on Fuel Oil 3.5% FOB Barges at 475$/MT for 25$/MT. The premium of the option is deducted from the level of the swap. Hence, SeaHorse has effectively entered into a swap at 350$/MT (capped at 475$/MT). This is within the 325 + 10% = 357.5$/MT limit defined by the hedging policy.

Pros. SeaHorse has reached its targeted hedging level (as long as the market does not move above the call strike level).

Cons. As a result of selling the call option, SeaHorse loses the protection of the swap whenever the market settles above the strike level of the call option. It is important to remember that the customer is not completely losing its price protection, since even in the event that the fuel oil market moves above the strike level of the call option, SeaHorse will benefit from a

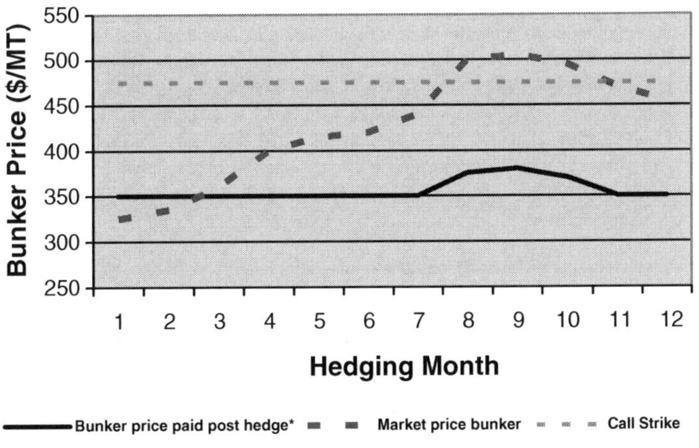

FIGURE 1.6 Fuel oil capped swap

cash flow from the risk management structure equal to the difference between the call option's strike and the swap level.

Payoff analysis Swap and option markets situation on 1 June 2014:

FO 3.5 FOB swap ($/MT)	FO 3.5 FOB call @ 475 ($/MT)
Jan15–Dec15	
375	25

SeaHorse buys a January 2015 to December 2015 fuel oil 3.5% barges swap at 375$/MT and SeaHorse sells a call option on fuel oil 3.5% barges for the period January 2015 to December 2015 at a strike of 475$/MT for 25$/MT.

The average fuel oil price during February 2015 is 330$/MT:

FO 3.5 FOB swap ($/MT)	FO 3.5 FOB call @ 475 ($/MT)
Feb15	
–45	Premium +25$/MT

SeaHorse pays 330$/MT to its physical supplier but also has to pay 45$/MT from the swap and receives +25/MT from the option's premium. The actual cost of fuel for SeaHorse is then 330 + 45 – 25 = 350$/MT.

The average fuel oil price during May 2015 is 405$/MT:

FO 3.5 FOB swap ($/MT)	FO 3.5 FOB call @ 475 ($/MT)
May15	
+30	Premium +25$/MT

SeaHorse pays 405$/MT to its physical supplier but receives +30$/MT from the swap and +25$/MT from the option's premium. The actual cost of fuel for SeaHorse is 405 – 30 – 25 = 350$/MT.

The average fuel oil price during August 2011 is $495/MT:

FO 3.5 FOB swap ($/MT)	FO 3.5 FOB call @ 475 ($/MT)
Aug11	
+120	Premium +25$/MT Settlement –20$/MT

SeaHorse pays 495$/MT to its physical supplier but receives +120$/MT from the swap and +25$/MT from the option's premium. SeaHorse also pays 20$/MT from the call option being exercised. The actual cost of fuel for SeaHorse is 495 – 120 – 25 + 20 = 370$/MT (e.g., above the target level but still cheaper than the market price).

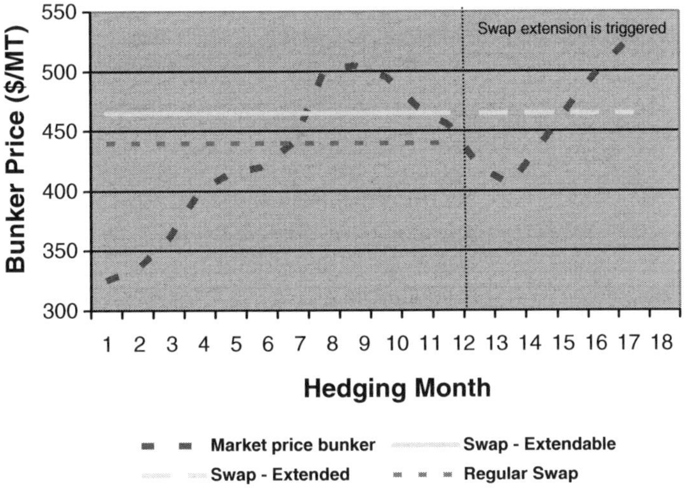

FIGURE 1.7 ICE Brent extendable swap

Brent Extendable: Accommodating Operational Issues *Situation.* SeaHorse has entered into a contract to transport goods for a customer from Hong Kong to Los Angeles. The contract is at a fixed price for one year with an option (for the customer) to extend it for another six months at the same rate (see Figure 1.7). SeaHorse is exposed to the bunker's price volatility (priced on a Singapore 380 IFO reference) and would like to lock in the profitability of the contract by locking the bunker's cost with a structure reflecting the potential time extension feature.

Strategy. SeaHorse can enter into an extendable swap structure on Singapore 380 where it would fix the price for a period of 12 months at a certain level with the right (to be exercised by SeaHorse before the end of the 12th month) to extend the maturity of the swap by an extra six months at the same level as that of the original 12-month structure. SeaHorse will exercise the option back to back, with its customer exercising its right to extend the shipping contract.

Pros. SeaHorse is able to match the risk deriving from the potential extension of the contract with a swap matching the extendibility of the shipping contract. In case the shipping contract is not extended beyond the 12th month, SeaHorse will not extend the swap and has no further obligations under the swap.

Cons. There is a cost associated with granting optionality to extend the swap beyond the 12th month for an extra six months. This cost is embedded in the level of the swap. Hence, a 'regular' 12-month swap will be at a better level compared with a 12-month swap with the option to extend for an extra six months.

1.2.4 Land Transportation: Risk Profile and Hedging Strategies

1.2.4.1 Introduction: Land Transportation and Exposure to Oil Prices The land transportation industry includes local and national road passenger services, passenger and freight railways, and commercial haulage. The economics are similar to that seen in the sections dedicated to the shipping and aviation industries, although the indexes used for risk

TABLE 1.3 Diesel sulphur content breakdown

	Sulphur content (ppm)
High-sulphur diesel	ppm > 500 (ppm > 0.05% by weight)
Low-sulphur diesel	15 < ppm < 500 (0.0015% < ppm < 0.05% by weight)
Ultra-low-sulphur diesel (ULSD)	10 < ppm < 15 (0.0010% < ppm < 0.0015% by weight)
Sulphur-free diesel	ppm < 10 (ppm < 0.0010% by weight)

management purposes are different. The oil products relevant to this industry are those used as fuel for the engines of buses, trucks and train engines, that is, diesel and occasionally gasoline.

Diesel is essentially the same product as gasoil, and from a practical standpoint there are only a few differences:

1. Diesel fuel, for road use, has a lower sulphur content than gasoil.
2. Gasoil is dyed with red dye.
3. During winter months, diesel fuel is cut or diluted with kerosene to improve its performance.

Demand for gasoline and diesel has a certain seasonality and tends to peak in summer during the so-called 'driving season'. *Diesel fuel* is the term used for fuels suitable for compression engines, also known as diesel engines, developed by Rudolph Diesel in 1892. Compression engines operate at a much higher pressure than gasoline engines and function without a spark plug. Diesel engines also offer the following advantages when compared with gasoline engines:

1. Diesel gets a higher mileage per gallon (20–30%) due to high compression and energy density.
2. Diesel, being a heavier hydrocarbon, has a higher energy content.
3. Diesel fuel is burned in a high-pressure/high-temperature environment, resulting in more efficient burning compared with gasoline.
4. Diesel engines are structurally easier to maintain and have a longer lifespan than gasoline engines.

The main feature examined when discussing and identifying diesel fuel with a customer is its sulphur content, identified in ppm. See Table 1.3.

Motor gasoline is the result of blending hydrocarbons from the naphtha family. The key specifications for gasoline are its octane rating, volatility, aromatics, olefins, lead and methyl tertiary butyl ether (MTBE) content.

1.2.4.2 Product Specifications The main oil references generally used by land transportation companies for risk management purposes are published by Platts and Argus.

Europe, Middle East and Africa Regions

1. ULSD 10 ppm CIF NWE (USD/MT).
2. Diesel 10 ppm Barges FOB ROT (USD/MT).

3. 10 ppm ULSD FOB MED Cargoes (USD/MT).
4. 50 ppm ULSD FOB MED Cargoes (USD/MT).
5. ULSD 10 ppm CIF MED Cargoes (USD/MT).
6. Gasoline Euro Bob Oxy NWE Barges (USD/MT).
7. Premium unleaded gasoline10 ppm Cargoes CIF NWE (USD/MT).
8. Premium unleaded gasoline 10 ppm Cargoes FOB NWE (USD/MT).
9. Premium unleaded gasoline 10 ppm Cargoes FOB MED (USD/MT).
10. Premium unleaded gasoline 10 ppm FOB Barges ARA (USD/MT).

Asian Region

1. Singapore Mogas 92 unleaded Mean of Platts Singapore (MOPS, in USD/bbl).
2. Singapore Gasoil Reg 0.5% Sulphur (USD/bbl).

Americas Region

1. ULSD US Gulf Coast (USGC) pipeline (USDc/gal).
2. Gasoline Reformulated Blendstock for Oxygenate Blending (RBOB) (based on the daily settlement price of the NYMEX gasoline futures contract, (USDc/gal)).

1.2.4.3 Risk Management Strategies for the Land Transportation Industry The land transportation industry can be divided into two subsections:

1. Regulated business, including metropolitan and some regional bus companies and regional train companies. These businesses often operate on a long-term concession basis from the government or local authority and operate in a regulated tariff environment. Hence, they need to protect their revenue margin by locking the variable costs (such as fuel) as much as possible. These companies are inclined to have very high hedging ratios for tenors as long as the tenor of the concession. Typical hedging ratios in this scenario are in the region of 75% or more for tenors of anywhere between 3 and 10 years.
2. Unregulated business, including regional and international bus and train passenger companies and road and train goods haulage. These businesses operate with dynamics more similar to those seen for shipping and aviation companies. Their hedging programmes follow the principle of a hedging envelope over a maximum period of five years, and its implementation will be on the back of budgeted fuel prices and fuel price market movements. A typical hedging envelope for a land transportation company is
   (a) up to 75% of expected fuel consumption for one year forward
   (b) up to 50% of expected fuel consumption for two years forward
   (c) up to 25% of expected fuel consumption for three years forward.

Diesel Differentials and Rolling Hedges: Optimizing the Liquidity of Financial Markets
Situation. A regional train company, Railmore, has won a seven-year concession for the London–Cardiff line, operating with diesel trains. The concession has a limited provision for fuel surcharge and Railmore needs to make sure the profit margin built into the concession price is not eroded by potential increases in the price of diesel. The fuel supply contracts are indexed to ULSD 10 ppm CIF NWE with an expected yearly consumption of 120,000 MT. After consultation with hedging counterparts, it becomes clear that there is no financial

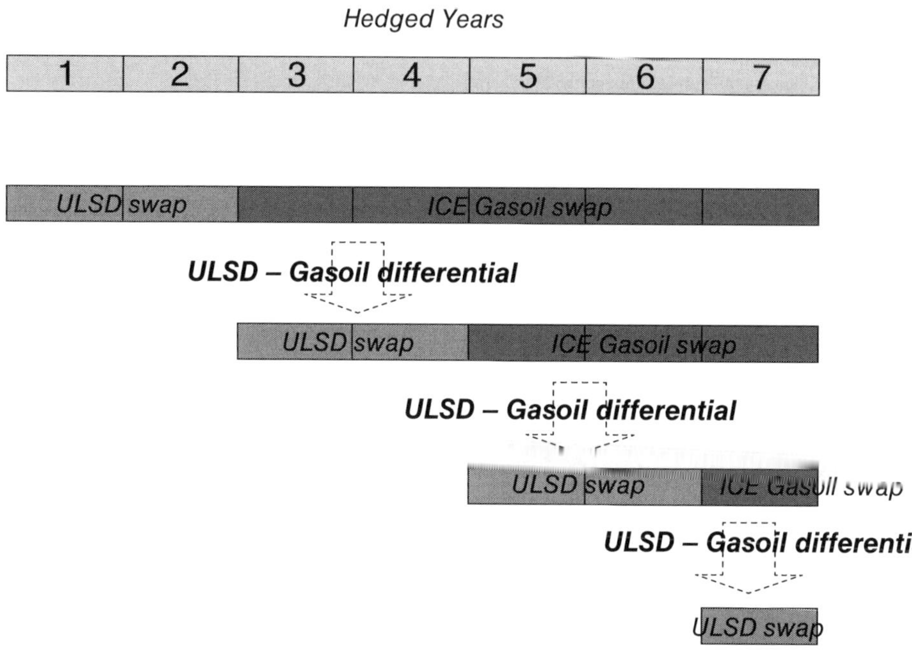

FIGURE 1.8 Rolling hedge structure

derivatives market for that ULSD reference for that tenor. The recommended strategy in this case is to enter into a two-step hedging strategy, also known as a rolling hedge (see Figure 1.8), where the company enters into a long-term hedge based on a liquid index correlated to ULSD 10 ppm CIF NWE (e.g., ICE gasoil) and into a short-term hedge based on ULSD 10 ppm CIF NWE.

Strategy. Railmore will initially enter into two swap transactions:

1. A swap on ULSD 10 ppm CIF NWE for 10,000 MT per month for two years.
2. A swap on ICE gasoil for 10,000 MT per month for five years, starting at the beginning of the third year.

Every month (or quarter) during the life of the hedging programme, Railmore will convert the forward ICE gasoil swap into ULSD 10 ppm CIF NWE swaps by buying the ULSD–gasoil differential (see the second hedging strategy for the aviation industry). This process will be repeated until all the outstanding volumes are covered by the ULSD swap:

$$\text{ULSD CIF NWE swap} - \text{ICE gasoil swap} = \text{ULSD CIF NWE differential}$$

Pros. By tapping the right liquidity pools, Railmore is able to lock in the long-term price level for gasoil, a product highly correlated to ULSD, and in the short to medium term the price for ULSD CIF NWE. Railmore can also take advantage of potentially favourable relative movements of ULSD against gasoil (e.g., a reduction in the ULSD differential). The ULSD price risk is effectively translated into a ULSD differential price risk.

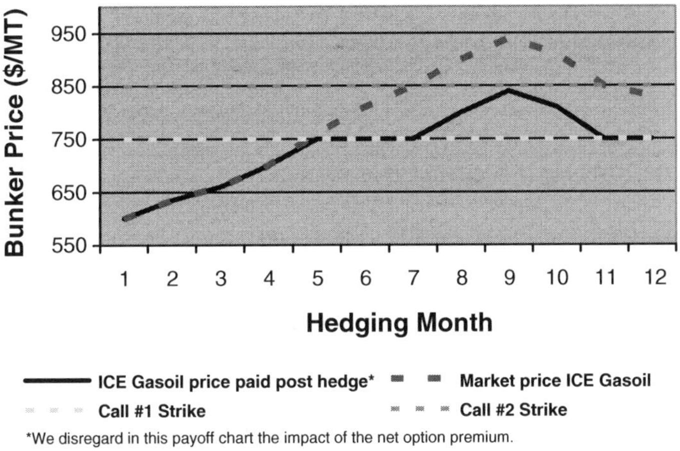

FIGURE 1.9 Gasoil call spread

Cons. This is not a perfect risk management structure, since during the life of the hedge the ULSD differential may move against Railmore (e.g., it may go up), resulting in the erosion of the rail concession contract's profitability.

Gasoil Call Spreads: Reducing the Cost of Option Strategies *Situation.* Railmore also operates a regional bus service and wants to protect against a perceived potential increase in the price of gasoil. The financial director decides against using swaps because the market is in steep contango and the forward levels are perceived to be too high when compared with the spot price of gasoil.

Strategy. Railmore enters into a call spread structure for the next year, where it buys a call option on ICE gasoil at a certain strike (strike #1 = $750/MT) and sells a call option on ICE gasoil at another strike (strike #2 = $850/MT), with strike #1 < strike #2 (see Figure 1.9).

Pros. Railmore gets full protection against price increases above strike #1 and partial price protection against price increases above strike #2. When gasoil prices move above strike #2, Railmore will always receive a net benefit equal to strike #2 – strike #1, compared with a no-hedge situation. The cost of this hedging strategy is lower than the simple purchase of a call option with strike #1 since the premium earned for strike #2 reduces the overall cost of the hedging structure.

Cons. This structure provides only partial market risk protection in case the gasoil markets move firmly above strike #2.

Payoff analysis The option market situation as of 1 June 2014 is as follows: Railmore buys a January 2015 to December 2015 ICE gasoil call at 750$/MT and sells ICE gasoil call at 850$/MT. The net premium paid is –45 + 20 = –25$/MT:

ICE GO +call @ 750 ($/MT)	ICE GO –call @ 850 ($/MT)
Jan15–Dec15	
–45	+20

The average gasoil price during February 2015 is 625$/MT:

ICE GO +call @ 750 ($/MT)	ICE GO –call @ 850 ($/MT)
Feb15	
0	0

None of the call options are exercised. Railmore is effectively paying 625$/MT for its gasoil plus the net premium of 25$/MT for a total of 650/$MT, thus worse than the spot market level.

The average gasoil price during the month of July 2015 is 800$/MT:

ICE GO +call @ 750 ($/MT)	ICE GO –call @ 850 ($/MT)
Jul15	
+50	0

Railmore exercises the option at $750, with the short second option not exercised. It is thus effectively paying 800$/MT for its gasoil plus the net premium of 25$/MT minus the settlement of the option (–50$/MT), for a total of 775$/MT, thus better than the spot market level.

The average fuel oil price during September 2015 is 925$/MT:

ICE GO +call @ 750 ($/MT)	ICE GO –call @ 850 ($/MT)
Sep15	
+175	–75

Railmore exercises the option at 750$/MT, with the short second option being exercised at 850$/MT. It is effectively paying 925$/MT for its gasoil plus the net premium of 25$/MT minus the settlement of the first option (–175$/MT) plus the settlement of the second option (+75$/MT), for a total of 850$/MT, thus better than the spot market level.

1.2.5 Utilities: Risk Profile and Hedging Strategies

1.2.5.1 Introduction: Utilities and Exposure to Oil Prices At the centre of nearly all power stations is a generator, a rotating machine that converts mechanical energy into electrical energy through the relative motion created between a magnetic field and a conductor. The energy source harnessed to turn such generators varies widely and depends chiefly on which fuels are easily available and the types of technology the power company can access.

Utilities have two different kinds of exposure to oil prices; namely, direct on the cost side and indirect on the cost and revenue side.

1. Direct exposure occurs when utilities use oil products as a combustible for power generation in thermal power stations. The fuels used are fuel oil and, to a less extent, gasoil.
   (a) In thermal power stations, mechanical power is produced by a heat engine that transforms thermal energy, produced by the combustion of fuel oil or gasoil generating steam via a boiler, into rotational energy.

   (b) Fuel-oil-based power plants are still used around the world, although due to their high operational costs, low efficiency and high environmental impact, their numbers have been declining over the past 10 years and they are progressively being replaced by natural gas-fired plants.
   (c) Gasoil-based power plants are less common. They are generally small and are typically used as back-up generation capability or whenever there is a need for small generation capabilities in remote areas (e.g., small islands or remote mining operations). In this context, gasoil has higher operational costs than fuel oil and similar environmental impact issues.
2. Indirect exposure occurs when utilities buy or sell gas (pipeline or LNG) or electricity, where prices are linked to oil products. Oil products generally used for energy pricing are fuel oil, gasoil and crude oil.
   - Indirect exposure can come in different shapes and forms. There are many different oil-linked pricing formulas for electricity and gas (pipeline and LNG), often including foreign exchange (FX) components and occasionally factors such as inflation and other macroeconomic indexes.
3. The actual exposure of an average utility company is fairly complex to calculate and represent, because in addition to direct and indirect exposure to oil products, it must also account for exposure to electricity and gas prices not linked to oil products, as well as exposure to fuels other than oil, such as coal and biofuels.

1.2.5.2 Product Specifications

Europe, Middle East and Africa Regions The main oil references generally used by utility companies for risk management purposes are published by Platts and include the following:

1. Fuel Oil 3.5% FOB Barges ARA (USD/MT).
2. Fuel Oil 3.5% Cargoes CIF NWE (USD/MT).
3. Fuel Oil 3.5% Cargoes FOB MED (USD/MT).
4. Fuel Oil 1% FOB NWE (USD/MT).
5. Fuel Oil 1% Cargoes CIF NWE (USD/MT).
6. Gasoil 0.1% Cargoes FOB NWE (USD/MT).
7. Gasoil 0.1% Cargoes CIF MED (USD/MT).
8. Gasoil 0.1% Cargoes CIF NWE (USD/MT).

In most cases exposure to these products derives from the fact that natural gas (used for power generation) is priced in many European markets by using pricing baskets containing the products above.

Utilities also use other crude oil and oil product references whenever the volume is too large or the tenor is too long to be accommodated within the liquidity of fuel oil or gasoil references. The main alternative references used by Europe-based utilities are the following:

1. ICE Brent (USD/bbl), based on the daily settlement price of the ICE Brent futures contract.
2. ICE gasoil (USD/MT), based on the daily settlement price of the ICE gasoil futures contract.
3. NYMEX WTI (USD/bbl), based on the daily settlement price of the NYMEX WTI futures contract.

4. Fuel oil crack (USD/bbl) = fuel oil/6.35 (conversion factor MT to bbl) – ICE Brent.
5. Gasoil crack (USD/bbl) = gasoil/6.35 (conversion factor MT to bbl) – ICE Brent.

Asian Region The main oil references generally used by utility companies for risk management purposes are published by Platts and include the following:

1. Singapore 180 cst (USD/MT).
2. Singapore 380 cst (USD/MT).
3. Singapore Gasoil Reg 0.5% Sulphur (USD/bbl).

Utilities also use other crude oil and oil product references whenever the volume is too large or the tenor is too long to be accommodated within the liquidity of fuel oil or gasoil references. The main alternative references used by Asian-based utility companies are the following:

1. ICE Brent (USD/bbl), based on the daily settlement price of the ICE Brent futures contract.
2. NYMEX WTI (USD/bbl), based on the daily settlement price of the NYMEX WTI futures contract.

Americas Region The main oil references generally used by utility companies for risk management purposes are published by Platts or NYMEX and include the following:

1. Residual fuel oil 1% CIF NWE York Harbour (USD/bbl).
2. NYMEX HO (USDc/gal), based on the daily settlement price of the NYMEX heating oil futures contract.

Utilities also use other crude oil and oil product references whenever the volume is too large or the tenor is too long to be accommodated within the liquidity of fuel oil or gasoil references. The main alternative reference used by Americas-based utility companies is

- NYMEX WTI, based on the daily settlement price of the NYMEX WTI futures contract.

1.2.5.3 Risk Management Strategies for the Utilities Industry Utilities are generally exposed to the full spectrum of energy price risks, from oil to natural gas, from electricity to coal and emissions certificates. They therefore tend to be among the largest and most experienced consumers of risk management products, with dedicated teams and well-defined risk management policies in place. For the purposes of this chapter, we focus only on transactions related to oil and oil product prices.

Gas Formula Swaps: Hedging an Oil Pricing Basket with Swaps *Situation.* A Belgian utility, Distriplus, has a portfolio of long-term pipeline gas supply contracts from Russia and Norway that are indexed to a basket of oil products. The total volume is 10 TWh (terawatt hours) per year, with the following pricing structure:

$$P_{\text{gas}}\,(\text{€c/MWh}) = 0.022 \times P_{\text{GO}} + 0.058 \times P_{\text{FO}}$$

where

- P_{gas} is the price in euro cents per megawatt hour (MWh) in a certain delivery month period
- P_{FO} is the monthly average Fuel Oil 3.5% FOB Barges (in \$/MT) daily settlement price during the P_{gas} delivery month period, published by Platts and converted into euros based on the monthly average of the daily euro and US dollar rates
- P_{GO} is the monthly average Gasoil 0.1% Cargoes FOB NWE (in \$/MT) daily settlement price during the P_{gas} delivery month period, published by Platts and converted into euros based on the monthly average of the daily euro and US dollar rates.

Distriplus pays its gas supplier every month based on the formula above, but for the next calendar year (e.g., 2015) it sells a total of 3 TWh to its customer on a fixed price basis. This exposes Distriplus to the risk that the price paid to the supplier will move above the price received in the fixed price contract.

Strategy. Distriplus will set the fixed price level based on the forward value for 2015 of the formula. The formula will then be hedged by its gasoil, fuel oil and FX components.

Step 1. Calculate the volume equivalents of fuel oil and gasoil for 3 TWh (3,000,000 MWh) of gas:

1. FO = 0.058 × 3,000,000 MWh = 174,000 MT over the calendar year => 14,500 MT per calendar month (pcm).
2. GO = 0.022 × 3,000,000 MWh = 66,000 MT over the calendar year => 5500 MT pcm.

Step 2. Using swaps, Distriplus hedges the underlying fuel oil and gasoil exposure (in euros per MT):

1. FO swap January 2015 to December 2015 for 14,500 MT pcm = 260 €/MT.
2. GO swap January 2015 to December 2015 for 5500 MT pcm = 519 €/MT.

Step 3. The pricing of the swap level for the formula for the period January 2015 to December 2015 is

$$P_{gas} = 0.058 \times 260 + 0.022 \times 519 = 26.50\text{€c/MWh}$$

Pros. Distriplus covers its pricing risk between the floating gas purchase price and its fixed gas sale price and locks in a margin.

Cons. If Distriplus decides not to hedge and the fuel oil and gasoil prices become cheaper during the life of the contract, Distriplus would be able to make a potentially larger margin.

1.2.6 Refineries: Risk Profile and Hedging Strategies

1.2.6.1 Introduction: What is a Refinery? In its basic structure, a refinery operation is composed of a distillation column (atmospheric or vacuum), where crude oil enters and the exiting oil products are gases (e.g., butane), gasoline, naphtha, kerosene, gasoil, fuel oil and residues. The distillation process is generally referred to as separation and it is the first step in the refinery process.

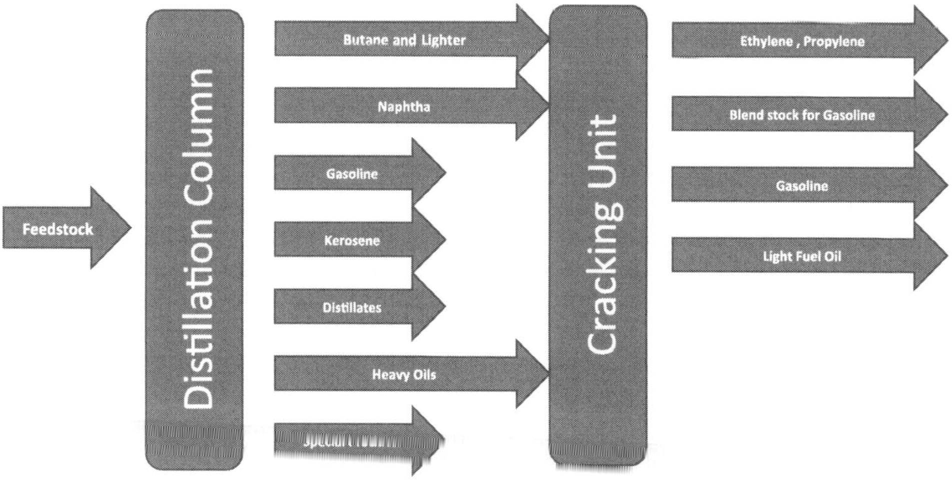

FIGURE 1.10 Distillation + cracking refinery

The section on crude oil and oil products at the beginning of this chapter shows the basic structure of a distillation column, but most modern refineries are more complex in structure than a simple distillation column. This is because over the years production technologies have been developed to maximize the production (yield improvement) of high-value products such as gasoline and jet fuel, as opposed to low-value products such as fuel oil and bitumen.

One of the most common ways of improving a refinery's yield is to extend the distilling column refining process with a 'cracking' process (see Figure 1.10). This involves processing naphtha, some light products and the heavy products produced by the distilling column with heat and pressure (thermal cracking) and/or placing them in contact with a catalyst (a chemical substance that facilitates a reaction) to promote cracking (catalytic, or cat cracking). The output of this process is the production of more gasoline, better quality fuel oil and light products for the petrochemical production process.

A variation and improvement of the cat cracking process is the hydrocracking process (see Figure 1.11). This involves technology similar to that in cat cracking, but with the addition

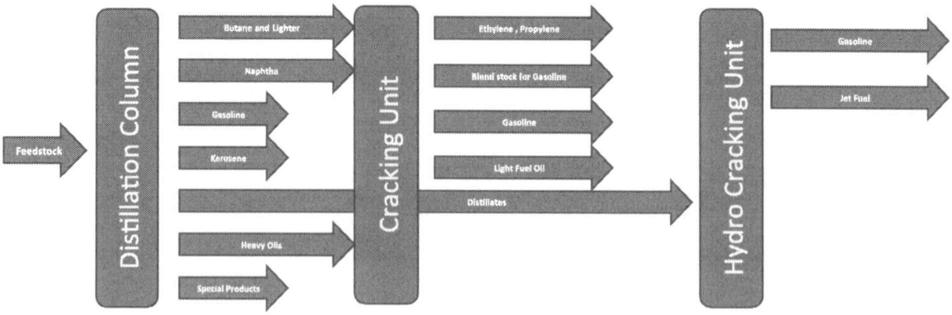

FIGURE 1.11 Distillation + cracking + hydro refinery

of hydrogen. This further improves the yield in terms of the production of gasoline and other high-end products (such as jet fuel).

The cracking process is part of the conversion process. The following are other elements of the conversion process:

1. Coking, a thermal cracking process specifically for the heavy-residue products of the refinery that yields additional naphtha, gasoline blend stock and coke (a product used as fuel in energy-intensive industries).
2. Combining and modifying, another process aimed at creating high-value-added products but this time by joining together smaller hydrocarbon molecules to produce larger, more valuable ones.

After the conversion, there are further steps in the refinery process:

1. Treatment/enhancement, involving the removal or reduction of unwanted elements such as sulphur and nitrogen.
2. Blending, where several semi-finished products are blended together to meet certain market specifications; for example, blending straight-run gasoline with other high-octane products to obtain a gasoline ready to be sold at the pump.

Oil refineries are large-scale plants, processing from about a hundred thousand to several hundred thousand barrels of crude oil per day. Because of their high capacity, many of the units are operated continuously at steady state, or approximately steady state, for long periods of time (from months to years). This high capacity also makes process optimization and advanced process control very desirable.

Refineries with secondary processing units typically have two modes of operation:

1. Maximum production of gasoline in the summer, during the so-called driving season.
2. Maximum production of middle distillates in the winter, during the so-called heating season.

All oil refineries are configured differently, according to the product needs and seasonality of their target market and according to the slate of crude oil feedstock they will likely end up buying. Complex, modern and large refineries can produce large amounts of gasoline and kerosene from heavy oil crude, while smaller, older refineries cannot produce as much high-value products from the same barrel of crude oil.

1.2.6.2 Product Specifications Refineries, by their very nature, are active across the full spectrum of oil and refined oil products, and the lists below present only the most active references at the time of this writing.

Europe, Middle East and Africa Regions The main oil references generally used by refineries for risk management purposes are the following and are published by Platts, Argus or are referenced to ICE futures contracts:

1. Fuel Oil 3.5% FOB Barges ARA (USD/MT).
2. Fuel Oil 3.5% Cargoes CIF NWE (USD/MT).

3. Fuel Oil 3.5% Cargoes FOB MED (USD/MT).
4. Fuel Oil 1% FOB NWE (USD/MT).
5. Fuel Oil 1% Cargoes CIF NWE (USD/MT).
6. Gasoil 0.1% Cargoes FOB NWE (USD/MT).
7. Gasoil 0.1% Cargoes CIF MED (USD/MT).
8. Gasoil 0.1% Cargoes CIF NWE (USD/MT).
9. ULSD 10 ppm CIF NWE (USD/MT).
10. Diesel 10 ppm FOB NWE (USD/MT).
11. Diesel 10 ppm Barges (USD/MT).
12. 10 ppm ULSD FOB MED Cargoes (USD/MT).
13. 50 ppm ULSD FOB MED Cargoes (USD/MT).
14. Gasoline 10 ppm Cargoes CIF NWE (USD/MT).
15. Premium Gasoline 10 ppm Cargoes FOB NWE (USD/MT).
16. Gasoline Euro Bob Oxy NWE Barges (USD/MT).
17. Premium Gasoline 10 ppm Cargoes FOB MED (USD/MT).
18. Premium Gasoline 10 ppm FOB Barges ARA (USD/MT).
19. Naphtha CIF NWE (USD/MT).
20. ICE Brent (USD/bbl), based on the daily settlement price of the ICE Brent futures contract.
21. ICE gasoil (USD/MT), based on the daily settlement price of the ICE gasoil futures contract.
22. Urals MED (USD/bbl) based on the Platts assessment.

Asian Region The main oil references generally used by refineries for risk management purposes are the following and are published by Platts or are referenced to ICE, Dubai Mercantile Exchange (DME) or NYMEX futures contracts:

1. Singapore 180 cst (USD/MT).
2. Singapore 380 cst (USD/MT).
3. Singapore Gasoil Reg 0.5% Sulphur (USD/bbl).
4. Singapore Kerosene (USD/bbl).
5. Singapore Gasoline 92 Unleaded MOPS (USD/bbl).
6. Singapore Naphtha FOB (USD/bbl).
7. NYMEX WTI (USD/bbl), based on the daily settlement price of the NYMEX WTI futures contract.
8. ICE Brent (USD/bbl), based on the daily settlement price of the ICE Brent futures contract.
9. DME Oman crude (USD/bbl), based on the daily settlement price of the Oman futures contract.

Americas Region The main oil references generally used by refineries for risk management purposes are the following and are published by Platts or NYMEX:

1. Residual Fuel Oil 1% CIF New York Harbour (USD/bbl).
2. NYMEX HO (USDc/gal), based on the daily settlement price of the NYMEX heating oil futures contract.
3. ULSD 15 ppm USGC Pipeline (USDc/gal).

4. Gasoline RBOB (USDc/gal), based on the daily settlement price of the gasoline NYMEX futures contract.
5. NYMEX WTI (USD/bbl), based on the daily settlement price of the NYMEX WTI futures contract.

1.2.6.3 Risk Management Strategies for the Refinery Industry Risk management activity in a refinery is closely linked to the planning of crude oil purchasing and its processing schedule to satisfy both specification and demand with the highest profit. The decision variables are crude oil supply purchase decisions, processing, inventory management and blending over various time periods. The lengths of these periods must be decided upon based on business cycles.

Most refineries are continuously involved in a full range of pricing risk management transactions, from short-term crude oil relative value optimization (more on this in Section 1.3) to short- to medium-term enhancement of the relative value of crude oil versus certain products (refinery crack swaps, similar in concept to the gasoil crack swaps in the section on aviation) to term locking in of the operational margin via the use of refinery margin swaps.

Refinery Margin Swaps: Locking the Forward Margin *Situation.* A refinery in Europe would like to take advantage of the favourable relative forward value of oil products versus crude oil and lock it in using financial OTC swaps.

Strategy. As seen in the previous section, refinery inputs are a blend of several kinds of crude oil and the output is comprised of different oil products. The large number of crude oil and oil products physical references used in the refinery process is unmatched by the relatively limited number of liquid OTC financial swap references. To find an effective hedge structure, the refinery needs to identify what OTC-traded products represent the best proxy for its crude and product slates. For the purpose of this example, we can assume the following.

1. The crude oils' slate supply is all indexed against the ICE Brent futures contract plus (or minus) certain premiums (or discounts).
2. The products' slate output can effectively be represented using the following proxy basket of OTC swaps:
   (a) 20% Fuel Oil 3.5% Barges
   (b) 30% Gasoil 0.1% Cargoes FOB NWE
   (c) 15% Jet Cargoes FOB NWE
   (d) 20% Premium Gasoline 10 ppm Cargoes FOB NWE
   (e) 15% Naphtha CIF NWE.
3. As seen before, the conversion from barrels (volume) to metric tonnes (weight) depends on the specific gravity, or density, of the oil or oil product. The lighter the oil or oil product, the more barrels per tonne. We assume the following conversion factors:
   (a) barrels per MT of fuel oil
   (b) barrels per MT of gasoil and jet fuel
   (c) barrels per MT of gasoline
   (d) 8.90 barrels per MT of naphtha.
4. If the refinery wants to lock in its refinery margin for 2015 for a volume of 100,000 barrels per month, it has to enter into the following transactions:
   (a) Buy a calendar 2015 monthly settled swap on ICE Brent for January 2015 to December 2015 for 100,000 barrels per month.

(b) Sell the following monthly settled swaps for January 2015 to December 2015
- **(i)** 20% × 100,000/6.35 = 3150 MT per month of 3,5% Fuel Oil Barges
- **(ii)** 30% × 100,000/7.45 = 4025 MT per month of Gasoil 0.1% FOB NWE
- **(iii)** 15% × 100,000/7.45 = 2015 MT per month of Jet Cargoes FOB NWE
- **(iv)** 20% × 100,000/8.33 = 2401 MT per month of Premium Gasoline 10 ppm Cargoes NWE
- **(v)** 15% × 100,000/8.90 = 1685 MT per month of Naphtha CIF NWE.

(c) The difference between the values of the crude oil swap and the basket of oil product swaps is the forward crack, which is generally measured in barrels.

Pros. By locking in the forward margin, the refinery is able to reduce the volatility of its operational margin.

Cons. The refinery may miss out on further potential positive movements in the margin level and there is an element of basis risk between the hedging instrument and the actual economics of the refinery that needs to be carefully evaluated and monitored

1.2.7 Industrial Consumers: Risk Profile and Hedging Strategies

1.2.7.1 Introduction: Energy-Intensive Manufacturing and Oil Prices This section discusses energy-intensive manufacturers with direct or indirect exposure to oil prices. These are typically paper mills, steel and aluminium mills, cement mills, ceramic and glass manufacturers, and any other industrial process requiring the production of large amounts of heat or steam. Direct exposure to oil markets comes from using fuel oil in furnaces or boilers or gasoil for localized power generation. Indirect exposure comes from using natural gas priced on a basket of oil products in the industrial process.

1.2.7.2 Product Specifications

Europe, Middle East and Africa Regions The main oil references generally used by manufacturing companies for risk management purposes are published by Platts and include the following:

1. Fuel Oil 3.5% Barges (USD/MT).
2. Fuel Oil 3.5% Cargoes CIF NWE (USD/MT).
3. Fuel Oil 3.5% Cargoes FOB MED (USD/MT).
4. Fuel Oil 1% Cargoes CIF NWE (USD/MT).
5. Gasoil 0.1% Cargoes FOB NWE (USD/MT).
6. Gasoil 0.1% Cargoes CIF MED (USD/MT).

Asian Region The main oil references generally used by manufacturing companies for risk management purposes are published by Platts and include the following:

1. Singapore 180 cst (USD/MT).
2. Singapore 380 cst (USD/MT).
3. Singapore Gasoil Reg 0.5% Sulphur (USD/bbl).

Americas Region The main oil references generally used by manufacturing companies for risk management purposes are the following and are published by Platts and NYMEX:

1. Residual Fuel Oil 1% CIF New York Harbour (USD/bbl).
2. NYMEX HO (USDc/gal), based on the daily settlement price of the NYMEX heating oil futures contract.
3. NYMEX WTI (USD/bbl), based on the daily settlement price of the NYMEX WTI futures contract.

1.3 OIL PHYSICAL MARKET HEDGING AND TRADING

1.3.1 The Actors, Futures and OTC Prices

The implementation of hedging strategies to protect against the movement of oil prices is an issue for many different industrial sectors. Corporate hedging strategies are not homogeneous across industrial sectors, and even within the same industrial sector the hedging strategies are substantially different across market participants, but they are usually implemented by a risk manager operating within a financial or supply department. However, there are other actors besides industrial risk managers active in the energy market. Indeed, we can rely on the presence of at least the following:

1. Speculators who attempt to gain from anticipated changes in the prices of commodities or financial instruments. Speculators aim primarily for a quick profit from a short-term trading strategy.
2. Traders who trade on different oil benchmarks. These traders are focused on gaining from their view. Therefore, they create different positions through a combination of the different derivatives described below.
3. Risk managers who trade the same type of financial derivative products as traders. However, risk managers are dedicated to optimizing the cost and results of their hedging strategies.

Contrary to expectations, risk management is not about the elimination of risk but concerns its management. Financial derivatives provide a powerful tool for limiting the risks that individuals and organizations face in the ordinary conduct of their business. Successful derivative risk management requires a thorough understanding of the principles that govern the pricing of financial derivatives that can save costs and increase returns.

For the sake of simplicity, both traders and risk managers are identified as traders. Traders can build portfolios and strategies by using and combining at least the following instruments:

1. Forwards are agreements where one party promises to buy an asset from another party at some specified time in the future and at some specified price. No money changes hands until the delivery date or the maturity of the contract.
2. Futures contracts are very similar to forward contracts. Futures contracts are usually traded through an exchange, which standardizes the terms of the contracts. The profit or loss from the futures position is calculated every day and changes in this value are paid from one party to the other. Thus, futures contracts involve a gradual payment of funds from initiation until expiry.

3. A swap is an exchange of a fixed price of a crude oil benchmark for a floating average of the same benchmark.
4. An option is an instrument that gives to the holder (buyer) the right to buy or sell a defined underlying at a certain price.

The energy market provides two main opportunities to create a profit:

1. Variations of oil prices – by way of an example, the movement of crude oil from \$80/bbl to \$85/bbl.
2. Variations of the differential, that is, the movement between two different oil benchmarks – by way of an example, the movement of the difference between European crude oil and American crude oil.

As a consequence, any energy underlying is calculated according to the following equation:

$$\text{final price} = \text{futures price} + \text{differential}$$

Thus, traders are generally focused on implementing strategies on flat prices and differentials separately.[1]

The flat prices are mostly traded on regulated markets, based on standardized contracts and defined rules. On the contrary, the differential risk is usually traded on OTC markets, which are based on bilateral negotiations. In these markets, the types of contracts and products traded are defined case by case. The prices are assessed by agencies on the basis of the information provided by different traders.

Futures contracts are usually traded through an exchange on a standardized contract. The most active exchanges are:

1. NYMEX, based in New York.
2. ICE, based in London.

The profit or loss from the futures position is calculated every day and the change in this value is paid from one party to the other. Thus, futures contracts involve a gradual payment of funds from initiation until expiry. This process is managed by a clearing house, which is a financial institution that stands between the parties to ensure that all market participants honour their trade settlement obligations. The clearing house secures market activity by the utilization of a margin methodology based on the following:

1. The initial margin or original margin is the amount necessary to start to trade.
2. The variation margin is the amount paid periodically (generally daily) by the market participant, according to the marking to market of their open position.[2]

---

[1]*Flat price* is a trading term that indicates the overall price of a commodity. The fluctuation between \$80/bbl and \$85/bbl of a futures on crude oil is defined as a flat price variation.

[2]Mark-to-market or fair value accounting refers to accounting for the fair value of an asset or liability based on the current market price of the asset or liability.

The initial margin should be considered the insurance necessary to guarantee the clearing house and its members from variations in price within a trading day. The variation margin is the mechanism necessary to restore the initial margin.

The futures contract is standardized, particularly for the following features:

1. Type of contract (physical or cash delivery).
2. Contract unit (barrel, metric tonnes, gallons, etc.).
3. Underlying (Brent, WTI, gasoil, etc.).
4. Trading hours (between 7:00 p.m. and 5:00 p.m. Chicago time, between 5:00 p.m. and 4:15 p.m. Chicago time, etc.).

Table 1.4 shows the specifications of the two contracts.

Table 1.4 compares the main futures contract. WTI was created on 02/01/1981 in New York by New York Mercantile, which was the first international energy regulated market. In recent years the rivalry between ICE Brent and NYMEX WTI has increased due to:

1. The development of a better electronic platform by ICE.
2. The rise of Far East demand.

However, the two contracts are very similar, except for settlement type. The difference between a physical delivery and a cash delivery is important, particularly for

1. US traders
2. arbitrageurs.

Physical delivery could be a risk for traders who have no physical asset to perform it (such as storage, pipeline capacity, etc.). For this reason, in recent years ICE has developed a WTI cash-settled contract. The futures contract is traded on ICE and, except for the price levels and expiry dates, which equal those of the NYMEX WTI, has the same features as ICE Brent.

Table 1.4 describes the settlement price for a futures contract, which is the closing price of the trading day for the futures, and it is necessary to mark the price of the market futures at the close. The settlement price is the official closing price of the exchange. However, NYMEX and ICE publish several other markers.

A marker is necessary to indicate the price of the futures at a defined period of the day. In this example, ICE Brent futures are characterized by several markers:

1. The ICE Brent futures crude afternoon marker is calculated by the weighted average of trades completed between 4:29 and 4:30 p.m. London time.
2. The ICE Brent futures crude Singapore marker is calculated by the weighted average of trades completed between 8:29 and 8:30 a.m. London time.

Markers represent points of contact between the regulated and OTC markets. The OTC markets are based on bilateral negotiations. In these markets, the types of contracts and products traded should be defined case by case between traders. The prices are

TABLE 1.4 A comparison of contract specifications between ICE Brent futures and NYMEX WTI

Specifications	ICE Brent futures	NYMEX WTI
Trading hours	**UK hours.** Monday to Friday. Open 1:00 a.m. (11:00 p.m. on Sundays). Closed 11:00 p.m. London time. **Chicago hours.** Monday to Friday. Open 7:00 p.m. (5:00 p.m. on Sundays). Closed 5:00 p.m. the following day.	**New York hours.** Sunday to Friday. Open 6:00 p.m. Closed 5:15 p.m., with a 45-minute break each day, beginning at 5:15 p.m. **Chicago hours.** Sunday to Friday. Open 5:00 p.m. Closed 4:15 p.m., with a 45-minute break each day, beginning at 4:15 p.m.
Comparison	**WTI has longer trading hours.**	
Listed contracts	A maximum of 72 consecutive months will be listed. In addition, six contract months comprising of June and December contracts will be listed for an additional three calendar years. Twelve additional contract months will be added each year on the expiry of the prompt December contract month.	Consecutive months are listed for the current year and the next five years. In addition, the June and December contract months are listed beyond the sixth year. Additional months will be added on an annual basis after the December contract expires.
Comparison	**WTI has more listed contracts.**	
Expiration date	Trading shall cease at the end of the designated settlement period on the business day (a trading day that is not a public holiday in England or Wales) immediately preceding either (i) the 15th day before the first day of the contract month, if such 15th day is a business day or (ii) if such 15th day is not a business day, the next one.	Trading in the current delivery month shall cease on the third business day prior to the 25th calendar day of the month preceding the delivery month. If the 25th calendar day of the month is not a business day, trading shall cease on the third business day prior to the last business day preceding the 25th calendar day.
Comparison	**Both contracts have defined expiry dates.**	
Price quotation	US dollars and cents per barrel.	US dollars and cents per barrel.
Daily margin	All open contracts are marked to market daily.	All open contracts are marked to market daily.
Settlement price	The weighted average price of trades during a 3-minute settlement period from 7:27 to 7:30 p.m. London time.	The weighted average price of trades during a 3-minute settlement period from 7:27 to 7:30 p.m. London time.
Minimum fluctuation	\$0.01 per barrel.	\$0.01 per barrel.
Contract security	ICE Clear Europe acts as the central counterparty for trades conducted on the London exchanges. This enables it to guarantee the financial performance of every contract registered with it by its members (the clearing members of the exchanges) up to and including delivery, exercise and/or settlement. ICE Clear Europe has no obligation or contractual relationship with its members' clients who are non-member users of the exchange markets or non-clearing members of the exchanges.	The CME Clearing House acts as the central counterparty for trades conducted on the CME exchanges. This enables it to guarantee the financial performance of every contract registered with it by its members (the clearing members of the exchanges) up to and including delivery, exercise and/or settlement. The CME Clearing House has no obligation or contractual relationship with its members' clients who are non-member users of the exchange markets or non-clearing members of the exchanges.
Comparison	**No difference**	
Settlement type	Cash	Physical

assessed by agencies on the basis of the information provided by different traders. The main agencies are

1. Platts
2. Argus
3. ICIS Heren.

The prices are calculated according to the methodology published on these agencies' respective websites.[3]

Of these agencies, the most important for crude oil and oil product assessment is Platts. Platts has defined a methodology called market on close (MOC). According to this methodology, Platts calculates the price of each commodity, considering the value of the physical cargo and derivatives traded during a defined period of the day. It is not the goal of this chapter to describe this calculation. However, the methodology is fundamental in pricing each physical and derivative contract based on an OTC benchmark.

Platts calculates its assessments during three defined periods:

1. The Singapore window, between 8:00 and 8:30 London time.
2. The European window, between 16:00 and 16:30 London time.
3. The US window, between 19:00 and 19:30 London time.

The MOC methodology provides an assessment based on the market condition of the futures market at the end of the window period. For this reason ICE decided to launch a series of their markers, the main ones of which were introduced above.

1.3.2 The Most Commonly Used Financial Instruments

Energy markets and financial markets have the following instruments in common, which are the most frequently utilized in trading strategies:

1. Futures traded in regulated markets.
2. Swaps traded in OTC markets.
3. Options.

The use of options is mainly a feature of risk manager strategies, which were considered previously. Trader strategies based on options are not a matter of concern for this chapter.

The distinction between futures and swaps is fundamental to evaluate the different trading strategies that could be selected. A swap agreement is a derivative where two counterparties exchange one stream of cash flows against another stream, calculated by reference to an underlying (e.g., a securities index, bond currencies, interest rates, commodities and even more intangible items). A swap represents a customized financial instrument that allows the

[3]The assessment methodologies of Platts, Argus and ICIS Heren are published at www.platts.com, www.argusmedia.com and www.icis.com, respectively.

trader to open a position on a quantity or a benchmark that is not possible to execute in the futures market. The underlying of the swap could be:

1. One of the futures markers indicated above.
2. One of the prices assessed and released by the agencies (Platts, Argus or ICIS Heren).

Traders combine futures and swaps with different underlyings to implement their strategies and maximize profit based on their market view. The combinations differ according to

1. Crude oil trader strategies.
2. Product trader strategies.

The differences are related to the different parts of the industry involved with crude oil and oil products. Crude oil is a commodity important for

1. Arbitrage.
2. Storage.
3. Refinery operations.

Oil products are important for

1. Arbitrage.
2. Storage.
3. Petrochemicals.
4. Utilities.
5. Automotive companies.
6. Industrial sectors.

1.3.2.1 Crude Oil The crude oil markets are characterized by a great number of benchmarks, the main ones being the following:

1. The ICE Brent futures is the benchmark for European crude oil markets and it is listed on the ICE exchange in London. The future contracts traded are monthly based. The contract does not settle with physical delivery.
2. The NYMEX WTI future is the benchmark for the US crude oil markets and is listed on the NYMEX in New York. The future contracts traded are monthly based. The contract settles with physical delivery.
3. The BFOE 21 days is a physical forward contract traded on the OTC markets of the North Sea.[4] The contract is similar to a futures and settles with physical delivery.
4. Dated Brent is the main benchmark for the OTC European, African and Mediterranean crude oil markets.

[4]21-day BFOE involves the actual cash market trade in the cheapest-to-deliver crude from the Brent, Forties, Osenberg and Ekofisk market. This historically was Brent itself, but that has changed with time to make Forties the cheapest-to-deliver crude oil more often than not. The 21-day BFOE index is used to compile the Brent Index on a daily basis and then used to cash-settle the Brent futures contract.

5. Exchange for physical (EFP) is a price that indicates the difference between the ICE Brent futures and the BFOE of the same delivery.
6. Dated to frontline (DFL) implies a differential between the daily Platts Dated Brent assessment for dated or physical cargoes and the ICE settlement for the front-month ICE futures for that day.
7. A contract for difference (CFD) implies a differential between the daily Platts Dated Brent assessment for dated or physical cargoes and the BFOE daily Platts assessment for that day.

The following equations are fundamental to understanding the trading strategies implemented in the European crude oil markets:

$$\begin{aligned}&\text{Dated Brent} = \text{BFOE}_{\text{t1}} + \text{differential}\\&\text{BFOE}_{\text{t1}} = \text{ICE Brent}_{\text{t1}} + \text{EFP}_{\text{t1}}\\&\text{Dated Brent swap}_{\text{t1}} = \text{ICE swap Brent}_{\text{t1}} + \text{DFL}_{\text{t1}}\end{aligned}$$

The Brent frontline swaps are calendar monthly swaps based on the ICE Brent futures contract. The swap is calculated using mean-adjusted values for the number of trading days, and each futures contract spends as the front month. This is done by calculating the exact number of trading days within each month, which varies according to the calendar month:

$$\text{ICE swap}_{\text{t1}} = (\text{ICE Brent futures}_{\text{t2}} \times g1 + \text{ICE Brent futures}_{\text{t3}} \times g2)/G$$

where $g1$ is the number of business days between the start of the month and the day before the expiry of the first line, $g2$ is the number of business days between the day before the expiry of the first line and the end of the month, and G is the total number of business days in the month $(g1 + g2)$.

Below is an example of an ICE Brent swap relating to June 2014.

The June 2014 swap is made up of 21 business days. The expiry date of the ICE Brent future is 13 June 2014 and the delivery month is July 14 (June 14 + 1). The first line from 16 June to the end of the month is August 14 (June 14 + 2). Here ICE Brent July 14 is the first line for 10 business days and ICE Brent August 14 is the first line for 11 business days. On the basis of the rule on the expiry date of the futures introduced above, we have to consider ICE Brent August and not ICE Brent July; therefore, there are 9 business days relating to ICE Brent July and 12 to ICE Brent August.

On the basis of the above, the following equation is obtained:

$$\text{ICE swap June 14} = (\text{ICE Brent future July 14} \times 9 + \text{ICE Brent future August 14} \times 12)\,/21$$

where $g1 = 10$, the number of business days between the start of the month and the day before the expiry of the first line; $g2 = 12$, the number of business days between the day before the expiry of the first line and the end of the month; and $G = (10 + 12) = 22$, the total number of business days in the month.

Suppose that:

1. The ICE Brent July 14 price is \$79.04/bbl.
2. The ICE Brent August 14 price is \$80.80/bbl.

Then the price of ICE Brent June 14 may be calculated as follows:

$$\text{ICE swap June 14} = (\$79.04/\text{bbl} \times 9 + \$80.80/\text{bbl} \times 12)/21 = 80.04\$/\text{bbl}$$

The ICE Brent swap is necessary to calculate the Dated Brent swap on the average of the month. To obtain the Dated Brent swap, the trader has to add the DFL to the ICE Brent swap, as indicated in the equation

$$\text{Dated Brent swap}_{t1} = \text{ICE Brent swap}_{t1} + \text{DFL}_{t1}$$

1.3.2.2 Products The product markets are characterized by too many different benchmarks to be listed in this chapter. The following futures and OTC benchmarks are defined, as utilized in the trading example:

1. The ICE gasoil future is the benchmark for European middle distillates and is listed on the ICE in London. The future contracts traded are monthly based. The contract settles with physical delivery.
2. The NYMEX heating oil futures is the benchmark for US middle distillates and is listed on the NYMEX in New York. The futures contracts traded are monthly based. The contract settles with physical delivery.
3. 10 ppm CIF MED is the main benchmark for the OTC Mediterranean middle distillate markets.[5]
4. The 10 ppm CIF MED differential is the differential between the daily Platts 10 ppm CIF MED assessment and the ICE settlement for the front-month ICE futures for that day.

The following equations are fundamental to understanding the trading strategies implemented in the European crude oil markets:

$$\text{10 ppm CIF MED} = \text{ICE gasoil futures} + \text{differential}$$
$$\text{10 ppm CIF MED swap}_{t1} = \text{ICE gasoil swap}_{t1} + \text{10 ppm CIF MED differential}_{t1}$$

The gasoil frontline swaps are calendar monthly swaps based on the ICE gasoil futures contract. The swap is calculated using mean-adjusted values for the number of trading days, and each futures contract is the front month. This is done by calculating the exact number of trading days within each month, which varies according to the calendar month:

$$\text{ICE gasoil swap}_{t1} = (\text{ICE gasoil future}_{t1} \times g1 + \text{ICE gasoil future}_{t2} \times g2)/G$$

where $g1$ is the number of business days between the start of the month and the day before the expiry of the first line, $g2$ is the number of business days between the day before the expiry of the first line and the end of the month, and G is the total number of business days in the month ($g1 + g2$).

Below is an example of an ICE gasoil swap relating to June 2014.

The June 2014 swap is made up of 21 business days. The expiry date of the ICE gasoil futures is 12 June 2014 and the delivery month is June 14. The first line from 13 June to the

[5] 10 ppm CIF MED means ULSD, a motor engine diesel with a sulphur content of 10 ppm. For the sake of clarity, we will continue to call it 10 ppm CIF MED.

end of the month is July 14 (June 14 + 1). Here ICE gasoil June 14 is the first line for nine business days and ICE Brent July is the first line for 12 business days. On the basis of the rule on the expiry date of the futures introduced above, it is necessary to consider ICE gasoil July and not ICE gasoil June; therefore, there are eight business days relating to ICE gasoil June and 13 relating to ICE gasoil July.

On the basis of the above, we obtain the following equation:

$$\text{ICE swap June 14} = (\text{ICE gasoil future June 14} \times 8 + \text{ICE gasoil future July 14} \times 13)/21$$

where $g1 = 8$, the number of business days between the start of the month and the day before the expiry of the first line; $g2 = 14$, the number of business days between the day before the expiry of the first line and the end of the month; and $G = (8 + 14) = 22$, the total number of business days in the month.

Suppose that:

1. The ICE gasoil June 14 price is \$902.25/MT.
2. The ICE gasoil July 14 price is \$898.75/MT.

The price of ICE gasoil June 14 may be calculated as follows:

$$\text{ICE swap June 14} = (\$902.25/\text{MT} \times 8 + \$898.75/\text{MT} \times 13)/21 = 900\$/\text{MT}$$

The ICE gasoil swap is necessary to calculate the 10 ppm CIF MED swap on the average of the month. To obtain the 10 ppm CIF MED swap, the trader has to add the 10 ppm CIF MED to the ICE gasoil swap, as indicated in the equation

$$\text{10 ppm CIF MED swap}_{t1} = \text{ICE gasoil swap}_{t1} + \text{10 ppm CIF MED differential}_{t1}$$

1.3.3 How to Monitor and Manage Risk

A trader has the opportunity to set his own risk strategy according to the following limits:

1. A stop loss is the level at which a trader has to close a position to avoid further losses.[6]
2. A take-profit strategy is the level at which a trader has to close a position to collect the gains.
3. Value at risk (VaR) calculates the worst expected loss over a given horizon at a given confidence level under normal market conditions. It provides a single number summarizing the organization's exposure to market risk and the likelihood of an unfavourable move. It provides a predictive tool to prevent portfolio managers from exceeding risk tolerances that have been developed in portfolio policies. It can be measured at the portfolio, sector, asset class and security levels. Multiple VaR methodologies are available and each has its own benefits and drawbacks. The three main methodologies are parametric (also called analytical), historical simulations and Monte Carlo simulations. To illustrate, suppose a \$100 million portfolio has a monthly VaR of \$8.3 million with a 99% confidence level.

[6]JP Morgan, *Product and Service Risk Disclosure*.

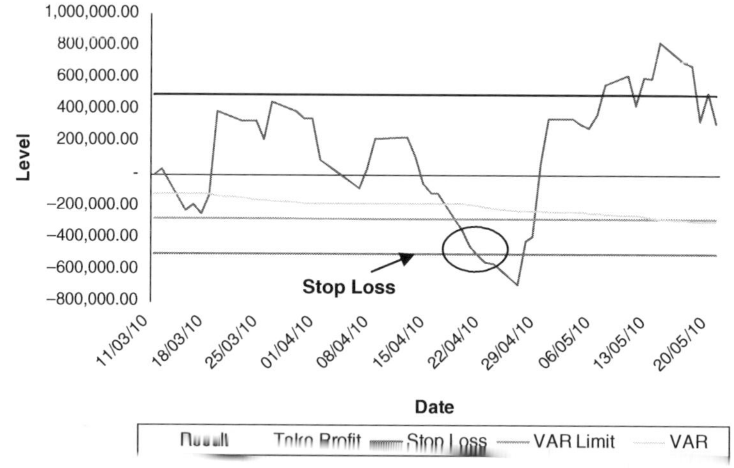

FIGURE 1.12 When the position hits the stop loss, the trader must close the position

The VaR simply means that there is a 1% chance of losses greater than \$8.3 million in any given month of a defined holding period under normal market conditions.[7]

The stop loss is the maximum level of loss that a trader can realize for a position. When the position has lost that amount, the trader must close the position and stop trading (see Figure 1.12).

The profit-taking strategy is the opposite of the stop-loss strategy and involves the level of profit a trader wants to realize for a position. When the position has gained that amount, the trader starts to close out the position and stops trading (see Figure 1.13).

The VaR is a measure of the maximum potential change in value of a portfolio of financial instruments with a given probability over a preset horizon. The VaR answers the question of how much one can lose with an *x*% probability over a given time horizon (see Figure 1.14).

If the position reaches the stop loss and VaR limits, the trader must close the position. The same types of obligation are not applicable when the strategy reaches the profit-taking level.

If the position does not hit any limits, the trader can decide to hold the position or to change it. The trader will decide according to his own view. If he strongly believes that his strategy will generate a profit he will hold it, otherwise he will close it and open another one (see Figure 1.15).

Below we have an example of how a monitoring system should be worked in the case of the following assumed variables:

- Underlying swap position indicated above at –\$0.10/bbl.
- VaR limit of \$275,000.
- Stop-loss strategy –\$500,000.
- Profit-taking strategy +\$500,000.

[7]Romain Berry, *Setting Up a Sound Risk Management Framework*, JP Morgan Investment Analytics and Consulting.

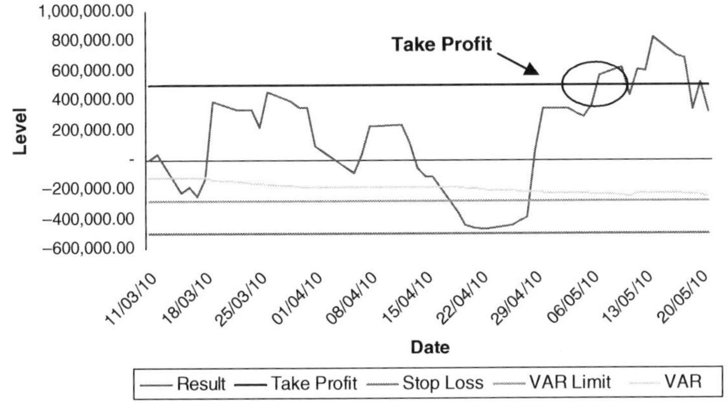

FIGURE 1.13 When the position hits the take profit, the trader must close the position

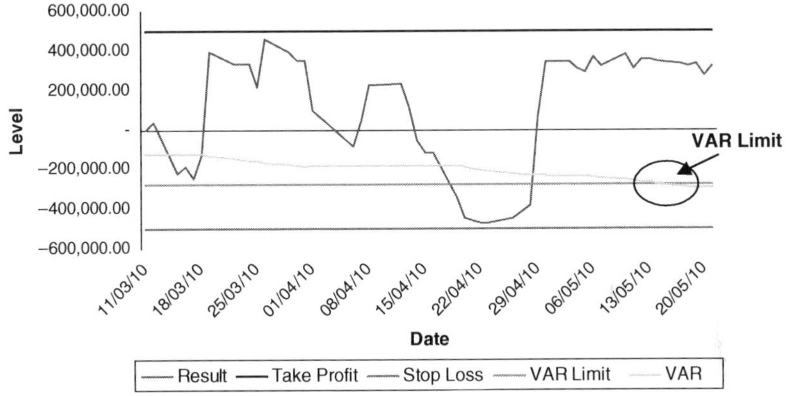

FIGURE 1.14 When the position hits the VaR limit, the trader must close the position

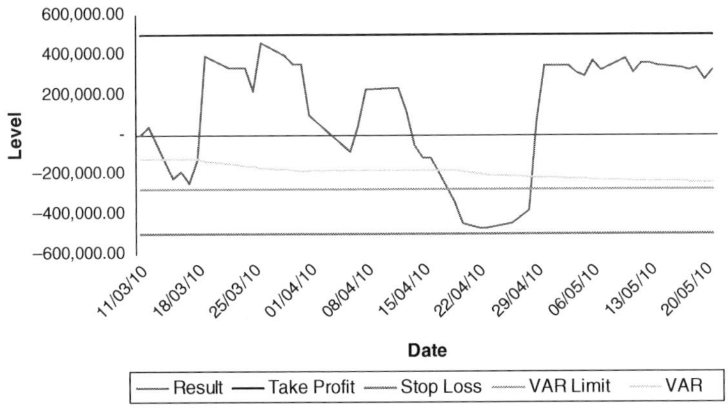

FIGURE 1.15 When the position does not hit any limits, the trader can elaborate another strategy

On this basis, a company can allow a trader to run the risk associated with the following strategies:

1. A wait-and-see strategy.
2. A breakdown strategy.

1.3.4 How to Create a Market View

The variables introduced above are influenced by the demand and supply of crude oil and refined products. The movement of demand is difficult to forecast but it is influenced by the seasons. For instance, the consumption of gasoline usually increases during the summer, with heightened consumer demand for travelling, while the consumption of heating oil is higher in the winter than the summer.

Reductions or increases in supply are easier to forecast because of their direct connection to the oil industry. The production of crude oil, and therefore its supply in the market, should be influenced by the following factors:

1. The decisions of Organization of the Petroleum Exporting Countries (OPEC) and non-OPEC producers to increase or reduce the production of crude oil.
2. The release of strategic reserves (US reserves are called the strategic petroleum reserve, or SPR).
3. Natural events (hurricanes, earthquakes, etc.).

The above example has an impact on the following price differentials:

1. Time spread structure.
2. Differential level.

In the analysis of a time spread, two market situations emerge (Figure 1.16):

1. *Contango*. This is the situation where today's price is lower than that of a subsequent period (weeks or months ahead). This is the classic situation in which an increase in price is expected. It is generally connected to current excess supplies in the physical markets.
2. *Backwardation*. This is the situation where today's price is higher than that of a subsequent period (weeks or months ahead). This is the classic situation in which a decrease in the price is expected. It is generally connected to current excess demand in the physical markets.

The differential level is the movement between two prices related to two different benchmarks or underlyings.

The most well-known differential is the spread between Dated Brent and ICE Brent first line, which is characterized by high volatility as indicated in Figure 1.17.

For instance, if OPEC and non-OPEC producers decide to increase the production of crude oil or the United States decides to release the SPR, the supply of crude oil will increase. The prices of physical crude oil benchmarks will drop and the contango structure will increase, because traders will expect demand to require a certain period to adjust and, as in any other market, if there is an excess of supply, current prices will start to drop.

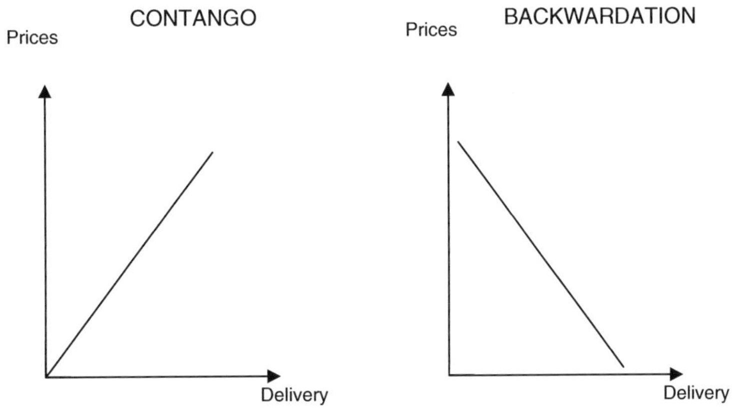

FIGURE 1.16 An example of contango and backwardation

On the contrary, if OPEC and non-OPEC producers decide to reduce the production of crude oil, the United States decides to increase the SPR or a hurricane stops production at the crude oil facilities in the Gulf of Mexico, the supply of crude oil will decrease. The prices of physical crude oil benchmarks will rise and the contango structure will decrease, because traders will expect demand to require a certain period to adjust and, as in any other market, if there is an excess of demand, current prices will start to rise.

The demand for crude oil is mainly influenced by the following:

1. Refinery maintenance, which is the period when a refinery is closed to carry out the maintenance of plants.
2. Refinery runs, which is the percentage of a refinery's total capacity that is active in a certain period.
3. Natural events.

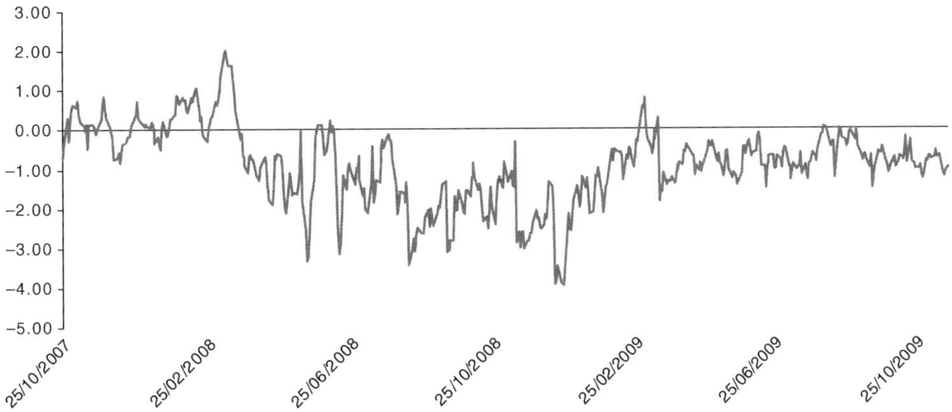

FIGURE 1.17 Sample of spread between the Dated Brent and ICE Brent first line
Source: Reuters.

TABLE 1.5 The main increase and supply events and their impact on crude oil and product prices

	Event	Impact on demand/supply	Price movement
Crude oil	Oil producers increase production	Increase in supply	Reduction
	Refineries reduce runs	Decrease in demand	Reduction
Crude oil	Oil producers reduce production	Decrease in supply	Increase
	Refineries increase runs	Increase in demand	Increase
Products	Refineries increase runs	Increase in supply	Reduction
	Decrease of industrial production	Decrease in demand	Reduction
Products	Hurricane stops refinery production in the Gulf of Mexico	Decrease in supply	Increase
	Increase of industrial production	Increase in demand	Increase

For instance, if US refineries decide to increase the production of products (i.e., the runs increase from 85% to 87%), the demand for crude oil will increase. The prices of physical crude oil benchmarks will increase and the contango structure will decrease, because traders will expect the supply to require a certain period to adjust and, as in any other market, if there is an excess of demand, current prices will start to increase.

On the contrary, if US refineries decide to reduce the production of products (i.e., the runs decrease from 85% to 83%), or decide on an extraordinary period of maintenance or a hurricane stops refinery activity in the Gulf of Mexico, the demand for crude oil in the market will decrease. The prices of physical crude oil benchmarks will decrease and the contango structure will increase, because traders will expect the supply to require a certain period to adjust and, as in any other market, if there is an excess of supply, current prices will start to decrease.

The events set out above affect not only the demand and supply of crude oil but also that of refined products. In addition, the events described have different impacts in different areas. The closure of a refinery in the United States has a strong impact on crude oil demand and the supply of products in the United States whereas the impact in Europe is minor and unimportant in the Far East.

The different impacts in the different geographical areas justify the greater importance of arbitrage trading strategies in the commodity market than in the equity and FX markets. Table 1.5 summarizes the most common events and their impacts on the level of the differentials (physical and swap) and the shape of the forward curve of crude oil prices. For the sake of simplicity, the events are identified as either having a reducing or an increasing effect on prices.

1.3.5 Trading Strategies to Maximize a Market View

1.3.5.1 Introduction This section describes possible trading strategies and how a trader can maximize a market view. The examples are divided as follows:

1. Crude oil hedging and crude oil storage (contango capture) strategies.
2. Arbitrage.
3. Product hedging and product storage strategies.

Each of these examples is introduced by means of a brief description of the hedging strategy involved. The hedging strategy is the right combination of financial derivatives that lets the trader neutralize risk and lock in a certain result. Knowledge of how to minimize or eliminate risk is necessary in order to mitigate effectively against all of the risk that goes against the particular market view.

1.3.5.2 Crude Oil Strategy

Hedging a Physical Crude Oil Cargo *Situation.* On 15 May 2014 a trader buys a cargo of 630 kb crude oil from a producer in the North Sea area.[8] The buy price is the average over June 2014 of the Dated Brent. The sell price of the cargo is 80.04$/bbl.

Strategy. The trader expects an increase in prices and decides to enter into two swap transactions for 630 kb each. The trader fixes the price of the ICE Brent swap (i.e., at 80.04$/bbl) and the DFL (i.e., at –50 cts/bbl). This way the trader locks in a margin against his or her physical operation, as indicated in Table 1.6.

However, the trader can hedge the risk by using a portfolio combination of swaps and futures. According to the equations introduced earlier, the trader knows that

$$\text{Dated Brent swap}_{t1} = \text{ICE Brent swap}_{t1} + \text{DFL}_{t1}$$
$$\text{ICE swap}_{t1} = (\text{ICE Brent future}_{t2} \times g1 + \text{ICE Brent future}_{t3} \times g2)/G$$

Strategy. The ICE June swap is calculated according to the above equation, yielding

$$\text{ICE swap June 14} = (\text{ICE Brent future July 14} \times 9 + \text{ICE Brent future August 14} \times 12)\,/21$$

Therefore, the ICE June swap is comprised of:

1. 270 lots of ICE Brent July.
2. 360 lots of ICE Brent August.

For this reason the trader buys 270 lots of ICE Brent July (i.e., at \$79.04/bbl) and 360 lots of ICE Brent August (i.e., at \$80.80/bbl) for an average buy price of the future of \$80/bbl:

$$\text{June dated Brent swap} = \text{June ICE Brent swap} + \text{June DFL}$$

TABLE 1.6

		COST	PROFIT
Physical		Avg. June 14 of Dated Brent	80.04$/bbl
Hedge	**ICE Brent Swap**	80.04 $/bbl	Avg. June 14 of ICE Brent
			Avg. June 14 of Dated Brent
	DFL Swap	**Avg. June 14 of ICE Brent**	50 cts/bbl
RESULT		**50 cts/bbl**	

[8] 1 kb = 1000 barrels.

TABLE 1.7

		COST	PROFIT
Physical			80.04 $/bbl
	Future July	Avg. June 14 of Dated Brent	
	Future Aug	270 lots @ 79.04 $/bbl	
	Average	360 lots @ 80.80 $/bbl	
		80.04 $/bbl	?
Hedge			Avg. June 14 of Dated Brent
	DFL Swap	Avg. June 14 of ICE Brent	50 cts/bbl
TARGET RESULT		**50 cts/bbl**	

Therefore, the trader buys a fixed swap on June DFL at a price of –0.50 cts/bbl. The portfolio leads to the trader's risk profile indicated in Table 1.7. Without any further action, the trader runs the risk that the average of the June settlement prices of ICE Brent will be lower than $80.04/bbl.

Therefore, during June, the trader will sell 30 lots per day at the ICE Brent settlement price, following the programme indicated in Table 1.8. By selling every day 1/21 of the total 630,000 barrels, the trader will be able to replicate the average of June's ICE Brent settlement prices.

TABLE 1.8

Trade Date	Lots	Expiry Date
02/06/2014	30	July14
03/06/2014	30	July14
04/06/2014	30	July14
05/06/2014	30	July14
06/06/2014	30	July14
09/06/2014	30	July14
10/06/2014	30	July14
11/06/2014	30	July14
12/06/2014	30	July14
13/06/2014	30	Aug14
16/06/2014	30	Aug14
17/06/2014	30	Aug14
18/06/2014	30	Aug14
19/06/2014	30	Aug14
20/06/2014	30	Aug14
23/06/2014	30	Aug14
24/06/2014	30	Aug14
25/06/2014	30	Aug14
26/06/2014	30	Aug14
27/06/2014	30	Aug14
30/06/2014	30	Aug14
Total Lots	**630**	

TABLE 1.9

		COST	PROFIT
Physical		Avg. June 14 of Dated Brent	80.04 $/bbl
	Future July	270 lots @ 79.04 $/bbl	
	Future Aug	360 lots @ 80.80 $/bbl	
	Average	**80.04 $/bbl**	**Avg. June 14 of ICE Brent**
Hedge			Avg. June 14 of Dated Brent
	DFL Swap	Avg. June 14 of ICE Brent	50 cts/bbl
RESULT		**50 cts/bbl**	

In this selling strategy, the average sell prices of the futures are equivalent to the monthly average of June's ICE Brent. The result of this strategy is exactly the same as that presented above, shown here in Table 1.9. For the sake of simplicity, no cost related to futures execution is assumed and it is further assumed that there are no bids or offers for swaps.

Crude Oil Storage or Contango Capture The most common practices are land storage and floating storage. For the sake of simplicity, the following identifies all land storage and floating storage as simply storage.

Storage is the practice of taking advantage of a price differential between two different time periods by using a combination of physical deals, physical facilities (storage or vessels) and derivatives. It is a widespread practice in physical and financial commodity trading. Such deals take advantage of a particular market situation, where there exists an excess of supply in which the spot prices are lower than the forward prices and the shape of the forward curve shows a steep contango. Since a large majority of the risk can be hedged, these deals carry a limited amount of commodity price risk.

For the sake of clarity, the following example does not consider the physical differential of the different crudes but only hedgeable underlyings. Typical storage activity for a cargo of crude oil is described below.

Situation. A trader buys, on 25 June 2014, a crude oil cargo of Forties with a bill of lading (b/l) of 23 July 2014[9] (and stores it for resale on 12 December 2014). The buy price is the average for Dated Brent over the week from 21 to 25 July, the cost of the storage is equal to $2/bbl and the sell price is the average over the month of December for Dated Brent.

The storage cost generally involves:

1. The physical cost to store the crude and rent the tank.
2. The financial cost of paying for the crude oil cargo in July and reselling it in December.
3. Possible loss of crude oil in storing and loading operations (loss).

For the sake of simplicity, these costs are considered to be linear and equal to 40 cts per month; therefore, the total cost from 23 July to 30 December is $2/bbl.

[9] A bill of lading is generated by a shipper; it details a shipment of merchandise, gives title to the goods and requires the carrier to deliver the merchandise to the appropriate party.

TABLE 1.10

		COST	PROFIT
Physical		Avg. Dated Brent from 21 to 25 of July Storage Cost – 2 $/bbl	Avg. December 14 of Dated Brent
Hedge Strategy 1	Dated Brent Swap	80 $/bbl	Avg. Dated Brent from 21 to 25 of July
Hedge Strategy 2	Dated Brent Swap	Avg. December 14 of Dated Brent	83 $/bbl
RESULT		**1 $ bbl**	

As discussed above, the trader executes an operation in the financial market that guarantees opposite flows of the physical contract. On 25 June, the trader executes the following operations:

1. Buys fixed at $80/bbl and sells the average for Dated Brent over the week from 21 to 25 July 600 kb.
2. Sells fixed at $83/bbl and buys the average over the month of December 2014 of Dated Brent for 600 kb.

On the basis of the combined operations above, the trader neutralizes any risk resulting from the fluctuation of prices and locks in a certain result, as indicated in Table 1.10.

In the following example, the market conditions change and the trader is interested in reselling the cargo before December.

Situation. A trader buys, on 25 July 2014, a crude oil cargo b/l 23 July 2014 and stores it for resale on 30 December 2014. The trader has already hedged the cargo but on 25 October 2014 sells it b/l 30 November 2014 because the market conditions are favourable. The buy price is the average month over July for Dated Brent, storage costs equal $2/bbl and the sell price expected is the average over the month of December for Dated Brent, but the sell price realized is the average over the month of November for Dated Brent + $1/bbl. In addition, the storage costs are lower, at $1.60/bbl, because the product is sold one month in advance.

On 25 June the trader executes the following operations:

1. Buys fixed at $80/bbl and sells the average for Dated Brent over the week from 21 to 25 July for 600 kb.
2. Sells fixed at $83/bbl and buys the monthly average over the month of December 2014 of Dated Brent for 600 kb.

On 25 October the trader executes the following operations:

1. Sells fixed at $82.75/bbl and sells the monthly average over the month of November 2014 of Dated Brent for 600 kb.
2. Buys fixed at $83.5/bbl and buys the monthly average over the month of December 2014 of Dated Brent for 600 kb.

TABLE 1.11

		COST	PROFIT
Physical		Avg. Dated Brent from 21 to 25 July Storage Cost – 1.6 $/bbl	Avg. December 14 of Dated Brent
Hedge Strategy 1	Dated Brent Swap	80 $/bbl	Avg. Dated Brent from 21 to 25 July
Hedge Strategy 2	Dated Brent Swap	Avg. December 10 of Dated Brent	83 $/bbl
Hedge Strategy 3	Dated Brent Swap	Avg. November 14 of Dated Brent	82.75 $/bbl
Hedge Strategy 4	Dated Brent Swap	83.5 $/bbl	Avg. December 14 of Dated Brent
RESULT		**1.65 $/bbl**	

On the basis of the combined derivative operations, the trader neutralizes any risk resulting from fluctuations in prices and locks in a certain result higher than the $1/bbl locked in on 25 June. Table 1.11 summarizes the details.

Arbitrage Opportunities: Geographical Arbitrage on Products and Crude Oil The following describes the most important arbitrage possibilities.

Arbitrage is the practice of taking advantage of a price differential between two or more markets by using a combination of physical deals and derivatives. It is a widespread practice in both the trading of financial instruments (especially Forex and international interest rates) and in commodity trading. Such deals take advantage of a particular market situation that presents itself irregularly, in which the commodity markets in a certain area place a higher premium on a commodity than the market in another area. Since a large majority of the risk can be hedged, these deals carry a limited amount of commodity price risk.

Typical major flows of arbitrage on oil-related commodities include the following:

1. Procure gasoil in the United States and move it to/sell it in European markets.
2. Procure crudes in West Africa on a Brent-related price base and sell in US markets at WTI-related prices.
3. Procure middle distillates in the Far East (Japan, Korea) and move them to/sell them in European markets.
4. Procure naphtha or fuel oil in European markets and move them to/sell them in the Middle East or the Far East.

These flows can form, depending on specific circumstances, a significant part of the activities of major oil and trading companies. However, the major flows are changing on the basis of the evolution of the supply and demand of crude oil and products. The following example tries to describe the main problems faced by a trader the moment he or she wants to take advantage of an arbitrage.

The characteristics of arbitrage opportunities are the following.

1. *Limited duration.* Arbitrages, being related to differences in market indices, 'open' and 'close' irregularly, according to the fluctuations of relative markets. Therefore, arbitrage

opportunities require a very rapid approach to lock them in. As an example, the arbitrage between Brent and WTI crudes has exhibited this recent historical trend.

2. *Involvement of multiple factors with different time scales.* A typical commodity arbitrage opportunity involves a physical buy, a physical sale, the structuring of a derivatives hedge/lock-in operation and chartering a ship. All these factors have different time dynamics, as follows:
   - **(a)** The derivatives operation (1) is essentially instantaneous in terms of execution; (2) can span several months and even exceed one year.
   - **(b)** Physical deals can require several days to assemble and must be executed within defined time frames before loading or delivering the cargo (a few weeks for crudes, 5 to 15 days for other products).
   - **(c)** The shipping component can require several days to charter, which is typically done relatively close to the actual date of travel (both in the case of a spot charter and in the case of dispatching a controlled ship, since scheduling is done as close as possible to the actual travel dates). Shipping operations, to an extent, may also be covered with derivatives (through freight forward agreements, or FFAs).

To understand better the hedging scheme connected with arbitrage strategies, we analyse the following:

1. The variables that concur with the result of the strategy.
2. The opportunities of a physical trader who is in charge of selling a cargo of West African Crude oil.
3. The possible result.

In fact, a trader must consider many different variables to implement an arbitrage, as indicated here:

1. ΔWTI = physical differential at which the physical trader sells the cargo in the United States.
2. ΔFOB = physical differential at which the physical trader buys or sells the cargo.
3. Freight = cost of the vessel to deliver the crude oil.
4. Other cost = lightening, loss, etc.
5. Financial cost = cost of the holding storage and FX hedging.
6. Paper result t_0 = for example, the differential at t_0 between Dated Brent and WTI.

For the sake of clarity, a strategy connected with the different geographical benchmarks (i.e., WTI and Dated Brent) is considered here. All other costs are defined just as transportation costs.

Situation. A trader buys, on 25 June 2014, a crude oil cargo of 1000 kb b/l 30 July 2014. The buy price is the average over the month of July for Dated Brent + \$1/bbl (ΔFOB). The trader can choose one of the following strategies:

1. Sell the cargo FOB at the Dated Brent average for July + ΔFOB.
2. Buy the cargo FOB on a Dated Brent basis and sell it delivered to the United States on a WTI basis.

TABLE 1.12

	COST	PROFIT
Physical	Avg. July 14 of Dated Brent + 1 $/bbl	
Physical		Avg. July 14 of Dated Brent + 1.5 $/bbl
RESULT	**0.5 $/bbl**	

In the first case the trader makes a profit if the buy price is lower than the sell price. There is no risk in this operation which could be eliminated with derivatives. The trader knows the quality of his or her own cargo and the demand of the market for that specific crude oil, but there are no derivatives to hedge the physical differentials of the different types of crude oil.

In the second case, the trader obtains a profit if the following holds:

$$(\text{Paper result } t_0) - \text{Transportation cost} + \Delta\text{WTI} - \Delta\text{FOB}_1 > \Delta\text{FOB}_1 - \Delta\text{FOB}_2$$

Situation. A trader buys, on 25 June 2014, a crude oil cargo of 1000 kb b/l 30 July 2014. The buy price is the average month of July for Dated Brent + $1/bbl (ΔFOB). The trader can choose one of the following strategies:

1. Sell the cargo at the Dated Brent average for July + $1.5/bbl (ΔFOB).
2. Sell the cargo in the United States at the price of the NYMEX October WTI of 20 August 2014.

In the first case the trader can lock in a certain margin of $0.5/bbl, as indicated in Table 1.12.

In the following case the trader decides that it is more profitable to deliver the cargo in the United States. Therefore, the trader implements the following trading strategies:

1. Buys fixed at $80/bbl and sells the monthly average over the month of July 2014 of the Dated Brent for 1000 kb.
2. Sells 1000 lots of NYMEX October futures at $84/bbl.
3. Buys 1000 lots of NYMEX October futures at the 20 August 2014 settlement price.
4. Fixes the cost to deliver the crude oil cargo in the United States at $2/bbl.
5. The physical differential at which the physical trader sells the cargo in the United States (ΔWTI) is 10 cts/bbl.

The result of this strategy is $1.1/bbl, which is higher than the 50 cts/bbl obtainable by reselling the crude oil cargo in the area. The results are summarized in Table 1.13.

1.3.5.3 Product Strategy

Hedging a Physical ULSD Cargo *Situation.* A trader buys, on 15 May 2014, a cargo of ULSD 10 ppm of 31.5 kt from a refinery in Italy. The buy price is the average for June 2014 of ULSD 10 ppm CIF MED. The sell price of the cargo is $935/MT.

Strategy. The trader expects an increase in prices and decides to enter into two swap transactions of 31.5 kt each and fixes the price of the ICE gasoil swap (i.e., at $900/bbl) and

TABLE 1.13

		COST	PROFIT
Physical		Avg. July 1 of Dated Brent + 1 $/bbl	
Physical		Transportation Cost 2 $/bbl	NYMEX October WTI 20/08/2010 + 0.1 $/bbl
Hedge Strategy 1	Dated Brent Swap	80 $/bbl	Avg. Dated Brent of July
Hedge Strategy 2	NYMEX Future	1000 lots of NYMEX October WTI @ 20/08/2010	1000 lots of NYMEX October WTI @ 84
RESULT		**1.1 $/bbl**	

the ULSD 10 ppm CIF MED differential (i.e., at $30/MT). In this way the trader locks in a margin against his or her physical operation, as indicated in Table 1.14.

However, the trader can hedge the risk by using a portfolio combination of swaps and futures. According to the equations introduced earlier, the trader knows that

$$\text{10 ppm CIF MED swap}_{t1} = \text{ICE gasoil swap}_{t1} + \text{10 ppm CIF MED differential}_{t1}$$
$$\text{ICE gasoil swap}_{t1} = \left(\text{ICE gasoil future}_{t1} \times g1 + \text{ICE gasoil future}_{t2} \times g2\right)/G$$

Strategy. The ICE June swap is calculated according to the above equation, yielding

$$\text{ICE swap June 14} = (\text{ICE gasoil future June 14} \times 8 + \text{ICE gasoil future July 14} \times 13)/21$$

Therefore, the ICE June swap is comprised of:

1. 120 lots of ICE gasoil June.
2. 195 lots of ICE gasoil July.

For this reason the trader buys 120 lots of ICE gasoil June (i.e., at $902.25/MT) and buys 195 lots of ICE gasoil July (i.e., at $898.75/MT) for an average buy price of the swap of $900/MT:

$$\begin{aligned}\text{June 10 ppm CIF MED swap} &= \text{June ICE gasoil swap}\\ &\quad + \text{10 ppm CIF MED differential June swap}\end{aligned}$$

TABLE 1.14

		COST	PROFIT
Physical		Avg. June of 14 ppm CIF MED	935 $/bbl
Hedge	Average 10 ppm CIF MED differetial	900 $/mt Avg. June 14 of ICE Gasoil 30 $/mt	Avg. June 14 of ICE Gasoil Avg. June of 14 ppm CIF MED
RESULT		**5 $/mt**	

TABLE 1.15

		COST	PROFIT
Physical		Avg. June of 10 ppm CIF MED	935 $/bbl
Hedge	Future June	120 lots @ 902.25 $/mt	
	Future July	195 lots @ 898.75 $/mt	
	Average	**900 $/mt**	?
	10 ppm CIF MED differential	Avg. June of ICE Gasoil	
		30 $/mt	Avg. June of 10 ppm CIF MED
RESULT			**5 $/mt**

Therefore, the trader buys a fixed swap on June 10 ppm CIF MED differential swap at the price of $30/MT. The portfolio gives the trader the risk profile indicated in Table 1.15. Without any further action, the trader runs the risk that the average June settlement price of ICE gasoil will be lower than $900/MT.

Therefore, during June the trader will sell 15 lots per day at the ICE gasoil settlement price, following the programme indicated in Table 1.16. By selling every day 1/21 of the total

TABLE 1.16

Trade Date	Lots	Expiry Date
02/06/2014	15	June14
03/06/2014	15	June14
04/06/2014	15	June14
05/06/2015	15	June14
06/06/2014	15	June14
09/06/2014	15	June14
10/06/2014	15	June14
11/06/2014	15	July14
12/06/2014	15	July14
13/06/2014	15	July14
16/06/2014	15	July14
17/06/2014	15	July14
18/06/2014	15	July14
19/06/2014	15	July14
20/06/2014	15	July14
23/06/2014	15	July14
24/06/2014	15	July14
25/06/2014	15	July14
26/06/2014	15	July14
27/06/2014	15	July14
30/06/2014	15	July14
Total Lots	**315**	

TABLE 1.17

		COST	PROFIT
Physical		Avg. June 14 of 10 ppm CIF MED	935 $/bbl
Hedge	Future June	120 lots @ 902.25 $/mt	
	Future July	195 lots @ 898.75 $/mt	
	Average	**900 $/mt**	**Avg. June of ICE Gasoil**
	10 ppm CIF MED differential	Avg. June 14 of ICE Gasoil	
		30 $/mt	Avg. June of 10 ppm CIF MED
RESULT			**5 $/mt**

31,500 metric tonnes, the trader will be able to replicate the average of June's ICE gasoil settlement prices.

With this selling strategy, the average sell prices of the futures are equivalent to the monthly average over June of the ICE gasoil price. The result of this strategy is exactly the same as that presented above, shown here in Table 1.17. For the sake of simplicity, the costs related to the futures execution are not considered and it is further assumed that there are no bids or offers for swaps.

Product Storage or Contango Capture As we have already seen in the crude oil section, the most common practices are land storage or floating storage. For the sake of simplicity, the following identifies both land storage and floating storage as simply storage.

Below is an example of typical storage activity for a cargo of diesel.

Situation. A trader buys, on 25 June 2014, a diesel cargo with b/l 23 July 2014 and stores it for resale on 30 December 2014. The buy price is the average for 10 ppm CIF MED over July, the cost of storage is equal to $5/MT and the sell price is the average over December for 10 ppm CIF MED.

The storage costs generally comprise the following:

1. The physical cost to store the diesel and rent the tank.
2. The financial cost to pay for the diesel oil cargo in July and resell it in December.
3. Possible loss of diesel in storing and loading operations (loss).

For the sake of simplicity, these costs are considered to be linear and equal to $2 per month; therefore, the total costs from 23 July to 30 December are $10/MT.

As discussed above, the trader executes an operation in the financial market that guarantees opposite flows of the physical contract. On 25 June the trader executes the following operations:

1. Buys fixed at $900/MT and sells the average for 10 ppm CIF MED over July for 33 kt.
2. Sells fixed at $920/MT and buys the monthly average over December of 10 ppm CIF MED for 33 kt.

TABLE 1.18

		COST	PROFIT
Physical		Avg. July 14 of 10 ppm CIF MED Storage cost – 10 $/mt	Avg. Dec 14 of 10 ppm CIF MED
Hedge Strategy 1	10 ppm CIF MED	900 $/mt	Avg. July 14 of 10 ppm CIF MED
Hedge Strategy 2	10 ppm CIF MED	Avg. Dec 14 of 10 ppm CFI MED	920 $/mt
RESULT		**10 $/mt**	

On the basis of the combined operations above, the trader neutralizes any risk resulting from fluctuations of the prices and locks in a certain result, as outlined in Table 1.18.

In the following example, the market conditions change and the trader is interested in reselling the cargo before December.

Situation. A trader buys, on 25 June 2014, a crude oil cargo b/l 23 July 2014 and stores it for resale on 30 December 2014. The trader has already hedged the cargo but on 25 October 2014 sells it b/l 30 November 2014 because the market conditions are favourable. The buy price is the average over July for 10 ppm CIF MED, with storage costs of $10/MT. The sell price expected is the average over December for 10 ppm CIF MED, but the actual sell price realized is the average over November for 10 ppm CIF MED. In addition, the storage cost is lower, at $8/MT, because the product is sold one month in advance.

On 25 June the trader executes the following operations:

1. Buys fixed at $900/MT and sells the average for the 10 ppm CIF MED over July for 33 kt.
2. Sells fixed at $920/MT and buys the monthly average over December for 10 ppm CIF MED for 33 kt.

On 25 October the trader executes the following operations:

1. Sells fixed at $920/MT and sells the monthly average over November of 10 ppm CIF MED for 33 kt.
2. Buys fixed at $915/MT and buys the monthly average over December for 10 ppm CIF MED for 33 kt.

TABLE 1.19

		COST	PROFIT
Physical		Avg. July 14 of 10 ppm CIF MED Storage cost – 8 $/mt	Avg. Nov 14 of 10 ppm CIF MED
Hedge Strategy 1	10 ppm CIF MED	900 $/mt	Avg. July 14 of 10 ppm CIF MED
Hedge Strategy 2	10 ppm CIF MED	Avg. Dec 14 of 10 ppm CIF MED	920 $/mt
Hedge Strategy 3	10 ppm CIF MED	Avg. Nov 14 of 10 ppm CIF MED	920 $/mt
Hedge Strategy 4	10 ppm CIF MED	915 $/mt	Avg. Dec 14 of 10 ppm CIF MED
RESULT		**17 $/mt**	

On the basis of this combination of derivative operations, the trader neutralizes any risk resulting from fluctuations in the prices and locks in a certain result of $17/MT higher than the $10/MT locked in on 25 June. See Table 1.19.

FURTHER READING

Downey, M. (2009) *OIL 101*, Wooden Table Press LLC, New York.

Geman, H. (2008) *Risk Management in Commodity Markets: From Shipping to Agriculturals and Energy*, Wiley Finance, Chichester.

Geman, H. and Amic, E. (2005) *Commodities and Commodity Derivatives: Modeling and Pricing for Agricultural, Metals and Energy*, Wiley Finance, Chichester.

Hermann, L., Dunphy, E. and Copus, J. (2010) *A Guide to the Oil and Gas Industry*, Deutsche Bank, Berlin.

Leffler, W.L. (2000) *Petroleum Refining in Nontechnical Language*, 3rd edn, Pennwell Publishing, Tulsa, OK.

Methodology and Specifications Guide – European Products, Platts.

Methodology and Specifications Guide – Asian Products, Platts.

Methodology and Specifications Guide – American Products, Platts.

CHAPTER 2

Coal Markets and Products

Lars Schernikau

2.1 INTRODUCTION

The world today depends on fossil fuels – oil, coal and gas (in that order of importance) – for over 80% of its primary energy. From the time early humans tamed fire, wood or biomass became their primary energy sources. Coal took over the leading role from biomass during the Industrial Revolution and accounted for over 60% of the world's primary energy by the early 1900s. The current age is often referred to as the 'Oil Age' (or the end thereof), which is somewhat appropriate considering that about 35% of the world's primary energy still comes from oil. However, today about 27% of the world's primary energy and more than 40% of the world's electricity comes from coal. In addition, about 66% of the world's steel is produced using coal (IEA – Statistics, 2012; VDKI, 2006, 2011, 2012) and coal is now expected to overtake oil again as the most important source of energy.

The World Coal Institute already projected a decade ago that coal will again become the primary source of energy in the future (see Figure 2.1). Despite the fact that the illustration may change slightly (especially the gas section) considering the recent shale gas revolution in North America, it does correspond to the global belief that future electricity demand will largely be met by coal as a fuel at least for decades to come.

The world's appetite for energy is still far from being met. Today, about 1.6 billion people (or almost one-quarter of the world's 7 billion inhabitants) are still without access to electricity. Of the remainder, over 2 billion people are dependent on primitive or erratic electricity supply. In 2030, the world's population is expected to have reached 8–9 billion. By then, about 1.4 billion people will still lack access to electricity (VDKI, 2006, 2011). Thus, it is expected that there will be over 1.5 billion new power customers in the next two decades. The international strategy consulting firm The Boston Consulting Group has tellingly named a series of its successful economic consumer studies *The Next Billion Consumers*, indicating the huge growth in demand that the energy industry is facing. The growth in energy demand is primarily driven by non-OECD countries such as China and India (see Figure 2.2).

Handbook of Multi-Commodity Markets and Products: Structuring, Trading and Risk Management. Edited by Andrea Roncoroni, Gianluca Fusai and Mark Cummins.

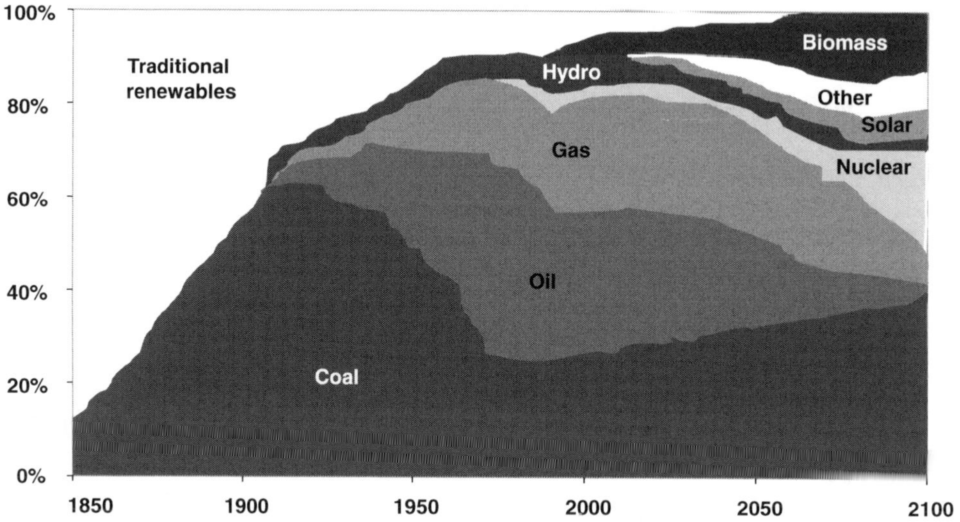

FIGURE 2.1 Historic and future world primary energy mix: scenario 2100
Source: World Coal Institute, www.wci-coal.org.

In the 1990s, certain events and market phenomena created a false sense of energy security in the Western world (see Yaxley, 2006). The Berlin Wall fell, and with it a decades-old enemy system. The victory of the international coalition in the first Gulf War and further European Union expansion deepened the false sense of geopolitical security. There was also a tendency to misinterpret energy policy as an extended arm of climate policy. Politics and modern environmentalism increasingly regarded coal and nuclear energy as a scapegoat. This attitude was coupled with an overestimation of the short- and mid-term potential of renewable energy. Overcapacity in coal, oil and gas led to low fossil commodity prices in the late 1990s and

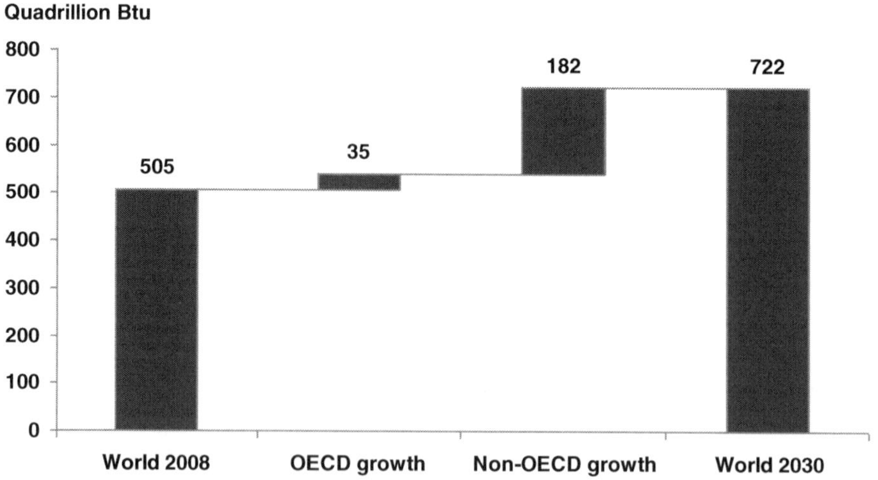

FIGURE 2.2 Comparison of energy demand growth up to 2030: OECD/non-OECD
Source: EIA, 2011. Author's analysis.

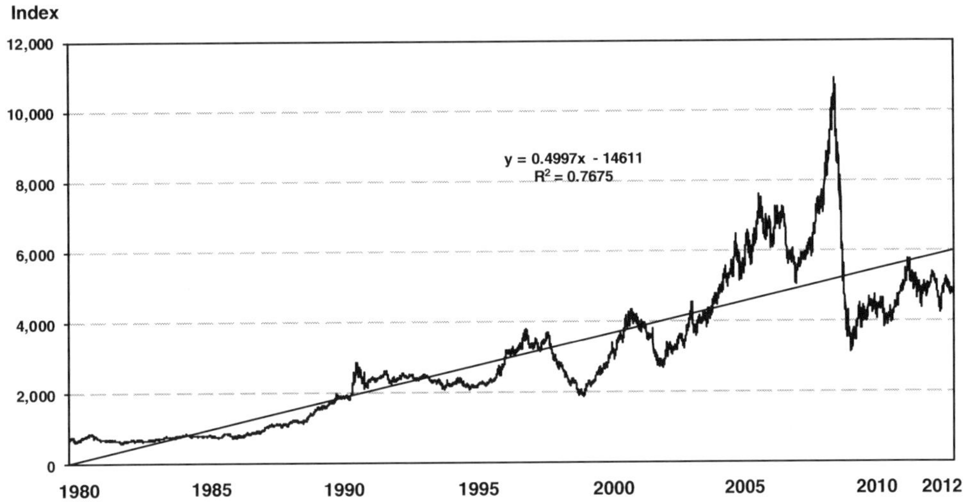

FIGURE 2.3 GSCI development 1980 to 2012
Source: Goldman Sachs Commodity Index, GSCI. Author's analysis.

the early 2000s, which in turn resulted in dangerous oversight of the unequal distribution of resources and the limitation of energy resources in the world. The resulting lack of investment by producers led to false expectations by consumers.

However, the new millennium also brought a set of new circumstances. In the following years, in the beginning of the third millennium, there was a growing need to reassess energy policy and to become aware of the importance of fossil fuels, especially coal, and our reliance on them. The threat of terrorism has increased dramatically, introducing a new type and concept of enemy for the West. Natural disasters such as Fukushima have raised questions about the viability of security of nuclear energy. Also, more political problems and rising instability in supplying countries have shaken the Western world. Oil, coal and gas prices have skyrocketed (even allowing for the price drops in 2008/2009 and 2012/2013), again raising questions about the impact of monopolistic and oligopolistic markets on the world economy and, as a result, the role of governments and protectionism. Renewable energy sources are being re-evaluated and their potential estimated more realistically than in the 1990s. In addition, the Chinese economic boom has affected every aspect of the world economy, including almost all commodities and logistical capacities.

As a result, commodity prices increased sharply (see Figure 2.3) up until the financial crisis in 2008 and have followed a long-term positive trend ever since (despite increased volatility). Along with this, coal prices reached unprecedented levels (see Figure 2.4) in 2008 before correcting in 2009 and then continuing a long-term rising trend.

Today, many voices claim that the commodity boom and with it the coal boom are over. There is no doubt that the abnormally high growth rates of the past 10 years will be a hindrance, but the reader can judge for him- or herself from the References whether the boom and the long-term story are really over.

The world seaborne steam coal market continues to be an interesting and, for the energy economy, a crucial playing field. A lack of investment since 2000 (Kopal, 2007), near-capacity export production and a new breed of market players influencing prices have ensured continued if not increased price volatility.

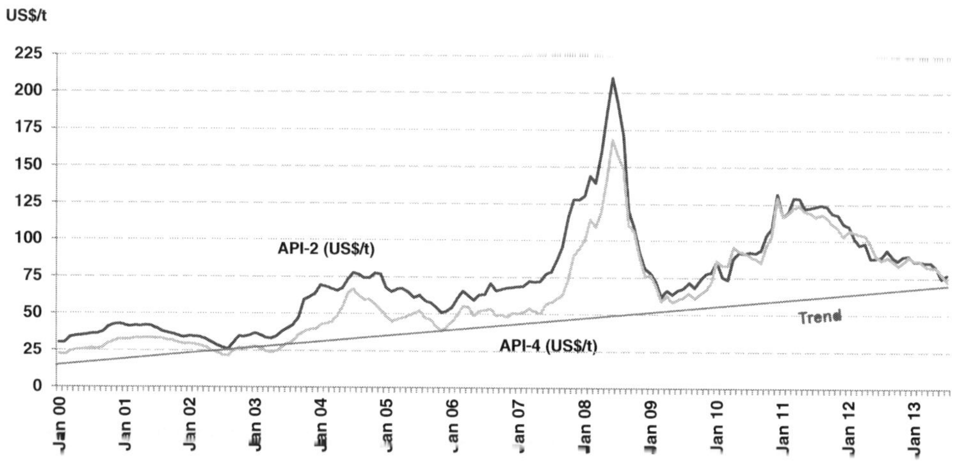

FIGURE 2.4 Coal price developments 2000 to July 2013
Source: McCloskey Coal Price Index. Author's analysis.

In the decades to come, despite slowing market growth, there will be no way around coal. Governments and organizations need to spend more time as well as financial and human capital on developing technologies to improve the world's power plant park and to find newer and better ways of producing and transporting fossil fuel resources rather than fighting coal (in Germany this opposition runs parallel to the fight against nuclear energy, which has now prevailed and it will be phased out. Such a phase-out will cost Germany a lot of money and does not make much economic sense). There is no question that the world needs every possible megawatt-hour sourced from renewable energy. However, for the foreseeable future, renewable energy will not satisfy the world's hunger for energy. Since coal's lifetime far surpasses that of other fossil energy resources (see Figure 2.5) it will become increasingly important, especially once the CO_2 problem of coal utilization can be managed.

There is increasing evidence that coal will not only remain one of the key sources for our energy demand, but actually gain in importance. Despite increased transparency, much of the coal market is still a very private and closed market with relatively little transparency, partly as a result of the general public antipathy towards coal. In fact, coal has only been traded on an international level since the early 1980s, a development that was sparked by the oil crises in 1973 and 1979. However, even today politicians and the scientific community lack the same level of knowledge about coal compared with oil, gas, nuclear and, increasingly, renewable energy sources.

Here we argue that coal will fill the gap between the Oil Age and the often-referred-to 'Solar Age' of the future, where renewable energy sources will satisfy the majority of the planet's hunger for electricity specifically and energy in general. In filling this gap, coal competes head-on with other sources of energy, but coal has the major advantage of being available in a relatively free market, with supply coming from developed and developing countries alike.

The Achilles' heel of coal is the justified environmental concern. Currently, coal generates more CO_2 per MWh of electricity produced than any other fossil fuel. With 43%, or 13 Gt of the total 30 Gt global CO_2 emissions stemming from coal, environmental risks demand 'clean coal' technology (IEA – CO_2, 2012). Independent of the need to step up efforts for cleaner production and use of coal, it is crucial that the world increases the speed at which renewable energy sources are being developed.

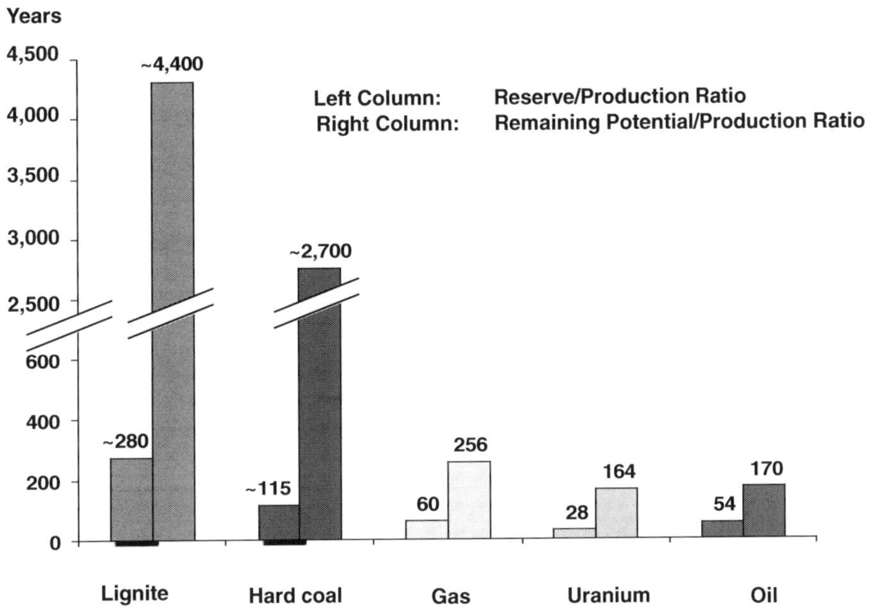

FIGURE 2.5 Statistical range of non-renewable energy sources
Source: Author's analysis based on BGR, 2011.

The world produced about 7.2 billion tons of hard coal in 2012, of which almost 1.2 billion tons was traded internationally. Green border trade totalled 79 million tons. The remaining 1082 million tons traded by sea comprised 256 million tons of coking coal and 826 million tons of steam coal – the focus of this study (VDKI, 2013). On a side note, the steam coal trade alone increased 12% from 739 million tons in 2011 to the numbers shown in Figure 2.6 in 2012, a phenomenal step up in one year when few would have expected it.

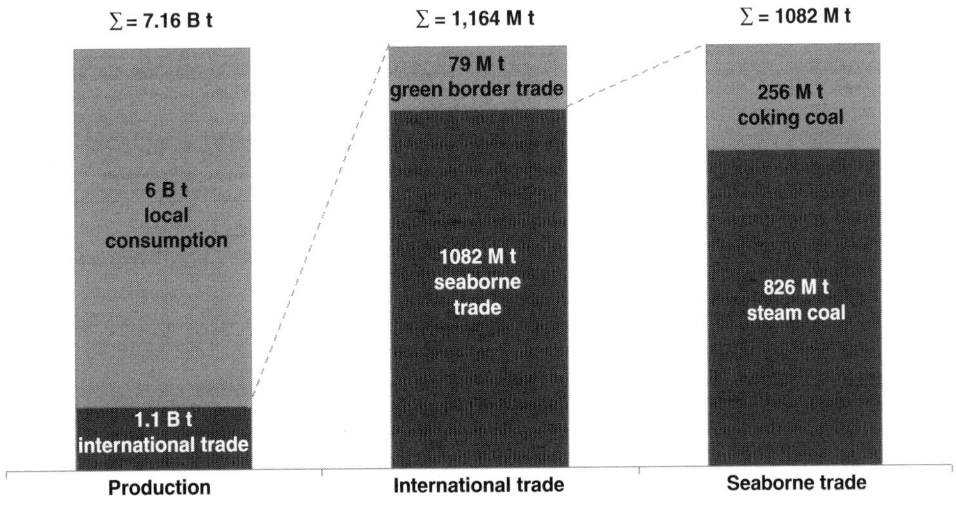

FIGURE 2.6 Overview of coal volumes 2012
Source: VDKI (2013). Author's analysis.

Steam coal includes all bituminous and most sub-bituminous coals as well as anthracite. Not included is coking coal or classic lignite coal.

The supply for the global seaborne steam coal market is measured by the production for export. The capacity is measured by the sum of all export mine capacities. The demand is measured by seaborne trade. Herein we focus on the power industry's coal consumption.

This research focuses on the global market. We can do this since Li (2008) and Warell (2007) have shown that the Atlantic and Pacific coal markets are co-integrated. As a result, the traditional separation of the Atlantic and Pacific steam coal markets is fading. In any case, today, the faster growing Pacific market has far surpassed the Atlantic market, a trend that will continue. The steam coal market has thus become a global market and is relatively unified in terms of economics. The law of one price acts as a guiding principle for defining the market.

2.2 SOURCE OF COAL – SYNOPSIS OF THE RESOURCE COAL

This chapter serves as an introduction to coal as a resource, examining the process of coal generation, coal classification and the key characteristics of coal, worldwide coal reserves, production methods, the competitive situation in the coal supply market, basic economic production costs and environmental and safety issues involved in the production of coal.

2.2.1 The Fundamentals of Energy Sources and Fossil Fuels

There are a number of energy sources available for human use. Table 2.1 summarizes these sources. Terrestrial sources of energy include the fossil fuels coal, oil and gas, as well as nuclear energy based on uranium. These terrestrial sources accounted for 87% of world primary energy production and 81% of world electricity production in 2010 (see Figure 2.7). Solar and other sources – including wind, hydro, biomass, tidal and geothermal energy – accounted for the remainder, less than 13%. Herein we refer to fossil fuels as primary energy, which is, scientifically speaking, not very precise. Wolf and Scheer (2005) have pointed out that fossil fuels are nothing but solar energy coupled with earth matter, water and CO_2, which have turned into biomass. In their very interesting and highly recommended book *Öl aus Sonne – Die Brennstoffformel der Erde* (*Oil from the Sun – the Earth's Fuel Formula*) they

TABLE 2.1 Overview of sources of energy for human use

Terrestrial sources	Solar sources	Other sources
Fossil fuels ▪ Hard Coal ▪ Lignite ▪ Oil ▪ Gas	Direct solar ▪ Solar radiation	Tidal energy Geothermal energy
Nuclear energy ▪ Uranium	Indirect solar ▪ Wind ▪ Hydro ▪ Biomass	

Source: *Energy: Long-Run Sustainability*, BCG Industrial Goods Alumni Meeting, Munich. Author's research.

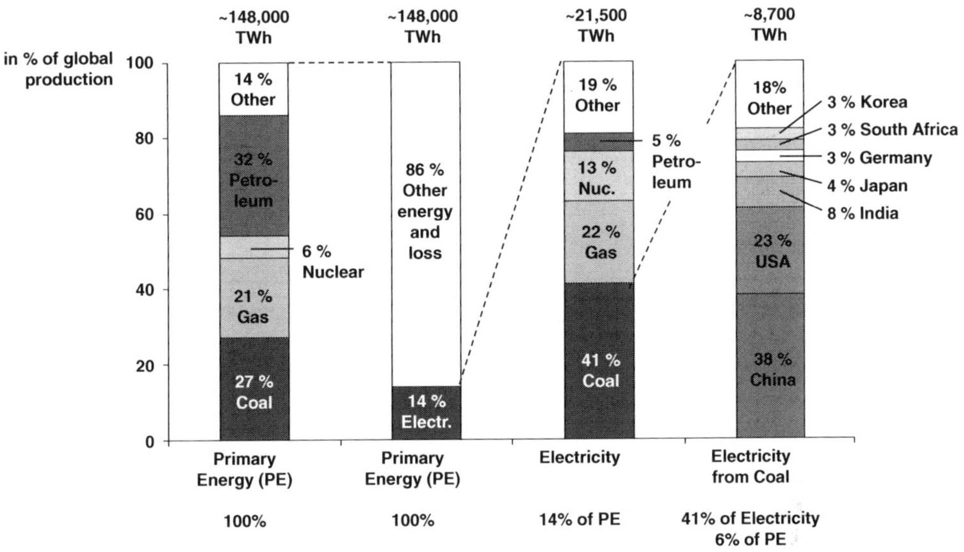

FIGURE 2.7 Global shares of primary and electricity energy 2010
Source: IEA – Statistics (2012). Author's analysis.

argue that, in the long run, the burning of fossil energy is a reversible process with solar energy required as the process energy.

When speaking about fossil energy sources, it is important to note that all carbon-based fossil energy sources are generated from biomass. Biological and physical processes in the form of heat and pressure are responsible for the generation of fossil fuels over millions of years. One could argue that even uranium is a fossil fuel; however, uranium does not develop through biological and physical processes, but rather during fusion processes in the final phase of certain stars (supernova).

Today, the majority of our electricity is generated using various industrial processes to oxidize (combust) the carbon contained in fossil fuels, and biomass for that matter. In this process, molecules develop in an exothermic reaction whose bonding force (the Coulomb force) is higher than that of the original molecules (Erdmann and Zweifel, 2008, pp. 15–19). The energy released in this combustion process is only released through heat.

Formula (2.1) summarizes the amount of energy released through combustion of 1 kg of carbon content. Formula (2.2) summarizes the theoretical complete combustion of fossil hydrocarbon fuels resulting in heat plus carbon dioxide and water.

$$1\ \text{kg C} + 2.7\ \text{kg } O_2 \rightarrow 3.7\ \text{kg } CO_2 + 32.8 \times 10^6\ \text{J} \tag{2.1}$$

$$C_xH_y + \left(x + \frac{y}{4}\right) O_2 \rightarrow \text{heat} + xCO_2 + \frac{y}{2}H_2O \tag{2.2}$$

Processes such as the steam turbine generator of a coal-fired power plant are required to generate energy in a form other than heat (i.e., mechanical or electromagnetic energy). Usually, only those fossil fuels whose energy content is economically utilized through the chemical reaction of some form of combustion are used for such energy sources. Fossil fuels are also finite. We are consuming them far faster than they can be produced. This is one key fact on which environmentalists base their protest. This is also a key fact for the coal industry to consider. However, coal reserves and resources will far outlast those of oil and gas, and mankind continues to find new reserves and resources. Nevertheless, the smart and economical use of our planet's fossil fuels will remain a key political and technological challenge until humans are able to satisfy their energy demand primarily from solar sources.

2.2.2 Process of Coal Formation

Today's hard coal resources were generated in the carboniferous era about 360–290 million years ago. The carboniferous era was named for the coalification process that took place at that time. During that era the continents had not yet reached their current position. The climate was mild, and morasses, swamps and large forests covered the land masses.

Two phases were required for the generation of coal:

1. Biochemical process – peat development under airtight conditions.
2. Geochemical process – coalification through heat and pressure exerted on the peat.

In the first phase, the climate as well as the flora and fauna were important for coal to develop. Biological remains of plants such as ferns and trees could not always decay or rot fully because they were compressed at the bottom of swamps or morasses. As a result, the usual aerobic process of rotting could not occur, and peat developed.

In the second phase, large amounts of heat and pressure were exerted on the peat-like material over hundreds of millions of years. The peat was covered by new oceans and land masses that developed over time. Geological movements of land masses, the creation of mountain ranges and tectonic eruptions were required to generate today's coal resources. Through heat and pressure the water and other 'impurities' in the peat slowly volatized.

Through the coalification process biomass obtains the properties shown in Figure 2.8. In the final stages, diamonds develop (Krüger, 2007). In the two extremes and for illustration, today's lignite resources first developed in the tertiary era about 65.2 million years ago, while diamonds that surface today are estimated to be between 1 and 3 billion years old.

Oil and gas differ from coal in their generation. Whereas coal developed mostly from terrestrial plants, most geologists support the biogenic theory in which oil and gas developed from small life forms and other ancient organic material. Here also compression and heat under oxygen-free conditions were required for the process to take place. This process also started over 300 million years ago.

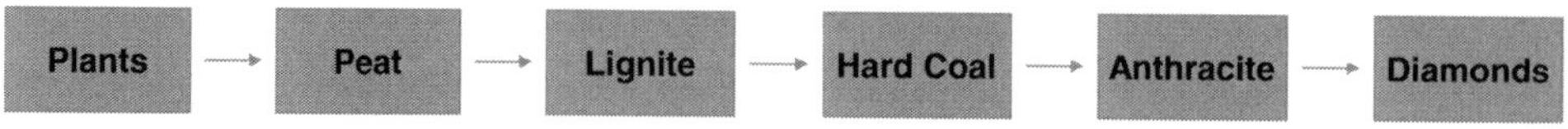

FIGURE 2.8 Coalification process

2.2.3 Coal Classification

Ever since coal replaced wood-based biomass as the primary source of energy in the early 1800s, various classifications of coal have been developed. Today, coal is generally divided into low-rank coal and high-rank coal, which is often referred to as hard coal.

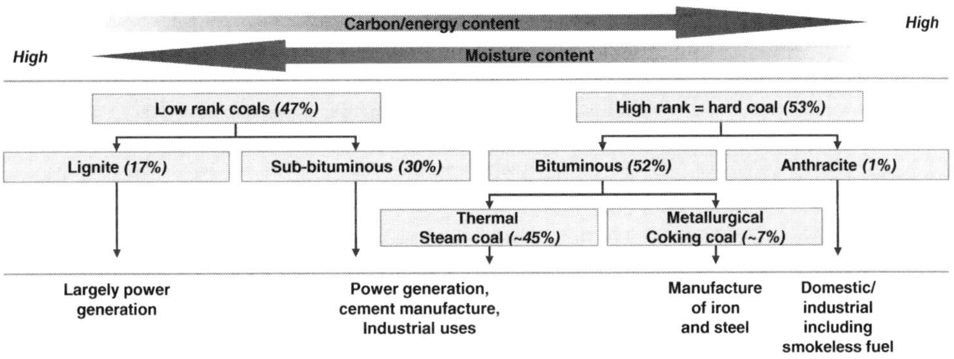

FIGURE 2.9 Coal classification: general overview
Note: XX% = approximate percentage share of proven, probable or indicated world coal reserves.
Source: European Association for Coal and Lignite (EURACOAL). Author's analysis.

Figure 2.9 provides a good overview of the general classification of coal products. Here, hard coal includes all bituminous coal and anthracite. Today, however, some sub-bituminous coal is also classified as hard coal (e.g., Indonesian sub-bituminous coal which is part of internationally traded steam coal).

Figure 2.10 provides a more detailed overview of various US-, UN- and German-based classification methods, including their official name. The classification of coal is generally derived from the key coal characteristics: (a) energy content or calorific value (in the coal industry, indicated by the abbreviation CV); (b) total moisture content (indicated by the abbreviation TM); and (c) volatile content.

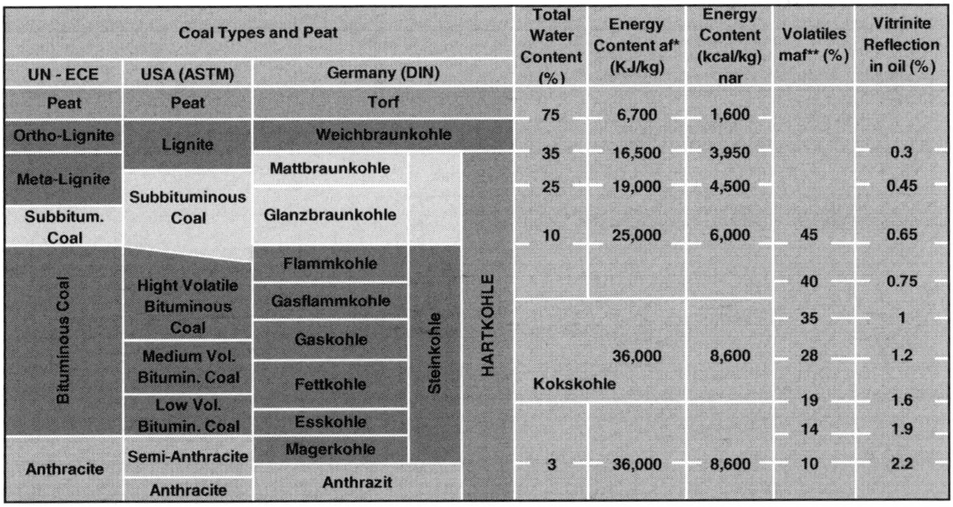
Coal Types and Peat
UN - ECE
USA (ASTM)
Germany (DIN)
Total Water Content (%)
Energy Content af* (KJ/kg)
Energy Content (kcal/kg) nar
Volatiles maf** (%)
Vitrinite Reflection in oil (%)
Peat
Peat
Torf
Ortho-Lignite
Lignite
Weichbraunkohle
Meta-Lignite
Mattbraunkohle
Subbituminous Coal
Subbitum. Coal
Glanzbraunkohle
Bituminous Coal
Hight Volatile Bituminous Coal
Flammkohle
Gasflammkohle
Gaskohle
Medium Vol. Bitumin. Coal
Fettkohle
Low Vol. Bitumin. Coal
Esskohle
Magerkohle
Steinkohle
HARTKOHLE
Anthracite
Semi-Anthracite
Anthracite
Anthrazit
75
6,700
1,600
35
16,500
3,950
0.3
25
19,000
4,500
0.45
10
25,000
6,000
45
0.65
40
0.75
35
1
36,000
8,600
28
1.2
Kokskohle
19
1.6
14
1.9
3
36,000
8,600
10
2.2

FIGURE 2.10 International coal classification: detailed overview
Note: *af = ash-free; **daf = dry ash-free.
Source: European Association for Coal and Lignite (EURACOAL). Author's analysis.

Herein we refer to hard coal and steam coal. Steam coal is usually treated as a subsection of hard coal. Steam coal for our purposes includes anthracite (even if not used in the power industry), but excludes coking coal. Hard coal includes all coking coal. However, many industry specialists regard hard coal as excluding sub-bituminous coals. For the purpose of this section, sub-bituminous coal is included in the category of steam coal. Later, when looking at reserves and resources, we will only refer to hard coal since it is currently close to impossible to differentiate coking coal and non-coking coal or steam coal when discussing global reserves and resources.

2.2.3.1 Calorific Value The calorific value (or CV) is stated in kcal/kg or MJ/kg (equal to GJ/t). The lower heating value (LHV) – also known as the net calorific value (net CV, or NCV) – of a fuel is defined as the amount of heat released by combusting a specified quantity of product (initially at 25°C or another reference state) and returning the temperature of the combustion product to 150°C. The NCV assumes that the latent heat of vaporization of the water in the fuel and the reaction products are not recovered. It is useful in comparing fuels when the condensation of the combustion products is impractical, or heat at a temperature below 150°C cannot be put to use. The NCV is generally used in the European coal trading business, which dominates the Atlantic coal trading market. Coal traded in the Atlantic market typically reaches a CV of 6000 kcal/kg net as received.

In contrast, the gross CV (GCV) or higher heating value (HHV) includes the heat of condensation of the water in the combustion products. The GCV is generally used in the Asian coal trading business, which dominates the Pacific coal trading market. Coal traded in the Atlantic market specifically for Asian customers typically reaches a GCV of 5500 to 6700 kcal/kg gross air dried. For converting gross into net or as received into air dried basis, please see below and refer to Table 2.2.

For comparison and to summarize, the NCV is the ‘net energy’ contained in coal that the power plant can use to generate electricity. The GCV is the ‘complete energy’ that coal contains. However, part of this energy is required to vaporize the water in the coal when generating heat.

The following formulas, especially the simplified ones, are used in the coal industry to convert GCV into NCV or NCV into GCV:

$$\text{NCV(ar)} = \text{GCV(ar)} - 50.6\text{H} - 5.85\text{TM} - 0.191\text{O}$$

$$\text{Simplification 1: NCV(ar)} = \text{GCV(ar)} - 6(9\text{H} + \text{TM})$$

$$\text{Simplification 2: NCV(ar)} = \text{GCV(ar)} - 260/300\ \text{kcal/kg}$$

where H = hydrogen content; TM = total moisture content; O = oxygen content. Note: Simplification 2 assumes typical bituminous coal with 10% TM and 25% volatile matter.

TABLE 2.2 Converting coal characteristics: ar, adb, db, daf

To obtain multiply	As received (ar)	Air dried basis (adb)	Dry basis (db)	Dry ash free (daf)
ar by		(100-IM%)/(100-TM%)	100/(100-TM%)	
adb by	(100-TM%)/(100-IM%)		100/(100-IM%)	
db by	(100-TM%)/100	(100-IM%)/100		100/(100-A%)

Note: IM = inherent moisture; TM = total moisture; A = ash.

The most frequently used simplified formulas for converting steam coal from the Atlantic market standard net as received (nar, or NCV(ar)) into the Pacific market standard gross air dried (gad, or GCV(adb)), and vice versa, are summarized below:

$$\text{NCV(ar)} = [1 - (\text{TM} - \text{IM}) \times \text{GCV(ad)}] - 260\ \text{kcal/kg}$$
$$\text{NCV(ar)} = \text{GCV(ad)} - 550/600\ \text{kcal/kg}$$

where IM = inherent moisture; TM = total moisture.

It should be noted that the CV is the key characteristic in the coal trade. This seems obvious, but the CV is not as simple as it first appears to be. It must be remembered that the coal customer in the end buys energy content per ton delivered to its power plant. Thus, a higher CV will not only reduce the relative cost of transportation per ton of coal transported but also have an impact on the efficiency reached in the power plant when measured per ton of input product. However, an overly high CV may result in overly high temperatures in the boiler and therefore cause technical problems. Even some veterans in the coal trading industry often forget these very important facts about CV.

In contrast, there is a general trend towards lower CVs when looking at international coal supplies. Indonesian export volumes have increased significantly and are often of lower CV content. South African exported coal products have also dropped in CV due to geological circumstances as well as for wash plant capacity reasons. Coal from Russia has also dropped in CV due to geological reasons. Long-term, it is expected that exported coal will continue to drop in CV. This will increase the relative cost of transportation and also pose challenges for old and new power plants. All else being equal, the falling CV will result in higher prices per delivered ton of coal. Thus, economically speaking, the trend towards lower CV coal does not make much sense; the relatively lower per ton cost is mostly offset by higher relative transport costs and lower power plant efficiencies. In mid-2013, when high-CV coal prices dropped faster than low-CV coal prices, for the first time in a decade power plants reconsidered their strategy of moving towards lower CV coal qualities and started shifting back to higher CV coal where possible.

2.2.3.2 Ballast: Moisture and Ash Content The key components in coal that do not carry calorific value are the moisture content and ash. Both together are referred to as ballast. The higher the ballast, the lower the carbon content and therefore the calorific value and vice versa.

Moisture. All mined coal is wet. When coal is mined, the product will include groundwater and other extraneous moisture – also referred to as adventitious moisture. The moisture that is held within the coal itself is called inherent moisture (IM). The total moisture content, both adventitious and inherent, is called just that: total moisture (TM).

Ash. This is an inorganic matter (i.e., sand crystals) and the residue left after coal is burnt. Thus, ash is non-combustible. It represents the bulk mineral matter after carbon, oxygen, sulphur and moisture (including from clays) have been driven off during the combustion process. High ash contents in bituminous coals can be 'washed out' in a chemical and mechanical process called coal washing. For instance, almost 100% of South African export coal (about 65 million tons p.a.) is first washed before shipping. Indonesian coal, on the contrary, tends to have very low ash content.

Ash fusion temperature (AFT). When considering ash in coal, it is also important to understand about fusion temperatures. Ash is a non-combustible component. However, at very high temperatures (i.e., above 1000°C), ash or the crystals held within it will melt. The temperature at which ash melts is called the ash fusion temperature.

2.2.3.3 Volatile Matter The volatile matter (also called volatiles, volatile content or VM) in coal refers to those components of coal, except for moisture, which are released at high temperature in the absence of air. VM is usually a mixture of short- and long-chain hydrocarbons, aromatic hydrocarbons and some sulphur. The volatile content is a key indication of how the coal will burn and what characteristic the flame will have. For instance, high-volatile coal tends to burn more quickly with a larger flame. Also, the coal self-ignites much quicker. Low-volatile coal, in contrast, tends to burn more slowly with a lower flame, but also at higher temperatures.

The volatile content can also be expressed on an as received (ar), air dried or dried basis. Typical volatiles of steam coal range from 20 to 40% ar. For example, Indonesian coal tends to have around 40% ar (therefore, it also self-combusts faster) and South African coal tends to have around 25% ar. Russian and Colombian coal tends to have 30 to 35% volatiles ar.

High-volatile coal with volatiles around or above 40% ar can slowly devolatize over time when exposed to oxygen. Since the volatiles also contain hydrocarbons, this also means that the calorific value of high-volatile coal can decline over time. This is especially a risk with lower calorific material, such as sub-bituminous, or younger, coal. As such, the ability to store low-CV/high-volatile coal is significantly reduced and such coal needs to be burnt quickly after it has been mined.

2.2.3.4 Fixed Carbon Content The carbon content of coal (called the ultimate carbon content) is responsible for the energy contained. The fixed carbon content of coal does not equal the ultimate carbon content. Fixed carbon is the carbon found in the material, which is left after volatile materials are driven off. This differs from the ultimate carbon content of the coal because some carbon is lost in hydrocarbons with the volatiles. Fixed carbon (FC) is used as an estimate of the amount of coke that will be yielded from a sample of coal and therefore is especially relevant for anthracite products or coking coal. The fixed carbon content is only of marginal importance for the power industry as the calorific value, ballast and volatile matter describe the coal well enough for power generation purposes. The ultimate carbon content, however, will determine the amount of CO_2 generated when burning the coal. Thus, the CV to C-content ratio is crucial when finding coal with the lowest CO_2 emission per MWh produced.

Fixed carbon is determined by removing the mass of volatiles determined by the volatility test above from the original mass of the coal sample. Often, fixed carbon is determined by difference:

$$\text{FC(db)} = 100 - \text{VM(db)} - \text{ash(db)}$$

Note that the above formula only works on a dried basis and not on an as received or air dried basis.

2.2.3.5 Sulphur, Size, Grindability, Nitrogen, Chlorine and Flour The sulphur content of coal is the last of the key coal characteristics important for the steam coal market. Coal quality and sulphur content are usually inversely related to each other. However, since most power plant consumers can blend the coal they utilize inside the boiler at their own storage facility, consumers often blend low-sulphur coal with high-sulphur coal, resulting in a better market potential for higher-sulphur material as well.

Less important for steam coal, but relevant for coking coal, is that sulphur comes in organic and inorganic, usually pyritic (FeS_2), forms. Besides pyrite there can be marcasite and sulphates, though the sulphate content is usually low unless the pyrite has been oxidized. The forms of organic sulphur are less well established and organic sulphur cannot be removed by physical means; existing chemical processes for removing organic sulphurs are usually very expensive. Inorganic sulphur (called 'pyritic sulphur' because it is combined with iron to form iron pyrite) washes out relatively easily when the ash of coal is reduced in washing processes.

The size of the coal in millimetres is another important factor for hard coal. Steam coal for power generation is usually offered in 0–50 mm size with maximum 5–10% above 50 mm. Since modern power plants work with pulverization, in theory, one could even supply 0–6 mm coal, however, here the risk of dust and environmental problems is very high. The grain size affects the transportation on belts and the choice of mills in the power plant. Sized coal (separated with screens) is traded at a significant price premium of around 10–40% compared with similar 'fine' coal. Such sized coal is used for domestic purposes and industrial uses, where some older ovens can only work with sized material. Run of mine coal (ROM, or coal straight from mining without crushing) usually has 0–300 mm size. However, surface mining can result in larger junks of up to 500+ mm in size. Harder coal is sometimes easier to handle than softer coal. Harder coal absorbs less moisture during transportation, tends to generate less dust and does not 'glue' to equipment.

Grindability is expressed through the Hardgrove grindability index (HGI). The HGI determines the hardness of the coal. A high HGI score means soft coal and a low HGI score means hard coal. Harder coal (i.e., HGI below 40) is more difficult to grind which causes larger coal particles to be supplied to the boilers. This in turn may result in an increased amount of unburned coal in the fly ash.

Nitrogen content is responsible for the NO_x emission of power plants. NO_x is especially carefully monitored in the UK and the USA. The relationship of the coal nitrogen with emissions of nitrogen oxides is not clearly understood to date, and thus is an area in which further research is needed (Davidson, 1994).

Chlorine and fluorine contents affect the performance of the wet flue gas desulphurization and the gypsum quality. The risk of corrosion increases with higher chlorine and fluorine values. Chlorine is one of the most troublesome components of coal in combustion applications, causing slagging, fouling and corrosion. There is substantial evidence that fouling and corrosion increase as the chlorine content in coal increases above 0.25 to 0.5% ar (IEA Clean Coal Center, 2008).

2.2.4 Reserves and Resources

The world's coal resources are widely distributed. One of the major advantages of coal compared with other fossil energy sources is that resources are not only available in developing countries but also in Europe, Australia, the USA and other countries that are generally considered part of the Western and more stable world. This is exemplified by Australia's status as one of the world's largest coal exporters.

We shall use the internationally accepted definitions of reserves and resources as detailed in Figure 2.11.

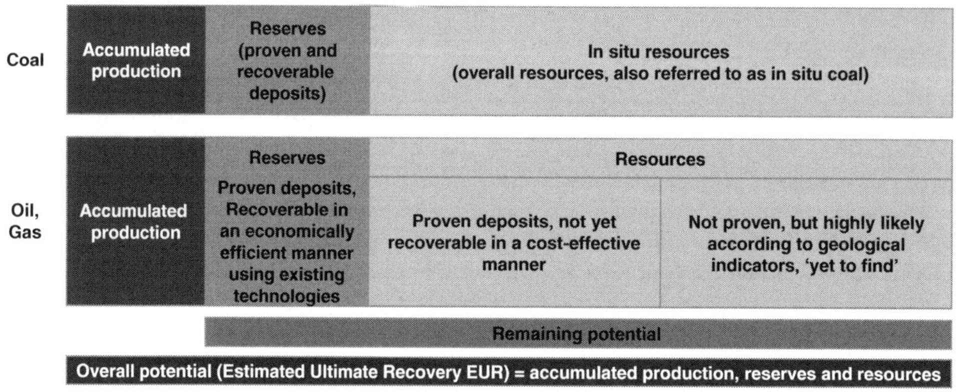

FIGURE 2.11 Definition of coal, oil and gas reserves and resources
Note: The above definitions may vary depending on the source used
Source: IEA Manual (2006).

Figure 2.12 summarizes the global distribution of hard coal. While total production in 2011 was 7 billion tons, of which about 1 billion tons were exported via sea, total hard coal reserves are estimated at 755 billion tons (lignite: 283 billion tons), resulting in a theoretical reserve/production ratio for hard coal of 114 years. The total remaining potential, combining reserves and resources, is about 17,874 billion tons of hard coal (lignite: 4,435 billion tons), resulting in a remaining theoretical potential/production ratio for hard coal of about 2,708 years (BGR, 2012). However, when interpreting these numbers it must be remembered that coal reserves and resources do not differentiate between raw coal and sellable coal. In many countries such as Australia and South Africa, where the coal is washed, only

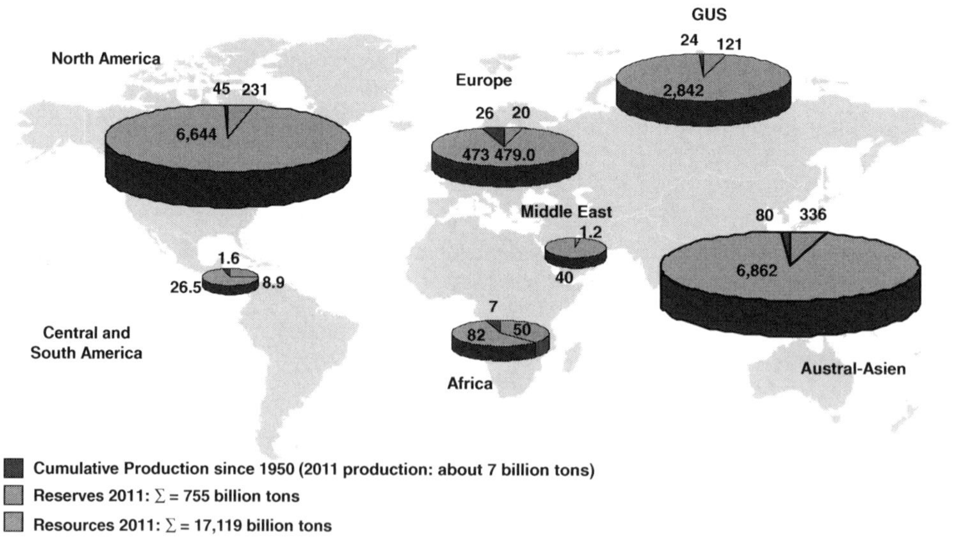

FIGURE 2.12 Global hard coal production, reserves and resources (in billion tons)
Source: BGR (2012). Author's research and analysis.

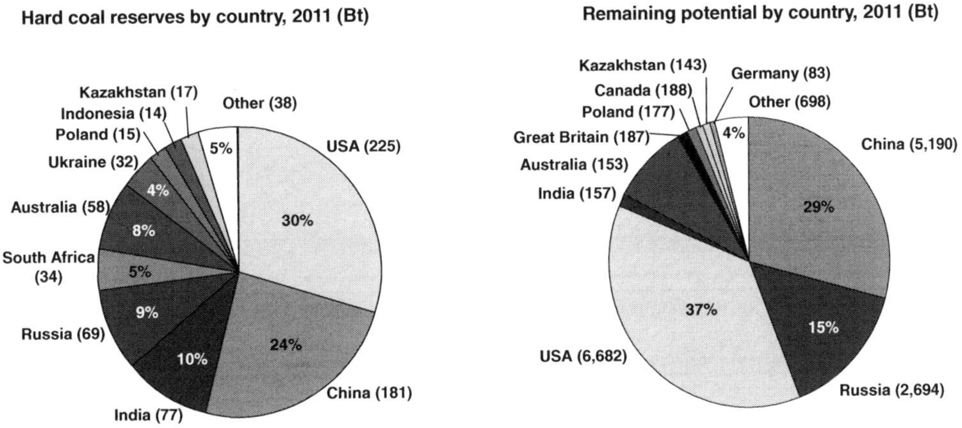

FIGURE 2.13 Global reserves and resources by country, 2011
Note: resources + reserves = remaining potential.
Source: BGR (2012). Author's analysis.

65–80% of raw coal translates into sellable coal. Kjaerstad and Johnsson (2008) argue that the reserve/production ratio is therefore meaningless. While it is agreed here that this factor makes the figures less reliable, they nonetheless demonstrate that coal is available in abundant quantities, which is the point we wish to discuss here.

Current production has only scratched the surface of the remaining potential of coal. The largest potential (reserves plus resources) in tons of hard coal exists in the USA and China (see Figure 2.13). The reserves of the USA are the largest in the world, which is most likely a function of the investments in and professional surveys done on US coal reserves.

Reserves are well distributed across the globe, with countries in Asia, Europe, North America and South America in the top 10. This fact is good news for the international coal market, in particular for steam coal consumers, since diversified sources translate into greater reliability of supply. Table 2.3 presents the 10 countries with the largest reserves. Indonesia is probably the most interesting case. According to the BGR, if it continues to produce at the current rate it will have exhausted its reserves in only 42 years. This, of course, will not happen. It indicates the difficulty with such statistics where the availability of data is limited. In fact, Schernikau World Coal (2013) – Myths and Realities, Indonesia – has clarified that Indonesia is expected to have over 150 years' reserves, but it is true that Indonesia's reserves are relatively modest considering its status as the largest steam coal exporter in the world. From Table 2.3 we can determine that the resource/reserve ratio for hard coal is 23:1. This ratio was 5:1 only 8 years ago according to Ritschel and Schiffer (2007). Thus, even though resources are reassigned to reserves, relatively speaking, known resources have increased at an extraordinary pace and are expected to continue to do so.

In general, the estimates of coal reserves and resources are subject to continuous adjustment, similar to the estimates concerning oil and gas. However, while figures for oil and gas are systematically updated, the same has not been true for coal deposits. The international community has historically spent much less time and capacity updating data on coal deposits than those on oil and gas. Also, relatively little effort has gone into researching new and long-term coal reserves. This has changed already in the past 5 years. For example, the BGR reported global coal resources almost doubled in 6 years from about 9,000 billion tons in 2006

TABLE 2.3 Hard coal reserves and resources of top 10 countries by reserves

No.	Country	Prod. 2011 (Mln mt)	Reserves (Mln mt)	%	Resources (Mln mt)	%	Remaining potential (Mln mt)	R/P (years)	RP/P (years)
1	USA	925	225,012	30%	6,457,386	38%	6,682,398	243	7,224
2	China	3,834	180,600	24%	5,010,000	29%	15,190,600	47	1,354
3	India	540	77,197	10%	175,352	1%	252,549	143	468
4	Russia	259	68,944	9%	2,624,612	15%	2,693,556	266	10,400
5	Australia	345	57,538	8%	1,521,732	9%	1,579,270	167	4,578
6	S. Africa	253	33,896	4%	n/a	0%	33,896	134	134
7	Ukraine	82	32,039	4%	49,006	0%	81,045	391	988
8	Kazakhstan	103	17,242	2%	125,890	1%	143,132	167	1,390
9	Poland	77	14,711	2%	162,317	1%	177,028	191	2,299
10	Indonesia	325	13,512	2%	73,299	0%	86,811	42	267
	…					–			
11	Colombia	86	4,881	1%	9,928	0%	14,809	57	172
	…					–			
12	Canada	57	4,346	1%	183,260	1%	187,606	76	3,291
	…								
56	Germany	13	48	0%	82,961	0%	83,009	4	6,385
	…								
	Total	6,640	754,595	1	17,119,082	1	17,873,677	114	2,692

Note: R/P = reserve/production; RP/P = remaining potential/reserves.
Source: BGR (2012).

to about 18,000 billion tons in 2012. We can expect that figures for coal reserves and resources will continue to increase significantly.

2.2.5 Coal Mining and Production

Understanding coal mining is important for the economic study of coal because coal mining costs are a key component of the marginal FOB costs relevant for global long-term pricing. Based on previous work on the international coal market, Schernikau (2010) estimates that mining costs account for almost 40% of total marginal FOB costs. Inland transportation accounts for 44% and trans-shipment about 16%. However, the mining companies have relatively little influence over inland transportation and trans-shipment costs.

2.2.5.1 Coal Mining Methods About 60% of global coal production is underground or deep mining, and the remaining 40% is surface mining (World Coal Institute – Resource Coal, 2005). Because of its inherent cost advantage surface mining is much more important for export coal mines, with an average share of about three-quarters and only about one-quarter extracted through underground mining (based on author's FOB cost analysis). The choice of coal mining method is largely determined by the geological location of the coal seams. Typically and depending on coal seam thickness, larger coal seams at a depth below 150–200 m are mined in underground mines (although this also varies from country to country). Figure 2.14 summarizes the stages of a typical mining project. The mining company decides whether the resource can be surface mined by the first exploration stage at the latest.

The methods of mining mentioned above differ not only in terms of marginal costs (export marginal mining costs of 15 USD/mt for deep mining versus 11 USD/mt for surface mining) but also in terms of investment costs (Schernikau, 2010). However, since only the marginal costs are relevant for the long-term competitiveness of a product, surface mining will always have an advantage. This is borne out by the prevalence of surface mining in the global seaborne steam coal market.

Underground mining is usually conducted in one of two ways:

1. Long-wall mining.
2. Room and pillar mining.

The long-wall mining method is much more efficient and used in the world's largest mines (i.e., in Russia, Australia and the USA). Here a mechanical extraction machine or shearers

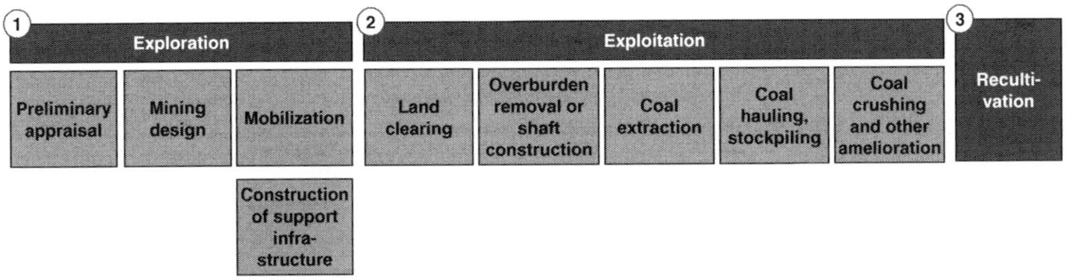

FIGURE 2.14 Process of a typical mining project
Source: Author's research and analysis.

extract entire seams of coal. The coal face from which the machines extract can vary in length from 100–400 m. Semi-automated (self-advancing) equipment supports the roof of the coal seams temporarily with hydraulically powered supports. In most cases, the coal roof collapses once the machine has moved on. These machines can extract from various seam thicknesses, between 3 m and 5 m or more. Seeing such equipment in operation is very impressive, but the mining company often has to spend tens of millions of US dollars just to procure one of these machines. Also, the planning, installation and training times involved are very long and costly.

Here lies the advantage of room and pillar mining. Mobile machinery that costs 1–5 million USD per mine can be used and set up very quickly. Here only 50–70% of the coal is mined in each seam; the remaining 30–50% of the coal remains in the mine and forms the pillars that support the roof. One moves through the seam from left to right leaving some coal unmined to form the pillars. The resulting pattern, when viewed from above, looks a bit like a chess board.

Surface mining is the oldest way of extracting coal from the ground. At its core is the very basic 'shovel and truck' exploitation system. One differentiates between continuous and discontinuous surface mining. Continuous mines often employ large-wheel bucket excavators, reclaimers and extensive systems of conveyor belts to move the overburden and coal. Discontinuous mining uses mostly excavators, bulldozers and trucks to extract and move overburden and coal. The basic surface mining exploitation system is accomplished in five stages: (1) the selected land area is cleared; (2) the overburden is removed; (3) the coal is extracted; (4) the coal is trucked to the intermediary stock piles at the mine; and (5) the coal is crushed or otherwise processed.

Stage 1: Land clearing. Depending on the size of the mine area and its location, this process may be as simple as removing trees and fauna from the land. In larger and more populated mine areas, for instance the large lignite mines in the Lausitz region in the East of Germany, this process may also involve relocating villages, houses and roads.

Stage 2: Overburden removal. During the exploration phase the mining company determines the mining plan and the size of the reserve. During this process the so-called overburden ratio (OB ratio – the average number of cubic metres of overburden that needs to be removed in order to extract one ton of coal) is determined. The overburden is removed either in a continuous or a discontinuous way, as explained above. The overburden needs to be replaced strategically so it does not have to be moved twice. Sophisticated mines use the overburden they remove from the start of the mine to refill the mining area after the coal has been extracted at the end of the mine. The OB ratio is the key economic factor determining mining cost, because removing one cubic metre of sand costs exactly as much as removing/extracting one cubic metre of coal (depending on its quality, one ton of raw coal usually equals between 0.9 and 1.3 cubic metres of sand).

Stage 3: Coal extraction. The coal is extracted either in a continuous or – more often in the case of hard coal – a discontinuous way, the same as the overburden. The key economic factor during coal extraction is to leave as little coal as possible unmined. In fact, some countries have regulations that determine how much coal can remain unmined in the ground. In the case of Russia, usually a maximum of 20% of the reserve may remain unmined, otherwise the mining company risks losing its exploitation licence.

With surface mining, most of the coal – usually 85–95% of the reserve – can be extracted. With underground mining, depending on the method, this figure is usually lower. The risk of extracting too high a percentage of the reserve is that the coal quality will decline for two reasons: (1) the coal closer to the roof of the seam often has higher sulphur contents or other impurities, because geologically the upper parts filter the water; and (2) the closer you come to the edge of the seam the higher the chance of extracting sand and other sediments including the ash content of the coal.

Stage 4: Coal hauling, stockpiling. A lot of very large trucks or extensive conveyor belt systems move the coal from the extraction site to the intermediary stockpiles. The key economic factor is to design a road and conveyor belt system that is inexpensive to maintain but minimizes distances. Especially with rising fuel costs, the design phase is therefore gaining importance. Smaller and less efficient mines will lose more and more competitive advantage in times of high fuel costs. An added layer of complexity is caused by the fact that the mine moves, thus requiring roads and any conveyor belt systems to move as well.

Stage 5: Coal crushing and other amelioration. The mined coal is extracted in what we call 'raw' or ROM form. All ROM coal needs to be treated in one or more ways, including but not limited to (a) crushing, (b) screening, (c) washing and (d) drying. For surface mining and for power plant use, all coal is crushed and often screened. In South Africa and much of Russia, exported coal is also washed.

2.2.5.2 Coal Mining Investment Costs Investment costs in coal mines can be significant and need to be analysed in order to understand the future economics of the industry. Especially in scarce times, even the most expensive producer in the world will want to recuperate his investment costs. Investment costs include expenditure on developing the deposits before or during actual production:

- Purchase costs for the land or mining rights.
- One-time licence costs.
- Prospecting and exploration costs.

It is still estimated today – and confirmed historically by Kopal (2007) and Ritschel and Schiffer (2007) – that total investment costs average about 60 USD for each annual production ton of coal mining capacity (see also Figure 2.15). Thus, when one develops a mine with one million tons of output per annum, one will pay on average 60 million USD upfront. Total financial costs are currently estimated at 6–7 USD per annual production ton, consisting of 2.5–3 USD/ton depreciation assuming a 20-year lifetime of the mine and 3.5–4 USD/ton interest (assuming 10% average debt service rate).

Investment costs vary widely. For mines with little or no existing infrastructure nearby (i.e., lacking roads, rail tracks, water, energy supply, accommodation, etc.) and high CV resources this cost can be substantially higher. Some greenfield coal projects (requiring large-scale investment in infrastructure) in remote and undeveloped areas may require specific investments of up to 160 USD for each annual production ton. From the author's own experience, however, some smaller coal mines in logistically superior locations can be developed with investments as low as 3–10 USD per annual production ton. This is especially true for small mines in Colombia, South Africa and, of course, Indonesia.

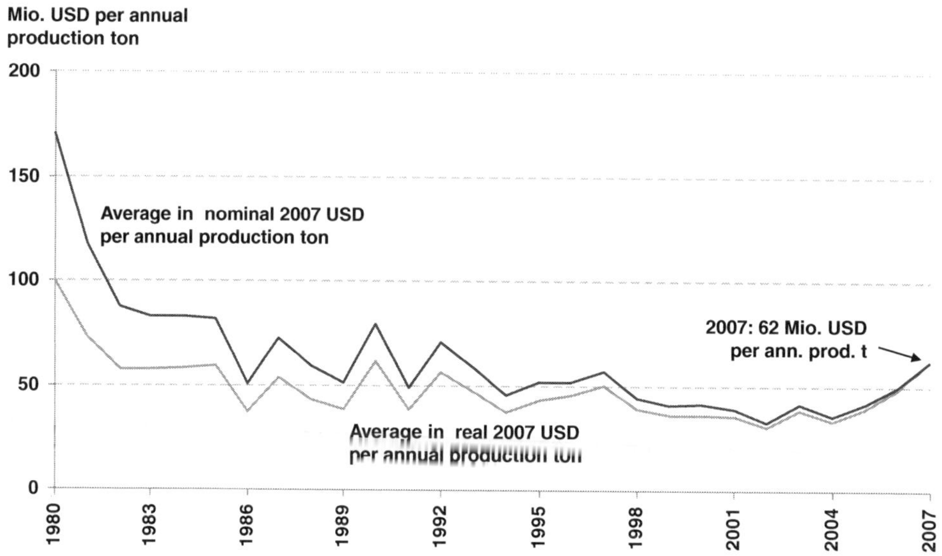

FIGURE 2.15 Specific investment costs in export mining 1980–2007
Source: Kopal (2007), p. 16.

Relatively speaking, coal has received a very small share of global investment in energy. This is astonishing, given the importance of coal. As discussed previously (Figure 2.7), 27% of world primary energy and 41% of world electricity generation is based on coal. However, as detailed by the IEA World Energy Investment Outlook (2011) and summarized in Figure 2.16, coal is projected to receive only 6% of global cumulative investments in fossil fuels between 2011 and 2035.

Kopal (2007) and Ritschel and Schiffer (2007) pointed out that this trend has been changing slowly. Coal has been and will continue to increase its investment share compared with gas and oil. When coal increases its global investment share, this will translate into higher investment costs per reserve ton, which in turn will result in higher prices, especially in scarcer times such as 2007/2008 and 2010/2011.

Nevertheless, the IEA has also determined and confirmed that coal is the least capital-intensive energy resource compared with oil and gas and has much room to remain competitive even when investment costs increase (IEA World Energy Investment Outlook, 2011). In fact, gas requires 4.5 times and oil 5.8 times as much investment as coal with all calorific values adjusted.

2.2.5.3 Coal Mining Operating Costs Variable or marginal coal mining costs depend on a number of factors: (1) the type of mining operation (i.e., opencast versus underground, continuous versus discontinuous); (2) the topography and available infrastructure (i.e., access to electricity and how hilly the region is); (3) the type of coal (i.e., steam coal versus coking coal); (4) labour costs; and (5) productivity per man year. The key components of average opencast mining costs are summarized in Table 2.4.

It is interesting to see that about two-thirds to three-quarters of the variable costs are driven by fuel and maintenance & repair. Thus, the kind of equipment used in any opencast mine will determine the efficiency of the mine.

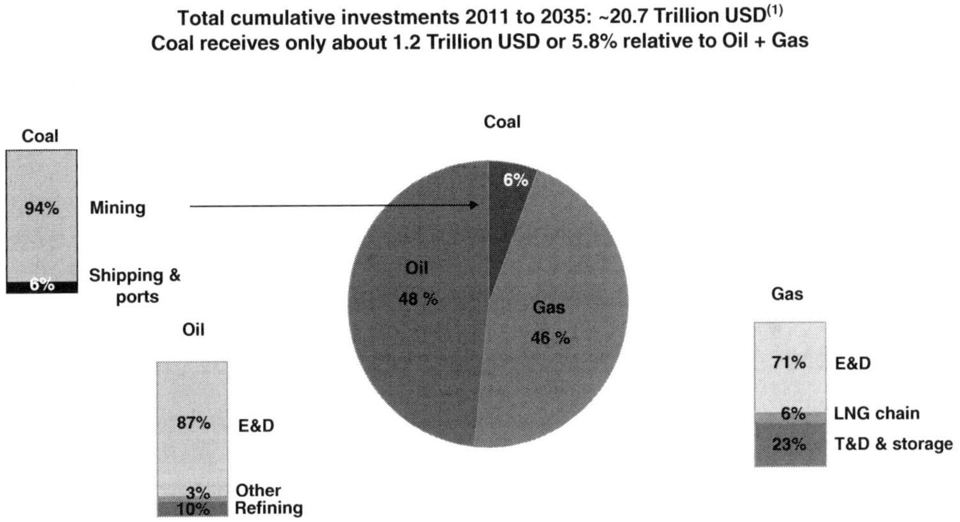

FIGURE 2.16 World energy investments, cumulative 2011–2035

(1) Global cumulative investment in energy 37.9 trillion USD, of which 44.6% or 16.9 trillion USD are investments in electricity generation and 20.7 trillion in coal, oil and gas.

Note: T&D = transmission and distribution; E&D = exploration and development.

Source: IEA World Energy Investment Outlook (2011); Schernikau (2010).

The outlook for operating costs is not positive. There is substantial rationalization and productivity improvement potential in many smaller and medium-sized mining operations. However, the key components of fuel and labour will likely increase further in cost. Coupled with higher investment and thus financing costs, it can be expected that coal production as a whole will become significantly more expensive in the future. The floor for coal prices on the international seaborne coal market will therefore increase further. Here is a brief summary of the drivers causing coal production costs to increase:

- New deposits require longer inland logistics.
- Overburden ratios increase.
- Fuel costs increase.
- Machinery costs increase.
- Royalties and other government charges are likely to increase.
- Coal qualities decrease.

TABLE 2.4 Percentage breakdown of variable mining costs

Category	Typical share of total variable cost (opencast mine in developing world)
Fuel	30–40%
Maintenance & repair (inc. tyres)	30–40%
Labour	10–20%
Other support functions and royalties	10–20%

Source: Author's research and analysis.

2.2.5.4 Coal Amelioration and Coal Washing Crushing, screening, washing and drying are typical ways of treating or ameliorating ROM coal after it has been extracted. Coal amelioration costs are an integral part of the total coal mining costs. It is important to note that all costs for the entire mining and logistics chain are paid on a per-ton basis. Thus, the earlier the coal is ameliorated the better, since all costs (usually only logistics related) are then lower per calorific unit. For instance, let's assume that a South African producer extracts and hauls the coal at a marginal cost of 8 USD/ton. The producer then washes the coal at a cost of 3 USD/feed ton to reduce the ash content, producing a yield of 65%. Thus, for each ton of ROM coal the producer gets 0.65 tons of washed product, yielding 6200 kcal/kg nar. The coal is then transported to the port and trans-shipped at a total marginal cost of 30 USD/ton. The coal is finally sold for 60 USD/mt. The sales basis of 6000 kcal/kg nar is the international standard for South African coal. The net margin achieved for this coal thus equals the sales price minus the true marginal FOB cost.

Washing means treating coal in order to reduce the ash content. Before washing, the coal is usually crushed and screened to remove the very fine material (for instance, 2 mm in size) because fine material does not wash very well and can clog the machinery. The coarser material is treated using a 'dense medium separation'. Here the coal is separated from other impurities by being floated in a tank containing a liquid of specific gravity. Usually, this liquid is a suspension of finely ground magnetite. The lighter coal floats and can be separated from the heavier rock and other impure materials that sink (World Coal Institute – Resource Coal, 2005).

Figure 2.17 shows a mobile wash plant capable of treating 100 tons of ROM coal per hour. Larger stationary wash plants are capable of treating 300 or more tons of ROM material per hour. Assuming 20-hour operation for 25 days a month over 12 months, you can process 600,000 tons of ROM coal per year for each 100 t/h washing capacity.

When washing coal, the yield is the most important factor. The more ash you wash out the lower is the yield and the more discard – the name of the washing by-product – you receive. Thus, relative costs increase and the need to find an outlet for the discard can also reduce your economic return. Therefore, mining companies take into consideration the increased sales

FIGURE 2.17 Mobile wash plant with 100 t/h feed capacity in South Africa

price for higher calorific value material, the cost of washing, the yield and the proceeds, if any, from discard material.

2.2.5.5 Environmental and Safety Issues Associated with Coal Production As with any industrial process, the production of coal strains the environment. State-of-the-art mine planning can minimize the environmental side-effects. The effect on the environment can be classified into four categories (see World Coal Institute – Secure Energy, 2005):

- Emissions from fuel-consuming equipment.
- Land disturbance and mine subsidence.
- Water, dust and noise pollution.
- Methane emissions.

Emissions from Equipment IEA – Oil (2007) estimates a total 2005 demand for motor gasoline and middle distillates of around 2.1 billion tons (compared with total oil product demand of around 3.9 billion tons during that year). Also, we discussed already that fuel accounts for about one-third of the operational costs in a typical non-continuous opencast mine. What this means in effect is that each ton of non-continuous opencast coal requires about 2–3 litres of fuel. So, 250 million litres of fuel are required to mine 100 million tons of non-continuous opencast coal. While this simplified figure may seem rather high, the calculation indicates that coal mining or mining in general will account for a significant share of global oil product demand. Thus, coal mining results in the emission of significant amounts of carbon dioxide due to fuel consumption, which is not accounted for when considering carbon dioxide emissions from coal combustion alone, as most statistics do.

Land Disturbance and Mine Subsidence Opencast mining requires land. During the mining process, vegetation, animal life, infrastructure and even housing can be affected. Some older underground mines are known to have caused land subsidence. Especially when mining beneath inhabited areas, modern mine planners carefully calculate how much coal can be taken out and how the roof has to be supported.

Water, Dust and Noise Pollution During mining a chemical reaction between water and rocks containing sulphur-bearing minerals can result in acid mine drainage (AMD), a metal-rich water. AMD is formed when pyrite reacts with air and water to form sulphuric acid and dissolved iron. This acid runoff dissolves heavy metals such as copper, lead and mercury that are emitted into the ground (World Coal Institute – Secure Energy, 2005). AMD can be minimized using water treatment plants and effective mine planning. Water can also be polluted during coal washing, which requires large amounts of water. Wash plant licences are therefore only granted with strict environmental requirements. Dust and noise pollution can be a problem when coal is surface-mined near inhabited areas. Also, mine workers are subject to dust and noise pollution, and so safety measures need to be installed in such mine operations.

Methane Emissions Methane emissions can occur during underground mining. Methane is 21 times more harmful to the planet (in terms of global warming) than carbon dioxide. Methane needs to be vented during underground mining in order to reduce the risk of methane explosions. Frondel *et al.* (2007) and Steenblik and Coronyannakis (1995) point out that about 15 tons of methane is emitted for each ton of coal production. They argue, therefore, that a number of older underground mines, especially in Europe, should be closed down immediately in order to substantially reduce greenhouse gas emissions. Three million tons of coal mined underground in Europe produces approximately one million tons of CO_2 equivalent.

Safety in Coal Production Larger mine accidents are regularly reported in the media. Many of these accidents occur in older mines in Eastern Europe and Asia. Historically, the majority of fatalities in coal mining accidents – according to statistics compiled by the Chinese State Administration of Work Safety (SAWS) – occurred in China, but this is changing. Mining operations in Australia, the USA and other countries also experience underground mine accidents with collapsing roofs or fumigation from time to time.

Modern mines rarely experience safety problems. Effective mine planning can greatly reduce and avoid safety hazards. Existing mines need to be reinvestigated and international treaties should be signed to make coal mining safer. International mining conglomerates have done a lot but need to do more to make mining safer.

Another factor to be considered with mining safety is the employment of inexpensive and often untrained labour in some of the world's underground mines. Today, however, most countries have laws regulating the hiring of untrained and trained personnel in mines.

2.3 USE OF COAL – POWER GENERATION AND MORE

Coal accounted for about half the increase in global energy use over the past decade (IEA – Energy Outlook, 2011). Electricity use was the key driver of this demand increase. Power or electricity is one of the most important elements of human life today. However, about 2.7 billion people still rely on primitive biomass fuels to meet their household energy and heat requirements. According to the World Health Organization (WHO), almost 2 million people die each year from the effects of burning solid fuels indoors. Dependable and affordable access to electricity is essential for improving people's health, providing education and information services, improving living conditions and freeing up time from gathering fuel. Electrification of rural areas and energy consumption growth are therefore not only environmental issues but also a necessity for the human race. Reliable access to electricity will allow (1) more people to work in agriculture and manufacturing jobs, freeing them from unproductive fuel-collecting tasks; (2) better use of agricultural or protected natural land; (3) improvement of public health; and (4) the use of modern appliances and lighting, which improves productivity. In short, electrification spurs a nation's GDP development (World Coal Institute – Resource Coal, 2005, p. 21).

Our ancestors tamed fire for the first time 300,000–800,000 years ago. Since then, light and warmth from burning biomass has fuelled – in the true sense of the word – the development of humankind. It took many thousands of years before humans discovered the advantages of burning coal rather than wood. Historians believe that the Chinese were at the forefront of this development. There are some reports that the Chinese were already using coal about 3000 years ago for casting coins and smelting metal products. It took about 500 years longer for Europeans to utilize coal for energy generation. The Greeks and Romans were first. In the Middle Ages, the use of coal was widespread and the first trading of coal apparently occurred between England and Belgium. The industrial revolution in the eighteenth and nineteenth centuries would not have been possible without coal. The steam engine, powered by coal, was invented by James Watt in 1769. In the nineteenth century, many cities – starting with

TABLE 2.5 Use of world hard coal by sector, 1980–2011

	1980		2011	
Consumption	**Bln tons**	**%**	**Bln tons**	**%**
Total hard coal consumed, of which:	2.8		7.0	
– Power plants	1.0	36%	4.6	66
– Steel industry	0.6	21%	1.1	15%
– Heat market, cement and other	1.2	43%	1.3	19%

Source: Estimate based on author's research and analysis. VDKI (2006–2013); Ritschel and Schiffer (2007); IEA Medium-Term Coal Market Report (2012); IEA Energy Outlook (2007, 2011).

London – produced so-called town gas from coal to light their city streets using the coal gasification process (World Coal Institute – Resource Coal, 2005, p. 19).

Today, coal is used in a variety of applications: (1) power generation, (2) steel production, (3) coal liquefaction, (4) cement production and (5) other applications including but not limited to household consumption, alumina refineries, paper manufacturers, chemical industry (such as for soda production), pharmaceutical industry and for specialist products, such as activated carbon, carbon fibre and silicon metal.

However, about two-thirds of the 7.0 billion tons of coal produced worldwide is used for power generation. The IEA (IEA Medium-Term Coal Market Report, 2012) estimates that about 78% of coal use is driven by demand for power in the OECD, while for non-OECD countries that figure is far lower at around 55%. The remainder is used for steel production and other applications. Table 2.5 summarizes the uses of all produced hard coal. Note that 6.1 billion tons of the total 7.0 billion tons of hard coal produced in 2011 was steam coal. Since about 4.6 billion tons of coal is used by power plants and since power plants mostly use steam coal, this results in power plants consuming about 85% of global steam coal production.

Hard coal, here mostly coking coal, is also a crucial ingredient for two-thirds of global steel production. Other industries, such as the alumina, paper and chemical industries, also rely heavily on coal. Coal liquefaction has been perfected by Sasol, the South African company that uses the famous German Fischer–Tropsch technology to generate fuel from coal. For example, Sasol already consumes one-quarter of South Africa's coal production for the purpose of CtL.

Since internationally traded steam coal is mainly used for power generation, we will focus on power generation and its implications for the global seaborne steam coal trade.

2.3.1 Steam Coal and its Role in Power Generation

Coal is used to generate over 41% of the world's electricity (see Figure 2.7). As such, coal is the single most important source of energy for all the world's electricity needs, outstripping gas (22%), nuclear (13%) and oil (5%). Based on market research, we estimate that over 85% of the global seaborne steam coal trade is used in power generation. This is confirmed by the German Coal Importers Association (VDKI, 2006, p. 8). Thus, power generation drives the demand for seaborne traded steam coal.

Efficient power generation requires availability and most importantly reliability of an energy resource. In addition to securing the raw material, power plants need to ensure they can get the produced electricity to the consumer. Coal, in many respects, is the most reliable

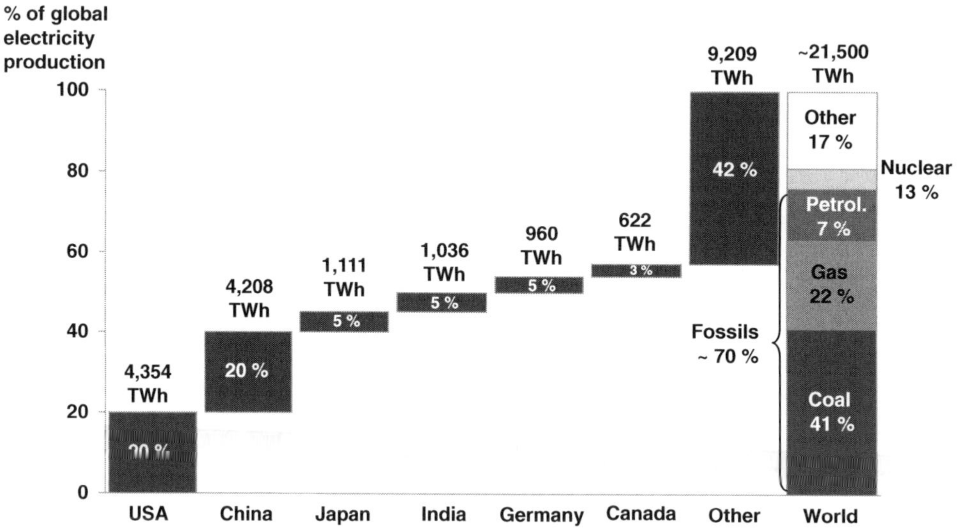

FIGURE 2.18 World's electricity energy share by region in 2010
Source: IEA – Statistics (2012). Author's analysis.

and widely available energy source for power generation. Major blackouts such as those that occurred in the last decade (for instance, in Brazil in 2001, California in 2000–2001, New Zealand in 2001 and 2003, Northeastern USA in 2003, Italy in 2003, China in 2008, South Africa in 2008, India in 2012, and so on) can be avoided in the future if steam coal is used more wisely, often in connection with renewable sources of energy (World Coal Institute – Secure Energy, 2005). Many countries that currently use little coal for power generation, such as New Zealand and Brazil, are advised to increase their coal share in order to reach higher levels of system reliability.

The world produced about 21,500 TWh of electricity in 2010. China has reached US levels and in fact overtook the USA in 2012. Figure 2.18 summarizes the global situation in more detail (2011 numbers).

More interestingly, Figure 2.19 shows the world's top ten electricity producers and their respective power generation mix. The top ten countries account for two-thirds of global power generation. China, India, the USA, Korea and Germany generate about half or more of their electricity using coal; in fact, China depends on coal for over 75% and India for almost 70% of power generated. The graph gives a good visual overview of the power generation mix. Canada and Brazil use a lot of hydro/biomass, while France is the country with the highest nuclear power generation share of almost 80%. Japan, the world's third largest power producer with almost one-quarter coal power generation share, has also been the largest steam coal importer in the world until 2012 when China overtook Japan for the first time. Remember, Japan has no significant coal reserves itself.

The graph also shows the compound annual growth rate (CAGR) for India and China, which illustrates how the importance of coal is continuously increasing globally, much driven by these two countries. However, one key factor changing or at least slowing this trend is the recent shale gas revolution in North America, reducing coal use in the USA, which used to be the largest power market in the world before China overtook it in recent years.

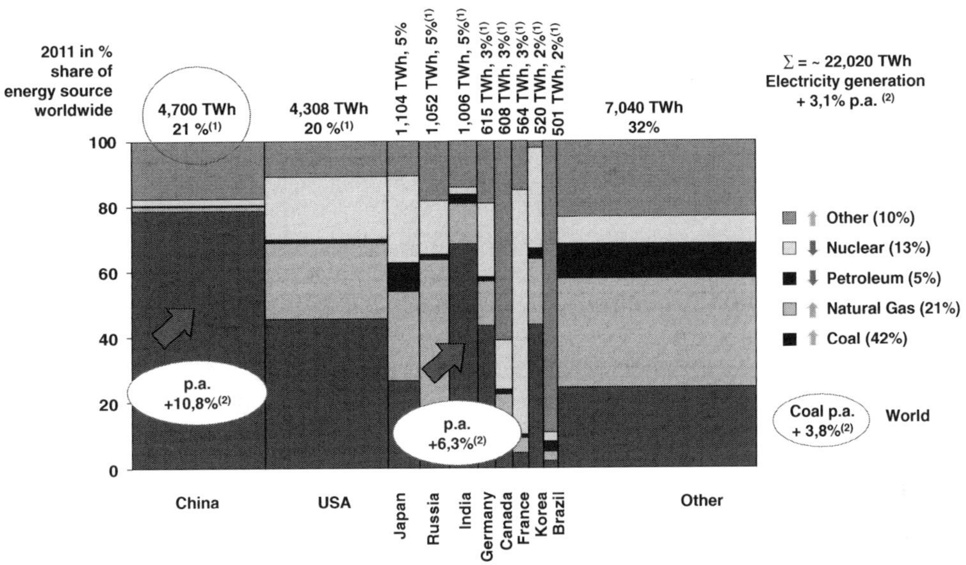

FIGURE 2.19 Global top ten electricity producers in 2011

(1) Share of total electricity production in various countries.

(2) CAGR 2005–2011 in %.

Source: Schernikau Research & Analysis; IEA Electricity Information (2011); BP Statistical Review of World Energy (2012).

Looking to the future one can visualize, based on Figure 2.19, that China's and India's columns will grow much wider and, thus, the world's use of coal will increase. Both countries rely more heavily than average on coal for their power generation mix, thus their use of coal will increase more than that of any other fossil or even nuclear energy resource.

2.3.2 Coal-Fired Power Plant Technologies

Coal power plant technology is considered one of the most stable technologies for generating electricity. This in fact is one of the many advantages of coal-based electricity over other energy sources. It is interesting, but in terms of efficiency unfortunate, that there are scarcely two coal power plants in the world of the same design. This means that almost every power plant is different and also works differently, resulting in varying efficiencies among power plants when burning various qualities of coal.

In a coal-fired power plant, the chemical energy stored in the coal is first converted into thermal energy in the boiler, then to mechanical energy in the turbine, and finally to electrical energy using generators. Figure 2.20 depicts the typical process of a coal-fired power plant.

Engineers are currently focusing on two principal means of optimizing coal-fired power plant technologies: (1) by increasing efficiency and (2) by reducing CO_2 emissions. However, these two aims compete to an extent; reducing CO_2 emissions always reduces efficiency, as energy is required to capture and process CO_2 for storage.

Figure 2.21 indicates current average efficiencies and the resulting CO_2 emissions. Previously, we discussed the amount of coal-fired electricity production in China. It can now

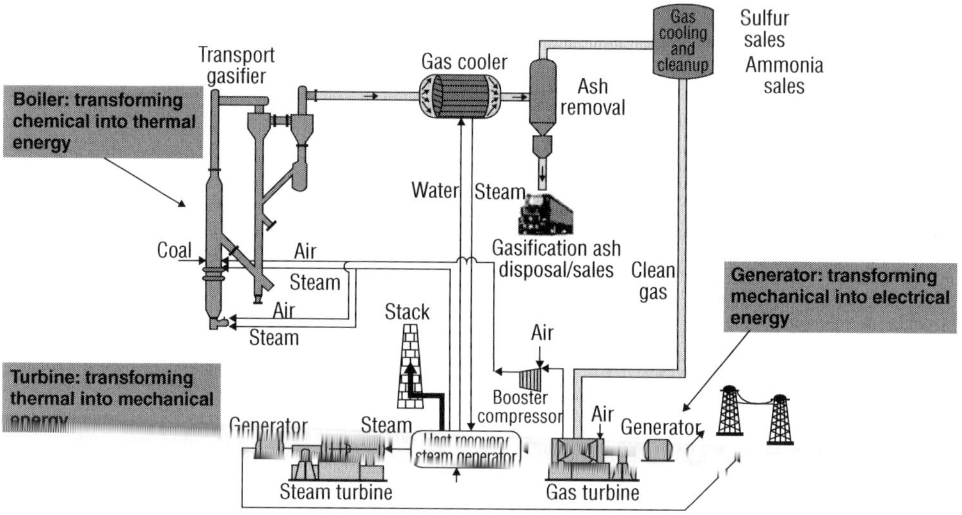

FIGURE 2.20 Typical process in a coal-fired power plant
Source: www.enr.com.

be derived that the driver for CO_2 reduction is not the Western world, but China and other developing countries. If China reached the same technological standard as Germany or the Western world, then CO_2 emissions in China from coal-fired power generation could almost be halved. Far over 1 billion tons of CO_2, or almost 5% of the 30 billion tons of CO_2 emitted globally through human activity, could be saved by this measure alone. I would like to remind the reader that to this day, China builds about one power plant every week of the year, and in this process of renewing its power plant park has also made amazing strides to improve its average efficiencies.

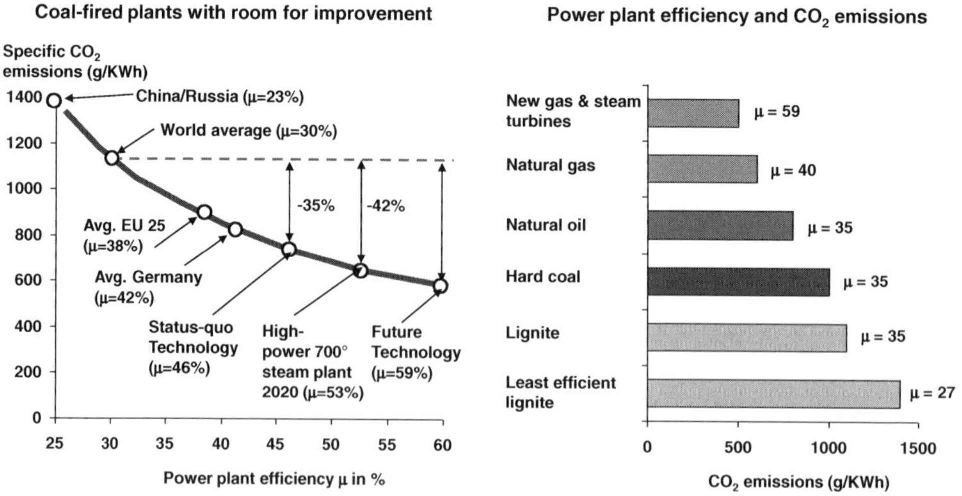

FIGURE 2.21 Efficiency and emissions of coal power plants
Source: Deutsche Bank Research (2007); UBS-Resources (2008). Author's research and analysis.

Future technologies are expected to increase conversion efficiencies to 60% or more. However, this has little impact on the present challenge of capturing and storing carbon dioxide. For a more detailed discussion of carbon capture and storage (CCS), please refer to a series of research papers from Stanford University (Rai *et al.*, 2008).

2.3.3 Cement and Other Industry

Demand for steam coal outside the power industry stems from the iron and steel industry, heat production for district and industrial processes, the cement industry, paper industry, textile industry and any other industry with large energy requirements that uses coal to generate the energy required – often using the steam generated in the process.

Such non-power coal demand correlates closely to GDP growth (similar to the power industry) and the construction industry economic cycle. In the OECD, where less than one-quarter of coal demand comes from this sector, it is projected that demand will be stable to slightly decreasing. Europe and Asia Oceania (here Japan) account for about 80% of such non-power OECD coal demand (IEA – Medium-Term Coal Market Report, 2012, p. 70). In China and other non-OECD countries, the proportion of non-power coal demand is much higher, over 40%. Industry is still more energy intensive here and coal is still used in some home heating. Growth focuses on China (accounting for over three-quarters of non-OECD non-power coal demand) and India, where infrastructure investments such as large railway systems, sea port capacity, airport capacity and the road network have been expanding and will continue to expand at remarkable speed.

2.3.4 Alternatives to Coal: Shale Gas and Other

As with any market, demand and prices for a product are also driven by the availability of substitutes and the costs of switching between substitutes. Key competitors for coal are other fuels and techniques for power generation; namely gas, nuclear, oil and alternatives such as hydro, wind, biomass and solar.

2.3.4.1 Natural Gas and Shale Gas Gas accounts for about 21–22% of the world's electricity production and is the second most important fuel for electricity generation after coal. Gas is also one of the most important sources of primary energy, accounting for 21% of primary energy in 2010 versus 32% for oil and 27% for coal (cf. Figure 2.7).

BGR (2011) estimates the remaining potential of natural gas to have increased substantially over the past 5 years, translating into approximately 60 years reserve/production ratio, and 256 years when taking the remaining potential into account. However, gas reserves and resources are spread very unevenly across the globe. Russia and the Middle East, and thanks to shale gas now North America, have the largest available reserves.

The shale gas revolution in the USA started in the years before 2010. It led to an oversupply of natural gas, which in turn reduced prices for natural gas from USD 6.00/MBTU in early 2010 to about USD 2.00/MBTU in 2012 (IEA – Medium-Term Coal Market Report, 2012, p. 73). Coal prices had increased after the sharp drop in 2009 and both these diverging price movements led to a switch from coal to gas in the USA. The IEA estimates that coal remains the backbone of power generation in the USA, but coal use will decrease further in the next 4 to 5 years by approximately another 15%. Gas, at the same time, will increase its share continuously.

Outside the USA it is predicted that the shale gas revolution will be more difficult to 'implement' itself. While large reserves are expected outside the USA, most mineral rights are owned by governments, giving local private entities little incentive for industrial drilling. It also suffices to say that the technology for fracking is anything but simple and also surprisingly energy intensive. For instance, Shell's technology is used a lot for shale gas production. They state that about 30% of the energy produced from shale gas has to be invested beforehand in its production. Keep in mind that much of this invested energy will in fact come from coal. Nevertheless, other countries in South America, Africa, Europe and Asia are exploring the possibilities of shale gas and are likely to succeed on a selective basis within the next 10 years.

Combusting gas versus coal is less CO_2 intensive. Assuming power plant efficiency of $\omega = 0.38$, with 1 MWh of coal power generation, each ton of standard 6000 kcal/kg nar coal emits 0.89 tons of CO_2. Gas-powered generators emit about 45% less carbon dioxide than coal. However, this does not take into consideration the energy-intensive production of shale gas as described above.

On a global scale, the key disadvantages for gas are its infrastructure requirements in the form of pipeline networks or LNG terminals.

2.3.4.2 Nuclear Energy Nuclear energy today plays an important role in our electricity production. In 2010, about 13% of global electricity was generated in nuclear power plants (down from 15% in 2005). Nuclear power accounts for approximately 6% of primary energy (cf. Figure 2.7). Since nuclear power production is virtually CO_2-neutral and is more economical for base load (see Figure 2.22), it would certainly be the technology for the future were it not for the risks involved.

Nuclear energy results from the splitting (fission) or merging (fusion) of the nuclei of atoms. The conversion of nuclear mass to energy is consistent with the mass–energy equivalence formula $\Delta E = \Delta mc^2$, in which ΔE equals energy release, Δm equals mass defect and c equals the speed of light in a vacuum. In the early 20th century, Albert Einstein

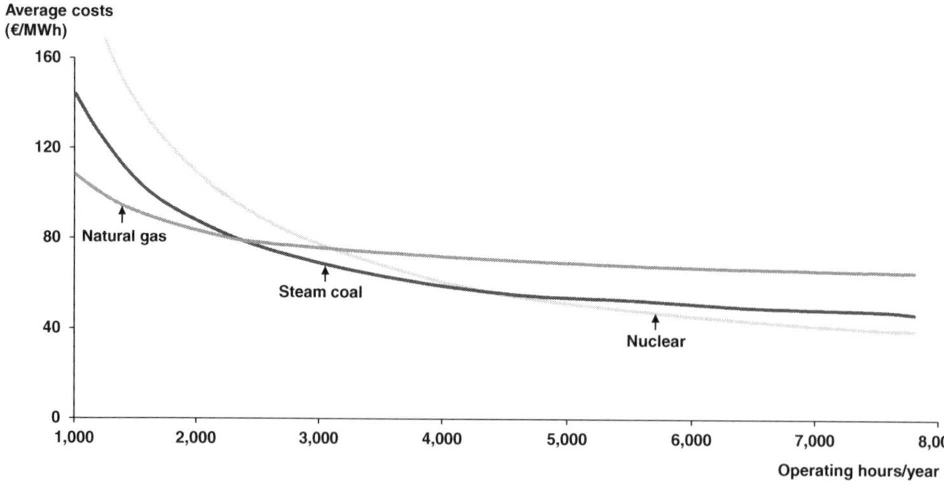

FIGURE 2.22 Exemplary average costs: gas vs. coal vs. nuclear
Source: Erdmann and Zweifel (2008), p. 301.

discovered that mass can be transferred to energy. In 1938, the German chemists Otto Hahn and Fritz Strassmann proved that nuclear fission is technically feasible. In 1945, the US Army exploded the first atomic bombs over Hiroshima and Nagasaki. Since the 1950s, nuclear energy has also been harnessed for peaceful purposes: to generate electricity. The use of nuclear energy for electricity generation expanded rapidly after the oil price shocks of the 1970s. However, at least three major incidents shattered confidence in nuclear energy: the accident at the Three Mile Island reactor in Harrisburg, USA in 1979; the Chernobyl catastrophe in the Ukraine in 1986; and the Fukushima tsunami catastrophe in 2011. After the first two incidents, no new nuclear power plants were built outside France and Japan until 2005 (Erdmann and Zweifel, 2008, p. 270). After Fukushima, Germany decided to step away from nuclear energy completely, with Japan planning to reduce its use and other nations becoming more careful.

The safety risks involved with nuclear energy, however, will politically stall development of new nuclear power plants. Leaving aside political and strategic games on the international diplomatic playing field, it is undeniably true that by their nature nuclear power plants can cause drastic catastrophes if something goes wrong. The reason for accidents or catastrophes can be terrorism, human error, natural disaster or any other cause. Another major environmental concern in relation to nuclear energy is how to deal with nuclear waste, which remains radioactive, and therefore hazardous to life, for tens and even hundreds of thousands of years.

The risks involved with nuclear energy are so large that one can argue in the interest of human survival that no nuclear power plants whatsoever should be built or operated. Germany followed this argument when it committed itself to decommissioning all of its existing nuclear power plants. It is clear that the three briefly discussed risk categories – (1) accidents in nuclear power plants, (2) disposal of radioactive waste and (3) potential misuse of nuclear fuel – cannot be carried by any one company or risk insurer. Risks 1 and 3 cannot even be quantified and the timeframes involved can go far beyond a human lifetime. Therefore, only laws and international regulation or collaboration can reduce and handle such risks, if at all. We doubt that is possible, and therefore predict that nuclear energy will not be the primary choice in the future, yet will remain part of the mix.

Fuelling nuclear power plants. Keep in mind that nuclear power does require a natural non-renewable, yet not fossil, resource. The uranium isotope uranium-235 (235U) is the most commonly used nuclear fuel. Naturally occurring uranium ore consists of 0.7% 235U and 99.3% 238U. The uranium isotope 235U can be split by bombarding it with neutrons of lower energy. The result of this nuclear fission is 3.2×10^{-11} joules of thermal heat and two to three new neutrons that can split more 235U atomic cores resulting in the well-known and often feared nuclear chain reaction.

BGR (2006, p. 23) estimates that nuclear power plants generated 390 GWe (gigawatts of electrical power) in 2006. The world's nuclear power plants thus required about 66,500 tons of uranium ore, of which about 40,000 tons (60%) came from normal uranium ore production. The other 40% came from earlier and sometimes quite old civil inventory and, most importantly, from strategic military inventory. As such, the production of uranium ore has been lagging behind consumption for many years.

Australia, Kazakhstan and Russia account for about 40% of global uranium production. The biggest importers – the USA, France, Japan, Germany and the UK – have virtually no domestic production. Total global uranium ore reserves at current production levels of 0.04 Mt (or 0.6 Gt tce) per year will last for only about 28 years (BGR, 2011). The remaining potential will last for 164 years (see Figure 2.5).

2.3.4.3 Oil and Power Generation In 2010, oil accounted for 32% of global primary energy but only 5% of electricity, down from 35% and 7%, respectively, in 2005. It has been argued in the press as well as by leading research institutions such as the IEA and others that coal will replace oil as the most important source of primary energy within the next 5 years.

Alternatively produced oil (heavy raw oil, oil sands, bitumen, tar, shale oil and possibly CtL and BtL technology) will ensure that there will be enough fuel for our cars, planes, vessels and other means of transportation. At the same time those alternatives are expensive and keep the price of oil at high levels.

Some countries, such as Indonesia (32% in 2005), Mexico (29%), Morocco (26%) and Japan (11%), and also Pakistan, rely heavily on oil for electricity generation. They are continuously reducing the share of petroleum in electricity generation, switching to coal and/or gas. Cumulative oil production almost equals currently known oil reserves. If we include currently known resources in the equation, experts expect that the 'depletion mid-point' (see also peak oil theory), where cumulative production equals the remaining potential, will be reached within the next 5 to 10 years. However, experts also argue that innovation and newly discovered resources will further extend the depletion mid-point into the future (see Figure 2.23). The current reserve/production ratio translates to 54 years as per BGR (2011), compared with 42 years in 2006 (Schernikau, 2010).

Prices for oil are driven by the fuel industry market and the oil producers. The electricity market plays only a minor role, unlike for gas and coal. With oil prices reaching above 140 USD/barrel in July 2008 before slumping back to 40 USD/barrel in November 2008 and climbing back up to consistently around 105–115 USD/barrel in 2013, the use of oil in the power industry will decrease even faster than expected.

When looking at oil versus coal it becomes clear that changes in oil consumption will only marginally impact coal. Heavy fuel oils, which have been used in power plants, can be used in

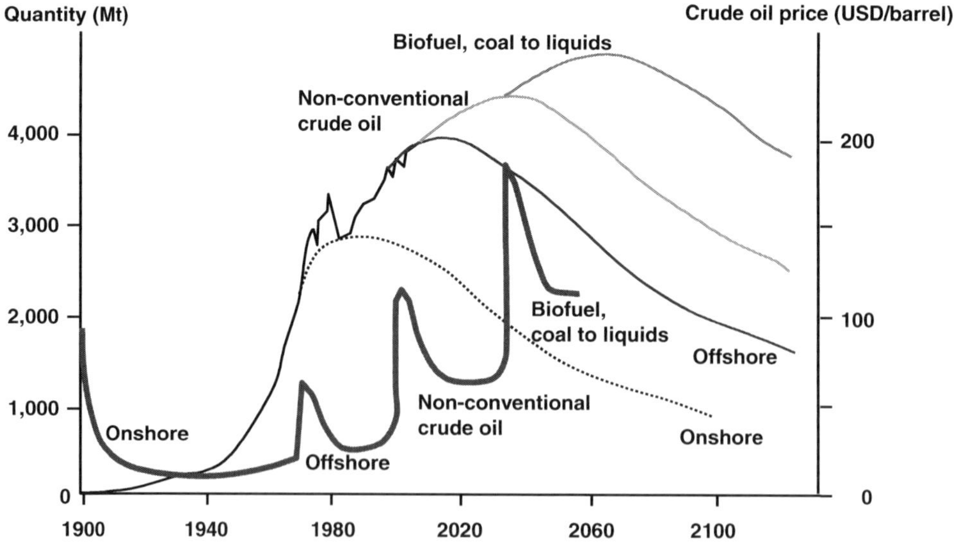

FIGURE 2.23 Exemplary: perspective on future oil supply
Source: Erdmann and Zweifel (2008), p. 207.

other fuel applications. The technology used for oil-fired power plants can be adapted to fire other fuels such as coal and gas. Many coal-fired power plants use oil to start up a power plant before switching to coal for fuelling combustion. Oil, however, is a key factor for the cost of coal production as much of global coal production uses truck-and-shovel methods which are very fuel intensive. Also, all transportation is heavily fuel intensive.

2.3.4.4 Alternatives: Hydro, Wind, Biomass, Solar and Other Sources The alternative, non-fossil and non-nuclear energy sources already accounted for 19% of total electricity production (21,500 TWh) in 2010. Of the about 4100 TWh classified as deriving from 'other sources', about 3400 TWh or 85% is hydroelectricity (IEA – World Energy Outlook, 2011; IEA – Statistics, 2012). Thus, non-hydro only accounted for approximately 650 TWh or less than 3% of global electricity production.

The IEA estimates that the non-hydro share of global electricity generation will increase five times by the year 2030. Because this starts from such a small base (650 TWh), this will only cover a relatively small portion of the increased electricity demand by that time. IEA predicts in its reference scenario that total electricity demand will increase to 35,500 TWh by 2030, thus increasing by 65% from 2010. The IEA estimates that by 2030 approximately 19% or 2700 TWh of the increased demand will be served by non-hydro alternative fuels; the remaining 81% or 11,300 TWh of increased demand will have to be filled by fossil fuels, nuclear and hydro (see Figure 2.24).

Hydroelectricity accounted for 16% of global electricity generation in 2010. The main hydroelectricity generators in terms of electricity share are many South American countries, Canada, China and Russia. Also, smaller countries such as Nigeria, Switzerland and Norway generate a large proportion of their electricity using hydro-technology. Importantly for this

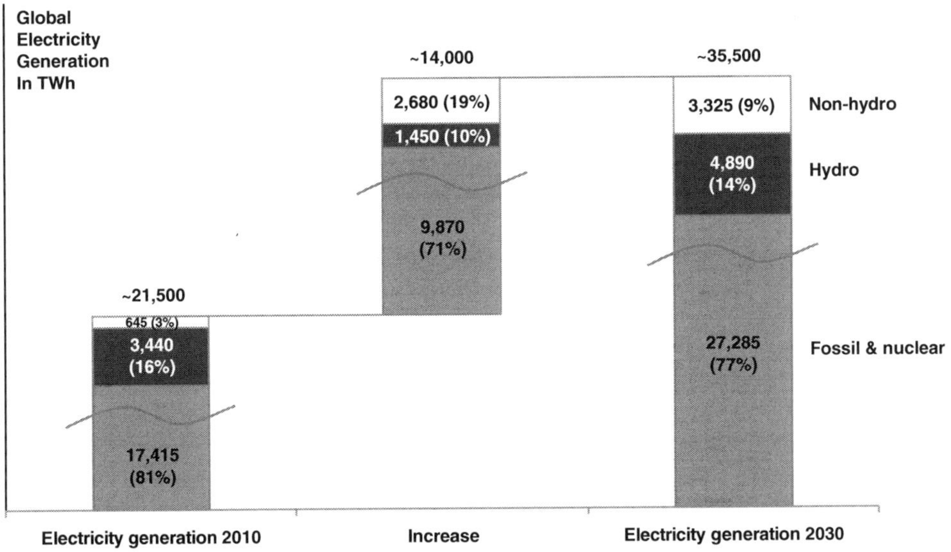

FIGURE 2.24 Non-hydro and hydro electricity growth up to 2030
Source: IEA – World Energy Outlook (2011); IEA – Statistics (2012); Schernikau (2010). Author's analysis.

study, the EIA predicts that hydro's share will drop to 14% of world electricity generation by 2030. This makes sense as hydro will not solve the world's energy problem nor can it keep up with the rise in global electricity demand.

Non-hydro alternative electricity accounted for about 3% of global electricity generation in 2010. While they are not yet relevant on a global scale, it is important to summarize these alternatives here as they will become more prominent in the future. Non-hydro alternatives include (1) wind, (2) biogenic products, (3) solar photovoltaic and other sources such as geothermal energy and hydrogen. We can safely assume that the 650 TWh generated by non-hydro alternatives in 2010 stem mostly from wind and maybe some biogenic products.

We view non-hydro alternatives as 'solar generated electricity'. In a way, this is where the world has to go after the Oil Age and Coal Age are over in perhaps 50–100 years. The goal is to find ways to capture the solar energy for CO_2-neutral electricity generation. However, this is less relevant for this study as its scope is merely the next 20–30 years. So far, non-hydro alternatives are not yet able to meet the majority of increased electricity demand in the next 20 years, but their share is increasing and in 30–50 years the situation will certainly look different. A technological breakthrough, today still unforeseen, is likely to shift the energy landscape when it happens. History has shown that such technological breakthroughs can very quickly alter the existing landscape. One recent example is certainly the fracking technology that allowed the shale gas revolution in the USA.

Wind Of the non-hydro alternatives, wind has developed the fastest. Some countries, such as Germany and certain other European countries, already generate a significant share (often more than 5%) of their electricity needs using wind power.

The problem with wind power is that much of it is still heavily subsidized and it requires a large area to generate any noticeable energy. Standard wind turbines today produce perhaps 2 MW of electricity; thus, 1500 onshore wind turbines would be required to replace a standard 1000 MW coal-fired power plant, assuming the turbines work only one-third as often and efficiently as a coal-fired power plant. Offshore wind power systems are expected to become more efficient and have less impact on the environment. The biggest problem with wind is that the wind cannot be predicted. Therefore, most countries have laws where wind power has priority over any other form of generation, often causing inefficiency with other power stations (i.e., when coal-fired power plants are switched on and off). These external factors, which also produce added inefficiency in existing power plants, are rarely, if ever, considered or quantified when talking about the effectiveness of wind power.

Biogenic Products Biogenic products can be divided into energy plants and residual plant products such as used wood. In order to process biogenic products into gaseous or liquid fuels, the industry uses (1) biochemical processes (i.e., fermentation to biogas or bio-ethanol), (2) thermochemical processes (i.e., Fischer–Tropsch synthesis used in BtL) and (3) physical/chemical processes (i.e., esterification of rape products to bio-diesel) (Erdmann and Zweifel, 2008, p. 254).

Biogenic products can support both the petroleum-based fuel industry and the coal- and gas-based electricity generation industries. Newer technology is also being developed to process biomass into coal products through biomass-to-coal (BtC) processes. These technologies promise to become more efficient, utilizing 100% of the carbon content and with 80% energy efficiency. However, the economic and energy community expects that biogenic energy products will play a small role in the future energy mix. Fuel product costs rise quickly as increasing quantities of the feed product (biomass) are required. Logistics for collecting, handling and storing high-energy plants are a further limiting factor. Economies of scale cannot be fully utilized because not enough feed product can be sourced. Subsidies in the form of tax breaks, direct investment or other financial support often distort the picture when comparing biogenic-based energy products to fossil-based products. However, for many farmers in the Western world, growing energy crops is a welcome change from cutting down crops or reducing planted areas. On a worldwide scale, though, using agricultural land to grow energy plants seems to have a limited future.

Solar, Photovoltaic, Geothermal, Tidal Power and Other Sources From a long-term perspective this third category of new technologies that don't rely on wind or biogenic products seems to have the brightest future. However, today it is difficult to say if and when such non-wind and non-biogenic products/technologies will play a more important role in the planet's electricity mix.

Solar, photovoltaic, geothermal and tidal power are currently being researched and already contribute, to some extent, to electricity needs. The use of such technologies will grow but it will take decades before they can economically satisfy a substantial share of the world's electricity needs. For example, about 3 GW of geothermal capacity was installed in the USA by December 2008; the goal is to reach 100 GW by 2050. This compares with a total globally installed capacity of 1000 GW in 2008 (Tester, 2009).

Longer-term future technologies may also include fusion power technology (see the current International Thermonuclear Experimental Reactor (ITER) project in Cadarache, South of France, www.iter.org) and other technologies that use hydrogen as an energy source. Currently there are five groups of technologies that have been selected for further research as they promise large-scale hydrogen production over the next 50 years: (1) steam reforming of natural gas, (2) gasification of coal, (3) gasification of biomass, (4) electrolysis of water and (5) thermolysis.

2.3.5 Future Trend: CtL and Coal Bed Methane

There are a number of new and not-so-new technologies that will further increase the efficiency of coal products in today's energy-hungry economies. First and foremost is the quest to further increase coal-fired power plant efficiencies. Second, carbon capture and storage is being explored to reduce CO_2 emission into the atmosphere (not only CO_2 resulting from coal combustion). Third, coal-to-liquid (CtL) and coal bed methane (CBM) allow more efficient and environmentally sustainable use of hard coal and sub-bituminous coals.

Coal-to-liquid technology expands the use of coal into fuel products, thus competing with oil. In 1913, Fritz Bergius patented the direct hydration of coal. In 1925, Franz Fischer and Hans Tropsch patented the indirect liquefaction method, which is still referred to as Fischer–Tropsch synthesis. Germany started using liquefied coal for strategic reasons before and during World War II. Towards the end of the war the country operated 27 CtL facilities, 9 Fischer–Tropsch indirect plants and 18 direct liquefaction plants. By the end of the war, 90% of Germany's fuel demand was being met by CtL. After the war the technology fell out of favour, as a result of a different energy policy and low oil prices (Deutsche Bank Research, 2007). South Africa picked up the technology to develop it further. Sasol, today's leading CtL company, converts over 40 million tons of coal into liquids using CtL technology and satisfies about 60% of South Africa's domestic fuel demand in this way, thus replacing oil imports. Germany's Lurgi is another CtL technology provider that is quite successful and is implementing and planning projects around the globe. CtL is, of course, more economical when oil prices are high.

The main disadvantages of CtL relate to the environment. CtL fuels cause significantly higher CO_2 emissions than standard fuels derived from oil. IEA CIAB-CtL (2006), p. 25 estimates that CtL fuel emits 2–2.5 times more CO_2 per km driven than standard fuel under similar conditions. Some experts argue that this figure is rather in the range 7–10 times. CtL plants also require 10–18 tons of water per ton of output (China Coal Monthly, 2006), are very expensive and require mine-mouth access to coal, which is possible in most larger coal-producing nations. Such projects exist in China, Russia and also in North America. Additionally, Mozambique is considering this technology to overcome the logistical disadvantages of its coal reserves. Technology is continuously improving and will reduce the environmental impact of CtL. Also, CCS will play a potentially large role when reducing the CO_2 impact of CtL.

Coal bed methane projects are supported under the Kyoto Protocol. Through so-called joint implementation projects investors can claim CO_2 credits, using them either to offset their own emissions or selling them on the open market. The idea is to capture otherwise wasted methane that is released (a) from abandoned underground coal fields, (b) from operating underground coal fields or (c) from bore holes on the surface. A combined heat and power station can be fuelled in this way. A case study in China, presented by Faizoullina (2006), shows that one such project capturing 15 million cbm of methane per annum can supply 10,000 houses with heat while generating electricity at the same time. In addition, the project accumulates 400,000 tons of CO_2 credits per annum. Recent projects in Australia and Indonesia will further optimize this technology. Also, new drilling technology will make this use of coal more economically viable in the future.

2.4 OVERVIEW OF WORLDWIDE STEAM COAL SUPPLY AND DEMAND

After having explored the source of coal and the use of coal we can now go to the traded coal market. The global steam coal trade market is ever changing and has gone through a decade of substantial transformation, moving from the Atlantic to the Pacific, with China emerging as the largest coal importer, the USA becoming a large exporter and new supply from Mozambique and Mongolia entering the market. This section will give an overview of the key demand and supply regions.

2.4.1 Atlantic Demand Market: Europe at its Core

Historically, the UK (2012 imports 45 million tons) and Germany (2012 imports 45 million tons) belonged to the top five steam coal importers globally. Despite Germany importing more now than 5 years ago, today the situation looks different. China, Japan, India, Korea and Taiwan are the top five and all are located in Asia, or the Pacific market. Europe, or the Atlantic market is supplied mainly by South Africa, Colombia, Russia and since the shale gas revolution also by the USA (VDKI, 2011, 2012).

While the Pacific and Atlantic markets have historically behaved differently, in recent years there has been more inter-market trade. For instance, Russian sales to Asia have increased, as has South African trade to India and China. Some Australian and Indonesian coal has found its way to Europe, subject to freight viability.

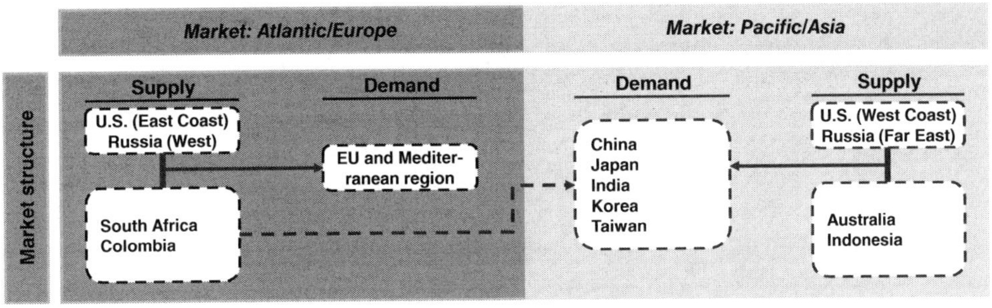

FIGURE 2.25 Market structure of Atlantic and Pacific coal trade
Source: Author's research and analysis, also based on BCG (2004).

Figure 2.25 depicts the market structure and how the Pacific and Atlantic markets interact.

The key importing gateways for European demand are ARA (Amsterdam/Rotterdam/Antwerp), the UK and north German ports. Another important market in the Atlantic is Poland. The country used to be one of the key exporters but in 2011 only exported seaborne about 3 million tons. In fact, Poland today imports more coal from Russia for its own use, much of it via rail.

Southern European imports via the Mediterranean are growing because Turkey is expected to import more coal in the years to come. Otherwise, Spain, Italy, Morocco and Israel are the key countries to be supplied in this region. The north European consumers are served by Russian coal and some small intra-European trade from Germany and ARA. Overall, it is expected that Atlantic demand will stagnate or grow very slowly. From 2011 to 2012, however, European imports (including Mediterranean imports) grew from 148 million tons to 193 millions tons (see Figure 2.26).

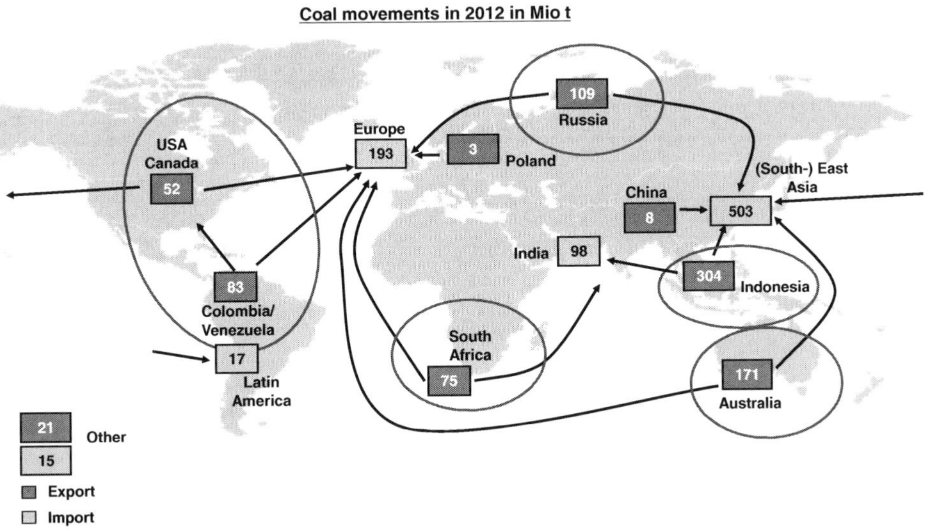

FIGURE 2.26 826 million tons traded steam coal, global seaborne trade flow 2013
Includes China (145), Japan (133), Korea (105), Taiwan (66), Hong Kong (12).
Source: Author's research and analysis, based on VDKI (2013).

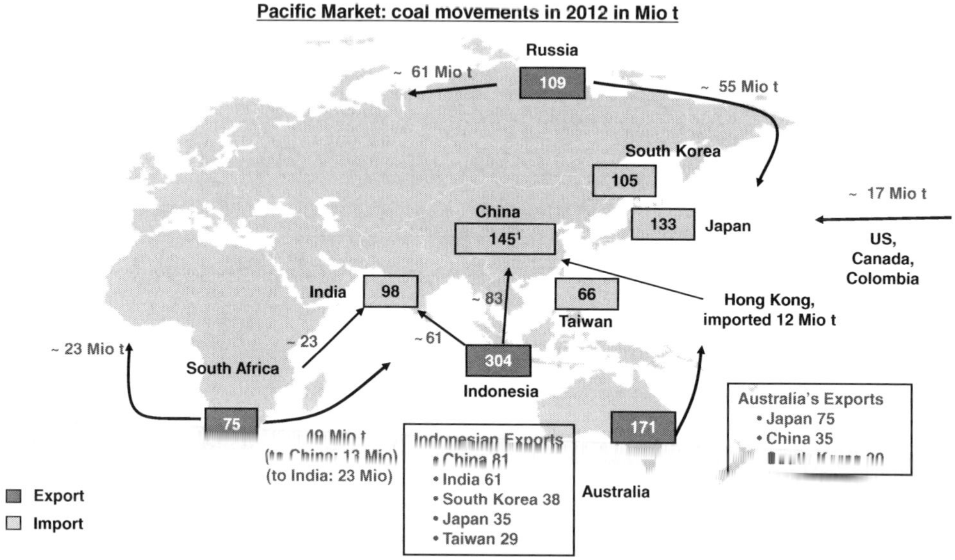

FIGURE 2.27 2012 Asian steam coal import distribution
Excluding approx. 34 million tons anthracite and approx. 54 million tons coking coal (total imports 235 million tons as per VDKI vs. 288 million tons as per import statistics).
Source: Author's research and analysis, based on VDKI (2012, 2013); Chinese customs data; RBCT export data and various market research.

2.4.2 Pacific Demand Market: China, India, Japan, Taiwan, Korea and SEA

Two new import powers have appeared in the Pacific market: China and India. Japan, Korea and Taiwan have already been part of the top five import nations for many years, but China has quickly moved to the top spot, for the first time becoming a net importer only in 2007/2008 after years of supplying Japan, Korea and Taiwan with steam coal. China became the largest steam coal importer only 4 years later in 2012 (see Figure 2.27).

2.4.2.1 China Undoubtedly, China plays a key role in the world market of any industry; and so it is with coal. Approximately 290 million tons of coal was imported into China in 2012, of which about 200 million tons was steam coal and lignite (VDKI puts China's steam coal imports of 2012 at 145 million tons) and the rest coking coal and anthracite. Indonesia alone supplied over 80 million tons of coal to China, up from 6 million tons in 2006 (VDKI, 2012, 2013; Platts, 2013). This means, today, that China is by far the largest steam coal importer, far surpassing Japan, the historic leader.

Some key facts about China (The Beijing Axis, 2012; National Bureau of Statistics of China, 2012; industry press) include the following:

- China has surpassed the USA as the largest energy-consuming nation, accounting for about 21% of global energy consumption. At the same time, China accounts currently for about 10% of global GDP on the way to making it 15% within 5 years.

- GDP per capita is still only 1/10th that of developed nations and still below Brazil, Russia and South Africa (but above India).
- GDP is concentrated in coastal regions, with growth spearheaded by more central regions.
- The Chinese workforce, and as a result heavy industry and coal demand, is expected to plateau within the next 10 years.
- China is the world's largest exporter (31% of China's GDP is exported, compared with Germany's 50% and Japan's around 15%).
- After the USA, China is the world's second biggest importer (almost 25% of its GDP).
- China accounts for 50% of global coal production or about 3.6 billion tons in 2011, only 5% import dependency.
- China consumes about 3500 kWh per capita per annum (compared with India's about 800 kWh).

China will remain a key influencing factor for the global coal market. Chinese policy is predicting that coal use will plateau. This is not only because of air pollution problems in Beijing and other cities (which, by the way, is mainly caused by old coal-fired power plant technology and insufficient filtering, which could easily be rectified). Chinese GDP growth is stabilizing.

In September 2013, China's domestic coal prices had dwindled to a 4-year low of 520 RMB/mt FOB QHD. Many industry experts are expecting a slight reduction in China's imports in 2013/2014. From China we can expect continued and regular imports, but volatility will remain high. China's relatively small import dependency and the power of its central planning system can quickly wipe out or add tens of millions of tons of imports, which would have a severe impact on the coal industry in Indonesia but also in South Africa and Australia at any given time.

China, currently relying on coal for almost 80% of its electricity generation, will have to reduce – and is in the process of reducing – this coal dependency. However, keep in mind that whatever China does, it will still pull up the global average of currently just over 40% coal dependency for decades to come.

2.4.2.2 India The third largest coal producer in the world, with about 580 million tons in 2012, is also continuously short of power and coal. Its internal infrastructure, logistics, the location of domestic coal reserves as well as quality constraints have resulted in India becoming the fourth largest importer after China, Japan and South Korea in 2012.

The industry estimates that about 105–110 million tons of steam coal will be imported in 2013, mostly from Indonesia and South Africa. Indonesia alone exported over 60 million tons to India in 2012. We can expect that India will become the largest steam coal importer in the world before the decade is over.

India is increasing its power plant park capacity by 88 GW, of which 64 GW is planned to come from coal. Total coal demand could surpass 750 million tons per annum, resulting in shortfalls of around 200 million tons per annum within the next 3 to 5 years. While it is difficult to predict exactly how Indian imports will develop, it is clear that India will remain a more stable and slowly growing importer of steam coal. With import dependency of around 20% it is also expected to be less volatile. According to the BP Statistical Review of World Energy (2012), India is even expected to overtake the USA as the second largest coal consumer in 2024. Import demand will continue to grow, maybe surpassing 200 million tons per annum later this decade, but long term it will tail off as India finds ways to become more self-sufficient with coal.

At the same time, power is still in extraordinarily short supply in India and will remain so for many years. One illustration is the low 800 kWh per capita per annum electricity consumption compared with China, where 3500 kWh per capita is consumed. Another illustration is that today it is not uncommon for the government to defer to load shedding rather than importing expensive coal from abroad.

Much of the power capacity is still in the government's hands. However, large private enterprises such as Tata, Reliance, Essar, Adani, JSW, Jindal and many more are constantly adding to their own capacity, increasing non-government imported coal demand. The key challenges that India face remain, such as: import port capacity, local logistical infrastructure, privatization of the power distribution networks and financial concerns of government agencies. In past years, private power companies such as those mentioned above have been continuously losing money since the power tariff does not cover the cost of coal. At the same time, the sharp depreciation of the Indian rupee (INR) in 2013 increased the strain on the Indian economy. While international coal prices dropped in 2013, the landed cost of coal in India in INR increased. The government will need to step in, but the 2014 election will seem to support more short-term rather than long-term thinking among many politicians.

2.4.2.3 Japan Japan is often credited with having engendered the 'Asian industrial revolution' in the second half of the last century. Because Japan does not possess any significant natural resources itself, it was able to accomplish this through building up long-lasting and successful trading relationships with most of the world's major natural-resource-exporting countries. This is also true for coal. Today, Japan is the second largest importer of steam coal after China. With 133 million tons of steam coal imports in 2011, Japan alone accounts for almost one-sixth of the global seaborne steam coal trade. Its share of the coking coal trade is even more substantial. Japan, which is the world's second largest steel producer after China, imported 52 million tons of coking coal, or one-quarter of all sea-traded coking coal (IEA – Statistics, 2005; Global Insight – Russia, 2007; VDKI, 2013).

Japan's electricity generation used to be based almost 30% on nuclear generation. After 2011's Fukushima tsunami accident, Japan has decided to phase out nuclear energy leaving room for coal, gas and of course renewable. At least 50% of Japan's steam coal imports come from Australia, and the rest mainly from Indonesia and Russia.

2.4.2.4 South Korea South Korea is now the third largest steam coal importer after China and Japan, sharing this place with India. Nevertheless, South Korea's demand was a key factor influencing the price spikes in 2007 and 2008 and has continuously lifted coal cargos during 2012, the difficult time of sharply dropping prices. In 2012, South Korea imported 105 million tons of steam coal. The country depends on coal for about 40% of its electricity generation. In the longer term, it is expected that the relative share of coal in South Korea's power generation mix will fall, and imports will stagnate or decline slightly. South Korea did not sign the Kyoto Protocol.

The key suppliers to South Korea are, as in the case of Japan, Australia, Indonesia and Russia. However, since 2007 a few cargos of South African coal have been imported each year. This means that Asian countries are now competing for coal that historically has been sold almost exclusively to Europe.

2.4.2.5 Taiwan Taiwan imported 66 million tons of steam coal in 2012. Coal accounts for over 50% of the country's power mix compared with about 18% for nuclear and about 17%

for gas. It is expected that Taiwan will continue to build up its coal-fired power plant park and further increase steam coal imports at a slow pace, reaching over 70 million tons by the end of the decade.

Taiwan holds a special position in the Pacific coal market. The country is logistically much better situated than Korea or Japan because of its proximity to Indonesia. Australian coal has also been a key source for Taiwan. Given its flexibility on quality, Taiwan, unlike Japan, can look to a wider range of import sources in the future. Taiwanese power companies have also started to invest into Chinese facilities and have started to import coal for their Chinese power plants.

2.4.2.6 Other Importers in South East Asia (SEA) Thailand, Malaysia, the Philippines and Vietnam (together SEA) are becoming increasingly a new importing region for steam coal. While data is difficult to get, it can be extracted from a number of industry sources that about 50 million tons were imported in 2012 (Malaysia, Thailand and the Philippines, in that order). Vietnam is expected to turn into a net importer by 2015 from being an historical net exporter (mostly anthracite). It is predicted that this will increase to about 90 million tons by the end of the decade, much driven by Vietnamese emerging steam coal imports. This would mean the SEA region importing more than Taiwan by that time, and getting closer to European levels. Much of the region has been supplied by Indonesia. However, some cargos from Australia as well as South Africa have been shipped in past years.

2.4.3 Steam Coal Supply Regions: ID, AU, USA, SA, RU, CO and Others

Figure 2.28 illustrates the top six coal exporters worldwide discussed in this chapter. The more detailed regional analyses below rely on information from various industry sources: VDKI (2011, 2012), IEA – Medium-Term Coal Market Report (2012), Schernikau (2010),

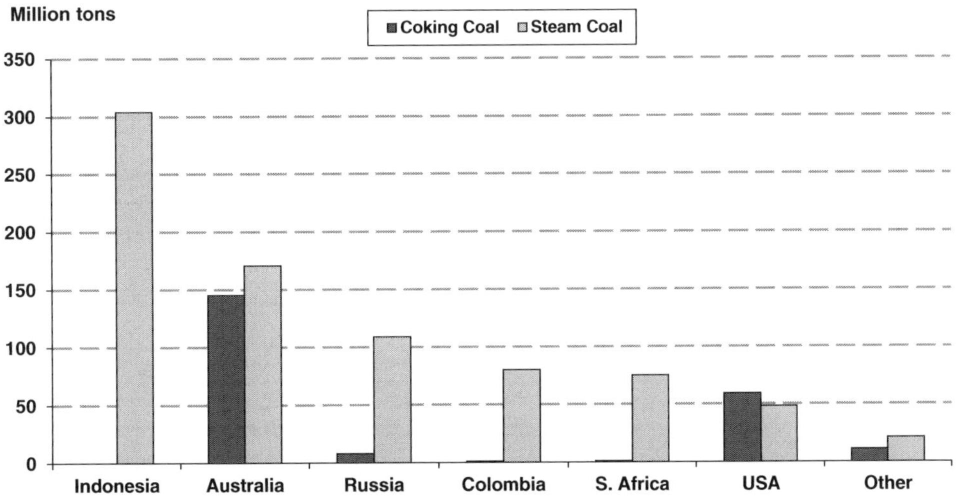

FIGURE 2.28 Top six steam coal and coking coal export countries 2012
Source: Author's analysis based on VDKI (2013).

Morse/Schernikau World Coal (2011), Schernikau World Coal (2012), Platts (2013) and various other publicly available articles and publications.

2.4.3.1 Indonesia Indonesia is the largest economy in South East Asia and the mineral sector including coal contributes 12% to the country's GDP, totalling about $93 billion. Indonesia has developed into the most important steam coal exporter, overtaking Australia for the first time in 2005. The country exported approximately 304 million tons of steam coal, more than 35% of global exports, in 2012 – much of it of lower quality. For example, in 2001 the country still exported only 67 million tons, resulting in a CAGR of about 15% from then until today. That is phenomenal growth, which is likely to slow now as the base has become so large. Indonesia is relatively new to the coal mining business, with modern coal mining only starting in the 1980s; according to the Indonesian Coal Mining Association (2006), in 1993 Indonesia's total coal production comprised only 27 million tons. Government policy up to now has prevented international standard consolidation in Indonesia's coal industry. Through a relatively complicated mining rights system, the government distributed state owned coal reserves in three tranches (referred to as coal contracts of work, CCOW) in the early 1980s (Ritschel and Schiffer, 2007). In 2009, the government redrafted the mining law introducing so-called intended use plans (IUPs). Mining laws and most importantly their implementation are often erratic with export bans, export tax and many other issues being discussed in government and industry on a regular basis. Some regulatory specialists in Indonesia expect the government to become less and less supportive of massive coal exports or at least continued export growth, resulting in continued road blocks along the way and appropriate regulation. At the same time, the government and its politicians depend a lot on a healthy coal export industry.

With about 250 million inhabitants, Indonesia is the world's fourth most populous country after China, India and the USA. Indonesia's electricity demand is still rising rapidly. Historically, Indonesia – until May 2008 a member of OPEC – has relied largely on oil and gas for its electricity production. In the near future, Indonesia will switch to coal and increase its own coal consumption within the next 20 years. Indonesians' domestic coal demand is currently expected to be around 65+ million tons per annum and is rising consistently every year.

The majority of Indonesia's coal reserves are located in Kalimantan and Sumatra, with Kalimantan being the historic exporter and Sumatra slowly catching up – although this is being hampered by logistics. Sumatra contributed only about 11 million tons to Indonesia's exports in 2011/2012 (see Figure 2.29), but the coal resources in South Sumatra alone total 60 billion tons, more than East and South Kalimantan combined. Sumatra is considered a 'new frontier' in Indonesian exports, but logistical infrastructure – here mostly rail – needs to improve for Sumatra to reach the realistically targeted 30–50 million tons of exports within the next 10 years. Central Kalimantan is still very small in terms of exports, but rail projects and foreign investments are ahead of Sumatra's despite the small resource base (Figure 2.30).

The top coal producers (Bumi with KPC and Arutmin, Adaro, Kideco, Banpu, Berau, Tanito, Bayan and Bukit Asam) control more than two-thirds of Indonesian exports and production. Foreign conglomerates have only limited control. Total production reached about 330 to 360 million tons in 2012 (numbers published vary), of which about 304 million tons were exported.

Indonesia's coal reserves are generally of lower quality compared with those of other exporting countries. Ash (1–9% ar) and sulphur (0.1–1% ar) contents are low, while TM contents are usually high (15–25% ar). The majority of the exported coal is bituminous and sub-bituminous. India, China and the South East Asian market are able to off-take Indonesia's

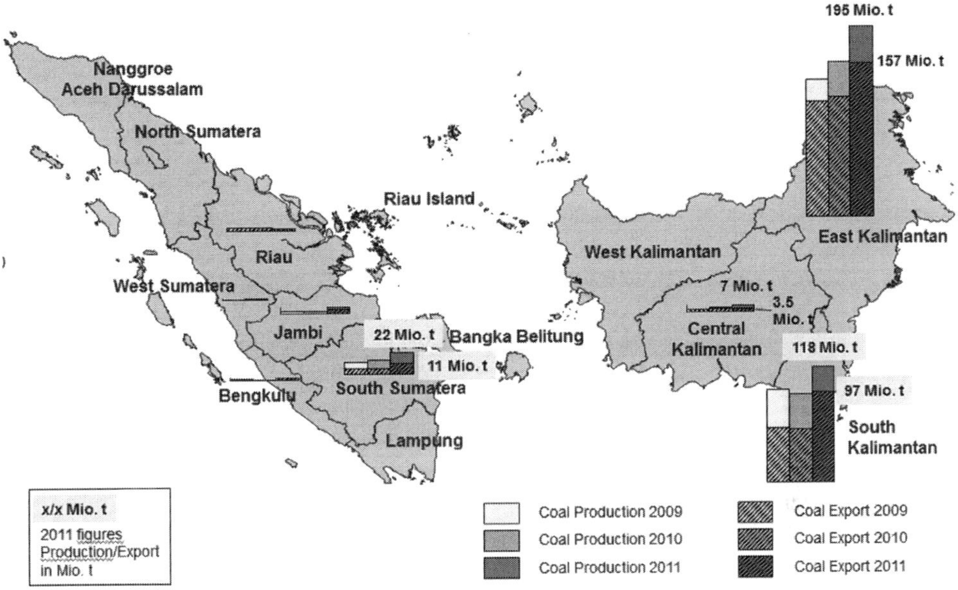

FIGURE 2.29 Indonesia's coal exports by province (total 2011: 273 million tons)
Source: Author's and PT HMS Bergbau Indonesia Research & Analysis; Indonesian Coal Mining Association; Ministry of Energy and Mineral Resources Republic Indonesia.

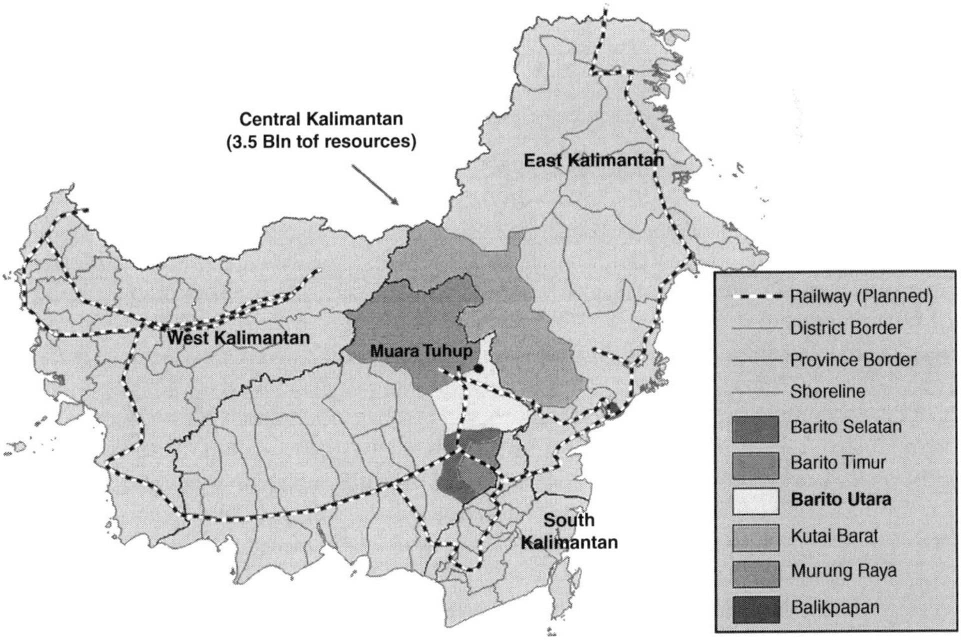

FIGURE 2.30 Rail projects in Kalimantan
Source: Author's and PT HMS Bergbau Indonesia Research & Analysis; Ministry of Transportation Republic Indonesia.

sub-bituminous coal qualities with TM running as high as 35–45% ar, while Japan, South Korea, Taiwan and Hong Kong generally prefer to buy coal of a higher calorific value. Where freight rates allow, Indonesian coal is also transported to Europe, but only in small quantities (such as to Italy, also driven by ENEL's investment in Indonesian coal mining).

Of the world's steam coal exporting countries, Indonesia is probably the country with the least worries about infrastructure. This, however, by no means infers a perfect inland transportation and trans-shipment system. By nature, and due to Indonesia being a country of many islands, Indonesia's coal mines are mainly located very close to the sea or rivers, with the exception of mines in Sumatra and Sumatra's key coal resource base around Lahat in South Sumatra. Trucks are used to transport the coal to river or sea ports. There are about 15 coal-loading ports and about 20+ offshore loading facilities (so-called anchorage points, where coal is trans-shipped via floating cranes or self-loading vessels from barges onto sea-going vessels). In Kalimantan, there are countless barge-loading facilities located along rivers or the seashore. Kalimantan has many rivers and almost every mine, even the smaller ones, has its own barge port facility. Barge loading capacities range from 3000 to 12,000 tons; some exports to nearby countries are handled purely by barge. In Sumatra, the situation is different. Here, 200–300 km of trucking is quite common.

Indonesia is probably the lowest-cost coal producer on a per-ton basis. The main reason for this, logistics, has already been discussed previously. Also, labour costs are still very low with an average mine worker earning maybe 100–300 USD per month. There is no productivity data available, but the many smaller mines work much less efficiently on a per-worker basis than in the rest of the world. However, one can assume that the big eight producers can compete with international productivity levels. The larger mines are managed by large Australian and other foreign mining contractors.

2.4.3.2 Australia In 2012, 21% of the world's exported steam coal was sourced from Australia, number two behind Indonesia. Australia's role in the supply of coking coal is even greater, as over 55% of the world's seaborne coking coal is sourced from Australia.

Australia's coal reserves are located in the East of the country, in the states of Queensland and New South Wales. Of the total production of about 366 million tons, about 316 million tons (171 million tons steam coal) or 86% were exported. Australia's largest customer, Japan, bought over 70 million tons of steam coal in 2012 followed by China with over 30 million tons, South Korea about 30 million tons and Taiwan 15 million tons (Platts, 2013; VDKI, 2013).

Of the total production, about three-quarters is produced in opencast mines and one-quarter underground. There are about 100 mines of various sizes in Australia. The coal is mined down to about 70 m in the opencast mines. Underground mines can reach depths of about 200 m. While Australia's mining operations are among the best in the world, productivity of 7–9 kt/employee per annum is far below the Western USA at 30–35 kt/employee per annum (IEA – Medium-Term Coal Market Report, 2012). Australia's coal production is almost entirely privately owned. The Australian Coal Report estimates that the four biggest Australian producers – BHP, Rio Tinto, Xstrata and Anglo – accounted for 53% of Australia's output and for 55% of the country's exports in 2006.

The Australian coal industry is likely to continue to be consolidated. In addition, Chinese, Indian and other new Asian entries have started purchasing smaller mine assets and are expected to continue to do so. It is expected that about half of all global coal investment projects are located in Australia. One example of a large project is GVK Hancock, which is expecting 60–85 million tons of new exports before 2020. Other large projects are centred around the Galilee Basin with large reserves. At the same time, mining has become financially less attractive in Australia with the Mining Resource Rent Tax (MRRT) coming into effect in July 2012, which basically taxes 30% above A$ 75 million earnings.

Australia's steam coal exports are known for their homogeneity and high quality. Since Australian coal is mostly washed in a similar way to South African coal, the high ash content of the raw coal is reduced sufficiently to supply a reliable 6000 and 5500 kcal/kg nar quality or even better. Water is scarce in Australian mining regions and the government has put a price on water. This may increase the cost of coal washing and as a result could lead to lower coal qualities in the future. Today, Australian coal has medium volatile matter (25–30% ar), average ash content (8–20% ar) and tends to be rather dry (7–9% ar). The sulphur content is below 1% ar and can go as low as 0.3% ar. The coal is also relatively soft (higher HGI). Overall, Australian steam coal quality is well suited for the export market. Japan, the world's second largest coal importer and also Australia's most important customer, is considered to be 'spoiled' by Australia's good coal qualities. International coal consumers have tended to prefer Australian coal over, for example, Indonesian and Russian coal, and are therefore often willing to pay a premium, especially in Japan.

Australia has been particularly hampered by a lack of infrastructure development. Both rail lines from the mines to the ports and port capacity have been and will continue to be expanded. Australia exports its coal resources through seven main ports; in order of importance these are Newcastle, Gladstone, Dalrymple Bay, Hay Point, NCIG, Abbot Point and Brisbane. All ports have expansion plans.

Australia is one of the world's most efficient and therefore also cost-effective coal producers. The distance from the mines to the ports ranges from about 100 to 400 km, and geologically the coal is situated advantageously with undisturbed deposits. Costs are likely to increase further for a number of reasons, including the following:

- Coal from newer deposits will be railed over longer distances.
- Overburden on coal ratios is expected to increase and drive up pure production costs.
- Machinery costs will go up because equipment suppliers lack the capacity to fulfil global mining requirements (this also affects iron ore and other mineral production in addition to coal).
- Fuel costs will rise, causing mining costs to rise with them.
- Australian royalties are linked to the sales price.
- The ash content of the coal will increase, reducing washing yields and exported qualities.
- Trained mining personnel are scarce and become more expensive.

Overall, Australia is expected to further increase its production and exports. Because of rising costs, high-value export products, such as coking coal, will be especially favoured. But also the development of a 5500 nar NEWC steam coal index has helped the export of higher ash material that is much sought after in China. In the author's view, Australia has the biggest long-term potential for sustainable steam coal and coking exports, total production (including coking coal) may reach as much as 500 million tons in the next 15 years.

2.4.3.3 Russia Russia accounts for about 13% of global steam coal exports, with 109 million tons of coal exported seaborne in 2012, and is the third largest steam coal exporter globally. Total steam coal production reaches about 279 million tons and coking coal production about 74 million tons per annum. Russian coal has a long history, though not in the international arena. Russia's own industry consumes the majority of the country's production output. In the early 1990s, following the collapse of the Soviet regime, small quantities of Russian coal started to appear on the international seaborne steam coal market. Russia's export growth really only began after 1997, but was not as spectacular as Indonesia's. The Russian coal industry was very quick to privatize in the 1990s, resulting in an immediate cut in large amounts of unprofitable production. In fact, Russian coal production (coking coal and steam coal) was cut by over 35% from 401 million tons in 1989 to 272 million tons in 1994 (see Global Insight – Russia, 2007).

Russia's reserves and resources are among the largest in the world and the country is one of the most important steam coal exporters. Europe and increasingly Asia rely on Russia's logistical proximity. Russia is especially important for the economics of the coal market, since it is the key marginal cost supplier. Thus, long-term global FOB prices will be close to Russia's FOB marginal cost.

Russia produced 353 million tons of hard coal in 2012 (VDKI, 2013). Of this, 279 million tons were steam coal. In total, Russia exported seaborne 117 million tons and 109 million tons of hard coal and steam coal, respectively. Another approximately 10 million tons was exported via the green border by rail. Production is centred in Kuzbass, Siberia where about 80% of Russia's coal is produced. About two-thirds of Russia's production is opencast. The production is concentrated in such a way that the top eight producers (SUEK, Kuzbassrazrezugol, Siberian Business Union, Yuzhkuzbassugol, Vostsibugol, Raspadskaya, Yuzhny Kuzbass and Yakutugol) account for about two-thirds of Russia's coal production, which has been decreasing from over 70% 6 years ago. Russia's coal production, unlike other industry sectors, is largely in private hands with little or no government involvement.

Two-thirds or just over 65 million tons of Russian hard coal is shipped to the European countries via the Baltic and the Black Sea. Another 50 million tons approximately is shipped to Japan, Korea, China and the Far East. Exports via the Far East are expected to rise to 85 million tons by 2020, a very sizable number. This is planned with increased rail and port capacity as well as a production increase to around 450 million tons. If this comes true, Russia will be competing head on with the USA, Australia and of course Indonesia in the Far East, but will have a logistical advantage especially for exports to Korea, Japan and Northern China.

Russian coal exports are of relatively high quality, with high enough calorific values and low sulphur contents. Much of Russia's coal for export is improved through washing programmes. The difficult and lengthy transportation on old rail cars results in some contamination of Russian coal with metal and other debris. The ports employ extensive metal cleaning technology, but often consumers still complain about problems with scrap and other decontamination. In wintertime, Russian coal is at risk of freezing, especially when shipped from Murmansk. The Kuzbass region is known for its low sulphur contents. This is probably the only advantage of being far from the sea. Also, the reserves were far removed from saltwater when the coal developed millions of years ago. Because of the low sulphur contents, Russian coal is often used for blending with higher-sulphur coal in European or Asian power stations. However, in times when the coal price is low, such as in mid-2013, it is expected that many exporters will move coal below their marginal cost of production.

Logistically speaking, Russian coal is very important for Eastern Europe, Turkey and the Nordic countries (i.e., Finland and Denmark). Despite being a very high-cost producer, this is another key reason why Russia will continue to play an important role in the Atlantic market, especially for the Nordic countries, Northern Germany and the UK. Riga, Ust-Luga and Murmansk are the most important Western ports for Russian coal, and Vostochny and

Muchka in the Far East. Russian coal needs to be transported by rail up to 5000 km from its Kuzbass-based production to the ports. Thus, the key infrastructural constraint is rail capacity. The rail company RhZD is still 100% government controlled (similar to the situation in South Africa). Some insiders claim that the increased government rail tariffs are one way for the government to recoup the money lost by the private producers' offshore marketing departments and low transfer pricing policies.

2.4.3.4 Colombia Colombia is ranked fourth in the world and is the key exporting country in Latin America, with 2012 exports reaching 81 million tons (up from 62 million tons in 2006) – 80 million tons of steam coal and 1 million tons of coking coal. Venezuela only exported 3 million tons in 2012, down from 9 million tons in 2006, and thus became less relevant. The USA and Europe consume most of Colombia's and Venezuela's coal. Virtually all of Colombia's coal produced is also exported.

The Colombian supply market is controlled by Cerrejon, Drummand and Glencore (Prodeco/Carbones de la Jagua), accounting for almost 90% of export volumes. Production in these countries is highly efficient and production costs are low and exports competitive. In fact, Colombia could still export profitably when prices fell sharply in 2012 and 2013 and the USA had to ship at a loss.

Colombia's coal generally has a very low ash content, which results in above-average calorific values. When buying some of the very high-CV Colombian coals on FOB terms, the buyer will benefit from reduced relative transportation costs and efficient coal burning. The drawbacks of the coal are – generally speaking – its relatively high moisture content, low HGI and thus hardness, and in some cases a proneness to self-ignition. However, this type of coal may be used as PCI coal for the steel industry.

The future will see rising export volumes from Colombia. Plans are in place to increase production to 150 million tons per annum by 2020. Reserves are large enough and various projects to improve rail and port infrastructure are underway, including a 1000-km railway from mines near Bogota to the Caribbean. Colombia and Venezuela do not yet consume much coal themselves and even if that consumption should increase, it would do so from a small basis. Demand in North, Central and South America is increasing and Colombia will remain a key supplier for these American markets as well as Europe and (in the future) Asia. The opening of the new improved Panama Canal in 2014, allowing mini-capes, will enable exports to Japan, China and Korea.

2.4.3.5 South Africa With about 9% share of world steam coal exports South Africa is slowly losing ground on the ever-growing world market (12% in 2006) and has become the number 5 exporter from formerly being the number 3. However, South Africa has a special position in the international steam coal business for the following reasons: (1) it runs the largest and most efficient single coal export terminal, Richards Bay Coal Terminal and (2) the FOB South African price is quoted daily in the form of the API4 Index, ensuring better market transparency and as such being a gauge for the global coal market. The country exported about 75 million tons (washed product) in 2012 and production has been relatively stable around 260 million tons (unwashed product). However, local coal demand and CtL demand is such that it is expected South Africa will increase production to about 350 million tons by 2020. Also, exports are expected to increase, driven by infrastructure investments in ports and rail.

For South Africa itself, the mining industry (and to a large extent coal) plays an above-average role in the health of the economy (Dlamini, 2007), accounting for almost 20% of GDP and 25% of employment (directly and indirectly). Coal and its industry accounts for 90% of electricity generation and 15% of electricity demand. Also, 30% of liquid fuels are produced from coal by Sasol, the world's market leader in CtL. Eskom, the country's government-owned power company, is increasing coal-fired power plant electricity output and requires more coal for the domestic market. Eskom has historically been buying on a very long-term contract basis at a cost-plus scheme (often below market price). This is slowly changing, as Eskom is tapping more into the junior coal market and has become open to pay market-relevant prices for the product.

In a drive for a fairer and more efficient use of South Africa's natural resources, and as part of its Black Economic Empowerment (BEE) programme, the South African government agreed to a new mining law in 2002. This law ensured that all of South Africa's natural resources were transferred from previous land ownership to state ownership. Thus, today, ownership of lands and mining rights can be separate. All previously operating mining companies had to reapply for their mining rights. New regulation also requires that older mining companies and new mining companies be partly black-owned. This has caused some problems due to an educational and financial gap between the black and white populations, but this gap is narrowing.

South Africa's reserves and resources are ample. With 38 billion tons of reserves and 115 billion tons of resources (BGR, 2006, 2011) the country has over 150 years of reserves and, additionally, over 600 years of resources at current production levels. The main reserves (about 20 billion tons) are located in the Highveld and Witbank areas just East of Johannesburg. South Africa's coal production is highly concentrated, with the top five producers controlling over 80% of exports. However, due to new mining regulations and increasing involvement of BEE companies, the consolidation process is shifting. It is for instance expected that BEE-controlled Exxaro will form alliances and take over other smaller BEE players, increasing its export share to 9–12 million tons within the next 3–5 years.

South Africa produces a high-ash, low-moisture coal. All exported coal volumes are mechanically and chemically washed, reducing the ash content from around 25% ar to 10–15% ar. The washing yield (typically in the 50–80% range) determines not only the washing capacity required but also the marginal cost, since all costs up to washing have to be divided by the washing yield in order to determine the true costs of exported coal, as discard material (left over from washing) has little or no value. South African coal otherwise has a very good reputation on the market, because washing guarantees a very homogenous output product.

The government-owned railroad system in South Africa has been a key capacity constraint for higher exports. COALlink, which operates the 600-km-long railway line from the key mining areas to Richards Bay Coal Terminal, has a capacity of 72 million tons, not enough to fill the 90-million-ton RBCT capacity. Trains running on this line can load more than 16,000 tons of coal in one load, for instance with 250 wagons of 64 tons each. Such trains are several kilometres long. The inefficiencies of a state-run rail operation also affect South Africa. While there is some talk about privatization, it is not clear when this will happen. Service philosophy and accountability are key problems at COALlink.

The outlook for South Africa is positive, as demand from the Pacific market, namely from India, China and even South Korea, is going to increase. In the past 5 years South Africa was unable to participate in the worldwide coal export growth and has been constantly exporting between 65 and 75 million tons while the world market grew. However, South Africa managed well to shift its customer base from Europe (the historic almost exclusive buyer of South African coal) to Asia. In 2012, two-thirds of all exports went to India and Asia (or outside Europe), an achievement for the country.

2.4.3.6 USA The US swing supply to the global steam coal market seems to be over. Since 2011, caused by the shale gas revolution, the USA has become a more consistent supplier to the global coal market. In 2012, it is estimated that the USA exported over 130 million tons: about 59 million tons coking coal, 48 million tons steam coal and maybe 30 million tons petcoke products (Platts, 2013; VDKI, 2013). For steam coal, the USA is therefore still relatively marginal (less than 5% of global supply) but the petcoke and coking coal products make the USA a serious contender globally. In fact, the price falls in 2012 were largely driven by increased exports of higher-CV and higher-sulphur US coal to the Asian markets (via the Pacific to China and the Atlantic to India). Most steam coal exports went to Europe and to a much lesser extent to Canada, China, Mexico and India/China.

Coal production reached just over 900 million tons, but has been reducing in the past 2 years because of much cheaper gas from shale gas production entering the market and replacing coal. Peabody and Arch Coal account for over 40% of US production and are two of the top five global producers. Production is of lower cost in the West, Powder River Basin (PRB) and of higher cost in the East, Appalachian and Interior. Some of the PRB coal has found its way to Asia via expanding ports in the West.

In the latter half of 2012 and the first few months of 2013, coal exports from the USA stabilized, stopping the 'disruptive' effect that low-cost, high-sulphur, high-CV coal had on the international coal arena. As a result, coal prices also stabilized despite the exchange rate effects disrupting prices again starting in June 2013. Today, fewer US producers are willing and able to export at a marginal loss. They were 'forced' to do so in 2011 and early 2012 because of long-term contracts with logistics providers and contractors when local coal demand in the USA fell too sharply. Many producers are still struggling. For instance, Patriot Coal filed for bankruptcy in July 2012.

We expect the USA to remain a sizeable exporter in the decades to come, while production will continue to decrease. The developments of PRB coal exports will largely determine the future of the USA as an exporter. If it is possible to set up the rail and port capacity as planned, we will get used to lower-CV coal, competing with Indonesian coal, arriving in Northern Asia. This would in fact be the first time that high-moisture coal would be available in significant quantities from a source outside Indonesia. On a macroeconomic level we expect that the USA is becoming again a new production hub for the developed world as low energy prices also mean lower production costs. Increased production/manufacturing (GDP growth) will again lead to increased power consumption, which in turn will stabilize coal production again – despite the current negativity in the USA about coal.

2.4.3.7 Other Producing Regions Relevant for Export Other countries and regions relevant for coal exports (hard coal and steam coal) are Mozambique/Southern Africa, Mongolia, Kazakhstan, Canada, Vietnam and Poland. These countries form a new frontier and will continue reshuffling the global coal trade business. It will be interesting to see the developments over the next 5 to 10 years.

Mozambique/Southern Africa. Vale, Rio Tinto (formerly Riversdale), Anglo American, Beacon Hill and Jindal are just a few names that are active in the Tete region to develop coking coal and steam coal exports out of Mozambique. The government has issued over 100 coal licences to 50+ national and international companies. Billions of US dollars have already been invested and more billions are about to be spent. The first shipments of coking coal and steam coal have been executed successfully. Port and rail capacity is still the limiting factor. Steam coal is only exported to reduce the cost of producing coking coal. In fact, it can be assumed that marginally much of the steam coal will not be economical because of transportation.

New Southern African rail and port projects are planned in the next 5 to 8 years and may, if successful, allow Botswana, Namibia and Mozambique coal to enter the international market.

Mongolia. One of the raw-material-richest countries in the world also claims 160+ billion tons of coal reserves. In 2012, it is estimated that between 15 and 22 million tons of coking coal was exported to neighbouring China. Plans are there to export up to 80 million tons of mostly coking coal per annum within 5 to 10 years. Mongolia is landlocked and has to rely on Russia or China for entering the seaborne trade market. As such, the author does not expect that Mongolian steam coal will enter the international seaborne market simply because of prohibitive logistic costs.

Kazakhstan/Ukraine/Poland. Kazakhstan does not have large coal reserves but still produced about 121 million tons of coal in 2012, about 30 million tons were exported in 2012 – most if not all via rail. The Ukraine produced about 84 million tons in 2012, of which about 62 million tons was steam coal. The Ukraine is mostly relevant for the international market because of its good anthracite and Yuzhny port operations that mostly exports Russian coal.

Poland used to be an important supplier to Western Europe. The country still produces shy of 80 million tons of high-quality thermal coal. However, the country requires large amounts of coal itself, now importing more from Russia and overseas. 2012 exports dwindled to 7 million tons, probably less than half of it via the sea.

Canada. An important supplier of coking coal, with 31 million tons of exports in 2012. Another 4 million tons of steam coal was also exported. The country produces about 67 million tons of coal and relies on hydropower and coal for its electricity generation. We do not expect large export increases to come from the Canadian coal industry, which is also struggling with cheap shale gas.

Vietnam. Vietnamese anthracite has been famous for decades because of its good and consistent quality. China still relies very much on anthracite imports from Vietnam for some of its steel heavy industry. Vietnam produced just below 45 million tons of coal in 2012 (another 10% reduction since 2011) and exported around 15 million tons of anthracite (about 12 of which went to China). Vietnam is expected to further reduce exports and in fact will be a key importer for steam coal in the decades to come.

2.4.4 Seaborne Freight

We have seen in previous sections that coal supply is very much about logistics. Logistics for any bulk raw material such as coal, iron ore or grain also includes shipping in bulk carriers across the world. Shipping not only costs money but also takes considerable time. For instance, a vessel travelling from Indonesia to Europe takes about 4 weeks and a vessel from South Africa to Europe more than 2 weeks. Thus, seaborne freight is a key CIF price determinant for coal.

Bulk carriers are divided into three categories: (1) Capesize vessels – named after the Cape because they have to ship around it – carrying 120 to 170 kt of bulk product; (2) Panamax vessels – so named because they are the largest vessels that can pass through the Panama Canal (prior to expansion) – carrying 60 to 80 kt of bulk product; and (3) supramax/handysize vessels carrying somewhere between 20 and 50 kt of bulk product. These smaller vessels are also typically geared versus the gearless Capesize and Panamax vessels that require shore

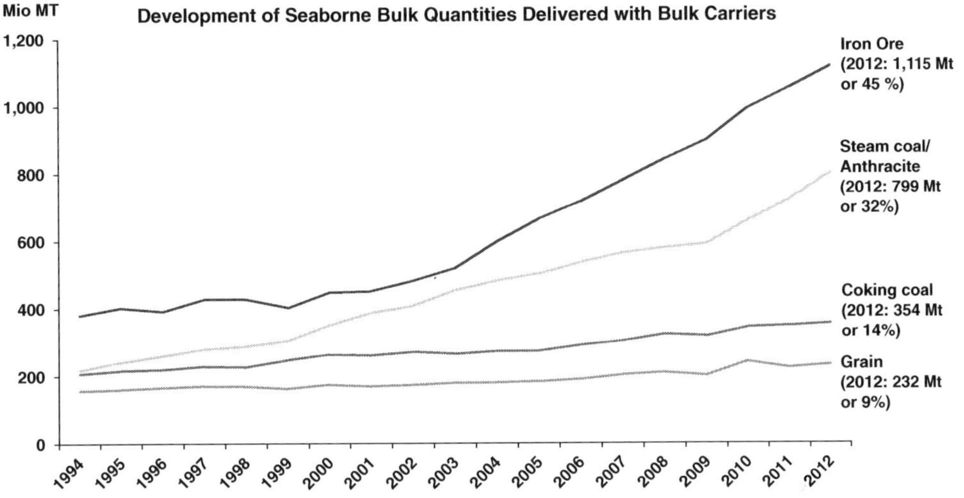

FIGURE 2.31 Iron ore, coal and grain determine sea freight demand, 1994–2012
Source: Frachtkontor Junge (2013). Author's analysis.

cranes for loading and unloading. Standard routes, such as Route 4 from Richards Bay, South Africa to ARA, Europe, are served by the largest Capesize and Panamax vessels. Less standard routes such as within Asia or from Baltic Russia to England tend to be served by smaller supramax and handysize vessels.

Coal is only one of many bulk products carried by such vessels. Ores – here mainly iron ore – make up the largest share, followed by steam coal, then coking coal and grain. Thus, ores, coal and grain are the so-called major bulk products. Minor bulk products include steel, scrap, cement, fertilizers and many others. Figure 2.31 shows the amount of major bulk products shipped with sea bulk carriers. The steam coal numbers do not add up to seaborne freight volume because this figure does not account for smaller handysize vessels or very small vessels.

The freight market is also nothing more than a normal global market with supply and demand. Based on research, we estimate the marginal cost of running a Capesize vessel from South Africa to Europe at around 9–14 USD/mt in 2012. But resource (or vessel) scarcity kept prices well above that until the staggering freight price drop in autumn of 2008. Since then the freight market has been hovering around very low numbers. On many occasions the freight was below the cost of running a vessel and barely covered bunker (fuel) costs. It is expected that freight rates will remain low for at least another 2 years. This is an important fact for the coal market: with low freight rates, it is economical to ship coal from faraway places such as the USA to Asia. Competition increases globally and FOB price levels will move more in sync across the coal world.

Freight capacity is influenced by the following basic determinants:

- Vessel stock.
- New builds that have about a 2-year lead time.
- Scrapped vessels.
- Vessels travelling empty.
- Asset utilization/port congestion.

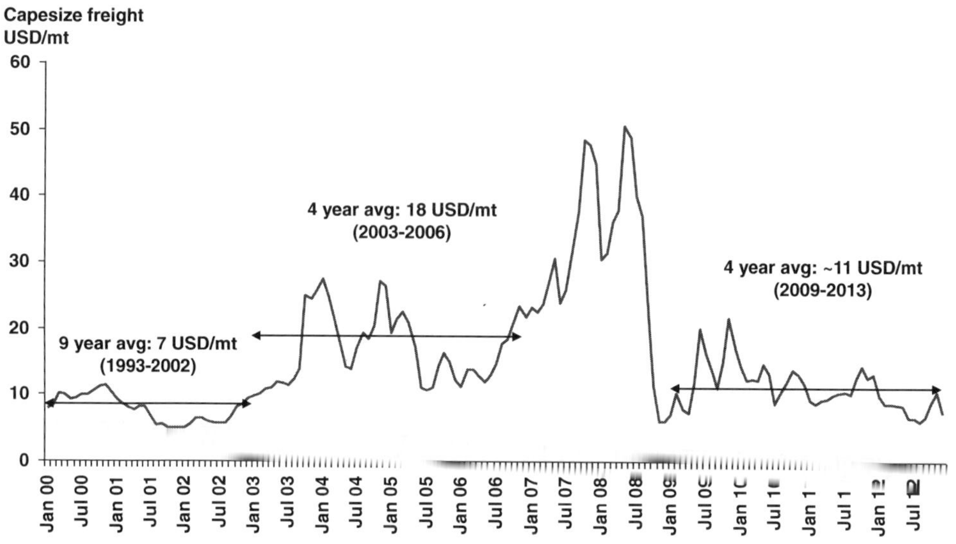

FIGURE 2.32 Capesize vessel freights 2001–2012
Source: Author's research and analysis. Data based on McCloskey (2012).

The outlook for freight rates is rather difficult. Freight rates went down from their peak levels in June 2008 to 8 USD/mt in October 2008 (see Figure 2.32) for a Capesize coal cargo from South Africa to Europe, similar to numbers in early 2013 when vessels were chartered below 7 USD/mt which is below cost. Experts expect generally weak freight prices in 2013 and 2014. In the longer term, it is expected that freight prices will be high enough to cover at least total costs while remaining highly volatile.

2.4.5 Geopolitical and Policy Environment

Before we look at the coal market, to pull all information together it is necessary to say a few words about the geopolitical and policy environment within which the coal market, and in fact most energy raw material markets, function.

This chapter is not a philosophical treatise on human existence; rather, it is about coal and therefore energy, or more specifically electricity. Humans have no doubt done to the atmosphere and the planet's environment what no other living creature has done in the past; however, in order to find solutions for the future, humans will need electricity. And coal, as we have seen, is the primary source of electricity and will continue to be so for many decades to come. Unfortunately, coal is also a main contributor to greenhouse gas emissions. Therefore, governments have a responsibility to create policy that enables safe and sustainable coal use.

It is the task of governments and the global community to find a framework and to decide on policy that guides the generation and use of energy and electricity. It is also their task to regulate monopolies. It is clear that no one single government can do much about the global population problem, energy crises and environmental issues on its own. These problems can only be solved if all nations participate. Western Europe may cut its CO_2 output by 50%, but that will be close to useless if China and India increase their CO_2 output by 10 times the amount saved in Western Europe. At the same time, it will be the utilities – the main coal

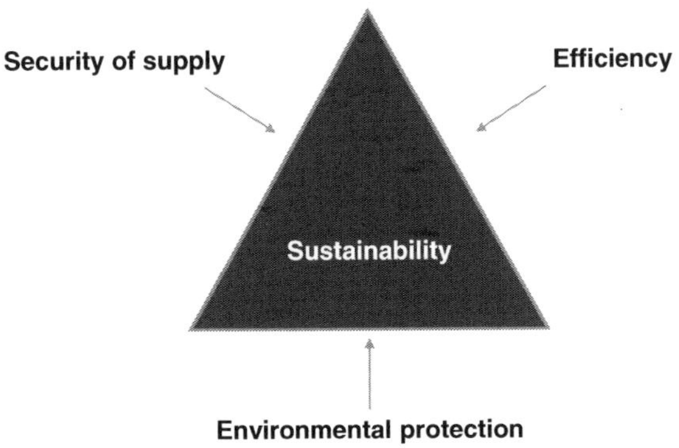

FIGURE 2.33 Triangle of objectives in energy policy

consumers – that can drive many technological and environmentally sensible changes. The large multinational energy corporations will not be able to avoid their growing responsibility for minimizing the effect of their choice of generation mix on the environment and for the development and use of modern technology.

The triangle of objectives depicted in Figure 2.33 summarizes the main objectives of energy policy. The same imperatives apply to the utilities. It is all about sustainability (financial and environmental), driven by security of supply, efficiency and environmental protection. What has been neglected in much of the past decade's environmental and sustainability debates is the application of sound economics in the face of enormous uncertainties when dealing with the environmental impacts of human activity in general, and more specifically the use of coal. The application of the simple Pareto efficiency concept could not only have prevented many misguided decisions that caused major environmental damage but also saved large amounts of money.

2.4.5.1 Greenhouse Gas, Kyoto and CO_2 Trading Greenhouse gases (GHGs) are harmful to the Earth's ozone layer and as a result will lead to increasing average temperatures, which in turn are likely to lead to climate change. At the World Climate Summit in Kyoto, 55 industrialized nations ratified the 1997 Protocol, including Annex I, and committed to reducing GHG emissions, first during the period 2008–2012. Kyoto covers the six main GHGs: carbon dioxide (CO_2), methane (CH_4), nitrous oxide (N_2O), hydrofluorocarbons (HFCs), perfluorocarbons (PFCs) and sulphur hexafluoride (SF_6). All gases are expressed as CO_2 equivalents, thus producing a single GHG reduction target. Unfortunately, the global climate conference in Durban in 2012 was not successful in starting a new era after Kyoto. Durban participants did, however, agree to a second commitment period of the Kyoto Protocol and a launch of a new platform of negotiations with the goal of legally binding GHG reductions by 2015 for the period beyond 2020.

The well-intended Kyoto Protocol was not, however, ratified by the most important nations when it comes to population, energy and raw material use: the USA, China and India. Vahlenkamp and McKinsey (2006) concluded that coal burning should decrease in Europe as a result of GHG-reduction policies, but will increase in the USA where it makes economic sense without the same GHG policy. As a result, Schernikau (2010) and Erdmann (2007) agree that Kyoto, as it is, has only a limited environmental effect, if any. In fact, it may result in higher emissions of GHGs. To illustrate this point, consider the following two scenarios which may result from the emissions trading scheme introduced in Europe in 2005 to comply with Kyoto:

1. Higher CO_2 prices in Europe could result in an avoidance strategy. But what if (as is most certainly the case) the area to which the CO_2-emitting activity is moved produces energy with much less efficiency than in Europe? The result would be an increase in global CO_2 emissions, which was certainly not the intention of Kyoto.
2. Higher CO_2 prices will, relatively speaking, push coal prices down and gas prices up, thus increasing the spread between gas and coal. Countries with no CO_2 avoidance obligations can now buy coal more cheaply than gas, thus they are incentivized to use CO_2-emitting coal rather than cleaner gas. As a result, global CO_2 emissions increase. This again was certainly not the intention of Kyoto.

Thus we can see that GHG policy only makes sense when all or at least the largest nations participate. International protocols can be useless or even harmful when nations such as the USA (18% of global CO_2 output), China (24% of global CO_2 output) and India (currently just 5% of CO_2 output) do not participate. By comparison, Germany contributes only 3% and the UK 2% of global CO_2 output (see IEA – CO_2, 2012).

In fact, the current Kyoto Protocol will rather support the increased global use of coal than reduce it. It is strongly suggested to find every energy alternative to coal, which accounts for 40% of all anthropogenic CO_2 emissions. However, we believe that there is no way around coal, and no matter what international policies are adopted they will not prevent the relative coal burn from increasing for at least the next three decades. They can, however, influence or reduce the level of this increase, and the impact of its GHG emissions.

2.4.5.2 Political Environment The political environment for coal in the industrialized world is not what I would call supportive. On first glance, this may seem predictable or even justified. However, politicians sometimes lack sound economic judgment, more often due to a lack of information or understanding than to unwillingness. The results are missteps such as those described previously. The problem with politics in a democracy is that politicians need to be elected every 4 to 5 years. It is argued that this system of democracy inherently favours short-term popular measures over long-term, initially unpopular approaches. The embracing of economic realities in democratic politics is required. There are certainly a number of politicians with very long-term views and sound analyses of the current situation, but inherently political systems are generally not well equipped to deal with long-term environmental and energy security issues. Populists in Germany, for instance, abandon nuclear power and at the same time want to stop all coal burning, yet together these sources currently account for about 70% of electricity generation. A result of Germany subsidizing wind and solar power is an unimaginable overcapacity of energy generation facilities in times of good wind and sun that strain the electricity networks and make conventional power plants uneconomical – which by law have to remain operational.

Domestic policies are about optimizing the nation's development and wealth. This is true for countries such as the USA, Russia, China, Indonesia or Middle Eastern countries. Experts argue that most countries lack a coherent energy policy (see PESD, 2009). Resources are used foremost to cover the country's domestic energy needs. But energy needs in developing countries are very large. As a result, prices for energy raw materials will tend to rise.

Politics is also responsible for subsidies, tariffs and quotas. These instruments are used by governments to either protect their resources from excessive export or to protect their industries from international competition that is harmful to the nation's security or long-term existence. For the global coal trade the use of such instruments has the effect of increased price volatility and, as a result, increased uncertainty for coal consumers. It can be expected that more coal-producing nations will use political means to protect the resources.

This section has discussed only limited aspects of the global geopolitical and policy context. We focus on less obvious aspects of the discussion rather than repeating what can be read in newspapers and magazines on a daily basis. In summary, politics and policy are all about compromises. The coal market is still a relatively unregulated arena. We expect that this market will be subject to greater regulation in the decades to come. Competitive issues will also be looked at much more closely. The attention of anti-competitive agencies is currently focused on coal consumers, such as power utilities, rather than coal producers. But we have shown that, in fact, the production of coal is already much more consolidated than the consumption of coal. It will therefore be interesting to see what the future brings.

2.5 THE GLOBAL STEAM COAL TRADE MARKET AND ITS FUTURE

Up to the late 1970s, steam coal was consumed near its site of production. If international trade occurred, it did so across green borders (i.e., in Europe or between Canada and the USA). Following the oil crises, the coal trade began to pick up. In 1980 only about 150 million tons of seaborne steam coal was traded globally (Ritschel and Schiffer, 2007, p. 23). By 2012 this figure had grown to 826 million tons (VDKI, 2013). This translates into a CAGR of 5.5%. Germany, for instance, also appeared very late on the international coal trading scene. The VDKI reported that in 1988 Germany imported only 6.5 million tons of steam coal. This figure grew to 48 million tons in 2012, and is likely to increase further as local production and nuclear power are phased out. Thus, while coal demand has grown at about 2% per annum since 1980, it can be deduced that trade has grown at more than twice the rate of underlying industry demand over the past three decades.

As with all raw material markets, the coal market is largely about logistics. Pure mining costs account for only a small fraction of total delivered costs, and 40% of FOB costs. We must consider that getting coal from the mine to the power plant involves the following logistical steps: (a) moving coal from the mine to the port; (b) trans-shipping the coal to bulk carriers; (c) shipping coal in vessels to the destination port; (d) unloading and storing the coal at the destination port; (e) moving the coal from the destination port to the power plant; and (f) storing the coal at the power plant. Even mining, as we have seen, is largely about logistics. For that reason, we have discussed key logistical issues, such as freight.

Trade flow has largely shifted from the Atlantic, with total imports of about 190 million tons to the Pacific, with total imports of about 550 million tons (including India), see Figure 2.26. This shift has occurred surprisingly quickly; in 2006 we were still at about 230 million tons versus 350 million tons respectively.

2.5.1 Current and Future Market Dynamics of the Coal Trade

2.5.1.1 Market Participants, Consolidation and Contract Behaviour Market participants in the global coal arena are of three types: (1) coal producers, (2) coal consumers and (3) physical coal traders. These three groups not only greatly influence pricing (as discussed below), but also product flow. Producers and consumers seemingly do not require traders to do business. However, since production and consumption are continuous and only correlate on a global scale, a buffer is required.

Producers Producers want to cover their investment and operational costs. Historically, they have a medium-term view but since coal price spikes in 2007 and 2008, and volatility thereafter, they are increasingly looking for spot deals. Only the biggest producers have their own freight departments. With a few exceptions, such as Peabody and more recently Anglo American, producers rarely act as traders – with some new developments expected in the coming years. However, some large traders participate in production.

Consumers Consumers tend to have a longer-term view driven by the larger relative investment in plant and equipment. Their storage capacity is limited and therefore just-in-time delivery is becoming increasingly important, especially with higher coal prices. Many larger consumers have built their own trading teams in order to utilize their inherent flexibility (especially where they have more than one power plant location) and to take advantage of logistical swap opportunities. Freight departments are also being built up. Japanese consumers still tend to buy mostly CIF. The author estimates that more than 50% (by volume) of European consumers are now flexible in terms of buying CIF or FOB, while the bulk of the volume is still sold to final consumers on CIF or DES terms.

Traders Traders serve several functions in the international coal market: they (a) act as a physical buffer, (b) finance cargos (i.e., prepay), (c) arrange freight and logistics, (d) act as outsourced purchasing or sales departments and (e) mitigate credit risk. Being a good and successful trader requires additional attributes to being a good and successful power generator or coal producer. Therefore, many producers or consumers utilize traders as an outsourced extension. Particularly larger utilities or producers have headcount budgets and are not as flexible in expanding or shrinking their teams. Trading, by nature, is a much more volatile business and requires flexibility that often consumers or producers, usually larger corporations, either cannot or do not want to offer.

Consolidation. Coal supply is being consolidated more and more. The largest coal merger in a long time, Glencore and Xstrata in 2012, illustrates this fact very well. Other mergers (not comprehensive, just illustrative) seen in the past 3 to 4 years include:

- Xstrata and Prodeco in Colombia in 2009.
- Yancoal and Felix Resources in Australia in 2009.
- Alpha Natural Resources and Massey Energy in the USA in 2011.
- Whitehaven and Aston Resources in Australia in 2011.
- Peabody and Macarthur Coal in Australia in 2011.
- Walter Energy and Western Coal in Canada in 2011.
- Exxaro and Total South Africa in 2014.

Each supply region tends to be dominated by three to five key producers that account for 50–80% of each region's production. The supply market is therefore neither monopolistic nor close to perfect competition. It is fair to say that it is oligopolistic and imperfect in nature. It is estimated that over 500 export mines supply the world coal trade. Coal demand is also being consolidated, but this development is slower and less relevant to the coal market. The demand

TABLE 2.6 Top 11 world hard coal producers

No.	Company	Resident	2012 production (Mln mt)
1	Coal India	India	554
2	Peabody*	SA	249
3	Shenhua	China	304
4	Arch	USA	141
5	China Coal	China	176
6	BHP Billiton	Australia	105
7	Anglo	UK	84
8	Suek	Russia	98
9	Xstrata	Switzerland	90
10	Bumi Group	Indonesia	79
11	Rio Tinto	Australia	32
Total			1.912
Share of world hard coal			27%
World hard coal (Mln Tons)			7.200

*Own production only.
Source: Author's market research and analysis based on VDKI (2012).

market is far more fragmented. For example, in Europe, despite consolidation, large utilities such as E.ON, EDF, RWE, Vattenfall, Drax and Enel account for a much smaller percentage of coal imports than do the largest producers.

There is an interesting trend that can be observed in the global coal trade: exporting countries, such as Indonesia, China, Russia and South Africa, will need to supply more and more to their own domestic coal power generators. Thus, exporting countries are being offered more competitive alternatives to pure exports. On the contrary, importing countries are relying more and more heavily on imports. This can be shown to be the case in Europe, where local production is declining. This trend underlines our finding that relative coal burn will increase as more countries turn to coal generation. Overall, one can expect the market power of producers to increase.

The coal supply market is becoming more concentrated on a global level, and even more so in the various supply regions. Historically the 25 top coal producers accounted for almost 55% of world hard coal exports, and one-third of world production. Today, the top 11 producers account already for 27% alone. Consolidation also makes economic sense as EBITDA margins and total shareholder returns are increasing (for more details, see Schernikau, 2010, p. 152).

Contract behaviour. The first transformation of the global coal trade occurred in the new millennium at the beginning of this decade. Becker and Ungethuem (2001), formerly of Enron, have already seen a change in the market, where historically long-term contract buying by utilities changed to increased spot buying due to the need for pricing close to current market levels. Utilities used to buy from one or two mines and purchasing was driven by technical rather than market considerations. Today, there is more spot buying and we are in the midst of a trend in which a real global commodity market for coal has developed or is still developing.

Contract behaviour has also changed, with the Pacific/Asian market taking a much larger percentage of steam coal imports. The Western, Anglo-Saxon understanding of contracts does not work 1:1 in countries such as China and India. Many large producers and traders were stuck with non-performing contracts in 2008/09 and again in 2012/13 when the markets fell.

These non-performances, even of large state-owned coal importers, also led to fewer long-term contracts as the supply side does not trust the demand side to perform in adverse situations. However, smaller Indonesian suppliers have also had problems with performance in times of rising markets. It is imperative that the industry counteracts such developments. The coal market, or any market for that matter, cannot function if contracts are not performed and simply become an option for either party rather than an obligation.

In the future, market participants will invest more and more in logistics and upstream assets. Coal remains a scarce raw material. This is supported by the conclusion that coal demand will continue to show higher growth rates than those for other traditional electricity generation methods such as nuclear, gas and oil. Less than 50% of global FOB costs are pure mining costs. Thus, of CIF costs, we can conclude that pure mining accounts for only 10–30% of total CIF costs, depending on freight. It is therefore evident that the coal market is largely about logistics and access to resources. This is apparent in the struggle for export port capacity, not only in South Africa but also in Russia, Australia, Colombia, the USA and even Indonesia.

2.5.1.2 Regional Developments Current industry sentiment is that world coal trade growth will slow in the years to come. While the author certainly sees a slow down in some countries, we still expect that trade growth will outpace demand growth on a global scale.

The six main export regions – Indonesia, Australia, Russia, Colombia, South Africa and the USA – will not benefit equally from the expected volume increase. Local demand in the various regions will curb export volume levels. The author considers Australia and Russia to be most likely to increase export volumes. However, Russia is more at risk because the national strategy is to increase gas exports and use indigenous coal more within the country and because its cost base is simply too high. Indonesia, relatively speaking, is expected to increase production most; but domestic demand will grow faster than production can grow. The USA and Colombia will increase their exports to Asia but increased volumes will still remain small compared with Australia and Russia. Demand will be driven by the Pacific market, here mostly China and India as well as the new developing South East Asian market. Thus, increased Russian volumes will be exported primarily to the Far East.

It is clear that African coal exports – outside of South Africa – will develop and increase in the next two decades. Africa is very rich in coal deposits, localized in Mozambique, Zimbabwe and Botswana in Eastern Africa, as well as Western Africa. The one key problem that African supplier countries have is a lack of logistical infrastructure. Inland transportation systems and port infrastructure need to be built, and wash plants need to be erected.

China is the wild card for global coal demand since it plays a special role as it developed from a fringe supplier to the largest importer in the world. The country produces about 50% of global coal volumes and historically has been an important supplier to Japan, South Korea and Taiwan. We predict that, over a longer period of time, China will remain a net importer but we don't see volumes increasing much beyond the current 200–300 million tons per annum for prolonged periods of time.

India is expected to increase coal imports more steadily, becoming number one importer worldwide (depending on Chinese developments) within this decade. The country is structurally short of coal and has to catch up with its per capita electricity consumption. Indigenous production is hampered by government inefficiencies.

2.5.1.3 Physical and Derivative Trading Volumes Steam coal is traded over large distances across the world to reach consumers in Europe and Asia. Currently less than 20% of globally consumed coal is traded; the remainder is consumed in the country of production.

Globalization translates into increased trade. For coal this also means that trading volumes will grow faster than the underlying growth of demand for coal. The resulting higher growth of the steam coal trade will further increase the significance of the market. The coal industry will become more professional – attracting new, well-educated talent – and will increase in transparency.

The growing importance of coal traders for financing and buffer purposes will also lead to more 'intra-trader' coal trading. Long trading chains of 10 or even more participants in one physical vessel delivery first developed during the price increases of 2007 and 2008. While price drops (in the autumn of 2008 caused by the financial crisis and the overheating of the coal market and in 2012/13 caused by the financial crisis and the shale gas revolution in the USA) will reduce these trading chains temporarily, the author expects that we will see each coal delivery go through more hands in the long term. As a result, the risk for any trader increases because default risk increases proportionally to the number of traders in one chain. These risks will also affect producers and consumers.

As price volatility increases, so does trading risk. As a result of the above developments, well-thought-out credit risk requirements and compliance are essential but probably not sufficient to keep trading as safe as it used to be. The development of physical and financial exchanges for coal will speed up with these developments. For example, the physical OTC coal exchange *globalCoal* represents one important step towards managing credit risks. But the market has to develop and implement true exchanges that manage default risks themselves. One step was the creation of coal swaps traded at the Chicago Mercantile Exchange (CME) in 2012, that reached *globalCoal* levels within less than a year. For financial derivatives, exchanges have become more common in the past years, but for physical coal there is still much to do.

We predict that only the large standardized coal volumes will be handled via exchanges in the next decade. This will include the standard RB and ARA as well as NEWC and API8 (CFR China) products. For the more fragmented trading routes that include 'off-spec' coal products, it will become much more difficult to standardize. Hence, the author predicts that at least 50% of the traded coal volume will continue being traded outside of exchanges, thus requiring physical coal traders to manage the product flow.

Increased trade volumes will also attract more financial traders, including but not limited to investment banks. Figure 2.34 depicts the growth of derivative coal volumes, which seem to have stagnated since 2007 but are likely to get a new boost from exchanges.

2.5.2 Future Steam Coal Price Trends

The trend for future steam coal prices in the medium term points towards higher prices for the following reasons:

- Electricity demand is rising.
- Coal's share of electricity generation is rising, mainly driven by China's and India's large coal share in electricity generation.
- Major export countries, such as South Africa, Indonesia and Russia, have increasing domestic coal demand.
- New demand coming from 'new' importers in South East Asia.
- FOB costs will increase because of labour and transportation costs. Machinery and experienced personnel will likely remain in short supply.
- Export mine capacity utilization will remain or go back to higher levels.

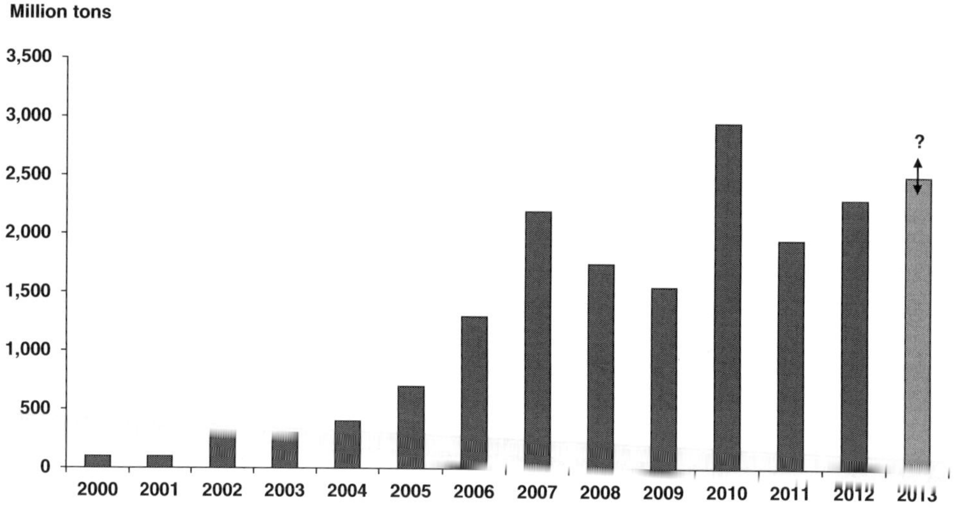

FIGURE 2.34 API2, API4 and NEWC FOB derivative coal trade volume
Source: Author's analysis based on VDKI (2013) and industry press.

- Coal asset prices will increase as relative coal investments slowly catch up with oil and gas investments (see Figure 2.16).
- Producers will continue to consolidate.

In contrast, we have factors keeping coal prices 'in check' and as such it becomes less likely that we will see price spikes such as in 2008 again.

- USA: low gas prices and new PRB coal.
- New supply sources (i.e., Mozambique, Mongolia and others).
- Increased supply from Australia.
- Freight rates are likely to remain low for a few years, increasing competition from global coal sources.
- Import demand growth will slow in China and India.

Figure 2.35 depicts historic average steam coal for CIF ARA (API2) and FOB Richards Bay (API4). It can be seen that the first price increase occurred in 2003/2004. In 2005 and 2006 the market consolidated at a relatively high level before peaking in 2008. The average price for 2008 is tainted by the intra-year peak of 210 USD/mt for API2 in July. By comparison, the API2 was at 130 USD/t in January 2008 and 62 USD/t in March 2009. After reaching the low point in early 2009 the market recovered until 2011 before retreating again in 2012 and 2013. At the time of writing this chapter (September 2013), the market has reached a low point and is likely to slowly increase again after a longer period of volatile low prices.

It can be seen by looking at Figure 2.35 that the 'low points' in 2002, 2006, 2009 and 2013 are touching higher and higher values. Long-term, pricing in a perfectly competitive market should equal the marginal cost of the marginal producer. In the coal market, the marginal cost is probably hit in the USA and Russia first. But we have also seen for several years now that, on average, price will remain above the marginal cost of production – allowing producers to earn scarcity rents. For a more detailed discussion about scarcity rents and marginal cost of production, please refer to Schernikau (2010), Chapters 5, 6 and 7.

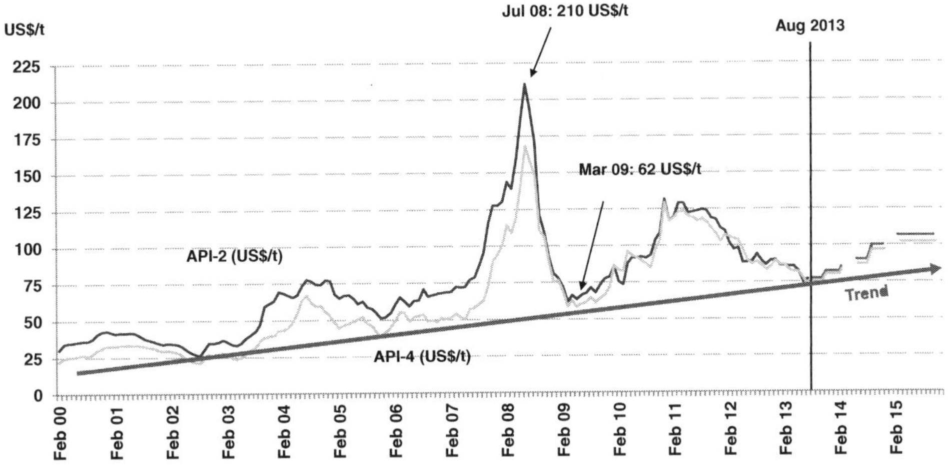

FIGURE 2.35 Steam coal prices 2000 until 2016
Note: API2 = coal price CIF Europe; API4 = coal price FOB South Africa. Forecast curve as per August 2013.
Source: McCloskey (2013), author's analysis.

Overall, basic demand growth is driven by population growth, GDP per capita growth and increasing electrification rates. Today, about 7 billion people inhabit our planet and by the middle of this century the number is expected to exceed 9–10 billion. At the same time, the average incomes of people in the so-called developing countries will continue to increase. The more money people have, the more they will spend on primary goods: water, food and energy.

We predict that coal prices will remain – on average – above the marginal cost of the marginal producers. In relative terms, we expect coal prices to slowly catch up with gas prices (in the USA gas prices have caught up and undercut coal prices). We believe that the basic economic principle of making a CO_2-friendly fuel less expensive than a non-CO_2-friendly fuel such as coal will win support from policymakers. This chapter has not considered exchange rates but they do remain an important driver for coal prices. Consider the rather steep depreciation of the South African rand, Indonesian rupiah and Indian rupee in the summer of 2013 and its impact on coal prices, which fell steeply as a result. In summary, the key long-term drivers for coal prices are (for a discussion on exchange rates, see also Schernikau World Coal, 2012):

1. Foremost demand/supply balanced including import dependency and domestic demand of coal-exporting countries.
2. Politics and government policy.
3. Cost of substitutes (gas, nuclear, renewables) and environmental concerns.
4. Supply costs including logistics.

2.5.3 Future Source of Energy: What Role Will Coal Play?

As can be seen in Figure 2.36, global primary energy consumption is growing at an average annual rate (1990–2030) of about 1.6% (CAGR). Electricity consumption, in contrast, has always grown much faster and will continue to do so at an average annual rate of 2.6% in the period 1990–2030. Growth is fuelled by non-OECD countries, most importantly China and

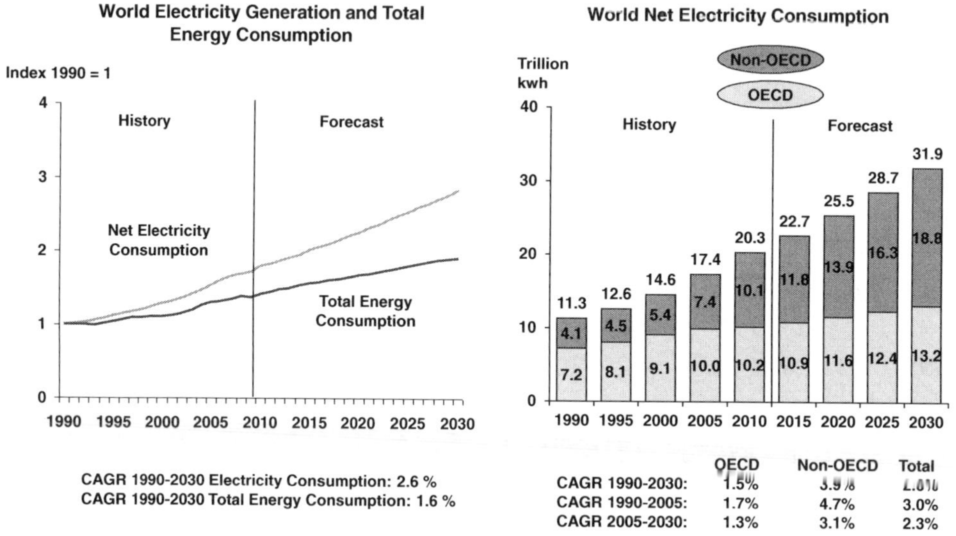

FIGURE 2.36 Growth in world power generation and consumption, 1990–2030
Source: EIA International Energy Outlook (2011). Author's analysis.

India. As such, electricity generation will grow at a CAGR (2005–2030) of 3.1% – slowing growth from 4.7% between 1990 and 2005 – in non-OECD countries versus 1.3% in OECD countries.

Global electricity demand will continue to outgrow GDP growth as developing nations catch up with per capita electricity consumption in addition to increased GDP. Coal will continue to be the most important energy source for power generation, and will increase its importance compared with oil and gas for primary energy in general. In fact, the IEA has already concluded that coal will surpass oil as the main source of energy in the next 10 years. Figure 2.37 illustrates how coal is expected to grow at a rate of 2.1% CAGR (2009–2030),

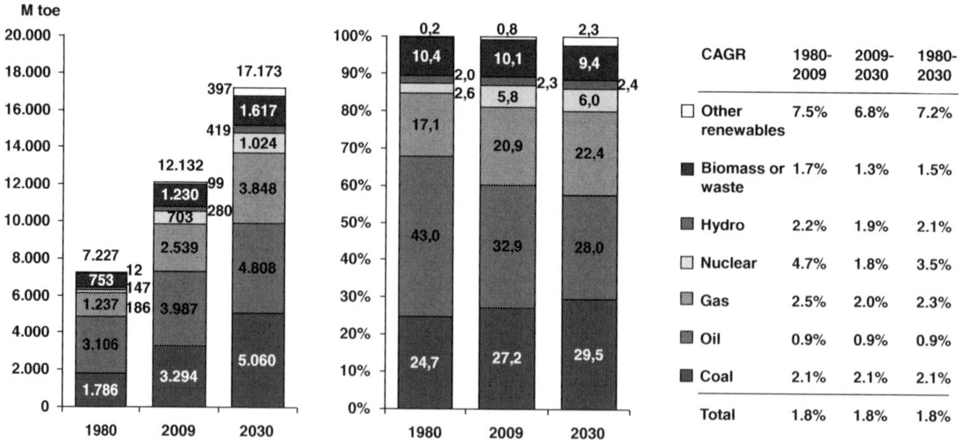

FIGURE 2.37 IEA forecast of world primary energy consumption up to 2030
Source: IEA World Energy Investment Outlook (2011). Author's analysis.

faster than gas at 2.0% CAGR or even hydro at 1.9% CAGR or biomass at 1.3% CAGR. Only 'other renewables' are expected to grow faster at 6.8% CAGR. Interestingly, renewable energy sources as a whole can increase their total 2009 share of 13% of primary energy just by 1% until 2030, to reach about 14%. For electricity generation total non-hydro and hydro renewable sources can increase their share from 19% in 2010 to 23% in 2013 (cf. also Figure 2.24). The shale gas revolution has increased the competitiveness of gas, which is good news for CO_2 emissions. This will mean that coal's growth is likely to reduce a bit, but the basic story of coal's renaissance remains unchanged.

2.6 CONCLUDING WORDS

Environmental concerns about emissions of CO_2 from increased burning of coal will need to be addressed by the global community. We have argued that there is no way around coal as a source of electricity and energy in the coming decades. More so, the use of coal will increase drastically. Thus, we predict that solar-based energy will only be able to reduce coal in the second half of this century. Politicians and scientists should, therefore, stop fighting coal and focus on improving technology to more efficiently burn coal. The best chances of reducing emissions lie in (a) more efficient power plants, (b) more efficient production of energy resources, (c) more efficient ways to transport energy resources and electricity and (d) more efficient use of energy and electricity in general (UBS – Resources, 2008; Schernikau, 2010).

In order to support more gas-fired electricity (gas-fired generation produces about 45% less CO_2/kWh than coal-fired generation) it is important to close the gap between coal and gas prices. The shale gas option has already improved the situation in North America. CO_2 trading schemes that penalize coal, which result in relative lower coal prices versus gas prices, in fact achieve the opposite. From a macroeconomic and geopolitical perspective, gas, the low-CO_2 fuel, should be priced below coal, the high-CO_2 fuel, and worldwide at that.

Independent of the current and future struggle to improve efficiencies, coal is likely to play an important role in replacing oil through CtL technologies. Coal may even play an important role in hydrogen production – a possible future source of energy – and for fracking and extracting gas from shale gas, coal will be required. However, using coal as a source of hydrogen production will require successful carbon capture and storage technologies. CCS is a much-hoped-for technology to solve the big CO_2 problem of coal use. We believe that CCS will come but do not think that it will be a long-term solution. In our view, the only long-term solution to all environmental problems associated with the burning of fossil fuels is solar energy.

The planet has access to enough energy in the form of solar radiation. The task for the future is not to develop new ways to release energy, but to discover how the primary needs of humankind (food, heat, electricity and fuel/process energy) can be met with regenerative or renewable sources of energy. Although this chapter is about coal, we would like to conclude it by repeating the formula proposed by Wolf and Sheer (2005) in their book *Öl aus Sonne – Die Brennstoffformel der Erde* (*Oil from the Sun – the Earth's Fuel Formula*), which illustrates that only solar energy is required to process carbon dioxide and water into a carbon-based fuel and oxygen:

$$\text{solar energy} + CO_2 + H_2O \Leftrightarrow CH_2 + 1.5O_2$$

ABBREVIATIONS AND DEFINITIONS

af	Ash-free
AFT	Ash fusion temperature
AMD	Acid mine drainage. A metal-rich water, resulting during mining from a chemical reaction between water and rocks containing sulphur-bearing minerals
API2	Physical coal price index published each week by McCloskey and Argus Media. API2 is the price for 1 metric ton of coal (6000 kcal/kg net as received, less than 1% sulphur as received) delivered CIF Europe (ARA = Amsterdam, Rotterdam, Antwerp) in Capesize vessels (approx. 150,000 mt)
API4	Physical coal price index published each week by McCloskey and Argus Media. API4 is the price for 1 metric ton of coal (6000 kcal/kg net as received, less than 1% sulphur as received) delivered FOB Richards Bay, South Africa
ASTM	American Society for Testing and Materials
ASX	Australian Securities Exchange
BCG	The Boston Consulting Group, international strategy consulting firm
BEE	Black Economic Empowerment or Black Economic Empowered (South Africa)
BtC	Biomass-to-coal, gasification of biomass to coal products
BtL	Biomass-to-liquid, liquefaction of biomass to fuel products
Btu	British thermal unit, a traditional unit of energy (1 Btu = approx. 1.06 kJ)
CAGR	Compound annual growth rate
CCGT	Combined cycle gas turbine
CCOW	Coal contracts of work, Indonesia
CCS	Carbon capture and storage
CDS	Clean dark spread, defined as base load electricity price minus coal price minus price of emission rights
CHP	Combined heat and power
CHPP	Combined heat and power plant
CIF	Price cost insurance freight (definition as per Incoterms, 2010)
CtL	Coal-to-liquid, liquefaction of coal to fuel products
CV	Calorific value
daf	Dry ash-free
Dark spread	Dark spread refers to the defined difference between cash streams (spread) for coal-fired power plants
DIW	Deutsches Institut für Wirtschaftsforschung (German Institute for Economic Research)
DS	Dark spread, defined as baseload electricity price minus coal price
EEX	European Energy Exchange in Leipzig, Germany
FC	Fixed carbon
FOB	Price free on board (definition as per Incoterms, 2000)
gad	Gross air-dried basis

gar	Gross as received
GCV	Gross calorific value
GDP	Gross domestic product
GHG	Greenhouse gas
Gtoe	Gigatons of oil equivalent (the amount of energy released by burning one gigaton of crude oil)
Hard coal	Hard coal is defined as the sum of steam coal and coking coal
HGI	Hardgrove index
HHV	Higher heating value
ICMA	Indonesian Coal Mining Association
IGCC	Integrated gasification combined cycle
IPO	Initial public offering
JSE	Johannesburg Stock Exchange
LHV	Lower heating value
LNG	Liquefied natural gas
MIT	Massachusetts Institute of Technology
nar	Net as received basis
Nash equilibrium	In game theory, Nash equilibrium is a solution concept of a game involving two or more players, in which each player is assumed to know the equilibrium strategies of the other players and no player has anything to gain by changing only his or her own strategy unilaterally
NCV	Net calorific value, as received basis (ar)
OECD	Organization for Economic Cooperation and Development
OTC	Over-the-counter
oxid. Atm.	Oxidizing atmosphere, relevant for ash fusion temperatures
PCI	Pulverized coal injection
PNG	Pipeline natural gas
RBCT	Richards Bay Coal Terminal – the world's largest coal export terminal located in Richards Bay, South Africa
red. Atm.	Reducing atmosphere, relevant for ash fusion temperatures
Remaining potential	Number of years that the coal in theory will last when taking current annual production, reserves and resources into account
Reserves	Proven and recoverable deposits of coal considering today's technology
Resources	Overall coal resources, also referred to as 'in-situ coal'. Resources include the known coal deposits that are currently not economical or technically recoverable
ROM	Run-of-mine coal; coal that comes directly out of the mines before it has been crushed, screened or otherwise treated
Spark spread	Spark spread is the theoretical gross margin of a gas-fired power plant from selling a unit of electricity
Steam coal	For the purpose of this study and in line with international practice I classify anthracite, bituminous and the majority of sub-bituminous coals as steam coal. Steam coal excludes coking coal and lignite
T&D	Transmission and distribution

tce	Tons of coal equivalent, assumes coal with a calorific value of 7000 kcal/kg net as received (SKE = Steinkohleeinheit in German)
toe	Tons of oil equivalent
TSR	Total shareholder return, a measure to determine profitability for an investor that includes share price and dividends
VDKI	Verein der Kohleimporteure (German Coal Importers Association)
VM	Volatile matter

ACKNOWLEDGEMENTS

This chapter was written by Dr Lars Schernikau with many hours of support and input from Raphael Braun and Wendelin Knauss of IchorCoal N.V. and HMS Bergbau AG in Berlin, Germany and Singapore. It is based on the *Renaissance of Steam Coal* (Schernikau, 2010) that summarizes the coal industry and international steam coal trade in more detail. We updated the information as best as possible and are open to any feedback.

REFERENCES

BCG (2004) Entwicklung eines Marktmodels für den Kohlemarkt. The Boston Consulting Group, Germany.

Becker, S. and Ungethuem, M. (2001) Der Kohlenmarkt im Wandel, Wirtschaftswelt: Energy, Enron.

BGR (2006) Reserven, Ressourcen und Verfügbarkeit von Energierohstoffen 2006, Bundesanstalt für Geowissenschaften und Rohstoffe (Federal Institute for Geosciences and Natural Resources), November.

BGR (2011) Reserven, Ressourcen und Verfügbarkeit von Energierohstoffen 2011, Bundesanstalt für Geowissenschaften und Rohstoffe (Federal Institute for Geosciences and Natural Resources), November.

BGR (2012) Reserven, Ressourcen und Verfügbarkeit von Energierohstoffen 2012, Bundesanstalt für Geowissenschaften und Rohstoffe (Federal Institute for Geosciences and Natural Resources), November.

BP Statistical Review (2012) Quantifying Energy – BP Statistical Review of World Energy, June.

China Coal Monthly (2006) China cracks down on coal-to-oil frenzy, McCloskey's ChinaCoalMonthly, Issue 31, August.

Davidson, R. (1994) Nitrogen in coal [Abstract], IEA paper, available at: www.caer.uky.edu/iea/ieaper08.shtml.

Deutsche Bank Research (2007) Technology to Clean up Coal for the Post-Oil Era, Deutsche Bank AG, Frankfurt am Main, 26th February.

Dlamini, K. (2007) Richards Bay Coal Terminal: Contributing to SA's Growth and Development, South African Coal Conference, Presentation by Executive Chairman of RBCT, Capetown, 30th January.

EIA (2007) EIA Annual Energy Review 2006, Energy Information Agency, Washington, DC, June.

EIA (2011) International Energy Outlook 2011, Energy Information Agency, Washington, DC, September.

Einstein, A. (1955) US (German-born) physicist (1879–1955), Quotations page, http://www.quotationspage.com/quote/9.html, accessed 18 February 2009.

Erdmann, G. (2007) Gut Gemeint – das Gegenteil von Gut Gemacht, Das Kyoto Protokoll und die Globalen CO_2-Emissionen, erschienen in Energiewirtschaftlichen Tagesfragen 1/2 2007, S. 92–94.

Erdmann, G. and Zweifel, P. (2008) *Energieökonomik: Theorie und Anwendungen*, Springer-Verlag, Berlin.

Faizoullina, T. (2006) Coal Mine Methane Projects under Kyoto Protocol, EcoSecurities Group plc, Athens, 27 September 2005.
Frachtkontor Junge (2007) Notizen zum Trockenmarkt, Frachtkontor Junge & Co., Hamburg, March.
Frachtkontor Junge (2013) Notizen zum Trockenmarkt, Frachtkontor Junge & Co., Hamburg, February.
Frondel, M., Kambeck, R. and Schmidt, C.M. (2007) Hard Coal Subsidies: A Never Ending Story?, Rheinisch-Westfälisches Institut für Wirtschaftsforschung RWI Essen, 16 January.
Global Insight – Russia (2007) Global Insight: Analysis of the Russian Coal Market 2007, Global Insight Inc., Boston.
IEA – CO_2 (2012), CO_2 Emissions from Fuel Combustion, 2012 Edition International Energy Agency, Paris.
IEA – Electricity Information (2011) Electricity Information 2011, International Energy Agency, Paris.
IEA – Manual (2006) IEA Handbuch Energiestatistiken, IEA Publications, Paris.
IEA – Medium-Term Coal Market Report (2012) Market Trends and Projections to 2017, 2012 Edition, International Energy Agency, Paris.
IEA – Oil (2007) IEA statistics – Oil Information 2007, International Energy Association, Paris.
IEA – Statistics (2005) Key World Energy Statistics 2005, International Energy Agency, 2005.
IEA – Statistics (2012) Key World Energy Statistics 2012, International Energy Agency, 2012.
IEA CIAB CtL (2006) CtL Workshop Results, IEA Coal Industry Advisory Board Workshop, IEA Headquarters, Paris, 2 November.
IEA Clean Coal Center (2008) Web Resource http://www.coalonline.org/catalogues/coalonline/81591/6247/html/6247_27.html, accessed 31 March 2008.
IEA Energy Outlook (2007) World Energy Outlook 2007: China and India Insights, International Energy Agency, Paris.
IEA World Energy Investment Outlook (2011) World Energy Investment Outlook 2011, International Energy Agency, Paris.
Indonesian Coal Mining Association (2006) Unternehmen Müssen in Kohlenbergbau Investieren, Indonesian Mining Association press article, October, http://www.ima-api.com.
Kjaerstad, J. and Johnsson, F. (2008) The Global Coal Market: Future Supply Outlook – Implications for the European Energy System, Department of Energy Conversions, Chalmers University of Technology, Sweden.
Kopal, C. (2007) Entwicklung und Perspektiven von Angebot und Nachfrage am Steinkohlenweltmarkt, ZfE Zeitschrift für Energiewirtschaft, no. 1.
Krüger, A. (2007) Neue Kohlenstoffmaterilien, Eine Einführung, Teubner, Abschnitt 1.3.2.
Li, R. (2008) International Steam Coal Market Integration, Macquarie University, Australia, Department of Economics.
McCloskey (2012) Weekly coal reports.
McCloskey (2013) Weekly coal reports.
Morse/Schernikau World Coal (2011) Asia's Changing Landscape, Richard Morse and Lars Schernikau, World Coal, October.
National Bureau of Statistics of China (2012) China Statistical Yearbook 2012.
PESD (2009) Global Coal Market Conference, 2009 PESD Annual Winter Working Seminar, Program on Energy and Sustainable Development, Stanford University, February.
Platts (2013) Publicly available industry press based on Platts ICR Coal Statistics Monthly, February 2013.
Rai, V., Victor, D.G. and Thurber, M.C. (2008) Carbon Capture and Storage at Scale: Lessons from the Growth of Analogous Energy Technologies, Program on Energy and Sustainable Development (PESD), Stanford University, November.
Ritschel, W. and Schiffer, H.-W. (2007) World Market for Hard Coal, 2007 Edition, RWE Power, Essen/Cologne, October.
Schernikau, L. (2010) *The Renaissance of Steam Coal – Economics of the International Coal Trade*, Springer-Verlag, Berlin.

Schernikau World Coal (2012) Thermal Coal: A Macroeconomic Perspective, Lars Schernikau and Cathryn Carlson, World Coal, October.

Schernikau World Coal (2013) Myths and Realities (Indonesia), Lars Schernikau and Daniel Goeckus, World Coal, June.

Steenblik, R.P. and Coronyannakis, P. (1995) Reform of coal policies in Western and Central Europe: Implications for the environment, *Energy Policy*, 23(6), 537–553.

Tester, J. (2009) A Pathway for Widespread Utilization of Geothermal Energy, Presentation at Stanford University by Professor Jefferson Tester from MIT, Stanford, February.

The Beijing Axis (2012) The China Compass – August 2012: Figures, Forecast and Analysis, August.

UBS-Resources (2008) UBS Research Focus – Knappe Ressourcen als Herausforderung und Chance, Wellershoff and Reiman, UBS AG Wealth Management Research, Zurich, August.

Vahlenkamp – McKinsey (2006) Integrated Power Perspective – Implications for Regulation, Thomas Vahlenkamp, McKinsey, Coaltrans Athens, October.

VDKI Annual Report (2006) Annual Report of the German Coal Importers Association (Verein der Kohlenimporteure e.V.), Hamburg, Spring 2007.

VDKI Annual Report (2007) Annual Report of the German Coal Importers Association (Verein der Kohlenimporteure e.V.), Hamburg, July 2008.

VDKI Annual Report (2011) Annual Report of the German Coal Importers Association (Verein der Kohlenimporteure e.V.), Hamburg, May 2011.

VDKI Annual Report (2012) Annual Report of the German Coal Importers Association (Verein der Kohlenimporteure e.V.), Hamburg, May 2012.

VDKI Annual Report (2013) Annual Report of the German Coal Importers Association (Verein der Kohlenimporteure e.V.), Hamburg, July 2013.

Warell, L. (2007) Market Integration in the International Coal Industry: A Cointegration Approach, Lulea University of Technology, Economics Unit, 2006, p. 38.

Wolf, B. and Scheer, H. (2005) *Öl aus Sonne – Die Brennstoffformel der Erde*, Bochum, Germany.

World Coal Institute – Resource Coal (2005) The Coal Resource: A Comprehensive Overview of Coal, First published in the UK in May 2005.

World Coal Institute – Secure Energy (2005) Coal: Secure Energy, First published in the UK in October 2005.

Yaxley, N. (2006) President Euracoal, Secure and Sustainable Energy from Coal, Presentation in Brussels, 23 January.

CHAPTER 3

Natural Gas Markets and Products

Mark Cummins and Bernard Murphy

3.1 PHYSICAL NATURAL GAS MARKETS

This first section is designed to give an introduction to natural gas as a fossil fuel and overview current levels of global reserves, production and consumption. It then goes on to discuss the physical structure and operation of the natural markets, presents the primary natural gas trading hubs and overviews the main market participants and then finishes with a discussion on the liquefied natural gas markets and recent shale gas developments.

Natural gas is a fossil fuel that when unprocessed is primarily composed of methane (CH_4), found in the typical range of 70–95%, but may also comprise other hydrocarbons such as ethane (C_2H_6), propane (C_3H_8) and butane (C_4H_{10}); often collectively referred to as the natural gas liquids that are used in the production of liquefied petroleum gases (LPGs) and which are found in the typical range of 0–8%. Additional components found in unprocessed natural gas may include nitrogen, carbon dioxide and hydrogen sulphide. Traces of mercury and rare gases such as helium, argon, neon and xenon may also be found. Natural gas may also include other impurities, such as water and sand, which contaminate deposits; such impurities are commonly referred to as bottoms, sediment and water (BS&W). Natural gas found with crude oil is referred to as associated gas, whereas in contrast natural gas found in a separate reservoir is referred to as non-associated gas. Associated gas may be found dissolved within the crude oil but may also be found next to the crude oil. In the past, associated gas was simply flared off while extracting crude oil. However, nowadays, in efforts to optimize reservoirs, the associated gas is extracted in parallel with the crude oil for commercial use. Methane may also be found associated with or within other substances such as coal, sandstone, shale, biomass, landfill materials and animal waste. Technologies exist and are being developed that allow for the extraction of such associated methane sources, with particular focus on unconventional shale gas in recent years.

The terms 'dry' and 'wet' are commonly used in classifying the quality of natural gas, with dry referring to natural gas that is almost pure methane and wet referring to natural gas that

Handbook of Multi-Commodity Markets and Products: Structuring, Trading and Risk Management. Edited by Andrea Roncoroni, Gianluca Fusai and Mark Cummins.

contains substantial amounts of other hydrocarbons, such as the liquefied petroleum gases of ethane, propane and butane. Given the relative purity of dry gas compared with wet gas, much less processing of this type of natural gas is required. Dry gas is typically non-associated and so found separate from crude oil or other substances. Like in the crude oil markets, the terms 'sweet' and 'sour' also apply to natural gas, with sweet referring to low hydrogen sulphide levels and sour referring to high hydrogen sulphide levels. Another dimension of interest in classifying natural gas is its energy output or calorific value. 'H-gas' refers to natural gas that has a high calorific value, while 'L-gas' refers to natural gas with a low calorific value.

As with other energy and commodity markets, there are a number of metrics for the measurement of natural gas within the industry. The metric used is typically determined by whether one is considering production and supply or sale and consumption. In the former case of production and supply, market participants are generally interested in volume and so measure on this basis. In the latter case of sale and consumption, market participants are generally more interested in energy content and so measure on this basis. The volumetric unit typically used in Europe is the cubic metre, while the typical unit used in the United States is the cubic foot. The volumetric measurement of natural gas must be done and quoted at a specified temperature and pressure. The reason for this of course is that given its gaseous state, the volume of natural gas may increase or decrease depending on the temperature and pressure. Three measurement conventions are typically used in the industry: (i) standard units, measured at 15°C and a pressure of 1.013 bar; (ii) normal units, measured at 0°C and a pressure of 1.013 bar; and (iii) Russian units, measured at 20°C and a pressure of 1.013 bar. Energy content is measured in terms of calorific value, which gives the amount of heat produced per unit of natural gas burned. The typical units of measurement used in North America, the United Kingdom and mainland Europe are as follows: (i) North America – British thermal unit (Btu); (ii) United Kingdom – therm (the equivalent of 100,000 Btus); and (iii) Continental Europe – kilowatt hours (kWh) or gigajoules (GJ).

To get an understanding of global levels of natural gas reserves, production and consumption, we refer to the annual BP Statistical Review of World Energy report series. This series is an excellent source of statistics pertaining to the key energy markets of oil, natural gas and coal, as well as nuclear, hydro and renewables. The 2013 report looks back at the 2012 energy markets and, of relevance here, gives important insights into the state of the natural gas market (BP Group, 2013).[1] In terms of total world primary energy consumption, Figure 3.1 shows that natural gas comes in third place to coal and oil, recording a consumption figure of approximately 3000 million tonnes oil equivalent. Figure 3.2 shows the distribution of proved reserves of natural gas for 2012 and for comparative purposes the same distributions for the earlier years of 2002 and 1992. Total proved reserves in 2012 were 187.3 trillion cubic metres, with this being dominated in the Middle East and Europe & Eurasia regions. Iran and Qatar take the top two positions in the Middle East region, with reported estimates of approximately 33.6 trillion cubic metres and 25.1 trillion cubic metres of reserves respectively. In the Europe & Eurasia regions, Russia dominates with approximately 32.9 trillion cubic metres of reserves, followed in second position by Turkmenistan with approximately 17.5 cubic metres. Total proved reserves are significantly higher than the 2002 and previous 1992 levels, but the geographic distribution of reserves has not changed much in the intervening years.

[1] Available at http://www.bp.com/content/dam/bp/pdf/statistical-review/statistical_review_of_world_energy_2013.pdf.

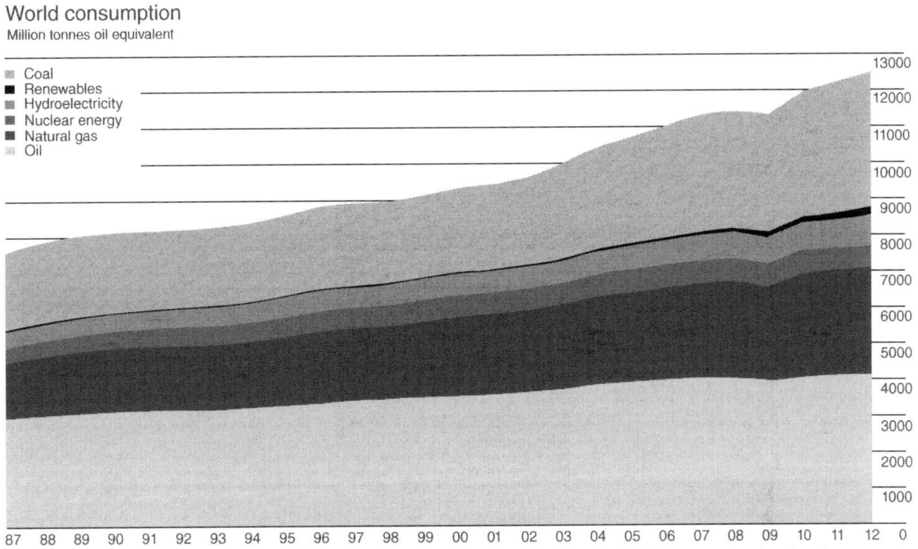

World primary energy consumption grew by a below-average 1.8% in 2012. Growth was below average in all regions except Africa. Oil remains the world's leading fuel, accounting for 33.1% of global energy consumption, but this figure is the lowest share on record and oil has lost market share for 13 years in a row. Hydroelectric output and other renewables in power generation both reached record shares of global primary energy consumption (6.7% and 1.9%, respectively).

FIGURE 3.1 World primary energy consumption 2012
Source: BP Statistical Review of World Energy 2013.

Further to this, Figure 3.3 gives production and consumption figures by region, with Figure 3.4 providing additional insight into consumption, showing the per capita figures by region. The analysis of BP reports that world natural gas consumption grew by 2.2% in 2012, which is below the historical average growth of 2.7%. Above average growth is reported to have occurred in South & Central America, Africa and North America, with the USA showing the greatest absolute increase (a 4.1% increase) in consumption to 722.1 billion cubic metres

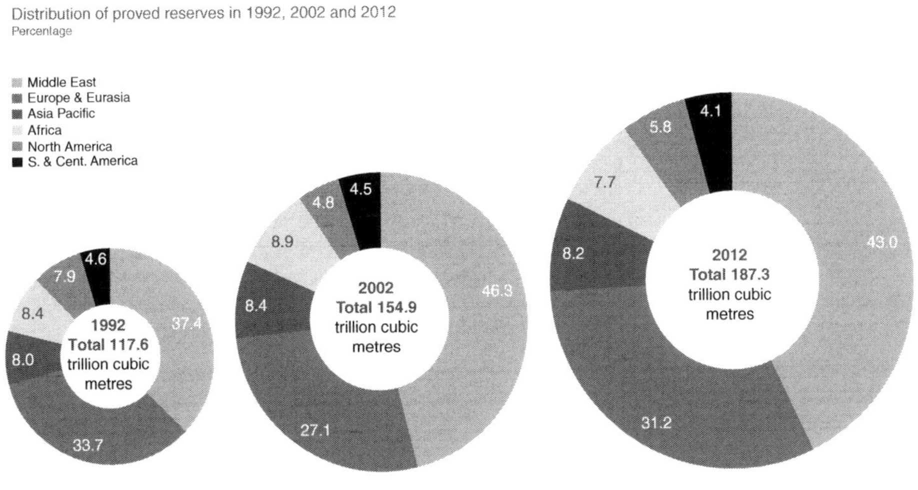

FIGURE 3.2 Natural gas proved reserves 1992, 2002 and 2012
Source: BP Statistical Review of World Energy 2013.

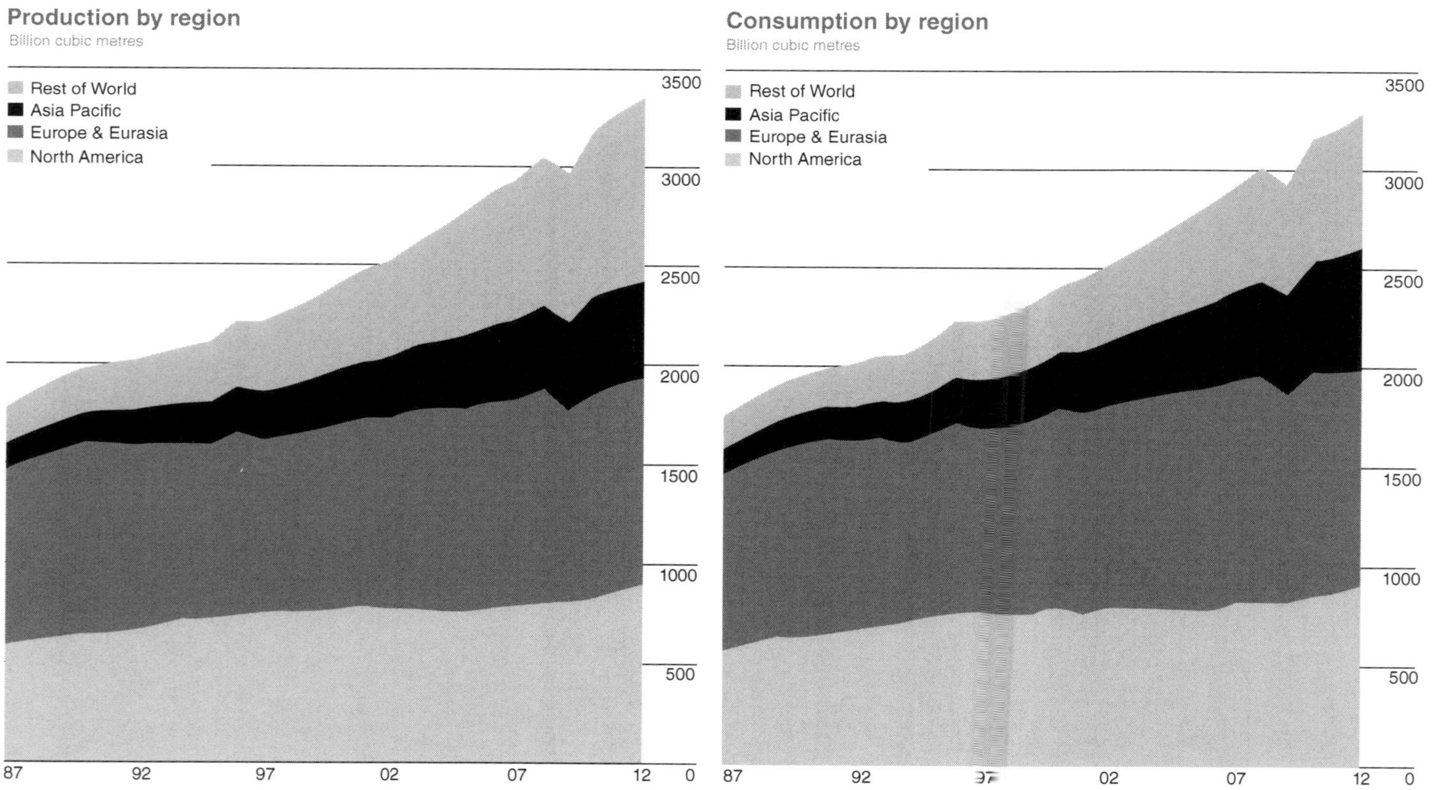

World natural gas production increased by 1.9% in 2012. The US once again recorded the largest national increase. Production grew in every region except Europe & Eurasia, where declines in Russia and the UK offset a gain in Norway. Natural gas consumption increased by a below-average 2.2%. As was the case with production, the US recorded the largest national increase and consumption rose in every region except Europe & Eurasia; EU consumption fell to the lowest level since 2000.

FIGURE 3.3 Natural gas production and consumption 2012
Source: BP Statistical Review of World Energy 2013.

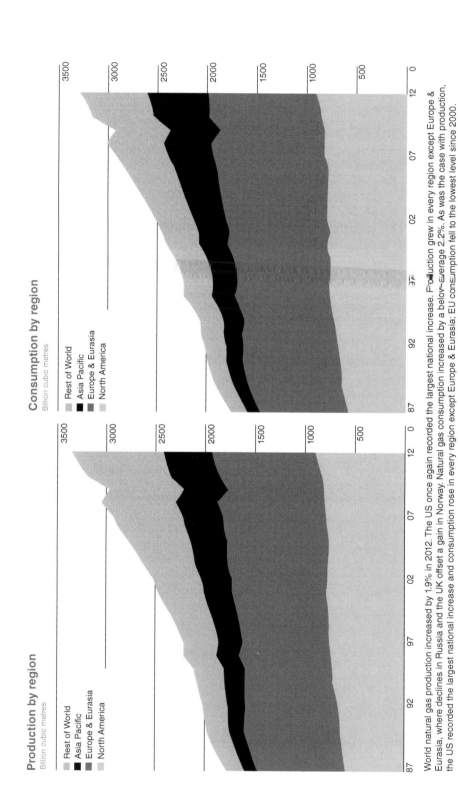

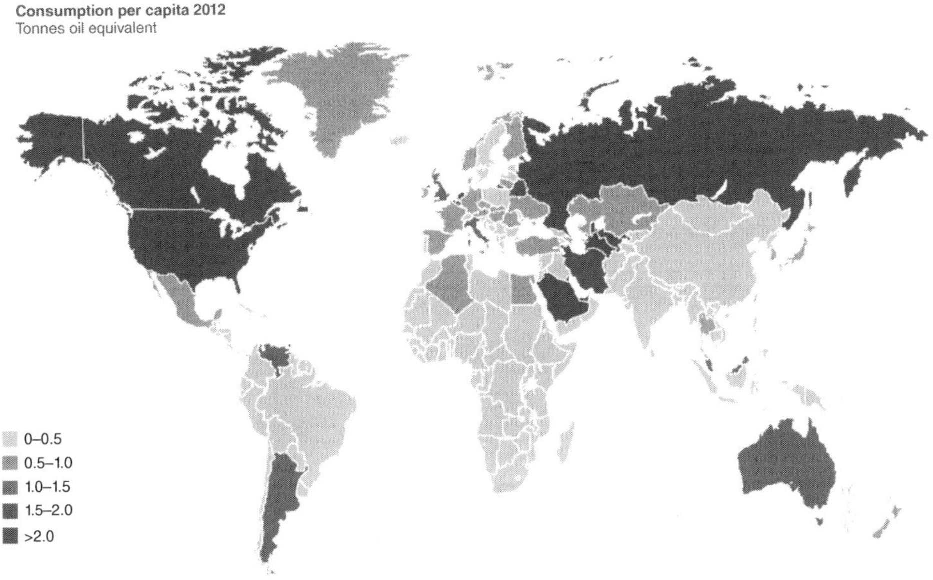

FIGURE 3.4 Natural gas consumption per capita 2012
Source: BP Statistical Review of World Energy 2013.

of natural gas. In Asia, China and Japan saw substantial increases in consumption totalling 143.8 billion (a 9.9% increase) and 116 billion cubic metres respectively. In contrast, the EU experienced a relative decline in natural gas consumption of 2.3%, with consumption in the former Soviet Union countries being down 2.6%. Of this latter figure, Russia as the second largest natural gas consumer saw its individual usage decline by 2.2% to 416.2 billion cubic metres. These significant declines in key global economies underlie the below average growth in natural gas consumption. In line with the modest growth in consumption, growth in natural gas production was relatively weak in 2012 with a 1.9% increase reported. The largest absolute increase occurred in the USA, with total production increasing to 681.4 billion cubic metres from 648.5 billion cubic metres the year previous. Although the largest global consumer of natural gas by far, it is also the largest natural gas producer by some margin. Norway, Saudi Arabia and Qatar saw significant relative increases in production of 12.6%, 11.1% and 7.8% respectively. Russia, as the second largest producer of natural gas, saw a non-negligible decline in its production, down from 607 billion cubic metres in 2011 to 592.3 billion cubic metres in 2012.

Natural gas is typically brought to market over pipeline networks, which are primarily regional in reach but are also international and transcontinental – to be discussed in the next section. However, it is also possible to convert natural gas into liquid form for transportation through a process referred to as liquefaction. Through the cooling process of liquefaction, natural gas becomes much denser and so its volume contracts significantly, with the conversion to liquefied natural gas (LNG) then allowing for efficient transportation via specialized freight vessels. This transportation of LNG has allowed for the globalization of natural gas markets and is often a viable solution for natural gas reserves where pipeline transportation is either not geographically possible or not economically viable. The LNG market has seen significant

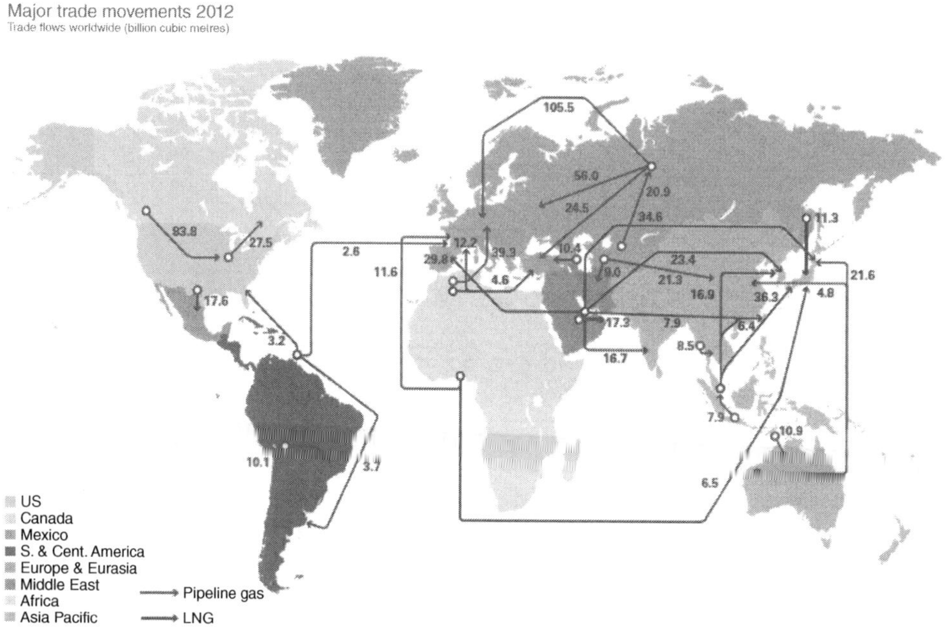

FIGURE 3.5 Natural gas and LNG: major trade routes 2012
Source: BP Statistical Review of World Energy 2013.

growth over recent years and will be discussed separately in Section 3.1.3. In terms of global natural gas trade, Figure 3.5 shows the major trade routes for natural gas and LNG, along with the volumes traded in 2012. Overall trade activity growth was very poor, with only a 0.1% increase recorded in the year. Massive declines of 12% in Russian pipeline exports were partly counterbalanced by an increase of 12% in Norwegian pipeline exports. The LNG share of global natural gas trade fell slightly over the period. A massive drop off in demand was seen in Europe, with a decline of 28.2% in LNG imports there. However, this was counteracted by a substantial increase in LNG imports into the Asia region, with a 22.8% increase recorded.

The face of the natural gas markets is also changing with the increasing prominence of shale gas, as the technology to exploit such unconventional natural gas deposits is developed and deployed. The USA in particular has undergone, what commentators refer to as a 'shale gas revolution' with significant penetration of shale gas reserves across a number of states in the USA. The introduction of shale gas reserves to the mix has dramatically altered the natural gas markets there, impacting on price dynamics and potentially positioning the USA as a net exporter of natural gas rather than a net importer in coming years. A previous focus on the development of regasification infrastructure for LNG imports has not changed to a focus on liquefaction infrastructure for LNG exports. To showcase this effect of the shale gas revolution in the USA, Figures 3.6 and 3.7 illustrate the change in natural gas reserve levels for the USA and UK respectively over the past two decades. Whereas a gradual decline has been seen in UK natural gas reserve levels with the depletion of deposits in the North Sea in particular, the USA in contrast has seen a dramatic rise in reserves generally since 2000 and in particular since 2006, driven primarily by the exploitation of shale gas basins. Shale gas and its current and future role in global natural gas markets will be discussed in Section 3.1.4.

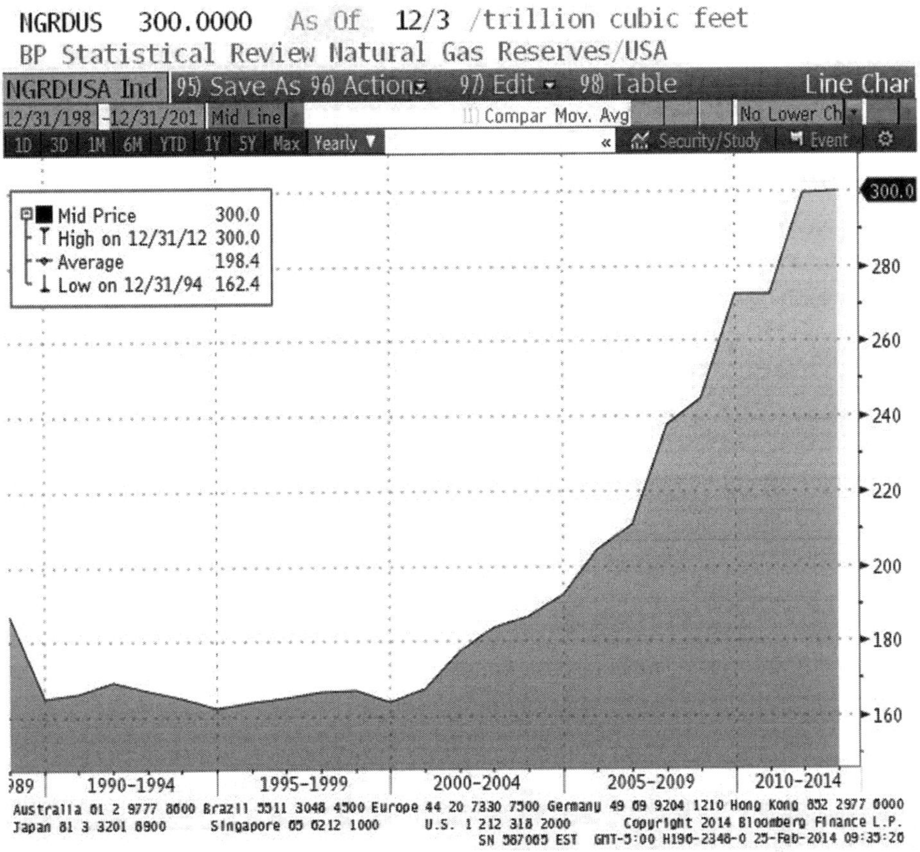

FIGURE 3.6 Natural gas reserve levels in the USA: 1994–2014
Source: © 2013 Bloomberg Finance L.P. All rights reserved. Used with permission.

3.1.1 Physical Structure

Natural gas is a key source of energy in all modern economies. Gas markets have evolved into a very complex network of physical and financial operations as a result of the following: (i) strong demand growth throughout the world; (ii) the need to transport gas from wells to final consumers; and (iii) the need to take financial positions for both physical and financial trading. We can divide the primary physical activities into exploration and production, processing, transportation, storage and local distribution.

Exploration and Production Natural gas fields are not easy to identify and access. The search for gas fields is costly and expected benefits are volatile because it is not known with absolute certainty how profitable the search and/or the extraction will be. The extraction activity could be a standalone project or could be a by-product of the extraction of crude oil. A detailed discussion of the latest technology underlying modern natural gas exploration and production is beyond the scope of this chapter.

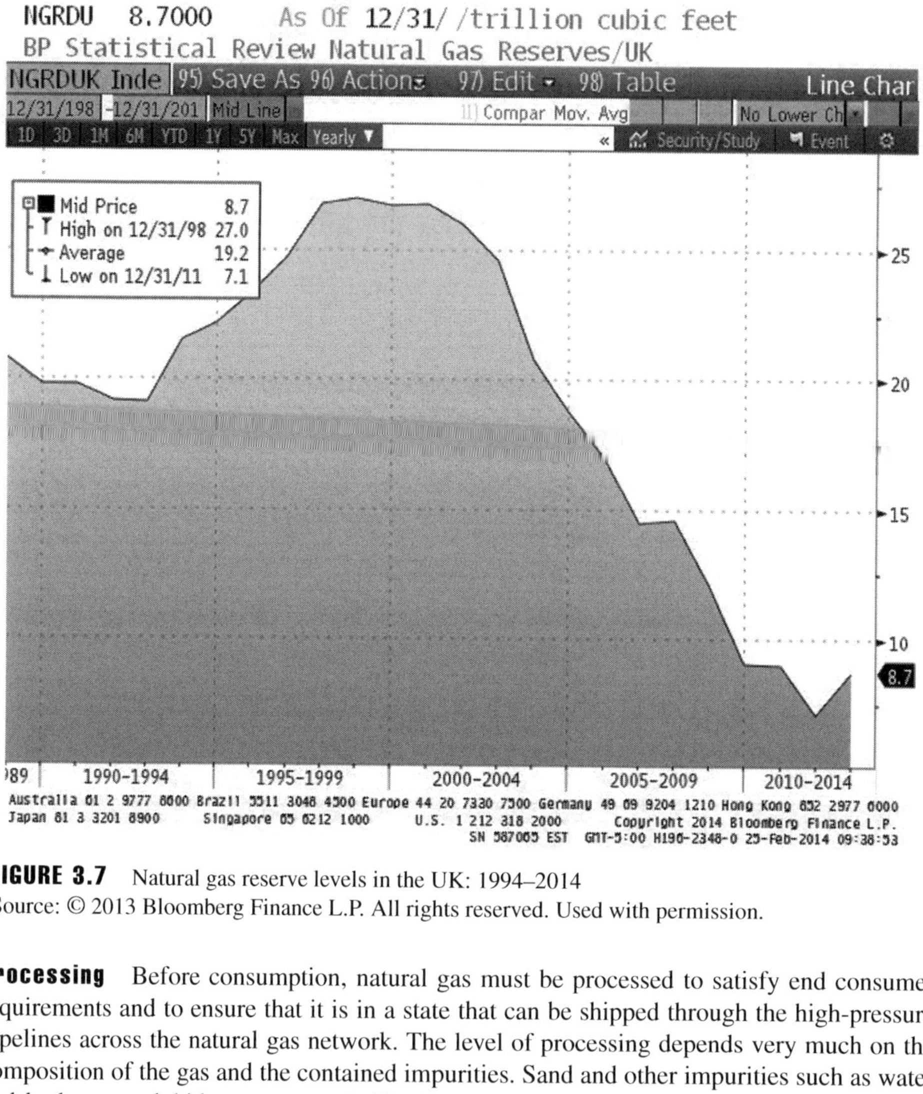

FIGURE 3.7 Natural gas reserve levels in the UK: 1994–2014

Processing Before consumption, natural gas must be processed to satisfy end consumer requirements and to ensure that it is in a state that can be shipped through the high-pressure pipelines across the natural gas network. The level of processing depends very much on the composition of the gas and the contained impurities. Sand and other impurities such as water and hydrogen sulphide are removed. Heavier gases or natural gas liquids, such as ethane, propane and butane, are also extracted as these have their own commercial value. There are three fundamental stages to processing: (i) dehydration; (ii) sweetening; and (iii) absorption. These process stages are together referred to as stripping and are described below.

- *Dehydration stage.* This process involves the removal of water content from natural gas by vaporization. It is important to remove such water traces in order to prevent the formation of hydrates and freezing in pipeline systems.
- *Sweetening stage.* This is the process of removing hydrogen sulphide impurities from natural gas, where the importance of this stage increases with the sourness of the natural gas. Carbon dioxide is also removed with the sweetening process, along with other gas contaminants, some of which may have commercial value in themselves.

- *Absorption stage*. This is the process whereby the natural gas liquids are separated from the natural gas. As mentioned previously, the natural gas liquids of ethane, propane and butane are used in the production of liquefied petroleum gases but may also be used as motor gasoline blending components and as raw material for the petrochemicals industry.

Transportation Once processed, natural gas must be transported to either large industrial users, storage facilities or local distribution companies. This is not a trivial part of the natural gas market because it adds a considerable cost to the commodity and results in price differentials between locations, underlining the need to be able to store gas at cost-effective prices. As gas fields tend to be in remote locations far away from the areas where the natural gas is ultimately consumed (e.g., urban areas, industrial centres, etc.), transportation distances can be substantial. Indeed, within the natural gas market, transportation between countries and between continents is also common. Natural gas is primarily transported over networks of pipelines that interconnect between the gas field sources and the end consumers. With LNG, shipping of natural gas using special freight vessels is a major but secondary transportation mechanism. High-pressure pipelines are typically made of welded steel, with low-pressure pipelines made of polyethylene. The pressure drops the further that the natural gas travels and so the longer the pipeline, the more the pressure drops as well. To deal with these pressure issues, pipelines are fitted with compression stations or compressors at regular intervals (80–100 km) that increase pressure within the pipeline. The overall objective of the compressor system is to maintain the flow of natural gas at as constant a rate as possible. In most cases, the compressors are powered by some of the flowing natural gas in the pipeline. Pipelines tend to operate at varying pressures depending on the time of year and the volume of natural gas in the pipeline. There are three main types of pipeline network, which are set out below.

- *Transmission system.* Delivers the upstream natural gas production to regional distribution networks or to large industrial centres.
- *Regional system.* Allows for the transportation of natural gas to local distribution grids.
- *Local grids.* Allow for the transportation of natural gas to end users in a locality that includes residential, commercial and industrial consumers. Local distribution companies own and operate these high-pressure networks.

Figure 3.8 illustrates the extensive natural gas pipeline network that services the US and Canadian regions. The Energy Information Administration reports that (as of 2007/2008) the natural gas pipeline network comprised:[2]

- More than 210 natural gas pipeline systems.
- 305,000 miles of interstate and intrastate transmission pipelines.
- More than 1,400 compressor stations that maintain pressure on the natural gas pipeline network and assure continuous forward movement of supplies.
- More than 11,000 delivery points, 5,000 receipt points and 1,400 interconnection points that provide for the transfer of natural gas throughout the United States.
- 24 hubs or market centres that provide additional interconnections.
- 400 underground natural gas storage facilities.

---

[2]See http://www.eia.gov/pub/oil_gas/natural_gas/analysis_publications/ngpipeline/index.html.

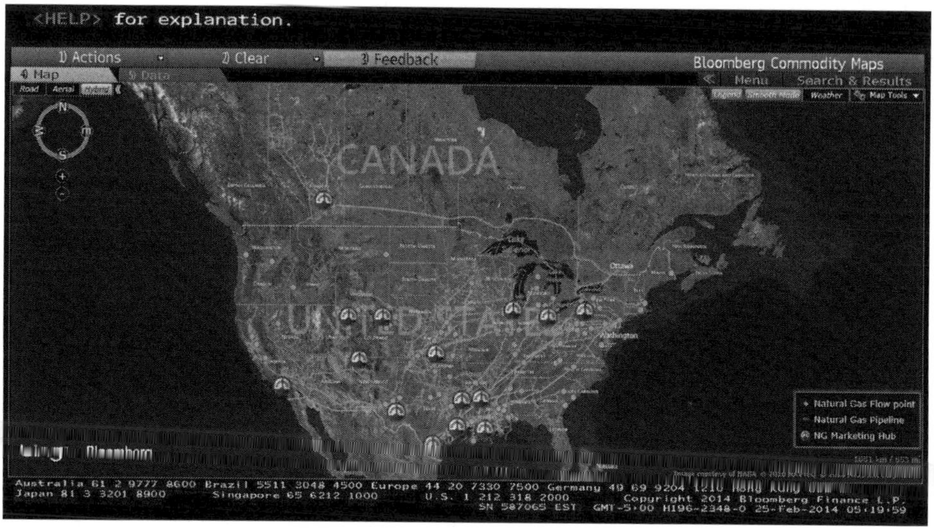

FIGURE 3.8 US and Canadian natural gas pipeline network map
Source: © 2013 Bloomberg Finance L.P. All rights reserved. Used with permission.

- 49 locations where natural gas can be imported/exported via pipelines.
- 8 LNG import facilities and 100 LNG peaking facilities.

Storage Natural gas demand is variable throughout the year but amongst the many fundamental drivers of natural gas markets, weather plays a key role. Although demand is volatile and unpredictable, natural gas prices tend to show a strong seasonal pattern: typically high demand in winter and low demand in summer, a feature which is usually accompanied by higher gas prices in winter and lower prices in summer. This strong seasonal component, coupled with the need to have a buffer to meet unexpected short-term demand and supply deviations, justifies the existence of storage capacity in developed natural gas markets. Natural gas storage facilities come in a variety of forms: caverns, depleted oil and gas fields, aquifers, and overground steel storage units. Storage facilities offer the market a mechanism for the efficient management of natural gas to deal with seasonal, daily and intra-daily fluctuations in demand. In this context, two classifications of storage exist: seasonal storage and peak storage.

- *Seasonal storage.* Incorporates large storage facilities with relatively low injection and withdrawal rates. Such facilities typically provide baseload winter supply to the natural gas markets. Market participants generally use such facilities to inject natural gas during summer months when demand and prices are lower and subsequently withdraw the gas later during winter months when demand and prices are higher. Seasonal storage facilities therefore allow for the temporal management of supply and demand differences between seasons. Seasonal storage facilities primarily comprise large-scale depleted oil and gas fields and aquifers.
- *Peak storage.* Incorporates smaller storage facilities with relatively high injection and withdrawal rates. Such storage facilities allow market participants to react to short-term variations in demand by means of quick injections and withdrawals of natural gas in and out of storage. Peak storage also allows market participants to balance their activity

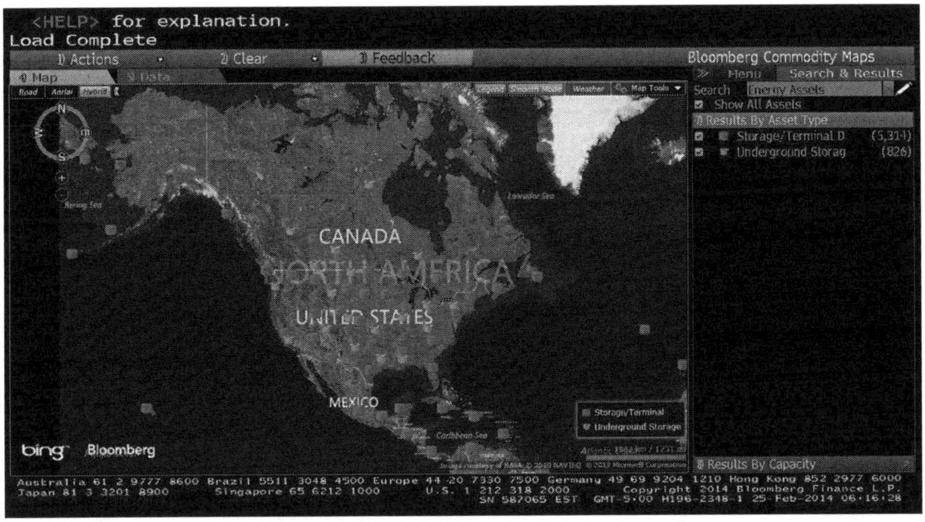

FIGURE 3.9 North American natural gas storage facility map
Source: © 2013 Bloomberg Finance L.P. All rights reserved. Used with permission.

on a transmission system, which is an integral part of maintaining the pressure within the pipeline network. Peak storage is therefore a mechanism through which daily and intra-daily fluctuations in demand may be managed. Peak storage facilities include salt and rock cavities, low-pressure tanks, linepack (i.e., pipeline storage) and LNG tanks.

Figures 3.9 and 3.10 provide maps of the major storage facilities in North America and North West Europe respectively. The Energy Information Administration (EIA), in its 2012 annual natural gas report (Energy Information Administration, 2012),[3] calculates that underground storage capacity in the USA, as of 31 December 2012, totalled approximately 9,000,000 million cubic feet of natural gas. The largest available capacity is in Michigan with just over 1,000,000 million cubic feet of capacity, followed closely by Illinois with just under 1,000,000 million cubic feet and then Texas with just over 830,000 million cubic feet. The types of storage capacity available include salt caverns, aquifers and depleted fields, with the latter being the dominant form of available capacity. Figure 3.11, drawn from the EIA natural gas annual report 2012, provides a detailed map of the regional distribution of natural gas storage capacity in the USA. The predominance of depleted fields is evident, with 330 depleted field sites identified compared with 44 aquifers and 40 salt caverns. Further to this, it is reported by the EIA that in terms of capacity utilization, US underground storage saw a net injection of 7,279 million cubic feet of natural gas, with total injection hitting 2,825,427 million cubic feet and total withdrawal 2,818,148 million cubic feet. LNG storage similarly saw net injection overall, by 1,560 million cubic feet in this case, although levels of LNG injection and withdrawal were less than 1% of their underground storage injection and withdrawal counterparts. The biggest total injection occurred in California (48,071 million cubic feet), with West Virginia leading the pole for withdrawals (26,959 million cubic feet).

[3]Available at http://www.eia.gov/naturalgas/annual/pdf/nga12.pdf.

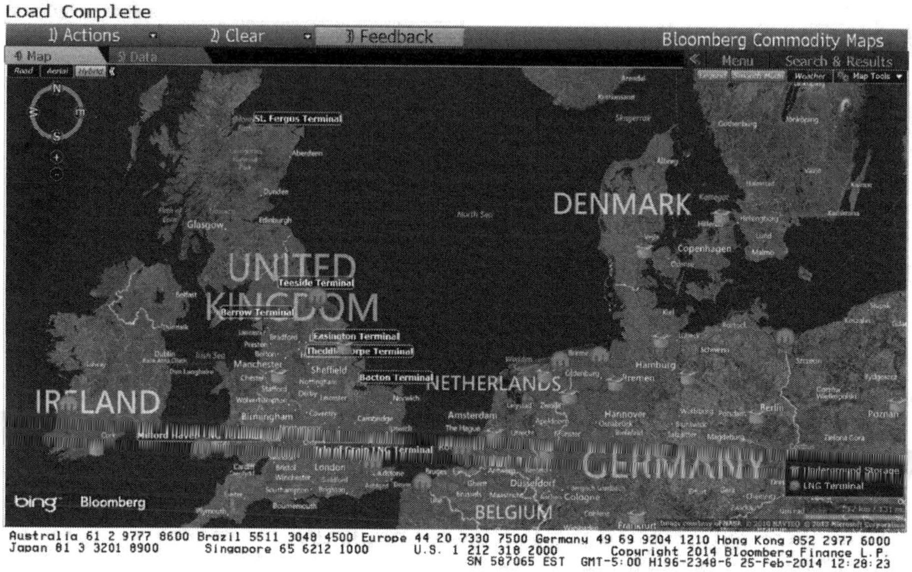

FIGURE 3.10 North West Europe natural gas storage facility map
Source: © 2013 Bloomberg Finance L.P. All rights reserved. Used with permission.

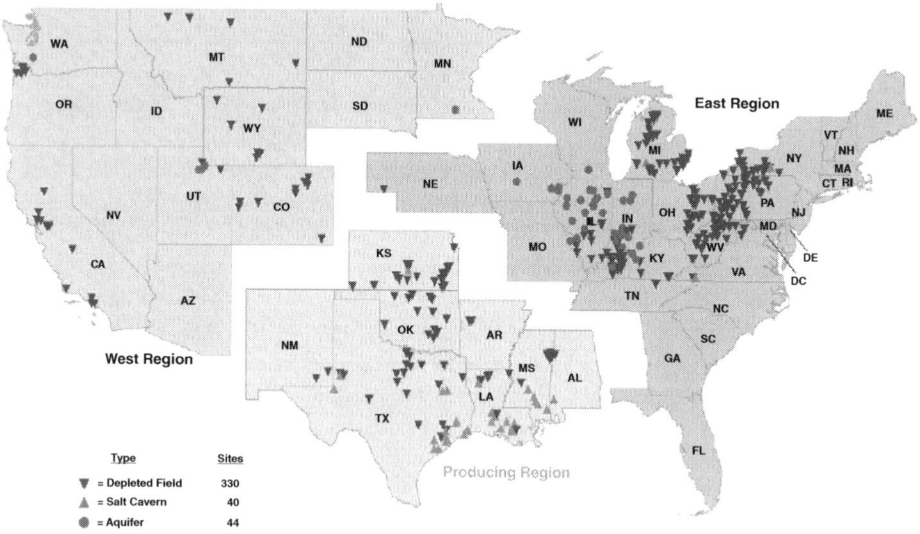

FIGURE 3.11 Detailed US natural gas storage facility map
Source: Energy Information Administration Natural Gas Annual Report 2012.

3.1.2 Natural Gas Market Hubs and Main Participants

The natural gas markets are centred around a number of prominent trading hubs, with much of the physical and financial-based trading indexed to or settled against the prices at these locations. Henry Hub is the primary natural gas hub in the United States and the main pricing point for natural gas transactions in North America. In Europe, the most liquid natural gas hub is by far the National Balancing Point in the United Kingdom. Other natural gas hubs have emerged in Continental Europe and continue to grow in importance. These include Zeebrugge in Belgium and the Title Transfer Facility in the Netherlands, in addition to Gaspool and NetConnect in Germany.

- *Henry Hub.* Distribution hub located at Erath, LA, which interconnects with nine interstate and four intrastate pipelines. It is the main pricing point in the United States and North America generally for physical and paper-based natural gas transactions.
- *National Balancing Point (NBP).* The NBP is the main pricing point for natural gas transactions in the United Kingdom, and indeed across Europe. It represents the most liquid natural gas market in Europe. The NBP differs from Henry Hub in that it is a virtual trading location rather than a physical location. All natural gas transactions in the United Kingdom are assumed to flow through this virtual hub for the purposes of price formation.
- *Zeebrugge.* Zeebrugge is a natural gas hub located in Belgium and like the NBP is a virtual trading location from a pricing perspective. However, Zeebrugge is the physical location where the UK interconnector pipeline to Continental Europe converges with the Norwegian Zeepipe. Hence, there is a close relationship between Zeebrugge and the NBP.
- *Title Transfer Facility (TTF).* A relatively new natural gas hub that was introduced in 2003 and located in the Netherlands. Once again it is a virtual trading location similar to the NBP and Zeebrugge. It is becoming an ever more important pricing point for European natural gas transactions.

The natural gas markets are comprised of a number of market participants, which include producers, consumers, wholesale suppliers and distributors, traders, transmissions system operators and shippers. These market participants are commonly classified into two levels: primary and secondary.

- Primary level
  - *Producers.* Extract and produce natural gas, selling it into the market.
  - *Power generators.* Buy natural gas from the market as an input fuel to the generation of electricity and, where a surplus of natural gas exists, sell natural gas into the market.
  - *Industrial consumers.* Large industrials that are sufficiently large to trade in the natural gas market on their own account rather than through a wholesaler.
  - *Suppliers and Distributors.* Buy and sell natural gas as part of ongoing supply and distribution activities to their customers.
- Secondary level
  - *Traders.* Concentrate on the buying and selling of natural gas using the financial paper-based markets rather than the physical buying and selling of gas. Such traders span banking and financial institutions, investment funds and energy trading houses.
  - *Operators.* Buy and sell natural gas as part of balancing activities and to ensure the reliable delivery of natural gas as demanded by network participants.

3.1.3 Liquefied Natural Gas

The process of liquefaction allows for the conversion of natural gas into LNG, which in its reduced volume liquid form may easily be transported globally by freight between locations not connected via pipelines. The liquefaction process involves cooling the natural gas – after first removing any trace gases and impurities – to about −162°C. This cooling condenses the natural gas into liquid form, reducing the volume dramatically to about 0.16% of its original volumetric size. The LNG is then in a suitable state that allows for it to be loaded into special refrigerated storage tanks on specially designed LNG freight vessels. This allows for the LNG to be transported to any location globally – although defined routes exist. Once the LNG freight vessel reaches a destination LNG terminal it is regasified, that is converted back into its original gaseous state, to be plugged into that regional natural gas network. The liquefaction and regasification processes are such that approximately 30% of the feedstock natural gas is consumed in the liquefaction process and about 10% in the regasification, although more efficient techniques are continuously being developed. The LNG process has opened up markets for gas fields in particularly remote locations where a pipeline network is either not logistically possible or economically viable. The benefits of the LNG market to the overall natural gas industry include the provision of emergency supplies and guaranteed pipeline system operation under extreme demand conditions and as a source of peak storage.

Referring to Figure 3.6 again, which is drawn from the BP Statistical Review of World Energy 2013, a selection of major trade routes and volumes of LNG moved are mapped out (BP Group, 2013). In terms of LNG imports, the Asia Pacific region dominates that market by a considerable margin, which is driven by imports into Japan primarily. Indeed, the BP assessment calculates imports into Asia Pacific at approximately 227 billion cubic metres, with imports into Japan alone amounting to almost 119 billion cubic metres; over 50% of the regional total. South Korea is the next largest importer in the region, with 2012 imports estimated to be just under 50 billion cubic metres. Indeed, Japan and South Korea depend exclusively on the LNG markets for their entire natural gas consumption (International Gas Union, 2013b). Europe & Eurasia is the next biggest import region for LNG, with a total of approximately 69 billion cubic metres across its countries. In terms of LNG exports, Qatar is the leading exporter by far based on the BP analysis, dwarfing other exporting countries with a total of approximately 105 billion cubic metres of natural gas.

The International Gas Union (IGU), in its World LNG Report 2013 (International Gas Union, 2013b), identifies that with the exception of a dip in 2012, the volume of LNG trade has grown year after year for the past three decades.[4] The number of exporting countries in 2012 dipped slightly to 17, while the number of importing countries rose to 25; the dip in exporting country numbers was due to Libya ceasing exports during the civil war period. The total export volume in 2012 is estimated to be in the region of 230 million tonnes. The number of re-exporters has continued to rise over the past number of years and in 2012 the list of LNG re-exporters has been extended with France and Portugal.[5] It is estimated that re-export volumes were in the region of 3.5 million tonnes of LNG in 2012, with the main re-exporters being Belgium, Spain and the USA.

The IGU further estimates in its World LNG Report 2013 (International Gas Union, 2013b) that regasification capacity globally has risen significantly over the past few years to over 600 million tonnes per annum of LNG, with the leading region being Japan with some 180 million tonnes of capacity, followed closely by the USA and South Korea. Indeed, if one includes Spain and the UK in this mix then all five nations account for over 74% of

[4]Available at http://www.igu.org/gas-knowhow/publications/igu-publications/IGU_world_LNG_report_2013.pdf.

[5]Re-exportation is the process whereby foreign LNG is offloaded to storage units within a given national jurisdiction, stored for a period of time and then later re-exported to foreign markets.

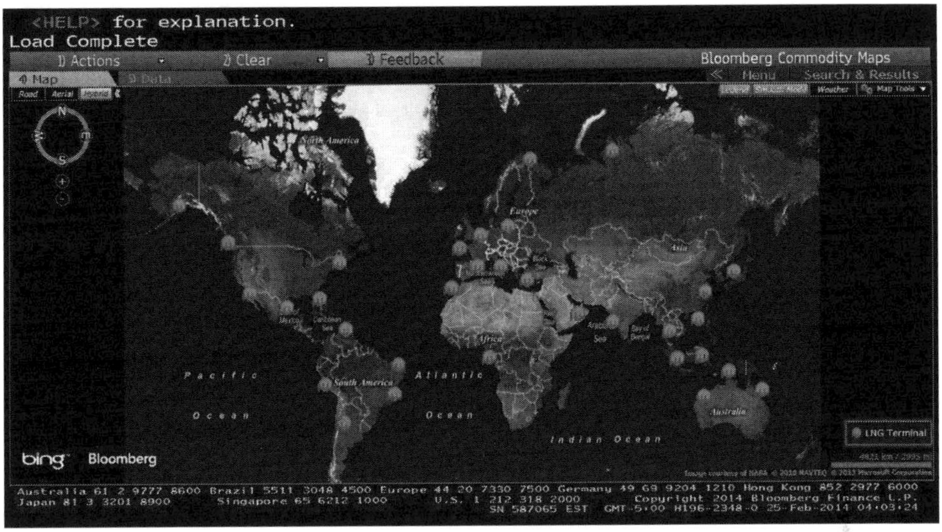

FIGURE 3.12 Major global LNG terminals
Source: © 2013 Bloomberg Finance L.P. All rights reserved. Used with permission.

global regasification capacity. Whereas utilization of regasification capacity is high in Japan and South Korea (and Asia generally), utilization in the USA was extremely low in 2012 at a reported figure of just 3%, reflecting the domestic production of natural gas in the USA, bolstered by its shale gas activities. In contrast, the IGU estimates that global liquefaction capacity across the main exporting countries in 2012 amounted to approximately 283 million tonnes per annum of LNG. Qatar as the main exporter globally has the largest liquefaction capacity at 77 million tonnes per annum of LNG and boasts a 100% utilization rate of this capacity. Indonesia, Malaysia, Nigeria and Australia follow in order after Qatar but with liquefaction capacity in each case that is less than half that of Qatar.

Figure 3.12 maps a selection of major LNG terminals globally, with Figures 3.13 and 3.14 providing more detailed maps for the USA and Europe respectively. Figures 3.15–3.17 respectively present snapshots of LNG vessel locations (as of the 27 March 2014) globally, in the Middle East and around Singapore.

3.1.4 Shale Gas

One of the most important changes to the landscape of the natural gas markets in recent years has been the rapid growth in shale gas exploitation since 2006. Shale gas is defined to be unconventional natural gas that is contained within shale gas formations that may be released through advanced fracturing techniques and is considered a subset of tight gas, which covers all unconventional gas deposits contained in rock formations such as sandstone, carbonates and shale (Energy Information Agency, 2013). Shale gas is released through hydraulic fracturing or fracking. In this process, a liquid mix that is 99% water and sand is injected into the rock formation at high pressure, resulting in the creation of fractures that allow the trapped natural gas to flow. The fracking fluid also keeps the formation more porous throughout the extraction process. Fracking as a technique is particularly controversial and opponents of the technology

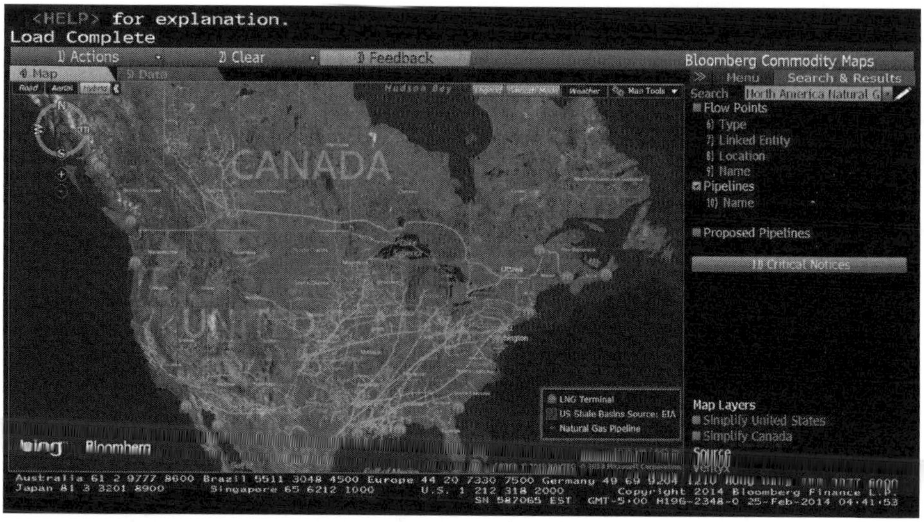

FIGURE 3.13 Major US LNG terminals
Source: © 2013 Bloomberg Finance L.P. All rights reserved. Used with permission.

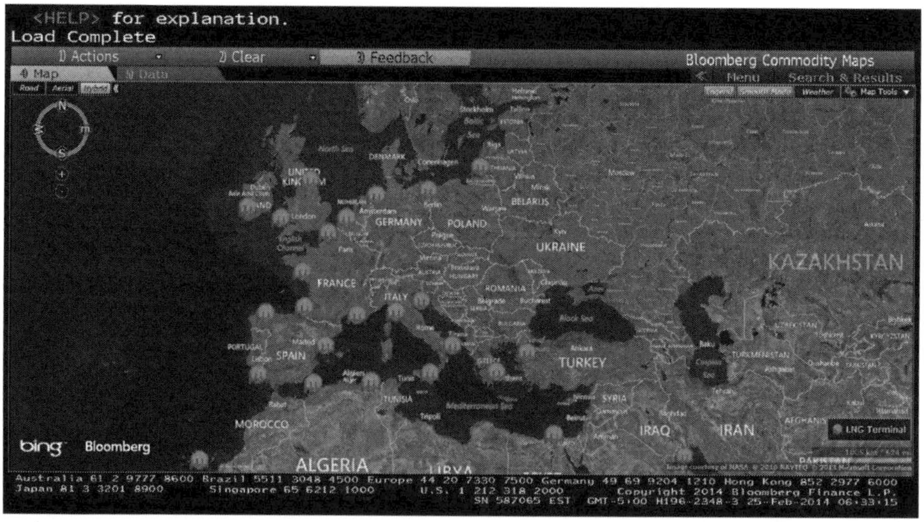

FIGURE 3.14 Major European LNG terminals
Source: © 2013 Bloomberg Finance L.P. All rights reserved. Used with permission.

point to the seismic disruption from the process and the environmental subsurface damage from chemicals added to the process.[6] This increased focus on shale gas has been driven by a number of economic factors, in particular the pursuit of energy security by sovereign nations, and has

[6]For further details of the fracking technology, and more generally on natural gas exploration and production technology, see the NaturalGas.org educational website at http://naturalgas.org/environment/technology/.

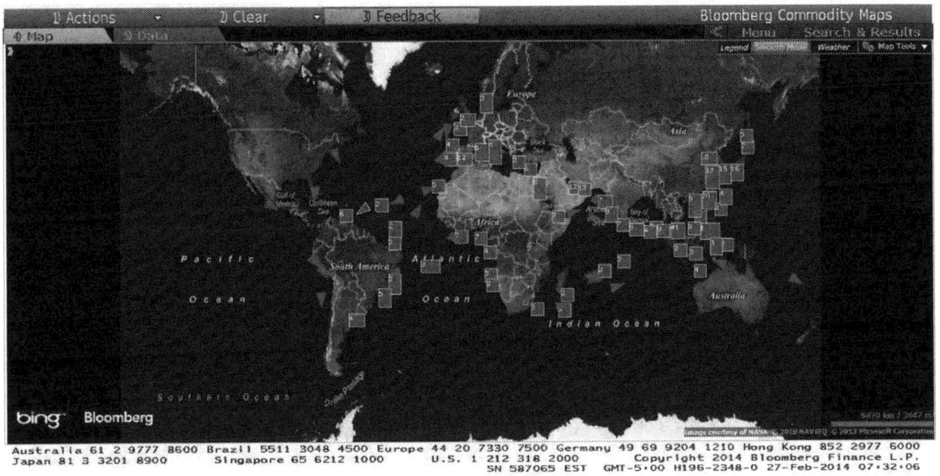

FIGURE 3.15 LNG freight vessel locations: global

been facilitated by progressive advances in exploration and production technology. The USA is experiencing what is commonly termed a 'shale gas revolution'. From a policy perspective, the USA (more specifically certain states such as Texas, Oklahoma and Pennsylvania) has reacted more rapidly than other countries in opening up its shale gas resources to the natural gas industry, notwithstanding continued controversy over the environmental impact of shale gas production techniques. This proactive strategy has included important policy measures such as incentive pricing, tax credits and supported R&D. The exploitation of shale gas reserves in the USA has dramatically altered the natural gas market landscape for the nation, leading

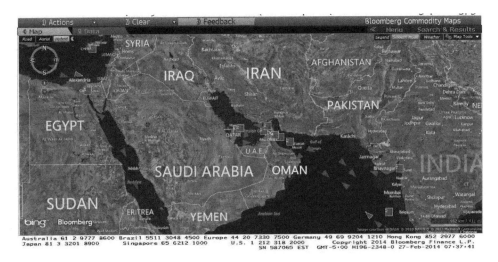

FIGURE 3.16 LNG freight vessel locations: Middle East

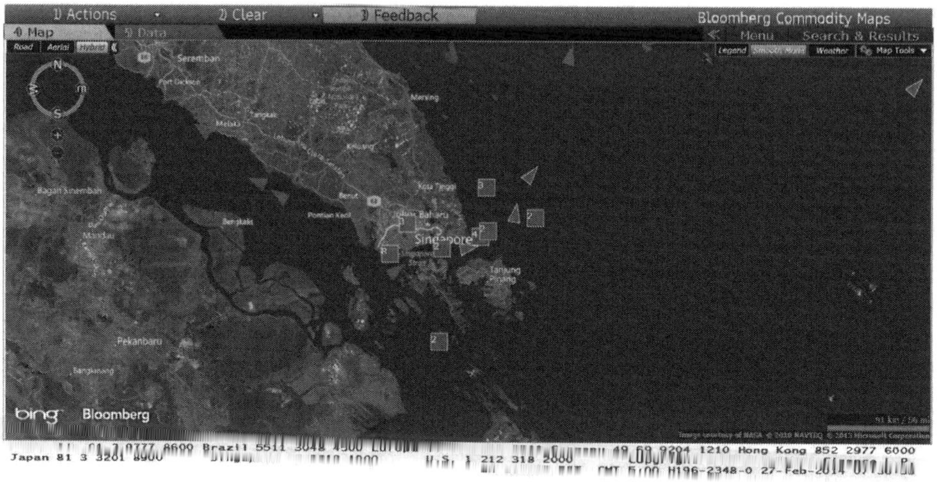

FIGURE 3.17 LNG freight vessel locations: Singapore
Source: © 2013 Bloomberg Finance L.P. All rights reserved. Used with permission.

to consistently low natural gas prices over the past few years and raising the real prospect for the USA to become a net exporter of natural gas. As noted earlier, a previous focus on the development of regasification infrastructure for LNG imports has now changed to a focus on building liquefaction infrastructure for natural gas exports. Indeed, the USA is currently in the process of constructing liquefaction capacity to the order of 18 million tonnes of LNG (International Gas Union, 2013b). Given this tangible success of shale gas in the USA, a greater focus is now being placed on available shale gas resources worldwide.

The EIA released a comprehensive report in 2013 that provides an assessment of the technically recoverable shale gas (and shale oil) resources worldwide (Energy Information Administration, 2013).[7] It is reported that total shale gas resources amount to 7,299 trillion cubic feet, spanning 41 countries, 95 basins and 137 individual shale gas formations. Indeed, it is estimated that 32% of global natural gas resources are now in shale gas form. Table 3.1 presents the top 10 countries by volume of shale gas resources as estimated by the EIA.[8] Three key factors are identified in the 2013 report that will drive the economic recoverability of the shale gas resources going forward. These three factors include: (i) cost of drilling and completing wells; (ii) amount of natural gas produced from an average well over its lifetime; and (iii) prevailing prices for natural gas (Energy Information Administration, 2013). In this respect, a number of key advantages that the USA has in its favour are not readily available to other jurisdictions. These advantages of the USA include, amongst others, the right of private owners to resources below the surface of lands owned, extensive exploration and production infrastructure, and relatively unconstrained access to water resources for the fracturing process (Energy Information Administration, 2013). Figure 3.18 shows the spread of shale gas deposits

[7] Available at http://www.eia.gov/analysis/studies/worldshalegas/pdf/fullreport.pdf.

[8] It is noted that based on estimates from Advanced Resources International, Inc., the USA would be the leading country with 1161 trillion cubic feet of shale gas (Energy Information Agency, 2013), some 500 trillion cubic feet more than assessed by the EIA.

TABLE 3.1 Top 10 countries by technically recoverable shale gas

Rank	Country	Shale gas (trillion cubic feet)
1	China	1115
2	Argentina	802
3	Algeria	707
4	USA	665
5	Canada	573
6	Mexico	545
7	Australia	437
8	South Africa	390
9	Russia	285
10	Brazil	245

Source: Energy Information Administration 'Technically Recoverable Shale Oil and Shale Gas Resources: An Assessment of 137 Shale Formations in 41 Countries Outside of the US' Report 2013.

in the USA, where particular concentrations can be seen to exist close to some of the main trading points.

The EU is currently in the process of assessing its potential and prospects for shale gas exploitation. According to the EIA statistics, shale gas in Europe (spanning Western and Eastern Europe, including Russia) extends across 14 countries, with 17 basins and 24 individual shale formations identified. The total amount of technically recoverable shale in Europe (based on figures from Advanced Resources International, Inc.) is estimated to be 883 trillion cubic feet as of 2013, with EU coverage including Poland, France, Norway and

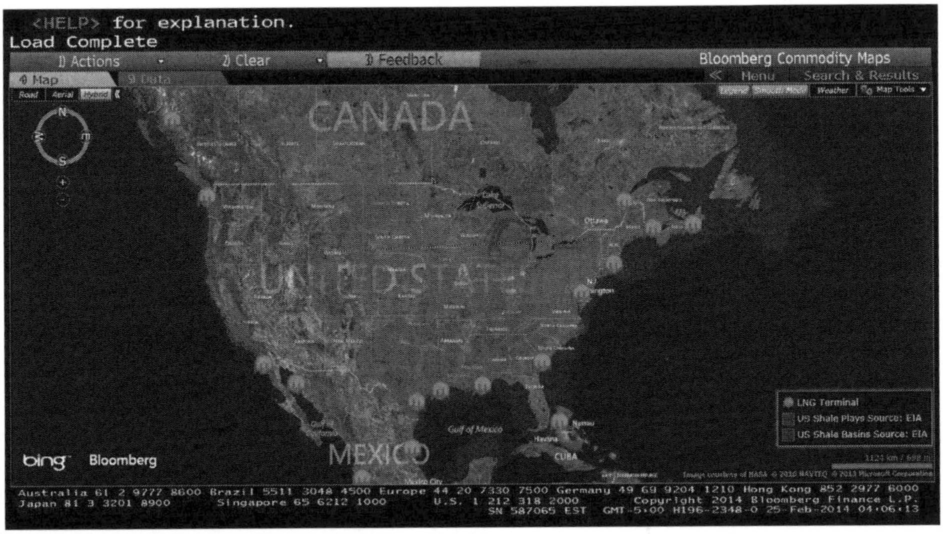

FIGURE 3.18 US shale gas deposit map
Source: © 2013 Bloomberg Finance L.P. All rights reserved. Used with permission.

the UK. The European Parliament issued a policy briefing in 2013 in which it considers the case for shale gas exploitation within the EU (European Parliament, 2013). The role of natural gas is prominent within the energy-mix proposals set out in the EU's 'Energy Roadmap 2050' and central to energy security efforts, while additionally, as the lowest greenhouse gas emitter of the main fossil fuels, natural gas is seen as a necessary transition fuel to a low carbon economy and fundamental to the EU's climate change objectives. The prospects for shale gas face a number of key challenges, not least environmental concerns around the fracking process. Indeed, France and Bulgaria have temporary bans in place on shale gas fracking, while other member states are considering similar lines of objection. The main proponents of shale gas in the EU include Poland (with the largest shale gas deposits), Romania and the UK (European Parliament, 2013). Energy security underlies much of the push for exploring shale gas resources; for example, the European Parliament briefing identifies that Poland is looking to reduce dependence on Russia, while the UK is looking to replace dwindling natural gas resources from its North Sea activities. A number of factors are set out by the European Parliament that create obstacles to large scale shale gas production. These obstacles include the following: the high density of populations across the EU member states, which constrains widespread fracking; EU land ownership laws, which differ significantly from those in the USA and are dominated by state ownership of subsurface resources; the availability of the requisite expertise to roll out a large-scale shale gas programme; and, finally and possibly most importantly, the strong environmental opposition that exists and continues to strengthen against shale gas fracking activities (European Parliament, 2013).

3.2 NATURAL GAS CONTRACTING AND PRICING

The natural gas market is characterized by the demand for reliable and continuous supplies of natural gas, which means that the market needs to be able to handle peaks in demand, supply disruptions and transmissions system failures. Hence, the market is structured with sufficient flexibility in order to deal with such eventualities. Much of the activity in the natural gas markets, particularly in the European market, involves long-term supply contracts of high volumes of natural gas. These contracts can span periods from 10 to 25 years, which provide significant levels of volumetric certainty for consumers but clearly expose suppliers to significant risks over the commitment period, not least the contractual requirement to meet the stated volume of supply but also the market price exposure from fluctuating prices. Contract provisions may be set down that provide market participants with the flexibility to manage the risks associated with the committed supply volumes, while financial contracts, such as those discussed in the forthcoming sections, provide mechanisms through which to manage the market price risk. These long-term contracts include take-or-pay conditions, swing optionality, index-based or formula pricing and/or interruptible supply provisions. These are briefly described.

- *Take-or-pay.* These contracts dominate the landscape of the European natural gas market in particular. Under the provisions of a take-or-pay contract, an annual contract quantity (ACQ) is set out that is typically fixed for the life of the contract and the seller commits to deliver this quantity to the buyer. The buyer in turn is committed to pay for a minimum amount of the ACQ, which is typically set in the 85–100% range depending on the contract negotiation. The minimum payment is required irrespective of the amount actually taken by the buyer. This structure places commitments on the seller and buyer and in so doing provides levels of certainty to both parties. Some take-or-pay contracts have additional clauses that allow for gas not taken by a buyer in one year to be taken in the next year, subject to the provision that the minimum payment has been met by the buyer first – this recovered gas is often referred to as 'free gas'.

- *Swing.* A swing contract is a type of take-or-pay contract that gives the buyer the right to nominate the amount of natural gas taken on a daily basis with prespecified maximum and minimum limits. Such contracts set out an average daily contract quantity (DCQ) and it is around this level that the minimum and maximum limits are set. The limits typically may be as narrow as the DCQ±10% or as wide as a minimum of 0% and a maximum of 200% around the DCQ. These contracts give the buyer significant levels of volumetric flexibility or optionality, essentially providing the holder with a multiple exercise right, multiple exercise date option.
- *Formula pricing.* These are contracts that link or index the natural gas to another energy product. Typically this is heating oil but may also be crude oil, fuel oil or coal. The indexing is set such that a specified lag of the indexing energy product is used in setting the natural gas price under the contract. The lag length typically ranges from 3 to 9 months. Contracts may also be written to protect against inflation and provisions are usually set out to allow for the resetting or renegotiation of the contract terms every 3 to 5 years. This allows these long-term contracts to respond and adjust to changing natural gas prices.
- *Interruptible contracts:* These long-term contracts allow the seller of the natural gas to disrupt and interrupt the supply of natural gas to the buyer. This provides the seller with flexibility to manage disruptions to its own supply source and make alternative arrangements without the same level of contractual penalty. There is normally a maximum duration set out for the interruption period, for example in the UK market this is typically a maximum of 45 days in any one year. The buyer is compensated for the disruption, which normally comes in the form of a discounted price for the natural gas ultimately supplied.

Long-term gas prices are affected by a number of factors that include the general state of the economy, external energy market influences (in particular, crude oil), long-term changes in supply and demand in the natural gas markets, the type of long-term supply contracts that dominate the market, prevailing pricing arrangements, the make-up of the regional power generation sector (i.e., to what extent this is based on gas), the level of seasonal capacity available and general competition in the natural gas markets.

3.2.1 Natural Gas Price Formation

The IGU provides prominent annual surveys and reports on the global wholesale natural gas markets. These reports provide particular insights into the global trading of natural gas, the drivers of natural gas prices and the key pricing mechanisms that exist in the natural gas markets. The IGU defines the main pricing mechanisms that prevail in the natural gas markets (International Gas Union, 2011, 2012, 2013a), which are reproduced in Table 3.2.

In its Wholesale Gas Price Survey 2013 report, the IGU provide statistics on natural gas contracting and price formation globally, discussing the evolution of the market over the period

TABLE 3.2 Pricing mechanisms in natural gas markets

Pricing mechanism	Definition
Oil price escalation	The price is linked, usually through a base price and an escalation clause, to competing fuels, typically crude oil, gas oil and/or fuel oil. In some cases coal prices can be used as can electricity prices.
Gas-on-gas competition	The price is determined by the interplay of supply and demand – gas-on-gas competition and is traded over a variety of different periods (daily, monthly, annually or other periods). Trading takes place at physical hubs (e.g., Henry Hub) or notional hubs (e.g., NBP in the UK). There are likely to be developed futures markets (NYMEX or ICE). Not all gas is bought and sold on a short-term fixed price basis and there will be longer-term contracts but these will use gas price indices to determine the monthly price, for example, rather than competing fuel indices. Spot LNG is also included in this category.
Bilateral monopoly	The price is determined by bilateral discussions and agreements between a large seller and a large buyer, with the price being fixed for a period of time, typically 1 year. There may be a written contract in place but often the arrangement is at the government or state-owned company level.
Netback from final product	The price received by the gas supplier is a function of the price received by the buyer for the final product the buyer produces. This may occur where the gas is used as a feedstock in chemical plants, such as ammonia or methanol, and is the major variable cost in producing the product.
Regulation cost of service	The price is determined, or approved, by a regulatory authority, or possibly a Ministry, but the level is set to cover the 'cost of service', including the recovery of investment and a reasonable rate of return.
Regulation social and political	The price is set, on an irregular basis, probably by a Ministry, on a political/social basis, in response to the need to cover increasing costs, or possibly as a revenue-raising exercise.
Regulation below cost	The price is knowingly set below the average cost of producing and transporting the gas, often as a form of state subsidy to its population.
No price	The gas produced is either flared, or provided free to the population and industry, possibly as a feedstock for chemical and fertilizer plants. The gas produced may be associated with oil and/or liquids and treated as a by-product.

Source: International Gas Union (2011, 2012, 2013a).

2005–1012.[9] These statistics form the basis of the discussion to follow. It is reported that of the total natural gas consumption in 2012 of 3,400 billion cubic metres, contracting based on gas-on-gas competition represented 40% of the entire market. This gas-on-gas-based contracting was twice the level of oil indexation-based contracting which only represented 20% of total

[9] Available at http://www.igu.org/gas-knowhow/publications/igu-publications/Wholesale%20Gas%20Price%20Survey%20-%202013%20Edition.pdf.

natural gas consumption. Gas-on-gas contracting has increased marginally from the 39% share it held in 2010 (International Gas Union, 2012) and significantly from the 32% share back in 2007 (International Gas Union, 2011). Oil indexation contracting has seen little relative change over the past decade or so, showing a market share of 20% in 2007 (International Gas Union, 2011) and 23% in 2010 (International Gas Union, 2012). The three regulation-based contracting categories collectively represented 35% of global natural gas consumption in 2012. The increasing share of gas-on-gas contracting reflects a significant change to the dynamic of the European natural gas markets in particular. North America traditionally has dominated the market in terms of gas-on-gas contracting, and continues to do so, which reflects the maturity of the liberalized US natural gas markets in particular and the extent of active Henry Hub and regional market trading (see Section 3.3 for more details). Indeed, of 2012 natural gas consumption in North America, 98% of all contracting was done on a gas-on-gas basis. This share has remained steady since 2007 (International Gas Union, 2011). The major change in gas-on-gas contracting has occurred in Europe. In 2007, contracting across Europe was dominated by oil indexation, with 72% of all consumption being transacted on this basis (International Gas Union, 2011). However, in the intervening years, the share of oil indexation has reduced dramatically, while gas-on-gas has increased significantly. In 2012, oil indexation fell to a 50% share of total European gas consumption, while gas-on-gas rose to a 45% share. A number of reasons underlie this shift in Europe, which includes an increase in active spot and hub-based natural gas trading and the renegotiation of contracts away from oil indexation to spot gas indexation (International Gas Union, 2013a). With the continued development of the natural gas markets outside North America, along with the increasing role of LNG, it is projected that gas-on-gas contracting will increase in importance in the formation of global natural gas prices.

Oil indexation continues to dominate gas transactions in the Asia Pacific region (54% share), while it represents a significant share of the Asian and Latin American markets (39% and 23% respectively). In terms of regulation-based contracting, this form tends to dominate transactions in Russia and the former Soviet Union countries, the Middle East and Africa. Regulation cost of service is the main price formation mechanism in Russia and the former Soviet Union countries, representing 48% of all consumption transactions, as well as being the main mechanism in Asia at 45% of total consumption in this region. Gas-on-gas contracting however is playing an ever-increasing role in Russia, driven by Gazprom in particular and a strategic move to compete for international business (International Gas Union, 2013a). The regulation social and political mechanism is central to the natural gas markets in the Middle East, while it also represents a significant share of transactions in Latin America and Asia Pacific. Africa is seen to be almost entirely dominated by regulation below cost, reflecting the lack of development in natural gas markets across the continent (International Gas Union, 2011).

In terms of price level achieved in alternative jurisdictions, there are significant differences in prices. These differences in prices reflect the price formation mechanisms that lead particular nations and that form the mix of pricing within regions. The IGU reports (International Gas Union, 2013a) that, based on 2012 data, prices were highest in Asia Pacific and Europe, at an average of $11 and $10.50/mmBtu respectively. In contrast, prices in North America were much lower at under $3/mmBtu, the lowest of the regions that operate competitive natural gas markets. Interestingly, in 2007, North America was the second most expensive region for gas, with prices transacting at an average price just under $7/mmBtu. The drop in price has largely been driven by the 'shale gas revolution' in the USA, as discussed in Section 3.1.4. The higher prices in Europe and Asia Pacific reflect, in addition to other important fundamentals, the leading role that oil indexation plays in these regions. Indeed, in 2012, the most expensive natural gas prices emerged from oil price escalation-based contracts. Average prices from this price mechanism are reported to be over twice the price commanded from gas-on-gas contracts. The interested reader is directed to the recent series of IGU natural gas reports (International Gas Union, 2011, 2012, 2013a) for further details on the above discussion and for a comprehensive treatment of the associated production and import figures.

3.3 FINANCIAL NATURAL GAS MARKETS

Given the liberalization of natural gas markets in the USA and continuing efforts in Europe towards liberalization, industry participants are increasingly exposed to uncertain and volatile natural gas prices in the course of their business activities. Effective risk management of such price exposure has become fundamental to modern-day natural gas markets. This section begins with a brief introduction to the two main exchange groups – CME Group and the Intercontinental Exchange – that offer a range of risk management products to participants within the natural gas markets. A detailed presentation then follows on the main derivatives products on offer, spanning futures and options. The section concludes with a brief overview of the over-the-counter (OTC) markets and points to some of the technical chapters in Part II of this book.

3.3.1 Exchange-Based Markets

The two major exchange conglomerates for natural gas derivatives markets are CME Group (CME) and the Intercontinental Exchange (ICE). Some key derivative products are traded on these exchanges that allow for the risk management of what have become highly volatile natural gas markets, with huge variations on a regional basis in market price dynamics. The contracts offered on these exchanges allow market participants to eliminate risk entirely (via futures contracts) or just downside risk (via options contracts), where it is possible to trade locational differentials, quality differentials and calendar (i.e., maturity-based) differentials. Both physically and financially settled contracts are offered so as to meet the broad range of trading and risk management requirements within the market.

CME generally provides access to a hugely diverse derivatives marketplace, reported to handle 3 billion contracts worth approximately $1 quadrillion annually (on average). The group controls a collection of prominent exchanges, including the Chicago Mercantile Exchange, Chicago Board of Trade, New York Mercantile Exchange and the Commodity Exchange. CME offers an extensive range of products across major asset classes such as interest rates, equity indexes, foreign exchange, energy, agricultural commodities, metals, weather and real estate. CME also offers a clearing service to the OTC markets. For the natural gas markets, CME manages the benchmark natural gas futures and options contracts that are linked to Henry Hub in the USA. The specifications of these derivative contracts will form the discussion in the forthcoming section, along with the futures and options contracts that span other key natural gas market locations in the USA. ICE is equally large with its network of regulated exchanges and clearing houses that span key global stock and derivatives markets. In total, ICE facilitates trading in 9,700 contracts across a similar range of major asset classes to CME: energy, interest rates, credit, currency, bonds, agriculture, precious metals, equities, exchange traded products and equity options. For the natural gas markets, ICE similarly offers an extensive range of futures and options derivatives contracts linked to key US, Canadian and European natural gas markets. The geographic coverage of the CME and ICE contracts is extensive, particularly for the USA, allowing market participants to manage regional price dynamics and cross-regional price differences.

3.3.2 Natural Gas Futures

The flagship natural gas futures contract offered by CME is the Henry Hub futures contract. It is the most liquid natural gas contract that trades globally. Table 3.3 provides a summary of the main features of the contract. It can be seen that the contract trades in standardized units of 10,000 mmBtus with a listing of up to 118 consecutive months available. Contracts expire with physical delivery of Henry Hub natural gas and must meet the particular specifications set out in the FERC-approved tariff of Sabine Pipe Line Company. Market participants not wishing to take physical delivery of the natural gas on long positions may sell the futures contracts prior to expiry. Final settlement of the Henry Hub futures contract follows the standard rules that

TABLE 3.3 CME Henry Hub physical futures contract specification

Code:	NG
Venue:	CME ClearPort, CME Globex, Open Outcry (New York)
Hours (all times are New York time/ET):	CME Globex. Sunday–Friday 6:00 p.m.–5:15 p.m. (5:00 p.m.–4:15 p.m. Chicago time CT) with a 45-minute break each day beginning at 5:15 p.m. (4:15 p.m. CT) CME ClearPort. Sunday–Friday 6:00 p.m.–;5:15 p.m. (5:00 p.m.–4:15 p.m. CT) with a 45-minute break each day beginning at 5:15 p.m. (4:15 p.m. CT) Open Outcry. Monday–Friday 9:00 a.m.–2:30 p.m. (8:00 a.m.–1:30 p.m. CT)
Contract unit:	10,000 mmBtus
Pricing quotation:	US dollars and cents per mmBtu.
Termination of trading:	Trading of any delivery month shall cease 3 business days prior to the first day of the delivery month. In the event that the official exchange holiday schedule changes subsequent to the listing of a natural gas futures, the originally listed expiration date shall remain in effect. In the event that the originally listed expiration day is declared a holiday, expiration will move to the business day immediately prior
Listed contracts:	118 consecutive months
Settlement type:	Physical
Grade and quality specifications:	Natural gas meeting the specifications set forth in the FERC-approved tariff of Sabine Pipe Line Company as then in effect at the time of delivery shall be deliverable in satisfaction of futures contract delivery obligations

Source: CME Group, http://www.cmegroup.com/trading/energy/natural-gas/natural-gas_contract_specifications.html.

TABLE 3.4 CME Henry Hub financial futures contract specification

Code:	HH
Venue:	CME Globex, CME ClearPort, Open Outcry (New York)
Hours (all times are New York time/ET):	CME Globex. Sunday–Friday 6:00 p.m.–5:15 p.m. (5:00 p.m.–4:15 p.m. Chicago time/CT) with a 45-minute break each day beginning at 5:15 p.m. (4:15 p.m. CT) CME ClearPort. Sunday–Friday 6:00 p.m.–5:15 p.m. (5:00 p.m.–4:15 p.m. CT) with a 45-minute break each day beginning at 5:15 p.m. (4:15 p.m. CT) Open Outcry. Monday–Friday 9:00 a.m.–2:30 p.m. (8:00 a.m.–1:30 p.m. CT)
Contract unit:	10,000 mmBtu
Price quotation:	US dollars and cents per mmBtus
Floating price:	The floating price for each contract month will be equal to the NYMEX (Henry Hub) natural gas Futures contract final settlement price for the corresponding contract month on the last trading day for that contract month
Termination of trading:	Trading shall cease on the third business day prior to the contract month
Listed contracts:	The current year and the next 5 years. A new calendar year will be added following the termination of trading in the December contract of the current year
Settlement type:	Financial
Final settlement:	Delivery under the NYMEX Henry Hub contract shall be by cash settlement. Final settlement, following termination of trading for a contract month, will be based on the floating price. The final settlement price will be the floating price calculated for each contract month

Source: CME Group, http://www.cmegroup.com/trading/energy/natural-gas/natural-gas-last-day_contract_specifications.html.

apply to a number of energy contracts on CME, including WTI futures, whereby settlement is based on the following two-tier system:[10]

- *Tier 1.* On the day of expiration, the expiring month will settle based on the volume weighted average price (VWAP) of the outright CME Globex trades executed between 14:00:00 and 14:30:00 ET.
- *Tier 2.* In the absence of outright or spread trades during this period, the settlement price will be the best bid or best ask in the expiring contract at 14:30:00 ET, whichever is closer to the last trade price. If there is not a bid/ask pair in the expiring contract at that time, the settlement price will be the best bid or ask implied by the bid/ask in the spread between the expiring and second-month contracts at 14:30:00 ET, whichever is closer to the last outright trade price in the expiring contract.

In addition to the benchmark physically settled Henry Hub futures contract, CME also offers a financially settled Henry Hub natural gas look-alike last day financial futures contract;

[10]See http://www.cmegroup.com/trading/energy/files/NYMEX_Energy_Futures_Final_Settlement_Procedure.pdf

TABLE 3.5 CME Henry Hub last day financial futures contract specification

Code:	NN
Venue:	CME Globex. CME ClearPort, Open Outcry (New York)
Hours (all times are New York time/ET):	CME Globex. Sunday–Friday 6:00 p.m.–5:15 p.m. (5:00 p.m.–4:15 p.m. Chicago time/CT) with a 45-minute break each day beginning at 5:15 p.m. (4:15 p.m. CT). Trade is flow per day CME ClearPort. Sunday–Friday 6:00 p.m.–5:15 p.m. (5:00 p.m.–4:15 p.m. CT) with a 45-minute break each day beginning at 5:15 p.m. (4:15 p.m. CT). Trade is flow per day or flow per month Open Outcry. Monday–Friday 9:00 a.m.–2:30 p.m. (8:00 a.m.–1:30 p.m. CT)
Contract unit:	2500 million mmBtus
Price quotation:	US dollars and cents per mmBtu
Floating price:	The floating price for each contract month will be equal to the NYMEX (Henry Hub) natural gas futures contract final settlement price for the corresponding contract month on the last trading day for that contract month
Termination of trading:	Posting of transactions shall cease on the third business day prior to the contract month
Listed contracts:	118 consecutive months
Settlement type:	Financial
Settlement procedure:	Delivery under the contract shall be by cash settlement. Final settlement, following termination of posting for a contract month, will be based on the floating price. The final settlement price will be the floating price calculated for each contract month

Source: CME Group, http://www.cmegroup.com/trading/energy/natural-gas/henry-hub-natural-gas-swap-futures-financial_contract_specifications.html.

referred to also as the Henry Hub swap futures contract. This contract is designed to allow market participants to trade without the prospect of physical delivery at expiry. As the Henry Hub financial futures contract is the same size as the physical contract at 10,000 mmBtus, it offers market participants the flexibility to trade out of the physical contract while holding a desired position in the natural gas market. The financial settlement of the contract is based on the physical Henry Hub natural gas futures first nearby contract settlement price on the last trading day for the delivery month. Table 3.4 sets out the main contract terms.

A third important contract in the CME Henry Hub futures series is the Henry Hub natural gas last day financial futures contract, which allows for the hedging of basis risk under the physical futures contract. The contract size is one-quarter the size of the physical and financial futures contracts described above, at 2500 mmBtus. It is characterized by high correlation with the physical futures contract. Table 3.5 presents the main features of the contract.

The Henry Hub futures contract series allows for the effective trading and risk management of Henry Hub natural gas, with either physical or financial exposure. Examples 3.1 and 3.2 present illustrative examples of how one would respectively hedge a physical purchase and physical sale of Henry Hub natural gas. Figure 3.19 presents the Henry Hub physical futures curve on 25 February 2014, along with the same curves for 5 years previous (2009) and 10 years previous (2004). The annual winter seasonal peaks in price are clearly evident in the term structure. Interestingly, it is very notable that Henry Hub prices are far below where they

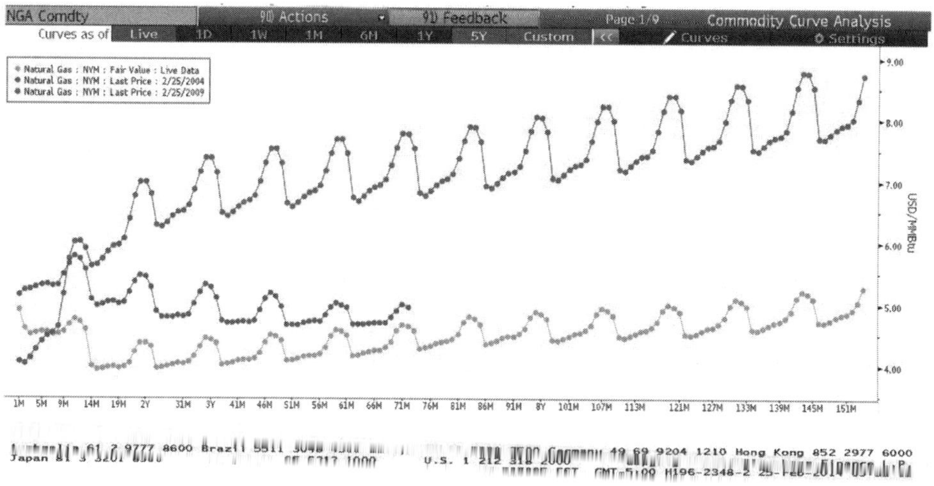

FIGURE 3.19 CME Henry Hub physical futures curves: Jan 2004, 2009 and 2014

were in 2009 and even below levels in 2004. This reduction in price reflects the impact of shale gas on the US natural gas markets and increased reserves (see Figure 3.7) and increased production that have resulted. Of interest as well in 2009 is the significant contango that was observable in the Henry Hub futures curve with market projections beyond 5 years greatly exceeding \$6.50/mmBtu. With current prices below \$5/mmBtu and a relatively flat futures curve along the term structure, the markets view is clearly for a long-term impact of shale gas on US natural gas markets.

Example 3.1 illustrates how a natural gas consumer would effectively hedge a future physical purchase of Henry Hub natural gas.

EXAMPLE 3.1 HEDGING A PHYSICAL PURCHASE OF HENRY HUB GAS

Consider a natural gas consumer who, on 26 February 2014, signs a gas sales agreement (GSA) to take a delivery of 100,000 mmBtus of Henry Hub natural gas in April 2014, with the payment terms based (simplistically for the purposes of illustration) on prevailing spot prices on 1 April 2014. To hedge itself from an expectation of *higher* spot prices in April, the natural gas consumer may take the following course of action: go long physical Henry Hub futures contracts to equal the GSA size and close out prior to the expiration of the contracts to avoid physical delivery commitments, using the payoff to offset the spot based payment under the GSA.

Assume the natural gas consumer takes a long position in 10 physical Henry Hub futures contracts, which are trading at 4.549 US\$/mmBtu. As the contract size for a single physical Henry Hub futures contract is 10,000 mmBtus, the long position in 10 futures contracts ensures the consumer covers its exposure under the GSA. On

26 March 2014, assume that natural gas prices have *risen* as per the expectation of the consumer and the physical Henry Hub futures contract is trading at 4.846 US$/mmBtu. The consumer decides to close out its long position by selling the contracts. The payoff for the consumer on the futures contracts is therefore 100,000 mmBtus × ($4.846–$4.549)/mmBtu = $29,700. On 1 April 2014, assume that spot prices have continued to rise and immediate delivery is priced at $4.850. The consumer is obligated to pay 100,000 mmBtus × $4.850/mmBtu = $485,000. Using the proceeds of the futures hedge as an offset for this purchase gives an effective purchase price of $4.850 – ($4.846–$4.549) = $4.553/mmBtu and so an overall effective cost of $455,300.

Example 3.2 illustrates how a natural gas producer would effectively hedge a future physical sale of Henry Hub natural gas.

EXAMPLE 3.2 HEDGING A PHYSICAL SALE OF HENRY HUB GAS

Consider a natural gas producer who, on 26 February 2014, signs a gas sales agreement (GSA) to make a delivery of 100,000 mmBtus of Henry Hub natural gas in April 2014, with the payment terms based (simplistically for the purposes of illustration) on prevailing spot prices on the 1 April 2014. To hedge itself from an expectation of *lower* spot prices in April, the natural gas consumer may take the following course of action: go short physical Henry Hub futures contracts to equal the GSA size and close out prior to the expiration of the contracts to avoid physical delivery commitments, using the payoff to offset the spot-based payment under the GSA.

Assume the natural gas producer takes a short position in 10 physical Henry Hub futures contracts, which are trading at 4.549 US$/mmBtu. As the contract size for a single physical Henry Hub futures contract is 10,000 mmBtus, the short position in 10 futures contracts ensures the producer covers its exposure under the GSA. On 26 March 2014, assume that natural gas prices have *fallen* as per the expectation of the producer and the physical Henry Hub futures contract is trading at 4.327 US$/mmBtu. The producer decides to close out its long position by selling the contracts. The payoff for the producer on the futures contracts is therefore 100,000 mmBtus × ($4.549–$4.327)/mmBtu = $22,200. On 1 April 2014, assume that spot prices have continued to fall and immediate delivery is priced at $4.320. The producer receives 100,000 mmBtus × $4.320/mmBtu = $432,000 from the sale. Using the proceeds of the futures hedge as an offset for this sale gives an effective sale price of $4.320 + ($4.549–$4.327) = $4.542/mmBtu and so overall effective proceeds of $454,200.

Before extending the discussion to the North American regional futures contract offerings, it is worth presenting the outright physically settled contracts that are offered on ICE and that span the European markets. The futures contracts cover the UK, Dutch and German natural gas markets. Contracts are for physical delivery through the transfer of rights in respect of natural gas at a given trading point in a given jurisdiction. Delivery is made equally each day at a given frequency throughout a specified delivery period (standard futures contract) or on a given date

TABLE 3.6 UK NBP futures contract specification

Code:	M
Expiration date:	Trading will cease at the close of business two business days prior to the first calendar day of the delivery month, quarter, season or calendar
Units of trading:	1000 therms of natural gas per day (1 therm = 29.3071 kWh)
Contract size:	1000 therms per day per delivery period (i.e., month, quarter, season or year)
	Delivery period
	Feb (non-leap year)
	Feb (leap year).
	Jan, May, Jul, Aug, Dec.
	Apr, Jun, Sep, Nov.
Quotation:	The contract price is in sterling and pence per therm
Settlement price:	The weighted average price of trades during a 15-minute settlement period from 16:00:00 to 16:15:00 London local time If there is low liquidity during this time, quoted settlement prices (QSPs) will be used to establish the settlement price
Delivery/settlement basis:	Matching acquiring and disposing trade nominations (buyer from ICEU, seller to ICEU) are input by buyer and seller to National Grid via Gemini before 18:30 on the business day prior to the commencement of the delivery period. Delivery takes place in kilowatt hours (29.3071 kWh therm).
	The EDSP will be the settlement price on the day the contract expires

Source: ICE, https://www.theice.com/productguide/ProductSpec.shtml?specId=910.

(daily futures contract). Taking the UK for example as the largest European natural gas market, ICE offers a range of futures contracts based on the NBP virtual hub. Table 3.6 outlines the contract specification for the standard NBP natural gas futures, where explicit reference to the physical delivery can be seen. For this contract, the trading period is broken into alternative monthly, quarterly, seasonal and yearly strips. Typically 78–83 consecutive month contracts, 11–13 consecutive quarters, 13–14 consecutive seasons and 6 consecutive years trade. Quarters are strips of three individual and consecutive contract months. Quarters always comprise a strip of Jan–Mar, Apr–Jun, Jul–Sep or Oct–Dec. Seasons are defined as strips of six individual and consecutive contract months. Seasons always comprise a strip of Apr–Sep or Oct–Mar. Years are defined as strips of 12 individual and consecutive contract months comprising Jan–Dec. The underlying unit of trade for the standard NBP futures contract is the therm, which is equivalent to 29.3071 kWh, with the currency of trade being pence sterling.

ICE also offers a variant of the standard futures contract that trades in units of 1 MWh of natural gas per hour per day over a specified delivery period, whether month, quarter, season or year, where the currency of trade for this contract is the euro. Based on the MWh unit of trade, the following monthly contract sizes can be specified: Feb (non-leap year), 28 days = 672 MWh; Feb (leap year), 29 days = 696 MWh; Mar, 31 days minus 1 hr = 743 MWh; Oct, 31 days plus 1 hr = 745 MWh; Jan, May, Jul, Aug, Dec, 31 days = 744 MWh; Apr, Jun, Sep, Nov, 30 days = 720 MWh. ICE additionally offers daily futures contracts that span a

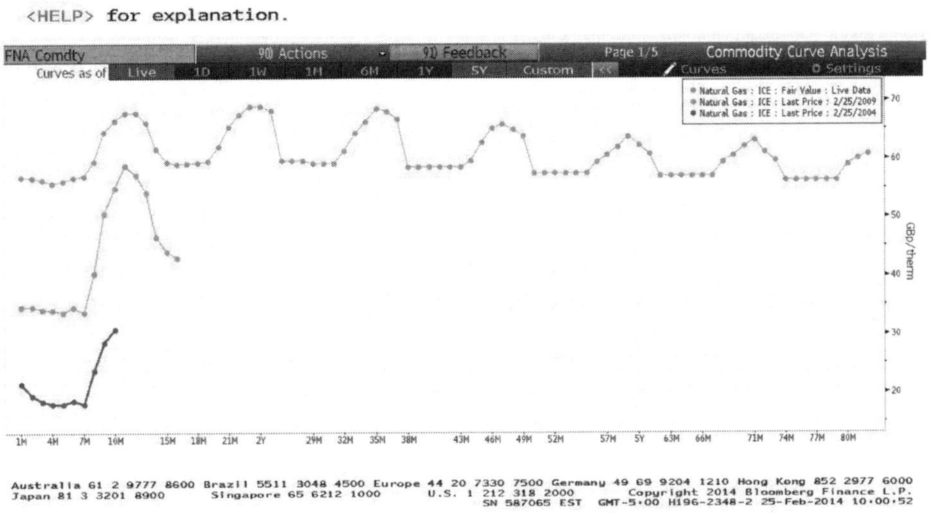

FIGURE 3.20 ICE UK NBP physical futures curves: Jan 2004, 2009 and 2014
Source: © 2013 Bloomberg Finance L.P. All rights reserved. Used with permission.

range of contract series, where all trading periods are strips of daily contracts and include the following:[11]

- Up to 42 daily contracts (from day ahead).
- 1 balance of week (BOW). A strip of daily contracts from day ahead to the end of the working week, business days only.
- 3 weekends (W/E) Weekends always comprise a strip of Saturday and Sunday contracts plus any UK bank holidays running sequentially either before or after the Saturday and Sunday.
- 5 working days next week (WDNW). WDNWs are strips of individual and consecutive contract days and will typically consist of Mon–Fri. UK Bank Holidays are not included in the WDNW contracts.
- 1 balance of month (BOM). The BOM contract is a strip of two or more days from two business days forward to the end of the contract month, where the first day of any period of non-trading days is considered to be a business day. On certain days at the end of a contract month there will not be a BOM listed.

Figure 3.20 presents the UK NBP physical futures curve on 25 February 2014, along with the same curves for 5 years previous (2009) and 10 years previous (2004). As with Henry Hub, annual winter seasonal peaks in price are observable. In complete contrast to the price discussion around Henry Hub prices though, it is intriguing to note that NBP prices increased significantly from 2004 to 2009 and have increased further over the intervening period to 2014. This reflects in no small part the gradual depletion of UK natural gas reserves (see Figure 3.8) and the lack of replacement reserves. Given that no such 'shale gas revolution' has

[11]See https://www.theice.com/productguide/ProductSpec.shtml?specId=20774967.

been experienced in the UK or indeed across Europe, and that the prospects for exploration and production of shale gas are hampered by a challenging political landscape (see Section 3.1.4), UK and European prices have traded persistently higher relative to the USA. The flat futures curve that prevails for NBP suggests that the market is not pricing in any such 'shale gas revolution' in the medium to long term.

To complete the discussion, a final comment is made about the Dutch TTF and the German Gaspool and NetConnect futures contracts. In contrast to the daily physical delivery under the standard UK NBP futures contract, these contracts provide delivery equally each hour throughout the specified delivery period. For the TTF futures contract, a number of trading periods are offered by ICE to market participants:

- Up to 83 consecutive month contracts or as otherwise determined and announced by the exchange from time to time.
- Up to 11 consecutive quarters or as otherwise determined and announced by the exchange from time to time. Quarters are strips of three individual and consecutive contract months. Quarters always comprise a strip of Jan–Mar, Apr–Jun, Jul–Sep or Oct–Dec.
- Up to 11 consecutive seasons or as otherwise determined and announced by the exchange from time to time. Seasons are strips of six individual and consecutive contract months. Seasons always comprise a strip of Apr–Sep or Oct–Mar.
- Up to 6 consecutive years or as otherwise determined and announced by the exchange from time to time. Years are strips of 12 individual and consecutive contract months comprising Jan–Dec.

For the Gaspool and NetConnect futures contracts the following trading periods are on offer:

- Up to 59 consecutive months.
- Up to 7 consecutive quarters. Quarters are strips of three individual and consecutive contract months. Quarters always comprise a strip of Jan–Mar, Apr–Jun, Jul–Sep or Oct–Dec.
- Up to 7 consecutive seasons. Seasons are strips of six individual and consecutive contract months. Seasons always comprise a strip of Apr–Sep or Oct–Mar.
- 4 consecutive years. Years are strips of 12 individual contract months comprising Jan–Dec.

3.3.2.1 USA and Canada: Regional Natural Gas Futures CME and ICE offer a vast array of futures contracts that span the regional US and Canadian natural gas markets. Three main futures contract types are tradable on these exchanges: (i) basis futures, (ii) index futures and (iii) swing futures. *Basis futures* contracts are structured to allow participants to manage basis risk. Basis trading is the fundamental trading approach in the USA whereby regional natural gas markets are traded as differentials off the benchmark Henry Hub market. Basis risk emerges from the use of the highly liquid Henry Hub futures contract to hedge natural gas prices in a different location. This mismatch between the futures contract used for hedging purposes and the underlying market price exposure forms the source of basis risk. The basis futures contracts allow market participants to lock in the price differential between Henry Hub as the key natural gas market index in the USA and the reported natural gas market location of interest. Specifically, the price differential is defined by means of subtracting the price of the CME Henry Hub natural gas futures contract from the monthly price published by Inside FERC for the specified location. In this way, basis futures allow for the trading and management of locational spreads, which may vary over time due to specific regional supply and demand factors, amongst other fundamental drivers such as weather. *Index futures* are the exchange-based equivalents of the OTC index swap, whereby an agreed fixed price is exchanged for a floating price defined as the average daily spot price over an agreed contract period. Given the highly volatile nature of the natural gas markets, the calculation of the floating price leg of the futures as an average mitigates exposure to large movements in price that may occur on a single date maturity contract. Such a contract is designed to allow natural gas producers to hedge physical contract obligations, whereby gas is delivered over a specified period on a daily basis to a given natural gas consumer. In this way, index futures allow for the effect management of natural gas price risk. *Swing futures*, in contrast to the two previous contracts, allow market participants to manage volumetric risk from ongoing production and consumption activities. These contracts facilitate market participants who need to enter the market at inopportune times to buy or sell natural gas in response to unexpected changes in demand and supply. The contracts are structured to exchange a fixed price for a published daily index price.

To provide further insights into the basis, index and swing futures series, specific contracts from CME will be examined. We begin with the basis futures contract and then extend the discussion to the index and swing futures contracts in turn.

Basis Futures Basis futures contracts allow participants to lock in the differential between Henry Hub prices and the prices in specific regional natural gas markets. Specifically, payoff is based on subtracting the price of the NYMEX Henry Hub natural gas futures contract from the monthly price published by Platts Inside FERC for a specified location. Table 3.7 outlines the main features of the Henry Hub basis futures contracts as traded on CME. This contract allows for the management of basis risk from exposure to underlying Henry Hub spot prices. It can be seen that the floating leg of this contract is specified as the difference between the Henry Hub index price as published by Platts Inside FERC and the final settlement price of the Henry Hub

TABLE 3.7 CME Henry Hub basis futures contract specification

Product symbol:	HB
Contract unit:	2500 mmBtus
Price quotation:	US dollars and cents per mmBtu
Minimum fluctuation:	$0.0001/mmBtu
Floating price:	The floating price for each contract month will be equal to the Platts Inside FERC's Gas Market Report ('Platts IFERC') Henry Hub Index ('Index') published in the table entitled 'Market Center Spot-Gas Prices' in the first regular issue of the contract month minus the NYMEX (Henry Hub) natural gas futures contract final settlement price for the corresponding contract month
Termination of trading:	Trading shall cease on the last business day of the month prior to the contract month
Listed contracts:	72 consecutive months
Settlement type:	Financial

Source: CME Group, http://www.cmegroup.com/trading/energy/natural-gas/henry-hub-natural-gas-basis-swap-futures-platts-iferc_contract_specifications.html.

TABLE 3.8 CME San Juan basis futures contract specification

Product symbol:	NJ
Venue:	CME Globex, CME ClearPort, Open Outcry (New York)
Contract unit:	2500 mmBtus
Price Quotation:	US dollars and cents per mmBtu
Minimum fluctuation:	$0.0001/mmBtu
Floating price:	The floating price for each contract month will be equal to the Platts Inside FERC's Gas Market Report ('Platts IFERC') El Paso Natural Gas Co., San Juan Basin Index ('Index') published in the table entitled 'Prices Of Spot Gas Delivered To Pipelines' in the first regular issue of the contract month minus the NYMEX (Henry Hub) natural gas futures contract final settlement price for the corresponding contract month
Termination of trading:	Trading shall cease on the last business day of the month prior to the contract month
Listed contracts:	CME Globex. 36 consecutive months
	CME ClearPort and Open Outcry. 72 consecutive months
Settlement type:	Financial

Source: CME Group, http://www.cmegroup.com/trading/energy/natural-gas/san-juan-basin-natural-gas-basis-swap-futures-platts-iferc_contract_specifications.html.

natural gas futures contract for the specified contract month. Now taking a regional contract, Table 3.8 provides the main features of the San Juan basis futures traded on CME. This contract allows traders to fix the price differential between Henry Hub and San Juan natural gas and in this way allow for the effective management of locational price differences between the two regions. The floating leg of this particular contract is specified as the difference between the San Juan index price as published by Platts Inside FERC and the final settlement price of the Henry Hub natural gas futures contract for the specified contract month. The Henry Hub–San Juan price differential can be seen as an East–West spread within the US natural gas markets and so the San Juan basis futures contract allows for the management of this spread. Example 3.3 illustrates the hedging of price and basis risk from a future physical purchase of natural gas in the San Juan (El Paso) region.

EXAMPLE 3.3 HEDGING PRICE AND BASIS RISK FROM A PHYSICAL PURCHASE OF NATURAL GAS IN THE SAN JUAN (EL PASO) REGION

Consider a natural gas consumer who, on 26 February 2014, signs a gas sales agreement (GSA) to take a delivery of 100,000 mmBtus of San Juan (El Paso) natural gas in June 2014, with the payment terms based (simplistically for the purposes of illustration) on prevailing spot prices on 1 June 2014. Spot prices in the San Juan region refer to FERC's Gas Market Report San Juan Basin Index. To hedge itself from an expectation of *higher* spot prices in June, the natural gas consumer may take the following course of action: (i) go long physical Henry Hub futures contracts to equal the GSA size and close out prior to the expiration of the contracts to avoid physical delivery commitments, using the payoff to offset the spot-based payment under the GSA; and (ii) go long San Juan basis futures contracts to equal the GSA size and either close out prior to expiry or hold until expiry (as the contract is financially settled) in order to hedge the basis risk from the exposure mismatch in using Henry Hub futures.

Assume the natural gas consumer takes a long position in 10 physical Henry Hub futures contracts, which are trading at 4.466 US$/mmBtu. As the contract size for a single physical Henry Hub futures contract is 10,000 mmBtus, the long position in 10 futures contracts ensures the consumer covers its exposure under the GSA. Assume the consumer also takes a long position in 40 financially settled San Juan basis futures contracts that are trading at −0.210 US$/mmBtu. As the contract size for a single basis futures contract is 2,500 mmBtus, the long position in 40 futures contracts ensures the consumer covers its exposure under the GSA. On 27 May 2014, assume that natural gas prices have *risen* as per the expectation of the consumer and the physical Henry Hub futures contract is trading at 4.933 US$/mmBtu. The consumer decides to close out its long position by selling the contracts. The payoff for the consumer on the futures contracts is therefore 100,000 mmBtus × ($4.933−$4.466)/mmBtu = $46,700. On the same date, the consumer decides to close out its long basis position, where the basis has now tightened to −0.150 US$/mmBtu. Given this appreciation in the spread, the basis position is closed out at a profit of 100,000 mmBtus × $0.060/mmBtu = $6,000. On 1 June 2014, assume that San Juan spot prices have continued to rise slightly and immediate delivery is priced at $4.765. The consumer is obligated to pay 100,000 mmBtus × $4.765/mmBtu = $476,500. Using the proceeds of the price and basis hedges as an offset for this purchase gives an effective purchase price of $4.765 – ($0.467+$0.060) = $4.238/mmBtu and so an overall effective cost of $423,800.

Figure 3.21 presents the term structure of basis prices for a selection of key trading locations in the USA. The magnitude of the differentials from Henry Hub can be seen to vary, while seasonal components to some of the basis price series can also be observed.

Index Futures An index futures contract is the exchange-based equivalent of an OTC index swap, whereby an agreed fixed price is exchanged for a floating price defined as the average daily spot price over an agreed contract period. The payoff of this contract is based on subtracting the monthly price published by Platts Inside FERC for a given reference natural gas quality from the average of the daily prices published by Platts Gas Daily for the same natural gas quality. The averaging over the contract period is designed to mitigate exposure to large movements in price that may occur on a single date maturity futures contract. Table 3.9 outlines the specific contract details for the Henry Hub index futures contract traded on CME. The payoff can be seen for each contract month to be the arithmetic average of the Platts Gas Daily Henry Hub midpoint price minus the Platts Inside FERC Gas Market Report Henry Hub Index for all flow dates during the contract month.

Swing Futures The swing futures contract allows market participants to manage volumetric risk from ongoing production and consumption activities, allowing entry into the market at

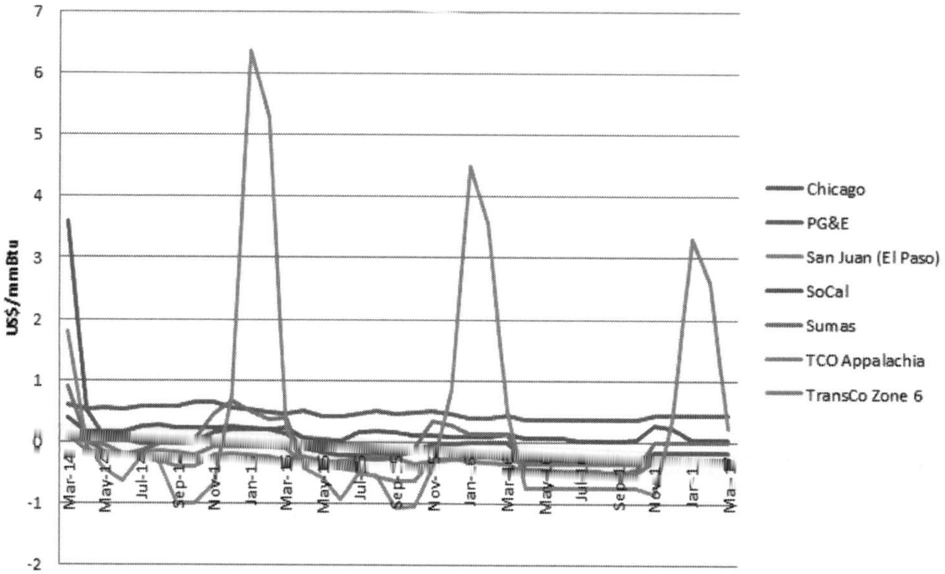

FIGURE 3.21 CME basis futures curves: selection of major US trading points
Source data: CME Group 2014.

TABLE 3.9 CME Henry Hub index futures contract specification

Product symbol:	IN
Contract unit:	2500 mmBtus
Price quotation:	US dollars and cents per mmBtu
Minimum fluctuation:	\$0.0001/mmBtu
Floating price:	The floating price for each contract month will be equal to the arithmetic average of the Platts Gas Daily Henry Hub Midpoint ('Midpoint') minus the Platts Inside FERC's Gas Market Report ('Platts IFERC') Henry Hub Index ('Index') published in the table entitled 'Market Center Spot-Gas Prices' for the corresponding contract month calculated for all flow dates during the contract month and rounded to the nearest hundredth of a cent. For the purposes of this chapter, 'flow date' shall mean a calendar date that corresponds to a published price used for determining the floating price
Termination of trading:	Trading shall cease on the last business day of the month prior to the contract month
Listed contracts:	CME Globex
	CME ClearPort and Open Outcry
Settlement type:	Financial

Source: CME Group, http://www.cmegroup.com/trading/energy/natural-gas/henry-hub-natural-gas-index-swap-futures-platts-gas-daily-platts-iferc_contract_specifications.html.

TABLE 3.10 CME Henry Hub swing futures contract specification

Product symbol:	CME Globex – SN Clearing – SN
Contract unit:	2500 mmBtus
Price quotation:	US dollars and cents per mmBtu
Minimum fluctuation:	\$0.0001/mmBtu
Floating price:	The floating price for each contract day is equal to the Platts Gas Daily Henry Hub Midpoint. The Platts Gas Daily Midpoint to be used can be found in the table entitled 'Daily Price Survey.'
Termination of trading:	Trading shall cease on the business day prior to the scheduled publication date. EFP and EFS transactions may be submitted up until the deadlines specified in Rules 6.21 and 6.21A
Listed contracts:	Days remaining in the current month and the following month
Settlement type:	Financial

Source: CME Group, http://www.cmegroup.com/trading/energy/natural-gas/henry-hub-natural-gas-swing-swap-futures_contract_specifications.html.

inopportune times to buy or sell natural gas in response to unexpected demand and supply. The contracts are structured to exchange a fixed price for a published daily index price, allowing a hedge against spot prices. Table 3.10 outlines the contract specifications for the Henry Hub swing futures contract on CME. It can be seen that the floating leg of this contract is defined to be the Platts Gas Daily Henry Hub midpoint price for Henry Hub.

3.3.2.2 Natural Gas Spread Futures A selection of calendar spread futures are traded on ICE that allow one to lock in the price differential between alternative tenors on the Henry Hub futures curve. ICE offers futures contracts on the spread between the first nearby month contract and respectively the second, fourth and seventh nearby month contracts. These contracts respectively allow one to trade the 1-, 3- and 6-month Henry Hub calendar spreads. The futures contracts are monthly cash-settled contracts based on the mathematical result of subtracting the monthly price published by NYMEX for the referenced nearby month contract from the monthly price published by NYMEX for the next nearby month contract. Table 3.11, for example, provides the contract specification for the Henry Hub penultimate 1-month calendar spread futures contract, which allows one to lock in the price differential between the first and second nearby month contracts. No such spread futures contracts appear to be offered by CME. However, both CME and ICE facilitate trading in a number of calendar spread options contracts, which will be discussed in the next section. Figure 3.22 shows the calendar spread term structure as of 25 February 2014 with March 2014 being the near-dated leg. A strong seasonal component is clearly observable reflecting the differences in prices between seasons.

Futures-based calendar spreads play an important role in exploiting the seasonal pattern in natural gas prices, with gas storage providing the physical structure to accommodate such trading. Market players may use gas storage to exploit seasonal spreads by means of buying gas at low prices over low-demand summer months and injecting the gas into storage and then withdrawing the gas again in high-demand winter months and selling at higher prices. Futures-based calendar spreads may be used to lock in prices today under such a strategy but this represents a static sub-optimal approach to storage utilization. This static sub-optimal

TABLE 3.11 ICE Henry Hub penultimate 1-month calendar spread futures contract specification

Contract symbol:	HHM
Settlement method:	Cash settlement
Contract size:	2500 mmBtus
Currency:	USD
Final settlement:	Reference price A minus reference price B
REFERENCE PRICE A	NATURAL GAS-NYMEX
(a) Ref price A–description	'NATURAL GAS-NYMEX' means that the price for a pricing date will be that day's specified price per mmBtu of natural gas on the NYMEX of the Henry Hub natural gas futures contract for the delivery date, stated in US dollars, as made public by the NYMEX on that pricing date
(b) Ref price A – pricing date	1 Business day prior to the last scheduled trading day of the NYMEX Henry Hub natural gas futures contract for the delivery date
(c) Ref price A – specified price	Settlement price
(d) Ref price A – pricing calendar	NYMEX
(e) Ref price A – delivery date	Contract period
REFERENCE PRICE B	NATURAL GAS-NYMEX
(a) Ref price B – description	'NATURAL GAS-NYMEX' means that the price for a pricing date will be that day's specified price per mmBtu of natural gas on the NYMEX of the Henry Hub natural gas futures contract for the delivery date, stated in US dollars, as made public by the NYMEX on that pricing date
(b) Ref price B – pricing date	1 business day prior to the last scheduled trading day of the NYMEX Henry Hub natural gas futures contract for the contract period
(c) Ref price B – specified price	Settlement price
(d) Ref price B – pricing calendar	NYMEX
(e) Ref price B – delivery date	Second nearby month

Source: ICE, https://www.theice.com/productguide/ProductSpec.shtml?specId=6590267.

approach captures the intrinsic value inherent in gas storage but ignores the changing intrinsic value that comes from market price changes and further ignores the extrinsic value that comes from the flexibility or embedded optionality that gas storage offers. The next section revisits gas storage in the context of the calendar spread options, which offer an instrument through which to capture extrinsic value in addition to intrinsic value.

3.3.3 Natural Gas Options

Whereas futures markets allow one to eliminate price risk, market participants often require greater flexibility to eliminate downside risk only while maintaining exposure to upside risk. Options contracts are designed to provide the holder with the right but not the obligation to buy or sell a specified quantity of a specified asset at a given date in the future. On CME, two main options contracts are offered on the Henry Hub natural gas market. The most heavily traded

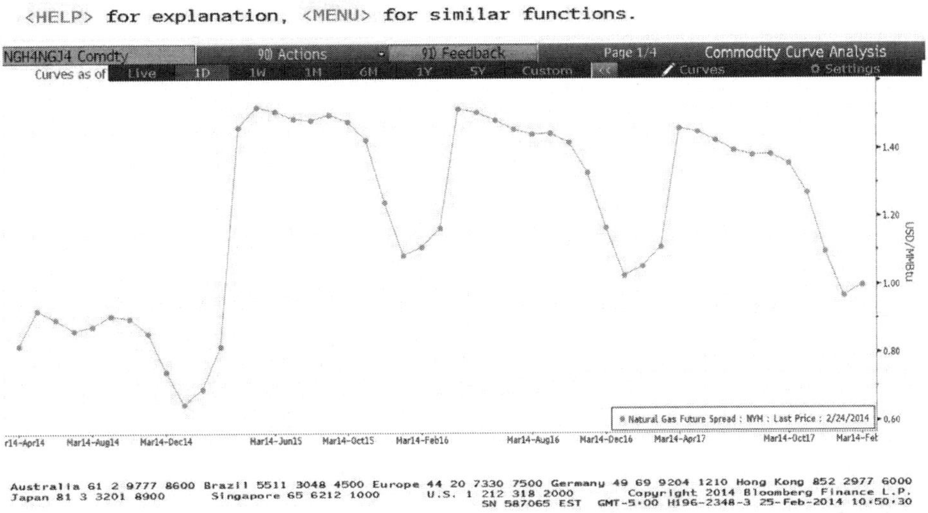

FIGURE 3.22 CME Henry Hub calendar spread term structure: March 2014 near-dated leg
Source: © 2013 Bloomberg Finance L.P. All rights reserved. Used with permission.

of the two by volume and open interest is the European-exercise natural gas options contract, which is written on the physical Henry Hub (NG) futures contract. The European-exercise feature of the contract allows only for exercise or settlement of the options contract on the date of expiration. Exercising a call option results in the holder taking a long position in the underlying physical futures contract, whereas exercising a put option results in the holder taking a short position in the underlying physical futures contract. The details of the European contract are provided in Table 3.12, where explicit reference can be seen to the European-exercise feature. The European call option contract will be exercised only when at expiration the difference between the settlement price for the underlying Henry Hub futures contract exceeds that of the stated exercise price or strike price. For the European put option contract, the decision to exercise will only be made when the strike price exceeds the settlement price of the underlying Henry Hub futures. A range of strike prices is offered on this contract with at least 201 strike price levels defined by increments of $0.01/mmBtu above and below the at-the-money (ATM) strike price; 100 strike prices below and 100 strike prices above this ATM strike.

Figure 3.23 presents the implied volatility surface for the European Henry Hub options contract, which plots implied volatility against option maturity and moneyness, with the latter defined in percentage terms as asset price over strike price. Along the maturity dimension, the implied volatility can be seen to decline in general with increasing time to expiration, in line with the usual Samuelson effect. However, annual winter seasonal peaks in the implied volatility are evident. This seasonal component to the implied volatility term structure of natural gas options is an important distinction from the implied volatility evidenced for other markets, such as oil and equities for instance. Along the moneyness dimension a smile-skew effect is clearly evident, with implied volatilities higher for low-strike and high-strike options relative to those options trading at- or near-the-money. Indeed, across the full span of moneyness, the high-strike options can be seen to trade at substantially higher volatility levels relative to the

TABLE 3.12 CME Henry Hub European options contract specification

Underlying futures:	Henry Hub natural gas futures (NG)
Product symbol:	LN
Contract unit:	On expiration of a call option, the value will be the difference between the settlement price of the underlying Henry Hub natural gas futures and the strike price multiplied by 10,000 mmBtu, or zero, whichever is greater. On exercise of a put option, the value will be the difference between the strike price and the settlement price of the underlying Henry Hub natural gas futures multiplied by 10,000 mmBtu, or zero, whichever is greater
Price quotation:	US dollars and cents per mmBtu
Option style:	European
Minimum fluctuation:	$0.0001/mmBtu
Expiration of trading:	Trading ends at the close of business on the business day immediately preceding the expiration of the underlying futures contract
Listed contracts:	Consecutive months for the balance of the current year plus 12 additional years
Strike prices:	100 strike prices in increments of $0.01/mmBtu above and below the ATM strike price, for a total of at least 201 strike prices. Strike price boundaries are adjusted according to price movements of underlying futures contract
Settlement type:	Financial

Source: CME Group, http://www.cmegroup.com/trading/energy/natural-gas/natural-gas_contractSpecs_options.html?optionProductId=1352#optionProductId=1352.

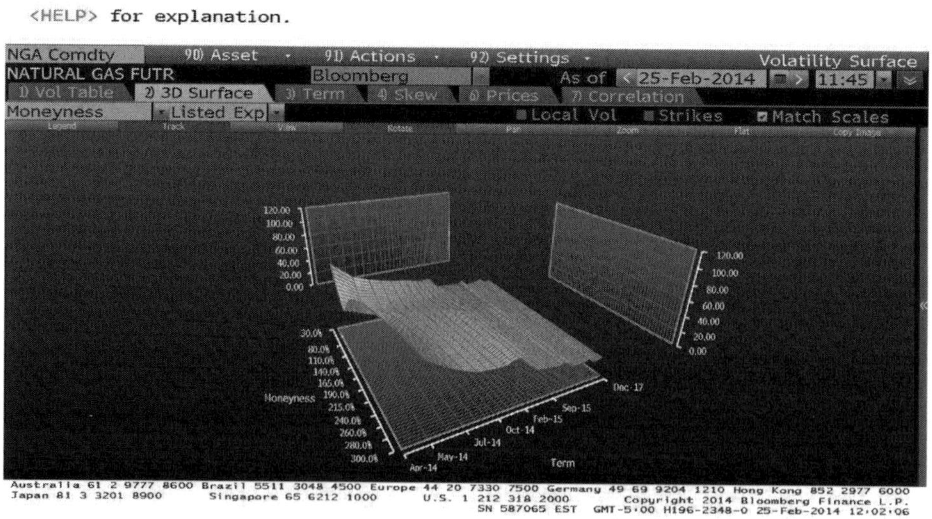

FIGURE 3.23 CME Henry Hub option implied volatility

Source: © 2013 Bloomberg Finance L.P. All rights reserved. Used with permission.

low-strike prices. This leads to a discernible positive skew, commonly referred to as the inverse leverage effect; an effect that is generally observed in energy and commodity markets. This inverse leverage effect reflects the fact that price volatility increases with rising energy and commodity prices, as concerns mount over the economic impact of these higher prices on the real economy. This pattern contrasts squarely with what we observe in the equity markets for instance, where we have a negative skew or leverage effect, whereby market participants are far more concerned with stock price declines and crashes and so price up out-of-the-money put options as a form of insurance against such events. This leads to higher implied volatility for low-strike options relative to high-strike options in these markets. The characteristics of seasonal volatility in the term structure and inverse leverage effect are important dynamics to the natural gas options markets.

The second key Henry Hub options contract offered by CME is the American-exercise counterpart to the European option. The American-exercise feature of this contract offers greater flexibility to the holder in allowing for exercise of the option on any date up to and including the expiration date. Table 3.13 provides the details for this options contract. The range of strike prices offered on this contract differs from the European contract. As quoted in the contract specification, 20 strike prices are offered in increments of $0.05/mmBtu above

TABLE 3.13 CME Henry Hub American options contract specification

Underlying futures:	Henry Hub natural gas futures (NG)
Product symbol:	ON
Contract unit:	A Henry Hub natural gas put (call) option traded on the exchange represents an option to assume a short (long) position in the underlying Henry Hub natural gas futures traded on the exchange
Price quotation:	US dollars and cents per mmBtu
Option style:	American
Minimum fluctuation:	$0.001/mmBtu
Expiration of trading:	Trading ends at the close of business on the business day immediately preceding the expiration of the underlying futures contract
Listed contracts:	Consecutive months for the balance of the current year plus 12 additional years
Strike prices:	20 strike prices in increments of $0.05/mmBtu above and below the ATM strike price in all months, plus an additional 20 strike prices in increments of $0.05/mmBtu above the ATM price will be offered in the first three nearby months, and the next 10 strike prices in increments of $0.25/mmBtu above the highest and below the lowest existing strike prices in all months for a total of at least 81 strike prices in the first three nearby months and a total of at least 61 strike prices for 4 months and beyond. The ATM strike price is nearest to the previous day's close of the underlying futures contract. Strike price boundaries are adjusted according to futures price movements
Settlement type:	Exercise into futures

Source: CME Group, http://www.cmegroup.com/trading/energy/natural-gas/natural-gas_contractSpecs_options.html?optionProductId=191#optionProductId=191.

and below the ATM strike price in all months, with an additional 20 strike prices in increments of \$0.05/mmBtu above the ATM price in the first three nearby months. A further 10 strike prices in increments of \$0.25/mmBtu above the highest and below the lowest existing strike prices in all months then gives a total of at least 81 strike prices in the first three nearby months and a total of at least 61 strike prices for 4 months and beyond.

Example 3.4 illustrates how a natural gas consumer might hedge downside risk relating to a future physical purchase of Henry Hub natural gas using a European natural gas option.

EXAMPLE 3.4 HEDGING DOWNSIDE RISK ON A PHYSICAL PURCHASE OF HENRY HUB GAS USING AN AMERICAN GAS OPTION

Consider a natural gas consumer who, on 20 February 2014, signs a gas sales agreement (GSA) to take a delivery of 100,000 mmBtus of Henry Hub natural gas in April 2014, with the payment terms based (simplistically for the purposes of illustration) on prevailing spot prices on the 1st April 2014. The consumer wishes to hedge itself from potentially higher spot prices in April but is unsure about where prices are going to go over the course of the coming weeks. The consumer does not wish to lock in a position using futures and would prefer instead to be in a position to protect itself from downside risk if spot prices rise but leave itself exposed to upside risk if spot prices fall. The natural gas consumer may take the following course of action: go long Henry Hub American options contracts, written on the April 2014 futures contract, to equal the GSA size and exercise these options at or close to expiry if in-the-money, using the payoff (under such a higher-price scenario) to offset the spot-based payment under the GSA. To complete the example, we consider a specific higher-price scenario, where the options are in-the-money close to expiry.

Assume the natural gas consumer decides to take a long position in 10 Henry Hub American options contracts. As a single options contract is written on a single physical Henry Hub futures contract of 10,000 mmBtus, the long position in 10 options ensures the consumer covers its exposure under the GSA. With the underlying futures contract trading at 4.549 US\$/mmBtu, the consumer opts to go for the option with strike price of \$4.600, which is slightly out-of-the-money and trading at 0.165 US\$/mmBtu. On 26 March 2014, assume that natural gas prices have risen and the physical Henry Hub futures contract is trading at 4.846 US\$/mmBtu. As the options are now well in-the-money (i.e., the prevailing futures price is higher than the strike price), the consumer decides to exercise its positions in the underlying futures contracts. It is assumed here for ease of exposition that the futures may be sold on immediately. The payoff for the consumer on the futures contracts is therefore 100,000 mmBtus × (\$4.846–\$4.600)/mmBtu = \$24,600. Taking account of the premium payment of 100,000 × \$0.165 = \$16,500 to set up the hedge, a total profit of \$8,100 is made. On 1 April 2014, assume that spot prices have continued to rise and immediate delivery is priced at \$4.850. The consumer is obligated to pay 100,000 mmBtus × \$4.850/mmBtu = \$485,000. Using the proceeds of the futures hedge as an offset for this purchase gives an overall effective cost of \$476,900 and so an effective purchase price of \$4.769/mmBtu.

If prices had fallen below the strike price level then the consumer would simply close out its long position in the options contracts, that is it would not exercise the options but simply sell out of its long position. Depending on the cost of the options at the point of this sale, the consumer would lose no more than the premium payment of $16,500 to set up the hedge. The consumer would then buy the gas under the GSA as per the spot-based payment terms at the prevailing price on 1 April.

Note that this options hedging example is static and presented for illustrative purposes. More dynamic trading of the consumer's exposure is possible but remains outside the scope of this chapter.

A range of other options contracts are offered on CME with varying degrees of volume and open interest. The next most prevalent type of options contract traded by US natural gas market participants are the Henry Hub calendar spread options. Physically and financially settled spread options are offered for a range of spread lengths. The 1-month contracts allow for the trading of the spread between the prices of the first nearby and second nearby Henry Hub physical futures contracts. Specifically, for the settlement of these options contracts, the floating spread price under the payoff function is defined to be the price differential between a long position in the second nearby futures and a short position in the first nearby futures. For the call option class, the payoff of the option is the difference between the spread price and the strike price, whereas for the put options class the payoff is the difference between the strike price and the spread price. Table 3.14 provides the contract details for the physically settled calendar spread option. The call options contract physically exercises into a long position in the spread, whereby the holder takes a short position in the far-dated futures contract and a long position in the near-dated futures contract. The put options contract conversely exercises into a short position in the spread, that is a short position in the near-dated futures contract and a long position in the far-dated contract.

As discussed in the previous section, futures-based calendar spreads have a role to play in exploiting the seasonal pattern in natural gas prices, with gas storage facilities being the physical infrastructure that allows such seasonal plays. As already identified, futures-based calendar spreads may be used to lock in prices today but this represents a static sub-optimal approach to storage utilization. This static sub-optimal approach captures the intrinsic value inherent in gas storage but ignores the changing intrinsic value that comes from market price changes and further ignores the extrinsic value that comes from the flexibility that gas storage offers market participants to trade and manage seasonal and indeed idiosyncratic regional weather-driven supply and demand. Dynamic rolling futures-based calendar spread positions allow market players to address this first issue, however extrinsic value is still not captured. Calendar spread options however offer a way to capture this extrinsic value, while rolling baskets of calendar spread options additionally allow one to dynamically adjust positions with changing market prices. Chapter 19 will present a technical treatment of gas storage valuation.

ICE also offers participants in the natural gas markets a range of options contracts for the US natural gas markets. Options are primarily offered on Henry Hub futures contracts, similar to the CME offering, although options contracts in regional markets are also available. For the European natural gas markets, the main options contracts offered on ICE are for the UK NBP and Dutch TTF markets. The NBP options are European exercise and at expiry the exercise

TABLE 3.14 CME Henry Hub 1-month spread options contract specification

Underlying futures:	Henry Hub natural gas futures (NG)
Product symbol:	IA
Contract unit:	A Henry Hub natural gas calendar spread put option on the exchange represents an option to assume a short position in the first expiring Henry Hub natural gas futures in the spread and a long position in the second expiring Henry Hub natural gas futures in the spread on the exchange. A Henry Hub natural gas calendar spread call option represents an option to assume a long position in the first expiring Henry Hub natural gas futures in the spread and a short position in the second expiring Henry Hub natural gas futures in the spread traded on the exchange
Price quotation:	US dollars and cents per mmBtu
Option style:	European
Minimum fluctuation:	$0.001/mmBtu
Expiration of trading:	A Henry Hub natural gas calendar spread option on the exchange shall expire at the close of trading on the business day immediately preceding the expiration of the first expiring futures contract in the spread
Listed contracts:	Options on 1 month calendar spread are available for the next 24 expirations. For 2-month spread, 3-month spread, 5-month spread, 6-month spread and 12-month spread, options are listed for the next 12-expirations
Strike prices:	Ten strike prices in increments of $0.01/mmBtu above and below the ATM strike price, and the next five strike prices in increments of $0.02/mmBtu above the highest and below the lowest existing strike prices for a total of at least 31 strike prices. Strike price boundaries are adjusted according to futures price movements
Settlement type:	Physical

Source: CME Group, http://www.cmegroup.com/trading/energy/natural-gas/natural-gas_contractSpecs_options.html?optionProductId=770#optionProductId=770.

is automatic for options in-the-money. Exercise is into the underlying physically settled NBP futures contract. A range of strike prices are offered on ICE, spanning 37.50–120.00 p/therm. In terms of trading period, up to 36 consecutive months, quarterly, seasonal and calendar contracts are offered. Indeed, any period of consecutive monthly contracts can be registered as a strip. An example of a strip is outlined in the ICE product documentation: a Q1 option, for example, is an option on the January futures, an option on the February futures and an option on the March futures, with each option expiring five calendar days before the start of the relevant contract month. Figure 3.24 shows the implied volatility surface for the NBP options contract, where similar dynamics to the Henry Hub contract can be seen, although the magnitude of the implied volatility is lower. The Samuelson type decline in the volatility term structure can again be seen with increasing maturity, although the discernible annual winter seasonal peaks of the Henry Hub implied volatility term structure are not replicated along the NBP surface. Indeed, a series of sharp peaks and troughs are observable, with the poorer quality of the surface likely reflecting lower liquidity and open interest at the various

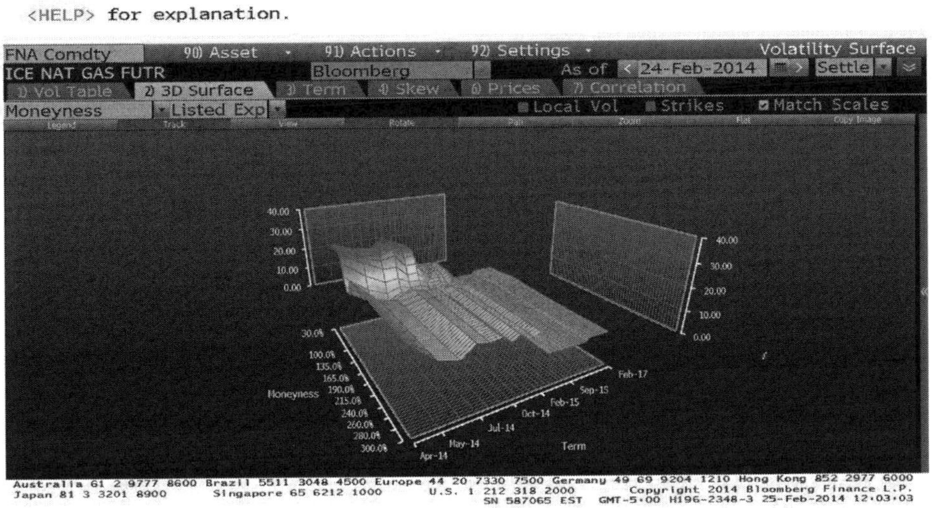

FIGURE 3.24 ICE UK NBP option implied volatility
Source: © 2013 Bloomberg Finance L.P. All rights reserved. Used with permission.

tenors. The inverse leverage effect is again evident in the NBP implied volatility surface, with high-strike options trading higher relative to low-strike options.

3.3.4 OTC Markets and Products

CME and ICE both offer clearing services for the OTC markets. The OTC operations of CME span the commodity markets, in particular energy, agriculture, metals and commodity indices, along with the financial markets, in particular interest rates swaps, credit default swaps and foreign exchange (non-deliverable forwards and cash-settled forwards). ICE has similar OTC operations spanning energy, agriculture, soft commodities, credit derivatives, foreign exchange and equity indexes. The OTC markets offer market participants the opportunity to structure non-standardized derivative structures that better suit individual hedging and risk management requirements. This non-standardization of products is what differentiates the OTC markets from the exchange-based derivatives markets. On the energy side, the OTC markets allow for customization based on contract size, location, grade or quality of the underlying energy, time of delivery and the form of delivery whether physical or cash settled. OTC markets have by their very nature lacked the transparency offered by exchange-based markets and expose market participants to higher levels of credit default risk. This has been due to the effective absence of regulation and oversight of OTC markets and hence lower reporting and governance standards around OTC transactions. However, with the emergence of the 2008 credit crisis, it was seen that the global financial downturn that followed was significantly compounded by the uncertainty in the financial system resulting from the opacity of the OTC credit derivatives markets. As a result, regulation pertaining to OTC markets in general has gradually been strengthened by regulatory bodies worldwide, with a concerted push to move OTC market transactions on exchange for clearing purposes. This move allows for greater system-wide transparency into the OTC markets and provides market participants with much lower credit default risk exposure in transactions.

In terms of the non-cleared OTC natural gas markets, tailored basis, index and swing forwards and swaps contracts are traded with full flexibility in negotiating the terms and conditions of the deals. As in other markets, a range of exotic options are structured to manage more complex risk exposures of natural gas participants. Examples of exotic options of relevance to the natural gas markets include spread options, Asian options and spread Asian options. As mentioned earlier, futures and options-based calendar spread trading allows for the exploitation of the strong seasonal component in the term structure of natural gas forward and futures prices. Such calendar spread plays are essential for the trading and optimization of gas storage, as discussed briefly in the previous sections. Locational spread plays are used by market participants to hedge and trade price differentials between regions. In this context OTC spread options offer a flexible trading and risk management tool to market participants. Spread options are covered in Chapter 17, where a technical discussion of pricing and hedging issues is presented.

Asian options are options contracts whereby the floating leg (which could possibly be the strike price if so defined) of the payoff function represents the average of a stated price series, whether spot, forward or futures. The process of averaging is important as it mitigates against volatile prices and in particular price jumps that may occur on single dates in a period. It also suits long-term contracting where delivery of natural gas will be provided over substantial periods of time or indeed rolling periods of time. The averaging inherently lowers the volatility exposure for the option holder and so often provides a much cheaper hedging option. Asian options are covered in Chapter 18, where a technical discussion of pricing and hedging issues is presented.

Finally, spread Asian options are also found in the natural gas markets, which combine the features of spread and Asian options. The spread is defined as the differential between the average price of one given natural gas grade and the average price of a second natural gas grade. Such contracts allow for calendar spread and locational spread plays as usual but offer the benefit of lower volatility exposure that results from the averaging.

REFERENCES

BP Group (2013). BP Statistical Review of World Energy.

Energy Information Administration (2012). Natural Gas Annual 2012.

Energy Information Administration (2013). Technically Recoverable Shale Oil and Shale Gas Resources: An Assessment of 137 Shale Formations in 41 Countries Outside of the US.

European Parliament (2013). The Shale Gas 'Revolution' in the United States: Global Implications, Options for the EU. Policy Briefing DG EXPO/B/PolDep/Note/2013_124.

International Gas Union (2011). Wholesale Gas Price Formation – A Global Review of Drivers and Recent Trends.

International Gas Union (2012). Wholesale Gas Price Formation 2012 – A Global Review of Drivers and Recent Trends.

International Gas Union (2013a). Wholesale Gas Price Survey – 2013 Edition.

International Gas Union (2013b). World LNG Report – 2013 Edition.

CHAPTER 4

Electricity Markets and Products

Stefano Fiorenzani, Bernard Murphy and Mark Cummins

4.1 MARKET STRUCTURE AND PRICE COMPONENTS

4.1.1 Spot and Forward Markets

The general scope of any liberalization process is to support a more efficient allocation of economic resources, especially when those resources are scarce. Efficient allocation means that resources are allocated to those subjects that are able to make the best economical use of them. This notion of economic efficiency should result in a higher degree of satisfaction for all market participants. The free interaction of demand and supply, which characterizes competitive markets, should produce such efficient allocation of scarce resources. However, perfect competition is just a theoretical notion and often the improvement of the final consumer's utility is not guaranteed at all.

The physical peculiarities of electric power influence greatly the process of power market liberalization. Electricity delivered at distinct times and at different places is a non-fungible and non-storable commodity for end users. In order to make the liberalization process effective, it is necessary to ensure that all market participants (producers and consumers) are granted non-discriminatory access to the market itself. Organized power spot and derivatives exchanges have emerged for this reason. Obviously, the internal organization of these exchanges cannot ignore the physical characteristics of electric power. Hence, peculiar rules have been devised for the purposes of facilitating electricity transactions.

Electricity spot markets are *day-ahead* markets, in the sense that physical quantities, expressed in megawatts per hour (MWh), and prices negotiated during a market session for each of the 24 hours in a day, will physically deliver on the specific hour of the following day. Recently, *within-day* market sessions have taken place up to 1 hour before physical delivery. These will be discussed further in Section 4.2 when we examine the implications of the mooted large-scale integration of renewables on the growth of intra-day trading volumes, and indeed for day-ahead or spot price volatility.

Handbook of Multi-Commodity Markets and Products: Structuring, Trading and Risk Management. Edited by Andrea Roncoroni, Gianluca Fusai and Mark Cummins.

One of the first examples of an electricity spot exchange was that of Nordpool (Nordic Power Exchange, Norway) in 1993. Nowadays, in almost all EU countries, in the USA and in Australia many exchanges are actively operating in short-term physical transactions.

The main goal of organized electricity exchanges should be that of facilitating electricity short-term physical transactions by improving market information, competition and liquidity. Power exchanges also represent neutral marketplaces, where deals can take place, reducing transaction costs and counterparty risk. The price reference may also represent an important benchmark for over-the-counter (OTC) transactions (financial or physical contracts).

Competitive power markets are usually organized around one or more auctions, but the specific way these auctions take place may be different from market to market. Power producers typically wish to sell their production, while consumers represent the buy side of the market. Suppliers' and demanders' bids (expressed in terms of price–quantity couples) are submitted to the market, ranked in economic merit order and combined together by the market operator in order to reach market clearing (equilibrium). Market models may differ substantially in terms of auction type and participation rules. As regards the latter, we may have mandatory or non-mandatory auctions, depending on whether market participants are obliged or not to submit their bids to the market.

Bidding sides represent a first criterion for auction type classification. If only power generators are asked to submit their bids, the market is called *one-sided*,[1] while if both buyers and sellers participate in the auction then the market is called *double-sided*. A second criterion for auction type classification is represented by price formation rules. We can have a *uniform pricing rule*, where all the participants get the same price independently of their price bid, or a *pay-as-bid pricing rule*, where the bidder pays or receives the price of his accepted offer (the pay-as-bid mechanism was adopted in the UK spot market in 2001 under the New Electricity Trading Arrangements (NETA)). Usually, the uniform pricing rule is associated with the classical system marginal price mechanism. This means that the uniform price that market participants pay or receive is the price of the last accepted bid in economic merit order.

As stated before, economic efficiency is not the only scope of electricity markets. Physical sustainability and grid balancing are essential issues that have to be ensured by a particular market framework. For this reason, the simple day-ahead or within-day auctions are not sufficient for a satisfactory allocation of installed and available power generation capacity. Dispatching services auctions and transmission rights auctions are essential elements of an efficient electricity market.

In liberalized regimes, the electricity spot price determined in organized exchanges varies a lot according to the interaction of power supply and demand. In the following sections we study this erratic behaviour, the magnitude of which may be substantial. Price uncertainty underpins economic risk for power generators, retailers and final consumers. Electricity derivative contracts and electricity derivative markets have been introduced for hedging out this risk. Electricity derivatives represent claims on the future delivery of electricity. Physical delivery can be replaced by a purely financial settlement rule referenced to the physical electricity spot price.

---

[1] One-sided auctions are present in early-stage phases of market evolution, and their scope is essentially that of creating a market model which can be easily understood by producers (e.g., Italian Spot Power Market 2004–2006 was without active demand).

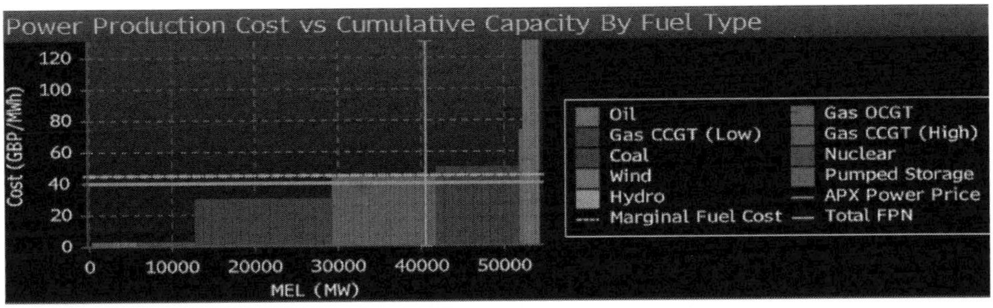

FIGURE 4.1 UK APX power exchange supply stack and marginal generation source (05/03/14)
Source: © 2013 Bloomberg Finance L.P. All rights reserved. Used with permission.

Standard derivative instruments are: forwards, futures and options. However, as will be seen later, power structured products represent a significant segment of the market.

Electricity derivatives can be either physically or financially settled. This feature, which is not usually shared by traditional commodity derivative products, makes electricity derivatives particularly interesting for financial market participants. Hence, the potential market liquidity is significantly enhanced. Market liquidity is further increased by instrument standardization. Liquidity is normally maximized when the number of contract clauses is limited through standardization.

Regarding the clearing mechanism and the daily settlement procedure, the way electricity derivatives markets work is not different from that of traditional derivatives ones. Hence, we usually find a clearing house which works as counterparty for every single trade and a margin call[2] system that prevents the credit risk embedded in any transaction.

4.1.2 Supply and Demand Interaction

Classical economic theory states that in a free and competitive market the price of any traded good or service is completely determined by the interaction between aggregated demand and aggregated supply. It is fundamental to understand and analyse the shape and dynamics of aggregated demand and supply in order to understand power price behaviour.

Even in 'pay-as-bid' markets, the concept of system marginal price has a fundamental importance. The system marginal price is exactly determined, hour by hour, by the intersection of the system merit order curve and system aggregated demand.

The merit order curve illustrated in Figure 4.1 is a map of the ability of the productive system to offer different quantities of electricity at different prices, in a given time. Consequently, it provides us with information about the marginal cost of production of the power generation units operating in the system (i.e., £40.10/MWh in Figure 4.1 corresponding to a CCGT generation technology and a capacity level of 40,000 MW for the fixed time interval 13.30–14.00 GMT) and about the bidding strategy of their managers. Very efficient but not extremely flexible plants contribute to the bottom left side of the curve shape, while less

[2]In some electricity derivatives markets the margin account system is structured in such a way that the additional risk related to the potential impact of unexpected physical outages or congestions on electricity price is considered.

efficient or very flexible generation units act in the top right corner. The stack curve is effectively a short-term supply function. The supply function defined is always upward sloping, by construction, but its shape will obviously depend on the internal physical characteristics of the productive system.

Aggregated electricity demand is typically price inelastic, at least in the short run. This feature can be graphically inferred from its steepness. In fact, the curve is almost vertical. In addition, in the case of aggregated demand the peculiarities of the system, in terms of electricity consumption structure, affect significantly the slope and shape of the demand curve. Typically, electricity demand can be divided into industrial demand and domestic demand. Industrial and domestic demands have a different behaviour and mostly display different price elasticity. Hence, the slope and shape of the aggregated demand curve of a certain country or geographic area are influenced by the proportion within aggregated demand of industrial and domestic consumption.

By observing Figure 4.1 it can be seen that demand fluctuations around the 'normal' level will cause price fluctuations. The ratio of the demand fluctuation amplitude and the price fluctuation amplitude depends on the slope of the supply curve in the normal load area. However, if the demand fluctuates in an area close to the maximum available capacity, a small demand shock can potentially lead to a significant price spike. Figure 4.1, for example, shows that the marginal cost of production for an open cycle gas turbine (OCGT) or oil peaking unit can lead to dramatic increases in the system marginal price if these technologies are required to be dispatched from the merit order.

Supply curve movements can also cause similar price effects. The supply curve can move up or down smoothly due to an increase or decrease in the production cost (fuel costs, taxes or other costs). More frequently, breaks in the supply curve appear for plant outages, which stop the production (Figure 4.2).

Also, bidding strategies can obviously affect the short-term shape of aggregate supply. Moreover, if the production system of a certain country or geographic area is intrinsically not sufficient to match the consumption needs of the same area (i.e., the system is intrinsically in a

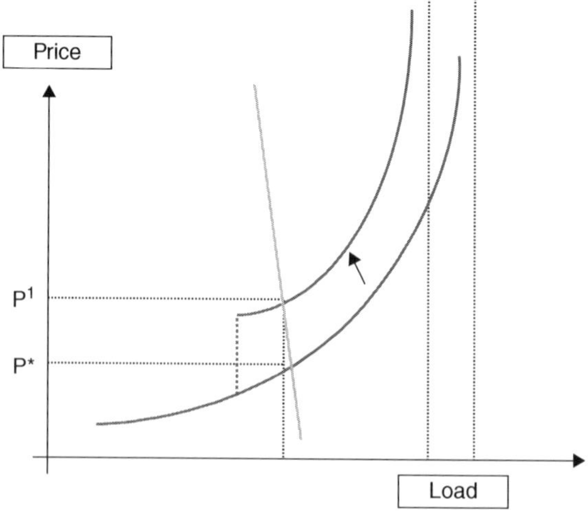

FIGURE 4.2 Supply local shock (upward supply price shock)

situation of under-capacity), then other factors such as congestion of transmission lines, used to import electricity, can play an important role in the determination of aggregate electricity supply.

Electricity aggregated demand is mainly composed of two principal components: industrial demand and domestic demand.

Industrial electricity consumption is driven by different economic factors, which differ sector by sector. Industrial electricity demand may reflect different cycles and seasonality. If the industrial structure of a certain country or geographic area is sufficiently diversified, then the idiosyncratic and seasonal components of the constituent sectors tend to balance themselves out within the consumption basket. Obviously, not all components are diversified away since some factors remain systematic.

In general, the main characteristic of industrial electricity demand is the relative insensitivity to electricity price in the short term. This naturally affects electricity procurement contracts and hedging strategies of large industrial players.

Domestic demand may be a significant and sometimes predominant component of aggregate electricity demand. Typical domestic consumption is concentrated on specific hours of the day when people use electricity for heating, freezing or cooking. This generates the typical intra-day load shape. Domestic electricity consumption related to heating or air conditioning is essentially related to weather conditions. In particular, many empirical studies prove that temperature and domestic consumption are closely related, especially in developed countries.

Industrial and domestic consumption merge together in different proportions in different countries and contribute to the typical shape of aggregated demand, with the usual hourly and monthly behaviour (see Figure 4.3 for example).

Electricity is not an intrinsically storable commodity. So, in analysing the drivers of electricity supply dynamics, the determinants of the available production capacity are mainly focused upon (more so than the installed capacity). The static shape of electricity supply, the merit order curve, depends on the characteristics of the plants which comprise the productive system. Thermoelectric power plants have patently different characteristics in terms of efficiency and flexibility relative to hydro or nuclear power plants. Hence, the structure of the production system in a given country strongly affects the dynamics of its electricity supply capability.

Obviously, installed capacity influences total supply. New entrant plants, characterized by more modern technology, have the effect of decreasing the price of offered electricity for

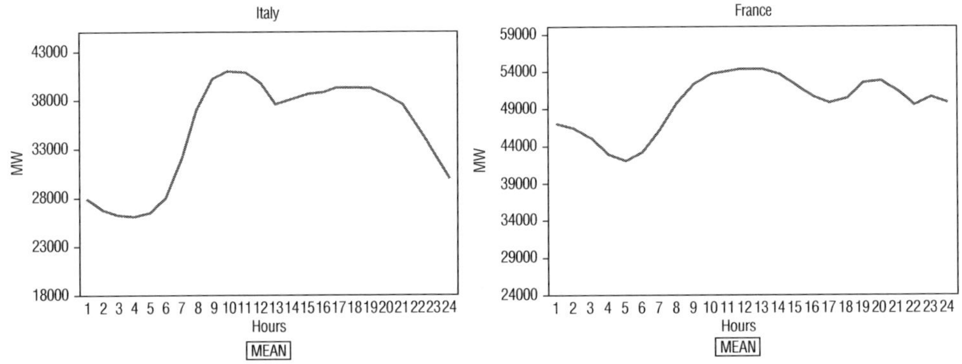

FIGURE 4.3 Schematic for mean hourly consumption of two European countries (Italy and France)

a given quantity. This effect may be described as a right parallel (or almost parallel) shift of the merit curve. In the short to mid-term, fuel costs have a strong impact on electricity supply. Fuel costs influence the marginal opportunity cost of production, and impact electricity prices through the short-term bidding strategy of electricity producers. Where a liquid market for the fuel exists, the opportunity cost and the real production cost tend to converge with the consequence of a more direct impact of fuel costs on final power prices. Another important long-term determinant of electricity supply is the dependence structure of different fuel prices. In fact, even in productive systems that are well-diversified technologically, fuel costs have a deeper impact on final prices if different fuel prices tend to move in the same direction (highly dependent fuel prices). Greater levels of diversification in the technology, efficiency and fuel consumed within a generation system mitigate against the impact of fuel costs on final power prices.

In the last few years the significant increase in renewable power generation (wind and solar in particular) and the corresponding economic incentive schemes adopted by different countries have sensibly affected power supply and supply price dynamics.

The relevant presence of non-programmable power generation units (units whose production load is not completely decided by the unit manager but by unpredictable external factors) within the system has increased the demand, and consequently the cost, of grid-balancing services. A within-day price volatility increase is the market price consequence of that situation. Moreover, economic incentive systems for renewable energy have introduced a competitive asymmetry between them and conventional generators.

Over a shorter time horizon, transmission constraints (international and regional interconnectors and merchant lines) play a very important role, particularly in countries or areas that are intrinsically under-supplied by installed capacity. The impact that transmission constraints have on prices (regional or national) can be fully understood by analysing price spreads between neighbouring countries or regions within the same country. If two neighbouring areas are well interconnected, electricity trading is more fluid between them and prices tend to be similar, according to no-arbitrage arguments. In the opposite situation, prices can potentially move in a very different way, both in the long, medium and short term. In the very short term, unpredicted plant outages and unit commitment strategies determine the shape of the supply function since they determine the capacity which is effectively available at that specific market moment.

In addition to the list of supply and demand dynamics determinants described so far, there are some economic drivers which jointly influence electricity demand and supply in the medium and long term. Such drivers include interest rates, country production and income trends. The impact of macroeconomic variables on electricity demand and supply is not within scope here. However, it is important to note that the impact of macroeconomic variables, such as interest rates and production level, on electricity market behaviour is not dissimilar to that on other, more traditional, financial markets.

4.1.3 Electricity Derivatives

Liberalized electricity markets are characterized by high volatility levels, which mean high risk for both electricity producers and consumers. This high level of risk is not always compatible with agents' risk attitudes. Hence, derivatives instruments are necessary in order to reconcile agents' economic exigencies with the natural characteristics of electricity markets.

Forwards and *futures* contracts are the simplest examples of derivative products. These contracts differ only by the associated settlement procedure, which for futures contracts involves 'marking to market' on a daily basis, while for forwards contracts it involves settlement at maturity.

Almost all energy exchanges worldwide actively trade futures contracts on baseload and peakload electricity prices. The actual contracts traded in different markets display different characteristics related to:

- delivery type
- payoff type.

Forwards and futures contracts can have a physical or a purely financial delivery type.

The standard payoff of a forward contract maturing at T for delivery over the period $[T(1), T(2)]$ is $(E(T) - K)$, where K is the forward price established at contract initiation and $E(T)$ is the average electricity spot price measured during the contract's delivery period. This *Asian-style* payoff feature makes the forward contract practically indistinguishable from the corresponding plain vanilla electricity swap. The plain vanilla swap is also known by the name 'contract for difference' (CFD). Basically, it is a contract to exchange a floating electricity price for a fixed one. Typically the floating leg of the contract is linked to the average spot electricity price calculated over a certain (usually quite long) period of time such as a month, quarter or year (i.e., calendar swap).

The unitary payoff of such an instrument is then given by the following formula:

$$\text{Swap payoff} = \left[\left(\frac{1}{N}\sum_{i=1}^{N} E_i\right) - K\right],$$

where E is the spot electricity price and K is a fixed swap price set at the contract's initiation.

Not many electricity exchanges regularly trade options (though the German EEX exchange is a notable exception). In general, exchange-traded options are purely financial (meaning financially rather than physically settled) *options written on forwards or futures* contracts with quite long maturities (i.e., a season or longer). However, the traded volume for such instruments is very low compared with that of OTC volumes. OTC markets enable the trading of not only plain vanilla options on futures but also exotic options such as swing options with flexible take characteristics. Such instruments include the following:

Block options. OTC options whose underlying is a block of hours (e.g., 17–20) of a certain day or of a certain group of days. They display typical option or swaption features in the sense that the opportunity to exercise can be limited to one period or to multiple periods.

Hourly options. OTC options whose underlying is a single hour of a single day or of a group of days. Such contracts display more or less the same characteristics as block options. They are important because they represent the maximum flexibility tradable in electricity markets. They are not intensively traded since they are extremely risky instruments.

Plain vanilla options can be further combined or bundled together to create derivative structures such as caps, floors or self-financing collars,[3] which are familiar to interest-rate and currency derivatives traders.

---

[3]A cap is a variable-price contract (typically a purchase contract) with a maximum purchase price. A cap can be synthetically replicated by a fully variable purchase contract and a call option. A floor is a variable-price contract (typically a sell contract) with a minimum sell price. A floor can be synthetically replicated by a fully variable sell contract and a put option. A collar is a combination of a cap and a floor.

Since electricity markets are typically highly connected with other commodity markets (through the generation process, for example) – such as gas or oil – it is common to trade commodity spread derivatives such as spark spread options or forwards. The spark spread is the spread between power and gas prices, once adjusted for the generation efficiency rate typical of modern gas-fired power plants. The spark spread is a good proxy for the gross margin associated with this kind of power generation. It is therefore natural that spark spread derivatives would be used to hedge and secure its variability.

Complex electricity derivatives are also typically embedded in traditional electricity supply contracts. Swing rights or tolling agreements are among the most important electricity structured products.

Swing rights are typical options embedded in physical gas and electricity contracts. In swing contracts, the buyer agrees to purchase up to a maximum volume of the underlying commodity (gas or electricity) in a given period of time and at a fixed price. The contract is often constrained by a minimum volume that the buyer has to take off in the same period. Long-term agreements are typically equipped with more than one swing opportunity during the global duration of the contract and often the global maximum and minimum volumes, which can be taken, are smaller or greater, respectively, than the simple sum of the period maximum and minimum volumes (representing non-trivial volume constraints). Penalty payments are typically imposed if the volume constraints are exceeded in order to incentivize the buyer to respect the limits imposed.

Swing contracts are normally defined by dividing the total delivery period $[0, T]$ into N sub-periods as follows:

$$0 \leq T_1 \leq T_2 \leq \ldots \leq T_{N-1} \leq T.$$

Over each of the N sub-periods, and over the entire duration of the contract, minimum and maximum delivery quantities are established as follows:

- SQ = sub-period quantity
- LSQ = lower sub-period quantity
- MSQ = maximum sub-period quantity
- LGQ = lower global quantity
- MGQ = maximum global quantity.

The following relations should be respected by the contract buyer:

$$LSQ \leq SQ \leq MSQ$$

and

$$LGQ \leq \sum_{i=1}^{N} SQ_i \leq MGQ.$$

The sub-period volume constraints are non-trivial with respect to the global volume constraints if

$$LGQ > N \times LSQ$$

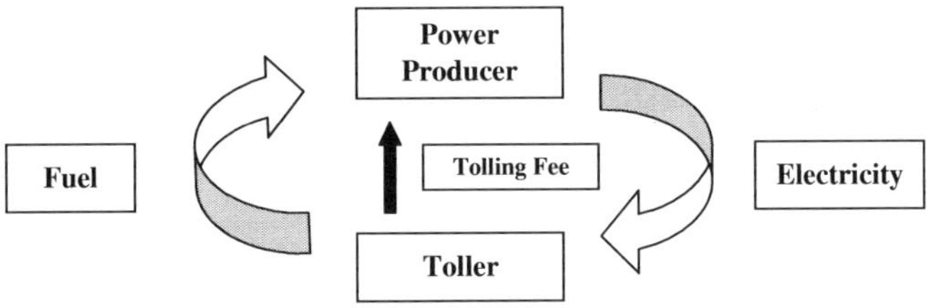

FIGURE 4.4 Tolling contract scheme

and

$$MGQ < N \times MSQ.$$

The purpose of the contract is to allow the buyer a certain degree of flexibility in the volume which can be taken, since typically the gas and electricity consumer is not always in a situation to know exactly, *a priori*, the quantity he is going to consume period by period or in total. Since the underlying commodity is usually costly to store, the volume flexibility that the swing right guarantees is very important and extremely valuable.

Tolling agreements are contracts which usually involve a power producer and a power marketer (toller). In general, in a tolling contract the toller has the right (the option) to use the power plant of the producer in order to transform a certain quantity of fuel into electricity. On the other side, for this service, the power producer is entitled to receive a fixed tolling fee, which is supposed to cover its fixed production costs and the energy transformation service price (see Figure 4.4 for a graphical representation of the general scheme of a tolling contract).

The term of the tolling agreement is divided into sub-periods. At the beginning of each sub-period the toller informs the power producer about the fuel quantity he wants to transform into electricity for that period. Minimum and maximum period quantity levels, in addition to swing rights, can be established in order to match the particular needs of both parties. Tolling contracts are typically physical contracts. Hence, they are usually equipped with ancillary clauses, which regulate rights and dues of the parties in case of asset default, fuel misprocurement, transportation problems, etc.

It is also possible for the tolling agreement to be a purely financial one. In such a case the toller does not physically take the electricity, but just receives the financial equivalent coming from selling the electricity in the spot market.

By subscribing to a tolling agreement, the power producer remains responsible only for the operational risks related to the generation activity, while the market risk due to the fluctuation of fuel and electricity prices belongs to the toller (spark spread risk).

Such products are actively traded in electricity markets because they represent a natural hedge to a power generation asset exposure. For this reason a tolling agreement typically supports project financing initiatives in power generation in order to stabilize the cash flow of the project.

4.1.4 Power Price Models

As power has become a commonly traded commodity with developed spot and derivatives markets, power price modelling is increasingly a fundamental exercise for pricing and risk assessment issues. Price modelling is also important for forecasting purposes but in this section the concentration will be on pricing and risk management needs, focusing on the presentation of the most commonly used probabilistic models to describe spot and forward electricity prices.

Typically, probabilistic models are reduced-form models, in the sense that the stochastic variables involved do not have a particular and exact economical or financial meaning but only a descriptive role. Purely probabilistic models are thought of and built to describe the probabilistic properties (trajectorial and distributional) that a certain measurable phenomenon displays. They have traditionally and extensively been used to model physical phenomena but by the early 1970s their use had become common also in financial analysis, especially in the fields of derivatives products and real asset valuation.

The class of stochastic processes which has been used until now for electricity price modelling can be divided into two main categories: traditional and more advanced models. Traditional modelling approaches have been inspired by and developed for financial modelling applications other than electricity. For this reason, often they do not provide a realistic description of typical electricity price features. In contrast, by advanced models is meant all those models which have been developed explicitly to model electricity prices. Such models are therefore able to provide a more realistic description even if their mathematical complexity is higher. It is also important to distinguish between models for spot electricity prices and those for forward prices, since price patterns and distributional features may be extremely different.

4.1.4.1 Electricity Spot Price Models

Traditional spot price models belong typically to the class of generic Itō processes:

$$dS_t = \mu(t, S_t)dt + \sigma(t, S_t)dW_t$$

where $W(t)$ is a standard Brownian motion; μ and σ are deterministic functions of time and price.

Among this very generic class of processes, mean reversion is typically recognized as one of the most important features that an electricity spot price model should be able to replicate. Lognormal mean-reverting models basically provide this feature, maintaining the simplicity of Itō processes.

$$\frac{dS_t}{S_t} = \vartheta\left[\mu(t) - \left(S_t\right)\right]dt + \sigma\left(t, S_t\right)dW_t.$$

According to this representation, the electricity log-price diffuses around a long-term attractor, which likely has a periodic behaviour, where the speed of the reversion is determined by the constant parameter ϑ. A generalized Brownian motion with a constant or locally deterministic volatility parameter generally represents the martingale stochastic component. The model of Lucia and Schwartz (2002) provides the first application of a lognormal mean-reverting process in the energy field. Despite its simplicity, the class of mean-reverting processes does not seem to be adequate for electricity spot price modelling mainly because the linear diffusive dynamics is not able to replicate the typical spiky behaviour.

Adding a jump component to the classical mean-reverting dynamics may help to improve the overall result. As suggested by Cartea and Figueroa (2005), the introduction of a compound Poisson stochastic jump component may improve the ability to replicate spikes:

$$\frac{dS_t}{S_t} = \vartheta[\mu(t) - \ln(S_t)]dt + \sigma(t, S_t)dW_t + dJ_t$$

$$\text{with } J_t = \sum_{j=1}^{N(t)} Y_j$$

where $N(t)$ is a Poisson counting process while $Y(.)$ models the jump size distributional properties.

This class of processes is considered by many people working in the electricity trading sector as good, since it merges together the two main features of electricity spot price dynamics: mean reversion and jumps. Unfortunately, the way in which this is done cannot be considered particularly realistic. In fact, the mean-reversion intensity is constant for both normal and spike regimes, while empirically we observe that the spike-reversion intensity is much more significant than the standard diffusive mean reversion. This implies that when a positive jump occurs, the reversion towards the normal regime is slower than that observed. Moreover, the simple compound Poisson process $J(t)$ is characterized by a constant jump frequency while it is known that the probability of a spike occurring is not constant over time but, in fact, is often cyclical since it depends on some price determinants, which are themselves periodical.

So, from the discussion to date, it is clear that electricity spot price dynamics are characterized by periods of either normal or spiky behaviour. Hence, a natural way of representing this feature mathematically is through the class of multiple regime processes. According to this modelling approach, the electricity spot price is assumed to follow two different and independent regimes. The first one, let us call it the 'mean-reverting regime', is intended to describe the non-spiky behaviour of the dynamics, while the second one is intended to replicate the 'spiky regime' of the process. The spikes in the second regime are modelled with a simple lognormal behaviour whose mean and standard deviation are much higher than those of the mean-reverting regime process:

$$\frac{dS_t}{S_t} = \begin{cases} \mu^L(t)dt + \sigma^L(t)dW_t^L \rightarrow P_L = 1 - \theta_{LU}dt \\ \mu^U(t)dt + \sigma^U(t)dW_t^U \rightarrow P_U = 1 - \theta_{UL}dt \end{cases}$$

where θ_{AB} represents the transition probability of switching from regime A to regime B in a given time interval, while P_A represents the probability of persisting in regime A within the same time interval.

The trajectorial and distributional characteristics of regime switching models make them extremely appealing for electricity spot price modelling, as well as the analytical tractability that can be nicely exploited to obtain closed-form derivative pricing formulas as shown by Deng (1999) and Kholodnyi (2001). However, in practice, parameter estimation is not that easy since we do not know which regime reigns in each single instant of time (the regime being a latent variable). Kalman's filtering methodology (see Fusai and Roncoroni (2008) for more details) may help to solve estimation problems, but any filtering procedure usually has a big impact on estimation results, which are difficult to control.

The models presented so far have not been developed explicitly for electricity markets, but have only been adapted to them. Some others have been thought of and built up specifically for modelling electricity spot prices. The Geman–Roncoroni model (2006) is a purely mathematical model whose probabilistic structure is particularly suitable to realistically model spiky behaviour. In this model, the electricity log-price process is represented by the unique solution of the following stochastic differential equation:

$$d\ln(S_t) = \mu_i(t)dt + \theta\left[\mu(t) - \ln(S_{t-})\right]dt + \sigma dW_t + h(t_-)dJ_t$$

where $\mu(t)$ is a periodic function of time; $h(t)$ is a sign function, which determines the jump direction; and $J(t)$ is the jump component.

The Geman–Roncoroni process is a marked point process, hence it is a semi-martingale and a Markov process. Note that it can also be thought of as a mean-reverting process with positive jumps and a level-dependent mean/jump-reversion attribute. In the original formulation, the jump reversion rate depends on the threshold level $T(t)$ of the sign function. The introduction of this particular form of 'jump-reverting' component allows the model to capture traditional mean reversion but also strong jump reversions which characterize spikes.

Another relevant contribution in this field is that provided by Barlow (2002). The Barlow model is a simple but attractive supply/demand model, which is able to reproduce spikes without introducing jumps as an external and independent source of randomness. The model assumes that supply is non-random and independent of time and that demand is very inelastic with respect to the price level. Assuming that demand can be expressed as an exponential function of price, an equilibrium price function can be obtained by equating supply and demand. Assuming demand has a traditional mean-reverting dynamics expressed by an Ornstein–Uhlenbeck process, Barlow derives electricity spot price dynamics of the following form:

$$S_t = (1 + \alpha X_t)^{1/\alpha}, \quad \text{if } 1 + \alpha X_t > \varepsilon_0$$
$$S_t = \varepsilon_0^{1/\alpha}, \quad \text{otherwise}$$

where

$$dX_t = -\lambda(X_t - a)dt + \sigma dW_t.$$

In its original form, Barlow's model cannot be considered a realistic model for electricity spot prices. Some corrections are necessary in order to better capture price and volatility seasonalities.

Fiorenzani (2007) proposed an extension of Barlow's approach. Exploiting the explanatory power that demand (load) has on price, Fiorenzani proposes the following modelling approach:

$$S_t = f(L_t) + Y_t$$
$$X_t = L_t - B(t)$$

where

$$dX_t = \lambda(a - X_t)dt + \sigma dW_t^1$$
$$dY_t = -\theta Y_t dt + \eta dW_t^2$$

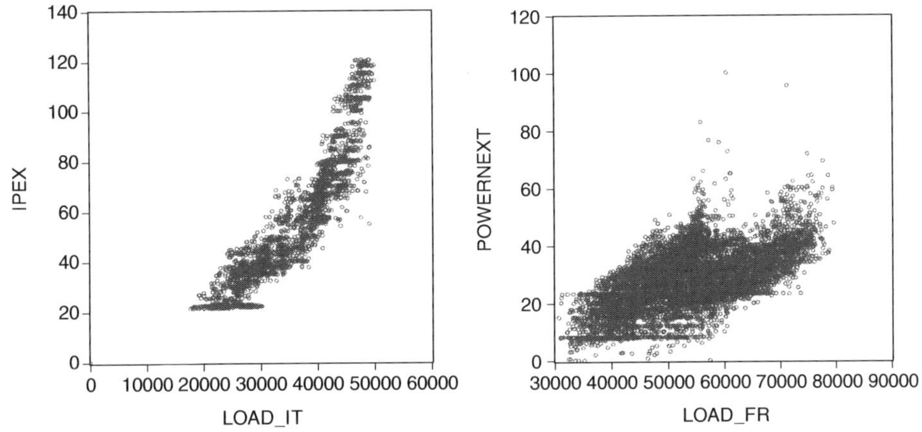

FIGURE 4.5 Load–price relation (Italian market IPEX and French market Powernext)

and *f* is a generic non-linear function that relates load ($L(t)$) to price and $B(t)$ is a non-parametric estimate of the load periodic component. Obviously, the model can also be expressed in a logarithmic form in order to avoid negative values.

A priori, the optimal functional form of *f* is not determined since its shape depends on the specific market we want to analyse, since it is supposed to represent the load versus price non-linear relationship. As can be inferred from Figure 4.5, different markets can display extremely different relationships between load and price. Moreover, *f* can also be assumed as a function of time, as suggested by Burger (2004). An econometric analysis is not in the scope of the present chapter. For an in-depth statistical analysis the interested reader can refer to Weron (2006).

Load-based models are relatively simple to estimate (via maximum likelihood, ML) and simulate by means of discretization schemes, producing nevertheless extremely realistic price paths. Figure 4.6 provides an example of the application of a load-based model. The model's parameters have been estimated via ML and are reported in Table 4.1. The empirical spot price path (upper graph) can be compared with a simulated path (middle graph) or an average simulated path over the same time period (lower graph).

4.1.4.2 Electricity Forward Price Models Electricity forward price modelling is as important as spot price modelling. Forward products in electricity markets represent the primary hedging and trading products, hence their realistic modelling is something more than an interesting exercise. If electricity spot price modelling deals with the stochastic representation of a single price signal, forward price modelling deals with the simultaneous description of different (per tenor and delivery period) electricity forward contracts.

Traditional electricity forward price modelling comes directly from interest rates models such as the HJM approach[4] or LIBOR models,[5] however some adjustments are needed in order to consider that electricity is delivered through a specific delivery period (see previous section). One of the main characteristics that a specific forward price modelling approach

[4]See Heath *et al.* (1992).

[5]See Brigo and Mercurio (2006).

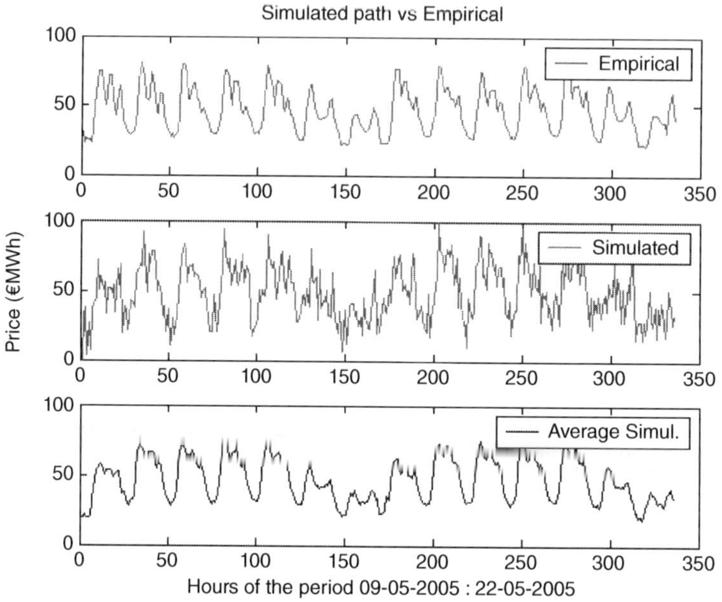

FIGURE 4.6 Simulated and empirical path (period II)

needs to have is inner consistency with the observed (and traded) forward prices, and for that reason market models such as HJM or LIBOR have been historically preferred.

According to the HJM approach, electricity 'instantaneous' forward prices $f(t, \tau)$ can be theoretically modelled with the following equation:

$$\frac{df(t,\tau)}{f(t,\tau)} = \mu(t,\tau)\,dt + \sum_{j=1}^{n} \sigma_j(t,\tau)\,dW_t^j$$

TABLE 4.1 Parameters vector estimates of Fiorenzani's model with $f(L) = (1 + \gamma_1 L)^{\gamma_2}$ on Italian spot market data

	a^*	λ	σ	θ	η	$\gamma(1)$	$\gamma(2)$
Period I	0	0.06353	192.81	0.37475	25.4083	0.000143	2.2799
		(0.002432)	(18.9147)	(6.48E-07)	(0.008414)	(1.584E-04)	(1.0995)
Period II	0	0.06046	187.9	0.87913	12.5984	0.00014	2.2221
		(0.00118)	(9.98)	(9.094E-07)	(0.009217)	(4.0E-04)	(0.5275)
Period III	0	0.24461	1387.96	0.357609	24.7663	0.000188	2.0081
		(0.02523)	(167.45)	(9.191E-07)	(0.007113)	(1.48E-04)	(1.0349)

Period I: from 07-02-2005 to 20-02-2005 (336 hourly observations).
Period II: from 09-05-2005 to 22-05-2005 (336 hourly observations).
Period III: from 24-10-2005 to 06-11-2005 (336 hourly observations).
*In the proposed estimation exercise the parameter a has been deliberately imposed equal to zero in coherence with the model specification and the short-term period of estimation proposed. In fact, in our load-based model parameter a is supposed to capture long-term linear drift.

Assuming only one stochastic factor and the absence of a non-zero drift function under the pricing measure, the following is obtained:

$$\frac{df(t,\tau)}{f(t,\tau)} = \sigma(t,\tau)\,dW_t$$

giving

$$f(t,\tau) = f(0,\tau)exp\left\{-\frac{1}{2}\int_0^t \sigma^2(u,\tau)du + \int_0^t \sigma(u,\tau)dW_u\right\}$$

with $f(0,\tau)$ being the initial forward curve observed in the market today.

Under these modelling assumptions, all forward prices have independent and normally distributed log returns with significant advantages for model parameter estimation and option pricing.

From instantaneous forward instruments it is possible to then price electricity forward contracts with discrete delivery period $[\tau(1),\tau(2)]$, following Benth *et al.* (2008), using the following relationship, and with $w(u) = 1$ or $w(u) = exp(-ru)$ depending on the contract's settlement rule:

$$F(t,\tau_1,\tau_2) = \int_{\tau_1}^{\tau_2} \hat{w}(u,\tau_1,\tau_2)f(t,u)du$$

where

$$\hat{w}(u,s,t) = \frac{w(u)}{\int_s^t w(v)dv}.$$

Despite its simplicity and tractability, the Gaussian assumption is not always appropriate for electricity forward price modelling. The sharp jumps in electricity spot price should be reflected in forward prices, at least for short-term maturity and short delivery period contracts. Hence, including jumps as follows is a natural extension of Gaussian HJM models:

$$\frac{df(t,\tau)}{f(t-,\tau)} = \sigma(t,\tau)\,dW_t + \eta(t,\tau)\,dJ_t$$

with $J(t)$ a generic jump process (typically a semi-martingale). Dealing with generic jump processes is not always practical since distributional and path properties of the overall forward price process may either be unknown or extremely complex. For that reason, usually Lévy-based jump processes are used (e.g., normal inverse Gaussian (NIG) processes or generalized hyperbolic processes) in order to reach a higher degree of mathematical tractability (see Benth *et al.* (2008)). However, the ability to model forward prices in a more realistic way allowed by non-Gaussian HJM models is often accompanied by increased complexity in parameter estimation and price simulation.

This added complexity becomes particularly significant when one needs to model simultaneously more than one electricity forward market (a pretty typical problem in industrial applications). In particular, it could be extremely difficult with multi-dimensional generic semi-martingale processes to correctly disentangle and represent the dependence structure associated with continuous and discontinuous parts. Despite the fact that electricity spot and forward prices may display different distributional and dynamic characteristics, which suggest the use of different modelling approaches for them, it is extremely important to guarantee their cross-consistency. It would be extremely dangerous to adopt a spot price modelling approach which is totally inconsistent (in its assumptions and properties) with its forward counterpart. As is known in general for commodity markets, spot and forward prices are related by no-arbitrage relationships involving storage costs and convenience yields:

$$F(t,T) = S(t)exp\left[(r+c-y)(T-t)\right]$$

where c is the instantaneous storage cost and y represents the convenience yield introduced by Geman and Vasicek (2001).

These parameters are almost impossible to estimate consistently in electricity markets, as suggested by Eydeland and Wolyniec (2003). This difficulty prevents the derivation of forward price dynamics from spot prices. On the contrary, some other approaches (see, e.g., Schwartz and Smith (2000)) aim to derive spot dynamics from forward prices, exploiting the following relationship:

$$\lim_{T \to t} F(t,T) = S(t)$$

Using this second approach, for example, it is possible to show that Gaussian HJM forward models, with time-decaying volatility functions, are consistent with traditional mean-reverting spot processes. However, it is worth considering that the above stated limit relationship between spot and forward prices is no longer valid if jump components are assumed present in spot and forward dynamics.

4.1.5 Spot Price Analysis (IPEX Case)

Hourly power prices (spot prices) usually display a complex structure, more complex than that of forward prices or spot prices of many other commodities and financial assets. Figure 4.7 shows characteristic spot price behaviour (for baseload power) across a number of European power as well as UD markets. The 'stylized facts' of the electricity spot price generating process are clear to see: namely, periodicity or seasonality (from calendar season down to weekday/weekend and intra-day granularity), strong mean reversion and occasional spikes (or double jumps), which can be well represented by the class of mean-reverting Lévy models (with subordinated jump processes) which have been used widely in the modelling and pricing of default risk in the credit markets.

The peculiar nature of power spot prices is intrinsically related to all those physical characteristics that were briefly described at the beginning of this chapter. Different from the typical dynamics of many financial assets, hourly power prices are not only characterized by a complex stochastic behaviour, but also tremendously impacted by a non-trivial periodic component. In general, one can write electricity spot price dynamics as the sum (or composition) of different components:

$$S_t = \alpha(t) + \mu(t) + W(t) + J(t)$$

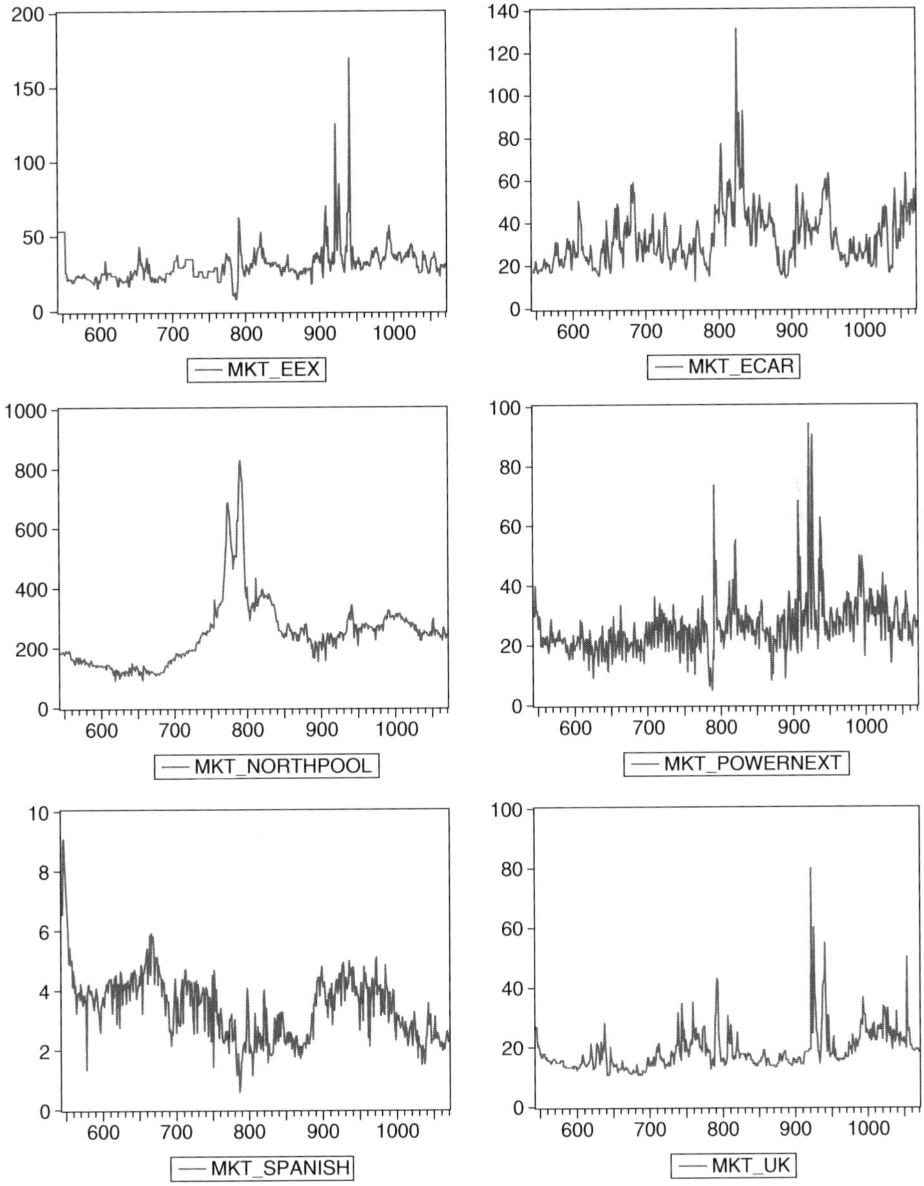

FIGURE 4.7 Daily baseload prices from major European and American electricity exchanges

where

$\alpha(t)$ is a linear drift component

$\mu(t)$ is a periodic component

$W(t)$ is a probabilistic noise component

$J(t)$ is a pure spike component.

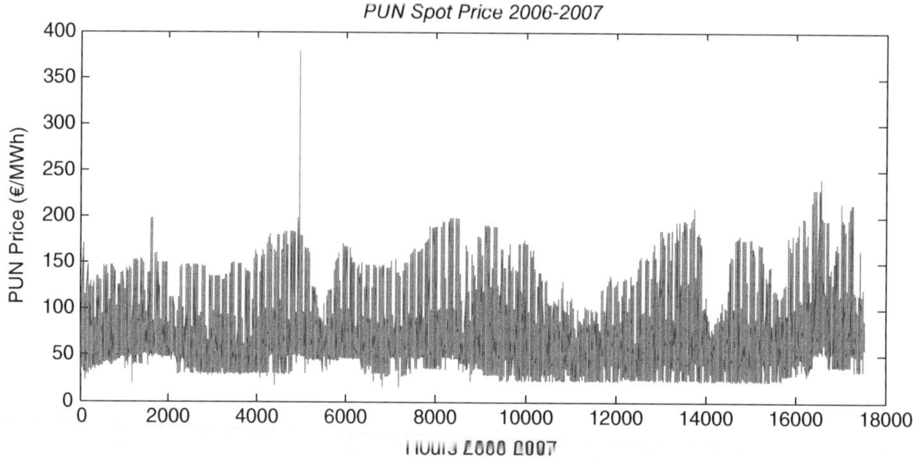

FIGURE 4.8 PUN (Italian electricity spot price) price plot

Each one of the generic components listed above is representative of a typical electricity price behaviour: a linear tendency, a periodic component for the micro and macro price frequency, a component for the description of the price variability (unpredictable behaviour) in the 'normal regime' and a component for the description of unpredictable price behaviour in extreme situations (spiky behaviour).

Quite often, in traditional financial data analysis, a lot of emphasis has been concentrated on the study of random components of financial asset prices. This is because the deterministic behaviour (especially the periodic behaviour) of financial asset prices is usually not significant from a statistical point of view. In complete contrast, electricity spot price dynamics are essentially characterized by a strong and complex periodic component, which has necessarily to be analysed with the appropriate instruments and filtered out from the data set before concentrating attention on the study of its statistical properties.

The detection of the periodic component of the price signal can be performed by classical Fourier analysis.[6] By means of the discrete Fourier transform one is able to analyse the original price signal (time series) in its frequency domain, being able to clearly determine its predominant periods. See Figure 4.8 for the example of a PUN (Italian electricity spot price) price plot.

Once the proper frequencies are detected, the periodic component can be extracted using parametric (e.g., by fitting the periodic component with a dummy equation or with a Fourier polynomial) or non-parametric filtering methods (such as wavelet methods). The effectiveness and impact of the filtering methodology can be appreciated by comparing the distributional behaviour of the price signal before and after the filtering.

Figure 4.9 shows how the shape of the Italian electricity spot price (PUN) changes after a simple dummy-based regression equation has been fitted to capture periodic behaviour and removed from the original time series.[7]

---

[6]The interested reader can refer to Howell (2001) for a comprehensive description of classical Fourier analysis.

[7]See Fiorenzani (2006) for more details about filtering methods applied to power price time series.

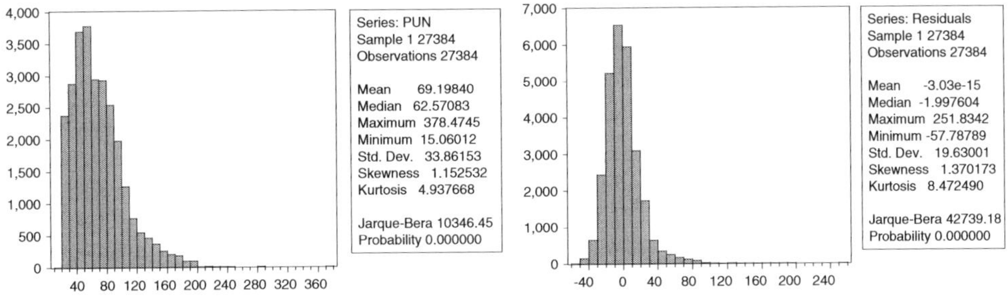

FIGURE 4.9 PUN statistics (left) vs. PUN filtered statistics (right)

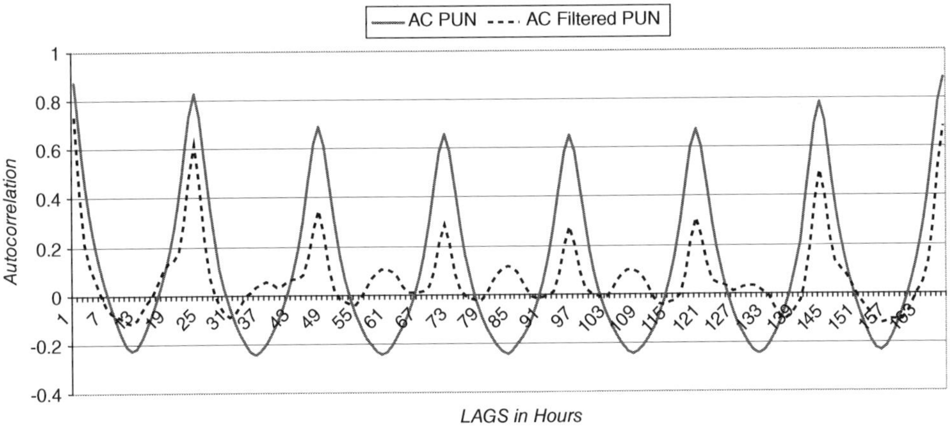

FIGURE 4.10 PUN vs. PUN filtered (autocorrelation functions)

Traditional correlogram analysis can also be used to detect and evaluate the presence of the periodic component within the price behaviour (see Figure 4.10). The analysis of the autocorrelation functions displayed by a certain price series has always been a useful signal for the presence of undetected periodic components or structural residual behaviours (such as ARMA behaving residuals).[8]

It is evident from Figure 4.10 that the filtering process previously adopted led us towards a non-trivial residual series, which has a clear autoregressive structure. ARIMA models can then be used to analyse this stochastic component further. Simply by introducing three autoregressive components of 1st, 24th and 168th order we are able to explain up to 90% of the realized variance of the signal with a significant reduction in the autocorrelation shape (see Figure 4.11).

The final residual is effectively quite 'white' but not really Gaussian (see Figure 4.12).

Fat tails behaviour can be explained as signalling the presence of an undetected jump component, which superposes the classical Gaussian random noise.

[8]See Verbeek (2000) for a detailed presentation of correlogram analysis of financial time series and ARMA/ARIMA models.

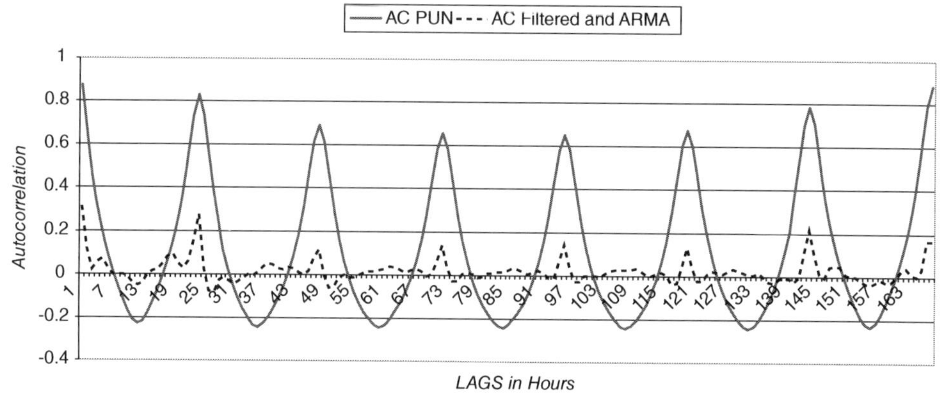

FIGURE 4.11 PUN vs. PUN filtered + AR (autocorrelation functions)

Obviously, the analysis performed here can also be done, by means of the same steps, on log prices (taking the natural logarithm of the price series). The results should not appear much different but, depending on the final scope of the analysis, the use of log prices can be preferred. In particular, if our scope is price modelling for forecasting or simulating purposes, price positivity is an essential feature we need to preserve. For that reason a direct analysis of log prices may be preferred in this case.

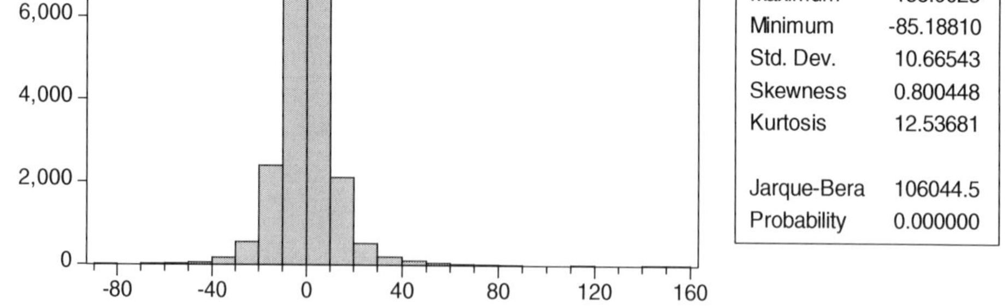

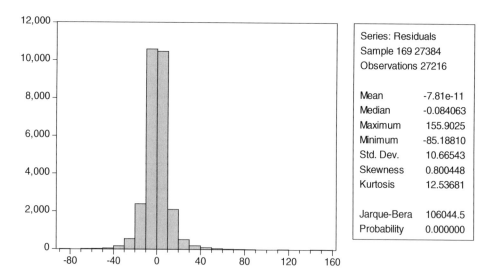

FIGURE 4.12 ARMA model residuals histogram

4.1.6 Forward Price Analysis (EEX Case)

Forward price analysis has an additional dimension on top of the time dimension – namely, the maturity dimension of the forward contracts. For this reason, before using traditional time

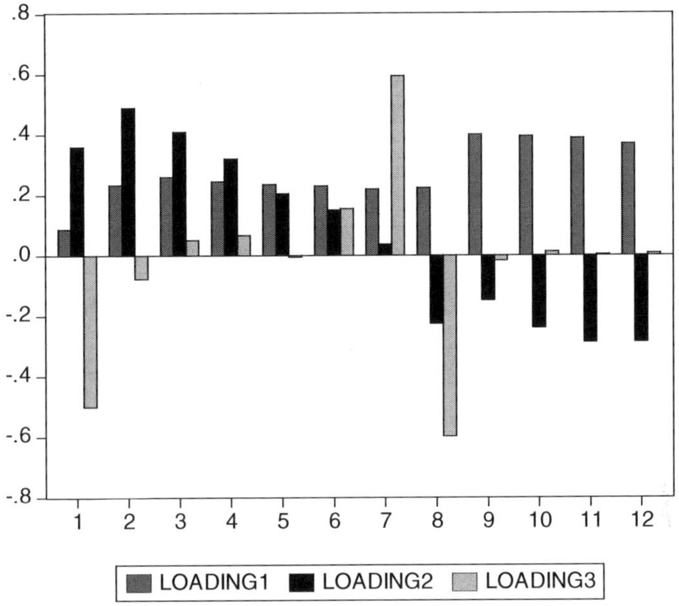

FIGURE 4.13 Factor loadings

series analysis methods, one needs to identify the main factors that affect the forward curve movement.

Principal components analysis (PCA) is a kind of analysis that applies well to groups of highly correlated market variables (see Fusai and Roncoroni (2008) for more details on PCA). PCA takes historical data on movements in the market variables and attempts to define a set of components or factors that explain the movements.

A futures term structure of 12 contracts has been considered; in particular, the closing prices of the first six monthly contracts, the third and fourth quarterly contracts, and the calendar contracts up to four years ahead. This amounts to a data set of 987 closing prices for each of the considered contracts. The start date for the data is 11/01/2005 and the end date 27/11/2008.

Figure 4.13 plots the factor loadings for the first three components identified using PCA, and from these it is possible to notice some classical features of the forward curve movements. The first component represents parallel shifts, all with the same signs – denoted by dark grey bars in the chart. The second factor – denoted by black bars in the chart – represents a *twist* of the term structure. Contracts between the first month and the third quarter move in one direction and contracts with longer maturities show opposite dynamics. The third factor – denoted by light grey bars in the chart – represents less structured dynamics. In particular, it is possible to notice a high level of correlation between the movements of the first month and the fourth-quarter power contract. In contrast, the third-quarter contract shows an uncorrelated movement with respect to the fourth quarter, and so against the first-month movement.

The importance of each factor is measured by the standard deviation of its factor score. The factors computed in this analysis are plotted in Figure 4.14, according to a ranking of importance by variance measures.

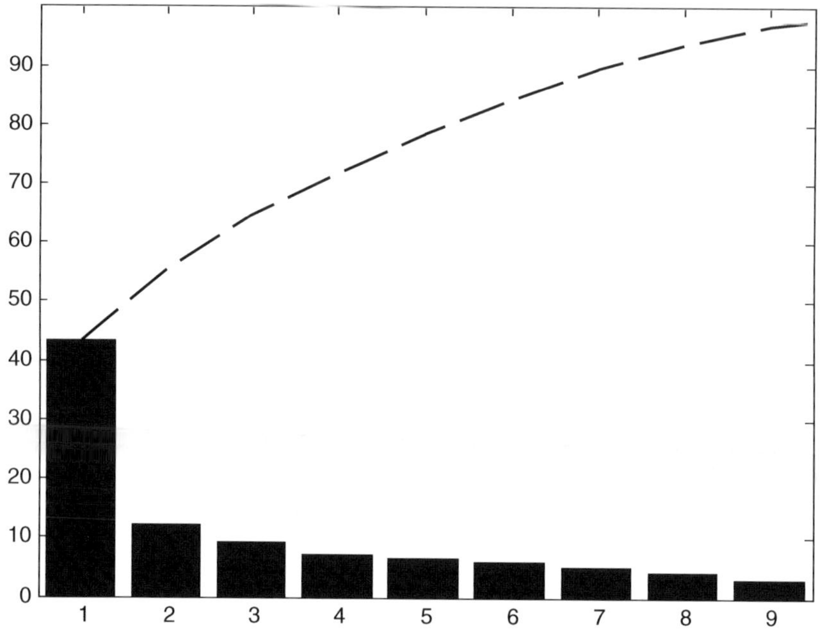

FIGURE 4.14 Proportion of curve's variance explained by each factor score

For this example, the first three factors analysed explain almost 70% of the total variance. It is not that much compared with a similar analysis that can be performed on other products or markets. This is proof that power price dynamics are more complex than those of other commodities or financial assets.

In particular, the presence of a seasonal component in the underlying price paths, as analysed in the spot price analysis of the previous section, or the non-Gaussian behaviour of the main risk factors of the curve may clarify why the PCA performed here shows that at least eight factors are needed to explain 90% of the realized curve's variance. In fact, the presence of an undetected seasonal component in the curve behaviour can erroneously induce the PCA analysis to attribute this unexplained movement to the stochastic behaviour of the curve itself, despite it just being a deterministic one. On the contrary, it is worth emphasizing that the main implicit distributional assumption of PCA is joint normality of all the factors. If this assumption is not supported by the empirical data, PCA results can be biased.

In the remainder of this section the scores series will be tested (for the first three meaningful components detected) in order to check for the hypothesis of normality of the main components and for the presence of seasonal behaviours in the autocorrelation paths. This analysis will be performed through classical distributional and statistical tests. Figure 4.15 is a scores histogram for the first principal component. The kurtosis value is above the zero level, denoting a leptokurtic distribution, while the level of skewness coefficient shows a lightly *left-skewed* distribution.

In testing the Gaussian hypothesis for the scores series through the Jarque–Bera statistical test, the hypothesis of normality is rejected. One may be interested to also outline any hidden recursive patterns, such as seasonal or autocorrelation effects, undetected by the PCA.

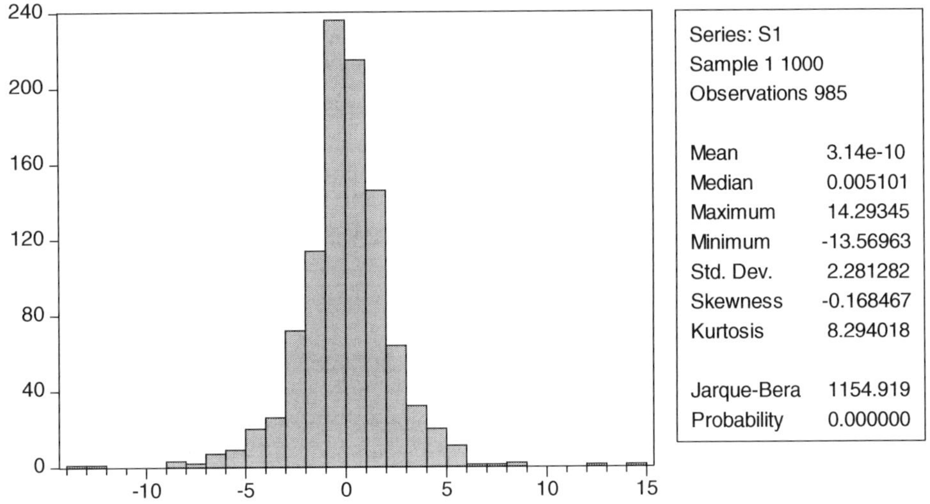

FIGURE 4.15 Histogram of score 1

So, autocorrelation analysis is performed to search for possible improvements in the PCA analysis.

The correlogram of the first principal component's scores does not show any meaningful structural breakdowns of the confidence interval level (computed at 95% confidence level), as reported in Figure 4.16.

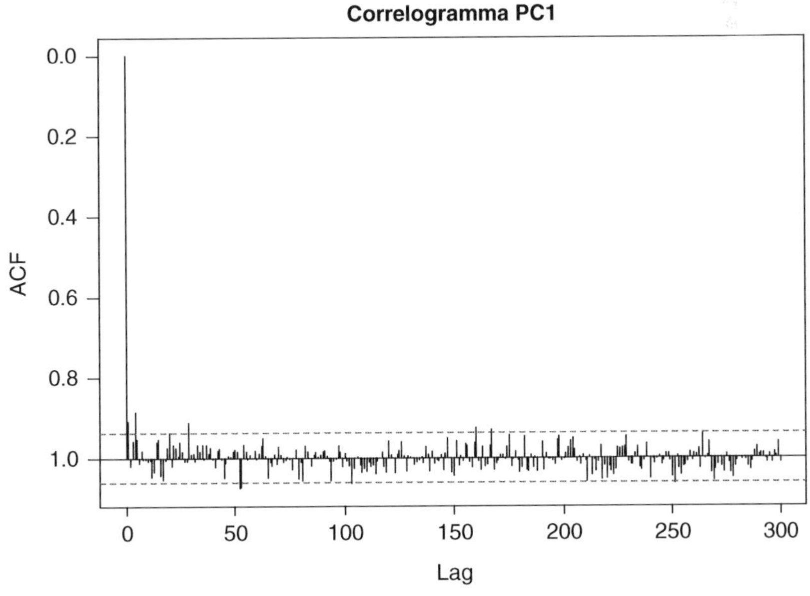

FIGURE 4.16 Correlogram of the first PC

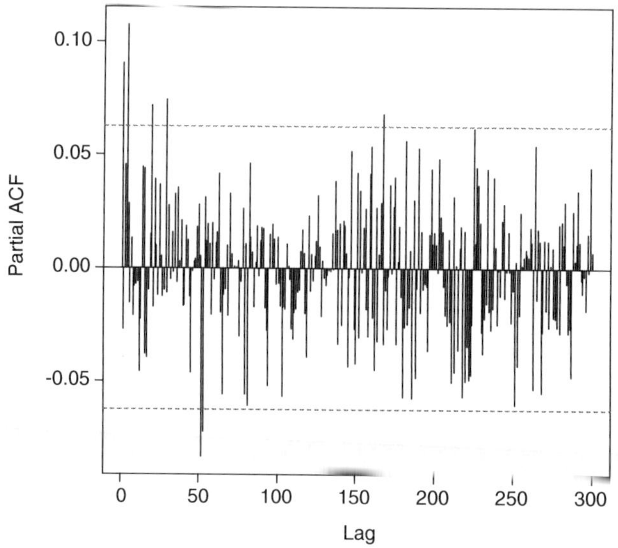

FIGURE 4.17 Partial autocorrelation path of the first PC

Partial autocorrelation analysis (that eliminates possible effects of linear dependence between overlapping lags) shows only the limited, and not meaningful, presence of breakdowns of the confidence interval level (computed at 95% confidence level), as reported in Figure 4.17.

Analytically powerful statistical tests such as the Box–Ljung test and the Box–Pierce test confirm the null hypothesis: the absence of linear autocorrelation through the scores of the first principal components (Table 4.2). This can also be interpreted as the absence of a potentially undetected seasonal component in the curve dynamic behaviour.

The same analysis and tests have been performed for the other two principal components. Similar results in terms of Gaussianity and absence of autocorrelation have been obtained for them.

The analyses presented to date are just simple examples of the kinds of statistical analyses that can be done on power price time series (both spot and forward) in order to understand their behaviour and their fundamental relationships with other economic variables. Depending on the scope of the analysis one wants to perform, different models can be constructed to predict, describe or risk assess power prices.

TABLE 4.2 Box–Ljung and Box–Pierce tests or PC1

Box–Ljung test
χ-squared = 278.2411, d.f. = 300, p-value = 0.8115
Box–Pierce test
χ-squared = 237.6254, d.f. = 300, p-value = 0.9967

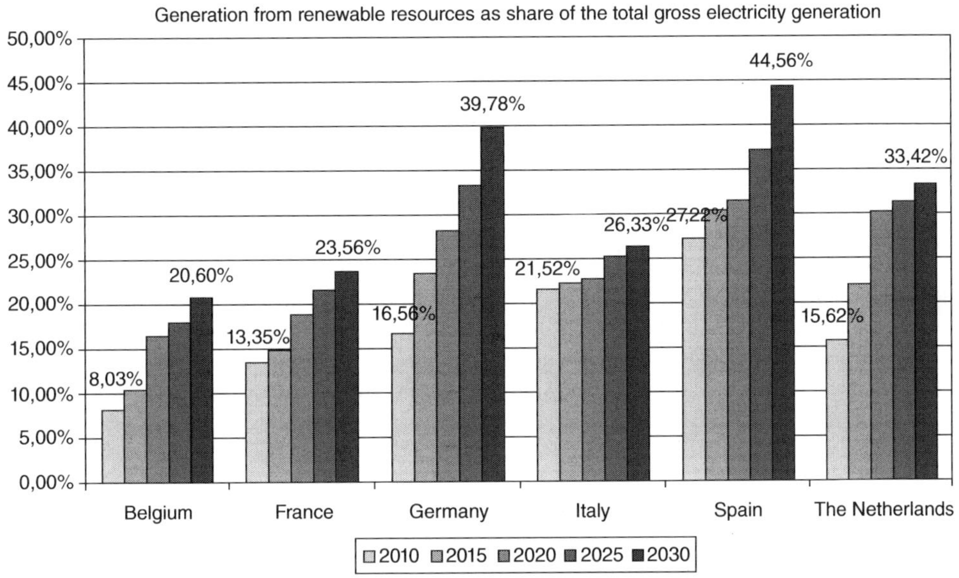

FIGURE 4.18 Expected evolution of the generation from renewable resources (% of total electricity generation)
Source: Cervigni and Niedrig (2011).

4.2 RENEWABLES, INTRA-DAY TRADING AND CAPACITY MARKETS

4.2.1 Renewables Expansion Targets

In this section we examine the implications of the large-scale integration and implicit 'firming'[9] of renewable electricity production, which has already been taking hold and which is mooted to gather pace over the next decade and beyond. Figure 4.18 (from Cervigni and Niedrig, 2011) shows the ambitious renewables electricity production targets which have been set for key European power markets over the next decade and beyond.

It is widely anticipated that the large-scale integration of renewables will lead to increased volatility in day-ahead or spot prices and will lead to a significant increase in market risk for legacy conventional thermal generators. The significantly increased but intermittent production from renewables sources (especially wind and photovoltaic) will additionally require that transmission control areas will increasingly have to adapt to the stochastic nature of renewables production at very short notice, resulting in increased intra-day up to real-time trading (e.g., growth in the trading of 15-minute contracts) and/or increased procurement (and possible

[9]We extend the definition of 'firming' beyond the traditional meaning of the large-scale integration of renewables production sources with, for example, large-volume CAES storage facilities or CCGT generators (see, e.g., Mason and Archer, 2012). We broadly define the 'firming' term to also include any capacity market innovation which encourages the provision of increased flexibility in dealing with the intermittency of supply problem, and hence which *accommodates* the uptake of supply (or firming) from the increasing share of renewables in the overall generation portfolio mix.

activation) of control power capacity, especially short-notice, short-duration 'minute reserve' capacity.

In this section we look at the implications for both day-ahead and intra-day electricity prices, as well as the effects on capacity market structures and prices. The objective is to better understand how these markets have already changed and how they need to evolve further if they are to fairly remunerate or incentivize developers for putting at risk the capital required for the inevitable increase in peaking and/or storage assets which will be required to provide the *flexibility* required in the renewables-dominated electricity markets of the future.

We also generalize our definition of 'prices' in both the electricity and capacity markets to mean an analysis of the changes in price levels, price profiles (or shapes) and price volatilities which have already occurred in both markets and which are expected to prevail into the future. Finally, we focus on the German market because the large-scale integration and accommodation of renewables electricity production underway is arguably the most 'politically prioritized' of the renewables policies being advocated across the various European power market control areas.

4.2.2 Growth in Intra-Day Trading

Figure 4.19 (from Cervigni and Niedrig, 2011) already shows a clear relationship being established between increased solar production levels and the growth in trading of 15-minute contracts during peak day-time hours in the German power market.

It is generally accepted that it is impossible to exactly forecast wind speed at the day-ahead stage, but that forecasts do improve significantly and can become quite accurate a few hours before real time. Given the priority feed-in and large-scale integration of renewables (principally wind but also photovoltaic in jurisdictions such as Germany) mooted over the next decade and beyond, it therefore seems likely that control areas/system operators will need to increasingly adapt to such information – resulting in the increased procurement (and possible activation) of control power capacity by system operators (in particular minute reserve) and

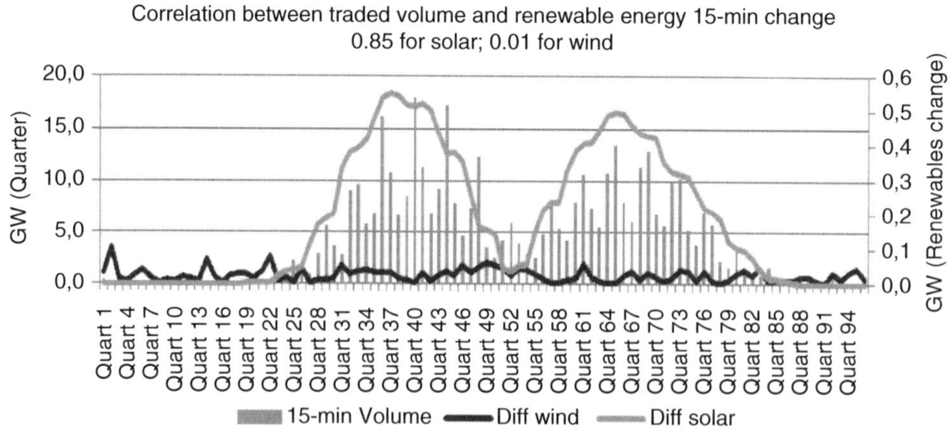

FIGURE 4.19 Correlation between growth in intra-day trading and increased PV production levels
Source: European Power Exchange.

increased intra-day up to real-time trading activity by generators. It seems inevitable therefore that there will continue to be a marked increase in trading of intra-day blocks and real-time electricity in order to mitigate the intermittency of this supply source (as illustrated in Figure 4.18 and also in Figure 4.22 below).

4.2.3 Implications for Future Price Volatility and Price Profiles

Figure 4.20 (from Cervigni and Niedrig, 2011) points to the likelihood that a significant proportion of conventional thermal plant capacity in Germany would not be needed in 2020 to cover off-peak demand in a high-wind environment.

In such periods Germany will likely be a net exporter of electricity (assuming a more interconnected EU transmission network) and German day-ahead electricity prices will likely trend very low (or perhaps even negative as long as renewable production continues to enjoy a priority feed-in). Day-ahead prices, both peak and off-peak, would inevitably become more volatile given the priority feed-in accorded to renewables production sources.

Figure 4.21 (from Cervigni and Niedrig, 2011) underscores the currently held wisdom that the sharp increase in installed photovoltaic capacity mooted for 2020 (incorporated in the solid red-coloured supply curve) has the potential to significantly lower German peak prices in summer. The day-ahead hourly peak price profile can be expected to shift downwards and indeed flatten under such a scenario, again making it difficult for legacy mid-merit and/or peaking thermal generators, as well as storage assets, to cover marginal costs of production in such a scenario.

Figure 4.22 points to a similar solar-driven flattening of day-time peak prices being likely across the winter weeks 49–52, where demand coverage in 2020 has been simulated based on the installed renewables capacity mooted for 2020 and based on 2003 weather data corresponding to the 4-week interval shown.

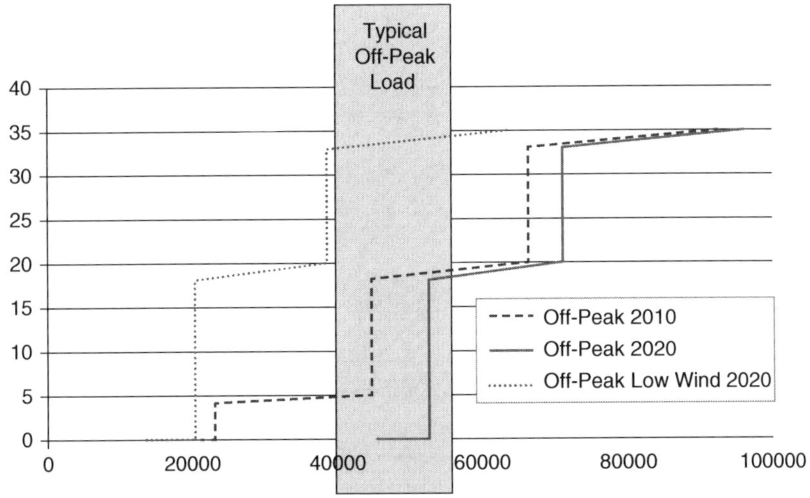

FIGURE 4.20 Supply stack in off-peak 2020 scenario
Source: Cervigni and Niedrig (2011).

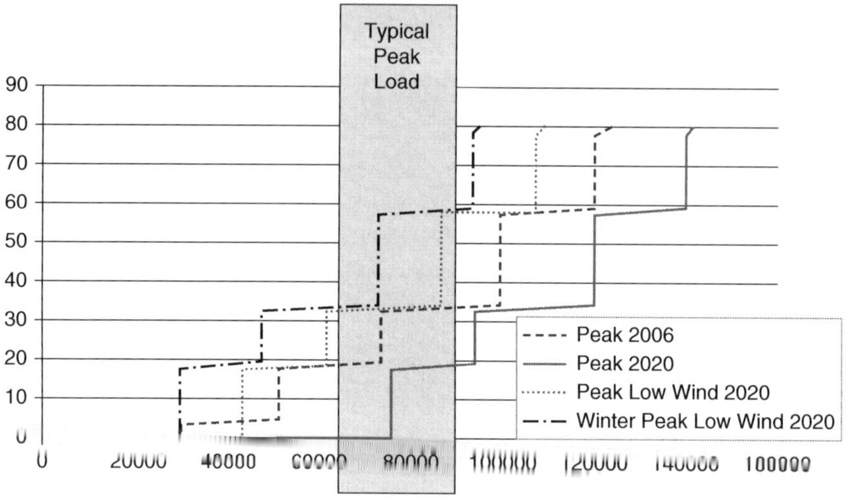

FIGURE 4.21 Supply stack in peak 2020 scenario
Source: Cervigni and Niedrig (2011).

Figure 4.23 in fact confirms that such a flattening in the hourly peak price profile is indeed already occurring, and is clearly being driven by increasing photovoltaic installed production capacities. This will have implications for the viability of storage assets such as pumped hydro or compressed air, which we discuss later in Section 4.2.5.

Hence, both the anticipated flattening of the hourly peak price profile and the increased volatility expected in day-ahead hourly prices are interconnected and are likely to be a direct

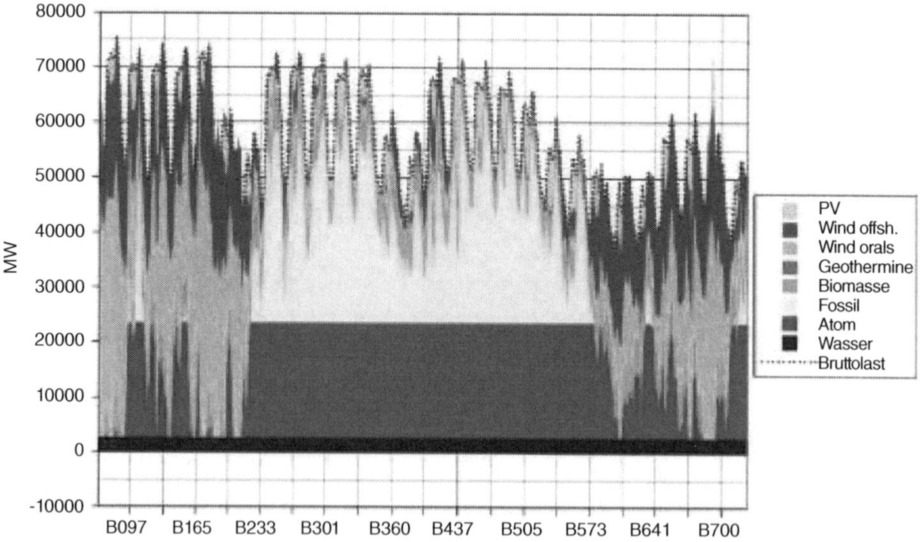

FIGURE 4.22 Simulation of 2020 demand coverage from intermittent renewables sources
Source: ISUSI.

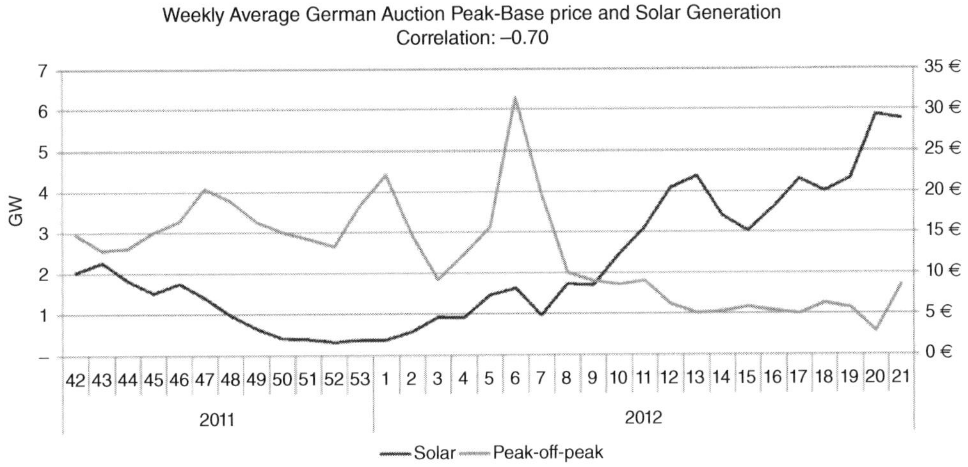

FIGURE 4.23 German peak–base spread as a function of solar production volumes
Source: European Power Exchange.

consequence of the increased integration of renewables production which has already been committed to across European electricity markets for 2020 and beyond.

4.2.4 Reforms and Innovations in Capacity Markets

As Figure 4.19 illustrates, while the intermittency of the increasing supply from renewables sources (in particular, wind and photovoltaic) has been a factor in explaining the significant growth observed in intra-day trading in Germany in recent years, there have also been significant reforms and innovations in the German capacity markets which have had an impact on the structure, levels and volatilities of capacity market prices, in particular the day-ahead market for short-duration ‘minute reserve’ capacity.

Haucap *et al.* (2012) conducted a vector autoregression (VAR) analysis of regulatory reforms implemented in Germany's minute reserve power market in the last 15 years. The launch of a common web-based tendering platform to synchronize and standardize the four separate control areas dates back to 1 December 2006, and this reform was followed by the gradual interconnection and increased cooperation of the country's four system operators between December 2008 and July 2010. The former reform was aimed at increasing capacity market efficiency by promoting competition and discouraging strategic bidding behaviour, whereas the second reform was aimed at delivering a more efficient cooperative style of ‘netting’ reserve capacity requirements across the four separate control areas in the German power market. By creating in effect a single market for control power in Germany, the overall amount and cost of control power required could therefore be kept to a minimum, and this reform objective appears to have been successful. Figure 4.24 shows that a clear ‘structural break’ (further verified by Chow test statistics) in the time series of negative-balancing reserve capacity prices occurred around the time of the first reform (1 Dec 2006). Although not clear from Figure 4.24, calculations show that the volatility of *absolute* changes in reserve capacity prices (i.e., in €/MW units) also fell in the period following the first reform.

Before discussing further the structure and profile of German capacity market prices, and identifying why they might need to evolve in such a way as to encourage the provision of

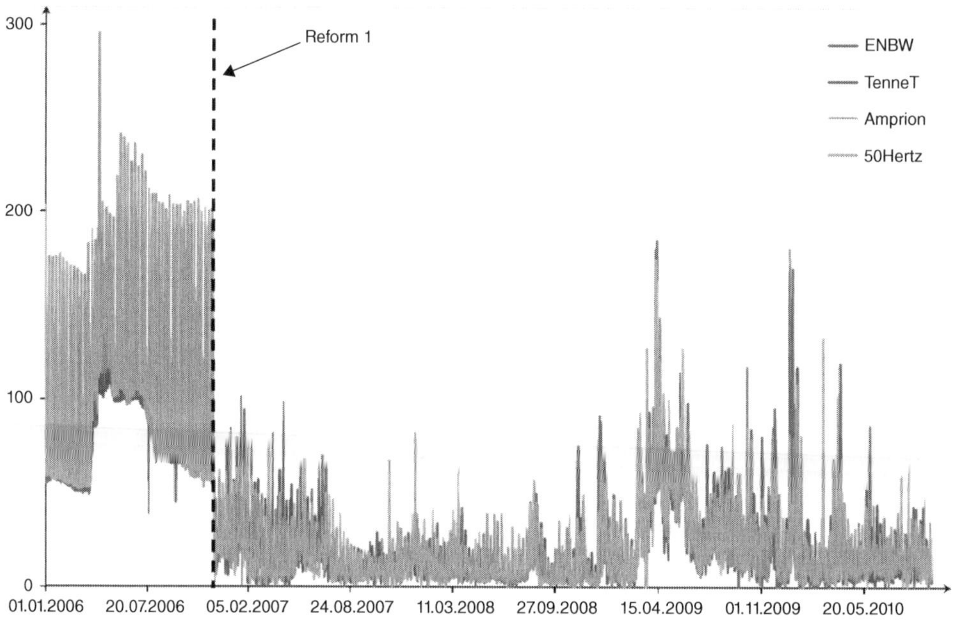

FIGURE 4.24 Average negative-balancing reserve capacity prices in Germany's four control areas Source: Haucap *et al.* (2012).

increased system flexibility in the face of the increasing integration of renewables, we first provide a general description of the various types of capacity market structures one might encounter in electricity markets.

4.2.4.1 Capacity Market Structures We need to distinguish between an energy-only market and an electricity market which is augmented by a parallel market for ancillary services such as the provision of operating reserve capacity and/or balancing power. In the former, the market-clearing energy price ostensibly reflects the marginal cost of generation of the marginal unit dispatched on the system, whilst additionally providing a margin sufficient to cover fixed costs. In such a market a generator is not explicitly compensated for keeping firm or declared capacity available as reserve – the generator is relying on potentially higher prices in the real-time market for balancing or control power. In the latter form of capacity market a capacity payment is paid separately for the provision of dedicated standby capacity which is declared available, which may or may not then be called upon to supply or take energy from the system. From the system operator perspective the capacity price is likely to be based on quantifying the probability and value of lost load, whereas from the generator's perspective the capacity price must reflect the opportunity cost of not using the capacity to generate electricity for sale in the day-ahead market. In the following discussion we focus on the latter type of ancillary services reserve market.

In Germany and in all other member states of the European Network of Transmission Operators for Electricity (ENTSO-E), three different types of reserve power/capacity exist. Secondary and minute reserve control power can be activated from successful capacity bids in regard to predetermined capacity which has been declared available, with a notice period ranging from seconds up to 15 minutes. Whereas secondary control power is procured in monthly cycles and can be activated within a 30-second up to 5-minute notice period for up to a 15-minute delivery intervals, minute reserve is procured by way of daily capacity auctions, activated within a 15-minute notice period and ranging from a 15-minute minimum delivery interval in quarter-hour intervals up to 4 contiguous hours for each of the 6 × 4-hour intervals or time blocks which can be tendered separately at auction for the following day. Primary control power capacity, which is called on first in the event of activation, is also tendered for in monthly cycles and can be activated within 30 seconds of the frequency event. The required volume of secondary control power and minute reserve which must be procured by the transmission system operators (i.e., for frequency stabilization purposes in the event of a real-time supply–demand imbalance) is defined in such a way that the defined residual risk probability of a power surplus or deficit that cannot be balanced is not exceeded.[10]

An interesting challenge resulting from the priority feed-in rights accorded to an increasing renewables stack, and the corresponding growth in intra-day and real-time trading, will be the optimization of within-day peaking or storage assets such as compressed air energy storage (CAES) or pumped hydroelectric storage (PHES) facilities. In the particular case of a storage asset, the primary source of revenue might well be the capacity market in the first instance, where in the case of Germany's capacity market described above the payment from the system operator can include a 'capacity price' compensation for the standby provision of positive or indeed negative-balancing reserve (which must be declared 'available') in the cases of secondary and minute reserve control and a separate tariff or 'energy price' for the 'delivery' of control power in the event of a 'successful'[11] capacity bid subsequently being 'activated'.

In the indicative levellized cost of energy (LCOE) calculations provided below we demonstrate that such facilities are not currently sufficiently incentivized by energy-only market system marginal prices (taking German day-ahead prices as the benchmark) and must additionally (or indeed principally) rely on day-ahead capacity markets combined with intra-day and real-time trading revenues for the return of their fixed costs (again pointing to a likely increase in future intra-day trading volumes).

4.2.4.2 Capacity Price Setting In liquid and well-developed bilateral markets (i.e., where liquid OTC and also exchange-based trading has long been established) capacity prices ought to reflect the fair value of ownership claims on 'firm' (i.e., 'declared available') generation capacity. The fair-value payment for a claim on peaking or storage asset capacity (for a particular block or hourly profile) ought to reflect the flexibility value, or optionality, of the asset to deliver/accept power at short notice and for possibly a short-lived duration (at a predetermined price) in the event a successful capacity bid is subsequently activated.

---

[10] http://www.amprion.net/en/control-energy.

[11] In Germany, offers for the day-ahead minute reserve auction must be submitted by 10.00 T-1 (i.e., day-ahead stage) and 'successful' bids for 6 × 4-hour blocks are then announced at 11.00 T-1. Depending on whether the deemed-successful bid (the decision of the system operator being made independent of the price offered for energy) is for positive or negative-balancing reserve, if activated (or deactivated subsequent to an earlier activation notice) on T0, power must then be delivered to (or taken from) the system in 15-minute granularity blocks. Given the 15-minute advance notification in either case, this underscores the high level of dynamic flexibility required to trade successfully in this segment of the capacity market.

In our subsequent discussion we highlight the fact that the prevailing capacity market price structure in markets such as Germany may not currently adequately reflect anticipated 'scarcity conditions' (see Cervigni and Niedrig, 2011). Moreover, as things stand it may not adequately reflect the future demands which could be placed on conventional thermal generators to more flexibly respond to supply–demand imbalances resulting from the intermittent but prioritized feed-in from an increasing share of renewable electricity sources in the overall generation portfolio.

4.2.5 Provision and Remuneration of Flexibility – Storage Assets

In addition to the anticipated and sustained increase in intra-day trading, highly flexible storage assets, such as CAES and PHES, will need to be commissioned if the inefficiencies associated with spinning reserve and short-notice ramping of conventional thermal plant are to be minimized. Consequentially, it is inevitable that there will need to be a corresponding increase in the procurement of short-notice, short-duration capacity market contracts for the provision of both positive and negative-balancing reserve, such as is facilitated in the German day-ahead 'minute reserve' market.

Anticipating the effect that increased German wind and photovoltaic production may have on the day-ahead peak versus off-peak spread by 2020 and beyond (Figure 4.23), a sizeable proportion of the investment return on a flexible CAES or indeed PHES storage asset will likely accrue from a strategy of bidding negative and/or positive capacity in the minute or secondary-reserve capacity markets. As alluded to already, such a strategy would additionally need to be flexibly combined with intra-day and real-time electricity trading to ensure energy storage inventory levels are always appropriately primed to respond to short-notice activation calls for negative or positive-balancing energy.

The intermittency of priority feed-in, renewable electricity sources therefore raises the question of how and where such storage assets are to be fairly remunerated. Even the somewhat crude analysis following will demonstrate that currently prevailing day-ahead electricity price profiles[12] do not offer a sufficient incentive for financiers to put at risk the capital necessary to commission and profitably operate such facilities. Notwithstanding the inherent ability of storage asset operators to be more attuned[13] than most market participants to balancing risk and corresponding system needs, we will show that even a daily cycled CAES storage facility cannot expect to rely on 'arbitraging' intra-day block spreads to cover its fixed as well as variable costs, both now and especially in the future.

4.2.5.1 CAES Storage Facility – A Levellized Cost of Energy Cost–Benefit Analysis

The 'cost-of-generation' calculation below uses actual closing prices for EEX off-peak power (€/MWh$_e$), EEX NCG Gaspool spot gas (€/MWh$_{th}$) and EUA CO_2 emissions allowance prices (€/tonne) for an indicative single day, 30 November 2012.

[12]As already alluded to, Cervigni and Niedrig (2011) convincingly argue that the spot or day-ahead price profile might be expected to flatten across most of the hours, and that in such an environment generators and storage operators should collect a greater part of their revenues from 'providing flexibility'.

[13]Harris (2006) cites the fact that the *ex-post* load duration price curve is much steeper than the *ex-ante* curve, and can be accessed by some participants *after* day-ahead prices have been set.

Assumptions The CAES compression and generation trains have been configured such that the rates of air compression and expansion are equal,[14] permitting an equal number of (continuous) compression and generation hours. Further assume the number of compression hours to be 12 so that one can reference the traded day-ahead off-peak electricity blocks (0.00–08.00 off-peak 1 and 20.00–24.00 off-peak 2) in the 'variable cost-of-generation' calculation which follows.

Cervigni and Niedrig (2011), in assessing the interaction between supply and demand for electricity in Germany for the future year 2020, conclude that there are strong grounds to believe that a significant capacity shortfall of 15,000 MW will prevail. However, the capacity shortfall will likely only be relevant for 10 hours/working day and for 30 days/year, since demand on those days during off-peak hours can still be covered by conventional thermal generators. Hence, the capacity shortfall is anticipated to relate to the 300 most expensive hours in the pro-forma price–duration curve for 2020, and the 'scarcity scenario' envisaged can be seen as in fact a 'storage problem'.

Therefore, in the following calculation we assume that the levellized cost of a CAES storage technology needed to yield a target internal rate of return of 10% over a 10Y investment period is given by the *sum* of the €/MWh all-in variable cost of generation *plus* the total capital expenditure or 'capex' requirement amortized over a 20Y operating period and then smeared over the 300 most expensive hours for each year of operation to give an equivalent €/MWh estimate.

All-In Variable Cost of Generation (€/MWh) Using, as an example, the actual EEX electricity and gas closing prices on 30 November 12, and the CAES heat rate and efficiency data cited in Lund *et al.* (2008), we can approximate the typical price differential of peak over off-peak which would be required for the CAES storage asset to just cover its variable costs of production.

Ignoring the cost of emissions[15] (which would have approximated out to a unit cost of €4/MWh_e on 30 November 2012), the marginal cost of generating 1 MWh_e from a CAES electricity storage facility is given as:

$$[(P_{\text{off-peak}} + MC_C)/(\eta_C \cdot \eta_T)] + P_{\text{gas}} \cdot \eta_{\text{ratio}} + MC_T$$

---

[14]Lund *et al.* (2008) use a 216-MW compressor, a 360-MW turbine and a 1478-GWh storage cavern to optimize a CAES facility in which the number of compression and expansion hours is equal.

[15]Using Bloomberg instrument codes, the following calculation defines the UK spark spread – the 'theoretical margin from producing power from natural gas'. The spread components include power (ELUBM V13 Index £/MWh), fuel (NBPGM V13 Index p/therm) and additionally the cost of carbon emissions (MOZ3 Comdty €/tonne). The formula used for the spark-spread calculation is (ELUBM V13 Index – NBPGM V13 Index * 34.129693 * 0.01/0.49131 – (MOZ3 Comdty * FX1MEUGB Index + UK_Co2Tax) * 0.42000). The efficiency and carbon values used are efficiency (0.49131), heat rate (6945 Btu/kWh), fixed cost (0) and CO_2 adj. (0.42). Following Table 2 in ETSAP 2010, the CO_2 emissions adjustment factor in the UK benchmark CCGT baseload spark-spread calculation would need to be increased by about 40% to approximate the CO_2 emissions impact of an open-cycle gas turbine configuration (rather than a combined-cycle gas turbine mid- to baseload generator) which is utilized in the generation train of a CAES facility. http://www.iea-etsap.org/web/E-TechDS/PDF/E02-gas_fired_power-GS-AD-gct.pdf.

where

$P_{\text{off-peak}}$ = cost of day-ahead off-peak electricity (€/MWh_e)

P_{gas} = cost of day-ahead gas (€/MWh_{th})

η_{ratio} = gas input to turbine (MWh_{th}) per unit electricity output (MWh_e)[16]

η_C = compressor efficiency (%), defined as the energy storage input divided by the power input to the compressor

η_T = turbine storage efficiency, defined as the power output of the turbine divided by the energy storage output[17]

MC_C = variable cost of compressor (€/MWh_e)

MC_T = variable cost of turbine (€/MWh_e)

If we take the day-ahead cost of the off peak electricity block on the EEX on 30 November 2012 to have been €36.52/MWh_e, €27.35/MWh_{th} for the day-ahead gas price and the various CAES compressor and turbine efficiency data used in Lund *et al.* (2008),[18] we can estimate the marginal cost of producing one unit of electrical energy from the CAES storage asset as approximately €59/MWh, an approximate 61% premium of peak over off-peak price.

Comparing this with the block price for peak power witnessed on 30 November 2012 of €54.0/MWh, it is clear that the CAES storage asset would have been unable to cover its marginal or variable cost of operation (at least on the representative date shown) by 'arbitraging' the intra-day spread between peak and off-peak electricity prices.

However, more striking evidence of the need for a storage asset to look to the capacity markets to recover its investment costs is provided in the following, which first estimates the levellized fixed cost of the investment required and then smears this cost over the 300 most expensive peak hours when 'scarcity conditions' are most likely to prevail in the day-ahead market for electricity.

Required 'Capex' Annuity This is the constant stream of *annual* free cash flows which are required to repay the total investment cost over say a 20-year investment recovery period, assuming an annualized internal rate of return of 10%. Taking an all-in estimate of €750/kW[19]

[16]This relates to the cost of the natural gas which is used to heat and expand the compressed air feed to the generator turbine.

[17]It should be noted here that a big advantage of the modified gas turbine used in the CAES generation train compared with a conventional open-cycle gas turbine peaking generator is that around two-thirds of the gross capacity or nameplate power rating of the latter is needed to compress air, with the remaining one-third driving the electrical generator. In the case of the CAES gas turbine, however, no compression is needed during turbine operation because the required enthalpy is already included in the compressed air.

[18]Lund *et al.* (2008) evaluated the financial performance of a CAES storage asset comprising a 216-MW capacity compressor, a 360-MW turbine and a 1478-GWh air storage cavern, designed to allow equal rates of air compression and expansion and an equal number of compression and expansion/generation hours.

[19]This is an estimate of the capital cost per installed unit of capacity, and is likely to be towards the mid- to high-end range of currently prevailing installed €/kW estimates for CAES plant. This admittedly contrasts with the open-cycle gas turbine peaking plant estimate of €350/kW cited in Cervigni and Niedrig (2011),

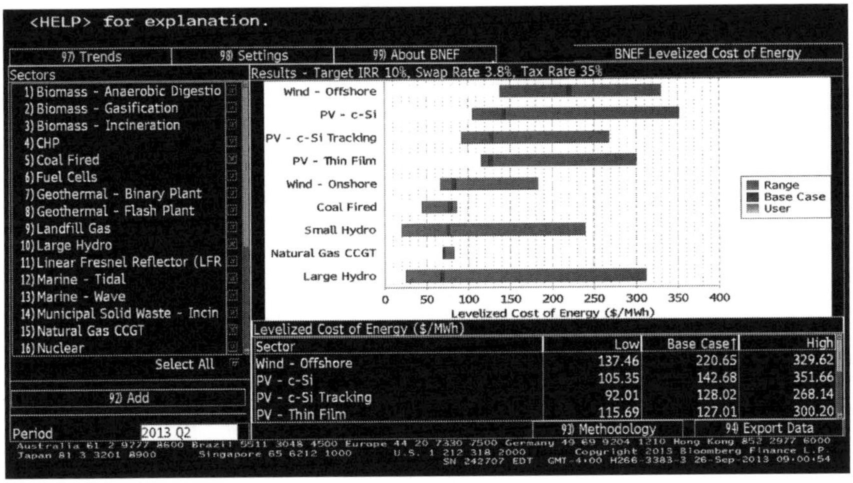

FIGURE 4.25 Levellized costs of energy for various renewables technologies.
Source:

installed to construct a CAES cavern plant and install its associated compression and generation train infrastructure, then using the Excel annuity pricing function we can estimate the required annual cash flow as

$$= -\text{PMT}(.10, 20, 750 \times 10^3) = €88,000/\text{MW p.a.}$$

If the required annual cash flow to cover fixed costs, or equivalently the internal cash return, is smeared over the most expensive 300 hours annually when scarcity conditions are likely to prevail, then this equates to an *additional* €293/MWh-equivalent.

Even from such a crude and incomplete analysis, it would appear that current day-ahead electricity price profiles (at least in the German power market) are quite some distance from pricing-in a sufficient incentive to encourage developers to invest in new-build storage facilities.[20] However, it should be noted that the 300-hour duration of 'scarcity conditions' mooted from 2020 onwards implies a very short load profile for the CAES to recover its fixed costs, and hence this should be borne in mind when comparing the LCOE estimate for the CAES storage asset with those estimates for the various renewable technologies shown in Figure 4.25.

Nonetheless the message appears clear. Both now and into the future, storage operators will likely have to look to the capacity markets as the natural way to earn the necessary

---

but the latter is considered the cheapest build option to deal specifically with the 300-hour scarcity conditions scenario depicted.

[20]This is sometimes referred to as the 'missing money' problem in that the revenues obtained by generators from selling electricity and ancillary services (such as reserve capacity or control power) in the short-term and/or forward markets are insufficient to attract an 'efficient' level of investment in generating and/or storage capacity. Another way of saying this is that the provision of flexibility is not encouraged by current market and/or regulatory structures.

revenues to make storage projects a viable proposition for investors. The calculations appear to show that the CAES storage asset would be unlikely to ever recover its fixed costs by trading in the day-ahead electricity markets alone.

Summary We have shown that the progressive large-scale integration of renewables in European electricity markets will likely lead to a sustained increase in intra-day electricity trading. With prices likely to become both increasingly volatile as well as showing significant changes from the current profile or shapes witnessed in day-ahead hourly prices across the off-peak and peak block periods in particular, there will be significant challenges and risks ahead for the operators of legacy thermal generators and indeed for the developers of new-build storage capacity.

In order that storage project financiers are sufficiently incentivized to provide the type of flexibility required in such an environment, the structure and pricing of contracts in the ancillary services reserve markets (for control power) in particular will need to reflect the new dynamics and risks posed by the intermittency of supply from renewables production sources. It can be expected that there will be an increase in the procurement of short-notice, short-duration control power, and hence a corresponding increase in the volume of successful bids activated by control area operators.

It is clear that current energy market prices do not appear to offer a sufficient incentive for the development of storage solutions which have the requisite dynamic flexibility to respond to the excess demand environment associated with scarcity conditions, or indeed to the excess supply environment likely to result in high-renewable, low-demand scenarios. Although the option of exporting excess supply is one possible solution, bidding near-zero or negative auction prices in the day-ahead markets is likely to prove to be an undesirable solution to the problems discussed. In short, what will be required is increased flexibility and dynamically flexible storage assets will have a particularly important role to play under such a market scenario.

4.3 RISK MEASURES FOR POWER PORTFOLIOS

This section is not intended to be a comprehensive presentation on risk measurement problems and techniques for power portfolios. Since many technical issues have already been considered and discussed, here the focus will just be on risk concepts and practical issues of electricity portfolios that are fundamental to understand and govern.

4.3.1 Value-Based Risk Measures

We concentrate on synthetic risk measures for portfolios made up of liquid physical or financial power products. In this situation, there is at any moment the possibility to liquidate or modify the composition of the portfolio without incurring large liquidity costs. Hence, the economic performance of this kind of business is determined mainly by the fluctuation of the portfolio's value more than by its realized payoff. Hence, the risk one runs is well represented by the maximum potential drop (or some function of it) in market value that the portfolio may incur in a given time horizon.

Synthetic risk measures that focus on this point are called 'value-based risk measures'. Of course, the discussion here will mainly concentrate on the classical value at risk (VaR) measure, as the most significant and intensively used value-based risk metric.

4.3.1.1 Value at Risk VaR has become widely used and popular among banks and financial institutions since the beginning of the 1990s. For this reason, in the energy field too it has become popular to evaluate the market risks embedded in open trading positions by means of VaR.

VaR effectively measures the market price risk exposure of an open position, condensing risk factors such as electricity market price, volatility and correlation and potentially, in more advanced cases, currency and interest rate risks. It is usually defined as 'the minimum potential loss that a trading portfolio may have over a holding period of m days, in the $x\%$ worst cases'. This means that we may expect to lose more than the VaR figure, in the given holding period of m days, only in $x\%$ of cases.

VaR is a simple and intuitive measure, which depends on two main arguments:

- the duration of the holding period (number of days); and
- the confidence interval level of $x\%$.

The holding period usually reflects the number of days necessary to liquidate completely the position without incurring any additional costs, and hence should be established proportionally to market liquidity. Usually, for portfolios of exchange-traded instruments, this period is something between 1 and 10 days. The level of the confidence interval reflects the level of conservativeness. In fact, the greater $x\%$ is then the higher the risk measure and consequently the lower the probability of having a worse economic result.

From a statistical point of view, VaR is a percentile measure. It measures the percentile of the portfolio value variations corresponding to the selected confidence level. Formally, if X is defined to be the portfolio fair value then

$$\{\text{VaR}(x\%) = c \in R_+ : \text{Prob}(-\Delta X > \text{VaR}(x\%)) = (1 - x\%)\}.$$

Typical confidence levels are 95%, 97.5% or 99%, since these levels correspond to well-known values in the Gaussian distribution tables.

As mentioned, the VaR calculation is based on the concept of fair value (market value) of the portfolio. Hence, VaR calculation methodologies are highly related to portfolio valuation methods – especially when options and non-linear derivatives are present in the portfolio.

Traditional VaR calculation methods can essentially be divided into two groups: analytical and numerical (simulation-based) methods. Analytical methods were first presented and used in traditional financial applications of VaR and are essentially based on some theoretical assumptions. The main one is the assumption of 'normality' of asset returns. The normality assumption is essential to obtain closed formulas for VaR calculations when managing a large and well-diversified portfolio of financial assets but it is clearly not realistic for electricity markets. However, the relaxation of this assumption makes the development of an analytical calculation method much more difficult and sometimes non-attainable. For this reason, numerical methods should be preferred in the case of electricity derivative portfolios even if the calculation time is much higher.

The best way to circumvent the problems of analytical models is by means of simulation. Using Monte Carlo simulation, one can price a wide range of derivative products and consequently obtain quite accurate estimates of the potential changes in a portfolio's value. One can simulate a large number of scenarios for the relevant risk drivers (forward prices and volatilities essentially) and for every scenario obtain a potential value change for the portfolio itself. Given the large number of scenarios performed, a probability distribution function can be estimated by means of parametric or non-parametric methods and the selected percentile measure can be extracted.

If the portfolio is mainly composed of linear positions, the VaR calculation may be quite quick since the simulation scenarios will reflect only forward curve shocks, while in the case of highly structured portfolios the calculation may complicate significantly. Realistic modelling of the joint stochastic behaviour of the relevant risk drivers is not a simple task. The main difficulty is modelling the dependence structure relating to the risk variables, and unfortunately there is not a simple solution for this.

The problem of simulating random draws from a multivariate and complex distribution may be solved with the substitution of Monte Carlo simulation with historical simulation. The historical simulation method consists of estimating VaR by means of historical daily market variable movements over a quite large and significant time horizon. Knowing the actual composition of the portfolio, it is possible to compute the VaR by means of calculating the theoretical portfolio value for every single day of the historical sample. The main advantage of the historical VaR method is that it is premised on an accurate estimate of the empirical distribution of the major risk factors. Hence, all the problems mentioned above regarding the correct simulation of realistic risk driver dynamics and dependence structure disappear. However, a number of disadvantages arise. The first is the size of the historical sample. In order to have a robust estimation of the distribution of portfolio value changes, a consistent database of historical prices is necessary but not always available. Secondly, this approach can only be applied to portfolios of liquid financial instruments, traded on organized exchanges, since only in this case are financial time series available. The third important disadvantage concerns the fact that historical VaR is a backward-looking measure, and the past does not always give a good indication of the future.

VaR is certainly the risk measure adopted as best practice in the financial industry but this does not mean that it always represents the best possible synthetic indicator of the economic risk embedded in portfolios.

4.3.2 Flow-Based Risk Measures

The economic performance of a portfolio made up exclusively of liquid financial products is fully determined by its day-by-day value change. This is because every single day it is possible to dynamically modify the structure of the portfolio itself, closing some positions or opening new ones without incurring enormous transaction costs.

When one manages a heterogeneous portfolio of non-standard physical deals, it is not often possible to liquidate a position without incurring expensive penalties or high liquidity costs. Hence, a non-profitable physical deal cannot be closed upfront, realizing a negative mark-to-market, but should be held in the portfolio till its natural maturity. The consequence of this fact is that the economic performance of the portfolio is not related to day-by-day portfolio value changes but is determined by its realized margin. Therefore, the risk of the portfolio cannot be expressed by the potential drop in the portfolio value over a short period of time, but should be measured by some indicator of the uncertainty which characterizes portfolio expected payoff over the whole portfolio tenor. Flow-based risk measures do this job.

4.3.2.1 Profit at Risk The characterizing feature of profit at risk (PaR) is that it assumes that markets are illiquid, and that as a consequence open positions are held to maturity. A formal definition of PaR can be given as 'the minimum potential loss that a portfolio may suffer in the $x\%$ worst cases if held to maturity'.

The focus is clearly on the economic flow (payoff) produced by the portfolio and not on its value. PaR is a risk measure suitable for monitoring and managing portfolios composed of medium to long-term structured contracts. The PaR time horizon should be chosen in line with the required purpose. Usually, the economic year is chosen by the management for a better comparison with budget values and balance sheet results.

The PaR calculation requires the assessment of economic margins coming from business activity that will generate economic results in the future. Typically, analytical methods are not available for the calculation of PaR and scenario-based simulation approaches should be used. Its assessment is done by simulating spot price scenarios for relevant commodities, evaluating their path evolution up to the selected time horizon. Then the portfolio margin relative to each of these scenarios is calculated and a probability distribution of the portfolio's margin obtained.

Since PaR measures the risk embedded in a portfolio of non-standard products, market risk variables may not be the only relevant drivers that should be simulated. Volumetric clauses and constraints should also be considered in order to have a fully comprehensive picture of the overall portfolio risk.

According to its calculation, PaR is a suitable risk measure for all ongoing activities for which the possibility of unwinding the position quickly is difficult. It may also be appropriate when measuring the risk of real asset management activities such as power generation, fuel procurement and storage origination, but in this case one has to remember that economic performance and risk are not affected exclusively by changes in market risk drivers but also by management strategy. Hence, the PaR calculation should also be based on simulation models capable of capturing the impact of operational and strategic decisions (real option models).

PaR is a fundamental control tool for the whole value-creation chain, measuring risk exposure and potential limit overruns, impacting on tactical decisions for risk reduction and hedging implementation. Moreover, it may be used as an indicator for top management in risk assessing medium to long-term investment decisions and commercial deals. PaR represents a coherent framework for strategic decisions.

4.3.2.2 Cash Flow at Risk The cash flow at risk (CFaR) approach answers the question of how large the deviation between actual cash flow and the planned value (or that used in the budget) is due to changes in the underlying risk factors. Effectively, it is a measure that is quite similar to PaR in terms of calculation methodology and time horizon, but it focuses on cash flow depreciation instead of economic margin depreciation. Sometimes the time delay, which characterizes the economic and financial manifestation of events within the firm's life, leads the choice between PaR and CFaR as the most appropriate risk measure.

Of course, in the case of CFaR, analytical calculation methodologies are again not available and simulation approaches (Monte Carlo or historical) prevail.

4.3.3 Credit Risk for Power Portfolios

Credit risk is the single most important risk for many power companies. In general, credit risk can be defined as the risk arising from an unexpected deterioration in the credit quality of one or more counterparties. Credit risk measurement and management is one of the main challenges facing industrial and financial companies today and it is not only related to trading activity. The consolidated approach to measuring credit risk is simply expressed by the so-called expected loss:

$$\text{expected loss} = \text{loss given default} \times \text{default probability}.$$

Loss given default (LGD) is technically the amount of money (exposure) one loses if a counterparty defaults today. In the power sector, especially when dealing with a portfolio made up of physical and financial positions, this quantity is typically composed of the settlement exposure and the replacement exposure. The settlement exposure is equivalent to the monetary amount of power delivered but not yet paid and is related to the fact that financial regulation of deals is usually temporally displaced with respect to physical delivery. If a counterparty defaults today, it may be the case that there are invoices related to past deals not yet executed. Settlement exposure is related to the payment terms of contracts and may be significant, especially for physical transactions where one is involved as the seller.

Replacement exposure is related to the situation where a counterparty defaults and the market value of the deal is positive for the company in question (i.e., negative for the counterparty). This means that the company faces a drop in P&L if the counterparty defaults on the contract. In physical contracts this amount is called the replacement exposure, just because it represents the opportunity cost the company faces from replacing in the market the physical power bought or sold. If settlement exposure is independent of market prices – since it only depends on the contract's price – replacement exposure is related to the mark-to-market of the defaulted contract. Hence, at least theoretically, the replacement exposure should be zero at the moment the deal closes.

Replacement exposure measures today's market value of a specific contract or of a bunch of contracts with a particular counterparty, but it does not reflect the potential value this contract may reach up to its natural maturity. In order to consider this dimension of the credit risk, one needs to replace the concept of replacement exposure with the concept of potential future exposure (PFE). PFE expresses a measure of how things can go against a certain counterparty and it is effectively the opposite to the concept of PaR.

Using PFE instead of replacement exposure, a higher value of expected loss is obviously reached, just because one is considering a risk dimension not considered previously. On its calculation, LGD can be modified by means of considering collateral that potentially guarantees a part of the portfolio or recovery amount. Recovery amounts are highly uncertain in size and time of effective settlement. Hence, it is prudentially better not to consider them. Collateral that can be executed upon request in the case of contract default reduces proportionally the exposure at default and consequently lowers the overall expected loss.

So, the previous equation can be reformulated as follows:

$$\text{expected loss} = (\text{loss given default} - \text{collateral}) \times \text{default probability}.$$

Time has not been spent on discussing the other important component of the expected loss, that is, the default probability. In the power sector, more than in other financial or non-financial fields, many typical trading or commercial counterparties are not big listed companies. Hence, traditional quantitative methods for the computation of the probability of default cannot be used straightforwardly. More commonly internal rating systems have to be employed, but this issue is outside the scope of the present discussion.

REFERENCES

Barlow, M.T. (2002) A diffusion model for electricity prices, *Mathematical Finance*, **12**(4), 287–298.

Benth, F.E., Benth, J.S. and Koekebakker, S. (2008) *Stochastic Modelling of Electricity and Related Markets*, World Scientific, Singapore.

Brigo, D. and Mercurio, F. (2006) *Interest Rate Models: Theory and Practice*, 2nd edn, Springer Finance, Heidelberg.

Cartea, A. and Figueroa, M.G. (2005) Pricing in electricity markets: A mean reverting jump diffusion model with seasonality, Birkbeck Working Papers in Economics and Finance 0507, Birkbeck, Department of Economics, Mathematics & Statistics.

Cervigni, G. and Niedrig, T. (2011) Capacity Markets: Relevant for Europe and appropriate for Germany? FORMAET Services GmbH.

Deng, S. (1999) Stochastic models of energy commodity prices and their applications: Mean reversion with jumps and spikes, Working paper, Georgia Institute of Technology.

European Power Exchange (2012) EPEX SPOT Markets and Products.

Eydeland, A. and Wolyniec, K. (2003) *Energy and Power Risk Management: New Developments in Modeling, Pricing and Hedging*, John Wiley & Sons, Hoboken, NJ.

Fiorenzani, S. (2007) Load based models for electricity prices, *Energy Risk*, June.

Fusai, G. and Roncoroni, A. (2008) *Implementing Models in Quantitative Finance: Methods and Cases*, Springer-Verlag, Berlin.

Geman, H. and Roncoroni, A. (2006) Understanding the fine structure of electricity prices, *Journal of Business*, **79**(3), 1225–1261.

Geman, H. and Vasicek, O. (2001) Forwards and futures on non storable commodities: The case of electricity, *Risk*, August.

Harris, C. (2006) *Electricity Markets: Pricing, Structures and Economics*, John Wiley & Sons, Chichester.

Haucap, J., Heimeshoff, U. and Jovanovic, D. (2012) Competition in Germany's minute reserve power market: An econometric analysis, Discussion paper, Dusseldorf Institute for Competition Economics.

Heath, D., Jarrow, R.A. and Morton, A. (1992) Bond pricing and the term structure of interest rates: A new methodology for contingent claims valuation, *Econometrica*, **60**(1), 77–105.

Howell, K.B. (2001) *Principles of Fourier Analysis*, CRC Press, Boca Raton, FL.

Kholodnyi, V. (2001) A non-Markov method, *Energy and Power Risk Management*, March.

Lucia, J. and Schwartz, E. (2002) Electricity prices and power derivatives: Evidence from the Nordic Power Exchange, *Review of Derivatives Research*, **5**, 5–50.

Lund, H., Salki, G., Elmegaard, B. and Andersen, A. (2008) Optimal operation strategies of compressed air energy storage (CAES) on electricity spot markets with fluctuating prices, *Applied Thermal Engineering*, **29**, 799–806.

Schwartz, E. and Smith, J.E. (2000) Short term variations and long term dynamics in commodity prices, *Management Science*, **46**(7), 893–911.

Verbeek, M. (2000) *A Guide to Modern Econometrics*, John Wiley & Sons, Chichester.

Weron, R. (2006) *Modelling and Forecasting Electricity Loads and Prices: A statistical approach*, John Wiley & Sons, Chichester.

FURTHER READING

Acerbi, C. and Tasche, D. (2001) On the coherence of expected shortfall, Working paper, www.gloriamundi.org/var/wps.html.

Bellini, F. and Frittelli, M. (2002) On the existence of the minimax martingale measure, *Mathematical Finance*, **12**, 1–21.

Black, F. and Scholes, M. (1973) The pricing of options and corporate liabilities, *Journal of Political Economy*, **81**, 637–659.

Breeden, D. and Litzenberger, R.H. (1978) Price of state contingent claims implicit in option prices, *Journal of Business*, **51**, 621–651.

Burger, M., Klar, B., Müller, A. and Schindlmayr, G. (2004) A spot market model for pricing derivatives in electricity markets, *Quantitative Finance*, **4**(1), 109–122.

Clewlow, L. and Strickland, C. (2000) *Energy Derivatives: Pricing and Risk Management*, Lacima Publications, London.

Cox, J., Ross, S. and Rubinstein, M. (1979) Option pricing: A simplified approach, *Journal of Financial Economics*, **7**, 229–264.

Davis, M. (1997) Option pricing in incomplete markets, *Mathematics of Derivative Securities*, pp. 216–226. Cambridge University Press, Cambridge.

Delbaen, F. and Schachermayer, W. (1994) A general version of the fundamental theorem of asset pricing, *Mathematische Annalen*, **300**, 520–563.

De Jong, C. and Huisman, R. (2002) Option formulas for mean reverting power prices with spikes, Working paper, Erasmus University of Rotterdam.

Fiorenzani, S. (2006) *Quantitative Methods for Electricity Trading and Risk Management*, Palgrave MacMillan, New York.

Foldes, L. (1990) Conditions for optimality in the infinite horizon portfolio cum saving problem with semimartingale investments, *Stochastics and Stochastics Reports*, **29**, 133–170.

Frittelli, M. (2000) Minimal entropy martingale measure and the valuation problem in incomplete markets, *Mathematical Finance*, **10**, 39–52.

Harrison, J.M. and Pliska, S.R. (1981) Martingales and stochastic integrals in the theory of continuous trading, *Stochastic Processes and their Applications*, **11**, 215–260.

Hull, J. (2000) *Options, Futures and other Derivatives*, 4th edn, Prentice Hall, Upper Saddle River, NJ.

Hull, J. and White, A. (1994) Numerical procedure for implementing term structure models I: Single factor model, *Journal of Derivatives*, **Fall**, 7–16.

Jacod, J. and Shiryaev, A. (2003) *Limit Theorems for Stochastic Processes*, 2nd edn, Springer-Verlag, Berlin.

Kaminski, V. and Gibner, S. (1997) Exotic options, in *Managing Energy Price Risk*, Risk Publications, London.

Keller, U. (1997) Realistic modelling of financial derivatives, PhD dissertation, University of Freiburg.

Longstaff, F. and Schwartz, E. (2001) Valuing American options by simulation: A simple least squares approach, *Review of Financial Studies*, **14**(1), 113–147.

Mason, J. and Archer, C. (2012) Baseload electricity from wind via compressed air energy storage (CAES), *Renewable and Sustainable Energy Reviews*, **16**, 1099–1109.

Merton, R. (1973) The theory of rational option pricing, *Bell Journal of Economics and Management Science*, **4**, 141–183.

Rockafellar, R.T. and Uryasev, S. (2002), Conditional value at risk for general loss distributions, *Journal of Banking and Finance*, **26**, 1443–1471.

Rodrigues, A. and Rocha Armada, M. (2006) The valuation of real options with the least squares Monte Carlo simulation method, Working paper available at www.fep.up.pt/conferencias/pfn2006/Conference%20Papers/540.pdf.

Ronn, E. (ed.) (2002) *Real Options and Energy Management*, Risk Books, London.

Saita, F. (2007) *Value at Risk and Bank Capital Management*, Academic Press, New York.

Tseng, C.L. and Bartz, G. (2001) Short term generation asset valuation, *Operations Research* **50**(2), 297–310.

CHAPTER 5

Emissions Markets and Products

Marc Chesney, Luca Taschini and Jonathan Gheyssens

5.1 INTRODUCTION

Climate change is one of the greatest challenges facing our planet in the coming decades and centuries. It has impacts on the environment, human health, our livelihoods, social relationships and the global economy. It is now scientifically accepted that human production of carbon dioxide and other greenhouse gases (GHGs) is directly related to global warming and therefore impacting virtually every aspect of economic activity from agricultural outputs to energy mix and consumption. In economic terms, air pollution and global warming are partially the consequence of an absence of tradable prices for certain 'public good' environmental resources, such as clean air. These would command the introduction of surrogate prices in the form of unit taxes or marketable emission permits in order to provide the necessary signal to use their resources optimally with limited negative externalities.

Emissions are not a traditional commodity. They cannot be stored like wheat or oil. They do not justify a positive price based on their marginal productivity in a production function, like metals or precious earth. Instead, their value (and price) is a human construct, an institutional way to impose a price on a negative externality. Where most commodity models price the commodity added value (from global demand), pricing models for emissions address the crucial issue of a just penalty, a cost that could make sense to negate, or at least mitigate, the social externalities borne by excessive GHG emissions.

The goal of this chapter is threefold:

1. Section 5.2 gives an overview of the science behind climate change and provides some numbers on the social costs created by excessive GHG emissions. The section provides a rapid introduction to the economics of externality and the fundamental concepts in use to justify a fair tax. The emergence of cap-and-trade solutions as an efficient mechanism to internalize the cost of carbon pollution is also described (in a perfect market, the least costly abatement techniques are promoted for a certain set of emission reduction goals).

Handbook of Multi-Commodity Markets and Products: Structuring, Trading and Risk Management. Edited by Andrea Roncoroni, Gianluca Fusai and Mark Cummins.

2. From Section 5.3 on the Kyoto Protocol to Section 5.5 on the current state of institutional regulations, we provide a detailed overview of the genesis and deployment of international regulations designed to internalize the emission constraints. These sections briefly describe the difficulty in choosing an appropriate strategy between command-and-control measures (strict regulations), taxes and markets for emissions. A particular emphasis is placed on the most successful scheme already implemented, the European Union Emissions Trading Scheme (EU ETS), with a look at its possible future. The future regional markets are also presented. They are, however, rapidly evolving and sometimes receding and are still not mature enough to draw a stable profile of the international scene, which changes every year. Compared with the much more mature markets depicted in the other chapters of this book, the market and regulations for GHG emissions are still very much driven by ever-changing political decisions. This adds a relatively unpredictable institutional component, which continues to play a strong role in the pricing mechanisms of this peculiar commodity.
3. Nonetheless, an array of current pricing models, acknowledging the commodity's idiosyncrasies, have emerged to assess the value and price of emission permits. In this new and promising field, approaches borrow from a large set of economic tools, ranging from macroeconomic models to econometric estimation and stochastic equilibrium models. Section 5.6 introduces the importance of the substitution principle between emission permits and abatement technology, a principle which may create partial price correlation between emissions, coal and gas (fuel switch). A short introduction is given to recent stochastic equilibrium models, which allow us to model the emission permit prices in a general and realistic uncertain setting with multiple firms. Readers interested in a more complete coverage of the environmental investment strategies and models in an uncertain context (including real options) should refer to the authors' companion book to this chapter, *Environmental Finance and Investments* (Chesney *et al.*, 2013. With kind permission of Springer Science+Business Media).

By the end of this chapter, the reader should have a better understanding of what sets emissions trading apart from other 'traditional' commodities (intrinsically, institutionally and in terms of pricing models) and the relationships between emissions permits and other energy-based commodities. It should also be clear that these markets are still in their infancy and very much dependent on political decisions that could modify certain principles or rules of valuation. Dealing with emissions certainly invites us to be cautious about sudden and unpredictable changes.

5.2 CLIMATE CHANGE AND THE ECONOMICS OF EXTERNALITIES

5.2.1 The Climate Change Issue

According to the Intergovernmental Panel on Climate Change (IPCC), global atmospheric concentrations of CO_2, CH_4 and N_2O have increased markedly as a result of human activity since 1750 and in 2005 exceeded by far the natural range of the last 650,000 years (IPCC,

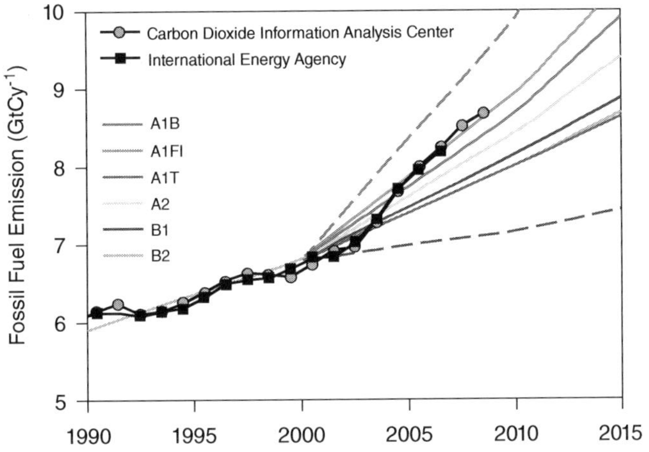

FIGURE 5.1 Actual fuel emission compared with IPCCC scenarios
Source: Global Carbon Project (2008).

2007). Between 1970 and 2005, GHG[1] emissions due to human activity increased by 70%. Global temperatures followed a similar pattern of increasing and accelerating warming. Eleven of the years between 2000 and 2012 rank amongst the warmest years in the instrumental record of global surface temperatures (since 1850), with almost permanent occurrences of positive temperature anomalies.

Among the different GHGs, CO_2 is the most important anthropogenic GHG responsible for global warming, in terms of volume and absolute impact. Annual emissions of CO_2 grew by about 80% between 1970 and 2004, as a consequence of increased use of fossil fuels and accelerated deforestation. Growth rates in CH_4 and N_2O emissions are mainly due to agricultural expansion.

For the purpose of comparison, the IPCC defined in its third assessment (AR3) (IPCC, 2001), and again in its fourth assessment (AR4) (IPCC, 2007) a set of scenarios exploring future developments for GHG emissions. According to the most recent estimates on fossil fuel emissions, global emissions are currently following the IPCC's most emission-intensive scenario (A1FI), with heavy reliance on fossil technologies combined with very rapid economic and population growth (see Figure 5.1).

To get a sense of the potential impact that the trend in past and future emissions could have on global temperatures, the IPCC computed in its fourth assessment possible stabilization levels in GHG concentration and the induced average increase in temperature associated with each of them, along with an estimate of global sea-level rise reproduced here in Table 5.1. According to the sensitivity projections of the IPCC, any commitment to limit the global average temperature increase within a $\pm 2°C$ limit would force the stabilization of CO_2 concentration around 350–400 ppm. At the end of 2012, the latest concentration was estimated to be 396 ppm, slowly increasing from the 375 ppm concentration recorded in 2005.

---

[1]The GHGs are carbon dioxide (CO_2), methane (CH_4), nitrous oxide (N_2O), hydrofluorocarbons (HFCs), perfluorocarbons (PFCs) and sulfur hexafluoride (SF_6).

TABLE 5.1 Concentration stabilization scenarios and impact on temperature increase and sea-level rise

Scenario	CO_2 concentration at stabilization	CO_2-e concentration at stabilization	Change in global CO_2 emissions in 2050 (% of 2000 emissions)	Global average temperature increase (in °C)	Global average sea-level rise (in m)
I	350–400	445–490	−85 to −50	**2.0–2.4**	0.4–1.4
II	400–440	490–535	−60 to −30	**2.4–2.8**	0.5–1.7
III	440–485	535–590	−30 to +5	**2.8–3.2**	0.6–1.9
IV	485–570	590–710	+10 to +60	**3.2–4.0**	0.6–2.4
V	570–660	710–855	+25 to +85	**4.0–4.9**	0.8–2.9
VI	660–790	855–1130	+90 to +140	**4.9–6.1**	1.0–3.7

Source: IPCC (2007)

In the current context of increasing emissions levels, achieving a 350–400 ppm stabilization level will require a set of mitigation measures, with different costs, areas of applicability and timing. The IPCC has introduced in the stabilization scenarios a set of usable mitigation strategies, with increasing marginal costs: technology efficiency improvement, source of energy switching (e.g., from coal to natural gas), development of renewable energies, demand reduction and carbon capture and storage. However, due to the long absence of a market and price for emissions, mitigation strategies have been difficult to adopt in the past. That is why understanding the negative impact of externalities and the economic instruments to prevent them is especially important.

5.2.2 The Economics of Externality and GHG Pollution

Environmental externality is the materialization of a simple market failure: when agents conduct economic activities that engage imperfectly priced environmental assets, either as inputs (excessive consumption) or outputs (pollution), they engage in socially excessive levels of harmful activities. The policy implication of this result is economically clear. The costs (at this stage, social or private) of polluting or depleting activities need to be internalized and agents benefiting from these externalities need to be confronted with a price equal to the marginal external cost of their polluting activities to induce a social optimum.

Such an incentive can take two main forms: either an institutionally forced control embodied in laws and regulations (command-and-control) or a price incentive that can be centralized (tax and subsidies, promoted first by Pigou (1920)) or decentralized through markets and permits as described by Coase (1960) (for more detailed discussions about the benefits of environmental instruments, see Baumol and Oates (1988) and Tietenberg (1985)).

Compared with the pure market approach devised by Coase, the promoted cap-and-trade market for CO_2 permits is a hybrid object: it combines a centralized component (the cap) and a decentralized one (the trade), and as such it benefits (as it is undermined by) both. The centralized component ensures the emergence of the market by creating a specific quantity scarcity that becomes valuable. Without a cap, problems involving public goods (such as global warming) would remain outside the market's reach due to a lack of global coordination, extremely high transaction costs and free-riding. The necessary creation of a quantity scarcity is the reason why the cap-and-trade market mechanism is often referred to as a quantity instrument.

Once the cap is set, quantities are exchanged through permits in a decentralized manner, as in a Coasian pure market. Companies are allocated initial permits, either through grandfathering or through auctions. They exchange them according to their respective needs and abatement costs. In the very hypothetical classical setting (atomized agents, pure and perfect market) the companies, as demonstrated by Coase,[2] reach the least costly optimum: at equilibrium, the exchange of permits ensures enforced quantities for a price equal to the least costly marginal cost of abatement. In different terms, whoever can reduce emissions at a lower cost always has the opportunity to abate more and sell unused permits to those who face higher abatement costs, without requiring governments to precisely know companies' cost functions. Moreover, by offering the opportunity to sell permits and generate profits, markets incentivize technology changes and competitiveness towards clean activities.

In the recent debates surrounding the recourse to a price mechanism to limit emissions, proponents of taxes and proponents of permits usually depict them as profoundly different, almost opposing, instruments. However, this is contrary to the economic theory that in a world of perfect knowledge, taxes are fully equivalent alternatives to marketable emissions. An environmental authority can set a price (i.e., a tax) and adjust it such that emissions are sufficiently reduced to prescribe environmental standards and reach the optimal pollution quantity. Alternatively, it can issue the requisite number of permits directly and allow the bidding of polluters to determine the market clearing price. The regulator can, in short, set either price (tax) or quantity (emission cap) and achieve the desired result. This short introduction does not, however, describe in enough detail some important differences between the two approaches, especially in situations of information asymmetry. Readers interested in a more detailed review of the 'quantity/price' debate are advised to refer to the seminal work of Weitzman (1974) or to the more recent Parsons and Taschini (2012) and references therein.

5.3 THE KYOTO PROTOCOL

5.3.1 The United Nations Framework Convention on Climate Change

The first scientific evidence of human activity affecting the world's climate emerged during the World Climate Conference (WCC) held in February 1979 in Geneva. For the first time, a large group of politicians were concerned about human interference with the climate and the environment. As a result of the global attention on climate change, the United Nations Environmental Programme and the World Meteorological Organization established the IPCC in 1988.

The key task of the IPCC was to assemble and assess scientific information on the impact of the human carbon footprint. In 1990, the IPCC issued its first assessment report (AR1), which reflected the views of 400 scientists on the threats posed by global warming. The report stated that global warming was a real problem caused by humans. Further, the IPCC urged the international community to take measures to curb GHG emissions. As a result, throughout the second meeting of the WCC held in Geneva later that year, the IPCC called

[2]See also Crocker (1966), Dales (1968) and Montgomery (1972).

TABLE 5.2 List of Annex I parties to the convention

Australia	Austria	Belarus	Belgium	Bulgaria
Canada	Croatia	Czech Republic	Denmark	Estonia
European Community	Finland	France	Germany	Greece
Hungary	Iceland	Ireland	Italy	Japan
Latvia	Liechtenstein	Lithuania	Luxembourg	Monaco
Netherlands	New Zealand	Norway	Poland	Portugal
Romania	Russian Federation	Slovakia	Slovenia	Spain
Sweden	Switzerland	Turkey	Ukraine	UK
USA				

Source: UNFCCC.

for an international treaty to tackle climate change. For this purpose, the IPCC formed the Intergovernmental Negotiation Committee (INC). The INC met first in February 1991 when its representatives discussed and established the United Nations Framework Convention on Climate Change (UNFCCC). The UNFCCC sets an overall framework for intergovernmental efforts to address the challenge posed by climate change and entered into force in March 1994. By that date it was signed by 166 countries and only 10 years later that number rose to 188 countries.[3] This almost worldwide membership makes the convention one of the most universally supported international agreements on the environment. Under this agreement, concerned parties claim that a substantial rise in GHG emissions will affect terrestrial and maritime ecosystems, resulting in an average rising of the temperature of the Earth's surface and atmosphere through an increase in the natural greenhouse-layer effect. Therefore, the ultimate objective of the convention is to stabilize GHG concentrations in the atmosphere at a level that will prevent dangerous anthropogenic interference with the climate system.[4] Further, all members should promote sustainable technologies to allow less harmful economic growth. The convention is only a proposal, with no time constraint or mandatory emission cap for the parties. Article 4 of the convention suggests that the parties should lower their emissions to the levels of 1990. Further, the convention holds provisions for updates and leaves to the Conference of Parties (COP) the task to set mandatory goals under the legal form of protocols. The convention divides country members into three groups. The first one is called Annex I parties. It includes industrialized countries which were members of the Organization for Economic Cooperation and Development (OECD) in 1992 and countries with economies in transition (EIT). Table 5.2 lists Annex I parties under the convention.

These countries should adopt climate change measures with the aim of reducing their GHG emissions to 1990 levels. However, no legally binding targets are set by the convention. The EIT countries are granted some flexibility in implementing commitments, in being allowed to choose a year other than 1990 as their base year.

The second group is called Annex II parties. This group consists of the Annex I members without the EIT countries. Members of this group can help developing countries finance emission reduction activities. The scope of such an opportunity is twofold: fight the adverse

[3]Please refer to the UNFCCC website for an updated and detailed list. As of November 2012, UNFCCC had 194 parties.
[4]UNFCCC – Article 2.

effects of climate change in other regions and enhance the transfer of environmentally friendly technology to EIT and developing countries. The third and last group, called Non-Annex I, consists mostly of developing countries. These countries have no commitment to reduce emissions under the convention. Developing countries are not part of these legally binding targets. The reason behind this exclusion is that it was considered that the climate change problems at the moment have been caused by the industrialization of developed countries in the last decades.

The institutional body of the UNFCCC (and the Kyoto Protocol) is the UNFCCC secretariat. It has been hosted in Bonn (Germany) since 1996. The secretariat is staffed by international civil servants and supports all institutions involved in the climate change process, particularly the COP (see Section 5.3.2), the subsidiary bodies and their bureau.

5.3.2 The Conference of Parties and the Subsidiary Bodies

The supreme body of the convention is the COP, which meets at least once a year to assess progress in dealing with climate change. The COP regularly reports progress in the implementation of the convention and makes public all policy instruments adopted under the convention. Further, the COP takes all necessary decisions to promote the effective implementation of the convention.[5] Beside the COP, two subsidiary bodies have been introduced with the aim of steering preparatory work for the COP:

- The Subsidiary Body for Scientific and Technological Advice (SBSTA), defined under Article 9 of the convention, assists the COP with scientific and technological matters. SBSTA identifies innovative technologies and provides assessments of the state of scientific knowledge relating to climate change. It promotes the transfer of environmentally friendly technologies and also carries out methodological work in specific areas (LULUCF, REDD, HFC) including adaptation and vulnerability.
- The Subsidiary Body for Implementation (SBI), defined under Article 10, reports to the COP about the overall effectiveness of the implementation of the convention. The SBI examines national communications and emission inventories submitted by parties. Furthermore, the SBI assists the COP during the preparation of its decisions with reviews of the environmental state of the art.

5.3.3 The Kyoto Protocol

At the first conference of the UNFCCC, the negotiations for a protocol with binding targets started. The Kyoto Protocol (KP) is the result of intensive negotiations at the third meeting held by the COP in 1997 in Kyoto, Japan. The KP commits Annex I countries to individual, legally binding targets to limit or reduce their GHG emissions.[6] The KP entered into force in February 2005 driven by Russia's ratification and the first commitment period ran from 2008 and ended in 2012. In fact, as specified by Article 25 of the KP, the criteria to make the protocol active is that at least 55 parties have signed the protocol. Or, under a different measure, at least

[5]Please refer to UNFCCC Article 7, 2.

[6]The KP covers six main GHGs: carbon dioxide (CO_2), methane (CH_4), nitrous oxide (N_2O), hydrofluorocarbons (HFCs), perfluorocarbons (PFCs) and sulfur hexafluoride (SF_6).

TABLE 5.3 Quantified emission limitation as contained in Annex B of the Kyoto Protocol

Annex I parties	Emission reduction or limitation (base year)
Australia, Austria, Belarus, Belgium, Bulgaria, Czech Republic, Denmark, Estonia, European Community, Finland, France, Germany, Greece, Ireland, Italy, Latvia, Liechtenstein, Lithuania, Luxembourg, Monaco, Netherlands, Portugal, Romania, Slovakia, Slovenia, Spain, Sweden, Switzerland, Turkey, UK and Northern Ireland	−8%
USA	−7%
Canada, Hungary, Japan, Poland	−6%
Croatia	−5%
New Zealand, Russian Federation, Ukraine	0%
Norway	+1%
Australia	+8%
Iceland	+10%

Source: UNFCCC.

55% of the total worldwide GHG emissions have to be covered. With the Russian ratification, both criteria have been fulfilled. At the time of writing, 191 countries had ratified the protocol.

Under the KP, countries are separated into two different main groups: those committed to binding targets (i.e., developed countries) and those that do not face mitigation targets, referred to as Non-Annex I countries. Quite interestingly, out of 191 countries only 41 plus the European Union (EU) are referred to as Annex I countries (see Table 5.2). However, these countries alone account for 61% of GHG emissions. As of November 2012, 40 of the 41 Annex I countries had ratified the KP (the exceptions being the USA and Canada, which decided in 2011 to stop fulfilling their obligations and withdraw from the KP).

Based on the claim that developed countries are largely responsible for past GHG emissions, the KP places a heavier burden on Annex I countries. More precisely, these countries commit to ensure that their GHG emissions do not increase above a certain percentage of a specified base year by 2012 (see Table 5.3).[7] As part of the quantified emission limitations, every country has assigned amount units (AAUs). These units are calculated in tons of CO_2 equivalent (CO_2-e) and are allocated at the beginning of each commitment period. To ease the accounting of the six different GHGs, offending gases are weighted by their global warming potential (GWP, see previous section). Besides strict policy regulations, the KP establishes three so-called flexible mechanisms in order to give the Annex I countries more flexibility to reduce emissions. The KP demands that the use of the mechanisms is supplemental to domestic actions and that these actions should constitute a significant element of the effort made by each party included in Annex I to meet its quantified emission limitation and reduction. The three flexible mechanisms of the KP are:

- *Emission trading* (as defined in Article 17 of the KP). Annex I parties can acquire AAUs from other Annex I parties and use them for compliance under the KP.

[7]The targets differ per country; see KP Articles 3, 5–8 for a more detailed description.

- *Joint implementation* (JI, as defined in Article 6 of the KP). The Annex B parties[8] can contribute to their emission targets by investing in emission reduction projects in other Annex B countries. These investments eventually result in emission reduction units (ERUs) that can be used for compliance in the KP.
- *Clean development mechanism* (CDM, as defined in Article 12 of the KP). Annex I parties can undertake emission reduction projects in developing countries (Non-Annex I), which lead to CER credits. These credits can be used for compliance in the industrialized countries. Contrary to AAUs and ERUs, CERs come from countries without emission reduction requirements, therefore augmenting defined emission capacities for Annex I countries.

These mechanisms should help all parties achieve GHG emission reductions at least cost.

5.3.4 The Road to Paris

In 2012, the Kyoto Protocol was extended for a second period by a limited group of countries, including the EU. However the recent ambition of UNFCCC negotiations has been to establish a new global agreement to succeed the Kyoto Protocol.

The general form of the agreement was settled in Durban in 2011. It would be 'a protocol, another legal instrument or an agreed outcome with legal force', applicable to all parties (i.e. developed and developing countries). The terms were to be agreed by 2015 and the agreement would enter into force by 2020.

Further details were negotiated at successive meetings in Doha (2012), Warsaw (2013) and Lima (2014). The agreement will be fundamentally different to the Kyoto Protocol. Countries will be able to delineate the extent and nature of their commitments (or 'Intended Nationally Determined Contributions' – INDCs), with no top-down review process, oversight or verification. Each country will submit its INDC by June 2015, before the final form agreement is negotiated in Paris in December 2015.

The shape of the Paris Agreement is likely to be soft and flexible, reflecting its bottom-up nature. In part this is because climate change negotiations are still dominated by the developing/developed country divide, arising from the UNFCCC's core principle of common but differentiated responsibilities between rich and poor countries. The developed world continues to argue for legally binding cuts, whilst the developing world argues for softer language, pointing to the developed world's historic emissions and for poorer countries' right to develop in the same manner.

However developing countries such as China and India, which were not required to make emission reduction commitments under the Kyoto Protocol, are now major emitters, even on a per capita basis, and it is becoming clear that the Paris Agreement cannot reflect the same structural divide between Annex I and non-Annex I parties. The joint announcement in 2014 that USA and China would limit their emissions within a clear time frame was groundbreaking; it is to be hoped that the announcement will create momentum for other developing countries to increase their ambitions in time for Paris.

---

[8]Annex B includes all KP countries that have agreed to a target for their greenhouse gas emissions, including all Annex I countries (as amended in 1998) except for Turkey and Belarus.

Finally, it is worth noting that a more flexible agreement could have some advantages. It will be easier for the international climate change dialogue to respond to structural changes in the world economy, such as the rise of the BRICs. Furthermore, it may be possible to scale up emissions cuts over time, to meet the 'ambition gap' between current pledges and the internationally agreed target of 2 degrees of warming.

5.4 THE EU ETS

5.4.1 Institutional Features

5.4.1.1 The European Directive Annex B signatories to the KP have a free hand to determine the tools they set up in order to achieve their emissions targets. So, in 1997 the EU engaged as a whole with an 8% reduction target of one of the most known anthropogenic greenhouse gases: CO_2. Because the EU was the legal entity in charge of achieving the KP target, the European Commission (EC) proposed in 2001 the creation of a European-wide instrument, the EU ETS, in order to help European countries to meet their national commitments. The legal framework of the EU ETS is laid down in Directive 2003/87/EC (see EUEPA (2003)). The EU ETS started in January 2005 and is divided into three phases. Phase I ran from 2005 to 2007 and had the function of a pilot phase in which the scheme was established. Phase II ran from 2008 to 2012, parallel to the Kyoto commitment period. Phase III corresponds to the post-Kyoto period and runs from 2013 to 2020.

5.4.1.2 The Contents of the EU ETS For the first phase, emissions were initially capped at 2.1 billion tons of CO_2 annually. The cap covered emissions from more than 12,000 installations with the highest GHG emission levels, in the 25 then 27 countries of the EU. These installations belonged to five industrial sectors: combustion (including electricity production, district heating, cogeneration and refineries), metal, cement, glass–ceramics and paper–board products. Emissions from households and transportation were notably not a part of the system. The EU ETS is a classic cap-and-trade system as described in Section 5.2.2.

Allowances for emissions equal to the total cap are distributed annually to each country (Section 5.4.2 describes in more detail the existing and employed allocation criteria). Then, each member state has to develop a National Allocation Plan (NAP) that states the total quantity of allowances allocated to each single installation. The NAPs are set at the beginning of each phase of the EU ETS. In order to homogenize the distribution of the permits among the different countries and industries and to increase supervision, an EU-wide target replaced the current 27 national targets (and NAPs). To reach the global EU target of reducing emissions by 21% below 2005 levels by 2020, allowances will be limited to a maximum of 1.72 billion units,[9] with total emission allowances cut by 1.74% annually as of 2013 and until 2020.

An allowance, called the emission unit allowance (EUA), gives the right to emit 1 ton of CO_2 during a specified period. Therefore, the amount of allowance allocated to each installation constitutes the amount of CO_2 emissions the installation can emit. Installations are then free to trade permits throughout the EU, creating a market in allowances. Installations have to report actual emissions annually by the end of March. By 30 April each year, each participating installation has to surrender a number of allowances equal to the total emissions

[9] To be compared with the current allocation of 2.08 billion tons for the second trading period.

from the installation during the preceding year. If the installation fails to surrender the necessary permits, it has to pay a penalty. In Phase I, this penalty was €40 for each ton of CO_2 emitted; in Phases II and III it was increased to €100 for each ton of CO_2. This penalty does not waive the obligation to submit the missing allowances.

Among others, Ellerman (2003), Tietenberg (2006), Convery and Redmond (2007), Kruger and Pizer (2004) and Chesney *et al.* (2013) provide a comprehensive discussion on the EU ETS setup. Zapfel and Vainio (2002) overview how the debate on greenhouse gas emissions trading has evolved in Europe since the adoption of the KP in 1997.

5.4.1.3 Banking and Borrowing Unused permits from Phase I have no redemption value. However, the subsequent phases are characterized by unlimited banking and one year borrowing. The bankability of emission permits is the ability to use them in periods subsequent to the one in which they were allocated. This means that any incumbent envisaging to emit less CO_2 than the amount of permits it owns has the possibility to store them instead of selling them directly on the market. Saving can be motivated by expectations of production growth or of an increase in the carbon constraints in the future that may bring about an increase in the price of emission permits. Banking permits smooth the price evolution over the long term by providing incentives to achieve early emissions reductions. Borrowing provisions allow regulated emitters to use part of their future allocations to cover their present emissions. In the environmental economics literature, banking and borrowing provisions have been proposed with the aim of enforcing the credibility of cap-and-trade schemes and allowing greater temporal flexibility. Interested readers can refer to Rubin (1996) or Schennach (2000) for an analysis of the consequences of banking and borrowing on the intertemporal trading of emission permits.

5.4.1.4 National Registries Each member state of the EU ETS is required to set up a national registry to record the creation, transfer and surrender of allowances. Member states report allocations and verified emissions at the installation level to a central registry in Brussels called the Community Independent Transaction Log (CITL). The role of the CITL is to gather information from national registries centrally to facilitate allowance tracking and the assessment of installation compliance each year. Each registry operates through a link established with the International Transaction Log (ITL) put in place and administered by the UNFCCC secretariat. The ITL verifies registry transactions in real time to ensure they are conducted in accordance with the set of rules agreed under the KP. In 2008, EU registries had to switch their connections from the CITL to the ITL. The ITL has to conduct Kyoto checks on transactions proposed by both EU and non-EU registries. In the case of transactions involving EU registries, the ITL forwards information to the CITL so that it can conduct supplementary checks defined under the EU scheme.

5.4.1.5 International Offsets With the aim of increasing the number of low-cost compliance alternatives within the EU ETS, European policy regulators recognized the use of certificates from project-based mechanisms for compliance purposes. This has been made possible by provisions for linking the EU ETS with the Kyoto flexible mechanisms, such as the CDM and the JI.[10] A second rationale behind such a linking directive is to stimulate

[10]CDM and JI mechanisms are described in the next sections.

the demand for CERs originated by CDM projects and thus assist developing countries hosting these projects in achieving their sustainable development targets. As a result, the linking directive opens the EU ETS to the CDM and JI projects, enabling relevant installation to use CERs for compliance purposes. However, the revisions of Phase III greatly changed this *modus operandi* in order to reduce the supply of ineffective (or hot air) offsets: the use of flexible mechanism units (CDM/JI) is now conditional on the passage of a global agreement pushing the required EU reduction to 30% by 2020. Without an agreement, the use of flexible credits may be limited to 3% of member states' total emissions in 2005.[11] Under Phase III, Kyoto credits are no longer de facto compliant with the EU ETS. CERs representing emission reductions occurring before January 2013 had to be swapped with EUA for full fungibility. CERs related to reductions occurring after December 2012 cannot be swapped but are considered fully equivalent with EUA of Phase III. Finally, future CERs coming from new projects (registered after 31 December 2012) will be eligible if they are located in a least-developed country.

5.4.2 Allocation Criteria

As mentioned, each member state is required to develop a NAP that specifies the total number of allowances that it intends to allocate for a specific period to every relevant installation. A NAP should be based on objective and transparent criteria. Allocation criteria can be divided into two groups: (i) allocation based on current or future activities (updating); (ii) allocation based on historical activities (grandfathering).

Updating is an approach that is based on current or future activities as opposed to historical activities. Basing future allocation on current emissions creates a disincentive to abate because every unit of abatement comes at a cost not only in the current period but also causing reductions in future allocations. Please refer to Böhringer and Lange (2005) for further discussion. Before an approach is introduced it must be decided which allocation base will be used for the allocation schemes, and upon which base year(s) the allocation schemes will be based. The choice of the base year(s) clearly has an effect on how relevant companies are affected, as discussed below. The allocation base determines which activities the allocations will be based upon. One can distinguish allocation bases into three groups, as follows: (i) input based; (ii) emission based; (iii) production or output based. Interested readers can refer to Aihman and Zetterberg (2005) for a more detailed discussion.

5.4.2.1 Input-Based Allocation Input-based allocations are based upon the input of resources for an installation. An example is the amount of energy that an installation uses. The advantage of input-based allocation is that it is easy to monitor. The biggest disadvantage of this approach is that it does not reward the efficiency of the installations. An efficient installation can produce, for instance, more electricity with the same amount of fossil fuel than a less efficient installation. But with an input-based approach both installations would be allocated the same amount of allowance for a given input unit.

[11]Provided that the additional quantity does not exceed 50% of EU-wide reduction between 2008 and 2020.

5.4.2.2 Emission-Based Allocation Emission-based allocation means that allocations are based upon emissions previously generated by the installation in a base year. This approach has the advantage that it is simple to implement. Also, emissions are relatively easy to monitor and measure once meters are installed. However, it does not reward early action by the installation if a late base year is used. It also does not take into account changes in installations which have taken place after the base year used for allocation.

The emission-based allocation for an installation is calculated as the installation's share of emissions in the whole sector multiplied by the total allocations to all installations in the sector:

$$N_{j,i}^{e} = \frac{E_j^{base}}{E_s^{base}} \times N_{s,i}$$

where $j = 1, \ldots, n$ is the jth installation and $i = 1, \ldots, T$ is the ith trading period of the allocation. $N_{j,i}^{e}$ corresponds to the amount of allocated permits at time i to installation j; E_j^{base} are the CO_2 emissions of installation j in the base year; and E_s^{base} are the total CO_2 emissions of the entire sector s in the base year. Unsurprisingly, the choice of the base year is an extremely (politically) relevant issue. On the one hand, early actions (abatement investments) implemented before the base year are not properly rewarded. On the other hand, business growth or economic boom after the base year may be severely penalized. In the EU ETS, historical-based allocation criteria have been used. In particular, most of the NAPs used the year 1990 as the baseline reference. Ellerman and Montero (2007) overview the political aspects associated with such a decision.

5.4.2.3 Production-Based Allocation In the production-based allocation, the output (production) of an installation or a group of installations is multiplied by an emissions factor. The result is then used as the base for the allocation of allowances. Emissions factors can be actor-specific or specific for a group of installations. For instance, in production-based allocation with actor-specific emissions factors, the allocation for an installation is calculated as

$$N_{j,i}^{p} = \frac{E_j^{base}}{P_s^{base}} \times P_j^{prod.year} \times f^j$$

where P_s^{base} and $P_j^{prod.year}$ are the production of installation j in the base year and in the current year, respectively. The total number of allocated allowances is adjusted with the scale factor f^j such that the total amount of allocated allowances corresponds to the allocation of the entire sector s. With this approach, if the installation has a current higher production output than in the base year, it receives more allowances.

5.4.2.4 Auctioning and Grandfathering Regardless of the allocation criteria, permits can be auctioned off or freely distributed, so-called grandfathering. The environmental economics literature typically prefers auctioning. The economic rationale behind such preference is threefold. First, auctioning can lead to a more equal and fair final allocation. Companies that have implemented abatement options in the past are rewarded for such early actions because they will possibly purchase fewer allowances. Also, new participants in the permit market are treated the same way as older participants. Second, auctioning should avoid windfall profits that are generally associated with grandfathering.[12] Third, under textbook assumptions, polluters reveal their abatement costs in an auctioning process. The fact that the revenues from auctioning can be invested in the public sector is in reality the political rationale behind auctioning.

Grandfathering was the most common allocation approach in Phases I and II of the EU ETS. In particular, in Phase I member states had to allocate at least 95% of the allowances free of charge. For the five-year period of Phase II, member states had to allocate at least 90% of the allowances free of charge. Therefore there was an auctioning limit of 5% of allowances in Phase I and of 10% of allowances in Phase II. However, most of the member states did not take full advantage of the auctioning limit since auctioned allowances were recorded well below the allowed limit in Phase I, as is similarly the case in Phase II.

5.4.3 Market Players and the Permit Markets

5.4.3.1 The Relevant Industries While the KP includes all the emissions of the six main anthropogenic GHGs, regulators of the EU ETS chose to cap on a mandatory basis only CO_2 emissions from major industrial installations belonging to five industrial sectors: combustion, metal, cement, glass–ceramics and paper–board production. In 2012, the aviation sector was added to increase the coverage of transport-based emissions. The sector represents the second-largest emitting sector covered by the scheme, after the power sector. An enlargement of the scope to include new sectors (petrochemical, ammonia and aluminium sectors) and two new gases (N_2O and PFCs) is highly probable. However, transport, shipping, agriculture and forestry remain outside the scope of Phase III.[13] In practice, the regulation does not apply to the sectoral or company level, but to individual industrial installations. The smallest industrial installations are not included. There follows a list of most of the relevant installations: combustion installations with a thermal input exceeding 20 MW; mineral oil refineries; coke ovens; metal ore roasting or siltering installations; installations for the production of pig iron or steel; installations for the production of cement clinker; installations for the manufacture of glass and glass fibre; installations for the manufacture of ceramic products; industrial plants for the production of pulp, paper and board; airlines.

Excluding the aviation industries, the covered installations emit approximately 2 gigatons of CO_2 per year, about 40% of European GHG emissions. However, each sector has a different pollution-intensity type of production. Table 5.4 lists the CO_2-equivalent intensity of some selected industrial sectors. The electricity sector is opportunely left out due to its different mix-generation capacity. It is evident how European industry is affected differently by the EU ETS. As a result, market players for permits are also quite different.

5.4.3.2 Market Players In general, one can distinguish four types of market players in the EU ETS: governments; industrial sectors; energy sector; financial institutions. In their role as regulators, governments organize the allocation of emission allowances. At the highest

[12]In theory, purchasing permits should oblige emitters to factor in the entire cost of permits and prevent them benefiting from undue profits incurred by pass-through of the permit costs to final consumers.

[13]Shipping is considered for inclusion at a later stage. For sectors not covered by the EU ETS, an average GHG reduction of 10% should be achieved, proportional to countries' GDP.

TABLE 5.4 GHG intensity from selected industrial processes in tons of CO_2-equivalent per ton of product

	GHG intensity (tCO_2-e/t prod.)
Steel	1.6–2
Aluminium	8.5
Cement	0.73–0.99
Ethylene	1.33
Ammonia	1.6–2.7
Petroleum refining	0.32–0.64
Pulp and paper	0.22–1.4

Source: Bernstein *et al.* (2007).

level, the EC approves or rejects NAPs. The EC also specifies guidelines for the flexibility mechanisms of the KP. At a lower level, national regulators control and operate the national registries that link into the central EU transaction log.

A prominent player is the energy sector. Due to the ongoing liberalization process of the European electricity industry, most of the utilities already have well-developed trading desks. Therefore, the inclusion of emission permits in their trading portfolios has been a relatively natural step. The rest of the industrial sectors covered by the EU ETS are instead less active on the market.

Because the access to the permit market is generally not restricted to covered installations, financial institutions have been quite active players in Phase I and II of EU ETS. Financial institutions include brokers, banks, insurers and private carbon funds. The rationale behind not restricting the market to compliance agents stems from the need for liquidity in the market. Financial institutions can play the role of intermediaries for a number of small emitters who are not familiar with the markets and prefer delegating their allowance management to a third party.

5.4.3.3 Markets for CO_2 Emission Permits Concerning market platforms, trading of EUAs on a forward basis began in spring 2003. A spot market was launched at the beginning of 2005 just prior to the launch of the first national registries in February 2005. Exchange-based futures trading began in mid-2005. The volume of transactions has been increasing steadily. In 2005, only 262 Mt trades were exchanged. In 2006, already 809 Mt were traded, with a steady increase to 1,500 Mt in 2007 and 4,400 Mt of exchanged allowances in 2011. EUAs are traded on several organized exchanges and outside them. In 2011, the market for allowances was split between the biggest exchanges, which represented 42% of all EUA, CER and ERU transactions, over-the-counter (OTC) (39%) and bilateral trades (12%):[14]

- *The European Climate Exchange (ECX) in London*, which is by far the biggest in terms of volume and value. ECX is part of the Climate Exchange plc, which also includes the

[14] Interested readers can refer to Chesney *et al.* (2013) for a detailed description of the market platforms in Europe.

Chicago Climate Exchange (see next section). Launched in 2005 and based in London, ECX uses the electronic trading platform and clearance services of ICE (the former International Petroleum Exchange). In addition to the traditional EUA and CER futures, the exchange offers spot prices (immediate settlement) for both types of contracts, option contracts (European call and put), spread trading (calendar spreads and CER–EUA spreads) and strip trading. To accommodate and lure OTC trading into the exchange, ECX also offers exchange-for-physical (EFP) facilities, as well as exchange-for-swap (EFS) and block trade facilities.

- *Nord Pool*, one of the largest power derivatives exchanges, provides marketplaces for trading in physical and financial contracts in the Nordic countries (it is based in Oslo and serves Finland, Sweden, Denmark and Norway). It was acquired by the NASDAQ OMX group in 2008 and now serves as a platform for the carbon and energy offers of NASDAQ OMX. Reflecting its precursory role in emission trading, the exchange was almost the sole provider of exchanged CERs and the second platform for EUAs after ECX during the first years that followed the launch of the EU ETS.
- *The European Energy Exchange (EEX)*, founded in 2002 as a result of the merger of the two German power exchanges Leipzig and Frankfurt. It trades spot and futures as well as coal and natural gas contracts. In an attempt to consolidate its position in Continental Europe, in 2007 EEX started a partnership with the derivative exchange EUREX to provide for its clients' emission trading capacities (using the EUREX electronic platform).

5.4.4 The Future of the EU ETS

In 2013, the EU ETS tightened its centralized cap. It is reduced by 1.74% each year of the average annual level of the Phase II cap. To ensure that adequate mitigation efforts are undertaken within European borders, access to UNFCCC project offsets is limited to no more than 50% of the reduction required in the EU ETS.

The EU ETS will also incorporate three new directives designed to increase the perimeter of regulation and to improve the mitigation process within the borders of the EU: (i) the partial auctioning of allowances; (ii) the inclusion of the aviation industry; and (iii) a practice of 'effort sharing' for sectors not included in the EU ETS, plus additional measures to improve the performance of the scheme.

- A proposed auctioning of around 30% of the total number of allowances in 2013. Furthermore, 100% of allowances for the power sector should be auctioned. The target is a progressive phase-out of the grandfathering practice, to reach a global 70% of allowances auctioned by 2020 and a 100% auctioning by 2020. However, certain energy-intensive sectors that are at risk of leakage (offshoring) continue to receive their allowances for free.
- An Energy Efficiency Directive (EED) was proposed by the European Commission on June 2011. This directive, whose aim is to save energy and to reach the EC's self-imposed target of a 20% cut in primary energy consumption by 2020, may create downward pressure on EUA prices by providing a competing command-and-control measure to reduce emissions.
- An enlargement of the scope of the scheme to include new sectors (petrochemical, ammonia and aluminium sectors) and two new gases (N_2O and PFCs).

- The use of flexible mechanism units (CDM/JI) will be conditional on the passage of a global agreement pushing the required EU reduction to 30% by 2020. Without an agreement, the use of flexible credits may be limited to 3% of member states' total emissions in 2005.
- With the conjunction of the financial crisis at international level and multiple European crises, verified emissions declined 2.4% year-on-year in 2011, after a significant and continuous decline of emissions in 2008 and 2009. The new EED proposes setting aside a certain share of EUAs to account for the weak demand for permits. According to the World Bank[15] and Deutsche Bank,[16] '*the decline translates into an additional surplus of about 380 million EUAs in the scheme, now expected to be oversupplied by about one billion tons until 2020*'. As such, the idea of setting aside permits touches upon two important limitations of the EU scheme: (i) the capacity to maintain a constant incentive towards mitigation; and (ii) the ability for the scheme to have dynamic and conditional rules instead of static ones.

5.5 REGIONAL MARKETS: A FRAGMENTED LANDSCAPE

5.5.1 Regional Markets

With the future international space partially left empty, countries and regions are in the process of developing domestic solutions that differ in their scope and pace but almost always combine elements of cap-and-trade schemes, baseline and credit mechanisms, carbon taxes, subsidies, emission standards and renewable energy and energy efficiency certificates. Along with the EU, which will remain the main player in the carbon field, multiple competing solutions will emerge in the near future at the national or regional levels, creating a fragmented regulatory environment with specific deadlines and requisites.

Here we provide a rapid overview of the most promising regulations in Annex B countries. Chesney *et al.* (2013) discuss in more detail the landscape of current and future carbon markets.

- **The United States**

  Considering the large uncertainties surrounding any new legislations for emission reductions, the US efforts are for now essentially spearheaded by the new AB 32 legislation in California and its role in the Western Climate Initiative.

  AB 32 requires California to cut greenhouse gas emissions to 1990 levels by 2020. It also identifies a cap-and-trade programme as one of the strategies the state will employ to reduce GHG emissions. During the programme's first compliance period (2013–2014), large stationary sources that emit at least 25,000 tCO_2-e per year in the industry and electricity sectors will be covered, including out-of-state generation (i.e., imports). As a cost-control measure, AB 32 allows entities covered by the scheme to purchase and use offsets for compliance purposes, but volumes are limited to 8% of annual emissions. Offsets will come from a domestic offsets programme with the possibility of importing international forest offsets. California also has a strong renewable energy mandate and a requirement that the carbon content of the state's vehicle fuels be cut by 10% by 2020.

[15] State and Trends of the Carbon Market 2012, World Bank.

[16] EU Emissions: 2011 VED Raises the Pressure, 4 April 2012.

California is the leading member of the Western Climate Initiative (WCI), an association of American and Canadian states which aim to reduce regional GHG emissions to 15% below 2005 levels by 2020. California and Québec (the other regional jurisdiction that passed a cap-and-trade regulation) have worked towards linking their systems from the start of their programmes in January 2013.

- **New Zealand**
  In early 2011, a review of the NZ ETS commenced, as required by the Climate Change Response Act 2002. The scope of the review included the following elements: coverage of agriculture, allocation mechanisms for New Zealand units, whether or not to keep the fixed-price cap of NZ$25 and the one-for-two obligation for emitters, and whether synthetic greenhouse gases should be included in the ETS.
- **Japan**
  The government of Japan considers the ETS component an important policy measure for Japan to achieve its announced target of reducing GHG emissions by 25% by 2020 compared with 1990 levels. However, Japan has tied the development of an ETS to broad international agreement, which has the foreseeable result of deferring its implementation. To compensate for the ETS deferral, other components (introducing a carbon tax and establishing a feed-in tariff for all renewable energy sources) were to be passed in 2011.
- **China**
  In March 2011, China released its 12th Five-Year Plan of National Economic and Social Development. This sets out a carbon-intensity reduction target of 17% and aims to cut energy intensity by 16% by 2015. These targets are consistent with the 40–45% reduction in carbon intensity from 2005 levels that was first announced at the Copenhagen Conference and reaffirmed at the Cancun Conference. As part of the 12th Five-Year Plan, China will increase forest cover by 12.5 million hectares by 2015, improve GHG emissions and energy monitoring systems, promote energy efficiency in industrial plants and buildings, support the expansion of public rail transport infrastructure and continue the development of non-fossil-fuel energy sources.

  China is introducing pilot emission trading schemes in two provinces (Guangdong and Hubei) and five cities (Beijing, Tianjin, Shanghai, Chongqing and Shenzhen) that may be expanded to a national scheme by 2015.

5.5.2 Voluntary Markets

In addition to the regional initiatives, voluntary carbon initiatives have emerged rapidly to offer companies and regional institutions a chance to offset their emissions. Benefiting from an increased awareness of companies and some marketing and compliance strategies to internalize carbon costs, the voluntary markets have progressed fast in terms of volume and value. According to a recent report by Ecosystem Marketplace and New Carbon Finance, the volume of voluntary permits went from 10 $MtCO_2$-e in 2002 to 123.4 $MtCO_2$-e in 2008 (doubling its size from 2007), for a 2008 market value of US$705 million. However, it receded due to the financial crisis and the numerous uncertainties surrounding the KP and the regulations of the EU ETS and stabilized in 2011 around 79 Mt for immediate or future delivery. Overall transaction volumes decreased 39% from 2010.

The voluntary market is somehow difficult to monitor closely because it encompasses a large number of small, ad hoc projects traded OTC. Therefore, the numbers reported above correspond to a low boundary for the real numbers of total voluntary units exchanged. OTC trades cover a large spectrum of projects, methodologies and purposes. Even with the help of several consolidations over the past years, several standards are still used for the origination of VERs. Among them, the prominent standards by order of volume importance were in 2011 the Verified Carbon Standard (49% of OTC trades), the Gold Standard (9%), the Climate Action Reserve Protocols (10%) and the American Carbon Registry Standard (4.5%). With a renewed interest in renewables, markets have been targeting Asia and Africa as the main sources of new energy and forestry projects.

Private companies are the primary buyers of voluntary units (66% of volume in 2008). As this new market matures, more and more intermediaries (investment companies and liquidity providers) have entered the markets, shifting the motivation from social responsibility to pure investment. According to the World Bank, 80% of credits were transacted by voluntary buyers (50% of them based in Europe) with the intent of retiring credits, while 59% were using the credits to communicate on their corporate environmental and sustainable policies; 6% of buyers used voluntary permits to 'green' their supply chain.

5.6 A NEW ASSET CLASS: CO_2 EMISSION PERMITS

CO_2 marketable permits can be considered as a *pseudo*-commodity whose price, as with any standard commodity, is a function of demand and supply. In particular, the price of CO_2 emission permits reflects the expectations regarding the evolution of the equilibrium in supply and demand. Supply in the EU ETS is determined by the allowances that result from the combination of three major components. The first component is the initial allocation of permits. Banking and borrowing provisions constitute the second component. Both of these components are controlled by a regulatory authority and, therefore, they are generally well assessed by the market. The third component involves the CDM credits (CERs) that could be converted into emission permits valid for compliance in the EU ETS. The demand side depends on the evolution of the CO_2 emissions drivers of those installations covered by the EU ETS. This includes (long- and short-term) pollution abatement options, economic growth, energy-related prices and weather conditions.

As described in Section 5.4.1, the state of compliance is achieved when a relevant installation surrenders as many permits as its emissions for a given period of time. Conversely, a penalty is levied. Keeler (1991) shows that the success of pollution control strategies, reliant on market permits, depends deeply on the enforcement structure. The penalty in the EU ETS, therefore, ensures a correct incentive to comply with the scheme. In a pollution-constrained economy where polluting companies are subject to environmental regulations, the tighter the cap (and the higher the penalty), the larger the amount of pollution abatement undertaken by relevant companies. In particular, each firm faces a basic choice from two main abatement alternatives: short-term or long-term abatement measures. In the short term, installations covered by the EU ETS have different compliance options. They can adjust their CO_2 emissions through a production adjustment in volume and the improvement of their production efficiency (the quantity of CO_2 emitted per unit produced). For instance, an electricity generator can switch from cheap-but-dirty coal-fired production to expensive-but-clean gas-fired production. Undertaking a pollution-abatement investment is justified if this strategy is cheaper than purchasing emission permits. On the contrary, installations can buy CO_2 emission permits on the market to cover emissions exceeding their permit holding. Long-term abatement options encompass major changes of the production technology that, typically, correspond to expensive and irreversible commitments lasting decades.

Currently, one can identify three main approaches in the literature for modelling the price of CO_2 emission permits in the EU ETS framework. The first focuses on the major macroeconomic factors that affect the demand of emission permits, such as economic growth, energy-related commodities and weather. A second approach is concerned with the tasks of developing and applying statistical methods to the study of the economic principles behind the price of CO_2 emission permits. One can readily list several univariate (and a few multivariate) unconditional and conditional econometric investigations of CO_2 price time series. Finally, stochastic equilibrium models have been proposed for describing the price dynamics of emission permits.

5.6.1 Macroeconomic Models

Several authors support the argument that permit prices respond to macroeconomic fundamentals. To prove this, they try to identify statistically which factors affect permit demand (economic growth, abatement options, energy-related prices and weather) and supply (allocation of permits).[17] Because the EU ETS regulates energy-intensive industries, the economic rationale behind such models is extremely intuitive. A rise in the demand of CO_2 permits typically follows an increase in the pollution emissions. Larger emissions are generally caused by positive economic cycles, the experience of extreme weather conditions or an increase in the (short- and long-term) abatement measures. Most of this literature has therefore concentrated on the demand side and can be divided into three major categories.

5.6.1.1 Economic Growth As discussed in Ellerman and Joskow (2008), in a cap-and-trade system, a deterioration of economic conditions reduces the demand for CO_2 permits. Consequently, the market for permits tends to be long. The installations can then sell their permit surplus or bank it into the next period. Unsurprisingly, this is reflected in the price of emission permits that should be relatively low. This is what we observed in the EU ETS during the 2009 economic slowdown.

5.6.1.2 Weather Factors that influence electricity generation are bound to affect the demand for allowances. For instance, a hot summer can lead to a higher demand for electricity because of air-conditioning. When electricity is produced by fuel-fired power plants, extremely hot summers or cold winters lead to higher CO_2 emissions, increasing the demand for permits. Using European weather data, Mansanet-Bataller *et al.* (2007) identify extreme weather events as CO_2 price drivers. Employing precipitations data, Houpert and de Dominicis (2006) argue that rain is a non-negligible price driver in the EU ETS. High precipitation makes it possible to use more non-CO_2-emitting power sources and therefore reduces emissions in energy production. When hydroelectric production is low, electricity has to be produced by other means that are generally quite CO_2 intensive, like coal or gas. In particular, most of the Scandinavian countries rely heavily on hydroelectric power production. When rainfall is scarce, a country like Norway for instance has to import electricity from neighbouring

[17] Most of this analysis is undertaken relying on principal components analysis or standard regression techniques. Please refer to Section 5.6.2 for a more technical discussion on such econometric tools.

countries, very likely Denmark. Danish electricity is in large part generated from coal-fired plants, implying higher emissions. Yet in Scandinavian countries, cold and dry weather can also lead to a water shortage in the winter because frozen water cannot be used for power production. Conversely, when hydroelectric production is high (because of an increase in rainfall or because of melting ice in spring), emissions are fewer compared with coal-fired power production. However, too much rainfall may also cause off-time for hydroelectric installations.

5.6.1.3 Energy Prices and Abatement Options Energy-related prices can unsurprisingly exert a great influence on the demand for emission permits. For instance, if gas prices are lower than coal prices, electricity will more likely be produced by gas-fired plants. The use of gas in power generation emits fewer GHGs than the use of coal; therefore, a switch from coal to gas implies a lower demand of emission permits. Looking at fuel switching, the studies of Convery and Redmond (2007), Alberola *et al.* (2008) and Creti *et al.* (2012), among others, highlight the importance of energy-commodity prices.[18] As discussed above, fuel switching may be considered a short-term abatement option. Installations may lower their emissions by implementing long-term pollution abatement measures and improve their energy-efficiency standards. Whether or not such measures are implemented also depends on the cost of these technologies compared with the projected cost of allowances.

5.6.2 Econometric Investigation of CO_2 Permit Price Time Series

Recently, in an effort to bridge the gap between theory and observed market price behaviour, an increasing number of empirical studies have investigated the historical time series of the price of emission permits. In the context of the EU ETS Phase I, the following classes of processes have been applied to the permit price series: GARCH models (Paolella and Taschini, 2008; Benz and Trück, 2008), regime-switching models (Benz and Trück, 2008), mix-normal GARCH-models (Paolella and Taschini, 2008), jump-diffusion models (Daskalakis *et al.*, 2009), and two-factor models (Cetin and Verschuere, 2009). Given the emphasis of this chapter on continuous-time stochastic processes, the major statistics relating to spot and futures prices are reported first. An overview of the findings obtained using a discrete-time model (Paolella and Taschini, 2008; Benz and Trück, 2008) is presented. Then, the findings of Daskalakis *et al.* (2009) are discussed and calibration results of two standard continuous-time dynamics (geometric Brownian motion and mean-reverting process) are reported.

5.6.2.1 Key Statistics for the EUA Price Table 5.5 reports the major statistics for the futures with maturity December 2010 and December 2012, respectively, and for the spot price in Phase I and Phase II, respectively, of the CO_2 emission permits. Similarly, Table 5.6 considers log-returns. Figure 5.2 represents visually the price evolution registered on Bluenext of the spot prices in Phase I from 24 June 2005 until 25 April 2008 and the spot prices in Phase II from 21 April 2008 until 9 May 2011. Similarly, Figure 5.3 depicts the price evolution registered on the European Climate Exchange of the futures with maturity December 2010 from 22 April 2008 until 29 November 2010 and futures with maturity December 2012 from

[18] Please refer to Chevallier (2011) for a more complete list of studies that investigate the allowance price drivers in Phase I and II of the EU ETS.

TABLE 5.5 Summary statistics of the futures and spot prices of the CO_2 emission allowances

	EUA10	EUA12	Spot I	Spot II
Mean	16.79	17.99	10.36	15.92
Standard deviation	5.13	5.17	10.32	4.25
Skewness	1.30	1.49	0.33	1.37
Kurtosis	0.37	0.97	−1.51	0.95

EUA10 is the futures contract with maturity December 2010; EUA12 is the futures contract with maturity December 2012; Spot I is the spot price in Phase I; and Spot II is the spot price in Phase II.
Source: ECX and Bluenext.

22 April 2008 until 9 May 2011. All prices are quoted in €/ton of CO_2. The futures and spot Phase I plots show an abrupt discontinuous shift in May 2006. At that time, after it became clear that the total amount of expected pollution was overestimated, a significant market price correction occurred. Then, due to banking restrictions, the spot price in Phase I decreased towards zero. Whether in Phase I or II, spot and futures prices have often been characterized by a relatively high degree of volatility. However, neither spot nor futures markets were characterized by a good level of liquidity.

Paolella and Taschini (2008) investigate both the CO_2 market related to the EU ETS and the SO_2 market related to the acid-rain programme in the USA. The SO_2 returns exhibit a high percentage of zero returns, which precludes the use of distributions like the Student's t or hyperbolic distribution in the GARCH case. A mixed-normal GARCH model for the SO_2 returns provides a good in-sample fit and competitive out-of-sample value at risk (VaR) forecasts.

In terms of likelihood-based goodness-of-fit measures, the mixture models perform better than the t-GARCH model, which in turn performs better than the standard normal-GARCH model. For the CO_2 price, the authors consider an AR(1)-GARCH(1,1) model with different innovation distributions: a Student's t, a symmetric and asymmetric stable Paretian distribution and a generalized asymmetric t distribution. The best likelihood-based goodness-of-fit is provided by the GARCH model with a generalized asymmetric t innovation distribution. When a VaR forecast is carried out, no model performs well at all risk levels. However, by using a parametric model which places more weight both on more recent returns and on negative returns,

TABLE 5.6 Summary statistics of the futures and spot log-returns of the CO_2 emission allowances

	EUA10 LR	EUA12 LR	Spot I LR	Spot II LR
Mean	0	0	−0.01	0
Standard deviation	0.02	0.02	0.1	0.02
Skewness	−0.13	−0.15	−0.67	−0.19
Kurtosis	1.91	2.53	15.82	2.31

EUA10 LR is the log-return of futures contracts with maturity December 2010; EUA12 LR is the log-return of futures contracts with maturity December 2012; Spot I LR is the log-return of spot price in Phase I; and Spot II LR is the log-return of spot price in Phase II.
Source: ECX and Bluenext.

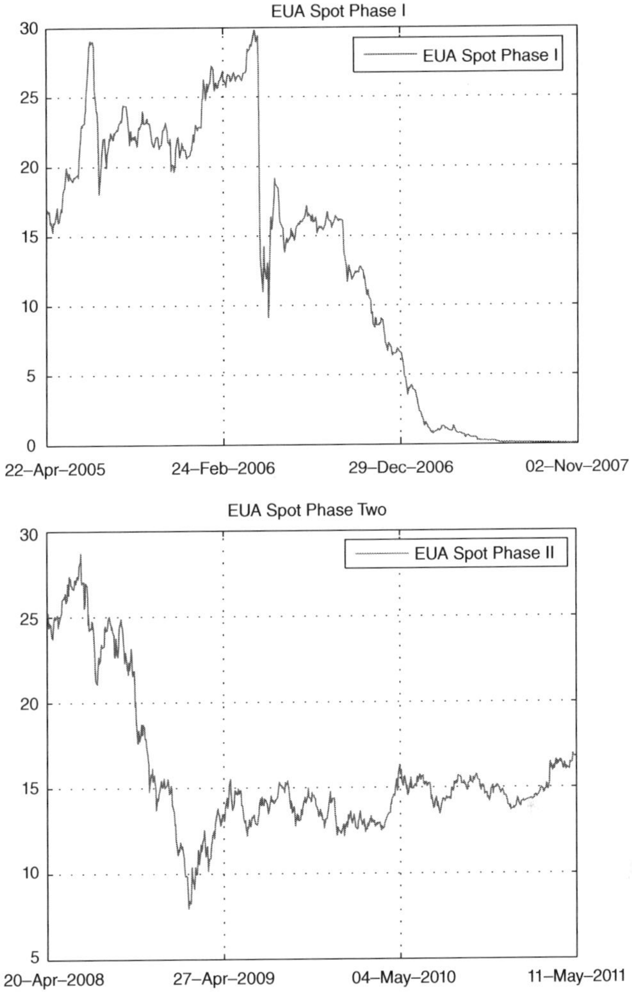

FIGURE 5.2 EUA Spot Phase I is the spot price of the emission allowances in Phase I from June 2005 until April 2008 (upper diagram). EUA Spot Phase II is the spot price of the emission allowances in Phase II from April 2008 until May 2011 (lower diagram)
Source: Bluenext.

a better VaR forecasting performance is achieved. Whereas Paolella and Taschini (2008) model the returns' time series, Benz & Trück (2008) analyse the adequacy of AR-GARCH and regime-switching models to represent the spot price time series of CO_2 emission permits in the first phase of the EU ETS. The best in-sample fit to the spot price process is offered by a regime-switching model with an autoregressive process for the base regime and a normal distribution for the spike regime. Performing an out-of-sample forecasting analysis for the CO_2 allowance log-returns in the different models, Benz and Trück (2008) detect only very minor differences for the evaluated mean absolute error and the mean-squared error

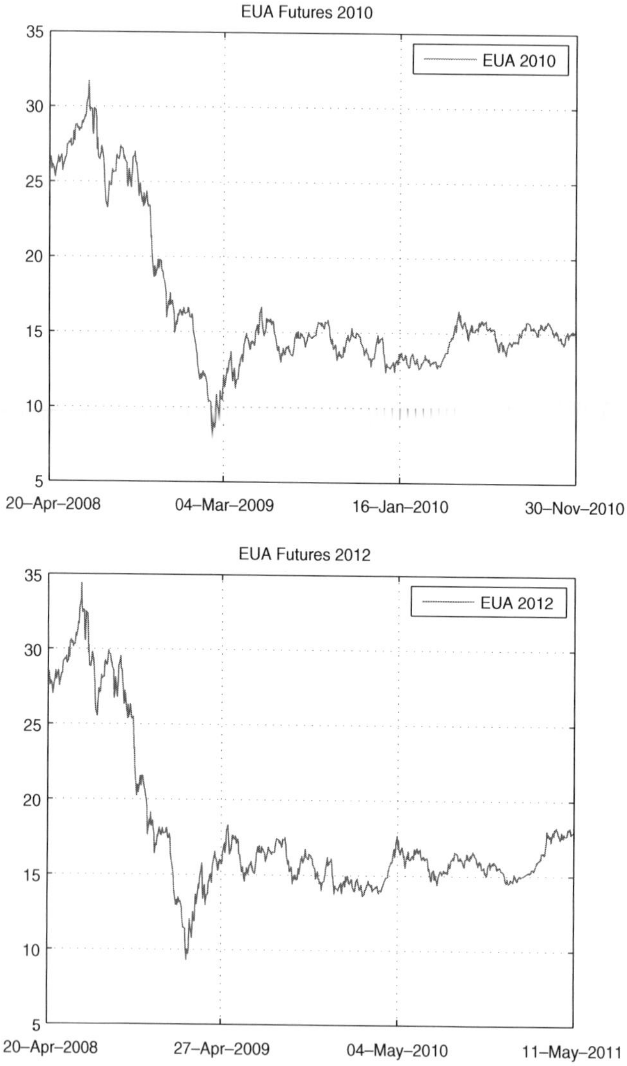

FIGURE 5.3 EUA 2010 is the futures price of the emission allowances with maturity December 2010 (upper diagram); EUA 2012 is the futures price of the emission allowances with maturity December 2012 (lower diagram). Time spans from April 2008 until November 2010 for futures with maturity December 2010; and from April 2008 until May 2011 for futures with maturity December 2012
Source: European Climate Exchange.

measures in terms of point forecasts. For risk managers, however, the density and interval forecasts are of more relevance. In this regard, the results showed that for one day-ahead density forecasts, the AR-GARCH and regime-switching models significantly outperform models with constant variance; thus, they reject the adequacy of a simple normal distribution and AR process.

Analysing the dynamics of the spot prices in Phase I, Daskalakis *et al.* (2009) compared six diffusion and jump diffusion continuous-time processes: geometric Brownian motion, mean-reverting square-root process, mean-reverting logarithm process, constant elasticity of variance, geometric Brownian motion process augmented by jumps and mean-reverting square-root process augmented by jumps. They determined that the geometric Brownian motion process augmented by jumps provides the best fit through maximum likelihood estimation. Given the abrupt spot price drop in May 2006, the addition of jumps unsurprisingly improves the performance significantly. Finally, the paper of Cetin and Verschuere (2009) exploits the arbitrage relationship existing in the EU ETS at the end of the first phase between CO_2 spot contracts and CO_2 forward contracts to derive the dynamics of the spot price of emission permits. The authors obtain such results by imposing exogenous dynamics on the forward contracts. Unfortunately, such a relation holds only when banking opportunities are not permitted (a situation which characterized only the transition time between the first and second phases of the EU ETS). Furthermore, the authors perform pricing analysis of digital options under incomplete information. In other words, they price digital options under the (realistic) assumption that the net amount of permits (i.e., the second factor) is not observable. For those readers interested in the growing market of emission derivative contracts, a simple closed-form pricing formula for European-style options is derived in Chesney and Taschini (2012).

5.6.2.2 Abatement in the Energy Sector: Fuel Switch Since Montgomery (1972), research on the theoretical price dynamics of emission permits has concentrated on the substitution principle between emission permits and abatement technology. After Montgomery (1972), such authors as Tietenberg (1985), Cronshaw and Kruse (1996) and Rubin (1996) also showed that, in a deterministic setup, the permit price corresponds to the marginal cost of abatement. In the context of the EU ETS, fuel switching is the cheapest abatement technology that can also be implemented easily in the short run. Fuel switching corresponds to the option to switch from coal- to gas-fired power generation. Gas-fired power production generates fewer emissions per MWh of electricity than coal-fired power generation; therefore, a fuel switch from coal to gas lowers emissions. Because coal and gas have different relative carbon intensities, rising CO_2 prices may make gas-fired power generation more competitive than coal-fired generation. A fuel switch from coal to gas yields a reduction of CO_2 emissions per MWh of produced electricity, which implies that fewer emissions have to be covered with EUAs. The price of gas compared with the price of coal affects the operating choices for the power generation industry. If coal prices are low compared with the price of gas, more coal will be used. Since coal produces more emissions than gas per 1 MWh of electricity, this leads to higher emissions, therefore raising the demand for EUAs. If gas prices are low compared with coal, then installations may switch to gas. Since gas has a lower carbon emission output than coal, the demand for EUAs would fall.[19]

Let us define e_c and e_g as the CO_2 emission factors of coal and gas, respectively. Also, let h_c and h_g be the heating rates of coal and gas, respectively. Heating rates measure how much

[19]Taschini and Urech (2010) investigate the opportunity of an energy producer to switch from cheaper but more emission-intensive coal to more expensive but less emitting gas-fired power plant when the utility is a price-maker and the CO_2 opportunity costs are explicitly internalized.

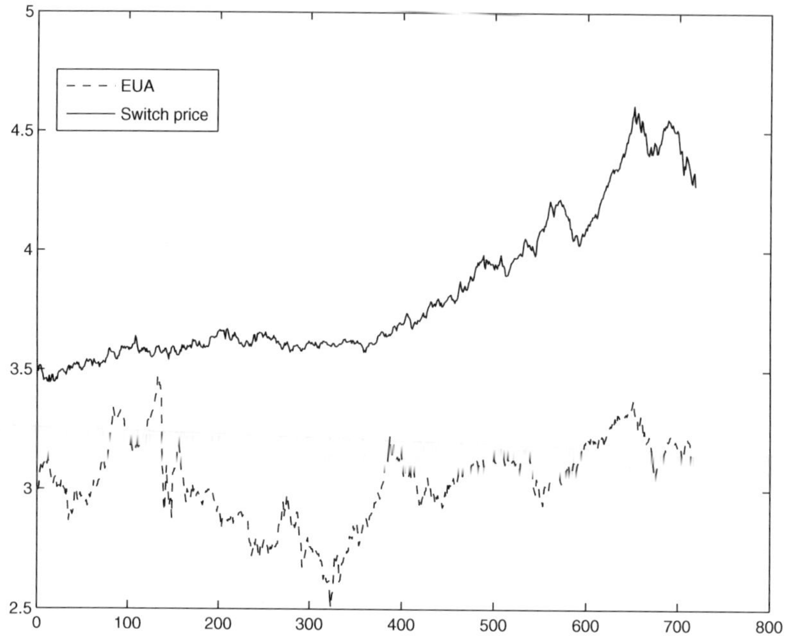

FIGURE 5.4 Log of the fuel switch and log-price of emission permits in the period from 29 September 2005 to 6 October 2008

fuel is consumed for the production of 1 MWh of electricity. Using these parameters and the coal C_t and gas G_t time series, we can derive the historical path of the coal-to-gas switch price E_t as

$$E_t = \frac{h_g G_t - h_c C_t}{e_c - e_g}, \quad t = 0, \ldots, T \tag{5.1}$$

Aligning to conventional results in environmental economics and assuming E_t to be the medium- and long-term CO_2 price benchmark, one can model it as being a proxy of the marginal cost to fuel switch. Figure 5.4 represents log E_t and the log-price of the emission permits in Phase I.

For the calculation of the fuel switch price, NBP gas futures and API#2 coal prices with maturity December 2008 are considered. The NBP gas prices are quoted in pence/therm and are converted to €/therm.[20] The API#2 coal contracts are quoted in \$/ton and converted to €/ton. The currency conversions are performed using exchange rates from the European Central Bank. The total length of the series is 717 observations and the time period is from 29 September 2005 to 6 October 2008.

[20]Therm stands for 100,000 British thermal units (Btu).

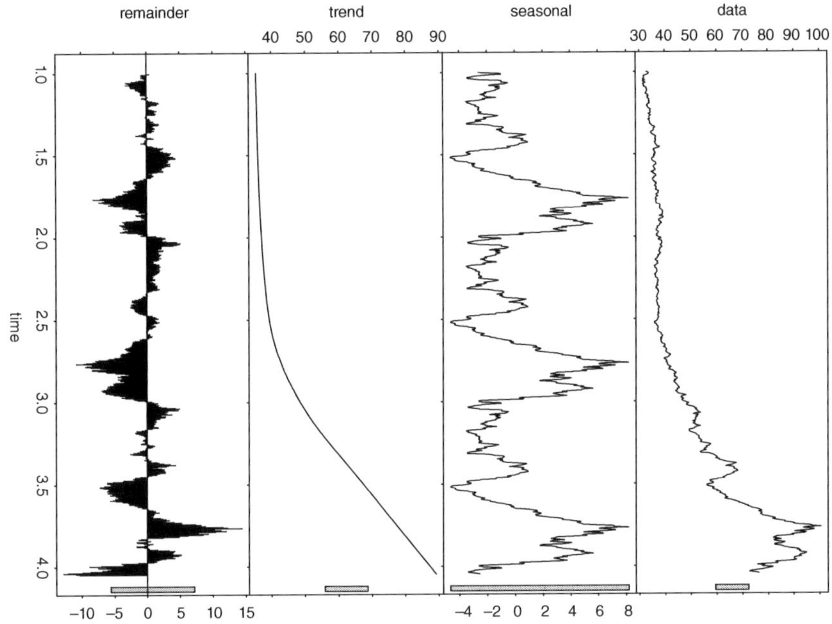

FIGURE 5.5 Plot of the time series, seasonality, trend and remainder

As mentioned, fuel switching is the most important short-run abatement measure for fuel-fired power plants in the context of the EU ETS. The continuous-time fuel switch price process can be modelled as a combination of two processes:

$$\varepsilon_t = P_t + X_t \tag{5.2}$$

where $P(t)$ is a deterministic process and $X(t)$ a stochastic process. The deterministic part models the trend and seasonal fluctuations. Gas prices have a marked winter–summer seasonality. Winter prices for gas are generally higher than summer prices. This is due to an increase in gas heating demand. Furthermore, cold weather renders the conditions for production and supply of gas difficult. Therefore, in general, the switching point is higher during the winter months and switching from coal to gas is less likely to occur. The fuel switch price is de-seasonalized using the seasonal trend loss (STL) procedure of Cleveland *et al.* (1990), which provides trend and seasonal components that are robust to outliers. In Figure 5.5 the decomposition of the series into seasonality, trend and remainder with the STL algorithm is shown. Table 5.7 shows parameters for the STL algorithm.

TABLE 5.7 STL parameters

	Value
Span (in lags) of loess window for seasonal extraction	7171
Span (in lags) of loess window for trend extraction	353
Span (in lags) of loess window for the low-pass filter	235

TABLE 5.8 Summary statistics of the de-seasonalized log-returns.

	Log-prices	Log-returns
Number of observations	717	716
Mean	−0.01	0
Standard deviation	0.05	0.01
Skewness	−0.15	−0.16
Kurtosis	3.4	3.82
Jarque–Bera (*p*-value)	0.02	0
Shapiro test (*p*-value)	0	0

TABLE 5.9 Parameters for the GBM and OU model

	GBM process	OU process
λ		2.2520
μ	−0.0002	−0.0030
σ	0.0114	0.0243

Once the trend and seasonal components are removed from the time series, we are left with the residual X_t:

$$X_t = \varepsilon_t - P_t, \quad t = 0, \ldots, T. \tag{5.3}$$

Table 5.8 reports the summary statistics of X_t. As expected, the Jarque–Bera and Shapiro–Wilk tests indicate the non-normality of the time series under investigation.

A geometric Brownian motion (GBM) process of the form

$$dX_t = \mu_1 X_t dt + \sigma_1 X_t dW_t \tag{5.4}$$

and an Ornstein–Uhlenbeck (OU) process of the form

$$dX_t = \lambda(\mu_2 - X_t)dt + \sigma_2 dW_t \tag{5.5}$$

are calibrated on the time series X_t, where W_t is a standard Brownian motion; μ_1 is the drift term; σ_1 and σ_2 are the volatility terms; λ measures the speed of adjustment to the long-run mean μ_2.[21] Table 5.9 reports the calibration results.

Industry routinely switches fuels in response to relative prices or allowance shortages. Fuel switching is a medium-term abatement option and, therefore, could be used as a proxy for the allowance price over such a horizon. As such, the fuel-switching process can be used for hedging and pricing purposes. For a review on pricing and hedging in the power industry, see Fusai and Roncoroni (2008) and the relevant chapters in this book.

[21] A comprehensive historical overview on the use of GBM and OU in the literature can be found in the last chapter of this book. A detailed description of the calibration procedure can be found in Brigo *et al.* (2009). We refer to Daskalakis *et al.* (2009) and Chevallier (2011) for a discussion of the model extensions.

5.6.3 Stochastic Equilibrium Models

There are numerous deterministic and stochastic models describing the equilibrium price dynamics of emission permits. A thorough discussion of selected models can be found in Chesney *et al.* (2013). General findings and the relation between these models are discussed in detail. The aim of this section is to provide an overview of the most recent stochastic equilibrium price models.

Allowing for stochastic production and abatement costs, revenues from selling electricity and emission quantities, Carmona *et al.* (2009) model the EU ETS in a general setting. In this setting, the equilibrium price of emission permits equals the discounted penalty multiplied by the probability of permit shortage (i.e., where the total pollution volume exceeds the total amount of permits). The models of Seifert *et al.* (2008), Chesney and Taschini (2012) and Grüll and Kiesel (2009) specify the process for the cumulative emissions in the framework of Carmona *et al.* (2009). In the first paper the emission rate of the representative agent follows an arithmetic Brownian motion, while in the other papers a firm's emission rate follows a geometric Brownian motion. This implies the total amount of pollution is described by the integral over an arithmetic and a geometric Brownian motion, respectively. The approaches of Chesney and Taschini (2012) and Grüll and Kiesel (2009) differ in the way such an integral is approximated. In all these models, the price of emission permits reflects the expectations regarding the evolution of the supply and demand dynamics. In particular, Carmona *et al.* (2009) analyse the effect of windfall profits, Chesney and Taschini (2012) investigate the effect of asymmetric information on the permit price and Grüll and Kiesel (2009) provide a theoretically sound discussion around the permit price slump in 2006 in the EU ETS. Taschini (2010) offers a comprehensive overview of other recent attempts at developing valid dynamic price models for emission permits.

These models realistically depict the dynamic price formation of emission permits in the EU ETS. However, they focus on showing theoretical properties of the cap-and-trade scheme implemented under the EU ETS rather than calibrating the model parameters to historical time series. With the objective of providing tractable pricing models for options on emission permits, Carmona and Hinz (2009) were the first to address the complexity of the calibration of the equilibrium model of Carmona *et al.* (2009). The authors introduce a simple risk-neutral reduced-form model for the price of emission permits and calibrate it to historical data. Grüll and Taschini (2011) extend the work of Carmona and Hinz (2009) by deriving estimation methods for the calibration to real data of those competing equilibrium models introduced in this paper. They first prove the existing relationship between the reduced-form model of Carmona and Hinz (2009) and the full model of Chesney and Taschini (2012). Then, they propose a new reduced-form model based on the full equilibrium models of Chesney and Taschini (2012). Using futures prices in the EU ETS with maturity December 2007 and December 2012, they calibrate reduced-form models and assess the in-sample performances of their reduced-form model and the one proposed by Carmona and Hinz (2009). With the aim of providing a comprehensive comparison among potentially competing models, they also calibrate and compare two quite popular continuous-time stochastic processes (geometric Brownian motion and normal inverse Gaussian).[22] In the current price evolution they show that reduced-form models perform relatively well at the end of a compliance period (Phase I) compared with standard stochastic processes. However, reduced-form models are

[22] Refer to Section 5.6.2.2 for a discussion about the calibration of continuous-time stochastic processes.

clearly outperformed by complex standard stochastic processes such as the normal inverse Gaussian, especially at the beginning of Phase I and Phase II, as shown by Grüll and Taschini (2011).

ABBREVIATIONS

AAU	assigned amount unit
CDM	clean development mechanism
CER	certified emission reduction
COP	conference of the parties
CO_2	carbon dioxide
EC	European Commission
ERU	emission reduction unit
EUA	emission unit allowance
EU ETS	EU Emission Trading Scheme
GHG	greenhouse gas
IPCC	Intergovernmental Panel on Climate Change
JI	joint implementation
NAP	national allocation plan
OECD	Organization for Economic Cooperation and Development
SO_2	sulfur dioxide
UNFCCC	United Nations Framework Convention on Climate Change

REFERENCES

Aihman, M. and Zetterberg, L. (2005) Options for emission allowance allocation under the EU Emissions Trading Directive, *Mitigation and Adaptation Strategies for Global Change*, **10**(4), 597–645.

Alberola, E., Chevallier, J. and Cëze, B. (2008) Price drivers and structural breaks in European carbon prices 2005–2007, *Energy Policy*, **36**(2), 787–797.

Baumol, W.J. and Oates, W.E. (1988) *The Theory of Environmental Policy*, Cambridge University Press, Cambridge.

Benz, E. and Trück, S. (2008) Modeling the price dynamics of CO_2 emission allowances, *Energy Economics*, **31**(1), 4–15.

Bernstein, L., Roy, J., Delhotal, K., Harnisch, J., Matsuhashi, R., Price, L., Tanaka, E., Worrell, E., Yamba, F. and Fengqi, Z. (2007) Industry. In Climate Change 2007: Mitigation. Contribution of Working Group III to the Fourth Assessment Report of the Intergovernmental Panel on Climate Change, Cambridge University Press, Cambridge.

Böhringer, C. and Lange, A. (2005) On the design of optimal grandfathering schemes for emission allowances, *European Economics Review*, **49**(8), 2041–2055.

Brigo, D., Dalessandro, A., Neugebauer, M. and Triki, F. (2009) A stochastic processes toolkit for risk management: Geometric Brownian motion, jumps, GARCH and variance gamma models, *Journal of Risk Management in Financial Institutions*, **2**(4), 365–393.

Carmona, R. and Hinz, J. (2009) Calibration and risk neutral dynamics of carbon emission allowances, Working paper.

Carmona, R., Fehr, M., Hinz, J. and Porchet, A. (2009) Market design for emission trading schemes, *SIAM Review*, **9**(3), 465–469.

Cetin, U. and Verschuere, M. (2009) Pricing and hedging in carbon emissions markets, *International Journal of Theoretical & Applied Finance*, **12**(7), 949–967.

Chesney, M. and Taschini, L. (2012) The endogenous price dynamics of emission allowances and an application to CO_2 option pricing, *Applied Mathematical Finance*, **19**(5), 447–475.

Chesney, M., Gheyssens, J. and Taschini, L. (2013) *Environmental Finance and Investments*, Springer-Verlag, Berlin.

Chevallier, J. (2011) *Econometric Analysis of Carbon Markets: The European Union Emissions Trading Scheme and the Clean Development Mechanism*, Springer-Verlag, Berlin.

Cleveland, R.B., Cleveland, W.S., McRae, J. and Terpenning, I. (1990) STL: A seasonal-trend decomposition procedure based on loess, *Journal of Official Statistics*, **6**(1), 3–73.

Coase, R. (1960) The problem of social cost, *The Journal of Law and Economics*, **3**, 1–44.

Convery, F.J. and Redmond, L. (2007) Market and price developments in the European Union Emissions Trading Scheme, *Review of Environmental Economics and Policy*, **1**(1), 88–111.

Creti, A., Jouvet, P. and Mignon, V. (2012) Carbon price drivers: Phase I versus Phase II equilibrium?, *Energy Economics*, **34**(1), 327–334.

Crocker, T. (1966) *The Structuring of Atmospheric Pollution Control Systems*, Vol. 1 of *The Economics of Air Pollution*, Harold Wolozin, New York.

Cronshaw, M.B. and Kruse, J.B. (1996) Regulated firms in pollution permit markets with banking, *Journal of Regulatory Economics*, **9**, 179–189.

Dales, J. (1968) *Pollution Property and Prices*, University of Toronto Press, Toronto.

Daskalakis, G., Psychoyios, D. and Markellos, R.N. (2009) Modeling CO_2 emission allowance prices and derivatives: Evidence from the European Trading Scheme, *Journal of Banking and Finance*, **33**(7), 1230–1241.

Ellerman, A.D. (2003) Lessons from Phase 2 compliance with the U.S. Acid Rain Program, Technical document, Center for Energy and Environmental Policy Research CEEPR – MIT.

Ellerman, A.D. and Joskow, P. (2008) The European Union's CO_2 cap-and-trade system in perspective, Technical report, Pew Center on Global Climate Change Report.

Ellerman, A.D. and Montero, J. (2007) The efficiency and robustness of allowance banking in the U.S. Acid Rain Program, *The Energy Journal*, **28**(4), 47.

EUEPA (2003) Directive 2003/87/EC of the European Parliament and of the Council of 13 October 2003 establishing a scheme for greenhouse gas emission allowance trading within the Community and amending Council Directive 96/61/EC.

Fusai, G. and Roncoroni, A. (2008) *Implementing Models in Quantitative Finance: Methods and Cases*, Springer-Verlag, Berlin.

Global Carbon Project (2008) Carbon budget 2008.

Grüll, G. and Kiesel, R. (2009) Pricing CO_2 permits using approximation approaches, Available at: http://ssrn.com/abstract=1527378.

Grüll, G. and Taschini, L. (2011) A comparison of reduced-form permit price models and their empirical performances, in Proceedings of the 58th World Statistics Congress.

Houpert, K. and de Dominicis, A. (2006) Trading in the rain, Technical report, Mission Climat, Caisse des Dépôts, Paris.

IPCC (2001) Third assessement report: Climate change 2001.

IPCC (2007) Fourth assessement report: Climate change 2007.

Keeler, A. (1991) Noncompliant firms in transferable discharge permit markets: Some extensions, *Journal of Environmental Economics and Management*, **21**, 180–189.

Kruger, J. and Pizer, W.A. (2004) The EU Emissions Trading Directive: Opportunities and potential pitfalls, Discussion paper, Resources for the Future, Washington DC.

Mansanet-Bataller, M., Pardo, A. and Valor, E. (2007) CO_2 prices, energy and weather, *The Energy Journal (Cambridge, MA)*, **28**(3), 73–92.

Montgomery, W. (1972) Markets in licenses and efficient pollution control programs, *Journal of Economic Theory*, **5**, 395–418.

Paolella, M.S. and Taschini, L. (2008) An econometric analysis of emission allowance prices, *Journal of Banking and Finance*, **32**(10), 2022–2032.

Parsons, J. and Taschini, L. (2012) The role of stocks & shocks concepts in the debate over price vs. quantity, *Environmental and Resource Economics*, **55**(1). Available at: http://ssrn.com/abstract=1784356.

Pigou, A. (1920) *The Economics of Welfare*, Macmillan Press, London.

Rubin, J.D. (1996) A model of intertemporal emission trading, banking, and borrowing, *Journal of Environmental Economics and Management*, **31**, 269–286.

Schennach, S.M. (2000) The economics of pollution permit banking in the context of Title IV of the 1990 Clean Air Act Amendments, *Journal of Environmental Economics and Management*, **40**, 189–210.

Seifert, J., Uhrig-Homburg, M. and Wagner, M. (2008) Dynamic behavior of CO_2 spot prices, *Journal of Environmental Economics and Managements*, **56**, 180–194.

Taschini, L. (2010) Environmental economics and modeling marketable permits: A survey, *Asia-Pacific Financial Markets*, **17**(4), 325–343.

Taschini, L. and Urech, S. (2010) The real option to fuel switch in the presence of expected windfall profits under the EU ETS, *The Journal of Energy Markets*, **3**(2), 27–47.

Tietenberg, T.H. (1985) Emissions trading: An exercise in reforming pollution policy, Working paper, Resources for the Future, Washington DC.

Tietenberg, T.H. (2006) *Emissions Trading: Principles and Practice*, Resources for the Future, Washington DC.

Weitzman, M.L. (1974) Prices vs. quantities, *The Review of Economic Studies*, **41**(4), 683–691.

Zapfel, P. and Vainio, M. (2002) *Pathways to European Greenhouse Gas Emissions Trading: History and Misconceptions*, Note di Lavoro Series 85, The Fondazione Eni Enrico Mattei.

CHAPTER 6

Weather Risk and Weather Derivatives

Alessandro Mauro

6.1 INTRODUCTION

Under the traditional view of neoclassical economics, the producible quantity of goods and services is considered to be known once we know the levels of inputs and their productivity. This assumption allows us to build a supply curve that defines, for any given price, the quantity of the good that the individual producer, and the aggregate production system, will be able to offer on the market. On the contrary, the demand curve is a mathematical function and therefore deterministic, which expresses the quantity demanded at any price, based on individual preferences. The market equilibrium will inevitably be reached at the intersection of the supply curve with the demand curve, the juncture where you determine the quantity traded and the market price. The price system then takes the role of market equilibrium setting in an economy described as neoclassical.

Economic theory has subsequently recognized the possibility of fluctuations in the price level, especially in markets where transactions occur frequently or where goods are even continuously exchanged. Models have been developed attempting to explain and predict the level of these prices, from which general modern risk management has evolved. Markets and financial instruments were created with the aim of reducing or amplifying the exposure of agents to the fluctuation of these prices. However, the economic discipline and risk management continued to ignore volumetric risk – that is, the possibility that produced and/or demanded quantities are not deterministic but random.

By using the theoretical apparatus of modern statistical theory, it is certainly possible to make random the demand curve and the supply curve, resulting in final market equilibrium uncertainty. This approach is ineffectual if we are unable to identify the causes that may determine this randomness. Such causal identification, however, is often not possible because of the complexity of the actions taken by agents in economic systems. An important exception to this is weather-based markets.

Weather conditions have always influenced human activities. This influence, sometimes positive and sometimes negative, has been reduced significantly in the modern era but still the

Handbook of Multi-Commodity Markets and Products: Structuring, Trading and Risk Management. Edited by Andrea Roncoroni, Gianluca Fusai and Mark Cummins.

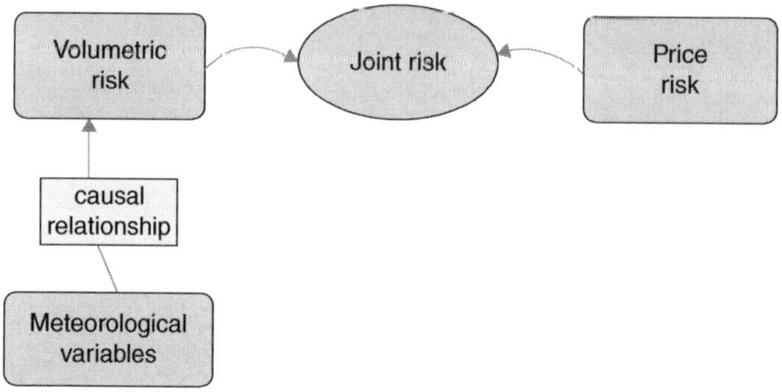

FIGURE 6.1 Price risk and volumetric risk

production and consumption of goods and services continue to be closely linked to atmospheric phenomena. Since meteorological conditions are characterized by (often extreme) uncertainty, the level of production is consequently uncertain. This uncertainty, however, is not confined to the production system because the demand for goods is also very often affected by weather conditions.

The objective of this chapter is to analyse the relationship between atmospheric phenomena and volumetric risk, focusing on the impact on the energy markets, which constitutes such an important part of the modern economy. By way of introducing briefly the topics to be discussed, it will be useful to refer to a schematic representation of the analysis we want to perform. See Figure 6.1.

Academic and operational attention has traditionally been given to the right side of Figure 6.1 – that is, the fluctuation of prices. For instance, it is possible nowadays to financially hedge the market risk on major oil products (e.g., WTI and Brent crude oils) up to 10 years ahead and beyond. In contrast to this usual focus, attention here will be on the left side of Figure 6.1.

In Section 6.2 we analyse how volumetric risk can be interpreted in terms of movements of demand and/or supply curves. We outline that such movements also have an effect on prices and therefore it is necessary to combine the two factors in order to fully understand the impact on revenues and costs.

In Section 6.3 we study the weather variable of atmospheric temperature. As suggested by the analytical framework presented in Figure 6.1, there are often some dependency relationships linking the meteorological events to volumetric risk, in the form of

- physical/technical laws, so basically deterministic
- statistical dependencies, hence random
- qualitative relationships, hence very random.

Still in Section 6.3 we clarify the type of dependency that links the atmospheric temperature to the consumption of gas for domestic purposes, which is a statistical dependency.

In Section 6.4 we present financial instruments, known as weather derivatives, which enable operators to reduce the potential impact of weather on supply or demand, especially in the energy markets.

PRICE VARIATION / VOLUME VARIATION	ΔQ : −10%	ΔQ : 0%	ΔQ : +10%
ΔP : −10%	25.2 * 90 = 2268 (case 1)	25.2 * 100 = 2520 (case 2)	25.2 * 110 = 2772 (case 3)
ΔP : 0%	28 * 90 = 2520 (case 4)	28 * 100 = 2800 (case 5)	28 * 110 = 3080 (case 6)
ΔP : +10%	30.8 * 90 = 2772 (case 7)	30.8 * 100 = 3080 (case 8)	30.8 * 110 = 3388 (case 9)

FIGURE 6.2 Interaction between price risk and volumetric risk

6.2 IDENTIFICATION OF VOLUMETRIC RISK

The process of identifying sources of risk is the essential first step in any business risk analysis. Often the process of identification cannot be separated from the analysis of market structure. This is particularly true in the scope of this chapter, whose aim is to add volumetric risk to the traditional analysis of price risk.

In this section, therefore, we undertake a theoretical analysis of the market structure in terms of a traditional supply and demand curve. This analysis will better clarify the object of study and avoid erroneous simplifications. For instance, a weather event can cause a reduction in quantity supplied or demanded, but this is not necessarily bad news for the producer. In fact, this may lead to an increase in the price of the good, hence offsetting the reduction in the traded quantity. Consequently total revenues, as a result of adverse weather events, could even increase.

From a neoclassical economic perspective, the goal is to maximize profits (i.e., the difference between revenues and costs). Without loss of generality we assume the costs to be fixed, in which case the firm must maximize revenues, or $R = Q \times P$, where Q stands for quantity and P for price. A simple example of the possible impact of volumetric risk on the balance sheet of a company is presented in Figure 6.2.

The figure shows the change in total value of a quantity of a generic good starting with a base case characterized by a quantity of 100 and a price of 28 (i.e., case 5). A variation in the unit price of the goods, equal to −10% or +10%, with the same quantity (cases 2 and 8), simply reduces or increases the total value by 10%. The same result is obtained when the quantity is reduced or increased by 10% at constant prices (cases 4 and 6). Therefore, in all cases in which only one of the two possible variations occurs, the variability of the total value is simply in the interval [−10%, +10%].

More interesting and realistic are the cases in which there is simultaneous realization of the two effects. In such cases the variability of the total value increases, standing outside the mentioned range. For example, the total result may be much lower if both changes are negative (−19% in case 1) or much higher if both changes are positive (+21% in case 9).

It is easy to prove that the particular cases mentioned in Figure 6.2 can be generalized with the following equation:

$$\Delta V = Q_0 \times \Delta P + \Delta Q \times P_0 + \Delta P \times \Delta Q \tag{6.1}$$

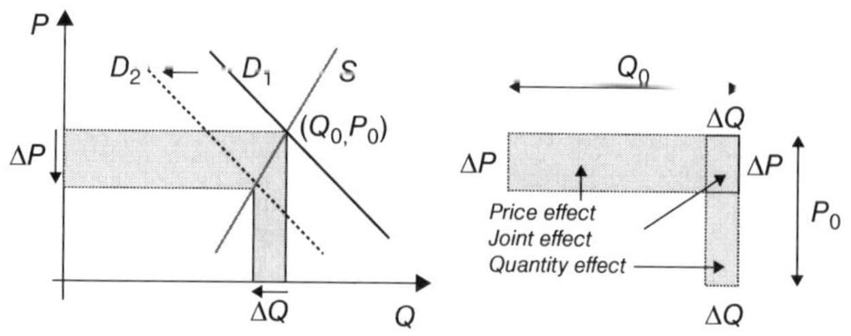

FIGURE 6.3 Price effect and quantity effect on the supply and demand curves

where Q_0 and P_0 are the initial values for price and quantity, respectively, and ΔQ, ΔP and ΔV are, respectively, the variations in the quantity, price and total value. The first term of the equation defines a price effect, from which, because of its variability and unpredictability, stems the price risk. The second term expresses a quantity effect, from which stems the volumetric risk. Finally, the third term defines a price–quantity joint effect, which usually has a negligible value when changes in the quantities and prices are not relevant. It is reiterated that the objective is to study the volumetric risk element. Price risk has instead been largely investigated in the past, both in theory and in practice. In fact, today many financial instruments are traded in order to reduce this type of risk borne by economic agents.

Equation (6.1) can be represented in graphical terms, using the demand and supply curves as shown in Figure 6.3.

Starting from the initial quantity–price pair (Q_0, P_0), the shaded area is representative of the total change in value due to the shift of the demand curve from D_1 to D_2 position. The three shaded areas represent the three effects mentioned above. It will soon be shown that a more precise identification of the relative importance of the price–quantity effects and risks depends on the characteristics of supply and demand curves, and the type of shocks to which the market is exposed. For the sake of clarity, the analysis will be split into two parts, distinguishing between shocks impacting the demand curve and the supply one.

6.2.1 Weather Events on the Demand Curve

The impact of a weather event on the demand curve is an exogenous factor with respect to the quantity–price relationship, and as such involves a horizontal movement of the demand curve.

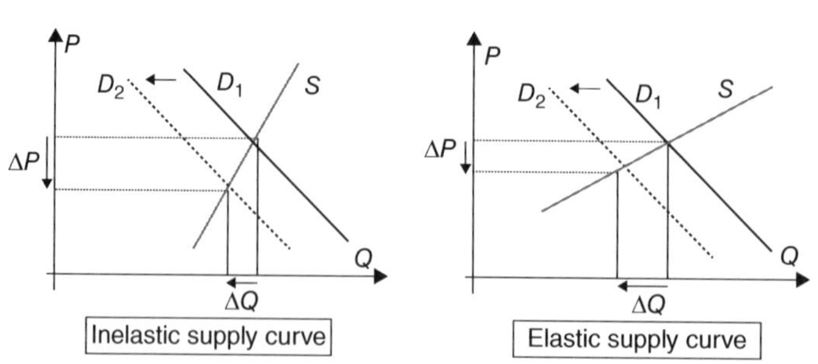

FIGURE 6.4 Demand curve shifting with inelastic (left) and elastic (right) supply

This situation is shown in Figure 6.4 where, without loss of generality, a contraction of the demand curve is presented relative to two different types of supply curves.

Some consequential effects are independent of the shapes of curves. In fact, the shift of the demand curve has an impact of the same algebraic sign on both the exchanged quantity and price. That is, if the demand curve is shifted from D_1 to D_2, both the quantity traded and the price will decrease. The opposite happens if demand expands. From the perspective of the producer, when ignoring the costs, the effect is unambiguous: if demand drops then revenues reduce, if instead demand expands then revenues will certainly increase.

Furthermore, it is necessary to analyse the shape of the supply curve. The left side of Figure 6.4 represents an inelastic supply curve.[1] The contraction in the demand curve leads to a reduction of the price that is higher than the reduction of the exchanged quantity. To the right instead is a more elastic supply curve. The contraction in the demand curve determines a reduction in the quantity that is greater than the reduction of the selling price. It is easy to adapt these findings, determined by the shape of the supply curve, to cases in which the demand curve moves to the right due to positive external shocks.

Ultimately, the foregoing observations can be summarized in general terms by saying that, if the demand curve moves, then:

- Price effect and quantity effect always have the same algebraic sign (cases 1 and 9 of Figure 6.2).
- If the supply is inelastic, then the price effect exceeds the quantity effect.
- If the supply is elastic, then the quantity effect exceeds the price effect.

It is also confirmed by the observation of the previous section that normally the two effects coexist. Only in two extreme cases does the prevalence of one of the two effects cancel the other completely, and this is the case when the supply curve is completely elastic (i.e., horizontal curve: the curve elasticity, ε, is infinite) or completely inelastic (i.e., vertical curve: the curve elasticity, ε, is zero). These cases are summarized in Table 6.1.

The first two lines (i.e., the case of the horizontal supply curve) represent the generalization of cases 4 and 6 of Figure 6.2. The last two lines instead generalize cases 2 and 8.

TABLE 6.1 The effects of extreme supply curves

Supply curve elasticity	Demand curve shift	Quantity change	Price change	Marginal revenue	Price risk	Volume risk
$\varepsilon \approx \infty$ (horizontal)	contraction	$\Delta Q < 0$		$MR < 0$	null	yes
	expansion	$\Delta Q > 0$	$\Delta P = 0$	$MR > 0$		
$\varepsilon \approx 0$ (vertical)	contraction		$\Delta P < 0$	$MR < 0$	yes	null
	expansion	$\Delta Q = 0$	$\Delta P > 0$	$MR > 0$		

[1]The elasticity of demand or supply curve is related to the change in quantity corresponding to a (small) change in the price of the good. For completeness, it should be noted that, apart from a particular class of curves (isoelastic curves), elasticity is a local measure and varies along the curve.

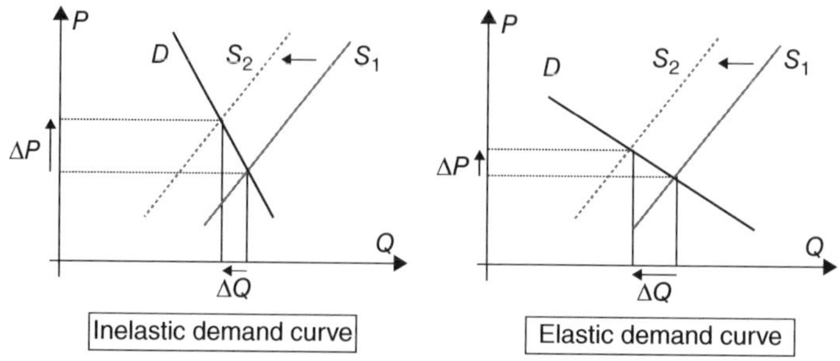

FIGURE 6.5 Supply curve shift with inelastic and elastic demand

6.2.2 Weather Events on the Supply Curve

In the previous section the impact of weather events on the demand curve was studied. Such events also represent exogenous shocks to the supply curve, and can again be represented by a horizontal shift of the supply curve. Figure 6.5 shows a contraction in the supply curve with respect to two demand curves of different shape.

The discrepancy with respect to what was previously shown regarding movements of the demand curve is immediately evident. The movements of the supply curve, whatever the form of the demand curve, determine a quantity effect and a price effect with different algebraic signs. In fact, they move in opposite directions: if the supply reduces, the market price increases as the quantity exchanged is reduced (case 7 in Figure 6.2). The opposite is true if the supply expands (case 3 of Figure 6.2). The total revenue is therefore uncertain and depends on the characteristics of the demand curve.

In order to better understand this point, neglect the third term in definition (1.1) and divide it by ΔQ, obtaining

$$\frac{\Delta V}{\Delta Q} = P \times \left[1 + \frac{Q}{P} \times \frac{\Delta P}{\Delta Q}\right]$$

In defining the elasticity of demand to price as

$$\varepsilon(Q) \equiv -\frac{P}{Q} \times \frac{\Delta Q}{\Delta P}$$

the definition of marginal revenue (MR) is obtained – that is, the change in revenue resulting from a small change in quantity:

$$MR \equiv P \times \left[1 - \frac{1}{|\varepsilon(Q)|}\right] \tag{6.2}$$

TABLE 6.2 The effects of different demand curve elasticities

Demand curve elasticity	Supply curve shifting	Quantity change	Price change	Marginal revenue	Price risk	Volume risk
$\lvert\varepsilon\rvert = 1$	indifferent	$\Delta Q = \lvert\Delta P\rvert$		$MR = 0$	equal	
$\varepsilon \approx \infty$ (horizontal)	contraction	$\Delta Q < 0$		$MR = -P < 0$	null	yes
	expansion	$\Delta Q > 0$	$\Delta P = 0$	$MR > 0$		
$\varepsilon \approx 0$ (vertical)	contraction		$\Delta P \gg 0$	$MR \gg 0$	yes	null
	expansion	$\Delta Q = 0$	$\Delta P < 0$	$MR < 0$		

It is clear that the evolution of marginal revenue depends on the price of the good and the elasticity of the demand curve.[2] We distinguish, for example, the following special cases:

- $\varepsilon = 1$. Marginal revenue is zero, so the change in revenue is still null. Hence, the contraction of the supply curve leads to a reduction of the sold quantity, which is exactly offset by an increase of the same size in the price ($\Delta Q = -\Delta P$). Therefore, price risk is equivalent, with an opposite algebraic sign, to the volumetric risk.
- $\varepsilon \approx \infty$. The demand curve is horizontal, that is infinitely elastic. This is the case of a perfectly competitive market structure in which individual producers cannot influence the market price, and therefore face a flat demand curve. In this situation, if the supply curve moves left there is no change in price, while the quantity sold is anyway reduced. Therefore, the marginal revenue is equal to P. That is, if the quantity sold is reduced by one unit, the revenue decreases obviously by a monetary amount which is equal to the unit price. In this case there is only volumetric risk in the market, and no price risk.
- $\varepsilon \approx 0$. The demand curve is completely inelastic, that is vertical. The decline of the supply curve leads to a change in quantity which is, however, null. On the contrary, the change in price is significant and depends only on the extent of displacement of the offer curve. In this case there is only price risk and zero volumetric risk.

Table 6.2 summarizes the three cases analysed.

Another special case, but still an interesting one, is that of a monopolistic market structure.[3] A monopolist will decide independently at which point of the demand curve to produce, in order to offer on the market an amount that maximizes his own profits. It is well known that this amount is lower than that offered in a competitive market. Therefore, the choice of a monopolist lies on an inelastic part of the demand curve, i.e. where $\lvert\varepsilon\rvert < 1$. In this situation, any shift of the supply curve leads to a reduction in profits, as the marginal revenue is below marginal cost. Therefore, any reduction or increase in sold quantities, due to weather events, leads to a sub-optimal result for the monopolist. In fact, the resulting change in the price of the goods is not worth the change in sold quantities, and therefore the profit is reduced while the unit cost stays the same. In practice, however, manufacturers hold inventories of the produced

[2]From a theoretical point of view, the absolute value of elasticity is between zero and infinity. Often the elasticity of demand for a good depends mainly on the existence (and the short-term availability) of substitutes for such good.

[3]At this point it is necessary to drop the assumption of fixed costs, as the analysis of monopoly requires the explicit consideration of profit (i.e., revenues and expenses simultaneously).

goods. Therefore, in the case of reduced production quantities due to a shock, there will be recourse to the stocks previously stored (i.e., reducing them). Conversely, if the shock is a positive one, the surplus production will be stored.

6.2.3 Risk Measurement and Weather-at-Risk

The measurement of risk is the second key stage of modern risk management and is aimed at evaluating the possible impact on the company accounts of the previously identified risks. Recently, statistical and probability measures have been introduced. The most used is known as value-at-risk (VaR) and measures the maximum possible loss at a given level of statistical confidence.[4] Even in the case of risk measurement, traditionally the focus has been solely on the impact of price risk. In terms of the fundamental equation (1.1), the study of price risk is only a particular case reducing the equation to $\Delta V = Q_0 \times \Delta P$. In this particular case, the definition of VaR in the so-called parametric formulation (i.e., modelled with use of the Gaussian probability distribution) is as follows:

$$\text{VaR}_P = \alpha_c \sigma_p Q_0 P \tag{6.3}$$

where P is the price of the asset, σ_p the volatility of the price returns, α_c is linked to the confidence level chosen and finally the amount Q_0 is fixed by assumption. This represents the special cases previously analysed, in which the demand curve or supply curve is infinitely inelastic – that is, vertical. In this case there is a possibility of change only in the price of the good, due to the movement of the supply or demand curve; the exchanged quantity is determined once and for all by the position of the other curve.

A symmetrical case is where there is volumetric risk but price risk is nil, as shown by the VaR formulation in this case:

$$\text{VaR}_Q = \alpha_c \sigma_Q Q P_0 \tag{6.4}$$

Here price is fixed, while the quantity may vary, and in fact the quantity volatility σ_Q appears in the equation. This case is applicable when, as we have seen previously, the demand curve or supply curve is infinitely elastic and movements in one of the two curves have the effect of only changing the quantity traded in the market but not the price, which remains instead fixed and determined by the position of the horizontal curve.

As noted previously, the most realistic case is the coexistence of volumetric risk and price risk – that is, when the demand curve and supply curve do not have extreme elasticities. In this case, in which the general equation (6.1) is again valid, it can be shown that the definition of VaR becomes:[5]

$$\text{VaR} = \sqrt{\text{VaR}_P^2 + \text{VaR}_Q^2 + 2\rho_{Q,P}\text{VaR}_P\text{VaR}_Q} \tag{6.5}$$

The VaR definition becomes more complex and takes into consideration the correlation between quantity effect and price effect, denoted here $\rho_{Q,P}$.

[4]For a general introduction to value-at-risk see Dowd (1998) and Jorion (1997).

[5]For a formal proof, see Mauro (1999a), p. 99.

This relationship again depends on the characteristics of the supply and demand curves. In fact:

- If the correlation is positive, an increase (or decrease) in price is accompanied by an increase (or decrease) in the exchanged quantity, as happens when the demand curve shifts (see Figure 6.4).
- If the correlation is negative, an increase (or decrease) in price is accompanied by a decrease (or increase) in the traded quantity, as happens when the supply curve shifts (see Figure 6.5).
- The extreme cases, represented previously in Tables 6.1 and 6.2, imply a zero correlation between price and quantity and a nil VaR for the quantity or price, leading to a simplification of equation (6.5) to the special cases referred to in equations (6.3) and (6.4).

The analysis of the preceding sections makes it clear that, beyond the special borderline cases, normally price risk and volumetric risk will coexist. The objective of risk measurement must then be to clarify and measure what can be the impact, in terms of probability, determined by the coexistence of the two identified risks. It should be noted that price risk measurement, through the use of statistical measures such as VaR, is widespread. Even in the market under consideration (i.e., the energy market) VaR has frequent applications.[6] Nothing however hinders the application of this approach to volumetric risk, provided that time series of volume evolutions are available, in order to gauge the volatility in equation (6.4).

Turning therefore to a more operational focus, global risk measurement must be done using equation (6.5) and also assuming the earlier estimate of equations (6.3) and (6.4) for the two standalone risks, plus the estimated correlation coefficient. These estimates require the availability of historical series of price and quantity traded – that is, timely ordered pairs (Q, P) are available.

Often, however, the evolution of the traded volume is a function of the level of another underlying factor, which in turn should be identified and measured. In fact, the aim of this chapter is to go one step further. The volumetric risk will not be considered in isolation or, in other words, as a mere series of values, but rather as influenced by weather events, with which causality is to be analysed. In the first instance this can be represented mathematically as

$$Q_i = f(x_i) \tag{6.6}$$

We therefore analyse weather events which can be measured (i.e., x_i) and where a functional dependence between weather and traded quantity of the good (i.e., $f(\cdot)$) can be identified. In this case, the 'visible' effect will be that of volumetric risk, but the real source of uncertainty in the market comes from meteorological factors. Consequently, when the existence of functional dependence as per equation (6.6) is shown, from the concept of volumetric VaR you should move to the concept of weather-at-risk.

[6] This is discussed in Mauro (1999a, b).

6.3 ATMOSPHERIC TEMPERATURE AND NATURAL GAS MARKET

In order to introduce the topics discussed in this section, it is useful to recall Figure 6.1. In Section 6.1 we analysed the volumetric risk, which depends on the characteristic features of the market, the latter being summarized by the characteristics of the supply and demand curves. It has also been shown that volumetric risk does not come alone, but usually along with price risk.

In this section we begin by analysing the nature and impact of weather (wind, rain, clouds, fog, snow, etc.) on energy markets, highlighting the volumetric risks created. More specifically, we study one particular atmospheric variable – air temperature. Other atmospheric variables are humidity, wind speed, barometric pressure, etc.

6.3.1 Characterization of the Air Temperature Meteorological Variable

There are several important physical phenomena that occur within the Earth's atmosphere, especially in the lower part called the 'Troposphere'. Among the most important of these are wind, precipitation (i.e., rain, snow, hail), sunshine and cloudiness, fog, hydrological phenomena (i.e., water level in reservoirs, river flow), etc.

In past centuries, the quantitative measurement of these phenomena was introduced in order to identify meteorological variables. Among these, for example, are barometric pressure, humidity, wind speed, the level of rain, etc. One of the fundamental meteorological variables for many human activities is the atmospheric temperature. This section is dedicated to the study of this weather variable, bearing in mind that the paradigm of the present study is also applicable to other meteorological variables.

In general, there is no unique measure of a weather variable. It is necessary to establish and use conventions in order to determine the terms and scales of measurement. These conventions are based, among other factors, on the *pro-tempore* available measuring instruments. Moreover, measurement is never absolute, but is necessarily related to a particular place and a specific moment in time at which the measurement takes place. Such measurement needs also to be subject to chronological measurement; namely, the simultaneous recording of the time when the survey and registration of the weather variable is taken.

As far as the atmospheric temperature is concerned, frequent observations are often made during the day but data commonly available are the maximum and minimum temperatures, measured during a predefined time interval. This interval may coincide with the solar day, from 00.00 to 24.00, but this choice is just the result of convention.[7] The use of algebraic

---

[7]In the UK, the *Met Office* measures the minimum temperature from 09.00am of the day before to 09.00am of the current day, and the maximum temperature from 09.00am of the current day to 09.00am of the following day. In France, *Météo-France* measures the minimum temperature from 06.00pm of the day before to 05:59pm of the current day, the maximum from 06.00am of the current day to 05:59am of the following day. In Germany, *Deutscher Wetterdienst* measures the minimum and maximum temperatures from 00.00am to 11.59pm in the same day, while a competing company measures the minimum temperature from 06.00pm of the day before to 06.00am of the current day and the maximum from 06.00am to 06.00pm in the current day – see Dischel (2002). All times are in coordinated universal time (UTC).

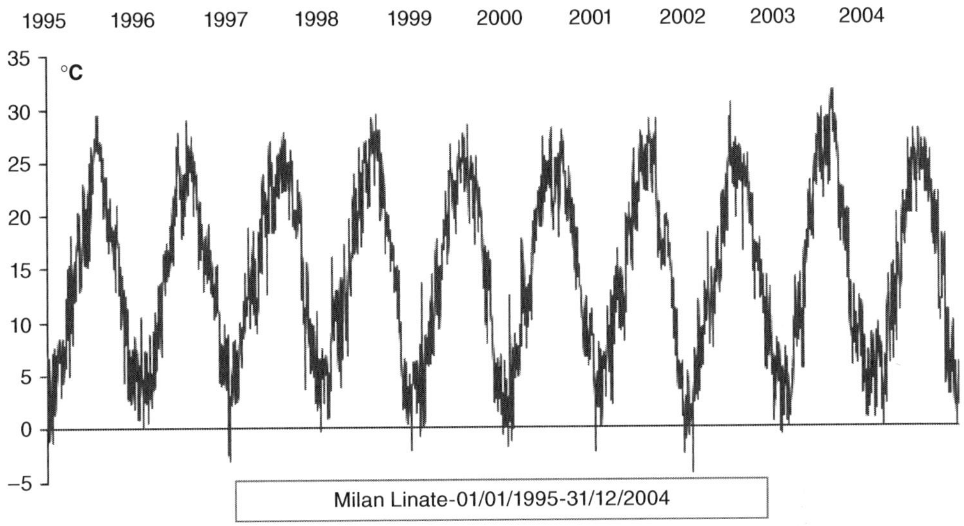

FIGURE 6.6 Average daily temperature recorded at Milan Linate weather station

transformations of measured temperatures is also very frequent, typically the daily average temperature (i.e., the arithmetic mean temperature between the recorded maximum and minimum values).

It is useful to represent the typical evolution of this measure through the seasons and years, as in Figure 6.6.

Figure 6.6 specifically shows the evolution of the average daily temperature recorded in Milan, in the meteorological station located at the airport of Linate. It is an obvious fact that, at similar latitudes, summer is hot and winter is cold. The smooth and sinusoidal shape depicted in Figure 6.6 is therefore not surprising. However, even with a superficial glance, it is noted that every season and every year is partly, but not entirely, different from the others. The single data points, and consequently the aggregated ones, are rather volatile. It is quite evident, for example, that there are winters colder than others, and summers warmer than normal. In order to further investigate these qualitative observations, in general it is very helpful to use quantitative analysis. In this chapter, the focus is on statistical methodologies. Particularly useful for the study of meteorological variables is time series analysis.[8] In this area a very important tool is the autocorrelation function (ACF), or rather the partial autocorrelation function (PACF), which establishes the strength of linear dependence between data points in the same series (hence the name 'autocorrelation' instead of 'correlation').[9] We show in Figure 6.7 the estimation of that function applied to the case of the daily average temperature measured at Milan Linate meteorological station over a decade.

The figure shows a significant and very strong autocorrelation at the 1-day lag, with a value that comes close to unity. This means that generally the level of the temperature today is highly correlated with the temperature recorded yesterday, and similarly the temperature tomorrow will be very well correlated with that today. However, in contrast, it is also clear

[8]For more information the reader is directed to, among other books, Pankratz (1991).

[9]The PACF allows the identification of the statistical significance of the lags in an autoregressive model.

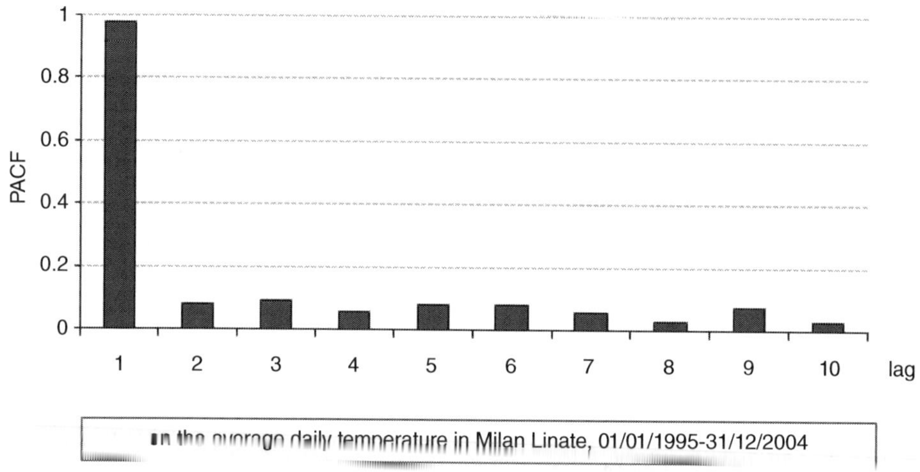

FIGURE 6.7 Partial autocorrelation function for the average daily temperature

from the figure that at the 2-day lag the linear dependence is very low, and probably not statistically different from zero.[10]

What is faced is what statisticians call a stochastic process with limited memory. Indeed, today's temperature depends almost solely on the value of the same variable on the immediately preceding day, but not that of 2 days earlier. Another relevant dependence, not shown in Figure 6.7, is between today's value and the values recorded at about the 365-day lag, that is observations distant about 1 year from each other. This correlation represents the existence of 'normal' seasonal temperatures and it is consistent with the periodical evolution highlighted in Figure 6.6. The characterization of the average atmospheric temperature has immediate implications for forecasting purposes. Indeed, based on the analysis carried out we can say that in order to get a prediction for the temperature 1 or 2 days forward, and based solely on statistical data, one may (and must) simply use the temperature recorded in the days immediately before and recorded about a year ago. Other values add no information and therefore should not be used.

It is possible to prove this hypothesis with statistical methods, estimating an autoregressive stochastic process.[11] An autoregressive model on the average daily temperature (ADT(t)), estimated on the basis of the data in Figure 6.6, takes the form

$$\mathrm{ADT}\,(t) = \underset{[99\%]}{14.28} + \underset{[99\%]}{0.87} \times \mathrm{ADT}\,(t-1) + \underset{[99\%]}{0.11} \times \mathrm{ADT}\,(t-365) \qquad (6.7)$$

The equation shows the values of estimated parameters. The model is composed therefore of a constant, a 1-day lag term and a 365-day lag term. The goodness-of-fit of the model

[10]This result, although generally true, also depends on the time horizon considered in the calculation and the meteorological station of your choice. In Nelken (2000) it is shown that for Chicago-O'Hare station the correlation is about 0.7 with 1-day lag and about 0.4 with 2-day lag. Hence, higher than in Milan Linate station.

[11]An autoregressive stochastic process is a random process explaining the current values of a variable using past values of the same variable.

is partially shown by the high statistical significance of all the estimated parameters. The estimated model helps explain much of the variability of the data, with a high R^2-value equal to 95.3%.[12] We can say that the atmospheric temperature is a variable which can be predicted with a low error, using purely statistical models, on a time horizon of 1 or 2 days.[13]

6.3.2 Degree Days

Having established these statistical properties of the average daily temperature, it is now useful to introduce a transformation of this data. This is the degree-days index,[14] an index widely used in meteorology. It is defined by the following equation:

$$\text{degree days} = 18°\text{C} - \text{ADT} \tag{6.8}$$

It is, in fact, a simple difference between the average daily temperature and a fixed value of 18°C. If this difference has a negative algebraic sign we have the cooling degree days (CDD) and, when positive, the heating degree days (HDD). More precisely, referring to the ith day, the two indices are defined as

$$\begin{aligned} \text{CDD}(i) &= \max\,[\text{ADT}(i) - 18°\text{C}; 0] \\ \text{HDD}(i) &= \max\,[18°\text{C} - \text{ADT}(i); 0] \end{aligned} \tag{6.9}$$

and therefore the equation is always $\text{CDD} + \text{HDD} = |\text{ADT} - 18°\text{C}|$. In order to better understand the features of these two indices, it is useful to compare the behaviour against daily temperature variation, as in Figure 6.8.

It appears that the HDDs may be a reference for the winter months. In fact, during the summer months, the HDDs would not normally arise as the ADT would normally be above 18°C. Conversely, the CDDs are the reference for the summer months, as usually there are no CDDs during the winter. Figure 6.9 shows the trend of daily HDDs and CDDs recorded during a calendar year in Milan Linate airport weather station.

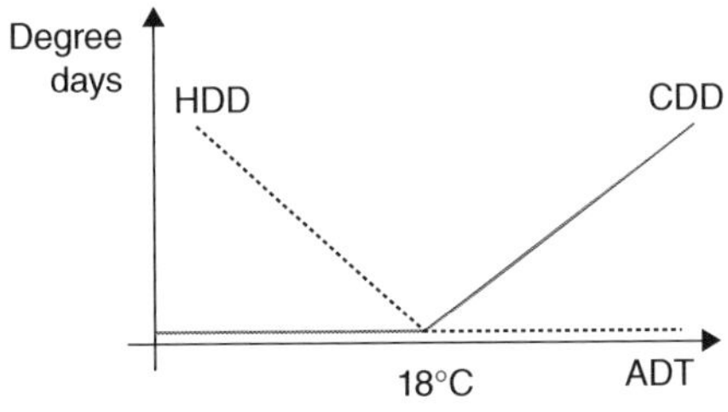

FIGURE 6.8 HDD and CDD compared with the average daily temperature

[12]Other models were estimated, but this is the one that represents the best estimate.

[13]Meteorological models provide estimates for a longer time horizon, but that still does not go beyond a week or two. In fact, weather forecasts made in the middle latitudes have large margins of error.

[14]It is worth noting that other temperature indexes could be proposed, measured and calculated.

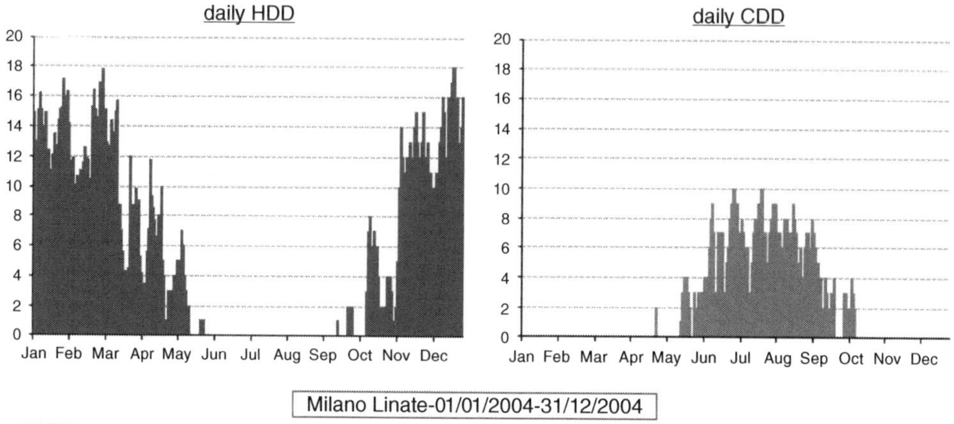

FIGURE 6.9 Daily HDDs and CDDs recorded in Milan's Linate airport in 2004

It can be seen that the number of HDDs is much higher than the CDDs, as the annual average temperature was below 18°C. Therefore, the 18°C level is just a chosen reference in definitions (6.8) and (6.9), and it is not the average atmospheric temperature.

The HDDs or CDDs are often not counted on a single day, but are instead cumulated over a time interval:

$$\text{HDD} = \sum_{i=1}^{T} \text{HDD}_i; \quad \text{CDD} = \sum_{i=1}^{T} \text{CDD}_i \tag{6.10}$$

where the interval $[1, T]$ may consist of one or more months, one or more seasons, or one or more years. Using the data of Figure 6.9, Figure 6.10 shows the cumulative HDDs (in winter) and CDDs (in summer) along year 2004 at Milan Linate airport weather station.

It can be seen from Figure 6.6 that each year presents a different weather pattern. In fact, Figure 6.11 shows the gradual build-up of HDDs during the period October–March in the years from 1960 to 2005.

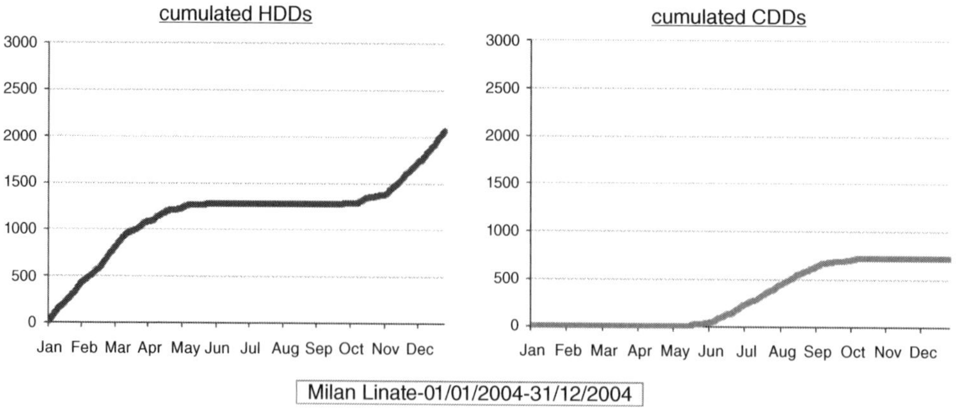

FIGURE 6.10 Cumulated HDDs and CDDs recorded at Milano Linate in 2004

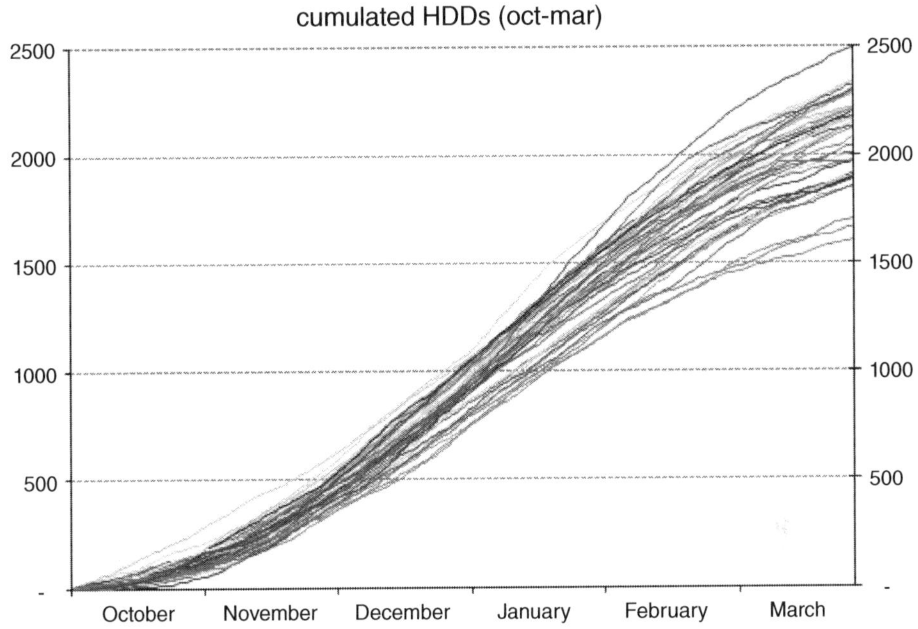

FIGURE 6.11 Cumulated HDDs in Milan Linate during the winters from 1960 to 2005

This representation of cumulated HDDs shows the variability of this index over the years, the difference becoming progressively stronger moving towards the final stage of the winter season. The two extreme curves represent the cumulatively coldest winter (2500 HDDs in total) and the cumulatively warmest one (slightly higher than 1500 HDDs in total) during the period, marking off a range nearly 1000 HDDs wide.

Even a shorter time horizon of observation does not subvert previous findings. Figure 6.12 reports the total value of the HDDs cumulated over the period 1 October to 31 March during the years 1995–2004.

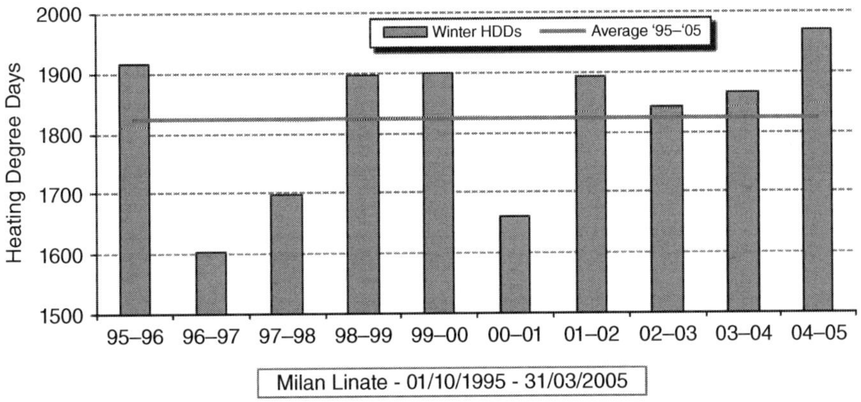

FIGURE 6.12 Cumulated HDDs in Milan Linate during winter from 1995 to 2005

Compared with the arithmetic average calculated over the period, amounting to about 1825 HDDs cumulated in each winter, the deviations are very significant in some years. Hence the analysis based on degree days adds relevant information, which cannot be detected from the raw data. In fact, from the average daily temperatures presented in Figure 6.6, yearly trends do not look so dissimilar. In conclusion, cumulated HDDs indicate in a synthetic way the extent to which a winter was warm or cold and allow quick comparisons of climate trends for consecutive years. The same applies to CDDs.

So far what has been analysed and presented are meteorological indicators for a single location only. It is often useful, as will be discussed in the next section, to create temperature indexes relating to a set of cities or entire regions. This aggregation can be achieved by taking into account simple arithmetic averages of temperatures, or average indices such as HDDs, CDDs, etc. Sometimes it is even more useful to calculate weighted averages of these indices, using variables representative of specific regions as weights. To name a few:

- the population living in cities or entire regions
- the number of people using heating oil or natural gas or electricity for home heating in a city or a region.

These weights are related to the energy markets and the motivation will be clarified in the next section.

6.3.3 Volumetric Risk in the Natural Gas Market

In Section 6.2 we studied how the impact of a weather event on demand and supply curves creates volumetric risk. Following this, atmospheric temperature was characterized as a meteorological variable. Recalling Figure 6.1, the intention here is to consider a specific volumetric risk and analyse its dependency on atmospheric temperature. The impact of this weather variable on household natural gas consumption will also be analysed. The nature and strength of this relation is summarized in Figure 6.13.

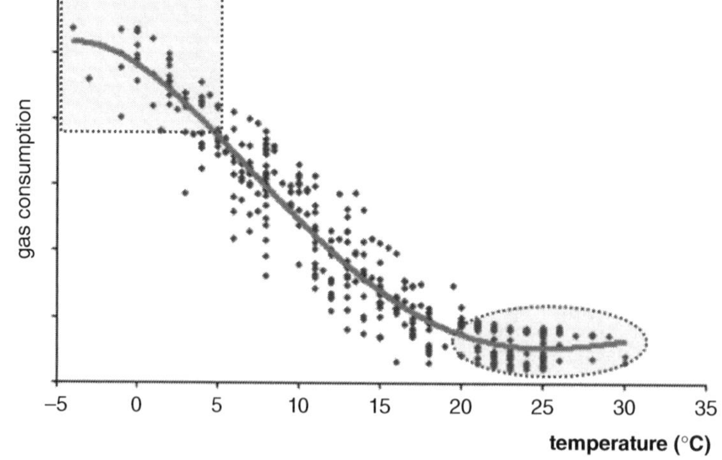

FIGURE 6.13 Relationship between temperature and gas consumption

The graph highlights a rather straightforward dependency relationship between temperature and natural gas consumption; namely, the lower the temperature, the greater the household consumption of gas. This is because natural gas is typically used for domestic space heating during the winter and much less in other uses such as cooking. The level of temperature is a key factor that drives the consumption of gas. Moreover, for this risk factor we can cover the entire paradigm of risk management (i.e., identification/measurement/hedging).[15]

From a statistical point of view, the relationship between temperature and gas consumption is in general quite significant, beyond the specific case represented here. The slope of this curve is one of the most prominent features and it is often called the 'thermal gradient'. It represents the increase (or decrease) in consumption corresponding to a decrease (or increase) by one degree in temperature. The gradient changes depend on the aggregation of the consumers under study and hence it is possible to estimate the gradient for a city, for a region or for an entire national market. In the latter case, one needs to consider aggregate indices of temperatures, as discussed previously.

As shown in Figure 6.13, if one considers the interpolation curve, the thermal gradient gradually lowers in the case of high temperatures and consequently the consumption–temperature correlation weakens (see the area highlighted with a dotted ellipse). The flattening of the interpolation curve indicates that, for high temperatures, the consumption of gas remains constant and becomes independent of the atmospheric temperature. In fact, during summer, natural gas is used primarily for purposes other than space heating. This is the main reason why the HDD calculation uses a reference temperature (i.e., 18°C) as a point of discontinuity between two quite different situations. In fact, the consumption–temperature correlation no longer warrants attention in the calculation of HDD if the temperature is above 18°C. Certainly a more accurate statistical approach could be built around the estimation of the exact 'borderline' temperature, thus changing and adapting the definition in equation (6.9) to specific cases. However, the widespread use of a single level set at 18°C enables the standardization and simplification of information flow.[16]

The square shaded area in Figure 6.13 is also worth mentioning. At very low temperatures the gradient is again reduced and often the correlation gets weaker. In fact, in the case of extreme events, the dispersion of observations around the interpolation line will increase and consequently the correlation between the two variables will decrease. The reason is that for very low temperatures, the technical limits of the logistic infrastructure for gas storage and transportation will be reached. This infrastructure is designed to meet pre-established maximum consumption levels and, indirectly, maximum temperature levels. Beyond these limits, gas supply must be interrupted to some users. There is also another consumption limit for individual users. Obviously they are unable to heat the same house for more than 24 hours a day!

It is possible to improve this analysis in many different directions. Especially for operational purposes it is important to conduct careful estimates of the consumption–temperature relation. Limiting the discussion to just one example, it is often meaningful to separate weekends from working days and conduct separate estimations with two interpolating lines and

[15]In fact, it will be shown later that financial instruments have been developed in order to hedge this 'temperature risk'.

[16]The cost of this simplification is a loss of information. For example, take into consideration two places where their points of discontinuity are different and indeed different from 18°C.

two different thermal gradients. In fact, it is likely that the consumption behaviour during the week is different from that during the weekend, as the number of hours spent at home may be quite different in the two cases.

6.4 MODIFICATION OF WEATHER RISK EXPOSURE WITH WEATHER DERIVATIVES

In order to introduce the topics covered in this section, it is useful to briefly summarize our previous findings. In Section 6.2, volume risk was discussed in general terms, placing it in relation to the features and movements of supply and demand curves. In Section 6.3, it was shown that volume risk, at least in the energy markets, can often be determined by the randomness of weather conditions. In particular, we have studied the atmospheric temperature as a weather variable and its impact on household consumption of natural gas. In terms of modern risk management, these two sections addressed the identification and measurement of risk. One last step is necessary to complete the process – that is, the modification in exposure to risk. As a starting point, the theoretical background to this topic is introduced.

J.K. Arrow, Nobel Laureate for Economics in 1972, clarified the importance of financial instruments in the optimal allocation of risk among economic agents.[17] Starting from the neoclassical theory of optimal resource allocation without uncertainty, Arrow extends these findings to the conditions of subjective uncertainty – that is, when agents assign different probabilities to the realization of different states of nature (i.e., possible future events). In a market where there are freely tradable financial securities – that is, securities whose payments are dependent on the state of nature realized ex-post – the optimal allocation of risk can be achieved. Indeed, the exchange of financial securities allows an ex-ante transferring of exposures to these states of nature. This will lead to a better allocation of risk exposures, consistent with individual preferences, until the Pareto optimum is reached.[18]

We have already demonstrated the importance of volumetric risk together with price risk. The lack of financial securities on weather-related volumetric risk would lead to a sub-optimal allocation of risk. In fact, an initial endowment of weather risk would leave some agents wishing to reduce their exposure and others instead wishing to increase it, and hence ultimately both of these groups would be dissatisfied. The introduction and development of financial instruments based on weather conditions (i.e., weather derivatives) is therefore based on sound economic theory and has found relevant operational applications.

Many commonly traded securities are primitive financial instruments. An example of such a type of security is the company share, which represents an ownership stake in a given company, and therefore the share price represents the market value of the company. This type of financial security cannot exist in the field of meteorology, as it makes no sense to even discuss the price or value of weather. However, in financial markets, financial derivatives instruments are also traded. The value of such derivative securities is linked to the value of random variables, often called underlyings. Weather derivative instruments are therefore derivatives for which the underlying is comprised of one or more meteorological variables.

---

[17]See Arrow (1964).

[18]Moreover, Arrow demonstrates that the existence and exchange of financial securities reduces the number of markets which are necessary in an economic system.

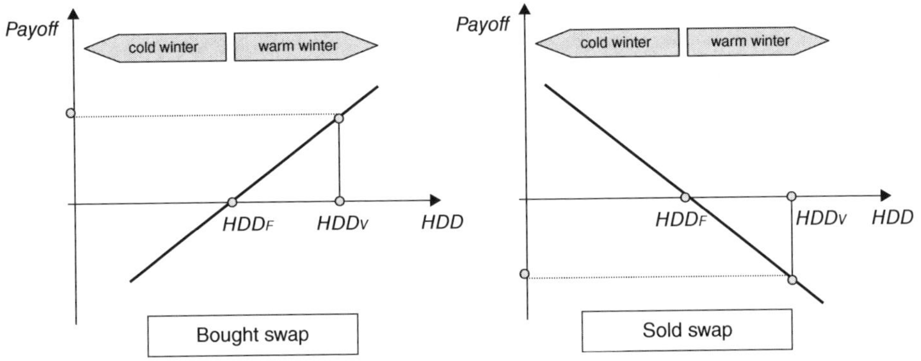

FIGURE 6.14 Monetary results for a HDD swap

6.4.1 Weather Derivatives for Temperature-Related Risk

The simplest weather derivative is the fix-variable swap on degree days. In this case two parties agree to exchange a monetary amount depending on the ex-post degree-days difference. Figure 6.14 gives a graphical representation of the evolution of ex-post performance of a swap on HDD.

On signing the contract, one party buys the swap while the other party sells the same swap. The counterparties agree on the fixed contractual level of the HDD or strike, as HDD_F in the figure. They will also negotiate and agree on the notional amount – that is, the amount of money to be exchanged ex-post for every HDD of difference against the predetermined HDD_F. Therefore, with K indicating the notional amount (here in EUR/HDD) and HDD_V the realized heating degree-days, it is possible to express the monetary result for the two counterparties mathematically as

$$\text{payoff} = K \times (\text{HDD}_V - \text{HDD}_F) \tag{6.11}$$

Very frequently the payoff profile (6.11) is not determined with the HDD on just a single date. Instead a cumulative HDD is used, that is the HDD summed over a period of time (e.g., a month, a season, multiple seasons or a whole year).

It is useful to show how such a financial instrument can be used in order to effectively hedge temperature risk. The analysis performed for Milan Linate station can once again be used, assuming that a gas seller, according to an analysis similar to that illustrated in Figure 6.13, has calculated that the temperature gradient for its sales is equal 10,000 scm/HDD. This means that, for each additional HDD, gas sales and consumption will increase by 10,000 scm.[19] Assuming also that the profit margin is 0.05 EUR/scm, the monetary gradient is 500 EUR/HDD. The seller gains 500 euros for each additional HDD, and vice versa. The seller, fearing a warm winter as occurred in 1996–1997 or 2001–2002 (see Figure 6.11), enters into a weather derivative with a bank under the following conditions.

- Financial instrument: Swap – the gas seller sells the swap, the bank purchases it.
- Reference weather station: Milan Linate airport.

[19]We use 'scm' to refer to a cubic metre measured under standard conditions.

- Period of observation: 1 October 20xx to 31 March 20xy.
- Underlying: HDD, calculated on the average daily temperature and compared with 18°C, summed over the period of observation.
- Fixed HDD (i.e., HDDF = 1825).
- Notional amount: EUR 500/HDD.

From this description, it may be noticed that the contractual conditions are independent of specific information/elements related to the business activities of the buyer or the seller, say for example the thermal gradient. The strike is negotiated, in this case, in correspondence with the average HDD in the period 1995–2004. Compared with this level, the profit margins expected on the gas sales amount to EUR 912,500 (1825 × 500) during each winter. For the sake of simplicity, a situation is considered whereby the volume risk, determined by weather risks, has no impact on price levels. In this framework, revenues, costs and trade margins will fluctuate only due to the uncertainty of the sold gas volume (see equation (6.4)). In Table 6.3, two scenarios are considered for the ex post registered HDD and the resulting payoff for both parties is presented in each case.

The example is a numerical representation of Figure 6.14. In case A, the difference between HDD_V and HDD_F is positive. The gas seller, having sold the swap, will have to pay the payoff to the bank. Instead, in case B, the difference between HDD_V and HDD_F is negative, and the gas seller will receive the payoff from the bank.

It is useful to correlate the HDD swap financial result with the business activity of the gas seller. To carry out this analysis, it is necessary to clarify how the thermal gradient (supposed to be 10,000 scm/HDD) can be calculated. Figure 6.13 will be used again, now placing the HDD on the horizontal axis and showing the statistical regression line interpolating the observations (Figure 6.15).

This estimation is done by means of a simple ordinary least squares (OLS) regression, calculating the line that best describes the phenomenon observed. The line has the following mathematical formulation:

$$\text{gas sales} = \alpha + \beta \times \text{HDD} + \text{error} \qquad (6.12)$$

The thermal gradient is simply the slope β of the line, which in the example we assumed equal to 10,000 scm for each HDD. We must bear in mind, however, that this is a statistical relationship and as such subject to variability. This can be seen from the cloud of points, which are scattered around the line but are generally not precisely on the line. Table 6.4 verifies the effect of such randomness on the previous example.

In the hypothetical case B, the change in consumption due to a warmer than average winter should be equal to –760,000 scm for a loss of profit equal to 38,000 euros for the gas

TABLE 6.3 Payoffs under two HDD scenarios

					Payoff in euro for	
	HHD_F	HHD_V	Delta HDD	Delta euro	Gas seller	Bank
Case A	1825	1937	112	56,000	–56,000	56,000
Case B	1825	1749	–76	–38,000	38,000	–38,000

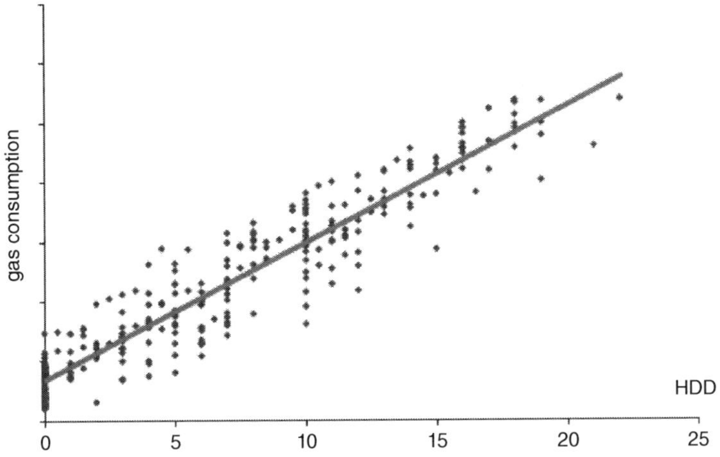

FIGURE 6.15 The relationship between HDDs and household gas consumption

seller. In a hypothetical situation under no uncertainty, the positive result of the swap, equal to 38,000 euros, would fully compensate the loss on the business activity. However, Figure 6.15 shows that the relationship between gas consumption and HDD is not a deterministic one: different levels of consumption may correspond to the same value of HDD. Cases B1 and B2 in Table 6.4 show two plausible examples, considering the uncertainty in the relationship between temperature and gas consumption. In fact it may happen that consumption is reduced, in response to a warm winter, but by an amount higher than that suggested by the linear relationship identified above; namely, the case of a combination of consumption and HDD below the interpolating line. In case B1 the loss of margin for the seller, that is 41,000 euros, exceeds the cash proceeds from the HDD swap, resulting in a residual loss of 3000 euros. In case B2, however, consumption is reduced by an amount lower than that suggested by the regression line, resulting in a residual income for the seller equal to 4500 euros.

These residual losses and gains are just two of the possible infinite outcomes of what is classified as basis risk. This risk is faced every time an exposure to a given source of risk is hedged with a derivative instrument whose underlying is different from this exposure, but whose price evolution is deemed sufficiently similar for hedging purposes. This situation is quite common in the financial world and particularly in commodity financial markets, as the number of available derivative instruments is lower than the number of existing physical commodities (and hence exposures) in the market.

TABLE 6.4 Payoffs under two HDD scenarios and basis risk

				Payoff in euro for the gas seller		
	HHD_F	HHD_V	Delta HDD	From SWAP	From consumption variation	Basis risk
Case B 1	1825	1749	−76	38,000	−41,000	−3,000
Case B 2	1825	1749	−76	−38,000	33,500	4,500

The best situation would be the use of financial instruments that directly meet the original exposure (i.e., uncertain gas consumption in this case). Failing that, the second best would be the use of derivative instruments that have a temperature index as the underlying. Under this second-best solution it becomes important to reduce, as far as possible, the mentioned basis risk in order to increase the efficiency of hedging activity. In terms of Figure 6.15, this is represented by the reduction of dispersion around the interpolating line.

This goal can be achieved by improving the quality of the data used for the statistical analysis. First of all, it is advisable to use a temperature index that can discriminate significant situations from insignificant ones. The use of HDD fits this purpose, excluding from consideration temperatures above 18°C. It is still possible to improve the significance of this index by using as the threshold a value different from 18°C, if statistical analysis shows that such a value can better discriminate significant cases (i.e., gas consumption driven by temperature) from insignificant ones. There are also various ways of improving the quality of the sample used in gas consumption estimation.

For example, it is often wise to separate estimates for weekdays and weekends, because the behaviour of households in these two cases will probably differ. Statistical estimation can also help to detect anomalies in consumption records. Examples are the erroneous inclusion of industrial gas users, or the non-constancy of the observed sample size. The latter can be the result of the gradual inclusion of a greater number of customers, giving rise to a consumption increase, which is of course not related to the atmospheric temperature.

6.5 CONCLUSIONS

Stemming from the clarification of the importance of volumetric risk together with price risk, this chapter has demonstrated that the assessment of the former is possible when volumetric risk is influenced by weather risk. In fact, we have conducted an in-depth study for a case of non-deterministic influence – that is, the impact of atmospheric temperature on the consumption of natural gas.

It is important to underline that there are many other cases in which weather conditions have an impact on the energy market in general. Atmospheric temperature will influence the consumption of other fuels used for heating, such as heating oil, but will also determine the amount of electricity that can be produced in any thermal power plant around the world. Moreover, other weather events are important in the context of energy transformation, and even in a more radical way. In fact, most renewable energy sources are just based on the availability of weather conditions and on the level of weather variables. It is almost obvious to note that wind power depends on the availability of sufficient wind strength, as hydroelectricity does not exist if water is not there.

Finally, through the linkage of weather events and variables to electricity production, weather is also connected to emissions and emissions trading schemes. Scarcity of water precipitation or lack of wind strength will imply, *ceteris paribus*, that a higher percentage of demanded electricity will have to be produced by burning fossil fuels, hence increasing CO_2 emissions.[20]

[20]These topics are summarized in Mauro (2007).

NOMENCLATURE

P	price
Q	quantity
V	value
ΔP	price variation
ΔQ	quantity variation
ΔV	value variation
P_0	initial price
Q_0	initial quantity
D	demand curve
S	supply curve
MR	marginal revenue
ε	elasticity of demand
VaR	value-at-risk
σ_p	volatility of price returns
$\rho_{Q,P}$	correlation between quantity and price
ACF	autocorrelation function
PACF	partial autocorrelation function
ADT	average daily temperature
CDD	cooling degree days
HDD	heating degree days

REFERENCES

Arrow, J.K. (1964) The role of securities in the optimal allocation of risk-bearing, *Review of Economic Studies*, **XXXI**, 91–96.

Dischel, B. (2002) Deutsches data duel, *Energy & Power Risk Management*, January, 34–37.

Dowd, K. (1998) *Beyond Value at Risk: The New Science of Risk Management*, John Wiley & Sons, Chichester.

Jorion, P. (1997) *Value at Risk*, McGraw-Hill, New York.

Mauro, A. (1999a) Price risk management in the energy industry: The value at risk approach, Proceedings of the XXII Annual Conference of the International Association for Energy Economics, June. Available at http://ssrn.com/abstract=1020917.

Mauro, A. (1999b) La gestione del rischio di prezzo nella industria energetica, Energia, no. 4-1999, available at http://ssrn.com/abstract=1992427.

Mauro, A. (2007) L'impatto di eventi meteorologici sulla produzione e lo scambio di energia, available at http://www.grin.com/en/e-book/195614/l-impatto-di-eventi-meteoreologici-sulla-produzione-e-lo-scambio-di-energia.

Nelken, I. (2000) Pricing for a rainy day, *Energy & Power Risk Management*, April, 40–44.

Pankratz, A. (1991) *Forecasting with Dynamic Regression Models*, John Wiley & Sons, New York.

CHAPTER 7

Industrial Metals Markets and Products

Alessandro Porru

7.1 GENERAL OVERVIEW

Industrial metals can be distinguished as *ferrous* or *non-ferrous* metals in relation to their iron content. They are defined as 'industrial' to address their end use and distinguish them from precious metals (gold and silver, platinum and palladium). The most important category market-wise is that of *non-ferrous* metals, also called *base metals*: aluminium and aluminium alloys, copper, lead, nickel, tin and zinc. Later in this book we will discuss the historical importance and the physical features of these metals, which contributed to the formation of a liquid market.

Other secondary metals will also be mentioned, as well as some recent efforts to develop a market based on ferrous and 'non-elemental' metals. We will nevertheless observe that steel (an alloy consisting of iron and carbon), which is heavily used in modern industry, also struggled to develop a liquid financial market.

Unlike most commodities, where several exchanges challenge each other to attract liquidity, base metals trading concentrates on the London Metal Exchange (LME). The history of the LME goes together with that of the base-metals market. Therefore, this chapter starts with a brief history of the LME. It follows with an overview of each metal's characteristics, consumption data and industry uses. Since the market is not based on non-ferrous metals alone, and not exclusively on the LME, the most promising newcomer contracts and exchanges will be discussed.

Sections 7.1.4 and 7.1.5 on instruments listed by the LME and traded over-the-counter (OTC) are introductory to the content covered in Sections 7.2 and 7.3. The reader will learn how trading is organized at the LME and how physical delivery takes place.

---

*Views expressed are those of the author and do not represent his employer.

Handbook of Multi-Commodity Markets and Products: Structuring, Trading and Risk Management. Edited by Andrea Roncoroni, Gianluca Fusai and Mark Cummins.

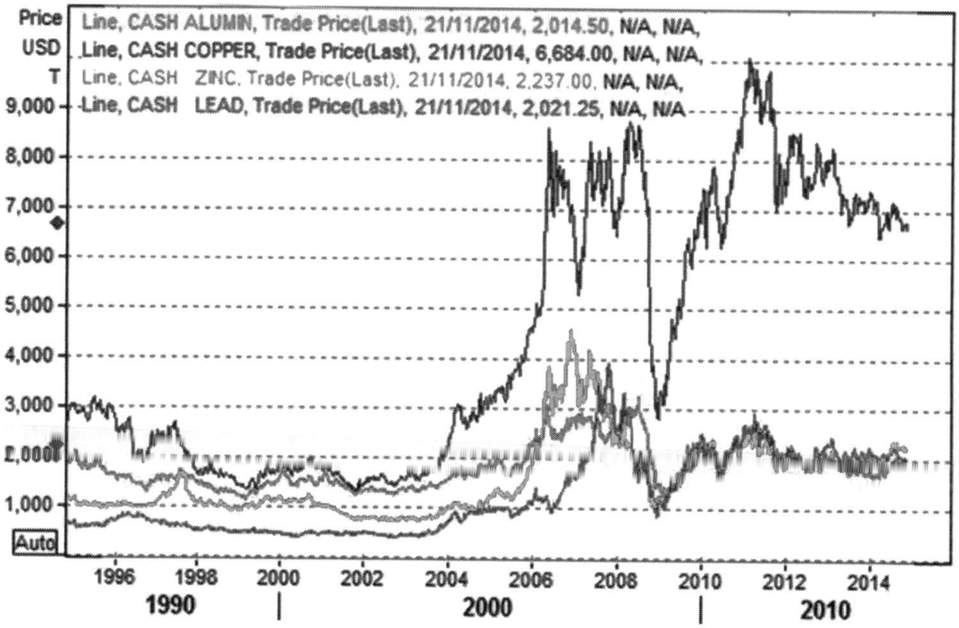

FIGURE 7.1 LME cash prices (a)

In the last decade, the market witnessed two important phenomena. First, the main role played by China and its fast-growing economy that boosted the demand for metals and energy products: the so-called 'China effect'. Second, the increasing presence of institutional and private investors that injected fresh money into the market: Section 7.1.6 is dedicated to these new players.

These factors help explain the rallies observed in Figures 7.1 and 7.2, where the time series are the LME official cash prices for the main six base-metal contracts.

At the end of 2005, the prices for all metals skyrocketed and, with the partial exception of aluminium, a very strong bull market lasted until mid-2008 when the credit crunch and the global crisis affected the markets. Starting from 2009, only copper prices recovered fast, breaking the record level of 10,000 USD/MT in February 2011.

7.1.1 Brief History of the LME

The LME, founded more than 130 years ago in 1877, has always been an example of both innovation and tradition. During the Roman Empire, copper and tin were extracted mainly in South Wales and the largest deposits were based in Britain. For centuries, until ca. 1850, the demand for copper and other metals grew at a slow pace and had always been satisfied by European supply. In such a scenario, metal prices were quite stable and at the beginning the primary role of traders was only to balance the local demand and supply. It was during the reign of Elizabeth I that the first metal traders started to deal on a regular basis. The practice was to draw a ring in the dust on the floor where merchants dealt and traded.

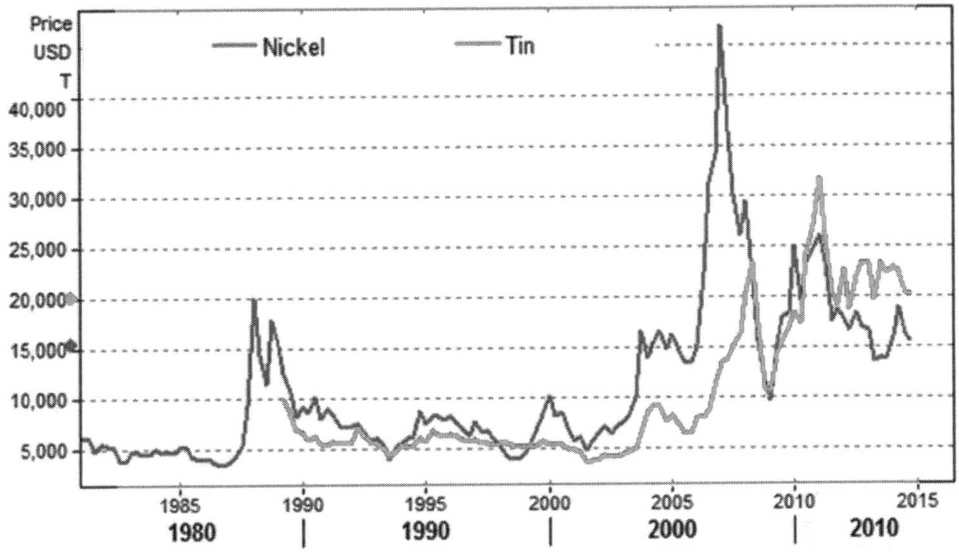

FIGURE 7.2 LME cash prices (b)

With the industrial revolution, Great Britain turned from a net exporter of base metals into the biggest importer from all over the world. This change further enhanced the development of trading to the extent that it became a real need given the different origins of the imports. Only in 1877 was the ring formalized, when the London Metals & Mining Company opened its exchange in Lombard Court.

Importing from all over the world meant long delivery times and the LME allowed merchants to forward-sell their loads in order to lock in their profits, thus guaranteeing their selling prices. Later on, the development of steam ships and the invention of telegraphy helped improve shipping times and the tracking of freight: the overall consequence was to improve the scheduling capabilities of merchants and the delivery of loads. At the time, the most traded metals were copper and tin and it took 3 months to ship the former from Chile and the latter from Malaysia to London.

- *The trading activity on the LME has hence concentrated on the 3-month forward: this is the reason why it is still the most liquid contract today.*

Since then, the LME has kept growing rapidly both in terms of volumes and popularity, with an increasing number of traders using the London marketplace as a world benchmark for metals prices. In addition to copper and tin, lead was introduced in 1903 and zinc in 1915.

The LME closed during the Great War and World War II. The Exchange reopened in 1954 with higher volumes and a more structured image, different categories of members were introduced: some of them pure brokers and others dealers. In the 1970s, new contracts were added to respond to the need for 'new' metals: aluminium first and then nickel were introduced in 1978 and 1979, respectively. The first European warehouse was opened in Rotterdam. Today, more than 400 warehouses are active all over the world.

The first problems came in the 1980s, with the 'tin crisis' caused by the International Tin Council (ITC). In order to avoid bankruptcy, the LME was forced to suspend tin trading for 6 months. The tin price collapsed because of the lack of demand, due to the limited uses of tin in the past few decades and the strong supply coming from emerging countries. The 1980s also brought positive changes as the LME developed its clearing functionality, thereby protecting its clearing members from the risk of bankruptcy of other members. These steps helped the LME to become a regulated market and grow in reputation, volume and confidence among the main metal traders.

The 1990s also saw changes in the market with the introduction of two regional contracts for aluminium alloy. The process of innovation at the LME is continuous and, in recent years, new contracts have been developed such as plastics, steel, cobalt and molybdenum.

In the year 2000, the corporate structure of the LME changed and LME Holdings Limited was founded: it incorporated the old LME Company and its members became shareholders in the new company. This new structure, coupled with technological advances, permitted the reduction of ring dealing members in favour of more non-ring-dealing members. The latter are players like investment banks or big manufacturing companies, which may operate from locations different from London. Today in fact, even though trading on the ring is still in use, trading can easily be done overseas through telephone and screens.

Although in most marketplaces the concept of a physical trading floor is no more in use, the LME is unique in its attempt to mix innovation and tradition in a perfect blend. The LME has been one of the first commodities exchanges to introduce an electronic trading platform: the LMEselect.

- *While LMEselect tracks the intra-day price movements of the main contracts (the 3-month or '3M'), the Ring is still the source of official prices and the City's last open-outcry market.*

In June 2012, the Board of LME Holdings Limited recommended the exchange shareholders to sell the entire issued share capital of LME Holdings Limited to HKEx Limited (Hong Kong Exchanges and Clearing) for £1388 million. The Board of LME Holdings Limited had received several bids, one of them notably being from the American giant, the Intercontinental Exchange (ICE). In July 2012 the large majority of LME shareholders voted in favour of acquisition by the HKEx: the change of ownership is expected to increase the LME's penetration in Asia and hence in one of the world's fastest growing economies: China. The following subsection will help us to understand how crucial China is in today's metals markets.

7.1.2 Non-ferrous Metals

When dealing with non-ferrous, base metals, generalizing can be very misleading. Often in the media, as well as in some analyst reports, the base metals are referred to as a 'complex'. In reality each metal, though correlated, displays unique chemical features, different production and consumption locations and specific industrial applications. In other words, the dynamics of supply and demand change a lot case by case.

The following pages report for each metal the Latin name of the element, the LME contract code (e.g., AHD for primary aluminium) together with some commonly used abbreviations (e.g., AL HG) and the regulated exchanges (worldwide) listing futures. Only the exchanges showing trading activity at present have been mentioned. In the forward curve and volatility sections, some of these markets will be compared in terms of arbitrage. Metals charts are shown with the percentage distribution of production and consumption by country and area. This is useful to get an idea of who are the biggest players in the market on the 'buy side' and the 'sell side'.

The role of China can easily be detected in these charts: the country very often holds first place as the biggest single buyer or producer. Chinese GDP in the last decade grew at an impressive pace and starting from 1998 the imports exceeded the exports. This is the consequence of the rapid process of industrialization that creates high demand for many commodities: oil, steel (and iron ore) and raw materials like base metals. The rallies observed in recent years are strictly linked to the impact of China on the market: the so-called *China effect*. It is no surprise that the Shanghai Futures Exchange is one of the most active trading venues for base metals, together with the LME.

Finally, the pie charts in Figure 7.3 provide an immediate insight into the relevance of each contract in the LME. In terms of *open interest* (the number of futures contracts outstanding for a metal across all maturities), primary aluminium has no competitors: it is by far the most traded metal followed by copper and zinc, lead and nickel. Aluminium alloys play a smaller role, together with the new contracts on steel and minor metals. This ranking could actually be misleading: the dollar value of these open interests should also be taken into account. In fact, taking the end of October 2012 quotations as a reference, while one lot (25 metric tons) of aluminium is worth 50,000 USD (at a price of 2000 USD/MT), one lot of nickel (6 metric tons) is worth 96,000 USD (at a price of 16,000 USD/MT). The result of such a wide price difference is that expensive metals like copper, nickel and tin have a higher relevance than that suggested by simple open interest, with copper being in fact the most important contract in terms of dollar value.

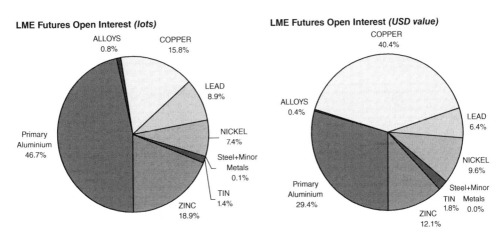

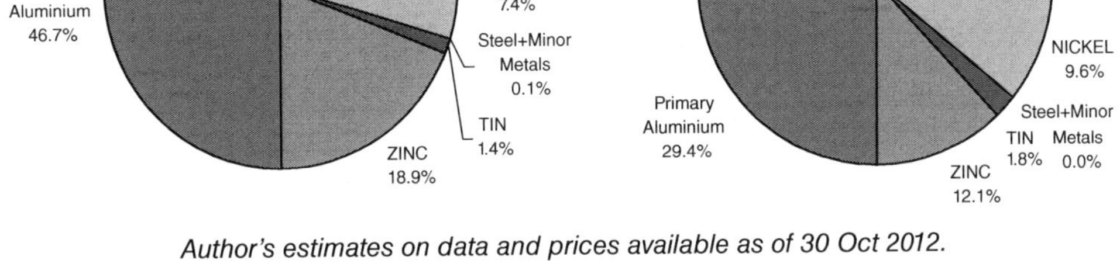

FIGURE 7.3 Futures open interest (lots and USD value)

High Grade Primary Aluminium
(Aluminium, AH, AL HG, 'ALI')

Main end uses:
Transportation, construction, packaging, electrical transmission lines, machinery, cooking utensils.

Exchanges listing liquid futures:
LME *(London Metal Exchange)*
SHFE *(Shanghai Futures Exchange)*
TOCOM *(Tokyo Commodity Exchange)*
MCX India *(Multi Commodity Exchange)*
NCDEX *(National Commodity & Derivatives Exchange, India)*

LME specifications *(from LME.com)*
Primary aluminium with impurities no greater than in the registered designation P1020A in the North American and International Registration Record.
Ingots, T-bars, sows.

Lot size: **25 MT**

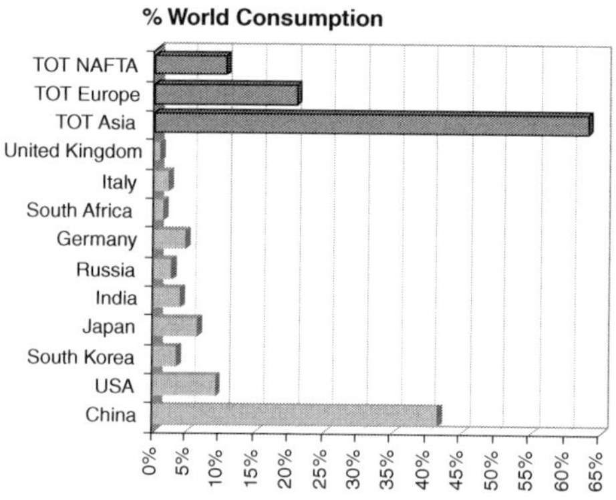

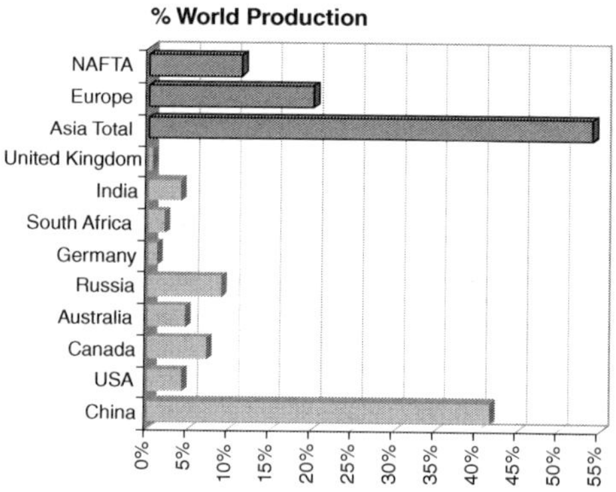

NAFTA stands for North American Free Trade Agreement, comprising the USA, Mexico and Canada. Author's elaborations on data from World Bureau of Metal Statistics (June 2010). Updated data to 2014 courtesy of Thomson Reuters Eikon.

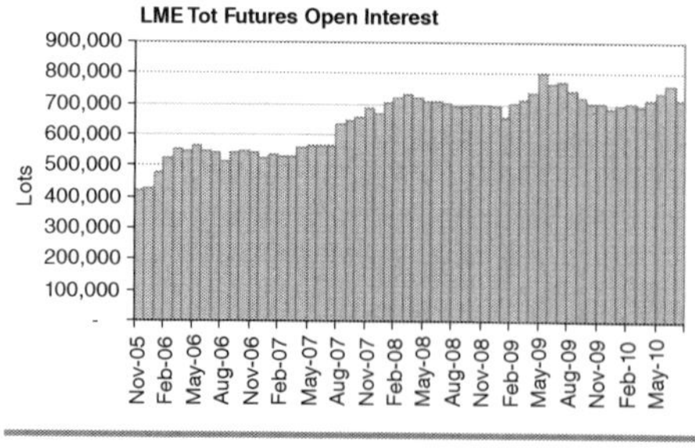

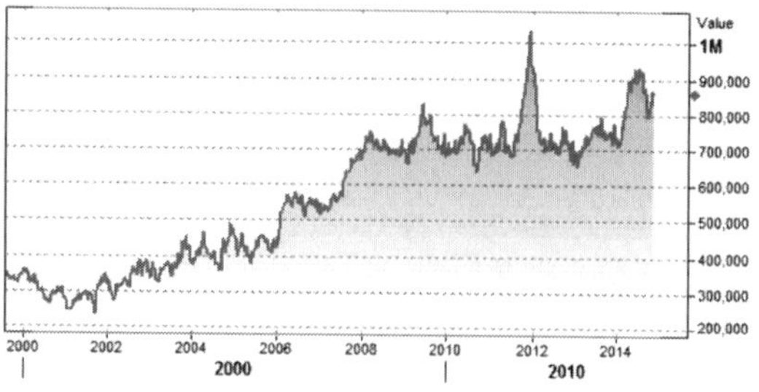

Alloy and NASAAC Aluminium
(AA and NA)

Main end uses:
Automotive engine parts, structural applications.

Exchanges listing liquid futures:
LME *(London Metal Exchange)*

LME specifications *(from LME.com)*
Alloy: Aluminium alloy conforming to A380.1, 226 or AD12.1.

NASAAC: North American Special Aluminium Alloy Contract. Aluminium alloy conforming to the 'LME NA380.1' specification.

Lot size: **20 MT**
Updated data to 2014 courtesy of Thomson Reuters Eikon.

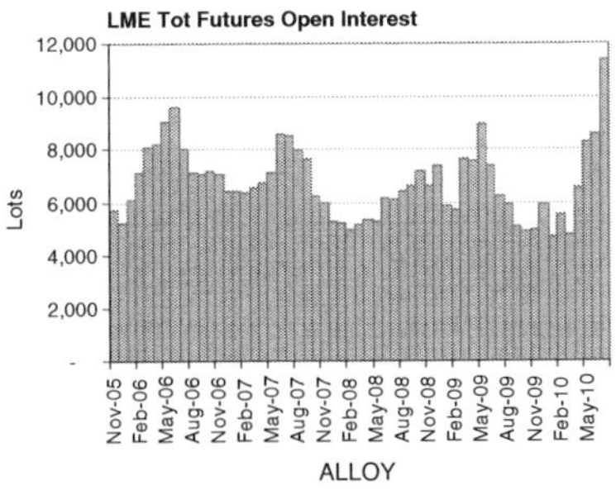

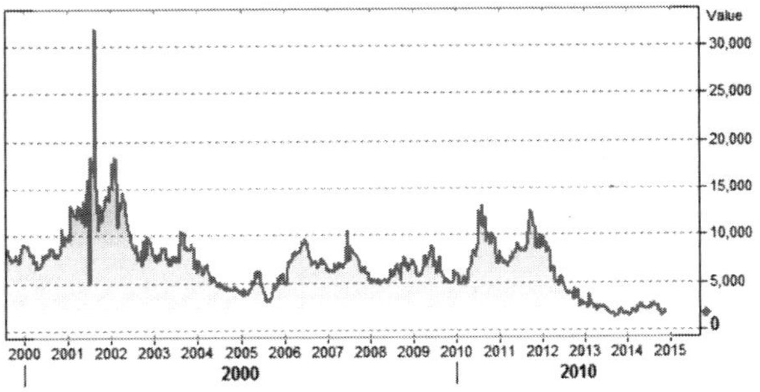

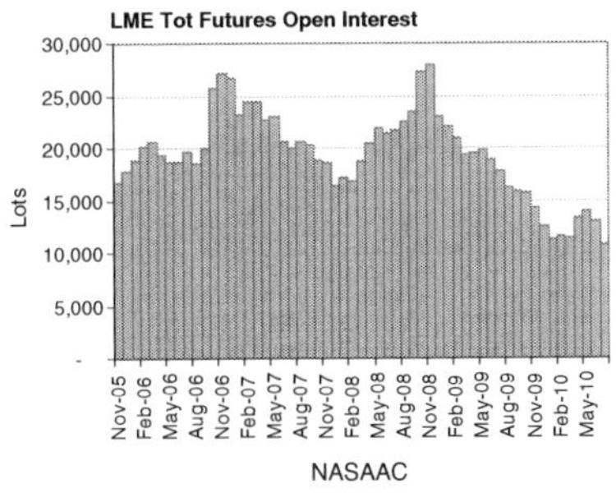

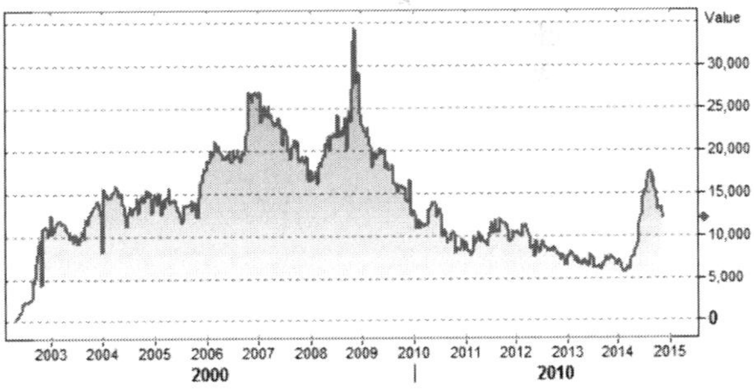

Copper
(Cuprum, CA)

Main end uses:
Electronic and electrical (wires, circuits, electromagnets), construction, transportation, machinery, piping, biomedical.

Exchanges listing liquid futures:
LME *(London Metal Exchange)*
COMEX *(a division of CME, New York)*
SHFE *(Shanghai Futures Exchange)*
MCX India *(Multi Commodity Exchange)*
NCDEX *(National Commodity & Derivatives Exchange, India)*

LME specifications *(from LME.com)*
Grade A copper conforming to BS EN 1978:1998 (Cu-CATH-1) .

Cathodes.

Lot size: **25 MT**

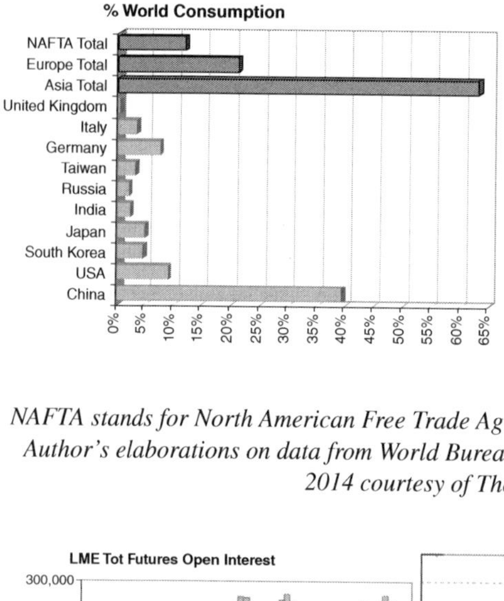

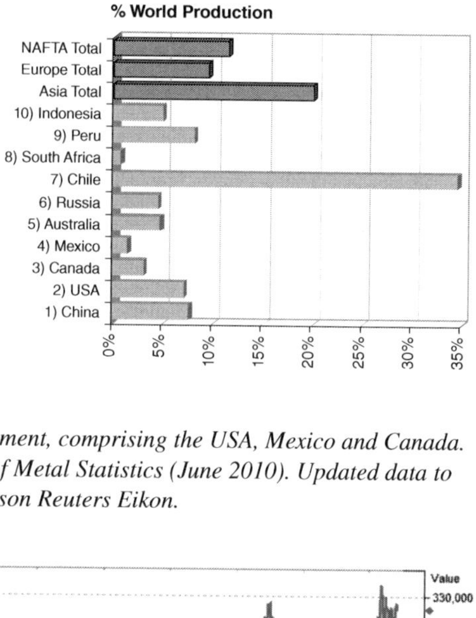

NAFTA stands for North American Free Trade Agreement, comprising the USA, Mexico and Canada. Author's elaborations on data from World Bureau of Metal Statistics (June 2010). Updated data to 2014 courtesy of Thomson Reuters Eikon.

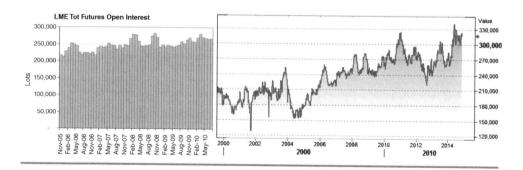

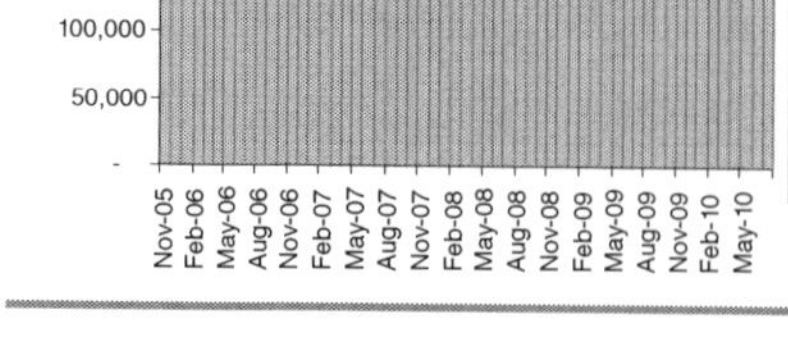

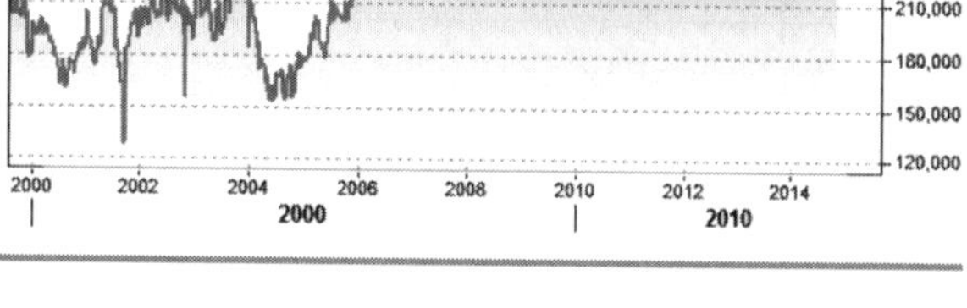

Lead
(Plumbum, PB)

Main end uses:
Batteries, chemicals, ammunitions, weight (elemental lead).

Exchanges listing liquid futures:
LME *(London Metal Exchange)*
MCX India *(Multi Commodity Exchange)*
NCDEX *(National Commodity & Derivatives Exchange, India)*

LME specifications *(from LME.com)*
Lead of 99.97% purity (minimum) conforming to BS EN 12659:1999.

Ingots.

Lot size: **25 MT**

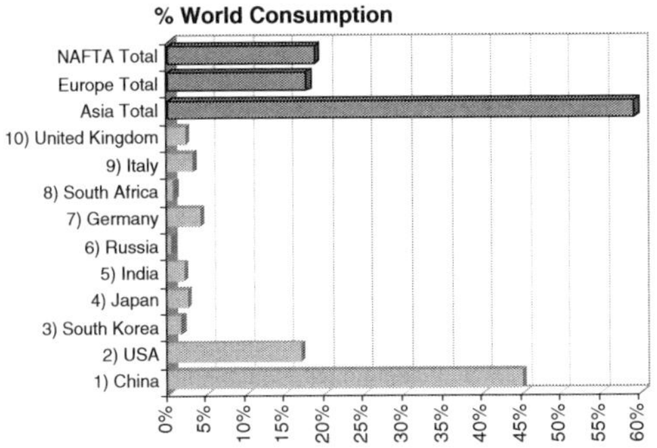

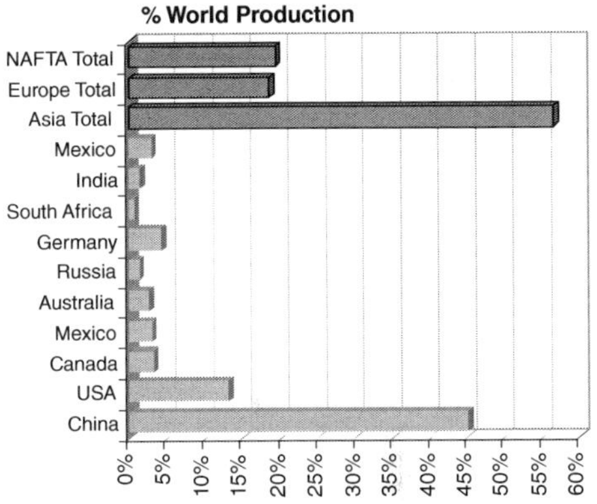

NAFTA stands for North American Free Trade Agreement, comprising the USA, Mexico and Canada. Author's elaborations on data from World Bureau of Metal Statistics (June 2010). Updated data to 2014 courtesy of Thomson Reuters Eikon.

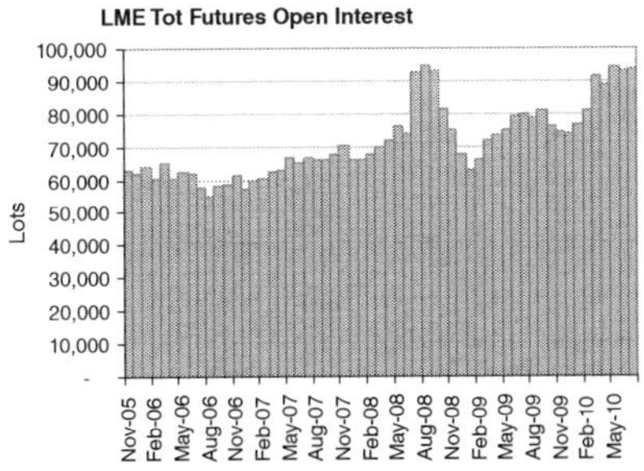

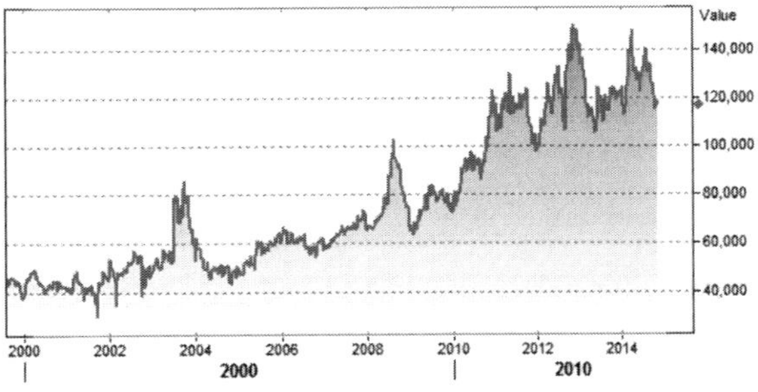

Nickel
(NI)

Main end uses:
Stainless steel, chemicals.

Exchanges listing liquid futures:
LME *(London Metal Exchange)*
MCX India *(Multi Commodity Exchange)*

LME specifications *(from LME.com)*
Nickel of 99.80% purity (minimum) conforming to B39-79 (2004).

Full plate cathode, cut cathodes, pellets, briquettes.

Lot size: **6 MT**

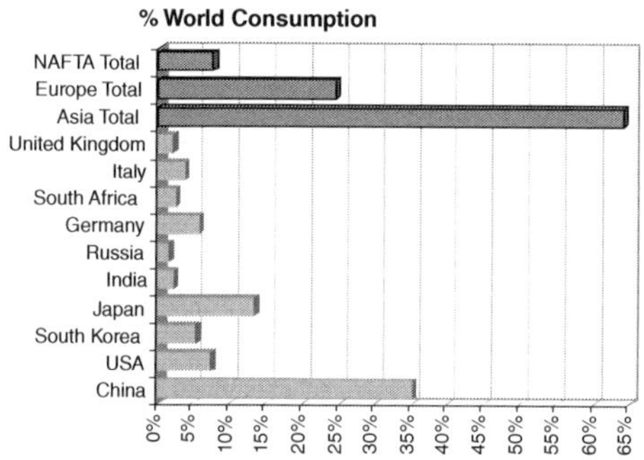

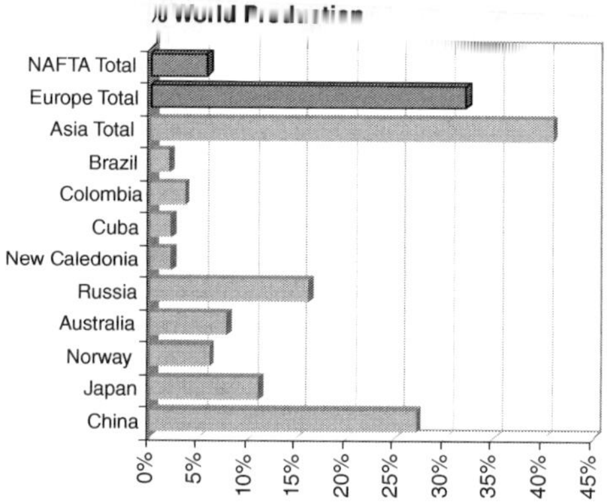

NAFTA stands for North American Free Trade Agreement, comprising the USA, Mexico and Canada. Author's elaborations on data from World Bureau of Metal Statistics (June 2010). Updated data to 2014 courtesy of Thomson Reuters Eikon.

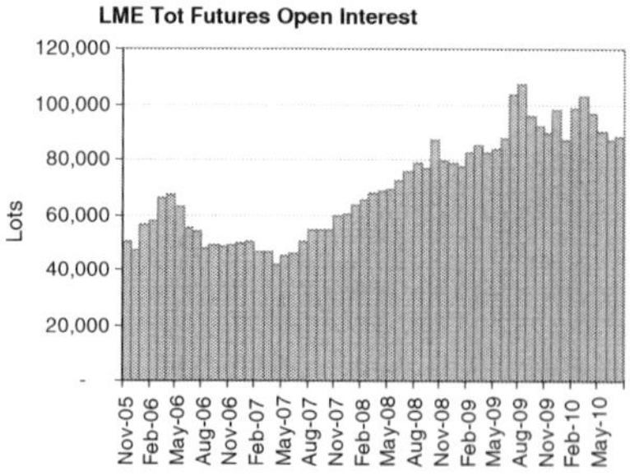

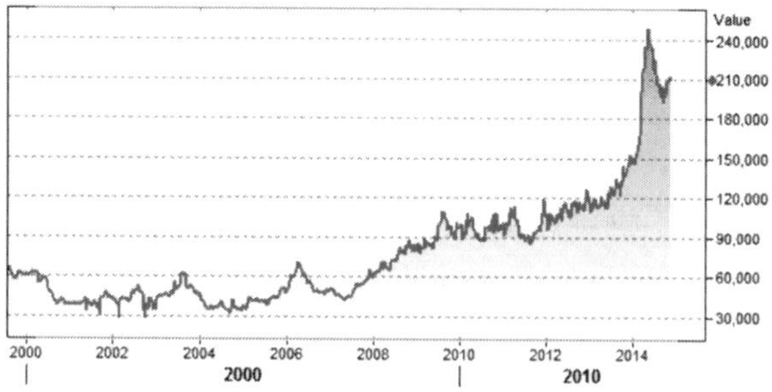

Tin
(Stannum, SN)

Main end uses:
Solders, tin plate, varnishes.

Exchanges listing liquid futures:
LME *(London Metal Exchange)*

LME specifications *(from LME.com)*
Tin of 99.85% purity (minimum) conforming to BS EN 610:1996.

Ingots.

Lot size: **5 MT**

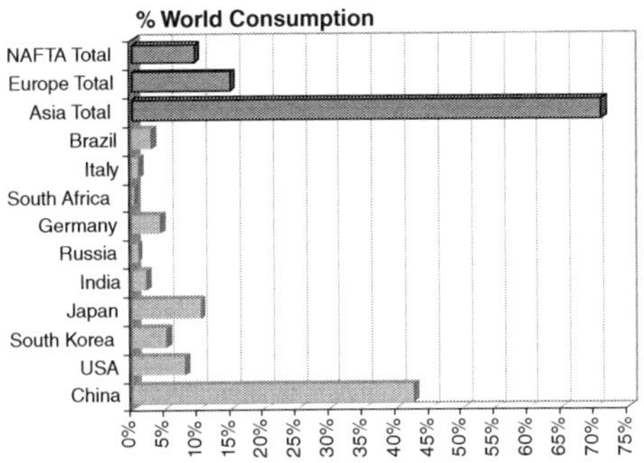

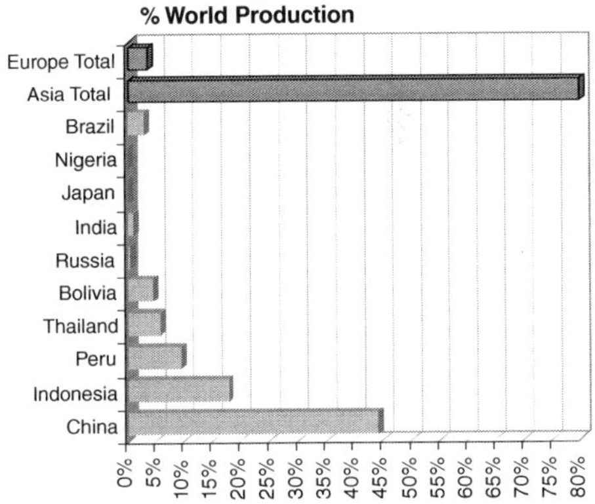

NAFTA stands for North American Free Trade Agreement, comprising the USA, Mexico and Canada. Author's elaborations on data from World Bureau of Metal Statistics (June 2010). Updated data to 2014 courtesy of Thomson Reuters Eikon.

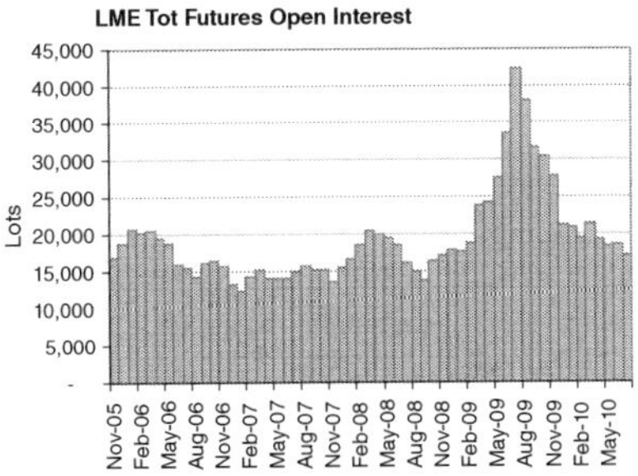

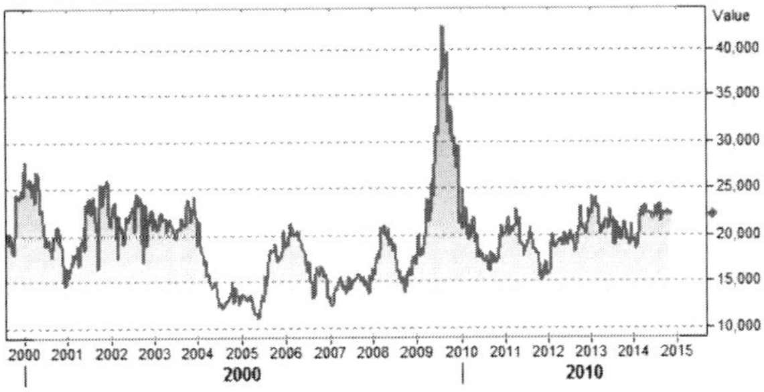

Zinc
(Zincum, ZS)

Main end uses:
Galvanizing, brass, bronze, chemicals, medicine (zinc compounds).

Exchanges listing liquid futures:
LME *(London Metal Exchange)*
SHFE *(Shanghai Futures Exchange)*
MCX India *(Multi Commodity Exchange)*

LME specifications *(from LME.com)*
Zinc of 99.995% purity (minimum) conforming to BS EN 1179:2003.

Ingots.

Lot size: 25 MT

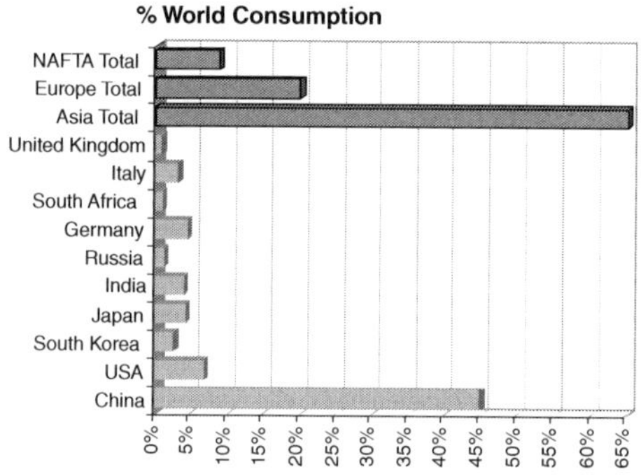

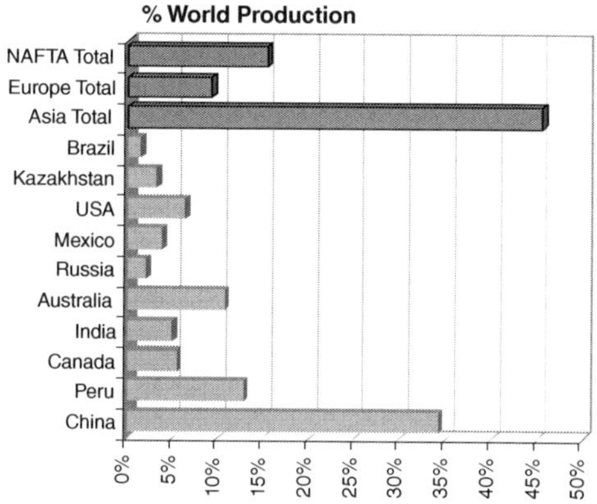

NAFTA stands for North American Free Trade Agreement, comprising the USA, Mexico and Canada. Author's elaborations on data from World Bureau of Metal Statistics (June 2010). Updated data to 2014 courtesy of Thomson Reuters Eikon.

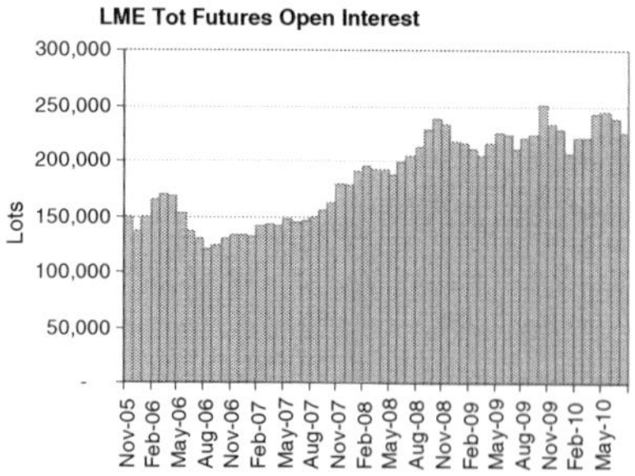

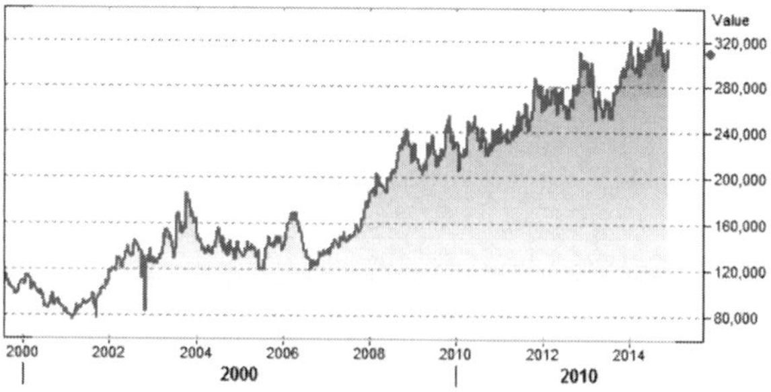

7.1.3 Other Metals

Steel is one of the most important commodities in the world in terms of dollar value of global transactions. Together with iron ore, which is used to produce steel, it is only second to oil. While the financial oil market is (amongst commodities) the biggest and most liquid in the world, historically there have not been equivalent futures contracts on steel or iron ore.

- *One reason is due to the so-called benchmark system: traditionally, the price of steel was fixed between sellers (miners) and buyers (steel producers) once a year.*

This system stood in place for over 40 years, almost eliminating price volatility. With fast-growing demand and the *China effect*, the benchmark system collapsed in favour of free spot prices. As the spot market on steel grew, the OTC forward market soon followed. Another reason is that steel is an alloy produced in hundreds of different variants. This has always represented an obstacle to contract standardization but, as the trading activity on the OTC market started growing, several attempts have been made towards standardization.

One constant between almost all new contracts on steel and iron ore is that they are cleared. In recent years, in fact, the OTC market on commodities has witnessed an unprecedented migration to cleared contracts. The credit crunch undermined the stability of the market, since OTC transactions are much less appealing compared with exchange-listed contracts if the counterparty risk of default is high. As a result, traders and brokers are increasingly posting OTC transactions on exchanges in order to benefit from the clearing house and offset their credit exposure.

7.1.3.1 Steel Steel futures are now listed on the MCX and NCDEX (India), NYMEX (New York), SHFE (Shanghai) and LME. The Shanghai-based exchange is probably the most successful so far: both list contracts, Deformed Bar Steel and Wire Steel, are considered quite liquid.

The LME initially introduced two contracts with different locations; namely, the Far East and Mediterranean. Since only one (the Med) gathered enough liquidity, the two contracts were merged (as of 2010) in the LME *Steel Billet Futures*. Approved warehouses for delivery are in the USA, Europe, Middle East and Far East. The contract displays the same maturity dates as for non-ferrous metals, and so the content of this section applies also to steel.

OTC activity is also rising in Europe around the *CRU European* hot rolled coil assessment.

7.1.3.2 Iron Ore The specification traded most on the OTC market is the *Iron Ore CFR China* (62% Fe fines). The instrument is the average swap cash settled against the Steel Index or the Platts steel assessments. Clearing of these contracts is provided by SGX AsiaClear (the clearing facility for the Singapore Exchange) and LCH (London Clearing House, the same clearer for the LME).

7.1.3.3 Minor Metals Cobalt and molybdenum are the latest newcomers on the LME. The exchange launched them in February 2010. Both have several industrial applications: alloys, batteries, catalysts and pigments. The contract displays the same maturity dates as for non-ferrous metals.

7.1.4 LME Instruments

On the LME, it is possible to trade both futures and options. As on most commodity exchanges in the world, for example the NY COMEX (now under the CME umbrella) on which copper futures and options are listed, the futures feature physical delivery and the options are American style. Unlike most exchanges, the LME contracts work in a different way as explained below.

7.1.4.1 Forwards Disguised as Futures Both forwards and futures contracts are the obligation to deliver a determined quantity of an asset or commodity at a fixed price at a specified date in the future. While a forward is a contract between two parties, futures are listed and traded on exchanges. A futures is highly standardized, and a clearing house stays between the parties to eliminate counterparty risk. The clearing house requires the holder of a futures position to submit an initial margin and, on a daily basis, variation margins to mark to market the value of positions. A forward, in contrast, is highly customizable to the needs of the two parties who have to bear the counterparty risk. It is only at the final payment date that the contract will be regulated if both the parties are solvent.

Futures on LME are a mix of two contracts. First of all, each operator's positions on futures remain open until the delivery date. Unlike on most futures exchanges, there is not in fact netting of opposite positions. If, for example, a trader has bought 10 lots of copper for delivery 1 year ahead, the subsequent sale of 10 lots on the same delivery date will be treated as a different contract. The LME hence is not a *cash-cleared* market (Crabb, 1999).

- *As a consequence, the variation margins of LME futures are discounted to take into account the time to maturity of the futures.*

The clearing of LME contracts is operated by the LCH, which applies the relevant discount factors computed on the basis of prevailing interest rates on the market. In the example above, if the 10 lots were sold 1 USD/MT higher than the purchase price, the trader would find in his clearing account 1 (USD) × 10 (lots) × 25 (MT per lot) × 1y *Df* (1-year discount factor). This is less than the 250 USD he would have on cash-cleared markets. The mark-to-market of LME futures, from a financial point of view, is then comparable with that of a forward. In the following sections we will see how this feature impacts on optimal hedging strategies and futures option pricing.

The calculation of margins is operated by the LCH using the *London SPAN® algorithm*. Initial margins are continuously updated on changing market conditions: absolute levels of prices and volatility are the main drivers. Table 7.1 reports the scanning range assessment (as of August 2010) for LME base metals futures. The scanning range is a worst-scenario measure of risk: the requested initial margins are a function of that risk. For example, an initial margin of 15,000 USD is roughly requested to enter in a position on one lot of copper (25 MT). With a 3M contract at 7000 USD/MT the total notional of one lot is 175,000 USD and the initial margin accounts for ~9% of it.

The SPAN algorithm distinguishes between outright futures positions, on which the above margins are requested, and calendar or inter-commodity spreads. With the latter positions being less risky, different parameters are used to take into account correlation.

The LME distinguishes between *clearing members* and *clients*. Only the clearing members interface with the clearing house and benefit from the full warranty operated by the LCH.

TABLE 7.1 LME futures size and margins

Commodity	Lot size	Code	Scanning Range (+/–) $ Per Tonne	$ Per Lot
Aluminium Alloy	20 tonnes	AAD	140	2,800
Aluminium HG	25 tonnes	AHD	165	4,125
Copper 'A' Grade	25 tonnes	CAD	600	15,000
Cobalt	1 tonnes	COD	4,500	4,500
Mediterranean Steel Billet	65 tonnes	FMD	60	3,900
Molybdenum	6 tonnes	MOD	6,000	36,000
NASAAC	20 tonnes	NAD	150	3,000
Primary Nickel	6 tonnes	NID	2,800	16,800
Lead	25 tonnes	PBD	260	6,500
Tin	5 tonnes	SND	1,600	8,000
Zinc	25 tonnes	ZSD	230	5,750

Source: LCH (2010).

Clients, basically most of the operators who are not brokers (notice that not all brokers are also clearing members), have contracts in place with clearing members. These contracts are not directly guaranteed by the LCH: in theory, clients still have counterparty risk towards their clearing brokers. In practice, the risk can be considered negligible since clearing members are selected on the basis of financial capabilities and strictly controlled by the LCH and LME. Besides, brokers are obliged to cross the trades done with clients on the LME matching system: this provides full transparency to the trades and indirectly protects the clients better.

Historically, the LME was an OTC market with a common fund established as the only protection against defaults. Only in 1987, after the so-called 'tin crisis' which resulted in the cascading default of many brokers, was the clearing house introduced. This feature explains another peculiarity of the LME in respect of the broker dealer. In most markets the role of the broker is limited to a third party which never bears market risk.

- *Since the relation between clients and brokers is that of principal-to-principal, some LME brokers are also dealers themselves and hold positions at risk.*

The structure of tradable delivery dates, called *prompt dates*, is also a clear example of the LME's industry-tailored standardization. On the LME it is possible to trade futures for delivery each business day up to 3 months. The first available delivery date is the *cash*, otherwise referred to as the *spot*. As on the foreign exchange rate (FX) markets, the cash delivers two business days after inception (i.e., $t+2$). The 3-month maturity (3M) is the most traded on the LME. After the 3M, for 3 months further along, weekly prompt dates are available on each Wednesday. After 6 months the monthly futures are listed that take delivery on the third Wednesday of each month.

- *Notice that the prompt dates are rolling maturity dates.*

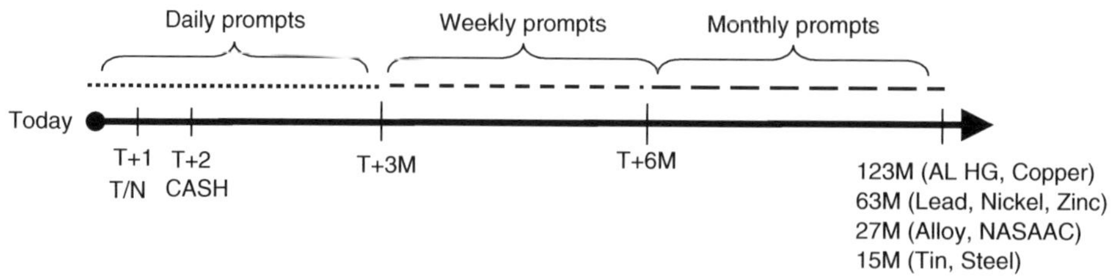

FIGURE 7.4 Delivery dates on LME.

Figure 7.4 displays the maturity set. This is valid for all dates except the monthly futures, which have fixed maturity. Notice that while the monthly maturities are typical of most commodity futures, the rolling maturities are typical of FX and interest rate markets.

- *In practice, only the 3M and the cash contracts are traded outright whereas all other maturities are traded as spreads to the 3M.*

The 3M is hence pivotal to assess prices of the whole forward curve. These spreads are called *carries*, referring to the action of carrying a position from one date to another. In LME jargon the carries are traded in the following way.

- *Borrowing* – the action of buying a short-term and selling a long-term maturity.
- *Lending* – the action of selling a short-term and buying a long-term maturity.

This jargon is linked to the physical trading: a naked short seller has in fact to borrow from someone else the metals to deliver, while the holder of stocks can instead lend metal to the market.

When forward prices increase with time to maturity, the forward curve is said to be in *contango*; when prices decrease with time the forward curve is instead in *backwardation*.

- *On the basis of the above considerations, LME futures can be considered as forward contracts that are cleared on a regulated market.*

7.1.4.2 Execution and Fixings On the LME, the execution of orders on futures can be done in several ways. Open outcry on the ring, which still preserves some of the LME's century-old practices, provides full transparency to the price-fixing process. Brokers sit in a small circle to form the ring: the trading day is divided into different scheduled phases, four ring sessions, with strict rules of engagement. The trading activity not only results in a fascinating old-school show for visitors but is also efficient and more organized than the classic pits. See Figure 7.5.

Table 7.2 reports the exact timing of all the sessions and intervals. During the *second ring session*, the *LME official prices* for each metal are fixed.

- *The official cash and 3-month (3M) prices are the most important assessments. The fixing is double: bid (buyer) and offer (seller) price. The offer price is also the official settlement price.*

FIGURE 7.5 The LME ring
Source: LME. © London Metal Exchange. Reproduced with permission.

The *inter-office trading* links the open-outcry to the rest of the world. Brokers provide price indications through electronic screens, chats and execution is often done via telephone. The LME was one of the first exchanges to couple these traditional methods of trading with electronic trading; *LMEselect* is the platform on which it is possible to trade the 3M contract directly and in real time.

At 16:35 (London time) the afternoon *Kerbs* start: a session where each broker can have more than one dealer seated or standing on the floor and all metals are traded together.

- *At the end of this session the evaluation prices (also named evening evaluations) are fixed. These are the assessments used by the LCH for the end-of-day margining of futures and options.*

The LME also runs the assessment of metal prices in other currencies: EUR, GBP and JPY. For these currencies the official LME exchange rate versus USD is published.

7.1.4.3 Delivery at LME A long/short position on the cash is subject to physical delivery. A standing position can also be offset after the official cash price is fixed (second morning ring) to avoid delivery: it is in fact possible to do this the next day, up until 12:20 (the so-called Tom-Next).

In Section 7.1.2 we saw for the main contracts some basic specifications: the lot size (number of metric tons) and the shape of deliverable material (ingots, bars, etc.). The standardization of LME futures is tailored to the needs of the industry and can display tolerance

TABLE 7.2 Trading sessions at the LME

SESSION	CONTRACT	TIME START	TIME END	FIXING
GLOBAL INTEROFFICE	ALL	24h/24h		
LME SELECT	**ALL**	**1.00 AM**	**7.00 PM**	
STOCKS WARNING	ALL	8.55 AM	9.05 AM	
1ST MORNING RING	STEEL	11.40 AM	11.45 AM	
1ST MORNING RING	NASAAC & ALUMINIUM A	11.45 AM	11.50 AM	
1ST MORNING RING	TIN	11.50 AM	11.55 AM	
1ST MORNING RING	ALUMINIUM PRIMARY	11.55 AM	12.00 PM	
1ST MORNING RING	COPPER	12.00 PM	12.05 PM	
1ST MORNING RING	LEAD	12.05 PM	12.10 PM	
1ST MORNING RING	ZINC	12.10 PM	12.15 PM	
1ST MORNING RING	NICKEL	12.15 PM	12.20 PM	
1ST MORNING RING	Cobalt and Molybdenum	12.20 PM	12.25 PM	
INTERVAL	ALL	12.25 PM	12.30 PM	
2ND MORNING RING	COPPER	12.30 PM	12.35 PM	**LME OFFICIAL PRICES** (Cash, 3M, 15M, 27M)
2ND MORNING RING	NASAAC & ALUMINIUM A	12.35 PM	12.40 PM	
2ND MORNING RING	TIN	12.40 PM	12.45 PM	
2ND MORNING RING	LEAD	12.45 PM	12.50 PM	
2ND MORNING RING	ZINC	12.50 PM	12.55 PM	
2ND MORNING RING	ALUMINIUM PRIMARY	12.55 PM	1.00 PM	
2ND MORNING RING	NICKEL	1.00 PM	1.05 PM	
2ND MORNING RING	STEEL	1.05 PM	1.10 PM	
INTERVAL	ALL	1.10 PM	1.20 PM	
KERB	ALL	1.20 PM	2.45 PM	
INTERVAL	ALL	2.45 PM	2.55 PM	
1ST AFTERNOON RING	NASAAC & ALUMINIUM A	2.55 PM	3.00 PM	
1ST AFTERNOON RING	LEAD	3.00 PM	3.05 PM	
1ST AFTERNOON RING	ZINC	3.05 PM	3.10 PM	
1ST AFTERNOON RING	COPPER	3.10 PM	3.15 PM	
1ST AFTERNOON RING	ALUMINIUM PRIMARY	3.15 PM	3.20 PM	
1ST AFTERNOON RING	TIN	3.20 PM	3.25 PM	
1ST AFTERNOON RING	NICKEL	3.25 PM	3.30 PM	
1ST AFTERNOON RING	STEEL	3.30 PM	3.35 PM	
INTERVAL	ALL	3.35 PM	3.40 PM	
2ND AFTERNOON RING	LEAD	3.40 PM	3.45 PM	
2ND AFTERNOON RING	ZINC	3.45 PM	3.50 PM	
2ND AFTERNOON RING	COPPER	3.50 PM	3.55 AM	
2ND AFTERNOON RING	ALUMINIUM PRIMARY	3.55 PM	4.00 PM	
2ND AFTERNOON RING	TIN	4.00 PM	4.05 PM	
2ND AFTERNOON RING	NICKEL	4.05 PM	4.10 PM	
2ND AFTERNOON RING	NASAAC & ALUMINIUM A	4.10 PM	4.15 PM	
KERB	ALL	4.15 PM	5.00 PM	**EVALUATIONS**

Times effective as of November 2012.

where needed to facilitate physical operations. For example, the weight of a deliverable lot of aluminium is 25 MT with a 2% (more or less) tolerance. At the same time, the admissible shapes are many: ingots weighing between 12 kg and 26 kg, T-bars weighing a maximum of 5% more than 750 kg, and so on.

Futures contracts are only rarely held until delivery: it happens for less than 5% of LME open positions. LME futures are in fact benchmarks used by producers and consumers to settle and hedge their physical contracts that could feature different qualities and locations. In particular conditions anyway, for example in a tight spot market, buyers and sellers can use the LME as a physical market of *last resort*. The operator having an open cash position already knows 'when' to deliver: he is concerned with 'what' and 'where'. It is possible to deliver the *brands* authorized by the LME. Each brand must reflect the metal's contract specifications, be formally guaranteed by the brand producer, pass a physical test run by a designated consumer and, finally, be approved by a committee.

- *The material has to be delivered into LME's approved warehouses.*

The LME neither holds nor manages the warehouses but instead designates and regulates them. The approved warehouses are many and located close to the biggest consumption regions all over the world: Antwerp, Barcelona, Bilbao, Geneva, Hamburg, Liverpool and Trieste are examples of European locations; Dubai, Singapore and Gwangyang are examples of Asian locations; Chicago, Detroit, Los Angeles and New Orleans are examples of American locations.

- *The brand and the warehouses where the metal is to be delivered are the seller's choice.*

The buyer could then be delivered unwanted brands or take delivery at unsuitable locations. This kind of uncertainty on the final delivery could in theory represent a threat to the status of the international benchmark of the LME's contracts. Warrants are used to mitigate this uncertainty. An LME warrant is a 'bearer' document giving the holder the right to withdraw a specified brand from a specified warehouse. When futures sellers deliver a brand into a warehouse, a warrant is issued. The futures buyer receives the warrant: at this point he could swap it with other holders, for example with one in a closer warehouse.

- *An active secondary market has arisen around the warrant system. A two-warrant swap is priced at a premium or discount in relation to the brand quality and the most requested locations.*

The LME, in order to regulate this market as well, has put in place LMEsword: an electronic system that manages the transfers of warrants and stock reporting. The robustness of the delivery process and the vast diffusion of delivery points all linked by the warrant system is one reason the LME is a consolidated world benchmark.

7.1.4.4 Options Two types of options can be traded on the LME: *futures options* and *TAPOs* (traded average price options). The futures options, introduced in 1987, are American style: the holder of the option has the right to exercise at any time before expiry. They are written on monthly futures, with delivery on the third Wednesday and expiry on the first Wednesday of the delivery month. When the option is exercised, the holder of the call (put) will buy (sell) the relevant futures at the option's strike price for the quantity (in tons) of the options held. In Section 7.3 we will outline the technicalities behind these types of options.

TAPOs were introduced in 1997 in response to the large success of Asian options in the OTC market to replicate corporate exposure. TAPOs are commodity Asian options automatically exercised and cash-settled. Asian options are described in more detail in Section 7.1.5.3.

7.1.5 OTC Instruments

The OTC market involves bilateral trading between counterparties. There is virtually no limit to the complexity of the derivative instruments traded, constrained only by the creativity and pricing capabilities of traders and financial engineers. Rather than analyse the wide range of complex structures, commonly referred to as exotics or exotic options, we will look at the most traded instruments by companies wishing to hedge their portfolios. OTC base-metal trades usually display a high degree of customization: as a consequence, investment banks are the main liquidity providers of the instruments described below.

7.1.5.1 Swaps The commodity swap is a contract where two parties agree to swap a fixed price for a floating price. One party will pay the fixed price and receive the floating price (and vice versa for the other party). The floating price is normally the *arithmetic* average, over a determined time period in the future, of the daily fixings of the commodity. The most used fixings for base metals are the LME official cash and 3M settlements. The standard time period is the monthly average: the daily average of the fixings on a calendar month.

- *Such instruments, either swaps or options, written on averages are referred to as Asian.*

In the limiting case where the pricing dates are reduced to one single day, the swap takes the form of a forward. The swap (or forward), on the cash fixing with pricing date two business days prior to the third Wednesday, replicates the LME monthly futures and is referred to as the LME *futures look-alike*. The swaps and forwards could also be physically settled, but the majority of trades on the OTC feature cash-settlement.

Asian swaps are very common also on energy markets, representing in many cases the ideal hedge for corporates. A metal producer, for example, who has a continuous production outflow, and hence an income from sales, is naturally *long* averages. At the same time, consumers prefer to index their purchases to monthly averages in order to protect themselves from the volatility of a single day fixing. For the same reason it is common between hedgers to trade calendar spreads: for example, swapping a cargo pricing on a single date versus a monthly average.

The payoff for the floating-price receiver, fixed-price payer (also referred to as the swap buyer) can be written as:

$$\text{Asian swap payoff (USD)} = \left[\left(\sum_{1}^{n} \frac{1}{n}\text{LME\_official\_fixing}_{\text{USD}}\right) - K_{\text{USD}}\right],$$

where n denotes the number of fixing days and K_{USD} is the strike expressed in USD. The left side of the formula is the floating price, while K is the fixed price. The payoff for a swap seller would be the reverse.

Two floating prices, instead of only one, could hold in the equation above: this would be the case of a *floating/floating* swap. An example is the already-mentioned calendar spread. In a floating/floating swap, the fixed price can be a premium or a discount of one leg against the other.

7.1.5.2 Cross-Currency Swaps Since the official currency on the LME is the US dollar, the operators having their balance sheets in different currencies have to hedge the associated FX risk. This induces demand for swaps denominated in other currencies, like the European euro (EUR), British pound (GBP) or Japanese yen (JPY). The floating price of the swap (in USD) is converted, applying the currency conversion (at monthly or daily level) taking, for example in the case of EUR, the European Central Bank (ECB) or LME official exchange rates.

The payoff for the floating-price receiver, fixed-price payer can be written as:

$$\text{Asian swap payoff (EUR)} = \left[\left(\sum_{1}^{n} \frac{1}{n} \frac{\text{LME\_official\_fixing}_{\text{USD}}}{\text{EUR/USD exchange\_rate}}\right) - K_{\text{EUR}}\right],$$

where n again denotes the number of fixing days, K_{EUR} is the strike expressed in EUR and EUR/USD is the number of USDs for 1 EUR. The payoff for a swap seller would be the reverse.

7.1.5.3 Asian options Although Asian options are exotic, their use is widespread between consumers and producers. In the Asian call (put) option the buyer has the right, but not the obligation, to receive (pay) the floating price and pay (receive) the fixed price (the strike). The option costs the buyer a premium, usually paid upfront, and the floating price is the arithmetic average with the same characteristics as the swap. In the limiting case of single-day maturity average, the Asian option becomes a European-style option. Asian options are, as a rule, automatically exercised and cash-settled.

The payoffs can be written as:

$$\text{Asian call payoff (USD)} = \max\left[0\,;\left(\sum_{1}^{n} \frac{1}{n}\text{LME\_official\_fixing}_{\text{USD}}\right) - K_{\text{USD}}\right],$$

$$\text{Asian put payoff (USD)} = \max\left[0\,; K_{\text{USD}} - \left(\sum_{1}^{n} \frac{1}{n}\text{LME\_official\_fixing}_{\text{USD}}\right)\right],$$

where n is again the number of fixing days and K_{USD} is the strike expressed in USD.

7.1.5.4 Cross-Currency Options Operators who do not want to bear the foreign exchange risk on base metals often trade in *composite* and *quanto* options. Such cross-currency options can be of any style, (European, American, Asian, etc.) and are collectively, and somewhat confusingly, referred to as quantos. The Asian euro composite on base metals, for example, is an option where both the premium and the strike are in EUR and the average price of the metal in USD is converted by applying the same conversions seen for the multi-currency swap.

The payoff for the call can be written as:

$$\text{Asian composite EUR call payoff (EUR)}$$
$$= \max\left[0\,;\left(\sum_{1}^{n}\frac{1}{n}\frac{\text{LME\_official\_fixing}_{\text{USD}}}{\text{EUR/USD exchange\_rate}}\right)-K_{\text{EUR}}\right],$$

where n as before is the number of fixing days, K_{EUR} is the strike expressed in EUR and EUR/USD is the number of USD for 1 EUR.

An Asian euro quanto option instead has the strike and average price in USD but the payoff is paid in EUR, applying a fixed exchange rate.

The payoff for the call can be written as:

$$\text{Asian quanto EUR call payoff (EUR)}$$
$$= \max\left[0\,;\left(\left(\sum_{1}^{n}\frac{1}{n}\text{LME\_official\_fixing}_{\text{USD}}\right)-K_{\text{USD}}\right)\times K_{\text{EUR/USD}}\right],$$

where $K_{\text{EUR/USD}}$ is the fixed exchange rate agreed by the parties.

If, for example, $K_{\text{EUR/USD}} = 1$ and the final average of the metal's fixings is 10 USD higher than the strike (expressed in USD), then the call buyer would receive 10 EUR.

The Asian composite mirrors the cross-currency swap and is preferred by companies for hedging purposes. The quanto option is instead more appealing for investors: it, in fact, totally eliminates the currency risk while instead the payoff of a composite is still a function of the foreign exchange rate. In Section 7.3 it will be considered how best to price and manage these options.

7.1.5.5 Contract Example The contractual standard most used for the OTC transactions, whether swaps or options, is the *Commodity Definitions* by the International Swaps and Derivatives Association (ISDA). The definitions regulate the terms of the contracts – like the price source, floating price description, disruption events and fallbacks; all of these rules are constantly reviewed and updated.

In the following an example of a real term sheet for a swap transaction on LME zinc is reported. The term sheet initially recalls the relevant ISDA definitions: in this case, those published in 1993. The two parties enter into a cross-currency Asian swap in EUR with *Company X* being the buyer (since it pays fixed price and receives floating price) and *Bank Y* being the seller. *Company X* buys 100 tons on the average of September, October and November, thus getting a total exposure on 300 tons. Each monthly swap is settled on the fifth business day after the pricing period (see 'settlement dates'). The underlying is the LME zinc cash settlement price (hence the offer assessment), converted into EUR using the ECB assessment. The agreed price is 2800 EUR/MT.

Lastly, note that the term sheet distinguishes between 'business' and 'commodity' days: the first are used to compute the payment dates (t+5 in the term sheet) and use the TARGET calendar, while the latter are used to identify the pricing days of the swap and use the LME calendar.

LME Zinc – Swap in EUR

Indicative Term Sheet

Indicative terms: Definitions contained in the 1993 ISDA Commodity Derivatives Definitions, as supplemented by the 2000 Supplement to the 1993 ISDA Commodity Derivatives Definitions (the 'Commodity Derivatives Definitions') are used herein, unless otherwise specified.

Total Notional Quantity:	300 MT (100 MT each month)
Unit:	Metric tonne
Commodity:	Zinc
Trade Date:	19 Aug 2010
Effective Date:	01 Sept 2010
Termination Date:	30 Nov 2010
Calculation Period(s):	Each month between, and including September and November
Settlement Date(s):	Five business days following the last day of each relevant calculation period
Fixed Amounts	
Fixed Price Payer:	Company X
Fixed Price:	2800 EUR/metric tonne
Floating Amounts	
Floating Price Payer:	Bank Y
Floating Price:	Means the unweighted arithmetic mean of the relevant price for each of the pricing dates during the relevant calculation period
Commodity Reference Price:	ZINC – LME CASH. Each relevant price shall be converted into EUR at the daily EUR/USD exchange rate
Specified Price:	Settlement price
EUR/USD Exchange Rate	Means for a pricing date the currency exchange rate between EUR and USD expressed as number of USD per EUR as published by the European Central Bank on Reuters Screen ECB37 on such pricing date
Pricing Date(s):	Each commodity business day during the relevant calculation period
Business Days:	TARGET settlement days
Calculation Agent:	Bank Y

7.1.6 A New Player: The Investor[1]

The traditional pattern of producers, sellers and traders dominating the LME arena has changed a lot in the last decade. The LME, created to meet the hedging needs of its members, has seen a huge increase of liquidity in the last few years, brought about by investment funds with investment and speculative aims. In fact, it has only been in the recent past that a wide range of investors have become interested in the LME, motivated mostly by speculation:

[1]The author wishes to thank Nicola Ventura for the contents of this section.

many investors pop up on the market just with the intention of riding the latest commodity supercycle. Investment funds that once were considered minor players in the commodity spectrum are now the most influential in terms of volumes negotiated and open interest. At the same time, commercial and investment banks started issuing base-metals-linked products (bonds, certificates and warrants) that experienced a great commercial success between private investors.

At the beginning of 2004, rumours circulated of investment funds (mostly based in the USA) investing a small percentage of their assets under management in LME base metals. Nowadays, fund managers are keener to disclose the amount of their yearly and periodical investments made in the commodity asset class, and in base metals in particular. What surprises more is not the willingness of fund managers to invest in commodities and in the LME specifically, but the size of their investments. In terms of volumes negotiated and open interest in futures and options, the weight of funds on the market today is huge: by comparing all volumes negotiated at the beginning of 2004 with the numbers of the previous two to three years, it is easy to spot the robust increase. There are different reasons behind this sudden interest in investing funds on the LME. One of the main reasons is the historical evidence of negative correlation between commodities and equities/bonds which underlines the diversification power of an investment in commodities; this is coupled with the positive correlation of commodity futures with inflation. The negative correlation between commodity futures and the other asset classes is due, in significant part, to their different behaviour over the business cycle (Gordon and Rouwenhorst, 2006). In addition, there is also a wide range of other fundamental and geopolitical reasons: the depreciation of the US dollar and the constant growth of emerging markets like China and India that pushed up the demand for commodities and reduced inventories at critical levels. The immediate consequence of these constant speculative money injections into the market is an unnatural increase in the quotations of the main LME metals. In the last few years, non-ferrous metals prices, struck by this wave of liquidity, jumped well over the value suggested by their fundamentals; the first one was copper, whose price skyrocketed reaching new highs in early 2006, followed by zinc and nickel quotations.

The increase in volumes brought by investment funds and banks is judged positively by some players in the market, bringing as it does higher levels of liquidity. At the same time others blame this kind of investment for being an obstacle to hedging, which is still the main reason for trading on the LME.

The funds that first invested a percentage of their liquidity in commodities were based in the USA, being followed a few years later by European and Asian funds. Since every single country has its own regulation of investment pools, a global classification would be hard to implement. In the US paradigm of investment funds, it is possible to distinguish two macro categories according to their corporate structure and the way they work: mutual funds and hedge funds. In addition to these two comprehensive groups, there are other classes of subjects that are likewise very active in commodities: commodity index funds, exchange-traded funds (ETFs) and exchange-traded commodities (ETCs); commodity trading advisors (CTAs); commodity pool operators (CPOs); and pension funds. The first category of funds that invested in LME in early 2004 were the CTAs, whose main feature is their active trading strategy (both long and short) and their brief time horizon; later on, mutual funds and index funds became active on the LME. Their main characteristics are the superior amount of money to invest, a longer time horizon (3–5 years) and a passive trading strategy. Pension funds were the last ones to enter the commodities market, playing an important role especially because of their size that permits them to invest large amounts of money, therefore impacting on a large scale the entire LME complex.

7.1.6.1 Mutual Funds Mutual funds were one of the first investment pools ever created. The first modern US mutual fund was founded in 1924, and today it is one of the most common investment tools. A mutual fund can be considered as a particular kind of company that pools money from many investors and invests collectively in a wide range of instruments and securities, complying with the rules and objectives of the fund. Mutual funds sell to their investors shares of the fund and in turn receive the money to invest in financial instruments. In the vast majority of mutual funds, the investors are free to sell their shares anytime. In mutual funds, differently from hedge funds, where there is no difference between the company that manages the fund and the portfolio invested, the company that manages money is separated from the assets managed and it is often able to manage more funds distinctly.

In the last few years the amount of investments made by mutual funds in commodities has grown dramatically.

- *They usually do not invest directly in commodity futures but use structured tools, for example commodity indexed notes, ETFs or ETCs, and bonds linked to the performance of a particular commodity or index.*

7.1.6.2 Commodity Index Funds Index funds are a particular kind of mutual fund whose aim is to benchmark the performance of an index. Commodity index funds are quite common and their objective is to passively replicate the performance of the most common commodity indexes (examples of commodity indexes are as follows: Standard & Poor's Goldman Sachs Commodity Index; Reuters Jefferies CRB Index; and Dow Jones UBS Commodity Index). The main advantages of commodity index funds are their low management costs and consequently lower fee structure. They recently became very popular amongst investors as their assets under management grew at a fast pace year after year thanks to their good return performance and transparency.

7.1.6.3 ETFs and ETCs An ETF, within the larger category of ETPs, is an investment fund freely traded on exchanges, much like stocks. An ETF holds assets such as stocks, commodities or bonds and trades at approximately the same price as the net asset value of its underlying assets over the course of the trading day. Most ETFs passively track an index, such as the S&P 500 or the Dow Jones UBS Commodity Index. The ETPs tracking a commodity index are also known as ETCs.

ETCs have grown in popularity in recent years because of their flexibility, low costs, tax efficiency and stock-like features that enable every investor to freely buy or sell them in real time on exchanges just like stocks (unlike shares of most mutual funds whose price is known once a day). They are open-end funds: this means that (unlike futures and options) they do not have a maturity date and are suitable for long-term investment periods. Figure 7.6 (elaborated on data from etfsecurities.com) displays the growth in the total number of shares of some ETCs in base metals issued by ETF securities.

7.1.6.4 Hedge Funds Hedge funds are a particular kind of fund whose main feature is their use of alternative methods, strategies and financial instruments, with the primary objective of achieving the highest possible absolute return. The universe of hedge funds is

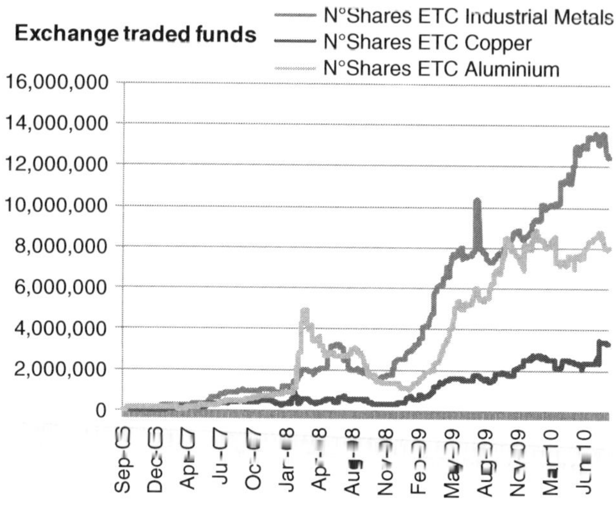

FIGURE 7.6 ETFs on base metals

potentially unlimited: they are typically classified according to the trading strategy they use or the underlyings in which they choose to invest.

Hedge funds, as a class, invest in a broad range of products including shares, debt and commodities. They are open to a limited range of professional or wealthy investors who meet certain criteria set by regulators, and are accordingly exempt from many regulations that govern ordinary investment funds. The exempted regulations typically cover short selling, the use of derivatives and leverage, fee structures and the rules by which investors can remove their capital from the fund. Light regulation and the presence of performance fees are the distinguishing characteristics of hedge funds. In Figure 7.7 the estimated value of assets under management by hedge funds is plotted.

7.1.6.5 CTAs and CPOs Another type of fund within the hedge funds paradigm is the so-called 'commodity trading pool'. These investments funds pool money from a multitude of investors and invest it in futures markets. They are structured in the same way as hedge funds but, unlike hedge funds, are managed by CPOs. CPOs are specific subjects involved in the administration and structuring of the fund. Usually they hire one or more CTAs in order to exploit their experience in the management of investments.

CTAs and CPOs can be single individuals or companies, specialized in the active management of their customers' money, and must be registered at the Commodity Futures Trading Commission (CFTC) and the National Futures Associations (NFA). Like hedge funds, CTAs also adopt a wide spectrum of strategies and investment tools; but unlike hedge funds their main feature is the massive use of listed futures. One of the main features of CTAs is their limited investment period (3–4 months) and a trading style mainly based on algorithmic and technical signals.

7.1.6.6 Pension Funds Pension funds are funds built with the aim of providing retirement income to employees. Amongst all the other investment funds, pension funds are probably the ones with the largest assets under management. Because of their nature, pension funds have

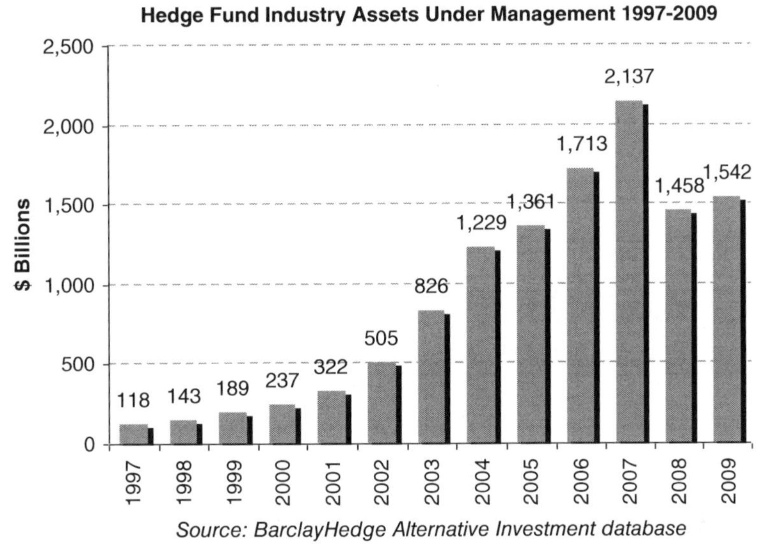

FIGURE 7.7 Hedge fund industry AUM

always invested in conservative assets and only recently are starting to invest a small part of their capital in commodities in order to exploit the diversification benefits of commodities as an asset class. Unlike CTAs and CPOs, whose main feature is their active trading style, pension funds have a long-term 'buy & hold' investment horizon (15–30 years) and their main purpose is to passively replicate the performance of the chosen asset class. Together with all the other investment funds, pension funds have particularly joined in on commodities bull market trends, particularly in the lead up to the financial crisis, giving such trends further momentum.

7.1.6.7 Commodity-Linked Products Mainly structured as bonds, these products have been issued and placed (both retail and private) in numbers by commercial banks and other financial institutions. These instruments usually feature an investment bank, which structures the embedded commodity option. The options are often exotic and written on several underlyings to increase the diversification of the investment: energy, agriculture, precious and base metals. Amongst the base metals, aluminium and copper are the most widely used; they are the only metals to guarantee sufficient liquidity on long-term forwards since bonds are usually issued on 3 to 6-year tenors. LME fixings are the most used assessment for the spot prices. As an alternative, sectorial sub-indices of the major commodity indices (e.g., S&P GSCI Industrial Metal Excess Return) can be used.

7.2 FORWARD CURVES

The construction of a reliable forward curve is, in most situations, an essential condition for taking trading and investment decisions as well as for corporate planning. The consumer who wants to take advantage of a market in backwardation, or the miner who wants to lock in a contango, needs the forward curve, often for very long-term maturities. The wholesaler who wants to match his buying and sales contracts needs to know exactly the time spreads between maturities. The options trader who wants to price a calendar month Asian option needs to know the metal price on every single day in the month to compute the average price.

These few examples give an idea of why the ideal forward curve assessment should have the following characteristics.

- Being extremely accurate on the *fair value*: 'mid' prices for the liquid maturities (from cash, to 3M to 15M at least).
- Being *continuous* at the *daily level*: the liquidity holes present in long-term futures must be filled using proper interpolation. Prices should be assessed for each business day on the curve.
- Being *real time*: continuous updating of prices during the trading day.
- Providing a realistic assessment of the *bid–ask* spread across the curve: the bid–offer is a function of the liquidity of each maturity and is therefore not constant. It can be considered a channel widening in long-term maturities.

The first two characteristics are relatively easy to achieve and represent daily practice for most practitioners. The third and fourth ones require instead a constant presence on the market.

At this stage, actual forward curve prices are being considered. Later, some considerations will be made on the evolution of the curves and price scenarios.

Two considerations are due before giving a detailed description of how to gather market information and build the necessary forward curve.

Bad news: each metal displays a unique forward curve

Although the base metals show high cross-correlation in spot prices, the forward curves rarely present similar patterns. This is somewhat counter-intuitive for commodities of the same class: for example, the oil trader knows that crude and his derivatives show similar characteristics in the shape of the forward.

The forward curve of two commodities in fact may show common forward dynamics when they have similar or derivative product specifications (e.g., gasoil is a distillate from crude oil), are exchangeable in the industrial process (as is the case for some bio-diesel feeders) or the market shares are the same (risk-adjusted) expectations for the future.

This is not the case for base metals. As already discussed, excluding the aluminium alloys (alloy and NASAAC), each metal has distinctive chemical features and market/industrial utilization.

Figures 7.8 and 7.9 depict the forward curves for aluminium HG, copper, nickel, lead, zinc, tin and NASAAC on the same business day. On the *x*-axis are the monthly maturities (third Wednesday). Each curve has a different length, given the different number of listed maturities on the LME (see Section 7.1.4).

There is a sharp contrast between metals being in contango (aluminium HG and NASAAC) and those in backwardation (copper, nickel). Zinc's forward curve is also interesting: the curve is in contango for the first 12 months and then in backwardation, almost reverting back to spot

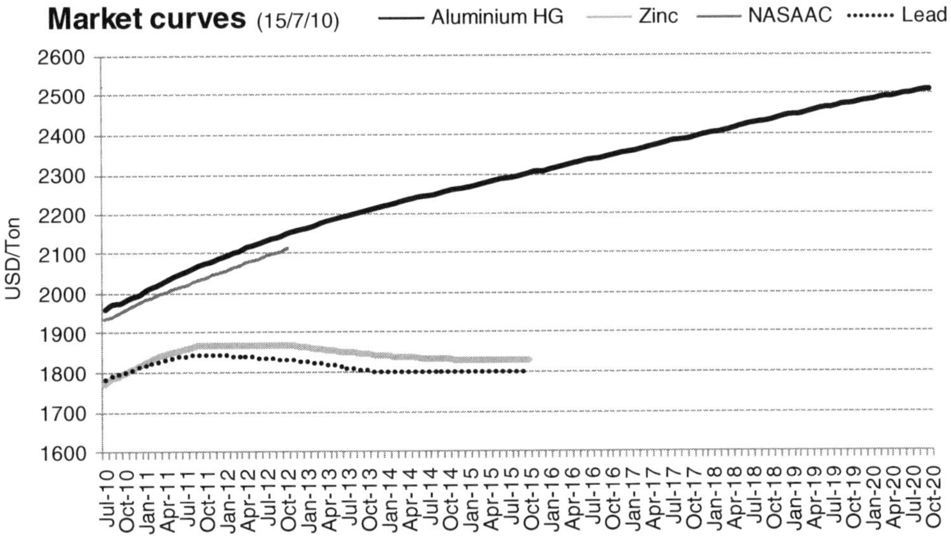

FIGURE 7.8 Market forward curves (a)

price levels. A very similar pattern is shared by lead, which in turn on the last part of the curve shows a flat shape, although this should not be considered reliable since it may be the result of poor open interest.

It is also interesting to compare aluminium HG and NASAAC: in this case, as one may expect, the curve of the latter is very similar to the parent contract but shifted to a lower level of price.

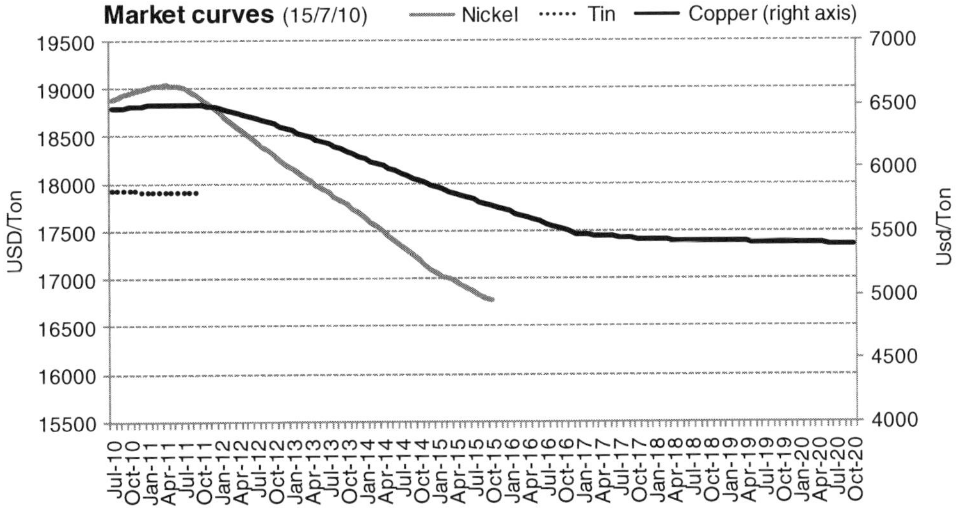

FIGURE 7.9 Market forward curves (b)

Good news: the process of construction of the curve is the same for all base metals
Actually, not only base metals but also steels, minor metals and plastics are traded in the same way on the LME. So, the rules and procedures covered in the following section can be applied to all contracts.

7.2.1 Building LME's Curves in Practice

If one had a live bid–ask quotation of outright prices for all the maturities, one wouldn't have to build the forward curve. This is actually rarely the case for most commodities markets (not only base metals) since liquidity typically concentrates on a few maturities (usually the shortest ones). Indeed, it is the exception where the exchange appoints one or more market-makers with the obligation to show continuous bids and offers. One example is gold futures traded on COMEX: not a coincidence that it resembles more a currency than a commodity. To build the forward curve, one should first gather all the market data available.

To summarize, we have the following possible inputs

7.2.1.1 3M Contract This is quoted as an outright price. It is tradable electronically through the *LMEselect*, via telephone through brokers and during ring sessions. The real-time electronic quotation on *LMEselect* is crucial in order to have a continuously updated curve. Indeed, the *LMEselect* attracts most volumes on the 3M, although some hedgers prefer to trade with brokers and banks. In fact, players are reluctant to show their orders on the screen (and hence to the whole market) when dealing large sizes.

The screen on 3M is also important to get a quick view of market depth. The screenshots below are an example of books for copper and aluminium taken from an electronic trading platform. At the time of the screenshot, it was possible to trade copper 3M with a bid–ask spread of only 2 USD/MT: amounting to an ~0.03% wide bid–ask. This is a very tight market and is valid for only two lots on the bid (50 MT) and one on the offer (25 MT). If, for example, one had to buy 30 lots (750 MT), one would have needed to buy at 6579.75, as shown in the 'Accum' column (accumulated volume). The difference between the first line price of 6577.00 and the volume-weighted average price accounts as *slippage*.

LME copper 3M book

Hit Bid	Join Bid		Join Offer	Take Offer	
BIDS			OFFERS		
Price	Volume	Accum	Price	Volume	Accum
6575.00	2	2	6577.00	1	1
6573.75	1	3	6577.50	1	2
6573.00	1	4	6577.75	1	3
6572.50	3	7	6578.00	3	6
6572.25	2	9	6578.25	10	16
6572.00	1	10	6578.50	5	21
6571.75	1	11	6579.00	3	24
6571.00	7	18	6579.50	1	25
6570.75	1	19	6579.75	5	30
6570.00	9	28	6580.00	20	50

LME AL HG 3M book

Hit Bid	Join Bid		Join Offer	Take Offer	
BIDS			OFFERS		
Price	Volume	Accum	Price	Volume	Accum
1956.50	4	4	1958.75	1	1
1955.50	1	5	1959.00	2	3
1955.25	5	10	1959.75	2	5
1955.00	12	22	1960.00	5	10
1952.00	5	27	1960.25	3	13
1951.00	2	29	1961.00	15	28
1950.00	15	44	1962.00	30	58
1949.50	6	50	1963.00	30	88
1949.25	19	69	1964.00	10	98
1948.50	3	72			

7.2.1.2 LME's Closing Prices This is a valuable source of information since it provides the evaluation (mid) prices for all the maturities. The LME runs this assessment daily for each prompt date after the close of the afternoon ring-trading session (16:15 London time) and communicates the prices to the clearing house after the close of kerb trading (17:00 London time). The LCH uses these prices as the basis for initial and variation margin calculations. The closing prices are also known as *evening evaluations*.

Brokers usually send to their customers the closing assessment and strip all the relevant spreads and carries out of it. Below is a sample report sent by brokers. In the left column there is the LME's closing assessment (outright prices) with the evidence of cash and 3M prompts, while the other columns show the calculated calendar month rolls and 3M carries.

BROKER XY DAILY REPORT **COPPER**

Monday dd/mm/yy

LME CLOSING PRICES	Price
CASH	**6.494,75**
3M	**6.510,00**
Jul-10	6.494,75
Aug-10	6.499,25
Sep-10	6.503,50
Oct-10	6.510,00
Nov-10	6.513,50
Dec-10	6.516,00
Jan-11	6.519,50
Feb-11	6.523,00
Mar-11	6.526,50
Apr-11	6.528,50
May-11	6.528,50
Jun-11	6.528,50
Jul-11	6.528,50
Aug-11	6.527,00
Sep-11	6.525,00
Oct-11	6.522,00
Nov-11	6.517,50
Dec-11	6.511,00
...	....

Month-to-month		Spread
Jul-10	Aug-10	4,50
Aug-10	Sep-10	4,25
Sep-10	Oct-10	6,50
Oct-10	Nov-10	3,50
Nov-10	Dec-10	2,50
Dec-10	Jan-11	3,50
Jan-11	Feb-11	3,50
Feb-11	Mar-11	3,50
Mar-11	Apr-11	2,00
Apr-11	May-11	-
May-11	Jun-11	-
Jun-11	Jul-11	-
Jul-11	Aug-11	- 1,50
Aug-11	Sep-11	- 2,00
Sep-11	Oct-11	- 3,00
Oct-11	Nov-11	- 4,50
Nov-11	Dec-11	- 6,50
Dec-11	Jan-12	- 12,00
Jan-12	Feb-12	- 12,00
Feb-12	Mar-12	- 13,00
...	....	....

3 Month		Spread
Jul-10	3 months	15,25
Aug-10	3 months	10,75
Sep-10	3 months	6,50
3 months	Oct-10	-
3 months	Nov-10	3,50
3 months	Dec-10	6,00
3 months	Jan-11	9,50
3 months	Feb-11	13,00
3 months	Mar-11	16,50
3 months	Apr-11	18,50
3 months	May-11	18,50
3 months	Jun-11	18,50
3 months	Jul-11	18,50
3 months	Aug-11	17,00
3 months	Sep-11	15,00
3 months	Oct-11	12,00
3 months	Nov-11	7,50
3 months	Dec-11	1,00
3 months	Jan-12	- 11,00
3 months	Feb-12	- 23,00
...	....	....

Dec to Dec		Spread
Dec-10	Dec-11	- 5,00
Dec-11	Dec-12	- 170,00
Dec-12	Dec-13	- 222,00
Dec-13	Dec-14	- 227,00
Dec-14	Dec-15	- 190,00
Dec-15	Dec-16	- 190,00
...	...	...

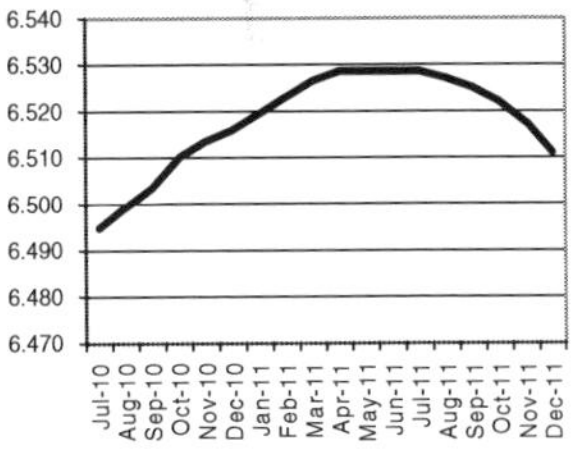

These spreads are likely to represent the reference for trading the following morning: the first bids and offers are likely to be around those 'mid' values.

- *Given this premise, and having a live feed of 3M quotes, it is possible to build the evaluation-adjusted forward curve: a 'quick and dirty' approximation of the actual forward curve.*

It will be enough to match the spreads present in the third column (3M spreads) with the updated 3M quotes to get a rough idea of the whole forward curve. The resulting curve will be consistent with the actual market curve in the absence of events changing its shape: for those familiar with principal component analysis (PCA), this means considering only the *parallel shift* in the curve movement.

7.2.1.3 Carries Although they can be quoted against any maturity pairs, most of the trading concentrates on 3M against the monthly (third Wednesday) maturities and the other 'pivot' maturities like the TOM and the CASH.

- *This reflects the common practice of trading outright the 3M, which is the most liquid contract also available on screen, and then rolling the position to other maturities through the carries.*

Carry	Price Source	Bid	Ask	Last Trade	Change (USD)		High	Low
Tom-Next	LMES	-3.0	-1.5	-3.50	**-3.10**	↓	-0.20	-3.50
Cash-3 Mth	RING	-16.0	-14.0	-16.50	**-1.25**	↓	-16.50	-16.50
Jul10-3 Mth	TRAF	-14.0	-14.0	-14.84	**0.41**	↑	-15.00	-16.00
Aug10-3 Mth	LMES	-8.0	-5.0	-10.38	**-0.13**	↓	-10.20	-11.00
Sep10-3 Mth	LMES	-6.0	-5.5	-6.00	**0.25**	↑	-6.00	-6.50
Oct10-3 Mth	LMES	0.0	0.3	0.25	**0.00**	↔	0.50	--
3 Mth-Nov10	LMES	-1.5	1.5	-3.50	**0.00**	↔	--	--
3 Mth-Dec10	RING	-7.0	-6.0	-6.00	**0.00**	↔	-6.00	-7.00
3 Mth-Jan11	RING	-8.5	-3.5	-9.75	**-0.25**	↓	--	--
3 Mth-Feb11	LMES	-12.3	-7.3	-12.75	**0.25**	↑	--	--
3 Mth-Mar11	RING	-15.3	-10.3	-15.50	**1.00**	↑	--	--
3 Mth-Apr11	SGEN	-20.5	-10.5	-17.50	**1.00**	↑	--	--
3 Mth-May11	LMES	-22.5	-12.5	-17.50	**1.00**	↑	--	--
3 Mth-Jun11	LMES	-16.5	-10.0	-16.00	**1.38**	↑	--	--
3 Mth-Jul11	ICA	-22.5	-12.5	-16.50	**2.00**	↑	-16.15	-17.20
3 Mth-Aug11	LMES	-21.5	-11.5	-14.50	**2.50**	↑	--	--
3 Mth-Sep11	LMES	-15.5	0.5	-11.50	**3.50**	↑	[illegible]	
3 Mth-Oct11	BCG	-19.0	-4.0	-8.00	**4.00**	↑	--	--
3 Mth-Nov11	LMES	-15.5	-0.5	-3.00	**4.50**	↑	--	--

FIGURE 7.10 Example of carries on copper

The market of carries is run by brokers and dealers, which can also show 'on demand' quotes for specific and illiquid carries. Software vendors and the brokers themselves offer screen tools that aggregate these quotes.

Figure 7.10 is a practical example of a typical screen displaying the market on carries.

Tom-Next (T/N). Tom stands for 'tomorrow'. This is the shortest tradable maturity: until first ring close (12:20 London time) it is possible to roll positions delivering tomorrow (i.e., the day before the cash prompt). Tom-next represents exactly the roll between tomorrow and the 'next' day, the cash. For those who forgot to roll their positions and do not want delivery, it is the last chance to avoid going physical.

Starting with the above inputs, it is possible to build the forward curve. This is done separately for maturities before and after the 3M.

Prompt dates before the 3M (date/3M) are quoted as prompt date vs. 3M

Example. A cash-3M quote (see the screenshot) –16.00/–14.00 (USD/MT) means that someone is bidding (borrowing) the cash prompt 16.00 USD lower than the 3M and someone is offering (lending) it 14.00 USD lower. This portion of the curve is hence in contango.

The 3M quotes shown previously are taken and used to calculate the cash outright prices:

	BID	ASK	BID/ASK
3M	6575	6577	2 Usd
Cash-3M	- 16,00	- 14,00	2 Usd
CASH	6.559,00	6.563,00	4 Usd

	BID	ASK
3M	+ ↕	↕ +
Cash-3M		

Cash bid: 3M bid + cash/3M bid = 6575.00 – 16.00 = 6559.00

Explanation. To sell the cash one must hit the bid on the carry (hence selling at –16.00). This will result in a short position on cash and a long on 3M. One now has to get rid of the long position on 3M and therefore sell the 3M by hitting the bid (hence selling at 6575). Finally, one will have a short position on the cash at a price level of 6559.

$$\text{Cash ask: 3M ask} + \text{cash/3M ask} = 6577.00 - 14.00 = 6563.00$$

Explanation. To buy the cash one must lift the offer on the carry (hence buying at –14.00). This will result in a long position on cash and a short on 3M. One now has to get rid of the short position on 3M. Therefore, buy the 3M taking the ask (hence buying at 6577). Finally, one will have a long position on the cash at a price level of 6563.

Prompt dates after the 3M (3M/date) are quoted as 3M vs. prompt date
Example. A 3M-Oct11 quote of –19.00/–4.00 (USD/MT) means that someone is bidding the Oct11 futures (third Wednesday) 4 USD higher than the 3M and someone is offering it 19 USD higher (so the curve is in contango).

The 3M quotes shown previously are taken and used to calculate the Oct11 outright prices:

	BID	ASK	BID/ASK
3M	6575	6577	2 Usd
3M-Oct11	- 19,00	- 4,00	15 Usd
Oct11	6.579,00	6.596,00	17 Usd

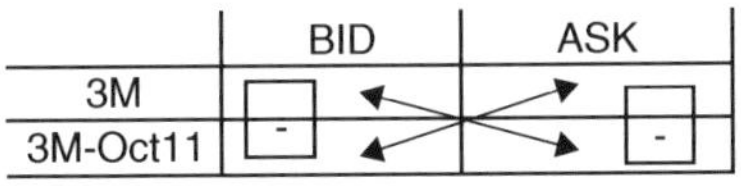

$$\text{Oct11 bid: 3M bid} - \text{3M/Oct11 ask} = 6575.00 - (-4.00) = 6579.00$$

Explanation. To sell the Oct11 contract one must take the ask on the carry (hence buying at –4.00): this will result in a short position on Oct11 and a long one on 3M. One now has to get rid of the long position on 3M. Therefore, sell the 3M hitting the bid (hence selling at 6575). Finally, one will have a short position on the Oct11 contract at a price level of 6579.

$$\text{Oct11 ask: 3M ask} + \text{3M/Oct11 bid} = 6577.00 - (-19.00) = 6596.00$$

Explanation. To buy the Oct11 one must hit the bid on the carry (hence selling at –19.00): this will result in a long position on Oct11 and a short on 3M. One now has to get rid of the short position on 3M. Therefore, buy the 3M taking the ask (hence buying at 6577). Finally, one will have a long position on the cash at a price level of 6596.

At the beginning of this section the importance of having the bid–ask across the curve was underlined. In the two examples above, it can be seen that starting from a bid–ask of 2 USD for the 3M, one obtained a 4 USD bid–ask for the cash and a 17 USD bid–ask for the Oct11 contract. Repeating the process for all maturities, one can build the whole current forward curve for copper. Figure 7.11 shows the curve obtained. The bid–ask gradually widens on

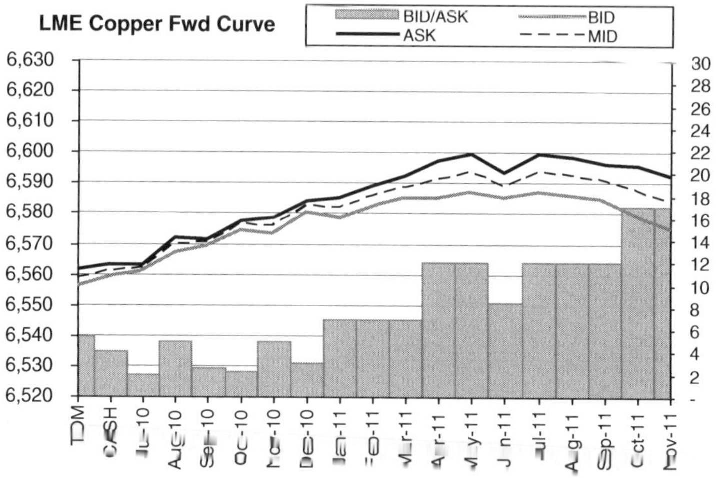

FIGURE 7.11 A complete forward curve on LME copper

the longest maturities, while being at the minimum at 3M (corresponding to Oct10). The mid curve is derived as the mean between the bid and the ask values.

Carries can be checked through a quote from a broker or a dealer that always comes with a size, giving an idea of slippage. This is even truer when it comes to the less liquid base metals. The carries screenshot seen above for copper would look something like that in Figure 7.12 for lead.

Carry	Price Source	Bid	Ask	Last Trade	Change (USD)		High	Low
Tom-Next	ADMI	-0.7	-0.3	-0.50	0.05	↑	-0.20	-0.60
Cash-3 Mth	LMES	-23.0	-22.0	-20.00	0.00	↔	--	--
Jul10-3 Mth	LMES	0.0	0.0	-20.00	-2.00	↓	-20.75	-20.75
Aug10-3 Mth	BIMI	-13.4	-13.2	-13.40	-0.15	↓	-13.00	-15.00
Sep10-3 Mth	MANF	-9.5	-8.3	-8.25	-0.25	↑	-8.00	-9.00
Oct10-3 Mth	RING	-5.0	-0.2	-0.19	0.00	↔	--	-1.00
3 Mth-Nov10	RING	-6.0	-5.5	-5.50	0.00	↔	-5.50	-5.50
3 Mth-Dec10	RING	-10.6	-11.0	-10.55	0.45	↑	-10.55	-10.55
3 Mth-Jan11	RING	-17.5	-17.0	-16.50	-0.50	↓	--	--
3 Mth-Feb11	YEST CLOSE	--	--	-21.00	-0.50	↓	--	--
3 Mth-Mar11	YEST CLOSE	--	--	-25.00	-0.50	↓	--	--
3 Mth-Apr11	YEST CLOSE	--	--	-29.00	-0.50	↓	--	--
3 Mth-May11	YEST CLOSE	--	--	-33.00	-0.50	↓	--	--
3 Mth-Jun11	YEST CLOSE	--	--	-34.00	-0.50	↓	--	--
3 Mth-Jul11	YEST CLOSE	--	--	-37.00	-0.50	↓	--	--
3 Mth-Aug11	YEST CLOSE	--	--	-40.00	-0.50	↓	--	--
3 Mth-Sep11	YEST CLOSE	--	--	-42.00	-0.50	↓	--	--
3 Mth-Oct11	YEST CLOSE	--	--	-44.00	-0.50	↓	--	--
3 Mth-Nov11	YEST CLOSE	--	--	-44.00	-0.50	↓	--	--

FIGURE 7.12 Example of carries on lead

It is observed that screen quotes are available only for the shortest maturities: liquidity for the longest ones would be given by brokers and dealers on demand.

- *Therefore, a fully reliable, bid–offer, continuously updated forward curve on base metals requires one operator to be constantly active on the market.*

7.2.2 Interpolation

At the beginning of this chapter it was suggested that the optimal forward curve should be continuous at the daily level. This is indeed important for many reasons. First of all the pricing of an average swap requires as input all the prices of the business days within the pricing period. Since on the exchange only the daily prompt dates up to the 3M are quoted, one must interpolate the daily prices for maturities beyond 3M. A very simple method is linear interpolation. The drawback of this method is that the first derivative is *discontinuous* on each node of the curve. For this reason the more sophisticated *spline interpolations* of degree >1, like the *cubic* and *natural cubic* spline, are often used.

Given a set of data points (x_i,y_i), for $i = 1, \ldots, k$, a continuous spline interpolation curve is obtained by concatenating interpolant functions of degree n between each pair of adjacent data points (x_i,y_i), (x_{i+1},y_{i+1}). The degree of n determines the type of interpolation. There are k–1 interpolants.

Where $n = 1$, the $k - 1$ interpolants are linear (i.e., of the form $y = mx + a$) and are equivalent to *piecewise constant* linear interpolation. Where $n = 2$, the $k - 1$ interpolants are quadratic (i.e., of the form $y = a + mx^2 + hx$) and the function is called a quadratic spline interpolation. Where $n = 3$, one has cubic spline interpolation, and so on. The cubic spline interpolation guarantees that the piecewise $k - 1$ cubic functions join each other smoothly at each node (the interpolant is twice continuously differentiable at the nodes). See Rouah and Vainberg (2007) for further details on Excel implementation.

In order to replicate the standard LME interpolation, it will be enough to use the piecewise linear interpolation with some specific caution: as a matter of fact, this is the method used by the LME. In our practical case, (x_i,y_i) would be the maturities (x_i) on which price quotations (y_i) are available.

The i functions are:

$$P_i(x) = a_i + m_i(x - x_i)$$

For each sub-interval (x_i, x_{i+1}) one must estimate the constants a_i (with $a_i = y_i$ being $P_i(x_i) = y_i$) and the coefficients m_i (with $m_i = \frac{y_{i+1}-y_i}{x_{i+1}-x_i}$).

The chart in Figure 7.13 plots the results of piecewise linear interpolation obtained for lead starting from the quotes available (main pillars).

The above interpolation would match the LME's evening evaluation under the observation of the following cautions.

- The curve has to start from a quotation of the cash.
- The quotation of 3M must also be included: notice that between Oct10 and Nov10 the interpolation is split into two pieces.

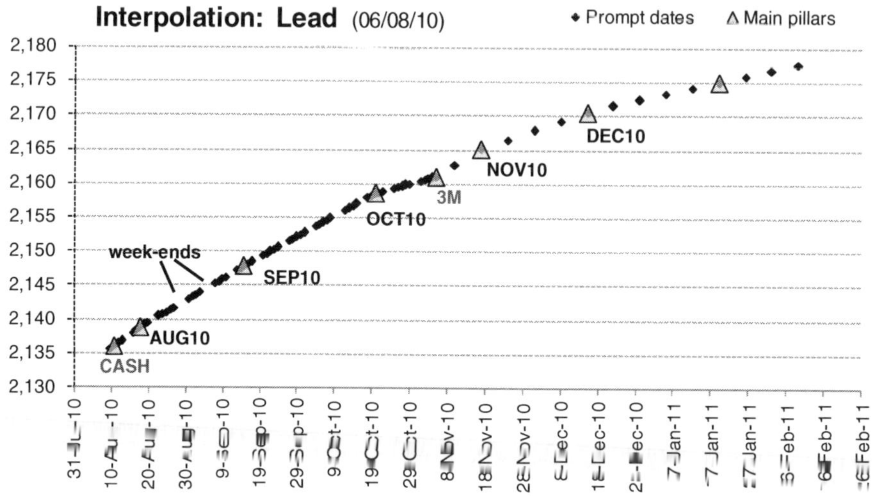

FIGURE 7.13 Price interpolation on lead curve

- The day count is based on calendar days within the month. The gaps in the curve are the weekends: during these days the price virtually increases.
- The non-LME prompt days must be treated like holidays.

7.2.3 LME, COMEX and SHFE Copper Curve and Arbitrage

Copper is privileged amongst metals: futures contracts are quoted and liquid on various markets across the world. Taking London time as reference, it is possible to trade early in the morning on SHFE until 08:00, then activity gradually rises on LME and at 13:10 the pit on COMEX also opens. These three markets nowadays are the most active but not unique: copper is listed also on the MCX and NCDEX, both based in India.

The chemical specifications of copper good-to-delivery are similar between the three futures contracts. SHFE also envisages the delivery of LME's brands. Contract specifications are instead different: this aspect, together with the different locations, may at times open up arbitrage opportunities. Forward quotations are in fact seldom perfectly identical. It will be shown how to build comparable forward curves. The arguments proposed can also be applied to the other metals listed on different exchanges.

Commodity unit quotation. LME and SHFE quote copper in metric tons (MT) with only a difference in the lot size (25MT for LME, 5MT for SHFE). COMEX copper is quoted in US cents per pound. The appropriate unit conversion is needed to convert the quote into metric tons:

$$1 \text{ lb} = 453.592 \text{ g}$$

Currency. LME and COMEX quote copper in USD, although COMEX prices are given in cents. SHFE quotes are in Chinese Renminbi (yuan): the official currency of China.

- *The exchange rate USD/CNY represents a first element of market distortion and a source of theoretical arbitrage opportunities.*

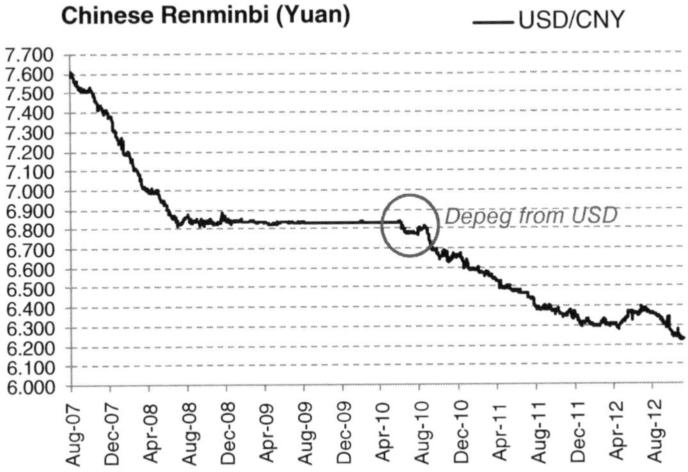

FIGURE 7.14 Chinese Renminbi price chart

These opportunities can only be theoretical since the Renminbi has been pegged to the USD for a long time and restrictions on currency transfers are in place. In June 2010 the People's Bank of China decided to de-peg the Renminbi from the USD and increase the rate flexibility. See Figure 7.14.

Delivery location. Each exchange approves warehouses for delivery. The LME can exploit several warehouses around the globe, which provides great logistic flexibility to operators and physical arbitrageurs. In the past, the copper arbitrage was between LME and COMEX: this arbitrage is very narrow though, since the contracts are both very liquid in USD and respective warehouses are located nearby. The arbitrage LME/SHFE is nowadays the one offering more opportunities: in this case warehouses are not so close and therefore freight costs are higher.

In Figure 7.15, copper spot prices on the three exchanges are converted to the LME standard: prices in USD/MT. The time series of Shanghai spot prices embeds VAT: this is removed in the chart to make prices comparable. As anticipated, LME and COMEX prices are pegged to each other. One should expect the same feature on the forward market. The spreads are plotted in the chart (right y-axis) and are a measure of the *gross* arbitrage. It is observed that LME/SHFE is more often in positive territory: LME at a premium to SHFE. This reflects the fact that China is a net importer of copper and the market is keener to import from LME (buy LME and sell SHFE) rather than exporting to LME (buy SHFE and sell LME). When the spread is negative (i.e., LME at a discount to SHFE), the imports rise and the arbitrage window is closed rapidly.

There is an arbitrage opportunity – in arbitrage jargon, the *window is open* – when the following holds:

$$\text{SHFE}_{\text{copper}} > (\text{LME}_{\text{copper}} + \text{CIF}) \times \text{USD/CNY} \times (1 + \text{taxes}),$$

where CIF is the cost of insurance and freight, taxes are VAT (value added tax) plus import taxes.

- *Differences in import/export taxes and VAT between countries can play a major role in determining the profitability, and hence the direction, of the arbitrage.*

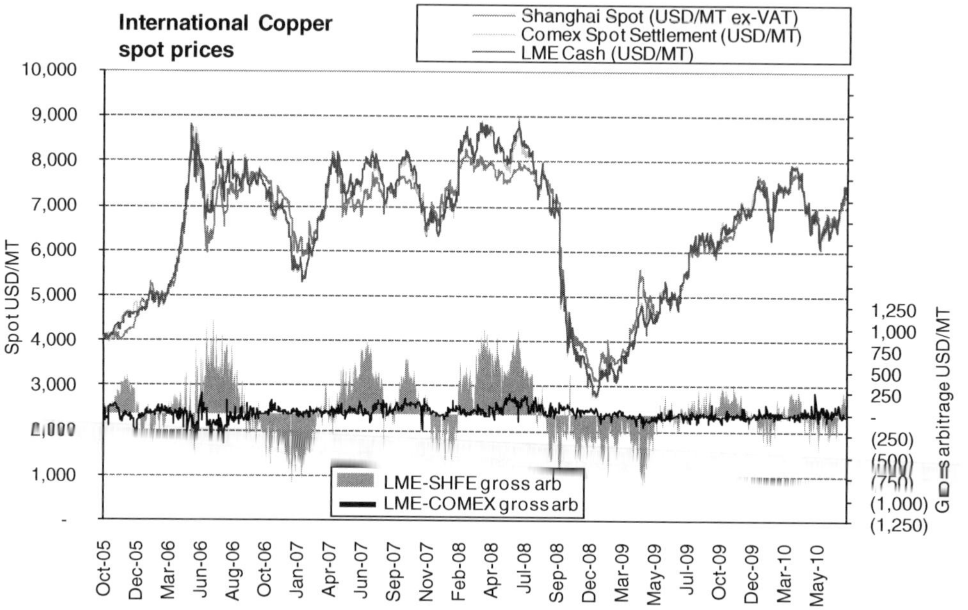

FIGURE 7.15 International copper spot prices

In particular, Chinese export tax and VAT policies (as well as the selective application of VAT rebates) on refined copper and scraps has changed quite often in recent years; as a matter of fact, they are used by the government as an effective tool to control the flow of exports from and to the country.

Delivery period. The three futures enclose different delivery periods. Since the goal is to build consistent forward curves, one must infer some hypothesis on the exact pricing day for each monthly futures. The LME monthly futures delivery rule leaves no doubt since the material is for delivery on a single day (the third Wednesday of the month). COMEX futures are for delivery on any business day within the month. SHFE futures are for delivery between the 16th and 20th business day of the month. Figure 7.16 represents visually the different deliveries.

Since the contracts encompass the feature of *seller's choice*, it is ultimately the seller's decision when to deliver. A rule of thumb is that the rational seller will deliver as soon as possible in contango and as late as possible in backwardation. Under this assumption the pricing date for COMEX futures can be set as the first business day of the month when in contango and the last of the month when in backwardation. Interpolation can then be applied to get all other maturity prices.

Finally, the three forward curves can be obtained. In Figure 7.17 COMEX and SHFE prices are converted to the LME standard with quotes expressed in USD/MT and the monthly prompts being the third Wednesday. Furthermore, SHFE prices are cleaned of the VAT effect. Prices are taken at 8:00 am London time. LME's forward curve is at a premium to SHFE's ex-VAT curve: this is consistent with the positive spread observable in the last part of Figure 7.15 on copper spot prices. COMEX copper is also slightly at a premium to LME: the differential widens with time while being very narrow at the front end of the curve.

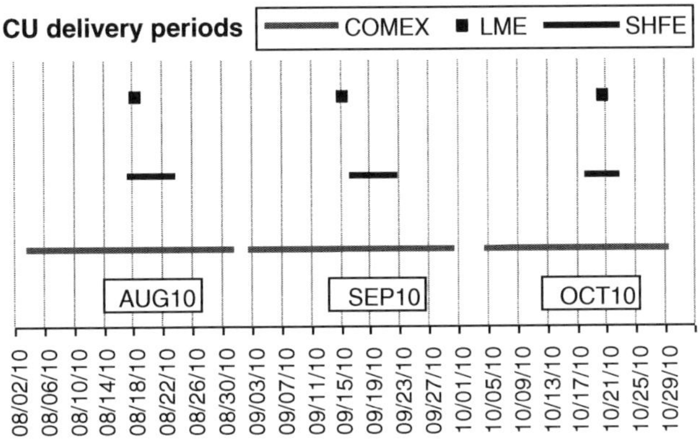

FIGURE 7.16 Copper delivery periods

This is just the starting point for the analysis of a potential arbitrage: CIF costs and taxes still have to be applied on top of these curves to identify real arbitrage opportunity.

Convexity bias. Since LME futures are actually forwards, the comparison with other, more standard, metals futures should account for the possible convexity bias. COMEX futures are in fact margined daily as the difference between the underlying's price and the initial strike without any discount factor. On margins, interest is accrued. A positive correlation between futures prices and interest rates would result in compounded proceeds for a long futures position: in fact, on rising (decreasing) metal prices both variation margins and the USD rate used to calculate interest would increase (decrease). This effect, called convexity bias, would make futures prices higher than forwards prices (with positive correlation). Nevertheless, since

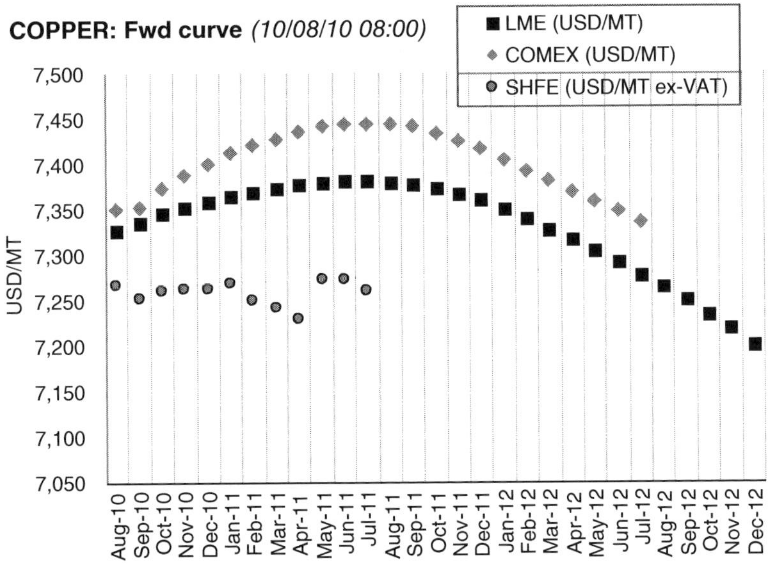

FIGURE 7.17 Copper international forward curves

there is little evidence of strong correlation between base metals prices and interest rates, this effect is often neglected.

7.2.4 Contango Limit...

Base-metals traders always monitor forward curves, trying to exploit any imperfection or mispricing. The presence of possible arbitrage is therefore very limited. At the same time, when a possible arbitrage is durable on the market it is hard, albeit impossible, to capitalize on this arbitrage.

In contango markets, a typical arbitrage trade is the *cash and carry arbitrage*. The trade consists of buying the metal at a prompt date t and at the same time selling it at a forward date $T > t$. If the forward price is higher than the spot price plus all the financing costs (assuming one borrows money to buy the metal spot) – the warehousing, insurance and transport costs (one needs to store the metal between t and T) – one would lock in a certain profit. This *gross* profit (the effect of different taxation regimes would alter the net result) attracts traders who, putting the trade on, progressively narrow the arbitrage until it disappears.

The cash and carry arbitrage hence represents the *upper limit* for the forward price:

$$F(t, T) < S_t\, e^{(r+u)(T-t)},$$

where $F(t, T)$ is the forward price at time t delivering at time T; $S(t)$ is the spot price in t; r is the risk-free rate; and u represents the storage costs in yield percentage terms (*inclusive of complementary costs like insurance and transport*).

It will be shown in detail if and how this concept finds practical application on the LME. As seen previously, the exchange provides a flexible and efficient way to manage physical delivery through warrants and the *LMEsword*. The arbitrageur who is long a metal on the cash will be delivered in t+2 the purchased tons into an authorized LME warehouse.

- *The fact that brand and warehouse location for delivery are the seller's choice does not represent an issue for the arbitrageur: he could in fact deliver back into the same warehouse at the forward date.*

Under the above hypothesis, one can neglect transportation costs and rather focus on storage costs at official warehouses. The above equation considers the storage costs as a function of the spot price $S(t)$ with costs increasing proportionally with prices. This may not be the best representation for base metals. Each authorized warehouse has freedom to fix the rates charged for each metal but, for the sake of transparency, the LME requires maximum rates to be communicated to the market. Any change in the maximum rates has to be notified 3 months in advance. Table 7.3 is an extract of maximum rates published by the LME.

Figure 7.18 shows the average rates (average of all authorized warehouses) expressed in USD per day from 2004 to 2010. It can be seen that the highest rates are charged for the most expensive metals (nickel and tin), with the exception of aluminium alloys. At the same time it is evident that rates are increasing year by year and are independent of market fluctuations.

These considerations lead us to prefer the formulation of storage costs as additive to the price:

$$F(t, T) < (S_t + U)e^{r(T-t)}.$$

TABLE 7.3 LME warehouse rates for location

Country	Location	Warehouse Company	Aluminium Alloy	Copper	Lead	NASAAC	Nickel	Primary Aluminium	Tin	Zinc
			40,55	35,61	34,01	40,33	43,88	39,60	40,85	35,48
Belgium	Antwerp	C. Steinweg NV	41	36	35	/	45	40	42	36
		CWT Commodities (Rotterdam) BV	41	36	34	/	45	40	42	36
		Henry Bath BV	40	35	34	/	43	40	41	35
		Metal Terminals International NV	41	35	33	/	44	40	41	35
		Pacorini Vlissingen BV	41	36	34	/	45	40	42	36
		Vollers Hamburg GmbH	41	35	32	/	42	39	38	34
		Zuidnatie NV	41	35	34	/	44	40	41	35
Germany	Bremen	BLG Cargo Logistics GmbH & Co. KG.	34	/	28	/	34	32	/	30
	Hamburg	C. Steinweg (Sud-West Terminal) GmbH & C	41	36	35	/	45	40	42	36
		CWT Commodities (Rotterdam) BV	41	36	34	/	45	40	42	36
		Vollers Hamburg GmbH	39	35	33	/	42	39	38	36
Italy	Genoa	Genoa Metal Terminal S.r.l.	41	/	35	/	45	40	42	36
		Pacorini Metals Italia S.r.l.	41	/	34	/	45	40	42	36
	Leghorn	F. lli Bartoli	/	35	35	/	37	35	/	35
		Genoa Metal Terminal S.r.l.	41	36	35	/	45	40	/	36
		Pacorini Metals Italia S.r.l.	41	36	34	/	45	40	/	36
	Trieste	Genoa Metal Terminal S.r.l.	41	36	35	/	45	40	42	36
		Henry Bath & Son Ltd	40	35	33	/	43	40	41	35
		Metro International Trade Services (Italia) S.r	40	36	34	/	43	40	39	36
		Pacorini Metals Italia S.r.l.	41	36	34	/	45	40	42	36
Japan	All Locations	All Warehouse Companies	/	/	/	/	/	29	/	/
Korea (South)	Busan	C. Steinweg Warehousing (FE) Pte Ltd	41	36	/	/	45	40	42	/
		CWT Commodities (Metals) Pte Ltd	41	36	/	/	45	40	42	/
		Henry Bath Singapore Pte Ltd	40	35	/	/	43	40	41	/
		Metro International Trade Services (UK) Ltd	40	36	/	/	43	40	40	/
		NEMS Singapore Pte Ltd	41	36	/	/	45	40	40	/
		Pacorini Toll Pte Ltd	41	36	/	/	45	40	42	/
...	...	...	...	...	/	/	...	...	...	...

Source: LME.com.
LME warehouse rates for single location: USD/MT/day as of June 2010.

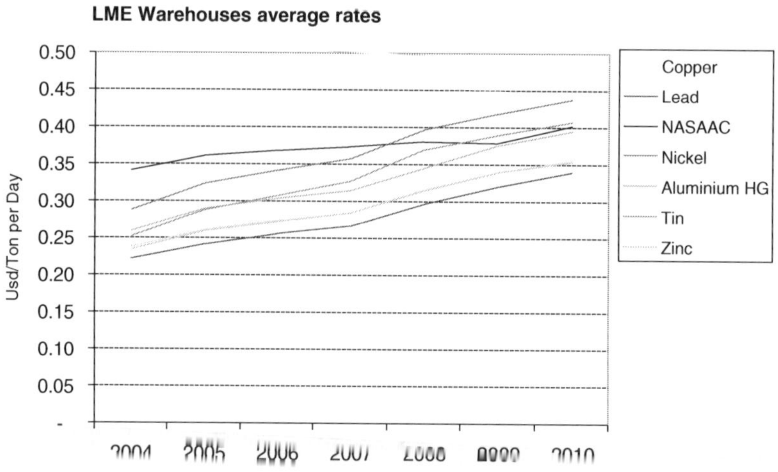

FIGURE 7.18 Warehouse average rates (USD/MT)

Combining the storage costs seen earlier together with the 1-year LIBOR rates (as proxy for the risk-free rate *r*) and the LME cash prices, it is possible to compute the 1-year contango limit in USD for each metal and compare it with the actual historical contango. In the following, this analysis is performed for the period from 2007 to 2010. Figures 7.19–7.24 compare the actual 1y contango (USD/MT – right axis) with the theoretical contango limit

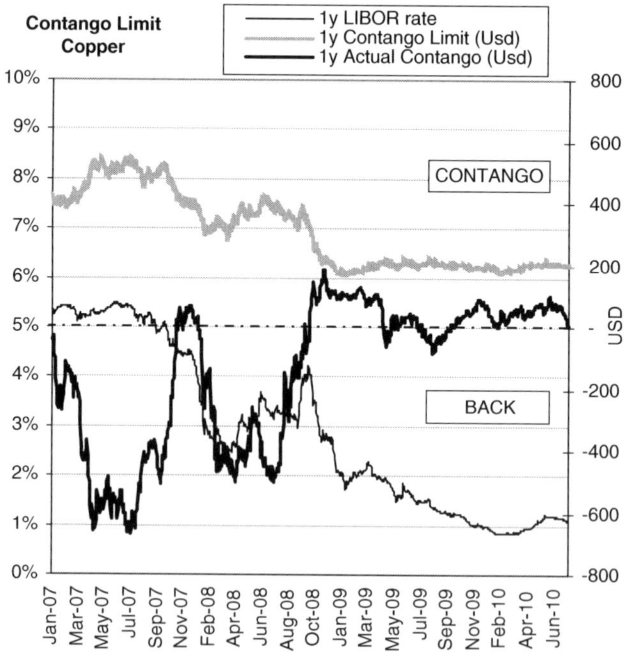

FIGURE 7.19 Copper contango limit

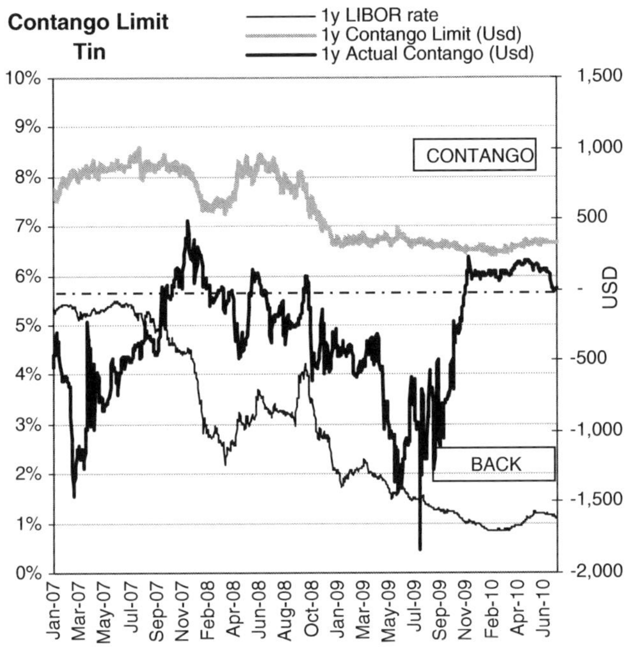

FIGURE 7.20 Tin contango limit

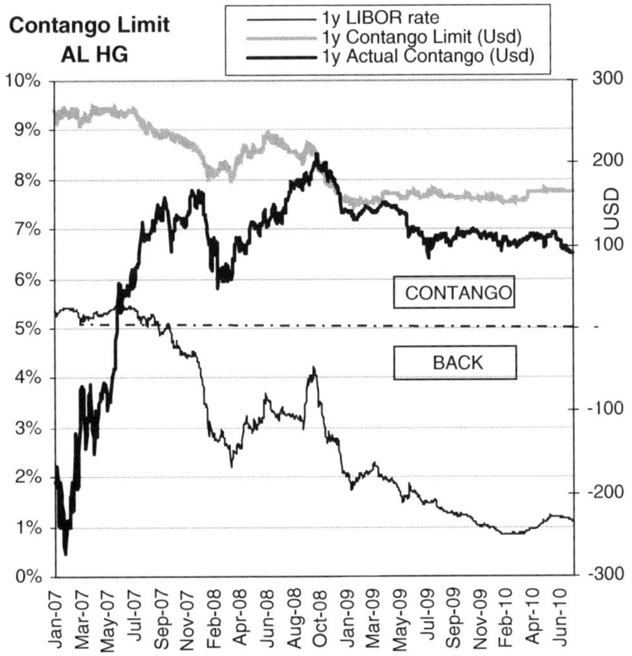

FIGURE 7.21 Aluminium HG contango limit

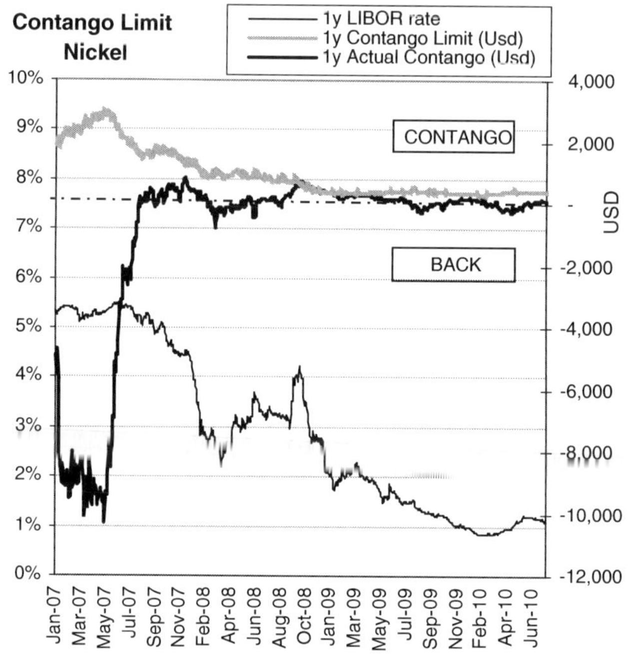

FIGURE 7.22 Nickel contango limit

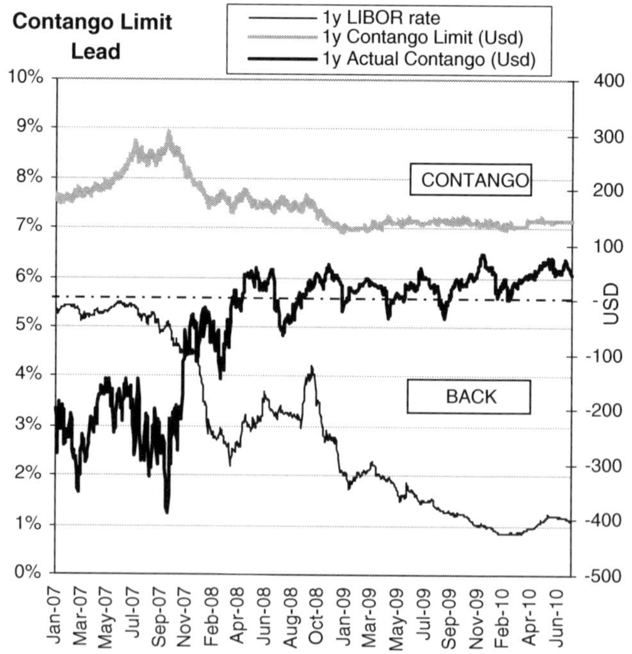

FIGURE 7.23 Lead contango limit

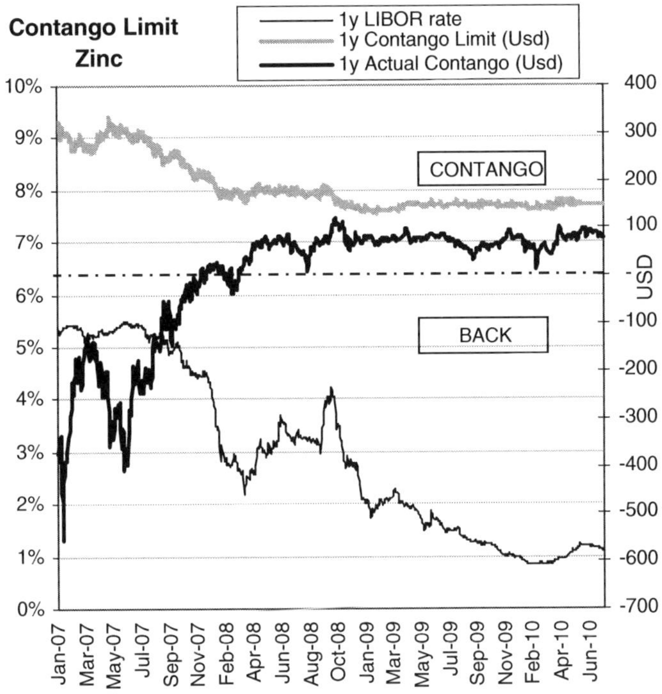

FIGURE 7.24 Zinc contango limit

(USD/MT – right axis) as well as the 1y Libor rate (% – left axis). When the actual contango is >0 USD/MT a contango market prevails, whereas when the actual contango is <0 USD/MT backwardation prevails.

The charts present some considerations:

- First of all, as anticipated at the beginning of the chapter, the forward curve fluctuations of each metal are unique and poorly correlated. Furthermore, the fluctuations of actual contango are random across all metals.
- In the sample considered (42 months) it is impossible to identify a 'structural' contango or backwardation. While metals like zinc and aluminium are in contango for most of the days, tin is mostly in backwardation. Copper instead shows significant changes in the curve's inclination.
- The contango limit in general seems to hold. There are nevertheless interesting exceptions.

There are exceptions to this in aluminium and nickel during the last quarter of 2008. During those days, actual contango was beyond the theoretical limit. But why did this apparent arbitrage opportunity last for several weeks? The answer is that in practice, the *cash and carry* trading was limited by the global credit crisis (i.e., the *credit crunch*), which culminated on 15 September 2008 with Lehman Brothers filing for Chapter 12 bankruptcy.

- *It is the condition r = risk-free rate that is violated: each company has different ratings and financing capabilities that result in an (r+premium) rate of financing.*

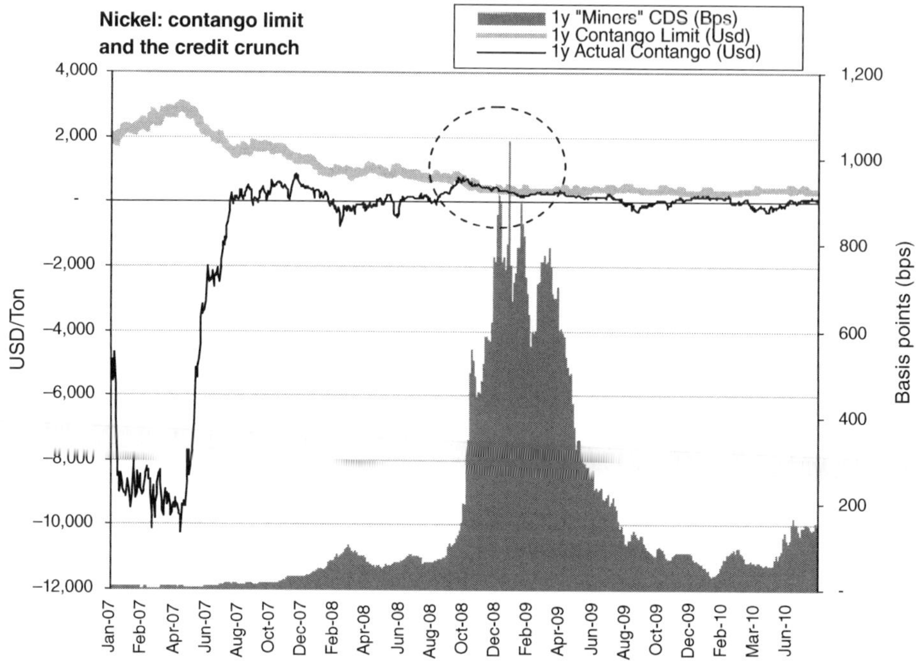

FIGURE 7.25 Contango limit and the credit crunch

To further investigate the impact of the credit crisis, an *ad-hoc* 'Miners' credit default swap (CDS) index is built. The index takes the unweighted average of the 1-year CDSs for three major international players active on industrial markets: Arcelor Mittal, Anglo American plc and BHP Billiton.[2] A CDS rate is not equal to a company's funding rate but provides a rough idea of its evolution: it is measured in basis points (bps). The higher the CDS, the higher the additional spread over LIBOR required by the interbank market to finance the company. Figure 7.25 shows the contango limit violation on nickel together with the 'Miners' CDS index rate.

In the fourth quarter of 2008 the credit crunch was at its peak: the companies who were long stocks started to sell their reserves in order to use the cash proceeds as an alternative (self-)financing system. At the same time, a requisite for arbitrage is full access to the physical market: often not the case for those financial institutions with the lowest funding rate.[3]

7.2.5 ...and No-Limit Backwardation

While it has been relatively easy to set a theoretical limit for contango, the same limit is impossible to calculate for backwardation. The holder of the physical commodity may yield some extra return that the holder of an equivalent forward position cannot. This is, for example,

[2]The choice of mentioned companies is purely indicative and based on their relevance in the physical market.

[3]For a detailed analysis of the topic, see Chris Harris in Geman (2005).

the case for companies who consume or transform base metals and create value added out of the production process. Even in situations of rising spot prices these companies sometimes just cannot stop consuming the metals: perhaps because stopping the industrial process may require too much time or because the finished products have already been sold.

The convenience of holding the physical commodity is called the *convenience yield.* Since the demand for spot consumption of a commodity could in theory infinitely inflate spot prices, the backwardation could, in theory, be infinite. When stocks are low, which means metal is scarce on the spot market, the market is usually in backwardation. The tighter the market is on spot, the more pronounced is the backwardation.

- *Backwardation is in fact more the consequence of the fast rising of spot prices rather than the lowering of forward prices.*

In Figure 7.26 the 3M–cash spread is plotted. When the spread is negative the market is in backwardation. The grey area shows the global inventories expressed in tons (right axis). In the summers of 2007 and 2008, the level of inventories was very low: the backwardation peaked. In the winters of 2006 and 2007, with stocks at reasonable levels, the market reverted temporarily to contango. Starting from the fourth quarter of 2008 the stocks increased steadily (part of the reason being linked to the aforementioned credit crunch) and the forward curve was in contango. The correlation between stock levels and contango/backwardation is sensible.

The same data used for the chart in Figure 7.26 can be used to plot a *scatter* chart: the *x-axis* is the 3M–cash spread (USD/MT) and the *y-axis* is the level of stocks (tons). The result is shown in Figure 7.27. The grey points are the actual spread levels while the dashed red line gives the calculated levels of the contango limit.

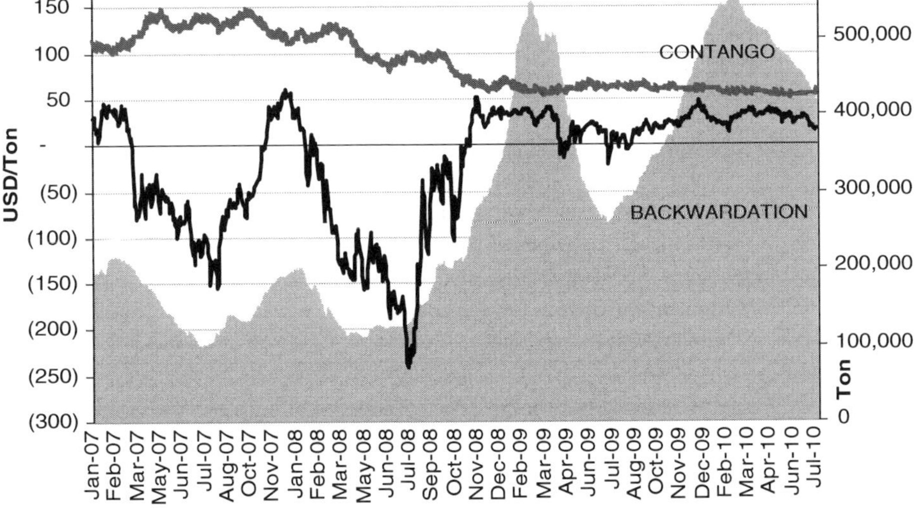

FIGURE 7.26 The role of inventories

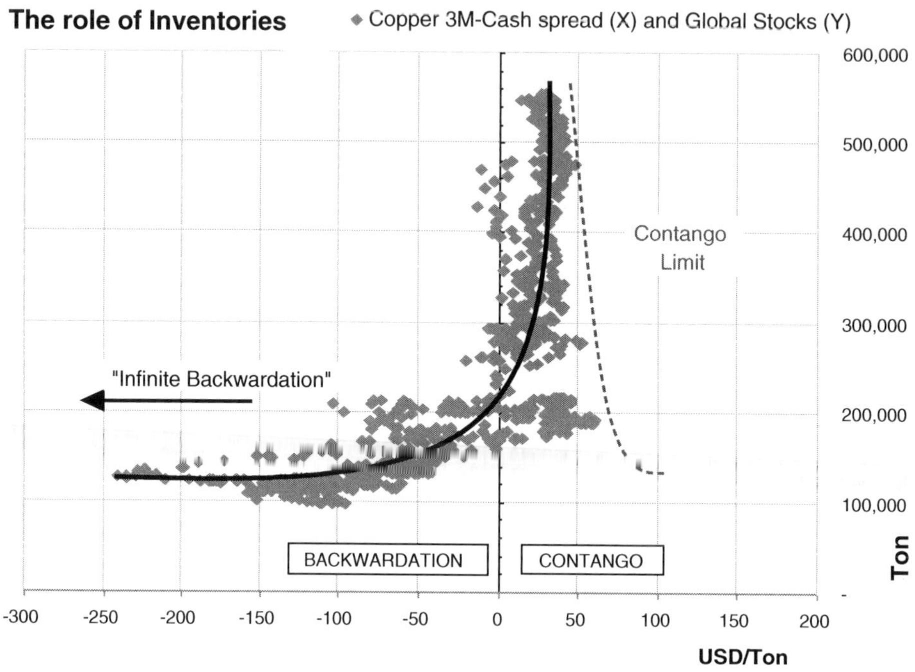

FIGURE 7.27 The role of inventories – dispersion chart

The chart in Figure 7.27 provides an illustration of the relation between stocks and the forward curve's inclination. It is also possible to identify the relation as an *exponential function* (solid black line), although the dispersion is not negligible. The resulting exponential function is indeed consistent with the considerations made.

- The function is unbounded on the left side: the backwardation could in theory be infinite.
- The function is bounded on the right side: the contango limit works as an asymptote of the function.

Looking back at recent years, one can find periods where the market on nickel experienced extreme backwardation. One clear example involved the T/N maturity. As seen at the beginning of the chapter, T/N is the shortest maturity on the curve: it is hence extremely sensitive to variations of stock levels. Figure 7.28 shows the nickel cash price (USD/MT, left axis) together with the level of T/N (USD/MT, right axis). The price of T/N, being the roll of just a single trading day, is normally within a +50/–50 USD range. In July 2007 and August 2008 the spread touched record levels of backwardation. As expected, this was happening in a scenario of wildly rising cash prices.

To explain this kind of situation, it must be remembered that it is the seller of a forward who has the obligation to deliver the metal. In a context of rising physical demand and general growth in the economy (as occurred in those years), cash prices go up and stocks are consumed. If sellers do not have the physical metal to deliver (also because of stock scarcity), when the forward date comes to expiration they must borrow it (buy cash, sell forward). The borrowing

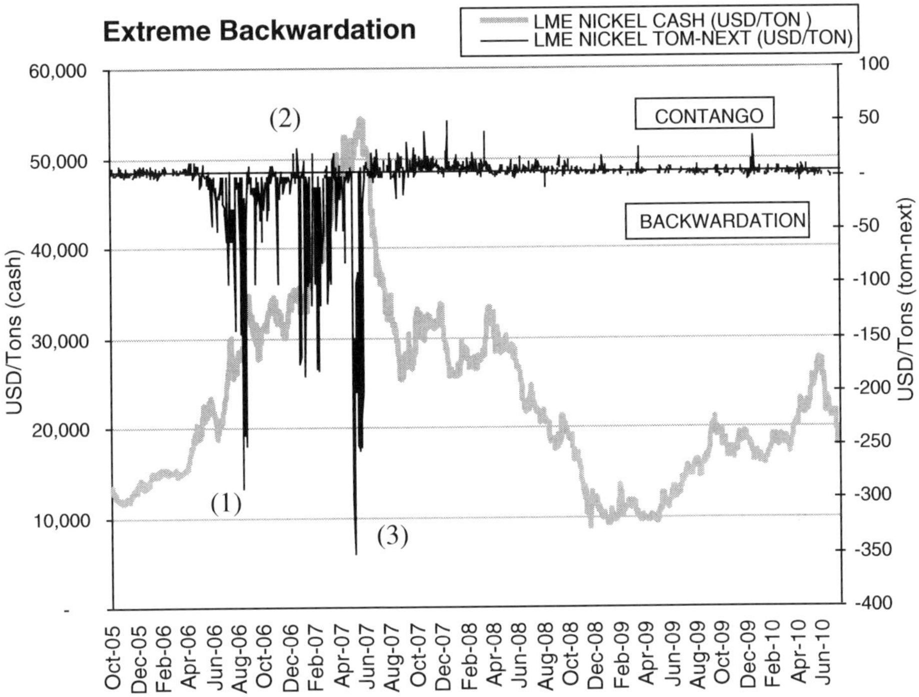

FIGURE 7.28 The role of inventories – dispersion chart

effect is then to widen further the backwardation. The holder of stocks is best positioned in this market scenario, explaining much of the 'convenience' behind the convenience yield.

Physical traders know very well that the market behaves in this fashion and can sometimes try to 'corner the market'.

- *If the majority of available stocks or the supply of metal is controlled by a single operator (or a cartel of operators), the market can be cornered. The operator, by simply not selling its stocks, can artificially inflate the cash prices, hence increasing the dollar value of his holdings.*

This strategy does not always work: Yasuo Hamanaka of Sumitomo Corporation failed and sunk in the attempt. For several years he tried to corner copper, to the extent that he gained the nickname of 'Mr Copper', until 1996, when the size of losses suffered became too big to be hidden. Sumitomo reported losses for 2.6 billion USD.

In order to prevent or limit such situations, the LME can adopt specific rules of lending and impose obligations on stock holders: the *Metal Lending Guidance*.

> Metal Lending Guidance paragraph 13.24 of Market Aberrations [...] setting out the behaviour required of the holders of dominant long positions in the Exchange's metal markets, including a clarification or explanation of that behaviour issued by the Exchange from time to time...
>
> LME Rulebook, Definitions

Looking back at the practical example on nickel, points (1), (2) and (3) in Figure 7.28 are the time steps of how in practice the exchange reacted to the aberrations on T/N.

1. **The exchange first decided to introduce a cap of 300 USD to daily backwardation**

   16/08/2006

   LME Imposes Backwardation Limit for Nickel

   At 1700 hours today, the London Metal Exchange (LME) announced that the Special Committee has imposed a backwardation limit of $300.00 per tonne per day in the nickel market and that there will be a suspension of the Lending Guidance in respect of those with nickel positions.

   (LME press release)

2. **Market reverted to normality and the cap was removed**

   10/11/2006

   LME Removes Nickel Backwardation

   The London Metal Exchange (LME) has today announced that the Special Committee has lifted the backwardation limit in the nickel market.

   (LME press release)

3. **In May 2007, the market was again in distress for nearby delivery: demand for nickel was fuelled by the substantial growth of stainless steel capacity in China. LME tightened the Lending Guidance on nickel**

   06/06/2007

   Modification of Lending Guidance

   The Special Committee has decided to modify the Lending Guidance in respect of those with nickel positions by introducing new levels at which the holder(s) of dominant long positions are required to lend nickel.

   (LME press release)

The new lending guidance dictates precise rules of lending and prices for holders of dominant positions on nickel cash dates and warrants. The holder can be forced to reduce his positions on warrant, TOM and cash (WTC) at a fixed price expressed as a percentage of the cash price per day. In Table 7.4 an abstract from the new lending guidance is reported.

After the release of the new lending guidance the nickel cash price dropped, while at the same time the backwardation reverted to normal levels. In those days, two players were rumoured to be responsible for the squeeze on the spot market. The exchange did not officially mention market abuses, but nevertheless the counter-measures taken worked well whatever the causes of market distress.

7.2.6 Hedging the Curve in Practice

At the beginning of LME's history, the only traded maturity was the 3-month. It subsequently became possible to trade all the dates from the cash to 14 days beyond the 3-month. When the

TABLE 7.4 LME lending guidance

Only one holder of 50% or more of WTC positions	Existing Lending Guidance Applies, i.e. 50% – <80% lend at $\frac{1}{2}$% (changes after 5 days)	Existing Lending Guidance Applies, i.e. 80% – <90% lend at $\frac{1}{4}$% (changes after 5 days)	Existing Lending Guidance Applies, i.e. = or >90% lend at level
Two holders of 25% or more each of WTC positions	25% – <40% lend at $\frac{1}{2}$%	40% – <45% lend at $\frac{1}{4}$%	= or >45% lend at level
Three holders of 25% or more each of WTC positions	16.66% – <26.66% lend at $\frac{1}{2}$%	26.66% – <30% lend at $\frac{1}{4}$%	= or >30% lend at level
Four holders of 25% or more each of WTC positions	12.5% – <20% lend at $\frac{1}{2}$%	20% – <22.5% lend at $\frac{1}{2}$%	= or >22.5% lend at level
Five holders of 25% or more each of WTC positions	10% – <16% lend at $\frac{1}{2}$%	16% – <18% lend at $\frac{1}{4}$%	= or >18% lend at level

Source: LME press release 06/06/07.

metal industry started concerning itself with risk management, the trading activity on long-term maturities rose. On the sell side of long-term contracts, there are for example mining companies and banks involved in project finance. Both aim to reduce the variance of future cash flows. On the buy side, there are big consumers like the motor industry. The objective is to fix the level of costs in their future budgets.

In order to meet these needs, the exchange progressively extended the listed maturities up to 15 months and 27 months: nowadays copper, primary aluminium and zinc are listed with up to 123 monthly prompts. Liquidity is nevertheless decreasing with maturity, with the only exception being the December contracts. Figure 7.29 shows this, taking the open interest as a benchmark of a contract's liquidity.

Although aluminium is the most traded metal on the LME, a hedger in 2010 looking for trading maturities after Dec12 would have difficulties. In the following, the possible alternatives for practical cases will be analysed.

7.2.6.1 Case 1: Hedging a Single Maturity Imagine being the trader in charge of hedging a big long position (25,000 tons, 1000 lots) with Dec14 aluminium futures. In this case, selling the monthly prompt Dec14 contract would be the perfect hedge, but the issues are the long tenor (and hence associated illiquidity) and the big position size. Table 7.5 shows some possible alternatives for the execution.

The possible execution alternatives can be divided into two groups: trading directly the required maturity or trading first a more liquid maturity (like the 3M in the example) and then working the carries. The first choice leaves no residual risks at all but the bigger the size then the higher the costs will be. The slippage would be the most relevant cost: in Section 7.2.1 it was shown how the bid–ask widens for longer maturities. The second choice should be cheaper but leaves the trader with the risk of curve movements. This macro choice is subject

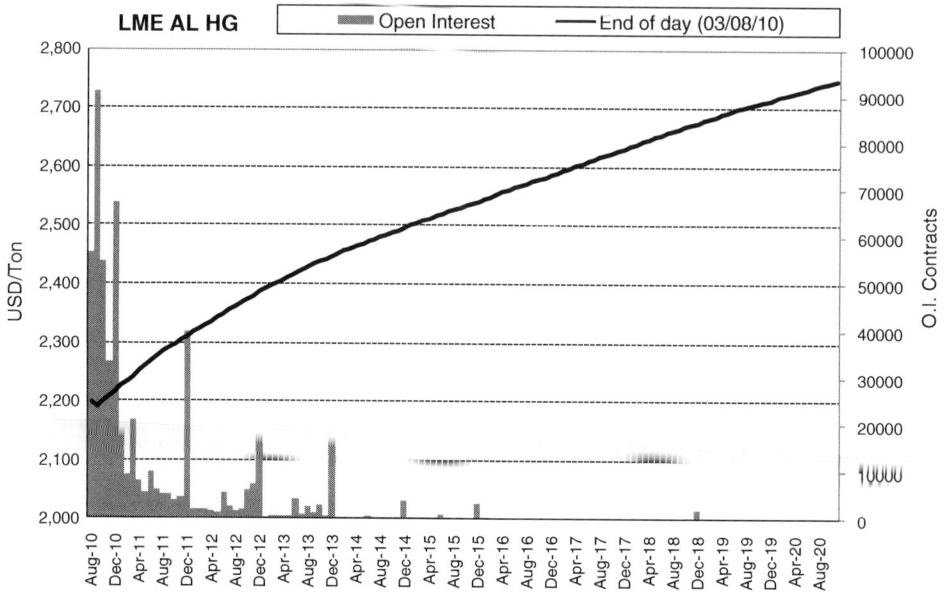

FIGURE 7.29 Open interest and futures maturities

to the risk management policies and risk attitude of an individual company. First of all, it is observed that the choice A3 is sub-optimal to other strategies: the directional risk is just too high to justify the saved slippage. Compared with B1/B2, the standard deviation of 3M daily changes is relatively higher than the standard deviation of the spread 3M–Dec14.

Figure 7.30 considers the generic rolling spread 3M–50M (one then gets a constant-maturity spread and avoids the effect of time decay on the spread). The standard deviation is computed over simple daily changes (USD) since it provides an immediate idea of the risk the trader is bearing each day in keeping a naked position.

The main difference between A1 and A2 is the legal nature of the trade: an LME futures contract versus an OTC swap. Execution of A1 leaves no counterparty risk but needs margins

TABLE 7.5 Hedging a single maturity

	Execution	Pros	Cons
A1	Sell the Dec14 on the market (brokers) the full size	No residual risks	Cost of slippage, partial fills, margins
A2	Sell the Dec14 OTC (banks/dealers) the full size	No residual risks, full size filled	Commissions, counterparty risk
A3	Sell the Dec14 on the market (brokers) in tranches	Slippage limited	Directional risk for not hedged tranches
B1	Sell the 3M the full size and work the 3M–Dec14 spread	Slippage limited, full size, anonymity	Basis risk 3M–Dec14
B2	Sell the 3M a proxy size and work the 3M–Dec14 spread	Slippage limited, full size, anonymity	Basis risk 3M–Dec14

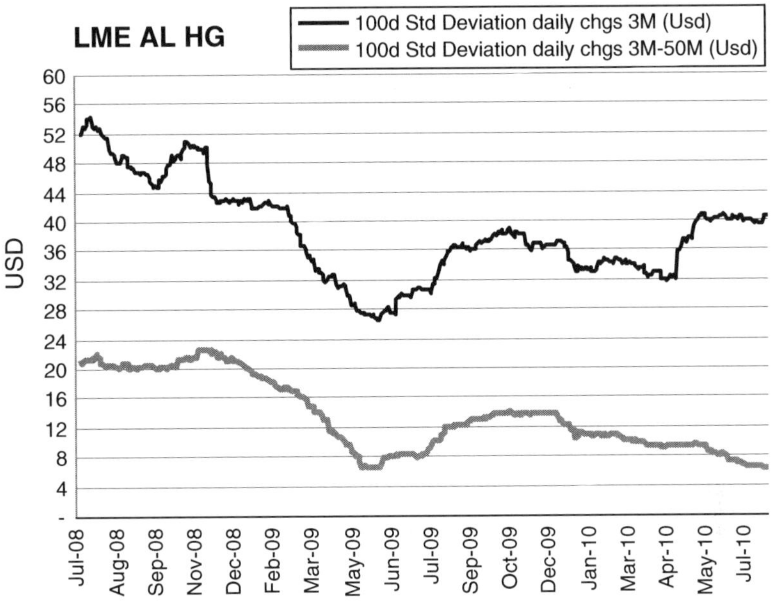

FIGURE 7.30 Standard deviations comparison

managing, whereas execution of A2 does not require initial margins but implies a bilateral deal with counterparty risk. The other pros and cons are more subtle and concern the trader's execution style.

Execution of strategies B1 and B2 shares the same approach: firstly, hedge as proxy on the 3M and then work the carry on Dec14. The only point of divergence is the percentage of the full size to hedge on the 3M: it is common practice to hedge 100% of the size since it is more straightforward than rolling the position on the 3M–Dec14. Nevertheless, this is not always the best solution.

- *When it is impossible to roll the proxy hedge to the proper maturity in a reasonably short time, it is more efficient to use a hedge ratio.*

One looks for the hedge ratio that minimizes the variance of a portfolio $\prod$ that is short a liquid asset x and long h_{tons} of an illiquid asset y: the peculiarity here is that the asset is the same (aluminium) on different maturities. The portfolio has variance $\prod_{\text{VaR}} = \sigma_x^2 + h^2\sigma_y^2 - 2h\rho_{xy}\sigma_x\sigma_y$, where ρ_{xy} is the correlation between the two underlyings and σ_x and σ_y are the respective standard deviations of price changes. The hedge ratio that minimizes variance is:

$$h = \rho_{xy}\frac{\sigma_y}{\sigma_x}.$$

In the practical example here, the hedge ratio in tons would be

$$h_{\text{tons}} = \rho_{\text{3M,Dec14}}\frac{\sigma_{\text{Dec14}}}{\sigma_{\text{3M}}}I_{\text{tons}},$$

where I_{tons} is the initial size (in tons) to hedge. This formula is commonly used for proxy hedging on commodity futures as well as on stocks (e.g., the hedge of an illiquid stock with a correlated stock index).

When dealing with LME futures, though, it must be remembered that they are more like forwards than standard futures. The main difference lies in the fact that LME futures margining is adjusted for the discount factor. The daily changes on a far maturity (like Dec14 in the example) will therefore be reduced by a far higher discounting. The optimal hedge ratio has to be adjusted for the ratio of the discount factors:

$$h_{\text{tons}} = \rho_{\text{3M,Dec14}} \frac{\sigma_{\text{Dec14}}}{\sigma_{\text{3M}}} \frac{Df_{\text{Dec14}}}{Df_{\text{3M}}} I_{\text{tons}},$$

where Df is the discount factor of the futures. This adjustment appears counter-intuitive at first sight. To understand the subtle impact of Df, consider the case where 3M and Dec14 are perfectly correlated (100%) and also have identical variance. In this case the hedge ratio would be 100%: if our long position on Dec14 is 1000 tons then the proxy hedge would be 1000 tons. Now assume Dec14 goes up 1 USD/ton on day 1 and as expected the 3M goes up 1 USD/ton as well: the market value of the positions would be +1000 USD on Dec14 and –1000 USD on the 3M that was sold for the hedge. The P&L is certainly not flat: in the clearer account, one will have +1000 USD × $Df_{\text{Dec14}} < -1000$ USD × Df_{3M} since the clearer (LCH) will apply different discount factors $Df_{\text{Dec14}} < Df_{\text{3M}}$ to the variation margin. Using the Df adjustment in the right part of the equation –1000 USD × $\frac{Df_{\text{Dec14}}}{Df_{\text{3M}}}$ × Df_{3M}, the P&L would effectively be zero.

- *The discount factor adjustment is not constant: it is a function of r (the higher r the more relevant the impact of Df adjustment) and time (as time passes the hedge ratio must be adjusted).*

Additionally, for the sake of precision, the rates r are not unique. Each discount factor should be calculated on the basis of the market rate for that specific maturity. Rates have indeed their own forward curves. Consider

$$Df_{\text{3M}} = e^{-r_{T_0-T_{\text{3M}}}(T_{\text{3M}}-T_0)},$$

where $r_{T_0-T_{\text{3M}}}$ is the interest rate applied in the period $(T_0 - T_{\text{3M}})$ compounded in the time period $(T_{\text{3M}} - T_0)$.

It is useful to emphasize a couple of concepts on the hypothesis behind the calculation of the hedge ratio before using it in practice. First, the estimates here are based on daily changes of price, hence USD/MT, instead of daily percentage changes (%). Therefore, the notation σ_x and σ_y is not to be confused with the common meaning of *volatility*, that is the annualized standard deviation of percentage return. Daily changes are used because the hedger is directly exposed to the variation in dollar value of the contracts: the volatility does not in fact account for the different contract dollar values of the position (Dec14) and the proxy hedge. The hedge ratio h^* with standard volatilities σ_x^* and σ_y^* as inputs should then be adjusted in the following way:

$$h^* = \rho \frac{\sigma_y^*}{\sigma_x^*} \frac{P_y}{P_x},$$

where P_y and P_x are the prices of y and x. If P_y and P_x are the average prices over the sample of y and x, then $h^* \cong h$.

Second, this kind of formula is meant to use *actual* parameters. Since it is impossible to know these values in advance, it is necessary to rely on *estimates.* It is common practice to use *historic* estimates: there are several methods and models in the academic literature, from the simplest moving average (used for the charts in this chapter) to the more complex family of GARCH models. Different models have different underlying hypotheses that impact the final output.

Another source of estimates could be the *implied* volatility and correlation. Starting from available market data it is possible to reverse-engineer a pricing model and extract the pricing parameters. In the example here, starting from the price of a European option on the Dec14 futures contract one could reverse-engineer Black's model and get the implied volatility of the forward. This second approach could actually be misleading since the implied volatilities and correlations can be more instable than the historic ones. *They are also generally considered biased estimators since they embed the risk aversion of the market.* Besides, an implied parameter is the result of a specific model's assumptions that, in practice, could be invalid. For example, some of Black's assumptions are: constant volatility, lognormal distribution of prices, zero cost of transactions, etc.

In both cases (historical or implied), when using these concepts in practice it is important to remember that the parameters are estimates and depend on the method of estimation and the sample of data.

- *The resulting hedge ratio is itself an estimate: the hedge ratio minimizes the variance in the sample of data used but will decrease the futures P&L variance of the portfolio only on average.*

Going back to the practical example here, assume that on a sample of 3 years of daily prices the following estimates are obtained:

$$\rho = 90\%$$
$$\sigma_{3M} = 40.50 \text{ (USD) and } \sigma_{\text{Dec14}} = 37.30 \text{ (USD)}$$
$$Df_{\text{Dec14}} = 0.84 \text{ and } Df_{3M} = 0.99$$
$$I_{\text{tons}} = 25{,}000 \text{ tons}$$

Therefore, the hedge ratio is

$$h_{\text{tons}} = 70.3\%\ I_{\text{tons}} = 17{,}582 \text{ tons}.$$

The result is not surprising in that since the 3M is much more volatile than the Dec14, and given the high correlation (which means that a great part of Dec14 variation is explained by the 3M), one will sell only 17,582 tons instead of the initial 25,000 tons. The hedge ratio without discount adjustment would have been 82.9%. The role of correlation is interesting. With $\rho = 0\%$ the hedge ratio would be zero since a proxy hedge would make no sense with two uncorrelated assets. The variance of the portfolio is at its maximum when the correlation is zero. At the opposite ends of the scale, a correlation of $\rho = +/-100\%$ would imply a hedge ratio equal to the ratio of the two volatilities since the dependent variable (Dec14) would be

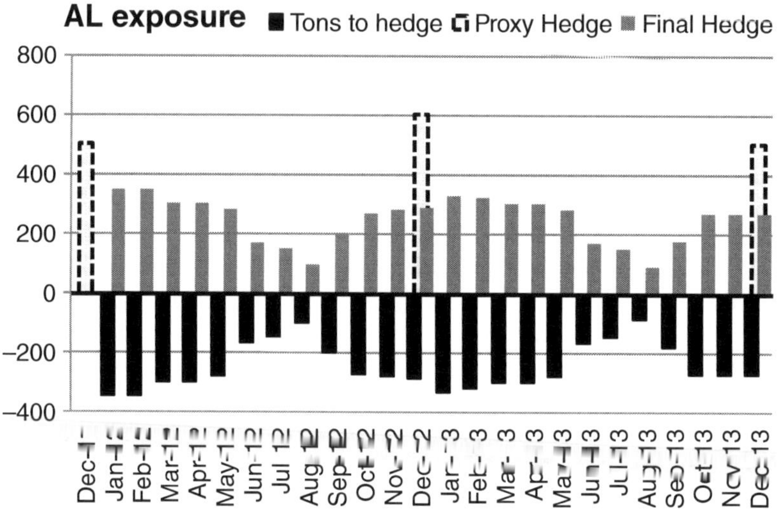

FIGURE 7.31 Hedging a volume profile in practice

totally explained by the independent (3M). This case is merely theoretical and would also imply a null variance of the hedged portfolio. While one can be wrong in estimating the two volatilities, one can be extremely wrong in estimating correlation.

7.2.6.2 Case 2: Hedging a Volume Profile

Consider now the situation, frequent between consumers, where the trader has the mandate to hedge a profiled consumption of aluminium on several months (a *strip*). A profiled volume on several months, like that shown in the bar chart of Figure 7.31, is common since the production processes can show seasonality: in August, for example, production slows down. The bars have negative sign since consumers naturally have a short exposure. For simplicity, in this example it will be assumed that the exposure is on the third Wednesday futures. More often, in practice, strips of Asian swaps are used. The core of the analysis would not change much.

Unlike in Case 1, here the trader has fewer alternatives: looking back at Table 7.5, A1 and A3 are excluded since it is unrealistic to work simultaneously on long-term market futures with different sizes. Option A2 instead remains available and in fact represents a typical request from customers to market-makers. Alternative B1 does not require any extra analysis, while B2 is more sophisticated. Since the initial hedge will be the proxy on the 3M, the proper hedge ratio must be worked out. This can be seen as a compound case of the hedge ratio of Case 1: more precisely, the sum of the hedge ratios of each maturity versus the 3M. The hedge ratio (in tons) of a volume profile is then

$$H_{\text{tons}}^{\text{strip}} = \sum_{i}^{n} h_i = \sum_{i}^{n} \rho_{3\text{M},i} \frac{\sigma_i}{\sigma_{3\text{M}}} I_i,$$

where h_i is the ith hedge ratio (already in tons) of the ith month versus the 3M. The volume profile is captured by each I_i (initial tons to hedge of ith month) and as a result the final $H_{\text{tons}}^{\text{strip}}$ is a volume-weighted average of the single hedge ratios.

7.2.6.3 Case 3: Better Hedging a Volume Profile Whatever the chosen execution between B1 and B2, the trader has to face another issue after the initial hedge on 3M is done – that is, on which maturities forward and how many tons to roll the initial hedge. In fact, the need to reduce the basis risk arising from the initial 3M hedge, together with the lack of liquidity on the entire strip, requires another (more refined) proxy hedge as a second step. The choice of the maturities is driven by liquidity: looking back at the open interest of aluminium one would pick Dec11, Dec12 and Dec13. Another proxy hedge will be put in place here: the objective being to minimize the risk arising from the profiled short position through the selective buying of the three maturities. This initial hedge, pictured in Figure 7.31 with the three long bars, will then be decomposed into the final hedge symmetric to the exposure.

Dec11 is included, although not a maturity within the exposure. However, it is very important since it allows one to hedge against movements in the more volatile part of the curve. Given that the volatility of metals futures normally decreases with longer tenors, using Dec12 as the first pillar would fail to capture the wild front-end fluctuations. To get a more general picture of the risks involved in taking positions on the forward curve, consider the changes in the curve's shape as the combination of three shifts: the parallel shift, the tilt (change of inclination or rotation) and convexity (bending of the curve). Under PCA, these movements account for the first three components. The components are ordered by importance: the first component (parallel shift) explains the majority of movements in a forward curve, while the third one (convexity) explains the residual part of them. The fourth-order shift is the sinusoid. In the graphs depicted in Figure 7.32, the sinusoid shift is given although it can be considered extremely unlikely for base metals: the fungibility of metals virtually prevents such patterns in reality. As a matter of fact, Cortazar and Schwartz (1994), analysing COMEX copper futures between 1978 and 1990, found that the three factors explain ~99% of total return variance.

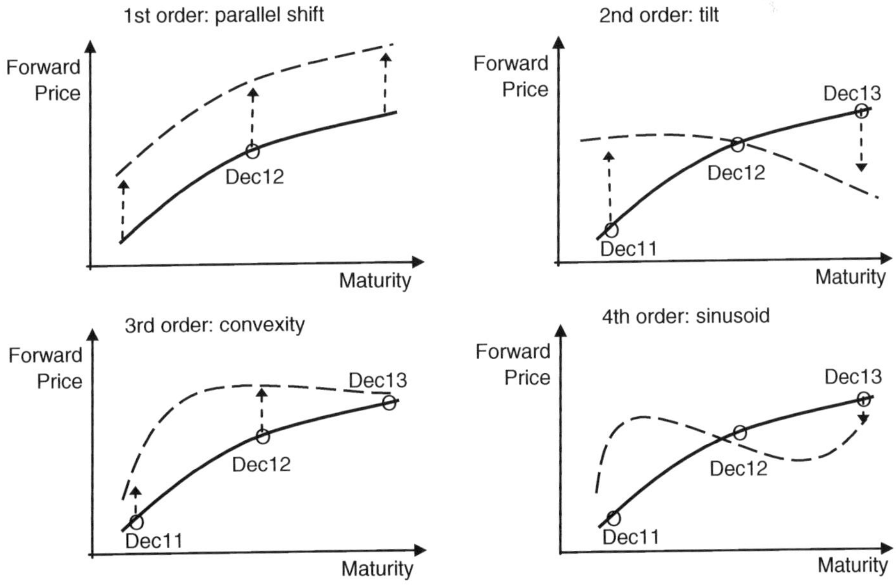

FIGURE 7.32 First four components of curve risk

The parallel shift can be hedged with a single contract: in the graph, the Dec12 contract is taken for example but any other could be used. The tilt of the curve cannot be hedged by a single contract: Dec11 and Dec13 are needed in order to capture the opposite movements on the head and tail of the curve. Notice also that the hedge on Dec12 is useless since the curve moves around that pillar. The convexity shift bends the curve centrally: the hedge on Dec12 is essential in contrast here. The three chosen contracts are hence the minimum hedge against the first three components of forward curve changes.

The objective is to find the hedge ratios on the three maturities that minimize the variance of the portfolio ($\prod$) composed of the strip (short) and the three contracts (long). Following the mean–variance analysis approach introduced by Markowitz in 1959, one can write the variance of the portfolio as

$$\prod\nolimits_{\text{VaR}} = w'\ V_R\, w,$$

where $w = (w_i, \ldots, w_n)$ is the vector of the n weights on the n months. Each weight is the total position for each month – that is, the profiled volumes plus the hedging tons. V_R is the $n \times n$ covariance matrix of the n forward returns.

The exercise is to find the weights (tons) on the contracts Dec11, Dec12 and Dec13 that are the solution of the minimization problem

$$\min_{\{w_{\text{Dec11}}, w_{\text{Dec12}}, w_{\text{Dec13}}\}} \quad w' V_R w.$$

Notice that the problem is unconstrained in that one is not interested in maximizing returns (a perfect hedge has zero returns) and that the sum of w_i is free. The covariance matrix V_R is symmetric and must be positive semi-definite (in order to always have non-negative variance of portfolio value).

$$V_R = \begin{Bmatrix} \sigma^2_{Dec11} & \sigma_{Dec11,Jan12} & \cdots & \sigma_{Dec11,Dec13} \\ \sigma_{\text{Dec11,Jan12}} & \sigma^2_{\text{Jan12}} & \sigma_{\text{Jan12,Feb12}} & \cdots \\ \cdots & \cdots & \sigma_i^2 & \cdots \\ \sigma_{\text{Dec11,Dec13}} & \cdots & \cdots & \sigma^2_{\text{Dec13}} \end{Bmatrix},$$

with σ_i^2 the variance of forward i and $\sigma_{i,k} = \rho_{i,k}\sigma_i\sigma_k$ the covariance between the forwards i and k. The matrix needs to be populated with the variance estimate for each forward and the correlation estimate for each pair. An analytical solution is not immediate: for each month i, a multiple regression should be run on the three hedging contracts, thus obtaining three betas $\beta_{i,\text{Dec11}}, \beta_{i,\text{Dec12}}, \beta_{i,\text{Dec13}}$. As a result, the $n \times 3$ betas would be estimated and used to compute the three final hedge ratios.

It is possible to run minimization routines on selected software (e.g., Matlab© or Excel Solver©): in this case, the portfolio variance would be set as a target to minimize, changing the variables $w_{\text{Dec11}}, w_{\text{Dec12}}, w_{\text{Dec13}}$.

The considerations made for parameter estimation in Case 1 are valid here as well.

7.3 VOLATILITY

This section is meant to be an introduction to base-metals volatility trading and analysis. The topic of volatility models is both a vast and complex field that is properly debated within academic literature. The applications range from pricing models for options to risk management tools for assessing portfolio value at risk (VaR). In the following, the focus will be on the specific features of metals options from the point of view of the trader rather than that of the risk manager or the quantitative analyst. Taking as reference the most common option models, some unique conventions of the LME will be pointed out, while also addressing how to build a volatility surface and deliver some implied volatility analysis.

In the last few years the hedging demand coming from companies, bounded by stringent accounting rules, has become more and more limited to the simplest of structures: that is why the focus here will be on European and Asian options only. Where more sophisticated instruments require more advanced models, it is common practice to refer to the much wider literature on energy models.

At this stage some preliminary clarification on the terms and conventions that will be used is useful. Volatility is meant generally as the measure of variability in the price of an asset. It is normally associated with the standard deviation of price returns (%) over a specified time period. In the following text, a time period of 1 year will be assumed and hence the focus will be on annualized volatility. When volatility is calculated on a past set of data, it is said to be actual or historical volatility. In what follows, the historical volatilities are calculated as the simple standard deviation of daily price returns (%) or daily changes (chgs) over a specified time range in the past. The focus will be on cumulative volatility only: the volatilities that refer to the standard deviation from t_0 to t_1. This is specified to distinguish them from the concept of local, instantaneous volatilities (Derman and Kani, 1994).

Implied volatility is the volatility that comes from the reverse-engineering of an option price given a specific model and with all the other model inputs known. As a consequence, different models could correspond to different implied volatilities. This point is expanded upon here.

When computing implied volatilities data one should always be sure of the prevailing model on the market: overlooking this will likely result in obtaining results that are not comparable with the market or, worse, results that are effectively useless.

- *This is crucial for the option trader since brokers sometimes directly quote implied volatilities instead of option premia.*

This practice, common in mature markets like that of currency options, is an advanced (and efficient) way of trading volatility: only after the trade is agreed will the broker communicate all the details together with the option premium. Imagine the unwise trader who buys an option at an agreed volatility and only afterwards realizes the premium (and hence the option model) is different from what he had figured out. This is the reason why on some markets the practice is to express option quotes directly in implied volatilities while in others premiums are quoted: the LME lies within the first category.

Where a prevailing pricing model is not available, options are quoted in premia to avoid 'modelistic misunderstandings': this is, for example, the case for WTI futures options. Those options listed on NYMEX are American style and as traders may use several models and methods to price them, quotes are given in premia terms.

The topic of model dependence of implied volatility has gathered the attention of some researchers. An example is the work of Britten-Jones and Neuberger (2000) that addresses a method to obtain model-free implied volatilities.

7.3.1 A European Disguised as an American

Futures options are the most traded options on the LME. The exchange also offers monthly average Asian options (TAPO), which show smaller traded volumes. It has already been established that technically the futures on the LME are instead forwards. The American nature of the LME options will be the focus here. The LME's futures (or forward) options are officially American – that is the buyer has the right, any time during the life of the option, to exercise the option. The exercise of a call (put) futures option gives the buyer a long (short) position on the underlying futures (the option month) at the option's strike price (K). As an example, the buyer of a Dec10 call on copper, with strike 7000 USD, could exercise the option any time and convert the option position to a long Dec10 futures position struck at 7000.

The European option can instead be exercised only at maturity. The early exercise could be convenient in some situations. Therefore, given the same characteristics (i.e., strike, maturity), the American futures option is worth more than the European.

To understand how early exercise can be convenient, consider the case of a generic put futures option with strike 1000 USD. If the underlying futures price goes down to 200 USD, the put is said to be deep *in-the-money* (ITM). If one decides to exercise early then a short position on the futures will be received at the level of 1000 USD. If the time to maturity is short enough, say 30 days, so that there is low probability that the futures price will rise back over the strike, the futures price changes will be equivalent to those of the option. In fact, if the price were to fall to zero, both the option and the futures would provide a gross gain of 1000 USD. In Figure 7.34 the price of the American put (before maturity) is the grey line: notice that below the threshold X the price of the put matches the final payoff line. Below X the put is in fact so much ITM that keeping the put or exercising it into the short futures is equivalent in terms of payoff.

At the date t_0 of early exercise, the short futures at 1000 USD would have a positive variation margin of 800 USD/MT (strike 1000 USD – price 200 USD). For a *standard* American futures option one will receive this variation margin as cash *upfront*. The early exercise will then yield 30 days of interest proceeds deriving from the cash received at t_0: below X the best strategy is hence to exercise the put early.

For a European futures option instead, one cannot exercise early by design. Therefore, the value of the deep ITM put option is the net present value of the strike minus the price. If in fact the price goes to zero, the option value is Ke^{-rt} – see Figure 7.33.

Going back to the LME's options, since the underlying futures is instead a forward, the exercise of a deep ITM option will result in a forward whose variation margin is paid discounted instead of upfront. In the example above, when the price of the futures falls to zero, the put option can be exercised early but the proceeds are discounted. The value of an LME put is therefore Ke^{-rt}, like a European-style option.

- *The LME's American futures option is actually a European forward option.*[4]

In practice, the LME's options are rarely exercised early.

[4] A formal demonstration can be found in Sartorelli (2010).

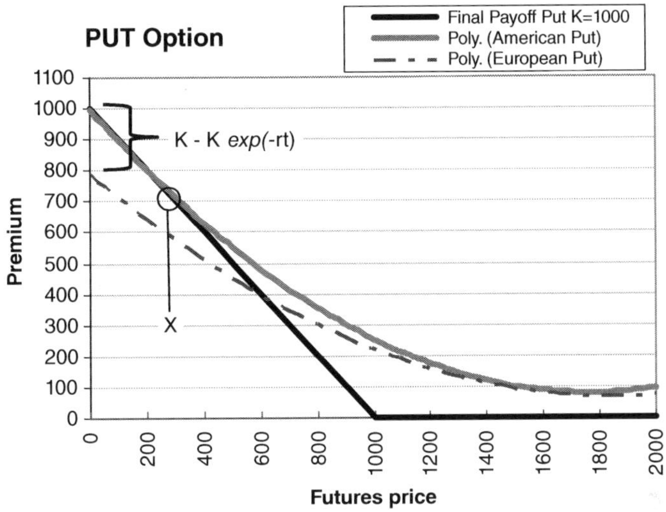

FIGURE 7.33 Exercise of a put option

7.3.2 LME's Closing Volatilities

The model commonly used to price futures options on the LME is the Black (1976) model for commodity contracts. Starting from the framework of the Black and Scholes (B&S) model for stock options, Fisher Black tailored the model to commodity contracts. The underlying process is no longer on the spot price (S) but rather on the futures price (F) on which the option is written. Most of the assumptions are common between the two models, such as the price of futures being lognormal but with zero drift. Black proves in fact that a futures price, under the risk-neutral measure, has an expected growth rate of zero from the intuition that a futures requires zero investment.[5] This approach is quite powerful: it can be applied to all futures and does not require any extra assumption on convenience yields. Black's model was the first model on European futures options and is still widely used by practitioners because of its simplicity. It has been shown in the previous section that futures options on the LME may be considered European.

- *Black's model can therefore be used on the LME, ignoring the fact that options are American style.*

This is the approach used by the LCH in the London SPAN for assessing option prices. The assessment process for LME options is quite unique. The exchange does not run an end-of-day assessment of the closing prices for the options as happens almost everywhere else.

- *The LME runs instead the assessment of closing volatilities for each metal on each maturity. The LCH uses these volatilities as input for Black's model to obtain option prices and calculate margins.*

[5]Actually, initial margin is required to enter into a futures position: incidentally, the clearing brokers normally give up the interest proceeds on the margins.

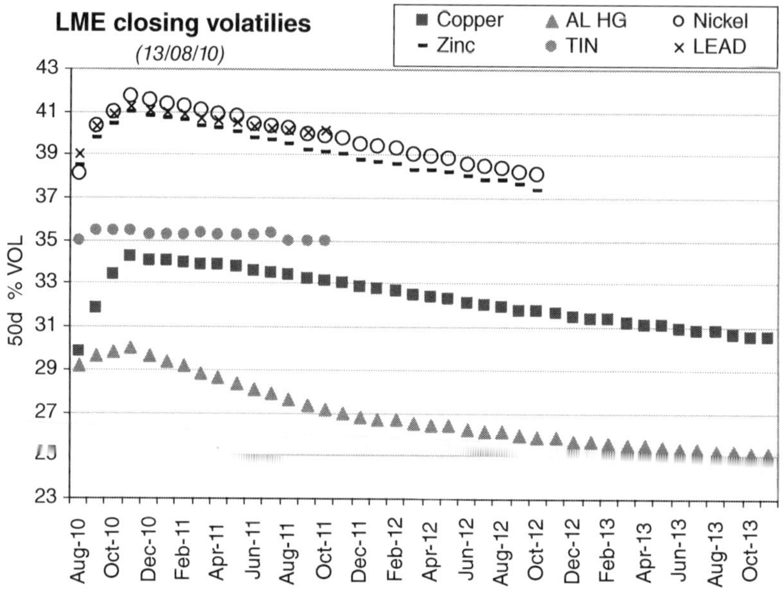

FIGURE 7.34 LME closing volatilities

This is a consequence of the fact that the LME option market is a volatility market rather than a premium market. The exchange collects data from brokers expressed in volatilities. In the following, some practical examples of broker quotes will be presented. Interestingly enough, the option assessment has historically been based only on *at-the-money* (ATM) options: the volatility skew was not considered. The *volatility skew* is, where present, the difference between ATM implied volatility and implied volatilities on other strikes. One of the strongest hypotheses of the Black and Scholes model (as well as Black's) is that of constant volatility. In reality, what is observable is both a non-flat volatility skew and a non-constant term-structure of volatility.

Figure 7.34 shows an example of LME closing volatilities used for margining on major metals. The same considerations as for the forward curve are valid here as well. Each metal has in fact its own implied volatility curve, with some key differences. The main difference is the absolute level of implied volatility, with nickel and primary aluminium being respectively the most and least volatile metals. Nickel, zinc and lead show similar shape and absolute levels of volatility. Long-term (cumulated) volatility is expected to be lower than the front-end: this is due to the viscosity of demand and supply in the short term. Any production disruption or news hitting the market has an immediate impact on the front-end of the forward curve, while the longer maturities are less affected since the market is expected to slowly adjust to the new conditions. This is known as the *Samuelson effect*. It is observable in Figure 7.34, where all of the term-structures show an initial rise of implied volatility and then a subsequent decline. As a matter of fact, the data are taken after a period of particularly low volatility.

Figure 7.35 is an example of the volatility skew (across strike) observable on Dec10 copper. The flat skew used by the LCH for margining has the effect of distorting the official option prices from the effective prices observable on the market. This implies that the requested variation margins are different from those expected by traders: in fact, it is unlikely that there are still traders pricing options (or calculating the mark-to-market of their books) using the

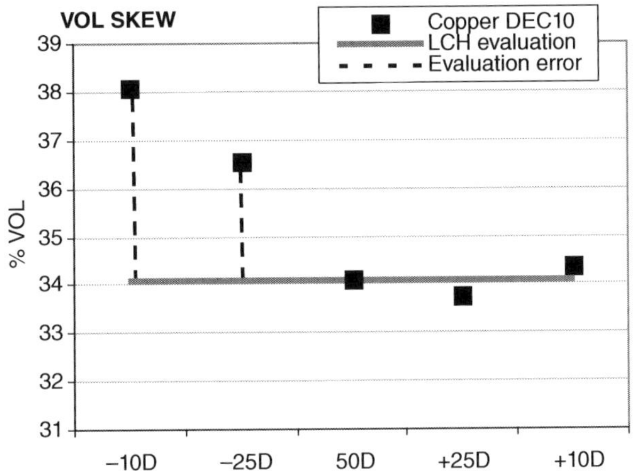

FIGURE 7.35 The volatility skew

constant volatility assumption. The mispricing is proportional to the vega of the option. The *vega* is the sensitivity of an option price or a portfolio value to changes in the underlying's volatility σ_x. When the option, or the portfolio, is written on metals, common practice is to measure it as the variation in USD of the option value at the 1% variation of implied volatility.

This issue was not neglected by the LME. After a (long) period of consultation with operators and the analysis of different proposals, the exchange decided in 2008 to undertake the following enhancements:

- To pass from ATM assessment to 50Δ (50% delta).
- To collect and publish option volatility wings. The published volatilities are now on the delta space:

$$-10\Delta \quad -25\Delta \quad +/-50\Delta \quad +25\Delta \quad +10\Delta$$

In February 2011 the LCH implemented the skew for margining purposes (LCH, 2011). The exchange decided to change the assessment from the ATM to the 50Δ: this is the volatility for an option that is struck at a level such that the sensitivity of the option price to the underlying (Δ) is 50%. Practically speaking, if for example the option is written on 100 tons, the delta hedge (under the B&S model) will be exactly 50 tons. The delta is generally meant as the *delta forward* (the forward hedge ratio) and not the *delta spot* (the spot hedge ratio). Similarly, ATM means ATM forward.

- *The 50Δ strike is considered pivotal in option trading because it corresponds to the option with maximum vega.*

The two quotations (ATM and 50Δ) are sometimes considered the same thing since in some cases the option with strike ATM has delta of 50%. This is actually a rough approximation since the ATM delta may be substantially different from 50%. As evidence, Figure 7.36 shows the computed Δ% for call and put ATM options on copper (data set as of 13/08/10).

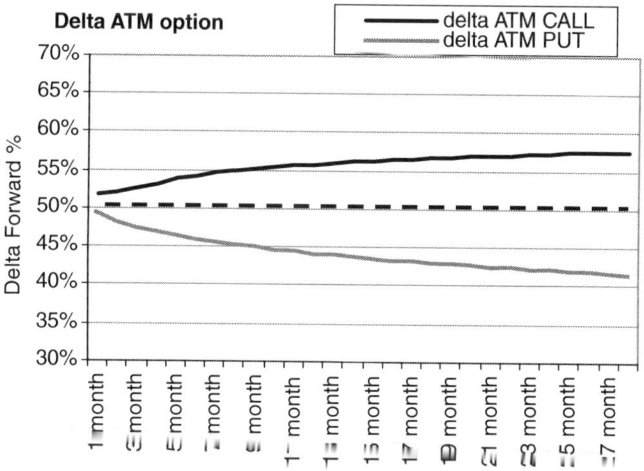

FIGURE 7.36 Delta of ATM option

7.3.3 Sticky Strike, Sticky Delta and Skew

The closing volatilities for each metal, each maturity and the five delta gradations are now available from the LME. This represents a suitable starting point to build a volatility surface. Table 7.6 is a practical example. Here, for example, a Dec10 copper option, with a delta of

TABLE 7.6 Copper closing implied volatilities

LME COPPER closing volatilities (as of 13/08/10)					
Contract	**−10Δ**	**−25Δ**	**50Δ**	**+25Δ**	**+10Δ**
Sep-10	3.95	2.37	29.86	(0.48)	0.09
Oct-10	3.96	2.45	31.85	(0.47)	0.16
Nov-10	4.06	2.51	33.40	(0.44)	0.20
Dec-10	4.07	2.55	34.26	(0.43)	0.22
Jan-11	4.01	2.48	34.09	(0.34)	0.28
Feb-11	4.02	2.46	34.02	(0.31)	0.46
Mar-11	4.01	2.45	34.01	(0.31)	0.48
Apr-11	3.95	2.44	33.91	(0.30)	0.48
May-11	3.92	2.42	33.83	(0.28)	0.34
Jun-11	3.90	2.42	33.78	(0.27)	0.36
Jul-11	3.81	2.38	33.59	(0.25)	0.39
Aug-11	3.77	2.34	33.52	(0.24)	0.41
Sep-11	3.75	2.34	33.39	(0.23)	0.41
Oct-11	3.70	2.33	33.21	(0.23)	0.42
Nov-11	3.68	2.32	33.13	(0.21)	0.44
Dec-11	3.65	2.30	33.08	(0.20)	0.44
Jan-12	3.48	2.15	32.88	(0.15)	0.47
Feb-12	3.45	2.13	32.77	(0.14)	0.47
[...]	[...]	[...]	[...]	[...]	[...]

50%, would be priced on a volatility of 34.26%, while an option with a delta of 10% would be priced with a 34.26% + 4.07% = 38.33% volatility. The 'Vol skew' given in Figure 7.35 is obtained from these data: the Dec10 volatility is particularly skewed on the left (i.e., lowest strikes).

The LME publishes volatilities across deltas for each third Wednesday monthly maturity (remember, implied volatilities are deducted from monthly futures options). This is indeed not the only possible choice. The volatility surface is a three-dimensional space (x, y, z) whereby

i. the *strike* (x-)axis can be expressed in terms of
- $x1$ – deltas (as per LME choice)
- $x2$ – moneyness (usually as percentage moneyness in respect of ATM)
- $x3$ – USD strike (the final USD strike of the underlying option)

ii. the time (y-)axis can be expressed in terms of
- $y1$ – third Wednesdays (as per LME choice)
- $y2$ – rolling forward maturities (e.g., 1 day, 1 week, 1 month, 3 months, 6 months, 1 year, 2 years, etc.)
- $y3$ – other customized configurations

iii. the z-axis gives the volatilities, normally expressed in annualized percentage volatility.

The configuration choice should not only correctly reflect the actual volatility market but also minimize the daily routine of updating the surfaces. The surface should in fact reflect the expected behaviour of implied volatility in respect of the underlying price movements. Consider that at t_0, when the surface is initially fitted to actual market data, the $x1$, $x2$ and $x3$ configurations must be consistent with each other. Ideally one could (and most commercial risk-management software includes this feature) switch the volatility from one configuration to another. Imagine that one is now at a later time t_1 and the underlying price has moved 1% up: how would one expect the volatility skew to change? Obviously now the ATM strike is 1% higher and also the 50Δ strike is higher.

If the whole skew is supposed to shift to the right, so that the ATM and 50Δ volatility at t_1 is the same as at t_0, the volatility is said to be *sticky delta*. The assumption is that implied volatility is indifferent in the short term to price changes and follows the delta. Said another way, if the ATM volatility level changes between t_0 and t_1, the driver is a change in the supply/demand of implied volatility. The sticky delta approach is equivalent for volatility in deltas and in moneyness.

If the skew is supposed to stand unchanged at the same strikes, so that the ATM volatility at t_1 is the same as at t_0, the volatility is said to be *sticky strike*. The assumption is that any strike has its 'own' volatility level. Said another way, if the ATM volatility level changes between t_0 and t_1, it could be the consequence of the underlying price change.

If a market belongs strictly to one of the two regimes (i.e., sticky delta or sticky strike), failing to configure the volatility accordingly will imply extra work to adjust the volatilities as the underlying moves. Moreover, the change of σ (volatility) in t_1 directly affects both portfolio P&L (through the vega) and portfolio sensitivity to the underlying (since Δ is itself a function of σ). Traders are very careful of this effect: the change of B&S delta induced by changes in implied volatility or the skew (also known as *shadow gamma*) can in fact undermine the effectiveness of delta hedging under the B&S framework.

To distinguish whether it is the volatility changing or the price moving is not an easy task, since both change continuously in parallel with changes in the other model parameters. An

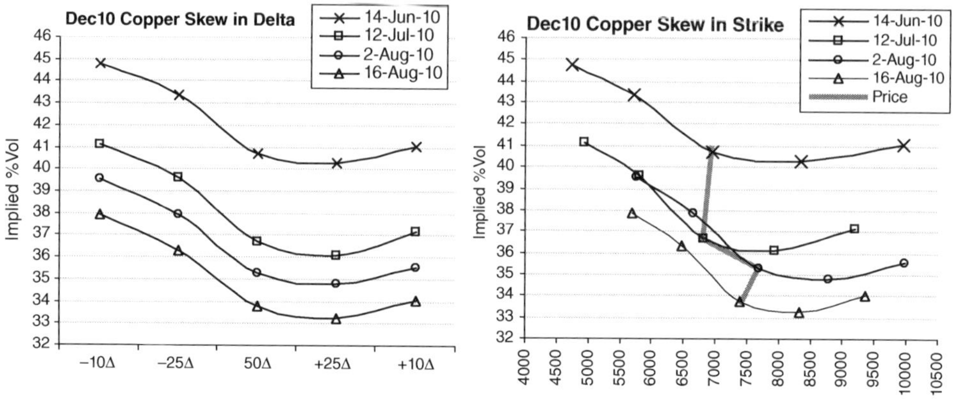

FIGURE 7.37 Copper skew in delta (left) and strike (right)

analysis of the evolution of the implied volatility skew in the past can suggest which, if any, regime is prevailing.

The two charts in Figure 7.37 are built on the basis of the same set of data: the implied volatility skew of copper Dec10, published by the LME, on four different dates. The left chart plots the skews with deltas on the x-axis while the right chart plots the same volatilities with absolute (USD) strikes on the x-axis. The sample period experienced a progressive drop of implied volatilities: the 50Δ volatility passes from 40.68% to 33.75%. The vertical grey line on the right chart identifies the Dec10 absolute prices: the volatility falls at any step regardless of whether the price goes up or down. We could not therefore ascribe this behaviour to any of the regimes but rather to a global weakening of the volatility market. Looking at the right chart, it is quite hard to identify a pattern in the evolution of the skew in terms of the falling volatility. Also, the shape of the floating skew is not constant: the first observation is flatter than the last one. The situation in the left chart seems completely different. The shape of the skew is clearly constant across the four observation dates: the whole skew is shifted progressively lower as the ATM (or better, 50Δ) volatility drops. In this example, while both sticky strike and delta regimes fail to capture the movement of ATM volatility, the skew is constant in the delta space with changing ATM volatility.

The choice of how to configure the y-axis is linked to the behaviour of the volatility term-structure as time passes. If, in the absence of news affecting in any way the option market, the whole term-structure of volatility is expected to roll on – passing from t_0 to t_1 – the optimal configuration is $y2$ as given earlier. Said another way, one would expect the volatility, for example of the 3M *rolling* maturity, to be constant.

If instead the higher volatility of the spot, in the absence of news affecting the option market, is supposed to converge to the lower levels of the long term, the correct configuration is $y1$. Said another way, one would expect the volatility, for example of the Dec10 maturity, to be constant. The correct configuration allows the trader to capture (and hence manage) the sensitivity of his option or portfolio to time decay. The change of an option premium (or a portfolio P&L) from t_0 to t_1 is called *theta* and it is also a function of σ. Figure 7.38 provides a graphical explanation of the alternatives. Here again, perhaps even more than in the case of the skew, it is quite hard to distinguish which regime, if any at all, is being followed by volatility. The choice is therefore up to the trader's perception and sometimes is reduced to a

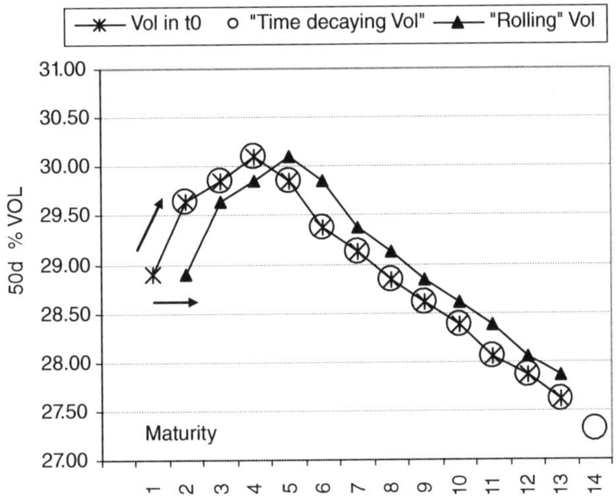

FIGURE 7.38 Volatility term structure and time

matter of mere convenience: $y1$ is already consistent with LME closing volatilities while $y2$ has to be deduced.

The charts seen so far, on copper, display a *negative skew*: implied volatilities increase at lower strikes (with the exception of deep out-of-the-money (OTM) $+10\Delta$ calls). This is the result of a strong demand for buying OTM put options. The market is more scared of price falls than price jumps and looks to put contracts for protection. The higher probability of large price falls is called the *leverage effect*. This is a phenomenon typical of stock markets where a decrease of price, reducing the market capitalization of a company and hence worsening its debt/equity ratio, could initiate further selling. The stock markets are also subject to panic selling at falling prices. Commodity markets are instead expected to feature the opposite behaviour, with volatility increasing at higher prices (*inverse leverage effect*). Previously, in fact, it was shown that the level of stocks is inversely correlated to spot prices, such that low stocks spark higher volatility. Under this hypothesis, one would expect the skew to be positive or at least a *smile* (implied volatility is higher on both the left and the right of ATM). The analysis of correlation between prices and implied volatility helps to solve the puzzle. Figure 7.39 shows copper 3M prices over the period (late) 2005–(early) 2009, together with the implied ATM volatility and the correlation between the two series. Until mid-2007 the correlation was constantly positive. At the top of the credit crunch (i.e., last quarter of 2008) prices dropped and the volatility reached the highest levels (70%). The 100-day rolling correlation (computed on % changes) reached –60% in that period. Again in 2010 the correlation became negative: the negative skew observed for June and August 2010 is therefore consistent with this behaviour.

7.3.4 Building the Surface in Practice

Similar to what was seen in Section 7.2.1, the surface has to be continuous both on time and on strikes to make it possible to price any kind of option. The Asian option, for example, needs as input (in most non-toy pricing models) the volatilities for each business day in the pricing period. Taking the closing volatilities by the LME as initial input, one has to deal with

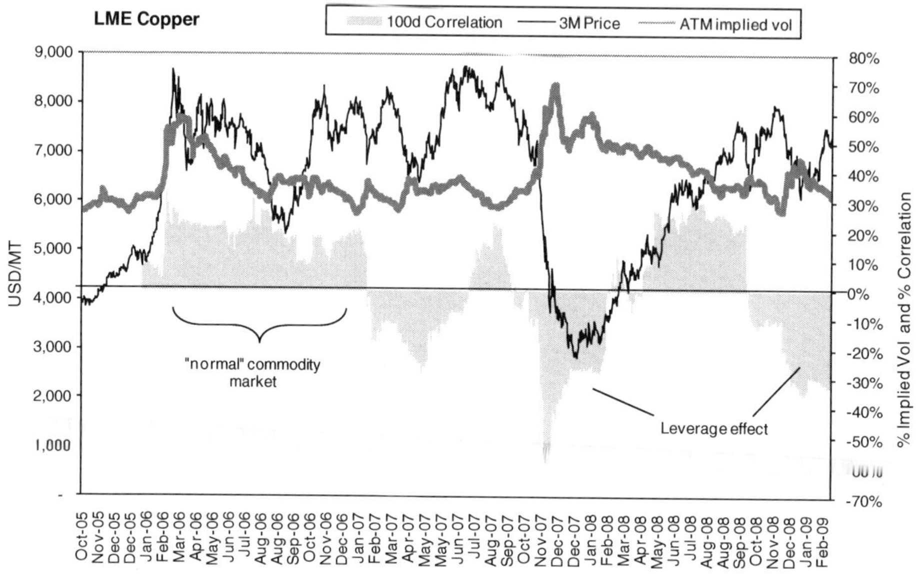

FIGURE 7.39 Copper prices and implied volatility

interpolation to build the volatility surface. The LME had itself considered developing the interpolation method for the surface. However, since there are many available methodologies and since none has been identified as best, the LME finally decided to leave it to the preference of single operators.

The interpolation can be implemented with the moneyness x-axis in terms of strikes or deltas: in both cases the volatility is just a means to the final goal of evaluating the option premiums. In order to prevent the building of an inconsistent volatility surface, the resulting premiums should not be arbitrageable. The basic arbitrage bounds to respect are:

- The premium of a zero-strike call ($K = 0$) is the discounted value of the underlying forward while the premium of a zero-strike put is zero: call $(K = 0) = F_T Df_T$ and put $(K = 0) = 0$.
- Between two options of the same type (call/put) with the same maturity, the one with the strike that is more in-the-money has the highest premium. This is also called the non-negative *vertical spread.*
- Between three options of the same type (call/put) with the same maturity, with three different strikes $(K, K + x, K - x; x > 0)$, the total premium of the options struck at $K + x$ and $K - x$ is higher than twice the premium of the option struck at K. This is also called the non-negative *butterfly spread.* In respect of the calls, the condition is: call $(K + x) +$ call $(K - x) - 2 \times$ call $(K) \geq 0$.
- Between two options of the same type (call/put) and the same moneyness, the one with the longest maturity has the highest premium. This is also called the non-negative *calendar spread.*

The last condition is based on the consideration that option prices should not decrease with increased time to expiration. This condition can be weaker, or even not hold at all, on

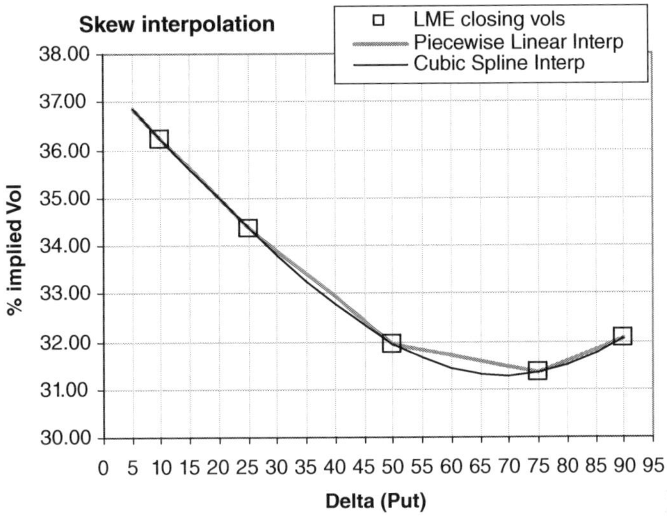

FIGURE 7.40 The skew

commodity markets since it relies on the fungibility of the underlying across the different maturities. Where the commodity is not fungible, each futures maturity has to be treated as a separate instrument with its own skew.

- *Base metals show a certain degree of fungibility across time and space since they can be stored and are not perishable goods.*

As a consequence, the no-arbitrage condition above is normally respected by market quotations: in practice, volatilities can also be interpolated across maturities.

Piecewise linear interpolation, splines and parameterized models, like the widely used SABR and SVI (Gatheral, 2004) are between the methods commonly used to interpolate a skew through the available quoted volatilities for a maturity. The interpolation can be run on option premia (an easy way to respect non-arbitrage conditions), strikes, moneyness and delta. Figure 7.40 shows an application on LME closing volatilities. The interpolation methods used are those described in Section 7.2. The original deltas of the LME (–10Δ, –25Δ, 50Δ, +25Δ, +10Δ) are converted into put deltas (10Δ, 35Δ, 50Δ, 75Δ, 90Δ) in order to implement the interpolation.

Volatility can also be interpolated across maturities between the traded pillars. In this case, one method involves interpolating the ATM term-structure first and then building the skews as functions of the closer pillars (e.g., applying the same SVI parameterization fitted on the closest traded maturity). The straight interpolation across maturities for each delta (or for moneyness) is to be avoided since the skew for prompt dates is normally much more convex than long-term ones; it is likely to produce arbitrageable volatilities.

Once the favoured interpolation method is chosen and the volatility surface set up, it is necessary to keep the volatilities up-to-date.

- *All the volatility trading activity on the LME is 'on voice'. There are no available quotes 'on screen'.*

The intra-day volatility changes must therefore be tracked via broker or dealer quotes. The following are some real quotes from brokers:

Broker John Smith (1): Dec10 Zn ATMs 38.5/40.5 100 × 200

Broker John Smith (2): Dec10 Zn ATMs 39.5/40.5 100 × 200

Broker John Smith (3): Dec10 v Dec11 Zn ATM 2.75/3.25

These are basic quotes on ATM options on zinc. The maturity is Dec10 and the quotes refer to futures options (TAPO would otherwise be stated for Asian options). The quote is expressed in implied volatility terms: 38.50% bid and 40.50% offer. Observe that between (1) and (2) there is an improvement on the bid. 100 × 200 refers to the size in lots. For zinc, the broker always quotes (3) a calendar spread option: Dec10 vs. Dec11. Both options are ATM. Volatility on Dec10 is higher than on Dec11.

Broker Mario Rossi: Jun11 Ali 25d rr 0.20/1.00 (puts)

This is a quote for a risk reversal (rr) – that is, a long call and short put – both written at the 25Δ strike. '(puts)' means the put is over, that is the volatility of the put is higher than the volatility of the call by 0.20% on the bid and 1.0% on the offer.

Broker John Doe: Dec 10 Cu 7300 straddle 33/33.75 50 × 100 per leg

This quotation refers to a straddle – that is, a long call and short put – both written at the same strike of 7300 USD. The volatility is 33% bid and 33.75% offer.

7.3.5 Considerations on Vega Hedging

In the following, some practical considerations will be made on the pricing of OTC options and their impact on vega hedging. In Section 7.3.5.4 an example of volatility arbitrage will be shown, together with the practical obstacles to implementing the strategy.

7.3.5.1 Asian Options The pricing of Asian options represents a challenging task. The source of problems lies in the fact that the B&S assumption of lognormal prices cannot be applied to arithmetic averages. The average of lognormally distributed variables is, in fact, not lognormal: its true distribution is yet to be found. A vast literature is available on this issue, proposing solutions under different approaches: approximations of the true distribution and numerical methods[6]. One example is the famous Kemna and Vorst (1990) approximation, one of the first models for Asians. The arithmetic average option is approximated using the geometric average since the latter is lognormally distributed. Under this approach the Asian can be priced with Black's formula with modified mean and reduced variance. This model is too simplistic and in practice the models used are far more sophisticated. Practitioners commonly use Monte Carlo methods as a way to get round the problem.

[6] A review of pricing procedures for Asians, together with VBA algorithms, is presented by the editors (Fusai and Roncoroni, 2008).

In the choice of model or method, the option trader aims to reach a compromise between pricing accuracy and operative efficiency. The option's fair value should be as accurate as possible in order to avoid the risk of being arbitraged by the market. At the same time, for many base metals the volatility market is quite illiquid: implied volatility bid–ask spreads of 3% and 4% are not unusual, for example, on metals like nickel and tin. Such a wide bid–ask makes the fair value of an option difficult to identify since traders do not trade at mid-volatility. The pricing error induced by an approximation model could therefore be negligible compared with the difference in price using the bid instead of the offer implied volatility. This could be the case for options displaying high vega: for example, long-term ATM options (which are also illiquid on the LME). At the same time, the pricing of deep OTM options, which in turn display lower vega, can be distorted by uncertainty on the skew: in fact, options with $\Delta < 25\%$ are rarely traded on any of the base metals. Under this framework, the operator who trades frequently might prefer the faster (in terms of computational speed) model over the more accurate one. For this reason, closed-form formulas are preferred over Monte Carlo simulations that are quite time-consuming.

The Asian option is considered, between the exotic options, one of the easier to hedge. This is true under the condition that the model outputs correct sensitivities. The option practitioner is in fact also concerned with the sensitivities coming from the model: delta and vega *in primis*.

As seen, the base-metal Asian option is written on spot (LME cash fixings): it can be viewed as an option on a basket of n underlyings, where n is the number of pricing days. Each pricing day can be considered a lognormally distributed *independent forward* date to which, as seen previously, is assigned a specific volatility. The n independent forwards are correlated with each other and, since they are points on the curve of the same metal, the correlation is usually very high (>90%). With these inputs it is possible to compute the first two moments of the average (that is the basket): mean and variance. These two moments can be used to fit a lognormal density function, which can then be used to price the Asian option with the usual B&S tools. This is Levy's (1992) version of the moment-matching method. Other versions use different density functions to be fitted on more moments.

The moment-matching approach helps to explain some of the essential features one would expect from a proper model:

- The entire term-structure of forwards is an input of the model.
- The option delta is broken down across all the n fixing days. This result can be obtained if the previous condition is satisfied. The delta of calendar month Asian options is roughly constant across the fixing days: the option can then easily be delta hedged using the corresponding Asian swap.
- The entire term-structure of volatility, within the option pricing period, is an input of (or fitted by) the model. Models are sometimes formulated taking as input a single volatility parameter σ under the assumption of constant volatility. It is crucial to consider instead the σ_n volatilities of the n independent forwards to take into account the term-structure of volatility.
- The skew should also be taken into account. Because of the slope of the forward term-structure, the n forwards feature different moneyness to the strike. An ATM Asian, for example, is only on average ATM: if the curve is in backwardation, the front-end maturities will be ITM while the back-end ones will be OTM.

- The option vega is divided across all the n forwards. If the single volatility parameter σ were used, the model would mistakenly assign the vega exposure, typically, to the last fixing date.
- Correlation between the forwards is also an input of (or fitted by) the model. The cross-correlation of base-metal forwards is normally quite high and constant compared with other, less fungible, commodities. Nevertheless, as the pricing period of the Asian lengthens, the correlation between the front end and the back end decreases. The result is the increased variance of the average. Models with constant 100% correlation tend to underestimate premiums.

Notice that vega is not necessarily constant across the n forwards. Consider the case where both the metal forward curve and volatility curve are in backwardation: the front end of the pricing period would feature both higher prices and higher volatilities than the back end. A change in volatility would hence impact the variance of the average much more in the front than the back end.

The main drawback of Levy's moment-matching is the lognormal approximation. In recent years there have been some more advanced models proposed that find the exact fair value of Asians under the true density function. Of these, notably Fusai *et al.* (2007) proposed a closed-form formula for Asian options on spot prices that captures term-structure effects. A possible way to hedge vega is represented by LME monthly futures options. The single-day vegas can thus be bucketed into the third Wednesday maturities.

7.3.5.2 Composite Options The most common solution used to price composite options is that of adjusting the volatility of the underlying to take into account the change of currency (Rainer, 1992):

$$\sigma_{S,FX} = \sqrt{\sigma_{S,USD}^2 + \sigma_{FX}^2 - 2\rho_{S,FX}\sigma_{S,USD}\sigma_{FX}}$$

where $\sigma_{S,FX}$ is the volatility of the commodity expressed in another currency, $\sigma_{S,USD}$ is the original volatility in the domestic currency, σ_{FX} is the volatility of the exchange rate and $\rho_{S,FX}$ is the correlation between the commodity and the exchange rate. The FX rate is quoted as the number of domestic currency units for one unit of foreign currency (for a metal composite in EUR, this would be the number of USDs for 1 EUR). The composite option will then be priced normally as if the commodity were expressed in the other currency. For example, to price a composite EUR on copper, one may input the forward price of copper converted into EUR, the strike in EUR, the EUR interest rate and the modified volatility above. The role of correlation is crucial in the determination of volatility in a composite. A positive correlation, between the metal and FX rate, decreases the metal's volatility in the foreign currency. Figure 7.41 pitches the shape of volatility in EUR at different correlation levels. The metal's starting volatility is 25%, while the EUR/USD volatility is 12%. Point A indicates a break-even point – that is, the correlation level (20%) at which the composite volatility is the same as the metal's volatility in USD.

Hedging the vega of this option implies hedging the commodity volatility and two additional parameters: the exchange volatility and the correlation. While the market on FX volatility is extremely liquid, almost no market at all exists on the correlation of base metals versus FX rates. Moreover, the option features two deltas: on the underlying and on the FX rate. The FX

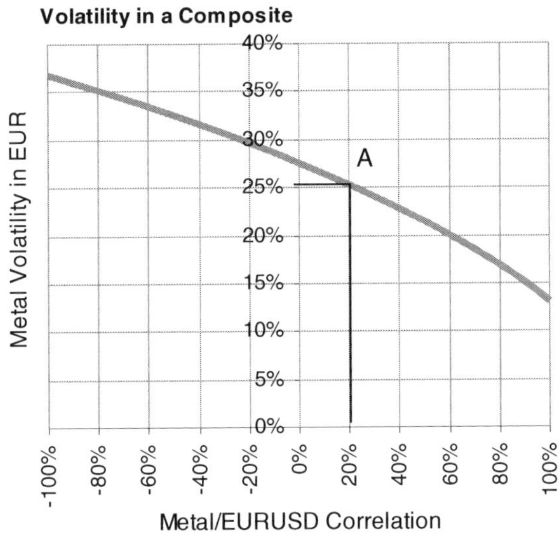

FIGURE 7.41 Volatility and currency correlation

rate is not negligible at all: it is proportional to the currency equivalent of the underlying delta (so that for a 25Δ option, it would be roughly half that of a 50Δ option).

- *The delta hedging should hence be dynamic both on the commodity and the FX rate.*

7.3.5.3 Quanto Options In the pricing of a composite, in addition to the volatility, all the parameters have to be converted into EUR. This is not the case for a quanto option since the floating price in USD will be compared with the strike in USD. The input parameters in the pricing model would be in the domestic currency for the volatility and the strike while the payoff would be discounted by interest rates on the foreign currency. To take into account that the payoff is paid at a fixed FX rate, it is the forward price of the underlying that needs to be adjusted:

$$F_T^{\text{quanto}} = F_T e^{\rho_{\text{S,FX}}\sigma_{\text{S,USD}}\sigma_{\text{FX}}T}$$

where F_T^{quanto} is the quanto adjusted forward of the commodity in respect of a foreign currency, F_T is the forward price quotation in the domestic currency, $\sigma_{\text{S,USD}}$ is the volatility in the domestic currency, σ_{FX} is the volatility of the FX rate, $\rho_{\text{S,FX}}$ is the correlation between the commodity and the FX rate, and T is the time to maturity of the forward. The FX rate is given as the number of domestic currency units for one unit of foreign currency. Since all parameters, except $\rho_{\text{S,FX}}$, are by definition positive then in case of positive correlation, $F_T^{\text{quanto}} > F_T$, while for negative correlation, $F_T^{\text{quanto}} < F_T$. As a consequence, a quanto call option struck ATM in respect of F_T would instead be ITM for $\rho_{\text{S,FX}} > 0$ or OTM for $\rho_{\text{S,FX}} < 0$. Here again there will be sensitivities to σ_{FX} and $\rho_{\text{S,FX}}$: in this case though they will not directly impact on the underlying volatility, which remains in USD for LME's base metals, but rather on the level of the forward. Increasing volatilities or correlation will make the forward steeper and the option more in-the-money or out-of-the-money.

- *Interestingly, the FX rate does not appear either in the final payoff or the quanto forward: at inception there is no delta to hedge on the FX rate.*

7.3.5.4 COMEX–LME Volatility Arbitrage In Section 7.2 an analysis was performed on the arbitrage opportunities in trading spot and forward copper between COMEX, SHFE and LME. COMEX also lists copper futures options. The option trader could hence try to exploit possible arbitrage opportunities on implied volatilities. COMEX and LME spot prices are highly correlated with each other, giving little or no room for physical arbitrages: the volatility of the price process should then be considered the same for both contracts. Where the implied volatility for the same maturity could diverge significantly, the arbitrageur could bet on volatility convergence by buying options on the cheapest exchange and selling options on the other. This kind of trade is in practice far more complex than it may seem. There are several issues to face.

- The bid–offer spread: imagine that the Dec10 implied volatility on COMEX is 2% higher than LME's. One therefore sells options in NY and buys in London, both ATM (in order to get the maximum exposure to vega). Thus the bid–offer is paid. If the bid–offer is >2%, the expected gain goes to zero. Additionally, copper options are less liquid on COMEX than LME.
- The option style: LME's options are European while COMEX's are American. So one is trying to arbitrage not only two different exchanges but also two different financial instruments.
- The delta hedging effectiveness: the sold and bought options must be delta hedged continuously, otherwise risk from price differentials is introduced. Delta hedging in the real world is discrete. It is effective in replicating the option premium only *on average*. In practice, the variance of the strategy could be several times higher than 2%.
- The skew: movements in the underlying cause options to go in or out-of-the-money. The strategy is therefore also sensitive to the skew of the markets. Moreover, American options behave differently from European when deep ITM.

The considerations above require the observed implied volatility differences to be sufficient to justify the risk of the trade.

ACKNOWLEDGEMENTS

The author is particularly grateful to Giulio Sartorelli whose comments and deep knowledge of financial mathematics led to significant improvements in the technical sections of this chapter. Special thanks are due also to Nicola Ventura (who is also co-author of a paragraph) and fellow traders Carlo Macchiaroli, Andrei Mariani and Stefano Martina who reviewed the original manuscript.

REFERENCES

Black, F. (1976) The pricing of commodity contracts, *The Journal of Financial Economics*, **3**, 167–179.

Britten-Jones, M. and Neuberger, A. (2000) Option prices, implied price processes, and stochastic volatility, *The Journal of Finance*, **55**, 839–866.

Cortazar, G. and Schwartz, E. (1994) The valuation of commodity-contingent claims, *Journal of Derivatives*, **1**(4), 27–39.

Crabb, P. (1999) *Metals Trading Handbook*, Woodhead Publishing, Cambridge.

Derman, E. and Kani, I. (1994) The volatility smile and its implied tree, *Risk*, **7**(2), 139–145.

Fusai, G. and Roncoroni, A. (2008) *Implementing Models in Quantitative Finance: Methods and Cases*, Springer-Verlag, Berlin.

Fusai, G., Marena, M. and Roncoroni, A. (2007) Commodity Asian options: A closed-form formula, EFA 2008 Athens Meetings Paper.

Gatheral, J. (2004) *The Volatility Surface: A Practitioner's Guide*, Wiley-Finance, Chichester.

Geman, H. (2005) *Commodities and Commodity Derivatives*, Wiley Finance, Chichester.

Gordon, G. and Rouwenhorst, G. (2006) Facts and fantasies about commodity futures, *Financial Analysts Journal*, **62**(2), 47–68.

Kemna, A.G.Z. and Vorst, A.C.F. (1990) A pricing method for options based on average asset values, *Journal of Banking and Finance*, **14**, 113–129.

LCH (2010) *Circular No. 2761*. LCH Clearnet Ltd, London.

LCH (2011) *Circular No. 2763*. LCH Clearnet Ltd, London.

LCH Clearnet Ltd Circular 2671, 25 August 2010.

Levy, E. (1992) Pricing European average rate currency options, *Journal of International Money and Finance*, **11**(5), 474–491.

Rainer, E. (1992) Quanto mechanics, *Risk*, **March**.

Rouah, F.D. and Vainberg, G. (2007) *Option Pricing Models & Volatility Using Excel-VBA*, John Wiley & Sons, Chichester.

Sartorelli, G. (2010) A short note on LME's forward contracts and options, available at: http://ssrn.com/abstract = 1616080.

FURTHER READING

Alexander, C. (2001) *Market Models*, John Wiley & Sons, Chichester.

Boesch, R. (2002) The front month proxy hedge, Kiodex.com.

Derman, E. (1999) Regimes of volatility, *Risk*, **12**(4), 55–59.

Hull, J.C. (2002) *Options, Futures and Other Derivatives*, Prentice Hall, Englewood Cliffs, NJ.

LME 130th Anniversary Supplement, Newsdesk Communications Ltd, 2007.

LME Rulebook, London Metal Exchange Rules & Regulations.

Ventura, N. (2006) Una simulazione del ruolo della speculazione sul London Metal Exchange, Università Bocconi.

CHAPTER 8

Freight Markets and Products

Manolis G. Kavussanos, Ilias D. Visvikis and Dimitris N. Dimitrakopoulos

8.1 INTRODUCTION

The market agents operating in the international shipping market face substantial business risks due to the high volatility, cyclicality and seasonality in rates and prices. These risks may be classified broadly into the following categories: business risk, credit risk, technical risk and financial risk. The purpose of this chapter is to outline the major business and financial risks that principals (ship owners and charterers) in the various sectors of the shipping industry are facing and highlight the modern methods and products that are currently available for efficient risk management in shipping.

The chapter starts with an overview of the shipping industry in terms of market segmentation (dry bulk, tanker and container ship), the different types of cargo transported under the different trading freight routes and the supply and demand economics of each subsector. The empirical regularities in the freight markets are then presented as: (a) seasonality is distinct between different submarkets, between contracts of different duration and between different market conditions prevailing in shipping markets; (b) freight rates of larger vessels are more volatile and bear higher relative risks compared with smaller vessels; and (c) freight contracts of longer duration are less volatile compared with shorter period contracts.

These regularities point to some 'traditional' risk management strategies, such as: (a) freight rate risks in the larger sectors may be mitigated by investing in smaller vessels; (b) freight rate risks can be reduced by operating vessels under long-term time-charter rather than spot contracts; and (c) the mix of investors' portfolios in terms of both charter contracts and investments in different ship segments should be reviewed constantly. However, as the above strategies are useful but may prove to be expensive, non-existent or inflexible at times, it is concluded that derivatives products can provide more efficient solutions to such problems.

The shipping derivatives markets are then introduced, as their existence makes risk management cheaper, more flexible and available to parties exposed to adverse movements in freight rates, bunker fuel prices, vessel prices, exchange rates, interest rates and other variables affecting the cash-flow positions of shipping companies. More specifically, the high

Handbook of Multi-Commodity Markets and Products: Structuring, Trading and Risk Management. Edited by Andrea Roncoroni, Gianluca Fusai and Mark Cummins.

fluctuations (volatility) of freight rates constitute a major source of business risk for both ship owners and charterers. The chapter continues by presenting the underlying assets that can be used to write dry-bulk, tanker and container-ship freight derivatives products. An introduction to forward freight agreements (FFAs), freight futures, cleared ('hybrid') FFAs and freight options is given, presenting the various contracts, markets and uses of these products. Two practical examples on the application of freight derivatives are also given.

The chapter next describes the pricing of freight derivatives, as well as their hedging effectiveness and risk measurement (including value-at-risk and expected shortfall). The non-storable nature of the underlying asset (freight service) of freight derivatives implies that spot and derivatives prices are not linked by a cost-of-carry (storage) relationship, as in financial and agricultural derivatives markets. Thus, derivatives prices on freight rates are driven by the expectations of market agents regarding the spot prices that will prevail at the expiry of the derivative contract. It is shown that freight derivatives prices are equal to the expected value of the spot (underlying) freight asset at the settlement date plus a stochastic error term. It is also shown that the FFA market satisfies its price discovery function, as forward prices today can help discover spot prices at the expiry of the FFA contract. In terms of optimal hedge ratios, the results for out-of-sample hedging effectiveness indicate that naïve hedge ratios produce the highest variance reductions. The chapter then presents the application of value-at-risk and expected shortfall techniques in measuring freight rate risk in the shipping industry, through some practical examples. Finally, the previous published empirical work in the area of freight derivatives is presented in order to give the reader an overview of the available literature.

The chapter concludes with an overview of the remaining shipping derivatives products; namely, the bunker fuel, vessel value, foreign exchange and interest rate derivatives. Of course, there are many more issues that remain unexplored and it is hoped that this chapter will help researchers focus on the relevant issues for further work in this area. Moreover, given the practical illustrations, it should also be of value to practitioners dealing with shipping markets.

8.2 BUSINESS RISKS IN SHIPPING

8.2.1 The Sources of Risk in the Shipping Industry

The purpose of this chapter is to outline the major business risks that principals (ship owners and charterers) in the various sectors of the shipping industry are facing and highlight the modern methods and products that are currently available for efficient risk management in shipping. Market agents operating in the international shipping market face substantial business risks due to the high volatility, cyclicality and seasonality in rates and prices. These risks may be classified broadly into the following categories (adapted from Kavussanos and Visvikis, 2006a):

- **Business risk** depends of the volatility of freight rates, voyage costs (including brokering commission, fuel costs, port charges, tugs, canal dues), operating costs (including manning, repairs and maintenance, stores and lubes, insurance and administration), vessel and scrap prices, interest rates and foreign exchange rates. Figure 8.1 presents the Baltic Dry Index (BDI), which shows that freight rates in the dry-bulk sector of the shipping industry

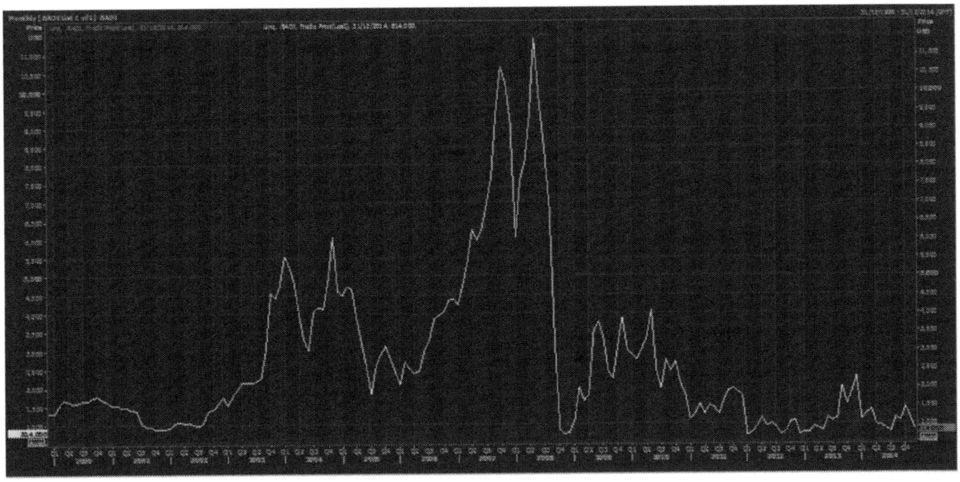

FIGURE 8.1 Baltic Dry Index (2000–2014)
Source: Thomson Reuters Eikon.

have fluctuated significantly from 10,844 in May 2008 down to 703 in February 2012; which recovered somewhat in the latter part of 2013 but dropped back again in 2014. This high volatility in freight rates constitutes the largest source of risk in the industry, as it represents the main income for ship owners and the major transportation cost for charterers.

- **Credit (or counterparty) risk** occurs when the counterparty does not fulfil its legal obligations that arise for a contractual agreement (e.g., loan, bond, derivative contract, etc.).
- **Technical risk** arises when a vessel breaks down, which could lead to environmental (pollution) risks.
- **Financial risk** depends on the way the company's investments are financed and on its financial leverage (gearing) level.

Consider an international investor who wants to enter the shipping industry. He must take the following investment decisions.

(i) First, he has to compare the risks and returns of alternative investments and different assets when formulating his portfolio. He can choose to enter shipping due to the possibility of high returns and/or portfolio diversification.

(ii) He then has to decide if he will enter shipping by buying or leasing vessels. If he buys the assets (vessels) and becomes a ship owner, then he also assumes operational risk by owning the assets.

(iii) The next decision to be taken is on the types of vessel to be purchased; that is, tankers, dry bulk, container ships, gas carriers or other. The choice of vessel requires the identification of market opportunities, the comparative advantage of this type of vessel, as well as the risk appetite of the investor.

(iv) Once he owns the vessels, a ship owner must decide which shipping routes and geographical areas (Atlantic or Pacific) to operate them in and what kind of charter party contracts (voyage, time charter, other) to agree upon.[1]

(v) Market timing – when to buy the vessels and when to sell them – is another important decision. The 'buy low/sell high' asset play paradigm has dominated shipping for decades.

(vi) How to finance the purchased vessels is the next decision. Besides the traditional bank shipping loans, which constitute the majority of funding in the industry, other alternative ways of ship finance include public and private issue of equity and/or debt, mezzanine finance, etc.

(vii) Finally, following the fluctuations of freight and bunker prices, the investor must decide on a risk management strategy in order to minimize the risks. Decisions must also be taken on whether to use financial derivatives products to hedge those risks.

8.2.2 Market Segmentation in the Shipping Industry

It is argued that 95% of world trade, volumetrically, is carried by ocean-going vessels. Figure 8.2 presents the development of international seaborne trade, with major commodities transported by sea, from 1986 to 2012. As can be seen, total seaborne trade has approximately trebled during this period.

The maritime industry contains several sectors, according to the cargos transported and the types of vessel that carry those cargos. Such sectors include dry bulk, wet bulk (tanker), cruise ship and liner, among others. In each sector, different types of vessel operate, corresponding to the different economic conditions that exist, which generate the demand for the shipping service. The liberalization of international trade and the discovery of new sources of material have led to the construction of specialized types of vessel of various sizes, which carry different types of commodity between different parts of the world. As argued by Kavussanos

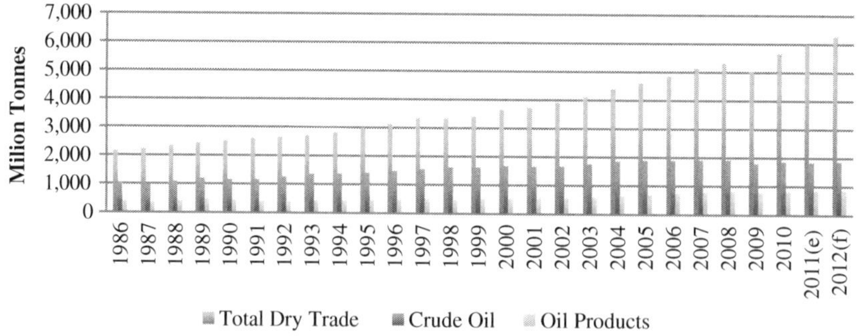

FIGURE 8.2 World seaborne trades (1986–2012)
Source: Clarkson's Research Studies.

[1] In voyage charters the ship owner is paid in US$/ton to transport commodities from port A to port B and all costs are paid by the ship owner. In time charters the ship owner earns hire, in US$/day, every 15 days or every month and operates the vessel under the instructions of the charterer who pays the voyage costs.

and Visvikis (2006a), 'specialized markets have developed for each of these vessels, with common driving forces, but also distinct features in terms of factors affecting demand, supply, and as a consequence risk and return profiles'.

Therefore, bulk cargos include liquid and dry cargos, where liquid cargos include crude oil, oil products and chemicals and dry cargos include: (i) majors (iron ore, grain, coal, bauxite and phosphates); (ii) minors (steel, steel products, sugar, cement, salt, gypsum, sulphur, non-ferrous metal ores, forest products, wood chips and chemicals; and (iii) specialist bulk cargos (refrigerated cargo, heavy lift, cars, timber, etc.).

The economics of the different shipping sectors are different. In the liner sector, oligopolistic conditions exist as the suppliers of the freight service are organized in conferences, producing tariffs which shippers have to accept. Shippers, in contrast, are many but with small cargo transportation needs and, as such, do not have the power to negotiate and fix freight rates. In the dry-bulk and tanker markets, on the contrary, conditions of perfect competition exist as there are many buyers (charterers) and sellers (ship owners) of freight services, with no barriers to entry or exit, transacting in well-organized and homogeneous freight markets. The charterers compete among themselves to fix (hire) vessels, which will transport their cargos. Equally, there are many ship owners and ship managers that compete among themselves to secure employment for their vessels. Tables 8.1 and 8.2 present the submarkets that are distinguished for dry-bulk and tanker shipping, respectively.

8.2.3 Empirical Regularities in Freight Rate Markets

A number of regularities regarding freight markets have been documented in the economic literature for the first time in a series of papers by Kavussanos (1996a,b, 1997, 1998, 2003). These include the findings that: (i) freight rates are determined by the interaction of demand and supply for freight services and as a consequence are highly volatile; (ii) they are cyclical and seasonal; (iii) seasonality is distinct between different submarkets of dry-bulk and tanker sectors, between contracts of different duration and between different market conditions prevailing in shipping markets – see Kavussanos and Alizadeh (2001, 2002); (iv) broadly speaking, freight rates of larger vessels are more volatile and bear higher relative risks compared with smaller vessels in both the dry-bulk and tanker sectors; and (v) freight contracts of longer duration are less volatile compared with shorter-period contracts.

8.2.3.1 Freight Risks and Returns in Shipping Subsectors Table 8.3 presents the mean values and relative volatilities[2] of monthly freight rate data for spot, 1-year and 3-year time-charter rates for different vessel sizes in the dry-bulk and in the tanker sector of the shipping industry.

It can be observed that almost all relative volatilities of spot (voyage) rates and of 1 and 3-year time-charter (period) rates are smaller (less volatile) for smaller-sized vessels compared with those of larger ones. This is true for both the dry-bulk and tanker sectors. This is expected, as smaller vessels are more flexible in terms of the number of trades they are involved in and the number of ports they can approach and, as a consequence, this flexibility translates into lower relative volatility in the freight rates of smaller compared with larger ones. In the dry-bulk sector, a clear ranking of freight volatilities seems to exist according to the duration of the

[2]Relative volatility is defined as the standard deviation of the variable divided by its own mean value.

TABLE 8.1 Cargo and routes of different size dry-bulk vessels

	Commodities (percentage of total shipments)				
Class of bulk carriers	Iron ore	Coal	Grain	Bauxite and alumina	Phosphate rock
Capesize	70%	45%	7%	–	–
Panamax	22%	40%	43%	45%	20%
Handy	8%	15%	50%	55%	80%
	Major routes				
	Iron ore	Coal	Grain	Bauxite and alumina	Phosphate rock
Capesize (100,000–180,000 dwt)	Brazil to West Europe, Japan and China W. Australia to West Europe, Japan and China	E. Australia to Far East, Japan and West Europe South Africa to West Europe and Far East	Argentina and River Plate to Near East and East Europe		
Panamax (50,000–79,999 dwt)	Brazil to West Europe and Japan Australia to West Europe and Japan	North America to Japan and West Europe E. Australia to Far East, Japan and West Europe	North America to Far East, West Europe and Near East		
Handy (25,000–49,999 dwt)	India to Japan, China and Korea Canada to USA and Japan Liberia and Mauritania to West Europe	South Africa to Far East and Europe	Australia to Far East, Japan and Middle East North America to Africa and West Europe	Caribbean to North America and West Europe West Africa to West Europe and Japan Australia to Japan and West Europe	Morocco to West Europe Russia to West Europe The USA to Japan and West Europe

Source: Fearnleys, World Bulk Trades, Lloyd's Shipping Economist and Baltic Exchange (taken from Kavussanos and Visvikis, 2006a).
Note: Deadweight tonnage (dwt) measures how much weight a vessel can safely carry and is the sum of the weights of cargo, fuel, ballast water, fresh water, crew, provisions and passengers.

TABLE 8.2 Cargo and routes of different size tanker vessels

	Commodities (percentage of total shipments)		
Class of tankers	**Crude oil**	**Dirty products**	**Clean products**
ULCC/VLCC	60%	–	–
Suezmax	30%	5%	0%
Aframax	10%	35%	20%
Panamax and Handy	0%	60%	80%
	Major routes		
	Crude oil	**Dirty products**	**Clean products**
ULCC (320,000+ dwt) VLCC (200,000–319,999 dwt)	Middle East to USEC, W. Europe and Far East		
Suezmax (120,000–199,999 dwt)	Middle East to USEC, W. Europe and Mediterranean via Suez Middle East to Far East North Sea to USEC West Africa to USA and Europe	Middle East to USEC, W. Europe and Far East	
Aframax (75,000–119,999 dwt)	North Sea to USEC West & North Africa to USA and Europe Indonesia to Japan Venezuela to US Gulf	Middle East to USEC, W. Europe and Far East US Gulf to different destinations Other routes around the world	Middle East to USEC, W. Europe and Far East US Gulf to different destinations Mediterranean and West Europe Other routes around the world
Panamax (50,000–74,999 dwt) Handy (10,000–49,999 dwt)		Middle East to USEC, W. Europe and Far East US Gulf to different destinations Mediterranean and West Europe Other routes around the world	Middle East to USEC, W. Europe and Far East US Gulf to different destinations Mediterranean and West Europe Other routes around the world

Source: Fearnleys, World Bulk Trades, Lloyd's Shipping Economist and Baltic Exchange (taken from Kavussanos and Visvikis, 2006a).
Notes: *Dirty* vessels carry the *black* (or *dirty*) cargos such as crude oil, heavy fuel oils, asphalt, etc.
Clean vessels carry the refined *white* (or *clean*) products such as gasoline, jet fuels, diesel oil, kerosene, naphtha, leaded and unleaded oil, etc.

TABLE 8.3 Summary statistics of spot, 1-year and 3-year time-charter rates for dry-bulk and tanker vessels

Panel A: Dry-bulk vessels

	Voyage (spot) rates		1-Year T/C rates		3-Year T/C rates	
	Mean ($/ton)	Relative volatility	Mean ($/day)	Relative volatility	Mean ($/day)	Relative volatility
Capesize	12.35	84	20,872	43	19,902	32
Panamax	17.50	64	14,521	35	12,390	21
Handy	29.78	62	13,032	26	12,347	16

Panel B: Tanker vessels

	Voyage (spot) rates		1-Year T/C rates		3-Year T/C rates	
	Mean (WS)	Relative volatility	Mean ($/day)	Relative volatility	Mean ($/day)	Relative volatility
VLCC	59.20	25	27,064	26	29,846	15
Suezmax	82.48	19	20,773	21	22,210	13
Aframax	101.42	15	15,069	13	16,201	9
Handysize	157.40	14	12,601	5	13,398	5

Note: Sample covers September 2009 to September 2012. Mean is the arithmetic average. Relative volatility is the standard deviation over the mean value ×100. WS stands for Worldscale rate.

freight contract for each vessel size. Specifically, it seems that the longer the duration of the contract, the smaller the volatility of the freight rate, indicating that longer-duration contracts bear less risk compared with shorter ones. The results are not so clear-cut in the tanker sector.

8.2.3.2 Vessel Value Risks and Returns in Shipping Subsectors The mean and relative volatility measures for different types of new-build and 5-year-old second-hand vessels, as well as for their scrap prices and earnings for the dry-bulk and tanker sectors, are computed in Table 8.4. Volatilities of earnings for larger vessels are higher than those of smaller ones, within the dry-bulk and tanker sectors. Moreover, new-build, second-hand and scrap prices for larger vessels seem to show higher relative volatilities than prices of smaller vessels. Smaller-sized vessels are geared so that they can load and unload cargo in ports without sophisticated handling facilities and they can approach more ports compared with larger vessels. Moreover, smaller vessels can switch between different trades more easily. Thus, risk-averse investors that wish to reduce their investment risk may wish to invest in smaller (larger) vessels – for example, Panamax or Handysize (Capesize) – if they want to reduce (increase) the risk in their portfolio of assets.

Kavussanos (1997, 2003) introduced the concept of time-varying volatilities (risks) in freight rates and vessel prices and compared them between the different sectors of shipping, but also between contracts of different duration. In each market, not only is the average value of freight rates affected by the state of the market, but also the risks vary with changing market conditions. Moreover, the risks of vessel prices are also time-varying and are affected, apart

TABLE 8.4 Risk comparisons of prices of new-build, 5-year-old, scrap prices and earnings for dry-bulk and tanker vessels

Panel A: Dry-bulk vessels

	Capesize		Panamax		Handy	
	Mean	**Relative volatility**	**Mean**	**Relative volatility**	**Mean**	**Relative volatility**
Earnings	19,684	75	11,388	65	10,789	54
New-build prices	35.74	20	26.42	16	23.00	14
Second-hand prices	30.29	35	20.57	28	17.95	22
Scrap prices	3.60	40	2.30	37	1.33	25

Panel B: Tanker vessels

	VLCC		Suezmax		Aframax	
	Mean	**Relative volatility**	**Mean**	**Relative volatility**	**Mean**	**Relative volatility**
Earnings	33,770	68	24,750	67	21,456	58
New-build prices	82.67	18	54.15	15	42.55	12
Second-hand prices	62.15	21	41.53	20	33.52	18
Scrap prices	6.32	38	4.53	35	3.21	35

Source: Kavussanos and Visvikis (2006a).
Note: Mean figures for second-hand, scrap and new-build prices are in US million dollars.

from their own past values and past values of shocks to long-run equilibrium in each market, by factors such as time-charter rates, interest rates and oil prices.

8.2.3.3 Freight Rate Seasonality in Shipping Subsectors Freight rate seasonality arises because of factors that influence the demand for shipping services. Kavussanos and Alizadeh (2001, 2002) show that these seasonalities are transmitted to dry-bulk and tanker freight rates. More specifically, in dry-bulk shipping spot freight rates increase significantly during the spring months of March and April for all sized vessels. During the autumn months of October and November, Panamax spot rates rise, while during the summer months of June and July, there is a seasonal decline in spot rates across all three vessel sizes.

The seasonal pattern in 3-year and 1-year time-charter rates shows that there is a seasonal increase in time-charter rates during spring and a decline in rates for all sizes during June and July. Moreover, the results suggest that the degree of seasonal fluctuation of shipping freight rates declines as the duration of contract increases. When seasonality is compared between different market conditions, results for all types of charter indicate that seasonal fluctuations are or become significant in 'good' market conditions. However, such differences become smaller as the duration of the contract rises from 1 to 3 years. Finally, Kavussanos and Alizadeh (2002) present similar results for seasonal patterns in the tanker market. They find that there are significant seasonal patterns in tanker freight rates, which vary by market condition.

8.2.3.4 Correlation and Portfolio Diversification in Shipping Subsectors All the above indicate that there are significant risk–return differences in freight rates and shipping prices in different subsegments of dry-bulk and tanker shipping. This points to possibly significant risk reductions in portfolio formations of vessels from different sectors of bulk shipping. To establish this we consider next the correlation coefficients in freight rates between different segments of dry-bulk and tanker shipping. We know from Markowitz (1952) that if the correlation coefficients between returns on assets are low, inclusion of these assets in a portfolio reduces the total risk of the portfolio, thereby achieving significant diversification effects.

Consider Table 8.5, which presents freight rate correlations in levels (panel A) and in logarithmic first differences (panel B) between the three major subsegments of the dry-bulk sector – namely, the Baltic Capesize Index (BCI), the Baltic Panamax Index (BPI) and the Baltic Supramax Index (BSI) and those of the tanker sector – namely, VLCC, Suezmax and Aframax vessels carrying crude oil (dirty) and Panamax and Handysize vessels carrying products of crude oil (clean). These are described in detail in Section 8.3.

TABLE 8.5 Freight rate correlations in segments of dry-bulk and tanker markets

Panel A: Correlations of freight rates in levels

	BCI	BPI	BSI	VLCC dirty	Suezmax dirty	Aframax dirty	Panamax clean	Handysize clean
BCI	1							
BPI	0.965	1						
BSI	0.962	0.988	1					
VLCC dirty	0.325	0.267	0.289	1				
Suezmax dirty	0.171	0.124	0.139	0.832	1			
Aframax dirty	0.210	0.169	0.193	0.736	0.878	1		
Panamax clean	0.086	0.104	0.135	0.456	0.386	0.380	1	
Handysize clean	0.310	0.322	0.344	0.542	0.542	0.591	0.552	1

Panel B: Correlations of freight rates logarithmic first differences

	BCI	BPI	BSI	VLCC dirty	Suezmax dirty	Aframax dirty	Panamax clean	Handysize clean
BCI	1							
BPI	0.513	1						
BSI	0.372	0.512	1					
VLCC dirty	0.111	0.070	0.115	1				
Suezmax dirty	−0.011	−0.020	0.028	0.419	1			
Aframax dirty	−0.123	−0.034	0.109	0.297	0.421	1		
Panamax clean	0.016	0.023	0.004	0.013	0.013	0.020	1	
Handysize clean	0.013	0.031	0.044	0.071	0.044	0.113	0.025	1

Note: BCI, Baltic Capesize Index; BPI, Baltic Panamax Index; BSI, Baltic Supramax Index.

As expected, the strongest correlations are exhibited in freight rate levels between the different segments of the dry-bulk sector, with correlations ranging between 96.5% and 98.8%. This is an expected outcome, as a Panamax vessel for instance can substitute a Capesize vessel and a Supramax vessel can substitute a Panamax vessel in most trades. The corresponding correlation coefficients between the 'dirty' tanker trades range from 73.6% to 87.8%, while between the Panamax and Handysize 'clean' trades the value is much lower, standing at 55.2%. In contrast, correlation coefficients between dry-bulk and tanker subsegments are rather low and only range in value from 8.6% to 34.4%, pointing to very different behaviour between the dry-bulk and tanker segments of the shipping industry. However, when considering the corresponding correlation coefficient figures for the logarithmic changes in freight rates, their values are reduced significantly and are very low in most cases compared with correlations examined for levels of freight rates. Specifically, between subsectors of dry-bulk shipping these correlations take values between 37.2% and 51.3%. Between tanker dirty trades the coefficients are even lower, while when these correlation coefficients are examined between tanker and dry-bulk trades they are close to zero or even negative in some cases.

It seems that the dry-bulk sector freight rates are not related so much to the tanker sector rates. This is expected, as each of these two sectors represent distinct market segments of the shipping industry. As a consequence, a ship owner investing in more than one segment of dry-bulk shipping brings about risk diversification effects to the income part of his investments, arising from his portfolio of vessels. Moreover, if he decides to include vessels from the tanker sector in his portfolio these risk reductions are even greater.

8.2.4 Traditional Risk Management Strategies

The results so far suggest that:

(i) Freight rate risks in the larger sectors of the dry-bulk and tanker sectors of the shipping industry may be mitigated by investing in smaller vessels. This is because freight rates and prices of ships for larger vessels seem to show higher volatilities than smaller ones, and correlation coefficients of freight rates and vessel prices amongst segments of shipping are low.

(ii) Spot (voyage) rates are more volatile than time-charter (period) rates. As a consequence, owners and ship management companies can reduce freight rate risks by operating vessels under long-term time-charter rather than spot contracts.

(iii) Freight and ship price risks are time-varying. As a consequence, the mix of the investors' portfolios in terms of both charter contracts and investments in different ship segments should be reviewed constantly to create optimal solutions that fit their risk–return profiles.

(iv) There are seasonal movements of dry-bulk and tanker rates. For instance, on average, the dry-bulk freight rates increase in certain months (March and April) and drop in others (June and July). This information may be used to dry-dock vessels in periods when rates are expected to fall and adjust speeds to increase productivity during peak seasons.

The above strategies are useful but may prove to be expensive, non-existent or inflexible at times. For instance, it consumes time and resources to buy and sell vessels and go in and out of freight contracts of different duration in order to switch between segments of shipping and charter parties. Long-term charters may be difficult for ship owners to find when the market is in decline. The opposite is true for the charterers when the market is improving. In addition, the counterparties (ship owner or charterer) may decide to discard the agreement when the conditions turn too much against them, damaging their reputation and brand name. Derivatives products, analysed next, can provide more efficient solutions to the above problems.

8.3 FREIGHT RATE DERIVATIVES

8.3.1 Risk Management in Shipping

Derivatives instruments are financial contracts, creating rights and obligations, the effect of which is to transfer risk to some other party willing to bear it. These contracts are determined by reference to or derived from underlying spot or physical markets. By using derivatives, market participants can secure (stabilize) their future income or costs and reduce their uncertainty and unforeseen volatility. The existence of financial derivatives contracts has helped to alleviate the problems of the previous section with respect to risk management in the business of shipping. They have provided real gains for market participants in shipping, as their existence has made risk management cheaper, more flexible and available to parties exposed to adverse movements in freight rates, bunker fuel prices, vessel prices, exchange rates, interest rates and other variables affecting the cash-flow position of the shipping company (see Kavussanos and Visvikis, 2006a, 2007, 2011).

More specifically, the high fluctuations (volatility) of freight rates constitute a major source of business risk for both the ship owner and the charterer. For the charterer wishing to hire in vessels for transportation requirements, increasing freight rates lead to higher costs. In contrast, for the ship owner seeking employment for his vessels, lower freight rates involve less income from hiring out the vessels. Freight derivatives contracts can be used to hedge this freight rate risk. Freight derivatives contracts, compared with time-chartering a vessel, are more effective instruments for managing freight market risks. This is because ship owners retain operational control of their vessels and at the same time are benefiting from favourable spot market conditions. Charterers, in contrast, are free from any operational risks which are present in time-charter agreements. Also, there is no physical delivery involved with freight derivatives. They simply settle in cash upon conclusion of the agreed terms (Kavussanos and Visvikis, 2008).

8.3.2 The Underlying Indices of Freight Rate Derivatives

8.3.2.1 Dry-Bulk Freight Rate Indices For derivatives contracts to be written on an underlying asset, an independent price for this asset must exist. This is important in order to enable the derivatives contracts to be settled against this price. The Baltic Exchange has undertaken the task of constructing such indices for the industry. Freight derivatives are cash-settled against the value of a freight index. The Baltic Exchange appoints panellists, which are major ship brokers. They are assigned the task of reporting actual or estimated freight rates on individual routes, where vessels are employed on a daily basis. These primary data are then utilized by the Baltic Exchange to build the freight indices. Provision is made that the composition of these indices could be altered over time, in line with developments in world trades and shipping, in order to continue to reflect changing trading patterns.

The Baltic Exchange has gradually launched a number of distinct sectoral indices. These indices include: the BPI, launched in 1998; the BCI, introduced in 1999; the BSI, launched

TABLE 8.6 BCI route definitions, 2012

Routes	Vessel size (dwt)	Cargo	Route description	Weights
C2	160,000	Iron ore	Tubarao (Brazil) to Rotterdam (Netherlands)	10%
C3	160,000	Iron ore	Tubarao to Qingdao (China)	15%
C4	150,000	Coal	Richards Bay (S. Africa) to Rotterdam	5%
C5	160,000	Iron ore	W. Australia to Qingdao	15%
C7	150,000	Coal	Bolivar (Colombia) to Rotterdam	5%
C8_03	172,000	T/C	Gibraltar/Hamburg transatlantic round voyage	10%
C9_03	172,000	T/C	Continent/Mediterranean trip to Far East	5%
C10_03	172,000	T/C	Pacific round voyage	20%
C11_03	172,000	T/C	China–Japan trip Mediterranean/Continent	15%

Source: Baltic Exchange.

in 2005; and the Baltic Handysize Index (BHSI), introduced in 2006 for the dry-bulk sector. Tables 8.6 to 8.9 show the compositions of the dry-bulk sector indices (BCI, BPI, BSI and BHSI) as they stood in 2012.

Table 8.6 shows the composition of the BCI. It comprises spot and time-charter routes, coded C2 to C11, involving vessel sizes which range from 150,000 dwt to 172,000 dwt, carrying iron ore and coal in the routes described fully in the fourth column of the table. The latter correspond to seaborne trade patterns. Moreover, the weights assigned to each route (shown in the last column of the table) reflect the importance of the route in the composition of the index.

The composition of the BPI is shown in Table 8.7. Just as with the BCI, the table shows the vessel sizes, the cargos carried, the routes that the vessels engage in, as well as the weights assigned to each route, reflecting the state of the Panamax market as it stood in 2012.

Table 8.8 presents the composition of the BSI. The Supramax vessels (as well as the Handysize and Handymax vessels) can carry on the different routes all bulk cargos, including grains, coal and iron ore. Typically, Handysize vessels can also carry steel products.

Table 8.9 shows the composition of the BHSI. It comprises smaller Handysize vessels of 28,000 dwt and as such covers a different market segment from the BSI.

8.3.2.2 Tanker Freight Rate Indices In an effort to create an independent index for the tanker freight markets, the Baltic Exchange launched in January 1998 the Baltic International Tanker Route (BITR) index. By October 2001, the BITR was split into two separate indices

TABLE 8.7 BPI route definitions, 2012

Routes	Vessel size (dwt)	Cargo	Route description	Weights
P1A_03	74,000	T/C	Transatlantic round voyage	25%
P2A_03	74,000	T/C	Skaw/Gibraltar to Far East	25%
P3A_03	74,000	T/C	Japan–South Korea to Pacific round voyage	25%
P4_03	74,000	T/C	Far East/NOPAC–Australia/South Korea pass	25%

Source: Baltic Exchange.

TABLE 8.8 BSI route definitions, 2012

Routes	Vessel size (dwt)	Route description	Weights
S1A	52,000	Antwerp/Skaw trip Far East	12.5%
S1B	52,000	Canakkale (Turkey) trip Far East	12.5%
S2	52,000	Japan–South Korea/NOPAC or Australia round voyage	25%
S3	52,000	Japan–South Korea trip Gibraltar/Skaw range	25%
S4A	52,000	US Gulf–Skaw/Passero	12.5%
S4B	52,000	Skaw/Passero range–US Gulf	12.5%
S5	52,000	West Africa via ECSA to Far East	0%
S9	52,000	West Africa via ECSA–Skaw/Passero	0%

Source: Baltic Exchange.
Note: Supramax vessels carry bulk cargos, such as grains and coal.

TABLE 8.9 BHSI composition, 2012

Routes	Vessel size (dwt)	Route description	Weights
HS1	28,000	Skaw/Passero trip Recalada–Rio de Janeiro	12.5%
HS2	28,000	Skaw/Passero trip Boston–Galveston	12.5%
HS3	28,000	Recalada–Rio de Janeiro trip Skaw/Passero	12.5%
HS4	28,000	US Gulf trip via US Gulf or NCSA to Skaw/Passero	12.5%
HS5	28,000	SE Asia trip via Australia to Singapore–Japan	25%
HS6	28,000	South Korea–Japan via NOPAC to Singapore–Japan	25%

Source: Baltic Exchange.

which exist until today – the Baltic Dirty Tanker Index (BDTI) and the Baltic Clean Tanker Index (BCTI) – bundling separately the *dirty* and *clean* routes, respectively. This modification came in recognition of the fact that *dirty* and *clean* markets are separate entities and must be treated accordingly.

The BDTI includes *dirty* vessels which carry the *black* or *dirty* cargos, such as crude oil, heavy fuel oils, asphalt, etc. The BCTI includes *clean* vessels which carry the refined *white* or *clean* products, such as gasoline, jet fuels, diesel oil, kerosene, naphtha, leaded and unleaded oil, etc. Tables 8.10 and 8.11 present the BDTI and BCTI compositions as they stood in 2012, respectively.

8.3.2.3 Container Freight Rate Indices The underlying assets of the container freight derivatives consist of the routes of the Shanghai Containerized Freight Index (SCFI) of the Shanghai Shipping Exchange (SSE) and of the World Container Index (WCI), which is a joint venture between Drewry Shipping Consultants and Cleartrade Exchange.

The SSE, on 16 October 2009, launched a revised version of the SCFI, replacing the original index published by the exchange on 7 December 2005.[3] The new index, as seen in

[3]In 1998 and 2001 the SSE, respectively, issued China (Export) Containerized Freight Index (CCFI) and China (Coastal) Bulk Freight Index (CBFI). In 2005, for the purpose of reflecting the momentum of the Shanghai container liner service market more accurately, the SSE further developed the SCFI.

TABLE 8.10 BDTI composition, 2012

Routes	Vessel size (mt)	Type of vessel	Route description
TD1	280,000	VLCC	Middle East to US Gulf; Ras Tanura (South Arabia) to Loop (USA)
TD2	260,000	VLCC	Middle East Gulf to Singapore; Ras Tanura to Singapore
TD3	260,000	VLCC	Middle East Gulf to Japan; Ras Tanura to Chiba (Japan)
TD4	260,000	VLCC	West Africa to US Gulf; Off Shore Bonny (Nigeria) to Loop
TD5	130,000	Suezmax	West Africa to USAC; Off Shore Bonny to Philadelphia (USA)
TD6	135,000	Suezmax	Black Sea/Mediterranean; Novorossiyk to Augusta
TD7	80,000	Aframax	North Sea to Continent; Sullom Voe (UK) to Wilhelmshaven (Germany)
TD8	80,000	Aframax	Kuwait to Singapore; Mena al Ahmadi (Kuwait) to Singapore
TD9	70,000	Panamax	Caribbean to US Gulf; Puerto La Cruz (Venezuela) to Corpus Christi (USA)
TD10D	50,000	Panamax	Caribbean to USAC; Aruba (Antilles) to New York
TD12	55,000	Panamax	ARA to US Gulf; Antwerp (Belgium) to Houston (USA)
TD14	80,000	Aframax	South East Asia to EC Australia; Seria to Sydney
TD15	260,000	VLCC	West Africa to China; Serpentina FPSO and Off Shore Bonny to Ningpo
TD16	30,000	Handysize	Black Sea to Mediterranean; Odessa to Augusta
TD17	100,000	Aframax	Baltic to UK Continent; Primorsk to Wilhelmshaven
TD18	30,000	Handysize	Baltic to UK Continent; Tallinn to Amsterdam
TD19	80,000	Aframax	Cross Mediterranean/Ceyhan to Lavera
VLCC-TCE	–	VLCC	Time-charter equivalent average of the rates derived from TD1 and TD3
Suezmax-TCE	–	Suezmax	Time-charter equivalent average of the rates derived from TD5 and TD6
Aframax-TCE	–	Aframax	Time-charter equivalent average of the rates derived from TD7, TD8, TD9, TD11, TD14 and TD17

Source: Baltic Exchange.

TABLE 8.11 BCTI composition, 2012

Routes	Vessel size (mt)	Type of vessel	Route description
TC1	75,000	Aframax	Middle East Gulf to Japan; Ras Tanura to Yokohama (Japan)
TC2_37	37,000	Handysize	Continent to USAC; Rotterdam to New York
TC3_38	38,000	Handysize	Caribbean to USAC; Aruba to New York
TC5	55,000	Panamax	Middle East to Japan; Ras Tanura (South Arabia) to Yokohama
TC6	30,000	Handysize	Algeria/Euromed; Skikda (Syria)/Lavera (France)
TC9	22,000	Handysize	Baltic to UK Continent; Ventspils to Le Havre
TC8	65,000	Panamax	AG to UK Continent, Jubail to Rotterdam
TC14	38,000	Handysize	US Gulf to Continent; Houston to Amsterdam
Baltic Exchange tanker routes (BITR-Asia)			
TC4	30,000	Handysize	Singapore to Japan; Singapore to Chiba (Japan)
TC7	30,000	Handysize	Singapore to EC Australia; Singapore to Sydney
TC10	40,000	Handysize	South Korea to NOPAC West Coast
TC11	40,000	Handysize	South Korea to Singapore
TC12	35,000	Handysize	Naptha Sikka (WCI) to Japan

Source: Baltic Exchange.
Note: TC4, TC7, TC10, TC11 and TC12 routes are excluded from BCTI and reported as standalone routes (BITR-Asia) with a publishing time of 16:00 hrs Singapore time.

Table 8.12, is based on spot ocean freight rates (including surcharges), quoted in US$/TEU (twenty foot equivalent units) and US$/FEU (forty foot equivalent units – for the US West Coast and East Coast services) of the Shanghai export container transport market. The rates are collected and published every Friday at 15:00 (Beijing time) from 30 panellists (15 from liner companies[4] and 15 from shippers and freight forwarders[5]) and include 15 individual shipping routes. According to the market, the new SCFI met the needs of carriers, freight

[4]The liner companies are: CMA-CGM, COSCO, China Shipping, Hanjin, Shanghai Haihua Shipping Co., Hapag-Lloyd, Jin Jiang Shipping, 'K' Line, Maersk, MOL, NYK Line, OOCL, Pacific International Lines, Sinotrans Shipping and SITC Shipping.

[5]The shippers/freight forwarders are: Orient International Logistics, UBI Logistics (China), JHJ International Transportation Co., SIPG Logistics Co., Shanghai Orient Express International Logistics Co., Shanghai Huaxing International Container Freight Transportation Co., Shanghai Jinchang Logistics Co., Shanghai Shenda International Transportation Co., Shanghai Viewtrans Co., Shanghai Richhood International Logistics Co., Shanghai Ever-leading International, Shanghai Asian Development Int'l Trans Pu Dong Co., Sunshine-Quick Group, COSCO Logistics (Shanghai) and Sinotrans Eastern Co., Ltd.

TABLE 8.12 SCFI composition, 2012

Line service	Unit	Weighting	Route description
1	USD/TEU	20%	Europe (base port)
2	USD/TEU	10%	Mediterranean (base port)
3	USD/FEU	20%	USWC (base port)
4	USD/FEU	7.5%	USEC (base port)
5	USD/TEU	7.5%	Persian Gulf and Red Sea (Dubai)
6	USD/TEU	5.0%	Australian/New Zealand (Melbourne)
7	USD/TEU	2.5%	East/West Africa (Lagos)
8	USD/TEU	2.5%	South Africa (Durban)
9	USD/TEU	2.5%	South America (Santos)
10	USD/TEU	5.0%	West Japan (base port)
11	USD/TEU	5.0%	East Japan (base port)
12	USD/TEU	5.0%	Southeast Asia (Singapore)
13	USD/TEU	2.5%	Korea (Pusan)
14	USD/TEU	2.5%	Taiwan (Kaohsiung)
15	USD/TEU	2.5%	Hong Kong (Hong Kong)

Source: Shanghai Shipping Exchange.
Notes: The freight rate includes ocean freight and surcharges.
Base port: Mediterranean Sea – Barcelona/Valencia/Genoa/Naples; Europe – Hamburg/Antwerp/Felixstowe/Le Havre; USWC – Los Angeles/Long Beach/Oakland; USEC – New York/Savannah/Norfolk/Charleston; West Japan – Osaka/Kobe East Japan, Tokyo/Yokohama.

owners and forwarders and traders, while at the same time providing the underlying asset of container derivatives.[6]

WCI is one of the two indices (together with SCFI) that are used for container FFAs. The WCI, assessed by Drewry Shipping Consultants and published by Cleartrade Exchange, reports actual spot container freight rates for major East–West trade routes. The WCI, as shown in Table 8.13, consists of 11 route-specific indices, representing individual routes expressed in US$/FEU. The 12 panellists are transport intermediaries (freight forwarders) based in Europe, North America and Asia. The panellists report the freight rates on which they are moving cargo, with a number of major shipping lines. Panellists provide up to four market assessments each (the rate which that panellist has agreed with a major carrier) per week and for each route.

The methodology for estimating the route-specific indices of the WCI is as follows (www.worldcontainerindex.com): (i) the median of all rates submitted is calculated; (ii) any rate more than 20% above or below this median is discarded; (iii) the remaining rates are sorted into reports for the specific carriers monitored; (iv) the mathematical average rate for each carrier monitored is reported; (v) the mathematical average of all individual carrier averages is calculated, which is the final WCI for that route for that week. According to WCI, besides being used for the settlement of container FFAs, facilitating risk management and price discovery, the index can also be used for index-linked container contracts (ILCCs), which are long-term contracts whose rates fluctuate with market conditions and for benchmarking spot rates and trends.

[6]On 18 January 2010, Clarkson Securities Limited announced the trade of the first OTC container freight swap agreement (CFSA), settled against the SCFI.

TABLE 8.13 WCI composition, 2012

Line service	Route	Weighting	Representative trade
1	Shanghai–Rotterdam	23.5%	Far East to North Europe
2	Rotterdam–Shanghai	10.7%	North Europe to Far East
3	Shanghai–Genoa	13.0%	Far East to Mediterranean
4	Genoa–Shanghai	4.4%	Mediterranean to Far East
5	Shanghai–Los Angeles	22.7%	Far East to US West Coast
6	Los Angeles–Shanghai	11.0%	US West Coast to Far East
7	Shanghai–New York	8.3%	Far East to US East Coast
8	Los Angeles–Rotterdam	0.30%	US West Coast to North Europe
9	Rotterdam–Los Angeles	0.50%	North Europe to US West Coast
10	New York–Rotterdam	2.5%	US East Coast to North Europe
11	Rotterdam–New York	3.0%	North Europe to US East Coast

Source: Cleartrade Exchange.

8.3.3 The Freight Derivatives Market

8.3.3.1 Forward Freight Agreements (FFAs) The FFA contracts, which appeared in 1992, were the first over-the-counter (OTC) freight derivatives products. They are private principal-to-principal *contracts-for-difference* (CFDs) between a seller and a buyer to settle a freight rate, for a specified quantity of cargo or type of vessel, for usually one or a combination of the major trade routes of the dry-bulk or tanker sectors of the shipping industry. Since FFAs are tailor-made to suit the needs of their users, they have become very popular with market participants wishing to hedge freight rate fluctuations (see, e.g., Kavussanos and Visvikis, 2003a,b).

The underlying instruments of FFA contracts are routes or baskets of routes from the BCI, BPI, BSI and BHSI for the dry-bulk sector, routes from BCTI and BDTI for the tanker sector and routes from the SCFI and WCI for the container sector. In OTC derivatives markets each party accepts credit (counterparty) risk from the other party. The primary advantage of an OTC market is that the terms and conditions of the contract are tailored to the specific needs of the two parties. This gives investors flexibility by letting them introduce their own contract specifications in order to cover their specific needs.

Voyage-based dry-bulk freight derivatives contracts on a particular route of the Baltic indices are settled on the difference between the contracted price and the average spot price of the route over the last seven working days of the settlement month. Time-charter-based dry-bulk contracts are settled on the difference between the contracted price and the average price over the calendar settlement month. If freight rates fall below the agreed rate, the buyer of FFAs (charterer) pays the difference between the agreed FFA price and the settlement spot price; if rates increase, then the buyer of FFAs receives the difference. The opposite is true for the seller of FFAs (ship owner).

In the tanker market, a tanker FFA contract is an agreement between two parties to fix a freight rate in Worldscale units (or in a time-charter equivalent – TCE) on a predetermined tanker route, over a time period, at a mutually agreed price. Settlement takes place at the end of each month, where the fixed forward price is compared against the monthly average of

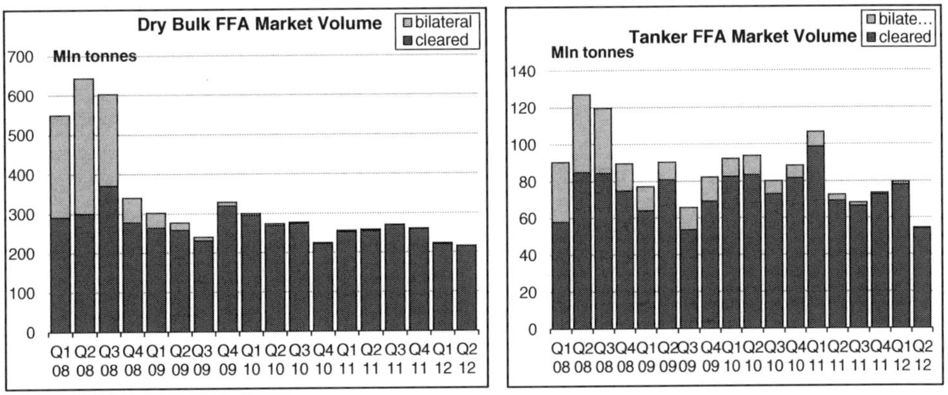

FIGURE 8.3 Dry-bulk and tanker FFA trading volume (Q1 2008–Q2 2012)
Source: ICAP Shipping, Baltic Exchange. Reproduced with permission.

the spot price of the tanker route selected. Yet again, if the seller's price is lower than the settlement price then the seller will compensate the buyer of the FFA contract.

Principals with physical exposure to container box rates can utilize container swaps (CFSAs) to manage the volatility in the container market. A CFSA is a cash-settled agreement between two parties to transport a specific volume of containers on a particular trade route at a specified future date, but at a box rate agreed today. The settlement price at expiry of the contract is calculated as the average index-measured box rate over the contract period. For end-users and commodity traders (shipping liners and operators), CFSAs hedge the risk of increasing (decreasing) box-rate costs (revenues) in a rising (falling) market. CFSA rates are published in US$/FEU for the US routes and US$/TEU for all other routes, these are 'all in rates' that include ancillary fees such as bunker surcharge (for more information, see the website of the Container Freight Derivatives Association – CFDA).

To see how FFAs can be used for hedging purposes, assume that a ship owner (or charterer) feels that the freight market in a specific route, with a specific vessel/cargo size, might move adversely in the near future. He can approach a freight derivatives broker to sell (buy) FFA contracts, written on the route–vessel/cargo type. The ship owner's broker will search to find a charterer with opposite expectations to the ship owner, thereby wishing to buy (sell) FFAs and negotiate the terms of the contract. If an agreement is reached then the FFA contract is fixed.

Figure 8.3 shows the evolution of cleared and OTC FFA trades. The growth in cleared FFAs (in comparison with OTC) over the period is clear, as currently all FFA trades are cleared. The bilateral (non-cleared) dry-bulk trading volume from more than 200 million tons in Q3 2008 goes close to nothing in Q4 2008. The shift is smoother for the tanker FFA market, but the result is the same as from about 40 million tons it goes to almost nothing. In other more mature markets, such as exchange rate markets, derivatives trading is several times higher than that of the underlying commodity. This reflects the potential in the freight derivatives market.

8.3.3.2 Freight Futures Freight futures contracts are also available, and currently trade in the organized exchange of the Chicago Mercantile Exchange (CME Group – formerly New York Mercantile Exchange, NYMEX); they are cleared in its associated clearing-house

TABLE 8.14 CME Group freight futures

Baltic routes	Coding	Sector	Route description	Cargo size (mt)	Type of contract	Settlement index
Panel A: Dirty tanker futures						
TD3	TL	VLCC	Middle Eastern Gulf to Japan	260,000	Futures	Baltic
TD5	TI	Suezmax	West Africa to USAC	130,000	Futures	Baltic
TD7	TK	Aframax	North Sea to Europe	80,000	Futures	Baltic
Panel B: Clean tanker futures						
TC2	TM	MR	Europe to USAC	37,000	Futures	Baltic
TC4	TJ	MR	Singapore to Japan	30,000	Futures	Platts
TC5	TH	LR 1	Ras Tanura to Yokohama	55,000	Futures	Platts
TC6	TCS	MR	Algeria to Euromed	30,000	Futures	Baltic
TC12	FRS		Sikka (West Coast India) to Chiba	35,000	Futures	Baltic
Panel C: Dry-bulk futures						
–	CFU	Capesize	Time-charter Average	–	Futures	Baltic
–	PFU	Panamax	Time-charter Average	–	Futures	Baltic
–	SFT	Supramax	Time-charter Average	–	Futures	Baltic
–	HFT	Handysize	Time-charter Average	–	Futures	Baltic

Source: CME Group.

(ClearPort).[7] In May 2005, tanker freight derivatives were launched and since 2010, dry-bulk freight derivatives have been traded on the electronic platform of the CME Group. These contracts are cleared in ClearPort, and as such, transactions executed on the exchange do not carry credit risk. They use as underlying commodities the freight routes of the Baltic Exchange and of Platts in some cases.[8] Table 8.14 presents the specifications of the underlying indices: they are the three *dirty* tanker routes TD3, TD5 and TD7, shown in panel A of the table; the four *clean* tanker routes TC2, TC4, TC5 and TC6, presented in panel B; and the four time-charter average baskets, presented in panel C of the same table.

---

[7]The International Maritime Exchange (IMAREX) in Oslo, which has traded and cleared freight futures and options since 2001, is another organized freight derivatives exchange. Marex Group acquired IMAREX's Spectron Group Ltd to become Marex Spectron in May 2011 and NASDAQ OMX Stockholm AB, which is a part of NASDAQ OMX Group Inc., acquired the Norwegian Options and Futures (NOS) clearing-house in July 2012.

[8]Platts is a provider of energy news, price benchmarks, energy intelligence and decision-support services to the industry. It covers the petroleum, petrochemical, electricity, natural gas, coal, metals, nuclear power, bunker fuels and freight rate markets.

TABLE 8.15 LCH.Clearnet cleared hybrid forwards

Routes	Sector	Route description	Cargo size (mt)
Panel A: Tanker forwards			
TD3	VLCC	Middle Eastern Gulf to Japan	250,000
TD5	Suezmax	West Africa to USAC	130,000
TD7	Aframax	North Sea to USAC	80,000
TD19	Aframax	Cross Mediterranean	80,000
TC2	MR	Continent to USAC	37,000
TC4	MR	Singapore to Japan	30,000
TC5	LR1	ME to Japan	55,000
TC6	MR	Algeria to Euromed	30,000
Panel B: Dry voyage routes			
C3E	Capesize	Tubarao to Qingdao	150,000
C4E	Capesize	Richard Bay to Rotterdam	150,000
C5E	Capesize	West Australia to Qingdao	150,000
C7E	Capesize	Bolivar to Rotterdam	150,000
Panel C: Dry time-charter basket routes			
CTC	Capesize	Capesize 4 T/C routes average	–
PTC	Panamax	Panamax 4 T/C routes average	–
STC	Supramax	Supramax 6 T/C routes average	–
HTC	Handymax	Handymax 6 T/C routes average	–
Panel D: Dry trip time-charter routes			
P1A	Panamax	Transatlantic round voyage	
P2A	Panamax	Continent trip Far East	–
P3A	Panamax	Transpacific round voyage	–
Panel E: Dry Time-charter voyage routes			
S7	Supramax	East Coast India to China	–
Panel F: Index			
BDI	–	Baltic Exchange Dry Index	–

Source: LCH.Clearnet.

8.3.3.3 Cleared Hybrid FFAs One way to deal with the credit risk issue of the OTC FFA contracts is to clear them in a clearing-house, while retaining their trading OTC. These contracts are *hybrid* FFAs, in the sense that they are OTC agreements but cleared through a clearing-house. Thus, they maintain the flexibility of the FFAs and, for a fee, have credit risk eliminated through mark-to-market clearing, like in freight futures. These hybrid FFAs are cleared in the London Clearing House Clearnet (LCH.Clearnet) and in the Singapore Exchange AsiaClear (SGX AsiaClear).

In December 2003, LCH Limited merged with Clearnet S.A. to form LCH.Clearnet Group. During September 2005, LCH.Clearnet launched a clearing and settlement platform for OTC FFAs. Table 8.15 presents the hybrid FFA contracts cleared on LCH.Clearnet. They include tanker FFAs (crude and refined products) written on four *dirty* and four *clean* routes, presented in panel A of the table.

In the dry-bulk sector, there are four dry-bulk voyage FFAs, written on Capesize voyage routes C3E, C4E, C5E and C7E, presented in panel B of the table; four dry-bulk time-charter baskets on Capesize, Panamax, Supramax and Handysize vessels, shown in panel C; three

TABLE 8.16 SGX AsiaClear cleared hybrid forwards

Routes	Sector	Route description	Cargo size (mt)
Panel A: Tanker forwards			
TD3	VLCC	Middle Eastern Gulf to Japan	260,000
TC4	MR	Singapore to Japan	30,000
TC5	LR 1	Middle Eastern Gulf to Japan	55,000
Panel B: Dry voyage forwards			
C3	Capesize	Tubarao/Beilun and Baoshan	150,000
C4	Capesize	Richard Bay/Rotterdam	150,000
C5	Capesize	West Australia/Beilun-Baoshan	150,000
C7	Capesize	Bolivar/Rotterdam	150,000
Panel C: Dry time-charter basket forwards			
CTC	Capesize	Capesize T/C routes average	–
PTC	Panamax	Panamax T/C routes average	–
STC	Supramax	Supramax T/C routes average	
HTC	Handysize	Handysize T/C routes average	–
Half-day CTC	Capesize	Capesize T/C routes average	–
Half-day PTC	Panamax	Panamax T/C routes average	–
Half-day STC	Supramax	Supramax T/C routes average	–
Half-day HTC	Handysize	Handysize T/C routes average	–
Panel D: Dry trip time-charter forwards			
P2A	Panamax	Skaw to Gibraltar/Far East	–
P3A	Panamax	Transpacific round to Japan	–

Source: SGX AsiaClear.
Note: A full-day contract refers to 1 day, while a half-day contract refers to 1/2 day = 1 lot.

dry-trip time-charter FFAs on Panamax time-charter P1A, P2A and P3A routes, shown in panel D; one dry time-charter voyage FFA on Supramax S7 route, shown in panel E; and a contract written on BDI, shown in panel F of the table.

In May 2006, SGX launched SGX AsiaClear, its OTC clearing facility for energy and freight derivatives. Clearing for the SGX AsiaClear facility is supported by Singapore Exchange Derivatives Clearing Limited. Table 8.16 presents the FFA contracts cleared on SGX AsiaClear. They include three tanker FFAs written on the *dirty* TD3 route and the *clean* TC4 and TC5 routes, presented in panel A of the table; four dry voyage FFAs written on Capesize voyage routes C3, C4, C5 and C7, presented in panel B of the table; four full-day and four half-day dry-bulk time-charter baskets on Capesize, Panamax and Supramax vessels (launched on November 2007) and on Handysize vessels (launched on June 2009), shown in panel C of the table; and two dry-trip time-charter FFAs written on Panamax time-charter P2A and P3A routes, shown in panel D of the table. These hybrid FFAs seem to combine the best of futures and forwards into one contract. That is, counterparty risk is removed and yet they retain their flexibility in terms of adjusting their terms according to the needs of the counterparties.[9]

[9]It should be noted that, at the time of writing, according to market sources more than 95% of FFA trades are cleared in one of the available clearing-houses for freight derivatives.

TABLE 8.17 CME Group tanker freight options

Baltic routes	Coding	Sector	Route description	Cargo size (mt)	Type of contract	Settlement index
TD3	TDT	VLCC	Middle Eastern Gulf to Japan	260,000	Options	Baltic
TC2	TCW	MR	Europe to USAC	37,000	Options	Baltic
TC5	TCF	LR 1	Ras Tanura to Yokohama	55,000	Options	Platts
TC12	FRS		Sikka (West Coast India) to Chiba	35,000	Options	Baltic

Source: CME Group.

TABLE 8.18 LCH.Clearnet dry-bulk freight options

Routes	Sector	Route description
CTO	Capesize	T/C average
PTO	Panamax	T/C average
STO	Supramax	T/C average
HTO	Handysize	T/C average

Source: LCH.Clearnet.

8.3.3.4 Freight Options Freight options contracts are available either in OTC or in organized exchanges on individual routes of the dry-bulk and tanker indices, as well as on baskets of time-charter routes. These options are Asian-type puts (floors) or calls (caps), as they settle on the difference between the average spot rate over a defined period of time and an agreed strikeprice.[10] A ship owner anticipating falling freight rates will buy a put option, agreeing thus to sell his freight service in the future at a strike or exercise price agreed today. He would exercise the option to sell at the agreed price if the market freight rate falls below the agreed price, otherwise he will let the option expire worthless and vice-versa for the charterer. Both the charterer and the ship owner would pay a premium to purchase these options. The downside cost is known in advance and is equal to the option's premium. The upside potential in a call option is unlimited, just as in the case of FFAs and freight futures.

The CME Group offers one *dirty* tanker freight option on route TD3 and three *clean* tanker freight options on routes TC2, TC5 and TC12, as shown in Table 8.17. Tanker freight options are settled against the Baltic Exchange quotes, with the exception of route TC5, where a Platts assessment is used.

During February 2008, LCH.Clearnet launched its dry freight options clearing service, by offering time-charter basket contracts on Capesize, Panamax, Supramax and Handysize vessels. Table 8.18 presents the three option contracts at LCH.Clearnet. The dry-bulk options

[10]An Asian option is an option that is exercised against an average over a period of time. Asian options are often used in thinly traded, volatile commodity markets to avoid problems with price manipulation of the underlying commodity near or at maturity.

TABLE 8.19 Baltex freight derivatives

Routes	Sector	Route description
Panel A: Dry-bulk voyage		
C3	Capesize	Tubarao to Qingdao
C4	Capesize	Richards Bay to Rotterdam
C5	Capesize	West Australia to Qingdao
C7	Capesize	Bolivar Roads to Rotterdam
Panel B: Dry-trip time-charter		
P1A (P1E)	Panamax	Transatlantic round voyage
P2A	Panamax	Skaw/Gibraltar to Far East
P3A	Panamax	Japan-SK/Pacific round voyage
C8	Capesize	Gibraltar/Hamburg transatlantic round voyage
C9	Capesize	Continent/Mediterranean trip to Far East
S7	Supramax	East Coast India to China
Panel C: Dry-bulk time-charter average baskets		
–	Capesize	4T/C time charter
–	Panamax	4T/C time charter
–	Supramax	6T/C time charter
–	Handysize	6T/C time charter

Source: Baltic Exchange.
Note: P1E refers to the mean of the daily Baltic Exchange spot price assessments in the expiry month.

at LCH.Clearnet are European style and are exercised automatically on the expiry day if they are 'in-the-money'. They are cash-settled and are measured in US$/day (1 lot = 1 day).

8.3.3.5 Freight Derivatives Trading Screens One of the latest developments in the market is the establishment of online trading screens for freight derivatives contracts. Such examples are the Baltic Exchange trading screen (The Baltex) in London and the Cleartrade Exchange (CLTX) in Singapore, both launched in June 2011. Baltex is a multilateral trading facility (MTF) for dry-bulk freight derivatives, created by the Baltic Exchange and approved and regulated by the UK's Financial Service Authorities (FSA) and the Swiss financial authority (FINMA). A change in derivatives regulation, as well as an increase in liquidity and transparency, brought about the need to create such solutions. Baltex has been developed to be used by both traders and brokers. Traders can nominate brokers on individual trades, or set up a default broker and allow their broker to input prices on their behalf, or work prices nominated to them. The Baltex facilitates a straight-through-clearing (STC) process at LCH.Clearnet and NOS Clearing.

Table 8.19 presents the instruments that trade on Baltex, which constitute individual routes, time-charter baskets, spreads, combos and options. More specifically, Capesize routes C3, C4, C5 and C7; time-charter trip forward routes C8, C9, P1A, P2A, P3A and S7; and Capesize 4T/C, Panamax 4T/C, Supramax 6T/C and Handysize 6T/C time-charter average baskets are shown in panels A to C, respectively.

The CLTX offers an execution venue for OTC cleared freight derivatives. It is regulated by the Monetary Authority of Singapore (MAS) and operates as a recognized market operator

TABLE 8.20 Cleartrade Exchange freight derivatives

Routes	Sector	Route description
Panel A: Dry-bulk voyage		
C3E	Capesize	Tubarao to Qingdao
C4E	Capesize	Richards Bay to Rotterdam
C5E	Capesize	West Australia to Qingdao
C7E	Capesize	Bolivar Roads to Rotterdam
Panel B: Dry-trip time-charter		
P1A (P1E)	Panamax	Transatlantic round voyage
P2A (P2E)	Panamax	Skaw/Gibraltar to Far East
P3A (P3E)	Panamax	Japan-SK/Pacific round voyage
S7	Supramax	East Coast India to China
Panel C: Dry-bulk time-charter average baskets		
CTC	Capesize	T/C time charter
PTC	Panamax	T/C time charter
STC	Supramax	T/C time charter
HTC	Handysize	T/C time charter
Panel D: SCFI container routes		
CNW (US$/TEU)	–	Shanghai to North West Europe
CMD (US$/TEU)	–	Shanghai to Mediterranean
CSW (US$/FEU)	–	Shanghai to US West Coast
CSD (US$/FEU)	–	Shanghai to US East Coast
Panel E: WCI container routes (US$/FEU)		
CSL	–	Shanghai to Los Angeles
CSN	–	Shanghai to New York
CSR	–	Shanghai to Rotterdam
CSG	–	Shanghai to Genoa
CLS	–	Los Angeles to Shanghai
CRS	–	Rotterdam to Shanghai
CGS	–	Genoa to Shanghai
CNR	–	New York to Rotterdam
CRN	–	Rotterdam to New York
CLR	–	Los Angeles to Rotterdam
CRL	–	Rotterdam to Los Angeles

Source: Cleartrade Exchange.
Notes: P1A, P2A, P3A refer to the mean of the last seven Baltic Exchange spot price assessments in the expiry month.
P1E, P2E, P3E refer to the mean of the daily Baltic Exchange spot price assessments for every trading day in the expiry month.
C3E, C4E, C5E, C7E refer to the mean of the daily Baltic Exchange spot price assessments for every trading day in the expiry month.

(RMO). CLTX works on a membership basis and is open to participation from inter-dealer brokers, traders/principals and general clearers. Table 8.20 presents the available dry-bulk derivatives (panels A to C), which can be cleared on LCH.Clearnet and NOS Clearing; the container derivatives on SCFI (panel D), which can be cleared on LCH.Clearnet; and the container derivatives on WCI (panel E).

TABLE 8.21 The two possible outcomes of an FFA time-charter hedge

April	
Physical market	FFA market
Freight rate of route P2A: $77,500/day	FFA December price: $77,500/day
Freight income/cost: $3,487,500 (= $77,500/day × 45 days)	Value of FFA: $3,487,500 (= $77,500/day × 45 days)
First scenario: Freight rates increase	Second scenario: Freight rates decrease
June: Physical market	
Freight rate: $298,500/day	Freight rate: $70,500/day
Freight income: $4,432,500 (= $98,500/day × 45 days)	Freight income: $3,487,500 (= $70,500/day × 45 days)
The ship owner (charterer) gains (loses) $945,000 (= $4,432,500 – $3,487,500)	The ship owner (charterer) loses (gains) $315,000 (= $3,172,500 – $3,487,500)
June: FFA market	
FFA February price: $99,500/day	FFA February price: $69,500/day
Value of FFA: $4,477,500 (= $99,500/day × 45 days)	Value of FFA: $3,127,500 (= $69,500/day × 45 days)
The ship owner (charterer) loses (gains) $990,000 (= $3,487,500 – $4,477,500)	The ship owner (charterer) gains (loses) $360,000 (= $3,487,500 – $3,127,500)
Portfolio of spot and FFA positions	
Net loss (profit) for ship owner (charterer): $45,000 (= $945,000 – $990,000)	Net profit (loss) for ship owner (charterer): $45,000 (= $360,000 –$315,000)
Brokerage fees: $8719 (= 0.25% × $3,487,500)	

8.3.4 Examples of Freight Derivatives Trading

This section presents examples of how FFAs and freight options contracts may be used in practice to hedge freight rate risk.

8.3.4.1 FFA Time-Charter Trade Suppose, in April, a ship owner sees FFA rates at higher levels than initially anticipated. As he will have a vessel available for fixture at the end of June, the owner wants to lock into a bid of $77,500/day in the FFA market for a Skaw/Gibraltar to Far East time charter (BPI Route P2A) for 45 days. His physical exposure is $3,487,500 (= $77,500/day × 45 days). On the other side of the transaction, there might be a charterer who aims to manage his risk of rising freight rates. Table 8.21 presents the two possible outcomes, two months later, in June.

Under the first scenario, presented in the first column of the table, freight rates increase against the ship owner's expectations to $98,500/day. In this case, the ship owner gains $945,000 (= $4,432,500 – $3,487,500) in the physical time-charter market, while in the FFA market he realizes a loss of $990,000 (= $3,487,500 – $4,477,500). From the other side, the charterer loses $945,000 in the physical time-charter market, while in the FFA market he realizes a gain of $990,000. Thus, the net loss of this portfolio for the ship owner is $45,000 (= $945,000 – $990,000), which is equal to the profit of the charterer.

Brokerage fees of $8719 (= $3,487,500 × 0.25%) are paid by both parties to the broker. Thus, when FFA transactions costs are also taken into account, the ship owner's loss becomes $53,719 (= $45,000 + $8719), while the charterer's gain is reduced to $36,281 (= $45,000 – $8719).

Under the second scenario, shown in the second column of the same table, the ship owner's expectations are correct; that is, freight rates fall to $70,500/day. In this case, the ship owner (charterer) loses (gains) $315,000 (= $3,172,500 – $3,487,500) in the spot market, while in the FFA market he realizes a gain (loss) of $360,000 (= $3,487,500 – $3,127,500). From the other side, the charterer gains $315,000 in the spot market, while in the FFA market he realizes a loss of $360,000. Thus, the net profit of this portfolio position, of spot and FFA trades, for the ship owner is $45,000 (= $360,000 – $315,000), which is equal to the loss of the charterer. When FFA transactions costs are also taken into account, the ship owner's gain is reduced to $36,281 (= $45,000 – $8719), while the charterer's loss is increased to $53,719 (= $45,000 + $8719).

If the ship owner had not decided to execute this FFA trade, he would have lost $315,000. Instead, not only did he manage to cover the losses from the physical market, but he also ended up making a gain of $36,281 from the overall portfolio position after transactions costs. From the charterer's point of view, who decided to hedge in the FFA market against possible freight rate increases, his expectations did not materialize, yielding a loss in the combined portfolio position of $53,719. However, by covering these losses from the gains in the physical market, he managed through the FFA trade to stabilize his costs at more or less today's levels.

8.3.4.2 Freight Options Trade Suppose that during February a ship owner knows that he will have a Capesize vessel of 150,000 dwt open for fixture in late June on route C4 of the BCI (Richards Bay to Rotterdam). He is likely to transport 140,000 mt of coal to receivers in Rotterdam. The current freight rate is $33.5/ton. If the ship owner is able to charter his vessel immediately, his freight income would be $4,690,000 (= $33.5/ton × 140,000 mt). However, as the actual fixture will take place during June, he decides to hedge freight rate risk by buying a June put option for route C4.

His broker advises him that there is a suitable counterparty (such as a bank or financial institution) willing to *write* him a June put option with a strike price of $40.0/ton at a premium of 70 cents/ton. Therefore, the total premium that the ship owner will pay to the seller of the put is $98,000 (= $0.70/ton × 140,000 mt). Table 8.22 presents the outcomes of the hedge under two market scenarios.

Under the first scenario, suppose that freight rates increase to $42.6/ton at the end of June. The ship owner experiences gains in the spot market of $1,274,000 (= $5,964,000 – $4,690,000). Since the spot price ($42.6/ton) is higher than the strike price ($40.0/ton), the put option is not exercised. A loss of $98,000 results in the paper market, which is equivalent to the option's premium. Thus, the overall portfolio position of the ship owner yields a freight income of $5,866,000 (= $5,964,000 – $98,000).

Under the second scenario, suppose that freight rates decrease to $32.5/ton. As a consequence, the ship owner experiences a loss in the spot market of $140,000 (= $4,550,000 – $4,690,000). Because the spot price ($32.5/ton) is lower than the strike price ($40.0/ton), the put option is exercised giving a payoff of $952,000 [= ($40.0/ton – $32.5/ton) × 140,000 mt – $98,000].

Combining the freight income of $4,550,000 received in the physical market with the profit of $952,000 made in the options market results in an overall portfolio position for the

TABLE 8.22 Ship owner's freight options hedge

4-Month hedge using options	
Physical market	Options market
February	
Freight rate: \$33.5/ton Cargo size: 140,000 mt Freight income: \$4,690,000 (= \$33.5/ton × 140,000 mt)	Action: Buy June put option Put strike price: \$40.0/ton Premium: 70 cents/ton
Ship owner buys June put at a total cost of \$98,000 (= 0.7/ton × 140,000 mt)	
30 June: Rising market	
Freight rate: \$42.6/ton Freight income: \$5,964,000 (= \$42.6/ton × 140,000 mt) Gain in the physical market: \$1,274,000 (= \$4,690,000 – \$5,964,000)	Spot price (\$42.6/ton) > strike price (\$40.0/ton) Action: Put option is not exercised Payoff from option: \$98,000 (premium)
Total freight income (including option premium): \$5,964,000 – \$98,000 = \$5,866,000	
30 June – alternative scenario: Falling market	
Freight rate: \$32.5/ton Freight income: \$4,550,000 (= \$32.5/ton × 140,000 mt) Loss in the physical market: \$140,000 (= \$4,690,000 – \$4,550,000)	Spot price (\$32.5/ton) < strike price (\$40.0/ton) Action: Exercise the put option Payoff from option: \$952,000 [= (\$40.0/ton – \$32.5/ton) × 140,000 mt – \$98,000]
Total freight income (including option premium): \$4,550,000 + \$952,000 = \$5,502,000	

ship owner of \$5,502,000. As can be seen from these payoffs, if the freight market moves against the ship owner, the purchased put option reduces his losses in the physical market by a substantial amount. If the freight market remains firm, the put option is not exercised and his cash-flow is simply reduced by the option's premium.

8.4 PRICING, HEDGING AND FREIGHT RATE RISK MEASUREMENT

8.4.1 Pricing and Hedging Effectiveness of Freight Derivatives

8.4.1.1 Pricing of FFAs As argued in Kavussanos and Visvikis (2006a, 2008), a special feature of the freight derivatives market is that the underlying commodity is a service, which cannot be stored. Working (1960), amongst others, developed the theory governing the relationship between spot and derivatives prices of continuously storable commodities, while Eydeland and Geman (1998), Geman and Vasicek (2001) and Bessembinder and Lemmon (2002) developed the theory of non-storable commodities, by examining the electricity derivatives markets. The non-storable nature of the FFA market implies that spot and FFA prices are not linked by a cost-of-carry (storage) relationship, as in financial and agricultural derivatives markets. Thus, derivatives prices on freight rates are driven by the expectations of market agents regarding the spot prices that will prevail at the expiry of the derivative contract.

For a storable commodity, it is argued that the price of a forward contract, written on the commodity, must be equal to the spot price of the commodity today plus the financial and other costs (e.g., storage and insurance) to carry it forward in time:

$$F_{t,T} = S_t + C_{T-t} \tag{8.1}$$

where $F_{t,T}$ is the price of a forward contract at time t, maturing at time period T; S_t is the spot price of the underlying commodity in period t; and C_{T-t} are the costs of carrying the commodity forward in time between period t and T. If the forward price is overpriced (underpriced) then arbitrageurs can simultaneously sell (buy) the forward contract, buy (sell) the underlying commodity and store it until the expiry of the contract. At expiry, reversing these positions will produce a risk-free profit. However, in practice this equality may break for a number of market factors, such as the existence of regional supply and demand imbalances, regulatory changes, market microstructure effects, market distortions created by market participants with large positions, etc. Such a situation would thus create arbitrage opportunities for market participants.

Kavussanos and Visvikis (2004, 2006a) point out that freight services, as the underlying commodity of freight derivatives, are not storable. This violates the usual arbitrage arguments, presented above, that led to the pricing of derivatives contracts in storable commodities. In fact, it is shown that in this case, the pricing of FFA and freight futures contracts takes the following form:

$$F_{t,T} = E(S_T) + u_t;\, u_t \sim \text{i.i.d.}(0, \sigma^2) \tag{8.2}$$

where $F_{t,T}$ is the FFA price formed at period t for settlement at period T, $E(S_T)$ denotes the expected value of the spot (underlying) freight asset at the settlement date and u_t is an independent and identically distributed stochastic error term with a mean value of zero and variance σ^2.

Kavussanos and Visvikis (2004) show that the FFA market satisfies its price discovery function. That is, forward prices today can help discover spot prices at the expiry of the FFA contract. Thus, the identification of riskless arbitrage opportunities in non-storable commodities, and therefore market efficiency, becomes a research issue.

8.4.1.2 Hedging Effectiveness of FFAs Financial derivatives have been introduced in order to provide instruments for businesses to reduce or control the unwanted market risk of price changes, by transferring it to others more willing to bear it. This function of derivatives markets is performed through hedging the spot (physical) position by holding an opposite position in the derivatives (paper) market. An important issue, in this process of hedging risks, is the calculation of the correct number (the hedge ratio) of forward contracts to use for each cash position held.

Kavussanos and Visvikis (2010) answer this issue for principals wishing to engage in freight rate risk management in the Capesize sector, through the use of the FFA markets on Capesize route C4 (Richards Bay to Rotterdam) and on the Capesize average time-charter basket (CTC). This is achieved by estimating different models that produce both constant and time-varying hedge ratios and comparing the hedging outcomes, so as to select the model which takes into account the properties of both spot and FFA prices. The hedging effectiveness of dynamic (time-varying) hedge ratios is compared and contrasted both in-sample and out-of-sample with that of constant hedge ratios. The selection criterion for the optimum model to use is the variance (risk)-reduction statistic, which compares the variance of the hedged portfolio from each model with that of the unhedged position.

Results for in-sample hedging effectiveness indicate that both in route C4 and in the CTC basket time-varying hedge ratios perform better, in terms of increasing hedging effectiveness, in comparison with constant hedge ratio models. These results reveal that the arrival of new information affects the relationship between spot and FFA prices, and therefore, time-varying hedging models display better performance. In contrast, the results for out-of-sample hedging effectiveness indicate that both in route C4 and in the CTC basket naïve hedge ratios (taking an FFA position with the same size as the spot position – i.e., setting the hedge ratio equal to 1) produce the highest variance reductions. This result validates the practice of using positions in the FFA markets, which are equal in magnitude with the underlying freight rate exposures.

Overall, the results reveal that shipping companies with Capesize vessels operating worldwide and trading companies that transport commodities to different parts of the world can use the FFA contracts effectively to reduce their freight rate risk, since the variability of their cash-flows can be explained significantly by the fluctuations of the FFA rates.

8.4.2 Value-at-Risk (VaR) in Freight Markets

8.4.2.1 Introduction to VaR Shipping is a particularly risky industry with its prices being significantly volatile. To this end, economic agents active in shipping cannot afford to ignore the financial risks associated with their activities. The management of these risks should be an integral part of the economic decision process of shipping market participants. This is because, through the practice of risk management, market agents can reduce uncertainty in their economic activities and optimize investment decisions by setting limits, mitigating losses through diversification and optimizing the timing of their investments. Additionally, companies may increase the shareholders' wealth by reducing the volatility in their cash-flows; this aids the better allocation of resources and reduces the probability of default. Consequently, with the use of risk management, corporate threats such as catastrophic losses, misallocation and under-utilization of resources can be minimized. A fundamental step towards the management of risks is the measurement of risk.

Although risk management offers many tools for expressing the downside risk[11] due to adverse market movements, during the last decade the evolutions in the risk management landscape have led to the development and establishment of a representative and informative measure of market risk – that is, the VaR framework. VaR is a simple and intelligible summary statistic that quantifies the downside risk exposure of an asset or portfolio to market factors. VaR expresses the maximum expected loss over a given time horizon, under normal market conditions, attributable to changes in the market price of the financial instruments.

More specifically, VaR is the loss corresponding to the $(100 - X)$th percentile of the distribution of the change in value of the portfolio over the next N days. VaR is therefore a technique for measuring the market risk of a particular position or portfolio of instruments, such as cash instruments, derivative instruments and borrowing and lending. By VaR analysis,

[11]Such tools include the variance, which expresses the deviations of outcomes over a mean, the semi-variance, which measures the variability of returns below the mean and the expected absolute deviation.

financial institutions, corporate treasurers, fund/portfolio managers and companies have a rigorous and straightforward-to-understand method for quantifying and reporting their risk.

Currently, the methodology of VaR is adopted by most financial institutions, investment and commercial banks, institutional investors and regulators. In 1995, the Basel Committee on Banking Supervision and in 1996, the Capital Adequacy Directive (CAD) of the European Union allowed banks to use their internal VaR models to calculate their capital requirements for market risk. Basel II still promotes the use of VaR models and extends their use in calculating capital reserve requirements.

It is worth noticing that the risk metric of VaR is not limited to the estimation of risk but is interrelated tightly with other layers of the risk management process, such as those of risk reporting, limit setting, performance evaluation and risk budgeting. Thus, VaR can become a valuable tool for controlling and managing market risk.

8.4.2.2 Calculation of VaR The methodologies for calculating VaR can be grouped into two broad categories: parametric and non-parametric methodologies. Parametric methods make a parametric assumption regarding the evolution of risk factors, such as normally distributed or Student's *t*-distributed risk factors, whereas non-parametric methods are free from parametric assumptions. Most parametric VaR models make inferences about the projected losses by imposing the assumption that risk factors belong to a location scale distribution – that is, distributions which are defined completely by their first two moments. Under this framework VaR is defined by

$$\text{VaR}_{t+1}^{1-a} = \hat{\mu}_{t+1} - \Phi^{-1}(a) \cdot \hat{\sigma}_{t+1} \cdot \sqrt{T} \tag{8.3}$$

where Φ^{-1} denotes the standardized quantile of the assumed distribution, $\hat{\mu}_{t+1}$, $\hat{\sigma}_{t+1}$ are the estimated/forecasted location and scale parameters, respectively and T is the investment horizon. Thus, under the parametric umbrella of VaR modelling, the estimation of VaR reduces to choosing a proper distribution for the projected risk factors or returns and estimating the moment parameters.

Figure 8.4 illustrates graphically the parametric 99% VaR estimate of a portfolio whose profit/loss probability distribution function follows a standard normal distribution.[12] Assuming that one currency unit is invested in this portfolio (i.e., 1 dollar), the 99% VaR of the portfolio equals 2.33 dollars; that is, the probability mass left to the vertical line of 99% VaR is equal to 1%.

8.4.2.3 Examples of Parametric Estimation of VaR in Shipping The systematic measurement of risk in the shipping industry was introduced by Kavussanos and Dimitrakopoulos (2007a,b, 2011), who analysed thoroughly the most appropriate models of risk measurement in the various segments of the dry-bulk and tanker subsectors of ocean shipping. Other studies in the literature considering the issue of risk measurement, in a less systematic manner, include Angelidis and Skiadopoulos (2008) and Tsolakis (2005). Here we provide examples of the use of VaR to measure freight rate risk for single vessels and for more than one vessel under ownership or management.

[12]The standard normal distribution has unit variance and zero mean, thus according to equation (8.3) the 99% VaR equals the first percentile of the standard normal distribution, which is equal to 2.33.

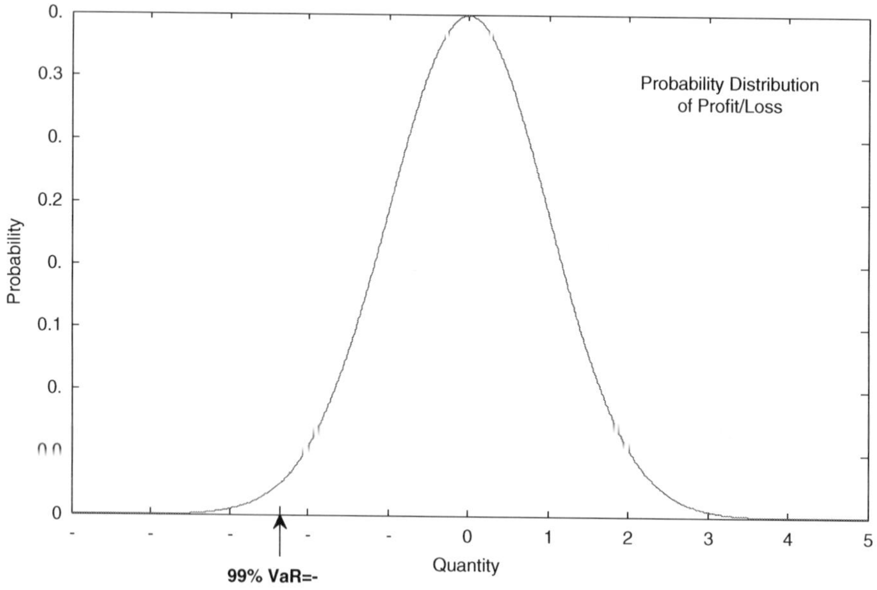

FIGURE 8.4 Parametrically specified 1-day-ahead 99% VaR of a standard normally distributed portfolio.

Case 1. VaR Estimation for a Freight Exposure Reciprocating from the Ownership of a Single Vessel A simple method for the estimation of VaR is the random walk method, which assumes that the sample period's volatility estimate (σ) is the best proxy of next period's volatility ($\hat{\sigma}_{t+1}$). That is,

$$\hat{\sigma}_{t+1} = \sigma \tag{8.4}$$

Normality of the distribution of returns is assumed, and hence σ is obtained from

$$\sigma = \sqrt{\frac{1}{T-1} \sum_{t=1}^{T} (r_t - \bar{r})^2} \tag{8.5}$$

where r_t is the return on the asset at time t, $\bar{r}$ is the sample mean return and N is the number of observations in the sample.

To see how this works, consider the following example. Assume that on 24 December a ship owner finds a spot fixture on his Capesize vessel operating on route C3 (Tubarao to Baoshan) at 8.85 \$/ton. Thus, his initial exposure is \$1,327,500 (= 150,000 mt × 8.85 \$/ton). At the same time, he is interested in estimating a threshold for the possible decline in his revenues after 15 days, when the fixture will terminate, and a new fixture will be negotiated, say on 8 January at the prevailing freight rate. For this purpose, he decides to estimate VaR, in order to obtain an estimate for the potential decline in his revenues. As the previous year was particularly lucrative and the ship-owner has a high tolerance towards risk, he decides to estimate a relatively high threshold corresponding to a 99% VaR.

Assuming that the date 24 December corresponds to time t and that the time point on 8 January corresponds to time $t+T$, where T is the journey time, according to the random walk VaR method the 99% VaR on 8 January, estimated on 24 December, is obtained as follows. First, a historical sample of the most recent 50 freight rate changes (i.e., $r_t, r_{t-1}, \dots, r_{t-49}$) is used to estimate the standard deviation. This is then plugged into equation (8.3) in order to obtain the VaR. For instance, assume that the standard deviation forecast obtained from the equation equals 1.4%. Then the 99% VaR for the Capesize vessel is:

$$\text{VaR}_{t+15}^{0.99} = \Phi_{0.01}^{-1} \cdot \hat{\sigma}_{t+1}\sqrt{T} = -2.33 \times 0.014 \times 150{,}000\sqrt{15} = \$19{,}271.55$$

That is, the maximum potential decline in revenues that shall not be exceeded 99% of the time is \$19,271.55. This does not represent a substantial decline in the income of the owner; he is likely not to use derivatives for hedging purposes.

However, assume that, according to the ship owner's calculations, such a decline is not sustainable, as he could not cover the operating costs or the debt undertaken for the funding of the purchase of the vessel and the ship owner anticipates a large decline in freight rates in the near future. In order to avoid such distressing circumstances the ship owner may resort to the shipping derivative markets to hedge in full or partially the exposure. For instance, the ship owner could sell dry voyage forward contracts on route C3 or buy put options. Additionally, the VaR could be used as a criterion for the selection of the routes to operate vessels that fit the risk profile of the ship owner best. For example, if the employed vessel can be used for the transfer of commodities in different routes, the ship owner may estimate VaR on each of these routes and choose those which yield sustainable VaR with reasonable profit opportunities.

Case 2. VaR Estimation for a Freight Exposure Reciprocating from Vessel Portfolio Ownership In order to estimate VaR for a portfolio of vessels there are principally two approaches. The first involves using covariances (as the standard deviation alone does not take into account the correlations and the possible diversification effects) and employing freight rate changes with frequency equal to the duration of the corresponding trip. The second approach involves combining the freight cash-flows reciprocating from the operation of the vessels to derive the net cash-flow and estimate VaR by applying the procedure illustrated in Case 1 on the net cash-flow series. According to the first approach, the VaR for a portfolio of vessels can be estimated from

$$\text{VaR}_{t+1}^{1-a} = W' \times \Sigma \times W * \Phi^{-1}(a) \times \text{position} \tag{8.6}$$

where W is a vector of weights consisting of the dwt of each vessel as a percentage of the total dwt of the fleet, W' is the transpose of W and Σ is the variance–covariance matrix of the series of freight price changes corresponding to the routes that each vessel is engaged in.

To illustrate, assume that the ship owner owns two Capesize vessels operating on routes C3 (Tubarao in Brazil to Baoshan in China) and C12 (Gladstone in Australia to Rotterdam in the Netherlands). Further, assume that on 6 February the ship owner agrees spot fixtures on the Capesize vessels operating on route C3 at 23.19 \$/ton and on route C12 at 14.45 \$/ton. Thus, his initial exposure is \$5,646,000 [= 150,000 mt × (23.19 \$/ton + 14.45 \$/ton)]. Then the 99% VaR when the fixture will terminate and a new fixture will be negotiated is obtained from

$$\begin{aligned}\mathrm{VaR}_{t+15}^{1-a} &= \sqrt{(\%\mathrm{dwt1} \quad \%\mathrm{dwt2}) \times \begin{pmatrix} \sigma_{11} & \sigma_{12} \\ \sigma_{21} & \sigma_{22} \end{pmatrix} \times \begin{pmatrix} \mathrm{dwt1} \\ \mathrm{dwt2} \end{pmatrix}} \times \Phi_{0.01}^{-1} \times 300{,}000 \\ &= \sqrt{(0.5 \quad 0.5) \times \begin{pmatrix} 0.0517 & 0.0243 \\ 0.0243 & 0.0255 \end{pmatrix} \times \begin{pmatrix} 0.5 \\ 0.5 \end{pmatrix}} \times -2.33 \times 300{,}000 \\ &= -\$21{,}966.6\end{aligned}$$

where σ_{11} and σ_{22} are the variances of freight rate changes of each of the vessels operating on routes C3 and C12, respectively; $\sigma_{12} = \sigma_{21}$ is the covariance between freight rate changes of the vessels operating on routes C3 and C12; and dwt1 and dwt2 are the weights (proportions) of each vessel employed on routes C3 and C12, respectively. Variance estimates are obtained from equation (8.5) and covariance estimates are obtained from

$$\sigma_{ij} = \sum_{t=1}^{T} (r_{it} - \bar{r}_i)(r_{jt} - \bar{r}_j)/T - 1 \tag{8.7}$$

where, i, j refer to vessels operating on routes C3 and C12, respectively. Note that when estimating VaR for many vessels, the frequency of the freight price changes of each series used corresponds to the duration of the trip that the corresponding vessel is engaged in. That is, for the vessel operating on route C3, 15-day freight price changes are used and for the vessel operating on C12, 12-day freight price changes are used. That is, the last observation of the sample of returns used for the estimation of VaR according to equation (8.6) is – for route C12 – the return for the period t until t–15 and – for route C3 – the return for the period t until t–12, where t corresponds to 6 February. The previous period's return observation for route C12 is the return for the period t–15 until t–30 and for route C3 the return for the period t–15 until t–27 and so on until a sample of 50 returns for each of the route series is obtained.

The above example could be extended to a multivariate setting, including many vessels in the portfolio. Specifically, VaR for a portfolio of n assets can be estimated as follows:

$$\mathrm{VaR}_{t+15}^{1-a} = \sqrt{(\%\mathrm{dwt1} \quad \%\mathrm{dwt2} \quad \ldots \quad \%\mathrm{dwt}n) \times \begin{pmatrix} \sigma_{11} & \cdots & \sigma_{1n} \\ \vdots & \ddots & \vdots \\ \sigma_{n1} & \cdots & \sigma_{nn} \end{pmatrix} \times \begin{pmatrix} \%\mathrm{dwt1} \\ \%\mathrm{dwt2} \\ \vdots \\ \%\mathrm{dwt}n \end{pmatrix}} \times \Phi_{0.01}^{-1} \times \mathrm{position} \tag{8.8}$$

According to the second approach, VaR is estimated from equation (8.3) but, instead of using freight price changes of each of the vessels employed, a single series of net cash-flows reciprocating from the payoff of the vessels employed is used, in order to obtain VaR according to equation (8.8). Beyond the uses of VaR illustrated in the first example, VaR can also be used to evaluate different investment plans. For instance, the VaR can be used to aid the choice between alternative vessel portfolios with the same expected return or evaluate the efficiency of different freight managers. Finally, investments can be allocated according to their VaR and expected returns.

8.4.3 Expected Shortfall (ES) in Freight Markets

During the past decades, VaR has proliferated in the financial industry as a market risk metric that has gained general acceptance and widespread adoption from market agents and regulators. Despite its acceptance, VaR has also received criticism. Specifically, it has been criticized heavily on two main fronts: first, for having limited informational content and second, for not being a coherent risk metric.

The limited information content of the VaR metric relates to the fact that it does not provide risk-taking agents with information regarding loss when the loss exceeds the VaR level. For example, assume that the estimated daily 99% VaR of a vessel portfolio is \$1.2m. Then, according to VaR, the risk-taking agent is 99% confident that the daily maximum loss will not exceed \$1.2m. However, VaR provides no information on the magnitude of the loss for the 1% probability that the loss will exceed the VaR.

The incoherency of the VaR metric relates to the work of Artzner *et al.* (1997), who put forth some desirable properties that risk metrics should have. Risk metrics which have these properties are known as coherent. VaR is not a coherent risk metric, as in some cases it fails to fulfil one of these properties known as the property of sub-additivity. The property of sub-additivity requires the risk measure of a portfolio to be equal to or less than the sum of the individual VaRs of the portfolio's assets. This property is violated when the profit and loss distribution is extremely fat tailed or when very low confidence levels are used for the estimation of VaR. In such cases the overall VaR of the portfolio may appear to be larger than the sum of individual assets' VaRs, creating in this way a delusive sense of security.

The ES risk metric[13] has been developed as a response to the above criticism of the VaR metric. The ES rectifies the aforementioned two problems associated with the risk metric of VaR, as ES constitutes a coherent risk metric that answers the question: 'if VaR is breached, then how much would we lose on average?' ES measures the expected value of the shortfall of portfolio returns, with respect to some benchmark, under the condition that a shortfall occurs. Analytically,

$$ES = E_t(r_t \,|r_t < Th_{t,a}) \tag{8.9}$$

where E is the expectations operator and $Th_{t,a}$ a threshold of interest. Possible choices for the specification of the threshold are the required rate of return for liabilities or the estimated VaR.

In the case where VaR is used for specifying the threshold, ES can be estimated analytically by taking the expectation of the respective VaR model conditional on a shortfall occurring. However, there is not always a closed-form solution for the estimation of ES. To make the estimation of ES possible, when there is no closed-form solution Dowd (2002) proposes an alternative procedure, which can be followed in order to estimate the ES. According to this procedure, the tail of the projected profit and loss distribution is sliced n times and a single VaR is estimated for each slice. ES is then calculated as the arithmetic average of the VaR of

[13]Different names have been given to the expected shortfall, such as conditional VaR, expected tail loss and tails conditional VaR, among others.

all slices. In order to increase the accuracy of ES estimation a large number of slices has to be used. An example of ES estimation is presented next.

8.4.3.1 An Example of ES Estimation Assume that the risk manager of Case 2 expects that due to adverse market conditions the estimated 99% VaR will be breached. Thus, the loss over the investment horizon of the exposure will exceed the –$21,966.6, leading to a shortfall in the estimation of market risk. By calculating the risk metric of ES the risk manager may have an estimate of the average of this shortfall. In other words, with ES the risk manager will have available an estimate of the expected loss if the loss exceeds the estimated VaR. In order to estimate ES the following procedure can be used:

(i) Slice the tail in n pieces of equal probability. Let n be 5000 then increments of 0.0002% have to be used to curtail the tail. The first slice is on 99%, the second on 99.0002%, the third on 99.0004% and the 5000th on 99.9998%.

(ii) Estimate VaR for each slice by following the procedure illustrated in Case 2. In place of the 99th percentile of the standard normal distribution, the relevant percentile of each slide is used. For example:

99% VaR (for the first slice): $21,966.6

99.0002% VaR (for the second slice): $21,967.3

...

99.9998% VaR (for the 5000th): $43,543.1

Thus, 5000 VaRs need to be estimated starting from a confidence level of 99% and ending at 99.9998%, with increments of 0.0002%.

iii. ES is estimated as the average of these 5000 VaRs. Taking the average of the 5000 estimated VaRs yields an ES of $25,163.9. Thus, the risk-taking agent expects that the average loss (if the loss exceeds the 99% VaR level) will be $25,163.9.

8.4.4 Empirical Evidence on Freight Derivatives

Relatively limited research has been conducted on freight derivatives in comparison with derivatives on other 'commodities', partially due to the unavailability of data until recently. The aim of this section is to present the previous published work in the area and not to analyse each paper exhaustively. For thorough surveys of the available empirical literature on freight derivative markets, see Kavussanos and Visvikis (2006b, 2008).

8.4.4.1 Market Surveys on the Use of FFAs Dinwoodie and Morris (2003) surveyed the attitudes of tanker ship owners and charterers towards freight hedging and their risk perceptions of FFAs. They argue that although FFAs are widely viewed as an important development, some respondents are unaware of their function and the majority had not used them. Many ship owners also fear that FFAs might expose their risk management policies to counterparties. Finally, most argue that improved 'technical' education is essential for widespread acceptance of FFAs.

Kavussanos *et al.* (2007) explored the importance of hedging by analysing the general attitudes and common perceptions of the use of shipping derivatives by Greek ship owners involved both in dry-bulk and tanker trades. The results indicate that: (i) risk management and shipping derivatives are at an early stage of development and understanding in the Greek shipping market; (ii) the traditional ways of thinking must be changed and replaced with modern risk management concepts; (iii) liquidity and credit (counterparty) risk are considered to be major obstacles in the use of shipping derivatives; (iv) they consider education to be of paramount importance; and (v) there seems to be a positive view of the future of shipping derivatives in Greece.

8.4.4.2 Price Discovery in FFA Markets Kavussanos *et al.* (2004a) examined the first aspect of the price discovery function[14] of the Panamax FFA market, namely if FFA contract prices are unbiased estimators of the spot prices of the underlying asset that will be realized at the expiration date of the contract. They report that FFA prices 1 and 2 months prior to maturity are unbiased predictors of the realized spot prices in all investigated routes. However, the efficiency of FFA prices 3 months prior to maturity gives mixed evidence, with some Panamax routes being unbiased estimators while others are biased estimators of the realized spot prices.

Kavussanos and Visvikis (2004) investigated the second dimension of the price discovery role of derivatives markets; that is, the lead–lag relationship between FFA and spot freight markets, both in terms of returns and volatilities. Return results indicate that there is a bidirectional causal relationship between spot and FFA prices in all routes, implying that FFA prices can be equally important sources of information as spot prices are. However, the results from causality tests suggest that causality from FFA to spot returns is stronger than in the other direction in most investigated Panamax routes. Moreover, the results of volatility spillovers indicate that on most routes FFA rates contribute to the volatility of the relevant spot rates. Overall the results indicate that market participants can have a better assessment of risk-management, ship-chartering and budget-planning decisions by utilizing the information available on the FFA market as a price discovery vehicle.

Alizadeh *et al.* (2007) examined if the implied forward 6-month time-charter rates in the dry-bulk freight market, which are derived through the difference between time charters with different maturities based on the term-structure model, are efficient and unbiased predictors of actual future time-charter rates. They report that implied forward rates are found to be unbiased predictors of future time-charter rates. However, despite the finding of unbiasedness, on average, chartering strategies based on technical analysis are able to generate economic profits.

Kavussanos *et al.* (2010) examined cross-market linkages and spillover effects between FFAs and futures contracts on the commodities transported by Panamax vessels. Results indicate that there are significant spillover effects between freight and commodity derivatives markets. These relationships run stronger from the commodity futures markets to FFA markets. Market participants can monitor changes in the futures markets of the commodities transported by Panamax vessels to enhance their decisions on FFA markets.

8.4.4.3 Hedging in FFA Markets Besides the aforementioned study of Kavussanos and Visvikis (2010), Samitas and Tsakalos (2010) investigated the significance of the use of financial derivatives in shipping firms and their impact on firm value. Results indicate that

[14] Price discovery refers to the use of one price series (e.g., derivatives returns) for determining (predicting) another price series (e.g., spot returns).

derivatives minimize the risk exposure of shipping firms and guarantee their growth. In another study, Prokopczuk (2011) considered the pricing and hedging of single-route dry-bulk freight futures contracts on the IMAREX market. Results show that the inclusion of a second stochastic factor significantly improves the pricing and hedging accuracy. Goulas and Skiadopoulos (2012), after examining if the IMAREX freight futures market is efficient over daily and weekly time horizons, concluded that IMAREX is not efficient over the shorter daily horizon. Finally, Tezuka *et al.* (2012) derived equilibrium spot price and forward curve formulae for shipping markets, allowing for non-storability. From the forward curve formula, the authors obtain forward hedge ratios that can explain the risk attitude of non-homogeneous market participants.

8.4.4.4 Forecasting Performance of FFAs Batchelor *et al.* (2007) tested the performance of several time-series models in predicting Panamax spot and FFA rates. The results indicate that FFA prices can enhance the forecasting performance of spot prices, as conditioning spot returns on lagged FFA returns generates more accurate forecasts of spot prices for all forecasting horizons (up to 20 days ahead). Thus, market participants can design more efficient investment trading strategies by selecting the appropriate time-series model for forecasting purposes.

8.4.4.5 The Impact of FFA Trading on Spot Market Volatility The issue of whether derivatives trading increases or reduces volatility in the spot market has been the subject of considerable empirical analysis. Kavussanos *et al.* (2004b) investigated the impact of FFA trading on spot Panamax market price volatility. The results suggest that FFA trading has reduced the spot price volatility of all investigated routes, had a decreasing impact on the asymmetry of volatility (market dynamics) and substantially improved the quality and speed of information flow. Thus, it appears that there has been an improvement in the way that news is transmitted into prices following the onset of FFA trading.

8.4.4.6 Microstructure Effects in FFA Markets Batchelor *et al.* (2005) examined if there is a positive relationship between expected volatility and bid–ask spreads in the FFA Panamax market as the greater the variability in price, the greater the risk associated with performance of the function of the brokers.[15] The results indicate that there is a positive relationship between bid–ask spreads and expected price volatility in most investigated Panamax routes. Market participants using information on the behaviour of bid–ask spreads can have a better insight into the timing of their FFA transactions and the future direction of the FFA market as a widening bid–ask spread corresponds to an anticipation of increased future volatility.

8.4.4.7 Measuring Freight Market Risk Kavussanos and Dimitrakopoulos (2007a,b, 2011) formalized a market risk measurement framework for the shipping business. Two alternative risk metrics were proposed: VaR and ES. They provide an evaluation assessment of alternative VaR and ES forecasting models for short- and medium-term freight risk exposures for the tanker sector. The comparative analysis of the alternative VaR and ES forecasting

[15] One significant transaction cost in derivatives trades is the bid–ask spread (= buy (bid) price – sell (ask) price).

models indicates that the GARCH and the historical or filtered historical simulation approaches perform best for forecasting short-term (daily) risk. On the contrary, the most reliable method for estimating long-term risk exposures is the empirically scaled historical simulation model.

Angelidis and Skiadopoulos (2008) applied several parametric and non-parametric VaR methods in the dry-bulk and wet-bulk sectors and argued that the simplest non-parametric methods can be used to measure freight market risk and that the freight rate risk is greater in the wet-bulk market. Lu *et al.* (2007), using index data from the dry-bulk market, found the generalized error distribution (GED) exponential E-GARCH-VaR model to be able to efficiently measure market risk.

8.4.4.8 Forward Freight Rate Dynamics Koekebakker and Adland (2004) investigated the forward freight rate dynamics by modelling them under a term-structure model. They transformed time-charter rates into average-based forward freight rates. They then assumed that there exists a continuous forward freight rate function that correctly prices the average-based forward freight rate contracts. Results indicate that the volatility of the forward curve is bumped, with volatility reaching a peak for freight rates with roughly 1 year to maturity. Moreover, correlations between different parts of the term structure are in general low and even negative.

Adland *et al* (2007) investigated the volatility structure of the forward freight rate function in the IMAREX tanker freight futures market. They report a volatility structure that is increasing over a horizon of several weeks and then sharply declining in the time to maturity of the contracts. It is suggested that this is a reflection of the expected short-term positive autocorrelation and long-run mean reversion of tanker spot freight rates.

8.4.4.9 Pricing Freight Options Koekebakker *et al.* (2007) proposed a mathematical framework for Asian freight options modelling, which is an extension of the framework put forward in Black (1976). It is argued that FFAs are lognormal prior to the settlement period, but this lognormality breaks down in the settlement period. They suggest an approximate dynamics structure in the settlement period for the FFA, leading to closed-form option pricing formulae for Asian call and put options written on the spot freight rate indices.

8.5 OTHER DERIVATIVES FOR THE SHIPPING INDUSTRY

8.5.1 Bunker Fuel Derivatives

Ship owners (when the vessel is under a voyage contract) and charterers (when the vessel is operated under a time-charter contract) are not only exposed to the risk of changes in freight rates, but are also affected by fluctuations in operational costs. These costs include fuel, manning, repairs and maintenance, stores and lubes, insurance, administration, broking commission, fuel costs, port charges, tugs, canal dues, etc. However, fuel costs represent around 50–60% of the total costs of running a vessel. The rest of the costs are fairly predictable as they rise in line with inflation. Thus, the bunker fuel price is the most important variable (due to its high volatility) to control on the cost side for risk management purposes as changes in this variable could have a significant impact on ship owners' cash-flows.

Figure 8.5 shows the historical fluctuations in price for IFO380cst bunker fuel in three major ports from January 2005 to December 2012. It can be observed than bunker prices move

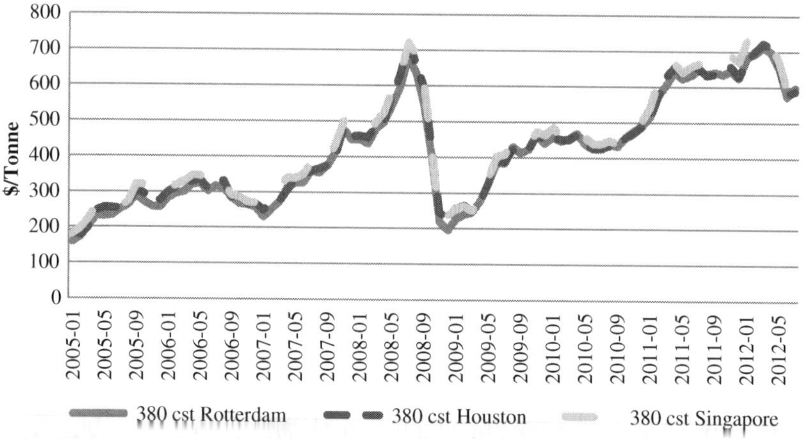

FIGURE 8.5 Bunker fuel IFO380 prices in three major ports (Jan 2005–Aug 2012)
Source: Clarkson's Research Studies.

together, indicating that they are driven by the world oil price. However, there are differences in price fluctuations between ports as local market conditions determine prices in each location.

Ship owners, vessel operators and charterers can use forward bunker agreements, bunker futures, bunker swaps and bunker options to manage bunker price risk. A forward bunker contract is an OTC agreement between a seller and a buyer to exchange a specified quantity of a certain quality of bunker, at an agreed price, at a certain delivery location and time in the future. Settlement is made on the difference between the forward price and the price of bunkers at the delivery point, although physical delivery is also possible. Since the contracts are OTC, each party accepts credit risk from the other party.

Since September 2006, SGX AsiaClear has cleared bunker fuel derivatives contracts on: Singapore fuel oil 180cst (3.5% sulphur), Singapore fuel oil 380cst (4.0% sulphur), balance-of-month Singapore fuel oil 180cst (3.5% sulphur) and Singapore fuel oil 380cst (4.0% sulphur). Balance-of-month fuel oil forwards are traded as individual day contracts in the current month. The final settlement price of these contracts is derived from the arithmetic average of Platts' daily spot assessment prices from the contract date till the last business day of the contract month. The contract size for bunker derivatives is 1000 mt, the minimum price fluctuation is US$0.01/mt and the position limits are set to 300 contracts. The regular-sized full-month Singapore fuel oil 180cst and Singapore fuel oil 380cst contracts are cash-settled using the arithmetic average of Platts' daily spot assessments in the contract month.

Alternatively, a bunker swap contract can be used whereby a floating price for bunkers is exchanged for a fixed price for bunkers, over a specified period, for a defined volume per period. There, the buyer exchanges a floating price for a fixed price. This is an OTC arrangement, which involves no transfer of the physical commodity but credit risk is an important issue. Swaps on bunkers are typically written against assessments of the spot bulk market supplying the relevant bunkering ports. The difference between the floating price (usually Platts' rates) and the fixed price is settled in cash. The net result, when combined with transactions in the physical market, is the outcome of hedging through the swap market.

Finally, OTC bunker Asian options can be used to hedge fuel oil risk. Asian options are popular within bunker hedging because the averaged settlement moderates short-term fluctuations and price spikes, common within the bunker market. Suppose a ship owner wants to protect himself against rising bunker prices and at the same time he wants the flexibility to buy bunkers at a lower price if they fall. He can buy a call option, at a premium, giving him the right to buy bunkers in the future at the fixed (exercise) price of the option. In contrast, bunker suppliers may want to protect themselves against a drop in bunker prices but also wish to retain the flexibility to capitalize on price increases. By buying a put option they secure the right to sell at a predetermined strike price.

8.5.2 Vessel Value Derivatives

Because vessels are the main asset which ship owners hold in order to provide their freight service to the market, and since the sums involved in holding these assets are the largest item in the ship owner's cash-flow, changes in their value can make all the difference to running a shipping company with a profit or loss.

The sale and purchase forward agreements (SPFAs) are OTC forwards contracts. These contracts are settled in cash against the Baltic sale and purchase assessments (BSPAs), which cover three dry-bulk (Capesize, Panamax, Super Handy) and three tanker (VLCC, Aframax, MR Product Tanker) model vessel types. All BSPA valuations are made on 5-year-old vessels and are based on professional assessments made by panellists assigned by the Baltic Exchange. BSPA prices are reported every week following the same procedures developed by the Baltic Exchange for the dry and tanker freight indices. SPFAs can be traded in multiples of lots, where one lot represents 5% of the vessel's value, with one vessel representing 20 lots of 5% each. Settlement of the SPFA contracts is against the 4-week average of the BSPA prices of the expiration month of the contract. However, according to market sources, the SPFA market, until the time of writing, remains illiquid with no trades at all.

8.5.3 Foreign Exchange Rate Derivatives Contracts

Another source of risk, which affects the ship owner's cash-flow, is the exchange rate risk. This emanates from fluctuations in the value of an asset or liability as a consequence of changes in exchange rates. In the shipping industry, because of its global nature, cash-flow transactions involve more than one currency somewhere. For example, payments to a Japanese yard for a new-build vessel are in yen but the reserves of the ship owner are in US$; the payment of a loan, for a vessel acquisition, may be issued in a different currency from the ship owner's reserves; management costs are typically paid in some domestic currency, whereas revenues are in US$. Thus, large fluctuations in exchange rates constitute a considerable source of risk for market agents operating in the shipping industry. In order to hedge foreign exchange rate risk, the following derivatives contracts may be used:

(i) Currency forwards are tailor-made contracts, with quantities and time to maturity matched to the needs of the company.
(ii) Currency futures are traded on exchanges and are highly liquid. They have the benefit of there being a secondary market, which allows for positions to be closed before the maturity date of the contract. They are standardized in terms of time to expiration and contract sizes.
(iii) Currency swaps offer companies the ability to borrow against long-term foreign currency exposures when direct access by the company to foreign debt markets is costly.

(iv) Currency options allow companies to hedge against currency movements in one direction while retaining exposure in the other. There are strategies with combinations of options that can cover many other situations.

8.5.4 Interest Rate Derivatives Contracts

Companies in the highly capital-intensive shipping industry can borrow from banks up to 80% of the value of a vessel or issue public or private debt (say in the form of bonds) in order to be able to finance their fleet investment plans. The cost of capital borrowed changes as interest rates in the world economy change. This, in turn, brings about fluctuations in the cash-flow positions of the shipping company. This interest rate risk relates to the management of liabilities for the shipping company. Interest rate derivatives, irrespective of whether they are exchange-traded (such as interest rate futures and options on underlying cash instruments like T-bonds, T-notes, T-bills or Eurodollars) or OTC traded (such as forward rate agreements – FRAs, interest rate swaps and options) involve the exchange of cash payments based on changes in market interest rates. Market participants in shipping may use interest rate derivatives to protect the value of their financial assets and to lock in favourable interest rates for the finance of their investments through loans and bonds.

8.6 CONCLUSION

This chapter has presented the various sources and ways of measuring and managing risks – including freight rate, bunker fuel price, vessel value, exchange rate and interest rate risks – for shipping companies with ocean-going vessels. Following an exposition of the market segmentation of shipping markets, their empirical characteristics investigated in the literature are presented. They point to there being significant opportunities of risk reduction by investments in different vessel sizes and types and by choosing to operate vessels in several types of freight contracts. However, the traditional strategies for risk management presented here can be costly and have been argued to be less flexible and less efficient compared with using derivatives for risk management purposes.

Following a presentation of the underlying to freight derivative contracts – freight rate indices constructed by the Baltic Exchange – the various freight derivatives contracts have been presented. They include both exchange-traded and OTC futures, forwards and options contracts, with settlement mainly on values of the Baltic indices. Examples are provided on how they can be used in practice for risk management purposes. A decision tool for using freight derivatives constitutes the VaR class of models. Their use in shipping freight markets is illustrated. Section 8.5 is devoted to a literature review and an outline of the empirical regularities revealed through a number of research papers. Of course, there are many more issues that remain unexplored and it is hoped that this chapter can help researchers focus on the relevant issues for further work in this area. Moreover, given the practical illustrations, it should also be of value to practitioners dealing with shipping markets.

ACKNOWLEDGEMENTS

The present chapter draws from the book *Derivatives and Risk Management in Shipping* by Kavussanos and Visvikis (2006a).

REFERENCES

Adland, R., Koekebakker, S. and Sodal, S. (2007) Forward curve dynamics in the tanker futures market, Proceedings of the International Association of Maritime Economists (IAME) Conference, Athens, Greece, 4–6 July 2007.

Alizadeh, A.H., Adland, R. and Koekebakker, S. (2007) Predictive power and unbiasedness of implied forward charter rates, *Journal of Forecasting*, 26(6), 385–403.

Angelidis, T. and Skiadopoulos, G. (2008) Measuring the market risk of freight rates: A value-at-risk approach, *International Journal of Theoretical and Empirical Finance*, 11(5), 447–469.

Artzner, P., Delbaen, F., Eber, J.M. and Heath, D. (1997) Thinking coherently, *Risk*, 10, 68–71.

Batchelor, R., Alizadeh, A.H. and Visvikis, I.D. (2005) The relation between bid–ask spreads and price volatility in forward markets, *Journal of Derivatives & Hedge Funds (formerly Derivatives Use, Trading & Regulation)*, 11(2), 105–125.

Batchelor, R., Alizadeh, A.H. and Visvikis, I.D. (2007) Forecasting spot and forward prices in the international freight market, *International Journal of Forecasting*, 23, 101–114.

Bessembinder, H. and Lemmon, M.L. (2002) Equilibrium pricing and optimal hedging in electricity forward markets, *Journal of Finance*, 57, 1347–1382.

Black, F. (1976) The pricing of commodity contracts, *Journal of Financial Economics*, 3, 167–179.

Dinwoodie, J. and Morris, J. (2003) Tanker forward freight agreements: The future for freight futures, *Maritime Policy and Management*, 30(1), 45–58.

Dowd, K. (2002) *Measuring Market Risk*, John Wiley & Sons Ltd, New York.

Eydeland, A. and Geman, H. (1998) Pricing power derivatives, *Risk*, 11, 71–73.

Geman, H. and Vasicek, O. (2001) Plugging into electricity, *Risk*, 14, 93–97.

Goulas, L. and Skiadopoulos, G. (2012) Are freight futures markets efficient? Evidence from IMAREX, *International Journal of Forecasting*, 28(3), 644–659.

Kavussanos, M.G. (1996a) Comparisons of volatility in the dry-bulk shipping sector: Spot versus time-charters and small versus large vessels, *Journal of Transport Economics and Policy*, 30(1), 67–82.

Kavussanos, M.G. (1996b) Price risk modelling of different size vessels in the tanker industry using autoregressive conditional heteroskedasticity (ARCH) models, *Logistics and Transportation Review*, 32(2), 161–176.

Kavussanos, M.G. (1997) The dynamics of time-varying volatilities in different size second-hand ship prices of the dry-cargo sector, *Applied Economics*, 29, 433–443.

Kavussanos, M.G. (1998) Freight risks in the tanker sector, *Lloyd's Shipping Economist*, specially commissioned article, June, 6–9 (also July, 9).

Kavussanos, M.G. (2003) Time-varying risks among segments of the tanker freight markets, *Maritime Economics and Logistics*, 5(3), 227–250.

Kavussanos, M.G. and Alizadeh, A.H. (2001) Seasonality patterns in dry-bulk shipping spot and time-charter freight rates, *Transportation Research Part E, Logistics and Transportation Review*, 37(6), 443–467.

Kavussanos, M.G. and Alizadeh, A.H. (2002) Seasonality patterns in tanker shipping freight markets, *Economic Modelling*, 19(5), 747–782.

Kavussanos, M.G. and Dimitrakopoulos, D.N. (2007a) Value at risk models in dry bulk ocean freight rates, Conference Proceedings, International Workshop on Economics and Finance, Tripolis, Greece, 14–16 June 2007.

Kavussanos, M.G. and Dimitrakopoulos, D.N. (2007b) Measuring freight risk in the tanker shipping sector, Proceedings of the 17th International Association of Maritime Economists (IAME) Conference, Athens, Greece, 4–6 July, 2007.

Kavussanos, M.G. and Dimitrakopoulos, D.N. (2011) Market risk model selection and medium-term risk with limited data: Application to ocean tanker freight markets, *International Review of Financial Analysis*, 20(5), 258–268.

Kavussanos, M.G. and Visvikis, I.D. (2003a) Financial derivative contracts in the shipping industry and the price discovery function of freight forward agreements (FFA), *Lloyd's Shipping Economist*, February.

Kavussanos, M.G. and Visvikis, I.D. (2003b) FFAs can stabilize revenue, *Lloyd's Shipping Economist*, July.

Kavussanos, M.G. and Visvikis, I.D. (2004) Market interactions in returns and volatilities between spot and forward shipping markets, *Journal of Banking and Finance*, 28(8), 2015–2049.

Kavussanos, M.G. and Visvikis, I.D. (2006a) *Derivatives and Risk Management in Shipping*, Witherbys Publishing Limited & Seamanship International, UK.

Kavussanos, M.G. and Visvikis, I.D. (2006b) Shipping freight derivatives: A survey of recent evidence, *Maritime Policy and Management*, 33(3), 233–255.

Kavussanos, M.G. and Visvikis, I.D. (2007) Derivatives in freight markets, Special report commissioned by *Lloyd's Shipping Economist*, November.

Kavussanos, M.G. and Visvikis, I.D. (2008) Freight derivatives and risk management: A review, in Geman, H. (ed.), *Risk Management in Commodity Markets: From Shipping to Agriculturals and Energy*, John Wiley & Sons Ltd, New York.

Kavussanos, M.G. and Visvikis, I.D. (2010) The hedging performance of the Capesize forward freight market, in Cullinane, K. (ed.), *The International Handbook of Maritime Economics and Business*, Edward Elgar Publishing, Cheltenham.

Kavussanos, M.G. and Visvikis, I.D. (2011) *Theory and Practice of Shipping Freight Derivatives*, Risk Books, London.

Kavussanos, M.G., Visvikis, I.D. and Menachof, D.A. (2004a) The unbiasedness hypothesis in the freight forward market: Evidence from cointegration tests, *Review of Derivatives Research*, 7(3), 241–266.

Kavussanos, M.G., Visvikis, I.D. and Batchelor, R. (2004b) Over-the-counter forward contracts and spot price volatility in shipping, *Transportation Research – Part E, Logistics and Transportation Review*, 40(4), 273–296.

Kavussanos, M.G., Visvikis, I.D. and Goulielmou, M.A. (2007) An investigation of the use of risk management and shipping derivatives: The case of Greece, *International Journal of Transport Economics*, XXXIV(1), 49–68.

Kavussanos, M.G., Visvikis, I.D. and Dimitrakopoulos, D.N. (2010) Information linkages between Panamax freight derivatives and commodity derivatives markets, *Maritime Economics and Logistics*, 12(1), 91–110.

Koekebakker, S. and Adland, R. (2004) Modelling forward freight rate dynamics – empirical evidence from time charter rates, *Maritime Policy and Management*, 31(4), 319–336.

Koekebakker, S., Adland, R. and Sodal, S. (2007) Pricing freight rate options, *Transportation Research – Part E, Logistics and Transportation Review*, 43(5), 535–548.

Lu, J., Wei, F. and Want, H. (2007) Value-at-risk on dry bulk shipping freight index, Proceedings of 17th International Association of Maritime Economists (IAME) Conference, Athens, Greece, 4–6 July 2007.

Markowitz, H. (1952) Portfolio selection, *Journal of Finance*, 7(1), 77–91.

Prokopczuk, M. (2011) Pricing and hedging in the freight futures market *Journal of Futures Markets*, 31(5), 440–464.

Samitas, A. and Tsakalos, I. (2010) Hedging effectiveness in shipping industry during financial crises, *International Journal of Financial Markets and Derivatives*, 1(2), 196–212.

Tezuka, K., Ishii, M. and Ishizaka, M. (2012) An equilibrium price model of spot and forward shipping freight markets, *Transportation Research Part E, Logistics and Transportation Review*, 48, 730–742.

Tsolakis, S. (2005) Econometric analysis of bulk shipping markets implications for investment strategies and financial decision making, PhD thesis, Erasmus University, Rotterdam.

Working, H. (1960) Price effects of futures trading, Reprinted in Peck, A.E. (ed.), *Selected Writings of Holbrook Working*, Chicago Board of Trade, Chicago, pp. 45–75 (1997).

CHAPTER 9

Agricultural and Soft Markets

Francis Declerk

9.1 INTRODUCTION: STAKES AND OBJECTIVES

9.1.1 Stakes

Agricultural and soft product prices have strong business and social impacts: decisions of production, consumption and trade; food prices and world hunger. Beyond professionals (producers, manufacturers, distributors and retailers), consumers and particularly poor people are very sensitive to increases and volatility in agricultural commodity prices.

9.1.2 Objectives

The objective is to explain the dynamics of market prices and the management specificity of hedging tools.

9.1.2.1 Price Volatility is Common Volatility in agricultural commodity prices is common, while price stability is rare. Risks taken by commodity producers and processors are high.

Commercial agreements following the World Trade Organization (WTO) framework and agricultural policies (such as the US Farm Bill and the EU Common Agricultural Policy) affect commodity price mechanisms. When agricultural commodity prices are quoted in US dollars, a professional operating outside the USD zone bears some risk due to the volatility of currency rates.

9.1.2.2 Different Ways to Manage Price Fluctuation Risks In addition to the political protection afforded by the Common Agricultural Policy (CAP), such as the intervention price for grain, producers and processors have devised several ways to mitigate the impacts of commodity price volatility:

- securing public regulation with an adequate trade policy, farming policy (CAP in the EU, Farm Bill with loan rates in the USA), and/or anti-dumping policy;
- self-absorbing volatility through reserves, credit lines and/or product diversification;

Handbook of Multi-Commodity Markets and Products: Structuring, Trading and Risk Management. Edited by Andrea Roncoroni, Gianluca Fusai and Mark Cummins.

- using insurance against weather problems (hail, floods, etc.);
- pooling risk in forming cooperatives or sales groups in order to sell a given commodity collectively every week and thus ensure they trade at the season's average price;
- subscribing to insurance;
- using over-the-counter (OTC) contracts such as forward contracts at a fixed price negotiated with suppliers and clients, options and/or swaps;
- using the futures markets, which are organized and regulated.

The first grain exchange futures market was the Chicago Board of Trade (CBOT), which offered forward contracts as early as 1848. A wheat futures contract was launched in 1865. Grain exchanges then began to open in Europe. Since the CAP protection was lowered in 2000, agricultural futures markets have expanded tremendously in the EU.

The first objective is to understand how price mechanisms are formed on international markets and are influenced by commercial and agricultural policies. The second objective is to understand commercial techniques used on international commodity wholesale markets. The third objective is to identify the principles, role and mechanisms of futures markets and to understand how hedgers, arbitragers and speculators may use futures markets.

This chapter focuses on agri-food physical commodity (spot/cash) markets and hedging with futures markets.

9.2 AGRICULTURAL COMMODITY SPECIFICITY AND FUTURES MARKETS

This section provides an overview of agri-food futures markets. It focuses mainly on agricultural commodity markets. It defines commodity markets and competition, forward and futures contracts. It provides a short history of futures markets, price volatility and supply–demand balance.

9.2.1 Agricultural Commodity Specificity

Agricultural commodities have unique specificity: long-term production process, impact of weather on harvests, perishability and storability of living products, sanitary conditions, short-term inelastic supply and demand.

Long-term production process. It takes quite a long time to produce agricultural commodities: most grains require 6 to 9 months from sow to harvest, while, cow starts producing milk when it is 2 years old. So, producers bear supply risk (quantity and price) over a long time. Furthermore, they always adjust supply to demand with a long delay.

Impact of weather on supply. Weather has a major impact on the quantity and quality of harvest and then supply to markets. Uncertainty about forthcoming weather up to harvest increases supply risks.

Perishability of living products. A lot of agricultural and food products, such as fruit and vegetables or milk, are so perishable that they must be processed quickly: they are not appropriate for futures contracts since products cannot be transferred to any purchaser, just to a nearby processor. Alternatively, grains and oilseeds are among the less perishable agricultural products: they are easily storable and may be preserved for food safety purposes with appropriate equipment. They are traded on futures markets.

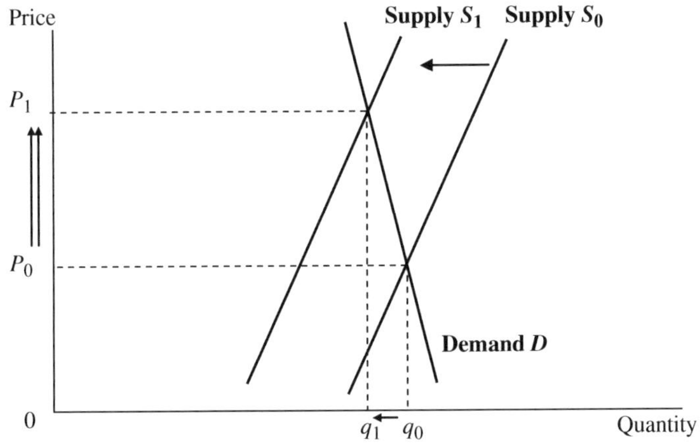

FIGURE 9.1 King effect: short-term inelastic demand leading to high price increase when supply is reduced

Sanitary conditions. Food safety laws must be conformed with in order to produce safe food. So, agricultural products must be preserved from deterioration. Grains must be preserved from humidity, insects and any chemical products. Epidemics may impede the trade of animals: for instance, any country without foot and mouth disease does not allow imports of cattle from countries where the disease has been reported.

Inelastic short-term supply and demand. These lead to strong price movements in case of an unexpected quantity supplied or demanded. For example, when a small harvest involves supply reduction then prices increase strongly. Similarly, when a large harvest leads to supply increase then prices tumble.

This phenomenon is the King effect (see Figure 9.1). Charles Davenant (1699) quoted King's calculation in 1696 (King, reprinted in 1936). For goods facing inelastic demand, such as staples without a good substitute, maximizing sales on the market implies restrictions on the quantity supplied. This explains policies decided in agriculture for sugar in 1968 and milk in 1984 according to the CAP of the European Economic Community (EEC) in order to stabilize farmers' revenues.

Observing a high agricultural price most producers will produce more, leading to a strong decrease in price and vice-versa. The long delay in supply adjustment to demand leads to production cycles, like the cobweb phenomenon mentioned by Ezekiel (1938) – see Figure 9.2. After harvesting grain in July, farmers form their production decisions in observing current market prices: they must decide quickly since most grains must be sowed in early autumn. The time lag between planting and harvesting may be about 8 to 10 months: so, production decisions are made according to the previous harvest without modification according to forthcoming market prices, except for non-harvesting decisions. The quantity produced in a given year depends on decisions made the previous year. The quantity demanded in a given year depends on the current price at that time. Nerlove (1958) expresses the hypothesis of adaptive expectations made by producers who learn from their historical experience. However, producers' forecasts are not systematically wrong as mentioned by Muth (1961), who provided the hypothesis of rational expectations. Producers are able to understand the impact of their feedback in the future. However, history (weather, policy decisions) never repeats itself exactly, new errors are made leading to cyclical price variation.

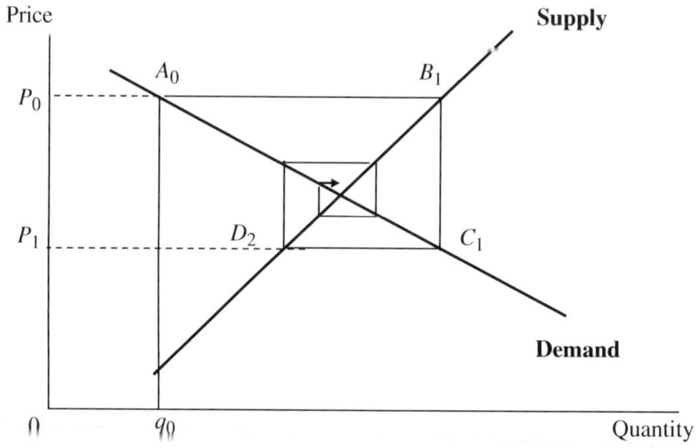

FIGURE 9.2 Cobweb phenomenon, due to lagged supply adjustment to demand

The cobweb phenomenon due to lagged supply adjustment is illustrated as follows. Assume that the initial quantity supplied, q_0, differs from the equilibrium quantity as a consequence of weather conditions such as drought or floods. The initial price, p_0, is such that the quantity supplied, q_0, is also the quantity demanded, p_0A_0. The price, p_0, is a signal for producers who will supply p_0B_1 for the next period. Then, the market price falls to p_1, and the quantity demanded is p_0C_1. This equals the quantity supplied, p_0B_1. Again, the price, p_1, is a signal for producers who will supply p_1D_2, for the next period. The process goes on, forming a cobweb.

At every period, the quantity demanded equals the quantity supplied. There is no unsold supply and there is no shortage. However, the price varies from period to period. Convergence towards price equilibrium is shown, because the slope of the demand curve is inferior, in absolute value, to the slope of the supply curve. This means that the slope of the demand curve is less steep than the slope of the supply curve. If the slope of the demand curve is steeper than the slope of the supply curve, the price will diverge as shown in Figure 9.3.

9.2.2 Volatility of Agricultural Markets

Prices on commodity markets fluctuate widely (see Figure 9.4), roughly by a factor of 1 to 3. The price volatility of agricultural commodities is structural, chiefly because of the weather uncertainty that affects production, but there are several other factors of uncertainty – such as the level of commodity inventories, changes in demand, sudden political decisions (embargoes, subsidies, taxes, quotas, etc.) – and sometimes excessive speculation which is not adequately monitored.

9.2.3 Forward Contract and Futures Contract

A lot of commodity futures contracts are derived from forward contracts used by commodity operators, for example for grain or edible oil. Futures contracts may exist for a commodity because there is an underlying product on the physical market (spot or cash). The price of

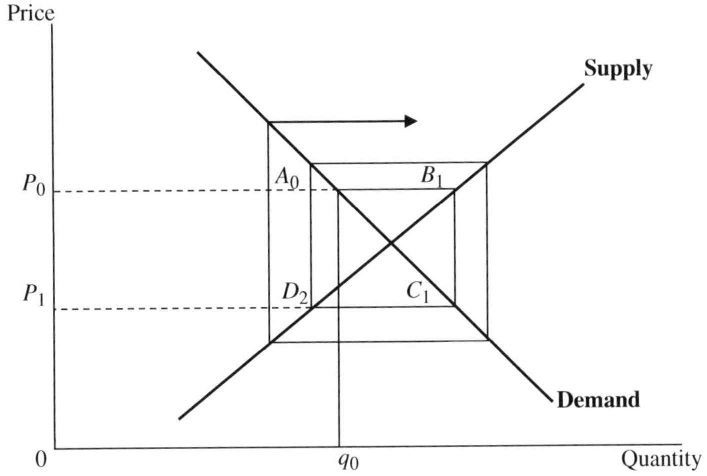

FIGURE 9.3 Diverging cobweb

the futures contract depends on prevailing conditions on the physical market. Commercial agreements following the WTO framework and agricultural policies (US Farm Bill, EU CAP etc.) may also affect commodity price mechanisms on markets.

A forward contract is an OTC contract by which two parties (a given seller and a given buyer) agree upon a price (fixed today) for delivery of a given quantity of goods in the future (at a given date).

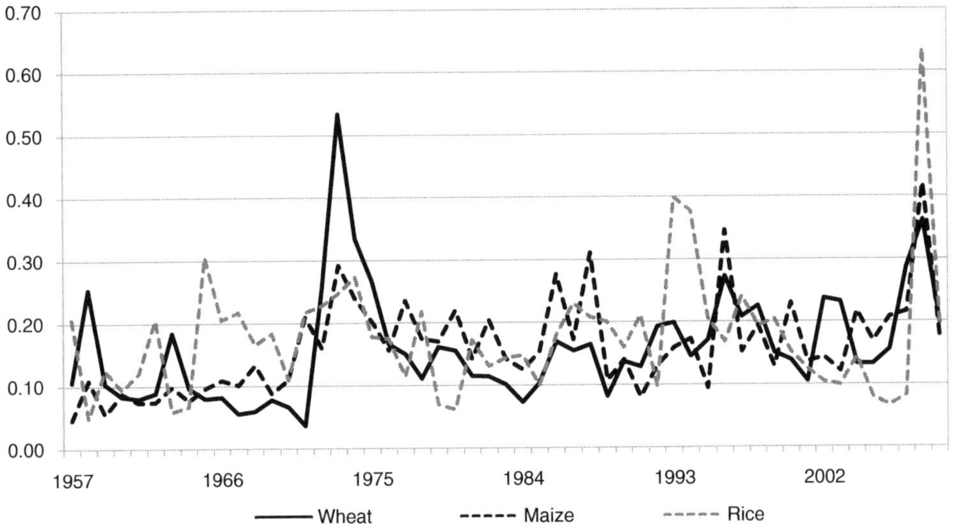

FIGURE 9.4 Nominal annualized historic volatility: cereal commodities 1957–2009 (Jan–May average)
Source: OECD/FAO 2010 (Figure 2.3, p. 58).

TABLE 9.1 Forwards and futures contracts: similarities and differences

	Forward contract	Futures contract
Terms of the contract	Freely written by the two contractors	Standardized contracts by the exchange organization
System of negotiation	By phone	Electronic system
Termination	Difficult before the delivery date of the contract	Easy to sell or buy back before the delivery date because of the liquidity in a formally organized market where suppliers and demanders meet
Manipulation	Quite easy, depending on the strength of market operators	Very difficult because huge volumes are traded
Guarantee of payment	None	Payment guaranteed by the market organization's clearing house
Transaction information	Private	Public
Prices	Unknown, not released	Publicly released

A futures contract is a contract by which an operator agrees with any counterparty contacted through a futures market organization upon a price (set today) for buying or selling a given quantity of goods for delivery at a specified date in the future (the delivery date). For the operator, the futures market organization substitutes its name for the counterparty's name. Futures markets are organized and regulated to avoid manipulation. At all times, supply and demand meet in order to determine prices and execute quick transactions.

See Table 9.1 for a comparison of forwards and futures contracts.

9.2.4 Major Agricultural Futures Markets and Contracts

Futures markets originated in the 17th century with the rice market in Osaka.

The first futures markets for agricultural commodities were established in the USA in the 19th century.

- 1848: Opening of the CBOT with forward contracts.
- 1865: Wheat futures contract introduced at the CBOT.
- 1885: Corn (maize) futures contract introduced at the CBOT; opening of the *Bourse de Commerce de Paris.*

A futures markets revival started in 1972.

- 1972: Financial futures contract on currencies introduced at the Chicago Mercantile Exchange (CME).
- 1977: US T-bond futures contract introduced at the CBOT to manage interest rate risks.
- 1982: Opening of the London International Financial Futures Exchange (LIFFE).
- 1986: Opening of the *Marché à Terme International de France* (MATIF) in Paris.

- 1988: Incorporation of the *Bourse de Commerce de Paris* into MATIF.
- During the 1980s: Launch of futures contracts on indices, freight, etc.

Since 1990 several futures exchanges have merged.

- 1999: Paris Bourse was formed through a merger between MATIF, SBF and MONEP.
- 2000: Amsterdam, Brussels and Paris futures exchanges merged to form Euronext Futures Exchange.
- 2001: Euronext bought Lisbon and the LIFFE.
- 2007: NYSE acquired Euronext to form NYSE-Euronext.
- 2007: The CME acquired the CBOT to form the CME group.
- 2008: The CME group acquired the New York Mercantile Exchange (NYMEX).
- 2013: The ICE–NYSE merged, selling Euronext in 2014 but keeping LIFFE. Then the LIFFE soft commodity (sugar, coffee and cocoa) contracts now belong to the ICE group.

The current major agricultural futures exchanges are:

- CME group (Globex electronic platform), USA, with contracts on soybean, corn, cotton, wheat, rice, milk, butter, cheddar, feeder cattle, live cattle, lean hogs, frozen pork bellies.
- Multi-Commodity Exchange (MCX) at Mumbai, India, set up in 2003 with contracts on cotton, Robusta coffee, oils, sugar, soybean, maize, wheat, barley, potatoes, peas, etc.
- Dalian Commodity Exchange, China, set up in 1993 with contracts on non-GMO soybean, palm oil.
- NYSE Euronext, UE, with contracts on Robusta coffee, cocoa, rapeseed grain and rapeseed oil, milling wheat, feed wheat, raw sugar, white sugar.
- ICE group, USA/Canada, including the New York Board of Trade (NYBOT) and Winnipeg Commodity Exchange, with contracts on soft commodities such as Arabica coffee, frozen concentrated orange juice (FCOJ), canola, barley, cotton.
- Zhengzhou Commodity Exchange, China, set up in 1990 with contracts on rice, corn, cotton, soybean.
- Risk Management Exchange at Hanover, Germany, set up in 2008 with contracts on hogs, piglets, potatoes, wheat.

9.2.5 Roles of Futures Markets

Futures markets have four major roles: they transfer price fluctuation risks, they discover a single price, they are a source of public information for decision-making and they guarantee delivery and payment.

9.2.5.1 Transfer of Price Fluctuation Risks Futures markets provide tools (contracts) to transfer price fluctuation risks between commodity producers, commodity processors, traders (merchants) and speculators.

9.2.5.2 Discovery of a Single Price Futures markets are economic tools to discover a single price for all operators (sellers and buyers) of a given product.

Supply and demand for a commodity is centralized by the futures market. The futures market synthesizes the expectations of operators (sellers and buyers) for a given product. It provides the best anticipation of future prices.

9.2.5.3 Source of Information for Decision-Making The volumes traded and prices formed on futures exchanges are publicly released immediately. The futures markets derive from physical cash markets. In order to understand futures markets, it is necessary to understand the physical cash markets for the underlying assets.

Public information about prices and volumes on futures markets may thus be used by everyone worldwide, even non-users of futures markets.

9.2.5.4 Guarantee of Delivery and Payment For every transaction undertaken on an organized market:

- buyers are afraid that sellers will not deliver the goods,
- sellers are afraid that buyers will not pay.

The futures markets guarantee delivery by sellers and payment by buyers. To achieve this, an initial deposit and a margin call system are enforced for every operator in the market

9.2.6 Institutions Related to Futures Markets

The futures market encompasses several organizations which fulfil different and complementary functions.

9.2.6.1 Futures Exchange A futures exchange is the (possibly virtual) place where the trading of contracts is organized (with pits in the case of auctions). It operates under the regulation of the state where it is registered.

9.2.6.2 Clearing House The clearing house of a futures exchange has several different functions:

- It is a back-office for management of all the payments (initial deposit and margin calls) in order to guarantee proper execution of recorded transactions.
- Then it becomes the counterparty for every transaction.
- It checks deliveries of products.
- It monitors transaction compliance, paying particular attention to speculation.

9.2.6.3 Regulatory Institutions Regulatory institutions are responsible for launching and controlling contracts. Contracts are supervised by national authority: the *Commodity Futures Trading Commission* (CFTC) in the USA, the *Financial Services Authority* (FSA) in the UK, the *Autorité des Marchés Financiers* (AMF) in France, etc.

9.2.7 Commodity Futures Contracts

Commodity futures contracts are designed as tools to be used by commercial sellers and buyers to mitigate their risks of commodity price volatility.

9.2.7.1 Standardized Contracts Futures exchanges provide standardized commodity futures contracts in order to attract large volumes and obtain market liquidity and depth. Liquidity refers to buyers' and sellers' ability to find a counterparty easily. Market depth means that an operator may enter and exit the market without a major change in price. Futures exchanges organize the launching and trading of contracts. When a contract goes to delivery, the futures exchange organizes the delivery of underlying commodities.

Futures contract trades:

- a given (large) quantity of a product;
- a given quality of a product, often the most standard quality on the physical market;
- at given dates of delivery (maturity dates);
- at given places of delivery.

9.2.7.2 Quotation Anyone wishing to buy and sell futures must contact a registered broker appointed by the clearing members at the futures exchange. For an auction market, every order is shouted out in the pit: everybody must be able to hear every price announced, see the type of order (buy or sell) and know when a transaction is made.

The main information shown on the quotation screen is:

- 'open' = first price traded
- 'last' = last price traded
- 'settlement price' = official closing price
- 'open interest' = total amount of contracts in existence after the close of trading that day. These contracts may go to delivery.

9.2.7.3 Margin Calls and Clearing The clearing house is responsible for balancing the transactions and flows of money between buyers and sellers. It organizes the security of all transactions up to their clearing of contracts. It assumes the financial responsibility as if it was the opposite side of every transaction: payment is guaranteed for sellers and delivery is guaranteed for buyers.

In order to secure every transaction, every operator has to pay initial deposit and margin calls. An initial deposit is required as a security or performance bond. Its amount depends on the type of operation (hedging, arbitrage or speculation) and price volatility. It may be worth 3–10% of the value of the contract. This amount is usually the maintenance level. Furthermore, in case of negative evolution of price, the contract is riskier and some margin call is required to offset such additional risk. Margin calls are based on the last official price of the day, called the settlement price.

As an example, two operators may take positions on the milling wheat futures market, one going long in buying and the other going short in selling 10 contracts at €240 per ton. A milling wheat futures contract concerns 50 t. So the transaction amounts to €120,000.

A contract is cleared either before maturity in taking an opposite position on the market or at maturity in delivering/being delivered the goods.

9.2.7.4 Two Examples of Commodity Futures Contracts in Europe Two major agricultural commodity contracts in Europe are the rapeseed and milling wheat futures contracts.

Example 9.2.1 *Rapeseed futures contract at Euronext*

1. *Trading unit per contract: 50 metric tons quoted in €/t.*
2. *Underlying asset: rapeseed of double zero varieties, of any origin, of sound, fair & tradable quality with the following specifications.*

3. *Specifications: oil content = 40%, moisture = 10% max., impurities = 3% max., oleic acidity = 2% max., erucic acid = 2% max., glucosinolates = 25 micromoles max.*
4. *Delivery months: February, May, August, November (X), 6 delivery months any time with a quotation period over 14 to 18 months.*
5. *Delivery: FOB barge at Belleville, Metz-Frouard, Bülstringen, Vahldorf, Magdeburg/Mittelkanal, Wurzburg/Main and Gent.*
6. *Tick: the tick is the minimum price fluctuation. It is 0.2 €/ton, i.e. 12.5 €/contract.*

Example 9.2.2 *Milling wheat futures contract at Euronext*
Creation: 27 March 1998 by MATIF – Paris

1. *Trading unit per contract = 50 metric tons.*
2. *Underlying asset = milling wheat, of any origin, of sound, fair & tradable quality with the following specifications*
3. *Specifications:*
   specific weight = 76 kg/hl min.
   moisture = 15% max.
   broken grains = 4% max.
   sprouted grains = 2% max.
   impurities = 2% max.
4. *Electronic price quotation in euros per metric ton with instant conversion into US dollars.*
5. *Delivery months: August (Q), November (X), January (F), March (H), May (K) and July (N).*
6. *Delivery months any time, with a quotation period of 14 to 18 months.*
7. *Port authorized for delivery on expiry of a futures contract: Port of Rouen (Seine), incograin no. 23 & technical addendum no. 2.*
8. *Transfer of goods: river FOB.*
9. *Tick: the tick is the minimum price fluctuation. It is 0.2 €/tonne, i.e. 12.5 €/contract.*

9.2.8 The Operators

There are three types of operators on futures markets: hedgers, arbitragers and speculators. A given operator may be a hedger and/or an arbitrager and/or a speculator.

Hedgers are interested in the physical goods and spot markets, and use futures markets to reduce the risks arising from price fluctuations. They are afraid of commodity price volatility and want to mitigate risks by fixing a firm price on futures markets. Hedgers are risk-averse and enter the futures markets to secure their operating margins. They are usually commodity producers, processors or merchants acting on both spot and futures markets.

Arbitragers take advantage of price distortions on the market. They have a risk-neutral attitude. Many banks which provide services for clients on futures exchanges have developed strong information technology tools to observe market prices and use arbitrage techniques.

Speculators enter the futures markets to take risks with the sole aim of making profits. They are risk-takers and provide liquidity for the market. Every type of economic agent may speculate. Speculators are useful, as they make it easier for hedgers to find a counterparty. For example, rapeseed and wheat producers usually enter into futures contracts maturing just after harvest time because they want to clear their position when they sell their agricultural products at harvest. Processors, in contrast, buy agricultural products since they manufacture food every day, and therefore do not want to be counterparties in transactions involving large amounts of commodities at harvest time. Speculators are thus welcome as counterparties because they facilitate the formation of transactions. If a market is not liquid, it is dead.

As long as futures market prices are connected to spot markets, speculation is not excessive. When this is not the case, it may signal excessive speculation and the futures market is no longer useful to hedgers, since futures transactions could increase risks. Speculation may lead to market manipulation, which kills the market. Speculation must therefore be monitored by futures exchanges.

9.2.9 Monitoring Hedging: Settlement

A position on the futures market may be settled in one of two ways:

1. By clearing the position when the operator offsets his position by taking an opposite position:
   A short hedger, a commodity producer, sells and buys back his futures contract.
   A long hedger, a commodity processor, buys and sells back his futures contract.
   The futures contract is settled before maturity.
2. By delivery of the product at the places of delivery stipulated in the futures contract.

9.2.10 Accounting and Tax Rules

The International Accounting Standard (IAS 39) for derivatives – like futures contracts – was released in 2004, but some parts of the standard are still challenged by professionals. IAS 39 is similar to current US accounting standards.

In the USA, unrealized capital gains/losses are reported in the income statements when margin calls are paid because:

- Quotations on futures markets are known at all times.
- Contracts may be settled at any time.

9.3 DEMAND AND SUPPLY, PRICE DETERMINANTS AND DYNAMICS

This section focuses mainly on the determinants of demand and supply for agricultural commodities: determinants, the specificity and dynamics. It analyses the features of major agricultural markets.

9.3.1 Supply and Demand for Agricultural Commodities: The Determinants

The determinants of a commodity 'supply–demand' balance on physical markets can be considered on the following scales:

- On the world market, as is the case for oilseeds (soybean, rapeseed, sunflower, etc.).
- On the EU market, as is the case for milling wheat, with modification due to the CAP: certificates with export rights under exportation subsidies or taxes, and certificates with import rights subject to a levy (which may be positive, nil or negative).

On the supply side, the major factors of instability are the following.

- Changes in decisions concerning production: increase, reduction or stop.
- Variations in weather conditions (drought, frost, floods, tornadoes, etc.).
- Sanitary problems: plant diseases and animal epidemics.
- Farm methods and practices.
- Research in plant and animal biology/biotechnology.
- Changes in available arable soils: availability of water, damages (erosion, pollution), increase in urban and industrial areas.
- Variations in yields.
- Changes in transportation costs, preservation costs and storage costs.
- The political environment, which may involve incentives (minimum price, subsidies, aids), limits (tax, quotas, land set aside, etc.) and prohibitions (import threshold price, etc.).
- Agriculture, food and health policy decisions about food uses of agricultural products and international trade.
- Exchange rate volatility.
- Social and political risk in a region/country.

On the demand side, the major factors of instability are the following:

- Changes in demand for food, which depends on world demographics (variations in population size and population structure by age), type of diet (food habits, changes in preferences) and income of the population in every region.
- Changes in the demand for animal feed (epidemics, etc.).
- Food aid policies.
- Changes in non-food and non-feed demand: energy (biofuels), industries.
- Changes in costs of transportation, preservation and storage.
- Policy decisions to subsidize or tax, rules and regulations on international trade.
- Volatility of currency rates.
- Social and political risks in a particular region/country.

Several of these factors depend neither on demanders (industry especially) nor on suppliers (producers). Furthermore, producing agricultural products requires time – months, sometimes years – and supply adjusts with a time lag to sudden changes in demand. Consequently, price fluctuations cannot be avoided on agricultural markets. Agri-food commodity prices are very volatile, and price stability is very rare. Many factors contribute to fluctuation in market prices. (See Figure 9.5).

Owing to natural conditions (subsoil soil and climate), the size and purchasing power of the population, technological conditions of production and human education, some countries are global net importers or exporters. From 2010 to 2012, the USA was the largest agricultural and food world exporter followed by the EU. Brazil was the third largest supplier while China and Argentina competed for the fourth position (see Figure 9.6).

From 2010 to 2012, the EU was by far the largest agricultural and food world importer. The USA was second, followed immediately by China which strongly increased its imports. Japan and Russia are behind. See Figure 9.7.

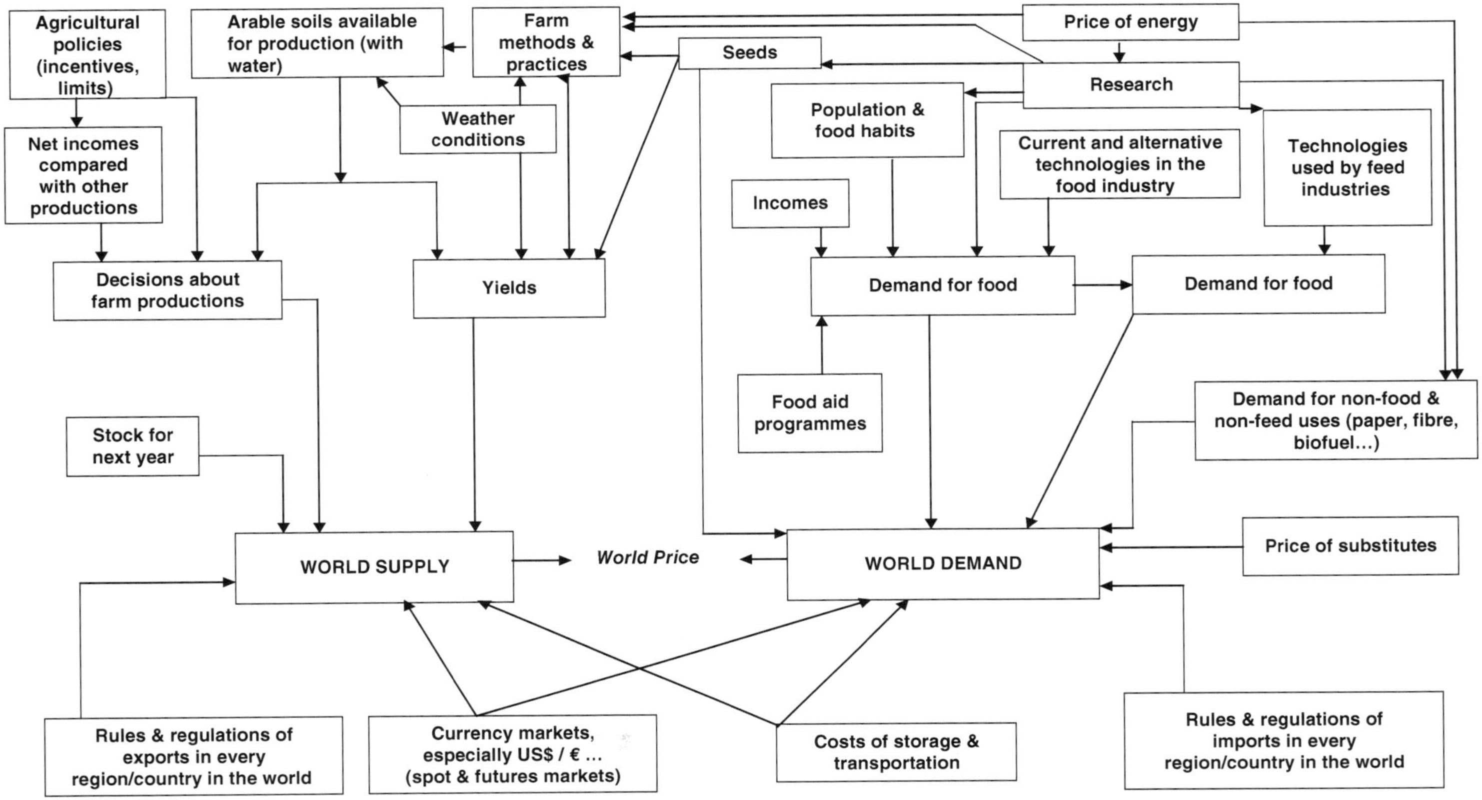

FIGURE 9.5 Determinants of world supply and demand for seasonal and storable agricultural commodities in the world market

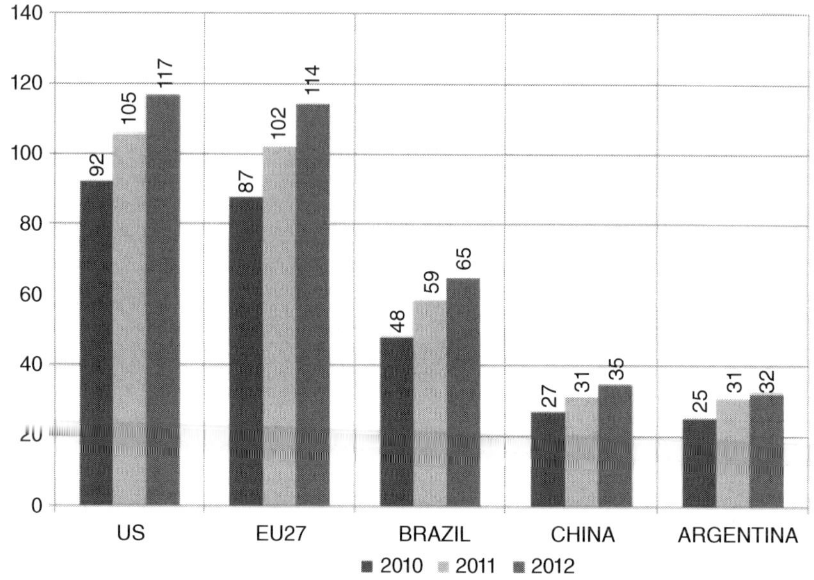

FIGURE 9.6 The top five world agricultural and food exporters
Source: EU Commission, 'Monitoring Agri-trade Policy – Agricultural trade in 2012: A good story to tell in a difficult year?' http://ec.europa.eu/agriculture/trade-analysis/map/2013-1_en.pdf.

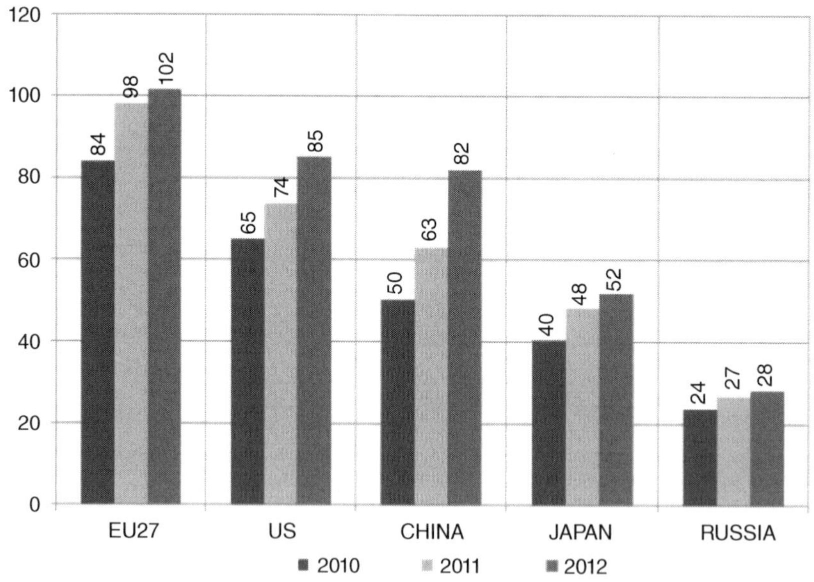

FIGURE 9.7 The top five world agricultural importers
Source: EU Commission, 'Monitoring Agri-trade Policy – Agricultural trade in 2012: A good story to tell in a difficult year?' http://ec.europa.eu/agriculture/trade-analysis/map/2013-1_en.pdf.

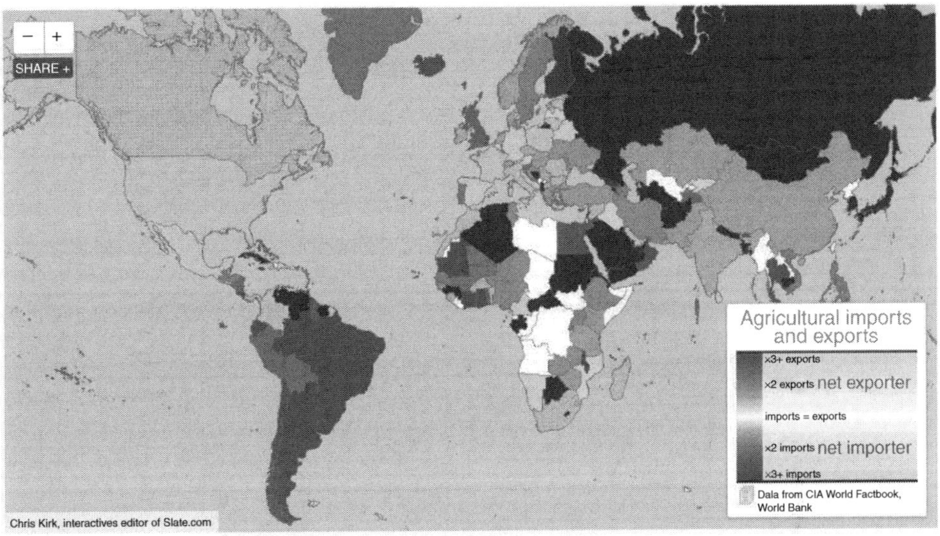

FIGURE 9.8 Net agricultural importing and exporting countries
Source: Kirk, C., *Maps: Agriculture in the US and around the world*, Slate, 2013. http://www.slate.com/articles/technology/future_tense/2012/06/a_map_of_farmers_in_the_u_s_and_world_.html; http://www.indexmundi.com/blog/wp-content/uploads/2013/02/agricultural-imports-and-exports.png.

As a result, over the 2010–2012 period the USA, Brazil and Argentina were large net exporters and the EU was also a net exporter while China, Japan and Russia were net importers of agricultural and food products (Figure 9.8).

Nearly all American countries are net food exporters. Argentina is the biggest net food exporter exporting about $23 in food for every $1 it imports. Major net food importers are Middle Eastern countries some, Asian countries, and developing African countries.

9.3.2 Agricultural Market Prices, Failures and Policies

Agricultural markets may not operate well and policy tools may be useful to fix failures. Agricultural and commercial policies may also influence market prices; and some policy tools may distort market prices.

The equilibrium market price is the price which clears the market. It means that every supplied product is demanded, no less and no more. A bid price is the highest price that a buyer (demander) is willing to pay for the commodity. An ask price is the lowest price accepted by a seller (supplier). When there is a difference between the bid price and the ask price, it is called the spread (see Figure 9.9).

Market failure exists in case of:

- lack of operators leading to risk of monopolistic power;
- lack of information about supply, inventories, demand leading to wrong price;
- lack of infrastructure to move the goods.

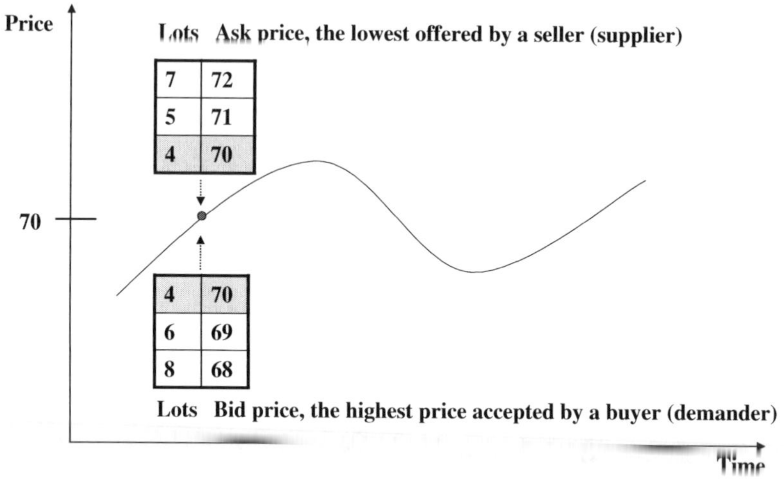

FIGURE 9.9 Formation of market price (related to orders made by suppliers and demanders)

Policy may be useful in case of market failure leading to market prices that are biased, and then wrong signals for suppliers to invest and produce and for demanders to buy and process. Prices on the agricultural commodity market may be distorted because of commercial and agricultural policies.

Commercial agreements may affect price formation on markets. Instruments such as import tariffs, export or import quotas and others lower or increase market prices. The right or not to use some of these tools may be negotiated in the framework of the WTO. For instance, according to WTO agreements, export subsidies are banned from January 2013.

Agricultural policies may also influence market prices. Investment and production subsidies, guaranteed floor prices (cf. payment-in-kind US programme or EU intervention price for grains), production quotas, embargoes, etc. affect market prices.

A major criterion focused specifically on price distortions is the producer nominal protection coefficient (NPC). The producer NPC is measured by the producer domestic prices (including support payments per unit of output) as a percentage of border prices. For the OECD countries it was 1.10 in 2010, indicating that OECD farmers received prices that were on average 10% above international levels. The indicator fell from 1.49 in 1987–88, indicating that OECD farmers were receiving prices 49% above world prices at that time, to 1.31 in 1995–97 and to 1.11 in 2008–10. See Figure 9.10. However, some OECD countries such as Norway, Japan, South Korea, Switzerland or Turkey have decreased their price support levels but their domestic prices still remain a lot higher than world prices. The USA, Australia and New Zealand have kept low price support levels over the period. The EU have decreased their price support level, with average domestic prices remaining slightly above average market prices.

Support levels in emerging countries are below the OECD average: Russia, Ukraine and China have taxed some domestic commodity producers. However, over the 2000s, Brazil, China, Russia and Ukraine have increased their price support levels to world level or above.

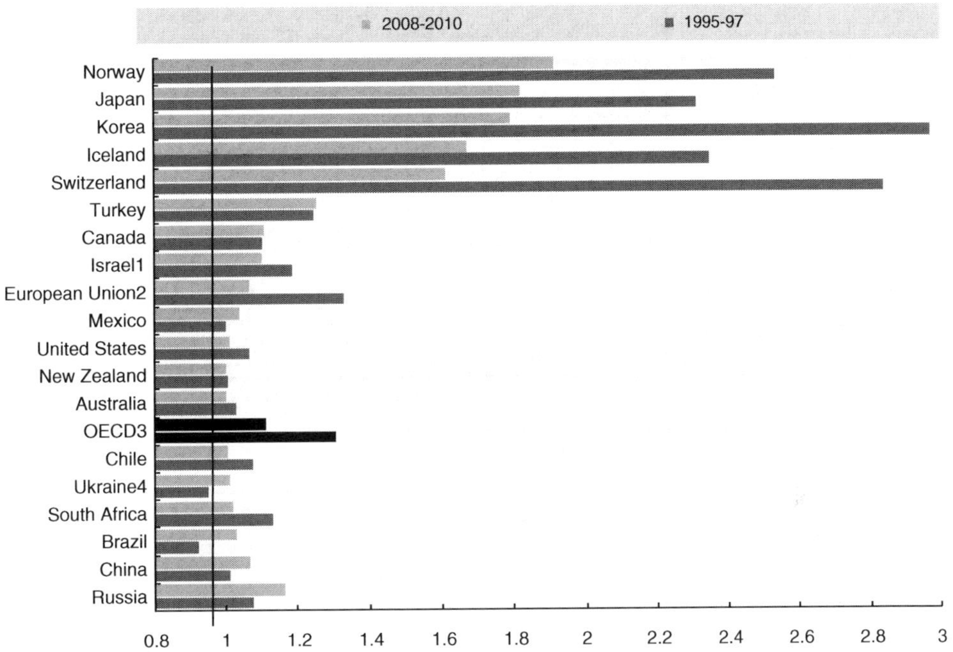

FIGURE 9.10 Producer nominal protection coefficient by country, 1995–97 and 2008–10
The producer NPC measures the producer domestic price (including support payments per unit of output) as a percentage of border price. Countries are ranked according to 2008–10 levels.

1. The statistical data for Israel are supplied by and under the responsibility of the relevant Israeli authorities. The use of such data by the OECD is without prejudice to the status of the Golan Heights, East Jerusalem and Israeli settlements in the West Bank under the terms of international law.
2. EU15 for 1995–2003; EU27 from 2007.
3. Austria, Finland and Sweden are included in the OECD total for all years and in the EU from 1995. The Czech Republic, Hungary, Poland and the Slovak Republic are included in the OECD total for all years and in the EU from 2004. Chile and Israel are included in the OECD total from 1995.
4. For Ukraine, 1995–97 is replaced by 1996–97.

Source: OECD, PSE/CSE database, in OECD (2011), Figure 2.7, p. 58.

Some commodities are affected more by policy measures and distortions as is the case for sugar, whose international trade accounts for about 28% of world production, and rice, whose international market is small since trade only represents less than 8% of world production. See Figure 9.11.

The milk market is also impacted by national policies to protect numerous breeders from the market power of a smaller number of dairy processors. Since milk is produced daily by milk cows or sheep or goats, it is high perishable; milk producers must transfer milk every day or every other day to the milk processor. Milk producers have a limited choice of dairy manufacturers with plant near enough to collect their milk. However, most protections were removed in the 2000s and the EU decided to remove its production quotas in 2015. Grains and oilseeds are impacted less by policies.

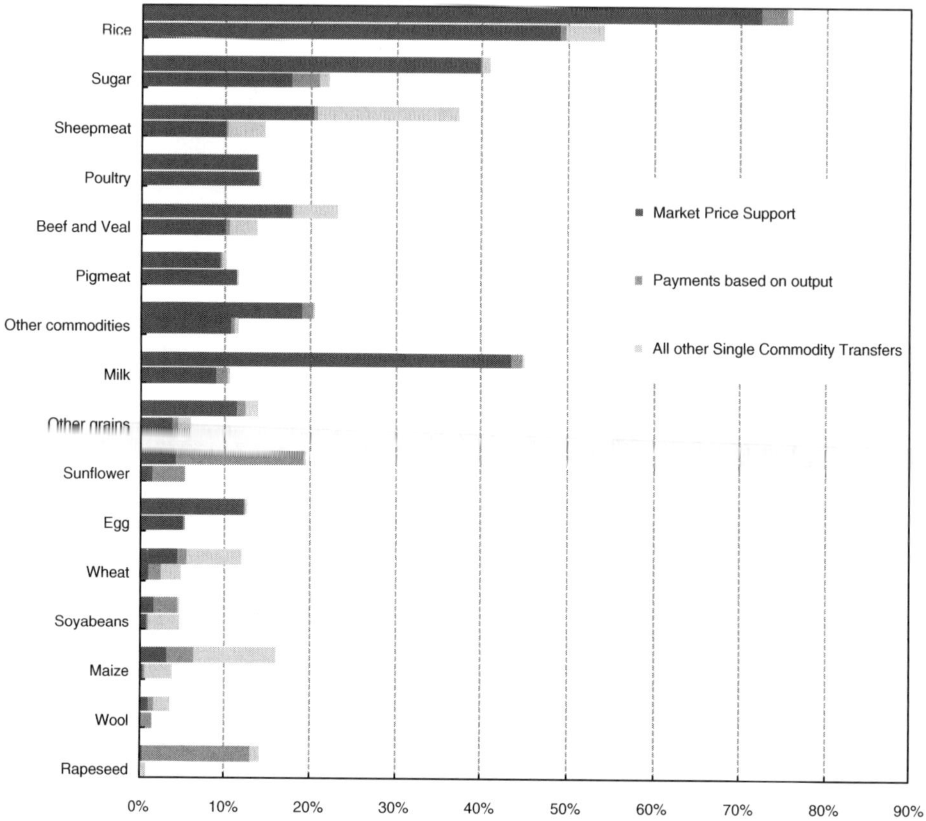

FIGURE 9.11 OECD: single commodity transfers, 1995–97 and 2008–10
Commodities are ranked according to 2008–10 levels. Top bar corresponds to 1995–97, bottom bar to 2008–10.
Source: OECD, PSE/CSE database, in OECD (2011), Figure 2.8, p. 60.

9.3.3 The Price Dynamics of Seasonal and Storable Agricultural Commodities

Major agricultural commodities traded on international markets are seasonal and storable, such as sugar, grains, oilseeds, coffee, cocoa, citrus, palm oil, etc. According to most economists (Haley, 2013), deviations around medium- and long-term pricing trends of seasonal and storable agricultural commodities should result from world surpluses and deficit computed as total production minus total consumption. However, things are more complex. Major determinants affecting price movements in the long-term are:

1. The production cost (including the effects of exchange rates) of the leading producing and exporting countries, so that return on cost of production must be positive most years.
2. The supply–demand imbalance measured by the year-to-year change in surplus/deficit, by change in inventory carry over and by stockholding dynamics.
3. The risks related to errors in forecasting supply and demand balances/imbalances in recent years.

The return on production cost of major operators in leading producing and exporting countries must be positive. According to neoclassical economic theory, long-term equilibrium price equals marginal cost of production. So, analysing the production costs in leading producing and exporting countries is helpful. Production costs include the effects of exchange rates when production costs are formed in countries whose currency differs from the selling currency on international markets, usually the US dollar. For illustration, the return on cost of production for Brazilian sugar (Haley, 2013) and for Vietnamese Robusta coffee and US corn (author's confidential source from an industry researcher) must be positive in the long term and provides an indication of long-term world price level. Over the 2000s, costs of agricultural production and logistics have increased strongly due to increases in energy prices. Changes in exchange rates also affect production costs, as observed for increasing costs of Brazilian sugar expressed in US dollars in comparison with costs expressed in Brazilian currency, the real, from 2002 to 2010. When there is a dominant exporter with constant returns to scale technology in production and with no other major exporter with lower cost, changes in its production costs expressed in world market currency are transmitted to the world market (Haley, 2013).

The supply–demand imbalance affects world market price. It may be characterized by two measures: the year-to-year change in surplus/deficit and by stockholding dynamics.

- The year-to-year change in surplus/deficit is expected to be inversely related to price changes. It is also affected by the ability of users to substitute a commodity for another.
- Stockholding behaviour influences the magnitude of surplus and deficit on international trade, imports and exports. Then, it is possible to measure the impact of stock depletion and replenishment on world price. Stockholding dynamics is featured by the stock/use ratio and the ability of producers to adjust to demand. The stock/use ratio is the stock of a given commodity as a proportion of world consumption. The dynamics of the stock/use ratio is impacted by the ability and decision of producers to adjust to demand in a context of competing crops. As a result, expected inventory carry over is also a key variable.

The risks related to errors in forecasting supply and demand balances/imbalances in recent years generate costs. Then, market prices include a premium when there is a recent history of deficit which is larger than initially forecasted. In opposition, when there is a previous not predicted surplus, there is a market price discount.

The three elements mainly explain the price dynamics of storable and seasonal agricultural commodities (Figure 9.12).

9.3.4 The Features of Major Agricultural and Soft Markets

Markets are platforms (electronic and/or physical places) where goods are traded. In the agricultural and food sector, beyond the farm input market, there are four types of markets: domestic commodity market, international commodity market, industrial goods market and fast-moving consumer goods market.

Agricultural production is achieved by millions of farmers dispersed in regions. When agricultural and soft commodities are harvested, they must be collected rapidly to be preserved in safe and sanitary conditions by processors. Sales are made on domestic commodity markets. Then a few large traders, usually carriers, will buy in regions with excess supply to sell in regions with excess demand. Sales are made on international commodity markets.

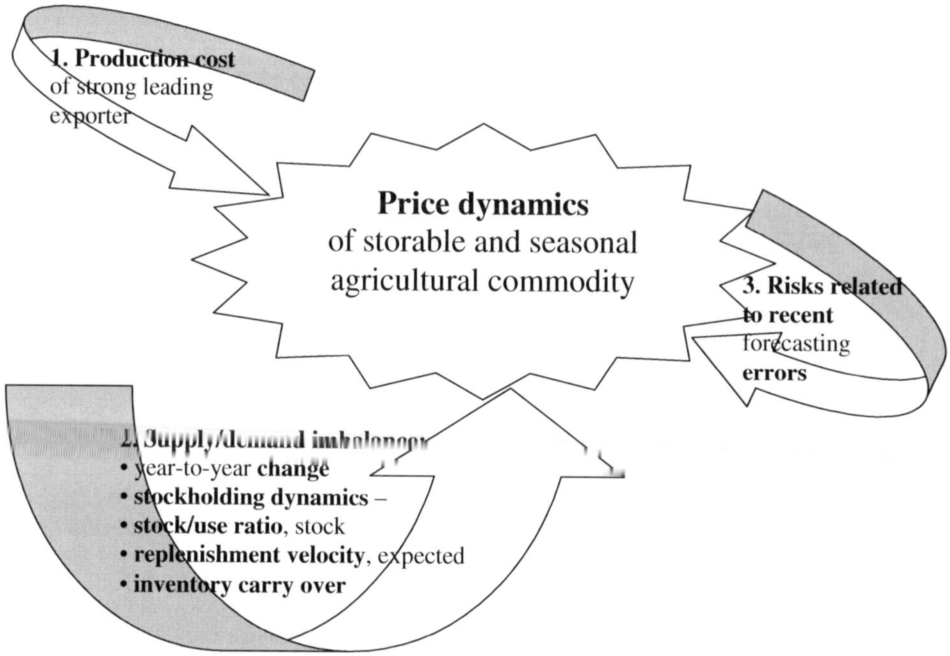

FIGURE 9.12 The price dynamic determinants of seasonal and storable agricultural commodities
Source: Author's figure from Haley (2013).

In a second processing stage, manufacturers process food ingredients that are sold for a third processing stage in order to produce packaged food goods. These fast-moving consumer goods will be sold to retailers in order to reach final consumers who are scattered in cities and villages.

Operators trade on markets along the agricultural and food chain where they are individually and collectively responsible for sanitary food conditions (Figure 9.13).

Since a given agricultural commodity is usually produced in different countries, it is also traded in different places. Investors have to take up the challenge of multiple trading platforms based on different regulatory environments. As a consequence, markets are fragmented.

International Traders and Carriers of Agricultural and Soft Commodities Among companies trading agricultural commodities on international markets, four leading groups – Archer Daniels Midland (ADM), Bunge, Cargill and Louis Dreyfus – known as the ABCD traders have prevailed for more than a century (see Table 9.2). They originate agricultural commodities from regions with excess supply to deliver in regions with excess demand. The ABCD companies buy, carry, store and sell mainly grain, oilseeds and sugar and some other commodities. So they have developed strong management skills and equipment in international trading, sourcing, transporting, storing and processing bulk agricultural commodities that are perishable and that must be maintained in good sanitary conditions. They are also more and more vertically integrated in the first processing stage of agricultural products into ingredients. Trading offices are usually in the USA and Geneva, Switzerland. The international market for grains and oilseeds is mainly oligopolistic.

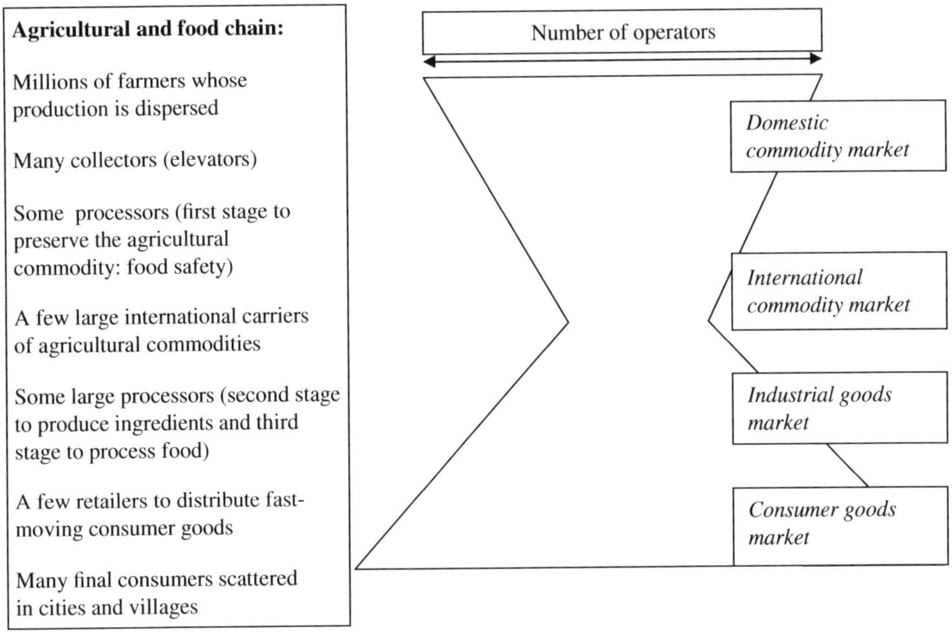

FIGURE 9.13 Operators trading on markets along the agricultural and food chain

Cargill is the largest world trader and processor of agricultural commodities, with about 140,000 employees in 65 countries. It generated net sales of US$136.7 billion, operational cash flows of US$4.2 billion and US$2.3 billion net earnings from continuing operations for the 2013 fiscal year ending in May (source: http://www.cargill.com). Founded in 1865 by Cargill and MacMillan, Cargill is a family-owned company whose 85% of equity capital belongs to the descendants of the two founders. It is headquartered in Minnesota, USA. It is involved in trading and processing grain, oilseeds, sugar, cocoa, cotton, beef meat, poultry and eggs. Its trading and risk management activities are located in the USA (Minneapolis and Miami) and Geneva, Switzerland.

ADM's net sales amounted to US$89 billion in 2012, from which it generated operating cash flows of US$2.9 billion and adjusted earnings before interest, taxes, depreciation

TABLE 9.2 ABCD, the largest traders and carriers of agricultural commodities

Company	Net sales in US$ billion	Year	Status
Cargill	137	ending in May 2013	family-owned company
ADM	89	2012	public company
Bunge	61	2012	public company
LDC	57	2012	family-owned company

ADM = Archer Daniels Midland.
LDC = Louis-Dreyfus Commodities.
Source: www.cargill.com, www.adm.com, www.bunge.com, www.ldcommodities.com.

and amortization (EBITDA) of US$1.7 billion (source: http://www.adm.com). It has 30,000 employees. It operates in more than 75 countries. ADM was founded in 1902 by Archer and Daniels. It is a public company listed and traded on the New York Stock Exchange and the Frankfurt Stock Exchange. Its headquarters are in Illinois, USA. It is involved in turning oilseeds, corn, wheat and cocoa into products for food, animal feed, industrial and energy uses with 265 processing plants.

Bunge's net sales amounted to US$61 billion in 2012 and it generated operating cash flows of US$2.9 billion, gross profit of US$2.6 billion and net income of US$36 million with over 35,000 employees in 40 countries (source: http://www.bunge.com). Founded in 1818 in the Netherlands, it is now headquartered in the USA. It is a public company listed and traded on the New York Stock Exchange. Bunge is the largest trader in South America.

Louis-Dreyfus Commodities delivered about US$57 billion in sales, US$2.3 billion in gross margin and US$1.1 billion in net income (excluding its sugarcane milling business Biosev's contribution) with 20,000 employees (38,000 with Biosev) in 53 countries in 2012 (source: http://www.ldcommodities.com and http://www.louisdreyfus.com). 80% of its equity capital belongs to Louis-Dreyfus group. Founded in 1851 in France by Léopold Louis-Dreyfus, Louis-Dreyfus group is a family-owned company whose business is run by descendants. Louis-Dreyfus Commodities is headquartered in Rotterdam, The Netherlands. In 2012, Louis-Dreyfus entered the capital of the Malaysian Felda and became the largest producer of palm oil. Biosev is the second largest producer of ethanol.

After World War II, other trading companies have emerged such as Glencore (founded in 1974 by Marc Rich and based in Switzerland), Noble, Wilmar International, Ed&F Man, Sucden, Ecom, Armajaro, Vitol, Mitsubishi, AgroTrade, Olam, Sinar Mas, etc.

Commodities Traded on International Markets The agricultural commodities most traded on international markets are grains (wheat and corn), oilseeds (soybean and palm), sugar, coffee and cocoa. Rice is the most widely consumed grain in the world, but less than 8% of rice production is traded on international markets (see Table 9.3).

Animal and meat products are not so exposed to international markets, mainly due to sanitary barriers and subsequent bans declared by governments. As sick animal which enters a country may be contagious and spread disease quickly to other animals. Furthermore, some

TABLE 9.3 World exports relative to production in 2012

Commodity	Export/production ratio
Raw sugar	27.6%
Soft wheat	29.6%
Corn	10.8%
Milled rice	7.6%
Soybean	35.9%
Rapeseed	19.5%
Green coffee bean	78.7%
Palm oil	71.0%
Cotton	38.0%

Source: Author's calculations from ERS-USDA data, 2013.

animal diseases may be transferred to human beings. So, the international market for animals is limited.

It is possible to analyse the features of major agricultural markets such as the sugar market, the wheat market and the coffee market.

In the present subsection, the top line on every figure with price quotes mentions the following information from left to right.

- The last day of quote: for example '01/31/2014'.
- The figure after the letter 'C' (for closing) indicates the closing price on that day.
- The figure after the letter '0' (for open) indicates the opening price on that day.
- The figure after the letter 'H' (for high) indicates the highest price on that day.
- The figure after the letter 'L' (for low) indicates the lowest price on that day.

On every figure with price quotes, thin curves crossing monthly price quotes provide moving averages.

- 12-week moving averages for the curve which is the closest to the thick monthly price curve.
- 6-month moving averages for the curve which is the middle of the thin 12-week and 1-year moving average curves.
- 1-year moving averages for the curve which is the most flattened price curve.

Small sticks at the bottom of every figure indicate the volume of transactions each month and the thin line shows the open interest that expresses the number of contracts that may go to maturity. They measure the importance of the activity on the contract.

On international markets, most agricultural and soft commodities are quoted in US dollars. While domestic production costs and processing costs are expressed in domestic currencies, exchange rates affect supply and demand.

The euro/US dollar rate moved between US$1.17 and 1.60 per euro over the January 2005 to December 2013 period (Figure 9.13). Such volatility was a lot lower than price fluctuations observed on agricultural and soft markets. However, some other currencies, such as the Brazilian peso and the Indian rupiah, experienced large fluctuations vis-à-vis the US dollar. Furthermore, agricultural production costs include fertilizers, pesticides and transportation costs that are strongly impacted by oil price and price volatility.

From January 2005 to December 2013, the oil price fluctuated with a low at US$35 a barrel in 2009 and a peak at US$147 a barrel in July 2008 (Figure 9.14a,b). So the oil price fluctuated from about 1 to 4, which was a lot more than the euro/US dollar fluctuation.

9.3.4.1 The Sugar Market, Strongly Impacted by Policies Among agricultural and soft markets, the sugar market may be the most impacted by national policies.

Products and Uses Sugar production may come from sugar beets in countries with temperate climate and from sugar cane in countries with temperate climate and warm climate countries. Beets and cane may also be used to produce biofuels like ethanol. Other co-products are alcohol and animal feeds.

Sugar from cane and beet is saccharose. It is used as 'table sugar' directly consumed at home or as an ingredient in agri-food (confectionery, pastry, cookies, etc.), chemical and

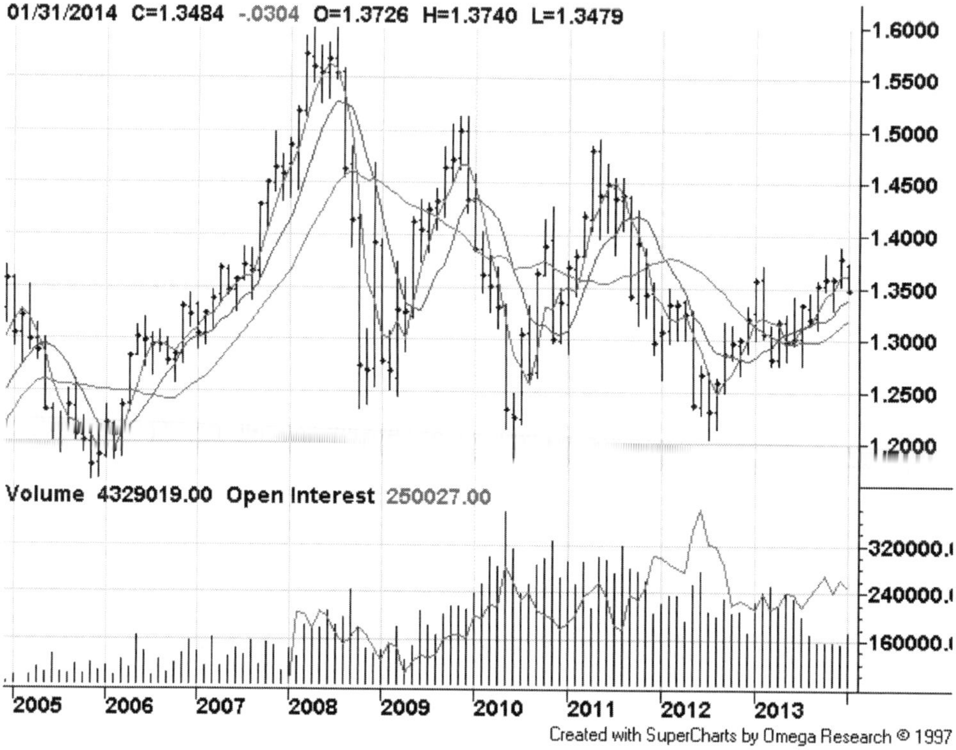

FIGURE 9.14A Value of one euro expressed in US dollars, on the CME
Source: http://futures.tradingcharts.com/chart/E6/M?anticache=1393575372.

pharmaceutical industries. However, mainly in the soft drink industry, sugar is in strong competition with isoglucose which is extracted from corn.

Consequently, since sugar may be used to produce ethanol, the sugar and petroleum markets are connected. And, since sugar and isoglucose are sweeteners, the sugar and corn markets are also connected. When corn prices increase, sugar market price is affected by incremental demand due to substitution and vice-versa.

Over the last 50 years, sugar production from cane has increased tremendously from 31 million tons in 1960–61 to 143 million tons in 2012–13, a 4.6-fold increases (Table 9.4; Figure 9.15). Over the same period, sugar production from beet only increased from 18 to 24 million tons, only a 1.5-fold increase. In 2012–13, 80% of world sugar production came from cane and 20% from beet. In 2005, only 74% of sugar was refined from cane. Up to now sugar cane production has been more efficient than sugar beet production. Sugar beets are mainly produced in Europe and France is the leading world producer. With the production quota and guaranteed prices for domestic consumption, the EU has constrained its production. However, strong efforts in sugar beet genetics and sugar refining have been made to decrease costs roughly 2% per year in order to be more competitive. With the removal of the EU production quota in 2015, EU sugar refining companies have announced a plan to increase production in order to reduce their average costs.

FIGURE 9.14B Light crude oil price at the NYMEX, in US dollars per barrel

Market Structure In 2012, production and exportation were dominated by Brazil while the USA and EU were net importers. However, the world market is strongly distorted by policies from most countries.

The International Sugar Organization (ISO, 2013) released key figures about the sugar sector in 2012:

- The 10 largest producers provided 77% of world production (Figure 9.16). The major producers were Brazil, India, the EU and China. Three countries (Brazil, India and

TABLE 9.4 World raw sugar production, in million tons

Year	Sugar from cane	Sugar from beet
1960–61	31	24
1970–71	42	30
1980–81	55	33
1990–91	73	42
2000–01	95	37
2010–11	134	32
2011–12	137	40
2012–13	143	38

Source: F.O. Licht, 2013.

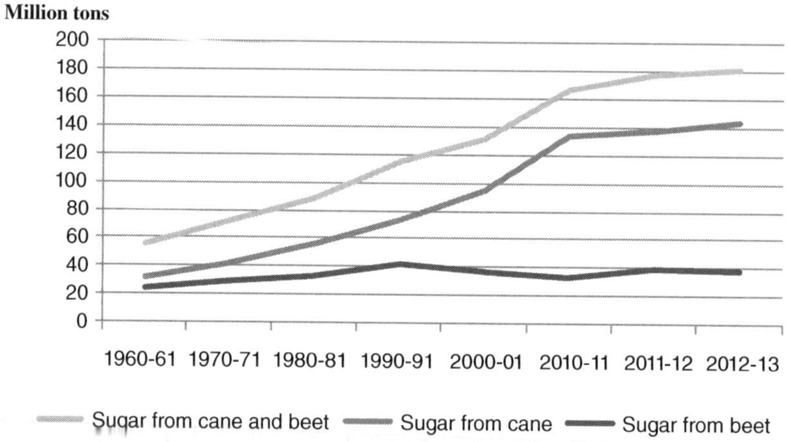

FIGURE 9.15 Raw sugar production from cane and beet
Source: Author's figure from F.O. Licht data, 2013.

the EU) produced 47% of world production and five countries (Brazil, India, the EU, China and Thailand) produced 60% of world production. Production is scattered over different continents.

- The 10 largest consumers accounted for 63% of world consumption (Figure 9.17). The major consumers were India, the EU, China, Brazil and the USA.
- The major importers were the EU, Indonesia, the USA and China (Figure 9.18).
- Brazil strongly increased its sales and exportations during the 2000s. Brazil has become by far the major exporter with 51% of all exports in 2012, which is about four times more than Thailand, the second largest exporter (Figure 9.19).

The leading world sugar trader is Sucden (France). Other major trading companies are Cargill, Bunge, Louis Dreyfus Commodities, etc.

Rank	Producer	Million tons	World market share
1	Brazil	40.3	22%
2	India	26.6	15%
3	EU	18.5	10%
4	China	14.6	8%
5	Thailand	9.5	5%
6	USA	8.4	5%
7	Mexico	6.0	3%
8	Pakistan	5.2	3%
9	Russia	5.2	3%
10	Australia	4.5	2%
	Top ten	138.7	77%
	Others	42.3	23%
	World	181.0	100%

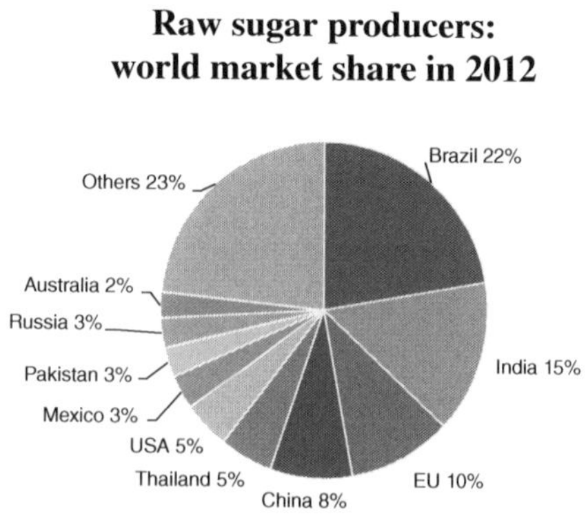

FIGURE 9.16 Raw sugar producers in 2012
Source: Author's calculations from ISO data, 2013.

Rank	Consumer	Million tons	World market share
1	India	24.6	14%
2	EU	19.6	11%
3	China	15.41	9%
4	Brazil	13.6	8%
5	USA	10.5	6%
6	Russia	5.9	3%
7	Indonesia	5.7	3%
8	Pakistan	5.1	3%
9	Mexico	4.4	3%
10	Egypt	3.1	2%
	Top ten	107.9	63%
	Others	62.8	37%
	World	170.7	100%

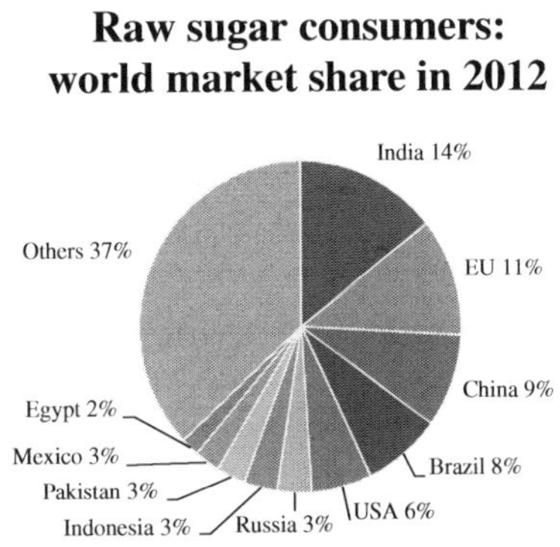

FIGURE 9.17 Raw sugar consumers in 2012
Source: Author's calculations from ISO data, 2013.

The major sugar refinery companies are SüdZucker AG (Germany), Associated British Foods plc, Raizen, (Brazil), Tereos (France), Mitr Phol Sugar Corp (Thailand), Nordzucker GmbH & Co. KG (Germany), Thai Roong Ruang Sugar Group (Thailand), Wilmar International Ltd (Singapore), Louis Dreyfus Commodities (The Netherlands), Pfeifer & Langen KG (Germany). Most companies operate in different countries. (Source: http://www.bloomberg.com/news/2011-11-04/suedzucker-leads-the-top-10-sugar-producing-companies-table-.html.)

Policy Sugar is a very policy-distorted commodity (Mitchell, 2004). Sugar markets are affected by production quotas, import controls and government-guaranteed prices in many parts of the world: the EU, Japan, the USA and many other countries. Protectionist policies originated from the early 1800s when European countries producing sugar beets could not compete with cane beet-producing countries in warmer areas. Up to now, EU, Japanese and US production is not competitive. Sugar is politically important since it is a basic staple

Rank	Importer	Million tons	World market share
1	EU	3.5	7%
2	Indonesia	3.1	6%
3	USA	2.6	5%
4	China	2.5	5%
5	UAE	1.9	4%
6	Algeria	1.6	3%
7	South Korea	1.6	3%
8	Malaysia	1.6	3%
9	Bangladesh	1.4	3%
10	Japan	1.4	3%
	Top ten	21.3	43%
	Others	28.7	57%
	World	50.0	100%

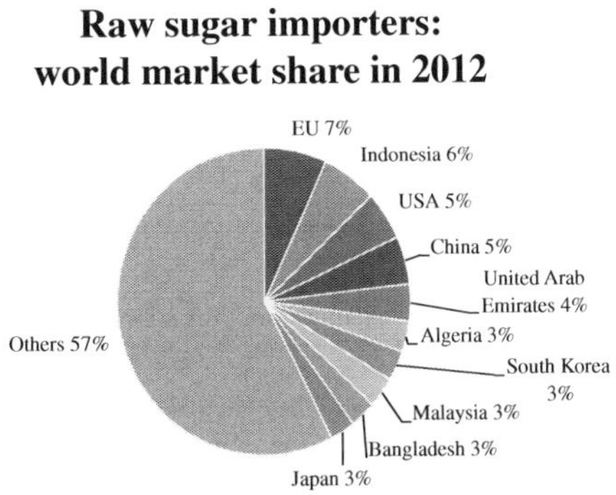

FIGURE 9.18 Raw sugar importers in 2012
Source: Author's calculations from ISO data, 2013.

Rank	Exporter	Million tons	World market share
1	Brazil	25.6	51%
2	Thailand	6.6	13%
3	Australia	3.5	7%
4	Guatemala	1.9	4%
5	UAE	1.8	4%
6	Mexico	1.7	3%
7	EU	1.5	3%
8	Cuba	0.9	2%
9	India	0.8	2%
10	Colombia	0.7	1%
	Top ten	45.0	90%
	Others	5.0	10%
	World	50.0	100%

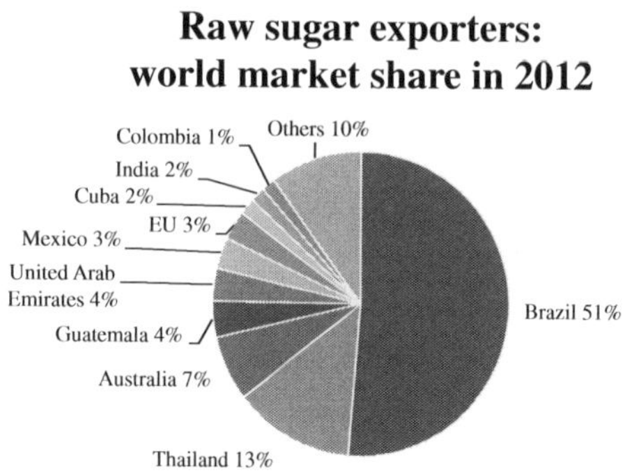

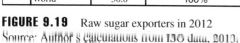

FIGURE 9.19 Raw sugar exporters in 2012
Source: Author's calculations from ISO data, 2013.

consumed by almost all the population. Some countries such as Turkey have adopted even higher protection. China keeps domestic sugar prices close to US prices with the help of import restrictions. India, the second largest producer and the third largest exporter in 2012 (ISO, 2013), protects its domestic producers mainly with import tariffs.

The USA protects its producers with a deficiency payment mechanism and allows import quotas mainly from Caribbean countries. The US sugar programme uses price supports, domestic marketing allotments and tariff-rate quotas to influence the amount of sugar available to the US market. The programme supports US sugar prices above comparable levels in the world market. The US Department of Agriculture (USDA) provides loans to sugar cane and beet producers and processors that guarantee a minimum price regardless of market conditions. At the maturity of the loan (often after 9 months), sugar producers and processors have to decide either to provide sugar to the government to repay the loan if the market price is low or sell their sugar on the market if the market price is higher than the USDA loan amount. Currently, the loan rate is 18.75 US cents per pound for raw cane sugar and 24.09 US cents per pound for refined beet sugar. See Figure 9.20.

In 2006, under pressure from the WTO, the EU decided to reform its production quota system, decreasing the minimum price by 36% over 5 years. As a result, from a net exporter the EU has become a net importer and among the two largest importers. In 2013, the EU production quota amounted to 13.3 million tons. The EU minimum price production under quota was fixed at:

- 335.2 €/ton (that is, 19.77 US cents/lb) for raw sugar while the world price fluctuated between 320 €/ton (that is, 18.87 US cents/lb) in September 2012 and 473 €/ton (that is, 27.93 US cents/lb) in October 2011 on the ICE;
- 404.4 €/ton (that is, 23.85 US cents/lb) for white sugar while the world price fluctuated between 424 €/ton (that is, 25 US cents/lb) on September 2012 and 539 €/ton (that is, 31.79 US cents/lb) in September 2012 on the LIFFE.

Out-of-quota sugar is sold at world market price. In 2011, the EU Commission observed that sugar beet growers and processors had strongly improved their productivity and could sustain their business with regard to sugar cane producers and processors. Finally, in 2013,

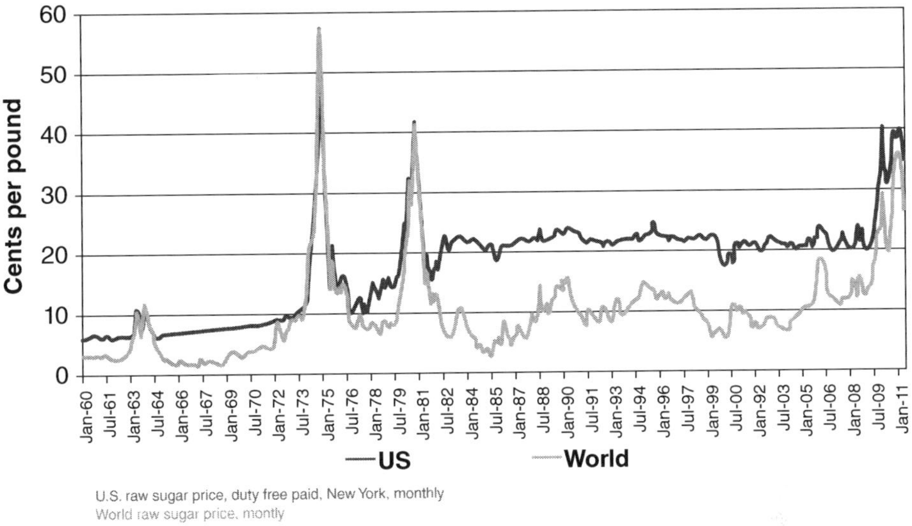

FIGURE 9.20 World vs. US sugar prices

the EU decided to remove its production quota system by the year 2017, but EU farmers and processors would like a 3-year delay to increase their competitiveness. Major EU producers are France, Germany, Poland and the UK. Furthermore, since 1975 less developed countries (LDCs) have benefitted from quota-free and duty-free access to the EU market. The removal of EU external trade protection will let African, Caribbean and Pacific (ACP) countries and LDCs compete with other exporters, mainly Brazil.

India, the first consumer and second largest consumer of sugar, became a net importer in the 2009–10 marketing year when the world price increased while its population was increasing strongly. To become a net exporter again maybe in 2013–14, India has encouraged domestic production with three types of minimum price paid to farmers. A minimum statutory price has been paid by processors to sugarcane farmers. Such minimum price is paid irrespective of the quality of the cane. It distorts market pricing. A state advised price (SAP) has taken differences in regional production costs and productivity into account. A fair and remunerative price (FRP) has been managed by the central government. Owing to different price support schemes per region, Zimmermann and Zeddies (2002) observed that the Indian market was partitioned into different sub-markets. Owing to domestic policy protections provided by most countries, they also estimated that only about 20% of world sugar production is traded under free market conditions.

Price Level and Volatility There are two major futures contracts trading sugar: raw sugar #11 on the ICE in New York (Figure 9.21) and the white sugar contract on the LIFFE (ICE group) in London. Other futures contracts exist, such as the National Commodity and Derivatives Exchange in Mumbai, India.

Brazil's production has played a major role in the world sugar market. Haley (2013) showed how higher production costs in Brazil and growing ethanol use in Brazil explained the higher world price during the 2000s.

FIGURE 9.21 Sugar #11 monthly prices on the ICE in US cents per pound
Source: Futures trading charts at http://futures.tradingcharts.com/chart/SU/M?anticache=1393575957.

Over the 2004–13 decade, sugar prices evolved from 8 to 35 US cents per pound, which is an increase from 1 to 4. Volatility may be very strong within a year. Price volatility was mainly due to policy-induced production swings in India (McConnell *et al.*, 2010).

Conclusion The world sugar market is strongly distorted by national sugar policies enforced in many countries. Over the 2000s, Brazil has increased its position as a dominant producer and exporter: its production and logistics costs are milestones for operators.

9.3.4.2 Grain Markets: Cooperation to Avoid Hunger? Grains are major sources of energy to feed human beings and animals. According to the USDA, the three major cereals in the world are corn (36% of total cereals), wheat (31%) and rice (20%): rice in Asia, corn in the Americas and wheat in Europe. Cereal production has shaped areas of population in the world. See Figures 9.22 and 9.23.

The 1929 economic crisis led to persistent problems of oversupply and low prices, and the spread of agricultural protectionism. Grains are so important to feed the world that multilateral grain cooperation started in 1934 with an International Wheat Agreement negotiated between wheat exporting and importing countries, involving mandatory price ranges and supply and purchase commitments. It was also decided to set up an international agency, which became the International Wheat Council in 1949. In 1985 it extended its activities to coarse grains (corn, barley, sorghum, rye, millet, triticale) and became the International Grains Council

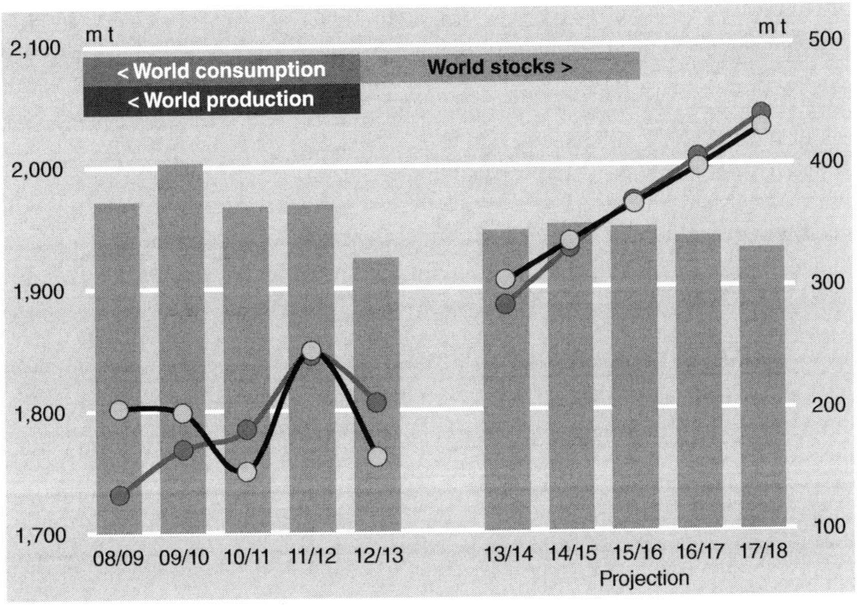

FIGURE 9.22 World production, consumption and stocks of grain
The left scale in million tons is used for the curves related to world grain production and consumption. The right scale in million tons is used for the bars related to world grain stocks.
Source: International Grains Council, December 2012, http://www.igc.int/en/Default.aspx.

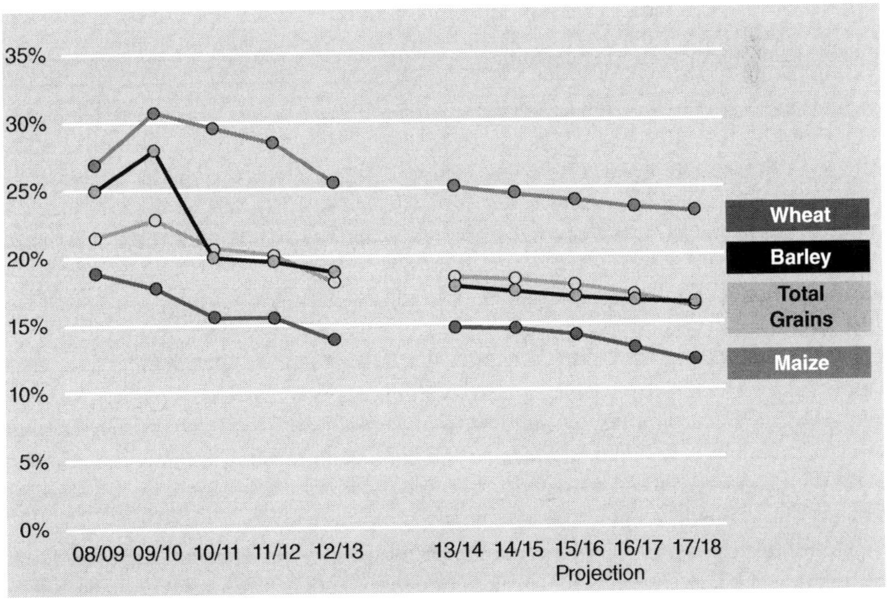

FIGURE 9.23 Total grain stock-to-use ratios
Source: International Grains Council, December 2012, http://www.igc.int/en/Default.aspx.

(IGC). Rice was added in 2009. Today, the IGC gathers and releases information about world production, consumption and trade in order to monitor and adjust grain policy. However, unlike the 1934 agreement, it places no limits on members' exports or production.

The 2008 and 2010 jumps in grain prices triggered new cooperation among the G20 countries in June 2011 with the setting up of the 'Agricultural Market Information System' (AMIS) in the hands of the Food and Agriculture Organization (FAO) to collect data for more agricultural commodities.

According to the International Grain Council (December 2012), 'For grains, the supply and demand trends result in a contraction in both the absolute level of inventories beyond 2014/15 and the stocks-to-use measure, changes in which give a very broad indication of market tightness. The stock-to-use ratio for total grains is expected to decline to 16% by 2017/18, from 18% at the end of 2012/13. The tighter outlook will leave markets more vulnerable to price gains, as well as volatility, in the event of poor crops.'

EU Policy for Grains With the implementation of the WTO Uruguay Round Agreement on Agriculture signed in 1994 in Marrakesh, Morocco, the EU reduced its expenditure on export subsidies by 36% and the volume of subsidized export by 21%. In 2005, the WTO agreement in Hong Kong required that all agricultural export subsidies should be strongly reduced by 2011 and phased out by the end of 2013. There are also some import tariffs that are compatible with the WTO agreements.

Within these constraints, the European Commission may fix refunds which enable EU exporters to compete on the lower-priced world market. These may also be fixed by tender. No export refunds have been granted on grains since September 2006 and grain-based processed products since 2007.

The EU may intervene in markets by purchasing grains from farmers and traders at an intervention price which is a minimum guaranteed price of €101.31 per ton between 1 November and 31 May for common wheat, barley, corn, sorghum and durum wheat. So, the EU intervention price is the price of last resort for farmers and traders. Grain held in intervention stores is sold by tender onto the domestic market or for export or released for EU food aid to people in distress.

The EU intervention system was abolished for rye in 2004–05. The EU reduced guaranteed intervention quantities to zero for corn from 2009–10, durum wheat from 2009–10, barley from 2010–11 and rice from 2009–10. The EU maintains the right to reintroduce intervention mechanisms. (http://gain.fas.usda.gov/Recent%20GAIN%20Publications/Grain%20and%20Feed%20Annual_London_EU-27_4-4-2013.pdf).

9.3.4.3 The Soft Wheat Market, Crucial to Feed Urban Populations Soft wheat – commonly called wheat – is a crucial staple providing energy to feed people in cities. It is used for food aid by western countries. In the past, the lack of wheat to feed the world led to riots (in several African capital cities in 2008) and was the immediate cause of several revolutions such as the 1789 French Revolution in Paris. Rural populations may cultivate fields and gardens to get enough food while urban populations cannot.

World wheat production and consumption has increased with the rise in urban population. According to the United Nations (2010), a major demographic shift occurred in 2010. For the first time in history, the world population was more urban than rural. In 2011 in China, after 30 years of strong economic development, the urban population surpassed the rural population. Furthermore, the UN anticipates that the world's urban areas will continue to draw some of the rural population and will absorb all the population growth over the next four decades, mainly in the developing world. 78% of the inhabitants of the more developed regions lived in urban areas in 2011, and just 47% of those in the less developed regions. From 2011 to 2050, the world population is expected to pass from 7.0 billion to 9.3 billion inhabitants. However, in 2050 it is expected to be 67% urban, passing from 3.6 billion in 2011 to 6.3 billion urban people (United Nations, 2012).

From 1934, the governments of major nations have paid a lot of attention to carry-over stocks in order to forecast prices and possible shortages to care for their urban populations.

Products and Use Wheat has become a critical staple in the world, not only in Northern America and Europe. Food aid usually includes wheat exports, so African countries which did not consume wheat have experienced a change of dietary habits.

There are two types of soft wheat: milling wheat and feed wheat. When its protein content is high because of the characteristics of varietals and dry weather conditions before harvest, wheat is called milling wheat. It may be processed into flour to make bread and pastry. Otherwise, wheat is used for animal feed and agro-industries. In Europe wheat is a major input to process starch and to produce biofuels. In the USA, due to its climate, corn is more productive than wheat. So, US starch-processing plants and biofuel plants use corn.

The major substitutes for soft wheat are:

- corn for animal feeds and the starch industry,
- oil for the fuel markets.

But wheat is the commodity used to feed urban populations.

Market Structure Wheat production is reaching 700 million tons per year. Wheat is the most important crop in Europe and Central Asia. However, due to strong weather differences from year to year (risk of drought or floods), production in the 'Black Sea countries' (including Russia, Ukraine and Kazakhstan, even if this last country does not have any border with the Black Sea) and Australia fluctuate a lot from year to year, so these countries may be big or small exporters… and disturb the strategies of operators in other exporting countries. In contrast, wheat production is a lot more regular in Western Europe, particularly within its French wheat loft. See Figure 9.24.

In 2009 the governments of Russia, Ukraine and Kazakhstan discussed the creation of the Black Sea grain pool to export a potential 70 million tons in good years. Up to now, the initiative has not been implemented.

In 2012 the top 10 wheat-producing countries accounted for 79% of world production (Figure 9.25). The EU, China, India and the USA were the largest producers. Those countries were also the largest consumers (Figure 9.26). In 2012 the top 10 wheat-consuming countries accounted for 71% of world consumption. The top three wheat consumers are China, the EU and India. Increasing urban populations and growing purchasing power in South Asia over the 2000s resulted in increasing consumption of grain and meat (chicken meat in India, chicken and pig meat in China)… and chicken and pigs are fed with wheat or corn.

From year to year, China and India consume their production and are net importers or exporters. In contrast, the USA and the EU are the two largest exporters.

From the mid-1990s the USA has produced about 10% of world wheat and has been the worlds leading wheat exporter (Figure 9.27). The EU and Canada also export every year. So,

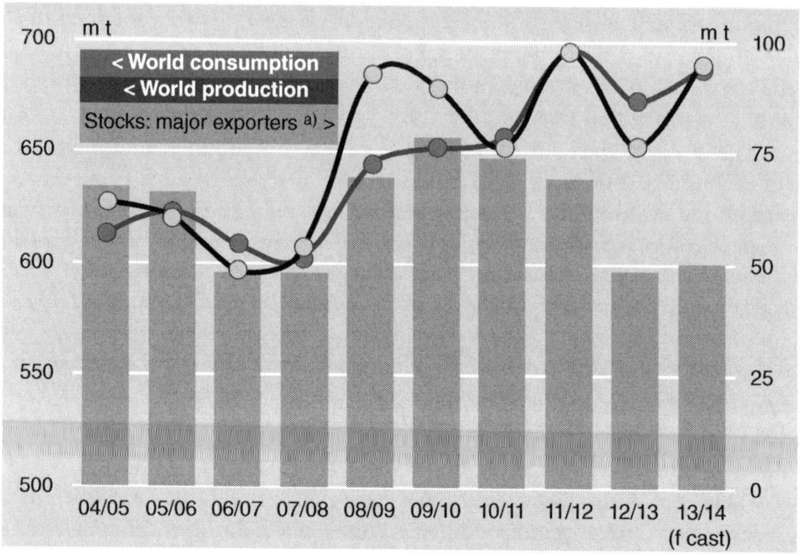

FIGURE 9.24 World production, consumption and stocks of wheat
The left scale in million tons is used for the curves related to world wheat production and consumption. The right scale in million tons is used for the bars related to world wheat stocks.
Source: International Grains Council, http://www.igc.int/en/Default.aspx.

the USA, the EU and Canada are the main competitors, disturbed by the erratic surpluses or deficits of Australia (due to a very irregular yield caused by severe droughts some years) and the three 'Black Sea countries' (due to extremely changeable weather with severe frosts, floods or droughts some years). In 2012 those seven countries accounted for 54% of world exports: competition is fierce.

Egypt is the largest importer of wheat (Figure 9.28). Brazil, Indonesia, Japan and Algeria follow.

Rank	Producer	Million tons	World market share
1	EU	133	19%
2	China	121	17%
3	India	95	14%
4	USA	62	9%
5	Russia	38	5%
6	Canada	27	4%
7	Australia	22	3%
8	Pakistan	23	3%
9	Turkey	16	2%
10	Ukraine	16	2%
	Top ten	552	79%
	Others	143	21%
	World	695	100%

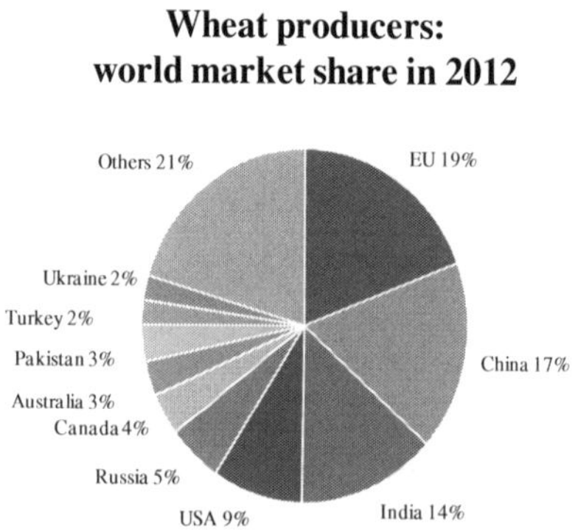

FIGURE 9.25 Wheat producers in 2012
Source: Author's calculations from ERS-USDA data, 2013.

Rank	Consumer	Million tons	World market share
1	China	125	18%
2	EU	121	17%
3	India	85	12%
4	USA	38	6%
5	Russia	34	5%
6	Pakistan	24	3%
7	Egypt	19	3%
8	Turkey	18	3%
9	Iran	16	2%
10	Ukraine	12	2%
	Top ten	491	71%
	Others	205	29%
	World	696	100%

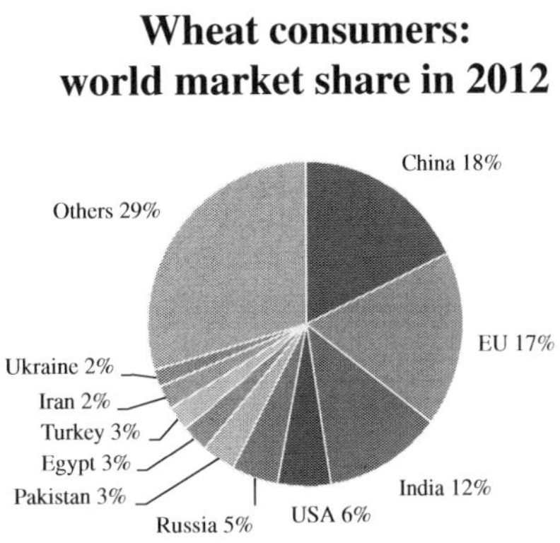

FIGURE 9.26 Wheat consumers in 2012
Source: Author's calculations from ERS-USDA data, 2013.

Rank	Exporter	Million tons	World market share
1	USA	27	13%
2	EU	22	11%
3	Canada	19	9%
4	Australia	19	9%
5	Russia	11	5%
6	Ukraine	7	3%
7	Kazakhstan	7	3%
8	India	7	3%
9	Argentina	4	2%
10	Turkey	3	2%
	Top ten	126	61%
	Others	80	39%
	World	206	100%

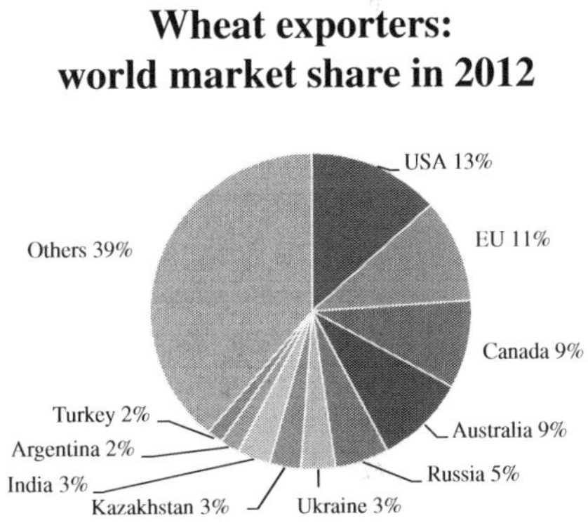

FIGURE 9.27 Wheat exporters in 2012
Source: Author's calculations from ERS-USDA data, 2013.

Rank	Importer	Million tons	World market share
1	Egypt	9	6%
2	Brazil	8	5%
3	Indonesia	7	5%
4	Japan	7	5%
5	Algeria	6	4%
6	EU	6	4%
7	South Korea	6	4%
8	Nigeria	4	3%
9	Mexico	4	3%
10	China	3	2%
	Top ten	58	41%
	Others	85	59%
	World	143	100%

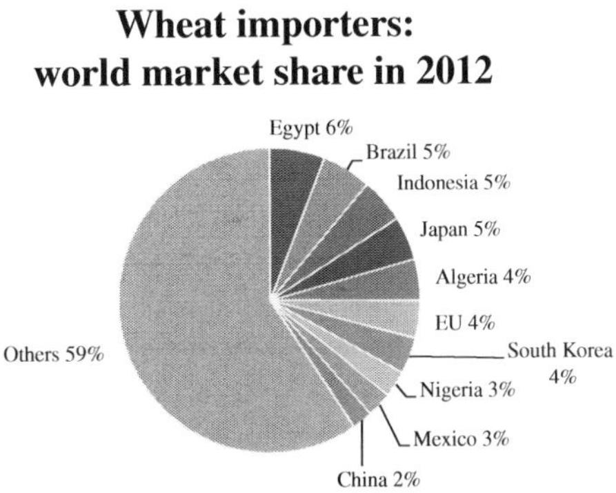

FIGURE 9.28 Wheat in importers in 2012
Source: Author's calculations from ERS-USDA data, 2013.

The ABCD traders are the main carriers in the wheat business. However in Europe, they source wheat from and also compete with French elevators. the French union of agricultural cooperatives In-Vivo, two grain coops Vivescia and Axereal and the Soufflet merchant family. Vivescia, Axereal and Souflet are heavily invested in the wheat milling industry and other cereal-processing industries such as the malt industry, throughout Europe and also around the world: the three groups Vivescia, Soufflet and Axereal belong to the top five malt processors.

Policy The US Food, Conservation and Energy Act of 2008 (2008 Farm Act) provides wheat producers access to marketing loan benefits, direct payments (DPs), counter-cyclical payments (CCPs) and average crop revenue election (ACRE) payments. In addition, many producers may benefit from subsidized crop and revenue insurance available under previous legislation, as well as from new permanent disaster assistance. Moreover, wheat producers are affected by conservation and trade programmes. US loan rates are set in the legislation. For wheat, the rate is \$2.75 per bushel for crop years 2008–09 and \$2.94 per bushel for crop years 2010–12. The US government provides direct payments to producers according to historical acreage at the rate of 52 cents per bushel for crop year 2008, for 85% of base acres in crop years 2008 and 2012 and 83.3% in crop years 2009–11, and a producer's historical payment yield for the farm.

Public support differs a lot among the biggest exporting countries: the EU, the USA and Canada provide substantial support while Australia removed almost all support systems. On the contrary, Argentina has taxed its grain exportations.

The EU intervention price for grains decreased from €163.49 per ton in 1992 to €101.31 per ton in 2002 and has remained at that level. As a result, the EU minimum wheat price went down and merged with the world price in 2002. Since 2002 the price has fluctuated from 1 to 2.5, especially in 2007–08 and 2010. Furthermore, wheat is a critical staple to feed people. So in the past, when governments feared some shortage to feed their population, they put embargoes on exports as India did in 2008 and Russia in August 2010. Such sudden policy decisions troubled market operators who feared shortages. Then, world wheat prices jumped immediately and tremendously.

Price Level and Volatility The above-mentioned political decisions strongly impacted wheat price and volatility. From an historical point of view, the wheat contract on the CBOT (CME group) was the first agricultural contract designed in 1865. For about 150 years, it has been a hedging instrument for wheat producers and users. CBOT wheat prices have prevailed, being a reliable signal first in the USA and then worldwide. With 27.4 million wheat contracts traded in 2012, the CBOT contract leads the market. Other wheat contracts have been launched during the last 15 years.

Hence, in 2012, 25.8 million wheat contracts were traded on the Zhengzhou Commodity Exchange in China. The contract was launched in 1993. 7.5 million contracts were made on the milling wheat #2 contract on the Paris (MATIF) NYSE-Euronext futures exchange (Figure 9.29). The contract opened in 1998 has become a leader in driving prices for food and animal feed world operators since the underlying wheat has a higher protein content than the CBOT contract. Furthermore, the Paris-based wheat contract (Figure 9.30) serves as a guidepost for other agricultural commodities produced and sold in Europe, such as barley, oats and rye.

On 6 June 2012, the CME group launched a wheat futures contract tied directly to milling wheat from the Black Sea region with 10 delivery ports in Russia, Ukraine and Romania

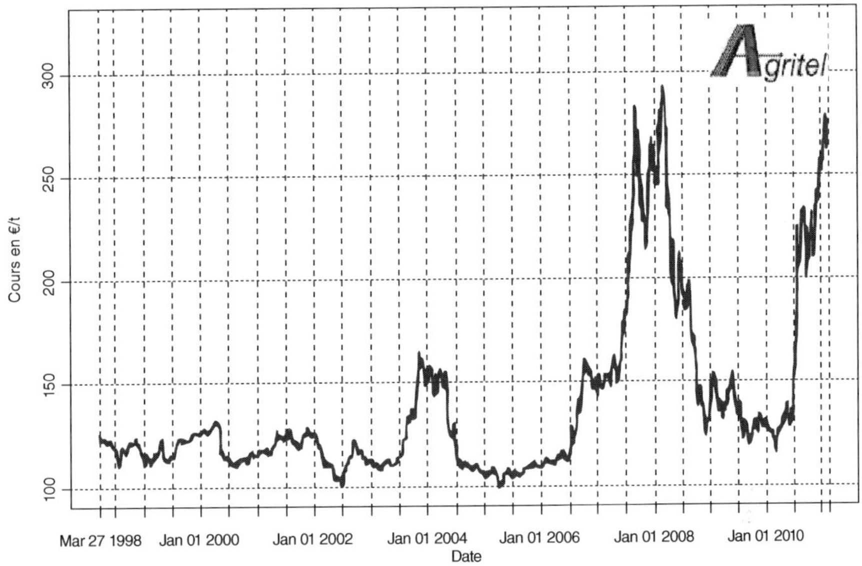

FIGURE 9.29 Milling wheat #2 contract prices over the 2000s on the Paris Euronext Futures Exchange, in euros per ton
Source: Agritel with data from NYSE-Euronext. Reproduced by permission of AGRITEL.

(Figure 9.31). But free trade conditions may be problematic to attract hedgers and speculators because of embargoes decided by governments in the region. Since 2007, Kazakhstan has suspended wheat exports once, Russia twice and Ukraine three times. It means that a buyer could not get delivery of the commodity during the period of embargo.

Conclusion On the supply side, the wheat market is much disputed on international markets among some regular exporting countries like the USA, Canada and Europe. Furthermore, sometimes these countries are troubled by large exports from the Black Sea countries (Russia, Ukraine and Kazakhstan) and Australia, whose production is very erratic due to climatic conditions.

On the demand side, the wheat market depends on the evolution of population size and dietary habits. Demand has also been affected by policy incentives to produce biofuels.

From a human and political viewpoint, wheat is a critical staple to feed people. In addition to permanent policy regulations enforced in several countries, when governments feared some shortage to feed their population they decided to introduce an embargo on exports and enforce it quickly. Such sudden policy decisions strongly impacted market price levels and volatility.

9.3.4.4 The Corn Market, with Brazilian Exports Overtaking US Exports in 2012

As mentioned above, corn is the most cultivated cereal but mainly located in the Americas.

Products and uses Corn is a major source of human food (tortillas, isoglucose, edible oil, gluten, etc.), animal feeds and non-food ingredients (ethanol, starch, etc.). If corn is central in the Mexican cuisine with sweetcorn and tortillas, it is used for many other types of food:

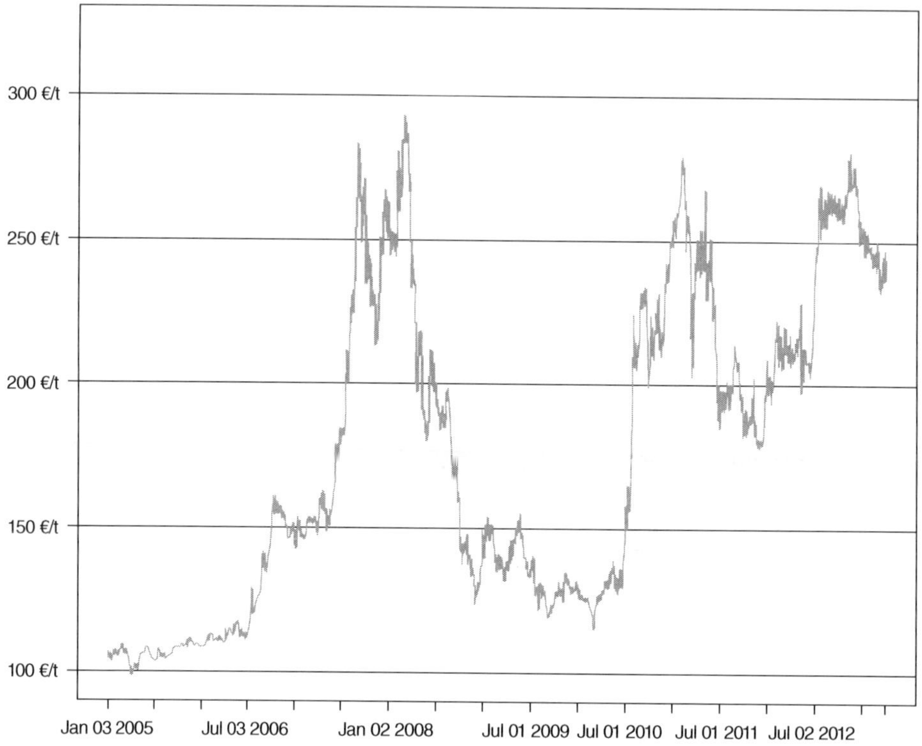

FIGURE 9.30 Milling wheat prices from 2005 to 2012 on the Paris Euronext Futures Exchange, in euros per ton
Source: Agritel with data from NYSE-Euronext. Reproduced by permission of AGRITEL.

popcorn, porridge, soft drinks and beer. Its hydrogenation leads to high-fructose corn syrup as a sweetener used in soft drinks. Corn is also fermented with other ingredients to produce beer. Corn is a major source of energy in animal feeds for cattle, pigs, chicken, etc. Over time, corn has become an ingredient for a lot of non-food uses in the paper industry, renewable plastic industry, biofuel (ethanol) industry, etc.

The major corn substitutes are:

- wheat for animal feeds and the starch industry;
- sugar cane and beet in the soft drink and ethanol industries;
- oil for fuel markets.

So the corn market is related to other commodity markets for food, feeds and biofuels.

Market Structure The world production of corn reached almost 950 million tons in 2012, even though the US harvest dropped by 13% in 2012 compared with 2011 (Figure 9.32).

In 2012 the USA and China accounted for 59% of world corn production. Brazil has become the third producer, with a strong increase from the mid-2000s. In 2012 the EU was the fourth producer, but consumes more than its production. Argentina was the fifth producer,

FIGURE 9.31 Milling wheat monthly price on the CBOT (CME group), in US cents per bushel
Source: Futures trading charts at http://futures.tradingcharts.com/chart/ZW/M?anticache=1393577462.

but is a small consumer so it exports a lot. The top five producers provided 79% of world production. See Figure 9.33.

In 2012 the USA and China accounted for 60% of world consumption of corn. The EU and Brazil followed. See Figure 9.34.

The international trade of corn represents 11% of world production. Before 2012, the USA was the largest exporter of corn in the world. But due to severe drought in the mid-west, US production was not sufficient to retain leadership on the international market. Brazil and Argentina exported more corn than the USA. Brazilian and Argentinean exports have increased strongly over the 2000s. However, in 2013 the US harvest seemed promising according to the IGC and the USA is expected to recover its leadership (Figure 9.35).

While those three American countries are the major exporters, Asian and European countries are major importers. In 2012 Japan, the EU and South Korea accounted for 39% of world imports. Japan accounted for 17% and has been quite stable since 1982 with volumes imported of 13 to 15 million tons per year. In contrast, Chinese imports have been erratic. In 2012 China was the second world producer and consumer, behind the USA (Figure 9.36).

Non-GMO corn is not much present on international markets, while the USA, Brazil and Argentina mainly produce GMO corn. Owing to some national legislation, most EU countries do not produce GMO corn, while they import GMO corn to feed animals. Notice that sweetcorn produced in Europe as food for people is GMO-free. In 2011, GMO sweetcorn appeared massively in the USA.

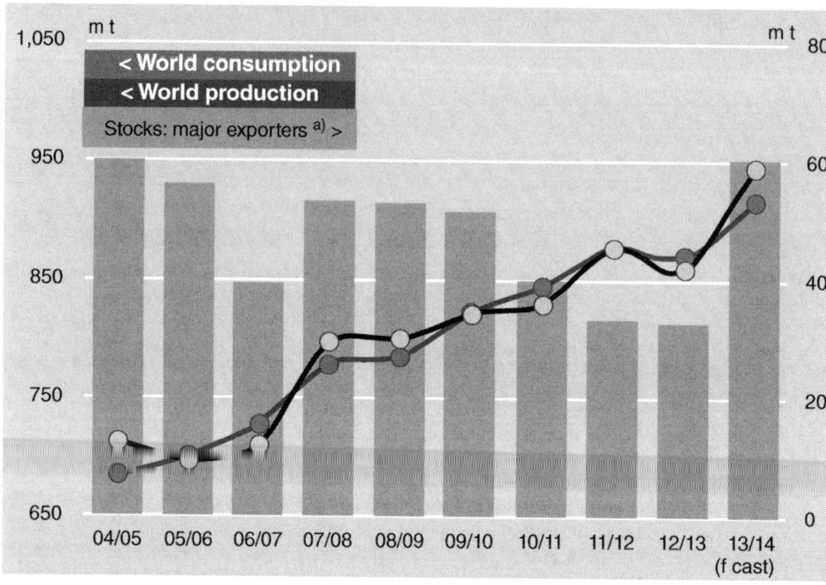

FIGURE 9.32 World production, consumption and stocks of corn
The left scale in million tons is used for the curves related to world corn production and consumption. The right scale in million tons is used for the bars related to world corn stocks.
Source: International Grains Council, http://www.igc.int/en/Default.aspx.

Policy The EU policy for grain is as mentioned above.

The US 2008 Farm Act provides quite similar policy tools for corn and wheat, except for the amount. For corn, the minimum effective corn price was \$2.23 per bushel – the sum of the direct payment (28 cents) and the national loan rate (\$1.95). The maximum payment rate for corn is 40 cents per bushel – the target price (\$2.63) minus the minimum effective price

Rank	Producer	Million tons	World market share
1	USA	274	34%
2	China	206	25%
3	Brazil	77	9%
4	EU	59	7%
5	Argentina	27	3%
6	Ukraine	21	3%
7	Mexico	22	3%
8	India	22	3%
9	Canada	13	2%
10	South Africa	12	2%
	Top ten	731	90%
	Others	80	10%
	World	811	100%

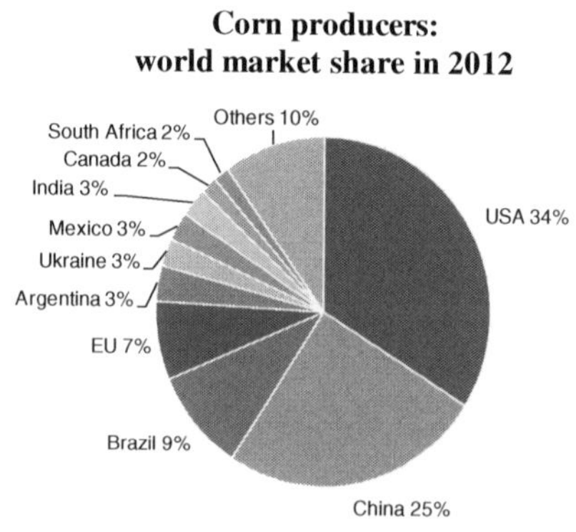

FIGURE 9.33 Corn producers in 2012
Source: Author's calculations from ERS-USDA data, 2013.

Rank	Consumer	Million tons	World market share
1	USA	267	34%
2	China	207	26%
3	EU	69	9%
4	Brazil	53	7%
5	Mexico	28	4%
6	India	17	2%
7	Japan	15	2%
8	Canada	12	2%
9	South Africa	11	1%
10	Indonesia	11	1%
	Top ten	688	88%
	Others	95	12%
	World	783	100%

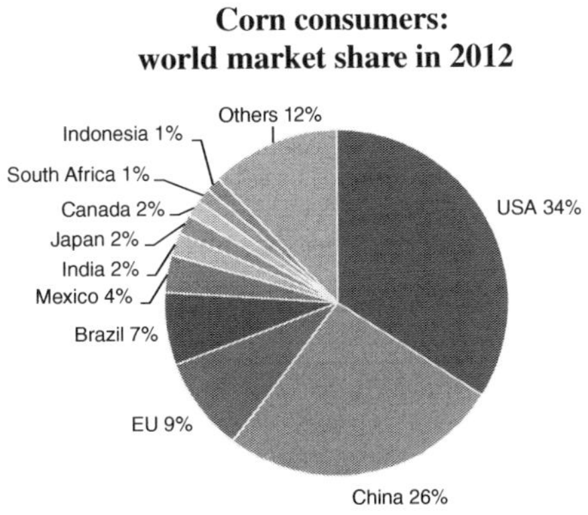

FIGURE 9.34 Corn consumers in 2012
Source: Author's calculations from ERS-USDA data, 2013.

Rank	Exporter	Million tons	World market share
1	Brazil	22	25%
2	Argentina	19	22%
3	USA	18	20%
4	Ukraine	14	15%
5	India	5	5%
6	Paraguay	2	2%
7	Russia	2	2%
8	EU	2	2%
9	South Africa	2	2%
10	Serbia	1	1%
	Top ten	85	97%
	Others	3	3%
	World	88	100%

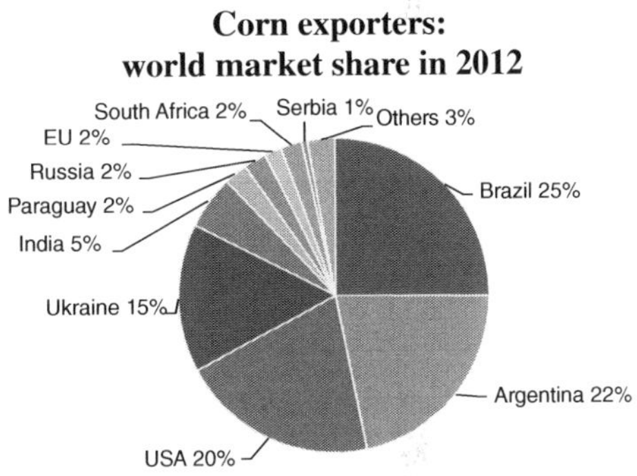

FIGURE 9.35 Corn exporters in 2012
Source: Author's calculations from ERS-USDA data, 2013.

Rank	Importer	Million tons	World market share
1	Japan	15	17%
2	EU	11	13%
3	South Korea	8	10%
4	Mexico	7	8%
5	Taiwan	4	5%
6	Iran	4	5%
7	Egypt	4	4%
8	Colombia	3	4%
9	Malaysia	3	4%
10	China	3	4%
	Top ten	61	72%
	Others	23	28%
	World	84	100%

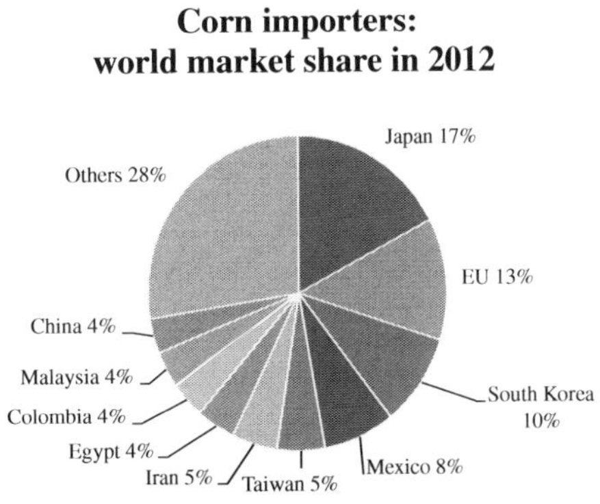

FIGURE 9.36 Corn importers in 2012
Source: Author's calculations from ERS-USDA data, 2013.

($2.23). The payment amount equals the product of the payment rate, a producer's historical payment acres (85% of base acres) and a producer's historical counter-cyclical payments yield, which may differ from the direct payment yield.

In contrast, Argentina, which was traditionally the second largest exporter, has a 20% tax on corn exports. The Argentinean government policies aim to keep 8–9 million metric tons in the country for domestic use. Any production beyond that will be exported under a licence system that gives Argentinean corn a price advantage over US exports. Limited grain storage infrastructure and tax on exports create a disincentive for farmers to hold grain and to increase corn plantings.

With the success of the extension programme to improve production practices, Brazilian farmers have increased plantings and yield over the 2000s to fulfil the objective of ethanol production. Furthermore, with the depreciation of their domestic currency against the US dollar, Brazilian competitiveness strongly increased fostering new plantings and exports.

There exists a controversy about environmental policy for biofuels for two major reasons:

1. Brazilian land dedicated to corn expanded at the expense of pasture and tropical forests, inducing less biodiversity. Brazilian forest is a large 'reservoir' for world biodiversity conservation.
2. US, Brazilian, Argentinean and EU farmland used to produce corn for biofuel could be used for food and make food prices lower, so more affordable for poor urban populations.

Price Level and Volatility For about 150 years, corn has been traded on the CBOT (CME group), which is by far the major corn market.

In 2012 the US harvest was poor, with a 13% decrease leading to a 55% decrease in US corn exports. In 2012, 6.5% of US corn production was exported instead of 12.5% in 2011 and about 15–18% previously. In 2012, Brazilian and Argentinean exports represented about 22% and 19% of their production, respectively.

So, US exports account for a relatively small portion of demand for US corn. But as the largest world exporter, except for the year 2012, the USA has dominated the world corn trade. International corn prices mainly reflect US prices, which are very dependent on weather in the mid-west around Chicago. In 2012, drought was responsible for a 17-year low yield in the USA. In August 2012, when traders realized that the harvest would be so poor, corn prices reached a record US$$8.43\frac{3}{4}$ a bushel on the CBOT. By September 2013, the corn harvest was expected to be excellent while government subsidies for biofuels were reduced. So prices went down below US$5 per bushel. See Figure 9.37.

Price volatility is mainly due to the uncertainty of weather impact on harvests and global demand for meat in Asia and subsidies for biofuels in the EU and the USA.

Conclusion Corn exports mainly originate from the Americas. The USA is the largest producer, with about 40% of world production. Brazilian production amounts to 20–26% of US production. Argentina only produces 7–10% of the volume produced by the USA. But Brazil and Argentina may continue to dispute the US leadership for exportation, as they did in 2012.

FIGURE 9.37 Corn monthly price on the CBOT (CME group), in US cents per bushel
Source: Futures trading charts at http://futures.tradingcharts.com/chart/CN/M?anticache=1393578051.

China is the second largest producer but mainly consumes its production. Japan, the EU and South Korea are the major importers.

9.3.4.5 The Rice Market, an Asian Market Disturbed by US Exports Rice is the major staple in Asia, the most populated continent.

Product and Use Rice is predominantly used to feed the population.

Market Structure The world production of rice amounted to about 475 million tons in 2012 (Figure 9.38). However, the international rice market only concerned 7–8% of the production, a very low rate compared with the 30% rate for wheat and 11% rate for corn.

Rice is mainly produced and consumed in Asia, even though African consumption has increased strongly during the 2000s. China, India, Indonesia, Bangladesh, Vietnam, Thailand, the Philippines and Myanmar are the top eight producers and consumers. See Figures 9.39 and 9.40.

Rice is mainly consumed in countries where it is produced, except for Thailand and the USA. In 2012 the USA was the 12th producing country, but the fourth exporter. Thailand was the sixth producing country, but the second exporter. Since 2011, Thailand has lost its 30-year

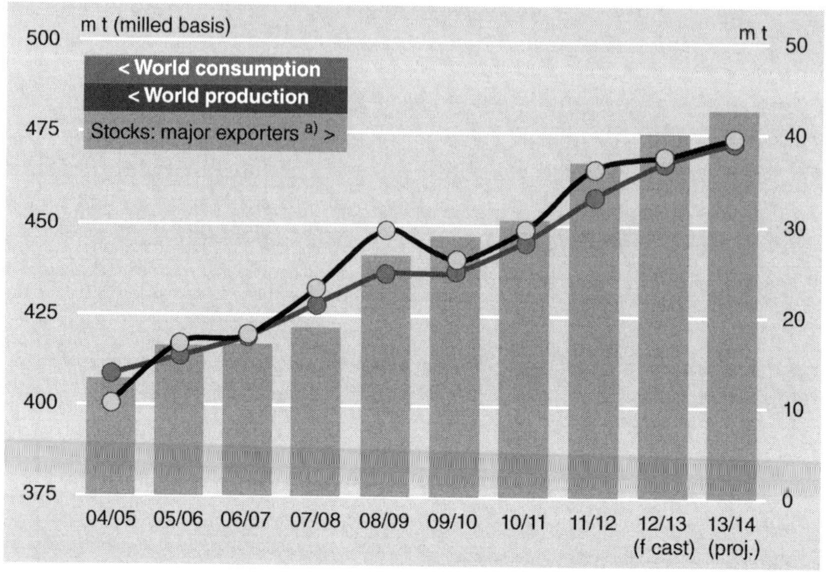

FIGURE 9.38 World production, consumption and stocks of rice
The left scale in million tons is used for the curves related to world rice production and consumption. The right scale in million tons is used for the bars related to world rice stocks.
Source: International Grains Council, http://www.igc.int/en/Default.aspx.

leadership as world top rice exporter mainly due to government domestic price support. The Thai government has purchased domestic rice at a higher price than the world price. It has stored rice. So, India has become the largest exporter. Notice that since 1998 Vietnam has strongly increased its production. In 2012 it became the third largest exporter. See Figure 9.41.

The major importers are Asian: China, Indonesia, Iran, Iraq, except for Nigeria which is the second largest importer. See Figure 9.42.

Rank	Producer	Million tons	World market share
1	China	143	30%
2	India	104	22%
3	Indonesia	38	8%
4	Bangladesh	34	7%
5	Vietnam	27	6%
6	Thailand	20	4%
7	Philippines	11	2%
8	Myanmar	11	2%
9	Brazil	8	2%
10	Japan	8	2%
	Top ten	404	85%
	Others	72	15%
	World	476	100%

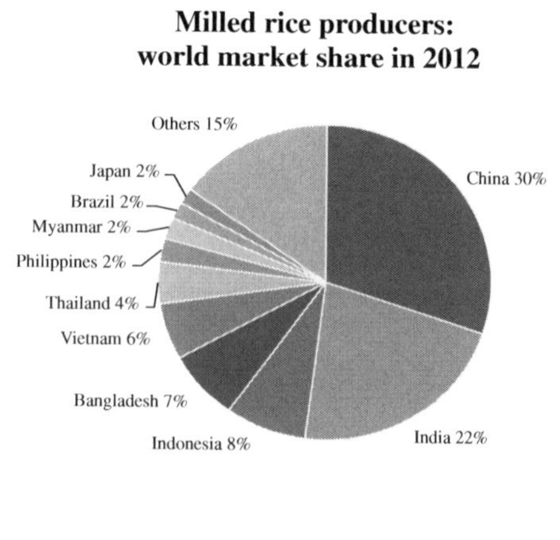

FIGURE 9.39 Milled rice producers in 2012
Source: Author's calculations from ERS-USDA data, 2013.

Rank	Consumer	Million tons	World market share
1	China	144	32%
2	India	96	21%
3	Indonesia	40	9%
4	Bangladesh	35	8%
5	Vietnam	20	4%
6	Philippines	12	3%
7	Thailand	11	2%
8	Myanmar	10	2%
9	Japan	8	2%
10	Brazil	8	2%
	Top ten	383	85%
	Others	70	15%
	World	453	100%

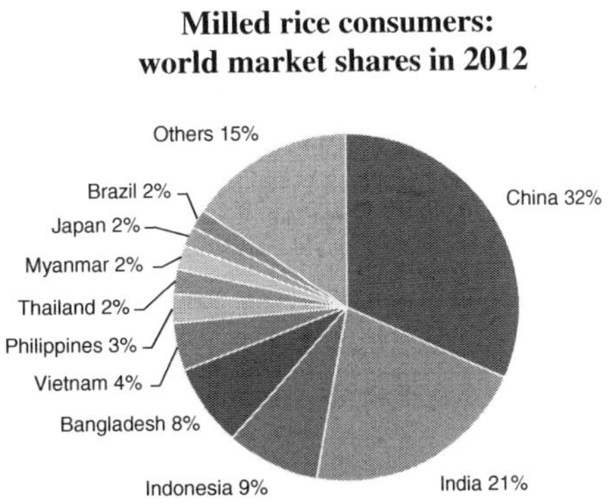

FIGURE 9.40 Milled rice consumers in 2012
Source: Author's calculations from ERS-USDA data, 2013.

Rank	Exporter	Million tons	World market share
1	India	9	25%
2	Vietnam	7	20%
3	Thailand	7	19%
4	USA	3	10%
5	Pakistan	3	8%
6	Cambodia	1	3%
7	Uruguay	1	2%
8	Egypt	1	2%
9	Brazil	1	2%
10	Myanmar	1	2%
	Top ten	34	94%
	Others	2	6%
	World	36	100%

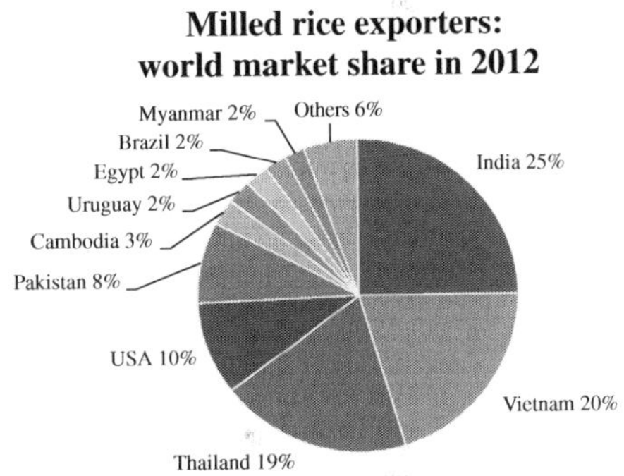

FIGURE 9.41 Milled rice exporters in 2012
Source: Author's calculations from ERS-USDA data, 2013.

Rank	Importer	Million tons	World market share
1	China	3	8%
2	Nigeria	3	7%
3	Indonesia	1	3%
4	Iran	2	4%
5	Iraq	1	4%
6	Saudi Arabia	1	3%
7	Philippines	1	4%
8	EU	1	3%
9	Ivory Coast	1	3%
10	Malaysia	1	3%
	Top ten	15	43%
	Others	21	57%
	World	36	100%

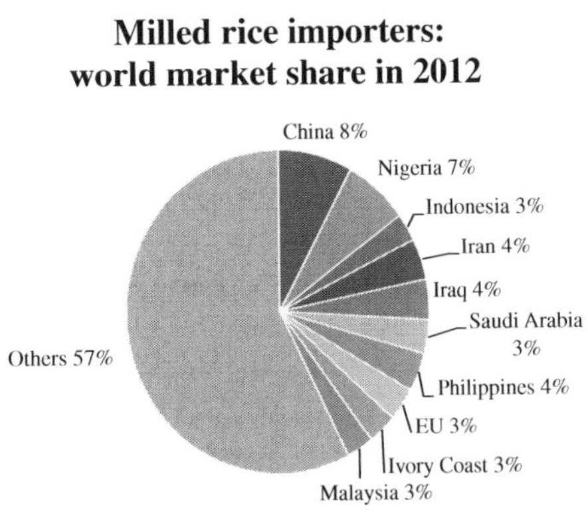

FIGURE 9.42 Milled rice importers in 2012
Source: Author's calculations from ERS-USDA data, 2013.

FIGURE 9.43 Rough rice monthly price on the CBOT (CME group), in US cents per bushel
Source: Futures trading charts at http://futures.tradingcharts.com/chart/RI/M?anticache=1393579221.

Policy The Asian countries learnt how to coordinate their policy in 2009 after their disorganized decisions on export embargoes in 2007–08.

Asian countries have adopted programmes to be self-sufficient (Dawe, 2010, 2013). With subsidies, they store rice to secure the food supply in their numerous and very populated urban areas.

Price and Price Volatility Rice is quoted mainly on the CBOT (CME group), see Figure 9.43, and also on the Zhengzhou Commodity Exchange and the Tokyo Grain Exchange.

In 2007–08, when wheat and corn prices increased, India and Vietnam – followed by Egypt and Cambodia – were afraid of an increase in rice domestic price and decided on an export embargo on rice. Also afraid of shortage, the Philippines imported more rice than expected. Speculators perceived a possible way to make profit by entering the rice market. Rice prices and price volatility went up from US$10 to 24 a bushel. Only in May 2008 – when China and Thailand indicated that they had a large surplus of rice – was there no longer uncertainty and fear of shortage. Prices went back near their previous level.

After the 2007–08 crisis, the ASEAN Food Security Information System (AFSIS) was set up by the FAO and Asian governments to prevent risks of misleading information that may trigger wrong governmental decisions. Furthermore, a programme of rice storage was decided on and implemented for local food security. Speculators were less attracted. Such governmental cooperation resulted in disconnecting world rice prices from other world grain (wheat and corn) prices over the 2010–12 period.

Conclusion The international rice market is small and dominated by China, Thailand and India. But it is troubled by the USA, which is the fourth exporter. Since 2009, Asian countries have increased their rice stocks and coordinated their policy actions with success over the 2010–12 years.

9.3.4.6 The Soybean Oilseed Market, with the USA and Brazil Exporting to China and the EU Oilseeds are major sources of protein to feed human beings and animals. Soybeans are the major protein crops, followed by rapeseed. Oilseeds are also sources of edible oil. In 2012, soybean oil was the second largest consumed edible oil after palm oil.

Products and Uses Soybeans provide protein and also edible oil and oil as biodiesel. Soybean as a food source of proteins is mainly consumed as soybean recipes such as tofu, miso, tempeh, etc. Soybean meal is also a major source of protein for animals: cattle, pigs, chickens, etc.

As a source of protein and edible oil, soybean is in competition with other oilseeds. Used for biodiesel, soybean is a substitute for ethanol coming mainly from corn, wheat and a substitute for other energies: oil petroleum, gas and coal.

Market Structure The world production of soybean amounted to about 268 million tons in 2012. The international market for soybean amounted to 36% of the world production: a high proportion. The three major producers – USA, Brazil and Argentina – accounted for more than 80% of world production in 2012. See Figure 9.44.

The four major consumers – China, the USA, Brazil and Argentina – accounted for 75% of world consumption in 2012. China imported almost two-thirds of world imports. The EU follows with a 5% world market share of consumption. See Figure 9.45.

Rank	Producer	Million tons	World market share
1	USA	82	31%
2	Brazil	82	31%
3	Argentina	50	19%
4	China	13	5%
5	India	12	4%
6	Paraguay	9	3%
7	Canada	5	2%
8	Uruguay	3	1%
9	Ukraine	2	1%
10	Bolivia	2	1%
	Top ten	261	97%
	Others	8	3%
	World	268	100%

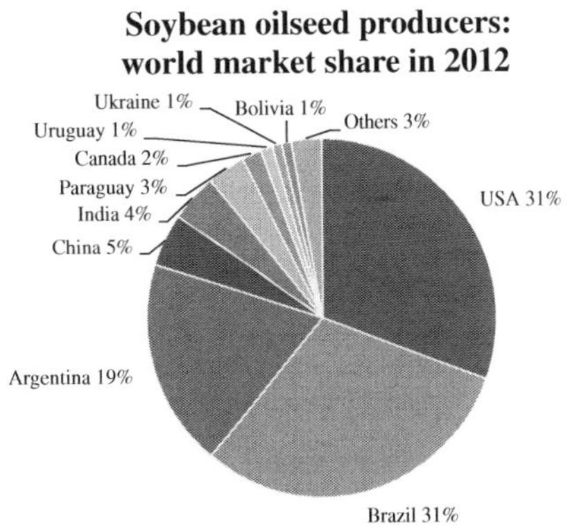

FIGURE 9.44 Soybean oilseed producers in 2012
Source: Author's calculations from ERS-USDA data, 2013.

Rank	Consumer	Million tons	World market share
1	China	76	29%
2	USA	48	18%
3	Brazil	39	15%
4	Argentina	36	14%
5	EU	13	5%
6	India	12	4%
7	Mexico	4	1%
8	Paraguay	3	1%
9	Japan	3	1%
10	Russia	3	1%
	Top ten	235	89%
	Others	30	11%
	World	265	100%

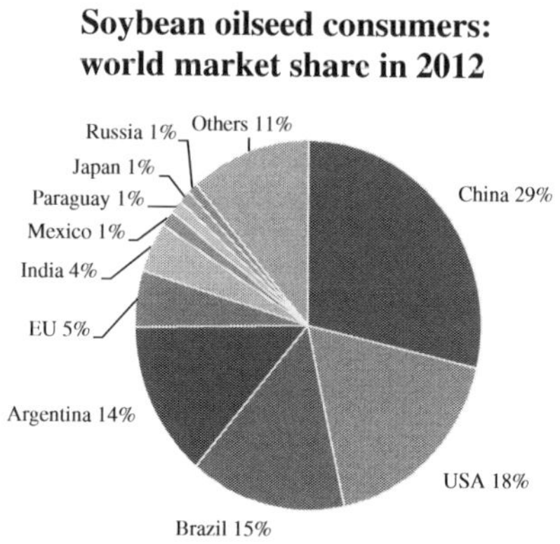

FIGURE 9.45 Soybean oilseed consumers in 2012
Source: Author's calculations from ERS-USDA data, 2013.

In 2012 the USA still produced more than Brazil but exported less and lost its world leadership for the first time. Brazil exported 39%, the USA 38% and Argentina 8% of world exports. Together, Brazil, the USA and Argentina accounted for 85% of world exports. See Figure 9.46.

China and the EU accounted for 75% of world imports. Both countries import soybean as a major source of protein for animal feeds. See Figure 9.47.

The ABCD traders are the major carriers of soybeans from the USA, Brazil and Argentina to China and the EU.

Policy The removal of price distortions for oilseeds was designed by the 'Blair House Agreement' – a memorandum of understanding on oilseeds – negotiated by the USA and the EU during the GATT Uruguay Round in 1992. So, for more than 20 years, the USA and the

Rank	Exporter	Million tons	World market share
1	Brazil	38	39%
2	USA	36	38%
3	Argentina	8	8%
4	Paraguay	6	6%
5	Canada	4	4%
6	Uruguay	3	3%
7	Ukraine	2	2%
8	China	0	0%
9	Bolivia	0	0%
10	Russia	0	0%
	Top ten	96	100%
	Others	0	0%
	World	96	100%

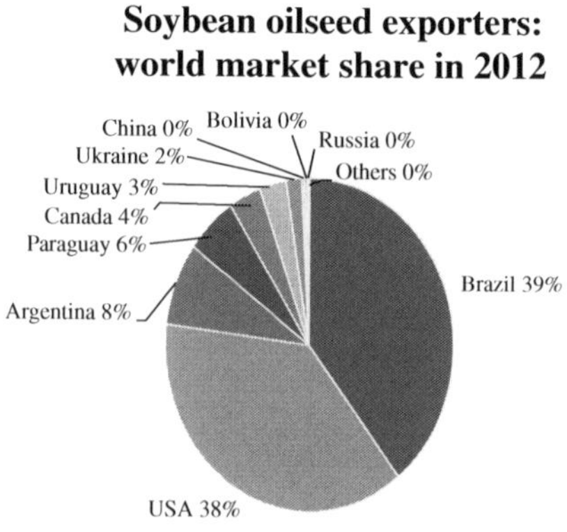

FIGURE 9.46 Soybean oilseed exporters in 2012
Source: Author's calculations from ERS-USDA data, 2013.

Rank	Importer	Million tons	World market share
1	China	59	62%
2	EU	12	13%
3	Mexico	3	4%
4	Japan	3	3%
5	Taiwan	2	3%
6	Thailand	2	2%
7	Indonesia	2	2%
8	Egypt	2	2%
9	Vietnam	1	1%
10	Turkey	1	1%
	Top ten	88	92%
	Others	3	3%
	World	95	100%

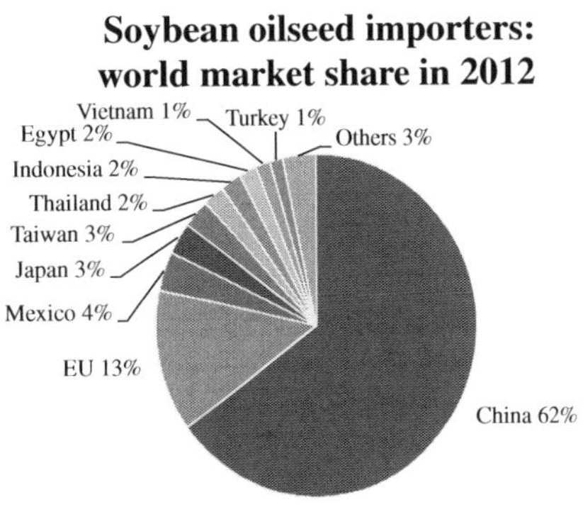

FIGURE 9.47 Soybean oilseed importers in 2012
Source: Author's calculations from ERS-USDA data, 2013.

EU have no longer had any specific support measures for oilseeds. Import tariffs for the main protein crops are set at zero. The only policies allowed are direct payments to farmers without any link to volumes produced and market prices.

As with corn, there is a controversy about the increase in Brazilian land planted with soybean at the expense of pasture and tropical forests, resulting in weaker biodiversity.

Price Level and Volatility Soybean grains have been quoted on the CBOT (CME group) since 1936, see Figure 9.48. Futures contracts of soybean oil and soybean meal were launched in 1950. So, oil crushers may mitigate the risks of fluctuating gross profit margin using the three futures contracts.

The prices of soybean grains is related to the price of other oilseeds as a source of protein and edible oil and the price of energy, via the demand for biodiesel as a substitute for other energies. Over the 2004–13 period, the price of soybean grains fluctuated between US cents 570 and 1800 a bushel, that is a fluctuation of 1 to 3. Price volatility was high in times of uncertainty about harvest in 2008 and 2010 and Asian demand for pig meat and chicken fed with soybeans.

Conclusion In 2012 for the first time, the US lost it corn export leadership. The USA and Brazil are competing for leadership on the international soybean market. Argentina is the third exporter. Corn is imported mainly by China, followed by the EU.

9.3.4.7 The Rapeseed Oilseed Market, in the Hands of Canadian Exporters The world production of rapeseed amounted to about 63 million tons in 2012, with a strong increase over the preceding decades. In 2012 rapeseed oil was the third largest consumed edible oil after palm oil and soybean oil.

Products and Uses Rapeseed is an oilseed mainly used as a source of protein for human beings and animals. It is also produced to make biodiesel.

FIGURE 9.48 Soybean oilseed monthly price on the CBOT (CME group), in US cents per bushel Source: Futures trading charts of http://futures.tradingcharts.com/chart/SB/M?anticache=1393580283.

Market Structure Contrary to soybean which is produced in warm areas, rapeseed is produced in regions with temperate climate. In 2012 the three largest producers – the EU, Canada and China – accounted for about 75% of the rapeseed production. India and Australia followed, and the top five producers generated 91% of rapeseed world production. See Figure 9.49.

The three largest consumers are the same countries – the EU, China and Canada – accounting for about 73% of rapeseed consumption in 2012. See Figure 9.50.

Canada dominates the international market. In 2012 Canada made 60% of world exports. Australia followed with 25%. So, Canada and Australia made 85% of rapeseed world exports. See Figure 9.51.

The major rapeseed importers were the EU and China, with about 26% and 25% of world imports, respectively. Japan followed with 20% and Mexico with 12% of world rapeseed imports. So, the top four importers accounted for about 83% of total imports in 2012. See Figure 9.52.

Policy As for soybeans the rapeseed markets are not very distorted by policy due to the Blair House Agreement already mentioned.

9.3.4.8 Price Level and Volatility The major futures contract is quoted on the IE Futures Canada (ICE group), mainly known by its former name until 2007 – the Winnipeg Commodity Exchange (Figure 9.53). The rapeseed futures contract started in 1963 at the heart of the region

Rank	Producer	Million tons	World market share
1	EU	19	31%
2	Canada	13	21%
3	China	14	22%
4	India	7	11%
5	Australia	4	6%
6	Ukraine	1	2%
7	Russia	1	2%
8	USA	1	2%
9	Belarus	1	1%
10	Pakistan	0	1%
	Top ten	62	99%
	Others	1	1%
	World	63	100%

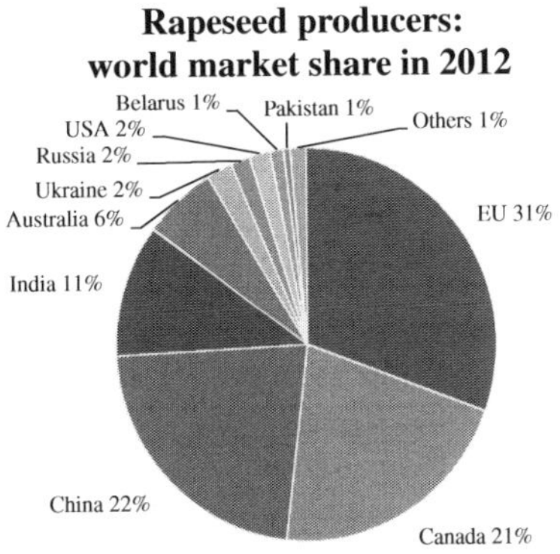

FIGURE 9.49 Rapeseed producers in 2012
Source: Author's calculations from ERS-USDA data, 2013.

Rank	Consumer	Million tons	World market share
1	EU	23	36%
2	China	17	27%
3	Canada	7	11%
4	India	7	11%
5	Japan	2	4%
6	Mexico	1	2%
7	Russia	1	2%
8	USA	1	2%
9	Pakistan	1	1%
10	United Arab Emirates	1	1%
	Top ten	61	96%
	Others	3	4%
	World	64	100%

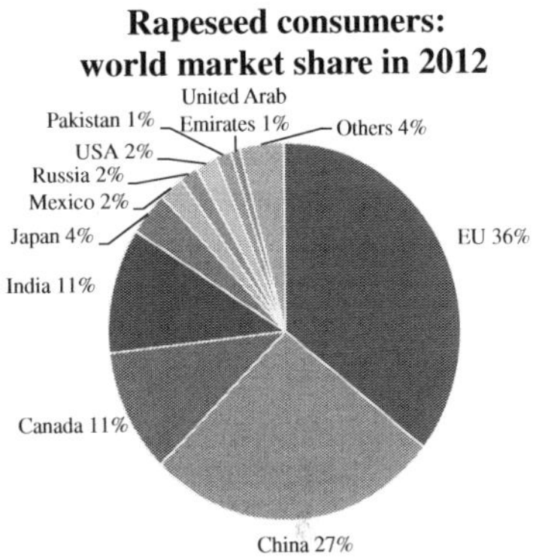

FIGURE 9.50 Rapeseed consumers in 2012
Source: Author's calculations from ERS-USDA data, 2013.

Rank	Exporter	Million tons	World market share
1	Canada	7.15	60%
2	Australia	2.90	25%
3	Ukraine	1.35	11%
4	USA	0.17	1%
5	EU	0.10	1%
6	Kazakhstan	0.05	0%
7	Paraguay	0.04	0%
8	Belarus	0.02	0%
9	Russia	0.02	0%
10	Chile	0.01	0%
	Top ten	11.83	100%
	Others	0.00	0%
	World	11.83	100%

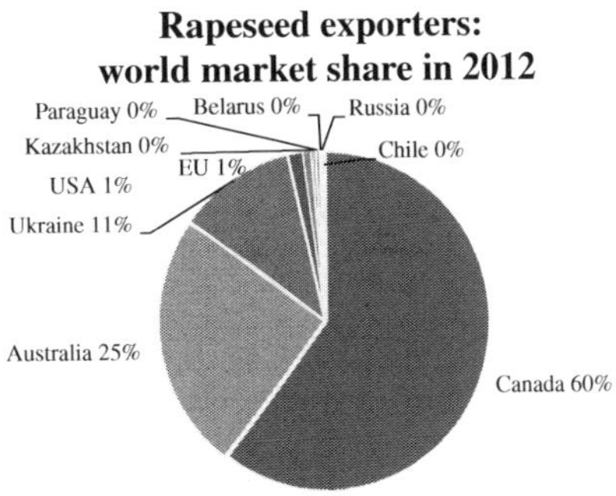

FIGURE 9.51 Rapeseed exporters in 2012
Source: Author's calculations from ERS-USDA data, 2013.

Rank	Importer	Million tons	World market share
1	EU	3.10	26%
2	China	2.90	25%
3	Japan	2.35	20%
4	Mexico	1.45	12%
5	United Arab Emirates	0.55	5%
6	Pakistan	0.50	4%
7	USA	0.39	3%
8	Canada	0.15	1%
9	Turkey	0.13	1%
10	Bangladesh	0.10	1%
	Top ten	11.62	99%
	Others	0.10	1%
	World	11.72	100%

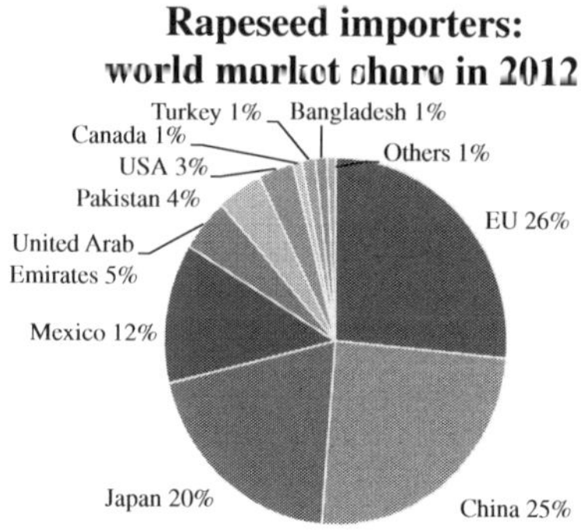

FIGURE 9.52 Rapeseed importers 2012
Source: Author's calculations from ERS-USDA data, 2013.

FIGURE 9.53 Rapeseed monthly price on the Winnipeg Commodity Exchange (ICE group), in Canadian cents per metric ton
Source: Futures trading charts. http://futures.tradingcharts.com/chart/CA/M?anticache=1393581103.

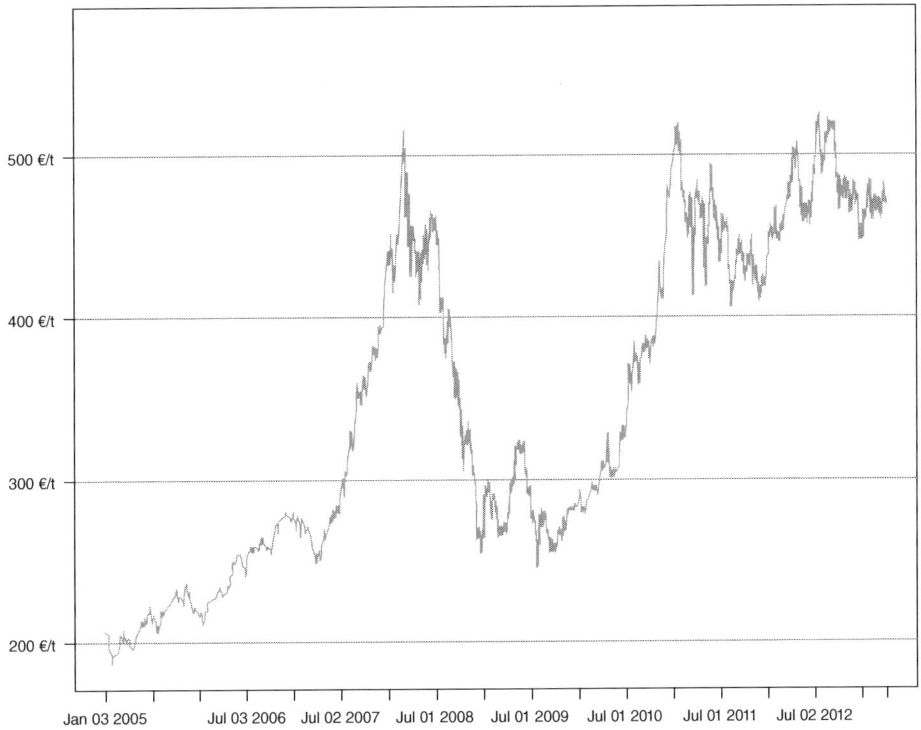

FIGURE 9.54 Rapeseed prices 2005–2012 in euros per ton
Source: AGRITEL. Reproduced by permission of AGRITEL.

in excess supply: Manitoba, Canada. A challenging futures contract is the NYSE-Euronext 'MATIF' rapeseed contract opened in 1994 in Paris, France when the EU removed its price protection policy. Then, EU farmers and crushers were motivated to ask for a local contract. The contract is now quoted in euros per metric ton (see Figure 9.54).

The price of rapeseed is strongly related to the price of soybean oilseed and also other oilseeds as a source of protein and edible oil and the price of energy. Over the 2004–13 period, the price of a metric ton of rapeseed grains fluctuated between Canadian cents 250 to 700 in Winnipeg, between €180 and €520 in Paris. That is a 1 to 3 price fluctuation, as with soybean oilseed.

Conclusion The rapeseed market depends mainly on the soybean market and Canadian exports.

9.3.4.9 The Palm Oil Market with 98% of Exports Made by Indonesia and Malaysia

Palm oil as an agricultural commodity is mainly produced in two countries, Indonesia and Malaysia.

Product and Uses Palm oil is a tropical plant. It is used for cooking, for the preparation of ready-to-eat dishes by food processors and to produce biodiesel. Palm oil is the most consumed of all edible oils. Substitutes for palm oil are other oils like soybean oil and rapeseed oil.

Palm oil is the most consumed oil in the world. It has replaced trans fatty acids (trans fats) during the 1990s and 2000s. However, palm oil has more saturated fat than soybean and rapeseed oil. Trans fatty acids and saturated fats may contribute to an increase in unfavourable levels of LDL cholesterol and apolipoprotein B. Soybean and rapeseed oils contain more monounsaturated and polyunsaturated fatty acids that are better against bad cholesterol. So, complementarities and substitutions among sources of edible vegetal oil are at stake in taking food-processing constraints into account.

Since the mid-1990s strong expansion of palm plantations in Indonesia and Malaysia has occurred at the expense of tropical forests. Monocultural crops are not favourable to biodiversity, while the biodiversity of tropical forests is high. So, deforestation has triggered environmental non-governmental organizations (NGOs) and media attention.

Market Structure From the 1990s, Indonesia and Malaysia have strongly increased their production to meet demand growth from final consumers who cook, food processors and biodiesel manufacturers. In 2012 Indonesia and Malaysia accounted for 52% and 34% of world palm oil production. Together they produced 86% of world production. Among the top 10 producing countries, they accounted for 53% and 35% of production (Figure 9.55).

The consumption of palm oil is widespread in the most populated countries. In 2012 India, Indonesia, China and the UE accounted for 54% of world consumption. The top four consuming countries accounted for 54% of world consumption: India accounted for 16%, Indonesia for 15%, China for 12% and the EU for 11%. Notice that the USA is not among the top 10 consumers since they mainly consume domestic soybean oil. See Figure 9.56.

In 2012 exports of palm oil represented 73% of world production. Indonesia accounted for 50% and Malaysia for 43% of world exports. With 93% of world exports, Indonesia and Malaysia dominate the palm oil market. See Figure 9.57.

In 2012 the top 10 importers represented 77% of all imports. Among them, India accounted for 39%, China for 7% and the EU for 7%. The other countries only accounted for 5% or less of world palm oil imports. See Figure 9.58.

The major palm oil processors are Cargill, Unilever and Agro Astra.

Policy The market for palm oil is free.

Rank	Producer	Million tons	World market share
1	Indonesia	29	52%
2	Malaysia	19	34%
3	Thailand	2	4%
4	Colombia	1	2%
5	Nigeria	1	2%
6	Papua New Guinea	1	1%
7	Ecuador	1	1%
8	Honduras	0	1%
9	Ivory Coast	0	1%
10	Brazil	0	1%
	Top ten	54	97%
	Others	2	3%
	World	56	100%

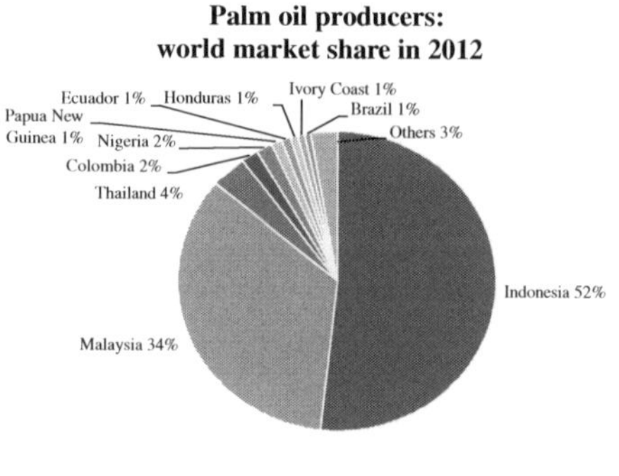

FIGURE 9.55 Palm oil producers in 2012
Source: Author's calculations from ERS-USDA data, 2013.

Rank	Consumer	Million tons	World market share
1	India	8	16%
2	Indonesia	8	15%
3	China	6	12%
4	EU	6	11%
5	Malaysia	3	6%
6	Pakistan	2	4%
7	Thailand	2	3%
8	Nigeria	1	3%
9	Egypt	1	2%
10	Bangladesh	1	2%
	Top ten	38	74%
	Others	14	26%
	World	52	100%

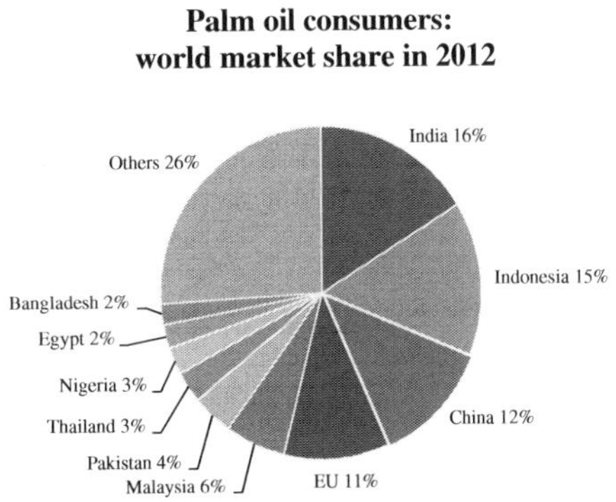

FIGURE 9.56 Palm oil consumers in 2012
Source: Author's calculations from ERS-USDA data, 2013.

Rank	Exporter	Million tons	World market share
1	Indonesia	20	50%
2	Malaysia	17	43%
3	Papua New Guinea	1	2%
4	Thailand	0	1%
5	United Arab Emirates	0	1%
6	Honduras	0	1%
7	Benin	0	1%
8	Ivory Coast	0	1%
9	Ecuador	0	1%
10	Guatemala	0	1%
	Top ten	40	100%
	Others	0	0%
	World	40	100%

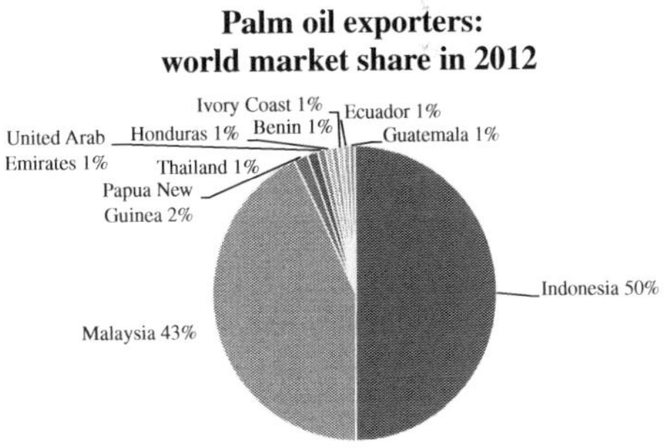

FIGURE 9.57 Palm oil exporters in 2012
Source: Author's calculations from ERS-USDA data, 2013.

Rank	Importer	Million tons	World market share
1	India	20	39%
2	China	4	7%
3	EU	4	7%
4	Pakistan	2	5%
5	Malaysia	2	4%
6	Egypt	2	5%
7	Bangladesh	2	3%
8	USA	2	3%
9	Singapore	1	3%
10	Iran	1	2%
	Top ten	40	77%
	Others	12	23%
	World	52	100%

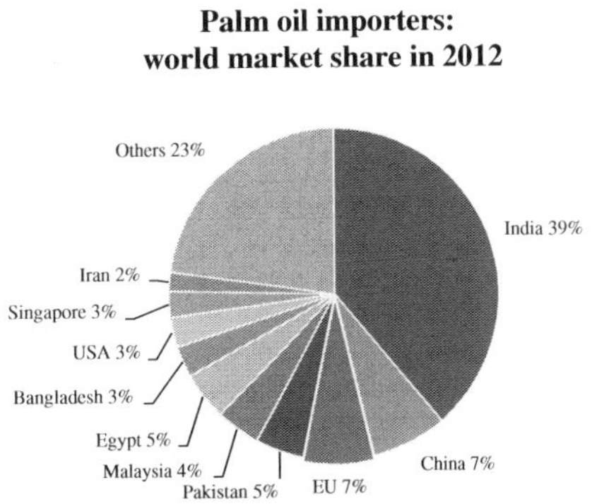

FIGURE 9.58 Palm oil importers in 2012
Source: Author's calculations from ERS-USDA data, 2013.

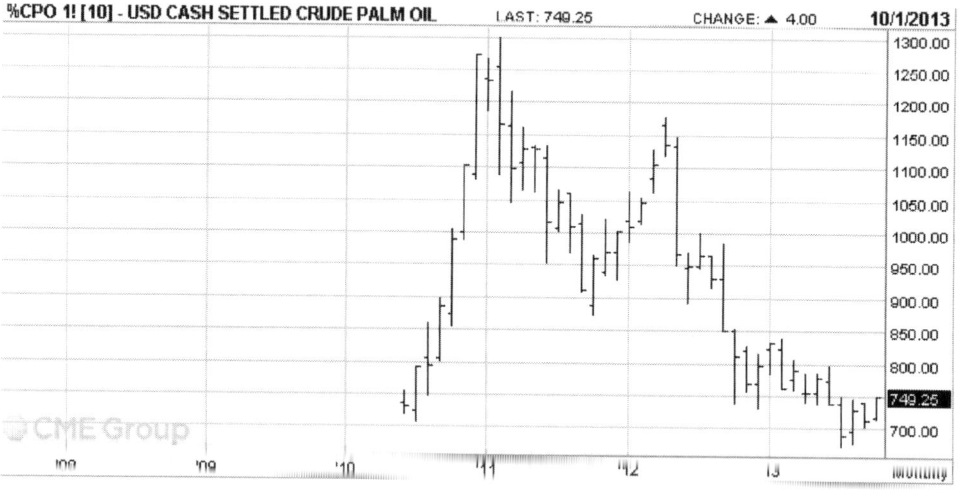

FIGURE 9.59 Palm oil monthly price on Bursa Malaysia Derivatives Berhad in US cents per metric ton
Source: CME group at http://www.cmegroup.com/international/partnership-resources/bursa-resources.html.

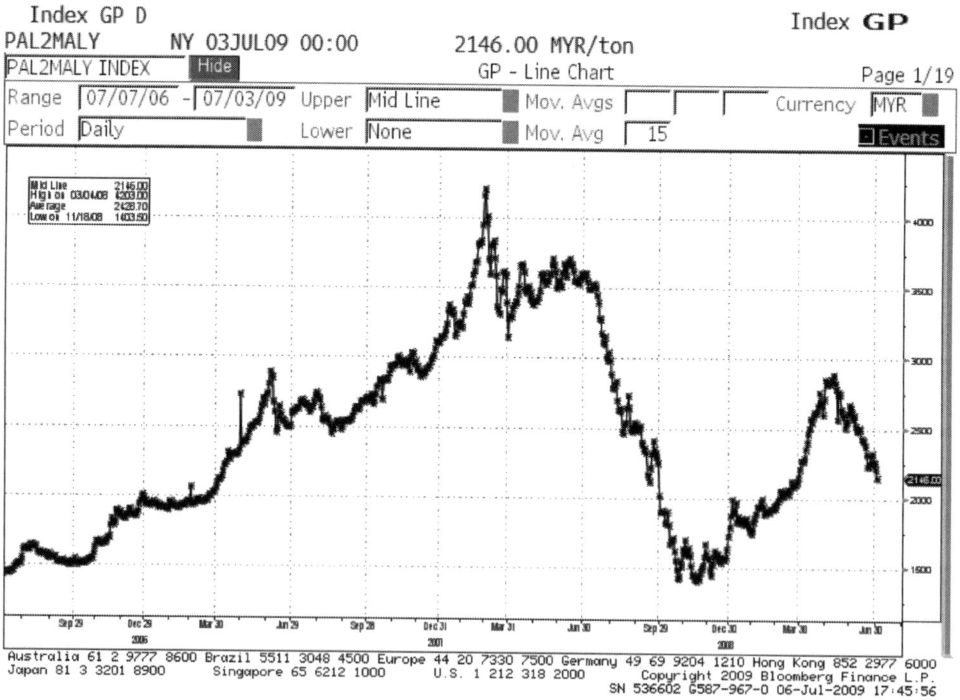

FIGURE 9.60 Palm oil price on Bursa Malaysia Derivatives Berhad in Malaysian ringgit per ton
Source: Bloomberg Finance L. P.

Price There exists a Crude Palm Oil Futures (CPO) contract at the Bursa Malaysia Derivatives Berhad (BMD). Since September 2010, it has been in partnership with the CME group which owns 25% of the shares. The final settlement of CPO contracts is determined by averaging the Bursa Malaysia Derivatives Berhad Crude Palm Oil Futures (FCPO) daily settlement prices for each of the last five trading days of the CPO futures contract. See Figure 9.59.

Conclusion The palm oil market has expanded strongly during the 1900s and 2000s. Its expansion is mainly constrainted by nutritional concerns and environmental issues about the right balance between monocultural crops and the biodiversity of tropical forests.

9.3.4.10 The Coffee Market, from Southern Exporters to Northern Importers

Coffee is only produced in tropical countries which export to the USA and Europe. Other major tropical agricultural products providing beverages are cocoa and tea.

Products and Uses There are two major varieties of coffee: Arabica making up about two-thirds of green coffee production and Robusta making up about one-third of green coffee production. Coffee is a tropical plant which is very sensitive to frost. Frost occurs occasionally in July and August on Brazilian mountains where many coffee plantations are located. Coffee beans are roasted to produce the most popular hot beverage, coffee.

Market Structure About 70 countries produce coffee beans in tropical countries. Among them, the exporting members of the International Coffee Organization (ICO) are responsible for over 97% of world production (source: The ICO, http://www.ico.org). The ICO provides statistics on the international coffee trade.

The coffee manufacturers buy green beans and roast them to produce coffee. The major manufacturers of coffee are Nestlé, Mondelez, Kraft and Sara Lee/Douwe Egbert, which dominate the market. Other processors are De Master Blenders, Smuckers, Massimo Zanetti, Starbucks, Tchibo, Lavazza, etc. Since consumption may evolve according to price, taste and forms of consumption, processors make arbitrage in blending Arabica and Robusta coffees whose price difference evolves over time. In order to secure their procurement, many of them have adopted programmes to train farmers in order to get a better quality of beans and a more regular yield.

Arabica is mainly produced and exported by Latin American countries (Brazil, Colombia, Honduras, etc.), but also Ethiopia. Robusta is mainly grown and exported by Asian countries (Vietnam, Indonesia) and Brazil.

In 2012 the top 10 countries producing green coffee accounted for 83% of world production. The two biggest producers were Brazil and Vietnam, which accounted for 33% and 18% of world production, respectively. Brazil is the traditional leader, while Vietnam is a relatively new producer whose massive plantations started in the 1990s. See Figure 9.61.

In 2012 the 10 largest countries consuming coffee accounted for 82% of world consumption. The major coffee consumers were the EU with 33%, the USA with 17%, Brazil with 14% and Japan with 5%. So, 50% of world coffee consumption was due to consumers living in the EU or US. See Figure 9.62.

International trade concerns about 85% of world production. In 2012 the major exporting countries were Brazil and Vietnam, which accounted respectively for 31% and 26% of the volume traded by the 10 largest exporters. In 2012 the major importing countries were the EU,

Rank	Producer	Million 60 kg bags	World market share
1	Brazil	49.2	33%
2	Vietnam	26.0	18%
3	Indonesia	8.3	6%
4	Colombia	7.7	5%
5	Ethiopia	6.3	4%
6	Honduras	5.6	4%
7	India	5.2	4%
8	Peru	5.2	4%
9	Guatemala	4.4	3%
10	Mexico	4.3	3%
	Top ten	122.2	83%
	Others	25	17%
	World	147.2	100%

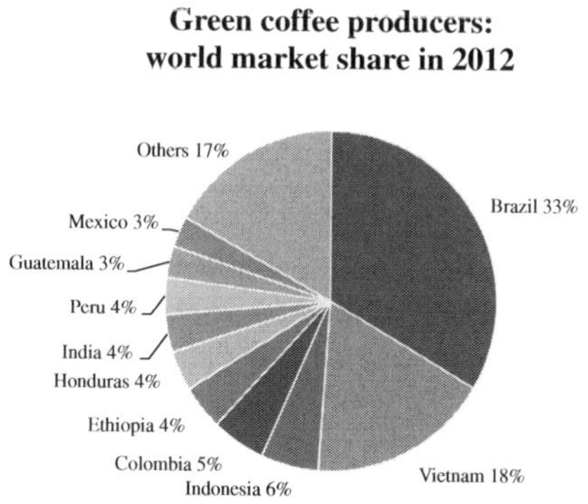

FIGURE 9.61 Green coffee producers in 2012
Source: Author's calculations from ERS-USDA data, 2013.

Rank	Consumer	Million 60 kg bags	World market share
1	EU	45.7	33%
2	USA	23.4	17%
3	Brazil	20.0	14%
4	Japan	6.96	5%
5	Russia	3.70	3%
6	Canada	3.39	2%
7	Philippines	3.66	3%
8	Ethiopia	3.05	2%
9	Indonesia	2.38	2%
10	Switzerland	2.17	2%
	Top ten	114.48	82%
	Others	25	18%
	World	139.48	100%

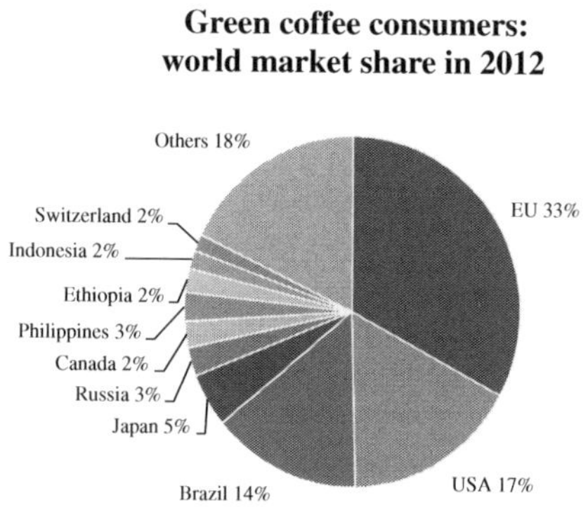

FIGURE 9.62 Green coffee consumers in 2012
Source: Author's calculations from ERS-USDA data, 2013.

Rank	Exporter	Million 60 kg bags	World market share
1	Brazil	29.8	26%
2	Vietnam	24.4	21%
3	Indonesia	7.4	6%
4	Colombia	7.3	6%
5	Honduras	5.3	5%
6	India	5.2	4%
7	Peru	5.2	4%
8	Guatemala	4.0	3%
9	Ethiopia	3.1	3%
10	Uganda	3.0	3%
	Top ten	94.9	82%
	Others	21.0	18%
	World	115.9	100%

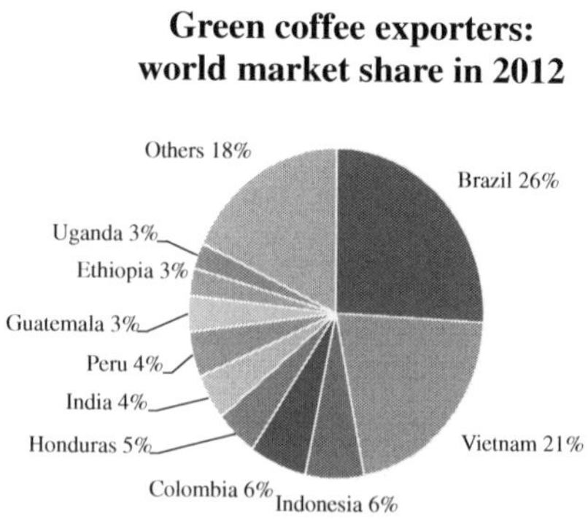

FIGURE 9.63 Green coffee exporters in 2012
Source: Author's calculations from ERS-USDA data, 2013.

Rank	Importer	Million 60 kg bags	World market share
1	EU	43.7	38%
2	USA	23.1	20%
3	Japan	6.6	6%
4	Russia	3.7	3%
5	Canada	3.4	3%
6	Philippines	3.3	3%
7	Algeria	2.3	2%
8	Switzerland	2.2	2%
9	South Korea	1.7	2%
10	China	1.0	1%
	Top ten	90.9	80%
	Others	23.0	20%
	World	113.9	100%

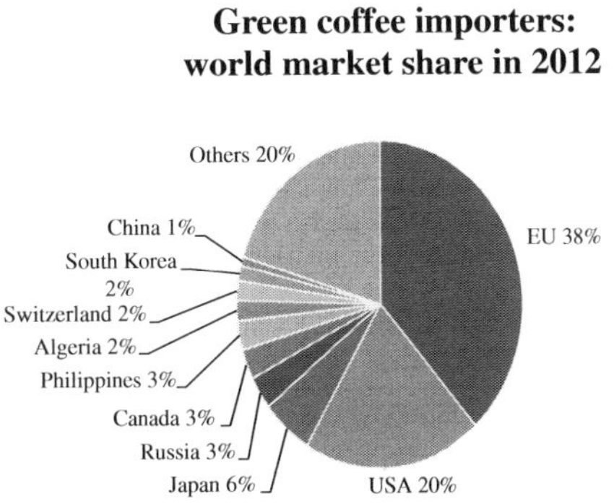

FIGURE 9.64 Green coffee importers in 2012
Source: Author's calculations from ERS-USDA data, 2013.

the USA and Japan, which accounted respectively for 38%, 20% and 6% of the volume traded by the 10 largest importers. So, Brazil and Vietnam export 47% of world exports to the EU, the USA and Japan, which import 64% of world imports. See Figure 9.64.

Policy Until the 1990s, centralized marketing systems organized by state agencies prevailed in major West and Central African countries producing coffee, cocoa and cotton. They were marketing boards in English-speaking countries and *caisse de stabilization* in French-speaking countries. Every government had an export monopoly, whilst it purchased commodities at a fixed price from domestic farmers. However, the system proved not to be as efficient as expected due to speculation and problems of organization.

The producing countries have almost fully liberalized the production and trade of coffee over the 1980s and 1990s. Only due to strong pressure from farmers, some large producing countries such as Brazil and Colombia subsidize farmers through purchasing programmes that were set up in years of oversupply and low price. Vietnam has enhanced the plantation of coffee trees.

Price Level and Volatility Coffee futures contracts are designed with warehouse delivery in harbours of consuming countries. Arabica coffee is mainly traded on the ICE in New York with delivery of green beans from one of 19 countries of origin in a licensed warehouse to one of several ports in the USA and Europe, with stated premiums/discounts for ports and growths (Figure 9.65).

Robusta coffee is traded on the LIFFE (ICE group) in London. Delivery is possible in 60 kg bags to a warehouse in London or other ports: Amsterdam, Antwerp, Barcelona, Bremen, Felixstowe, Genoa-Savona, Hamburg, Le Havre, Marseilles-Fos, New Orleans, New York, Rotterdam or Trieste.

The delivery process is as follows:

- Licensed warehouses are owned by private companies.
- Coffee has to be in a licensed warehouse before the delivery day as it has to go through the certification process (the grade of the bean is tested and the flavour is evaluated).

FIGURE 9.65 Arabica coffee monthly prices on the ICE, in US cents per pound
Source: Futures trading charts at http://futures.tradingcharts.com/chart/CF/M?anticache=1393582403.

- The issuer has until the last day of the month to deliver the certified coffee to the warehouse and the stopper has ownership of the coffee as soon as the issuer has notified the exchange of the delivery and the stopper has paid the amount required.
- The stopper can leave the coffee in the licensed warehouse but will have to pay the warehouse rent.
- A certain number of discounts and premiums are applied to the price received or paid for the coffee.

Consumption has increased over time. However, from 2011 production has exceeded consumption and world prices have decreased. By the end of 2013 Brazilian production is expected to soar above historic records while stocks are piling. So, Arabica coffee prices are depressed, amounting to 116 US cents per pound at the end of September 2013 from a peak of 300 US cents per pound at the beginning of 2011, that is a 60% decrease.

In 2013 Arabica prices were decreasing faster than Robusta prices. Over the years 2010–12, the production of Robusta coffee was greater than consumption and Vietnamese production was also expected to be excellent. However, Robusta carry-over stocks were less important than Arabica carry-over stocks. So, the premium for Arabica over Robusta was lower and lower.

Coffee price volatility depends mainly on the impact of summer frost in Brazil, the largest producer and exporter.

Conclusion Coffee is a commodity mainly produced by Southern countries and exported to Northern countries which are the largest consumers. Brazil is the major producer and holds a dominant position on Arabica coffee. Consequently, world price levels and volatility are very dependents on Brazilian harvests that are sensitive to frosts in summer. Vietnam has become the second largest exporter and leads the Robusta market.

9.3.4.11 The Cocoa Market where the Ivory Coast and Ghana Export to the EU and the USA Some agricultural commodities are mainly produced in one or two countries. This is the case with cocoa, which is mainly produced in the Ivory Coast and Ghana.

Product and Uses Cocoa is a tropical bean which is roasted to produce chocolate and cocoa butter. Chocolate is used in pastry, sweets, desserts and ice-cream. Also as a hot beverage.

Market Structure From 1990 cocoa production has increased over time to reach about 3500 tons in 2005–06 according to UNCTAD, based on International Cocoa Organization (ICCO) data (Figures 9.66 and 9.67).

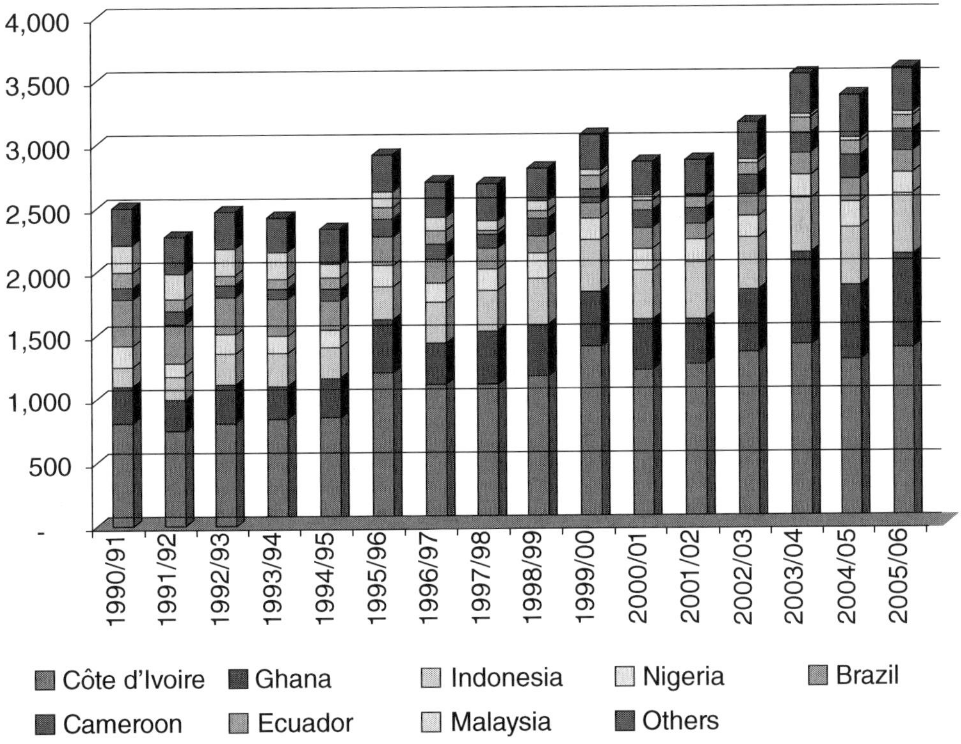

FIGURE 9.66 World production of cocoa beans, in thousand tons
Source: UNCTAD based on data from the International Cocoa Organization, quarterly bulletin of cocoa statistics.

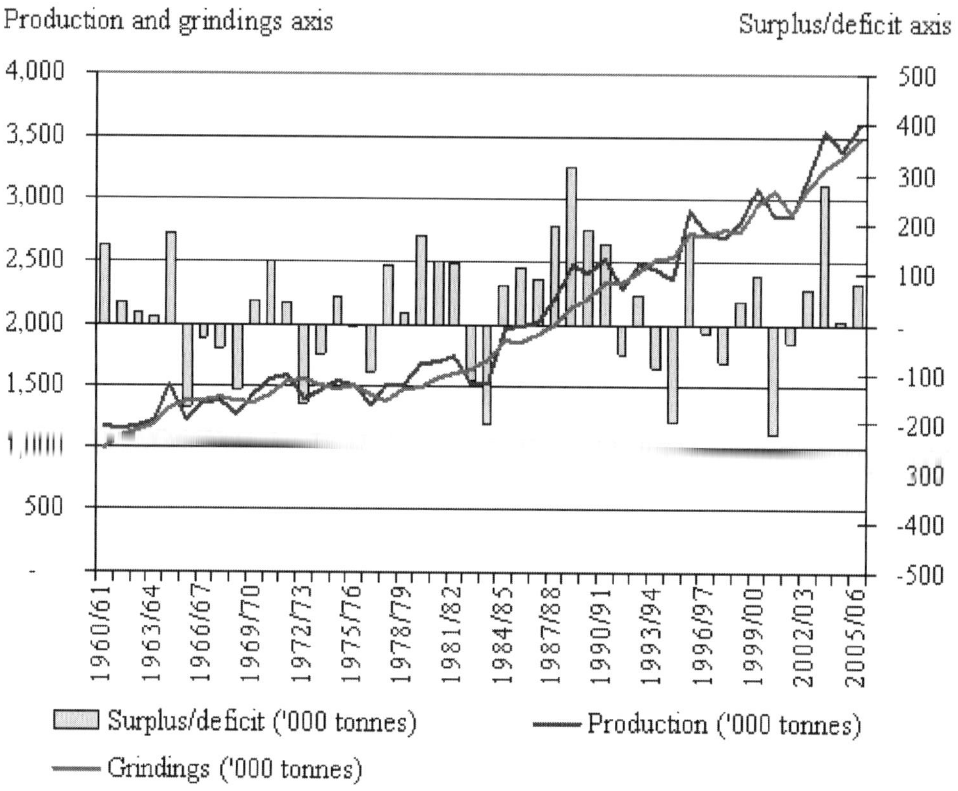

FIGURE 9.67 World cocoa bean production, grindings and supply/demand balance in thousand tons from 1960/61 to 2005/06
Source: UNCTAD based on data from the International Cocoa Organization, quarterly bulletin of cocoa statistics.

Cocoa statistics mainly come from the ICCO, which released its last report in 2010 with export–import data up to 2007–08. The ERS-USDA provides more recent data, but only about production.

In 2012 the Ivory Coast and Ghana harvested 37% and 22% of world production, respectively. Together, they accounted for 59% of world cocoa production and exports. The Ivory Coast and Ghana accounted respectively for 40% and 24% of the production of the top eight producing countries. The top four producers – the Ivory Coast, Ghana, Indonesia and Nigeria – accounted for 76% of world production in 2012 (source: ERS-USDA), see Figure 9.68. The same four countries were major exporters, with 82% of world exports in 2007–08 (Source: ICCO), see Figure 9.69.

On the demand side in 2007–08, the UE accounted for 53% of world imports and the USA 15%. Together, they accounted for 68% of all imports. Among the top six importers the UE accounted for 64% of imports and the USA 18%, followed by Malaysia, Russia, Canada and Japan (Figure 9.70).

The major traders and grinders of cocoa are Cargill, ADM, Armajaro, Barry-Callebaut and Cémoi, which have logistics facilities in West Africa. The market for industrial chocolates

Rank	Producer	Thousand tons	World market share
1	Ivory Coast	1486	37%
2	Ghana	879	22%
3	Indonesia	450	11%
4	Nigeria	235	6%
5	Brazil	220	5%
6	Cameroon	190	5%
7	Ecuador	190	5%
8	Papua New Guinea	39	1%
	Top 8	3689	91%
	Others	373	9%
	World	4062	100%

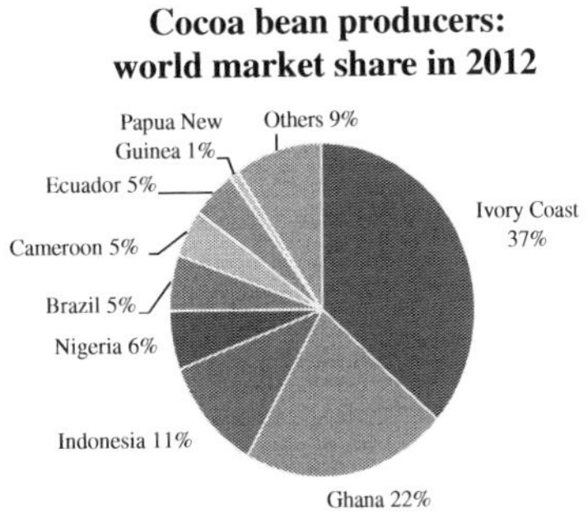

FIGURE 9.68 Cocoa bean producers in 2012
Source: Author's calculations from ERS-USDA data, 2013.

Rank	Exporter	Thousand tons	World market share
1	Ivory Coast	1247	38%
2	Ghana	675	21%
3	Indonesia	526	16%
4	Nigeria	217	7%
5	Cameroon	170	5%
6	Ecuador	111	3%
7	Togo	87	3%
8	Papua New Guinea	50	2%
9	Dominican Republic	36	1%
10	Guinea	18	1%
	Top ten	3138	96%
	Others	141	4%
	World	3279	100%

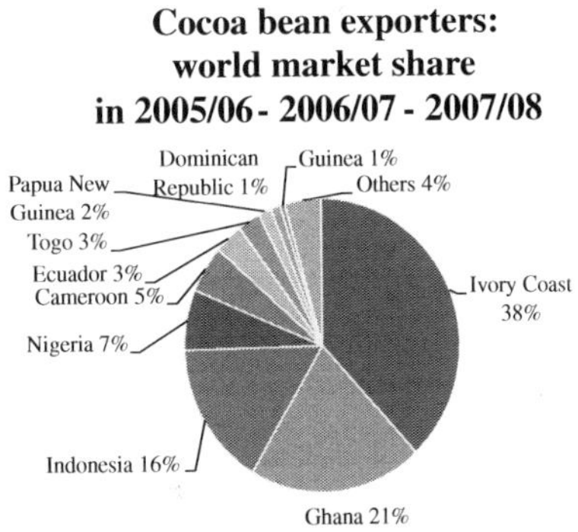

FIGURE 9.69 Cocoa bean exporters in 2012
Source: Author's calculations from ICCO data, 2010.

Rank	Importer	Thousand tons	World market share
1	EU	2623	53%
2	USA	719	15%
3	Malaysia	320	6%
4	Russia	179	4%
5	Canada	144	3%
6	Japan	116	2%
	Top 6	4101	83%
	Others	850	17%
	World	4951	100%

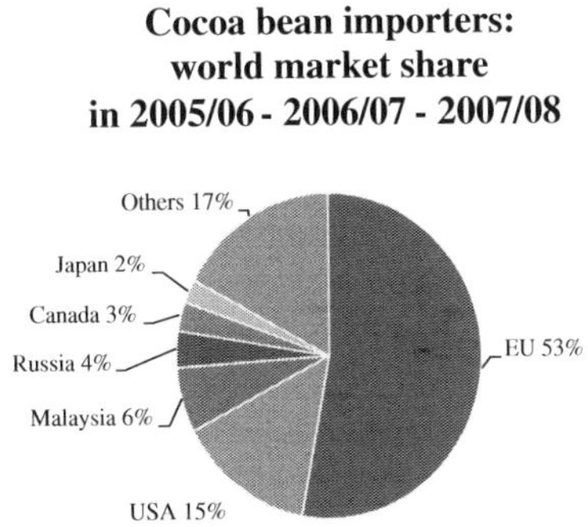

FIGURE 9.70 Cocoa bean importers in 2012
Source: Author's calculations from ICCO data, 2010.

and speciality cocoas is led by Barry Callebaut with a market share above 50%; the other major players are Cargill, ADM, Blommer, etc. (source: Barry Callebaut).

The consumer branded chocolate market is dominated by large international food companies such as Mondelez International, Kraft Foods, Nestlé, Mars and Hershey, which accounted for 64% of the market. The other main consumer chocolate manufacturers, such as Ferrero, Lindt & Sprüngli, Peter's Chocolate (Cargill group) and Valrhona (Soparind-Bongrain group), are major suppliers of high-quality and prestige chocolates.

Policy Until the 1990s, centralized marketing systems were dominant in major West and Central African cocoa-producing countries. From a peak price in 1984, the international market price of cocoa declined. It was decided to store cocoa in order to squeeze the market and push the world price upwards. The Ivory Coast maintained its domestic price at a constant level even though the international price went below this. The state had to borrow money to buy domestic cocoa beans and store them. However, near bankruptcy due to increasing debt, the Ivorian government had to sell its stored cocoa in 1987. Furthermore, the government agency could not avoid losses on the international market and surpluses used by ministries. So in 1999 the market was liberalized in the Ivory Coast, which fully privatized its marketing structures.

In 1992 Ghana partially liberalized its cocoa market, which was fully controlled by the state-owned Cocobod, a marketing board with fixed floor price paid for all domestic purchases. Ghana introduced competition in domestic marketing by allowing private licensed agents to purchase cocoa from farmers. Other cocoa-producing countries, such as Nigeria, Cameroon, Brazil, Indonesia and Malaysia, have liberalized their markets.

Price Level and Volatility Cocoa is traded on the NYMEX, which belongs to the CME group. The cocoa futures contract has settlement procedures at maturity. By contrast, the London based ICE cocoa contract proposes delivery in five US ports (Figure 9.71).

In the 2000s the cocoa price was sensitive to strong political disorders and in the Ivory Coast, civil war led to lack of production care and logistics disorder, making procurement difficult and more costly. Uncertainty about the ability to carry cocoa beans out of the country caused strong price volatility.

Conclusion With 59% of world production and exports, the Ivory Coast and Ghana dominate the export of cocoa beans to the EU and the USA. This does not mean that the price can be manipulated by their governments. In the 1980s, when export state agencies exported cocoa, the Ivory Coast stored cocoa beans in order to create a shortage and increase the price, but it failed to squeeze the market because the state could no longer borrow money to buy from domestic farmers and store beans.

9.3.4.12 The Cotton Market, with WTO Disputes about Subsidized US Production and Exports The cotton market is at the heart of policy issues between the USA and emerging countries.

Product and Uses Cotton is a tropical plant whose capsules contain cellulose fibre. Cotton provides natural, soft and fluffy textiles. Cotton competes with other natural fibres, like silk, flax or hemp, and synthetic fibres.

FIGURE 9.71 Cocoa monthly prices on the ICE, in US cents per pound
Source: Futures trading charts at http://futures.tradingcharts.com/chart/CC/M?anticache=1393583207.

Market Structure In 2012 China produced 29% of the world production of cotton. India followed with 22%. So, China and India accounted for 51% of world production and also used it for domestic consumption. The USA was the third world producer with 14%, but its production has declined since 2005 when the WTO agreement on cotton obliged the US government to reduce production subsidies. Pakistan and Brazil were the fourth and fifth world producers, with 8% and 5% of world production respectively. The top five producers accounted for 77% of world production. The other main producers are Australia with erratic production, Uzbekistan, Turkey, Turkmenistan and Burkina Faso. See Figure 9.72.

In 2012 China and India were the main consumers of cotton, with 50% of world consumption. Pakistan, Turkey and Brazil followed. The top five consumers accounted for 77% of world consumption (Figure 9.73).

In 2012 the international cotton market concerned 38% of production. The USA was the largest exporter of cotton with 13.3 million bales, a 34% market share. Since 2005, with a peak at 17.7 million bales, US exports have declined. In the USA the volume of cotton is measured in bales of about 17 cubic feet (0.48 cubic metres), weighing 480 pounds (226.8 kilograms). The other major exporters are India with 18%, Australia with 15%, Uzbekistan and Brazil. The top three exporters accounted for 57% of world exports and the top five for 74%. The other main exporters are Burkina Faso, Mali, Turkmenistan, Greece and Malaysia. See Figure 9.74.

Rank	Producer	Million 480 lb Bales	World market share
1	China	35	29%
2	India	27	22%
3	USA	17	14%
4	Pakistan	9	8%
5	Brazil	6	5%
6	Australia	5	4%
7	Uzbekistan	5	4%
8	Turkey	3	2%
9	Turkmenistan	2	1%
10	Burkina Faso	1	1%
	Top ten	108	89%
	Others	13	11%
	World	121	100%

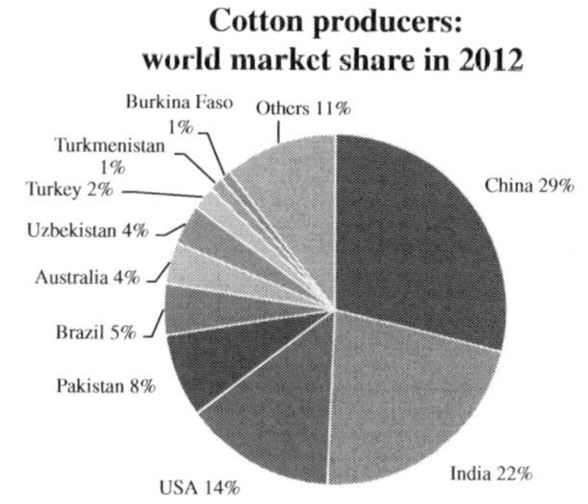

FIGURE 9.72 Cotton producers in 2012
Source: Author's calculations from ERS-USDA data, 2013.

Rank	Consumer	Million 480 lb Bales	World market share
1	China	36	31%
2	India	22	19%
3	Pakistan	22	19%
4	Turkey	6	5%
5	Brazil	4	3%
6	Bangladesh	4	3%
7	USA	3	3%
8	Vietnam	2	2%
9	Indonesia	2	2%
10	Mexico	2	2%
	Top ten	104	89%
	Others	13	11%
	World	117	100%

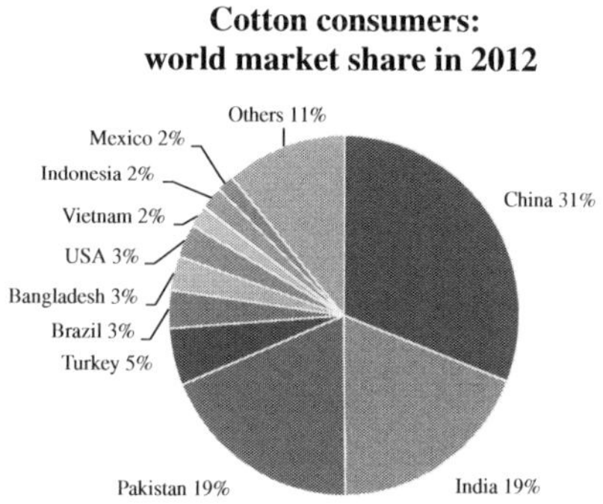

FIGURE 9.73 Cotton consumers in 2012
Source: Author's calculations from ERS-USDA data, 2013.

Rank	Exporter	Million 480 lb Bales	World market share
1	USA	13.3	29%
2	India	7.2	16%
3	Australia	6.0	13%
4	Brazil	4.3	9%
5	Uzbekistan	3.2	7%
6	Burkina Faso	1.2	2%
7	Turkmenistan	1.2	3%
8	Greece	1.1	2%
9	Mali	0.9	2%
10	Malaysia	0.9	2%
	Top ten	39.2	85%
	Others	7.0	15%
	World	46.2	100%

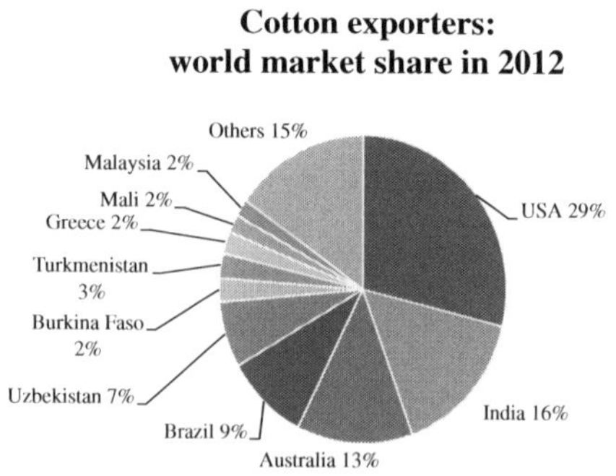

FIGURE 9.74 Cotton exporters in 2012
Source: Author's calculations from ERS-USDA data, 2013.

Rank	Importer	Million 480 lb Bales	World market share
1	China	20.0	43%
2	Turkey	3.8	8%
3	Bangladesh	3.6	8%
4	Vietnam	2.4	5%
5	Indonesia	2.4	5%
6	Pakistan	2.2	5%
7	Thailand	1.5	3%
8	India	1.5	3%
9	South Korea	1.3	3%
10	Mexico	0.9	2%
	Top ten	39.7	85%
	Others	7.0	15%
	World	46.7	100%

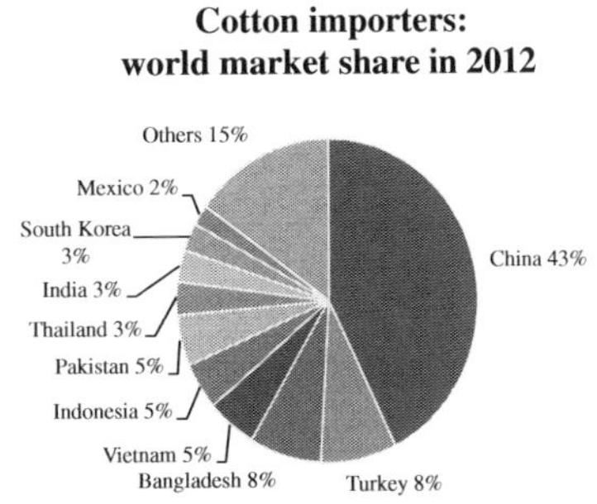

FIGURE 9.75 Cotton importers in 2012
Source: Author's calculations from ERS-USDA data, 2013.

In 2012 China was the major importer, with 43% of all world imports. China was followed by Turkey and Bangladesh, with 8% each of world imports. The top three importers accounted for 59% of world imports.

Policy Until the 1990s, major West and Central African countries had centralized marketing systems with state agencies with export monopoly.

In 2002 Brazil complained to the WTO about US domestic production subsidies. Furthermore, in 2003 a group of four least-developed African countries – Benin, Burkina Faso, Chad and Mali – also claimed for the reduction of US cotton subsidies through negotiations. In March 2005, at the WTO, the Dispute Settlement Body (DSB) adopted the Appellate Body Report, which is an Agreement on Subsidies and Countervailing Measures. In October 2005, the United States Commodity Credit Corporation (CCC) ceased issuing export credit guarantees under the supplier credit guarantee programme. So, since 2005, US production and exports have decreased. However, the USA may have continued to provide marketing loans and counter-cyclical payments to US upland cotton producers. Direct payments are provided to US cotton producers. In 2009 Brazil introduced a new complaint against US subsidies at the WTO. The dispute was still pending in 2013.

In addition to concerns over subsidies, the cotton industries of some countries are criticized for employing child labour and damaging workers' health by exposure to pesticides used in production. In Uzbekistan, men and children are forced to harvest cotton for free.

Price Level and Volatility Cotton futures contracts with settlement procedures at maturity are traded on the NYMEX.

Cotton #2 futures contracts, with delivery on five US ports, are traded on the ICE Figure 9.76, previously known as the New York Board of Trade, which leads the soft commodity exchange.

Conclusion The cotton market is very competitive. It involves economic development stakes for emerging countries in Asia, Africa and South America. Brazil asked the WTO to solve its dispute with the USA, which was accused of unfair production subsidies.

FIGURE 9.76 Cotton #2 monthly prices on the ICE, in US cents per pound
Source: Futures trading charts at http://futures.tradingcharts.com/chart/CT/M?anticache=1393584917.

9.4 HEDGING AND BASIS MANAGEMENT

This section presents short hedging and long hedging to illustrate how commercial operators deliver or use agricultural commodities. In hedging, price risk fluctuation is reduced to basis risk fluctuation. Basis risk fluctuation may be managed by operators.

9.4.1 Short Hedging for Producers

Short hedging is presented in order to assess the advantages and limitations of futures contracts for a milling wheat producer selling on the physical cash market.

9.4.1.1 The Principle of Short Hedging Any wheat seller on physical spot markets is afraid of a possible drop in wheat prices. He holds a long position on the physical market. In order to mitigate his price risk, he will take an opposite risk, a short risk on futures markets in going short: he makes a short hedge.

The producer will sell futures contracts to lock in his selling price:

Now	→	Later
To sell futures contracts	→	To buy futures contracts and to sell physical wheat on the physical spot market

9.4.1.2 Example: Context In October of year N a farmer sows milling wheat over 50 hectares (ha) and expects a minimum yield of 6 t/ha harvested in July $N+1$, i.e. 300 t. (For information, 1 t = 1 metric ton = 1000 kg.)

- Price on futures markets for delivery in August year $N+1$= 260 €/t.
- Expected price on the spot (physical) market in July year $N+1$ 'at the farm gate' = 245 €/t.

The basis is therefore:

$$\text{Basis} = \text{Futures price} - \text{Spot price} = +15€/\text{t}$$

The farmer thinks this price is good and is afraid of any drop in wheat prices. Because he wants to lock in the price, the farmer will undertake a short hedge by selling six futures contracts. Hence, the farmer goes short on the futures market in order to offset his long position on the physical spot market.

Four possible cases are described below.

Scenario 1: If the price of wheat decreases The price of wheat may decrease by 40 €/t as shown here.

Time	Spot Market	Futures Market	Basis
October year *N*	expected next July 245 €/t	**to sell August year *N*+1** **260 €/t**	expected basis +15 €/t
July year *N*+1	**to sell** **205 €/t**	**to buy August year *N*+1** **220 €/t**	actual basis **+15 €/t**

The hedging results in the following price received by the farmer:

Price on the physical spot market	205 €/t
+ Profit on futures contracts	40 €/t
= Net price received by the producer	245 €/t, which is the expected price.

A second explanation shows that the hedge may be viewed in another way, as follows:

Price locked in selling on the futures market	260 €/t
– Actual basis	–15 €/t
= Net price received by the producer	245 €/t, which is the expected price.

Scenario 2: If the price of wheat increases The price of wheat may increase by 30 €/t as shown here.

Time	Spot Market	Futures Market	Basis
October year *N*	expected next July 245 €/t	**to sell August year *N*+1** **260 €/t**	expected basis +15 €/t
July year *N*+1	**to sell** **275 €/t**	**to buy August year *N*+1** **290 €/t**	**actual basis** **+15 €/t**

The hedging results in the following price received by the farmer:

Price on the physical spot market	275 €/t
+ Profit on futures contracts	−30 €/t
= Net price received by the producer	245 €/t, which is the expected price.

A second explanation shows that the hedging may be viewed in another way, as follows:

Price locked in selling on the futures market	260 €/t
− Actual basis	−15 €/t
= Net price received by the producer	245 €/t, which is the expected price.

Scenario 3: If the basis decreases (by 4 €/t) The price of wheat may decrease by 40 €/t and the basis may decrease by 4 €/t as shown here.

Time	Spot Market	Futures Market	Basis
October year *N*	expected next July 245 €/t	**to sell August year *N*+1** **260 €/t**	expected basis +15 €/t
July year *N*+1	**to sell** **209 €/t**	**to buy August year *N*+1** **220 €/t**	**actual basis** +11 €/t

The hedging results in the following price received by the farmer:

Price on the physical spot market	209 €/t
+ Profit on futures contracts	40 €/t
= Net price received by the producer	249 €/t, which is 4 €/t more than expected.

It is also: the selling futures price minus the actual basis, as explained below:

Price locked in selling on the futures market	260 €/t
− Actual basis	−11 €/t
= Net price received by the producer	249 €/t

The extra 4 €/t, in comparison with the expected price, is the variation of the basis.

Scenario 4: If the basis increases (by 5 €/t) The price of wheat may decrease by 40 €/t and the basis may increase by 5 €/t as shown here.

Time	Spot Market	Futures Market	Basis
October year *N*	expected next July 245 €/t	**to sell August year *N*+1** **260 €/t**	expected basis +15 €/t
July year *N*+1	**to sell** **200 €/t**	**to buy August year *N*+1** **220 €/t**	**actual basis** **+20 €/t**

The hedging results in the following price received by the farmer:

Price on the physical spot market	200 €/t
+ Profit on futures contracts	40 €/t
= Net price received by the producer	240 €/t, which is 5 €/t lower than expected.

It is also the selling futures price minus the actual basis, as explained below:

Price locked in selling on the futures market	260 €/t
– Actual basis	–20 €/t
= Net price received by the producer	240 €/t

The missing 5 €/t, in comparison with the expected price, is the variation of the basis.

9.4.2 Long Hedging for Processors

The advantages and limitations of futures contracts for a wheat processor buying on the physical cash market: long hedging.

9.4.2.1 The Principle of Long Hedging Any purchaser of wheat on a physical market is afraid of a possible price increase. He holds a short position on the physical market. In order to mitigate his price risk, he will take an opposite risk, a long risk on futures markets in going long: he makes a long hedge.

The commodity user will buy futures contracts to lock in his buying price:

Now	→	Later
To buy	→	To sell futures contracts
futures contracts		and to buy physical wheat on the physical spot market

9.4.2.2 Example: Context In January of year *N*, a wheat miller plans to buy 6000 tons of wheat in April of year *N*:

- Price on futures market for delivery in May of year *N* = 250 €/t.
- Expected price on the physical spot market in January of year *N* for a delivery 'at the milling gate' in April of year *N* = 226 €/t.

The basis is therefore:

$$\text{Futures Price} - \text{Physical Spot Price} = 24€/t$$

The miller considers this a good price, and is afraid of any increase in wheat prices. He wants to lock in the price. Long hedging, to buy 120 wheat futures contracts.

Scenario 1: If the price of wheat increases The price of wheat may increase by 35 €/t as shown here.

Time	Spot Market	Futures Market	Basis
January year *N*	expected in April 226 €/t	**Buy May year *N* 250 €/t**	expected basis +24 €/t
April year *N*	**Buy 261 €/t**	**Sell May year *N* 285 €/t**	**actual basis +24 €/t**

Price paid on the physical cash market	261 €/t
– Profit on futures contracts	−35 €/t
Net price paid by the processor	226 €/t, which is the expected price at the wheat miller's gate.

Scenario 2: If the price of wheat decreases The price of wheat may decrease by 33 €/t as shown here.

Time	Spot Market	Futures Market	Basis
January year *N*	expected in April 226 €/t	**Buy May year *N* 250 €/t**	expected basis +24 €/t
April year *N*	**Buy 193 €/t**	**Sell May year *N* 217 €/t**	**actual basis +24 €/t**

Price paid on the physical cash market	193 €/t
– Profit on futures contracts	−(33) €/t
Net price paid by the processor	226 €/t, which is the expected price at the wheat miller's gate.

Scenario 3: If the basis increases (by 6 €/t) The price of wheat may increase by 35 €/t and the basis may increase by 6 €/t as shown here.

Time	Spot Market	Futures Market	Basis
January year *N*	expected in April 226 €/t	**Buy May year *N* 250 €/t**	expected basis +24 €/t
April year *N*	**Buy 255 €/t**	**Sell May year *N* 285 €/t**	**actual basis +30 €/t**

Price paid on the physical cash market	255 €/t
– Profit on futures contracts	−35 €/t
Net price paid by the processor	220 €/t, which is 6 €/t lower than expected.

It is also the buying futures price minus the actual basis:

Price locked in buying on the futures market	250 €/t
– Actual basis	−30 €/t
= Net price paid by the processor	220 €/t

The missing 6 €/t, in comparison with the expected price, is the variation of the basis.

Scenario 4: If the basis decreases (by 4 €/t) The price of wheat may increase by 35 €/t and the basis may decrease by 7 €/t as shown here.

Time	Spot Market	Futures Market	Basis
January year *N*	expected in April 226 €/t	**Buy May year *N*** **250 €/t**	expected basis +24 €/t
April year *N*	**Buy** **268 €/t**	**Sell May year *N*** **285 €/t**	**actual basis** **+17 €/t**

Price paid on the physical cash market	268 €/t
– Profit on futures contracts	−35 €/t
Net price paid by the processor	233 €/t, which is 7 €/t higher than expected.

It is also the buying futures price minus the actual basis:

Price locked in buying on the futures market	250 €/t
– Actual basis	−17 €/t
= Net price paid by the processor	233 €/t

The extra 7 €/t, in comparison with the expected price, is the variation of the basis.

9.4.3 Management of Basis Risk

This section focuses on the management of basis risk mainly for seasonal, storable agricultural commodities.

9.4.3.1 Hedging and Basis Risk Recall that in hedging, the basis is the difference between the futures market price and the physical cash price at the gate of the operator's facilities:

$$Basis = Futures\ price - Physical\ spot\ price$$

TABLE 9.5 Impact of changes in the basis on hedging

	Short Hedging (Producer)	Long Hedging (Processor)
Lower Basis	Price received is HIGHER	Price paid is HIGHER
Higher Basis	Price received is LOWER	Price paid is LOWER

When the price is locked in on futures markets, the product's price increases or decreases have no effect. Only a basis fluctuation can modify the price that has been locked in (See Table 9.5). Price risk is reduced to basis risk.

As the maturity of a contract approaches, the basis tends towards zero.

Any commodity producer who sells commodity on the physical market undertakes short hedging:

Net price received by the producer = Selling price on the futures market – Actual basis

For any short hedger, when the basis decreases the price received is higher than expected. A short hedger bears the risk that the basis goes up.

Any commodity user who purchases commodity on the physical market undertakes long hedging:

Net price paid by the purchaser = Buying price on the futures market – Actual basis

For any long hedger, when the basis increases the price paid is lower than expected. A long hedger bears the risk that basis goes down.

The risk of price fluctuation is reduced to some risks of basis fluctuation. A commercial operator using physical spot markets and hedging on futures contracts needs to know and monitor changes in the basis in order to anticipate future movements and mitigate risks further.

9.4.3.2 Meaning of Basis Risk for Seasonal and Storable Products Basis is specific to an operator in the cash market using futures contracts for hedging purpose. There are as many bases as operators on the market.

Basis is a spread due to space, time, form, convenience yield and speculation that may be excessive sometimes.

- Time causes storage costs: the time difference between the futures contract maturity and the date at which the operator locks in the cash market causes storage costs.
- Space causes transportation costs: the space difference between the futures contract place of delivery and the gate of the operator in the cash market causes transportation costs.
- Form causes quality costs: the form difference between the product quality required by the futures contract and the quality of the commodity in the cash market causes quality costs.
- Uncertainty in physical supply causes convenience yield: uncertainty in physical supply due to an unexpected lack of quantity or quality at the time of delivery of outstanding futures contracts leads to a high premium for available goods. Such a premium for holding the goods in a cash market is called the convenience yield.

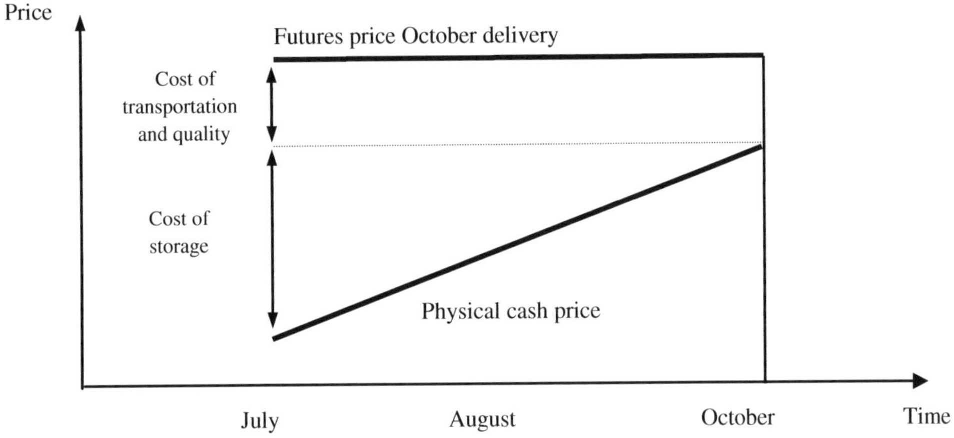

FIGURE 9.77 Basis convergence for seasonal and storable commodities between two crop years

- Uncertainty and rumours cause speculation on futures markets, which may not be related to cash markets. Financial investors may hold positions in futures markets due to rumours since it is easy to enter and exit such liquid markets in comparison with cash markets that are not liquid.

For seasonal and storable commodities such as cereals and oilseeds, between two crop years—as the month of delivery approaches – the basis converges towards zero (see Figure 9.77). The cost of storage goes down day after day and finally becomes null on the day of delivery of the futures contract. Theoretically, only the cost of transportation and quality may remain. For the place of delivery and on the day of delivery of the futures contract, only the quality cost may remain since the quality of the commodity harvested may differ from the standard quality of the futures contract.

Futures exchanges always check the basis convergence, particularly as the futures contract expires (see Figure 9.78). A persistent price gap and lack of convergence hurt hedgers who are no longer well protected. The ability of producers and commodity users to protect themselves from price volatility is then impaired. The operators on physical markets may no longer rely on futures markets to price their commodity and manage their price risks over time.

Large gaps are pricing disparities that may be due to speculation on futures contracts. Such speculation must be explained: the commodity quality in the potato case presented below, excessive long positions by financial investors or other reasons.

All futures exchanges pay strong attention to the basis gap and convergence. They may have to adapt their regulation (contract design, position limits, etc.) in order to preserve the effectiveness of futures contracts for hedgers.

The sugar basis for a MATIF contract maturing in October 1995 fits the theoretical model for seasonal storable agricultural products (see Figure 9.79).

Risk of Bad and Unstable Correlation: The Potato Case The potato futures contract seems problematic due to strong speculation about the preservation of tubers in case of dry weather in July. A dry early summer may cause the catalysis of starch in tubers to be harvested. Tubers that

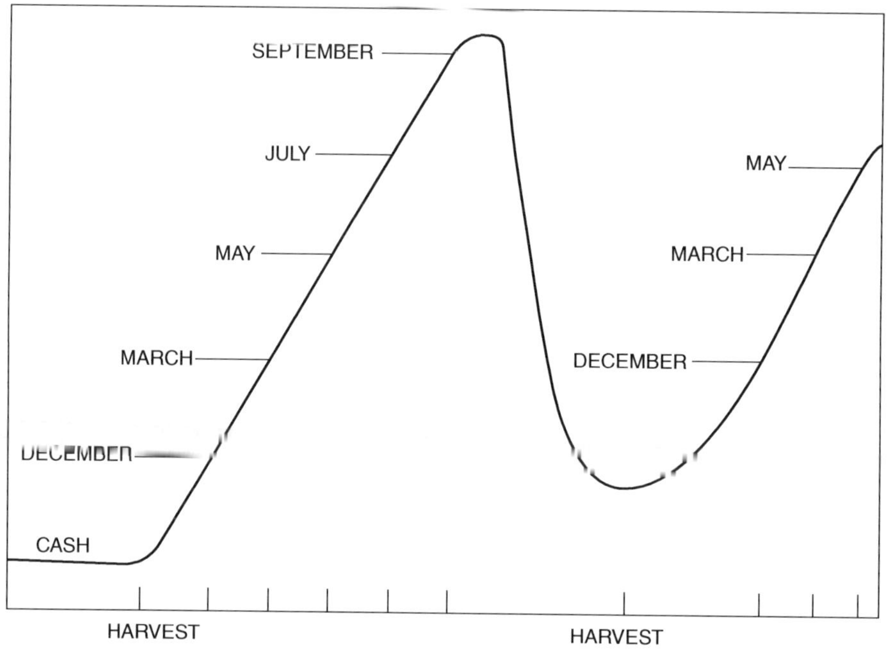

FIGURE 9.78 Futures and cash price between harvests
Source: Leuthold *et al.* (1989), Figure 7–1, p. 125.

are harvested in September or October may be rotten: uncertainty fuels speculation on futures markets for long maturity contracts because potato producers may have to sell their products quickly. So, the futures market price and spot price may evolve differently. The potato market may be subject to speculation on the preservation of tubers harvested. As a consequence, the potato futures market does not seem a good tool for hedging. See Figure 9.80.

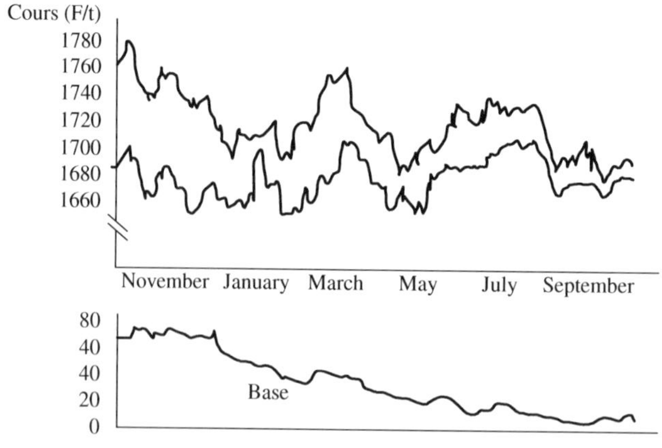

FIGURE 9.79 Futures price, spot price and basis for sugar on MATIF contract maturing in October 1995
Source: Voyer (1995), Figure 6.

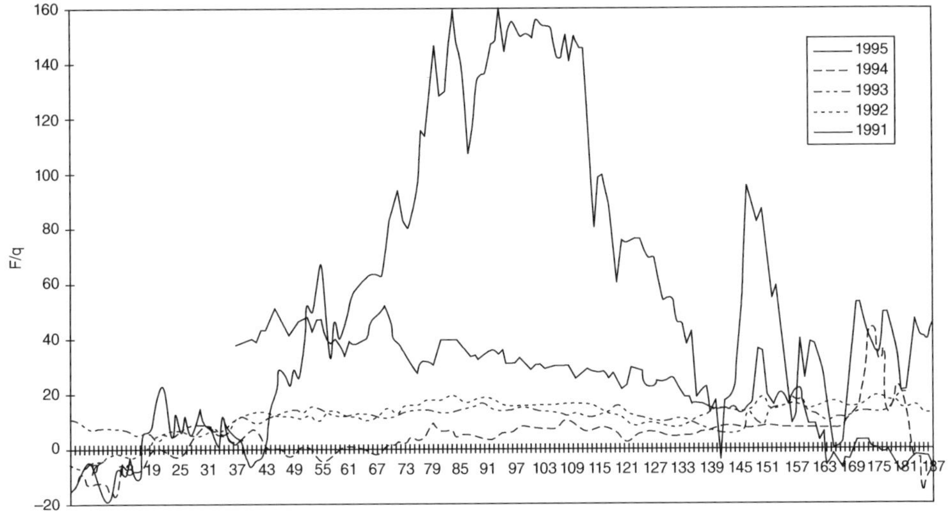

FIGURE 9.80 Potato futures (MATIF April contract) – spot prices, years 1991–95
Source: Voyer H. (1995), Figure 7.

Risk of Bad and Unstable Correlation when Using Other Product Futures Market For many products, there is no futures contract available. So, some professionals try to hedge their production of barley using milling wheat futures contracts, since they are substitutes. However, they are not perfect substitutes: their coefficient of correlation is low and unstable. As a consequence, such a practice is very risky. Milling wheat futures contracts are not a good tool for hedging barley price volatility. See Figure 9.81. When the basis is unstable, the basis risk becomes very strong.

Risk with Futures Contract whose Basis Convergence is Not Observable The observation of basis convergence depends on the characteristics of futures contracts with regard to products sold on cash markets at delivery points of futures contracts.

Most grain and oilseed futures contracts were designed according to local production features, including FOB delivery in local places. So, basis convergence may be tracked. However, soft commodities such as coffee and cocoa, traded with US and UK futures contracts, were designed for standard quality products stored in warehouses at various ports of destination with CIF delivery, not at tropical zones of production. Owing to progress in production and US/European consumers' demands, products on US and European cash markets are more and

HARVEST	2000	2001	2002	2003	2004	2005	2006	2007
Number of observations	124	247	251	251	256	254	250	134
Coefficient of correlation	–0.68	0.42	0.12	0.44	0.46	0.01	0.43	0.79

FIGURE 9.81 Correlation between milling wheat futures contract and barley spot market
Source: Declerk, ESSEC Business School.

more often premium quality and certified products. There are no longer basic quality products on export markets in the USA or Europe. So, basis convergence is not easily observable.

9.4.3.3 Contango and Backwardation Contango means a full carry market. The price difference between contracts with two different delivery months is the full cost of carrying the commodity from the delivery month of the first contract to the next.

For a non-perishable commodity, carrying costs include interest, insurance and storage, less income from leasing out the commodity if possible (for gold). This is the amount by which the price of a commodity for future delivery is *higher* than:

- the spot price,
- or a far future delivery price higher than a nearer future delivery.

Backwardation is the amount of money required for future delivery of an item if *lower* than the amount required:

- for immediate delivery of that item,
- for a nearer future delivery.

It leads to an inverted basis.

Which events may cause an inverted basis?

- Weather, such as frost in winter, may lead to very high spot prices when lorries are not allowed on roads, when boats are not allowed on rivers. Such an event is very temporary, futures market prices may not move. So, the basis may be inverted.
- Strikes on harbours may also lead to high spot prices and cause an inverted basis.
- A delayed harvest of wheat due to rain in England or Northern France leads to high spot prices and causes an inverted basis.
- The expectation of a large harvest also leads to an inverted basis.

9.4.3.4 Basis Variations for Seasonal and Non-storable Products The basis fluctuates every day according to cost fluctuations and operators' expectations. But day-to-day fluctuations are small and the basis varies only a little for a given day from year to year. The relative stability of the basis explains why futures markets are so helpful. *Note*: For non-storable products, the basis depends on the supply and demand at any moment.

9.4.3.5 Residual Risk: Hedge Ratio The risk of a wrong hedge ratio is a major residual risk when hedging. It is presented here.

Notations:

π	Return on a portfolio including the asset S and the asset F
$\boldsymbol{S}$	Asset negotiated on a (physical) spot market
$\boldsymbol{F}$	Asset negotiated on a futures market
$\boldsymbol{X_S}$	Quantity of S, number of assets S
$\boldsymbol{X_F}$	Quantity of F, number of assets F
$\boldsymbol{E(R_S)}$	Expected return per unit of the cash asset S, that is $E(S) - S$
$\boldsymbol{E(R_F)}$	Expected return per unit of the futures asset F, that is $E(F) - F$

The operator's objective is to maximize the expected utility of profit, here expressed in the form of return:

$$\text{Max } E(U(R_p) = E(R_p) + \lambda\sigma^2$$

with respect to X_S and X_F with:
λ = coefficient of risk aversion.

- When an operator is risk-averse, he does not like risk: λ is negative.
- When an operator accepts no risk, he is strongly risk-averse: λ tends to $-\infty$.
- When an operator is perfectly willing to bear risk: λ is very low and tends to 0.

$E(R_p)$ = expected return of the portfolio made up of the two assets S and F

$$E(R_p) = E(X_S R_S + X_F R_F)$$
$$E(R_p) = X_S E(R_S) + X_F E(R_F)$$

σ^2 = variance of the profit of the portfolio made-up of the two assets S and F

$$\sigma^2 = X_S^2\sigma_{R_S}^2 + X_F^2\sigma_{R_F}^2 + 2X_sX_F C\sigma_{R_S}\sigma_{R_F}$$

with:
variance of the profit from the asset on the (physical) spot market = Var $(R_S) = \sigma_{R_S}^2$
variance of the profit from the asset on the futures market = Var $(R_F) = \sigma_{R_F}^2$
C = coefficient of correlation between the profit from the asset on the spot market and the profit from the asset on the futures market

The covariance of the profit from the asset on the spot market and the profit from the asset on the futures market is thus

$$\text{Cov}(R_s R_F) = C\sigma_{R_S}\sigma_{R_F}$$

The objective function is thus

$$\text{Max } E[U(R_p)] = X_S E(R_S) + X_F E(R_F) + \lambda\left[X_S^2\sigma_{R_S}^2 + X_F^2\sigma_{R_F}^2 + 2X_sX_F C\sigma_{R_S}\sigma_{R_F}\right]$$

with respect to X_S and X_F.

The parameters X_S and X_F are found from the Lagrangian, that is the first derivative with respect to each parameter X_S and X_F is zero and the second derivative with respect to each parameter X_S and X_F is negative.

$$\frac{dE\left[U(R_p)\right]}{dX_S} = E(R_S) + 2\lambda X_S\sigma_{R_S}^2 + 2\lambda X_F C\sigma_{R_S}\sigma_{R_F} = 0 \quad (9.1)$$

$$\frac{dE\left[U(R_p)\right]}{dX_F} = E(R_F) + 2\lambda X_F\sigma_{R_F}^2 + 2\lambda X_S C\sigma_{R_S}\sigma_{R_F} = 0 \quad (9.2)$$

So,

$$X_S = \frac{-E(R_S)}{2\lambda\sigma^2_{R_S}} - \frac{C\sigma_{R_S}\sigma_{R_F}}{\sigma^2_{R_S}}X_F$$

$$X_F = \frac{-E(R_F)}{2\lambda\sigma^2_{R_F}} - \frac{C\sigma_{R_S}\sigma_{R_F}}{\sigma^2_{R_F}}X_S$$

The hedge ratio is

$$X_F = \frac{-E(R_F)}{2\lambda\sigma^2_{R_F}} - \frac{C\sigma_{R_S}\sigma_{R_F}}{\sigma^2_{R_F}}X_S = \frac{-E(R_F)}{2\lambda \mathrm{Var}(R_F)} - \frac{\mathrm{Cov}(R_S R_F)}{\mathrm{Var}(R_F)}X_S$$

It is the quantity X_F of asset F on the futures market which hedges (offsets, reduces) the price fluctuation risk of the quantity X_S of asset S on the physical spot market. The hedge ratio comprises two factors:

$$\left[-\frac{c\sigma_{RS}\sigma_{RF}}{\sigma^2_{R_F}}X_S\right] = \left[-\frac{\mathrm{Cov}(R_S, R_F)}{\mathrm{Var}(R_F)}X_S\right] \quad \text{pure hedge factor}$$

$$\left[\frac{-E(R_F)}{2\lambda\sigma^2_{R_F}}\right] = \left[\frac{-E(R_F)}{2\lambda \mathrm{Var}(R_F)}\right] = \text{speculative factor}$$

Conclusions:

1. Optimal hedge ratio: pure hedge

   When an economic agent wants no risk at all, he is totally risk-averse: λ tends to $-\infty$.

   Therefore the speculative factor tends to 0, so $X_F =$ the pure hedge factor.

$$X_F = \left[-\frac{\mathrm{Cov}(R_S, R_F)}{\mathrm{Var}(R_F)}X_S\right] = \left[-\frac{c\sigma_{R_S}\sigma_{R_F}}{\sigma^2_{R_F}}X_S\right] = \left[-\frac{c\sigma_{R_S}}{\sigma_{R_F}}X_S\right]$$

$$X_F/X_S = \left[-\frac{\mathrm{Cov}(R_S, R_F)}{\mathrm{Var}(R_F)}\right] = \left[-\frac{c\sigma_{R_S}\sigma_{R_F}}{\sigma^2_{R_F}}\right] = \left[-\frac{c\sigma_{R_S}}{\sigma_{R_F}}\right]$$

For a hedger wishing to minimize his price fluctuation risk, the hedge (X_F/X_S) depends on the relative variability (σ_{R_S}, σ_{R_F}) of $\sigma^2_{R_F}$ returns for the futures and physical cash market positions, and their correlation c.

A hedge $X_F = -X_S$ then (X_F / $X_S = -1$) is only appropriate if the f futures and physical cash market positions have the same standard deviation ($\sigma_{R_S} = \sigma_{R_F}$) and are perfectly correlated. The hedger takes a futures position of an equal amount to his physical position, but in the opposite direction. For example, a farmer who expects to harvest

50 tons of standard quality wheat will sell one futures contract for 50 tons of standard quality wheat.

Level of risk: pure hedging means minimizing the risk on the portfolio, $\mathrm{Var}(R_p)$

$$\mathrm{Var}(R_p) = X_S^2\sigma_{R_S}^2 + X_F^2\sigma_{R_F}^2 + 2X_sX_F C\sigma_{R_S}\sigma_{R_F}$$

$$\frac{\mathrm{Min\,Var}(R_p)}{X_S, X_F} \Rightarrow \frac{d\mathrm{Var}(R_p)}{dX_F} = 2X_F\mathrm{Var}(R_F) - 2X_S\mathrm{Cov}(R_S, R_F) = 0$$

So, $X_F = -X_S \frac{\mathrm{Cov}(R_S, R_F)}{\mathrm{Var}(R_F)}$ = pure hedge factor. The risk of price fluctuation is fully hedged that is reduced to zero.

2. Optimal hedge when the correlation is positive and lower than 1

When the price fluctuations on the spot market and the futures markets are positively correlated, that is, when $\mathrm{Cov}(R_s, R_F) = C\sigma_{R_s}\sigma_{R_F} > 0$. Then the hedge is undertaken by taking an opposite position on the futures market to the position taken on the spot (physical) market.

Example: An operator who holds a long position on the spot (physical) market (a producer) will enter the futures market with a short position in selling futures contracts.

The hedge ratio may differ for 1 ton on the futures market and 1 ton on the spot (physical) market. This situation may occur when there is no futures market for a given feed commodity. In such a case an operator who is considering buying/selling barley on the spot (physical) market may hedge his position on the futures market for fodder wheat since there is no futures contract for fodder barley.

3. Speculator's hedge ratio

The speculative factor may be larger than the pure hedge factor for an operator who loves risk: λ becomes small, slightly negative and tends to zero. The expected profit from the asset on the futures market is equal to its final value minus its initial value, that is $E(R_F) = [E(F_1) - F_0]$.

The speculative factor has the sign of $E(R_F) = [E(F_1) - F_0]$. If the price on the futures market is a lot higher than the price on the spot (physical) market, the expected profit on the futures market per unit of asset F is very positive, that is $[E(F_1) \gg F_0] \Rightarrow E(R_F) \gg 0$.

Sometimes, this expected profit may be so positive that the speculative factor is higher than the pure hedge factor. A speculator takes a position on the futures market which is similar to his position on the spot (physical) market. For instance, a farmer speculates twice when he buys futures contracts for potatoes. He is speculating both on his harvest to be sold on the spot (physical) market and on the contracts he has bought on the futures market. He holds a long position twice.

9.4.3.6 Residual Risks: Quantity and Quality Risks Due to Poor Harvest Mainly due to weather conditions, harvested volumes are uncertain until harvest is achieved. If producers have hedged more volumes than actual volumes harvested, they are in a speculative position for missing quantity in the cash market.

Mainly due to weather conditions, the quality of harvest may be below the requirements of futures contracts. For instance, a milling wheat contract requires a minimum specific weight of 76 kg/hl in both cash and futures markets. In case of rain at harvest time, as may be the case in European countries along the North Sea and the English Channel, wheat may not be suitable to make bread. Producers in those regions may harvest a product that cannot be sold as milling wheat. Such a good can only be sold as feed wheat whose price is a lot lower. Producers face speculative price risk, which is worth the difference between milling and feed wheat prices.

9.4.3.7 Other Residual Risks: Fret Risks and Financial Risks Commodity transactions may include fret management risk. Financial risks related to commodity transactions may include cash management risks, risks of exchange rate fluctuation and risks of interest rate fluctuation. Cash management risks arise from the financing of margin calls every evening. Credit lines must be secured with the banker. Usually, the banker only provides a limited amount of credit or asks for collateral: assets, cautions. So, in case of high price volatility, margin calls may reach such amounts. Risks of exchange rate fluctuation may be hedged by exchange rates futures contracts, options, etc. Risks of interest rate fluctuation (on inventories and cash) may be hedged by interest rate futures contracts, options, etc.

9.5 THE FINANCIALIZATION OF AGRICULTURAL MARKETS AND HUNGER: SPECULATION AND REGULATION

The financialization of the agricultural commodity markets has emerged in the second part of the 2000s. Financial investors have invested heavily in commodity futures contracts, directly or indirectly through index funds … The major question is: Did it affect agricultural prices so that the market price does not reflect supply and demand on physical markets? Did agriculture and food market prices become a false signal for producers and users? Did it contribute to a strong increase in price so that hunger and malnutrition increased over the world?

9.5.1 Factors Affecting the Volatility of Agricultural Commodity Prices

Volatility appears because of uncertainty when a price is formed on markets. According to Balcombe (2009), agricultural commodity market prices are volatile for many reasons, including natural shocks. The major factors of uncertainty are: fluctuating production output, lagged supply adjustment to demand, short-run price inelasticity in both demand and supply, poor quality of information about inventories, unexpected change in demand, sudden policy decisions, shocks on other markets, unstable exchange rates, the financialization of agricultural markets and, sometimes, rumours that lead to excessive speculation. These points are detailed below.

- Fluctuating production output: natural shocks such as weather, diseases, pests, etc., lead to variable agricultural production output. The impact of droughts, heavy rainfall and floods on production yield can cause a very significant increase or decrease in the level of inventory carry over.
- Lagged supply adjustment to demand: the long agricultural production cycle leads to lagged adjustment of supply to changes in demand.

- Very low price demand elasticity and price supply elasticity: this contributes to an amplification of price movements. In the short run, supply is almost stable but even if commodity prices fluctuate, it is not possible to produce more grain. All that can be done is to avoid harvesting. If the supply is abundant, it is only possible to set aside part of the production: policymakers do this with fruit and vegetables.

  Furthermore, commodities have few substitutes. Demand for agricultural staples is also inelastic: it does not fluctuate even if prices go up or down, since there is almost no substitute. For instance, wheat millers are willing to pay more for quality milling wheat and this contributes to high price fluctuations. Compound feeders and non-food users may find other commodities as substitutes, but the substitution rate may be low.
- Poor quality of information about inventories: this leads to uncertainty about inventories in terms of quantity, quality (degree of preservation) and availability (within a week or a month). Some countries do not provide reliable information on their grain inventories: asymmetric information leads to market failure. Furthermore, it is difficult to assess the preservation of some commodities such as potatoes. Information may be out-of-date or unreliable.
- Unexpected change in demand: the forecast demand for food and feed is usually accurate since it depends mainly on demography (which is quite well known), purchasing power and degree of malnutrition (hunger, obesity, etc.). However, the demand for biofuel may fluctuate since it depends mainly on policy decisions, particularly in the USA and Europe.
- Sudden policy decisions (embargoes, subsidies, quotas, etc.): these can strongly affect prices. New tax rules for biofuels will immediately modify the supply–demand balance. The Russian embargo on wheat exports announced on 5 August 2010, with effect from 15 August, disrupted markets: prices went up because of fears that harvests would be worse than anticipated, but also that inventories would be lower than expected. Such uncertainties and fears led to increasing price volatility.

  Market rules and regulations provide a framework to ease trade between suppliers and demanders. At the international level, the *Codex alimentarius* Commission defines minimum quality requirements, including sanitary quality, for agricultural and food products. International commodity agreements regulating supply through quotas and buffer stocks have been removed for most commodities. According to Tothova (2011, p. 26), national management of inventories is central, since low stocks often exacerbate uncertainties and make rumours of shortage more credible.

  Generally, during political negotiations, tensions between stakeholders are sources of volatility. The adjustment of supply to demand under new constraints and opportunities takes time, and this affects market prices.
- Shocks in other markets such as oil and currency markets influence agricultural markets (Balcombe, 2009). Oil prices are input costs for farm production. They have an effect on agricultural selling prices used to make biofuels: energy and agricultural markets are now linked. Co-movements of agricultural and oil prices are observed (Tothova, 2011, p. 23). Agricultural products are also more or less substitutes for each other. Consequently, the price volatility of a product impacts agricultural prices.
- Unstable exchange rates: most commodities are negotiated in US dollars on international markets, but outside the US dollar zone farmers sell their products in domestic currency, food processors buy agricultural products in domestic currency and exchange rates are volatile.

- The financialization of agricultural markets: these markets' assets have attracted financial investors since 2007. As a result, commodity markets are more closely linked to financial markets.
- In high uncertainty situations, suppliers and demanders do not have reliable information to approach equilibrium in forming prices. In times of uncertainty, rumours seem more credible and may lead to excessive speculation. Speculation may come from different types of operators: commercial operators (producers, manufacturers) actively involved in physical markets and non-commercial operators, i.e. 'speculators'.

From the moment he decides to sow grain until he sells it, a farmer holds a speculative long position. As soon as he decides to sow rapeseed, a farmer holds a speculative long position because he faces price fluctuation risks, with the hope of a higher price and fear of a price drop. Before purchasing agricultural products, food manufacturers face the speculative risk of price volatility, with the hope of a lower price and fear of an increase in prices. Farmers and manufacturers usually enter the futures markets to lock in their agricultural price in order to mitigate their price volatility risk: they are hedgers. But they may also sometimes speculate on the futures markets.

Operators with no activity in the physical cash commodity markets enter the futures markets and take risks in the hope of making profit. Such risk-takers are called speculators. High uncertainty about supply and demand – in terms of quantity and quality, in a given location at a given point in time in the future – is an incentive for speculators to enter markets and buy (or sell) contracts with distant maturity. They are effectively making a bet that they will be able to make a profit by buying back (or selling back) these contracts. They never intend to actually deliver or take delivery of the goods, since they have no business activity on physical cash markets.

When there is fear and risk of stock shortage before harvest time due to low carry-over levels, holding a commodity is a 'plus' which is subject to speculation. The risk raises commodity prices and provides a convenience yield for operators owning the goods. This happens when the harvest is uncertain in terms of quantity and quality. It also happens when the harvest is delayed due to bad weather and stock carry-over levels are low. In such situations uncertainty rises about the ability to manage low stock carry over in order to meet very short-term demand … and it is not possible to produce more agricultural products such as grain in the short run. Low-inventory periods are also periods of high volatility on commodity markets (Deaton and Laroque, 1992; Chavas and Kim, 2006; Balcombe, 2009).

Volatility appears because of uncertainty when a price is formed on markets. Uncertainty puts buyers and sellers in a situation where there is no consensus about price. Agricultural price volatility showed strong increases with high price spikes in 2008 and 2010. In 2008, specific new shocks affected grain markets:

- an unexpected surge in Asian demand for meat, and therefore for grain;
- the effect of EU and US policies subsidizing the production of biofuel even with high market prices for grain, contributing to further price increases;
- a poor grain harvest in many regions while inventories were at low levels of less than 80 days of consumption (IGC, 2010);
- the financialization of agricultural commodities as an asset class in investors' portfolios.

Volatility can concern price increases or decreases.

Speculation is Essential for Market Liquidity In bearing risks, speculators contribute to market liquidity. They provide counterparties for hedgers who are constantly seeking to reduce their price volatility risks. The role of speculators is to bring liquidity in order to ease transactions, which means the adjustment of supply and demand, particularly in commodity futures markets. However, this adjustment involves risks: prices may go up or down. Speculators help the market by bearing such risks.

Usually, farmers want to sell contracts with the earliest possible maturity after harvest in order to hedge (that is, reduce price fluctuation risk). Price volatility is reduced to basis fluctuation risk. Basis fluctuation risk is a residual risk due to the unstable correlation between the futures market price and the physical (cash) price for hedgers, here farmers. Food processors, however, do not want to buy futures contracts maturing just after harvest. They prefer to hedge commodities month after month, depending on their purchases of agricultural products on physical (cash) markets. A processor will thus seek to reduce his price fluctuation risk and his basis fluctuation risk.

A lack of counterparties for post-harvest maturities could therefore strongly depress prices. The market needs speculators taking risks by entering the futures market in hope of profit. Risk-takers are needed to help price formation such that supply and demand are balanced not only at that period, but also every day. Speculators bear price fluctuation risks and thus ease optimal allocation of the resources traded between suppliers and demanders.

A market is liquid or dead. Liquidity risk is the risk of not finding a counterparty easily, at a price close to the last transaction price. Such a risk results from a lack of operators on the futures market, and may be caused by:

- Small price fluctuations, which do not attract hedgers and speculators.
- Small volumes traded by commodity producers and processors on physical (cash) markets. In such a case there are not enough hedgers who could also enter futures markets. This means that the prices formed on futures markets do not show good correlation with the physical fundamentals of supply and demand. As a result, the risk of basis fluctuation could increase strongly.

A minimum level of speculation is essential to ensure the agricultural futures markets operate properly.

Speculation can be Excessive and Detrimental The market needs speculators, but not too many. Speculation may be excessive if the prices formed in futures markets no longer reflect the equilibrium between supply and demand in physical markets. A speculative bubble may occur, with prices based only on rumours and speculation. Agricultural producers and processors may no longer trust such a futures market, and be unwilling to enter the futures market. Excessive speculation can thus kill markets.

9.5.2 Financialization: Impact of Non-commercial Traders on Market Price

Many studies have focused on agricultural commodities. Some results are provided. As exhibited in Figure 9.82, in 2002 the Standard & Poor's Goldman Sachs Commodity Index (S&P GSCI) evolved differently from the Stoxx EU index and the WTI oil price.

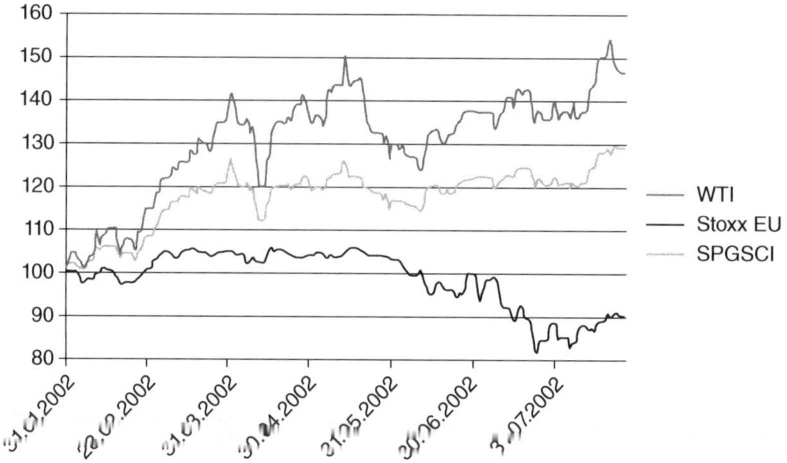

FIGURE 9.82 Evolution of commodity (oil and GSCI) vs. Stoxx EU in 2002, more than 10 years ago
Source: UNCTAD, http://unctad.org/en/PublicationsLibrary/presspb2012d1_en.pdf.

But in 2012, all the indices exhibited the same pattern: commodity prices and stock prices are moving together (Figure 9.83).

According to UNCTAD, financial investments in OTC commodity derivatives, and particularly oil, have increased over the 2000s (Figure 9.84).

According to UNCTAD, the coefficient of correlation between commodity and equity indices has become closer to 1 from the mid-2000s (Figure 9.85).

9.5.3 The Financialization of Grain Markets and Speculation

In 2011 the Permanent Subcommittee on Investigations of the US Senate reported observations made by the CFTC on the wheat futures contract on the CME, the largest wheat market in the

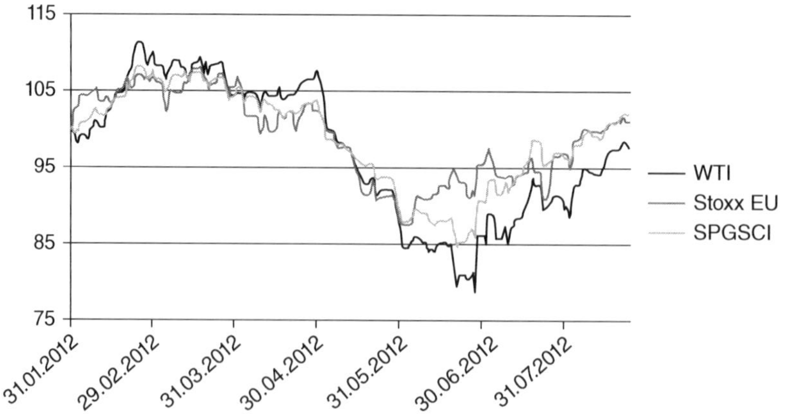

FIGURE 9.83 Evolution of commodity (oil and GSCI) vs. Stoxx EU in 2012
Source: UNCTAD, http://unctad.org/en/PublicationsLibrary/presspb2012d1_en.pdf.

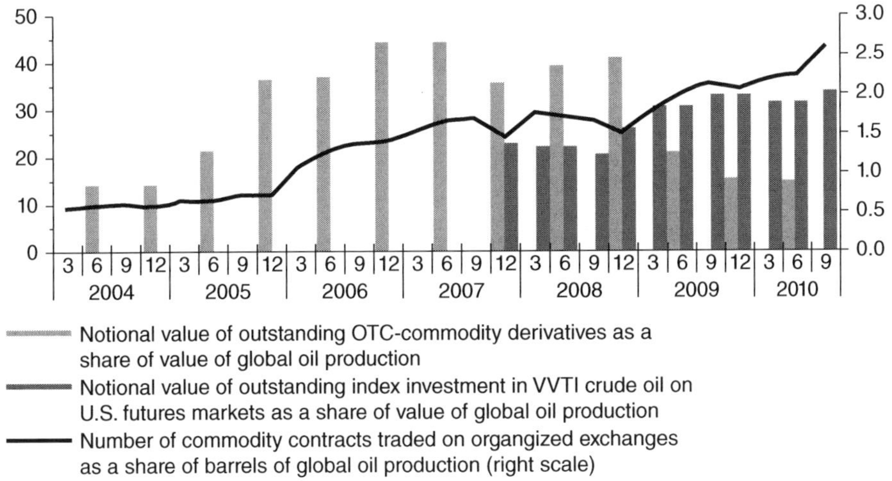

FIGURE 9.84 Financial investment in commodities as a proportion of global oil production, 2004–10
Source: UNCTAD, http://dgff.unctad.org/chapter2/2.6.html.

world. Focused on the open long interest, it observed that the amount of outstanding wheat futures contracts purchased by index traders (i.e., speculators) increased sevenfold from about 30,000 daily outstanding contracts at the beginning of 2004 to about 220,000 contracts in mid-2008. Index traders held 35–50% of the open long interest. They held 20–30% in the other US wheat markets.

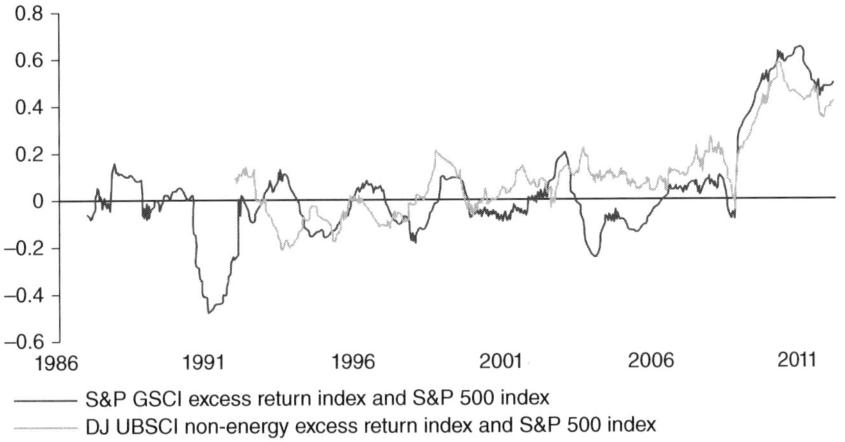

FIGURE 9.85 Coefficient of correlation between commodity and equity indices, 1986–2012
UNCTAD secretariat calculations, based on Bloomberg.
The data reflect 1-year rolling correlations of returns on the respective indices, based on daily data.
Source: UNCTAD, http://dgff.unctad.org/chapter2/2.6.html.

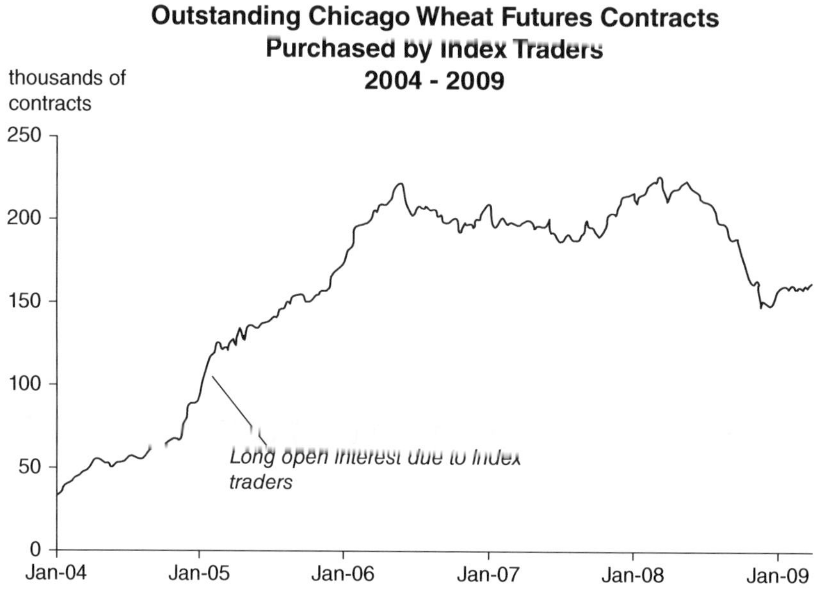

FIGURE 9.86 Growth in index fund purchases of Chicago wheat futures contracts. Chart prepared by Permanent Subcommittee on Investigations, with data from the CFTC

Source: Permanent Subcommittee on Investigations, US Senate, in IATP (2011), p. 78.

In 2011 the Permanent Subcommittee on Investigations of the US Senate reported that 'the large number of wheat futures contracts purchased by swap dealers and index traders is the prime reason for higher prices in the wheat futures markets relative to the cash market'. Since financial investors do not operate in the physical spot market, their investment in futures contracts has been so high that the gap between futures prices and spot prices, namely the basis, has become larger and more persistent over the 2000s. The basis did not converge as expected at contract maturity for places of delivery of futures contracts. For soft red winter wheat at Chicago, the average daily basis between the nearest maturity and the physical price on place of delivery was \$0.25 per bushel from 2000 to 2005. During the second semester of 2008, it was between \$1.50 and \$2.00 (see Figure 9.87). The analysis of supply and demand in the spot market alone cannot explain such a gap. In addition, the basis has not converged at futures contract expiration, but has increased from about \$0.13 per bushel in 2005 to \$0.35 in 2006 and \$1.53 in 2008 (see Figure 9.88), that is a 10-fold increase for a threefold price increase. The CFTC also noticed a larger presence of index traders: from 2006 to early 2008, they held between 33% and 50% of outstanding long positions. From mid-2008, they accounted for more than 55% of long open interest.

The Subcommittee pointed out that the CFTC did not monitor speculation properly during the late 2000s. The CFTC continued to waive some position limits for index traders and swap dealers over the 2000s, even though speculation was large enough and questions arose about possible excessive speculation. A position limit puts a maximum number of agricultural futures contracts that can be held by a single trader. A position limit is a tool to monitor market fairness and manage liquidity to avoid dominant positions by a single trader.

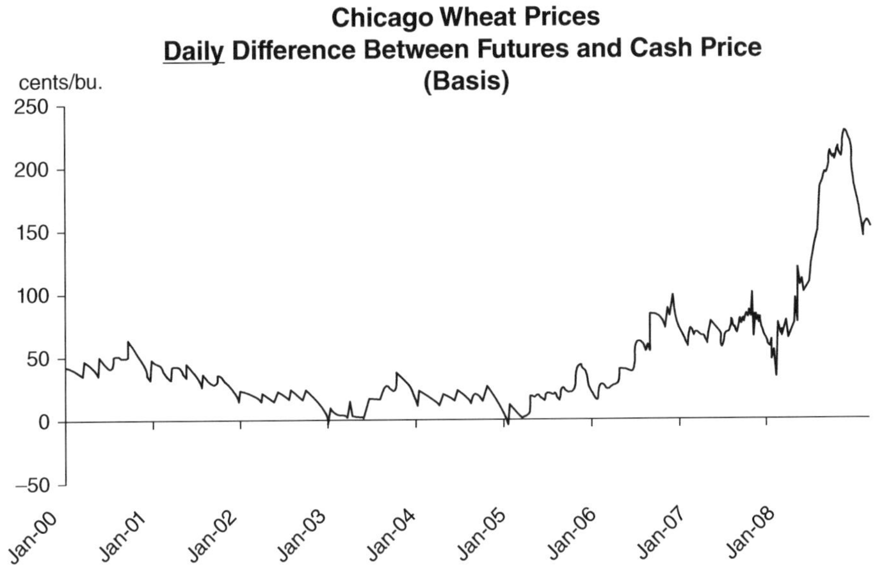

FIGURE 9.87 Increase in daily difference between futures and spot prices for Chicago wheat. Chart prepared by Permanent Subcommittee on Investigations with data sources from CME (daily futures prices) and MGEX (average daily spot prices)
Source: Permanent Subcommittee on Investigations, US Senate, in IATP (2011), p. 79.

Economic research on grain futures markets has resulted in the following findings:

- Uninformed traders adopt speculative investment strategies which bring liquidity to markets. They contribute to the price adjustment of supply and demand (De Long *et al.*, 1990).
- Often, volumes of speculation increase as volumes traded by hedgers (producers and manufacturers) increase. Working (1960) argues that the level of speculation must be compared with the level of hedgers. For nine agricultural commodities, Sanders *et al.* (2008) have shown that the level of speculation was not excessive on futures markets during the period 2006–08.
- Sanders *et al.* (2009) found that long-only index funds may be beneficial in markets traditionally dominated by short hedging and have no significant impact on agricultural commodity prices. However, over the period 2005–08, volumes traded by index funds increased 10-fold. With data from June 2006 and December 2009, Irwin and Sanders (2010, 2011) confirm that index funds have not impacted speculation significantly. Irwin and Sanders (2010, 2011) found no evidence of a direct empirical link between index fund trading and commodity futures prices, casting doubt on the common belief that index funds fueled the 2008 price spike.
- Financial investors may have amplified price movements for some period of time. Index funds are long only. Usually their prospectus mentions that they commit themselves in holding a balance of various commodities, often dominated by energy and minerals with agricultural commodities as a minor component. Agricultural commodities only account

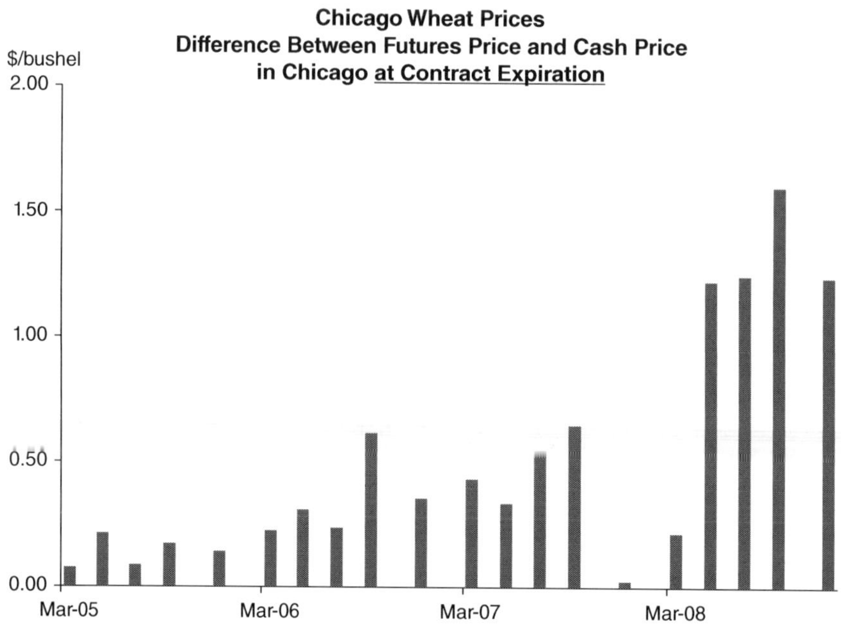

FIGURE 9.88 Increase in differences between futures and spot prices for Chicago wheat at futures contract expiration. Chart prepared by Permanent Subcommittee on Investigations with data sources from CME (daily futures prices) and USDA (spot prices at Chicago)
Source: Permanent Subcommittee on Investigations, US Senate, in IATP (2011), p. 79.

for 12.2% of the S&P GSCI (De Schutter, 2010). So their long position may influence grain markets, even though decisions are not related to market fundamentals.

- 'Herding behaviour' in periods of strong upward prices attracts many speculators since market access is easy.
- However, futures markets have worked with delivery of goods executed. Furthermore, in the late 2000s, investors were searching for better yields in an environment with low stock and bond returns. It is more difficult to get research results about the opaque and unregulated OTC trading (IATP, 2011).

Nevertheless, speculative bubbles exist: for a few weeks the price volatility is high, and prices may go up or down. Pricing seems difficult. Then the bubble bursts and the price reverts to reflecting supply and demand fundamentals in the physical market. A speculative bubble may be suspected when the market price rises or falls so rapidly that all operators are convinced such a movement can last, even though it cannot be explained by market fundamentals: harvest, inventories, demand. Sometimes, a price may rise very sharply before falling back. For instance in the EU, the milling wheat price was €181/t in early July 2007, went up to €290/t in February 2008 and then dropped to €200/t in April 2008 in a context of strong price volatility. Such price jumps for wheat harvested in July 2007 show that the market operators did not have appropriate information to form prices according to the fundamentals of demand and supply.

TABLE 9.6 2012 performance of the largest commodity hedge funds and stock markets

S&P 500 equities	16%
US Treasuries Index	2.10%
Commodity hedge funds (Newedge)	−3.70%
Hedge fund BCM	−5%
Hedge fund Clive Capital LLP	−9%
Hedge fund Vermillion	−10%

Source: *The Financial Times*, 7 February 2013, p. 25.

Speculation is Fueled by Uncertainty and Rumours Some market operators may benefit from rumours and uncertainty:

- Financial businesses earn fees on transactions, they need to attract operators. Hedge funds invest in trading in case of increasing or decreasing price: high price volatility is a helpful argument to attract investors. Brokers can take advantage of uncertainty and rumours as an incentive to attract investors who do not want to miss some expected profit that may seem quick to achieve.
- Producers, including exporting states, want price increases and may ease them in by communicating production risks.
- Consumers, including importing states, prefer price decreases and may ease them in by announcing possible product substitutions for other products or a reduction in commodity use due to new recipes and efficiency gains.

9.5.4 Bubble or Not, Agricultural Commodities have Become an Asset Class

In 2012, while stock markets recovered, several hedge funds experienced losses and decided to lower their exposure to commodities. See Tables 9.6, 9.7.

Ethics and reputation reasons have motivated some banks to stop their food commodity funds. Even though empirical research found little evidence of increase or greater volatility in food prices due to speculation, non-government organizations have exerted pressure on banks. They have told them that food commodity funds are 'speculating on hunger' on the premise that investment in such funds contribute to push up food prices and ultimately hunger, social and political instability. Some banks decided to shut their food commodity funds. The French BNP-Paribas, which shut three commodity funds exposed to agricultural commodities in 2011, closed its last one in 2012 even though it only accounted for 0.08% of its total assets. In early 2013 the French Crédit Agricole closed three agricultural funds and the UKs

TABLE 9.7 Commodity hedge funds, total annual returns from 2002 to 2012 (in %)

Year	2002	2003	2004	2005	2006	2007	2008	2009	2010	2011	2012
Annual total returns	44%	27%	23%	13%	22%	16%	3%	6%	8%	−1.5%	−3.7%

Source: *The Financial Times* 7 February 2013, p. 25.

Barclays Bank announced that it will stop speculating on food commodities. In 2012 several German banks, such as Commerzbank and Deka-Bank, reduced their activity in agriculture and food commodities while German LBB Invest stopped it. Since research found little empirical evidence that financial investors were responsible for increases in food prices and greater volatility, some banks decided to continue to offer commodity funds. Agricultural derivatives have become an asset class and will remain.

9.5.5 Price Volatility and Regulation

This section focuses on the management of price volatility through regulation. The 2008 financial crisis triggered regulatory financial reforms, with the Dodd–Frank act passed in 2010 in the USA and strong evolution of the European Market Infrastructure Regulation (EMIR) and the Market in Financial Instruments (MiFid) Directive 2004/39/EC in the EU. They provide general frameworks for comprehensive risk assessment and regulations to be designed for the different financial services and instruments, including agricultural commodity derivatives.

The Dodd–Frank act is being implemented. The CFTC is issuing regulations to diminish, eliminate or prevent excessive speculation on agricultural commodity derivative markets: position limits, clearing of OTC derivatives through central clearing houses, capital deposit for OTC dealers.

In August 2012 the EU regulation no. 648/2012 enforced similar rules on OTC derivatives with central counterparties (CCPs) and required trade repositories (TRs), including the duty to make certain data available to the public and relevant authorities. The EMIR was amended and enforced in March 2013. It imposed new rules for trading companies and for financial instruments. Financial counterparties and non-financial counterparties above some clearing threshold have clearing obligations, risk mitigation techniques and reporting obligations to the European Securities and Market Authority (ESMA). EU member states are harmonizing the rules and regulations of investment services and activities. Investment firms are required to be allowed to operate in the EU and are registered to the ESMA. Rules and regulations are being put in place.

Policymakers may improve operations on agricultural and soft futures markets by acting on the following levers:

1. **Harmonizing national regulations and agricultural commodity markets** The prices formed in agricultural commodity futures markets are the benchmark food prices for 7 billion people. Transaction security and food safety require harmonized regulation of the various futures exchanges. The G20 meeting on agriculture in June 2011 ended with such an agreement, but with no penalty for non-application. There is thus nothing to stop a government from introducing an embargo. The embargo on wheat exports decided by the Russian government in August 2010 immediately increased uncertainty about available supply on international markets and led to a sharp increase in price.
2. **Policies on biofuels** Some policy decisions distort the formation of market price. For example, subsidies or a lower tax rate on biofuels distort market price formation: the demand for agricultural products used for biofuels (corn, sugar cane, wheat) does not depend on price – even in case of increasing price due to supply shortfall, the demand for biofuel is similar. Governments could adjust their subsidies as a function of market price level and supply level. This is already done with water in the USA and Europe: in case of drought, irrigation is limited or forbidden for farmers and even washing cars

TABLE 9.8 Regulation and commitments of traders

	US futures contracts	EU futures contracts
Regulatory institution	A unique institution: the *Commodity Futures Trading Commission* (CFTC).	A governmental authority per country.
Commitment of traders (COT)	The first COT started in 1962. Weekly, every trader must declare its: ■ buy or sell side position or arbitrage ■ operation as commercial operator (producer/merchant/processor/user) or non-commercial operator by mentioning swap dealer or managed money or other. Transparency: the market institution releases traders' positions every week on its website.	No report by trader, except for NYSE Euronext futures contracts and options on coffee, cocoa, sugar and feed wheat since October 2011. For these contracts, every trader must declare its position and type of operation weekly as enforced by the CFTC.
Delivery or settlement at contract maturity	Delivery of the goods or cash settlement.	Delivery of the goods.

Source: CFTC, http://www.cftc.gov/MarketReports/CommitmentsofTraders/index.htm; NYSE Euronext, https://globalderivatives.nyx.com/en/nyse-euronext-publish-weekly-commitments-traders-reports.

may be forbidden for inhabitants in order to save water and use it for the primary needs: beverages. Similarly, in case of severe frost, electricity companies enforce some contracts made with plants who no longer consume electricity in order to save it and use it for more urgent demands. Furthermore, in case of high grain market prices the processing of biofuels could be reduced.

3. **Improving liquidity management** Futures exchanges must manage market liquidity adequately:
   - To attract sufficient risk-takers, speculators, so that each operator finds a counterparty easily without having to accept a less favourable price. Then price formation is easy.
   - To monitor the volatility level in establishing trading position limits on commercial operators and on non-commercial traders. This would help the price to reflect the balance between the supply and demand of the agricultural commodities underlying physical futures.

   Unfortunately, it is not possible to quantify the proportion of desired and undesired speculation, because acts of speculation cannot be distinguished from acts of hedging.

   The procedures used by futures exchanges can be improved with further requirements:
   - Mandatory weekly reporting of volumes and positions (long or short) by type of operator, to adjust the initial margin call (deposit) of collateral by type of operator – professional operators in the physical market (producers, processors, traders), swaps, index funds. This is the case in the USA, and since October 2011 for coffee, cocoa, white sugar and feed wheat contracts on the NYSE Euronext. However, an operator can intervene at times to hedge risk, sometimes involving risk-taking in speculating.

- Mandatory reporting of the type of transaction by each operator – hedging, arbitrage, risk-taking. This is not currently required, but would make it possible to adjust the initial deposit guarantee according to the degree of risk-taking.
- Banning operators from having a position equivalent to 30% or 40% or more of the open interest of a futures contract, at least in the 6 months leading up to expiry of the futures contract. This would ensure no operator can be in a position to influence the price. Currently, this is applied in the USA, but not necessarily elsewhere in Europe and Asia.
- Checking convergence between the price of a futures contract at maturity in the place of delivery of the product and the cash price of the product on the physical market in the same place at the same time.

A futures contract is governed by the rules of the country where it is established. Regulation differs from country to country (see Table 9.8). US commodity futures markets have existed for more than 150 years and are more regulated than most markets in Europe and Asia. Futures markets may thus have contracts subject to different regulations according to the country where they are established. Regulation could be harmonized across countries. There are major differences between US and EU regulations. The USA has tried to improve its regulations over more than 150 years since the CBOT set up a wheat futures market in 1865, while EU and Asian grain futures contracts are only 20 years old or less.

4. **Improving information and transparency on the quantity and quality of crops and inventories** Currently, there are many uncertainties about the quantities and qualities of commodity inventories. Uncertainty prevents operators from having accurate price expectations. It fuels speculation, which can lead to excessive volatility. Prices may then rise too high or fall too low, with poor signal quality, and become a source of speculation that could be detrimental to all, affecting production and investment in agriculture. Each country has a responsibility to its own people and the international community to make sincere and true information available in a transparent manner. In June 2011, the G20 focused on food security. The member countries committed to coordinated food production and information sharing. They decided to harmonize their international agricultural policy decisions and set up an 'Agricultural Market Information System' (AMIS). AMIS is a new instrument overseen by the FAO to collect data about agricultural production, inventories, demand and international trade. However, some countries do not have reliable records of harvests and stocks in terms of quantity, quality and availability. Furthermore, some may prefer to avoid transparency in order to develop their own import or export strategy.
5. **Improving knowledge to identify potentially excessive speculation** The seasonal products of the futures markets, such as cereals (especially corn and wheat in the USA, wheat in the EU) and oilseeds (including soybeans and rapeseed) are the commodities that work best, but there are imperfections. While prices may seem exaggerated – sometimes too high, sometimes too low – researchers have so far been unable to distinguish the impact of speculators from other explanatory factors, including among others: uncertainty over the volume and quality of crops and stock, uncertainty caused by potential changes in political decisions (quotas or export embargoes, subsidy/tax exemption for production of biofuels), uncertainty about changes in eating habits in emerging markets, thin markets with too few buyers and sellers. On 27 September 2012 the European Parliament voted in favour of introducing mandatory limits on speculation in commodity derivatives.

9.5.6 Ongoing Research about Speculation and Regulation

Ongoing research is done on speculation: is it excessive or not? This situation calls for further study:

- What is the impact of funds that invest in futures contract and the impact of algorithm trading, also known as high-frequency trading, on volatility?
- What is the impact of funds (particularly index funds investing in bundles of commodities) on the financialization of agricultural commodity markets?
- How can we secure the convergence of basis and the correlation of futures contracts prices and physical cash prices for commodities?
- What is the impact of position limits for commercials and non-commercials (financial investors) on price level and volatility?
- How can we improve the analysis of basis convergence for agricultural commodities?

Some types of volatility on agricultural markets are particularly problematic:

- What can we do for highly perishable products like fresh milk whose volatility hurts dairy farmers and processors? Furthermore, milk production quotas will be removed in 2015 so uncertainty will increase. Managing uncertainty and risk may be studied in such a context. Are other economic tools, such as contracting, better suited for fresh products like fresh milk, fresh fruit and vegetables?
- The futures markets for certain grains (e.g., malting barley) and oilseeds (e.g., sunflower) have low volumes because they concern only a small volume of production, mainly for own consumption in producing countries.

9.6 CONCLUSION ABOUT HEDGING AND FUTURES CONTRACTS

Commodity futures contracts provide useful tools to commercial operators to discover commodity price and to reduce their risks of price volatility.

9.6.1 Hedging Process

Commercial operators hedge to mitigate the risks of price volatility on physical markets. Then, they reduce price fluctuation risks to basis fluctuation risks and some residual risks. The hedging process may be summed up as follows.

1. Risk identification:
   - product risk (basis risk including time, transportation and quality risk, hedge ratio, quantity risk);
   - cash management risk when dealing with margin calls;
   - exchange rate risk;
   - interest rate risk.
2. Analysis of the overall economic situation in order to anticipate general trends affecting the identified risks.

3. Internal regulations to allow use of futures contracts for hedging purposes over 17 to 19 months.
4. Choice of hedging instruments and analysis of sensitivity to any change in the economic situation.
5. Execution of hedging and clearing of positions.
6. Monitoring of the operations (positions on physical spot markets and futures markets), sensitivity analysis.
7. Results of the operations.

9.6.2 Key Success Factors for Agricultural Commodity Futures Contracts

The key success factors for agricultural commodity futures contracts are as follows:

1. **Commodity price volatility and market transparency** Futures contracts are useful when there is commodity price volatility. Then, commodity commercials (producers and users) want to mitigate price volatility risks to protect their costs and profit margins. Speculators are keen on taking risks so that they provide counterparties on the market and contribute to market liquidity. Market transparency is crucial to get trust from investors, hedgers and speculators.
2. **Motivated, well-trained professionals** Motivated and well-trained professionals are ready to hedge using commodity futures contracts. For instance, during summer 1992 the French oilseeds industry organization (*Organisation interprofessionnelle des oléagineux*, ONIDOL), asked MATIF-Euronext to set up a futures contract for rapeseed. The contract was launched on 28 October 1994 and was successful because it met a need for risk reduction by sellers and buyers of rapeseed. ONIDOL organized a training programme to train those sellers and buyers.
3. **Fungible, undifferentiated, homogeneous, storable standardized commodity with established grades and standards** Contract is designed for the most common standard quality, at the most usual place of delivery on the physical market. It helps in gathering large amounts of supply and demand. Established grades and standards ease price quality differences to connect futures contracts delivery with the cash market. Furthermore, commodities of different qualities must be fungible in order to get large volumes, as is the case for grains. However, it is not possible to blend the wool with fibres of a different quality in order to obtain an intermediate quality: that explains why it may be difficult to set up successful contracts. When a commodity is not storable for some days, it is not easy to freely sell it everywhere without some process of preservation. That explains why there is no futures market for fresh milk while there are futures markets for milk powder.
4. **Existing forward contracts** A futures contract has the same general features as a forward contract. A futures contract is standardized and transacted through a futures exchange while a forward contract is customized by the two parties. A futures contract is a standardized forward contract in which an operator (buyer, seller) accepts the standardized terms of commodity product, grade, quantity of physical good per contract, location and maturity in the framework of a futures exchange: it only takes market price at a given instant. Consequently, commodity commercial operators, who use forward contracts, may adopt futures contracts easily as is the case in the grain sector.
5. Large volumes in competitive cash markets without any operator large enough to influence price

Large volumes of commodities are necessary to attract many buyers and sellers and get enough liquidity to trade.

6. No suitable existing futures contract as a substitute for cross-hedging
7. Free market without government interference or excessive regulation

9.6.3 Conclusion and Prospects

Agricultural commodity prices are volatile mainly due to the impact of weather, the long-term process of production and sticky demand to feed people and animals. Major determinants affecting price movements in the long term are: (1) the production cost of the leading producing and exporting countries, so that the return on cost of production must be positive most years; (2) the supply–demand imbalance measured by the year-to-year change in surplus/deficit and by stockholding dynamics measured by the stock-to-use ratio and producers' ability to adjust to demand; and (3) the risks related to errors in forecasting supply and demand balances in previous years. In conclusion, standardized, organized and regulated commodity futures contracts are extremely useful instruments for commodity professionals to reduce the risks of price volatility and then costs.

Regulation is crucial to monitor market liquidity: (1) speculation is a necessity for commodity price formation and to help hedgers find a counterparty and (2) speculation in excess must be avoided in managing position limits by non-commercial operators (index traders, swap dealers and other financial investors) through transparent commitments of traders. Regulation may be improved particularly in Asia and Europe, where regulatory institutions may take advantage of US experience over 150 years with the commitment of traders to declare their position limits every week and their types of trade (hedging, arbitrage or speculation).

Excessive speculation is not only the responsibility of futures exchanges. Agricultural markets would be more efficient if states could reduce uncertainty. The AMIS data bank can only collect relevant data about agricultural production, inventories, demand and international trade if states are transparent. Furthermore, states may avoid isolated policy decisions without harmonization with other states for decisions – such as export embargoes, subsidies or tax exemptions for biofuels – that may contribute to increasing uncertainty. Agricultural futures market prices must provide reliable signals to producers and commodity users to make appropriate decisions on investments and price volatility protection. They contribute to the efficiency of agriculture and food businesses. The efficiency of agricultural futures markets is crucial since it affects food prices for all human beings.

REFERENCES

Balcombe, K. (2009) The nature and determinants of volatility in agricultural prices: An empirical study from 1962–2008, in *The Evolving Structure of World Agricultural Trade*, FAO.

Chavas, J.P. and Kim, K. (2006) An econometric analysis of the effects of market liberalization on price dynamics and price volatility, *Empirical Economics*, **78**(2), 329–335.

Davenant, C. (1699) *Essay upon the Probable Methods of Making a People Gainers in the Balance of Trade*, James Knapton, London.

Dawe, D. (ed.) (2010) *The Rice Crisis, Markets, Policies and Food Security*, Earthsan, London, available at http://www.fao.org/docrep/015/an794e/an794e00.pdf.

Dawe, D. (2013) Geographic determinants of rice self-sufficiency in Southeast Asia, ESA Working Paper No. 13-03, Available at http://www.fao.org/docrep/018/aq656e/aq656e.pdf.

Deaton, A. and Laroque, G. (1992) On the behaviour of commodity prices, *Review of Economic Studies*, **59**(1), 1–23.

De Long, J.B., Shleifer, A., Summers, L.H. and Waldman, R.J. (1990) Noise trader risk in financial markets, *Journal of Political Economy*, **98**, 703–738.

De Schutter, O. (2010) Food commodities speculation and food price crises: Regulation to reduce the risks of price volatility, United Nations Special Report on the Right to Food, Briefing Note 02 – September 2010, available at http://www2.ohchr.org/english/issues/food/docs/Briefing_Note_02_September_2010_EN.pdf.

Ezekiel, M. (1938) The cobweb theorem, *Quarterly Journal of Economics*, **52**(2), 255–280.

Haley, S. (2013) World raw sugar prices: The influence of Brazilian costs of production and world surplus/deficit measures, ERS/USDA SS-M-297-01, available at http://www.ers.usda.gov/publications/sssm-sugar-and-sweeteners-outlook/sssm297-01.aspx.

IATP (2011) *Excessive Speculation in Agriculture Commodities*, Institute for Agriculture and Trade Policy.

IGC (2010) International Grains Council, Report for Fiscal Year 2008/09, available at http://igc.int/downloads/publications/fy/fy0009.pdf

Irwin, S.H. and Sanders, D.R. (2010) The impact of index and swap funds on commodity futures markets: Preliminary results, OECD Food, Agriculture and Fisheries Working Papers, No. 27, OECD Publishing, doi: 10.1787/5kmd40wl1t5f-en.

Irwin, S.H. and Sanders, D.R. (2011) Index funds, financialization, and commodity futures markets, *Applied Economic Perspectives and Policy*, **33**(1), 1–31.

ISO (2013) *Sugar Yearbook 2013*, International Sugar Organisation, http://www.isosugar.org/.

Leuthold, R.M., Junkins, J.C. and Cordier, J.E. (1989) *The Theory and Practice of Futures Markets*, Lexington Books.

McConnell, M., Dohlman, E. and Stephen H. (2010) World Sugar Price Volatility Intensified by Market and Policy Factors, *Amber Waves*, September. Available at: http://webarchives.cdlib.org/sw1tx36512/http://www.ers.usda.gov/AmberWaves/September10.

Mitchell, D. (2004) Sugar Policies: Opportunity for Change, *World Bank Policy Research Working Paper 3222*, 55 pages.

Muth, J.F. (1961) Rational Expectations and the Theory of Price Movements, *Econometrica*, **29**(3), 315–335. Stable URL: http://links.jstor.org/sici?sici=0012-9682%28196107%2929%3A3%3C315%3AREATTO%3E2.0.CO%3B2-G.

Nerlove, M. (1958) Adaptive expectations and cobweb phenomena, *Quarterly Journal of Economics*, **xxii**, 227–240.

OECD (2011) *Agricultural Policy Monitoring and Evaluation 2011: OECD Countries and Emerging Economies*, OECD Publishing, http://dx.doi.org/10.1787/agr_pol-2011-en.

OECD-FAO (2010) *Agricultural Outlook 2010–2019*, OECD Publishing.

Sanders, D.R., Irwin, S.H. and Merrin, R.P. (2008) The adequacy of speculation in agricultural futures markets: Too much of a good thing? Marketing and Outlook Research Report 2008_02, Department of Agricultural and Consumer Economics, University of Illinois at Urbana-Champaign, IL, June 2008, http://www.farmdoc.uiuc.edu/marketing/morr/morr_archive.html.

Sanders, D.R., Irwin, S.H. and Merrin, R.P. (2009) A speculative bubble in commodity futures prices? Cross-sectional evidence, Proceedings of the NCCC-134 Conference on Applied Commodity Price Analysis, Forecasting, and Market Risk Management, St. Louis, MO. http://www.farmdoc.uiuc.edu/nccc134.

Tothova, M. (2011) Main challenges of price volatility in agricultural commodity markets, in Piot-Lepetit, I. and M'Barek, R. (eds), *Methods to Analyze Commodity Price Volatility*, Springer, New York, pp. 13–29.

Voyer, H. (1995) Le marché à terme de la pomme de terre et la gestion du risque de prix, Mémoire IGIA ESSEC Business School, Cergy-Pontoise, France.

Working, H. (1960) Speculation on Hedging Markets, *Food Research Institute Studies*, **1**, 185–220.

Zimmermann, B. and Zeddies, J. (2002) International competitiveness of sugar production, in *International Competitiveness of Sugar Production*, City, London.

Further Reading

Cahill, C. *et al.* (2011) *Comment nourrir le monde?* (*How to feed the world?*) Under the direction of Jean-François Gleyzes, Les Editions de l'Aube, Paris.

Cluff, M. and Jones, W. (2010) *OECD and FAO Agricultural Outlook*, OECD/FAO, 250 pages. http://www.agri-outlook.org.

Declerck, F. and Portier, M. (2009) *Comment utiliser les marchés à terme agricoles et alimentaires*, 2ème édn, Editions France Agricole, Paris.

Dodd–Frank act/CFTC (2010) available on the US Commodity Futures Trading Commission (CFTC) website: http://www.cftc.gov/lawregulation/doddfrankact/index.htm; http://www.cftc.gov/ucm/groups/public/@swaps/documents/file/hr4173_enrolledbill.pdf.

EMIR (2013) Available at: http://www.esma.europa.eu/page/European-Market-Infrastructure-Regulation-EMIR; http://eur-lex.europa.eu/JOHtml.do?uri=OJ:L:2013:052:SOM:EN:HTML.

EU (2010) Investment Services Directive – Market in Financial Instruments Directive (MiFID), available at: http://ec.europa.eu/internal_market/securities/isd/mifid/index_en.htm; http://europa.eu/legislation_summaries/internal_market/single_market_services/financial_services_general_framework/l24036e_en.htm.

FAO (2011) The State of Food Insecurity in the World: How does international price volatility affect domestic economies and food security? FAO website, www.fao.org.

Natanelov, V., Alan, M.J., McKensie, A.M. and van Huylenbroeck, G. (2011) Is there co-movement of agricultural commodities futures prices and crude oil? *Energy Policy*, **39**(9), 4971–4984.

Piot-Lepetit, I. and M'Barek, R. (2011) Methods to analyse agricultural commodity price volatility, in Piot-Lepetit, I. and M'Barek, R. (eds), *Methods to Analyse Agricultural Commodity Price Volatility*, Springer, New York, pp. 1–11. http://www.springer.com/economics/agricultural+economics/book/978-1-4419-7633-8.

Scott, N. (2003) Agribusiness and commodity risk: strategies and management, Rabobank, Netherlands.

Thompson, W., Smith, G. and Elasri, A. (2012) World wheat price volatility: Selected scenario analyses, OECD Food, Agriculture and Fisheries Papers, No. 59, OECD Publishing, http://dx.doi.org/10.1787/5k8zpt62fs32-en.

United Nations, Department of Economic and Social Affairs, Population Division: *World Urbanization Prospects, the 2009 Revision* (highlights), New York, 2010. http://esa.un.org/unpd/wup/Documents/WUP2009_Highlights_Final.pdf.

United Nations, Department of Economic and Social Affairs, Population Division: *World Urbanization Prospects, the 2011 Revision* (highlights), New York, 2012, http://esa.un.org/unup/pdf/WUP2011_Highlights.pdf.

GLOSSARY, QUOTATIONS AND POLICY ON WEBSITES

Glossary

http://www.thectr.com/glossaries/english.php

http://www.euronext.com/common/glossary/glossary-2214-EN.html

Quotations

Futures markets sites: http://www.euronext.com, http://www.CBOT.com, http://www.CME.com, etc.

NYSE-Euronext: end of day files, http://globalderivatives.nyx.com/en/nyse-liffe/end-of-day-files

CME group: http://www.cmegroup.com/market-data/

Agritel: http://www.agritel.fr

Commodity futures charts: http://www.futures.tradingcharts.com/

Agricultural and Trade Policy

Agricultural Economics Virtual Library (the best site for agricultural issues, including access to market institutions such as the CME): http://www.aeco.ttu.edu/aecovl/index.htm

AMIS – Agricultural Market Information System: http://statistics.amis-outlook.org/data/index.html

CIRAD (tropical agriculture): http://www.cirad.fr

Codex alimentarius (world rules about agricultural and food product norms):

http://www.fao.org/catalog/interact/inter-f.htm

European Union

http://ec.europa.eu/agriculture

http://ec.europa.eu/agriculture/sugar/index_en.htm

http://ec.europa.eu/agriculture/cereals/factsheet-cereals_en.pdf

http://ec.europa.eu/agriculture/cereals/factsheet-oilseeds-protein-crops_en.pdf

FAO – Food and Agriculture Organization of the United Nations: http://faostat.fao.org/

UNCTAD: information about agricultural markets worldwide, http://r0.unctad.org/infocomm

USDA foreign food & agricultural server (US Department of Agriculture): http://ffas.usda.gov

USDA reports per country: http://ffas.usda.gov/agexport/

USDA Economic Research Service (USDA-ERS)

http://www.ers.usda.gov/about-ers.aspx

http://www.ers.usda.gov/topics/crops/sugar-sweeteners/policy.aspx

http://www.ers.usda.gov/topics/crops/corn/policy.aspx

http://www.ers.usda.gov/topics/crops/cotton-wool.aspx

http://www.ers.usda.gov/topics/crops/wheat/policy.aspx

http://www.ers.usda.gov/data-products/wheat-data.aspx

US Securities and Exchange Commission (activity report for public companies/USA, only):

http://www.sec.gov/index.html

OECD/OCDE: Organization for Economic Cooperation and Development http://www.oecd.org/

World Bank: http://www.worldbank.org/

CHAPTER 10

Foreign Exchange Markets and Products

Antonio Castagna

10.1 THE FX MARKET

The foreign exchange (FX) market is an over-the-counter (OTC) market where each participant trades directly with others; there is no exchange, though we can identify some major geographic trading centres: London (the primary centre, where majors market makers are located; its importance increased in the last few years), New York, Tokyo, Singapore, Sidney. This means that trading activity is 24 hours a day, though in practice during London working hours the market has the greatest level of liquidity. Needless to say, the FX market experiences fierce competition amongst participants.

10.1.1 FX Rates and Spot Contracts

Definition 10.1.1 ***FX rate***. *An exchange (FX) rate is the price of one currency in terms of another currency; the two currencies make a* ***pair***. *The* ***pair*** *is named by a label comprising two tags of three characters: each currency is identified by its tag. The first tag in the exchange rate is the* ***base currency***, *the second is the* ***numeraire currency***. *So the FX is the price of the base currency in terms of the numeraire currency.*

The numeraire currency can be considered as domestic: actually, in what follows we will refer to it as that. The base currency can be regarded as an asset whose trading generates profits and/or losses in terms of the domestic currency. In what follows, the base currency will also be referred to as the foreign currency. We would like to stress that these denominations are not made from the perspective of the trader, who can actually be located anywhere and for whom the foreign currency may turn out to indeed be the domestic currency, from a 'civil'

Handbook of Multi-Commodity Markets and Products: Structuring, Trading and Risk Management. Edited by Andrea Roncoroni, Gianluca Fusai and Mark Cummins.

point of view. To avoid any possible confusion, for an economic operator we will define the currency in which profits and losses and the balance sheet are denominated as *internal*; the remaining currencies other than the internal are defined as *external*, with respect to the same operator.

Example 10.1.1 *The euro/US dollar FX rate is identified by the label EURUSD and it denotes how many US dollars are worth 1 euro. The domestic (numeraire) currency is the US dollar and the foreign (base) currency is the euro.*

The FX rates are expressed as a five-digit number, without regard to the number of decimals; the fifth digit is named a *pip* – 100 pips make a *figure*. As an example, major FX rates for spot contracts (we will define 'spot' below) as of 29 October 2007 are shown in Figure 10.1. For benchmark purposes with more contemporary rates, the lower panel of Figure 10.1 gives key FX rates as of 5 November 2014. Regular trades, amongst professional market operators, are for fixed amounts of the base currency. We define the spot contract as follows:

Definition 10.1.2 ***Spot***. *Two counterparties entering into a spot contract agree to exchange the base currency amount against an amount of the numeraire currency equal to the spot FX rate. The settlement date is usually two business days after the transaction date (but it depends on the currency).*

10.1.2 Outright and FX Swap Contracts

Outright (or forward) contracts are a simple extension of a spot contract, as is manifest from the following definition:

Definition 10.1.3 ***Outright***. *Two counterparties entering an outright (or forward) contract agree to exchange, at a given expiry (settlement) date, the base currency amount against an amount of the numeraire currency equal to the (forward) exchange rate.*

It is quite easy to see that the outright contract differs from a spot only by the settlement date, which is shifted forward in time up to the expiry date in the future. An FX rate, at which the transaction will be executed, is different from the spot rate so the problem of its calculation arises. The calculation of the forward FX price can easily be tackled by means of the following arbitrage strategy.

Strategy 10.1.1 *Assume that we have an XXXYYY pair and that the spot FX rate is S_t at time t, whereas $F(t, T)$ is the forward FX rate for the expiry at time T. At time t, we execute the following:*

- *Borrow one unit of foreign currency XXX.*
- *Change one unit of XXX (foreign) against YYY and receive S_t YYY (domestic) units.*
- *Invest S_t YYY in a domestic deposit.*
- *Close an outright contract to change the terminal amount back into XXX, so that we will receive $S_t \frac{1}{P^d(t,T)} \frac{1}{F(t,T)}$ XXX.*
- *Pay back the loan of one YYY plus the interests.*

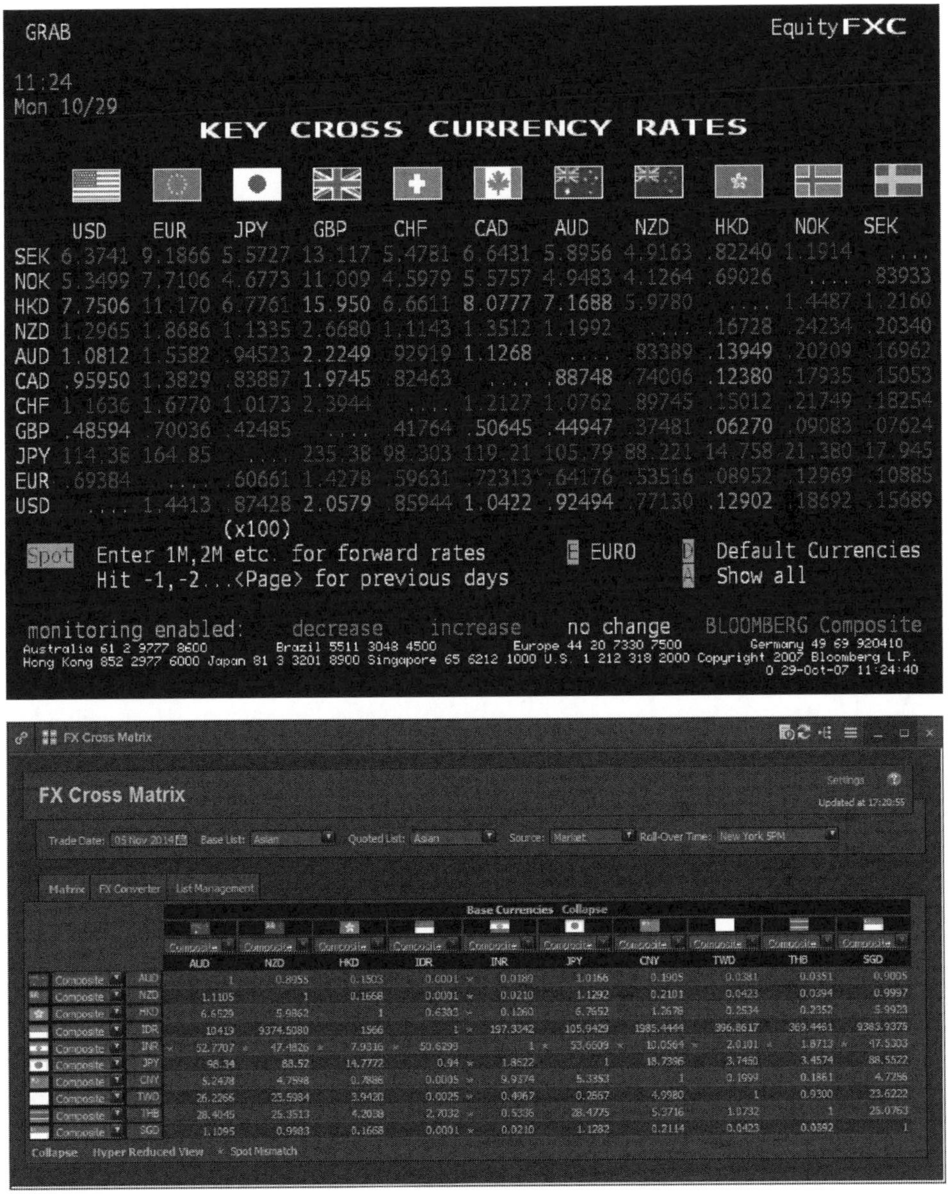

FIGURE 10.1 FX Spot Rates as of 29th October 2007 (upper panel; Source: Bloomberg) and 5th November 2014 (lower panel; Source: Thomson Reuters Eikon)

To avoid arbitrage the final amount $S_t \frac{1}{P^d(t,T)} \frac{1}{F(t,T)}$ *XXX must be equal to the value of the loan of 1 XXX at time* T, *which can be calculated by adding the interests to the notional amount.*

This strategy can be translated formally as:

$$S_t \frac{1}{P^d(t,T)} \frac{1}{F(t,T)} = 1 \frac{1}{P^f(t,T)},$$

which means that we invest the S_t YYY units in a deposit traded in the domestic money market, yielding at the end $S_t\frac{1}{P^d(t,T)}$ ($P^d(t,T)$ is the price of the domestic pure zero-coupon bond), and change it back into XXX currency at the $F(t,T)$ forward rate equal to 1 XXX units invested in the foreign money market ($P^f(t,T)$ is the price of the foreign pure zero-coupon bond). Hence

$$F(t,T) = S_t \frac{P^f(t,T)}{P^d(t,T)}. \tag{10.1}$$

In the market outright, contracts are quoted in forward points:

$$\mathbf{Fpts}(t,T) = F(t,T) - S_t.$$

Forward points are positive or negative, depending on the interest rate differential, and they are also a function of the level of the spot rate. They are added (algebraically) to the spot rate when an outright is traded, so as to get the fair forward FX rate. In Figure 10.2, forward points as of 6 November 2007 for a 3-month delivery are shown: they are also the same points used in FX swap contracts, which will be defined below. For benchmark purposes with more contemporary rates, the lower panel of Figure 10.2 gives key FX rates as of 5 November 2014. The base currency is the euro and forward points are referred to each (numeraire) currency listed against the euro: in the column 'Arb. rate' the forward implied no-arbitrage rate for the euro is provided. It is implied from equation (10.1) to calculate the forward FX rate so as to match the market level of the latter.

For the sake of clarity and to show how forward FX rates are actually calculated, we provide the following example.

Example 10.1.2 *Assume we have the market data as in Figure 10.2: we want to check how the forward points for the EURUSD are calculated. We use formula (10.1) to calculate the forward FX rate, but we apply the money market conventions for capitalization and for discounting (i.e., simple compounding):*

$$F(0,3M) = 1.4522\frac{\left(1 + 4.875\%\frac{92}{360}\right)}{\left(1 + 4.4435\%\frac{92}{360}\right)} = 1.45378$$

where 3M stands for '3-month expiry'. Hence, the FX swap points are straightforwardly calculated:

$$\mathbf{Fpts}(0,3M) = F(0,3M) - S_0 = 1.45378 - 1.4522 = 0.00158$$

so that both the forward FX rate and forward points are verified with what is shown in the figure.

The FX swap is a very popular contract involving a spot and an outright contract:

Definition 10.1.4 ***FX swap***. *Two counterparties entering into an FX swap contract agree to close a spot deal for a given amount of the base currency, and at the same time they agree to reverse the trade by an outright (forward) with the same base currency amount at a given expiry.*

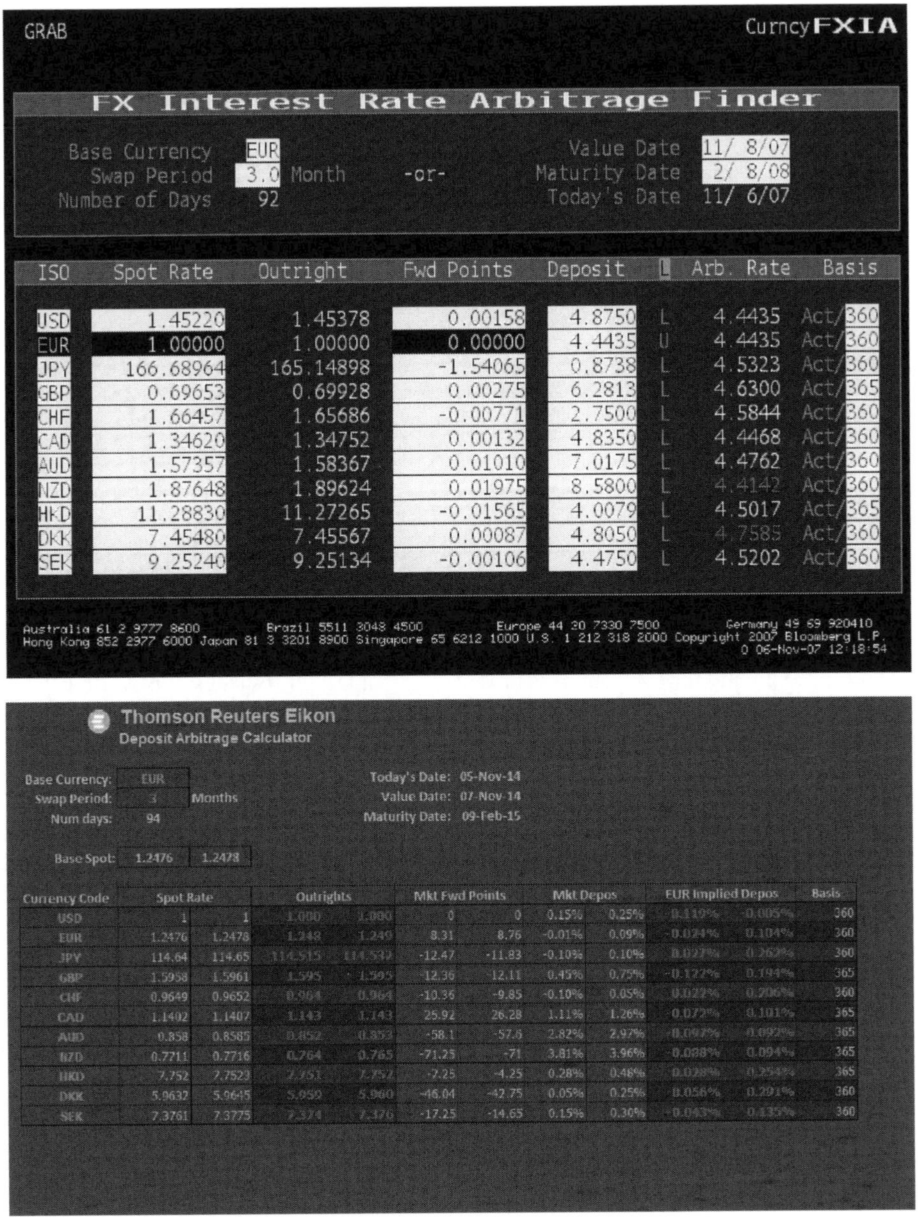
GRAB
Curncy FXIA
FX Interest Rate Arbitrage Finder
Base Currency EUR
Swap Period 3.0 Month
-or-
Number of Days 92
Value Date 11/ 8/07
Maturity Date 2/ 8/08
Today's Date 11/ 6/07
ISO Spot Rate Outright Fwd Points Deposit L Arb. Rate Basis
USD 1.45220 1.45378 0.00158 4.8750 L 4.4435 Act/360
EUR 1.00000 1.00000 0.00000 4.4435 U 4.4435 Act/360
JPY 166.68964 165.14898 -1.54065 0.8738 L 4.5323 Act/360
GBP 0.69653 0.69928 0.00275 6.2813 L 4.6300 Act/365
CHF 1.66457 1.65686 -0.00771 2.7500 L 4.5844 Act/360
CAD 1.34620 1.34752 0.00132 4.8350 L 4.4468 Act/360
AUD 1.57357 1.58367 0.01010 7.0175 L 4.4762 Act/360
NZD 1.87648 1.89624 0.01975 8.5800 L 4.4142 Act/360
HKD 11.28830 11.27265 -0.01565 4.0079 L 4.5017 Act/365
DKK 7.45480 7.45567 0.00087 4.8050 L 4.7585 Act/360
SEK 9.25240 9.25134 -0.00106 4.4750 L 4.5202 Act/360
Australia 61 2 9777 8600 Brazil 5511 3048 4500 Europe 44 20 7330 7500 Germany 49 69 920410
Hong Kong 852 2977 6000 Japan 81 3 3201 8900 Singapore 65 6212 1000 U.S. 1 212 318 2000 Copyright 2007 Bloomberg L.P.
0 06-Nov-07 12:18:54
Thomson Reuters Eikon
Deposit Arbitrage Calculator
Base Currency: EUR
Swap Period: 3 Months
Num days: 94
Today's Date: 05-Nov-14
Value Date: 07-Nov-14
Maturity Date: 09-Feb-15
Base Spot: 1.2476 1.2478
Currency Code Spot Rate Outrights Mkt Fwd Points Mkt Depos EUR Implied Depos Basis
USD 1 1 0 0 0.15% 0.25% 360
EUR 1.2476 1.2478 8.31 8.76 -0.01% 0.09% 360
JPY 114.64 114.65 -12.47 -11.83 -0.10% 0.10% 360
GBP 1.5958 1.5961 12.36 12.11 0.45% 0.75% 365
CHF 0.9649 0.9652 -10.36 -9.85 -0.10% 0.05% 360
CAD 1.1402 1.1407 25.92 26.28 1.11% 1.26% 365
AUD 0.858 0.8585 -58.1 -57.6 2.82% 2.97% 365
NZD 0.7711 0.7716 -71.25 -71 3.81% 3.96% 365
HKD 7.752 7.7523 -7.25 -4.25 0.28% 0.48% 365
DKK 5.9632 5.9645 -46.04 -42.75 0.05% 0.25% 360
SEK 7.3761 7.3775 -17.25 -14.65 0.15% 0.30% 360

FIGURE 10.2 FX Forward Points as of 6th November 2007 (upper panel; Source: Bloomberg) and 5th November 2014 (lower panel; Source: Thomson Reuters Eikon)

From the definition of an FX swap, the valuation is straightforward: it is the sum of a spot contract and a forward contact. So we just need the spot rate and the forward points. The outright is mainly traded by speculators and hedgers in the FX market, whereas the FX swap is more a treasury product, traded in the interbank market to move funds from one currency to another without any FX risk (for par contracts) and hedge or get exposure to the interest rate risks in two different currencies.

10.1.3 FX Option Contracts

FX options are no different from the usual options written on any other asset, apart from some slight distinctions in the jargon. The definition of a *plain vanilla European* option contract is the following:

Definition 10.1.5 ***European plain vanilla FX option contract.*** *Assume we have the pair XXXYYY. Two counterparties entering a plain vanilla FX option contract agree on the following, according to the type of option traded.*

- *Type* ***XXX call YYY put****: the buyer has the right to enter at expiry a spot contract to buy (sell) the notional amount of the XXX (YYY) currency, at the strike FX rate level K.*
- *Type* ***XXX put YYY call****: the buyer has the right to enter at expiry a spot contract to sell (buy) the notional amount of the XXX (YYY) currency, at the strike FX rate level K.*

The spot contract at expiry is settled on the settlement date determined according to the rules for spot transactions. The notional amount N in the XXX base currency is exchanged against $N \times K$ units of the numeraire currency. The buyer pays a premium at the inception of the contract for their right.

In the following sections we will examine how to calculate the fair premium of an option. A very rough taxonomy for FX options is presented in Table 10.1. Besides, it is worth noticing that the difference between first generation and second generation exotics is due to the time sequence of their appearance in the market rather than their level of complexity.

It is worth describing the option contract in more detail, and the market conventions and practices related to it.

10.1.3.1 Exercise The exercise normally has to be announced by the option's buyer at 10.00 am New York time: options are denoted *NY cut* in this case, and they are the standard

TABLE 10.1 Taxonomy of FX options

Group	Name	Exercise	Monitoring
Plain vanilla	Call/put	E/A	E
First generation exotic	Digital	E	E
First generation exotic	Knock in/out barriers	E/A	E/C/D
First generation exotic	Double knock in/out barriers	E/A	E/C/D
First generation exotic	One touch/no touch/ Double no touch/double touch	A	C/D
First generation exotic	Asian	E/A	D
First generation exotic	Basket	E/A	D
Second generation exotic	Window knock in/out barriers	E/A	E/C/D
Second generation exotic	First in then out barriers	E/A	E/C/D
Second generation exotic	Forward start plain/barriers	E/A	E/C/D
Second generation exotic	External barriers	E/A	E/C/D
Second generation exotic	Quanto plain/barriers	E/A	E/C/D

Exercise: European (E), American (A). Monitoring: At expiry (E), continuous (C), discrete (D).

options traded in the interbank market. The counterparties may agree also on a different time, such as 3.00 pm Tokyo time: in this case we have the *Tokyo cut*. The exercise is considered automatic when the option is in-the-money (i.e., is worth exercising) for a given percentage of the strike price at expiry (e.g., for a call option, the FX spot is higher than the strike by an amount of 1.5% of the strike level). These details are typically provided in the ISDA master agreement signed between two professional counterparties when they decide to start a relationship involving trading derivative contracts. In the other cases the exercise has to be announced explicitly.

10.1.3.2 Expiry Date and Settlement Date The expiry date for an option can be any date on which at least one market place is open: then the settlement date is set according to the settlement rules used for spot contracts. It is the date when the decision whether to exercise the option has to be announced.

10.1.3.3 Premium The option's premium is paid on the spot settlement date corresponding to the trade date. It can be paid in one of either currencies of the underlying pair and it can be expressed in four different ways, which we list below.

1. *Numeraire currency units* (p_{numccy}). For some pairs this is the standard way premiums are expressed for plain vanilla options in the interbank market after the closing of the deal. It is worth noting also that this is the natural premium one calculates by means of a pricing formula. The actual premium to pay is calculated by multiplying the currency units times the notional amount (in base currency units): $N \times p_{numccy}$.
2. *Numeraire currency percentage* ($p_{numeccy\%}$). This is the standard way premiums are expressed and quoted for exotic (one touch, double no touch, etc.) options in the interbank market, when the payout is a numeraire currency amount. It can be calculated by dividing the premium in numeraire currency units by the strike: $p_{numccy\%} = \frac{p_{numccy}}{K} \times 100$. The actual premium to pay is equal to the notional amount in numeraire currency units ($N \times K$) times the numeraire currency percentage premium: $N_{numccy} \times \frac{p_{numccy\%}}{100}$.
3. *Base currency units* ($p_{baseccy}$). This way of quoting may be useful when the numeraire currency amount is fixed for all the options to be entered in a given strategy (e.g., in a EUR call USD put spread). It can be calculated by dividing the premium in numeraire currency units by the spot FX rate and then by the strike: $p_{baseccy} = \frac{p_{numccy}}{S_t K}$. The actual premium to pay is equal to the notional amount, expressed in numeraire currency (that is $N \times K$) times the base currency units premium: $N_{numccy} \times p_{baseccy}$.
4. *Base currency percentage* ($p_{baseccy\%}$). This is the standard way premiums are expressed and quoted for exotic (barrier) options, and in the case of some pairs also for plain vanilla options, in the interbank market. It can be calculated by dividing the premium in numeraire currency units by the spot FX rate: $p_{baseccy\%} = \frac{p_{numccy}}{S_t} \times 100$. The actual premium to pay is equal to the notional amount times the base currency percentage premium: $N \times \frac{p_{baseccy\%}}{100}$.

In Table 10.2 we report some market conventions for option premiums: usually the numeraire currency premium is multiplied by a factor such that it is expressed in terms of pips (see above for the definition of pips). We will see later on that the way in which markets quote premiums has an impact on the building of volatility matrices, so that it is not just a curiosity one may lightly neglect.

TABLE 10.2 Market conventions for option premiums for some pairs

Pair	p_{numccy}	$p_{baseccy\%}$
EURUSD	USD pips	
EURCAD	CAD pips	
EURCHF		EUR%
EURGBP	GBP pips	
EURJPY		EUR%
EURZAR		EUR%
GBPCHF		GBP%
GBPJPY		GBP%
GBPUSD	USD pips	
USDCAD		USD%
USDCHF		USD%
USDJPY		USD%
USDZAR		USD%

Example 10.1.3 *Assume we want to buy* 2,000,000 *EUR call USD put struck at* 1.3500, *with a reference EURUSD spot rate equal to* 1.2800. *The notional amount in USD is* $2{,}000{,}000 \times 1.3500 = 2{,}700{,}000$. *The premium can be quoted in one of the four ways we have examined and we have:*

1. *If the premium is in numeraire currency units and* $p_{USD} = 0.0075$ *US dollars per one EUR unit of option, we will pay* $2{,}000{,}000 \times 0.0075 = 15{,}000$ *USD.*
2. *If the quotation is expressed as a numeraire currency percentage, the premium is* $p_{USD\%} = \frac{0.0075}{1.3500} \times 100 = 0.5550\%$ *(rounded to the nearest quarter of* 0.01%*) for one USD unit of option dollar, and we pay* $0.5550 \times \frac{2{,}700{,}000}{100} = 14{,}985$ *USD (the small difference from* 15,000 *is due to rounding conventions).*
3. *If the quotation is expressed as base currency units, the premium is* $p_{EUR} = \frac{0.75}{1.2800 \times 1.3500} = 0.00435$ *EUR per one USD unit of option dollar, and we pay* $0.55 \times \frac{2{,}700{,}000}{100} = 11{,}750$ *EUR.*
4. *Finally, if the premium is in base currency percent, it is* $p_{EUR\%} = \frac{0.0075}{1.2800} \times 100 = 0.5875\%$ *of the EUR notional (rounded to the nearest quarter of* 0.01%*) and we pay* $0.5875 \times \frac{2{,}000{,}000}{100} = 11{,}750$ *EUR.*

10.1.3.4 Market Standard Practices for Quoting Options FX options can be dealt for any expiry and also for any level of strike price. Amongst professionals, options are quoted according to some standards. We will briefly review these.

Firstly, options are usually quoted for standard dates, though it is possible to ask a market maker for an expiry occurring on any possible date. Secondly, quotations are not in terms of (any of the four above) premiums, but in terms of implied volatilities, that is to say in terms of the volatility parameter to plug into the Black–Scholes (BS) model (given the values of all other parameters and the level of the FX spot rate, retrievable from the market). Once the deal is closed, the counterparties may agree to actually express the premium in any of the four ways listed above, though the standard is in numeraire currency pips (p_{numccy}). Thirdly, strike prices are quoted in terms of Delta[1] of the option: this means that before closing the deal, the strike level is not determined yet in absolute terms. Once the deal is closed, given the level of the FX spot rate and of the implied volatility agreed upon (the interest rate levels will be taken from the money market), the strike will be set at a level yielding the BS Delta the two counterparties were dealing. If not otherwise specified when asking for a quote, the option is considered to be traded Delta-hedged ('with Delta exchange'), that is a spot trade offsetting the BS Delta exposure is closed along with the option's transaction.

For popular exotic options,[2] some other conventions are in force in ordinary market activity. For barrier options, contrary to the plain vanilla type, strikes and barrier levels are asked for in absolute terms by specifying the reference spot FX rate and also an ATM implied volatility level. The quote will be assumed to be valid for those levels and it will be provided in terms of premium as a percentage of the base currency notional. Also for barrier options it is assumed that the deal includes a Delta-hedge transaction and in most cases a Vega-hedge[3] transaction (by dealing a spot contract and an ATM straddle[4] to offset the related exposures). The amounts dealt in those transactions are calculated according to the BS model, using as inputs the reference FX spot and implied volatility levels.

Other very common exotics are the bet options[5], that is one touch, no-touch, double-no-touch, double touch, digitals. They are quoted as a percentage of the notional amount (which is the payout of the bet, usually in base currency), given reference levels of the FX spot and implied volatility. After agreement on the price, the deal will include the Delta-hedge and the Vega-hedge transactions (to be defined according to the BS model).

10.1.4 Main Traded FX Options Structures

Although the FX option market is very liquid for options with any kind of strike level and expiry, nonetheless it is possible to identify some structures that are very popular amongst professional market participants. We will understand why later on, when we examine how to manage the volatility risk of an options portfolio, and we will also study the features and behaviour of their risk exposure.

The first structure is the ATM *straddle* (**STDL** hereon): that is the sum of a (base currency) call and a (base currency) put struck at the at-the-money level. The strike is chosen so that, given the expiry, a put and a call have the same Delta but with different signs. This implies that no Delta-hedge is needed when trading the straddle. We will see later on how to retrieve this strike.

The ATM implied volatility quoted in the FX option market is that referred to a 0 Delta **STDL** strike and hence it is the implied volatility to plug in the BS formula when trading an ATM **STDL**. The amount of an ATM **STDL** is traded as the sum of the (base currency) amounts of two component options. In Figure 10.3, the payoff at expiry of a long ATM **STDL** position is shown.

---

[1]The Delta of an option will be defined in Section 10.2, where the BS model is presented.

[2]The definition for each of the options we mention below will be given in the sections devoted to their analysis.

[3]The Vega will be defined in Section 10.2.

[4]This structure is described later on in this section.

[5]More details about the definition of bet options can be found in Section 10.4.

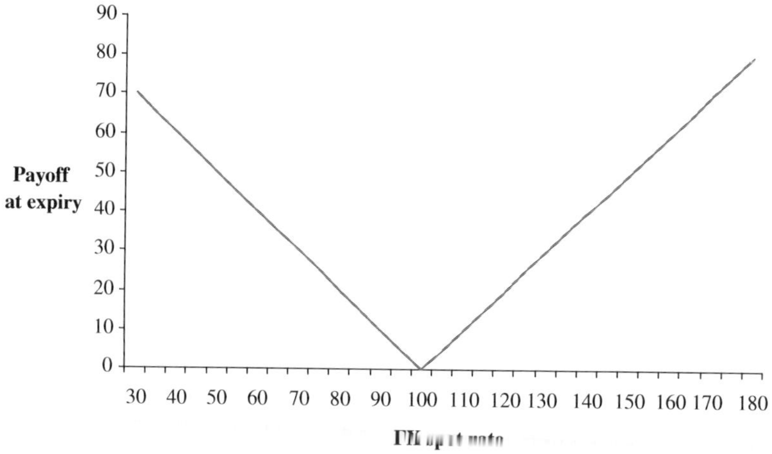

FIGURE 10.3 Payoff at expiry of a long ATM straddle, struck at $K_{ATM} = 100$

Besides ATM **STDL**, there are at least two other structures frequently traded: these are the 25% *Delta risk reversal* (**RR** hereon) and the 25% *Delta Vega-weighted butterfly* (**VWB** hereon).

The **RR** is a structure set up when one buys a (base currency) call and sells a (base currency) put, both featured with a symmetric Delta (long **RR**) or the reverse (short **RR**). The Delta can be chosen at any level, but 25% is the most liquid level: so the call and the put to be entered in the **RR** will have a strike level yielding a 25% Delta, without considering the sign (actually for puts it will be negative). The **RR** is quoted as the difference between the two implied volatilities required in the BS formula to price the two legs of the structure; we indicate this price in volatility as **rr**. A positive number means that the call is favoured and that its implied volatility is higher than the implied volatility of the put; a negative number implies the opposite. For example, if the 3-month 25% Delta **rr** for the EURUSD pair is −0.5%, then the implied volatility of the EUR call is 0.5% lower than the EUR put (both struck at a level yielding 25% in absolute terms). At time t, we can write the price (in implied volatility's terms) of a 25% Delta **RR** with maturity in T as:

$$\mathbf{rr}(t, T; 25) = \sigma_{25C}(t, T) - \sigma_{25P}(t, T), \tag{10.2}$$

where $\sigma(t, T)$ is the implied volatility at t for an option expiring at T and struck at the level indicated in the subscript.

The amount of an **RR** is typically denominated in terms of base currency units and is referred to the amount of base currency call that will be traded against the equal amount of base currency put. The payoff at expiry of a long position in an **RR** structure is shown in Figure 10.4.

The **VWB** is the other notable structure. It is built up by selling an ATM **STDL** and buying a symmetric Delta strangle, if one wishes to be long the **VWB**; on the contrary, by buying the straddle and selling the strangle, one is short the **VWB**. The strangle is just the sum of a (base currency) call and put, both struck at a level yielding the specified level of Delta (without

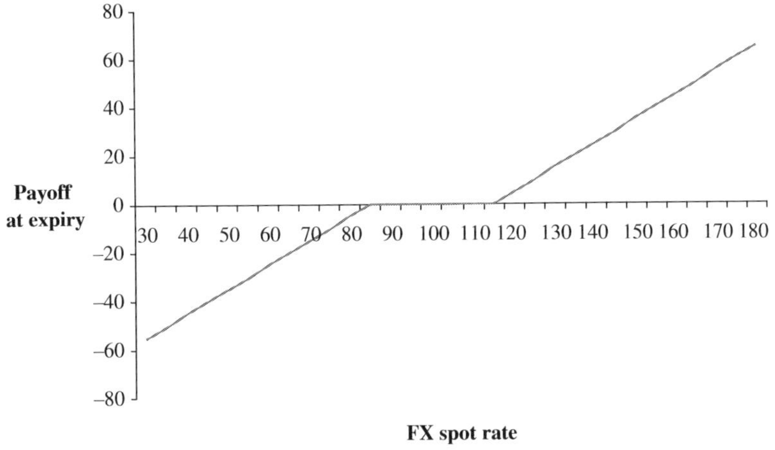

FIGURE 10.4 Payoff at expiry of a long risk reversal. Base currency call struck at $K_{25C} = 115$ and base currency put struck at $K_{25P} = 85$

any consideration of its sign); the 25% Delta is the most traded **VWB**. Since the structure, as already mentioned, has to be Vega-weighted and since the Vega of the straddle is greater than the Vega of the strangle, then the quantity of the former has to be smaller than the quantity of the latter. Indicating as **vwb** the butterfly's price in volatility terms, at time t we can write the price of a 25% Delta **VWB** expiring in T as:

$$\mathbf{vwb}(t, T; 25) = 0.5(\sigma_{25C}(t, T) + \sigma_{25P}(t, T)) - \sigma_{ATM}(t, T). \tag{10.3}$$

This is how quotations for **VWB** appear in the interbank market.

The amount of the **VWB** is, as usual, expressed in terms of base currency units and is referred to the amount of the ATM **STDL** (with the same convention as above) that is traded against the Vega-weighted amount of strangle (whose total is evenly split between the 25% Delta call and the 25% Delta put). Figure 10.5 shows the payoff at expiry of a long **VWB** position.

Later, we will use the ATM **STDL**, **RR** and **VWB** to build the volatility matrix.

10.2 PRICING MODELS FOR FX OPTIONS

The basic model to price FX options, which is also used extensively in market trading activity, is the Black–Scholes model. This is not a perfect model and it has to be replaced by the stochastic volatility model if one wants to properly take into account the volatility smile shown in the market by option quotes. We will not examine these models here, but refer to Castagna (2010) for a more in-depth analysis and also for some market approaches to include the smile in the price of exotic options.

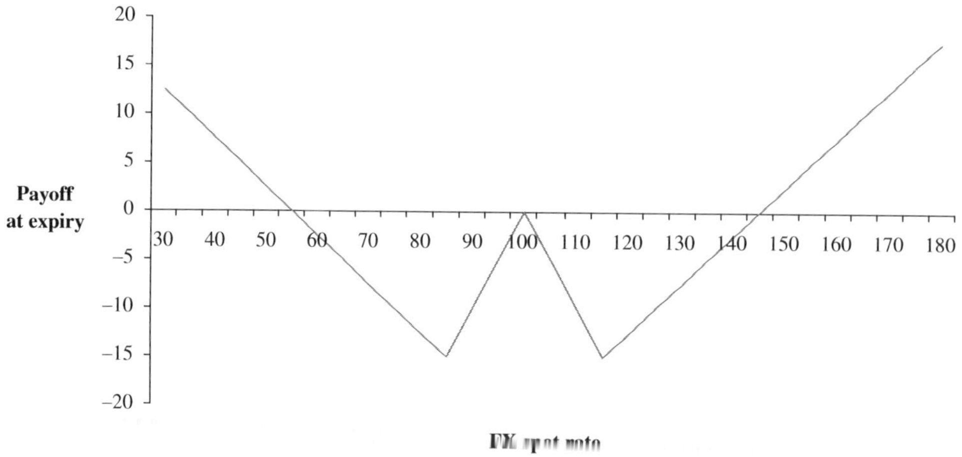

FIGURE 10.5 Payoff at expiry of a long Vega-weighted butterfly. The ATM straddle is struck at $K_{ATM} = 100$, the strangle's base currency call is struck at $K_{25C} = 115$ and base currency put struck at $K_{25P} = 85$. We assume that the strangle's amount is 1.5 times the straddle for the structure to have a Vega equal to zero

10.2.1 The Black–Scholes Model

The pricing formula for FX plain vanilla options within the BS economy was derived for the first time by Black and Scholes (1973), though it was generalized by Merton (1973) and this generalization is used to evaluate FX options (actually, just for historical precision's sake, the application of the BS framework to the FX markets was studied by Garman and Kohlhagen, 1983).

Assume that at time t we want to price a European FX option expiring at time T; the spot FX rate is S_t. Evaluating the present risk-neutral expectation of the terminal payoff (i.e., $\max[S_T - K, 0]$ for a call and $\max[K - S_T, 0]$ for a put), we have:

$$\begin{aligned} \mathcal{O}(S_t, t) &= \mathrm{Bl}(S_t, t, T, K, P^d(t,T), P^f(t,T), \sigma, \omega) \\ &= P^d(t,T)[\omega F(t,T)\Phi(\omega d_1) - \omega K \Phi(\omega d_2)] \end{aligned} \tag{10.4}$$

where

$$d_1 = \frac{\ln \frac{F(t,T)}{K} + \frac{\sigma^2}{2}(T-t)}{\sigma\sqrt{T-t}}$$

$$d_2 = d_1 - \sigma\sqrt{T-t}$$

and $\Phi(x)$ is the normal cumulative distribution function calculated in x.[6] We are still working in a deterministic interest rate setting, so that $D_t^n/D_T^n = P^n(t,T)$ for $n = \{d, e\}$. Formula (10.4)

[6]The evaluation of $\Phi(x)$ can be performed by means of numerical integration or analytical approximations, see for example Abramowitz and Stegun (1972).

can be used to price call options by setting the parameter $\omega = 1$; if one needs to price a put then $\omega = -1$. The FX spot rate enters into the formula via the FX forward price (outright):

$$F(t,T) = S_t \frac{P^f(t,T)}{P^d(t,T)}$$

where the prices of the zero-coupon bond maturing at the option's expiry can be retrieved and calculated from the money market rates. The parameter σ is the implied volatility and it is equal to

$$\sigma = \sqrt{\frac{\int_t^T \varsigma_s^2 ds}{T-t}}.$$

This is important because it is a tool to express the market prices of the options, since the BS formula is monotone in σ. In the next sections much room will be devoted to the analysis of the implied volatility and the implications of market practices related to it. In what follows, to lighten the notation, we will omit the arguments of the Bl function where this can be done with no loss of precision.

Although the BS model suffers from many flaws, it is still used very much for quoting purposes. In the FX options market, option prices are quoted in terms of implied volatilities; the Delta-hedge to be exchanged between counterparties is calculated according to the BS formula, and this is true also for the Vega-hedge for exotic options trading. Finally, in many cases, the model is also employed to run trading books. A detailed discussion on the derivatives and sensitivities of the BS formula for FX options is given in Castagna (2010).

10.3 THE VOLATILITY SURFACE

A stylized fact in the FX market is that options are quoted depending on their Delta, and not their strike as in other options markets. This basically reflects the *sticky Delta* rule, according to which implied volatilities do not vary, from one day to the next, if the related moneyness remains the same. To state it differently, when the underlying exchange rate moves, and the Delta of an option changes accordingly, a different implied volatility then has to be inserted into the corresponding BS formula.

If the sticky Delta rule is adopted, implied volatilities are mapped, for each expiry, with respect to the Delta of the option. An example of such a method to represent the volatility smile is given in Table 10.3: for a given expiry, implied volatilities are provided for given levels of (base currency) put and call Deltas.

TABLE 10.3 Example of sticky Delta matrix

	Δ Put					**Δ Call**			
	10.0%	**20.0%**	**30.0%**	**40.0%**	**ATM**	**40%**	**30%**	**20%**	**10%**
1m	10.30	10.20	10.10	10.00	9.90	10.00	10.10	10.20	10.30
2m	10.40	10.30	10.20	10.10	10.00	10.10	10.20	10.30	10.40
3m	10.50	10.40	10.30	10.20	10.10	10.20	10.30	10.40	10.50

TABLE 10.4 Taxonomy of barrier options

Barrier	Call/Put	Bets
w/r to moneyness	standard/reverse	–
w/r to the starting FX rate	up/down–in&out–first in then out	–
number	single/double	touch/double-touch
cancel/activate	in/out	/no
monitoring frequency	continuous/discrete	continuous/discrete
monitoring period	/window	/window

A method to build the volatility surface, based on market quotes of the ATM **STDL** and the 25% Delta **RR** and **VWB**, is given in Castagna (2010).

10.4 BARRIER OPTIONS

Barrier options are the most commonly traded kind of exotic options in the FX market. They are employed in structures devised for hedging the FX risk of the cash-flows of a corporate and as tools to take exposures on sophisticated views on the FX spot rates by speculators. We will start with a taxonomy of the different kinds of barrier options, including the touch-type exotics products in this broad category.

10.4.1 A Taxonomy of Barrier Options

Let us start with the barrier options. The main feature, common to all these kind of exotic contracts, is the presence of a barrier whose breaching triggers a given event (see Table 10.4).

Definition 10.4.1 ***Barrier FX option contract.*** *An XXXYYY barrier option is a contract in all respects equal to an otherwise identical plain vanilla option, the only difference being that the terminal payoff is contingent on the knocking of a predefined level by the underlying FX spot rate.*[7]

More specifically, *knock-in* options pay the terminal value only if during the life of the contract the barrier is breached at least once, whereas *knock-out* options pay their value at expiry only if the barrier level is never touched. If the barrier is set at a level in whose correspondence the terminal value of the option is out-of-the-money, the contract is considered a *standard* barrier, whereas if the terminal value is in-the-money then the contract is denoted as a *reverse* barrier. The position of the trigger level with respect to the starting FX rate identifies *up* or *down* barriers.

It is possible to set more barriers, both with a knock-in or a knock-out feature (respectively *double knock-in* and *double knock-out*), but nothing prevents setting one of the barriers as a knock-in and the other as a knock-out level (*knock-in knock-out*). Besides, the knock-out level can be contingent on breaching the knock-in level (*first-in-then-out*).

[7]Actually some second-generation barrier options have a payoff contingent on a second FX rate or another financial variable (*external barriers*).

The monitoring frequency of the barrier is generally *continuous*, although it can be preferred by some customers to set the monitoring on a *discrete* frequency, usually on the basis of a more or less official fixing. For example, for parity involving the euro, the daily ECB fixing can be used. Less frequent monitoring, such as weekly or monthly observations, is much less common. With respect to the life of the contract, the barrier can be monitored from the start-up to a given time or from a given time up to the expiry, or only for a specified period after the start and before the expiry. In these cases we have *window* barriers. When the trigger level is monitored only at the expiry of the contract, the barrier is named *at-expiry*: it is rather straightforward to realize that in this case the only meaningful position of the barrier is where the option expires in-the-money. More convoluted combinations of the observation period are possible, but extremely rare in the FX market.

The breaching of the barrier may also produce or cancel the payment of a given amount of money. This kind of contract is often referred to as a *bet*.

Definition 10.4.2 ***Bet FX option contract***. *An XXXYYY bet option is a contract paying a given amount denominated in one of the two currencies involved in the underlying pair*[8] *contingent on the knocking of a predefined level by the underlying FX spot rate. Payment may occur at the time the barrier is breached or at expiry.*

In *one-touch* and *double-touch* contracts the breaching of the barrier (or, respectively, one of the two barriers) triggers the payment of the notional amount. The payment may occur at the very time the level is touched (*at-hit*) or at the end of the contract (*at-expiry*). The no-touch and double-no-touch contracts pay the notional amount if during the life of the contract the level of the barrier has never been touched by the underlying FX rate (or, respectively, the levels of the two barriers have never been touched).

10.5 SOURCES OF FX RISK EXPOSURE

FX risk can be defined as the variation in value, in terms of the internal currency, of cash-flows, assets and liabilities denominated in an external currency. The sources of FX risk can be identified as follows:

- Cash-flows originated by international trades, for example sales and purchases of goods and services.
- Purchases of inputs and services employed in the production process paid in a foreign currency.
- Cash-flows related to financial contracts and obligations.
- Cash-flows deriving from assets and liabilities, denominated in an external currency, and the value of these in the balance sheet (we include here also the investments in foreign firms, in production plants located abroad, etc.).

A firm producing goods and/or services typically has exposures originated by international trades and by the purchase of commodities (e.g., raw materials, energy, etc.) and services, rather

[8] It is nevertheless possible to have a payment denominated in any other currency.

than by assets and liabilities, although the third and fourth sources of risk cannot be excluded totally since they may, for instance, negotiate a loan denominated in a foreign currency. For a financial institution, FX exposures are typically originated by financial contacts and assets and liabilities.

To hedge FX risk exposures, first a firm has to forecast:

- The future amount of goods and services exported or imported and the prices at which they are bought or sold.
- The costs of inputs (e.g., oil) and services and their quantities needed in the production process.
- The cash-flows and the value related to assets and liabilities and financial contracts and obligations.

Forecasts unfortunately may not always be precise and often they are based on assumptions that are more or less easy to define, especially for the first two points. It is beyond the scope of this work to examine the methodologies and the tools that a firm has at its disposal to perform such a task, so we assume that the forecasts are given and they are reliable within a reasonable degree of certainty. On the contrary, it is much easier to predict the cash-flows related to the third point (cash-flows related to financial contracts), since they may be inferred from the deals' clauses or somehow guessed with a given level of confidence. In what follows, we dwell on the FX risk a firm has to cope with, starting with some examples and then examining possible hedging strategies. We will somewhat arbitrarily name the firms involved in the production of goods and services as *companies* and the firms involved in the financial industry as *banks*. These names are just used to distinguish the economic operators needing to hedge the FX risk from those producing the tools to hedge it.

We classify companies operating in the international trade activity into two categories:

- *Importers.* They buy goods and services from international providers and producers, and they may be exposed to FX risk if the prices are denominated in an external currency. A typical example is a European importer that pays goods and/or services in US dollars. An importing company is short the external currency when the payment dates occur, since it will have to pay for goods and services in the external currency and will have to convert the internal currency to cover this shortage. The risk is that the external currency appreciates more than expected and hence the company will pay more than expected, in terms of internal currency.
- *Exporters.* They sell goods and services to international clients and they may be exposed to FX risk if the prices are denominated in an external currency. Similarly to the example above, a European exporter sells the goods and/or services it produces at a price set in US dollars. An exporting company is long the external currency when it receives the payments, since it will be paid for goods and services in the external currency and will have to convert them into the internal currency. The risk is that the external currency depreciates more than expected and hence the company will receive less than expected, in terms of internal currency.

Generally importing and exporting companies can predict, within a period of 1 year, the amount of goods and services they will buy or sell, normally on a quarterly basis (or even

TABLE 10.5 Forecasts of FX exposures in US dollars of an exporting company

Quarter	US$	Expected EURUSD	EUR
Mar	3,000,000	1.0825	−2,771,363
Jun	5,000,000	1.0875	−4,597,701
Sep	4,000,000	1.0900	−3,669,724
Dec	3,000,000	1.0925	−2,745,995

more frequently) and the paid or received cash-flows denominated in the external currency, so that it is possible to determine the FX exposures and hence the risks borne.

Example 10.5.1 *Assume an exporting company forecasts on 1 January to sell in the next year a given amount of its production to foreign clients and to receive an amount equal to* US$15,000,000, *which is bucketed at the end of each quarter as shown in Table 10.5, where expected levels of the EURUSD for the same dates are also shown: they could simply be set equal to the FX forward prices dealing in the market, or alternatively they can be rates predicted by the company.*

The company is long dollars at the end of each quarter and it has to hedge the risk related to these exposures. Assuming that the company is happy with the expected revenues given the predicted FX rates, if the US dollar depreciates (i.e., the EURUSD FX spot rate rises), then the company will lose money since it will convert the cash-flows by selling dollars and buying euros at higher levels. The amount of euros that have to be bought when converting from US dollars is shown in the final column of Table 10.5.

Assume now that the company is an importer so that it will pay the cost of the goods and services bought abroad in US dollars according to its forecasts shown in Table 10.6. The amount in dollars at risk has now the opposite sign with respect to an exporting company, since in this case the position is short dollars. The corresponding amount of euros, which is needed to buy the amounts of US dollars, is shown in the final column. If the EURUSD declines (i.e., the US dollar appreciates), then the company will lose money since it will need more euros than expected to buy the US dollar.

Example 10.5.1 can be paradigmatic also for companies that have to pay for production inputs denominated in external currency. In this case, they have a higher risk to bear since sometimes the prices of some inputs, such as commodities or energy, are typically less predictable than the value of the imports and the exports. In fact, while some prices can be set at a predefined level by an agreement between the provider and the client, some other prices are

TABLE 10.6 Forecasts of FX exposures in US dollars of an importing company

Quarter	US$	Expected EURUSD	EUR
Mar	−7,000,000	1.0825	6,466,513
Jun	−4,000,000	1.0875	3,678,161
Sep	−5,000,000	1.0900	4,587,156
Dec	−1,000,000	1.0925	915,332

TABLE 10.7 Forecasts of FX exposures in US dollars for a purchase of heating oil over 1 year

Quarter	Oil quantity	Expected oil price	US$ Cost	Expected EURUSD	EUR Cost
Mar	5,000,000	1.7706	−8,853,000	1.0825	8,178,291
Jun	6,000,000	1.7981	−10,788,600	1.0875	9,920,552
Sep	4,000,000	1.8746	−7,498,400	1.0900	6,879,266
Dec	6,000,000	1.9661	−11,796,600	1.0925	10,797,803

Quantity expressed in gallons; oil price in US dollars per gallon.

just set by all market participants and their volatility has to be considered as a risk of its own, to be managed as well. Consider the following example.

Example 10.5.2 *Assume a European company has to buy, for production purposes, 21 million gallons of heating oil in the next year, and it plans the purchase as shown in Table 10.7. The expected oil prices in each quarter can be based on company forecasts or, alternatively, taken from futures prices (e.g., trading on the NYMEX). The short exposure in US dollars at the end of the four quarters in this case is a function also of the price of the heating oil, so that the amount of dollars to hedge is more volatile than the amount of the exposures originated by the international trades. The FX exposures will change adversely for the company if both the US dollar appreciates with respect to the euro (i.e., the spot EURUSD declines) and the heating oil price increases.*

From Example 10.5.2 it is clear that a company which has to pay production inputs denominated in an external currency faces the same risks as an importing company, since it has to buy the amount of external currency to fulfil the payments. The difference is only in the higher or lower dispersion of the expected future exposures, which depend on the ability to accurately predict the quantities and prices.

When prices denominated in the external currency can only be partially controlled by the company, or are completely out of the company's control, as may be the case in Example 10.5.2, then the hedging can be performed in two steps, by combining a forward contract on the commodity (or energy product)[9] and a forward contract on the relevant FX pair. We first define a forward contract on a commodity.

Definition 10.5.1 ***Commodity forward contract****. The counterparty that is long in a forward contract will buy at the expiry a given amount of the underlying commodity at the fixed forward price. The short counterparty will be obliged to sell the amount at the predefined price.*

It is beyond the scope of this chapter to examine thoroughly how to derive a forward price on a commodity. Anyway, for completeness sake we give the formula without entering into details: let E_t be the price of the commodity at time t (denominated in YYY currency units), T

[9]From now on we will simply use the term 'commodity', on the understanding that it means either a commodity or an energy product.

the expiry date of the forward contract, r_t^Y and b_t respectively the instantaneous interest rates for the YYY currency and the convenience yield. Then, the fair forward price is:

$$F^G(t,T) = E_t e^{\int_t^T (r_s^Y - b_s)ds}. \tag{10.5}$$

The price can be derived via a no-arbitrage argument similar to that adopted to define an FX forward price. If we assume deterministic (although time-dependent) interest rate and convenience yield, then a forward price is equal to a futures price.

The hedging strategy when prices are out of the control of the company can now be described as follows:

1. Hedge the price, denominated in external currency, at which the transaction will be executed via a commodity forward or futures.
2. The resulting FX exposure is now fixed and its value in the internal currency is determined only by the level of the FX rate. Hedge this exposure by the available FX hedging strategies (e.g., an FX forward).

In the example above, the company can hedge the price of heating oil by buying futures on the NYMEX, thus locking in the purchase price at the end of each quarter. The US dollar exposures are now more stable and can be monitored and hedged separately.

The FX exposures originated by the other sources can be managed in a similar way, so that at the end we can always come up with a risk configuration corresponding to that of an importing or exporting company. It is for this reason that in what follows we only refer to these, and in each case one should refer to their typical exposures as shown in Example 10.5.1.

10.6 HEDGING FX EXPOSURES EMBEDDED IN ENERGY AND COMMODITY CONTRACTS

Commodity and energy prices are generally expressed in US dollars so that market operators, whose reference currency is a different one (e.g., the euros), have to deal with FX risk when they trade.

The FX risk can be hedged in different ways and some features have been devised so as to make contracts more or less FX risk-free. We define two of them, typically traded amongst commodity or energy traders.

Definition 10.6.1 ***Composite commodity forward contract.*** *A counterparty entering into a long position in a composite forward contract will buy at the expiry a given amount of the underlying commodity, whose price is denominated in YYY currency units, at the fixed forward price denominated in XXX currency. The other counterparty, being short, will sell the amount at the predefined price. The contract is generally, but not necessarily, cash settled.*

The composite contract will allow the buyer (or the seller), who is exposed to an FX risk when trading in the commodity, to remove the FX risk by implicitly setting at the inception the FX rate of the pair XXXYYY (or YYYXXX, depending on market convention) used to convert the commodity's price from YYY units to XXX units.

Definition 10.6.2 ***Quanto commodity forward contract.*** *A counterparty entering into a long position in a quanto forward contract will receive (pay) at the expiry the positive (negative) difference between the price of the underlying commodity prevailing in the market at that date and a defined forward price. The price of the underlying commodity and the forward price are denominated in YYY currency units, but their difference is considered denominated in XXX as for settlement purposes. The counterparty being short, in turn, will receive (pay) if the difference is negative (positive). The contract is cash settled.*

Given the three types of forward contracts we have defined above (standard, composite and quanto), we have three possible ways to convert the forward price denominated in a given currency YYY, into another currency XXX. We analyse these in the next paragraph.

10.6.1 FX Forward Exposures and Conversions

Assume we have a commodity whose price at time t is E_t, denominated in the currency YYY (e.g., US dollars). Its dynamics is given by:

$$dE_t = \left(r_t^Y - b_t\right) E_t dt + \varsigma_t^E E_t dz_t^E. \tag{10.6}$$

The notation is the same as defined above for r_t^Y and b_t, whereas ς_t^E is the instantaneous variance of the process E_t. Assume for simplicity that parameters are constant. Let S_t be the exchange rate, where the base currency XXX is the internal currency (e.g., euros) and the numeraire currency YYY is the external currency. We have seen the dynamics for S_t above.

Remark 10.6.1 *We assume that the exchange rate is XXXYYY, so that the internal (for the trader) currency XXX is the base currency of the pair. This means that the price E_t in YYY for a market operator whose profits/losses are denominated in XXX units is equal to E_t/S_t in XXX terms. We have chosen this situation in the following analysis since this is the (rather common) case of a trader located in Europe who has to deal in the EURUSD pair to convert commodities' US dollar prices. Thus we have made things slightly more complicated than the other possible case when the pair is YYYXXX and the YYY price E_t is E_tS_t in XXX terms.*

We buy one unit of the commodity at time T, and we should pay the price E_T. Assume we are market agents whose profits and losses are denominated in XXX currency: we are clearly exposed to FX risk[10] and we may deal with the conversion of the terminal value of the forward exposure into XXX by trading one of the three forward commodity contracts described, whose payoffs $\mathbf{CFw}(T,T)$ at time T are:

1. Standard conversion at the forward date T by a spot contract traded in T at the exchange rate S_T:

$$\mathbf{CFw}(T,T) = \frac{1}{S_T}(E_T - K_{YYY}). \tag{10.7}$$

[10] Besides, we are surely also exposed to the risk related to the movements of the price of the underlying commodity.

2. Conversion via a *composite* forward contract:

$$\mathbf{CFw}_C(T,T) = \left(\frac{1}{S_T}E_T - K_{XXX}\right). \tag{10.8}$$

The forward price K_{XXX} is in XXX units and set at the inception of the contract.

3. Conversion via a *quanto* forward contract, expressed in XXX units:

$$\mathbf{CFw}_{Qu}(T,T) = \frac{1}{S_0}(E_T - K_{YYY})\,\text{XXX}. \tag{10.9}$$

The forward price K_{YYY} is in YYY units, but the entire payoff is simply considered denominated in XXX units instead of YYY units. $\frac{1}{S_0}$ is a multiplier usually set equal to the FX spot rate at the contract's inception, although it can be equal to any value.

We examine separately each of the conversion methods and how to obtain them by dealing in FX and commodity forward contracts.

10.6.1.1 Standard Conversion at Expiry To obtain a standard conversion at expiry, we simply start the following replication strategy:

- buy at t (today) $e^{-b(T-t)}$ units of the commodity to end up with exactly one commodity worth E_T on the delivery date T;
- sell a zero-coupon bond of face value K_{YYY} maturing at time T (or, alternatively said, borrow the present value of K_{YYY}).

The value of the forward contract in YYY units at t is:

$$\mathbf{CFw}^Y(t,T) = e^{-b(T-t)}E_t - K_{YYY}e^{-r^Y(T-t)}$$

whereas its value in XXX units at t is obtained by converting it at the current FX rate S_t:

$$\mathbf{CFw}^X(t,T) = \frac{1}{S_t}(e^{-b(T-t)}E_t - K_{YYY}e^{-r^Y(T-t)}).$$

The commodity forward price that gives a zero value to the contract at inception is: $F^E(t,T) = E_t e^{(r^Y-b)(T-t)}$. So the value in XXX units at t of the forward contract converted at T at the rate S_T is simply the forward value in YYY units converted into XXX units:

$$\mathbf{CFw}^X(t,T) = \frac{1}{S_t}e^{-r^Y(T-t)}(F^E(t,T) - K_{YYY}). \tag{10.10}$$

It is easy to check also that the fair forward price converted at expiry is simply the standard forward price $F^E(t,T)$ converted into XXX units by dividing it by S_t.

The standard conversion implies no protection from the FX risk, as is clear from equation (10.10), where the dependence of the contract's value in XXX terms on the FX rate is manifest. In XXX terms both the commodity's forward price $F^E(t,T)$ and the amount to be paid are affected by the FX spot rate. In conclusion, the standard conversion is such that the sign of the terminal payoff is independent of the terminal FX spot rate, whereas the magnitude of the payoff depends upon it.

10.6.1.2 Composite Contract To obtain the payoff of a composite contract we need to implement the following replication strategy:

- a long position in one forward contract on the commodity;
- a long position in a forward contract to buy an amount $F^E(t,T)$ YYY and to sell an amount $F^E(t,T)/S_T$ XXX of currencies;
- a long position in a XXX zero-coupon bond with face value $F^E(t,T)/F^S(t,T)$;
- a short position in a XXX zero-coupon bond with face value K_{XXX}.

The value of the strategy in XXX units at T is:

$$(E_T - F^E(t,T))\frac{1}{S_T} + \left(\frac{1}{S_T} - \frac{1}{F^S(t,T)}\right)F^E(t,T) + \frac{F^E(t,T)}{F^S(t,T)} - K_{XXX} = \frac{E_T}{S_T} - K_{XXX},$$

which is exactly the payoff at T that we want to replicate (see equation (10.8)).

By recalling that forward contracts are worth zero at inception, at time t we have:

$$\mathbf{CFw}_C^X(t,T) = e^{-r^X(T-t)}\left(\frac{F^E(t,T)}{F^S(t,T)} - K_{XXX}\right). \qquad (10.11)$$

$F^E(t,T)$ has been derived above, whereas by Ito's lemma[11] we have that $1/F^S(t,T) = 1/S_T e^{[(r^X - r^Y - (\sigma^S)^2)(T-t)]}$ (where the FX rate's integrated variance is $\sigma^S = \varsigma^S$, since we assume constant parameters), so that the composite forward price making nil the value of the contract at inception is:

$$F_C^X(t,T) = K_{XXX} = \frac{F^E(t,T)}{F^S(t,T)} = \frac{E_t}{S_t}e^{(r^X - b - (\sigma^S)^2)(T-t)}. \qquad (10.12)$$

As is possible to imply from equation (10.11), the composite contract's value (expressed in XXX terms) partially depends on the FX spot rate in the sense that the commodity's forward price (in XXX terms) is affected by the FX rate, but the strike price K_{XXX} is specified in XXX terms from the inception and no FX risk is inherent in it. This means that the magnitude and sign of the terminal payoff both depend on the FX spot rate.

It may appear that the composite contract is not an effective hedging tool as far as FX risk is concerned. It should be stressed, though, that if we have an opposite position at the expiry T in the underlying commodity, then its value in XXX terms fully offsets the variable component of the composite forward contract's value ($\frac{F^E(T,T)}{F^S(T,T)} = \frac{E_T}{S_T}$), and we are left with a

[11] The FX rate dynamics is commanded by an SDE with a risk-neutral drift $\mu = r^Y - r^X$. We change the notation, slightly by adding a superscript S to the instantaneous variance, to distinguish it from the commodity's variance, which will be denoted by $\sigma^E = \varsigma^E$.

fixed price K_{XXX} to pay or to cash in. Then the composite forward contract offers complete FX protection when traded for hedging purposes.

10.6.1.3 Quanto Contract The quanto forward contract is more difficult to replicate since there is no simple buy-and-hold strategy producing a payoff of $(1/S_0)E_T$ XXX at expiration. The only viable strategy is to create a synthetic portfolio of traded assets such that it is always worth $(1/S_0)E$ XXX, having an exposure of $(1/S_0)$ XXX to the commodity and zero exposure to the YYY currency. To do that, at each time $t < s < T$ we rebalance the portfolio according to the following rules:

- invest $(1/S_0)E_s$ units of XXX currency;
- borrow $(S_s/S_0)E_s$ units of YYY currency;
- buy S_s/S_0 units of the commodity.

Thus, we have to implement a dynamic trading strategy which depends on the movements of the commodity and on the FX spot rate. This synthetic security is then used in a standard static strategy:

- a long position in $e^{-r^{Qu}(T-t)}$ of the synthetic security, where r^{Qu} is the yield granted by the synthetic portfolio worth $(1/S_0)E_s$ (we will discuss this below);
- a short position in an XXX zero-coupon bond with face value K_{YYY}/S_0.

The value of the contract in XXX units at time t is:

$$\mathbf{CFw}^X_{Qu}(t,T) = (1/S_0)(e^{-r^{Qu}(T-t)}E_t - K_{XXX}e^{-r^X(T-t)}). \tag{10.13}$$

It can be shown (see next remark) that $r^{Qu} = r^X - r^Y + b - \rho\sigma^S\sigma^E$ (where $\sigma^E = \varsigma^E$ is the constant commodity's price variance and ρ is the correlation between the FX spot rate and the commodity), so that the quanto forward price is:

$$F^X_{Qu}(t,T) = E_t e^{(r^X - r^{Qu})(T-t)}.$$

It is easy to check from equation (10.13) that the terminal value of the quanto forward contract (which is by definition in XXX units) is independent of the FX spot rate. Hence, both the sign and the magnitude of the quanto forward contract's payoff are totally protected from the FX risk.

It may appear that the quanto forward contract is the perfect instrument to hedge the FX risk related to the commodity's price denominated in YYY units. Nevertheless, this is not the case: if we are exposed at the expiry T to the underlying commodity, then its value in XXX terms depends on the terminal FX spot rate S_T used to convert it from YYY units. This means that if we have an opposite position in a quanto forward its variable part E_T XXX is not offsetting E_T YYY $= E_T/S_T$ XXX, so that the total position is not immune from FX risk. The quanto forward is not the best suited contract to hedge forward exposures to the commodity and it could be more useful for speculation.

10.6.2 FX-Linked Energy Contracts

As mentioned above, since commodity prices are US dollar denominated and many market operators have their profits and losses computed in another currency, typical commodity contracts have features intended to protect the counterparties from FX risk. We will examine two types of contract common in the commodity and energy markets. These contracts are generally traded with no FX protection but we will consider the variants with FX protection clauses.

10.6.2.1 FX-Linked Formula Contract In energy markets the underlying can be a formula that combines, according to given parameters, several distinct products. Then contracts can be written on this virtual underlying, such as forwards or swaps, and they can be *FX linked*, meaning that they include a protection from FX risk. An example of an FX-linked formula contract for gas is the following:[12]

Example 10.6.1 ***FX-linked formula contract***
Buyer: *A Inc.*
Seller: *B Inc.*
Quantity: *1200.00 GJ/d (gigajoules per day)*
Time Unit: *Daily*
Total Supply Period: *From 06:00 hours CET 01 OCT 09 to 06:00 hours CET 01 OCT 10*
The contract price P applicable to the quantities will be determined on a monthly basis according to the formula

$$P_m = P_0 + \Delta P_m + P_1$$

where

$$\begin{aligned}
P_0 &= P_{AUG08} = 694.555\ EURcent/GJ \\
P_1 &= 86.111\ EURcent/GJ \\
\Delta P_m &= 315.092 \times 0.95 \times (I_m - I_0)\ EURcent/GJ \\
I_0 &= I_{OCT08} = 2.038 \\
I_m &= 0.41 \times \frac{GASOIL_m}{21.914} + 0.46 \times \frac{BTZ_m}{14.107} + 0.13 \times \frac{BRENT_m}{18.250}
\end{aligned}$$

$GASOIL_m$ is the average, associated with the period elapsing between the ninth and the first month prior to the update, of the monthly averages of 'CIF Med Basis Genoa/Lavera quotations' of gas oil 02, published by Platt's Oligram Report, expressed in US dollars per metric tonne, converted into EUR/kg considering the exchange rate obtained as an arithmetic average of the daily values of the EUR/US$ exchange rate determined by the ECB in the supply month.

BTZ_m is the average, referred to the period elapsing between the ninth and the first month prior to the update, of the monthly averages of 'CIF Med Basis Genoa/Lavera quotations' of LSFO (low-sulphur fuel oil), published by Platt's Oligram Report, expressed in US dollars per metric tonne, converted into EUR/kg considering the exchange rate obtained as an arithmetic

[12]The example is based on the termsheet of a real contract.

average of the daily values of the EUR/US\$ exchange rate determined by the ECB in the supply month.

$BRENT_m$ is the average, with the period elapsing between the ninth and the first month prior to the update, of the monthly averages of 'Spot Crude Assessments International quotations' of Brent, published by Platt's Oligram Report–Price Average Supplement, expressed in US dollars per barrel changed into US dollars per metric tonne with a conversion factor of 7.4 barrels per metric tonne, converted into EUR/kg considering the exchange rate obtained as an arithmetic average of the daily values of the EUR/US\$ exchange rate determined by the ECB in the supply month.

Basically this contract allows the buyer to fix the price of a gas supply over a 1-year period according to the formula provided in the contract, by considering the average prices of the single components during the last 9 months. Additionally, there is a conversion rule to determine the conversion from US dollars to euros, thus offering FX protection to the buyer: the exchange rate used is the average of the ECB fixings over the last month. The average converted to euros is calculated each month and paid to the seller. One may notice that the averaging rules refer to two different periods for the energy products entering into the formula and for the EURUSD spot rate.

We would like to know which are the exact exposures to the energy components and to the EURUSD pair, embedded in the terms above. The best way to analyse the contract is to focus on a single component, disregarding for the moment all conversions and multiplying factors. Let E_t be one of the energy products entering into the formula (e.g., BRENT), and N_m^E be the number of observations needed for the average A_m^E. The average for the month m, at time t, can be written as:

$$A_m^E(t) = \overline{E}_m \frac{n_m^E}{N_m^E} + \frac{1}{N_m^E - n_m^E} \mathbf{E}^Q \left[\sum_{i=n_m^E+1}^{N_m^E} E_{t_i} \right] \frac{N_m^E - n_m^E}{N_m^E}$$

$$= \overline{E}_m \frac{n_m^E}{N_m^E} + \frac{1}{N_m^E} E_t \sum_{i=n_m^E+1}^{N_m^E} e^{(r^Y - b)(t_i - t)},$$

where n_m^E is the number of observations for the energy product already occurred and $\overline{E}_m$ is their average. A similar formula can be written for the FX rate (n_m^S is the number of past observations for the FX spot rate and $\overline{S}_m$ is their average):

$$A_m^S(t) = \overline{S}_m \frac{n_m^S}{N_m^S} + \frac{1}{N_m^S - n_m^S} \mathbf{E}^Q \left[\sum_{i=n_m^S+1}^{N_m^S} S_{t_i} \right] \frac{N_m^S - n_m^S}{N_m^S}$$

$$= \overline{S}_m \frac{n_m^S}{N_m^S} + \frac{1}{N_m^S} S_t \sum_{i=n_m^S+1}^{N_m^S} e^{(r^Y - r^X)(t_i - t)}.$$

According to the contract's rule for the conversion into EUR, the energy value in EUR units entering into the price formula is:

$$\overline{E}_m^{X,FC}(t) = A_m^E(t) / A_m^S(t). \tag{10.14}$$

This formula resembles slightly the forward price entering into a composite contract, although in this case the averaging period of the energy product's formula and of the EURUSD refer to two different ranges (previous 9 months for the former and previous 1 month for the latter). Additionally, the very mechanics of the rule imply that no correlation between the energy prices and the FX spot rate enters into the computation for $\overline{E}_m^{X,FC}$.

We can easily calculate the hedging quantities from the formula above (we still neglect all multiplying factors of the price formula). The quantity of energy product to hold is the (reverse sign) Delta with respect to the energy price:

$$\Delta_t^E = \frac{\partial \overline{E}_m^{X,FC}(t)}{\partial E_t} = \frac{1}{A_m^S(t)} \frac{1}{N_m^E} \sum_{i=n_m^E+1}^{N_m^E} e^{(r^Y-b)(t_i-t)}.$$

This quantity indicates the variation of the formula contract's value, in XXX currency, given a change in the energy product E_t, which is in YYY. If we trade in E_t to hedge/replicate the contract, then we have a P&L in YYY, so the Delta in YYY has to be multiplied by S_t to be equivalent to XXX units:

$$\Delta_t^E = S_t \frac{\partial \overline{E}_m^{X,FC}(t)}{\partial E_t} = \frac{S_t}{A_m^S(t)} \frac{1}{N_m^E} \sum_{i=n_m^E+1}^{N_m^E} e^{(r^Y-b)(t_i-t)}.$$

If futures are available on the product then we can perform the Delta-hedging by trading it. Assume the futures price is H_t and that its expiry is at time T'. As we are working with constant parameters, we have that the futures price is equal to the forward price, so that:

$$\Delta_t^H = \frac{\partial \overline{E}_m^{X,FC}(t)}{\partial H_t} = \frac{\partial \overline{E}^{X,FC}(t)}{\partial E_t} \frac{\partial E_t}{\partial H_t} = \Delta_t^E \frac{e^{b(T'-t)}}{e^{r^Y(T'-t)}}.$$

The Delta with respect to the FX spot price is:

$$\Delta_t^S = \frac{\partial \overline{E}^{X,FC}(t)}{\partial S_t} = -\frac{A_m^E(t)}{(A_m^S(t))^2} \frac{1}{N_m^S} \sum_{i=n_m^S+1}^{N_m^S} e^{(r^Y-r^X)(t_i-t)}.$$

We are calculating the Delta with respect to the FX spot rate of $\overline{E}^{X,FC}(t)$, which is expressed in the XXX currency (euros in our example) and is exposed to variations in the XXX currency (euros): so the Delta indicates the quantity of YYY currency (US dollars) to trade assuming that the exchange rate is $1/S_t$. Since in the market the actual traded exchange rate is S_t that generates profits and losses into YYY units (US dollars) we convert the Delta variations into YYY units (US dollars) so as to determine the amount of XXX units (euros) to trade for hedging purposes:

$$\Delta_t^S = -S_t \frac{A_m^E(t)}{(A_m^S(t))^2} \frac{1}{N_m^S} \sum_{i=n_m^S+1}^{N_m^S} e^{(r^Y-r^X)(t_i-t)}.$$

To make the hedging correct we have to take into account the conversions and multiplying factors. In the example above, if the energy component is BRENT we multiply each Delta quantity above by $315.092 \times 0.95 \times \frac{0.13}{18.250}$. The total hedge is performed for each component of the price formula.

10.6.2.2 FX-Linked Swap Contract The buyer of a commodity swap pays a fixed (swap) price against receiving the price of a commodity at a set of given dates. The difference is typically netted and the contract is cash settled. The floating price can also be an average of the commodity's prices over some specified period and it may offer FX protection by including predefined conversion rules as in the following example.

Example 10.6.2 ***FX-linked energy swap contract***
Trade Date: *01 Sep 09*
Commodity Type: *Oil Brent*
Total Quantity: *40,000.00 U.S. Bbl/Period*
Fixed Price Payer: *A Inc.*
Floating Price Payer: *B Inc.*
Effective Date: *01 Sep 2009*
Termination Date: *30 Nov 2010*

Start Date	*End Date*	*Payment Date*	*Size BBL*	*Start Date*	*End Date*	*Payment Date*	*Size BBL*
01/09/09	30/09/09	07/10/09	2430	01/05/10	31/05/10	07/06/10	2800
01/10/09	31/10/09	06/11/09	2850	01/06/10	30/06/10	07/07/10	2480
01/11/09	30/11/09	07/11/09	3275	01/07/10	31/07/10	06/08/10	2050
01/12/09	31/12/09	08/01/10	3670	01/08/10	31/08/10	07/09/10	1650
01/01/10	31/01/10	05/02/10	3675	01/09/10	30/09/10	30/10/10	1240
01/02/10	28/02/10	05/03/10	3650	01/10/10	31/10/10	05/11/10	820
01/03/10	31/03/10	09/04/10	3590	01/11/10	30/11/10	07/12/10	420
01/04/10	30/04/10	07/05/10	3250				

Calculation Period: *Each consecutive calendar month, from and including the effective date to the end including the termination date*
Fixed Price: *51 EUR per US barrel*
Floating Price: *For each determination period, the average of the closing settlement price(s) on the Intercontinental Petroleum Exchange for the nearby ICE Brent futures contract converted to EUR (referenced below). The daily floating prices will be converted to EUR/BBL using the daily USD/EUR conversion rate as published by the European Central Bank (currently Reuters page 'ecb37'). If, as of any pricing day, a USD/EUR conversion rate is unavailable, then for the purposes of this transaction the prior business day USD/EUR conversion rate shall be used to calculate the final daily floating prices. All such conversions shall be rounded to four decimal places. The final floating price to be rounded to three decimal places*
Commodity Reference Price: *OIL-BRENT-ICE*
Currency: *USD*
Roll Adjustment: *In order to use the correct floating price quotations, the nearby month quotation specified in the floating price will be used except for the expiration date of the*

cash commodity's underlying delivery month's futures contract. On such a date the applicable pricing quotation will be rolled to the following month's (the next nearby) quotation
Settlement Date(s): *The last trading day of each determination period*
Payment Date(s): *5 TARGET business days after each settlement date*

The contract has a duration of 13 months and each month the reference size of the underlying Brent oil is variable. The fixed price is set in EUR, although the oil price is in USD. For this reason, a conversion rule is also provided for the floating price: this is computed, at the end of each calculation period, as the average of the previous month's (futures settlement) prices converted into EUR every day at the ECB fixing for the EURUSD. The payments are netted and the contract is cash settled.

We analyse the contract focusing on a single swaplet (in our case it is the payment referring to a 1-month period) assuming a unit notional amount: N_m is the number of observations needed for the average $\overline{E}_m^{X,SC}$. It is easy to check that the FX linked swaplet is an average of composite forward contracts, as examined above. Actually the average for the month m, at time t, can be written as:

$$\begin{aligned}\overline{E}_m^{X,SC}(t) &= \overline{E}_m \frac{n_m}{N_m} + \frac{1}{N_m - n_m} \mathbf{E}^Q \left[\sum_{i=n_m+1}^{N_m} E_{t_i}/S_{t_i} \right] \frac{N_m - n_m}{N_m} \\ &= \overline{E}_m \frac{n_m}{N_m} + \frac{1}{N_m} \frac{E_t}{S_t} \sum_{i=n_m+1}^{N_m} e^{(r^X - b - (\sigma^S)^2)(t_i - t)},\end{aligned} \tag{10.15}$$

where n_m is the number of observations already occurred and $\overline{E}_m$ is their average.

We can calculate the hedging quantities from equation (10.15). The quantity of energy product to hold is the (reverse sign) Delta with respect to the energy price (considering also the fact that it has to be multiplied by S_t, see above the Delta for the formula contract):

$$\Delta_t^E = \frac{\partial E_m^{X,SC}(t)}{\partial E_t} = \frac{1}{N_m} \sum_{i=n_m+1}^{N_m} e^{(r^X - b - (\sigma^S)^2)(t_i - t)}.$$

If futures H_t are available on the product with expiry T', then we have that $\Delta_t^H = \Delta_t^E \frac{e^{b(T'-t)}}{e^{r^Y(T'-t)}}$.

The Delta with respect to the FX spot price, in the standard (according to market conventions) XXX amount, is:

$$\Delta_t^E = \frac{\partial E_m^{X,SC}(t)}{\partial S_t} = -\frac{1}{N_m} \frac{E_t}{S_t} \sum_{i=n_m+1}^{N_m} e^{(r^X - b - (\sigma^S)^2)(t_i - t)}.$$

Hence we have the amounts of underlying asset (in the contract in the example: Brent oil) and of the XXX currency to trade for hedging purposes, clearly each of them multiplied by the notional amount. The entire swap is hedged by summing over all individual swaplets.

We present an example of dynamic hedging of a formula contract and a swap contract.

Example 10.6.3 *We consider two stylized contracts: a formula contract and a swap contract, whose underlying is the BRENT oil futures; each contract's payoff is based on the average* *of the BRENT price, calculated over a period of 1 month (22 business days), converted into euros. The rule to convert the USD denominated average price into a EUR denominated price is the same as we have analysed above; we assume that each contract is based on the average price calculated over the same period.*

For simplicity, and without any loss of generality, we assume no conversion factors both in the formula and swap price and we set interest rates and convenience yield equal to zero, whereas the volatility of the EURSUD spot rate is 10% on a yearly basis: we need this to calculate the Delta with respect to the FX rate.

The dynamic replica/hedging is performed by setting up a portfolio of an amount of cash equal to the contract's fair price at inception and a continuously (actually, daily in our case) updated quantity of BRENT and EUR/USD spot contracts. The time series we use are from market prices for the month of August 2009 and they are shown in Table 10.8 with summary statistics regarding their average, volatility (expressed on a yearly basis) and correlation.

TABLE 10.8 Time series for EURUSD spot rate, inverse of the EURUSD, Brent oil in US dollars and converted into euros

Observation no.	EURUSD	USDEUR	BRENT Oil	BRNT/E-U
1	1.4342	0.6973	69.6500	48.5637
2	1.4232	0.7026	67.7300	47.5899
3	1.4287	0.6999	67.6600	47.3577
4	1.4259	0.7013	67.1200	47.0720
5	1.4307	0.6990	66.8200	46.7044
6	1.4336	0.6975	66.5300	46.4076
7	1.4519	0.6888	69.4200	47.8132
8	1.4573	0.6862	69.8300	47.9174
9	1.4591	0.6854	69.8600	47.8788
10	1.4576	0.6861	67.6900	46.4394
11	1.4623	0.6839	67.4400	46.1191
12	1.4636	0.6832	67.3500	46.0167
13	1.4701	0.6802	71.6700	48.7518
14	1.4715	0.6796	71.5500	48.6239
15	1.4724	0.6792	71.3200	48.4379
16	1.4677	0.6813	68.6900	46.8011
17	1.4781	0.6765	70.5300	47.7167
18	1.4775	0.6768	67.9900	46.0169
19	1.4684	0.6810	64.8200	44.1433
20	1.4676	0.6814	65.1100	44.3649
21	1.4616	0.6842	65.5400	44.8413
22	1.4581	0.6858	65.4900	44.9146

	Average	Yr. Volatility
EURUSD	1.4555	8.66%
USDEUR	0.0008	8.66%
BRENT Oil	68.1732	49.38%
Corr BRNT U-E		−8.16%
Covar BRNT U-E		−0.35%

TABLE 10.9 Performance of the dynamic hedging/replica of a formula contract

Observation no.	Delta FX EUR	Amount USD	P&L FX USD	P&L FX EUR	Delta Oil	P&L Oil USD	P&L Oil EUR
1	−48.5637	69.6500			1.0000		
2	−45.4534	64.6892	0.5342	0.3754	0.9542	−1.9200	−1.3491
3	−43.1121	61.5942	−0.2500	−0.1750	0.9091	−0.0668	−0.0468
4	−40.7326	58.0806	0.1207	0.0847	0.8634	−0.4909	−0.3443
5	−38.3659	54.8901	−0.1955	−0.1367	0.8185	−0.2590	−0.1810
6	−36.0734	51.7148	−0.1113	−0.0776	0.7733	−0.2374	−0.1656
7	−34.8165	50.5500	−0.6601	−0.4547	0.7304	2.2350	1.5393
8	−32.7278	47.6942	−0.1880	−0.1290	0.6855	0.2994	0.2055
9	−30.5438	44.5665	−0.0589	−0.0404	0.6401	0.0206	0.0141
10	−27.8421	40.5827	0.0458	0.0314	0.5941	−1.3890	−0.9529
11	−25.6408	37.4943	−0.1309	0.0895	0.5492	−0.1485	−0.1016
12	−23.4883	34.3774	−0.0333	−0.0228	0.5037	−0.0494	−0.0338
13	−21.9799	32.3127	−0.1527	−0.1039	0.4590	2.1759	1.4801
14	−19.7713	29.0934	−0.0308	−0.0209	0.4133	−0.0551	−0.0374
15	−17.5562	25.8498	−0.0178	−0.0121	0.3675	−0.0951	−0.0646
16	−15.1596	22.2498	0.0825	0.0562	0.3209	−0.9666	−0.6586
17	−12.3256	18.2185	−0.1577	−0.1067	0.2765	0.5905	0.3995
18	−10.8483	16.0284	0.0074	0.0050	0.2303	−0.7022	−0.4753
19	−8.5723	12.5875	0.0987	0.0672	0.1833	−0.7301	−0.4972
20	−6.4304	9.4372	0.0069	0.0047	0.1374	0.0532	0.0362
21	−4.2751	6.2484	0.0386	0.0264	0.0913	0.0591	0.0404
22	−2.1328	3.1098	0.0150	0.0103	1.5302	−0.0046	−0.0031
Total			−1.0372	−0.7079		−1.6811	−1.1961
Initial Cash	48.5637	EUR					
P&L + Initial Cash	46.6597	EUR					
Contract Payoff	46.8406	EUR					

The performance of the formula contract dynamic replica/hedging is shown in Table 10.9. It is started by an amount of cash equal to the fair contract price at inception (since we are assuming zero interest rates and convenience yield, this is simply equal to the price of the Brent oil converted into euros). It is easy to check that the dynamic hedging strategy yields a final result slightly lower than the actual payoff of the contract. We will examine in the next paragraph the sources of this replication error.

The dynamic replica/hedging performance is also tested for a swap contract and the results are given in Table 10.10. Also in this case the dynamic strategy underperforms slightly with respect to the final contract payoff: the reasons for this are also examined in the next paragraph.

10.6.2.3 Sources of Error in Dynamic Replica/Hedging The dynamic replica/hedging we showed in the previous example is not perfect due to the second-order derivatives, Gamma and cross-Gamma, of the contracts.

TABLE 10.10 Performance of the dynamic hedging/replica of a swap contract

Observation no.	Delta FX EUR	Amount USD	P&L FX USD	P&L FX EUR	Delta Oil	P&L Oil USD	P&L Oil EUR
1	−48.5441	69.6220			0.9996		
2	−45.4093	64.6266	0.5340	0.3752	0.9542	−1.9192	−1.3485
3	−43.0368	61.4867	−0.2498	−0.1748	0.9088	−0.0668	−0.0468
4	−40.6391	57.9473	0.1205	0.0845	0.8633	−0.4907	−0.3442
5	−38.2003	54.6532	−0.1951	−0.1363	0.8179	−0.2590	−0.1810
6	−35.8495	51.3938	−0.1108	−0.0773	0.7725	−0.2372	−0.1655
7	−34.7632	50.4728	−0.6560	−0.4519	0.7271	2.2325	1.5376
8	−32.6622	47.5986	−0.1877	−0.1288	0.6816	0.2981	0.2046
9	−30.4608	44.4453	−0.0588	−0.0403	0.6362	0.0204	0.0140
10	−27.4352	39.9895	0.0457	0.0313	0.5908	−1.3806	−0.9472
11	−25.1506	36.7777	−0.1289	−0.0882	0.5453	−0.1477	−0.1010
12	−23.0039	33.6685	−0.0327	−0.0223	0.4999	−0.0491	−0.0335
13	−22.1561	32.5717	−0.1495	−0.1017	0.4545	2.1596	1.4690
14	−19.8885	29.2660	−0.0310	−0.0211	0.4090	−0.0545	−0.0371
15	−17.6115	25.9312	−0.0179	−0.0122	0.3636	−0.0941	−0.0639
16	−14.8896	21.8534	0.0828	0.0564	0.3181	−0.9562	−0.6515
17	−13.0124	19.2336	−0.1549	−0.1048	0.2727	0.5854	0.3960
18	−10.4576	15.4511	0.0078	0.0053	0.2273	−0.6927	−0.4688
19	−8.0256	11.7848	0.0952	0.0648	0.1818	−0.7204	−0.4906
20	−6.0496	8.8784	0.0064	0.0044	0.1364	0.0527	0.0359
21	−4.0764	5.9581	0.0363	0.0248	0.0909	0.0586	0.0401
22	−2.0416	2.9768	0.0143	0.0098	0.0455	−0.0045	−0.0031
Total			−1.0302	−0.7031		−1.6654	−1.1853
Initial Cash	48.5441	EUR					
P&L + Initial Cash	46.6557	EUR					
Contract Payoff	46.8382	EUR					

For the formula contract we calculate the Gamma and cross-Gamma as the first and mixed derivatives of the 'pure' Deltas (i.e., without multiplying them by the FX spot rate, see the computations and the discussion above):

$$\Gamma_t^E = \frac{\partial^2 \overline{E}^{X,FC}(t)}{(\partial E_t)^2} = 0,$$

$$\Gamma_t^S = -\frac{\partial^2 \overline{E}^{X,FC}(t)}{(\partial S_t)^2} = -2\Delta_t^S \frac{1}{\left(A_m^S(t)\right)} \frac{1}{N_m^S} \sum_{i=n_m^S+1}^{N_m^S} e^{(r^Y - r^X)(t_i - t)},$$

$$\Gamma_t^{E,S} = \frac{\partial^2 \overline{E}^{X,FC}(t)}{\partial S_t \partial E_t} = -2\frac{S_t}{\left(A_m^S(t)\right)^2} \frac{1}{N_m^S} \sum_{i=n_m^S+1}^{N_m^S} e^{(r^Y - r^X)(t_i - t)} \frac{1}{N_m^E} \sum_{i=n_m^E+1}^{N_m^E} e^{(r^Y - b)(t_i - t)}.$$

Example 10.6.4 *With reference to the example of dynamic replica/hedging 10.6.3, we have that the FX Gamma, at the beginning of the contract, has the following values for different levels of the EURUSD rate:*

			EURUSD			
1.4042	*1.4142*	*1.4242*	*1.4342*	*1.4442*	*1.4542*	*1.4642*
50.31	*49.25*	*48.22*	*47.21*	*46.25*	*45.29*	*44.37*

The Gamma is also not constant as time goes by. The time evolution of the FX Gamma, as the number of observations increases, is:

	Days	
1	*10*	*20*
47.21	*13.00*	*0.3638*

The cross-Gamma at the beginning of the period and its time evolution is:

			EURUSD			
1.4042	*1.4142*	*1.4242*	*1.4342*	*1.4442*	*1.4542*	*1.4642*
−1.42	*−1.41*	*−1.40*	*−1.39*	*−1.38*	*−1.38*	*−1.37*

	Days	
1	*10*	*20*
−1.39	*−0.41*	*−0.01*

For the swap contract we have that Gamma and cross-Gamma, computed w.r.t. the 'pure' Deltas, are:

$$\Gamma_t^E = \frac{\partial^2 E_m^{X,SC}(t)}{(\partial E_t)^2} = 0,$$

$$\Gamma_t^S = \frac{\partial^2 E_m^{X,SC}(t)}{(\partial S_t)^2} = -2\frac{\Delta_t^S}{S_t},$$

$$\Gamma_t^{E,S} = \frac{\partial^2 E_m^{X,SC}(t)}{\partial S_t \partial E_t} = -\frac{1}{N_m}\frac{1}{S_t}\sum_{i=n_m+1}^{N_m} e^{(r^X-b-(\sigma^S)^2)(t_i-t)}.$$

Example 10.6.5 *We still refer to Example 10.6.3: we have that the FX Gamma of an FX-linked swap contract, at the beginning of the period, has the following values:*

			EURUSD			
1.4042	*1.4142*	*1.4242*	*1.4342*	*1.4442*	*1.4542*	*1.4642*
35.31	*34.81*	*34.32*	*33.85*	*33.38*	*32.92*	*32.47*

The time evolution of the FX Gamma, as the number of observations increases, is:

	Days	
1	*10*	*20*
33.85	*18.82*	*4.12*

The cross-Gamma at the beginning of the period and its time evolution is:

			EURUSD			
1.4042	*1.4142*	*1.4242*	*1.4342*	*1.4442*	*1.4542*	*1.4642*
−0.71	*−0.71*	*−0.70*	*−0.70*	*−0.69*	*−0.69*	*−0.68*

	Days	
1	*10*	*20*
−0.70	*−0.41*	*−0.09*

Remark 10.6.2 *It should be stressed that the Gamma and the cross-Gamma of both the formula and the swap contracts are different from zero because we are working in the case where the energy product has a price in YYY units and this has to be converted into XXX units via an FX rate XXXYYY: E/S. If the conversion involves an FX rate whose base currency is YYY, then the converted price is $E \times S$: this case would yield zero Gamma also with respect to the FX rate and clearly zero cross-Gamma as well. Such a situation would occur, for example, if the trader has a P&L in Japanese yen and the FX rate used to convert the energy price from US dollars to yen is the USDJPY.*

Remark 10.6.3 *The FX conversion provided for by the two contracts is such that while the formula contract shows no dependence on the volatility parameters associated with the energy price or the FX spot rate, the swap contract depends on the volatility of the exchange rate, as is manifest from equation (10.15). It should be noted, though, that the impact of the FX volatility on the swap price is rather limited, since it enters only in the exponential and it is multiplied by the time to expiry. Besides, the dependence would disappear should we be working in the situation where a YYYXXX FX rate is used for the conversion (see the considerations in Remark 10.6.2).*

10.6.2.4 Hedging the Formula with the Swap Contract It may happen in trading activity that you have a book containing both swap contracts and formula contracts (or even other kinds of more exotic contracts). If both types of contract have the same underlying commodity and offer protection against the same FX pair, it is interesting to analyse how a market operator may hedge one of them (say the formula contract) with the other one (the energy swap). To that end we assume a simplified situation where both contracts have the same averaging periods associated with the energy product and the FX. We also consider the formula contract with a single component. Needless to say this is not a typical situation, as the examples above show, but it allows us to point out the sources of hedging mismatch between the two types of contract. The analysis can readily be extended to incorporate increased complexity.

From the analysis above, we can infer that the (single-period, single-component) formula contract is a payoff of the kind[13]

$$\overline{E}_m^{X,FC}(T) = \mathbf{E}^Q[f(E)]\frac{1}{\mathbf{E}^Q[f(S)]},$$

where $f(x)$ is the average rule (basically the number of periods to consider for the average).

A (single-period) swap contract, with all other contract features equal to the formula contract, is a payoff of the kind

$$\overline{E}_m^{X,SC}(T) = \mathbf{E}^Q[f(E/S)].$$

Now, if we try to hedge the formula contract with a swap contract, we will experience hedging errors due to two causes: the first a relationship of probability theory

$$\mathbf{E}^Q[f(E/S)] = \mathbf{E}^Q[f(E)]\mathbf{E}^Q\left[\frac{1}{f(S)}\right] + \mathbf{cov}[f(E), 1/f(S)]$$

and the second Jensen's inequality

$$\mathbf{E}^Q\left[\frac{1}{f(S)}\right] \geq \frac{1}{\mathbf{E}^Q[f(S)]}.$$

We can write the inequality above as $\mathbf{E}^Q\left[\frac{1}{f(S)}\right] = \frac{1}{\mathbf{E}^Q[f(S)]} + \epsilon$, where ϵ is a positive quantity.

Considering these two relationships, we can then rewrite the formula contract price as

$$\overline{E}_m^{X,FC}(T) = \mathbf{E}^Q[f(E)]\mathbf{E}^Q\left[\frac{1}{f(S)}\right] - \mathbf{E}^Q[f(E)]\epsilon.$$

We substitute in the swap price formula and finally get

$$\overline{E}_m^{X,SC}(T) = \overline{E}_m^{X,FC}(T) + \mathbf{E}^Q[f(E)]\epsilon + \mathbf{cov}[f(E), 1/f(S)]. \tag{10.16}$$

The hedging performance can easily be inferred by inspection of (10.16):

- If the realized covariance between the average of the inverse FX spot rate and the average of the energy product E is zero ($\mathbf{cov}[f(E), 1/f(S)] = 0$), then the swap contract over-hedges the formula contract by the additive factor $\mathbf{E}^Q[f(E)]\epsilon$, whose magnitude depends on the actual average of the inverse FX spot rate S and of the energy product E.
- If the realized covariance between the average of the inverse FX spot rate and the average of the energy product E is positive ($\mathbf{cov}[f(E), 1/f(S)] > 0$), then the swap contract over-hedges the formula contract.

[13]We do not consider any conversion and multiplying factors.

- If the realized covariance between the average of the inverse FX spot rate and the average of the energy product E is negative ($\mathbf{cov}[f(E), 1/f(S)] < 0$), then the swap contract under-hedges, perfectly hedges or over-hedges the formula contract if, respectively, $\mathbf{E}^Q[f(E)]\epsilon < |\mathbf{cov}[f(E), 1/f(S)]|$, $\mathbf{E}^Q[f(E)]\epsilon = |\mathbf{cov}[f(E), 1/f(S)]|$ or $\mathbf{E}^Q[f(E)]\epsilon > |\mathbf{cov}[f(E), 1/f(S)]|$.

After this brief review of the methods to deal with the FX exposure embedded in commodity contracts we examine a number of structures specifically designed to hedge an FX exposure, in a way completely independent of the source. Recalling what we have said before, it is always possible to hedge the forward commodity exposure with a standard commodity forward contract and then manage the forward FX exposure independently. The following structures can be traded when this strategy is adopted.

10.7 TYPICAL HEDGING STRUCTURES FOR FX RISK EXPOSURE

In this section we examine several alternative structures to hedge FX exposures. For each of them we provide the building blocks (i.e., plain vanilla or exotic options) underlying it; a description of the payoff and the different events affecting it, the specific needs it satisfies, the main variations if they exist, a practical example and finally the pros and the cons. In the examples, the hedging performance of the different structures will be related to an FX exposure revalued at the FX forward rate traded in the market for the relevant expiry: this allows us to appraise the structure's profits and losses compared with the simplest possible hedge operated by an FX forward contract. We assume that the (either exporting or importing) company will hedge its FX risks by trading with a bank, that will produce and sell the structures.

We would just like to stress that the list below of possible hedging strategies is not at all exhaustive. Many other structures can be devised, with a higher degree of complexity and also with other kinds of exotic options involved. We chose the strategies below because they are the most commonly proposed by banks to their customers and also because in most cases they do meet the needs of customers in hedging FX risk. They can be considered *evergreen*, compared with others that are linked more to fads and contingent economic situations.

10.7.1 Collar Plain Vanilla

10.7.1.1 Description The plain vanilla collar is the name usually adopted in the non-professional market for risk-reversal. As such, when one buys this structure, there is a long (buy) position of a base currency call option, struck at level K_1 and a simultaneous short (sell) position of a put option, struck at level K_2 ($< K_1$). Both options expire on the same date and have the same notional amount. If one is selling the structure, the bought option should be sold and the sold one should be bought.

The structure is typically negotiated at zero cost, so that no premium payment is due by either party at inception. To make this possible, strike levels have to be higher (K_1) and lower (K_2) than the forward rate at the expiry date. The payoff at maturity of a long (short) collar can be identified by the following events related to the terminal value of the FX spot rate S_T:

- If the underlying FX spot rate is lower than K_2 ($S_T < K_2$), then the company buys (sells) the underlying base currency notional amount at K_2.

- If the underlying FX spot rate is between K_2 and K_1 ($K_2 < S_T < K_1$), then no obligation exists between the bank and the company.
- If the underlying FX spot rate is higher K_1 ($S_T > K_1$), then the company buys (sells) the underlying base currency notional amount at K_1.

10.7.1.2 Needs the Structure Satisfies The plain vanilla collar is specifically suited to exporting companies that wish to reduce their exposure to FX risk related to the future incoming foreign denominated cash-flows. In this case, the profits and losses originating from the hedged position have a lower and an upper limit determined by the options' strikes (K_1 and K_2). Clearly a short collar position (i.e., short the base currency call option and long the base currency put option) matches the needs of an importing company that has to hedge a future outgoing cash-flow (the opposite of the exporting company's one).

10.7.1.3 Main Variations If the strike levels are inverted ($K_1 < K_2$), that is equivalent to saying that both options building the structure are ITM at the inception of the contract, one may get the same result as before but the resulting hedged position is different from the standard case. In fact, the hedged position for an exporting company will be equivalent to a long base currency call spread (compared with the long put spread). Similarly, the hedged position of an importing company will be a long put spread in the inverted collar (compared with the long call spread).

Example 10.7.1 *Assume that an exporting company wants to hedge its future FX exposure in 3 months in EURUSD, since it will receive US dollars (and hence it will have to buy euros). It opens a long position in a plain vanilla collar, with the following conditions.*

- *FX spot price at expiry (S_T): 1.0800.*
- *FX price for a 3-month expiry forward contract $F(0, 3M)$: 1.0765.*
- *Long position: EUR call USD put, strike $K_1 = 1.1150$, expiring in 3 months.*
- *Short position: EUR put USD call strike $K_2 = 1.0450$, expiring in 3 months.*

The payoff at expiry of the collar is shown in Figure 10.6. No profit or loss occurs within the range delimited by the two strike levels. The company starts earning a profit above 1.1150 *and on the opposite side it starts losing money below* 1.0450. *In Figure 10.7 the payoff at expiry of the hedged position is shown. It is easily recognizable, with the profile being similar to that of a long EUR put USD call spread position.*

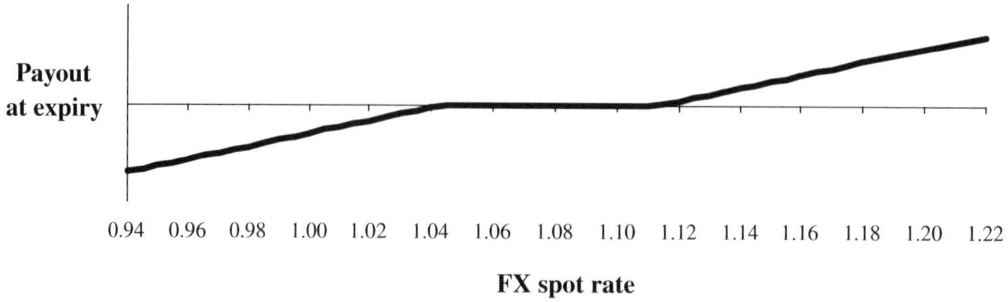

FIGURE 10.6 Payoff at expiry of a long plain vanilla collar

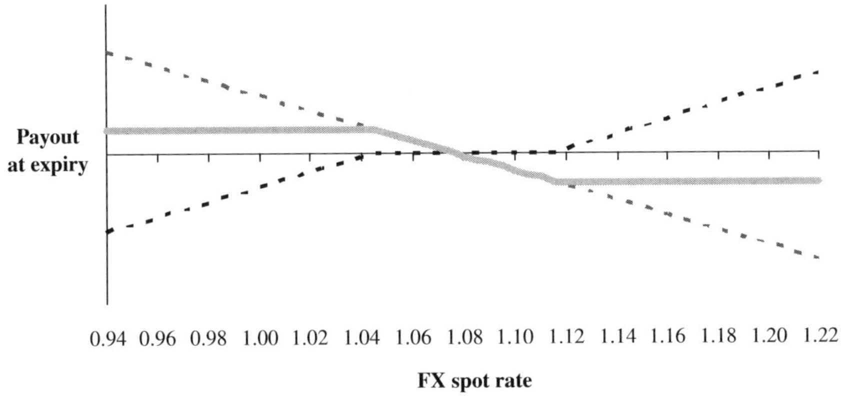

FIGURE 10.7 Payoff at expiry of an FX spot exposure of an exporting company hedged by a plain vanilla collar payoff. Red dotted line: FX exposure. Blue dotted line: collar payoff. Green line: hedged position

Assume now that the same exporter wants to hedge its position by a collar with inverted strikes, at the following conditions.

- *FX spot price at expiry (S_T): 1.0800.*
- *FX price for a 3-month expiry forward contract $F(0, 3M)$: 1.0765.*
- *Long position: EUR call USD put, strike $K_1 = 1.0450$, expiring in 3 months.*
- *Short position: EUR put USD call strike $K_2 = 1.1150$, expiring in 3 months.*

The payoff at expiry of such a variation of the plain vanilla collar is shown in Figure 10.8: the main difference with respect to the standard collar case is that within the range delimited by the two strikes, the profits and losses are not nil. The payoff resulting from the hedged position is shown in Figure 10.9 and it is manifestly similar to a EUR call USD put spread position this time.

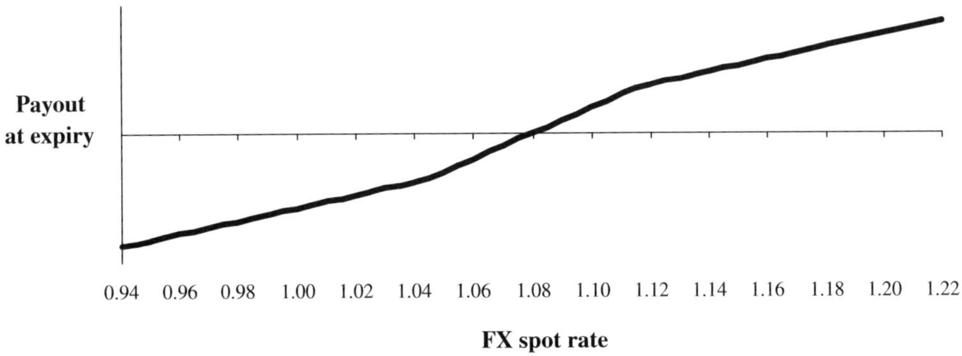

FIGURE 10.8 Payoff at expiry of a long inverted strike plain vanilla collar

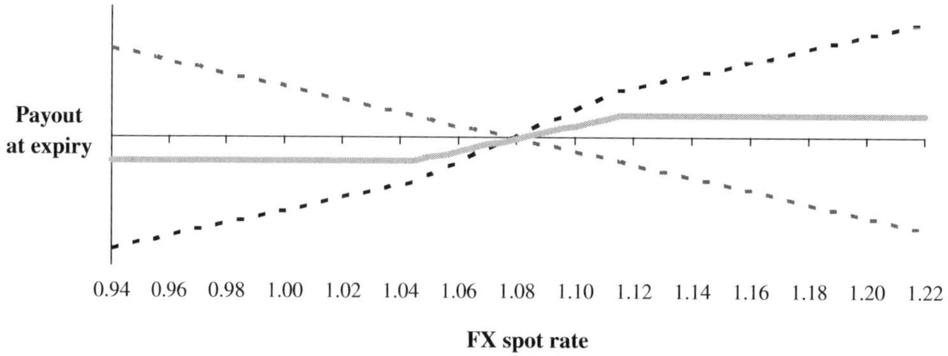

FIGURE 10.9 Payoff at expiry of an FX spot exposure of an exporting company hedged by an inverted strike plain vanilla collar. Red dotted line: FX exposure. Blue dotted line: collar payoff. Green line: hedged position

The preference to hedge by means of a standard collar or an inverted strike collar depends on the counterparty's expectations on the future levels of the FX spot rate.

10.7.1.4 Pros and Cons

- The plain vanilla collar, compared with a simple (buy or sell) forward contract, allows the buyer (or seller) to keep some profits arising from a favourable variation of the FX spot rate, but the hedging operates at levels worse than the FX forward rate at inception if the movement is adverse.
- The strategy can be traded at zero cost (though this is not required and some combinations of strikes entailing a net premium payment, due by the bank or by the company, can be negotiated as well).
- When one observes the profit and loss profile at expiry of an exporting company's hedged position (i.e., long the collar and an incoming (outgoing) numeraire (base) currency cash-flow), it is similar to a long position in a put spread, which allows limited profits when the base currency depreciates and limited losses when it appreciates. The hedged position of an importing company (i.e., short the collar and an outgoing (incoming) numeraire (base) currency cash-flow), on the contrary, is similar to a call spread, giving the company the possibility to earn limited profits if the base currency appreciates, with limited losses in the opposite case.

10.7.2 Leveraged Forward

10.7.2.1 Description A long *leveraged forward* is built from a long (buy) position in a base currency call option and a short (sell) position in a base currency put option, both struck at the same level K but with a different base currency notional amount equal to, respectively, N_1 and N_2, with $N_1 < N_2$. Since the structure is usually traded at zero cost, the strike level will be lower the greater is the amount of the sold option. A short leveraged forward is built by reversing the bought (sold) option to a sold (bought) one. The strike in this case will be higher, the greater is the amount of the sold option.

The following events may occur at the expiry of a long (short) leveraged forward:

- If the terminal FX spot rate is lower than the strike ($S_T < K$), the company buys (sells) the amount N_2 of base currency at a level equal to K.
- If the terminal FX spot rate is higher than the strike ($S_T < K$), the company sells (buys) the amount N_1 of base currency at a level equal to K.

10.7.2.2 Needs the Structure Satisfies The leverage forward is suitable for exporting/importing companies that need to attain a terminal FX spot rate more favourable than the FX forward rate prevailing in the market at the inception of the contract. This is counterbalanced by an asymmetric hedging of the FX spot exposure, which is a function of the difference between the two notional amounts N_1 and N_2.

The future exposure of the company is normally between the two amounts N_1 and N_2. In one extreme case, if the future cash-flow is equal to N_1, then the buyer (seller) of the structure has a perfect hedge against upward (downward) movements of the FX spot rate, but they are exposed to downward (upward) movements of the FX spot rate by an amount equal to $(N_2 - N_1)$. In the other extreme case, if the future cash-flow is equal to N_2, then they are partially hedged against a rising (declining) FX spot rate by an amount $N_1 < N_2$, but they have no exposure to a declining (rising) FX spot rate. An exposure lower than N_2 and greater than N_1 will produce a mixed result between the two extreme cases.

Example 10.7.2 *An exporting company hedges its future FX exposure in 3 months, when it will have to buy N_1 EUR against USD, by a long position in a leveraged forward as follows.*

- *FX spot price at expiry (S_T): 1.0800.*
- *FX price for a 3-month expiry forward contract $F(0, 3M)$: 1.0765.*
- *Long position: EUR call USD put strike $K = 1.0600$ expiring in 3 months, with a base currency notional amount N_1.*
- *Short position: EUR put USD call strike $K = 1.0600$, expiring in 3 months, with a base currency notional amount $N_2 = 2 \times N_1$.*

The payoff at expiry of the leveraged forward is shown in Figure 10.10: it is like a long position in the EURUSD opened at the level K, for an asymmetric amount equal to N_1 when the FX spot

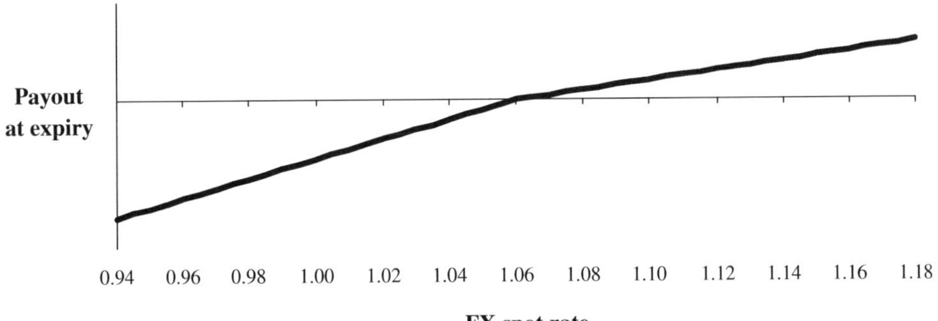

FIGURE 10.10 Payoff at expiry of a long leveraged forward

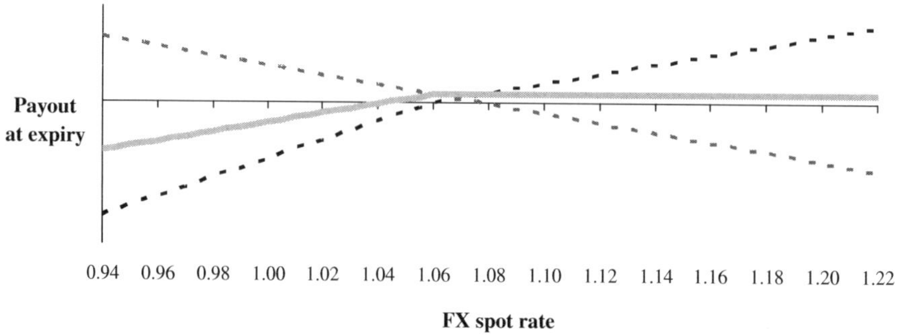

FIGURE 10.11 Payoff at expiry of an FX spot exposure of an exporting company hedged by a leveraged forward. Red dotted line: FX exposure. Blue dotted line: leveraged forward payoff. Green line: hedged position

rate is above the strike ($S_T > K$) and the double when it is below ($S_T < K$). In Figure 10.11 the payoff at expiry of the hedged position is shown: its profile resembles a short EUR put USD call position.

10.7.2.3 Pros and Cons

- The leveraged forward allows the company to fix a spot rate at maturity better than the market forward rate for the same date, at the cost of an asymmetric hedge of the exposure.
- The structure can be (not necessarily) dealt at zero cost.
- If we examine the profit and loss profile at expiry of the company's hedged position, we observe that for an exporter it is similar to a short contract in a (base currency) put option if the notional amount of the FX exposure is equal to N_1, or to a short (base currency) call option if the FX exposure is equal to N_2. For an importer, analogous considerations can be made, with the position this time being similar but with a short call option profile.

10.7.3 Participating Forward

10.7.3.1 Description A long (short) *participating forward* is built from a long position in a base currency call (put) option and a short position in a base currency put (respectively, call) option, both expiring on the same date and struck at the same level K, but with different base currency notional amounts N_1 and N_2, with $N_1 > N_2$. Since the structure is usually traded at zero cost, the strike K will be higher (lower, for a short position in the structure), the greater is the notional amount of the bought option.

At expiry the following events may occur for a long (respectively, short) position in a participating forward:

- If the terminal FX spot rate is lower than the strike ($S_T < K$), then the company buys (respectively, sells) the base currency notional amount N_2 at a level K.
- If the terminal FX spot rate is higher than the strike ($S_T > K$), then the company buys (respectively, sells) the base currency notional amount N_1 at a level K.

10.7.3.2 Needs the Structure Satisfies This structure is suggested for those companies wishing to eliminate their FX risk related to future cash-flows, yet keep open opportunities to gain profit from favourable movements of the FX spot rate, at least for a fraction of the original FX exposure.

Example 10.7.3 *Assume an exporting company wants to hedge its future FX exposure, short N_1 EUR against USD, in 3 months with a long position in a participating forward as follows.*

- *FX spot price at expiry (S_T): 1.0800.*
- *FX price for a 3-month expiry forward contract $F(0, 3M)$: 1.0765.*
- *Long position: EUR call USD put strike $K = 1.0900$ expiring in 3 months, with a base currency notional amount $N_1 = 2 \times N_2$.*
- *Short position: EUR put USD call strike $K = 1.0900$, expiring in 3 months, with a base currency notional amount N_2.*

The payoff at expiry of the participating forward is shown in Figure 10.12: it is very similar to a leveraged forward in that it is like a long position in the EURUSD opened at the level K, for an asymmetric amount equal to N_2 when the FX spot rate is below the strike ($S_T < K$) and the double when it is above ($S_T > K$). In Figure 10.13 the payoff at expiry of the hedged position is shown: its profile resembles a long EUR put USD call position.

Assume now that the same company wants to hedge its FX exposure in 3 months when it has to buy N_2 euros against US dollars. The payoff of the hedged position is in Figure 10.14 and it is equivalent to one of a EUR call USD put option.

10.7.3.3 Pros and Cons

- The participating forward forces the company to fix an FX spot rate worse than the FX forward rate prevailing in the market for the same expiry. This cost is compensated by a residual positive exposure to favourable variations of the underlying FX rate.
- The strategy is usually zero cost, but it is possible for the company to even receive a net premium.

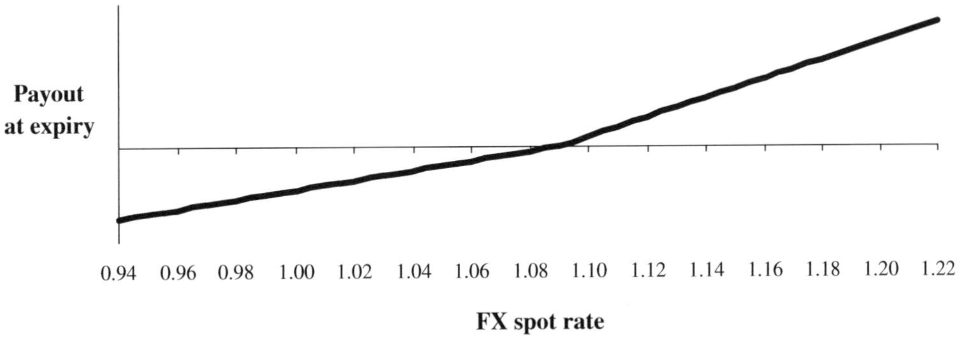

FIGURE 10.12 Payoff at expiry of a long participating forward

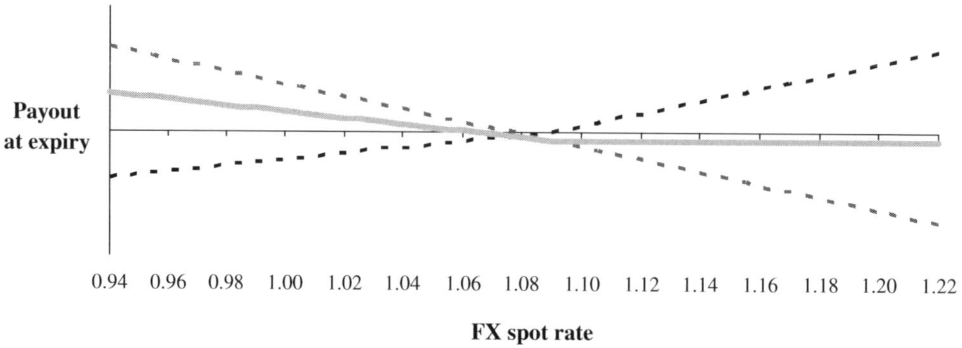

FIGURE 10.13 Payoff at expiry of an FX spot exposure (equal to the sold EUR put USD call notional amount) of an exporting company hedged by a participating forward. Red dotted line: FX exposure. Blue dotted line: participating forward payoff. Green line: hedged position

- If we examine the profit and loss profile of the hedged position at expiry, it is immediately obvious that for an exporter (importer) it corresponds to that of a long base currency put (respectively, call) option in the case that the notional amount of the FX exposure is equal to N_1, or to one of a base currency call (put) in case the FX exposure is equal to N_2.

10.7.4 Knock-Out Forward

10.7.4.1 Description A long (short) position in a *knock-out forward* is set up by buying a base currency call (put) option and simultaneously selling a base currency put (respectively, call) option, struck at the same level K and both with a knock-out barrier set at the same value B above (below) the strike level, $B > K$ ($B < K$). The base currency notional amount is equal for both options. As usual, since the structure is meant to be sold at zero cost, the enhancement of the buying (selling) price of the base currency amount at expiry, with respect to the forward price prevailing in the market at inception, is greater, the nearer to the starting FX spot rate the barrier level is set.

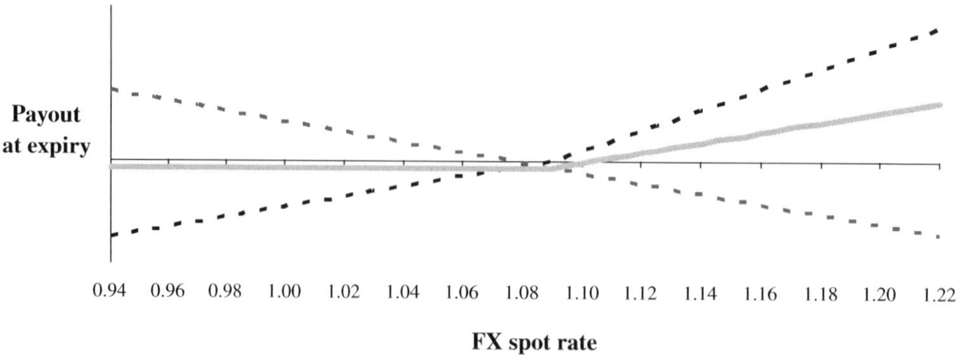

FIGURE 10.14 Payoff at expiry of an FX spot exposure (equal to the bought EUR call USD put notional amount) of an exporting company hedged by a participating forward. Red dotted line: FX exposure. Blue dotted line: participating forward payoff. Green line: hedged position

At the expiry of the contract, for a long (respectively, short) position in the knock-out forward, the following events may occur:

- If the underlying FX spot rate never breaches the barrier level B until expiry, then the company buys (respectively, sells) the base currency notional amount at the strike price K.
- If the underlying FX spot rate breaches the barrier level B at least once, any time up until the expiry of the contract, then the company cannot buy (sell) the base currency amount at strike level K, but it will have to trade at the market level prevailing on the maturity date. Hence it will be exposed to the original FX risk.

10.7.4.2 Needs the Structure Satisfies The long knock-out forward is suitable for exporting companies that wish to appreciably enhance the terminal buying price with respect to the forward rate prevailing at the inception of the contract. This remarkable enhancement is counterbalanced by the risk of losing the hedge if the barrier level is breached at any time during the life of the contract. The short knock-out forward satisfies the same needs, with the same counterbalancing risks, for importing companies.

Example 10.7.4 *An exporting company wants to hedge its future FX exposure, short EUR against USD, in 3 months with a long position in a knock-out forward as follows.*

- *FX spot price at expiry (S_T): 1.0800.*
- *FX price for a 3-month expiry forward contract $F(0, 3M)$: 1.0765.*
- *Long position: EUR call USD put strike $K = 1.0600$ expiring in 3 months, with a knock-out barrier at $B = 1.1000$.*
- *Short position: EUR put USD call strike $K = 1.0600$, expiring in 3 months, with a knock-out barrier at $B = 1.1000$.*

The payoff at expiry of the knock-out forward is shown in Figure 10.15: the sudden drop in gains above the barrier level 1.1000 is a consequence of the fact that after the barrier is touched, the company has no right to buy euros at 1.0600. Actually, we should consider that if the structure has been knocked-out before the expiry date, the gains in the range defined

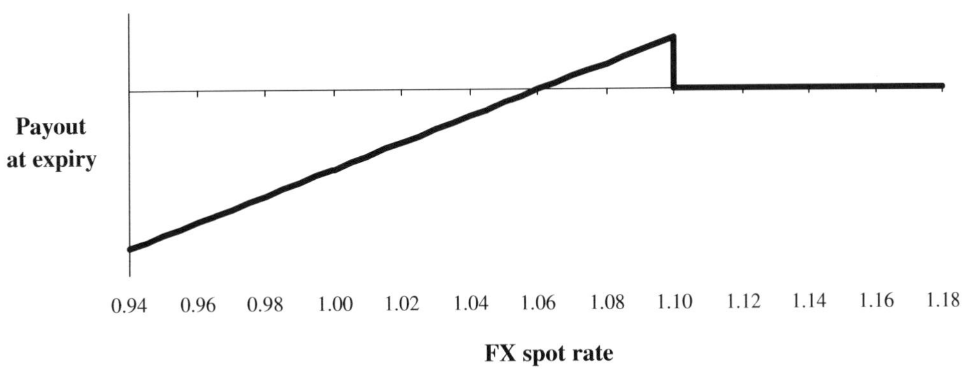

FIGURE 10.15 Payoff at expiry of a long knock-out forward

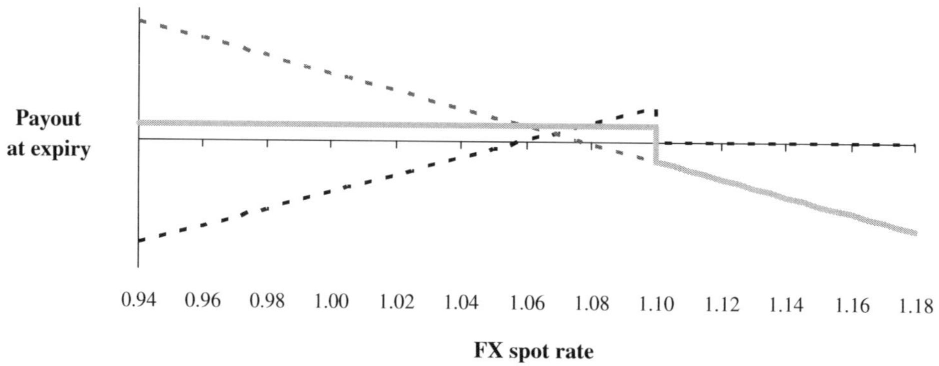

FIGURE 10.16 Payoff at expiry of an FX spot exposure of an exporting company hedged by a knock-out forward. Red dotted line: FX exposure. Blue dotted line: knock-out forward payoff. Green line: hedged position

by the strike and barrier (i.e., between 1.0600 and 1.1000), do not exist. In Figure 10.16, we observe the the payoff profile at expiry of the hedged position: the profit is limited and above the barrier 1.1000 *it drops to negative levels, that is a loss is incurred, due to the vanishing of the protection. The same considerations as above also apply here: if the knock-out occurs before the expiry, the profit below the barrier level* 1.1000 *does not exist and the company is just fully exposed to the original FX risk.*

10.7.4.3 Main Variations

- The knock-out forward can be designed so that the monitoring of the barrier level breaching is not continuous (i.e., at any time until expiry) but discrete according to a predefined schedule. As an example, rather common in reality, we may consider, for the FX spot rate against the euro, the daily European Central Bank fixing (the so-called ECB37 fixing) and monitor the long (short) position in the structure as follows:
  - If the daily ECB37 fixing never prints a value above (below) the barrier level, every day until the expiry of the contract, then the company buys (sells) the euro notional amount at the strike level K.
  - If the daily ECB37 fixing prints a value above (below) the barrier level, at least one day up until the expiry of the contract, then the company loses the right to buy (sell) at the strike level K and in this case it will have to trade at the FX spot rate prevailing on the maturity date.
- It is possible to monitor the barrier only at expiry, so that for a long (short) knock-out forward the following may occur on the expiry date:
  - If the terminal FX spot rate level is below (above) the barrier level B, then the company buys (sells) the euro notional amount at the strike level K.
  - If the terminal FX spot rate level is above (below) the barrier level B, then the company loses the right to buy (sell) at the strike level K and in this case it will have to trade at the FX spot rate prevailing on the maturity date.

10.7.4.4 Pros and Cons

- The knock-out forward allows the company to set a terminal FX spot rate remarkably more favourable than the forward rate dealing in the market at inception, but the hedging of FX risk is limited in that it may vanish if the barrier level is breached (according to the predefined monitoring schedule).
- The structure may be traded at zero cost, though this is not necessarily required.
- The greater risk borne by the company is due to the fact that, in order to achieve a terminal rate much better than the forward price, the barrier level must be set at an 'in-the-money' level, relating to the long option in the structure. In this way the protection from adverse FX spot movements disappears just when it is needed most.

10.7.5 Knock-In Forward

10.7.5.1 Description A long (short) *knock-in forward* is built with a long (buy) position in a base currency plain vanilla call (put) option and a short (sell) position in a base currency put (call) option, struck at the same level K and expiring on the same date as the first option, but with a knock-in barrier set at the level B. This structure is commonly sold at zero cost, so that the strike rate is increasingly worse than the forward price prevailing in the market, the further the knock-in level is set from the starting level of the FX spot rate at inception.

At expiry, for a long (short) position in a knock-in forward, the following events may occur:

- If the underlying FX spot rate is greater (lower) than the strike level $S_T > K$ ($S_T < K$), then the company buys (sells) the base currency notional amount at the strike level K.
- If the underlying FX spot rate is lower (greater) than the strike level $S_T < K$ ($S_T > K$) **and** it never reaches the barrier level B during the life of the contract, then the company buys (sells) the base currency notional amount at the terminal FX spot rate level S_T.
- If the underlying FX spot rate is lower (greater) than the strike level $S_T < K$ ($S_T > K$) **and** it reaches at least once the barrier level B any time during the life of the contract, then the company buys (sells) the base currency notional amount at the strike level K.

10.7.5.2 Needs the Structure Satisfies The knock-in forward is recommended for companies aiming to hedge FX risk on a given date and have a chance to profit from favourable movements of the FX spot rate, up to the breaching of the barrier level. To achieve this goal the company is keen on setting a strike level worse than the forward price available in the market at the start of the contract.

Example 10.7.5 *An exporting company wants to hedge its future FX exposure, short EUR against USD, in 3 months with a long position in a knock-out forward as follows.*

- *FX spot price at expiry (S_T): 1.0800.*
- *FX price for a 3-month expiry forward contract $F(0, 3M)$: 1.0765.*
- *Long position: EUR call USD put strike $K = 1.0900$ expiring in 3 months.*
- *Short position: EUR put USD call strike $K = 1.0900$, expiring in 3 months, with a knock-in barrier at $B = 1.0000$.*

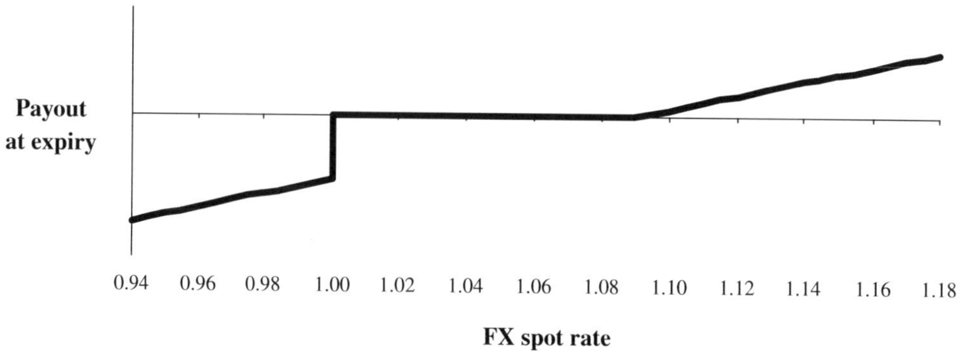

FIGURE 10.17 Payoff at expiry of a long knock-in forward

Figure 10.17 shows the payoff at expiry of the knock-out forward. The profile is flat at zero value in the range delimited by the strike price ($K = 1.0900$) and the knock-in barrier ($B = 1.0000$). For terminal FX spot values above the upper limit, the structure yields profits, whereas it suffers losses below the barrier level. In Figure 10.18, the profit and loss profile is shown for the hedged position: it is easy to see that the company takes advantage of downward FX spot movements in the range between the strike and the barrier, earning increasing profits up to the barrier level and then losing all gains below the barrier. In any case, the protection is guaranteed since for any other FX spot level a fixed and small cost is borne by the company.

10.7.5.3 Main Variations

- The knock-in forward can be designed so that the monitoring of the barrier level breaching is not continuous (i.e., at any time until expiry) but discrete according to a predefined schedule, similar to a knock-out forward. As an example, we may still consider, for the

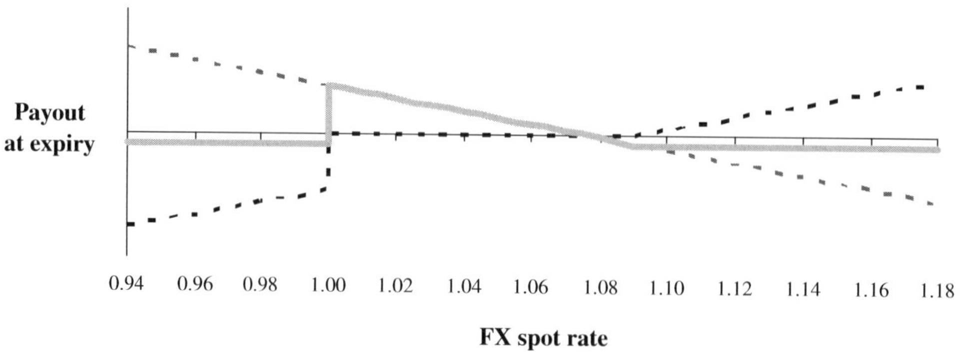

FIGURE 10.18 Payoff at expiry of an FX spot exposure of an exporting company hedged by a knock-in forward. Red dotted line: FX exposure. Blue dotted line: knock-in forward payoff. Green line: hedged position

FX spot rate against the euro, the daily European Central Bank fixing and monitor a long (short) position in the structure as follows:
- If the underlying FX spot rate is greater (lower) than the strike level $S_T > K$ ($S_T < K$), then the company buys (sells) the base currency notional amount at the strike level K.
- If the underlying FX spot rate is lower (greater) than the strike level $S_T < K$ ($S_T > K$) **and** the ECB37 fixing never prints below the barrier level B, any day up until the expiry, then the company buys (sells) the base currency notional amount at the terminal FX spot rate level S_T.
- If the underlying FX spot rate is lower (greater) than the strike level $S_T < K$ ($S_T > K$) **and** the ECB37 fixing prints below the barrier level B at least one day during the life of the contract, then the company buys (sells) the base currency notional amount at the strike level K.

- It is possible to monitor the barrier only at expiry, so that for a long (short) knock-in forward the following may occur on the expiry date:
  - If the underlying FX spot rate is greater (lower) than the strike level, $S_T > K$ ($S_T < K$), then the company buys (sells) the base currency notional amount at the strike level K.
  - If the underlying FX spot rate is lower (greater) than the strike level and greater (lower) than the barrier level $B < S_T < K$ ($K < S_T < B$), then the company buys (sells) the base currency notional amount at the terminal FX spot rate level S_T.
  - If the underlying FX spot rate is lower (greater) than the barrier level $S_T < B$ ($S_T > B$), then the company buys (sells) the base currency notional amount at the strike level K.

10.7.5.4 Pros and Cons

- The knock-out forward allows the company to keep open opportunities to gain profits from favourable movements in the FX spot rate.
- The structure may be traded at zero cost, though this is not necessarily required and the Company may also receive (or pay) a net premium.
- The main drawback of the knock-in forward is that the company has to accept a terminal FX spot rate worse than the forward price prevailing in the market at inception.

10.7.6 Knock-In Knock-out Forward

10.7.6.1 Description A long (short) position in a *knock-in knock-out forward* is attained by buying (selling) a base currency call option with a knock-out barrier B_1 above (below) the strike level K and by simultaneously selling a base currency put (call) option struck at the same level as before K, but with a knock-in barrier B_2 below (above) the strike level. Both options have the same expiry date and the same base currency notional amount.

At expiry the long (short) position in the structure will produce the following outcomes:

- If the underlying FX spot rate is greater (lower) than the strike level $S_T > K$ ($S_T < K$) **and** it never reaches the upper (lower) knock-out barrier level B_1 during the life of the contract, then the company buys (sells) the base currency notional amount at the strike rate level K.
- If the underlying FX spot rate is greater (lower) than the strike level $S_T > K$ ($S_T < K$) **and** it reaches at least once the upper (lower) knock-out barrier level B_1 any time during

the life of the contract, then the company buys (sells) the base currency notional amount at the terminal FX spot rate level S_T.

- If the underlying FX spot rate is lower (greater) than the strike level $S_T < K$ ($S_T > K$) **and** it never reaches the lower (upper) knock-in barrier level B_2 during the life of the contract, then the company buys (sells) the base currency notional amount at the terminal FX spot rate level S_T.
- If the underlying FX spot rate is lower (greater) than the strike level $S_T < K$ ($S_T > K$) **and** it reaches at least once the lower (upper) knock-in level barrier level B_2 any time during the life of the contract, then the company buys (sells) the base currency notional amount at the strike level K.

10.7.6.2 Needs the Structure Satisfies The knock-in knock-out forward is advisable for those companies that wish to hedge their FX exposures and at the same time keep open opportunities to gain from favourable movements up to the knock-in barrier level B_2. Different from the knock-in case, the knock-in knock-out forward does not necessarily force the company to accept a terminal FX rate worse than the forward rate available in the market at inception, but to counterbalance this benefit the knock-out feature will make the hedging ineffective if the level B_1 is breached.

Example 10.7.6 *An exporting company wishes to hedge its future FX exposure, short EUR against USD, in 3 months with a long position in a knock-in knock-out forward as follows.*

- *FX spot price at expiry (S_T): 1.0800.*
- *FX price for a 3-month expiry forward contract $F(0, 3M)$: 1.0765.*
- *Long position: EUR call USD put strike* $K = 1.0700$, *with a knock-out barrier* $B_1 = 1.1500$, *expiring in 3 months.*
- *Short position: EUR put USD call strike* $K = 1.0700$, *with a knock-in barrier* $B_2 = 1.0000$, *expiring in 3 months.*

Figure 10.19 shows the payoff at expiry of the knock-in knock-out forward: the profile is rather complex, being flat when the terminal FX spot rate is between the strike level $K = 1.0700$

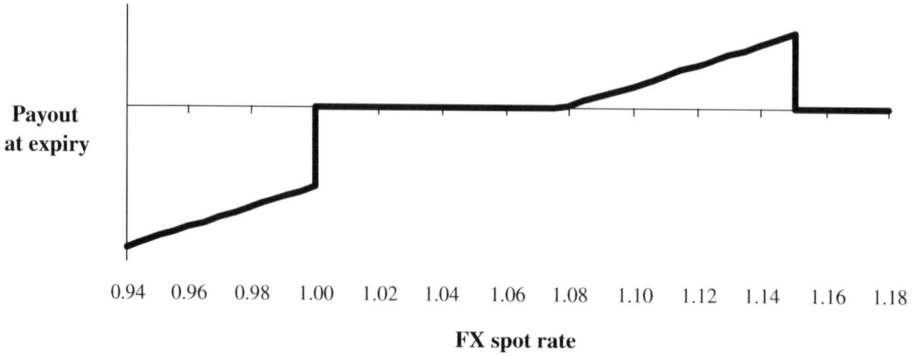

FIGURE 10.19 Payoff at expiry of a long knock-in knock-out forward

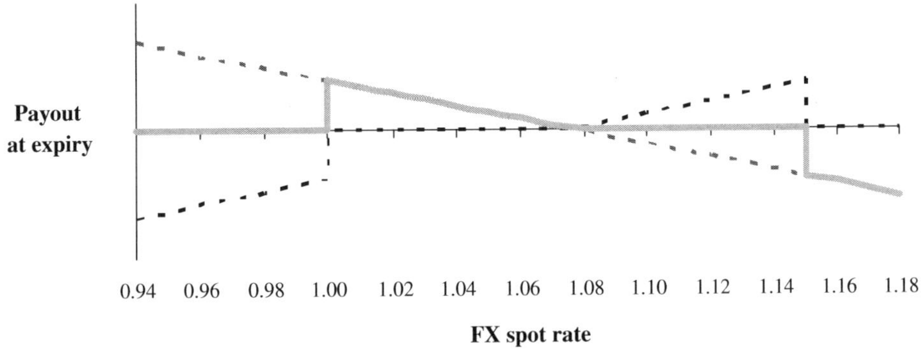

FIGURE 10.20 Payoff at expiry of an FX spot exposure of an exporting company hedged by a knock-in knock-out forward. Red dotted line: FX exposure. Blue dotted line: knock-in knock-out forward payoff. Green line: hedged position

and the knock-in barrier $B_2 = 1.0000$, *and positive between the strike level* $K = 1.0700$ *and the knock-out barrier* $B_2 = 1.1500$. *If the spot rate breaches the upper barrier, then the profit disappears, whereas below the knock-in barrier the structure suffers a sudden loss that increases as the FX spot rate declines. In Figure 10.20, the profit and loss profile of the hedged position similarly looks complex: the company takes advantage of downward FX spot movements in the range between the strike and the lower barrier, earning increasing profits up to the barrier level and then losing all gains below the barrier. In the region above the strike price, no profits and losses occur until the upper barrier is reached, then the hedged position starts losing money as a consequence of losing its hedging effectiveness.*

10.7.6.3 Main Variations

- The knock-in knock-out forward can be designed so that the monitoring of the barrier level breaching is not continuous (i.e., at any time until expiry) but discrete according to a predefined schedule, similar to the previous structures involving barrier options. As a common example we consider, for the FX spot rate against the euro, the daily European Central Bank fixing and monitor the long (short) position in the structure as follows:
  - If the underlying FX spot rate is greater (lower) than the strike level $S_T > K$ ($S_T < K$) **and** the ECB37 fixing never prints above (below) the knock-out barrier level B_1, any day up until expiry, then the company buys (sells) the base currency notional amount at the terminal FX spot rate level K.
  - If the underlying FX spot rate is greater (lower) than the strike level $S_T > K$ ($S_T < K$) **and** the ECB37 fixing prints above (below) the knock-out barrier at least one day during the life of the contract, then the company buys (sells) the base currency notional amount at the terminal FX spot rate level S_T.
  - If the underlying FX spot rate is lower (greater) than the strike level $S_T < K$ ($S_T > K$) **and** the ECB37 fixing never prints below the knock-in barrier level B_2, every day up until the expiry, then the company buys (sells) the base currency notional amount at the terminal FX spot rate level S_T.
  - If the underlying FX spot rate is lower (greater) than the strike level $S_T < K$ ($S_T > K$) **and** the ECB37 fixing prints below the knock-in barrier level B_2 at least one day during

the life of the contract, then the company buys (sells) the base currency notional amount at the strike level K.

- It is possible to monitor the barrier only at expiry, so for a long (short) knock-in knock-out forward the following may occur on the expiry date:
  - If the underlying FX spot rate is greater (lower) than the strike level $S_T > K$ ($S_T < K$), then the company buys (sells) the base currency notional amount at the strike level K.
  - If the underlying FX spot rate level is greater (lower) than the knock-out barrier level B_1, then the company buys (sells) the euro notional amount at the terminal FX spot rate level S_T.
  - If the underlying FX spot rate is lower (greater) than the strike level and greater (lower) than the barrier level $B_2 < S_T < K$ ($K < S_T < B_2$), then the company buys (sells) the base currency notional amount at the terminal FX spot rate level S_T.
  - If the underlying FX spot rate is lower (greater) than the knock-in barrier level $S_T < B_2$ ($S_T > B_2$), then the company buys (sells) the base currency notional amount at the strike level K.

10.7.6.4 Pros and Cons

- The knock-in knock-out forward allows the company to keep open opportunities to gain profits from favourable movements of the FX spot rate.
- The structure may be traded at zero cost.
- The strike price is not necessarily worse than the forward price dealing in the market at inception.
- The main drawback of the structure is that the company may lose the hedging of its FX exposure if the knock-out barrier is breached according to the monitoring schedule.

10.7.7 Resettable Forward

10.7.7.1 Description A long (short) position in a *resettable forward* is built by buying (selling) a base currency call option (put) and by simultaneously selling (buying) a base currency put (call) option, both struck at the same level K_1 and with a knock-out barrier B above (below) the strike level K_1. Additionally, the structure entails buying (selling) one more base currency call option (put) and simultaneously selling (buying) one more base currency put (call) option, both struck at the same level K_2 and with a knock-in barrier level equal to the previous knock-out one B. All options have the same expiry date and the same base currency notional amount.

The barrier level B is set at the same level so that, when breached, the structure as a whole is still alive with the strike price K_1 switching to K_2. More specifically, for a long position in a resettable forward we may have the following outcomes at expiry:

- If the underlying FX spot rate never breaches the upper (lower) barrier level B during the life of the contract, then the company buys (sells) the base currency notional amount at the strike rate level K_1.
- If the underlying FX spot rate reaches at least once the upper (lower) barrier level B any time during the life of the contract, then the company buys (sells) the base currency notional amount at the strike level K_2.

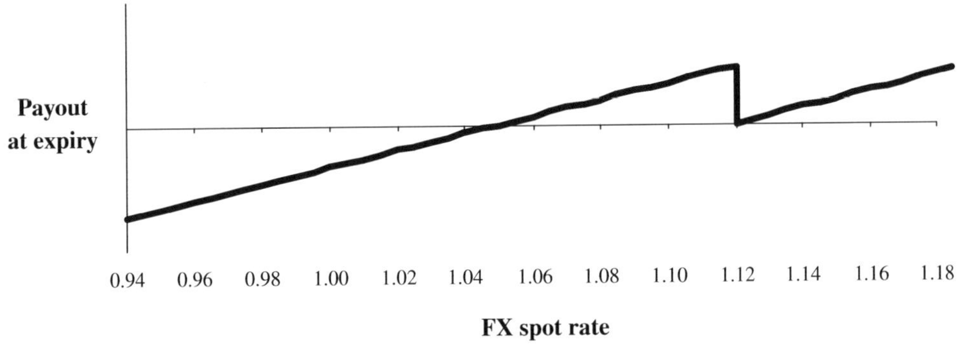

FIGURE 10.21 Payoff at expiry of a long resettable forward

10.7.7.2 Needs the Structure Satisfies The resettable forward is suitable for those companies that wish to improve their terminal spot rate with respect to the forward price prevailing in the market at the start of the contract. To achieve this result, they are willing to accept a worse terminal spot rate compared with the forward price if the FX spot rate touches the barrier level during the life of the contract.

Example 10.7.7 *An exporting company hedges its future FX exposure, short EUR against USD, in 3 months by a long position in a resettable forward as follows.*

- *FX spot price at expiry (S_T): 1.0800.*
- *FX price for a 3-month expiry forward contract $F(0, 3M)$: 1.0765.*
- *Long position: EUR call USD put strike $K_1 = 1.0500$, with a knock-out barrier $B_1 = 1.1200$, expiring in 3 months.*
- *Short position: EUR put USD call strike $K_1 = 1.0500$, with a knock-out barrier $B_1 = 1.1200$, expiring in 3 months.*
- *Long position: EUR call USD put strike $K_2 = 1.1000$, with a knock-in barrier $B_1 = 1.1200$, expiring in 3 months.*
- *Short position: EUR put USD call strike $K_2 = 1.1000$, with a knock-in barrier $B_1 = 1.1200$, expiring in 3 months.*

In Figure 10.21, we can see the payoff at expiry of the resettable forward: basically it is similar to a long position in EUR, with a 'restart' of the profits when the FX spot rate is above the barrier level $B = 1.1200$. This is reflected in a rather simple profit and loss profile of the hedged position, shown in Figure 10.22: a constant profit up to the barrier level and, for higher FX spot rate levels, a limited and constant loss.

10.7.7.3 Main Variations

- The resettable forward, like all other structures involving barrier options examined above, can be designed so that the monitoring of the barrier level breaching is not continuous (i.e., at any time until expiry) but discrete according to a predefined schedule, similar to before.

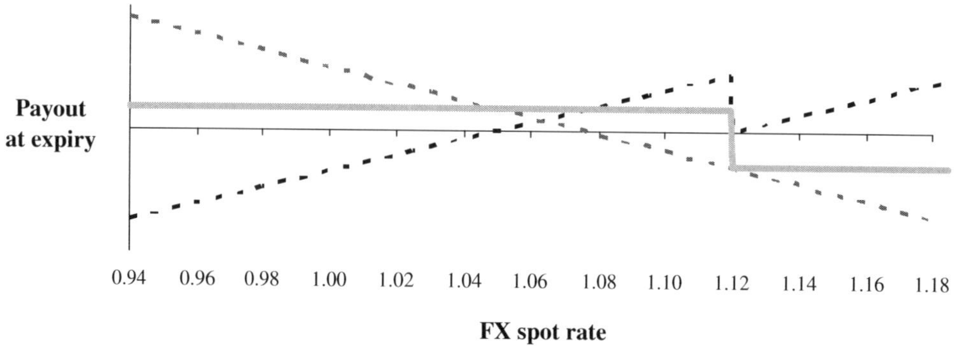

FIGURE 10.22 Payoff at expiry of an FX spot exposure of an exporting company hedged by a resettable forward. Red dotted line: FX exposure. Blue dotted line: resettable forward payoff. Green line: hedged position

For the FX spot rate against the euro, the typical option is to observe the daily European Central Bank fixing and monitor the long (short) position in the structure as follows:
- If the ECB37 fixing never prints above (below) the barrier level B, any day up until the expiry, then the company buys (sells) the base currency notional amount at the strike rate level K_1.
- If the ECB37 fixing prints above (below) the barrier at least one day during the life of the contract, then the company buys (sells) the base currency notional amount at the strike rate level K_2.

- It is possible to monitor the barrier only at expiry, so for a long (short) resettable forward the following may occur on the expiry date:
  - If the underlying FX spot rate is lower (greater) than the barrier level $S_T < B$ ($S_T > B$), then the company buys (sells) the base currency notional amount at the strike level K_1.
  - If the underlying FX spot rate level is greater (lower) than the barrier level $S_T > B$ ($S_T < B$), then the company buys (sells) the euro notional amount at the strike level K_2.

10.7.7.4 Pros and Cons

- The resettable forward allows the company to set a terminal FX rate better than the forward rate available at the inception of the contract.
- The main drawback is that the terminal rate worsens with respect to the forward rate if the barrier level is breached according to the monitoring schedule.
- Compared with other structures allowing for an improved terminal FX spot rate with respect to the forward, the resettable forward never loses its hedging effectiveness, even when the barrier is touched (although in this case the strike switches to a less favourable level).
- The structure can be traded at zero cost.

10.7.8 Range Resettable Forward

10.7.8.1 Description A long (short) position in a *range resettable forward* is set up by buying (selling) a base currency call (put) option and by simultaneously selling (buying) a base currency put (call) option, both struck at the same level as before (K_1) and with double knock-out barrier levels B_1 and B_2 above and below the strike level K_1. Additionally, the company should buy (sell) one more base currency call option (put) and it should simultaneously sell (buy) one more base currency put (call) option, both struck at the same level K_2 and with double knock-in barriers set at levels equal to the previous knock-out ones B_1 and B_2. All options have the same expiry date and the same base currency notional amount.

The barrier levels B_1 and B_2 are set at the same levels so that, when either of them is breached, the structure as a whole is still alive with the strike price K_1 switching to K_2. We have the following outcomes at expiry for a long position in a range resettable forward:

- If the underlying FX spot rate breaches neither the upper barrier B_1 nor the lower barrier B_2 during the life of the contract, then the company buys (sells) the base currency notional amount at the strike rate level K_1.
- If the underlying FX spot rate reaches at least once the upper barrier B_1 or the lower barrier B_2 any time during the life of the contract, then the company buys (sells) the base currency notional amount at the strike level K_2.

10.7.8.2 Needs the Structure Satisfies The range resettable forward is very similar to the resettable forward and so it is recommended for those companies that wish to improve the terminal spot rate with respect to the forward price prevailing in the market at the start of the contract. Also in this case, this result implies that the company will trade at a worse terminal spot rate compared with the forward price if the FX spot rate touches one of the barrier levels during the life of the contract.

Example 10.7.8 *We consider the case of an exporting company wishing to hedge its future FX exposure, short EUR against USD, in 3 months with a long position in a range resettable forward as follows.*

- *FX spot price at expiry (S_T): 1.0800.*
- *FX price for a 3-month expiry forward contract $F(0, 3M)$: 1.0765.*
- *Long position: EUR call USD put strike $K_1 = 1.0400$, with double knock-out barriers $B_1 = 1.0000$ and $B_2 = 1.1200$, expiring in 3 months.*
- *Short position: EUR put USD call strike $K_1 = 1.0400$, with double knock-out barriers $B_1 = 1.0000$ and $B_2 = 1.1200$, expiring in 3 months.*
- *Long position: EUR call USD put strike $K_2 = 1.1100$, with double knock-in barriers $B_1 = 1.0000$ and $B_2 = 1.1200$, expiring in 3 months.*
- *Short position: EUR put USD call strike $K_2 = 1.1100$, with double knock-out barriers $B_1 = 1.0000$ and $B_2 = 1.1200$, expiring in 3 months.*

Figure 10.23 shows the payoff at expiry of the range resettable forward: it is similar to a long position in a resettable forward, with the only difference that losses are generally lower between the strike price K_1 and the lower barrier B_1. Profits are zeroed when the FX spot rate is above the upper barrier level $B_2 = 1.1200$, then they start to increase with higher levels of the terminal spot rate S_T. The profit and loss profile of the hedged position, shown in Figure 10.24, is very simple to interpret: a limited constant gain within the range delimited by the two barrier levels and a limited constant loss outside the same range.

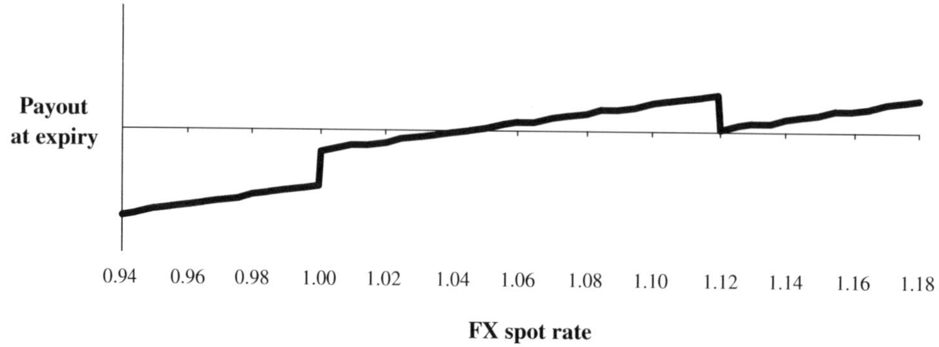

FIGURE 10.23 Payoff at expiry of a long range resettable forward

10.7.8.3 Main Variations

- The monitoring of the barrier levels breaching can be continuous (i.e., they can be touched at any time until expiry) or discrete according to a predefined schedule. For the FX spot rate against the euro, the monitoring frequency can be daily and linked to the European Central Bank fixing; in this case a long (short) position in the structure produces the following outcomes.
  - If the ECB37 fixing never prints above the upper barrier B_1 or below the lower barrier B_2, any day up until the expiry, then the company buys (sells) the base currency notional amount at the strike rate level K_1.
  - If the ECB37 fixing prints above the upper barrier B_1 or below the lower barrier B_2 at least one day during the life of the contract, then the company buys (sells) the base currency notional amount at the strike rate level K_2.
- It is possible to monitor the barrier only at expiry, so for a long (short) range resettable forward we have the following on the expiry date:
  - If the underlying FX spot rate is within the range delimited by the two barrier levels $B_2 < S_T < B_1$, then the company buys (sells) the base currency notional amount at the strike level K_1.

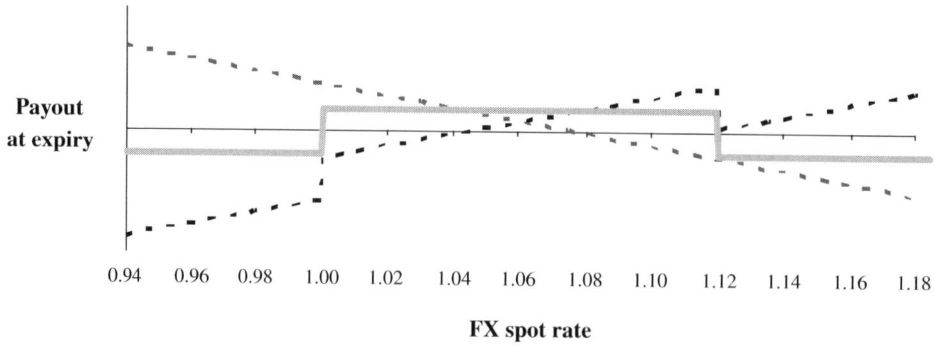

FIGURE 10.24 Payoff at expiry of an FX spot exposure of an exporting company hedged by a resettable forward. Red dotted line: FX exposure. Blue dotted line: range resettable payoff. Green line: hedged position

– If the underlying FX spot rate level is outside the range delimited by the two barrier levels, $S_T > B_1$ or $S_T < B_2$, then the company buys (sells) the euro notional amount at the strike level K_2.

10.7.8.4 Pros and Cons

- The range resettable forward allows the company to set a terminal FX rate better than the forward rate available at the inception of the contract.
- One of the drawbacks is that the terminal rate worsens with respect to the forward rate if one of the barrier levels is breached according to the monitoring schedule.
- Compared with a resettable forward, the range resettable forward improves the terminal FX spot rate more since there are two barriers triggering the switch of the strike price and hence a greater probability of trading at the expiry date at a level worse than the forward rate available at inception.
- The structure can be traded at zero cost.

REFERENCES

Abramowitz, M. and Stegun, I.A. (1972) *Handbook of Mathematical Functions*, National Bureau of Standards, Applied Mathematics Series No. 55, 10th edition.

Black, F. and Scholes, M. (1973) The pricing of options and corporate liabilities, *Journal of Political Economy*, **81**, 637–654.

Castagna, A. (2010) *FX Options and Volatility Smile*, John Wiley & Sons, New York.

Garman, M.B. and Kohlhagen, S.W. (1983) Foreign currency option values, *Journal of International Money and Finance*, **2**, 231–237.

Merton, R.C. (1973) Theory of rational option pricing, *Bell Journal of Economics and Management Science*, **1**(4), 141–183.

Part Two

Quantitative Topics

CHAPTER 11

An Introduction to Stochastic Calculus with Matlab® Examples

Laura Ballotta and Gianluca Fusai

Given the technical nature of the quantitative applications covered in Part II, we open with a comprehensive introduction to stochastic calculus. Readers who are competent in stochastic calculus are encouraged to proceed and explore the chapters that follow. Those less competent with stochastic calculus will find this chapter beneficial before progressing.

The aims of this chapter are:

1. To introduce the concept of Brownian motion.
   - What are $W(t)$ and $dW(t)$?
   - What are the properties of $W(t)$?
2. To explain the meaning of the stochastic differential equation

$$dX = \mu(X,t)dt + \sigma(X,t)dW(t).$$

3. To explain the meaning of the stochastic integral. For example:
   - To give meaning to

$$X(t) = X(0) + \int_0^t \mu(X_s, s)ds + \int_0^t \sigma(X_s, s)dW_s.$$

   - The properties of $X(t)$: distribution, expected value, variance.
   - How to construct a (continuous) martingale.
4. To explain Itô's formula.
   - For example, how to relate

$$dS = \mu S dt + \sigma S dW$$

to

$$d\ln S = \left(\mu - \frac{\sigma^2}{2}\right)dt + \sigma dW.$$

Handbook of Multi-Commodity Markets and Products: Structuring, Trading and Risk Management. Edited by Andrea Roncoroni, Gianluca Fusai and Mark Cummins.

5. Examples of common stochastic differential equations:
   - arithmetic Brownian motion;
   - geometric Brownian motion;
   - mean-reverting Gaussian model (Vasicek);
   - mean-reverting square-root model (CIR);
   - constant elasticity of variance model (CEV);
   - stochastic volatility model (Heston).
6. Examples of jump processes:
   - Poisson process;
   - Poisson compound process;
   - Gamma process;
   - jump diffusion process (Merton);
   - jump diffusion process (Kou double exponential);
   - time changed Brownian motion (variance Gamma model)

11.1 BROWNIAN MOTION

In this section we define Brownian motion (BM) and present its main properties. Let us recall that a stochastic process (s.p.) is a family of indexed random variables (r.v.'s). Usually, but not necessarily, the index refers to time. If we use the time index, as we will do, this means that at each instant of time (if the stochastic process is continuous in time) or at discrete times (if the stochastic process is discrete in time) we have to draw a r.v. Once we have extracted them, we observe a path or a trajectory of the s.p. We also remark that to fully characterize the s.p., we have to specify the distribution of the r.v.'s at different times as well as their time-dependence properties, that is how the r.v. that will be extracted in 1 month will affect the value of the r.v. that will be extracted in 2 months. The simplest process in continuous time is Brownian motion. We start by considering this process.

A comprehensive introduction to the BM, SDEs and their properties with a range of financial applications can be found in Stochastic Calculus for Finance II by Shreve.

11.1.1 Defining Brownian Motion

Fact 11.1.1 (Brownian Motion) *The stochastic process* $W := \{W(t) : t \geq 0\}$ *is called* Brownian motion *if:*

(i) $W(0) = 0$.

(ii) For $s \leq t$, $W(t) - W(s)$ *is independent of the past history of* W *until time* s, *that is the Brownian motion has increments which are independent of the* σ*-field* $\mathcal{F}(s)$ *generated by the process up to time* s.

(iii) For $0 \leq s \leq t$, $W(t) - W(s)$ *and* $W(t-s)$ *have the same distribution, which is Gaussian with mean zero and variance* $(t-s)$, *that is*

$$W(t) - W(s) \sim W(t-s) \sim \mathcal{N}(0, t-s).$$

Hence, the Brownian motion has stationary increments.

(iv) W *has continuous sample paths:* $W(t)$, $t \geq 0$ *is a continuous function of* t *(a.s.).*

11.1.1.1 The Odd Properties of Brownian Motion

- $W(t)$ is continuous in t (by definition), that is its trajectories do not show sudden jumps.
- $W(t)$ is not monotone in any interval, no matter how small the interval is (like in a fractal structure). This property means that, even over very small time intervals, we cannot say if the BM is increasing or decreasing.
- $W(t)$ is nowhere differentiable. This property means that we cannot predict what the change in BM will be over the next time interval.
- $W(t)$ is a process of unbounded variation, that is the length of its path is infinity. This property is a consequence of the two previous properties. BM paths are so irregular that if you try to measure their length you do not obtain a finite measure.
- $W(t)$ is a process of bounded quadratic variation. Quadratic variation, as we will see shortly, is a measure of the volatility of the process. Therefore, even being a very irregular process, BM at each finite time has a finite volatility.
- Brownian motion has the Markov property. In practice, this means the process does not remember how it got to the current state.
- $\mathbb{E}(W(t)W(s)) = \min(s,t)$. This property, discussed later, is telling us that the time dependence of the Brownian motion depends on what happened up to $\min(s,t)$.
- The BM will eventually hit any and every real value no matter how large, or small. The BM paths are so dispersed that the BM can reach any desired level in finite time with positive probability.
- Once a BM hits a value, it immediately hits it again infinitely often.

11.1.1.2 Density of Brownian Motion at Different Time Horizons

Fact 11.1.2 (Density Function of Brownian Motion) *We have:*

$$W(t) - W(s) \sim \mathcal{N}(0, t-s).$$

Therefore, the density function of the increment of the BM between time s and time t is

$$\phi_{0,\sqrt{t-s}}(x) = \frac{1}{\sqrt{2\pi(t-s)}} \exp\left(-\frac{1}{2}\left(\frac{x}{\sqrt{t-s}}\right)^2\right), x \in \Re.$$

Remark 11.1.1 *We observe that $W(t) = W(t) - W(0)$, from which it follows that $W(t) \sim \mathcal{N}(0,t)$. The dispersion of the BM, as measured by the variance, increases with the time horizon $t-s$. This is shown in Figure 11.1.*

11.1.1.3 The (Auto)-Covariance Function

- The (auto)-covariance function of a stochastic process X having expectation μ_X is defined as

$$c_X(t,s) = cov(X_t, X_s) = E((X_t - \mu_X(t))(X_s - \mu_X(s))), t, s \in T.$$

- The variance function of X is just $c_X(t,t)$.

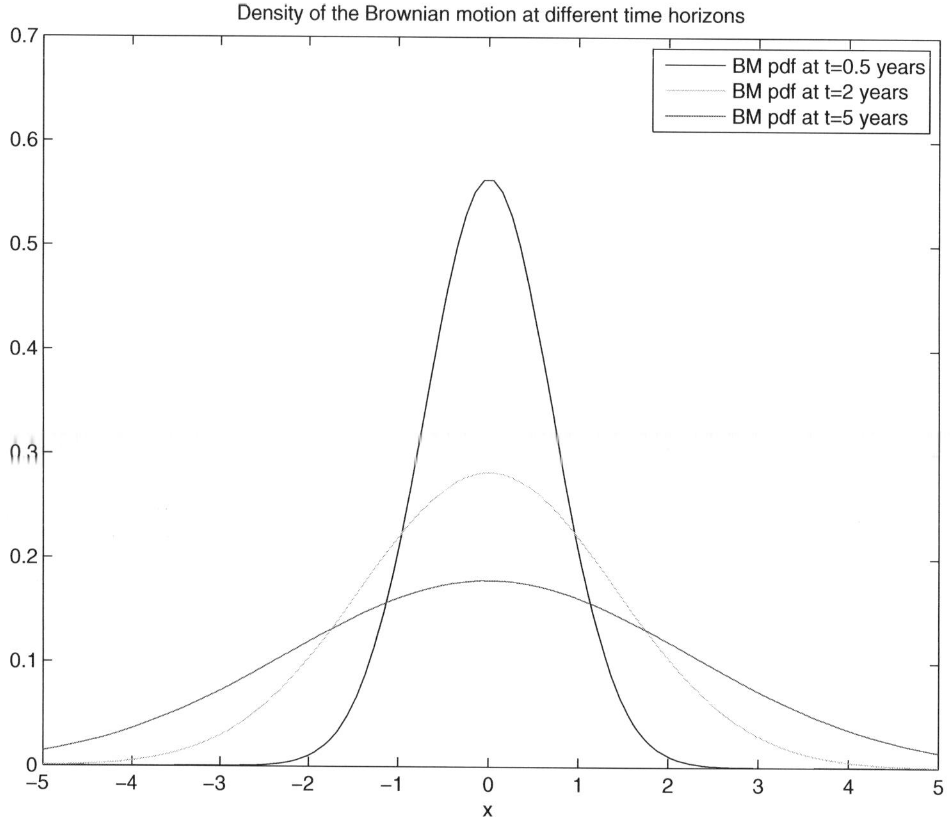

FIGURE 11.1 Density of Brownian motion at different time horizons.

Fact 11.1.3 (Covariance Function of Brownian Motion) *A Brownian motion has covariance function given by*

$$c_W(t,s) = min(t,s).$$

Proof: The (auto)-covariance function of the BM

- Let us consider two time instants, t and s, $t < s$. We have

$$\begin{aligned} c_W(t,s) &= cov(W(t), W(s)) \\ &= cov(W(t), (W(s) - W(t)) + W(t)) \\ &= cov(W(t), (W(s) - W(t))) + cov(W(t), W(t)) \\ &= 0 + c_W(t,t) \\ &= t. \end{aligned}$$

- With a similar reasoning, if we take t and s with $s < t$, we have

$$c_W(t,s) = s.$$

- Therefore

$$c_W(t,s) = min(t,s).$$

11.1.1.4 Martingale Property

Remark 11.1.2 *A stochastic process $X = (X(t) : t \geq 0)$ is a martingale relative to the probability measure $\mathbb{P}$ if the following conditions are satisfied:*

(i) $\mathbb{E}|X(t)| < \infty$ *for all* $t \geq 0$;
(ii) $\mathbb{E}[X(t)|\mathcal{F}(s)] = X(s)$ *for all* $s \leq t$.

- In other words, a martingale is a random process whose future variations are completely unpredictable given the current information set.
- For this reason, the best forecast of the change in X over an arbitrary interval is zero, that is $\mathbb{E}[X(t) - X(s)|\mathcal{F}(s)] = 0$.
- A martingale represents a fair game: given the knowledge we have, on average the return produced by the bet is what we invested in it.

Fact 11.1.4 (Martingale Property) *The Brownian motion is a martingale.*

Proof: The martingale property of the BM We check that the Brownian motion satisfies the two properties of a martingale process. Hence:

- For the first property, direct calculations show that

$$\begin{aligned}\mathbb{E}|W(t)| &= \int_{-\infty}^{0} \frac{-y}{\sqrt{2\pi t}} \exp\left(-\frac{1}{2}\left(\frac{y}{\sqrt{t}}\right)^2\right) dy + \int_{0}^{\infty} \frac{z}{\sqrt{2\pi t}} \exp\left(-\frac{1}{2}\left(\frac{z}{\sqrt{t}}\right)^2\right) dz \\ &= 2\int_{0}^{\infty} \frac{z}{\sqrt{2\pi t}} \exp\left(-\frac{1}{2}\left(\frac{z}{\sqrt{t}}\right)^2\right) dz \\ &= \sqrt{\frac{2t}{\pi}} < \infty.\end{aligned}$$

- Let us consider two time instants, s and t, $s < t$. We have

$$\mathbb{E}[W(t)|\mathcal{F}(s)] = \mathbb{E}[W(t) - W(s) + W(s)|\mathcal{F}(s)] = \mathbb{E}[W(t) - W(s)] + W(s) = W(s).$$

11.1.1.5 Markov Property

Remark 11.1.3 *Let $\mathcal{F}(t)$ denote the σ-field generated by the process up to time t. The process $\{X\}_{t\geq 0}$ has the Markov property if, for $t \geq s$, the conditional distribution of $X(t)$ given $\mathcal{F}(s)$ is the same as the conditional distribution of $X(t)$ given $X(s)$:*

$$P(X(t) \leq y|\mathcal{F}(s)) = P(X(t) \leq y|X(s)), \quad a.s.$$

- In practice, this means the process does not remember how it got to the current state x.

Fact 11.1.5 (Markov Property) *Brownian motion has the Markov property.*

- This property is also important for simulating Brownian motion, because we can iteratively add to the last simulated value of the Brownian motion a new simulated increment. The increment of the BM in the time interval $(t, t+dt)$ does not depend on the past history up to t. Therefore, the value of the process at time $t+dt$ will be given by the value up to time t plus the independent increment in $(t, t+dt)$.

11.1.1.6 Simulation of Brownian Sample Paths In order to simulate a Brownian motion sample path $W(t)$ on the interval $[0, T]$:

1. Choose an integer n and let $\Delta t = \frac{T}{n}$, so that $t_i = i\Delta t$, for $i = 0, 1, \ldots, n$.
2. Generate a sequence $\varepsilon_1, \ldots, \varepsilon_n$ of i.i.d. standard normal r.v.'s
   (a) Generate a sequence $U_1, \ldots, U_n$ of uniform r.v.'s in the interval $(0, 1)$.
   (b) Set $\varepsilon_i = \Phi^{-1}(U_i)$, where $\Phi^{-1}(x)$ is the inverse cumulative distribution of the standard Gaussian distribution.
   (c) Set $dW_i = \varepsilon_i\sqrt{\Delta t}$.
3. Finally recursively construct the sample path of the BM letting
   - $W(0) = 0$,
   - $W(t_i) = W(t_{i-1}) + dW_i, \quad i = 1, \ldots, n.$

Remark 11.1.4 *Notice that the simulation of the BM as described above is convenient if you are using a spreadsheet or programming language like C, VBA. This is illustrated in Figure 11.2. If you are using Matlab a different approach, avoiding cycles, is preferred, see Figure 11.3 and the accompanying code.*

Simulating a Brownian motion path

	A	B	C	D	E
2	dt	0.004	This cell has been named dt		
3	Time	U(0,1)	N(0, 1)	dW(t)	W(t)
4	0				0
5	0.004	0.170564	-0.95194	-0.06021	-0.06021
6	0.008	0.16364	-0.97961	-0.06196	-0.12216
7	0.012	0.441049	-0.14831	-0.00938	-0.13154
8	0.016	0.112407	-1.21383	-0.07677	-0.20831
9	0.02	0.536748	0.092245	0.005834	-0.20248
10	0.024	0.965861	1.823174	0.115308	-0.08717
11	0.028	0.882031	1.185202	0.074959	-0.01221
12	0.032	0.603845	0.263312	0.016653	0.004443
13	0.036	0.218079	-0.7787	-0.04925	-0.04481
14	0.04	0.407958	-0.2328	-0.01472	-0.05953
15	0.044	0.458369	-0.10454	-0.00661	-0.06614
16	0.048	0.042483	-1.72258	-0.10895	-0.17509
17	0.052	0.838807	0.989568	0.062586	-0.1125
18	0.056	0.960449	1.755922	0.111054	-0.00145
19	0.06	0.239008	-0.7095	-0.04487	-0.04632
20	0.064	0.633115	0.340114	0.021511	-0.02481
21	0.068	0.839474	0.992299	0.062759	0.03795
22	0.072	0.063243	-1.52811	-0.09665	-0.0587
23	0.076	0.844169	1.011739	0.063988	0.005292
24	0.08	0.104906	-1.25408	-0.07932	-0.07402
25	0.084	0.784708	0.788192	0.04985	-0.02417
26	0.088	0.483031	-0.04255	-0.00269	-0.02686
27	0.092	0.78869	0.801885	0.050716	0.023851
28	0.096	0.276293	-0.59389	-0.03756	-0.01371
29	0.1	0.911414	1.349517	0.085351	0.071641

G	H	I	J	K
Time	U(0,1)	N(0, 1)	dW(t)	W(t)
=A4+dt	=RAND()	=NORM.S.INV(B5)	=C5*dt^0.5	=E4+D5
=A5+dt	=RAND()	=NORM.S.INV(B6)	=C6*dt^0.5	=E5+D6
=A6+dt	=RAND()	=NORM.S.INV(B7)	=C7*dt^0.5	=E6+D7
=A7+dt	=RAND()	=NORM.S.INV(B8)	=C8*dt^0.5	=E7+D8
=A8+dt	=RAND()	=NORM.S.INV(B9)	=C9*dt^0.5	=E8+D9
=A9+dt	=RAND()	=NORM.S.INV(B10)	=C10*dt^0.5	=E9+D10
=A10+dt	=RAND()	=NORM.S.INV(B11)	=C11*dt^0.5	=E10+D11
=A11+dt	=RAND()	=NORM.S.INV(B12)	=C12*dt^0.5	=E11+D12

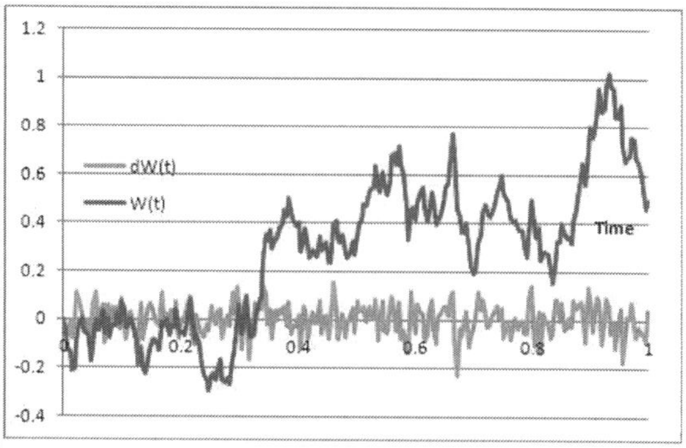

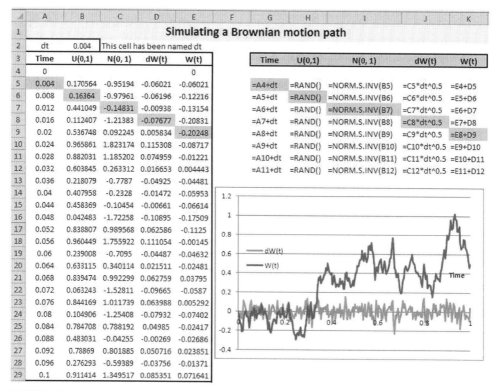

FIGURE 11.2 Simulating the Brownian motion: Excel example.

Matlab Code

```
%%%%%%%%%%%%%%%%%%%%%%%%%%%%%%%%%%%%%%%%%%%%%
%%%%SIMULATING THE BROWNIAN MOTIONS%%%%%%%%
%%%%%%%%%%%%%%%%%%%%%%%%%%%%%%%%%%%%%%%%%%%%%
nsimul=500; %Assigning the number of simulated paths
%time to maturity (expiry), number of steps,
%time step (dt) and observation times (timestep)
expiry=1, nsteps=250;
dt=expiry/nsteps; timestep=[0:dt:expiry]';
%Simulate increments of the BM setting:
dw=randn(nsteps,nsimul) * dt0.5;
%Simulate Wiener process:
%(use cumulative sum of the increments):
cdW=[zeros(1,nsimul); cumsum(dw)];
%Plot simulated paths:
h=figure('Color', [ 1 1 1]); plot(timestep, cdW)
title('Simulated Paths of the Wiener Process');
xlabel('Time (years)')
%print the figure
print(h,'-dpng','FigBMPaths.jpg')
```

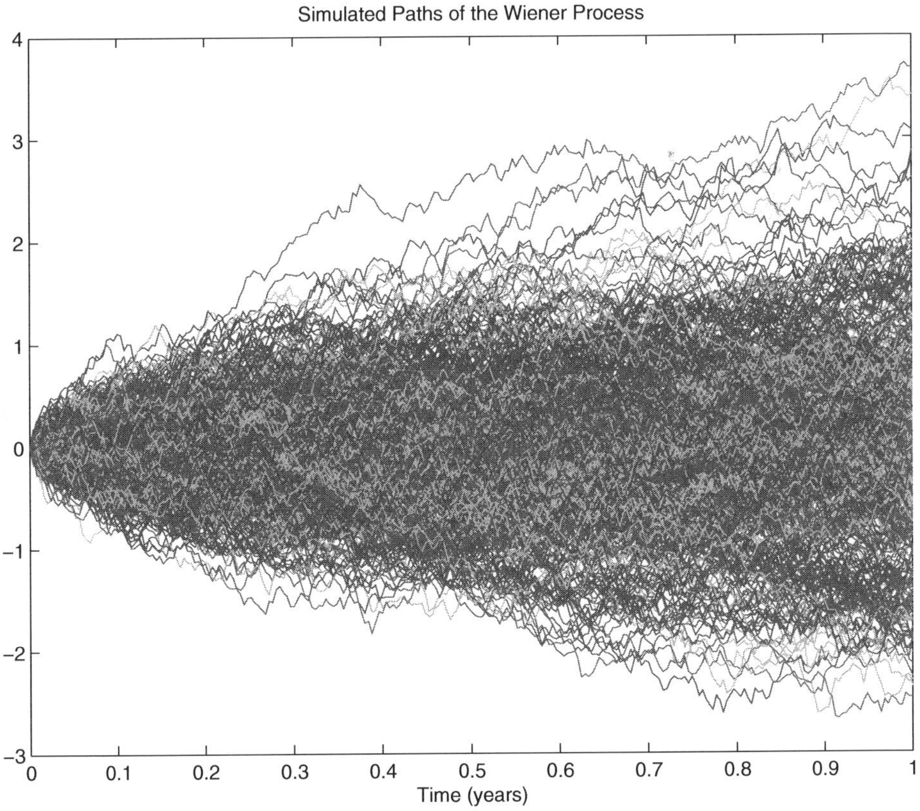

FIGURE 11.3 Simulated paths of the Brownian motion.

11.1.1.7 Total Variation

- Given a partition of the interval $[x_0, x_n]$, the variation of a function $f(x)$ measures the total amount of up and down motion:

$$TV(f) = \sum_{i=0}^{N} |f(x_i) - f(x_{i-1})|.$$

- The notion of unbounded variation plays an important role in stochastic calculus since continuous stochastic processes used to represent asset prices have trajectories with unbounded variation, that is they are very irregular.
- Heuristically, functions of bounded variation are not excessively irregular. In fact, any smooth function will be of bounded variation.

Fact 11.1.6 (Total Variation of Brownian Motion) *The Brownian motion has unbounded total variation, that is*

$$TV(W) = \sum_{i=1}^{N} |\Delta W(t_i)| \to +\infty$$

as $N \to +\infty$, *where* $t_0, t_1, ..., t_N$ *represent a discrete partition of the interval* $[0, t]$.

11.1.1.8 Quadratic Variation

- Quadratic variation is a measure of volatility.
- Given a partition of the interval $[t_0, t_n]$, the quadratic variation of a function $f(t)$ is given by

$$QV(f) = \sum_{i=0}^{N} (f(t_i) - f(t_{i-1}))^2.$$

- QV plays a major role in stochastic calculus, but is hardly ever met in standard calculus due to the fact that smooth functions have zero quadratic variation. This makes sense if QV is a measure of volatility.
- For example, if we consider a continuously differentiable function, QV is zero. The function $X(t) = at$ has QV equal to $\sum_{i=1}^{N} (a\Delta t_i)^2 = a^2 N \Delta t^2 = a^2 N \left(\frac{t}{N}\right)^2 \to 0$ as $N \to \infty$.

Fact 11.1.7 (Quadratic Variation of Brownian Motion) *The quadratic variation of BM over the time interval* $[0, t]$ *tends to* t*:*

$$QV(W) = \sum_{i=1}^{N} (\Delta W(t_i))^2 \to t$$

as $N \to +\infty$, *where* $t_0, t_1, ..., t_N$ *represent a discrete partition of the interval* $[0, t]$.

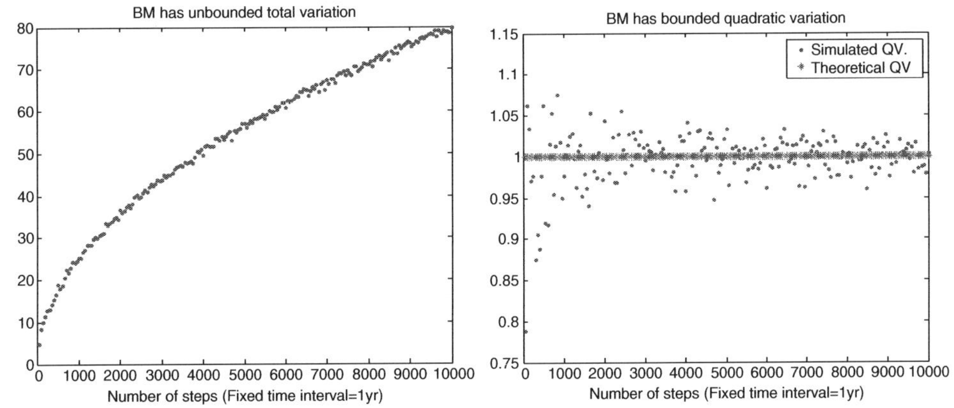

FIGURE 11.4 Total variation (left) and quadratic variation (right) of the BM.

Simulating the Total Variation and Quadratic Variation of BM

- Figure 11.4 illustrates, by simulation, that:
  - The total variation of the BM grows without limits as we refine the partition of the interval (0,1) (left panel).
  - The quadratic variation converges to the length of the interval as we refine the partition of the interval (0,1) (right panel).
- The Matlab code to generate Figure 11.4 is as follows.

Matlab Code

```
%%%%%%%%%%%%%%%%%%%%%%%%%%%%%%%%%%%%%%%%%%%%%%%%%%%%%%%%%%%%%%%%%%%
%%%%COMPUTING BY SIMULATION TOTAL VARIATION        %%%%%%%%%%%%%%%%%%%
%%%%AND QUADRATIC VARIATION OF THE BM                  %%%%%%%%%%%%%%%
%%%%%%%%%%%%%%%%%%%%%%%%%%%%%%%%%%%%%%%%%%%%%%%%%%%%%%%%%%%%%%%%%%%
clear all;
i=1; expiry=1;
for jstep=50:50:10000   %increase the number of steps (refine the partition)
    dt=expiry/jstep;    %reduce the time step
    dW=[zeros(1,nsimul); randn(jstep,1)*dt^0.5];    %simulate BM
    TV(i)=sum(abs(dW));     %compute total variation
    QV(i)=sum(dW.^2);           %compute quadratic variation
    i=i+1;
end
h = figure('Color',[1 1 1]);
plot([50:50:10000], TV,'.')
title('BM has unbounded total variation'); xlabel('Number of steps (Fixed
time interval=1yr)')

h = figure('Color',[1 1 1]);
plot([50:50:10000], QV,'.',[50:50:10000], expiry,'*')
legend('Simulated QV', 'Theoretical QV')
title('BM has bounded quadratic variation'); xlabel('Number of steps (Fixed
time interval=1yr)')
```

TABLE 11.1 The cell contents represent the product of the quantities appearing in the first row and in the first column. We have set equal to 0 the quantities that are of order $dt^n, n > 1$

$\times$	dt	$dW(t)$
dt	0	0
$dW(t)$	0	dt

11.1.1.9 Properties of the Increments of BM In the following we set equal to 0 quantities that are $o(dt)$, that is go to zero faster than dt:

1. $dW(t) = \mathcal{N}(0, dt)$ (by definition);
2. $\mathbb{E}_t(dW(t)) = 0$ (by definition);
3. $\mathbb{E}_t(dW(t)dt) = 0$ (by the linearity of the expectation);
4. $\mathbb{E}_t(dW^2(t)) = dt$ (this is the second moment of the increment of the BM, that is Gaussian);
5. $\mathbb{V}ar_t(dW^2(t)) = \mathbb{E}_t(dW^4(t)) - \mathbb{E}_t(dW^2(t))^2 = 3dt^2 - dt^2 = o(dt)$ (by the normality of dW);
6. $dW^2(t) = dt$ (this follows by (4) and (5));
7. $\mathbb{E}_t((dW(t)dt)^2) = \mathbb{E}_t(dW^2(t))dt^2 = dt^3 = o(dt)$ (this follows by (4));
8. $\mathbb{V}ar_t(dW(t)dt) = \mathbb{E}_t((dW(t)dt)^2) - \mathbb{E}_t((dW(t)dt))^2 = \mathbb{E}_t(dW^2(t))dt^2 - o(dt) = o(dt)$;
9. $dW(t)dt = o(dt)$ (this follows by (3) and (8)).
10. We can synthetize the above results using Table 11.1

11.2 THE STOCHASTIC INTEGRAL AND STOCHASTIC DIFFERENTIAL EQUATIONS

11.2.1 Introduction

- The Itô or stochastic integral is one way of defining sums of uncountable and unpredictable random increments over time:

$$\underbrace{\int_0^T \sigma(X(s), s)dW(s)}_{\text{sum of i.i.d. noises}} \approx \sum_{j=0}^{n-1} \underbrace{\sigma(X(t_j), t_j)}_{\text{vol scaling factor in } t_j} \underbrace{[W(t_{j+1}) - W(t_j)]}_{\text{noise in } [t_j, t_{j+1}]}.$$

- Recall that the sample paths of BM are nowhere differentiable and have unbounded variation.
- This has major consequences for the definition of a stochastic integral with respect to Brownian sample paths.

Fact 11.2.1 (Problem in Defining the Stochastic Integral) *If $\int_0^T f(s)dg(s)$ exists as a Riemann–Stieltjes integral for all continuous functions f on $[0, T]$, then g necessarily has bounded variation. Unfortunately, the BM has unbounded variation.*

11.2.2 Defining the Stochastic Integral

- The last observation tells us that if our aim is to define the stochastic integral $\int_0^T f(s)dW(s)$ for all continuous deterministic functions f on $[0, T]$, the pathwise integration suggested by the Riemann–Stieltjes integral approach fails since it does not allow the integration of a large class of integrable functions f.
- We will define the integral as a probabilistic average. This will lead us to the so-called Itô stochastic integral.
- We define the Itô stochastic integral as a mean square limit of suitable Riemann–Stieltjes sums. This is equivalent to saying that the variance of the random error $\varepsilon_n = X_n - X$ goes to zero as we refine the partition.
- This has the disadvantage that we lose the intuitive interpretation of an integral which is naturally provided by a pathwise integral.

Definition 11.2.1 (Mean Square Convergence) *Let us consider a sequence of random numbers $X_1, X_2, \ldots, X_n$, with $X_n \in L^2$, that is $\mathbb{E}(X_n^2) < \infty$. We say that the sequence of r.v. X_n converges in mean square to the random variable X, and we write $X_n L^2. \to X$ iff $\lim_{n\to\infty} \mathbb{E}(| X_n - X |^2) = 0$.*

11.2.3 The Itô Stochastic Integral as a Mean Square Limit of Suitable Riemann–Stieltjes Sums

- Let:

  1. $\sigma(u)$ be an adapted process, that is $\sigma(u)$ is known once we know the whole history of the Brownian motion up to time t;
  2. $\sigma(u)$ be square integrable, that is $E(\int_0^T \sigma^2(u)du) < \infty$.

- Then the following limit:[1]

$$\lim_{\|\Pi\|\to 0} \sum_{j=1}^{n} \sigma(t_{j-1})[W(t_j) - W(t_{j-1})] = I_\sigma(0, T)$$

  exists (in the mean square sense) and is independent of the partitions used to take the limit.
- By definition, this limit is the Itô integral of σ with respect to BM over $[0, T]$.

Example 11.2.1 *Let us consider the Itô integral of the identity function with respect to BM over $[0, T]$. Given a partition $\tau_n = 0 = t_0 < t_1 < \ldots < t_{n-1} < t_n = t$, we define the Riemann–Stieltjes sums*

$$S_n = \sum_{j=1}^{n} (W(t_j) - W(t_{j-1})).$$

[1] In the limit here, the notation $\| \Pi \| \to 0$ means that we are refining more the partition of the interval $(0, T)$.

As S_n is a telescopic sum, then $S_n = W(T)$ and therefore

$$\int_0^T dW(u) = W(T) - W(0) = W(T).$$

11.2.4 A Motivating Example: Computing $\int_0^t W(s)dW(s)$

- Given a partition $\tau_n = 0 = t_0 < t_1 < ... < t_{n-1} < t_n = t$, let us define the Riemann–Stieltjes sums

$$S_n = \sum_{j=1}^{n} W(t_{j-1})(W(t_j) - W(t_{j-1})).$$

- Using the binomial formula for $(W(t_j) - W(t_{j-1}))^2$, S_n can be written as

$$S_n = \frac{W^2(t)}{2} - \frac{1}{2}\sum_{i=1}^{n}(W(t_j) - W(t_{j-1}))^2 = \frac{W(t)}{2} - \frac{1}{2}QV_n(W)(t).$$

- But if we refine the partition τ_n, then $QV_n(W)(t) \to t$, so that

$$\mathbb{V}ar\left(S_n - \frac{W^2(t) - t}{2}\right) \to 0,$$

that is S_n converges in mean square to $\frac{W^2(t)-t}{2}$, which we can take as the value of the integral $\int_0^t W(s)dW(s)$.

11.2.4.1 Example: Computing $\int_0^t W(s)dW(s)$ by Simulation

The following code illustrates the one-to-one relationship between $\int_0^t W(s)dW(s)$ and its value $\frac{W^2(t)-t}{2}$. See also Figure 11.5: the line in the plot has a unit slope and goes through the origin. This confirms, by simulation, that the integral, albeit being a random variable, can be written as $\frac{W^2(t)-t}{2}$.

```
%%%%%%%%%%%%%%%%%%%%%%%%%%%%%%%%%%%%%%%%%%%%%%%%%%%%%%%%%%%
%%%Computing Integral[W(s) dW(s),fs,0,Tg]%%%%%%%%%
%%%%%%%%%%%%%%%%%%%%%%%%%%%%%%%%%%%%%%%%%%%%%%%%%%%%%%%%%%%
clear all;
expiry=1;
nstep=10000;
nsimul=100;
dt=expiry/nstep; %reduce the time step
dW=randn(nstep,nsimul)*dt0.5; %simulate BM
W=[zeros(1,nsimul); cumsum(dW)];
[sum(W(1:end-1,:).*dW)' (W(end-,:).2-expiry)'/2]
h = figure('Color',[1 1 1]);
plot(sum(W(1:end-1,:).*dW)', (W(end-1,:).2-expiry)'/2,'.')
xlabel('(W(t)2-t)/2')
title('nint 0tW(s)dW(s)')
print(h,'-dpng','FigStocIntegral.jpg')
```

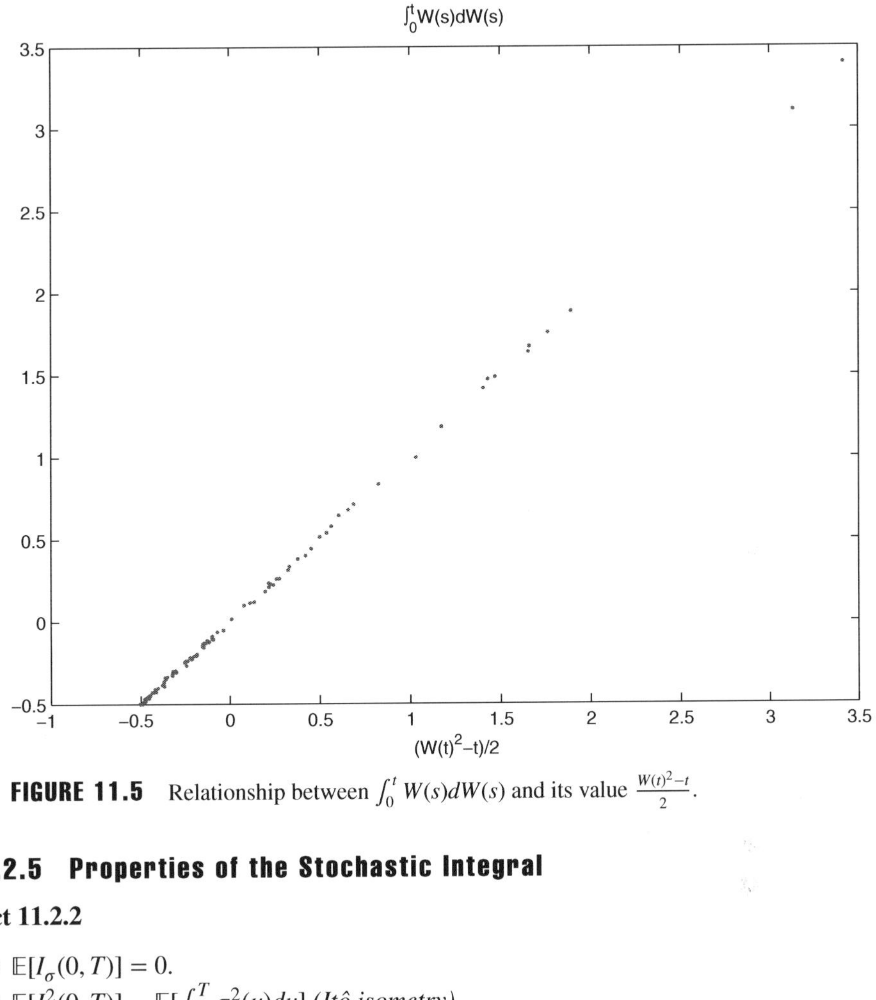

FIGURE 11.5 Relationship between $\int_0^t W(s)dW(s)$ and its value $\frac{W(t)^2-t}{2}$.

11.2.5 Properties of the Stochastic Integral

Fact 11.2.2

- $\mathbb{E}[I_\sigma(0,T)] = 0.$
- $\mathbb{E}[I_\sigma^2(0,T)] = \mathbb{E}[\int_0^T \sigma^2(u)du]$ *(Itô isometry).*
- *The Itô integral is Gaussian, for any deterministic integrand function* $\sigma(t) = \sigma(t)$ *(by definition).*
- $I_\sigma(0,T)$ *is a* $\mathbb{P}$*-martingale.*

Proof: Properties of the stochastic integral The above-mentioned properties can be shown using the definition of Brownian motion, the fact that the integrand function is an adapted process and the properties listed in Section 11.1.1.9.

- We use the tower property of the conditional expectation, so that

$$\begin{aligned}\mathbb{E}[I_\sigma(0,T)] &= \int_0^T \mathbb{E}[\sigma(u)dW(u)]\\ &= \int_0^T \mathbb{E}[\mathbb{E}_u(\sigma(u)dW(u))]\\ &= \int_0^T \mathbb{E}[\sigma(u)\mathbb{E}_u(dW(u))] = 0,\end{aligned}$$

where the last equality follows from property 2 of Section 11.1.1.9.

- Given a partition $\tau_n = 0 = t_0 < t_1 < ... < t_{n-1} < t_n = t$, consider the Riemann–Stieltjes sums

$$S_n = \sum_{j=1}^{n} \sigma(t_{j-1})(W(t_j) - W(t_{j-1})).$$

It follows that

$$S_n^2 = \sum_{j=1}^{n} \sigma^2(t_{j-1})(W(t_j) - W(t_{j-1}))^2 + \sum_j \sum_{i \neq j} \sigma(t_{j-1})\sigma(t_{i-1})(W(t_j) - W(t_{j-1}))(W(t_i) - W(t_{i-1})).$$

Without loss of generality, assume $t_i < t_j$. We note that

$$\begin{aligned}\mathbb{E}\left(S_n^2\right) &= \mathbb{E}\left[\sum_{j=1}^{n} \mathbb{E}_{t_{j-1}}\left(\sigma^2(t_{j-1})(W(t_j) - W(t_{j-1}))^2\right)\right] \\ &+ \mathbb{E}\left[\sum_j \sum_{i \neq j} \mathbb{E}_{t_{j-1}}\left(\sigma(t_{j-1})\sigma(t_{i-1})(W(t_i) - W(t_{i-1}))(W(t_j) - W(t_{i-1}))\right)\right] \\ &= \mathbb{E}\left[\sum_{j=1}^{n} \sigma^2(t_{j-1})(t_j - t_{j-1})\right],\end{aligned}$$

where the last equality follows from the definition of Brownian motion. The result follows.

- We note that $I_\sigma(0,T) = I_\sigma(0,t) + I_\sigma(t,T)$. Then

$$\begin{aligned}\mathbb{E}_t[I_\sigma(0,T)] &= I_\sigma(0,t) + \mathbb{E}_t[I_\sigma(t,T)] \\ &= I_\sigma(0,t) + \mathbb{E}_t\left[\int_t^T \mathbb{E}_u(\sigma(u)dW(u))\right] \\ &= I_\sigma(0,t).\end{aligned}$$

Remark 11.2.1 *As the Itô integral is a zero mean process, the Itô isometry implies that*

$$\mathbb{V}ar\left(I_\sigma(0,T)\right) = \mathbb{E}\left[\int_0^T \sigma(u)^2 du\right].$$

Why is this result relevant in finance? It is related to the interpretation of the implied volatility of an option as the average variance of the underlying stock return over the remaining life of the option!

Important Properties of the Stochastic Integral

$I_\sigma(0,t)$ is a stochastic process with continuous sample paths	
$I_\sigma(0,t)$ is a martingale w.r.t. to Brownian filtration	
$I_\sigma(0,t)$ has zero expectation	$\mathbb{E}(I_\sigma(0,t)) = 0$
$I_\sigma(0,t)$ satisfies the isometry property	$\mathbb{V}ar(I_\sigma(0,t)) = \mathbb{E}\left[\int_0^t \sigma^2(u,w)du\right]$
For constants α and β, $I_\sigma(0,t)$ is linear	$I_{\alpha\sigma_1+\beta\sigma_2}(0,t) = \alpha I_{\sigma_1}(0,t) + \beta I_{\sigma_2}(0,t)$
For adjacent intervals $0 \le t \le T$	$I_\sigma(0,T) = I_\sigma(0,t) + I_\sigma(t,T)$

11.2.6 Itô Process and Stochastic Differential Equations

Fact 11.2.3 *An Itô process is a stochastic process of the form*

$$X(t) = X(0) + \int_0^t f(X(u), u)du + \int_0^t \sigma(X(u), u)dW(u),$$

where $X(0)$ is a random variable and $f(X(t), t)$, $\sigma(X(t), t)$ are adapted processes satisfying some regularity conditions.

The Itô process $X(t)$ can also be written in differential form (as a shorthand notation)

$$\begin{cases} dX(t) = f(X(t), t)dt + \sigma(X(t), t)dW(t), \\ X(0) = X. \end{cases}$$

Meaning of $f(X(t), t)$ and $\sigma(X(t), t)$

- We observe that

$$\mathbb{E}_t(dX(t)) = f(X(t), t)dt,$$
$$\mathbb{V}ar_t(dX(t)) = \sigma^2(X(t), t)dt,$$

hence we can interpret
  - $f(X(t), t)dt$ as the expected instantaneous change in X over the time period $(t, t + dt)$; $f(X(t), t)$ is called the DRIFT COEFFICIENT.
  - $\sigma^2(X(t), t)dt$ as the variance of the instantaneous changes; $\sigma(X(t), t)$ is called the DIFFUSION COEFFICIENT.

11.2.6.1 Example: ABM with Deterministic Volatility

- Arithmetic Brownian motion is an Itô process defined as

$$X(t) = X(0) + \int_0^t \mu(s)ds + \int_0^t \sigma(s)dW(s).$$

- By virtue of the properties of the stochastic integral, it follows that

$$X(t) \sim \mathcal{N}\left(X(0) + \int_0^t \mu(s)ds, \int_0^t \sigma^2(s)ds\right).$$

- The conditional distribution of $X(t)$ given $\mathcal{F}(s)$ is

$$X(t)\,|\mathcal{F}(s) \sim \mathcal{N}\left(X(s) + \int_s^t \mu(s)ds, \int_s^t \sigma^2(u)du\right).$$

- The expressions of the variance obtained above are obtained using the Itô isometry.
- The corresponding stochastic differential equation is

$$dX(t) = \mu(t)dt + \sigma(t)dW(t).$$

Example 11.2.2 *Let us assume that $\mu(t) = \mu \in \mathbb{R}$ and $\sigma(t) = \sigma > 0$, then the ABM is given by*

$$X(t) = X(0) + \mu t + \sigma W(t)$$

or, equivalently,

$$dX(t) = \mu dt + \sigma dW(t).$$

From the above, the facts listed in the following table hold.

Arithmetic Brownian Motion: Facts	
The SDE	$dX(t) = \mu dt + \sigma dW(t), X(0) = x_0$
The solution	$X(t) = X(0) + \mu(t-0) + \sigma(W(t) - W(0))$
The distribution of $X(t)$	$X(t) \sim \mathcal{N}(X(0) + \mu t, \sigma^2 t)$
The moments of $X(t)$	$\mathbb{E}_0(X(t) - X(0) - \mu t)^p = (\sigma\sqrt{(t)})^p\,(p-1)!!$ *if p is even*
The auto-covariance of $X(t)$	$c_X(t,s) = \sigma^2\, min(t,s)$

11.2.6.2 Matlab: Simulating Arithmetic Brownian Motion Sample paths of the ABM are presented in Figure 11.6 (see also the accompanying code). Figure 11.7 shows the distribution of the ABM at different time horizons.

Matlab Code

```
%%%%%%%%%%%%%%%%%%%%%%%%%%%%%%%%%%%%%%%%%%%%%%%%%%%%%%%%%
%%%%SIMULATING THE ARITHMETIC BROWNIAN MOTIONS%%%%%%%%%
%%%%%%%%%%%%%%%%%%%%%%%%%%%%%%%%%%%%%%%%%%%%%%%%%%%%%%%%%
%Assigning the number of simulated paths
%(nsimul), time to maturity (expiry), number of steps
%(nsteps), time step (dt) and observation times (timestep):
%and model parameters
nsimul=10000, expiry=1, nsteps=250;dt=expiry/nsteps;
timestep=[0:dt:expiry]'; mu=0.2; sigma=0.3;
%Simulate increments ABM dX:
dX=mu*dt+sigma*randn(nsteps,nsimul)*dt\^0.5;
%Simulate ABM process: cumulate increments
cdX=[zeros(1,nsimul); cumsum(dX)];
%Compute Expected Value
EcdX=timestep*mu;
%Plot simulated paths:
plot(timestep, cdX, timestep, EcdX)
title('Simulated Paths of the Arithmetic Brownian Process ABM(0.2, 0.3)')
xlabel('Time')
```

```
%Plot distribution of the ABM at different dates:
bmmin=-0.8; bmmax=1.5;
```

```
subplot(3,1,1); hist(cdX(50,:),100);xlabel('ABM')
xlim=[bmmin,bmmax];title('Density at time 0.2 years')
subplot(3,1,2); hist(cdX(125,:),100);xlabel('ABM')
xlim=[bmmin,bmmax];title('Density at time 0.5 years')
subplot(3,1,3); hist(cdX(end,:),100);xlabel('ABM')
xlim=[bmmin,bmmax];title('Density at time 1 years')
```

11.2.7 Solving Stochastic Integrals and/or Stochastic Differential Equations

- We have shown the equivalence between stochastic integrals and stochastic differential equations.
- Consequently, finding the solution to a stochastic integral is equivalent to finding a solution to the corresponding stochastic differential equation.
- As illustrated in Section 11.2.4, finding this solution can be quite complicated.
- However, there is a very useful tool for this task: Itô's lemma. This will be introduced in Section 11.3.
- In the remainder of this section, we want to summarize some useful facts about SDEs and their solution.

11.2.7.1 Deterministic vs. Stochastic Differential Equations

Deterministic

- Differential form

$$dx(t) = f(x(t), t)dt.$$

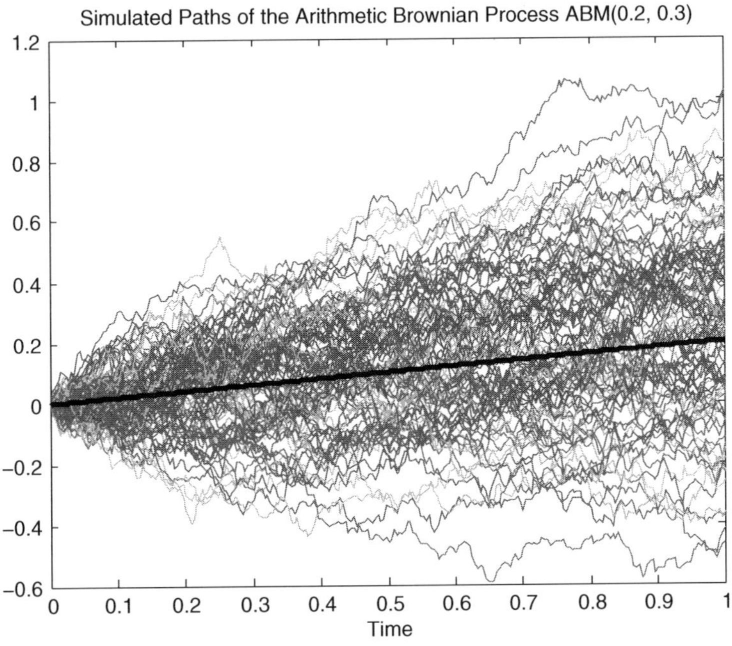

FIGURE 11.6 Example: Sample paths of the ABM(0.2,0.3).

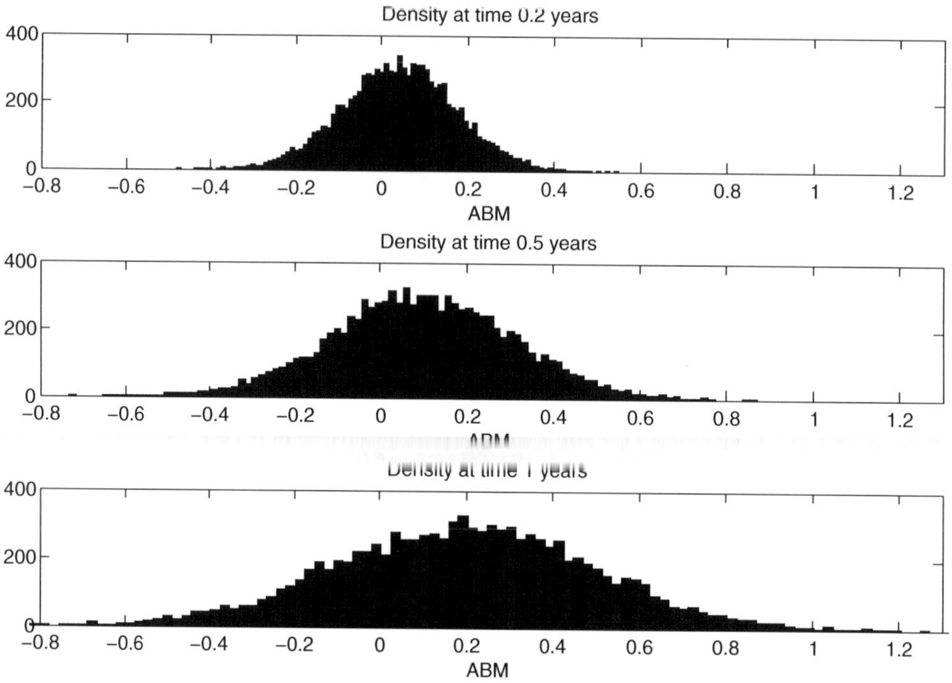

FIGURE 11.7 Simulated distribution of the ABM(0.2,0.3) at different horizons.

- Integral form

$$x(t) = x(0) + \underbrace{\int_0^t f(x(u), u)du}_{\textit{Riemann Integral}}.$$

Stochastic

- Differential form

$$dX(t) = f(X(t), t)dt + \sigma(X(t), t)dW(t). \tag{11.1}$$

- Integral form

$$X(t) = X(0) + \underbrace{\int_0^t f(x(u), u)du}_{\text{Riemann Integral}} + \underbrace{\int_0^t \sigma(X(u), u)dW(u)}_{\text{Stochastic Integral}}. \tag{11.2}$$

11.2.7.2 Examples of Stochastic Differential Equations A few examples of SDEs are given in Table 11.2, where we also provide the deterministic version.

TABLE 11.2 Examples of deterministic and stochastic differential equations

Deterministic	Stochastic	Name
$dx = \mu dt$	$dX(t) = \mu dt + \sigma dW(t)$	arithmetic Brownian motion
$dx = \mu x dt$	$dX(t) = \mu X(t)dt + \sigma X(t)dW(t)$	geometric Brownian motion
$dx = \mu x dt$	$dX(t) = \mu X(t)dt + \sigma X^{\beta+1}(t)dW(t)$	constant elasticity of variance (CEV)
	$dX(t) = \alpha(\mu - X(t))dt + \sigma dW(t)$	Ornstein–Uhlenbeck (Vasicek)
$dx = \alpha(\mu - x)dt$	$dX(t) = \alpha(\mu - X(t))dt + \sigma\sqrt{X(t)}dW(t)$	square root (Cox–Ingersoll–Ross)
	$dX(t) = \alpha(\mu - X(t))dt + \sigma X(t)dW(t)$	lognormal with mean reversion
$dx = \mu x dt$	$dX(t) = \mu X(t)dt + \sqrt{v(t)}X(t)dW(t)$	
	$dv(t) = v(t)dt + \kappa v(t)dW(t)$	stochastic volatility (Hull–White model)
	$dv(t) = \alpha(\mu - v(t))dt + \kappa\sqrt{v(t)}dW(t)$	stochastic volatility (Heston model)

11.2.7.3 Existence and Uniqueness of the Solution

Remark 11.2.2 (Definition of Solution) *$X(t)$ is called a strong solution of the SDE (11.1) if for all $t > 0$, $X(t)$ is a function $F(t, (W(s), s \le t))$ of the given Brownian motion $W(t)$, integrals $\int_0^t f(x(u), u)du$ and $\int_0^t \sigma(X(u), u)dW(u)$ exist and the integral equation (11.2) is satisfied.*

Fact 11.2.4 (Existence and Uniqueness) *Assume the initial condition $X(0)$ has finite second moment, $\mathbb{E}(X^2(0)) < \infty$, and is independent of $W(t), t \ge 0$ and that, for all $t \in [0, T]$ and $x, y \in R$, the coefficient functions $f(x, t)$ and $\sigma(x, t)$ satisfy the following conditions:*

1. *They are continuous.*
2. *They satisfy a Lipschitz condition with respect to the first variable:*

$$|f(x, t) - f(y, t)| + |\sigma(x, t) - \sigma(y, t)| \le K|x - y|.$$

Then the Itô stochastic differential equation (11.1) has a unique solution X on $[0, T]$.

In the following, we will assume that the considered SDEs also admit a unique solution.

11.3 INTRODUCING ITÔ'S FORMULA

- The main tool in stochastic calculus is Itô's formula, a stochastic Taylor formula.
- Given the Itô process $X(t)$:

$$dX = \mu(X, t)dt + \sigma(X, t)dW,$$

let $g \in C^2$ (i.e., g is a function whose second-order partial derivatives are continuous):

$$Y = g(t, X).$$

- We can think of g as the price of a derivative written on $X(t)$, and we aim to find the dynamics of the derivative price.
- What is the stochastic differential of the process $Y(t)$?
- In order to answer this question, let us recall the basic calculus rules with BM:

$\times$	dt	$dW(t)$
dt	0	0
$dW(t)$	0	dt

- Therefore, we have

$$\begin{aligned}(dX)^2 &= (\mu dt + \sigma dW)^2 \\ &= \mu^2(dt)^2 + 2\mu\sigma dt dW + \sigma^2(dW)^2 \\ &\quad 0(dt) + 0(dt) + \sigma^2 dt \\ &= \sigma^2 dt.\end{aligned}$$

11.3.1 A Fact from Ordinary Calculus

- Let us consider the function $x = f(t)$ with f a continuously differentiable function. We can write

$$dx(t) = f'(t)dt.$$

- Let us now introduce $y = g(x)$ with g also being a continuously differentiable function. Then

$$y'(t) = \frac{dy}{dt} = \frac{dg}{dx} \times \frac{dx}{dt} = g'(x(t))f'(t).$$

- We are looking for the dynamics of dy. We have

$$dy(t) = y'(t)dt = g'(x(t))f'(t)dt = g'(x(t))dx(t),$$

and over a time period $[0, T]$, we have

$$y(T) = y(0) + \int_0^T dy(t) = y(0) + \int_0^T g'(x(t))dx(t).$$

- How does this result translate when we deal with stochastic differential equations? We derive Itô's formula.

11.3.2 Itô's Formula when $Y = g(x), g(x) \in C^2$

- Let us consider the SDE $dX(t) = \mu(X, t)dt + \sigma(X, t)dW(t)$, and let us set $y = g(x)$.
  – **What is the SDE for Y?**

- Considering the second-order Taylor series expansions (and using the fact that $(dX)^2 = \sigma^2 dt$):

$$\begin{aligned} dY &= g'(X)dX + \frac{1}{2}g''(X)(dX)^2 \\ &= g'(X)dX + \frac{1}{2}g''(X)(\sigma^2(X,t)dt) \\ &= g'(X)(\mu(X,t)dt + \sigma(X,t)dW(t)) + \frac{1}{2}g''(X)(\sigma^2(X,t)dt) \\ &= \left(g'(X)\mu(X,t) + \frac{1}{2}\sigma^2(X,t)g''(X)\right)dt + \sigma(X,t)g'(X)dW(t). \end{aligned}$$

- The additional term in the drift is due to the rule $(dW)^2 = dt$.

Therefore, we can say that

Fact 11.3.1 (Itô's Lemma for $Y = g(X)$) *The SDE for $Y = g(X)$ when $dX(t) = \mu(X,t)dt + \sigma(X,t)dW(t)$ is given by*

$$dY(t) = \left(g'(X)\mu(X,t) + \frac{1}{2}\sigma^2(X,t)g''(X)\right)dt + \sigma(X,t)g'(X)dW(t).$$

Remark 11.3.1 *In contrast to the deterministic case, when $X(t)$ is a Brownian motion or an Itô process, the contribution of the second-order term in the Taylor expansion is not negligible since Brownian motion has finite quadratic variation. This fact is the reason for the deviation from the classical chain rule.*

11.3.3 Guiding Principle

- Write out the Taylor series expansion of g with respect to all its arguments:
  1. Take this Taylor series expansion out to first order for every argument that has zero quadratic variation.
  2. Take the expansion out to second order for every argument that has nonzero quadratic variation.
  3. Since the variation of order three of each argument is zero and the covariation of $W(t)$ and t is zero, the other terms can be neglected.

11.3.4 Itô's Formula when $Y(t) = g(t, X), g(t, X) \in C^{1,2}$

- Let us consider $dX(t) = \mu(X,t)dt + \sigma(X,t)dW(t)$, and let us set $Y(t) = g(t, X)$.
- Considering the second-order Taylor series expansions, we have

$$\begin{aligned} dY(t) &= \frac{\partial g(t,X)}{\partial t}dt + \frac{\partial g(t,X)}{\partial x}dX + \frac{1}{2}\frac{\partial^2 g(t,X)}{\partial x^2}(dX)^2 \\ &= \frac{\partial g(t,X)}{\partial t}dt + \frac{\partial g(t,X)}{\partial x}(\mu(X,t)dt + \sigma(X,t)dW) + \frac{\sigma^2(X,t)}{2}\frac{\partial^2 g(t,X)}{\partial x^2}dt. \end{aligned}$$

- We can now formulate the general form of Itô's lemma.

Fact 11.3.2 ***(Generalized Itô's Lemma for*** $Y(t) = g(t, X)$***)*** *The SDE for* $Y(t) = g(t, X) \in C^{1,2}$ *when* $dX(t) = \mu(X, t)dt + \sigma(X, t)dW(t)$ *is:*

$$dY(t)(t) = \left(\frac{\partial g(t,X)}{\partial t} + \mu(X,t)\frac{\partial g(t,X)}{\partial x} + \frac{1}{2}\sigma^2(X,t)\frac{\partial^2 g(t,X)}{\partial x^2}\right)dt + \sigma(X,t)\frac{\partial g(t,X)}{\partial x}dW(t).$$

$$\mathbb{E}(dY(t)) = Drift(dY(t))dt = \left(\frac{\partial g(t,X)}{\partial t} + \mu(X,t)\frac{\partial g(t,X)}{\partial x} + \frac{1}{2}\sigma^2(X,t)\frac{\partial^2 g(t,X)}{\partial x^2}\right)dt.$$

$$Volatility(dY(t)) = Diffusion(dY(t))\sqrt{dt} = \sigma(X,t)\frac{\partial g(t,X)}{\partial x}\sqrt{dt}.$$

- Itô's lemma gives us a tool to derive stochastic differential equations of stochastic processes obtained as a function of another Itô process.

Example 11.3.1 *Let us consider the process* $Y(t) = W^2(t)$*, where* $W(t)$ *is a BM. By Itô's lemma, the SDE of* $Y = g(W) = W^2$ *is*

$$dY(t) = 2W(t)dW(t) + dt.$$

- At the same time, Itô's lemma can provide a way to solve a given SDE by suitably choosing an auxiliary process with a simpler SDE.

Example 11.3.2 *Let us consider the process* $X(t) = \int_0^t W(t)dW(t)$*, or equivalently* $dX(t) = W(t)dW(t)$*. From the SDE of the process* $Y(t) = W^2(t)$ *obtained above, it follows that*

$$dX(t) = \frac{1}{2}(dY(t) - dt).$$

By integrating both sides, it follows that $X(t) = W^2(t)/2 - t/2$*, which verifies the result given in the example of Section 11.2.4. Indeed*

$$\begin{aligned} X(t) &= X(0) + \int_0^t dX(s) \\ &= X(0) + \frac{1}{2}\left(\int_0^t dY(s) - \int_0^t ds\right) \\ &= X(0) + \frac{1}{2}(Y(t) - Y(0) - t) \\ &= 0 + \frac{1}{2}(W^2(t) - t). \end{aligned}$$

11.3.5 The Multivariate Itô's Lemma when $Z = g(t, X, Y)$

- Let us consider two Brownian motions $W_1(t)$ and $W_2(t)$.
- Their increments $dW_1(t)$ and $dW_2(t)$ satisfy

$$\mathbb{E}(dW_1(t)dW_2(t)) = \rho dt.$$

- Here the coefficient ρ is interpreted as the instantaneous correlation coefficient between the increments of the two Brownian motions.
- The multiplicative rules in the multivariate case become

$\times$	dt	$dW_1(t)$	$dW_2(t)$
dt	0	0	0
$dW_1(t)$	0	dt	ρdt
$dW_2(t)$	0	ρdt	dt

- We have

$$dX(t) = \mu(X,t)dt + \sigma(X,t)dW_1(t),$$
$$dY(t) = \mu(Y,t)dt + \sigma(Y,t)dW_2(t).$$

We consider a function of time t, and of the two variables X and Y, $Z = g(t, X, Y)$ *say*.

- **What is the SDE for** $Z = g(t, X, Y)$**?**

- Considering the multivariate second-order Taylor formula, we have

$$\begin{aligned} dZ = &\frac{\partial g(t,x,y)}{\partial t}dt + \frac{\partial g(t,X,Y)}{\partial X}dX + \frac{\partial g(t,X,Y)}{\partial Y}dY \\ &+\frac{1}{2}\frac{\partial^2 g(t,X,Y)}{\partial X^2}(dX)^2 + \frac{1}{2}\frac{\partial^2 g(t,X,Y)}{\partial Y^2}(dY)^2 \\ &+\frac{\partial^2 g(t,X,Y)}{\partial Y \partial X}dXdY. \end{aligned}$$

- Let us use the multiplicative rules of the above table:

$$(dX)^2 = \sigma^2(X,t)dt,$$
$$(dY)^2 = \sigma^2(Y,t)dt,$$

and

$$dXdY = \rho\sigma(X,t)\sigma(Y,t)dt.$$

Fact 11.3.3 (Multivariate Itô's Lemma) *Given* $Z = g(t, X, Y)$*, the SDE for* Z *is*

$$dZ = \mu(Z,t)dt + \frac{\partial g(t,X,Y)}{\partial X}\sigma(X,t)dW_1(t) + \frac{\partial g(t,X,Y)}{\partial Y}\sigma(Y,t)dW_2(t),$$

where

$$\begin{aligned} \mu(Z,t) = &\frac{\partial g(t,x,y)}{\partial t} + \frac{\partial g(t,X,Y)}{\partial X}\mu(X,t) + \frac{\partial g(t,X,Y)}{\partial Y}\mu(Y,t) \\ &+\frac{1}{2}\frac{\partial^2 g(t,X,Y)}{\partial X^2}\sigma^2(X,t) + \frac{1}{2}\frac{\partial^2 g(t,X,Y)}{\partial Y^2}\sigma^2(Y,t) \\ &+\rho\frac{\partial^2 g(t,X,Y)}{\partial X \partial Y}\sigma(X,t)\sigma(Y,t). \end{aligned}$$

11.3.5.1 Examples

- Let us consider two examples of the multivariate Itô's formula:
  - the product XY;
  - the ratio Y/X.
- These are important when X and Y are GBM processes and for example we model oil prices, quoted in USD, and the USD/EUR currency rate and we are interested in the dynamics of oil prices expressed in EUR.

Fact 11.3.4 (Product $Z = XY$)

$$\frac{dZ}{Z} = \frac{dX}{X} + \frac{dY}{Y} + \left(\frac{dX}{X}\right)\left(\frac{dY}{Y}\right).$$

Fact 11.3.5 (Ratio $Z = Y/X$)

$$\frac{dZ}{Z} = \frac{dY}{Y} - \frac{dX}{X} - \left(\frac{dX}{X}\right)\left(\frac{dY}{Y}\right) + \left(\frac{dX}{X}\right)^2.$$

Example 11.3.3 (Volatilities of Products) *We have two processes under the same measure:*

$$\frac{dX}{X} = \mu_X + \sigma_X dW_X,$$
$$\frac{dY}{Y} = \mu_Y + \sigma_Y dW_Y.$$

The SDE for the product $Z = XY$ is given by

$$\frac{dZ}{Z} = \left(\mu_X + \mu_Y + \rho\sigma_X\sigma_Y\right) dt + \sigma_X dW_X + \sigma_Y dW_Y.$$

$$\mathbb{E}\left(\frac{dZ}{Z}\right) = \left(\mu_X + \mu_Y + \rho\sigma_X\sigma_Y\right) dt,$$
$$\mathbb{V}ar\left(\frac{dZ}{Z}\right) = \left(\sigma_X^2 + \sigma_Y^2 + 2\rho\sigma_X\sigma_Y\right) dt,$$
$$\mathbb{V}ol\left(\frac{dZ}{Z}\right) = \sqrt{\sigma_X^2 + \sigma_Y^2 + 2\rho\sigma_X\sigma_Y}\sqrt{dt}.$$

Example 11.3.4 (Volatilities of Ratios) *We have two processes under the same measure:*

$$\frac{dX}{X} = \mu_X + \sigma_X dW_X,$$
$$\frac{dY}{Y} = \mu_Y + \sigma_Y dW_Y.$$

The SDE for the ratio $Z = Y/X$ is given by

$$\frac{dZ}{Z} = \left(\mu_Y - \mu_X - \rho\sigma_X\sigma_Y\right) dt + \sigma_Y dW_Y - \sigma_X dW_X.$$

$$\mathbb{E}\left(\frac{dZ}{Z}\right) = \left(\mu_Y - \mu_X - \rho\sigma_X\sigma_Y\right) dt,$$
$$\mathbb{V}ar\left(\frac{dZ}{Z}\right) = \left(\sigma_X^2 + \sigma_Y^2 - 2\rho\sigma_X\sigma_Y\right) dt,$$
$$\mathbb{V}ol\left(\frac{dZ}{Z}\right) = \sqrt{\sigma_X^2 + \sigma_Y^2 + 2\rho\sigma_X\sigma_Y}\sqrt{dt}.$$

11.4 IMPORTANT SDEs

In this section we review the most important SDEs in finance, such as:

- geometric Brownian motion (GBM);
- Vasicek mean-reverting process;
- Cox–Ingersoll–Ross mean-reverting process;
- constant elasticity of variance (CEV) model;
- stochastic volatility (SV) Heston model;
- Brownian bridge (BB).

11.4.1 The Geometric Brownian Motion $GBM(\mu, \sigma)$

Fact 11.4.1 (Geometric Brownian Motion) *The SDE with drift μX and diffusion coefficient σX (i.e., $\mu(X,t) = \mu X$ and $\sigma(X,t) = \sigma X$) given by*

$$dX(t) = \mu X(t)dt + \sigma X dW(t)$$

is said to be the geometric Brownian motion with coefficients μ and σ and is denoted by $GBM(\mu, \sigma)$.

- Compared with the ABM process, which has constant coefficients, the GBM process has affine coefficients.
- In particular, this guarantees that the process remains always positive if it starts from a positive value (good news if you need to model market prices!).
- Our aim is to use Itô's lemma to solve the above SDE.

11.4.1.1 Solving the ODE $dX(t) = \mu X(t)dt$

- We would like to solve the SDE $dX(t) = \mu X(t)dt + \sigma X(t)dW(t)$.
- Let us see what's happening with the **ordinary differential equation**, that is the deterministic version:

$$dx(t) = \mu x(t)dt.$$

  - We let $y(t) = \ln x(t)$.
  - Then, $dy(t) = \frac{1}{x(t)}dx(t)$.
  - Therefore $dy(t) = \mu dt$, that is $y(t) = y(0) + \mu t$.
  - It follows that $\ln x(t) = \ln x(0) + \mu t$.

Fact 11.4.2 (Solving the ODE $dx(t) = \mu x(t)dt$) *The solution of the ODE $dx(t) = \mu x(t)dt$ is*

$$dx(t) = \mu x(t)dt \Rightarrow x(t) = x(0)e^{\mu t}.$$

11.4.1.2 Solving the SDE $dX = \mu X dt + \sigma X dW$

- We want to solve the SDE $dX(t) = \mu X(t)dt + \sigma X(t)dW(t)$.
- By analogy with the ODE $dX(t) = \mu X(t)dt$, let us look for the SDE of $Y(t) = g(x) = \ln X(t)$.
- Using Itô's lemma, we have

$$\begin{aligned} dY(t) &= \left(\frac{\partial g(t,X)}{\partial t} + \mu X \frac{\partial g(t,X)}{\partial X} + \frac{\sigma^2 X^2}{2}\frac{\partial^2 g(t,X)}{\partial X^2}\right) dt + \sigma X \frac{\partial g(t,X)}{\partial x} dW(t) \\ &= \left(0 + \mu X \frac{1}{X} - \frac{1}{2}\sigma^2 X^2 \frac{1}{X^2}\right) dt + \sigma X \frac{1}{X} dW(t) \\ &= \left(\mu - \frac{1}{2}\sigma^2\right) dt + \sigma X dW(t). \end{aligned}$$

- This means that $Y(t)$ follows an ABM$(\mu - \frac{1}{2}\sigma^2, \sigma)$ process, with solution

$$Y(t) = Y(0) + \left(\mu - \frac{1}{2}\sigma^2\right) t + \sigma(W(t) - W(0)),$$

and therefore

$$\begin{aligned} \ln X(t) &= \ln X(0) + \left(\mu - \frac{1}{2}\sigma^2\right) t + \sigma(W(t) - W(0)), \\ X(t) &= X(0) e^{\left(\left(\mu - \frac{1}{2}\sigma^2\right)t + \sigma(W(t) - W(0))\right)}. \end{aligned}$$

- It follows that

$$\ln X(t) \sim \mathcal{N}\left(\ln X(0) + \left(\mu - \frac{1}{2}\sigma^2\right) t, \sigma^2 t\right)$$

and

$$X(t) \sim \mathcal{LN}\left(\ln X(0) + \left(\mu - \frac{1}{2}\sigma^2\right) t, \sigma^2 t\right).$$

- In particular, we have

$$\mathbb{E}_0(x(t)) = X(0) e^{\mu t}.$$

Remark 11.4.1 *Notice that the SDE*

$$dX(t) = \mu X(t) + \sigma X(t) dW(t)$$

is equivalent (e.g., they have the same solution) to the SDE

$$d \ln X(t) = \left(\mu - \frac{1}{2}\sigma^2\right) dt + \sigma dW(t).$$

In general, the first SDE is useful to model prices, whilst the second one is used to model log-returns.

Simulated trajectories of the GBM are shown in Figure 11.8 (see accompanying code); the resulting distribution originated at different time horizons are presented in Figure 11.9.

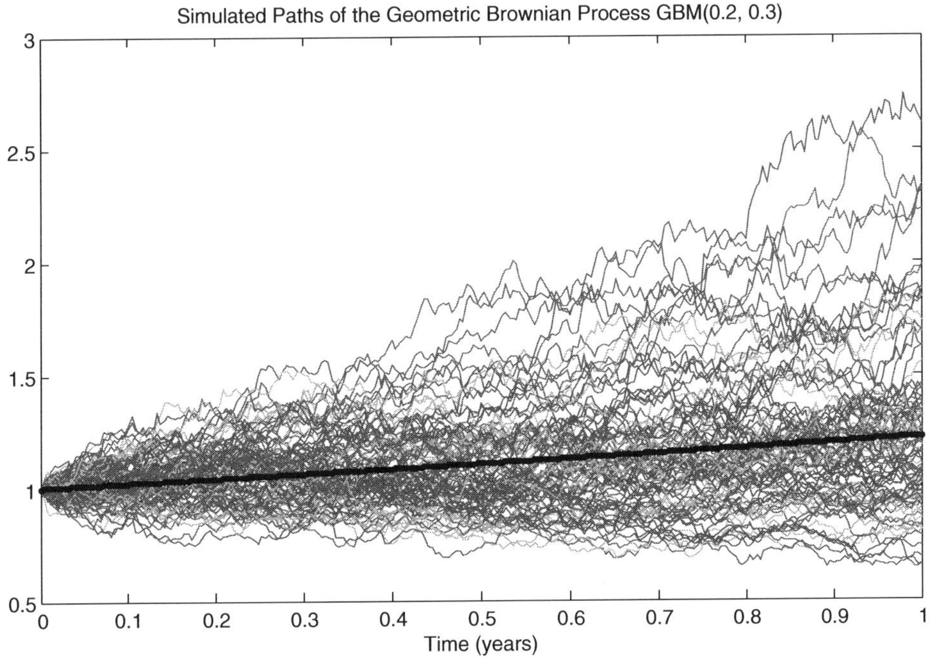

FIGURE 11.8 *Sample paths of the GBM(0.2,0.3).*

Geometric Brownian Motion: Facts

The SDE

$$dX(t) = \mu X(t)dt + \sigma X(t)dW(t), X(0) = x_0$$

The solution

$$X(t) = X(0)e^{\left(\mu-\frac{1}{2}\sigma^2\right)t+\sigma(W(t)-W(0))}$$

The distribution of $X(t)$

$$X(t) \sim \mathcal{LN}\left(\ln X(0) + \left(\mu - \frac{1}{2}\sigma^2\right)t, \sigma^2 t\right)$$

The moments of $X(t)$

$$\mathbb{E}_0\left(X(t)^n\right) = X(0)^n e^{n(\mu-\frac{1}{2}\sigma^2)t+\frac{n^2\sigma^2}{2}t}$$

In particular, if $n = 1$

$$\mathbb{E}_0(X(t)) = X(0)e^{\mu t}$$

11.4.1.3 Matlab Implementation: Simulating GBM

Matlab Code

```
%%%%%%%%%%%%%%%%%%%%%%%%%%%%%%%%%%%%%%%%%%%%%%%%%
%%%%SIMULATING THE GEOMETRIC BROWNIAN MOTIONS%%%
%%%%%%%%%%%%%%%%%%%%%%%%%%%%%%%%%%%%%%%%%%%%%%%%%
```

```
%Assigning the number of simulated paths
%(nsimul), time to maturity (expiry), number of steps
%(nsteps), time step (dt) and observation times (timestep):
%and model parameters
nsimul=100, expiry=1, nsteps=250;
dt=expiry/nsteps;
timestep=[0:dt:expiry]';
mu=0.2; sigma=0.3;
%Simulate increments ABM dX:
dX=mu*dt+sigma*randn(nsteps,nsimul)*dt^0.5;
%Simulate ABM process: cumulate increments
cdX=[zeros(1,nsimul); cumsum(dX)];
gbm=exp(cdX);
%Compute Expected Value
Egbm=exp(timestep*mu);
%Plot simulated paths:
plot(timestep, gbm, timestep, Egbm,'black.')
title('Simulated Paths of the Geometric Brownian Process GBM(0.2, 0.3)')
xlabel('Time (years)')
```

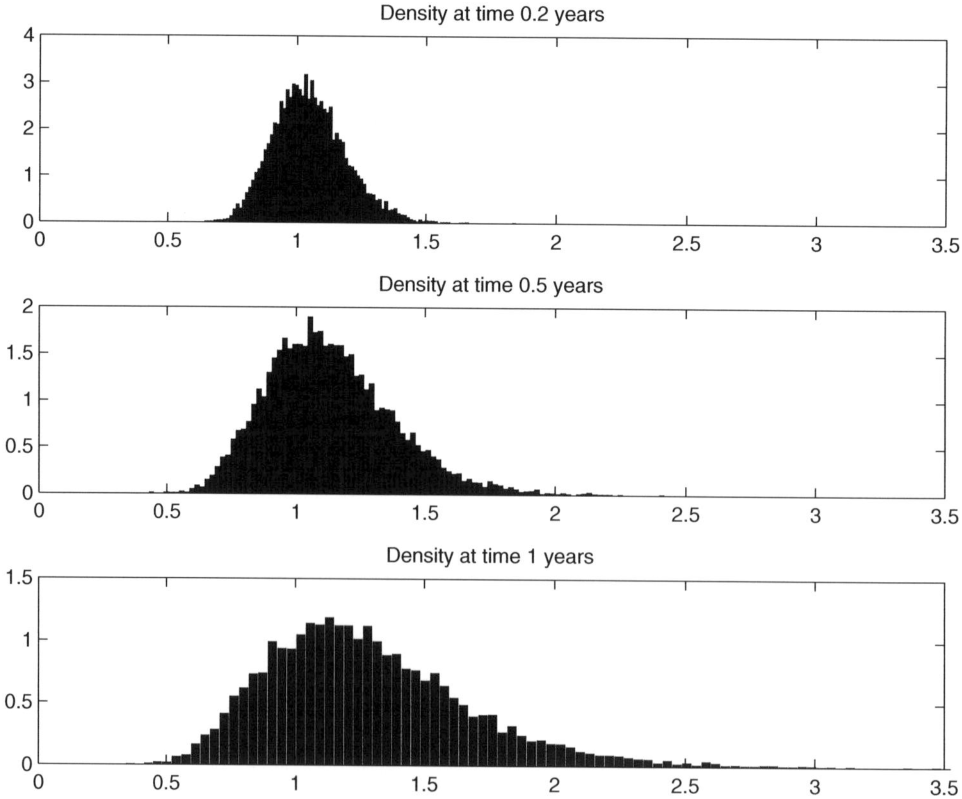

FIGURE 11.9 Density of the GBM(0.2,0.3) at different horizons.

```
%%%%%%%%%%%%%%%%%%%%%%%%%%%%%%%%%%%%%%%%%%%%%%%%%%%%
%%%%Plot GBM densities at different time horizons%%%%
%%%%%%%%%%%%%%%%%%%%%%%%%%%%%%%%%%%%%%%%%%%%%%%%%%%%
gbmmin=0; gbmmax=3.5;
[N, X]=hist(gbm(50,:),100);
pdfgbm50=N/(sum(N)*(X(2)-X(1)));
h=figure('Color',[1 1 1])
subplot(3,1,1); bar(X, pdfgbm50)
xlim([gbmmin,gbmmax]);title('Density at time 0.2 years')

[N, X]=hist(gbm(125,:),100);
pdfgbm125=N/(sum(N)*(X(2)-X(1)));
subplot(3,1,2); bar(X, pdfgbm125)
xlim([gbmmin,gbmmax]);title('Density at time 0.5 years')

[N, X]=hist(gbm(end,:),100);
pdfgbmend=N/(sum(N)*(X(2)-X(1)));
subplot(3,1,3); bar(X, pdfgbmend)
xlim([gbmmin,gbmmax]);title('Density at time 1 years')
print(h,'-dpng','LecBMFigGBMDens.jpg')
```

11.4.1.4 Remark: GBM with Deterministic Drift and Volatility

- The SDE

$$dX(t) = \mu(t)X(t)dt + \sigma(t)X(t)dW(t)$$

is equivalent to the SDE

$$d\ln X(t) = \left(\mu(t) - \frac{1}{2}\sigma^2(t)\right)dt + \sigma(t)dW(t).$$

- The solution of both equations is

$$X(t) = X(0)e^{\int_0^t\left(\mu(s)-\frac{1}{2}\sigma^2(s)ds\right)+\int_0^t\sigma(s)dW(s)},$$

or equivalently

$$\ln X(t) = \ln X(0) + \int_0^t \left(\mu(s) - \frac{1}{2}\sigma^2(s)\right)ds + \int_0^t \sigma(s)dW(s).$$

- Moreover

$$\ln X(t) \sim \mathcal{N}\left(\ln X(0) + \int_0^t \left(\mu(s) - \frac{1}{2}\sigma^2(s)\right)ds, \int_0^t \sigma^2(s)ds\right),$$

$$X(t) \sim \mathcal{LN}\left(\ln X(0) + \int_0^t \left(\mu(s) - \frac{1}{2}\sigma^2(s)\right)ds, \int_0^t \sigma^2(s)ds\right).$$

- In particular, we observe that

$$\mathbb{E}(X(t)) = X(0)e^{\int_0^t \mu(s)ds}.$$

- This result can be useful if we interpret $X(t)$ to be the price of some commodity and we observe in the market a term structure of futures prices written on X, say $F_0(t)$.
- Maybe we are interested in a GBM process for X that takes the observed futures curve as expected value, that is

$$\mathbb{E}(X(t)) = F_0(t).$$

- This is possible if we impose

$$X(0)e^{\int_0^t \mu(u)du} = F_0(t).$$

- Therefore, we can write

$$X(t) = F_0(t)e^{-\frac{1}{2}\int_0^t \sigma^2(s)ds + \int_0^t \sigma(s)dW(s)}.$$

- If we are interested in the differential form, we observe that it must also hold that

$$\int_0^t \mu(s)ds = \ln\left(\frac{F_0(t)}{X(0)}\right),$$

and then by differentiating with respect to t:

$$\mu(t) = \frac{F_0'(t)}{F_0(t)}.$$

- The SDE of $X(t)$ now becomes

$$dX(t) = \frac{F_0'(t)}{F_0(t)}X(t)dt + \sigma(t)X(t)dW(t).$$

Example: Simulation of the oil price according to a GBM fitting the futures term structure

- To make concrete the discussion, let us consider Table 11.3 containing the term structure of futures prices on Light Sweet Crude Oil traded at CME on 12 March 2013.
- Given the very short maturity of the April contract (only 8 days), we can set

$$X(0) = 91.94.$$

- Then we can iteratively simulate X according to

$$X(t_i) = \frac{F_0(t_i)}{F_0(t_{i-1})}X(t_{i-1})e^{-\frac{1}{2}\sigma^2(t_i - t_{i-1}) + \sigma(W(t_i) - W(t_{i-1}))}, i = 1, \ldots,$$

where t_i refers to the expiry dates of different futures contracts, so that $t_0 = 8/365$, $t_1 = 41/365$, $t_2 = 70/365$, …, $t_{13} = 373/365$.

TABLE 11.3 Light Sweet Crude Oil (WTI) futures prices quoted at CME as of 12 March 2013. The first column refers to the contract month; the second to the product code; the third provides the exact expiry date of the contract; the fourth column gives the quoted futures price the last column contains the actual number of days to expiration.

Contract Month	Product Code	Settlement	Open	Days
APR 2013	CLJ13	20-mar	91.94	8
MAY 13	CLK13	22-apr	92.46	41
JUN 13	CLM13	21-may	92.75	70
JLY 13	CLN13	20-jun	92.79	100
AUG 13	CLQ13	22-jul	93.2	132
SEP 13	CLU13	20-aug	93.13	161
OCT 13	CLV13	20-sep	92.76	192
NOV 2013	CLX13	22-oct	92.13	224
DEC 13	CLZ13	20-nov	91.99	253
JAN 14	CLF14	19-dec	91.91	282
FEB 2014	CLG14	21-jan	92	315
MAR 2014	CLH14	20-feb	91.25	345
APR 2014	CLJ14	20-mar	91.11	373

- As volatility parameter, let us set

$$\sigma = 0.2284,$$

corresponding to the annualized volatility of log-oil price increments in 2012.

- If we run 100,000 MC simulations, we can verify that the restriction imposed by the futures term structure is satisfied. In Table 11.4 we compare, for each future date t, the futures price $F_0(t)$ with the expectation $\mathbb{E}_0(X(t))$. The agreement is very good.
- A sample of simulated paths is illustrated in Figure 11.10.

TABLE 11.4 The first column refers to the time to maturity (in days) of the different futures contracts; the second column refers to the expected value of the GBM process, i.e. $\mathbb{E}(X(t))$; the third column is the futures price quoted today for maturity t

t (days)	$\mathbb{E}_0(X(t))$	$F_0(t)$
8	91.94	91.94
41	92.445	92.46
70	92.7386	92.75
100	92.7702	92.79
132	93.1911	93.2
161	93.1345	93.13
192	92.7703	92.76
224	92.1132	92.13
253	91.9431	91.99
282	91.8659	91.91
315	91.951	92
345	91.2335	91.25
373	91.0994	91.11

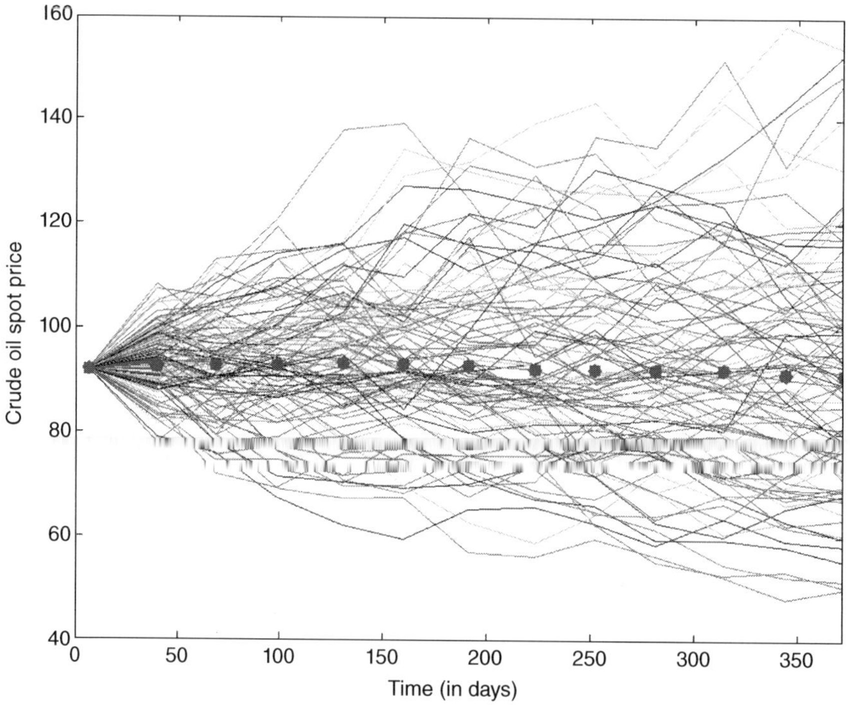

FIGURE 11.10 Simulated GBM paths fitting on average the term structure of futures prices (blue dotted points).

11.4.2 The Vasicek Mean-Reverting Process

- An empirical property of several economic variables such as interest rates, inflation rates and even commodity prices is the tendency towards lower levels (higher levels) when they are too high (low).
- This property is called **mean reversion** and can be modelled using a so-called **mean-reverting (MR) process**. The effect of mean-reversion is described in Figure 11.11.
- A Gaussian mean-reverting process is described by the following SDE:

$$dX(t) = \alpha(\mu - X(t))dt + \sigma dW(t), \alpha > 0.$$

- This model has been introduced in finance by Vasicek to model the instantaneous short rate. It is also named the Ornstein–Uhlenbeck process.
- We observe that

$$\mathbb{E}_t[dX(t)] = \alpha(\mu - X(t))dt,$$

so that, assuming $\alpha > 0$, $\mathbb{E}_t[dX(t)] > 0$ when $X(t) < \mu$. That is, we expect an increase (decrease) in the interest rate level when we are below (above) the level μ.
- The higher the value of α, the faster the return towards the level μ. α is called the speed of reversion, whilst μ determines the long-run mean level.

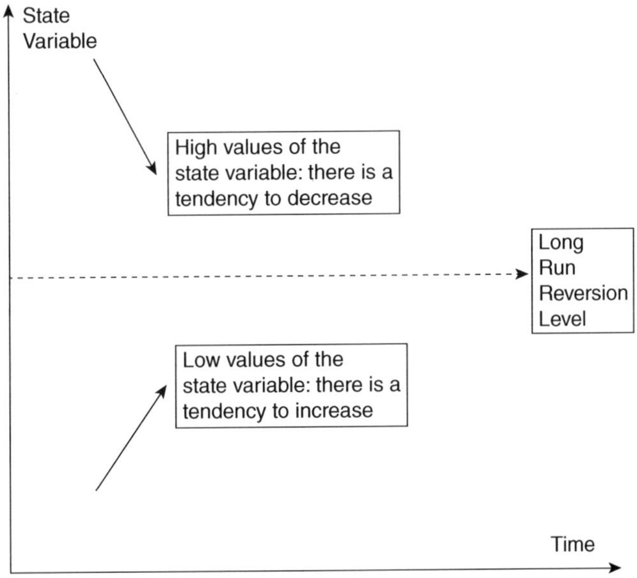

FIGURE 11.11 Mean reversion and expected change in the state variable (here an interest rate).

- The distribution of X at any future time is Gaussian, so it allows for negative values.
- An extension that guarantees positive interest rates has been proposed by Cox, Ingersoll and Ross (CIR model).

11.4.2.1 A Note: The Ordinary Differential Equation $dx(t) = \alpha(\mu - x(t))dt$

- We would like to solve the SDE in the Vasicek model. Let us start by considering the deterministic version:

$$dx(t) = \alpha(\mu - x(t))dt.$$

- This is a first-order ordinary differential equation. The procedure to solve it is standard. We recall it here.
- We proceed through the following steps:
  - Let $y(t) = g(t, x) = e^{\alpha t}x(t)$.
  - Then, $dy(t) = \alpha e^{\alpha t}xdt + e^{\alpha t}dx(t)$.
  - Therefore, $dy(t) = \alpha e^{\alpha t}x(t)dt + e^{\alpha t}\alpha(\mu - x(t))dt$.
  - Therefore, $dy(t)(t) = e^{\alpha t}\alpha\mu dt$.
  - Finally, $y(t) = y(0) + \alpha\mu\int_0^t e^{\alpha s}ds = y(0) + \mu(e^{\alpha t} - 1)$.

Fact 11.4.3 (Solving the ODE $dx(t) = \alpha(\mu - x(t))dt$**)** *The ode $dx(t) = \alpha(\mu - x(t))dt$ admits solution*

$$x(t) = e^{-\alpha t}y(t) \Rightarrow x(t) = e^{-\alpha t}x(0) + \mu(1 - e^{-\alpha t}).$$

This is illustrated in Figure 11.12 and the accompanying Matlab code.

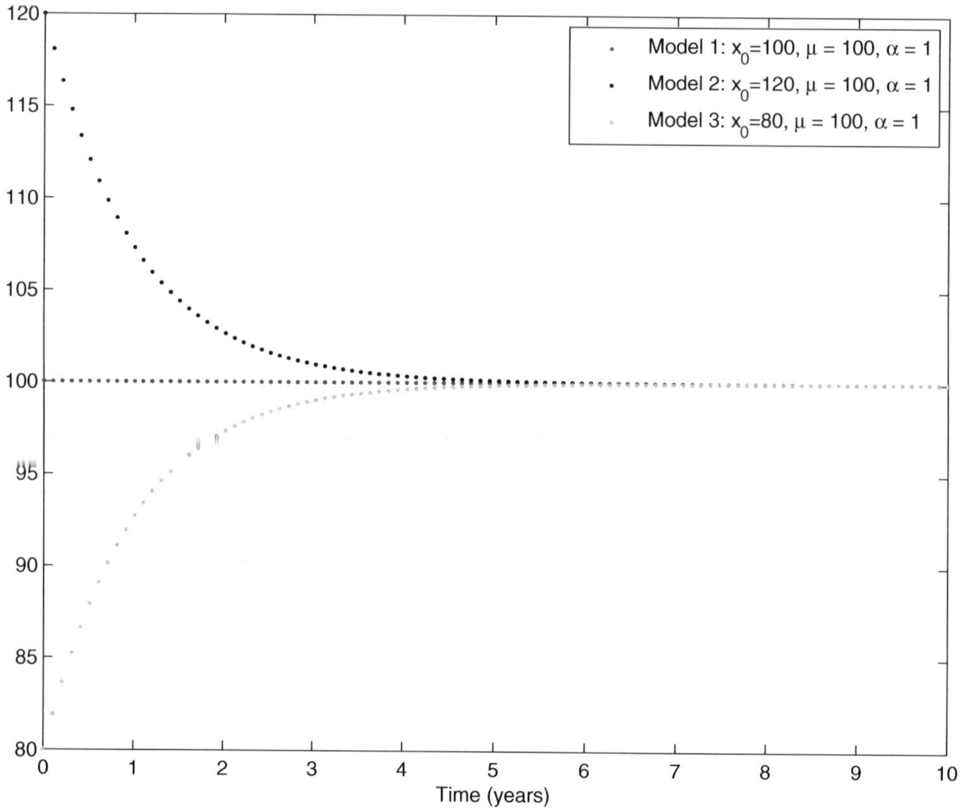

FIGURE 11.12 Solution of the equation $dx = \alpha(\mu - x)dt$ changing the initial condition x_0.

Matlab Code

```
%%%%%%%%%%%%%%%%%%%%%%%%%%%%%%%%%%%%%%%%%%%%%
%%%%MEAN REVERSION%%%%%%%%
%%%%%%%%%%%%%%%%%%%%%%%%%%%%%%%%%%%%%%%%%%%%%
clear all;expiry=10;
timestep=linspace(0,expiry,100)';
mu=100; alpha=1;
X0=100; sol1=mu+(X0-mu)*exp(-alpha*timestep);
X1=120; sol2=mu+(X1-mu)*exp(-alpha*timestep);
X2=80; sol3=mu+(X2-mu)*exp(-alpha*timestep);
%Plot solutions:
h=figure('Color', [ 1 1 1])
plot(timestep', [sol1, sol2, sol3],'.')
xlabel('Time (years)')
legend('Model 1: x 0=100, nmu = 100, nalpha = 1', ...
       'Model 2: x 0=120, nmu = 100, nalpha = 1 ',...
       'Model 3: x 0=80, nmu = 100, nalpha = 1')
print(h,'-dpng','LecBMFigMeanReversion.png')
```

11.4.2.2 Solving the SDE $dX(t) = \alpha(\mu - X(t))dt + \sigma dW(t)$

- We need to solve

$$dX(t) = \alpha(\mu - X(t))dt + \sigma dW(t). \tag{11.3}$$

- By analogy with the previous ODE, let us define

$$Y(t) = g(t, Xt) = e^{\alpha t}X(t)$$

and apply Itô's lemma.
- Then

$$\begin{aligned} dY(t) &= \left(\underbrace{\frac{\partial g(t,X)}{\partial t}}_{\alpha e^{\alpha t}X} + \alpha(\mu - X)\underbrace{\frac{\partial g(t,X)}{\partial X}}_{e^{\alpha t}} + \frac{1}{2}\sigma^2 \underbrace{\frac{\partial^2 g(t,X)}{\partial X^2}}_{0} \right) dt + \sigma \underbrace{\frac{\partial g(t,X)}{\partial X}}_{e^{\alpha t}} dW(t) \\ &= (\alpha e^{\alpha t}X + \alpha(\mu - X)e^{\alpha t})dt + \sigma e^{\alpha t}dW(t) \\ &= \alpha\mu e^{\alpha t}dt + \sigma e^{\alpha t}dW(t). \end{aligned}$$

- Therefore

$$\begin{aligned} Y(t) &= Y(0) + \int_0^t \alpha\mu e^{\alpha s}ds + \int_0^t \sigma e^{\alpha s}dW(s) \\ &= Y(0) + \mu(e^{\alpha t} - 1) + \int_0^t \sigma e^{\alpha s}dW(s). \end{aligned}$$

Fact 11.4.4 *The solution of the SDE (11.3) is*

$$X(t) = e^{-\alpha t}Y(t) = e^{-\alpha t}X(0) + \mu(1 - e^{-\alpha t}) + \sigma \int_0^t e^{-\alpha(t-s)}dW(s).$$

In addition, we also have that

$$X(t) \sim \mathcal{N}\left(\mathbb{E}_0(X(t)), \mathbb{V}ar_0(X(t))\right),$$

$$\mathbb{E}_0(X(t)) = e^{-\alpha t}X(0) + \mu(1 - e^{-\alpha t}),$$

$$\mathbb{V}ar_0(X(t)) = \sigma^2 \int_0^t e^{-2\alpha(t-s)}(s)ds = \frac{\sigma^2}{2\alpha}\left(1 - e^{-2\alpha t}\right),$$

where, in order to compute the variance, we have exploited the Itô isometry.

11.4.2.3 The (Auto)-Covariance Function

- Let us consider two time instants, t and s, $t < s$. We have for $t < s$ (but similarly for $s < t$) that $c_X(t,s)$ is given by

$$
\begin{aligned}
c_X(t,s) &= cov\left(\sigma \int_0^t e^{-\alpha(t-u)} dW(u), \sigma \int_0^s e^{-\alpha(t-u)} dW(u)\right) \\
&= \sigma^2 cov\left(\int_0^{min(t,s)} e^{-\alpha(t-u)} dW(u), \int_0^{min(t,s)} e^{-\alpha(s-u)} dW(u)\right) \\
&= \sigma^2 e^{-\alpha(t+s)} cov\left(\int_0^t e^{\alpha u} dW(u), \int_0^t e^{\alpha u} dW(u)\right) \\
&\quad \text{by the isometry property} \\
&= \sigma^2 e^{-\alpha(t+s)} \int_0^t e^{2\alpha u} d(u) \\
&= \sigma^2 \frac{e^{-\alpha(s-t)}}{2\alpha}.
\end{aligned}
$$

- With a similar reasoning, if we take t and s with $s < t$, we have

$$
c_X(t,s) = \sigma^2 \frac{e^{-\alpha(t-s)}}{2\alpha}.
$$

Fact 11.4.5 *The auto-covariance function of the Vasicek model is given by*

$$
c_X(t,s) = \sigma^2 \frac{e^{-\alpha|t-s|}}{2\alpha}.
$$

This result can be exploited to generate simultaneously the entire trajectory of the Vasicek model: we can simulate the full path by drawing samples from a multivariate normal distribution with the above covariance matrix.

11.4.2.4 Matlab: Simulation of the Vasicek Model Here we simulate the Vasicek model exploiting the solution in Fact 11.4.4. A sample of simulated paths is illustrated in Figure 11.13, whilst distributions originated at different time horizons are presented in Figure 11.14.

Matlab Code

```
%%%%%%%%%%%%%%%%%%%%%%%%%%%%%%%%%%%%
%%%%SIMULATING THE VASICEK MODEL%%%%
%%%%%%%%%%%%%%%%%%%%%%%%%%%%%%%%%%%%
clear all;close all
%Model: dr = a * (b - r ) * dt + sg * dW
%Assign Inputs
r0=0.05; a=10; b=0.07; sg=0.1; nstep=200; horizon=1;
nsimul=1000; dt=horizon/nstep;
%Compute the variance of the increments
vol2=(1-exp(-2*a*dt))/(2*a);
```

```
rall=[];
for j=1:nsimul
    %Initialize the interest rate vector
    r=zeros(nstep+1,1); r(1)=r0;
    %Simulate the increments
    dW=randn(nstep,1)*vol2^0.5;
    %Start iteration
    for i=1:nstep
        r(i+1)=b+exp(-a*dt)*(r(i)-b)+sg*dW(i);
    end
    %store the simulated path
    rall=[rall, r]
end
%Plot the sample path
h=figure('Color',[1 1 1])
plot([0:nstep]*dt,[rall, b+(r0-b)*exp(-a*[0:nstep]*dt)']);
xlabel('Time')
legend('Simulated path','Expected path')
title('Simulated path of the Vasicek model dr=a(b-r)dt+sg*dW')
print(h,'-djpg','LecBM SimVasicek new.jpg')
```

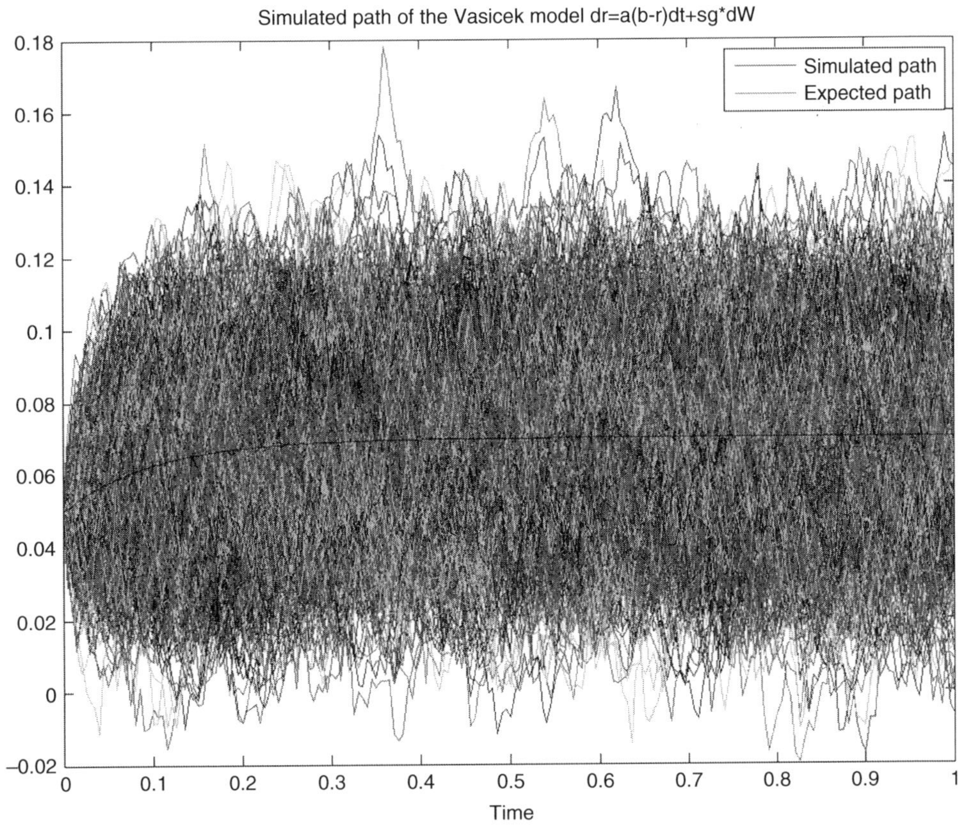

FIGURE 11.13 Parameters: $r_0 = 0.05$; $\alpha = 10$; $\mu = 0.07$; $\sigma = 0.1$; nstep = 200; horizon = 1.

Matlab Code

```
%%%%%%%%%%%%%%%%%%%%%%%%%%%%%%%%%%%%%%%%%%%%%%%%%%%
%%%%VASICEK densities at different time horizons%%%%
%%%%%%%%%%%%%%%%%%%%%%%%%%%%%%%%%%%%%%%%%%%%%%%%%%%
clear all
%Assign parameters
mu=0.09; sg=0.05; alpha=0.8;rt=0.04;
horizon=[0.25 0.5 0.75 1 5];
%Compute Exp. Value and variance
meanVas=mu+exp(-alpha*horizon).*(rt-mu);
varVas=sg*sg*(1-exp(-2*alpha*horizon))/(2*alpha);
range=linspace(mu-3*sg/(2*alpha)^0.5,...
            mu+3*sg/(2*alpha)^0.5,200);
pdfV=[];
for i=1:length(horizon)
meanV=meanVas(i);
stdV=varVas(i).^0.5;
pdfVas=pdf('norm', range,meanV,stdV);
pdfV=[pdfV;pdfVas];
end
h=figure('Color',[1 1 1])
plot(range,pdfV)
title('Pdf of the short rate at different times')
legend('0.25 yrs','0.5 yrs','0.75 yrs','1 years','5 yrs')
print(h,'-dpng','LecBMFigpdfVasicek.jpg')
```

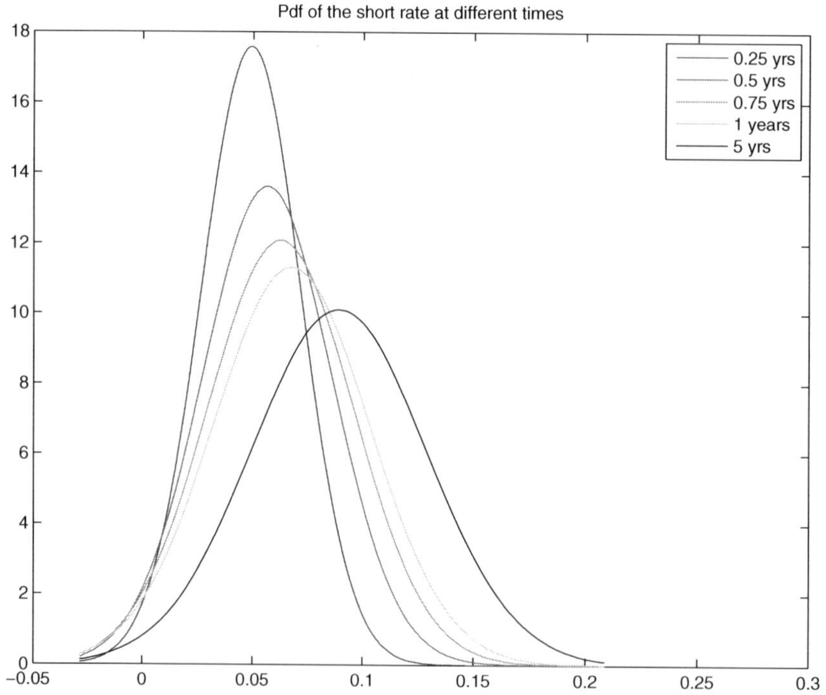

FIGURE 11.14 Density of the MR(0.09,0.8,0.05) at different horizons.

Mean-Reverting process MR(α, μ, σ): Facts

The SDE	$dX(t) = \alpha(\mu - X(t))dt + \sigma dW(t), X(0) = x_0$
The solution	$X(t) = e^{-\alpha t}X(0) + \mu(1 - e^{-\alpha t}) + \sigma \int_0^t e^{-\alpha(t-s)}dW(s)$
The distribution of $X(t)$	$X(t) \sim \mathcal{N}(\mathbb{E}_0(X(t)), \mathbb{V}ar_0(X(t)))$
The mean of $X(t)$	$\mathbb{E}_0(X(t)) = e^{-\alpha t}X(0) + \mu(1 - e^{-\alpha t})$
The variance of $X(t)$	$\mathbb{V}ar_0(X(t)) = \sigma^2 \int_0^t e^{-2\alpha(t-s)}(s)ds = \frac{\sigma^2}{2\alpha}(1 - e^{-2\alpha t})$
The stationary distribution of $X(t), (t \to \infty)$	$X(t) \sim \mathcal{N}\left(\mu, \frac{\sigma^2}{2\alpha}\right)$ if $\alpha > 0$
The auto-covariance of $X(t)$	$c_X(t, s) = \frac{\sigma^2}{2\alpha}e^{-\alpha\lvert t-s\rvert}$

11.4.2.5 Extension: MR with Deterministic Volatility

- We can generalize the Vasicek model to a deterministic time-varying volatility.
- The SDE becomes

$$dX(t) = \alpha(\mu - X(t))dt + \sigma(t)dW(t).$$

- It has solution

$$X(t) = X(0) + \mu(1 - e^{-\alpha t}) + \int_0^t \sigma(s)e^{-\alpha(t-s)}dW(s).$$

- The solution has the following properties (variance and covariance are computed using the isometry property):

$$\begin{aligned} X(t) &\sim \mathcal{N}\left(\mathbb{E}_0(X(t)), \mathbb{V}ar_0(X(t))\right), \\ \mathbb{E}_0(X(t)) &= X(0) + \mu(1 - e^{-\alpha t}), \\ \mathbb{V}ar_0(X(t)) &= \int_0^t \sigma^2(s)e^{-2\alpha(t-s)}ds, \\ \mathbb{C}ov_0(X(t), X(s)) &= \int_0^{min(t,s)} \sigma^2(u)e^{-2\alpha(t+s-2u)}du. \end{aligned}$$

11.4.3 The Cox–Ingersoll–Ross (CIR) Model

The SDE is given by

$$dX(t) = \alpha(\mu - X(t))dt + \sigma\sqrt{X(t)}dW(t).$$

This model has been introduced by Cox, Ingersoll and Ross to model the dynamics of the instantaneous interest rate. The peculiar form of the diffusion coefficient has been chosen to ensure that the process does not achieve negative values, still preserving the analytical tractability.

A detailed discussion of the properties of the square-root process can be found in: A. Cairns, *Interest Rate Models. An Introduction*. Princeton University Press, Princeton, NJ, 2004.

11.4.3.1 Solving the SDE $dX(t) = \alpha(\mu - X(t))dt + \sigma\sqrt{X(t)}dW(t)$

- The SDE for the short rate is given by

$$dX(t) = \alpha(\mu - X(t))dt + \sigma\sqrt{X}dW(t).$$

- This model shares with the Vasicek one the form of the drift term, so that it allows for mean reversion and interest rates cannot explode.
  - The mean-reversion property implies also that the interest rate displays a steady-state distribution.
- The difference with respect to the Vasicek model is the appearance of the square root term $\sqrt{X}$ in the diffusion term:
  - this ensures that the process remains non-negative in every instant of time and a zero rate of interest can become positive again.
  - The level of absolute variance increases with increasing interest rates.
- Unfortunately, this SDE does not admit an explicit solution, such as for the Vasicek model.
- This model is less tractable than the Vasicek one: the distribution of X is related to the non-central chi-square distribution.
- We can obtain a few properties of the solution such as expected value, variance and distribution.
- To do this, we exploit Itô's lemma.

11.4.3.2 Computing the Expectation of the CIR Model

- In particular, the expectation of $X(t)$, $\mu_X(t) = E(X(t))$, is the same as in the Vasicek model and is obtained by solving the ODE

$$d\mu_X(t) = \alpha(\mu - \mu_X(t))dt.$$

- Therefore, we have

$$\mu_X(t) = \mathbb{E}_0(X(t)) = e^{-\alpha t}X(0) + \mu(1 - e^{-\alpha t}).$$

- We observe that for large times t, we have

$$\mu_X(t) \to \mu.$$

11.4.3.3 Computing the Variance of the CIR Model

- To compute $\mathbb{V}ar_0(X(t))$, we proceed as follows:
  1. Let us define

$$Y(t) = X^2(t).$$

2. Let us find the SDE for $Y(t)$ by applying Itô's lemma:

$$dY(t) = (2X(t)\alpha(\mu - X(t)) + \sigma^2 X(t))dt + 2X(t)\sigma\sqrt{X(t)}dW(t)$$
$$= (2X(t)(\alpha\mu + \sigma^2) - 2\alpha Y(t))dt + 2X(t)\sigma\sqrt{X}dW(t).$$

3. Let us compute $\mu_Y(t) = \mathbb{E}_0(Y(t))$ by solving the ODE

$$d\mu_Y(t) = \left(2\mu_X(t)(\alpha\mu + \sigma^2) - 2\alpha\mu_Y(t)\right) dt.$$

4. This can be done by writing

$$d\mu_Y(t) + 2\alpha\mu_Y(t)dt = 2\mu_X(t)(\alpha\mu + \sigma^2)dt$$

and recognizing in the first term the derivative of $e^{2\alpha t}\mu_Y(t)$.
5. So, multiply both sides by $e^{2\alpha t}\mu_Y(t)$, integrate and get $\mu_Y(t)$.
6. Finally, the variance of $X(t)$ is obtained as $\mu_Y(t) - \mu_X^2(t)$:

$$\mathbb{V}ar_0(x(t)) = X(0)\left(\frac{\sigma^2}{\alpha}\right)\left(e^{-\alpha t} - e^{-2\alpha t}\right) + \mu\left(\frac{\sigma^2}{2\alpha}\right)(1 - e^{-\alpha t})^2.$$

7. Observe that for large times, we have

$$\mathbb{V}ar_0(x(t)) \to \mu\frac{\sigma^2}{2\alpha}.$$

11.4.3.4 The Distribution of the Short Rate in the CIR Model

- In order to get an intuition on the distribution of the short rate, let us consider the SDE

$$dX(t) = -\frac{\alpha}{2}X(t)dt + \frac{\sigma}{2}dW(t).$$

- The properties of $X(T)$ are known, being Gaussian with mean $m(T) = e^{-\frac{\alpha(T-t)}{2}}X(0)$ and variance $s^2(T) = \sigma^2(1 - e^{-\alpha(T-t)})/(4\alpha)$.
- Therefore, we can write $X(T) = s(T)Z(T) + m(T)$, where $Z(T)$ is a standard Gaussian random variable.
- Therefore, if we define

$$R(t) = X^2(t) = s^2(t)\left(Z(t) + \frac{m(t)}{s(t)}\right)^2,$$

we can say that $R(t)/s(T)$ will have a non-central chi-square distribution with 1 degree of freedom and parameter of non-centrality $m(t)/s(t)$ (see Appendix A).
- Now, let us apply Itô's lemma to $R(t)$:

$$dR(t) = \alpha(\mu - R(t))dt + \sigma\sqrt{R}dW(t),$$

where $\mu = \sigma^2/(4\alpha)$. Therefore, $R(t)$ follows a square-root process.

- This shows that the distribution of the solution of the square-root process above will have a non-central chi-square distribution with 1 degree of freedom and parameter of non-centrality $m(T)/s(T)$.
- However, if we generalize to

$$R(t) = \sum_i^d X_i^2(t),$$

where the X_i are d i.i.d. processes like above with coefficients α_i and σ_i, R will still have a non-central chi-square distribution but now with d degrees of freedom.
- The definition can be generalized to a non-integer number d.

Fact 11.4.6 (Distribution of X in the CIR Model) *Given $X(t)$, the distribution of*

$$X(T)/k$$

is a non-central chi-square distribution with d degrees of freedom and non-centrality parameter λ, where

$$d = \frac{4\alpha\mu}{\sigma^2}, \lambda = \frac{4\alpha X(t)}{\sigma^2(e^{\alpha(T-t)} - 1)}, k = \frac{\sigma^2(1 - e^{-\alpha(T-t)})}{4\alpha}.$$

The distribution of the CIR process is shown in Figure 11.15 (see also accompanying Matlab code).

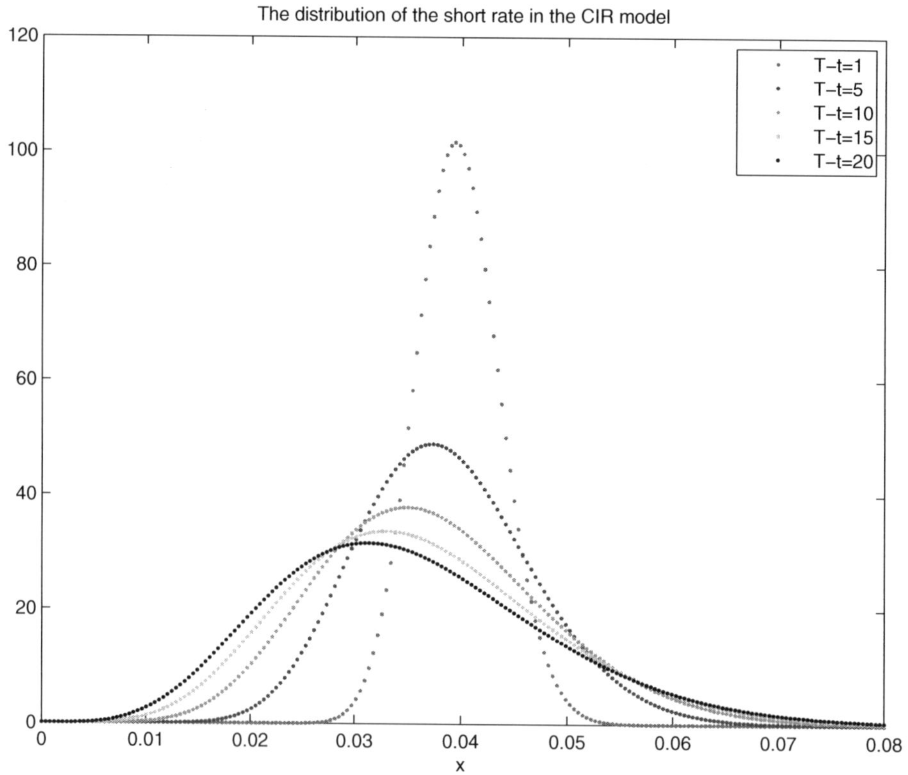

FIGURE 11.15 Density of the short rate in the CIR model at different horizons T. $\alpha = 0.1$, $\sigma = 0.01$, $r(t) = 0.03$, $\mu = 0.05$.

Fact 11.4.7 (Stationary Distribution of X in the CIR Model) *The stationary distribution of $X(t)$ for large t is Gamma, with density function*

$$\frac{\omega^\nu X(t)^{\nu-1} e^{-\omega X(t)}}{\Gamma(\nu)},$$

where

$$\omega = \frac{2\alpha}{\sigma^2}, \nu = \frac{2\alpha\mu}{\sigma^2}$$

and $\Gamma(x)$ is the Gamma function. In addition, the stationary mean and variance are respectively equal to μ and $\sigma^2\mu/(2\alpha)$.

Fact 11.4.8 (The Feller Positivity Condition) *If*

$$\frac{2\kappa\mu}{\sigma^2} > 1 \tag{11.4}$$

then X will never reach zero.

See Figure 11.16 for an illustration.

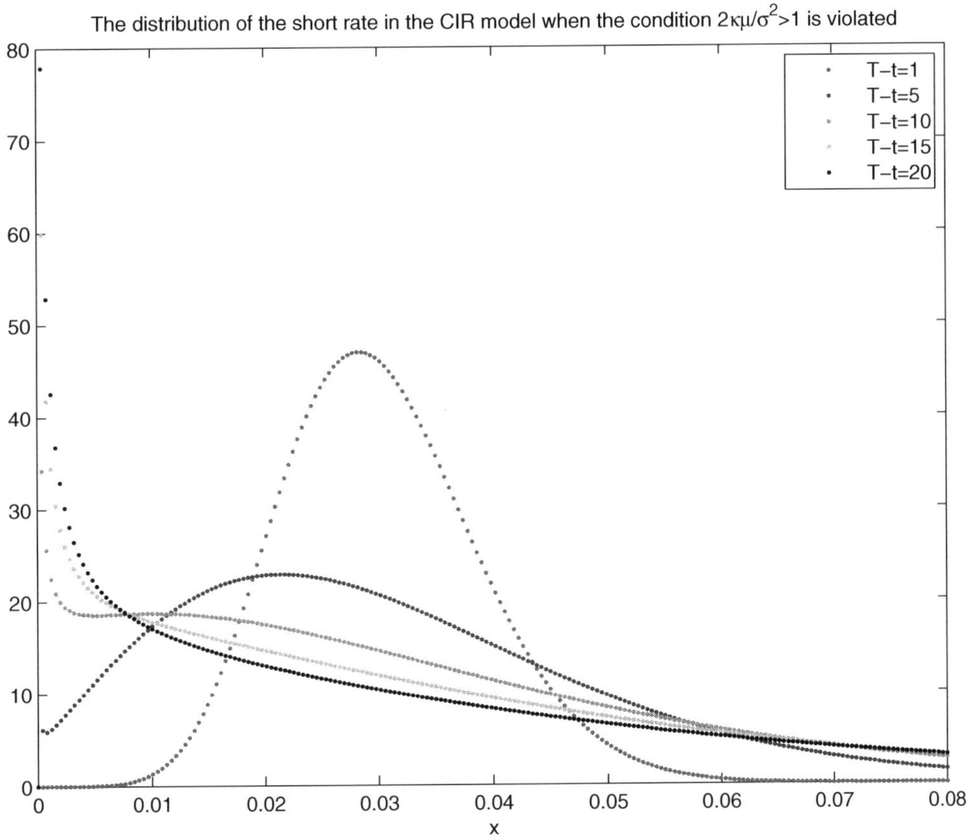

FIGURE 11.16 Short rate density in the CIR model when the Feller condition (11.4) is violated. $\alpha = 0.01$, $\sigma = 0.05$, $r(t) = 0.03$, $\mu = 0.05$.

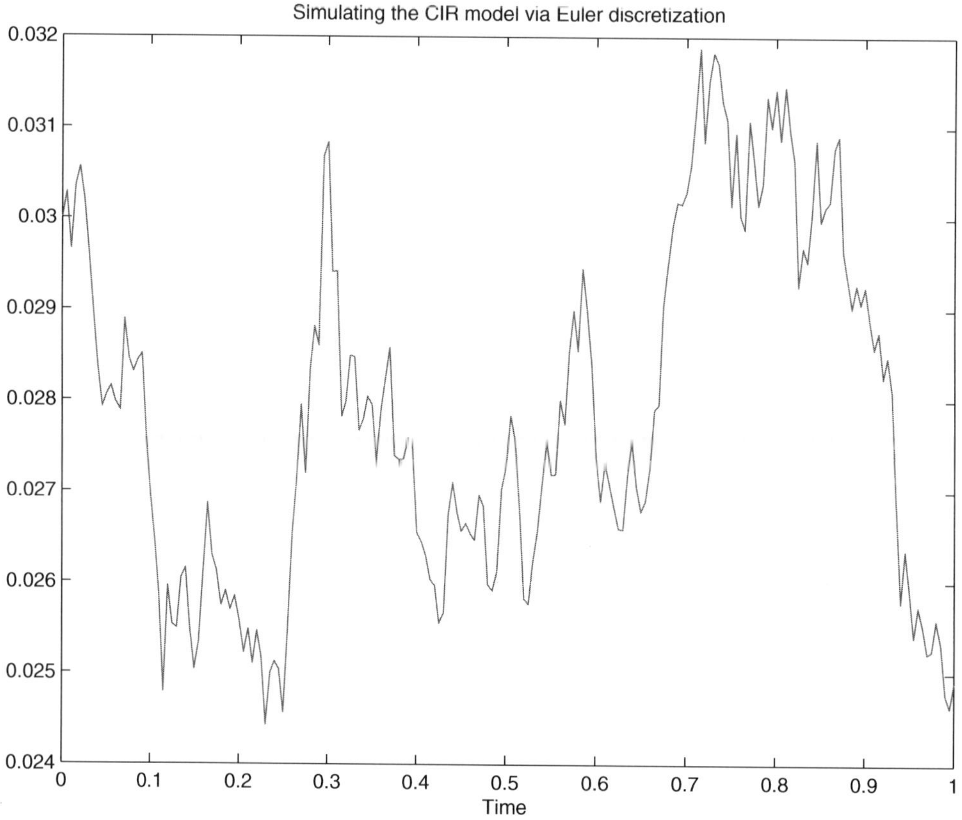

FIGURE 11.17 Simulated paths of the CIR model. Parameters: $\alpha = 0.01$, $\sigma = 0.05$, $r(t) = 0.03$, $\mu = 0.05$.

11.4.3.5 Simulating the CIR Model

- We can simulate the CIR model in at least three different ways.
  1. **Euler simulation**: we replace $dW(t)$ by $\epsilon(t)\sqrt{dt}$, where $\epsilon(t)$ is a standard Gaussian random variable:

$$X(t + dt) = X(t) + \alpha(\mu - X(t))dt + \sigma\sqrt{X(t)dt}\epsilon(t). \tag{11.5}$$

A sample trajectory is shown in Figure 11.17 (see also accompanying Matlab code).

Matlab Code

```
%%%%%%%%%%%%%%%%%%%%%%%%%%%%%%%%%%%%%%%%%%%%%%%%%%%%%%%%%%%
%%%%%%THE PDF OF THE SHORT RATE IN THE CIR MODEL%%%%%%%%%
%%%%%%%%%%%%%%%%%%%%%%%%%%%%%%%%%%%%%%%%%%%%%%%%%%%%%%%%%%%
%CIR Parameters
alpha=0.03; sigma=0.02; rt=0.04; mu=0.03;
```

```
tau=[1 5 10 15 20]; %time horizon
%compute d,k
d=4 *alpha *mu/sigma^2;
rT=linspace(0,0.08,200);
for i=1:length(tau)
    lambda=4*alpha* rt/(sigma2 *(exp(alpha*tau(i))-1));
    k=sigma2 *(1-exp(-alpha*tau(i)))/(4*alpha);
    pdfncchi2(i,:)=pdf('ncx2',rT/k,d,lambda)/k;
end
h=figure('Color', [ 1 1 1])
plot(rT,pdfncchi2,'.')
xlabel('x')
legend('T-t=1','T-t=5','T-t=10','T-t=15','T-t=20')
title('The density of the short rate in the CIR model')
print(h,'-djpeg','FigshortrateCIR.jpg')
```

2. **Gaussian approximation using exact moments**: in the Euler discretization we use the exact mean and the exact standard deviation, rather than the discretized version of the drift and diffusion coefficient:

$$X(t+dt) = e^{-\alpha dt}X(t) + \mu(1 - e^{-\alpha dt}) + \sqrt{\mathbb{V}ar_t(X(t+dt))}\epsilon(t), \tag{11.6}$$

where

$$\mathbb{V}ar_t(X(t+dt)) = X(t)\left(\frac{\sigma^2}{\alpha}\right)(e^{-\alpha dt} - e^{-2\alpha dt}) + \mu\left(\frac{\sigma^2}{2\alpha}\right)(1 - e^{-\alpha dt})^2.$$

A sample trajectory is shown in Figure 11.18 (see also accompanying Matlab code).

3. **Exact simulation**: we iteratively simulate from a non-central chi-square distribution changing the non-centrality parameter according to the current level of X:

$$X(t+dt) = k\chi^2_{d,\lambda}, \tag{11.7}$$

where

$$d = \frac{4\alpha\mu}{\sigma^2}, \lambda = \frac{4\alpha X(t)}{\sigma^2(e^{\alpha dt} - 1)}, k = \frac{\sigma^2(1 - e^{-\alpha dt})}{4\alpha}.$$

So at each time step, we have to simulate a non-central chi-square distribution. This can be done using the Matlab command icdf ('ncx2', rand, d, lambda). A sample trajectory is shown in Figure 11.19 (see also accompanying Matlab code).

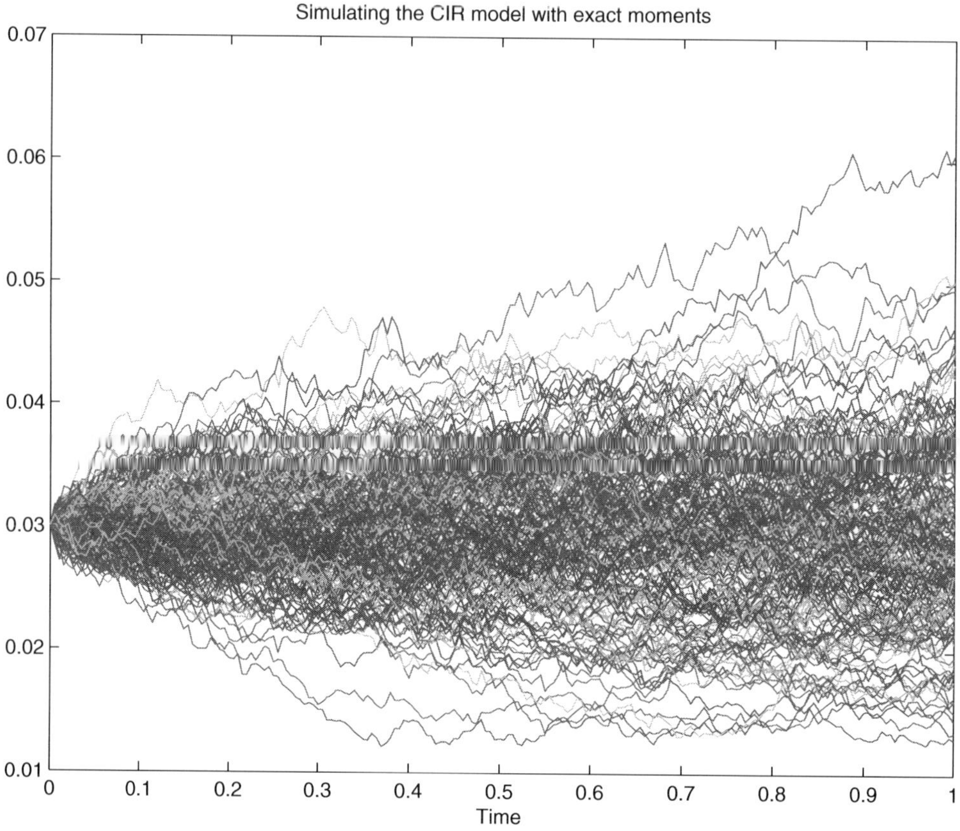

FIGURE 11.18 Simulated paths of the CIR model with exact moments. Parameters: $\alpha = 0.01$, $\sigma = 0.05$, $r(t) = 0.03$, $\mu = 0.05$.

- The third method, albeit exact, is the most expensive and is very slow, as shown in the following table where we provide the CPU time (in seconds) to simulate one path with 200 time steps:

Method	CPU (s)
Euler	0.008382
Gaussian	0.010881
Exact	61.87

- Therefore, we suggest using the second method, Gaussian discretization with exact moments. It allows us to achieve a good trade-off between accuracy and computational time.

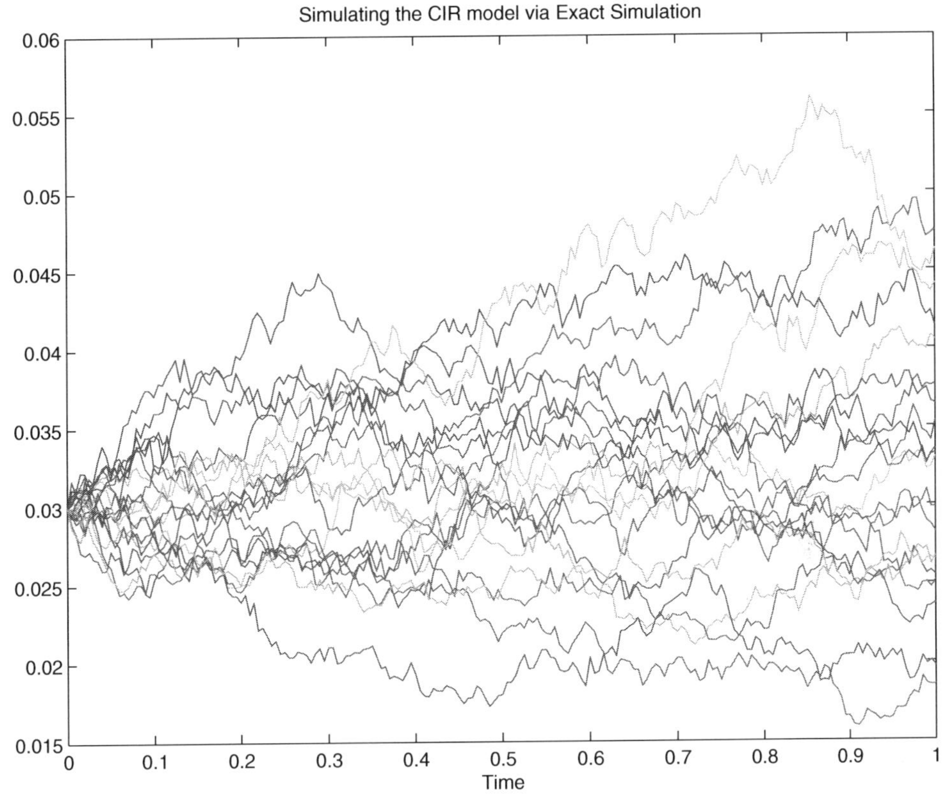

FIGURE 11.19 Simulated paths of the CIR model sampling from the non-central chi-square distribution. Parameters: $\alpha = 0.01$, $\sigma = 0.05$, $r(t) = 0.03$, $\mu = 0.05$.

Square-Root Mean-Reverting Process MR(α, μ, σ): Facts

The SDE	$dX(t) = \alpha(\mu - X(t))dt + \sigma\sqrt{X(t)}dW(t), X(0) = x_0$
The solution of the SDE	is not explicit
The distribution of $X(t)$	$X(t) \sim k \times \chi^2_{d,\lambda}$
The mean of $X(t)$	$\mathbb{E}_0(X(t)) = e^{-\alpha t}X(0) + \mu(1 - e^{-\alpha t})$
The variance of $X(t)$	$\mathbb{V}ar_0(X(t)) = X(0)\left(\frac{\sigma^2}{\alpha}\right)\left(e^{-\alpha t} - e^{-2\alpha t}\right) + \mu\left(\frac{\sigma^2}{2\alpha}\right)(1 - e^{-\alpha t})^2$
If $2\alpha\mu > \sigma^2$, the stationary distribution ($t \to \infty$) of $X(t)$ is Gamma	$X(t) \sim \frac{\omega^\nu X(t)^{\nu-1} e^{-\omega X(t)}}{\Gamma(\nu)}$, if $\alpha > 0$
The stationary mean of $X(t), (t \to \infty)$.	μ
The stationary variance of $X(t), (t \to \infty)$	$\mu \frac{\sigma^2}{2\kappa}$

Matlab Code

```
%%%%%%%%%%%%%%%%%%%%%%%%%%%%%%%%%%%%%%%%%%%%%%%%%%%%%%%%%%%
%%%%%SIMULATING THE CIR MODEL: EULER DISCRETIZATION %%%%%
%%%%%%%%%%%%%%%%%%%%%%%%%%%%%%%%%%%%%%%%%%%%%%%%%%%%%%%%%%%
nstep=200; horizon=1; nsimul=100
dt=horizon/nstep;
rall=[];
for j=1:nsimul
    r=zeros(nstep+1,1); r(1)=rt;
    for i=1:nstep
        r(i+1)=r(i)+ alpha*(mu-r(i))*dt+...
                   sigma *sqrt(r(i)*dt)*randn;
    end
    rall=[rall, r];
end
h=figure('Color',[1 1 1])
plot(dt*[0:nstep]',rall)
xlabel('Time')
title('Simulating the CIR model via Euler discretization')
print(h,'-djpeg','FigshortrateCIR Euler.jpg')
```

11.4.4 The Constant Elasticity of Variance (CEV) Model

- The CEV model has dynamics

$$dX(t) = \mu X(t)dt + \sigma X^{\beta+1}(t)dW(t). \tag{11.8}$$

- For $\beta > 0$ ($\beta < 0$) the local volatility, defined as $\frac{SDev(dX)}{X} = \sigma X^{\beta}$, increases (decreases) monotonically as the asset price increases.
- Therefore, the so-called leverage effect, that is the inverse relationship between spot price and volatility, can be recovered by taking $\beta < 0$.
- For example, Rubinstein and Jackwerth (1996) find that typical values of the CEV elasticity implicit in the S&P 500 stock index option prices are strongly negative and as low as $\beta = -4$. They term the corresponding model unrestricted CEV.
- The unrestricted CEV process is used to model the volatility smile effect in the equity index options market.

Matlab Code

```
%%%%%%%%%%%%%%%%%%%%%%%%%%%%%%%%%%%%%%%%%%%%%%%%%%%%%%%%%%%
%%%SIMULATING THE CIR MODEL: GAUSSIAN APPROXIMATION %%%%%
%%%WITH EXACT MEAN AND VARIANCE%%%%%%%%%%%%%%%%%%%%%%%%%%%
%%%%%%%%%%%%%%%%%%%%%%%%%%%%%%%%%%%%%%%%%%%%%%%%%%%%%%%%%%%
clear all
```

```
clc
alpha=0.01; sigma=0.05; rt=0.03; mu=0.05;
nstep=200; horizon=1;nsimul=100
dt=horizon/nstep;
rall=[];
for j=1:nsimul
    r=zeros(nstep+1,1); r(1)=rt;
    for i=1:nstep
        m=exp(-alpha*dt)*r(i)+mu*(1-exp(-alpha*dt));
        v=r(i)*(sigma*sigma/alpha)*...
          (exp(-alpha*dt)-exp(-2*alpha*dt))...
          +mu*(sigma*sigma/(2*alpha))*...
          (1-exp(-alpha*dt))^2;
        r(i+1)=m + sqrt(v)*randn;
    end
    rall=[rall, r];
end
h=figure('Color',[1 1 1])
plot(dt*[0:nstep]',rall)
xlabel('Time')
title('Simulating the CIR model with exact moments')
```

Matlab Code

```
%%%%%%%%%%%%%%%%%%%%%%%%%%%%%%%%%%%%%%%%%%%%%%%%%%%%%%%%%%%%%%%%
%%%%%SIMULATING THE CIR MODEL: EXACT METHOD%%%%%%%%%%
%%%%%%%%%%%%%%%%%%%%%%%%%%%%%%%%%%%%%%%%%%%%%%%%%%%%%%%%%%%%%%%%
clear all; clc
%CIR Parameters
alpha=0.01; sigma=0.05; rt=0.03; mu=0.05;
nstep=200; horizon=1; nsimul=20;
dt=horizon/nstep;
r=zeros(nstep+1,1); r(1)=rt;
rall=[];
%compute d,k
d=4 *alpha *mu/sigma^2;

k=sigma^2 *(1-exp(-alpha*dt))/(4*alpha);

for j=1:nsimul
    r=zeros(nstep+1,1); r(1)=rt;
    for i=1:nstep
        lambda=4*alpha* r(i)/(sigma^2 *(exp(alpha*dt)-1));
        r(i+1,:)=icdf('ncx2',rand,d,lambda)*k;
```

```
    end
    rall=[rall, r];
end

h=figure('Color', [ 1 1 1])
plot(dt*[0:nstep]',rall)
xlabel('Time')
title('Simulating the CIR model via Exact Simulation')
```

- The CEV name is due to the fact that if we define the elasticity of a function $f(x)$ as

$$E_f(x) = \frac{\partial f(x)}{\partial x}\frac{x}{f(x)}$$

and we set

$$f(x) = \mathbb{SD}ev\left(\frac{dX}{X}\right) = \sigma X^{\beta},$$

then

$$E_f(x) = \beta,$$

in other words, it does not depend on X (i.e., it is constant).
- The CEV model admits as particular cases:
  - The O–U Gaussian process when $\beta = -1$.
  - The GBM process when $\beta = 0$, i.e. the elasticity is zero.
  - The squared root (SR) process when $\beta = -1/2$.
- The CEV SDE does not admit a closed-form solution, however the transition probability density over a time frame of length Δ

$$p(X, \xi; \Delta) := e^{-r\Delta}\, p_0\left(X, e^{-r\Delta}\xi; \frac{1}{2r\beta}\left(e^{2r\beta\Delta} - 1\right)\right),$$

with

$$p_0(X, \xi; \Delta) = \frac{\xi^{-2\beta-\frac{3}{2}} X^{\frac{1}{2}}}{\sigma^2|\beta|\Delta}\, e^{-\frac{X^{-2\beta}+\xi^{-2\beta}}{2\sigma^2\beta^2\Delta}}\, I_{\frac{1}{2|\beta|}}\left(\frac{X^{-\beta}\xi^{-\beta}}{\sigma^2\beta^2\Delta}\right),$$

where I_ν is the modified Bessel function of the first kind of order ν.
- In Figure 11.20 we plot the density function of the CEV process for different values of β. In Figure 11.21 we plot the corresponding implied volatility curve. In particular, large negative values of β generate very steep implied volatility curves, as often observed in the option market.

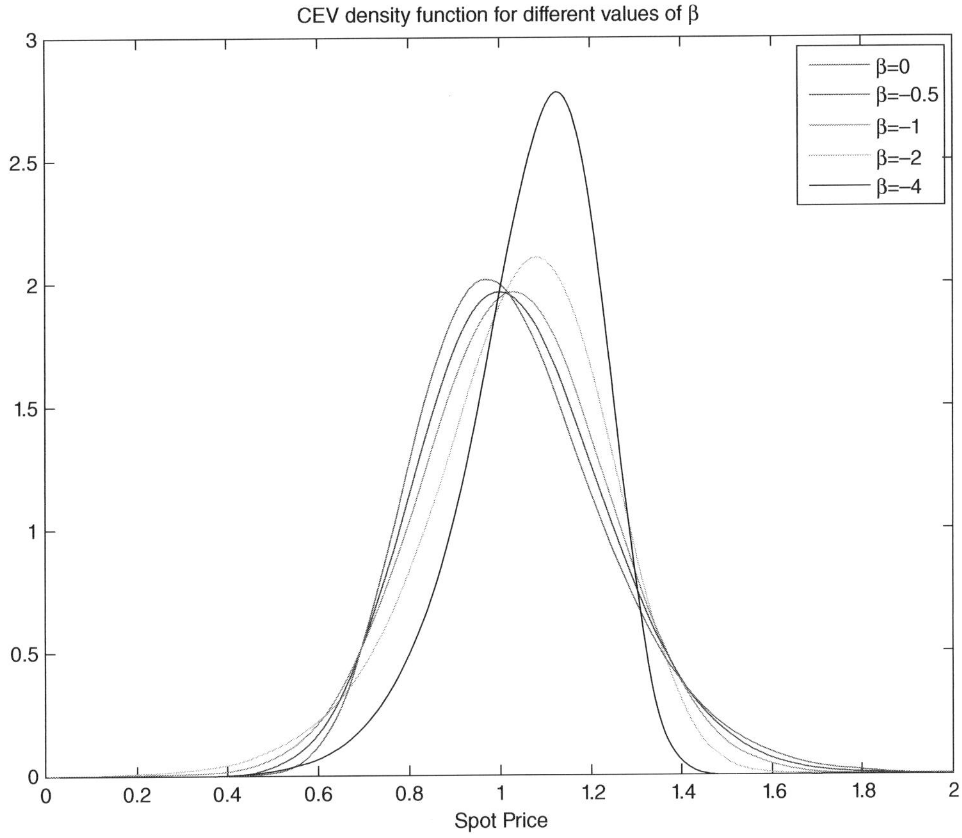

FIGURE 11.20 Density function of the CEV model for different values of β.

11.4.5 The Brownian Bridge

Fact 11.4.9 (Brownian Bridge) *Let $W(t)$ be a Brownian motion. Fix $s > 0$ and $T > 0$ with $s < T$, $a \in \mathbb{R}$ and $b \in \mathbb{R}$. We define the Brownian bridge from a to b on $[s, T]$ to be the process $B(t)$ satisfying the SDE*

$$dX_t = \frac{b - X(t)}{T - t}dt + dW(t), \tag{11.9}$$

with initial condition at time s $B(s) = a$.

11.4.5.1 A Note: The Ordinary Differential Equation $dx(t) = (b - x(t))/(T - t)dt$

- We would like to solve the SDE of the Brownian bridge. Let us start by considering the deterministic version:

$$dx(t) = \frac{b - x(t)}{T - t}dt.$$

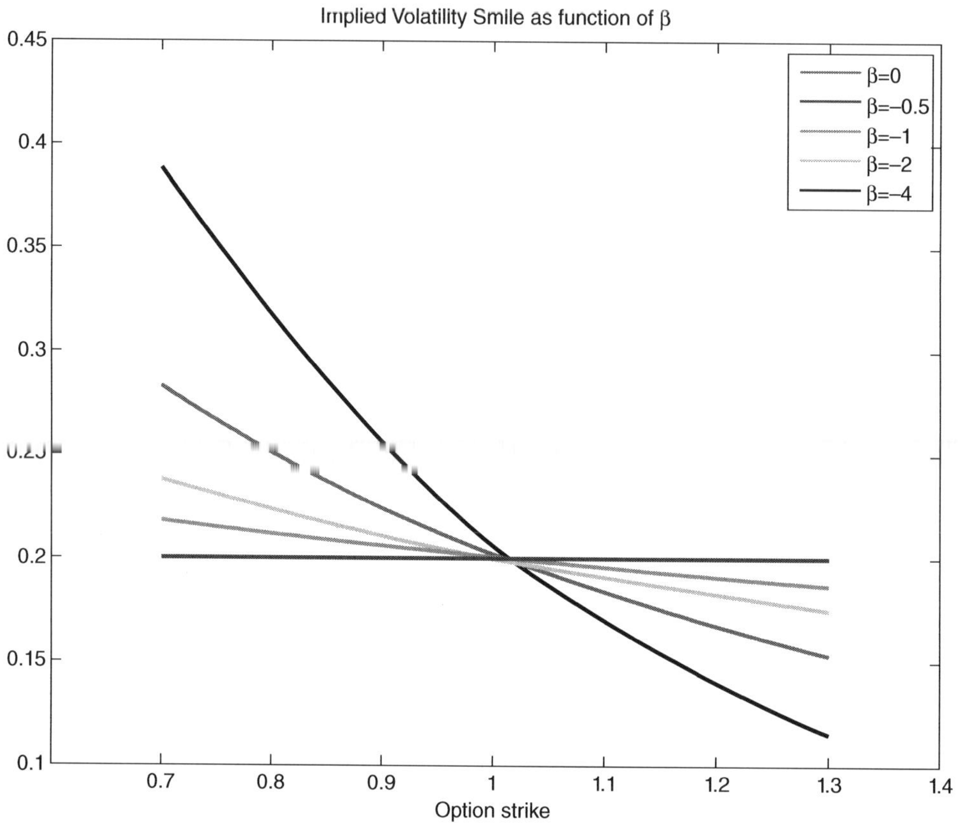

FIGURE 11.21 Implied volatility in the CEV model for different values of β.

- We proceed through the following steps:
  - Let $y(t) = g(t,x) = (T-s)/(T-t)x(t)$.
  - Then, $dy(t) = b(T-s)/(T-t)$.
  - Finally, $y(t) = y(s) + b(t-s)/(T-t)$.

We can conclude:

Fact 11.4.10 (Solving the ODE $dx(t) = (b - x(t))/(T-t)dt$**)** *The ODE* $dx(t) = (b - x(t))/(T-t)dt$ *admits the solution*

$$x(t) = a + (b-a)\frac{t-s}{T-s}$$

11.4.5.2 Solving the SDE $dX_t = (b - X(t))/(T-t)dt + dW(t)$

- We need to solve

$$dX_t = \frac{b - X(t)}{T-t}dt + dW(t).$$

- By analogy with the previous ODE, let us define

$$Y(t) = g(t, X(t)) = \frac{T-s}{T-t} X(t)$$

and apply Itô's lemma. Then it follows that:

$$\begin{aligned} dY(t) &= \left(X(t)\frac{T-s}{(T-t)^2} + \frac{T-s}{T-t}\frac{b-X(t)}{T-t} \right) dt + \frac{T-s}{T-t} dW(t) \\ &= b\frac{T-s}{(T-t)^2} + \frac{T-s}{T-t} dW(t). \end{aligned}$$

- Therefore

$$Y(t) = a + b\frac{t-s}{T-s} + (T-s)\int_s^t \frac{1}{T-u} dW(u).$$

Fact 11.4.11 (Solving the SDE $dX_t = \frac{b-X(t)}{T-t}dt + dW(t)$) *The solution of the SDE (11.9) is*

$$X(t) = a + \frac{t-s}{T-s}(b-a) + (T-t)\int_s^t \frac{1}{T-u} dW(u).$$

Further

$$\begin{aligned} X(t) &\sim \mathcal{N}\left(\mathbb{E}_0(X(t)), \mathbb{V}ar_0(X(t))\right), \\ \mathbb{E}_0(X(t)) &= a + \frac{t-s}{T-s}(b-a), \\ \mathbb{V}ar_0(X(t)) &= \frac{(t-s)(T-t)}{T-s}, \\ c_X(t,z) &= \frac{(t\wedge z - s)(T - t\vee z)}{T-s}. \end{aligned}$$

- The function $a + \frac{t-s}{T-s}(b-a)$, as a function of t, is the line from (s, a) to (T, b).
- To this line, we add the Brownian bridge from 0 to 0 on $[s, T]$.
- This generates a process that begins at a at time s and terminates at b at time T.

Remark 11.4.2 *Notice that the process*

$$X(t) = a + \frac{t-s}{T-s}(b-a) + (T-t)\int_s^t \frac{1}{T-u} dW(u)$$

is equivalent (e.g., they have the same distribution, mean, variance and (auto)-covariance) to

$$X(t) = a + \frac{t-s}{T-s}(b-a) + (W_t - W_s) - \frac{t-s}{T-s}(W_T - W_s).$$

11.4.5.3 Matlab Implementation: Simulating Brownian Motions (Part 2) The primary use for the Brownian bridge in finance is as an aid to Monte Carlo simulation, since the Brownian bridge $X(t)$ represents a Brownian motion on the time interval $[s, T]$, starting at $W_s = a$ and conditioned to arrive at b at time T.

- To see this, consider a time partition such that $t_i < t_j < t_k$.
- Let

$$\begin{aligned} X &= W(t_j) - W(t_i), \\ Y &= W(t_k) - W(t_j), \\ Z &= W(t_k) - W(t_i) = X + Y. \end{aligned}$$

- Then X and Y are independent; moreover, $X \sim \mathcal{N}\left(0, \sigma_X^2\right)$, $Y \sim \mathcal{N}\left(0, \sigma_Y^2\right)$ and $Z \sim \mathcal{N}\left(0, \sigma_Z^2\right)$, where $\sigma_X^2 = t_j - t_i$, $\sigma_Y^2 = t_k - t_j$ and $\sigma_Z^2 = t_k - t_i = \sigma_X^2 + \sigma_Y^2$.
- Therefore, the conditional density of X given Y is

$$\begin{aligned} f_{X|Z}(x) &= \frac{f_X(x) f_Y(y)}{f_Z(z)} \\ &= \frac{1}{B\sqrt{2\pi}} e^{-\frac{1}{2}\left(\frac{x-Az}{B}\right)^2}, \end{aligned}$$

  where $A = \sigma_X^2/\sigma_Z^2$ and $B = \sigma_X \sigma_Y / \sigma_Z$.
- Hence, we can claim conditioning on the knowledge of the process value at time t_k, $W_{t_j} - W_{t_i} \sim \mathcal{N}(Az, B^2)$.
- From this, it follows that

$$W_{t_j} = \frac{t_k - t_j}{t_k - t_i} W_{t_i} + \frac{t_j - t_i}{t_k - t_i} W_{t_k} + \sqrt{\frac{(t_k - t_j)(t_j - t_i)}{t_k - t_i}} \varepsilon, \qquad \varepsilon \sim \mathcal{N}(0, 1). \tag{11.10}$$

- But this is the Brownian bridge from W_{t_i} to W_{t_k} on $[t_i, t_k]$.

Hence, we can simulate the value of the Brownian motion at each time step over $[0, T]$ by using the Brownian bridge according to the following steps:

- Simulate first the value of Brownian motion at time T. Set b equal to this value and set $a = 0$.
- Simulate $W(t_1)$, using (11.10).
- Set $a = W(t_1)$ and repeat for all $t_j \in (0, T)$.

Resulting sample trajectories are shown in Figure 11.22 (see also accompanying Matlab code).

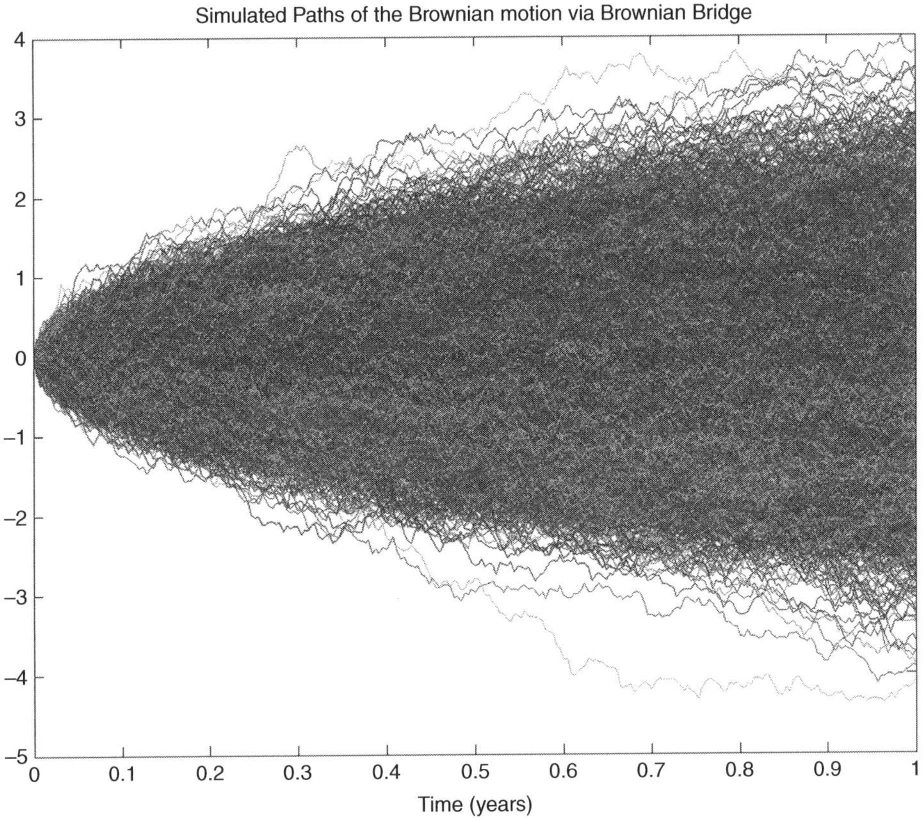

FIGURE 11.22 Brownian motion via Brownian bridge.

11.4.6 The Stochastic Volatility Heston Model (1987)

- Stochastic volatility models are widely used in investment banks and financial institutions.
- The model is sufficiently complex to explain the volatility smile in the option market.
- The dynamics of the log-price is

$$s(t) = \log S(t),$$

$$ds(t) = \left(\mu - \frac{1}{2}v(t)\right) dt + \sqrt{v(t)}dW_s(t),$$
$$dv(t) = k\,(\theta - v(t))\, dt + \varepsilon \sqrt{v(t)}dW_v(t).$$

- The correlation between the two Brownian motions affecting the dynamics of the two state variables is

$$\mathbb{E}(dW_s(t)dW_v(t)) = \rho dt.$$

- The model parameters are:

  k = mean-reversion speed

  θ = long-run variance

  ε = volatility of variance

  ρ = correlation coefficient between the underlying and volatility.

- The parameter restrictions are

$$S_0, v_0, k, \theta, \varepsilon > 0, \quad \rho \in [-1, 1].$$

Matlab Code

```
%%%%%%%%%%%%%%%%%%%%%%%%%%%%%%%%%%%%%%%%%%%%%%%%%%%%%%%%%%%%%%%%
%%%%SIMULATING THE BROWNIAN BRIDGE                    %%%%%%%%%%
%%%%%%%%%%%%%%%%%%%%%%%%%%%%%%%%%%%%%%%%%%%%%%%%%%%%%%%%%%%%%%%%
%Assigning the number of simulated paths
%(nsimul), time to maturity (expiry), number of steps
%(nsteps), time step (dt) and observation times (timestep)
clear all;
nsimul=10000, expiry=1, nsteps=250;
dt=expiry/nsteps;
timestep=[0:dt:expiry]';
Wt=zeros(nsteps+1,nsimul);
%Simulate the Brownian motion at T:
eY = randn(1,nsimul);
Wt(nsteps+1,:)= sqrt(expiry).*eY;
%Simulate the Brownian motion W(t):
for j=2:nsteps
    deltat1=(nsteps+1-j)/(nsteps+1-j+1);
    eYt = randn(1,nsimul);
    Wt(j,:)=deltat1*Wt(j-1,:)+...
    (1-deltat1)*Wt(nsteps+1,:)+...
    sqrt(deltat1*dt)*eYt;
end
Bb=Wt;
%Plot simulated paths:
h=figure('Color',[1 1 1])
plot(timestep, Bb)
title('Simulated Paths of the BM via Brownian Bridge')
xlabel('Time (years)')
```

- The variance process is always positive and cannot reach 0, if:

$$\varepsilon^2 \leq 2\kappa\theta \quad \text{(Feller condition)}.$$

11.4.6.1 The Characteristic Function of the Log-Price

- The Heston model fits in the class of affine models: drift and covariance are linear in the state vector (x, v).
- The Heston model has no jump component.
- Heston's characteristic function can be computed in closed form:

$$\psi^H(u; s_t, v_t, r, T-t) = \mathbb{E}_t\left[e^{ius_T}\right] = e^{C(u,T-t)+D(u,T-t)v+i\phi s_t},$$

$$C(u,\tau) = iu(r-q)\tau + \frac{k\theta}{\varepsilon^2}\left((k - i\rho\varepsilon u - d)\tau - 2\ln\frac{1-ge^{-d\tau}}{1-g}\right),$$

$$D(u,\tau) = \frac{1}{\varepsilon^2}(k - i\rho\varepsilon u - d)\frac{1-e^{-d\tau}}{1-ge^{-d\tau}},$$

  where

$$\begin{aligned} i &= \sqrt{-1}, \\ \tau &= T - t, \\ d &= \sqrt{(i\rho\varepsilon u - k)^2 + \varepsilon^2(iu + u^2)}, \\ g &= \frac{k - i\rho\varepsilon u - d}{k - i\rho\varepsilon u + d}. \end{aligned}$$

- The density function is given by

$$f_H(s(T), v(t), \tau) = \frac{1}{\pi}\int_0^\infty Re\left[e^{-ius(T)}\psi^H(u; s(t), v(t), r, \tau)\right] du.$$

  This is illustrated in Figures 11.23–11.26 for different value of the model parameters.

- The call option price is given by

$$c_H\left(S, v = \sigma_t^2\right) = SP_1 - KP(t,T)P_2,$$

  where

$$P_j = \frac{1}{2} + \frac{1}{\pi}\int_0^\infty Re\left[\frac{e^{-iu\ln K}f_j(x, v, \tau; u)}{iu}\right] du, j = 1, 2.$$

  Here S = stock price, $\tau = T - t$ = time to maturity, K = strike price, $Re()$ is the real part of a complex variable, $x = \ln(S)$ and $P(t,T) = e^{-r(T-t)}$ is the discount factor,

$$f_j(x, v, \tau, \phi) = \exp(C_j(\phi, \tau) + D_j(\phi, \tau)v + iux),$$

  $i = \sqrt{-1}$, $C_j(\phi, \tau)$ and $D_j(\phi, \tau)$ are functions (given in the Heston paper) that depend on τ and the model parameters, but not on x and v.
- The put option price can be computed via put–call parity.

The resulting implied volatilities are shown in Figures 11.27–11.30 for different values of the model parameters.

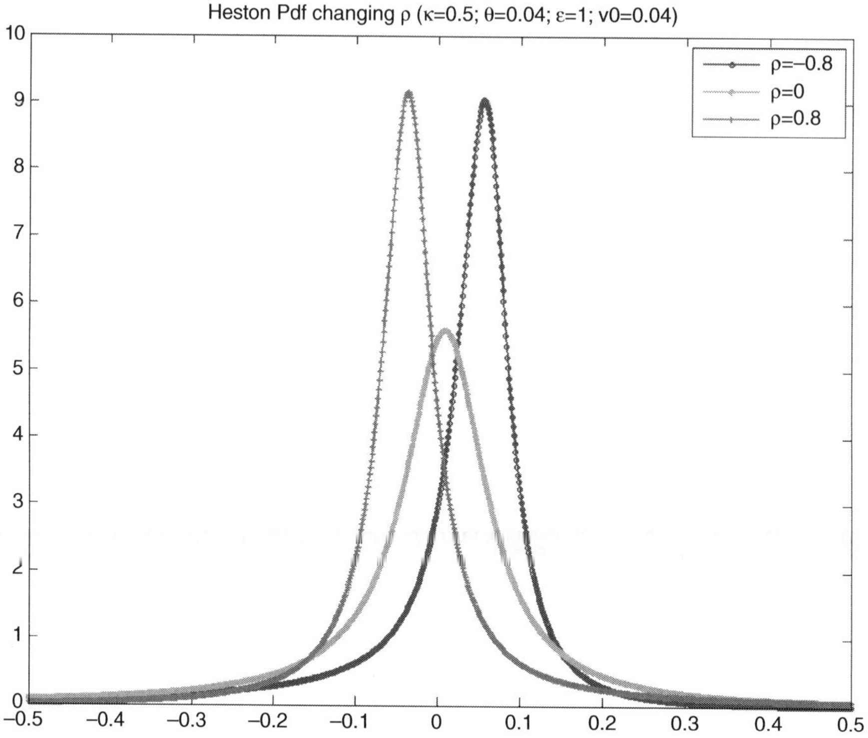

FIGURE 11.23 Heston pdf changing ρ.

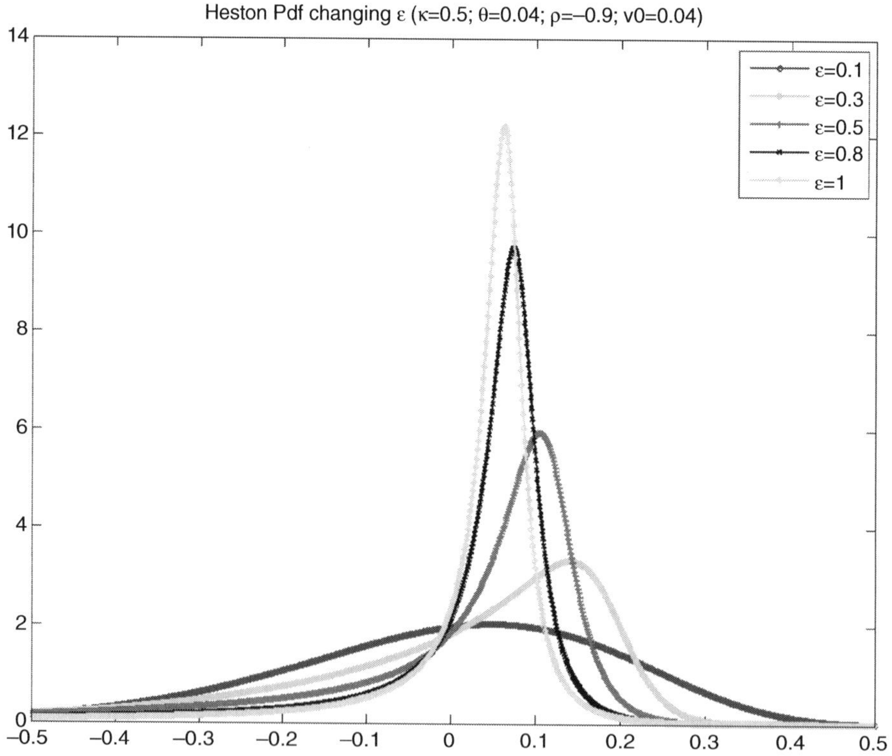

FIGURE 11.24 Heston pdf changing ε.

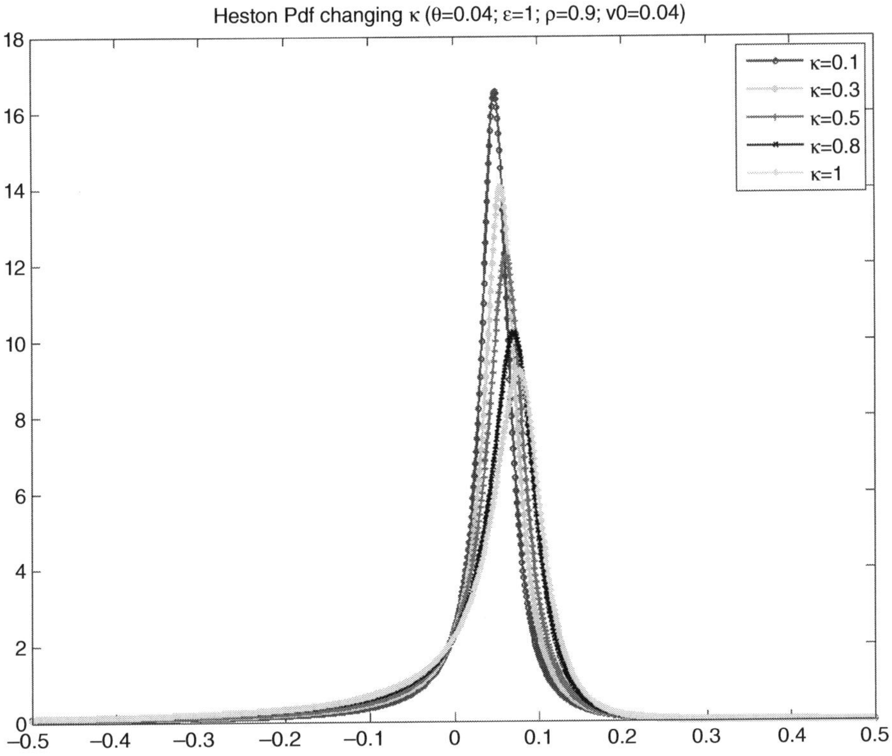

FIGURE 11.25 Heston pdf changing κ.

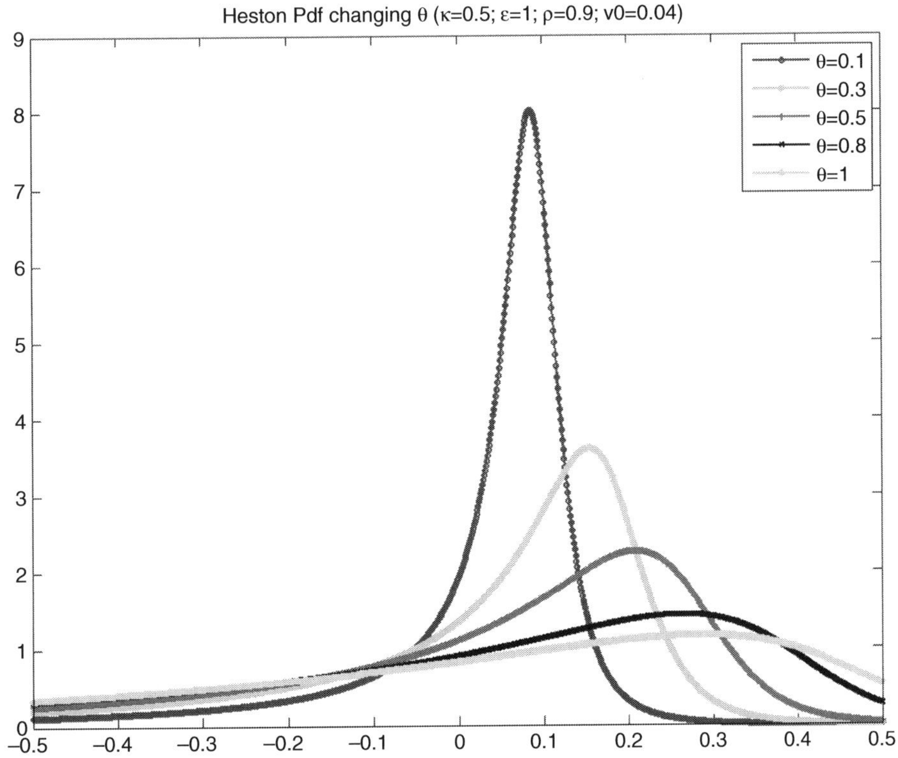

FIGURE 11.26 Heston pdf changing θ.

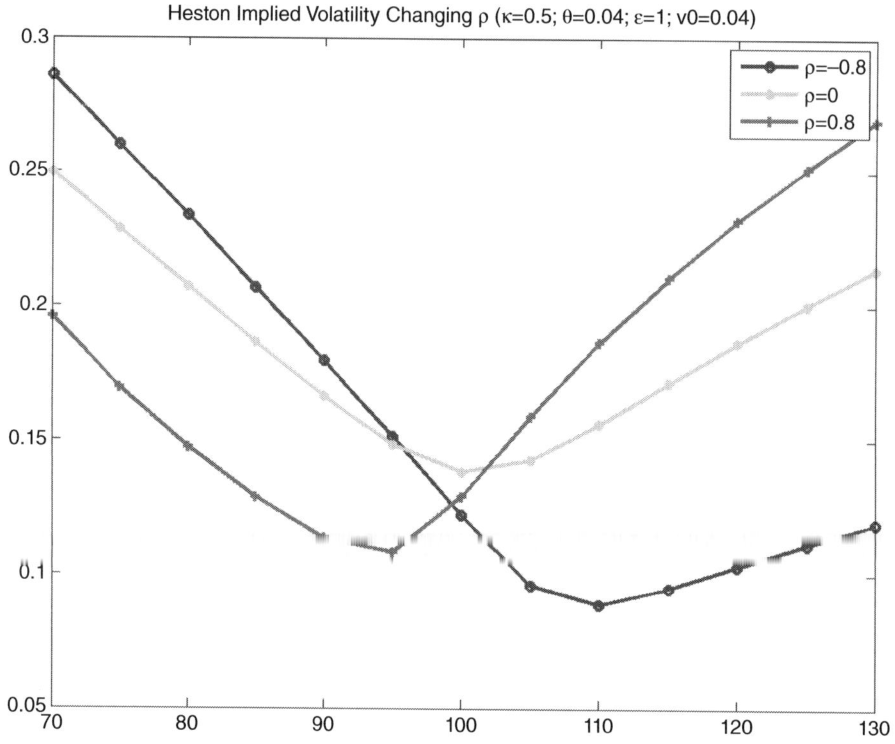

FIGURE 11.27 Black–Scholes implied volatility changing ρ in the Heston model.

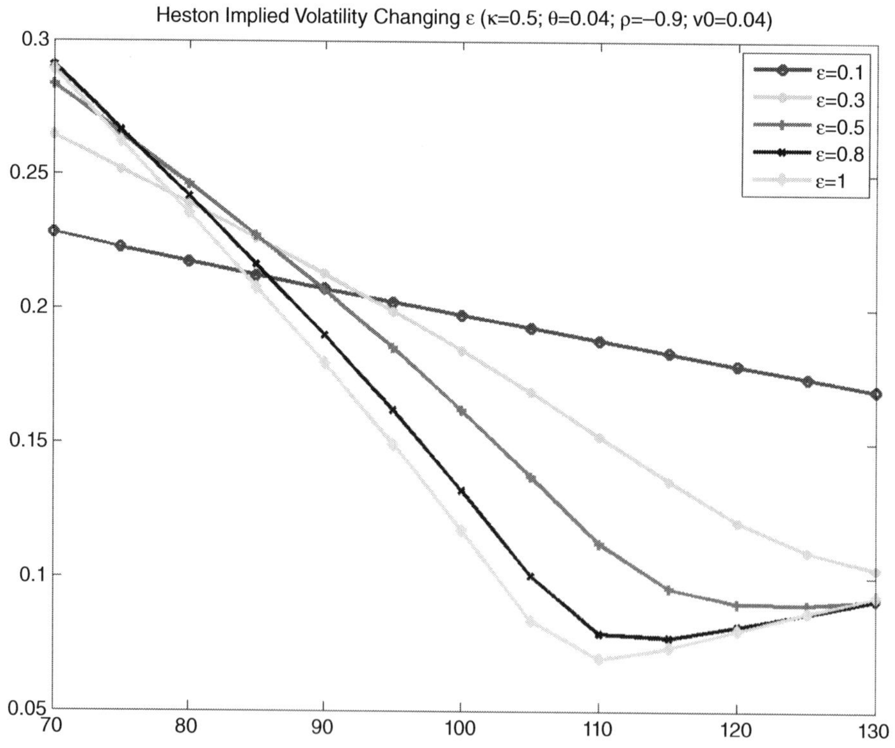

FIGURE 11.28 Black–Scholes implied volatility changing ϵ in the Heston model.

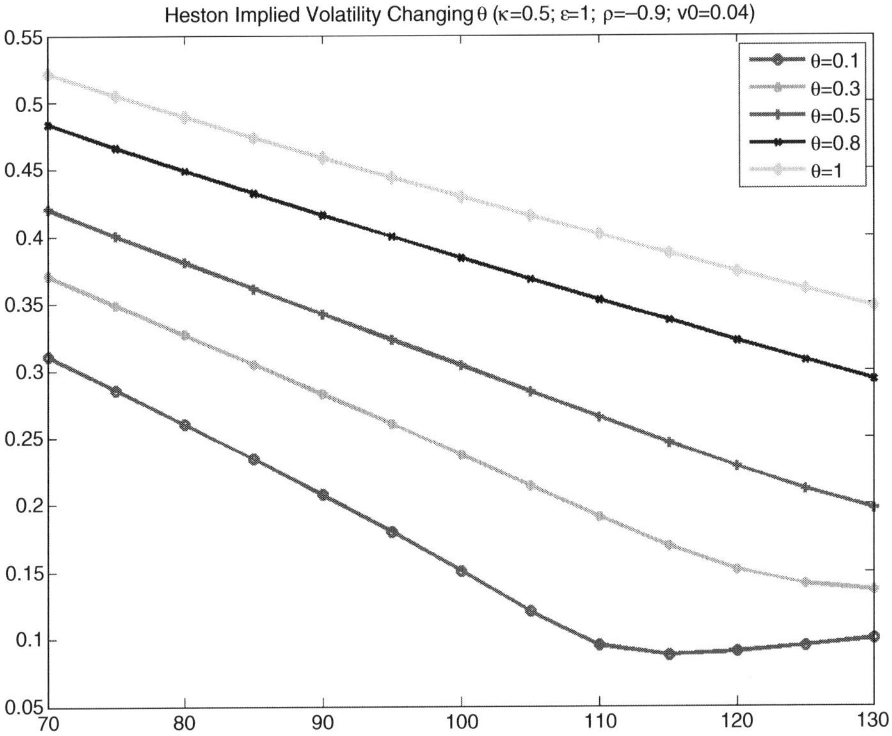

FIGURE 11.29 Black–Scholes implied volatility changing θ in the Heston model.

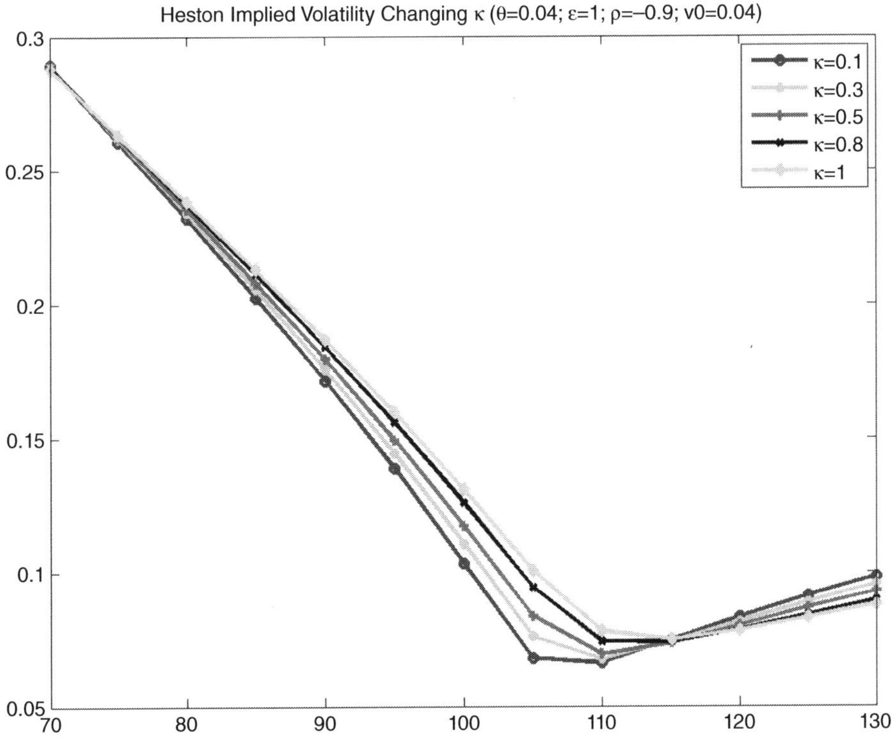

FIGURE 11.30 Black–Scholes implied volatility changing κ in the Heston model.

11.4.6.2 Heston Model: Main Findings

- For ATM options, the SV model gives the same result as the BS model.
- We need
  - a negative correlation between the two processes in order to generate an asymmetric distribution;
  - a higher volatility of volatility to give a higher kurtosis in the distribution.
- Introducing a non-zero correlation, the mispricing of OTM options is considerably reduced. This is also true in terms of hedging error.
- The SV model does not generate considerable kurtosis and skewness in a short period.
- To accurately fit short-term options we need to add a jump component to the return equation.

11.5 STOCHASTIC PROCESSES WITH JUMPS

- Brownian motion is a process which is continuous in time and space.
- As a consequence, it cannot capture extreme movements.
- Brownian motion is, in fact, Gaussian – that is, it has symmetric distribution with zero excess kurtosis.
- Extreme movements, originating skewness and excess kurtosis, can be captured by allowing, for example, discontinuity in space (i.e., introducing jumps).
- Possible examples of such processes are:
  - jump diffusion processes, like the Merton JD or Kou JD;
  - time-changed Brownian motions, like the VG process.
- The construction of these processes requires some preliminary facts, listed in the following section.

In the rest of this chapter, we assume the following:

- The dynamics of the log-price is

$$s(t) = \log S(t),$$

where

$$s(t) = at + X(t).$$

- $X(t)$ is the stochastic process of interest.

11.5.1 Preliminaries

11.5.1.1 The Poisson Process

Fact 11.5.1 *A Poisson process is an increasing, positive stochastic process $N(t)$ on $\mathbb{N}$ with independent and stationary increments which are Poisson distributed with instantaneous rate of arrival $\lambda > 0$. In other words, for any $0 < s < t$ the following hold:*

1. $N(0) = 0$;
2. *$N(t) - N(s)$ is independent of the information set $\mathcal{F}(s)$ generated up to time s;*

3. $N(t) - N(s) \sim N(t-s) \sim Poi(\lambda(t-s))$.

Moreover, the characteristic function of $N(t)$ is

$$\phi_N(u;t) = e^{\lambda t(e^{iu-1})},$$

where $i = \sqrt{-1}$ is the imaginary unit. Further,

$$\mathbb{E}(N(t)) = \lambda t$$

and

$$\mathbb{V}ar(N(t)) = \lambda t.$$

Hence, we note the following:

- It follows from properties 1 and 3 above that $N(t) \sim Poi(\lambda t)$.
- It follows from the definition of the Poisson distribution (see Appendix A) that the increments can only take values 1 or 0 according to whether an arrival occurs or not.
- Hence, the Poisson process counts the arrivals in a system, like calls at a call centre or shocks in the market.
- By definition of a Poisson distribution, there cannot be more than one jump per time period.
- Hence, the Poisson process can only generate a finite number of jumps over a finite time horizon.
- For this reason, the Poisson process is said to have finite activity.

11.5.1.2 The Compound Poisson Process In order to gain some additional flexibility in modelling the size (severity) of the jumps, the Poisson process can be used to construct a more flexible process by assigning a specific distribution to the severities.

Fact 11.5.2 *A compound Poisson process is a stochastic process $Y(t)$ of the form*

$$Y(t) = \sum_{k=1}^{N(t)} Z_k,$$

where $\{Z_k\}_{k\in\mathbb{N}}$ is a sequence of i.i.d. random variables which are assumed independent from the Poisson process $N(t)$.

Moreover, the compound Poisson process has characteristic function

$$\phi_Y(u;t) = e^{\lambda t(\phi_Z(u)-1)},$$

where $\phi_Z(u)$ denotes the characteristic function of the random variable Z. It follows that

$$\mathbb{E}(Y(t)) = \lambda\mathbb{E}(Z)t$$

and

$$\mathbb{V}ar(Y(t)) = \lambda\mathbb{E}(Z^2)t.$$

We can think of the compound Poisson process as follows:

- At time t a jump occurs.
- When this happens, the Poisson process increases by 1 unit.
- At the same time, a random draw Z is taken from a given distribution to quantify the jump size and it is summed up to the value of the process at the previous time point.
- The compound Poisson process has finite activity, like the Poisson process.

11.5.1.3 The Gamma Process Alternative processes which capture jump arrivals and size simultaneously, like the compound Poisson process, are available. One example is given by the Gamma process.

Fact 11.5.3 *A Gamma process is a positive, non-decreasing stochastic process $Y(t)$ with independent and stationary increments which follow a Gamma distribution (see Appendix A), that is:*

- $Y(0) = 0$;
- *$Y(t) - Y(s)$ is independent of the information set up to time $s < t$;*
- $Y(t) - Y(s) \sim Y(t - s) \sim \Gamma(\alpha(t - s), \lambda)$.

The characteristic function of the Gamma process is

$$\phi_Y(u; t) = \left(\frac{\lambda}{\lambda - iu}\right)^{\alpha t},$$

therefore

$$\mathbb{E}(Y(t)) = \frac{\alpha}{\lambda} t$$

and

$$\mathbb{V}ar(Y(t)) = \frac{\alpha}{\lambda^2} t.$$

Remark 11.5.1 *The Gamma process differs from the compound Poisson process in two aspects.*

1. *The Gamma process has infinite activity, as there can be an infinite number of jumps of very small size in a finite time period.*
2. *In the Gamma process case it is not possible to separare the rate of arrival of the jumps from their distribution.*

Sample trajectories of the Poisson process and Gamma process are illustrated in Figure 11.31 (see also accompanying Matlab code).

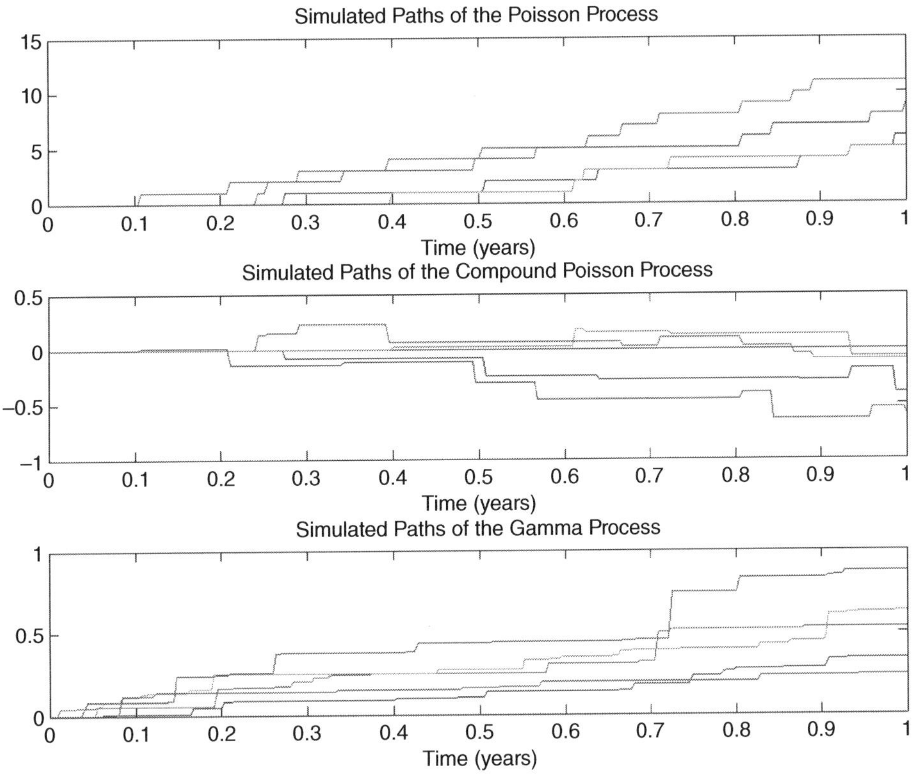

FIGURE 11.31 Simulated paths of the Poisson process $N(t) \sim Poi(\lambda t)$ for $\lambda = 5$ (top panel); the compound Poisson process with Gaussian jump severities with parameters $\lambda = 5$, $\mu_Z = -0.05$, $\sigma_Z = 0.1$ (middle panel); the Gamma process $G(t) \sim \Gamma(\alpha t, \lambda)$, with parameters $\alpha = 5$, $\lambda = 10$ (bottom panel).

Matlab Code

```
%%%%%%%%%%%%%%%%%%%%%%%%%%%%%%%%%%%%
%%%% SIMULATING JUMP PROCESSES %%%%%
%%%%%%%%%%%%%%%%%%%%%%%%%%%%%%%%%%%%
%Assigning the number of simulated paths
%(nsimul), time to maturity (expiry), number of steps
%(nsteps), time step (dt) and observation times (timestep):
clear all; nsimul=5, expiry=1, nsteps=250;
dt=expiry/nsteps; timestep=[0:dt:expiry]';
%Assigning parameters
lambdaP=5; muZ=-0.05; sigmaZ=0.1; alpha=5; lambdaG=10;
%Simulate increments of the Poisson process
dN=poissrnd(lambdaP*dt,[nsteps,nsimul]);
%Simulate Poisson process (use cumulative sum of the increments):
cdN=[zeros(1,nsimul); cumsum(dN)];
```

```
%1. Simulate increments of the CPP for Gaussian jump sizes
dJ=muZ*dN+sigmaZ*sqrt(dN).*randn(nsteps,nsimul);
%2. Simulate CPP process (use cumulative sum of the increments):
cdJ=[zeros(1,nsimul); cumsum(dJ)];
%3. Simulate increments of the Gamma process:
dG=gamrnd(dt*alpha,1/lambdaG,[nsteps,nsimul]);
%4. Simulate Gamma process (use cumulative sum of the increments):
cdG=[zeros(1,nsimul); cumsum(dG)];
%Plot simulated paths:
h=figure('Color', [ 1 1 1])
subplot(3,1,1); plot(timestep, cdN);xlabel('Time (years)')
title('Simulated Paths of the Poisson Process')
subplot(3,1,2); plot(timestep, cdJ);xlabel('Time (years)')
title('Simulated Paths of the Compound Poisson Process')
subplot(3,1,3); plot(timestep, cdG); xlabel('Time (years)')
title('Simulated Paths of the Gamma Process')
```

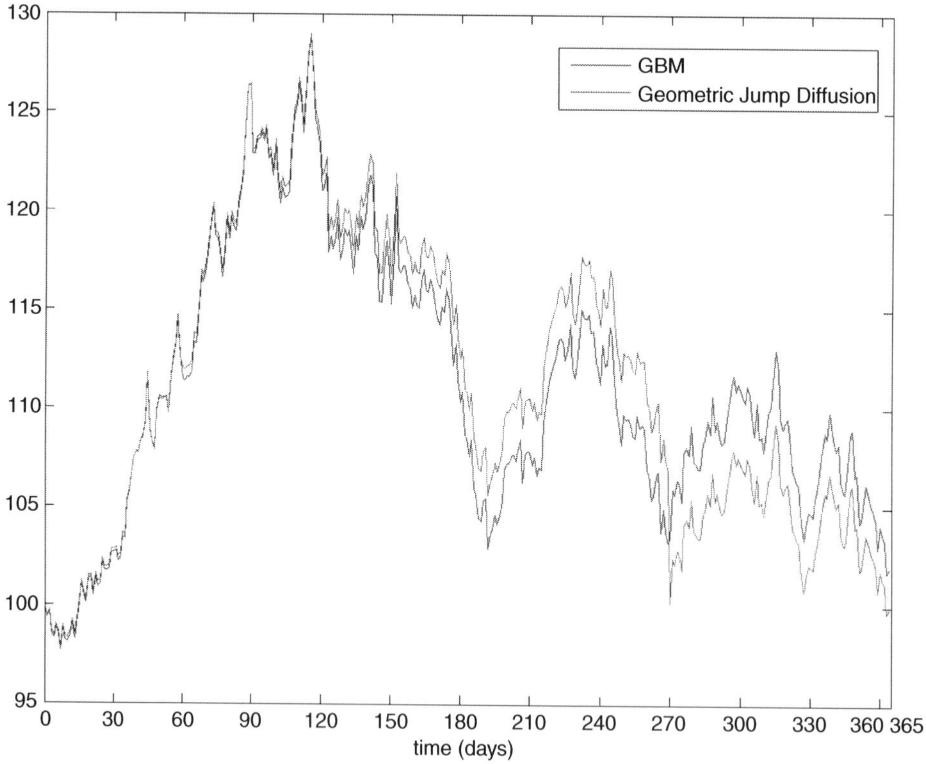

FIGURE 11.32 Sample trajectories of a stock price $S(t)$ in the cases in which $X(t)$ is either an arithmetic Brownian motion or a jump-diffusion process of the form $X_t = \mu t + \sigma W_t + \sum_{k=1}^{N_t} Z_k$. In this example, the jump size Z is Gaussian (Merton, 1976). The process X is obtained from the arithmetic Brownian motion (the continuous parts are identical) by superimposing the compound Poisson process.

11.5.2 Jump Diffusion Processes

Fact 11.5.4 (Jump Diffusion Process) *A jump diffusion process is a stochastic process $X(t)$ with independent and stationary increments which is obtained as the sum of an arithmetic Brownian motion and an independent compound Poisson process, that is*

$$X(t) = \mu t + \sigma W(t) + \sum_{j=1}^{N(t)} Z_k,$$

where $\mu \in \mathbb{R}$, $\sigma > 0$ and

- *$W(t)$ is a Brownian motion,*
- *$N(t)$ is a Poisson process with instantaneous rate of arrival $\lambda > 0$ and independent of $W(t)$,*
- *$\{Z_k\}_{k\in\mathbb{N}}$ is a sequence of i.i.d. random variables, which are independent of both the Brownian motion and the Poisson process.*

We can further 'specialize' the compound Poisson part of the JD process by specifying the distribution of the jump severities. Common choices for this distribution in financial applications are the Gaussian distribution and the exponential distribution.

A simulated path of the geometric Brownian motion and of the same process by superimposing a compound Poisson process is given in Figure 11.32.

11.5.2.1 The Merton Jump Diffusion Process

Fact 11.5.5 *Let us assume that the jump severities follow a Gaussian distribution, that is $Z \sim \mathcal{N}\left(\mu_Z, \sigma_Z^2\right)$. Then, the JD process $X(t)$ is a Merton JD process.*

- The process takes its name from Robert Merton who first used it for financial applications.
- The choice of modelling dynamics using a JD process is quite common in financial applications due to the following observation:
  - stock prices appear to have small continuous movements most of the time (due, for example, to a temporary imbalance between demand and supply);
  - sometimes though they experience large jumps upon arrival of important information with more than just a marginal impact.
- By its very nature, important information arrives only at discrete points in time and the jumps it causes have finite activity.

Properties of the Merton JD process

- $\mathbb{E}X(t) = (\mu + \lambda\mu_Z)t$.
- $\mathbb{V}ar(X(t)) = \left(\sigma^2 + \lambda\left(\mu_Z^2 + \sigma_Z^2\right)\right)t$.

- The indices of skewness and excess kurtosis are respectively

$$\mathbb{S}kew(t) = \frac{\lambda\mu_Z\left(\mu_Z^2 + 3\sigma_Z^2\right)}{\left(\sigma^2 + \lambda\left(\mu_Z^2 + \sigma_Z^2\right)\right)^{3/2}\sqrt{t}},$$

$$\mathbb{EK}urt(t) = \frac{\lambda\left(\mu_Z^4 + 6\mu_Z^2\sigma_X^2 + 3\sigma_Z^4\right)}{\left(\sigma^2 + \lambda\left(\mu_Z^2 + \sigma_Z^2\right)\right)^{2} t}.$$

- The Matlab script get_moments_JD allows the user to compute these quantities.

Interpretation of the parameters

- μ = drift of the process.
- σ = volatility of the Brownian motion.
- λ = rate of arrival of the jumps; it controls the level of excess kurtosis.
- μ_Z = mean of the jump sizes; it controls the sign of the skewness index. Hence, the Merton jump diffusion has a distribution which is skewed to the left if $\mu_Z < 0$ and skewed to the right if $\mu_Z > 0$.
- σ_Z = volatility of the jump sizes.

Matlab Code

```
function m=get_moments_JD(mu, sg, lambda, muZ, sgZ, t)

m(1,:)= (mu+lambda*muZ)*t; %mean
m(2,:)= (sg*sg+lambda*(muZ.^2+sgZ.^2))*t; %variance
numsk= lambda.*muZ.*(muZ.^2+3*sgZ.^2);
densk=(sg.^2+lambda.*(muZ.^2+sgZ.^2))^1.5*t.^0.5;
m(3,:)=numsk./densk;%skewness
numk= lambda.*(muZ.^4+6*muZ.^2.*sg.^2+3*sgZ.^4);
denk=(sg.^2+lambda.*(muZ.^2+sgZ.^2))^2*t;
m(4,:)=numk./denk;%excess kurtosis
```

Parameter fitting

- The simplest method (straightforward but not very accurate) to fit the parameters is to use the method of moments procedure.
- It consists of minimizing the distance between sample moments (such as sample mean, sample variance, sample skewness and sample kurtosis) with theoretical ones.
- For example, over year 2012, the log-return series of crude oil prices was characterized by the sample moments in Table 11.5.

TABLE 11.5 Sample moments of daily log-price changes in oil price in year 2012

Mean	Variance	Skewness	Excess Kurtosis
−0.0003	0.0144	0.1417	4.3605

- We can solve for the MJD parameters such that theoretical moments fit those in Table 11.5. This can be done through the following commands in the Matlab command window:

Matlab Code

```
%fitting parameters
>>x0(1)=0; x0(2)=0.05; x0(3)=0.5; x0(4)=0.01; x0(5)=0.17
>>[xopt fval]= fminsearch(@(x) sum(((get_moments_JD(x(1), x(2), x(3),
  x(4), x(5),1)-ms').^2)),x0)
>>mJD=get_moments_JD(xopt(1), xopt(2), xopt(3), xopt(4), xopt(5),1)
```

We obtain the parameter estimates as in Table 11.6.

Simulating the Merton JD process

- The simulation procedure for the trajectories of the Merton jump diffusion process is based on the following two observations:
  1. The increments of the Poisson process are independent and follow a Poisson distribution with rate $\lambda(t_{j+1} - t_j)$.
  2. Conditioned on the number of jumps occurring from t_j to t_{j+1}, the sum of the jump severities is Gaussian with given mean and variance.
- Hence, the simulation algorithm can be organized as follows:

  Step 1. Simulate the continuous part of the JD diffusion process, that is the ABM, on the given time partition.

  Step 2. Simulate the number of jumps occurring from t_j to t_{j+1}, that is $N \sim Poi(\lambda(t_j, t_{j+1}))$.

  Step 3. Generate $Z \sim \mathcal{N}(0, 1)$; set $J = \mu_Z N + \sigma_Z \sqrt{N} Z$.

  Step 4. Sum the ABM and J.

- Simulated paths are illustrated in Figure 11.33. A comparison between the density of the MJD model and the Gaussian with the same mean and variance is given in Figure 11.34.

TABLE 11.6 Calibrated parameters of the MJD model to sample moments of daily log-price changes in oil price for year 2012

μ	σ	λ	μ_Z	σ_Z
−0.0037	0.0407	0.5373	0.0064	0.1541

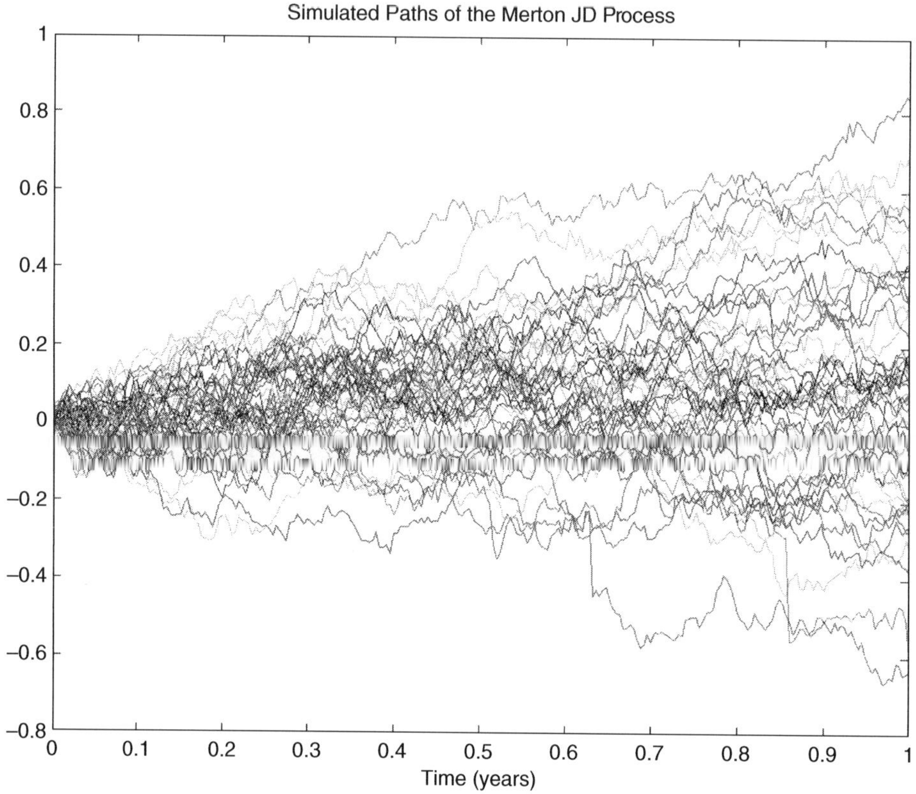

FIGURE 11.33 Simulated paths of the Merton jump diffusion process. Parameters: $\mu = -0.0003$, $\sigma = 0.0425$, $\lambda = 0.5175$, $\mu_Z = 0.0064$, $\sigma_Z = 0.1520$.

Matlab Code

```
%%%%%%%%%%%%%%%%%%%%%%%%%%%%%%%%%%%%%%%%%%%%
%%%% SIMULATING THE MERTON JD Process %%%%%
%%%%%%%%%%%%%%%%%%%%%%%%%%%%%%%%%%%%%%%%%%%%
%Assigning the number of simulated paths
%(nsimul), time to maturity (expiry), number of steps
%(nsteps), time step (dt) and observation times (timestep):
clear all; nsimul=50, expiry=1, nsteps=250;
dt=expiry/nsteps; timestep=[0:dt:expiry]';
%Assigning parameters
mu=-0.0003; sigma=0.0425; lambda=0.5175;
muZ=0.0064; sigmaZ=0.1520;
%Simulate increments of the ABM
dW=mu*dt+sigma*sqrt(dt).*randn(nsteps,nsimul);
%Simulate increments of the CPP
```

```
dN=poissrnd(lambda*dt,[nsteps,nsimul]);
dJ=muZ*dN+sigmaZ*sqrt(dN).*randn(nsteps,nsimul);
dX=dW+dJ;
%Simulate MJD process (use cumulative sum of the increments):
cdX=[zeros(1,nsimul); cumsum(dX)];
%Plot simulated paths:
h=figure('Color', [ 1 1 1])
plot(timestep, cdX);xlabel('Time (years)')
title('Simulated Paths of the Merton JD Process')
```

11.5.2.2 The Kou Process In the case of the Kou process, the jump sizes follow a double-exponential distribution with parameters (p, η_1, η_2), that is their density function is given by

$$p\eta_1 e^{-\eta_1 y} 1_{(y \geq 0)} + (1-p)\eta_2 e^{\eta_2 y} 1_{(y<0)}, \quad \eta_1, \eta_2 > 0, p \in [0, 1].$$

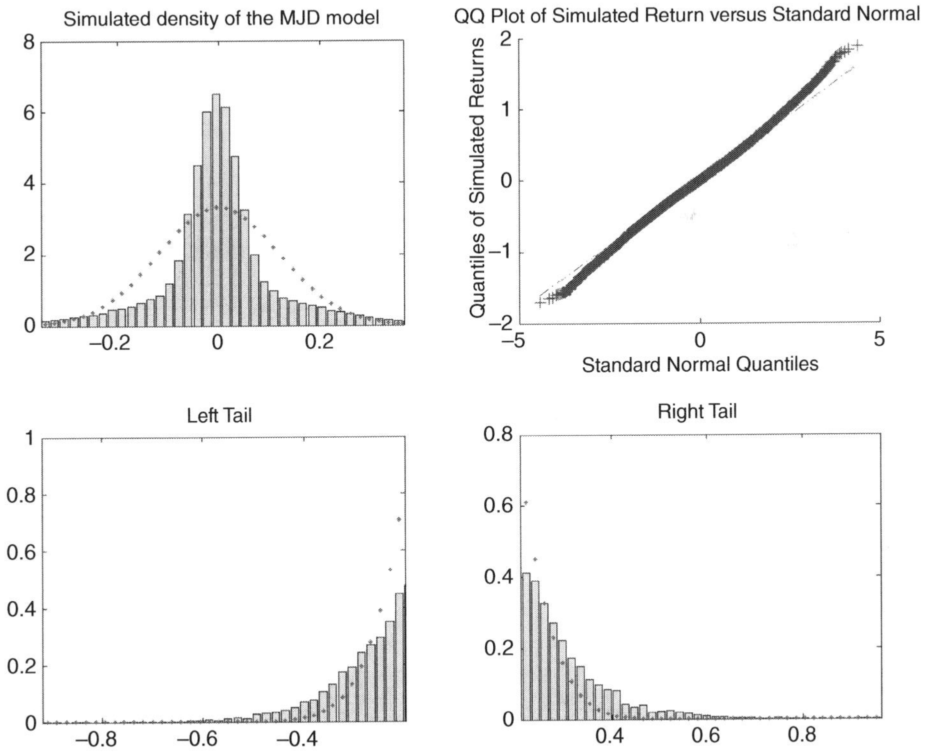

FIGURE 11.34 Top left: Simulated density of the Merton jump diffusion process at 1-day horizon and superimposed Gaussian density with the same mean and variance. Top right: QQplot of simulated returns. Bottom left: Left tail of the simulated returns versus Gaussian tail. Bottom right: Right tail of the simulated returns versus Gaussian tail. Parameters as in Table 11.6.

Properties of the Kou JD process

- $\mathbb{E}(X(t)) = (\mu + \lambda(p/\eta_1 - (1-p)/\eta_2))t$.
- $\mathbb{V}ar(X(t)) = \left(\sigma^2 + 2\lambda\left(p/\eta_1^2 + (1-p)/\eta_2^2\right)\right)t$.
- The indices of skewness and excess kurtosis are respectively

$$\mathbb{S}kew(t) = \frac{6\lambda\left(p/\eta_1^3 - (1-p)/\eta_2^3\right)}{\left(\sigma^2 + 2\lambda\left(p/\eta_1^2 + (1-p)/\eta_2^2\right)\right)^{3/2}\sqrt{t}},$$

$$\mathbb{EK}urt(t) = \frac{24\lambda\left(p/\eta_1^4 + (1-p)/\eta_2^4\right)}{\left(\sigma^2 + 2\lambda\left(p/\eta_1^2 + (1-p)/\eta_2^2\right)\right)^2 t}.$$

Interpretation of the parameters

- μ = drift of the process.
- σ = volatility of the Brownian motion.
- λ = rate of arrival of the jumps; it controls the level of excess kurtosis.
- p = probability of an upward jump.
- η_1 = parameter of the exponential distribution controlling the upward jumps; therefore, the upward jumps have mean $1/\eta_1$.
- η_2 = parameter of the exponential distribution controlling the downward jumps; therefore, the downward jumps have mean $1/\eta_2$.

11.5.3 Time-Changed Brownian Motion

An alternative way of constructing stochastic processes with jumps is to consider an arithmetic Brownian motion on a time scale which is not governed by the standard calendar time, but by a random clock. These processes are called time-changed Brownian motion.

Fact 11.5.6 *A time-changed Brownian motion is a process of the form*

$$X(t) = \theta G(t) + \sigma W(G(t)), \qquad \theta \in \mathbb{R}, \sigma > 0,$$

where $W(t)$ is a Brownian motion and $G(t)$ is a positive, increasing stochastic process independent of W. The law of increments of the process G is what allows us to characterize the resulting process X.

Constructing time-changed Brownian motion has particular economic appeal as:

- This construction finds its rationale in the following – uncertainty in price changes is originated by the time at which the next investor enters the market with a transaction altering the current price values, and the amount by which this current price is changed. The random clock models the time at which the next transaction will take place; the 'size' of the price change is instead captured by the Brownian motion component.
- Empirical evidence shows that stock log-returns are Gaussian but only under trade time, rather than standard calendar time.

- Further, the time-change construction recognizes that stock prices are largely driven by news, and the time between one piece of news and the next is random as is its impact.
- Finally, this construction offers a high degree of mathematical tractability as, once we operate under business time, log-returns are once again Gaussian and therefore the results derived for the Black–Scholes model still hold.

A time-changed Brownian motion commonly used in finance is the variance Gamma process.

11.5.3.1 The Variance Gamma Process

Fact 11.5.7 *Let us assume that G is a Gamma process with parameters $\alpha = \lambda = k^{-1}$, for any positive constant k, so that $\mathbb{E}G(t) = t$ and $\mathbb{V}ar(G(t)) = kt$. Then, $X(t)$ is a VG process.*

We note the following:

- The parameters of the Gamma process are chosen so that $\mathbb{E}(G(t)) = t$, that is the process chosen as random clock is an unbiased representation of calendar time.
- The VG process has infinite activity; specifically it is characterized by an infinite number of jumps of small size in a finite time period.
- The VG process has finite variation, so it is characterized by a finite number of jumps of big size in a finite time period.

Other examples of time-changed Brownian motion used for financial applications are the normal inverse Gaussian and the CGMY process.

Properties of the VG process

- The probability density function is

$$2\frac{e^{\theta x/\sigma^2}}{k^{t/k}\sigma\sqrt{2\pi}\Gamma(t/k)}\left(\frac{x^2}{\theta^2+2\sigma^2/k}\right)^{\frac{t}{2k}-\frac{1}{4}} K_{\frac{t}{k}-\frac{1}{2}}\left(\frac{|x|}{\sigma^2}\sqrt{\theta^2+2\sigma^2/k}\right). \tag{11.11}$$

- The characteristic function of the VG process is

$$\phi_X(u;t) = \left(1 - iu\theta k + u^2\frac{\sigma^2}{2}k\right)^{-\frac{t}{k}}. \tag{11.12}$$

- The expected value is

$$\mathbb{E}(X(t)) = \theta t.$$

- The variance is

$$\mathbb{V}ar(X(t)) = (\sigma^2 + \theta^2 k)t.$$

- The indices of skewness and excess kurtosis are respectively

$$\mathbb{S}kew(t) = \frac{(3\sigma^2 + 2\theta^2 k)\theta k}{(\sigma^2 + \theta^2 k)^{3/2}\sqrt{t}},$$

$$\mathbb{E}\mathbb{K}urt(t) = \frac{(3\sigma^4 + 12\sigma^2\theta^2 k + 6\theta^4 k^2)k}{(\sigma^2 + \theta^2 k)^2 t}.$$

- The above quantities are computed via the Matlab function get_moments_VG.

Interpretation of the parameters

- $\theta \in \mathbb{R}$: mean of the VG process; it also controls the sign on the skewness index. Hence, the VG process has distribution skewed to the left if $\theta < 0$ and skewed to the right if $\theta > 0$. If $\theta = 0$, the process has symmetric distribution.
- $\sigma > 0$: controls the variance of the VG process. If $\sigma = 0$, the VG process reduces to the Gamma process.
- $k > 0$: variance rate of the Gamma process. It controls the level of excess kurtosis.

Matlab Code

```
function m=get_moments_VG(theta, sg, kappa,t)

m(1,:)= theta*t; %mean
m(2,:)= sg*sg*t+theta*theta*kappa*t; %variance
numsk= (3*sg^2+2*theta^2*kappa)*theta*kappa;
densk=(sg^2+theta^2*kappa)^(3/2)*t.^0.5;
m(3,:)=numsk./densk%skewness
numk=(3*sg^4+12*sg^2*theta^2*kappa+6*theta^4*kappa^2)*kappa;
denk=(sg*sg+theta*theta*kappa)^2*t;
m(4,:)=numk./denk;%kurtosis
```

Simulation of the VG process The simulation procedure of the variance Gamma process is based on the following two observations:

1. The increments of the Gamma process are independent and follow a Gamma distribution $\Gamma((t_{j+1} - t_j)/k, 1/k)$.
2. Conditioned on the increments of the Gamma clock, the increments of the VG process are Gaussian with given mean and variance.

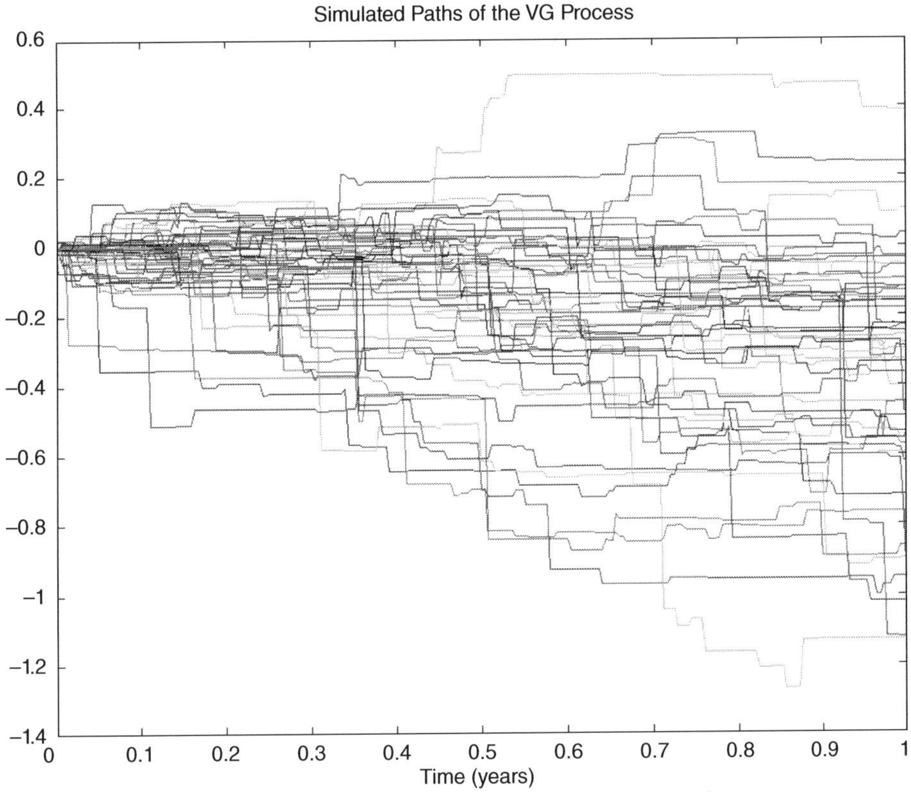

FIGURE 11.35 Simulated paths of the VG process. Parameters: $\theta = -0.4$, $\sigma = 0.3$, $\kappa = 0.25$.

Hence, the simulation algorithm can be organized as follows:

Step 1. Simulate the increments from t_j to t_{j+1} of the Gamma clock, that is $G \sim \Gamma((t_{j+1} - t_j)/k, 1/k)$.

Step 2. Generate $Z \sim \mathcal{N}(0, 1)$; set $X = \theta G + \sigma\sqrt{G}Z$.

A sample trajectory is shown in Figure 11.35 (see also accompanying Matlab code).

Matlab Code

```
%%%%%%%%%%%%%%%%%%%%%%%%%%%%%%%%%%%%%%%%%%%%
%%%% SIMULATING THE VARIANCE GAMMA %%%%%%%%
%%%%%%%%%%%%%%%%%%%%%%%%%%%%%%%%%%%%%%%%%%%%
%Assigning the number of simulated paths
%(nsimul), time to maturity (expiry), number of steps
%(nsteps), time step (dt) and observation times (timestep):
clear all;
nsimul=50, expiry=1, nsteps=250; dt=expiry/nsteps;
timestep=[0:dt:expiry]';
%Assigning parameters
```

```
theta=-0.4; sigma=0.3; kappa=0.25;
%Simulate increments of the Gamma process:
dG=gamrnd(dt/kappa,kappa,[nsteps,nsimul]);
%Simulate increments of the ABM on the Gamma clock scale
dX=theta*dG+sigma*sqrt(dG).*randn(nsteps,nsimul);
%Simulate VG process (use cumulative sum of the increments):
cdX=[zeros(1,nsimul); cumsum(dX)];
%Plot simulated paths:
h=figure('Color', [ 1 1 1])
plot(timestep, cdX)
title('Simulated Paths of the VG Process')
xlabel('Time (years)')
```

11.5.4 Final Remark: Lévy Processes

- All the processes presented in this section share the feature of independent and stationary increments.

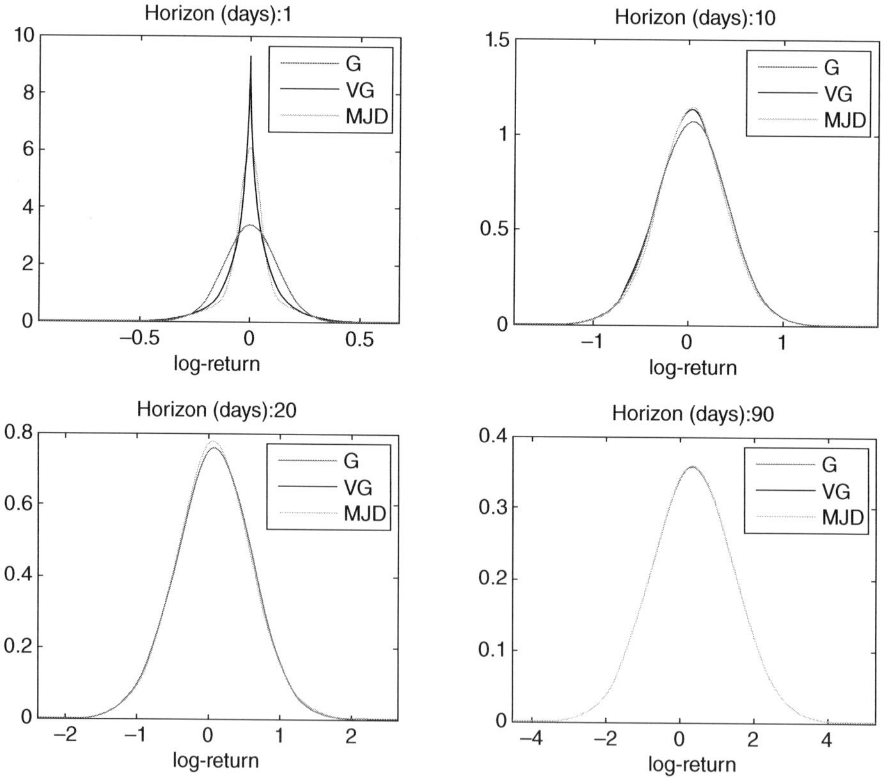

FIGURE 11.36 The pdf of Gaussian (G), variance-Gamma (VG) and Merton jump-diffusion (MJD) processes at different time horizons. Parameters are chosen to fit sample moments of daily log-returns of oil prices in 2012.

- Brownian motion shares the same feature as well.
- They differ in the distribution chosen to model these increments.
- A process with independent and stationary increments is called a Lévy process.
- Lévy processes are widely used in financial applications.
- All processes can be made more rich in terms of features they can capture by assuming, for example, time-dependent parameters, or by using more complex processes as stochastic clocks.
- For example: the instantaneous volatility of any of the processes presented above is constant. This assumption can be relaxed by assuming time-dependent parameters. However, the resulting more general process will no longer have independent and stationary increments.
- The main problem with Lévy processes is that they cannot capture the volatility clustering effects, which can be captured by other models such as stochastic volatility models.
- Lévy processes and the stochastic volatility model complement each other: jump processes have a relative advantage in analytical tractability and they better capture short-term behaviour of financial time series, whilst stochastic volatility models have a richer time-dependence structure and are more useful to model long-term behaviour.
- Figure 11.36 compares the MJD, the VG and the Gaussian pdf at different horizons (1, 10, 20 and 90 days). We can see that the three densities approach one another as the time horizon lengthens. This is due to the nature of independence of the increments of the three processes. This allows the central limit theorem to operate: in practice, the skewness and the kurtosis fade away very quickly.

REFERENCES

Merton, R. (1976) Option pricing when underlying stock returns are discontinuous, *Journal of Financial Economics*, 125–144.

Rubinstein, M. and Jackwerth, J. (1996) Recovering probability distributions from option prices, *Journal of Finance*. **51**(5).

FURTHER READING

Barndorff-Nielsen, O.E. (1995) Normal inverse Gaussian distributions and the modeling of stock returns, Research report no. 300, Department of Theoretical Statistics, Aarhus University.

Carr, P. and Wu, L. (2004) Time-changed Lévy processes and option pricing, *Journal of Financial Economics*, **71**, 113–141.

Carr, P., Geman, H., Madan, D.B. and Yor, M. (2002) The fine structure of asset returns: An empirical investigation, *Journal of Business*, **75**, 305–332.

Cox, J. (1975) Notes on option pricing I: Constant elasticity of variance diffusions, Working paper, Stanford University (reprinted in *Journal of Portfolio Management,* 22, 15–17, 1996).

Cox, J. and Ross, S. (1976) The valuation of options for alternative stochastic processes, *Journal of Financial Economics* **3**, 145–166.

Emanuel, D. and MacBeth, J. (1982) Further results on the constant elasticity of variance call option pricing model, *Journal of Financial and Quantitative Analysis*, **17**, 533–554.

Kou, S.G. (2002) A jump-diffusion model for option pricing, *Management Science*, **48**(8), 1086–1101.

Madan, D.B. and Milne, F. (1991) Option pricing with VG martingale components, *Mathematical Finance*, **1**, 39–45.

Madan, D.B. and Seneta, E. (1990) The variance gamma (VG) model for share market returns, *Journal of Business*, **63**, 511–524.

Madan, D.B., Carr, P. and Chang, E. (1998) The variance gamma process and option pricing, *European Finance Review*, **2**, 79–105.

Shreve, S. (2004) *Stochastic Calculus for Finance II*, Springer Finance.

Schröder, M. (1989) Computing the constant elasticity of variance option pricing formula, *Journal of Finance*, **44**, 211–219.

CHAPTER 12

Estimating Commodity Term Structure Volatilities

Andrea Roncoroni, Rachid Id Brik and Mark Cummins

12.1 INTRODUCTION

This chapter introduces two leading methods used in estimating the term structure of volatility in energy and commodity futures markets. The first of these methods is the Kalman filter and the second is principal components analysis. Technical definitions are provided and the methods are illustrated using historical futures data.

12.2 MODEL ESTIMATION USING THE KALMAN FILTER

The literature in financial modelling offers a large number of models to draw on in determining commodity prices. Several papers are based on spot prices, where the spot price is for immediate delivery of a commodity, while others are based on forward or futures prices, where delivery or cash settlement occurs at a date in the future. The no-arbitrage relationship between futures and spot prices introduces the concept of convenience yield. This new variable allows us to reproduce the term structure of futures prices from a spot price model. However, this variable is not observable in the market and so must be measured from observable market price information. The convenience yield only has an economic interpretation and can be linked with the level of inventories. Spot price and convenience yield as a pair have been well studied by Gibson and Schwartz (1990), Schwartz (1997), Casassus and Collin-Dufresne (2005) and many others. In this context, since the convenience yield is unobservable, and indeed for some markets a liquid spot price may not be readily observable either, one may need to introduce filtering techniques in order to estimate the parameters of a given price model specification. Our first objective in this chapter is to describe the Kalman filter through an estimation of the parameters of the Gibson–Schwartz model.

Handbook of Multi-Commodity Markets and Products: Structuring, Trading and Risk Management. Edited by Andrea Roncoroni, Gianluca Fusai and Mark Cummins.

Studies of systems in signal processing, where signals can be determined by non-observable variables, led to the development of state-space methods such as the Kalman filter (Kalman, 1960). Such methods provide optimal estimation of the value of a state vector from noisy observations for linear dynamic systems. Hence, these methodologies differentiate between two kinds of variables: observed variables and hidden or latent variables. State-space methods allow us to estimate the latent variables of the system as a function of the observed variables, with some noise measures. The Kalman filter is a powerful mathematical tool since it can be applied in many fields. More specifically, researchers in energy finance utilize it in estimating the parameters of spot price/convenience yield commodity price models – with convenience yield being the unobservable. In particular, the application of Kalman filter methods to the estimation of term structure models has been investigated by Schwartz (1997), Schwartz and Smith (2000) and many others. Indeed, the logarithm of the futures price which is observable is often considered to be a linear function of spot price, convenience yield and interest rates. In this context, it is natural to introduce this filtering technique. We detail the general concept and apply it for illustrative purposes to the Gibson Schwartz model as described in Schwartz (1997).

In general, the Kalman filter consists of detecting information represented by a signal polluted by some noise. More precisely, it aims to optimally estimate the state of a linear system given information linked to this system. This is why the Kalman filter is often used to estimate non-observable parameters. In particular, the filtering problem involves considering a non-observable process $\mathbf{x}_k$ that describes the state of a system and, at time t_k, trying to collect information on an observable process $\mathbf{z}_k$, which is a combination of a function of the non-observable process and some noise. That is,

$$\mathbf{z}_k = h(\mathbf{x}_k) + \mathbf{v}_k.$$

The statistical characteristics of $\mathbf{v}_k$ are known and, at time t_k, we have all the information from $(\mathbf{z}_0, \ldots, \mathbf{z}_k)$; our goal is then to get the most information on $\mathbf{x}_k$ by deriving its estimator.

The model considers a causal and a deterministic evolution. Causal evolution is the change of the system due to past and present phenomena. Deterministic evolution corresponds to a given initial condition, giving the model a unique scenario. This evolution can be represented by an ordinary differential equation taking account of some perturbations.

12.2.1 Description of the Methodology

We introduce the Gibson–Schwartz model under the historical measure, with $s(t)$ the spot price and $\delta(t)$ the instantaneous convenience yield according to the standard theory of storage:

$$\begin{aligned} ds(t)/s(t) &= (\mu - \delta(t))dt + \sigma_1 dw_1(t), \\ d\delta(t) &= \kappa(\alpha - \delta(t))dt + \sigma_2 dw_2(t), \\ \rho dt &= dw_1(t) \times dw_2(t), \end{aligned}$$

where w_1 and w_2 are two Brownian motions with correlation ρ. Moreover, the coefficient μ, the volatility of the logarithm of the spot price σ_1, the mean reversion speed κ, the long-run equilibrium level α, the volatility of the convenience yield σ_2 and the correlation ρ are constant. This model exhibits an important behaviour which can be observed in commodity markets, called backwardation. We say that a market is in backwardation when for two futures contracts with different maturities in this market, the futures price with shortest maturity is greater than the one with longest maturity. When the opposite occurs, we say that the market is in contango. One of the main assumptions of this model is the mean-reversion pattern of the spot price $s(t)$, which has been exhibited in different commodity markets in Gibson and Schwartz (1990) and Schwartz (1997). The mean-reversion feature is indirectly induced by the dynamics of the instantaneous convenience yield $\delta(t)$. Indeed, commodity markets exhibit high correlation ρ on the Brownian motions of the two factors. When the spot price $s(t)$ is high, the convenience yield $\delta(t)$ is high. Since the convenience yield factor is mean-reverting, the spot price tends to return a long-run equilibrium value.

Transitioning to the risk-neutral probability measure, the two factors can be written as follows:

$$\begin{aligned} ds(t)/s(t) &= [r - \delta(t)]dt + \sigma_1 d\omega_1(t), \\ d\delta(t) &= \kappa[\hat{\alpha} - \delta(t)]dt + \sigma_2 d\omega_2(t), \end{aligned} \tag{12.1}$$

where r is the interest rate assumed to be constant; $\hat{\alpha} := \alpha - \lambda\sigma_2/\kappa$, where λ is the market price of risk for the convenience yield; and ω_1 and ω_2 are two Brownian motions with correlation ρ, defined under the risk-neutral measure.

We introduce the Kalman filter to the Gibson–Schwartz model, whereby the state variables are assumed to be the spot price (which in practical market terms may be assumed to be illiquid and effectively unobservable) and the convenience yield, with the observed data assumed to be readily available liquid futures prices. We consider the following general framework. Let $\mathbf{x}(t) \in \mathbb{R}^p$ and $\mathbf{z}(t) \in \mathbb{R}^m$, respectively representing the state and measure variables. The couple $(\mathbf{x}(t), \mathbf{z}(t))$ is a continuous stochastic process. Hence, the variable $\mathbf{x}(t)$ is not observable and the process $\mathbf{z}(t)$ is available from the market at time t with some noise. Moreover, we link the two processes as follows:

$$\mathbf{z}(t) = h(\mathbf{x}(t)) + \mathbf{v}(t),$$

where $\mathbf{z}(t)$ is the observation, $\mathbf{x}(t)$ is the state process and $\mathbf{v}(t)$ is some known noise. This aligns with the representation of the previous section. This equation is called a measure equation and describes the dependence between the observations $\mathbf{z}(t)$ and the state variables $\mathbf{x}(t)$. In general, $\mathbf{x}(t)$ follows a dynamic system. The objective is to find an optimal estimator $\hat{\mathbf{x}}(t)$ of the state vector from the available measure over a period $[0, t] : \{\mathbf{z}(\tau), \tau \in [0, t]\}$.

We now derive the relationship between the spot price and convenience yield and the futures prices under the Gibson–Schwartz model. Since r is supposed to be constant, futures and forward contracts are equal. The futures prices satisfy a partial differential equation which has an explicit solution.

Proposition 12.2.1

$$F(t, T) = s(t)e^{-\delta(t)\frac{1-e^{-\kappa T}}{\kappa} + A(T)} \tag{12.2}$$

where T is the time-to-maturity of the futures contract and

$$A(T) := \left(r - \hat{\alpha} + \frac{\sigma_2^2}{2\kappa^2} - \rho\frac{\sigma_1\sigma_2}{\kappa}\right)T + \frac{\sigma_2^2}{4}\frac{1 - e^{-2\kappa T}}{\kappa^3} + \left(\hat{\alpha}\kappa + \rho\sigma_1\sigma_2 - \frac{\sigma_2^2}{\kappa}\right)\frac{1 - e^{-\kappa T}}{\kappa^2}.$$

TABLE 12.1 Variables under the Gibson–Schwartz model

Variables	Formula
State variables	$\begin{pmatrix} \log(s(t)) \\ \delta(t) \end{pmatrix}$
Observed variables	$\begin{pmatrix} \log(F(t,T_1)) \\ \vdots \\ \log(F(t,T_m)) \end{pmatrix}$

Proof. See Jamshidian and Fein (1990). □

It is natural to introduce the logarithm of the futures prices $F(t,T)$ since this is a linear function of the spot price $s(t)$ and the convenience yield $\delta(t)$ in Eq. (12.2). Table 12.1 summarizes the application of the Gibson–Schwartz model for a set of fixed times to maturity, $T_1,\dots,T_m$.

Remark 12.2.1 *Notice that the dimension of the state variable, which we denoted by p in the general framework, is equal to 2 in this case since we only have the spot price s(t) and the convenience yield δ(t) as the latent variables.*

For the sake of simplicity, we now work with discrete models. The discrete version of the previous model can be written as follows. We consider the following discretization of time: $0 = t_0 < \cdots < t_k < \cdots < t_n = t$. Define $\mathbf{x}_k \in R^p$ and $\mathbf{z}_k \in R^m$ as respectively representing the state and measure variables at t_k. The goal is to estimate the state of a dynamic system from partial observations with some noise,

$$\mathbf{z}_k = h(\mathbf{x}_k) + \mathbf{v}_k,$$

where $\{\mathbf{z}_k, k = 0,\dots,n\}$ is available and $\mathbf{v}_k$ are some additional noise.

We assume that measurement errors are additive and normally distributed. The variance–covariance matrix of the measurement errors can take various forms. We only focus on the following Gaussian linear system:

$$\begin{aligned} \mathbf{x}_{k+1} &= F_k\mathbf{x}_k + \mathbf{f}_k + \mathbf{w}_k, \\ \mathbf{z}_k &= H_k\mathbf{x}_k + \mathbf{h}_k + \mathbf{v}_k. \end{aligned}$$

The process $\mathbf{w}_k$ is a Gaussian white noise with covariance matrix Q_k^W. The initial condition of the state variable $\mathbf{x}_0$ is Gaussian, whereby its mean is equal to $\bar{\mathbf{x}}_0$ and its covariance matrix is Q_0^X. The process $\mathbf{v}_k$ is also a Gaussian white noise with covariance matrix Q_k^V. More precisely, we assume that $Q_k^V = \chi' Id$, where Id is the identity matrix χ. We also suppose that the initial conditions of the state variable $\mathbf{x}_0$ and the noise $(\mathbf{v}_0, \mathbf{w}_0)$ are independent. Moreover, the following information $(\mathbf{z}_0,\dots,\mathbf{z}_k)$ is available at each t_k. In particular, for the Gibson–Schwartz model, let $x(t) := \log(s(t))$. We discretize Eq. (12.1). The transition equation becomes

$$x(t+\Delta t) = x(t) + \left(r - \delta(t) - \frac{\sigma_1^2}{2}\right)\Delta t + \sigma_1 \epsilon_1(t)\sqrt{\Delta t},$$

$$\delta(t+\Delta t) = \delta(t) + \kappa(\hat{\alpha} - \delta(t))\Delta t + \sigma_2 \epsilon_2(t)\sqrt{\Delta t},$$

$$\rho = Corr(\epsilon_1, \epsilon_2),$$

where $\begin{pmatrix}\epsilon_1(t)\\ \epsilon_1(t)\end{pmatrix} \rightsquigarrow N\left(\mathbf{0}, \begin{pmatrix}1 & \rho\\ \rho & 1\end{pmatrix}\right)$.

The equation measurement applying the Euler discretization of Eq. (12.2) becomes

$$\log(F(t,T)) = x(t) - \delta(t)\frac{1-e^{-\kappa T}}{\kappa} + A(T).$$

Now, we can write the system of measurement and the system of state variables. The observed variables are the logarithm of the futures prices

$$\mathbf{z}_t = \begin{pmatrix}\log(F(t,T_1))\\ \vdots \\ \log(F(t,T_m))\end{pmatrix}.$$

The state variables are the logarithm of the spot price and convenience yield

$$\mathbf{x}_t = \begin{pmatrix}x(t)\\ \delta(t)\end{pmatrix}.$$

Hence, the parameters of the measurement equation are

$$H_k = \begin{pmatrix}1, & -\frac{1-e^{-\kappa T_j}}{\kappa}\\ \vdots & \vdots \\ 1, & -\frac{1-e^{-\kappa T_m}}{\kappa}\end{pmatrix}, \quad \mathbf{h}_k = \begin{pmatrix}A(T_1)\\ \vdots \\ A(T_m)\end{pmatrix}.$$

The system equation has the following parameters:

$$F_k = \begin{pmatrix}1 & -\Delta t\\ 0 & 1-\kappa\Delta t\end{pmatrix},$$

$$\mathbf{f}_k = \begin{pmatrix}\left[r - \sigma_1^2/2\right]\Delta t\\ \kappa\alpha\Delta t\end{pmatrix}.$$

The covariance matrices of the errors are

$$Q_k^V = diag(\chi_1, \ldots, \chi_m),$$

$$Q_k^X = \begin{pmatrix}\sigma_1^2\Delta t & \rho\sigma_1\sigma_2\Delta t\\ \rho\sigma_1\sigma_2\Delta t & \sigma_2^2\Delta t\end{pmatrix}.$$

Remark 12.2.2 *The previous matrices do not depend on time t_k.*

The parameters to estimate in the Gibson–Schwartz model are the coefficient μ, the volatility σ_2 of the spot price $s(t)$, the mean-reversion speed κ of the convenience yield $\delta(t)$, the long-run equilibrium level α of $\delta(t)$, the volatility σ_2 of $\delta(t)$, the market price of risk λ, the correlation ρ and the variance generated from the noise errors $\chi_1, \chi_2, \ldots, \chi_m$.

We consider θ as the set of all these parameters to be estimated. The filtering method consists of optimally and recursively estimating the stochastic process $\mathbf{x}_k$ from the available information $\mathbf{z}_k$ at time t_k. The problem requires giving some initial conditions and a set of observations $\mathbf{z}$, finding the conditional law of $\mathbf{x}_k$ given all the past information $\{\mathbf{z}_0, \ldots, \mathbf{z}_k\}$. The optimal value is found by applying the minimum of the variance criterion using the partial information we have about $\mathbf{x}_k$ on $(\mathbf{z}_0, \ldots, \mathbf{z}_k)$. Since we suppose that the processes are Gaussian, we only need the first two moments: the mean $\hat{\mathbf{x}}_k$ and covariance P_k to define its law. We wish $\hat{\mathbf{x}}_k$ to be a function depending only on the observation from the previous estimation of $\hat{\mathbf{x}}_k$ and covariance matrices. Therefore,

$$\hat{\mathbf{x}}_k := \mathbb{E}[\mathbf{x}_k | (\mathbf{z}_0, \ldots, \mathbf{z}_k)],$$
$$P_k := \mathbb{E}[(\mathbf{x}_k - \hat{\mathbf{x}}_k) \times (\mathbf{x}_k - \hat{\mathbf{x}}_k)' | (\mathbf{z}_0, \ldots, \mathbf{z}_k)],$$

and

$$\hat{\mathbf{x}}_k^- := \mathbb{E}[\mathbf{x}_k | (\mathbf{z}_0, \ldots, \mathbf{z}_{k-1})],$$
$$P_k^- := \mathbb{E}[(\mathbf{x}_k - \hat{\mathbf{x}}_k^-) \times (\mathbf{x}_k - \hat{\mathbf{x}}_k^-)' | (\mathbf{z}_0, \ldots, \mathbf{z}_{k-1})].$$

Supposing knowledge of the conditional law of the process $\mathbf{x}_{k-1}$ given $(\mathbf{z}_0, \ldots, \mathbf{z}_{k-1})$, the Kalman filter considers two steps in order to evaluate $\mathbf{x}_k$ given $(\mathbf{z}_0, \ldots, \mathbf{z}_k)$. The first step is called the prediction step, whereby the conditional law of $\mathbf{x}_k$ is derived from the past information $(\mathbf{z}_0, \ldots, \mathbf{z}_{k-1})$. The second step, named the correction step, brings new information to the past information $(\mathbf{z}_0, \ldots, \mathbf{z}_{k-1})$ by introducing $\mathbf{z}_k$. Let us introduce the innovation $\mathbf{i}_k \in \mathbb{R}^m$,

$$\mathbf{i}_k = \mathbf{z}_k - \mathbb{E}[\mathbf{z}_k | (\mathbf{z}_0, \ldots, \mathbf{z}_{k-1})],$$
$$= \mathbf{z}_k - [H_k \hat{\mathbf{x}}_k^- + \mathbf{h}_k].$$

One can show that:

Proposition 12.2.2 *The innovation $\mathbf{i}_k$ is a Gaussian process independent of the observations $(\mathbf{z}_0, \ldots, \mathbf{z}_{k-1})$. Its mean and covariance are respectively $\mathbf{0}$ and*

$$Q_k^I = H_k P_k^- H_k' + Q_k^V.$$

Proof. See Appendix. □

The next proposition details the conditional law of $\mathbf{x}_k$.

Proposition 12.2.3 *Under the condition that Q_k^I is invertible for all k, the processes $\{\hat{\mathbf{x}}_k\}$ and $\{P_k\}$ are defined as follows.*

1. *Prediction step:*

$$\hat{\mathbf{x}}_k^- = F_k\hat{\mathbf{x}}_{k-1} + \mathbf{f}_k,$$
$$P_k^- = F_kP_{k-1}F_k + Q_k^W.$$

2. *Correction step:*

$$\hat{\mathbf{x}}_k = \hat{\mathbf{x}}_k^- + K_k[Z_k - (H_k\hat{\mathbf{x}}_{k-1} + \mathbf{h}_k)],$$
$$P_k = [\mathbf{i}_k - K_kH_k]P_k^-,$$

where

$$K_k = P_k^-H_k'\left[H_kP_k^-H_k' + Q_k^V\right]^{-1}.$$

K_k is called the Kalman gain with the initial condition and

$$\hat{\mathbf{x}}_0^- = \hat{\mathbf{x}}_0$$
$$= \mathbb{E}[\mathbf{x}_0],$$
$$P_0 = Q_0^X.$$

Proof. See Kalman (1960). □

Since $\mathbf{i}_k$ is Gaussian, we can apply the maximum likelihood estimator.

Proposition 12.2.4 *The log-likelihood function is given by*

$$L(\theta) = -\frac{NM}{2}\log(2\pi) - \frac{1}{2}\sum_{k=1}^{N}\left[Mk\log(2\pi) + \log\left|Q_k^I\right| + \mathbf{i}_k'\left[Q_k^I\right]^{-1}\mathbf{i}_k\right].$$

Proof. Prediction errors $\mathbf{i}_k$ of the Kalman filter are normally Gaussian distributed with zero mean and covariance matrix Q_k^I. Hence, parameters can be estimated with the maximum likelihood method. Since $\mathbf{i}_k$ and Q_k^I depend upon θ, the optimal parameter is chosen to maximize the likelihood function. Therefore, $\mathbf{i}_k$ can be used to evaluate the likelihood function. □

The estimation procedure is recursive and it is calculated at each time t_k as part of the Kalman filter. The next proposition highlights an important property on P_k and P_k^- and reduces the complexity of the algorithm.

Proposition 12.2.5 *The conditional covariances P_k and P_k^- are independent of* $(\mathbf{z}_0, \ldots, \mathbf{z}_{k-1})$.

Proof. Consequence of Proposition 12.2.2. □

P_k and P_k^- are independent of the observation. Therefore, P_k can easily be computed from the beginning since its expression does not depend on the observations.

We summarize the algorithm. The Kalman filter differentiates two kinds of variables: observed and latent variables. Under the Gibson–Schwartz model, the latent variables are the spot price and convenience yield. The filter consists of estimating the state of a dynamic system governed by the following equations: one or several measure equations, describing how the observable variables denoted $\mathbf{z}_k$ are generated by the non-observed variables denoted $\mathbf{x}_k$ and some noise. The transition equation is the next discrete-time distribution of the state variables, where θ contains the unknown parameters of the model, (i.e., the set of parameters). One or several state equations describing how the latent variables are generated: the measurement equation. The Kalman filter aims to obtain information on $\mathbf{x}_k$ from the observed data. The algorithm is divided into two steps: the prediction (update of time) and the correction (update of measures) of the state variable. At time $k-1$, we have an estimation of the hidden variable $\mathbf{x}_{k-1}$ and its variance P_{k-1} with some value for θ. During the prediction step, we find an estimation of $\hat{\mathbf{x}}_k^-$ and P_k^-. At time t_k, we get information on the data: $\mathbf{z}_k$. Using this information, we derive $\hat{\mathbf{x}}_k$ and P_k. To estimate the parameter θ, we maximize the log-likelihood function L of the previous proposition.

Remark 12.2.3 *The initial parameters $\mathbf{x}_0$ and P_0 are not determined. However, many books give some insights into deriving the initial values. In general, $\mathbf{x}_0$ is chosen from an understanding of the state variable. P_0 represents confidence on $\mathbf{x}_0$. In the literature it is shown that a large coefficient on this matrix increases the convergence speed of the algorithm.*

12.2.2 Case Study: Estimating Parameters on Crude Oil

Crude oil dominates the energy market. The oil futures market is one of the most mature and liquid energy markets. Its price exhibits high volatility and a mean-reverting pattern. Our data consists of West Texas Intermediate (WTI) futures contracts for physical delivery of crude oil quoted on the New York Mercantile Exchange (NYMEX) in 2005.[1] We use daily data ($\Delta t = 1/252$) for the period between 2 January 2005 and 29 December 2005. More precisely, we consider futures contracts with the first 18-month maturities. Figure 12.1 illustrates the WTI futures prices. One can observe three broad regimes: low price from January to March 2005; high price from April to September 2005; low price for the remainder of the year. Figure 12.2 shows the price of the 1-month and 9-month futures contracts. Comparing the two futures contracts, the figure suggests that the market is in contango for most of the period.

The Kalman filtering algorithm is implemented in Matlab. Table 12.2 describes the estimation of the Gibson–Schwartz parameters on four futures contracts in 2005: 1-month, 3-month, 9-month and 18-month futures contracts.

Figures 12.3 and 12.4 respectively plot the state variables spot price $s(t)$ and convenience yield $\delta(t)$ extracted from the Kalman filter. The two figures suggest a high correlation between the couple $(s(t), \delta(t))$, which is confirmed by the value of the correlation $\rho = 0.8635$. Figures 12.5 and 12.6 provide the distribution of the volatilities σ_1 and σ_2 estimated from simulated data of the model using the estimated parameters of Table 12.2.

[1]The year 2005 is chosen as it draws on previous work done by the authors and the case study is presented purely for illustration of the Kalman filtering technique. This year is also characterized by three broad regimes in the price series (see Figure 12.1): low price from January to March 2005; high price from April to September 2005; low price for the remainder of the year.

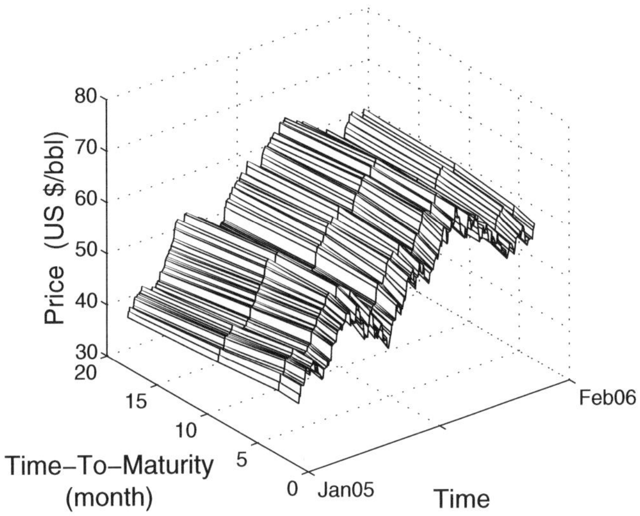

FIGURE 12.1 Term structure of WTI (2005)

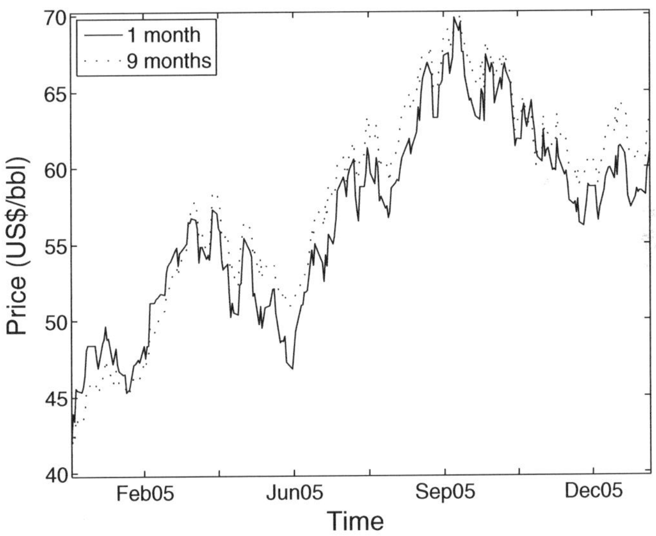

FIGURE 12.2 1-Month and 9-month WTI futures contracts (2005)

TABLE 12.2 Estimated parameters

Parameter	σ_1	σ_2	ρ	κ	μ	λ	α
Estimated value	0.3000	0.2099	0.8635	1.1973	0.4250	0.0126	0.0843

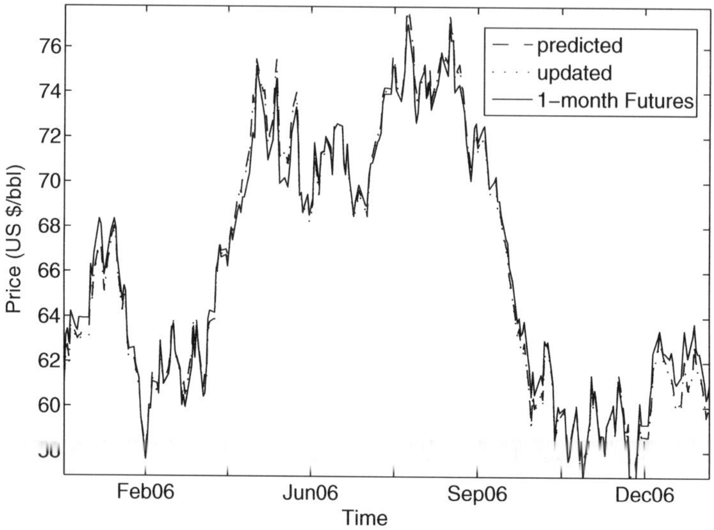

FIGURE 12.3 Estimated spot price from Kalman filter vs prompt futures contract (2005)

We wish to plot the volatility term structure and compare it with the empirical volatility. The next proposition allows us to compute the volatility term structure under the Gibson–Schwartz model.

Proposition 12.2.6 *The variance of the log return of the futures price, denoted $\sigma^2(t,T)$, is*

$$\sigma^2(t,T) = \sigma_1^2 - 2\rho\sigma_1\sigma_2\left[\frac{1-e^{-\kappa T}}{\kappa}\right] + \sigma_2^2\left[\frac{1-e^{-\kappa T}}{\kappa}\right]^2.$$

Proof. See Appendix. □

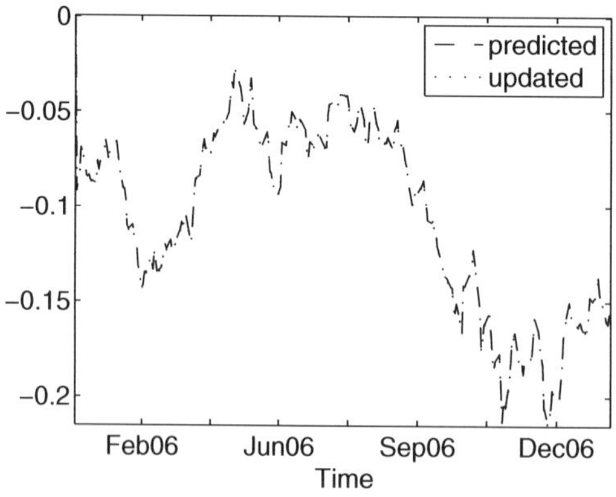

FIGURE 12.4 Estimated convenience yield from Kalman filter (2005)

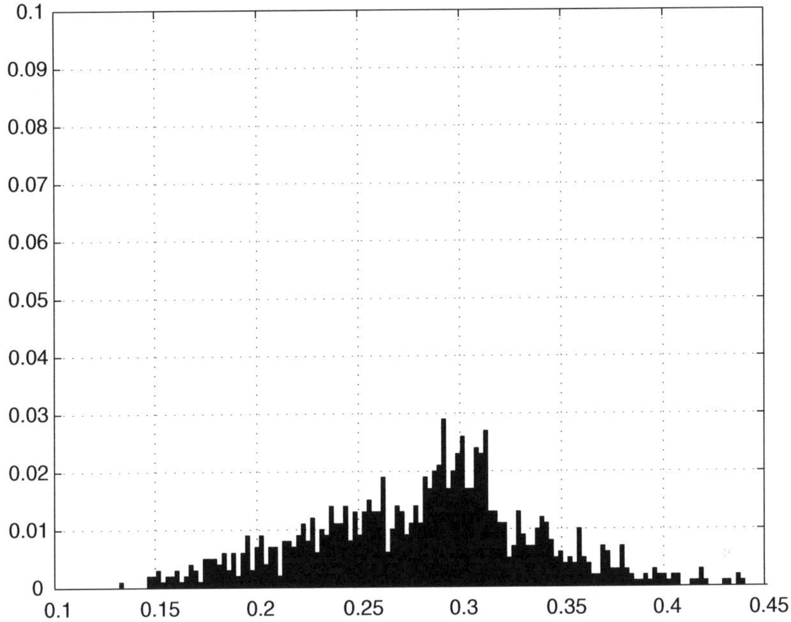

FIGURE 12.5 Distribution of spot price volatility σ_1 (2005)

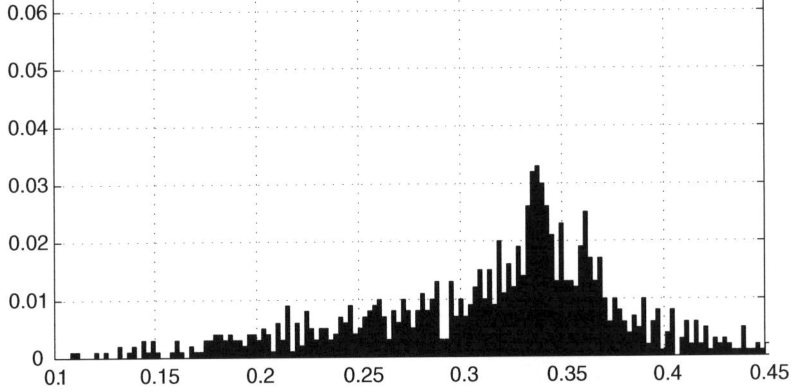

FIGURE 12.6 Distribution of convenience yield volatility σ_2 (2005)

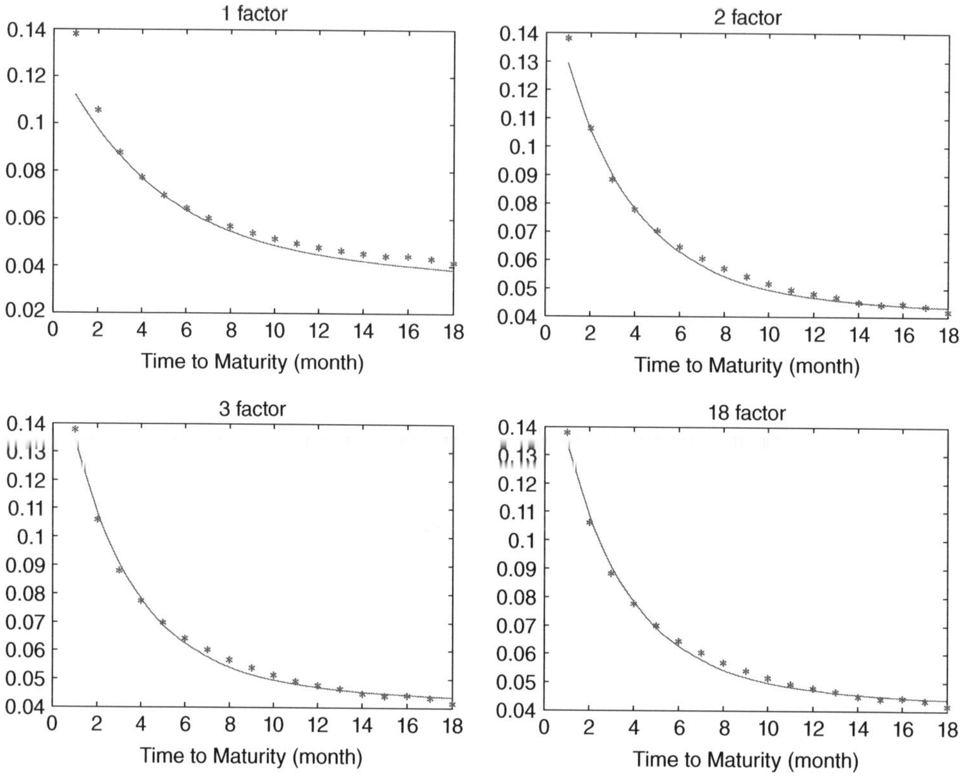

FIGURE 12.7 WTI volatility term structure (2005)

The variance of the log return of the empirical futures $\sigma^2_{emp}(t,T)$ can easily be computed as follows:

$$\sigma^2_{emp}(t,T) = Var[\log F(t+\Delta t, T) - \log F(t,T)].$$

Figure 12.7 shows the recovery of the volatility structure of the futures return from the Gibson–Schwartz model in 2005 and compares this to the empirical term structure. Both term structures can be seen to match very closely. Oil futures exhibit an important pattern: the Samuelson effect, whereby as the time-to-maturity increases, the volatility of the log-return decreases, since the trading volume is much higher for short contracts.

12.3 PRINCIPAL COMPONENTS ANALYSIS

In the section we focus on the determination of risk factors in the volatility term structure. In many cases, we face a large number of time series with no readily available information on the dependencies in the data. Data analysis provides us with a suite of robust techniques that allow us to explore the data. Principal components analysis (PCA) belongs to the group of descriptive techniques within the factorial framework. PCA transforms any large sample into a smaller sample with fewer variables. It is then easier to work with the reduced number of variables and to understand the sample summarized by these reduced factors. In particular,

PCA allows us to build orthogonal factors from the correlation matrix of the multidimensional time series. Working with a matrix $X \in M(n, m)$ having m observations and m variables, PCA aims to determine a reduced number of factors which are a linear combination of X. The idea is to build a number of factors lower than the number of variables m.

In finance, PCA was applied first in interest rate theory. More generally, unpredictable prices, indices or interest rates represent sources of risk for an agent who works in the financial markets. Measuring these risks explicitly needs a very large numbers of factors. However, many financial instruments are correlated and so the risk factors can be reduced. PCA has become an important tool to reduce risk factors. It has been applied in interest rate markets, commodity markets and also more generally in asset management. The aim here is to describe PCA and illustrate its use with an example.

12.3.1 PCA: Technical Presentation

We consider a set of data $\{F(t_i, x_j)\}_{i=1\ldots n, j=1\ldots m}$. For example, assume $F(t, x)$ is a crude oil futures price at time t and maturing in x months. We define its return (r_{ij}) as follows:

$$r_{ij} := \frac{F(t_i, x_j) - F(t_{i-1}, x_j)}{F(t_{i-1}, x_j)}.$$

The return can be represented by the matrix $R \in \mathbf{M}(n, m)$, where

$$R = \begin{pmatrix} r_{11} & \cdots & r_{1m} \\ \vdots & \vdots & \vdots \\ r_{n1} & \cdots & r_{nm} \end{pmatrix}.$$

PCA disentangles two elements. Each column of R represents futures price returns for a given maturity over time, whereas each row corresponds to the futures price returns for all the maturities at a given point in time. Hence, we introduce $\mathbf{u}_j \in \mathbb{R}^n, j \in \{1, \ldots, m\}$, such that

$$\mathbf{u}_j = \begin{pmatrix} r_{1j} \\ \vdots \\ r_{nj} \end{pmatrix},$$

and $\mathbf{v}_i \in \mathbb{R}^m$, $i \in \{1, \ldots, n\}$, such that

$$\mathbf{v}_i = \begin{pmatrix} r_{i1} \\ \vdots \\ r_{im} \end{pmatrix}.$$

The vectors $\{\mathbf{v}_1, \ldots, \mathbf{v}_n\}$ and $\{\mathbf{u}_1, \ldots, \mathbf{u}_m\}$ are respectively called the population and the variables. One individual within the population is represented by a given futures returns term structure at a given point in time. The futures price returns maturing in a given number of months correspond to a variable.

PCA introduces an important element that measures the dispersion of the total population around its centre of mass, called inertia and defined as follows:

$$\tilde{\imath} := \frac{1}{m} \sum_{j=1}^{m} ||\mathbf{u}_j||^2,$$

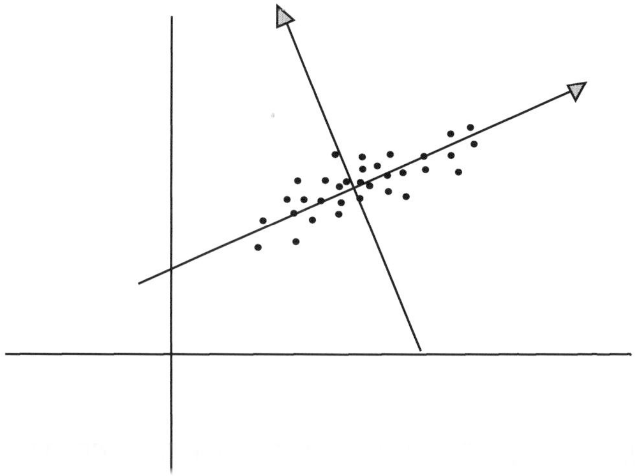

FIGURE 12.8 Examples of axes that minimize distortions

where $||\mathbf{u}||$ denotes the Euclidean norm of the vector $\mathbf{u}$. If the inertia $\tilde{i}$ is high, the population is scattered. If the value is low, the population is concentrated. When the inertia is equal to zero, individuals are almost the same. By rewriting the previous equation that defined the inertia, one can easily show that

$$\tilde{i} = \frac{1}{m}\sum_{j=1}^{m}\left(\sum_{i=1}^{n} r_{ij}^2\right),$$

which can be written as the sum of the empirical variance of $\mathbf{v}_i$,

$$\tilde{i} = \sum_{i=1}^{n} Var(\mathbf{v}_i).$$

Remark 12.3.1 *Note that for the covariance of futures returns matrix* Σ,

$$\tilde{i} = Trace(\Sigma).$$

Inertia with respect to an axis Δ can be defined as the sum of the distance between individuals and the axis Δ. Projected data on a subspace defined by some axes may imply a distorted reality and may lose some information. The role of PCA is to find a subspace that minimizes this distortion. The idea is to propose a methodology which finds axes that minimize inertia with respect to these axes. Figure 12.8 illustrates this idea and shows the axes that we have to define in order to capture the maximum independent information. One can show the following result:

Proposition 12.3.1 *The axes realizing the previous conditions are the eigenvectors of* Σ. *Moreover,*

$$\Sigma = \Pi \times \Lambda \times \Pi'$$

where Π *and* $\Lambda := diag(\lambda_i)$ *are respectively the set of eigenvectors and the set of eigenvalues such that* $\lambda_1 > \lambda_2 > \cdots > \lambda_m$.

Proof. See Jolliffe (2002). □

The inertia is exactly the sum of the eigenvalues,

$$\tilde{i} = \sum_{j=1}^{m} \lambda_j.$$

The kth contribution of the new variable can be represented as

$$\frac{\lambda_k}{\sum_{j=1}^{m} \lambda_j}.$$

Hence, the contribution of the first p factors is defined as

$$\frac{\sum_{k=1}^{p} \lambda_k}{\sum_{j=1}^{m} \lambda_j}.$$

To build the volatility term structure of the futures price, we suppose that the futures prices follow a defined stochastic differential equation. The next proposition allows us to express the volatilities of the futures price return as a function of the eigenvalues $\{\lambda_j\}$ and eigenvectors $\{\pi_{kj}\}$.

Proposition 12.3.2 *Suppose that* $F(t,x)$ *is governed by the following stochastic differential equation:*

$$\frac{dF(t,x)}{F(t,x)} = \sum_{k=1}^{p} \sigma_k(x) \times d\omega_k(t),$$

for independent Wiener processes $\omega_k(t)$, $k = 1, \ldots, p$. *Therefore,*

$$\sigma_k(x_j) = \pi_{kj}\sqrt{\lambda_j},\ j = 1, \ldots, m, k = 1, \ldots, p.$$

Proof. See Basilevsky (1994). □

Remark 12.3.2 *p is generally chosen for a given contribution of the first p risk factors.*

FIGURE 12.9 First axis of PCA: level

To summarize, we disentangle three important steps for the PCA. First, we compute the correlation matrix Σ. Second, we compute its eigenvalues and eigenvectors, $\Pi := (\pi_{kj})$ and $\Lambda := (\lambda_j)$ such that $\lambda_1 > \lambda_2 > \cdots > \lambda_m$. Finally, we derive the volatilities.

PCA studies in finance generally highlight three main factors: (i) the first is commonly referred to as the 'level' factor, determining the trend of the term structure and typically interpreted as capturing parallel shifts (Figure 12.9); (ii) the second is commonly referred to as the 'slope' factor, characterized by opposite signs on the extrema and interpreted as the slope of the term structure (Figure 12.10); and (iii) the third is commonly referred to as the

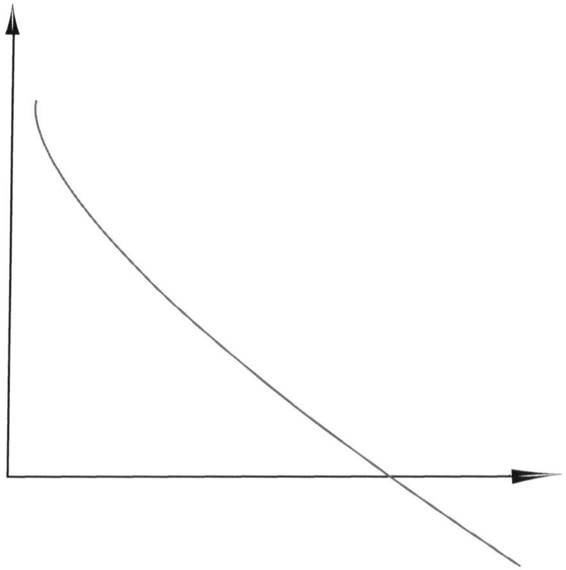

FIGURE 12.10 Second axis of PCA: slope

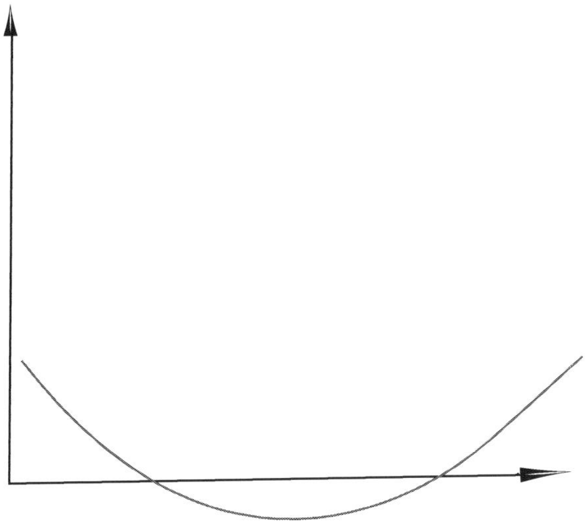

FIGURE 12.11 Third axis of PCA: curvature

'curvature' factor, characterized by identical signs at the extrema of the term structure but an opposite sign in the middle and determining the twisting or bending of the term structure (Figure 12.11).

12.3.2 Case Study: Risk Analysis on Energy Markets

Our data consists of two samples.

Sample 1: WTI futures contracts for physical delivery crude oil quoted on NYMEX. The units of trade are US dollars per barrel. We use daily data between 1 January 1990 and 31 May 2007 as illustrated in Figures 12.12 and 12.13. The market clearly alternates between contango and backwardation.

Sample 2: Henry Hub natural gas futures contracts for physical delivery natural gas traded on NYMEX. The units of trade are US dollars per million British thermal units. We use daily data between 1 January 1990 and 31 May 2007 as illustrated in Figure 12.14.

We perform the PCA on both markets. Figures 12.15 and 12.16 respectively show the first three factors on the oil and gas markets.

Table 12.3 provides the cumulative contributions of the three factors for each of the two samples. For WTI, it can be seen that 95% of the volatility term structure is explained by the first factor, while the contribution reaches 99.22% for the first two factors and reaches the even higher value of 99.71% when the first three factors are considered. In contrast, for the Henry Hub futures, the contribution of the first three factors comes to less than 90%.

This low contribution may be due to the seasonality pattern on the volatility, as exhibited in Figure 12.16. Hence, we propose to apply the PCA on the different months. We perform the PCA on the two samples for each month. Tables 12.4 and 12.5 give the results for the WTI and Henry Hub markets respectively.

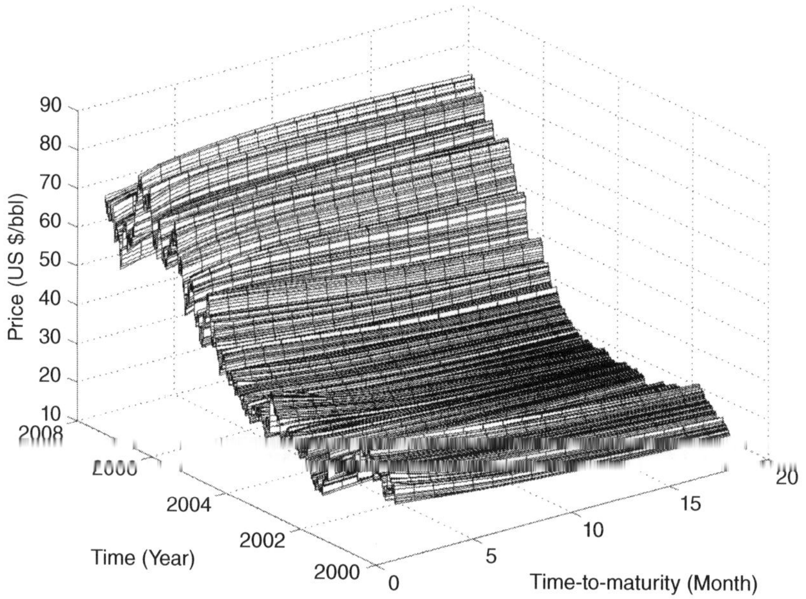

FIGURE 12.12 WTI futures prices (2000–2007)

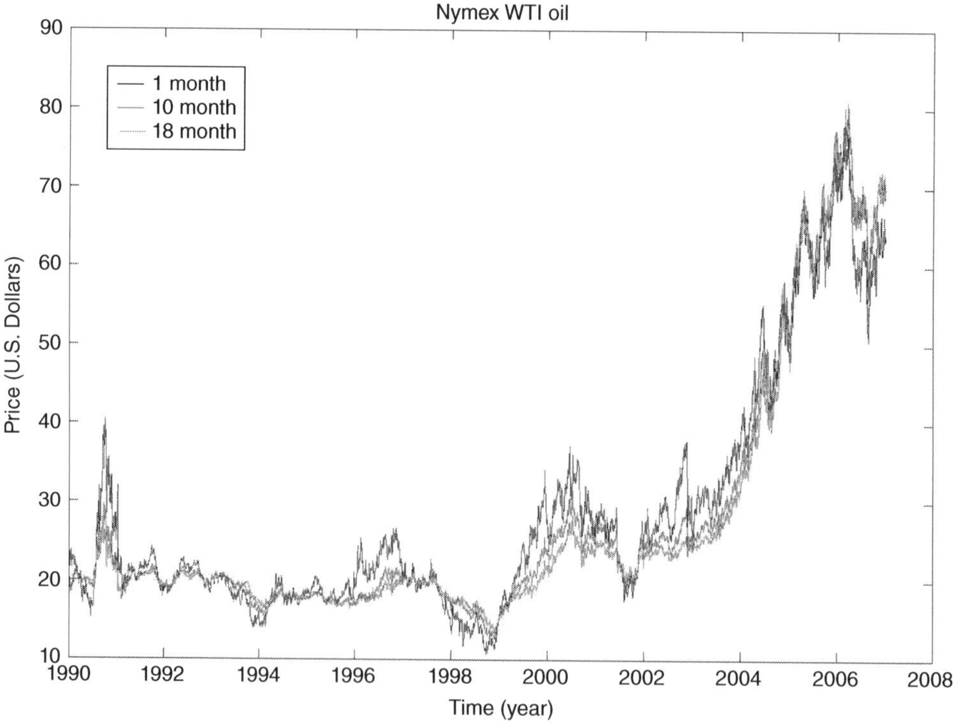

FIGURE 12.13 1-Month, 10-month and 18-month WTI futures

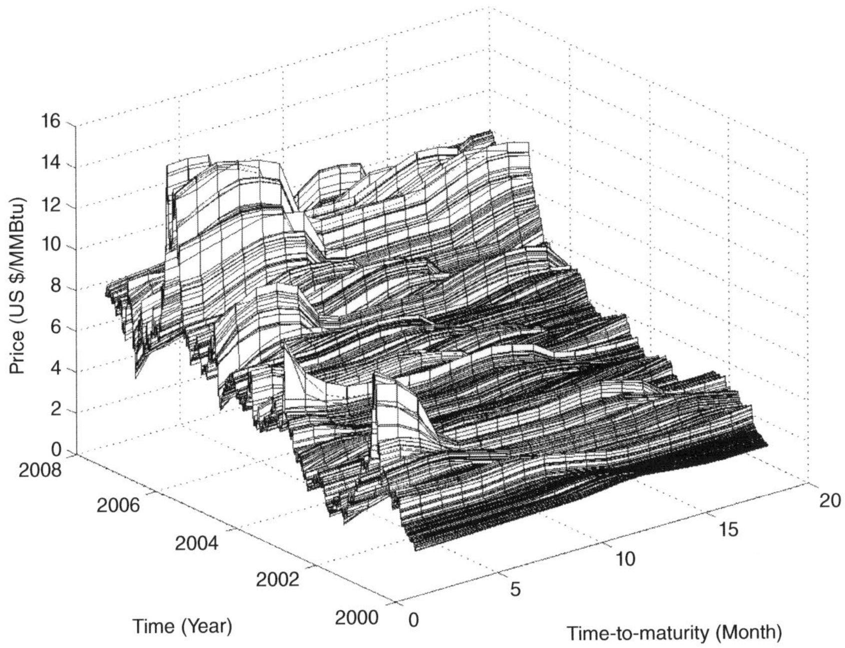

FIGURE 12.14 Henry Hub futures prices (2000–2007)

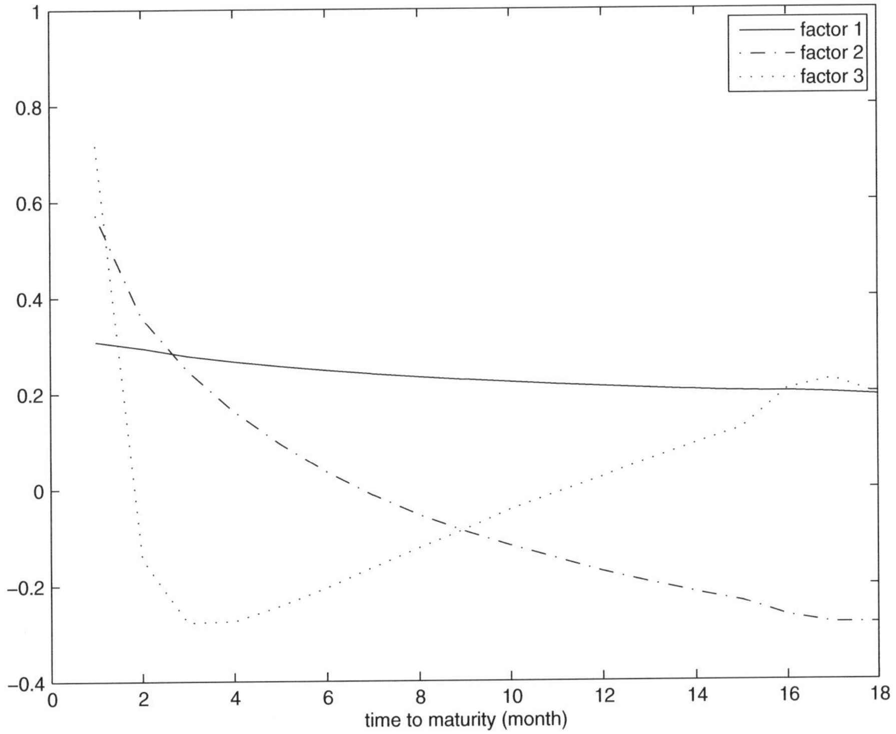

FIGURE 12.15 First three risk factors of WTI (2000–2007)

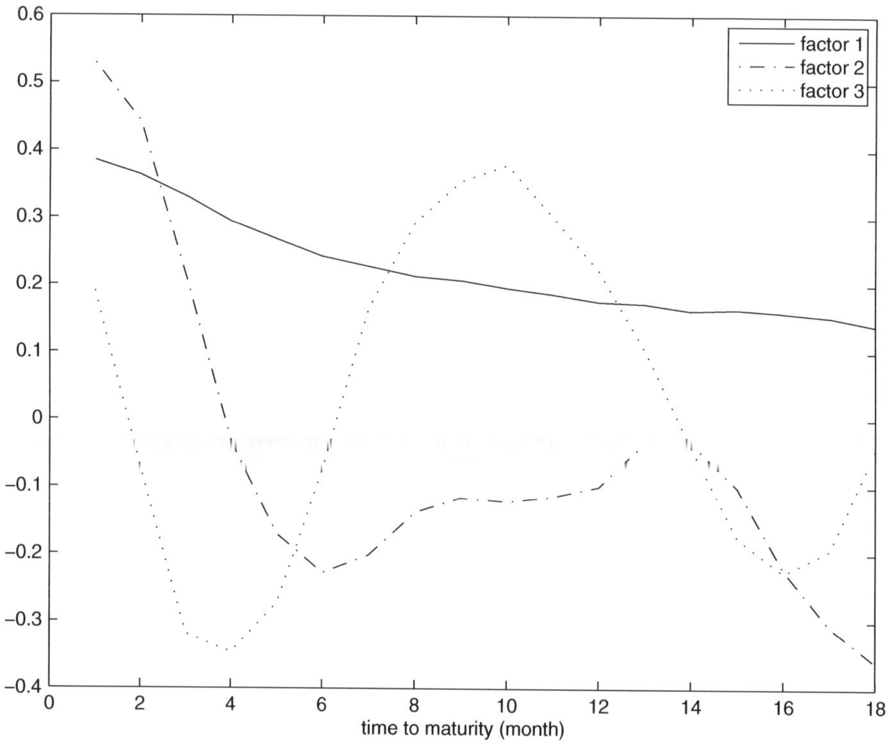

FIGURE 12.16 First three risk factors of Henry Hub (2000–2007)

TABLE 12.3 Cumulative contributions of the two samples

Cumulative contribution	Factor 1	Factor 2	Factor 3
Sample 1 (WTI)	0.9564	0.9922	0.9971
Sample 2 (Henry Hub)	0.7779	0.8421	0.8813

TABLE 12.4 Monthly cumulative contributions: WTI

Factor	1	2	3
January	0.9492	0.9946	0.9983
February	0.9455	0.9907	0.9981
March	0.9474	0.9909	0.9982
April	0.9487	0.9825	0.9948
May	0.9612	0.9934	0.9984
June	0.9584	0.9945	0.9984
July	0.9582	0.9915	0.9982
August	0.9582	0.9915	0.9982
September	0.9604	0.9930	0.9978
October	0.9510	0.9949	0.9989
November	0.9666	0.9954	0.9988
December	0.9737	0.9957	0.9987

TABLE 12.5 Monthly cumulative contributions: Henry Hub

Factor	1	2	3
January	0.8476	0.9298	0.9789
February	0.7682	0.8785	0.9514
March	0.8089	0.9486	0.9744
April	0.7858	0.9566	0.9794
May	0.7728	0.9370	0.9783
June	0.8143	0.9418	0.9852
July	0.8054	0.9323	0.9830
August	0.7603	0.9357	0.9689
September	0.7003	0.9285	0.9641
October	0.7962	0.9362	0.9769
November	0.8007	0.9292	0.9741
December	0.8066	0.9107	0.9697

Contributions are higher and change over the months for the two markets. Moreover, the first three factors explain at least 95% of the futures price movements in both samples in each month.

12.4 CONCLUSION

In this chapter, we describe two methods commonly used in estimating the volatility term structure in energy and commodity markets. The first tool aims to estimate the parameters of a spot price–convenience yield model using the Kalman filter. In particular, we describe the method on the Gibson–Schwartz model. An application is given for WTI crude oil. In this case study, the volatility term structure generated by the model and the empirical term structure are shown to match closely.

The second tool captures the risk factors of price movements using a data reduction technique. The methodology is based on PCA and allows us to reduce the dimensionality of the data. This is achieved by transforming into new variables that are uncorrelated and ordered in terms of their contribution. A case study on WTI and Henry Hub futures is presented, showcasing the strength of this estimation tool.

APPENDIX

Proof. (Proposition 12.2.2).

$$\begin{aligned}\mathbf{i}_k &= \mathbf{z}_k - [H_k\hat{\mathbf{x}}_k^- + \mathbf{h}_k]\\ &= H_k[\mathbf{x_k} - \hat{\mathbf{x}}_k^-] + \mathbf{v}_k.\end{aligned}$$

Hence, its mean and covariance are respectively 0 and

$$\begin{aligned}Q_k^I &= Cov(\mathbf{i}_k, \mathbf{i}_k)\\ &= H_k P_k^- H_k' + Q_k^V.\end{aligned}$$

□

Proof. (Proposition 12.2.6).

We write the dynamics of the futures price under the historical measure (Id Brik, 2011)

$$\begin{aligned} d\log F(t,T) = {} & \left[\mu - r + \frac{\lambda}{\kappa}\frac{e^{-\kappa T}-1}{\kappa}\right] dt \\ & - \frac{1}{2}\left(\sigma_1^2 - 2\rho\sigma_1\sigma_2\left[\frac{1-e^{-\kappa T}}{\kappa}\right] + \sigma_2^2\left[\frac{1-e^{-\kappa T}}{\kappa}\right]^2\right) dt \\ & + \sigma_1 d\omega_1(t) - \sigma_2\left[\frac{1-e^{-\kappa T}}{\kappa}\right] d\omega_2(t). \end{aligned}$$

By discretizing the previous formula, we obtain

$$\begin{aligned} \log F(t+\Delta t,T) - \log F(t,T) = {} & \left[\mu - r + \frac{\lambda}{\kappa}\frac{e^{-\kappa T}-1}{\kappa}\right] \Delta t \\ & - \frac{1}{2}\left(\sigma_1^2 - 2\rho\sigma_1\sigma_2\left[\frac{1-e^{-\kappa T}}{\kappa}\right] + \sigma_2^2\left[\frac{1-e^{-\kappa T}}{\kappa}\right]^2\right) \Delta t \\ & + \sigma_1 \epsilon_1(t)\sqrt{\Delta t} - \sigma_2\left[\frac{1-e^{-\kappa T}}{\kappa}\right] \epsilon_2(t)\sqrt{\Delta t}, \end{aligned}$$

where $\epsilon_1(t)$ and $\epsilon_2(t)$ are two normal processes and $Cov(\epsilon_1(t), \epsilon_2(t)) = \rho$. Therefore, the first two moments are

$$\begin{aligned} \mathbb{E}[\log F(t+\Delta t,T) - \log F(t,T)] = {} & \left[\mu - r + \frac{\lambda}{\kappa}\frac{e^{-\kappa(T-t)}-1}{\kappa}\right] \Delta t \\ & - \frac{1}{2}\left(\sigma_1^2 - 2\rho\sigma_1\sigma_2\left[\frac{1-e^{-\kappa T}}{\kappa}\right] + \sigma_2^2\left[\frac{1-e^{-\kappa T}}{\kappa}\right]^2\right) \Delta t, \end{aligned}$$

$$\begin{aligned} \mathbb{V}ar[\log F(t+dt,T) - \log F(t,T)] &= E\left[\left(\sigma_1\epsilon_1(t)\sqrt{\Delta t} - \sigma_2\left[\frac{1-e^{-\kappa T}}{\kappa}\right]\epsilon_2(t)\sqrt{\Delta t}\right)^2\right] \\ &= E\left[\begin{matrix} \sigma_1^2\epsilon_1^2(t) - 2\rho\sigma_1\sigma_2\left[\frac{1-e^{-\kappa T}}{\kappa}\right]\epsilon_1(t)\epsilon_2(t) \\ -\sigma_2^2\left[\frac{1-e^{-\kappa T}}{\kappa}\right]^2\epsilon_2^2(t) \end{matrix}\right]\Delta t \\ &= \left[\begin{matrix} \sigma_1^2\mathbb{E}\left\{\epsilon_1^2(t)\right\} - 2\rho\sigma_1\sigma_2\left[\frac{1-e^{-\kappa T}}{\kappa}\right]\mathbb{E}\{\epsilon_1(t)\epsilon_2(t)\} \\ -\sigma_2^2\left[\frac{1-e^{-\kappa T}}{\kappa}\right]^2\mathbb{E}\left\{\epsilon_2^2(t)\right\} \end{matrix}\right]\Delta t. \end{aligned}$$

Using the properties of white noises, $\mathbb{E}\{\epsilon_1^2(t)\} = \mathbb{E}\{\epsilon_2^2(t)\} = 1$ and $\mathbb{E}\{\epsilon_1(t)\epsilon_2(t)\} = \rho$, we conclude. □

REFERENCES

Basilevsky, A. (1994) *Statistical Factor Analysis and Related Methods: Theory and Applications*, John Wiley & Sons, New York.

Casassus, J. and Collin-Dufresne, P. (2005) Convenience yields implied from interest rates and commodity futures, *The Journal of Finance*, **60**(5), 2283–2331.

Gibson, R. and Schwartz, E. (1990) Stochastic convenience yield and the pricing of oil contingent claims, *Journal of Finance*, **45**, 959–976.

Id Brik, R. (2011) Modélisation du risque dans les marchés de commodités: théorie et applications, Doctoral Thesis, Université Paris Dauphine.

Jamshidian, F. and Fein, M. (1990) Closed-form solutions for oil futures and European options in the Gibson–Schwartz model: A note, Working Paper, Merrill Lynch Capital Markets.

Jolliffe, I.T. (2002) *Principal Component Analysis, Springer Series in Statistics*, Springer-Verlag, Berlin.

Kalman, R.E. (1960) A new approach to linear filtering and prediction problems, *Journal of Basic Engineering*, **82**(1), 35–45.

Schwartz, E.S. (1997) The stochastic behavior of commodity prices: Implications for valuation and hedging, *The Journal of Finance*, **LII**(3), July.

Schwartz, E. and Smith, J.E. (2000) Short-term variations and long-term dynamics in commodity prices, *Management Science*, **46**(7), 893–911.

CHAPTER 13

Nonparametric Estimation of Energy and Commodity Price Processes

Gianna Figà-Talamanca and Andrea Roncoroni

13.1 INTRODUCTION

Random changes in several financial figures such as stock data market indices and commodity prices are commonly represented by a diffusion process X of the following form:

$$dX(t) = \mu(X(t))dt + \sigma(X(t))dW(t), \qquad (13.1)$$

where W is a one-dimensional standard Brownian motion, $\mu(\cdot)$ and $\sigma(\cdot)$ are assumed to be regular functions in order to guarantee the existence and uniqueness of a weak solution to equation (13.1). Most model specifications assume parametric forms for both these functions, which are called the drift and the diffusion coefficient of process X, respectively. A possible extension of the above model is obtained by adding a jumping part in the dynamics of process X, that is

$$dX_t = \mu(X(t^-))dt + \sigma(X(t^-))dW(t) + YdJ(t). \qquad (13.2)$$

Here J is a compensated jump process with intensity $\lambda(x)$, that is, $J(t) - \lambda(X(t))$ is a martingale, and Y is a random jump size whose distribution p_Y is assumed to be independent of that of J and W.

We aim at testing the consistency of the diffusion model described in equation (13.1) with changes in the log-price of several commodities; this is done by applying kernel methods to estimate the infinitesimal conditional moments of the process, as suggested by Stanton (1997), and computing confidence intervals based on simulations for these estimated moments. Our empirical analysis proves that continuous diffusion models are unable to describe the features displayed by commodity data in several cases. We then resort to the model in equation (13.2)

Handbook of Multi-Commodity Markets and Products: Structuring, Trading and Risk Management. Edited by Andrea Roncoroni, Gianluca Fusai and Mark Cummins.

and use the results of Johannes (1999, 2004) and Bandi and Nguyen (1999, 2003) to estimate the drift, the diffusion and the intensity function of the process in a nonparametric form.

We organize the chapter as follows. Section 13.2 introduces the main issue of estimating diffusion processes by finite sample data and describes the estimation techniques for both continuous and mixed-jump models. Section 13.3 resumes the outcomes of the nonparametric estimation for crude oil, corn, copper and gold log-prices.

13.2 ESTIMATION METHOD

Assume at first that the dynamics of the process X is described by the continuous diffusion process in equation (13.1); it is shown in Stanton (1997), as well as in several other papers, that the drift coefficient represents the instantaneous average speed of the process at each point in time, conditional on its value. That is:

$$\lim_{\Delta t \to 0} \frac{1}{\Delta t} \mathbb{E}[X(t+\Delta t) - X(t) | X(t) = x] = \mu(x). \tag{13.3}$$

Similarly, the diffusion coefficient represents the instantaneous average centred moment of order two of the process at each point in time, conditional on its value:

$$\lim_{\Delta t \to 0} \frac{1}{\Delta t} \mathbb{E}[(X(t+\Delta t) - X(t))^2 \big| X(t) = x] = \sigma^2(x). \tag{13.4}$$

Further, higher-order moments for these figures are null. That is:

$$\lim_{\Delta t \to 0} \frac{1}{\Delta} \mathbb{E}[(X(t+\Delta t) - X(t))^r \big| X(t) = x] = 0, \qquad r > 2. \tag{13.5}$$

On the contrary, if the dynamics of process X is described by a mixed-diffusion process as in equation (13.2), the corresponding relations between model coefficients and process properties are (see Johannes, 1999, 2004)

$$\lim_{\Delta t \to 0} \frac{1}{\Delta t} \mathbb{E}[X(t+\Delta t) - X(t) | X(t) = x] = \mu(x), \tag{13.6}$$

$$\lim_{\Delta t \to 0} \frac{1}{\Delta t} \mathbb{E}[(X(t+\Delta t) - X(t))^2 \big| X(t) = x] = \sigma^2(x) + \lambda(x)\mathbb{E}_Y[Y^2], \tag{13.7}$$

$$\lim_{\Delta t \to 0} \frac{1}{\Delta} \mathbb{E}[(X(t+\Delta t) - X(t))^r \big| X(t) = x] = \lambda(x)\mathbb{E}_Y[Y^r], \qquad r > 2. \tag{13.8}$$

The key point in these expressions is that jumps allow us to model time series displaying instantaneous increments with nonzero moments of order $r > 2$.

Statistical estimation of both diffusion processes such as (13.1) and jump-diffusion processes such as (13.2) aims to obtain the functions $\mu(\cdot)$, $\sigma(\cdot)$ and $\lambda(\cdot)$ as well as the jump size distribution $p_Y(y)$, which are consistent with observed data with respect to some criterion to be defined. In particular, nonparametric estimation derives these functions in a pointwise manner, that is, for each value x chosen in a suitable interval of the real line, without any reference to parametric families. Of course, the functions $\mu(\cdot)$, $\sigma(\cdot)$ and $\lambda(\cdot)$ are required to satisfy suitable regularity conditions to ensure that the resulting process is well-defined as the unique solution of the corresponding stochastic differential equation (see, e.g., Øksendal, 2003 and Protter, 1995, among others).

A possible method to estimate a diffusion process nonparametrically, introduced by Stanton (1997), is to define its coefficients by means of a finite-sample version of the left-hand sides in expressions (13.3), (13.4) and (13.5). To this end we assume that each available time series $x_1, x_2, \ldots, x_n$ is collected at a sufficiently small time span Δ and estimate infinitesimal conditional moments by their finite-sample counterparts obtained by kernel methods.

More precisely, we obtain finite-sample estimates for the conditional moments by kernel convolutions

$$M_1(x) = \frac{\sum_{t=1}^{n} K\left(\frac{x_t - x}{h}\right)(x_{t+1} - x_t)}{\Delta \sum_{t=1}^{n} K\left(\frac{x_t - x}{h}\right)}, \tag{13.9}$$

$$M_2(x) = \frac{\sum_{t=1}^{n} K\left(\frac{x_t - x}{h}\right)(x_{t+1} - x_t)^2}{\Delta \sum_{t=1}^{n} K\left(\frac{x_t - x}{h}\right)} \tag{13.10}$$

and, in general, for $r > 2$:

$$M_r(x) = \frac{\sum_{t=1}^{n} K\left(\frac{x_t - x}{h}\right)(x_{t+1} - x_t)^r}{\Delta \sum_{t=1}^{n} K\left(\frac{x_t - x}{h}\right)}. \tag{13.11}$$

In the above expressions, the kernel function K is a symmetric probability density on the real axis expressing the influence a point at zero has on all other points in its domain; the mean variation of the process starting at a level x, for instance, is obtained by weighting all sample variations $x_{t+1} - x_t$ obtained in the past. If we define

$$\omega_t(x) = \frac{K\left(\frac{x_t - x}{h}\right)}{\sum_{t=1}^{n} K\left(\frac{x_t - x}{h}\right)}, \qquad t = 1, 2, \ldots, n,$$

we can write the approximate moments in equations (13.9), (13.10) and (13.11) as

$$M_r(x) = \sum_{t=1}^{n} \frac{(x_{t+1} - x_t)^r}{\Delta} \omega_t(x), \qquad r \geq 1.$$

Hence, the kernel function provides weights which depend on the level x and on a parameter h, called the bandwidth, which determines the smoothing behaviour of the kernel (see Silverman, 1986 and James and Webber 2000 for more details).

Usually K is assumed to be a standard Gaussian density so that the larger the distance between x_t and x, the lower the impact of sample increment $x_{t+1} - x_t$ on the average increment of the process starting at level x. Conversely, the closer x_t to the actual level x, the higher the importance of the sample increment $x_{t+1} - x_t$ in explaining the average increment from x.

In case the sample is generated by a continuous diffusion process, M_r should be zero for $r > 2$ and M_1 and M_2 are estimates of the drift and the squared diffusion coefficient, respectively. That is:

$$\widehat{\mu}(x) = M_1(x),$$
$$\widehat{\sigma}^2(x) = M_2(x).$$

For a mixed-jump diffusion, M_2 is the sum of the instantaneous squared diffusion term and the product of the jump size second-order moment times the jump intensity, according to expression (13.7); higher moments may be nonzero and should be computed to complete the estimation procedure. In this case we still have

$$\widehat{\mu}(x) = M_1(x).$$

If we further assume that the jump size Y has a centred normal distribution with variance σ_Y^2, formulae (13.7), (13.8), (13.10) and (13.11) lead to the following approximated equalities for finite-sample conditional moments:

$$M_2(x) \simeq \sigma^2(x) + \lambda(x)\sigma_Y^2, \tag{13.12}$$
$$M_4(x) \simeq 3\lambda(x)\sigma_Y^4, \tag{13.13}$$
$$M_6(x) \simeq 15\lambda(x)\sigma_Y^6, \tag{13.14}$$

where $\sigma^2(x)$, $\lambda(x)$ and σ_Y^2 are the true coefficient function values at x.

By taking the ratio between the sixth and the fourth sample kernel moments, we get

$$\widehat{\sigma}_Y^2(x) = \frac{M_6(x)}{5M_4(x)}$$

which depends on the value x; as a first-order estimate for the constant variance of the jump size we take the sample average of this quantity, namely

$$\widehat{\sigma}_Y^2 = \frac{1}{n}\sum_{t=1}^{n} \frac{M_6(x_t)}{5M_4(x_t)}.$$

Given this value, the jump intensity may be derived by equality (13.13) as

$$\widehat{\lambda}(x) = \frac{M_4(x)}{3\widehat{\sigma}_Y^4}$$

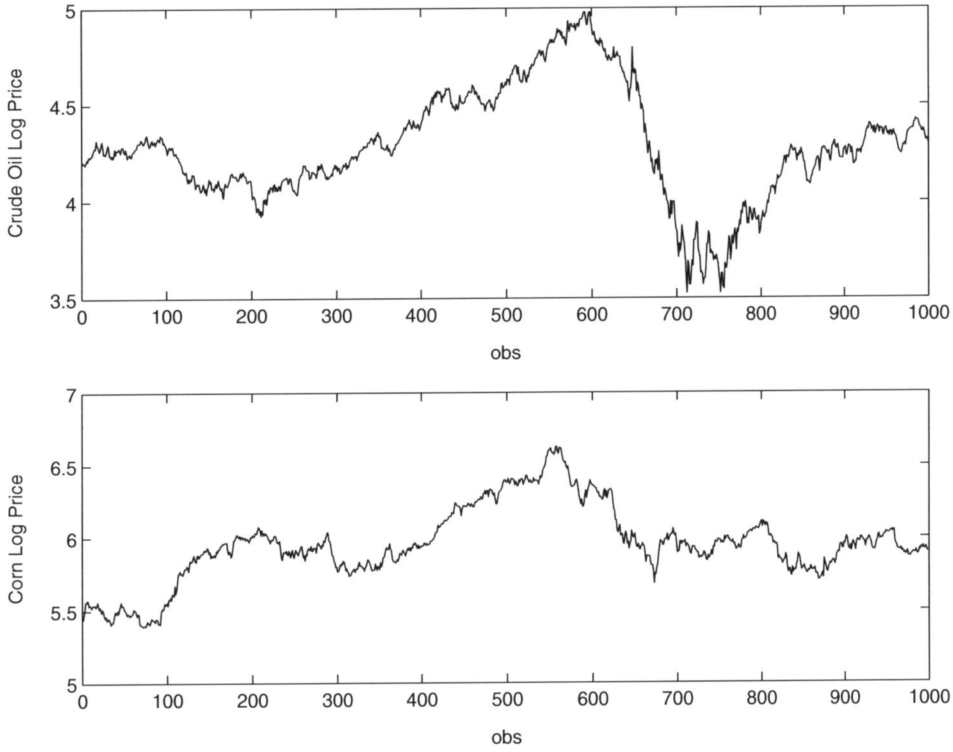

FIGURE 13.1 Crude oil (top) and corn (bottom) log-prices from May 2006 to March 2009

and the squared diffusion term is finally obtained as

$$\widehat{\sigma}^2(x) = M_2(x) - \widehat{\lambda}(x)\sigma_Y^2,$$

from relation (13.12).

Under technical assumptions reported in Bandi and Nguyen (2003), these estimators can be proven to be consistent and asymptotically normal.

13.3 EMPIRICAL RESULTS

We apply the above estimation procedure to daily prices of crude oil, corn, copper and gold from May 2006 to March 2009 (1000 observations) – see Figures 13.1 and 13.2. The selected commodities are representative of different sectors in the commodity market: crude oil, traded on the NYMEX, is an example of energy commodities; corn, traded on the CBOT, is an example of agricultural products; copper and gold, traded on the COMEX, are examples of industrial and precious metals, respectively.

Our aim is to simultaneously detect whether daily time series of the price of such commodities are generated by a continuous diffusion model and to identify the functional forms in the dynamics of the corresponding log-price process X.

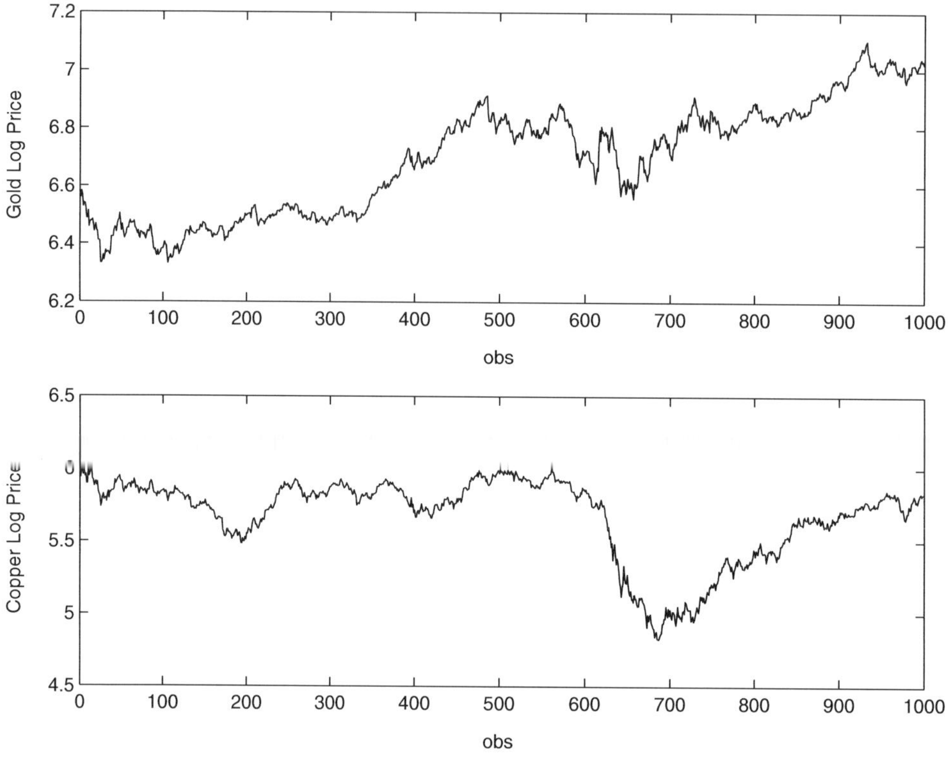

FIGURE 13.2 Gold (top) and copper (bottom) log-prices from May 2006 to March 2009

For each time series $x_1, x_2, \ldots, x_n$, with $n = 1000$ and $\Delta = 1/252$, we compute kernel sample moments $M_1(x)$, $M_2(x)$, $M_3(x)$ and $M_4(x)$ for all values x in the interval $[x_{\min}, x_{\max}]$, where $x_{\min}$ and $x_{\max}$ denote respectively the minimum and maximum values for observed log-prices. For the calculation of the above sample moments we adopt a Gaussian kernel defined as

$$K(x) = \frac{1}{\sqrt{2\pi}} \exp(-\frac{x^2}{2})$$

and select a different bandwidth, depending on the standard deviation s of log-price daily changes, for each moment to be computed, as suggested by Johannes (1999, 2004). These values are reported in Table 13.1

The above choice for the bandwidth is consistent with Chapman and Pearson (2000) and Bandi and Nguyen (1999, 2003), where the authors suggest oversmoothing the drift function with respect to the diffusion coefficient.

High-order sample moments can be used to test for a continuous diffusion process against a jump-diffusion one; if these estimates lie inside the corresponding confidence bands obtained, as described below, by simulation, the null hypothesis of a continuous diffusion may not be rejected.

TABLE 13.1 Bandwidth values, where s is the annualized standard deviation of the Euribor daily changes

Moment M_k	**Bandwidth h**
M_1	$1.25s$
M_2	$0.4s$
$M_{3,4,5,6}$	$0.75s$

In order to obtain confidence bands we simulate m paths of the continuous diffusion process defined by equation (13.1) with $\mu(x) := M_1(x)$ and $\sigma^2(x) := M_2(x)$; each path, for $j = 1, 2, \ldots, m$, is treated as a single sample from which we compute kernel sample moments $M_1^{(j)}(x)$, $M_2^{(j)}(x)$, $M_3^{(j)}(x)$ and $M_4^{(j)}(x)$ by applying equations (13.9), (13.10) and (13.11), respectively. A shortcut aimed at avoiding an excessively intensive computation is to evaluate kernel weights once for all paths, for example, by using the original data set. We thus end with m values for $M_1^{(j)}(x)$, $M_2^{(j)}(x)$, $M_3^{(j)}(x)$ and $M_4^{(j)}(x)$ with $j = 1, 2, \ldots, m$; the 10th and 90th percentiles of these values give the lower and upper band for the corresponding sample moments of a diffusion, that is whether our time series comes from a diffusion process with drift $M_1(x)$ or

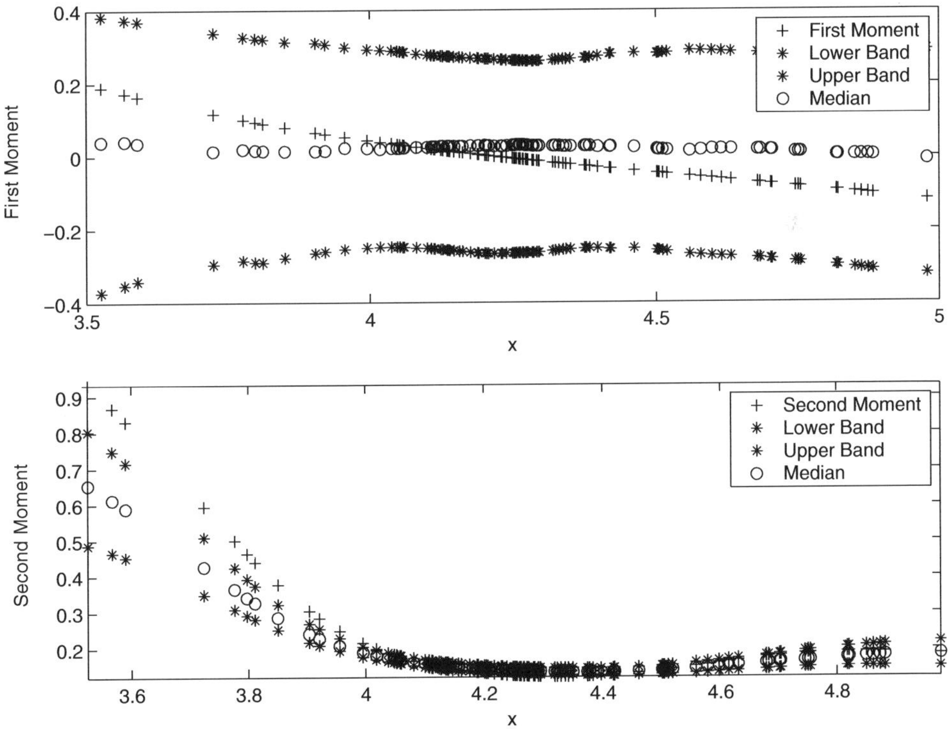

FIGURE 13.3 First (top) and second (bottom) sample conditional moment estimates (+) for crude oil log-prices with simulated confidence bands (∗) for the null of a diffusion. The simulated median value (○) is reported as a benchmark

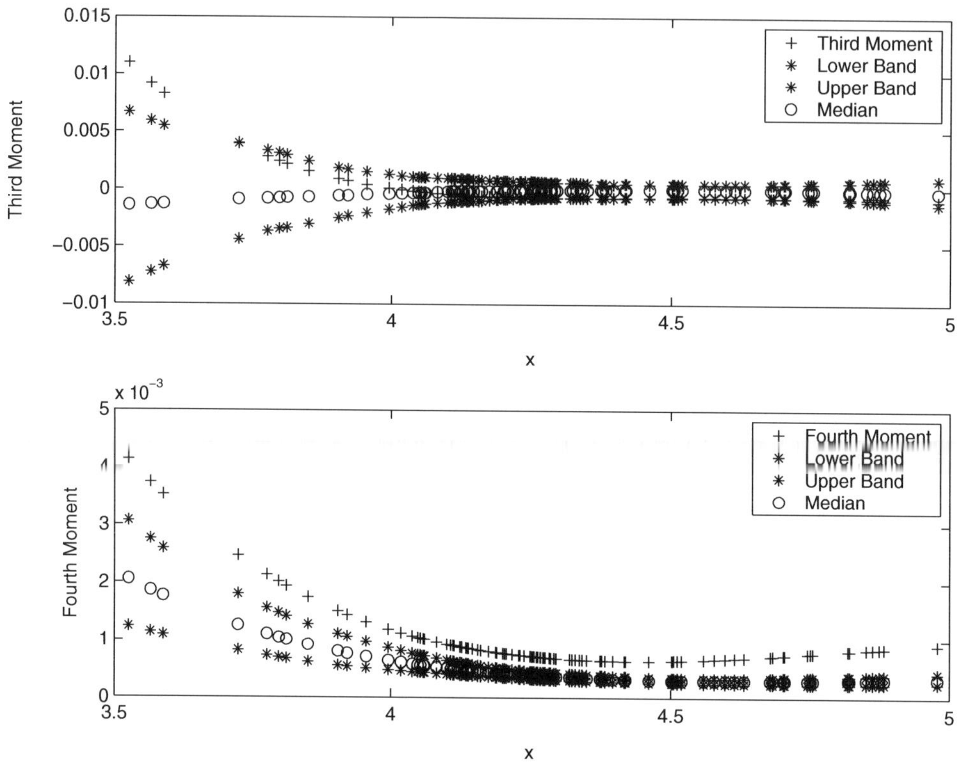

FIGURE 13.4 Third (top) and fourth (bottom) sample conditional moment estimates (+) for crude oil log-prices with simulated confidence bands (∗) for the null of a diffusion. The simulated median value (o) is reported as a benchmark.

a squared diffusion $M_2(x)$ we expect the sample moments to lie within the lower and upper band with probability 0.8. The median of the simulated sample moments is also computed as a benchmark.

In Figures 13.3 to 13.10 sample moment estimates of order 1 to 4 are reported with corresponding simulated confidence bands, respectively, for crude oil, corn, copper and gold log-prices.

It is evident from Figures 13.4, 13.6, 13.8 and 13.10 that the simple diffusion model is rejected for all analyzed data sets since both the third and fourth sample moments lie outside the confidence bands for several values of the log-price x.

In Figures 13.11 to 13.14 we report the estimated values for the drift function $\mu(x)$, the diffusion function $\sigma(x)$ and the jump intensity function $\lambda(x)$ assuming that the dynamics of the log-prices is described by model (13.9). The drift function is well represented by a linear decreasing function for all analysed commodities. In particular, a linear fitting gives a slope of −0.19, −0.38, −0.24, and −0.12 for the crude oil, corn, copper and gold log-price drift functions, respectively. The jump intensity function is decreasing for corn and copper, while it decreases at first and then increases for crude oil, with a minimum attained in middle values of the log-price and the converse for gold log-prices, where a maximum is attained for middle values of x. The diffusion function shows the highest variability across the analysed data sets.

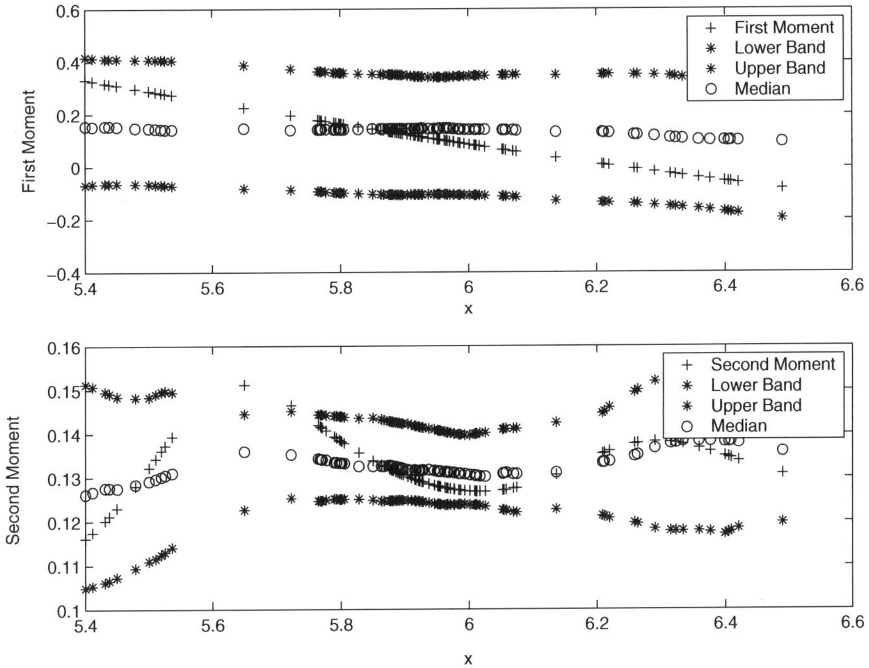

FIGURE 13.5 First (top) and second (bottom) sample conditional moment estimates (+) for corn log-prices with simulated confidence bands (∗) for the null of a diffusion. The simulated median value (∘) is reported as a benchmark

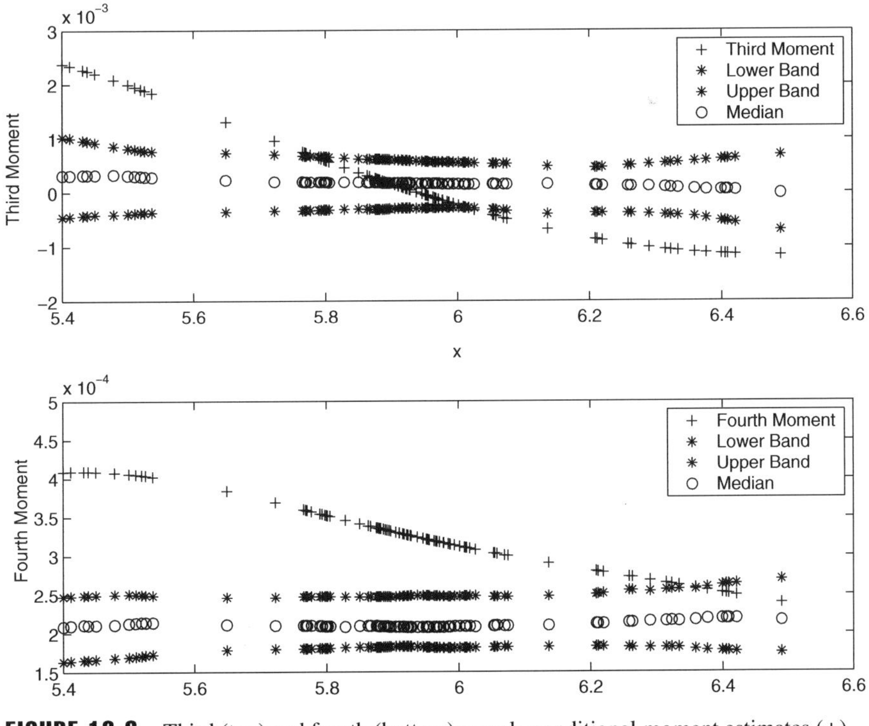

FIGURE 13.6 Third (top) and fourth (bottom) sample conditional moment estimates (+) for crude oil log-prices with simulated confidence bands (∗) for the null of a diffusion. The simulated median value (∘) is reported as a benchmark

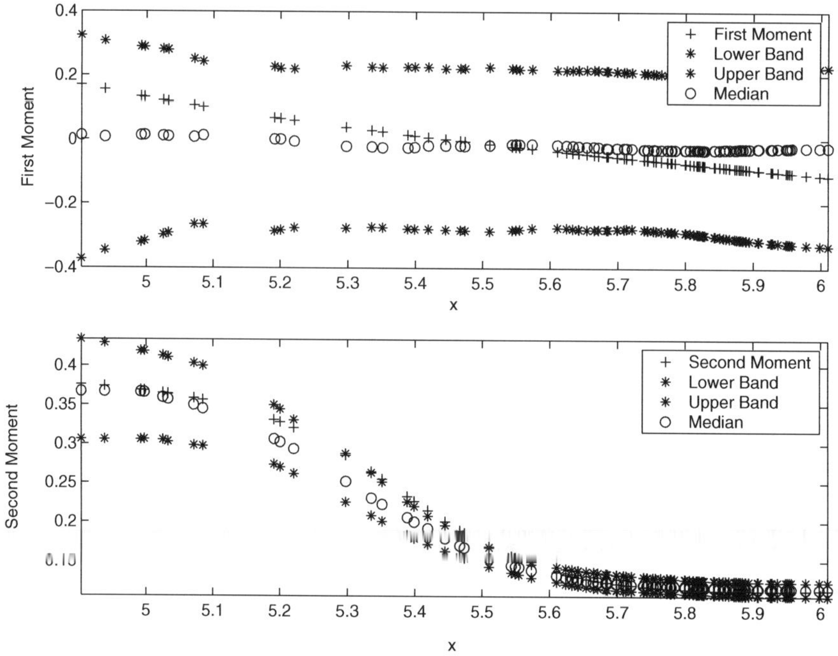

FIGURE 13.7 First (top) and second (bottom) sample conditional moment estimates (+) for copper log-prices with simulated confidence bands (∗) for the null of a diffusion. The simulated median value (∘) is reported as a benchmark

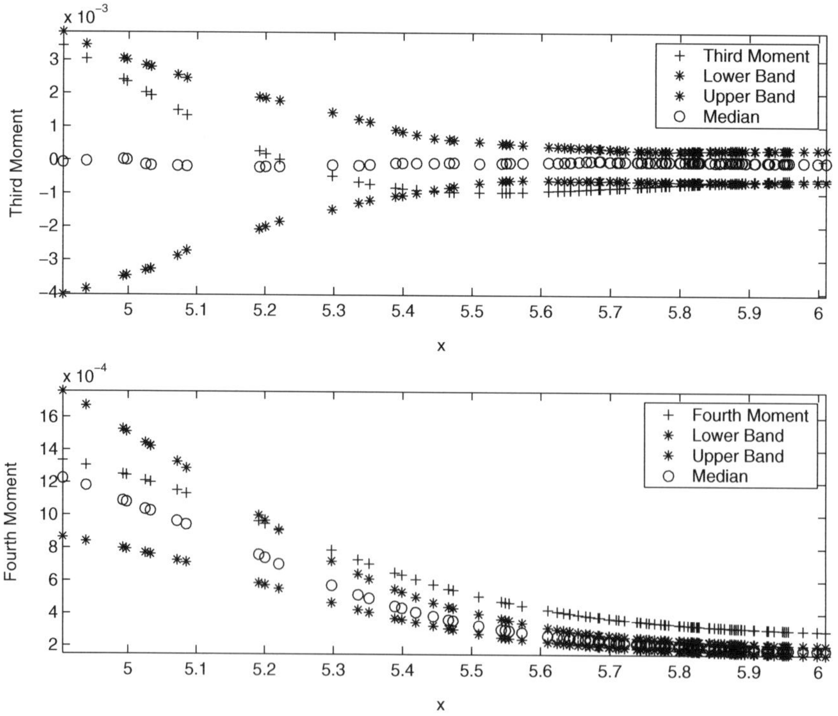

FIGURE 13.8 Third (bottom) and fourth (bottom) sample conditional moment estimates (+) for copper log-prices with simulated confidence bands (∗) for the null of a diffusion. The simulated median value (∘) is reported as a benchmark

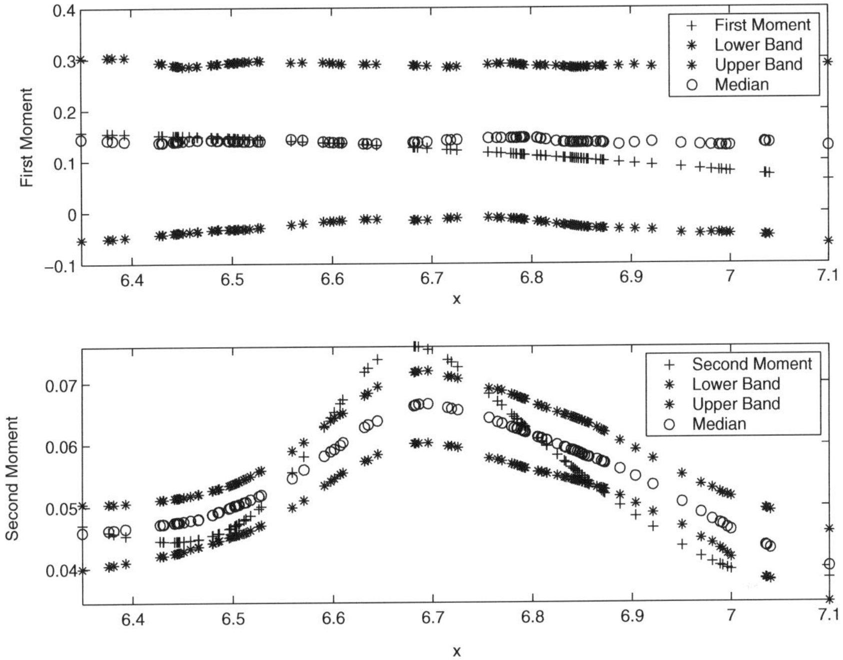

FIGURE 13.9 First (top) and second (bottom) sample conditional moment estimates (+) for gold log-prices with simulated confidence bands (∗) for the null of a diffusion. The simulated median value (∘) is reported as a benchmark

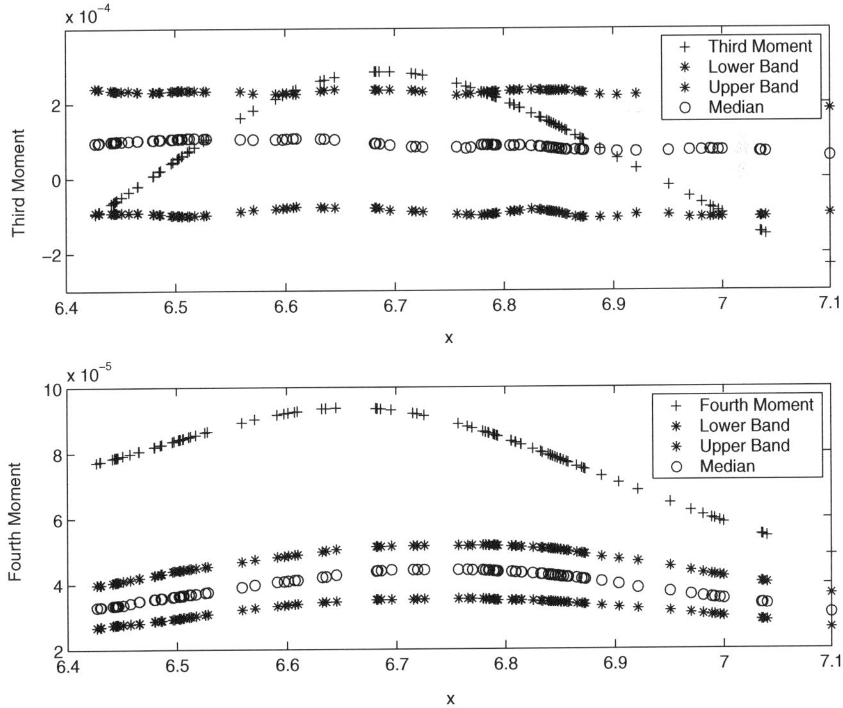

FIGURE 13.10 Third (top) and fourth (bottom) sample conditional moment estimates (+) for gold log-prices with simulated confidence bands (∗) for the null of a diffusion. The simulated median value (∘) is reported as a benchmark

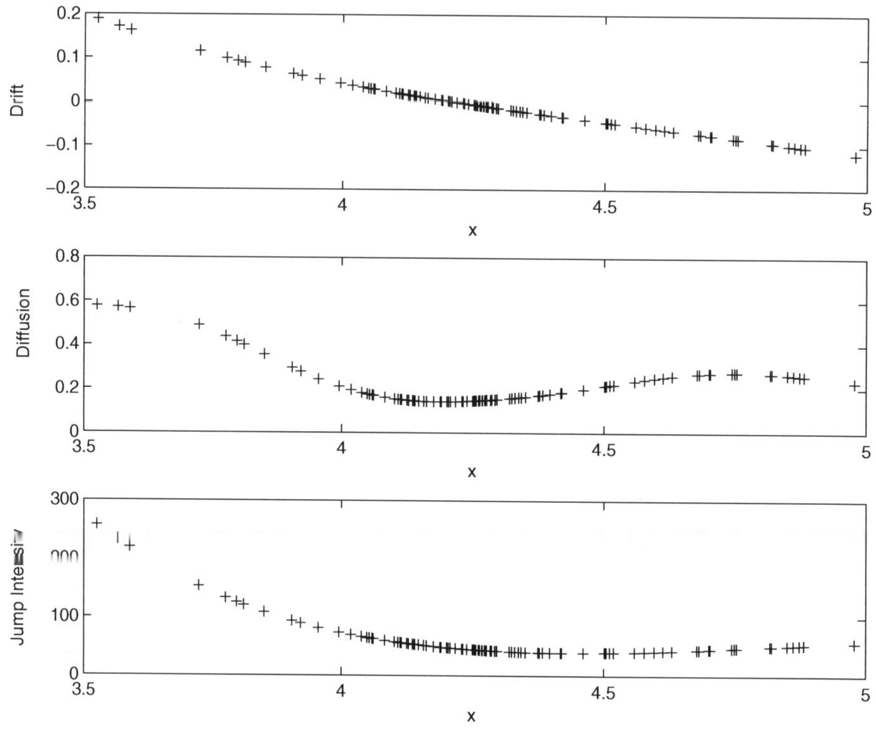

FIGURE 13.11 Nonparametric estimates for the drift function (top), the diffusion function (middle) and the jump intensity (bottom) for the crude oil log-price process

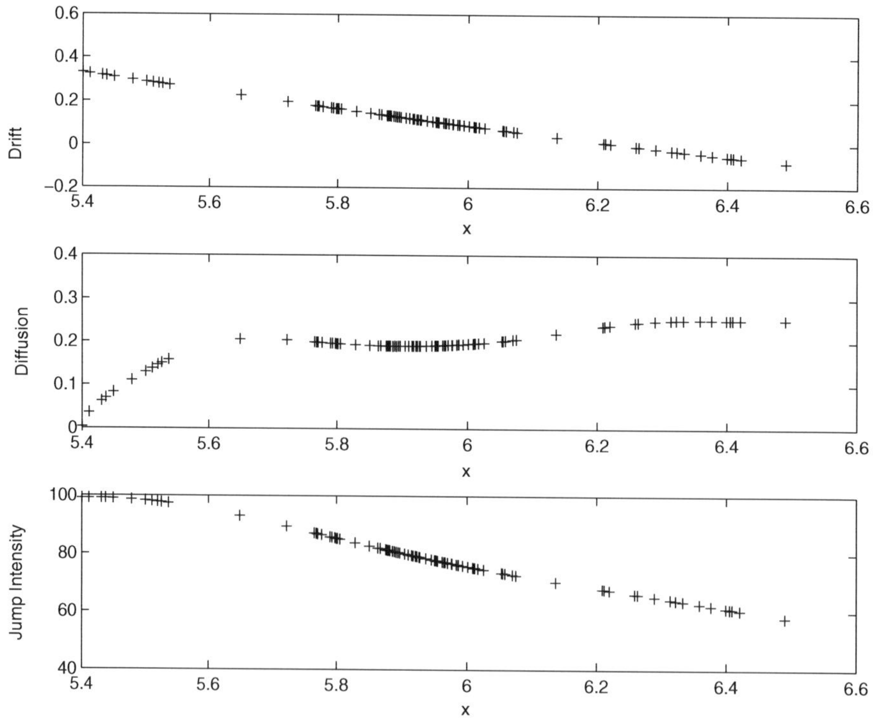

FIGURE 13.12 Nonparametric estimates for the drift function (top), the diffusion function (middle) and the jump intensity (bottom) for the corn log-price process

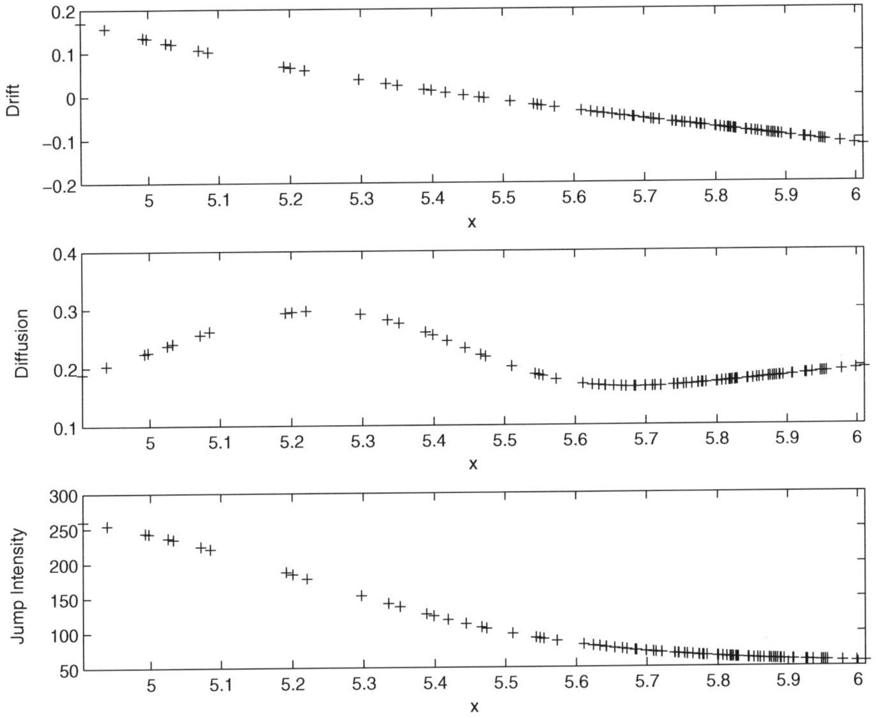

FIGURE 13.13 Nonparametric estimates for the drift function (top), the diffusion function (middle) and the jump intensity (bottom) for the copper log-price process

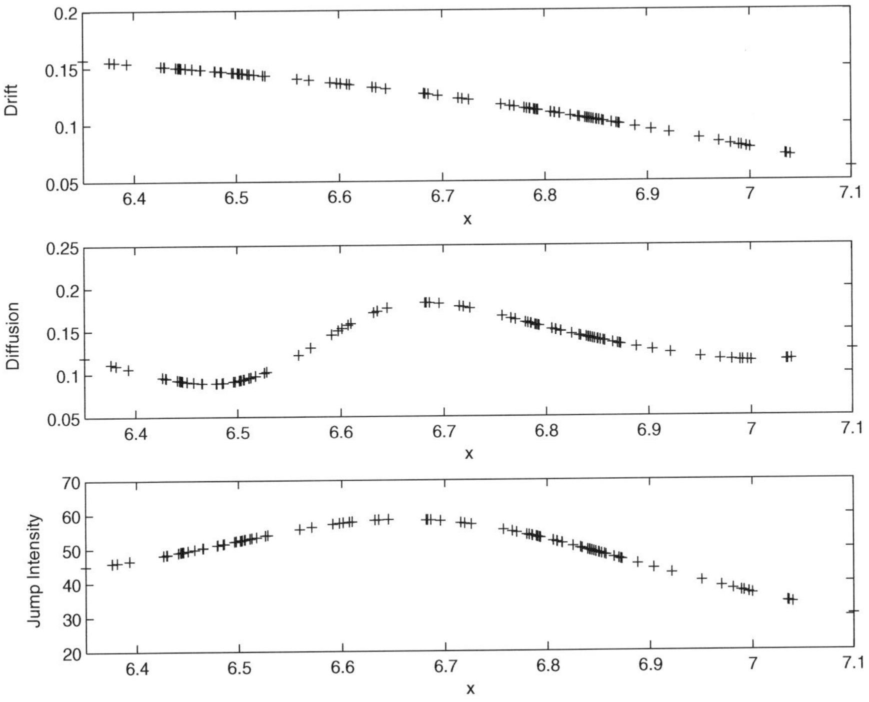

FIGURE 13.14 Nonparametric estimates for the drift function (top), the diffusion function (middle) and the jump intensity (bottom) for the gold log-price process

In the case of crude oil log-prices the diffusion function attains its minimum at centre values for x as one would expect from a stock. For corn log-prices the diffusion function, after a small increase for small values of x, remains almost constant around 0.22; this is indeed reasonable for an agricultural product the variability of which is probably due to weather anomalies generating jumps rather than to market activities. For the two analysed metals, our outcomes show an oscillating diffusion coefficient. It may be of interest to notice that in the case of gold data a maximum is attained around middle values of the log-prices x both for the diffusion coefficient and the jump intensity function.

The estimated deviation $\widehat{\sigma}_Y$ of the jump size is 0.0066, 0.0342, 0.0059 and 0.0270 for crude oil, corn, copper and gold log-prices, respectively. These estimates are reliable since the ratio $\frac{M_6(x)}{5M_4(x)}$ does not vary much with respect to x. The highest absolute jumps are evidenced in the corn data set, followed by gold log-prices.

REFERENCES

Bandi, F.M. and Nguyen, T.H. (1999) Fully nonparametric estimators for diffusions: a small sample analysis, Working Paper, University of Chicago.

Bandi, F.M. and Nguyen, T.H. (2003) On the functional estimation of jump-diffusion processes, *Journal of Econometrics* **116**, 293–328.

Chapman, D. and Pearson, N. (2000) Is the short rate drift actually non linear? *Journal of Finance* **55**(1), 355–388.

James, J. and Webber, N. (2000) *Interest Rate Modelling*. Wiley Series in Financial Engineering, John Wiley & Sons, Chichester.

Johannes, M. (1999) Jumps in interest rates: A nonparametric approach, Working Paper, University of Chicago.

Johannes, M. (2004) The statistic and economic role of jumps in interest rates. *Journal of Finance* **59**, 227–260.

Øksendal, B. (2003) *Stochastic Differential Equations*, 6th edn, Springer-Verlag, Berlin.

Protter, P. (1995) *Stochastic Integration and Differential Equations*, Springer-Verlag, Berlin.

Silverman, B.W. (1986) *Density Estimation for Statistics and Data Analysis*. Chapman & Hall, New York.

Stanton, R. (1997) A nonparametric model of term structure dynamics and the market price of interest rate risk. *Journal of Finance* **7**(5), 1973–2002.

CHAPTER 14

How to Build Electricity Forward Curves

Ruggero Caldana, Gianluca Fusai and Andrea Roncoroni

14.1 INTRODUCTION

The *electricity forward curve* (EFC) $f_t(\cdot)$ quoted in a given market at a point in time t is a mathematical function associating with each day in the future a price for the commitment to deliver one megawatt-hour for every hour of that specific day. In other terms, it is the term structure of electricity forward prices as quoted with daily granularity across the maturity dimension, which is represented by the dotted argument "·" in the expression $f_t(\cdot)$.[1]

EFCs are particularly useful for marking to market (i.e., pricing compatibly with market quotes) a standing portfolio of electricity-related positions of an industrial company or financial institution. Another important instance is the modelling of electricity price dynamics for the purpose of pricing contingent claims or monitoring the net exposure of a company. *Strictu sensu* any EFC is a purely mathematical abstraction in that actual market quotes refer to commitments to deliver over a time period as opposed to a single day. Popular maturities for which electricity exchanges provide traders with quotes are:

- full day
- week

[1]We here use the term "maturity" to mean either a specific point T in future time, that is $T > t =$ standing time, or the time period $x := T - t$ elapsing between standing time t and a future time T. The exact connotation of the term usually appears clear from the context. In case of ambiguity, we will distinguish between "maturity" T and "time-to-maturity" x. Correspondingly, an electricity forward curve may be defined either on the maturity or on the time-to-maturity axis. The relation of the two possible representations is $f_t^{\text{maturity}}(T) = f_t^{\text{time-to-maturity}}(T - t)$.

Handbook of Multi-Commodity Markets and Products: Structuring, Trading and Risk Management. Edited by Andrea Roncoroni, Gianluca Fusai and Mark Cummins.

- month
- quarter
- calendar year.

We may shortly say that each of these maturities is "*quoted by the market*". However, several tailor-made contracts which trade over-the-counter (OTC) actually involve maturities other than those quoted by exchanges. Moreover, OTC quotes provided by brokers may refer to overlapping delivery periods. These facts make it arduous, if not impossible, to model price or valuing contracts consistently with available market quotes.

The most popular strategy to solve the issue has been borrowed from fixed income markets. There it is common practice to build a term structure of interest rates compatible with a number of instruments, usually coupon bond prices or money market and interest rate swaps, and then use it as a primitive source of information to carry out the task in hand. In the case of electricity markets, one may build an EFC playing the role of "middleman", conveying market information embedded in quoted contracts into a single source of information. However, implementing this strategy on electricity price data requires tackling a number of issues idiosyncratic to electricity markets – such as daily granularity, spikes in the observed price and time periodicity pattern at varying frequencies, among others.

Disposing of a rational assessment of an EFC with daily granularity allows the user to accomplish a wide variety of tasks, including:

1. Pricing forward contracts for arbitrary delivery times or periods.
2. Calibrating arbitrage models of electricity prices aimed at pricing contingent claims.
3. Forecasting spot price evolution up to assessing a market price of risk.
4. Defining trading rules based on market price discrepancies.

This chapter illustrates a practical and effective algorithm to build an electricity forward curve with daily granularity compatible with market quotes stemming from exchange-traded as well as OTC quotations. The outline is as follows. Section 14.2 briefly reviews the literature in the field, focusing on the elements lacking in existing methodologies for the purpose of accomplishing the task in hand. Section 14.3 introduces us to the energy markets, focusing on the electricity segment, and describes the mechanics of electricity forward contracts. Section 14.4 provides the reader with a self-contained description of the method put forward by Benth *et al.* (2007). Section 14.5 delves into the core of the subject by explaining how to estimate a periodical price component and convey this piece of information into a quantitative assessment of a term structure forward price with daily granularity. Section 14.6 concludes the discussion. The power of our method is illustrated through a detailed example based on market data referring to the European Energy Exchange (EEX).

14.2 REVIEW OF THE LITERATURE

Fitting a yield curve to market data is a topic that has been studied extensively in the fixed income market. The two most popular approaches are either to fit to observed yields a parametric function by regression, or by a spline. A thorough analysis of estimation techniques and a survey of yield curve interpretation in fixed income markets are provided by Anderson and Deacon (1996). The seminal paper in this field is that of McCulloch (1971), who develops a cubic spline technique of fitting a smooth discount function to observations on the price of bonds with varying maturities and coupon rates. Adams and van Deventer (1994) improved on this, introducing a new approach. By defining the criterion for the best fitting yield curve to be "maximum smoothness" for the forward rate curve, they arrived at a powerful curve-fitting technique. Lim and Xiao (2002) shows that the result in Adams and van Deventer (1994) was sub-optimal and provide a correct solution for the maximum smoothness fitting problem.

Fleten and Lemming (2003) first applied a curve-fitting method in the energy market: they smoothened an electricity futures curve based on a bottom-up model called the MPS model. The MPS model calculates weekly equilibrium prices and production quantities based on fundamental factors for demand and production (e.g., temperature, fuel costs, snow levels, capacities). The approach of Fleten and Lemming (2003) is nonparametric, in the sense that they derive a sequence of daily (or any other appropriate time resolution) forward prices minimizing the least-squares distance to the output from the MPS model. The optimization is constrained on the bid–ask spreads of market prices and the curve is appropriately smoothened by a penalty term. Hildman *et al.* (2011) propose a practical framework to estimate hourly, daily and yearly energy price profiles, based on the median estimation, instead of the mean value. Some statistical methods are used in the curve-fitting procedure: hourly and daily data used for the estimation are normalized in order to minimize the seasonality bias and the LAD-Lasso method to prevent overfitting.

To the best of our knowledge, the most important work concerning how to fit forward price curves in the energy market is that of Benth *et al.* (2007). The authors combine a seasonal specification with smoothing techniques in line with existing work from fixed income markets. Using the "maximum smoothness" criterion of Adams and van Deventer (1994), they derive a smooth curve modelling the forward price as the sum of a seasonality function and a polynomial spline. The method of Benth *et al.* (2007) will be described briefly in Section 14.4.

14.3 ELECTRICITY FORWARD CONTRACTS

Electricity is often referred to as a *flow commodity* due to its highly limited storability: electrical power is useful for practical purposes provided it can be delivered over a whole period of time. Deregulated power markets have internal mechanisms aimed at balancing supply and demand. For day-ahead delivery, these take the form of daily auctions for delivering power over a specified hour on the next day. Some contracts prescribe physical delivery, that is others are cash settled.

We consider electricity contracts with physical delivery, that is contracts with actual energy delivery as part of the contract fulfilment. Physical markets split into three segments. One is the day-ahead market, where power trades for each of the 24 hours of the next day. The second is the real-time market, used to balance energy injections and withdrawals in real time. The third segment somewhat closes the gap between the day-ahead market and the real-time market and is called the intra-day market. Once the day-ahead market is closed for bids, the day-ahead price is derived for each hour next day. Since this price plays the role of a common reference variable for many financial energy contracts, we briefly describe the mechanics of the day-ahead market.[2]

[2]For a detailed discussion of day-ahead, real-time and intra-day markets, with particular attention to the case of the Nordic market, see Benth *et al.* (2008).

On day-ahead markets, hourly power contracts are traded daily for physical delivery in the next day's 24-hour period, from midnight to 1 a.m., from 1 a.m. to 2 a.m. and so on until 11 p.m. to the midnight of the following day. In the morning of day n, say, agents submit their bids for either purchasing or selling electricity on the following day. Each bid consists of price, volume and hour of delivery. Upon closing at noon, a day-ahead price is announced for each hour on the following day. From a financial viewpoint, that is the forward price negotiated on day n for delivery at a specific hour h within day $n + 1$. Financial contracts on electricity are cash-settled contingent claims written on the day-ahead price. The day-ahead price is monitored over a specified delivery period. The contract is settled in cash against the day-ahead price during, or at the end of, the delivery period. Trading occurs until the last day prior to delivery starting. In general, market participants typically close their positions beforehand.

We now move to a formal description of electricity forward contracts. In standard financial markets, a forward contract is a security whereby the holder receives full delivery of some underlying S on a future day T for a price $f_t(T)$ negotiated at inception, say time $t < T$. That price is fixed in such a way that the initial value of the commitment is zero. This is referred to as the time t forward price.

Let $S(t)$ denote the electricity day-ahead price quoted at time t. A standard financial argument leads to the following relation between spot and forward prices:

$$f_t(T) = \mathbb{E}_t[S(T)],$$

where the expectation is taken under a risk-neutral measure and is made given the information available at t. However, prices $f(T) := f_t(T)$ are not quoted in electricity markets. Instead, quotations are posted for forward prices related to delivery occurring over time periods, much like it occurs in a swap agreement.

Consider a forward contract settled over a time period $[\tau^b, \tau^e]$ and paying at maturity. In a settlement at maturity the payment of the whole amount is due at the end of the delivery period τ^e. By definition of a forward contract, the strike F has to be set so that the contract is of zero cost at the time t we enter into it. So for settlement at maturity,[3] and assuming deterministic interest rates, we have

$$e^{-r(\tau^e - t)}\mathbb{E}\left[\int_{\tau^b}^{\tau^e} (S(u) - F)du\right] = 0,$$

which leads to

$$F(\tau^b, \tau^e) = \frac{1}{\tau^e - \tau^b}\int_{\tau^b}^{\tau^e} f(u)du.$$

[3]There is another kind of payout possible for forward contracts, called instant settlement. In an instant settlement the contract pays $(S(u) - F)\Delta u$ at time $u \in [\tau^b, \tau^e]$. However for small delivery periods, it makes a small difference whether the money is settled at the end of the period or on a daily basis, as proved in Benth *et al.* (2008).

From now on, we refer to f and F as (instantaneous) *financial forward* and *average forward* prices, respectively. This continuous-time description ought to be modified to account for discrete-time settlement. This latter may involve a number of days or blocks of hours. Baseload forward contracts refer to settlement periods comprising all the hours in a given day. *Baseload forward* contracts are the most popular kind of electricity forward contract. Another typical time block consists of peak hours, namely those on which electricity demand is the highest in a day. *Peakload forward* contracts refer to settlement periods comprising peak hours between a starting day and an ending day. Despite the importance of the peakload forward in energy markets, we do not consider this kind of contract to build the EFC.

Let S denote the set of days defining a delivery period. We may express the baseload average forward price F in terms of financial forward prices for daily delivery:

$$F = \frac{1}{\sharp S} \sum_{T \in S} \hat{f}(T),$$

where:

- The operator "$\sharp$" counts the number of elements in its argument.
- $\hat{f}(T)$ is the standing financial forward price for delivering 1 megawatt-hour over the entire day T. This number represents the arithmetic average of the hourly forward quotes over the 24 hours in the day:

$$\hat{f}(T) = \frac{1}{1 \text{ day}} \int_{T}^{T+1 \text{ day}} f(u)du.$$

14.4 SMOOTHING FORWARD PRICE CURVES

We describe the Benth *et al.* (2007) method for building an instantaneous financial forward price curve $\left(f(u), u \geq t_0\right)$ compatible with average forward prices observed in the markets at a point in time t_0. Assume one observes m baseload average forward prices $F(\tau_k^b, \tau_k^e)$ $(k = 1, \ldots, m)$. Delivery periods can be gathered in a set:[4]

$$\mathcal{A} = \left\{ \left[\tau_1^b, \tau_1^e\right], \left[\tau_2^b, \tau_2^e\right], \ldots, \left[\tau_m^b, \tau_m^e\right] \right\}.$$

As long as these intervals may overlap, we order time endpoints and relabel them as increasing $t_1, \ldots, t_n$, where the time unit is the day. If forward contract settlement periods are long (e.g., a calendar year), the seasonality may be obscured in the quoted market price. This means we must specify a seasonal function based on more information than can be read off from the market prices.

[4]Benth *et al.* (2007) propose a procedure to constrain the curve between the bid and ask prices. We do not treat this case, limiting our description to a curve obtained from mid or closing price quotations.

We model the standing financial forward price curve as the sum of two components: one is a function Λ meant to reproduce overlapping periodical patterns (e.g., seasonal components) exhibited by the curve; the other an adjustment function ε allowing for the curve to fit observed average forward prices. The (instantaneous) financial forward price for maturity $u \in [t_0, t_n]$ reads as

$$f(u) = \Lambda(u) + \varepsilon(u; \mathbf{x}),$$

where both Λ and ε are suitable continuous functions and $\mathbf{x}$ denotes a vector of parameters identifying a specific ε within a set of regular functions. These latter are assumed to be twice continuously differentiable polynomial splines of order four with zero-valued first-order derivative at the rightmost endpoint of the domain. That is:

$$\varepsilon(u; \mathbf{x}) = \begin{cases} a_1 u^4 + b_1 u^3 + c_1 u^2 + d_1 u + e_1 & u \in [t_0, t_1], \\ a_2 u^4 + b_2 u^3 + c_2 u^2 + d_2 u + e_2, & u \in [t_1, t_2], \\ \vdots & \\ a_n u^4 + b_n u^3 + c_n u^2 + d_n u + e_n, & u \in [t_{n-1}, t_n], \end{cases}$$
$$\varepsilon'(t_n; \mathbf{x}) = 0.$$

Moreover, the splines are assumed to be twice continuously differentiable and with zero derivative in t_n. A specific ε is determined by the vector

$$\mathbf{x} = \begin{pmatrix} a_1 \\ b_1 \\ \cdot \\ \cdot \\ d_n \\ e_n \end{pmatrix}$$

solving the maximal smoothing quadratic programming problem:

$$\min_{\mathbf{x}} \int_{t_0}^{t_n} [\varepsilon''(u; \mathbf{x})^2] du \tag{14.1}$$

subject to continuity and smoothness constraints at knots points:

$$\begin{aligned} (a_{j+1} - a_j)u_j^4 + (b_{j+1} - b_j)u_j^3 + (c_{j+1} - c_j)u_j^2 + (d_{j+1} - d_j)u_j + e_{j+1} - e_j = 0, \\ 4(a_{j+1} - a_j)u_j^3 + 3(b_{j+1} - b_j)u_j^2 + 2(c_{j+1} - c_j)u_j + d_{j+1} - d_j = 0, \\ 12(a_{j+1} - a_j)u_j^2 + 6(b_{j+1} - b_j)u_j + 2(c_{j+1} - c_j) = 0, \end{aligned} \tag{14.2}$$

with $j = 1, \ldots, n-1$, as well as average forward price-fitting conditions:

$$F(\tau_i^b, \tau_i^e) = \frac{1}{\tau_i^e - \tau_i^b} \int_{\tau_i^b}^{\tau_i^e} (\varepsilon(u; \mathbf{x}) + \Lambda(u))\, du, \tag{14.3}$$

for $i = 1, \ldots, m$. Benth *et al.* (2007) show that this problem can be cast as a linear system of algebraic equations whose solution $\mathbf{x}^*$ leads to uniquely identifying the instantaneous financial forward curve

$$f(u) = \Lambda(u) + \varepsilon(u; \mathbf{x}^*)$$

for all $u \in [t_0, t_n]$.

14.5 AN ILLUSTRATIVE EXAMPLE: DAILY FORWARD CURVE

We describe the construction of a daily forward curve of electricity prices in the German market (EEX). Assume the evaluation date is set to t_0 = 22 May 2012. Baseload forward quotations refer to traded contracts for a variety of delivery periods. These include days, weeks, weekends, months, quarters and calendar years. Prices are expressed in euros per megawatt-hour (€/MWh). We report these data in Table 14.1.

The key idea is to estimate the periodical component Λ of the forward curve by using information on periodical patterns exhibited by time series of spot prices.

We begin by recording EPEX German day-ahead daily prices over the time period ranging from 1 January 2005 to 22 May 2012. This set, which we denote by $\mathcal{T}$, comprises 2579 days. Next, we devise a procedure to detect data outliers in such a way that the OLS analyses to follow are as robust as possible to input data. Following Truck *et al.* (2007), we apply the nonparametric filter proposed in Hodrick and Prescott (1997), henceforth HP, to the time series of daily prices. Any HP filter depends on a numerical parameter λ whose setting is left to the user. In our case, we adopt the optimal selection put forward in Pedersen (2001) for the

TABLE 14.1 EEX forward market data

Start date	End date	F^{mkt}
22/05/12	22/05/12	42.750
23/05/12	23/05/12	42.450
24/05/12	24/05/12	38.380
25/05/12	25/05/12	36.980
26/05/12	27/05/12	28.350
02/06/12	03/06/12	27.500
28/05/12	03/06/12	35.125
04/06/12	10/06/12	36.850
11/06/12	17/06/12	39.400
18/06/12	24/06/12	40.625
25/06/12	01/07/12	40.210
01/07/12	31/07/12	40.175
01/08/12	31/08/12	38.775
01/09/12	30/09/12	44.475
01/09/12	31/12/12	50.600
01/01/13	31/03/13	51.900
01/01/13	31/12/13	48.725

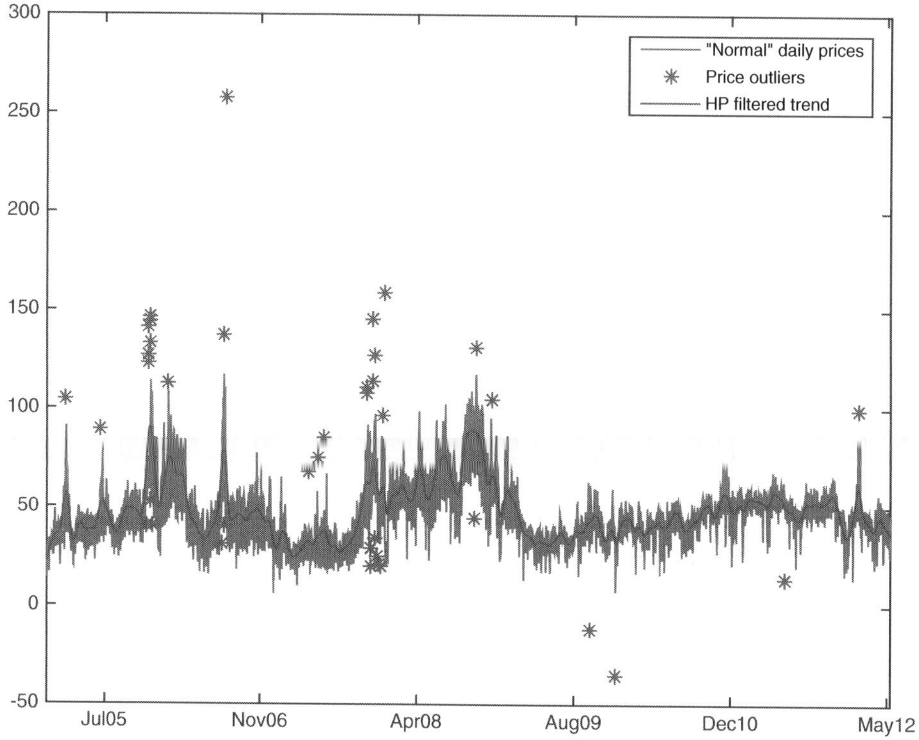

FIGURE 14.1 Hodrick–Prescott filtered trend, price outliers, and resulting time series of "normal" daily spot prices

purpose of filtering out any component exhibiting periods exceeding a selected number. We decided to set this latter equal to one month. The resulting filtered series is then compared with the input series.

An outlier is any market quote deviating from the value indicated by the filtered trend at the same time by more than three times the standard deviation of the sample set comprising all the discrepancies between observed prices and values of the filtered trend at the same dates. If this is the case for one datum, then this latter is replaced by a "normal" value defined as the value of the HP filtered series at the same point in time. We note that this filtered trend serves the sole purpose of identifying data outliers: in particular, no use is made of determining the actual trend of quoted prices. Figure 14.1 reports all the outliers that have been detected in the EPEX German market for the period under consideration. From this graph, we clearly see that the number of outliers fades away with the level of maturity of the market. The time series of 'normal' daily spot prices $S(t)$ resulting from the replacement procedure described is now represented as the sum of three components:

$$S(t) = trend\,(t) + seasonality\,(t) + noise\,(t). \tag{14.4}$$

We want to extract the seasonality component to analyse and estimate it using a suitable parametric function $\Lambda(t)$. To do so, we first estimate the trend component and then fit $\Lambda(t)$ to the detrended series. The trend component is assumed to reproduce cyclical paths related

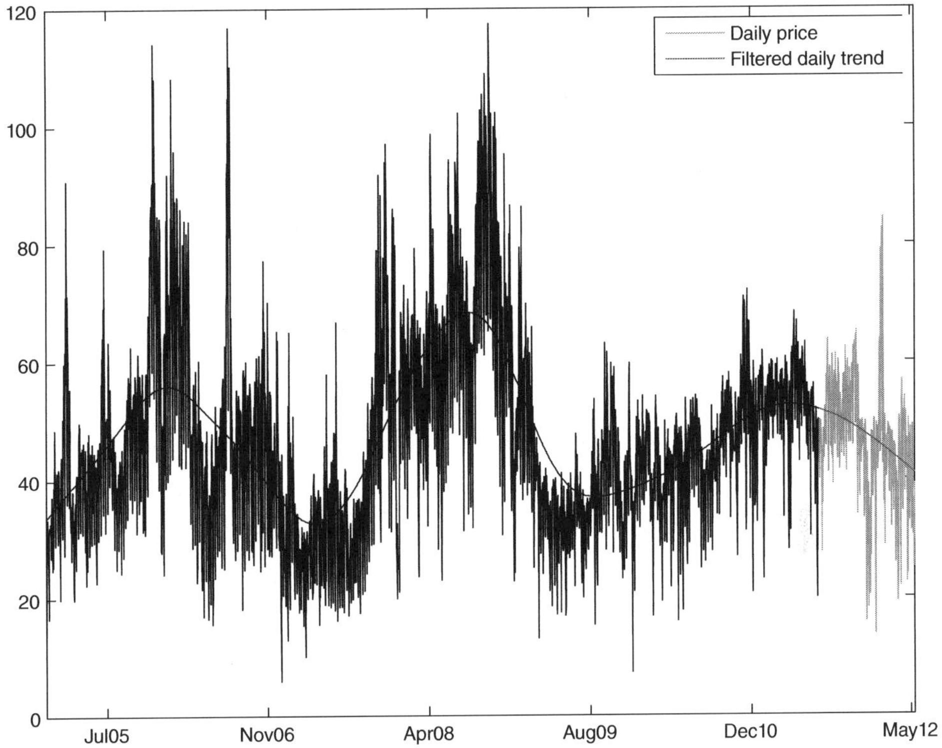

FIGURE 14.2 Filtered trend $H(t)$ and EPEX German daily price time series $S(t)$

to macroeconomic events affecting electricity price movements. For this reason, it can be estimated conveniently by using an HP filter with parameter λ compatible with filtering out frequencies with period exceeding one year and a half. Figure 14.2 exhibits the cyclical trend we estimated on EPEX German market price data, which we denote by H. The resulting detrended series

$$Z(t) := S(t) - H(t),$$

for $t \in \mathcal{T}$, feeds our seasonal components analysis.

We consider a parametric set of functions aimed at reproducing components with period up to one year. We perform a periodogram analysis delivering and ranking periods of recurrent components exhibited by the time series of detrended prices $Z(t)$. Figure 14.3 shows results for the EPEX German market. A suitable class comprises a semiannual component paired with dummy variables for days in the week and months:

$$\Lambda(t) = a \cos\left(\frac{4\pi}{365}t + b\right) + \mathbf{D}_{day}(t)\mathbf{d} + \mathbf{D}_{month}(t)\mathbf{m}. \tag{14.5}$$

Hereby **d** and **m** denote the corresponding parameter vectors for the daily ($day = 1, \ldots, 7$) and monthly ($month = 1, \ldots, 12$) dummy variables $\mathbf{D}_{day}(t)$ and $\mathbf{D}_{month}(t)$. For the purpose of estimation, official holidays are treated as a "Sunday". As long as the seasonality function $\Lambda(t)$

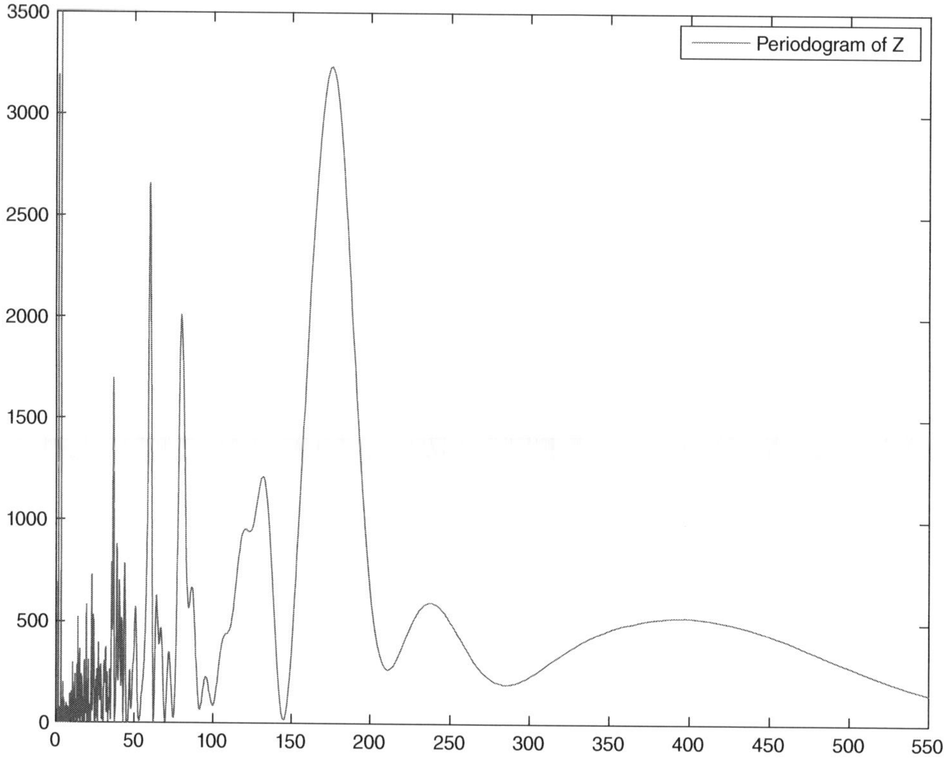

FIGURE 14.3 Periodogram of the detrended time series Z

is defined based on a continuous representation of time, as in Benth *et al.* (2007), we need to integrate this quantity to allow for fitting data on a finite set of dates $\mathcal{T}$. The daily seasonality reads as

$$\hat{\Lambda}(t) := \frac{1}{1 \text{ day}} \int_t^{t+1 \text{ day}} \Lambda(u) du$$

for day $t \in \mathcal{T}$. Let θ gather all parameters identifying a specific function $\hat{\Lambda}(t)$ within the proposed class. The fitting problem delivering a numerical assessment for the periodical trend may be cast as the least-squares minimization problem

$$\min_{\theta} || e^{-\alpha(\max(\mathcal{T})-t)}(Z(t) - \hat{\Lambda}(t))||^2_{2,\mathcal{T}}, \tag{14.6}$$

for a suitable weighing coefficient α. A few experiments not reported here show that a reasonable value for this quantity is 0.4. The resulting periodical trend is shown in Figure 14.4. This figure shows a few interesting properties of the electricity price series under investigation:

1. On average, monthly prices are lower during December, January, July and August. Analysing the time series, we observe that the values estimated for February are heavily affected by the persistence of high spot prices during February 2012.

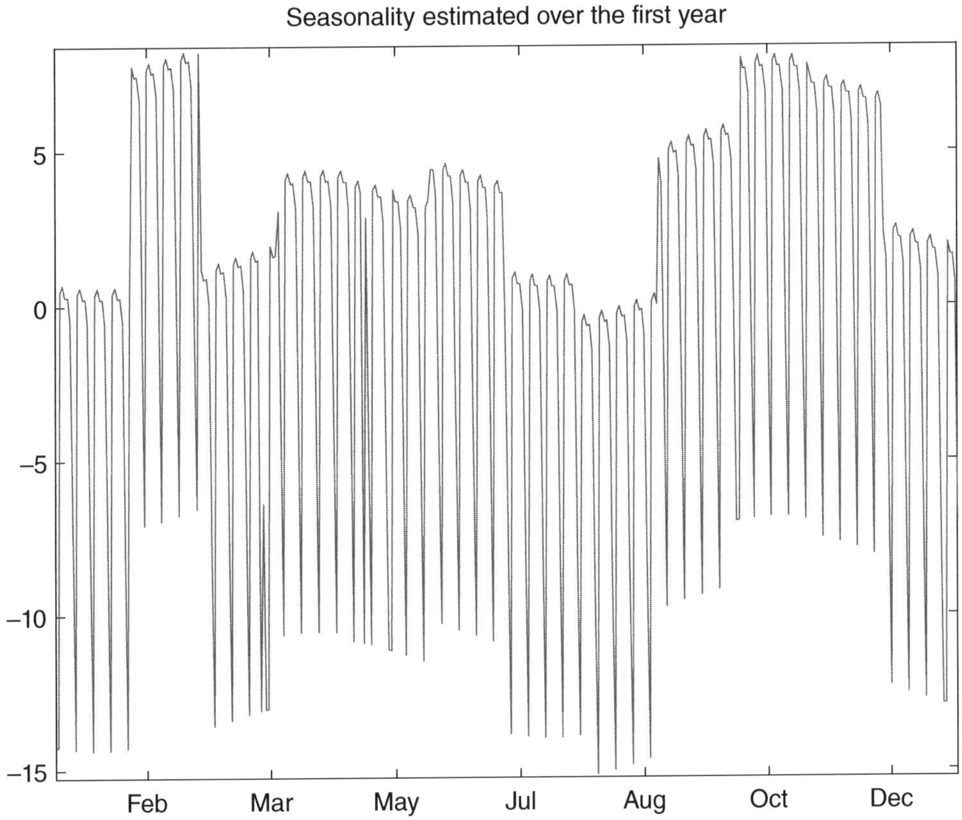

FIGURE 14.4 The periodic function $\hat{\Lambda}(t)$ computed over a calendar year

2. The weekly seasonality is well captured by the chosen seasonality function, showing a lower price during Sundays and holidays than during weekdays.

The estimated seasonality function Λ enters the optimization problem (14.1)–(14.3), which in turn delivers an instantaneous forward curve f. We remark that base load forward contracts have been considered as input to the problem. The corresponding daily forward price curve computes by averaging over single days, as in

$$\hat{f}(t) = F(t, t + 1\text{ day}) = \frac{1}{1\text{ day}} \int_{t}^{t+1\text{ day}} f(u)du. \tag{14.7}$$

Observe that (14.7) represents a prediction under a risk-neutral probability measure of the future daily spot price, so $\hat{f}(t)$ can also be used to estimate the daily risk premia. The daily curve computed for the EEX market example with data in Table 14.1 is shown in Figure 14.5, which exhibits the daily forward price curve compared with the baseload average forward quotations. The latter are easily seen as the average of the values taken from the former, as we pointed out earlier.

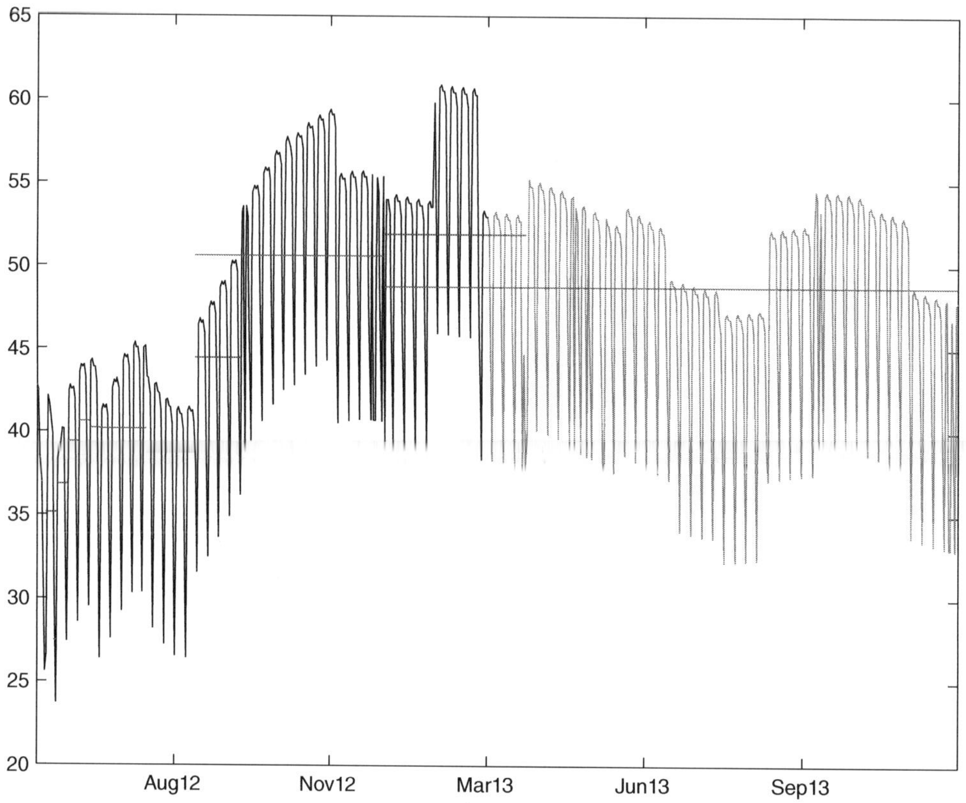

FIGURE 14.5 Daily forward price curve (oscillating path) and baseload average forward quotes (piecewise constant path)

14.6 CONCLUSION

We propose a method to build a rational estimate of the electricity forward price curve. This method combines the proposal of Benth *et al.* (2007) with a skilled analysis of the periodical patterns exhibited by daily price time series. Our analysis shows that historical price path provides relevant information improving estimation of forward price curve with daily granularity. The method proposed here nests inside the general scheme put forward by Caldana *et al.* (2015), who provide forward price curves construction under varying granularity with solid foundation.

REFERENCES

Adams, K.J. and van Deventer, D.R. (1994) Fitting yield curves and forward rate curves with maximum smoothness, *Journal of Fixed Income*, **4**, 53–62.

Anderson, F.B. and Deacon, M. (1996) *Estimating and Interpreting the Yield Curve*, John Wiley & Sons, Chichester.

Benth, F.E., Koekebakker, S. and Ollmar, F. (2007) Extracting and applying smooth forward curves from average-based commodity contracts with seasonal variation, *Journal of Derivatives*, **15**(1), 52–66.

Benth, F.E., Benth, J.S. and Koekebakker, S. (2008) *Stochastic Modelling of Electricity and Related Markets*, Word Scientific Publishing, Singapore.

Caldana, R., Fusai, G. and Roncoroni, A. (2015) *On the Rational Construction of Electricity Forward Curves with Hourly Granularity*, Energisk.org WP Series.

Fleten, S. and Lemming, J. (2003) Constructing forward price curves in electricity markets, *Energy Economics*, **25**, 409–424.

Hildmann, M., Cornel, J., Stokic, D., Andersson, G. and Herzog, F. (2011) Robust calculation and parameter estimation of the hourly price forward curve, Available at http://www.eeh.ee.ethz.ch/uploads/tx ethpublications/Hildmann PSCC2011.pdf.

Hodrick, R.J. and Prescott, E.C. (1997) Postwar U.S. business cycles: An empirical investigation, *Journal of Money, Credit and Banking*, **29**(1), 1–16.

Lim, K.G. and Xiao, Q. (2002) Computing maximum smoothness forward rate curve, *Statistics Computing*, **12**, 275–279.

McCulloch, J.H. (1971) Measuring the term structure of interest rates, *Journal of Business*, **44**, 19–31.

Pedersen, T.M. (2001) The Hodrick–Prescott filter, the Slutzky effect, and the distortionary effect of filters, *Journal of Economic Dynamics & Control*, **25**, 1081–1101.

Truck, S., Weron, R. and Wolff, R. (2007) Outlier treatment and robust approaches for modeling electricity spot prices, Technical report, Hugo Steinhaus Center, Wroclaw University of Technology, Available at http://mpra.ub.uni-muenchen.de/4711/.

CHAPTER 15

GARCH Models for Commodity Markets

Eduardo Rossi and Filippo Spazzini

15.1 INTRODUCTION

In this chapter we focus on volatility modelling with special attention paid to the features of volatility of commodities. In general, an important contribution to the understanding of modern financial markets has been the study of the volatility of asset returns. Volatility is considered a measure of risk, and the riskiness of any financial asset is a crucial element in determining its equilibrium price. In its broader sense, volatility can be interpreted as a measure of variability over a period of time. This chapter is devoted to present models for the expectation of volatility.

The autoregressive conditional heteroscedasticity (ARCH, hereafter) class of models have been developed to provide a convenient and accurate methodology to forecast volatility. In particular, this class of models is able to capture several empirical regularities observed in financial data. In brief, some stylized facts common to many financial time series are:

- Asset prices are generally nonstationary. Returns are usually stationary. Some financial time series are fractionally integrated.
- Return series usually show no or little autocorrelation.
- Serial independence between the squared values of the series is often rejected, pointing towards the existence of nonlinear relationships between subsequent observations.
- Volatility of the returns series appears to be clustered.
- Normality has to be rejected in favour of some thick-tailed distribution.
- Some series exhibit the so-called *leverage effect*, that is changes in stock prices tend to be negatively correlated with changes in volatility. A firm with debt and equity outstanding typically becomes more highly leveraged when the value of the firm falls. This raises equity returns volatility if returns are constant. Black, however, argued that the response of stock volatility to the direction of returns is too large to be explained by leverage alone. It is now widely agreed that this asymmetry has little to do with actual financial leverage.
- Volatilities of different securities very often move together.

Handbook of Multi-Commodity Markets and Products: Structuring, Trading and Risk Management. Edited by Andrea Roncoroni, Gianluca Fusai and Mark Cummins.

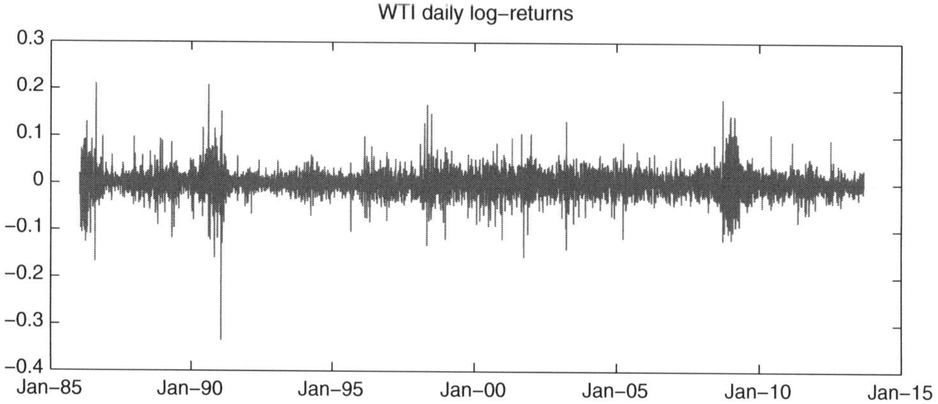

FIGURE 15.1 WTI front-month futures daily log-returns

To provide an example of the empirical regularities mentioned above, we display in Figure 15.1 the daily log-returns of West Texas Intermediate (WTI) front-month futures. As is apparent, the log-returns exhibit periods of low and high variability coupled with the presence of some outliers. This produces higher kurtosis than that observed in the Gaussian case, as is also evident from the kernel density plot in Figure 15.2. Further, the sample autocorrelation function, in Figure 15.3, of log-returns and squared log-returns makes it evident that daily returns are uncorrelated whereas squared returns appear to be significantly correlated.

The ARCH model and its generalizations are employed to model the processes of returns volatility of a large set of financial assets, like: fixed-income products, exchange rates, individual stocks and stock index returns, commodity derivatives. In the discrete-time ARCH class of models, the expectations are formulated in terms of directly observable variables, while the discrete- and continuous-time stochastic volatility models both involve latent state

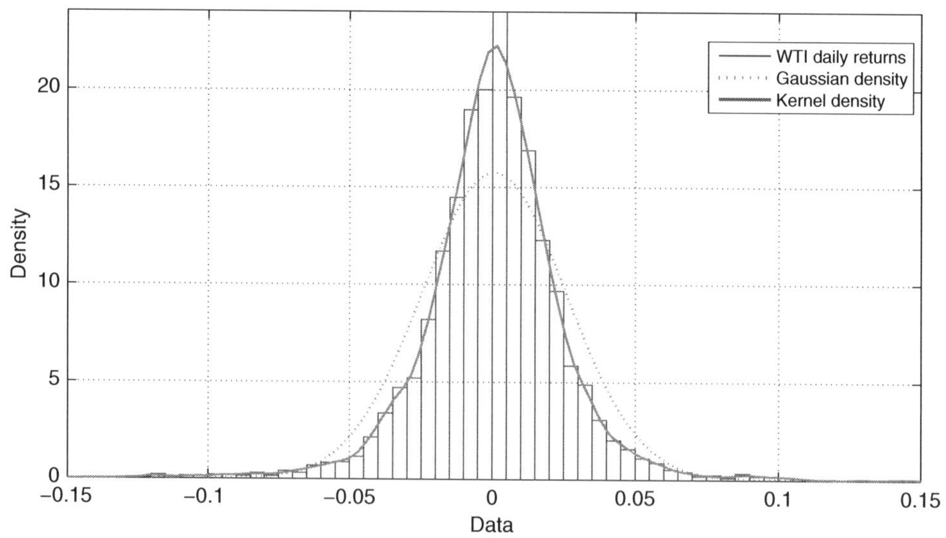

FIGURE 15.2 WTI daily log-returns kernel and Gaussian densities

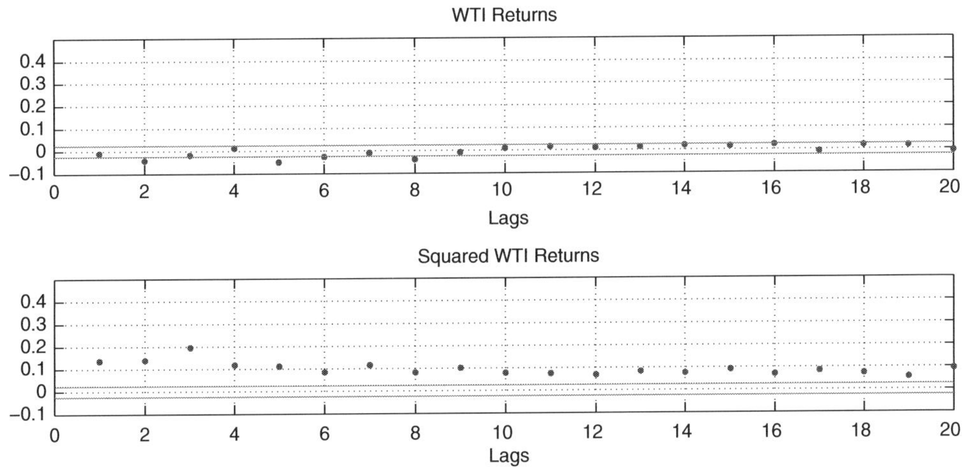

FIGURE 15.3 Sample autocorrelation function of WTI daily log-returns and squared log-returns

variable(s). In recent years, the number of new proposed ARCH models has grown dramatically, and new parameterizations are still being proposed. However, Engle (2002b) identifies as the most influential models the generalized autoregressive conditional heteroscedasticity (GARCH) model by Bollerslev (1986) and the exponential GARCH (EGARCH) model by Nelson (1991). Numerous surveys of the extensive ARCH literature also exist; for example, Andersen and Bollerslev (1998), Andersen *et al.* (2006), Bauwens *et al.* (2006), Bera and Higgins (1993), Bollerslev and Ghysels (1996), Bollerslev and Mikkelsen (1996), Degiannakis and Xekalaki (2004), Diebold (2004), Diebold and Lopez (1995), Engle (2001, 2004), Engle and Patton (2001), Pagan (1996), Palm (1996), Shephard (1996) and Teräsvirta (2009).

These reviews and the textbook treatments reveal an ever-increasing list of acronyms and abbreviations used to describe the plethora of models and procedures that have been developed over the years. For instance, Bollerslev (2009) – as a complement to these more traditional surveys – provides a reference guide to the long list of ARCH acronyms.

Initial developments in econometric modelling of volatility were tightly parametric, but the recent literature has moved in less parametric, and even fully nonparametric, directions. We don't discuss this line of research here. However, it should be noted that the nonparametric approaches to volatility modelling, which are generally free from functional form assumptions, afford estimates of notional volatility that are flexible yet consistent (as the sampling frequency of the underlying returns increases) (for a survey, see Andersen *et al.*, 2009).

GARCH models have also been successfully employed for the analysis and forecasting of commodity returns volatility. Kroner *et al.* (1995), using daily data for cocoa, corn, cotton, gold, silver, sugar and wheat, found that volatility forecasting with market-based information combined with a GARCH(1,1) specification of the volatility yields better forecasts of commodity prices than can be obtained from market expectations or time series models alone.

Baillie *et al.* (2007) find that the volatility of daily futures returns for six important commodities (corn, soybeans, cattle, hogs, gasoline and gold) is well described as fractionally integrated GARCH, whereas the mean returns exhibit very small departures from the martingale difference property. Several years of high-frequency intraday commodity futures returns are also found to have very similar long memory in volatility features as the daily returns.

Kang *et al.* (2009) evaluated the forecasting capability of a number of GARCH-class models, like the integrated GARCH (IGARCH), the component GARCH (CGARCH) and the FIGARCH for better capturing volatility persistence and concluded that CGARCH and FIGARCH models better capture persistency over other models.

Alom *et al.* (2012) examine the asymmetry and persistency in the volatility of a set of petroleum futures price returns – namely crude oil, heating oil, gasoline, natural gas and propane – within the framework of a set of nonlinear GARCH-type models. The study reveals that over the sample period (1995–2010), all futures price returns show persistent and asymmetric effects of shocks to the volatility but the level of persistency and degree of asymmetry differ from product to product.

Furthermore, volatility modelling has important consequences for risk management. For example, Giot and Laurent (2003) calculated Value-at-Risk (VaR) measures for daily spot prices of Brent crude oil and WTI crude oil covering the period 20 May 1987 to 8 March 2002. Focusing on market risk over a 1-day time horizon, they found that the skew student absolute power ARCH (APARCH) model performed best on these data.

Another interesting example is provided by Hung *et al.* (2008). They adopt the GARCH model with heavy-tailed distribution to estimate 1-day-ahead VaR for WTI crude oil, Brent crude oil, heating oil, propane and New York conventional gasoline regular, and further compare the accuracy and efficiency with alternative GARCH specifications.

The rest of this chapter is organized as follows. In Section 15.2 we illustrate ARCH and GARCH models and their main features. The IGARCH model is introduced in Section 15.3 while the component model is discussed in Section 15.4. Asymmetric GARCH models and periodic extensions are presented in Sections 15.5 and 15.6, respectively. Section 15.7 is dedicated to the nesting parameterizations. In Section 15.8, long memory is briefly introduced and long-memory GARCH models are discussed. Estimation and inference are illustrated in Sections 15.9 and 15.10, respectively. The multivariate models are presented in Section 15.11. Section 15.12 contains two empirical applications, one analyses and estimates the volatility of electricity prices while the second focuses on risk management application of GARCH models. In Section 15.13 we present the GARCH modelling with Eviews® and Matlab®.

15.2 THE GARCH MODEL: GENERAL DEFINITION

Let $\{\varepsilon_t(\theta)\}$ denote a discrete-time stochastic process with conditional mean and variance parameterized by the finite-dimensional vector $\theta \in \Theta \subseteq \Re^m$, where θ_0 denotes the true value. We assume, for the moment, that $\varepsilon_t(\theta_0)$ is a scalar. Let $E_{t-1}[\cdot] \equiv E[\cdot|\Phi_{t-1}]$ denote the conditional expectation when the conditioning set is composed of the past values of the process along with other information available at time $t-1$ (denoted by Φ_{t-1}) and analogously for the conditional variance, that is $\text{Var}_{t-1}[\cdot] \equiv \text{Var}[\cdot|\Phi_{t-1}]$.

Definition 15.2.1 *(Bollerslev et al., 1996) The process $\{\varepsilon_t(\theta_0)\}$ follows an ARCH model if*

$$E_{t-1}[\varepsilon_t(\theta_0)] = 0 \qquad t = 1, 2, \ldots \tag{15.1}$$

and the conditional variance

$$\sigma_t^2(\theta_0) \equiv \text{Var}_{t-1}[\varepsilon_t(\theta_0)] = E_{t-1}\left[\varepsilon_t^2(\theta_0)\right] \qquad t = 1, 2, \ldots \tag{15.2}$$

depends nontrivially on the σ-field generated by the past observations: $\{\varepsilon_{t-1}(\theta_0), \varepsilon_{t-2}(\theta_0), \ldots\}$.

Let $\{y_t(\theta_0)\}$ denote the stochastic process of interest with conditional mean

$$\mu_t(\theta_0) \equiv E_{t-1}(y_t) \qquad t = 1, 2, \ldots \tag{15.3}$$

By the time convention, both $\mu_t(\theta_0)$ and $\sigma_t^2(\theta_0)$ are measurable with respect to the time $t-1$ information set. Define the $\{\varepsilon_t(\theta_0)\}$ process by

$$\varepsilon_t(\theta_0) \equiv y_t - \mu_t(\theta_0). \tag{15.4}$$

It follows from equations (15.1) and (15.2), that the standardized process

$$z_t(\theta_0) \equiv \varepsilon_t(\theta_0)\,\sigma_t^2(\theta_0)^{-1/2} \qquad t = 1, 2, \ldots \tag{15.5}$$

will have conditional mean equal to zero ($E_{t-1}[z_t(\theta_0)] = 0$) and a time-invariant conditional variance equal to one.

We can think of $\varepsilon_t(\theta_0)$ as being generated by

$$\varepsilon_t(\theta_0) = z_t(\theta_0)\,\sigma_t^2(\theta_0)^{1/2}$$

where $\varepsilon_t^2(\theta_0)$ is an unbiased estimator of $\sigma_t^2(\theta_0)$. Let's suppose $z_t(\theta_0) \sim NID(0, 1)$ and independent of $\sigma_t^2(\theta_0)$:

$$E_{t-1}\left[\varepsilon_t^2\right] = E_{t-1}\left[\sigma_t^2\right] E_{t-1}\left[z_t^2\right] = E_{t-1}\left[\sigma_t^2\right]$$

because $z_t^2|\Phi_{t-1} \sim \chi^2_{(1)}$. The median of a $\chi^2_{(1)}$ is 0.455, so $\Pr\{\varepsilon_t^2 < \frac{1}{2}\sigma_t^2\} > \frac{1}{2}$. The proxy ε_t^2 introduces a potentially significant error into the analysis of small samples of $\sigma_t^2, t = 1, 2, \ldots, T$, although the error diminishes as T increases.

If the conditional distribution of z_t is time invariant with a finite fourth moment, the fourth moment of ε_t is

$$E\left[\varepsilon_t^4\right] \geq E\left[z_t^4\right] E\left[\varepsilon_t^2\right]^2$$

by Jensen's inequality.[1] The equality holds true for a constant conditional variance only. If $z_t \sim NID(0, 1)$, then $E[z_t^4] = 3$ and the unconditional distribution for ε_t is therefore leptokurtic:

$$E\left[\varepsilon_t^4\right] \geq 3E\left[\varepsilon_t^2\right]^2,$$
$$E\left[\varepsilon_t^4\right] / E\left[\varepsilon_t^2\right]^2 \geq 3.$$

[1]Jensen's inequality. Let X and $g(X)$ be integrable random variables, then

$$E[g(X)] \leq g(E[X])$$

if $g(\cdot)$ is concave, or

$$E[g(X)] \geq g(E[X])$$

if $g(\cdot)$ is convex.

Furthermore, the kurtosis can be expressed as a function of the variability of the conditional variance. In fact, if $\varepsilon_t|\Phi_{t-1} \sim N(0, \sigma_t^2)$:

$$\begin{aligned}
E_{t-1}\left[\varepsilon_t^4\right] &= 3E_{t-1}\left[\varepsilon_t^2\right]^2, \\
E\left[\varepsilon_t^4\right] &= 3E\left[E_{t-1}\left(\varepsilon_t^2\right)^2\right] \\
&= 3\left[E\left(\varepsilon_t^2\right)\right]^2 + 3E\left[E_{t-1}\left(\varepsilon_t^2\right)^2\right] - 3\left\{E\left[E_{t-1}\left(\varepsilon_t^2\right)\right]\right\}^2.
\end{aligned}$$

It follows that the kurtosis can be expressed as

$$\begin{aligned}
k = \frac{E\left[\varepsilon_t^4\right]}{\left[E\left(\varepsilon_t^2\right)\right]^2} &= 3 + 3\frac{E\{E_{t-1}\left[\varepsilon_t^2\right]^2\} - \left\{E\left[E_{t-1}\left(\varepsilon_t^2\right)\right]\right\}^2}{\left[E\left(\varepsilon_t^2\right)\right]^2} \\
&= 3 + 3\frac{\mathrm{Var}\left\{\sigma_t^2\right\}}{\left[E\left(\varepsilon_t^2\right)\right]^2}.
\end{aligned}$$

Another important property of the ARCH process is that it is conditionally serially uncorrelated. Given that

$$E_{t-1}[\varepsilon_t] = 0$$

we have that, with the law of iterated expectations:

$$E_{t-h}[\varepsilon_t] = E_{t-h}[E_{t-1}(\varepsilon_t)] = E_{t-h}[0] = 0.$$

This orthogonality property implies that the $\{\varepsilon_t\}$ process is conditionally uncorrelated:

$$\begin{aligned}
\mathrm{Cov}_{t-h}[\varepsilon_t, \varepsilon_{t+k}] &= E_{t-h}[\varepsilon_t \varepsilon_{t+k}] - E_{t-h}[\varepsilon_t]E_{t-h}[\varepsilon_{t+k}] \\
&= E_{t-h}[\varepsilon_t \varepsilon_{t+k}] = E_{t-h}[E_{t+k-1}(\varepsilon_t \varepsilon_{t+k})] \\
&= E[\varepsilon_t E_{t+k-1}[\varepsilon_{t+k}]] = 0.
\end{aligned}$$

15.2.1 The ARCH(q) Model

The ARCH(q) model introduced by Engle (1982) is a linear function of past squared disturbances:

$$\sigma_t^2 = \omega + \sum_{i=1}^{q} \alpha_i \varepsilon_{t-i}^2. \tag{15.6}$$

In this model, to assure a positive conditional variance, the parameters have to satisfy the following constraints: $\omega > 0$ and $\alpha_1 \geq 0, \alpha_2 \geq 0, \ldots, \alpha_q \geq 0$. Defining

$$\sigma_t^2 \equiv \varepsilon_t^2 - v_t$$

where $E_{t-1}(v_t) = 0$, we can write equation (15.6) as an $AR(q)$ in ε_t^2:

$$\varepsilon_t^2 = \omega + \alpha(L)\varepsilon_t^2 + v_t$$

where $\alpha(L) = \alpha_1 L + \alpha_2 L^2 + \ldots + \alpha_q L^q$ (with L the lag operator, i.e. $x_{t-1} = Lx_t$). The process is weakly stationary if and only if $\sum_{i=1}^{q} \alpha_i < 1$; in this case the unconditional variance is given by

$$E\left(\varepsilon_t^2\right) = \omega/(1 - \alpha_1 - \ldots - \alpha_q). \tag{15.7}$$

The process is characterized by leptokurtosis in excess with respect to the normal distribution. In the case, for instance, of ARCH(1) with $\varepsilon_t|\Phi_{t-1} \sim N(0, \sigma_t^2)$, the kurtosis is equal to

$$E\left(\varepsilon_t^4\right)/E\left(\varepsilon_t^2\right)^2 = 3\left(1 - \alpha_1^2\right)/\left(1 - 3\alpha_1^2\right) \tag{15.8}$$

with $3\alpha_1^2 < 1$; when $3\alpha_1^2 = 1$ we have

$$E\left(\varepsilon_t^4\right)/E\left(\varepsilon_t^2\right)^2 = \infty.$$

In both cases we obtain a kurtosis coefficient greater than 3, characteristic of the normal distribution.

15.2.2 The GARCH(p,q) Model

In order to model in a parsimonious way the conditional heteroscedasticity, Bollerslev (1986) (and Taylor (1986) independently) proposed the GARCH(p,q) model

$$\sigma_t^2 = \omega + \alpha(L)\varepsilon_t^2 + \beta(L)\sigma_t^2, \tag{15.9}$$

where $\alpha(L) = \alpha_1 L + \ldots + \alpha_q L^q$, $\beta(L) = \beta_1 L + \ldots + \beta_p L^p$. GARCH(1,1) is the most popular model in the empirical literature:[2]

$$\sigma_t^2 = \omega + \alpha_1 \varepsilon_{t-1}^2 + \beta_1 \sigma_{t-1}^2. \tag{15.10}$$

In order to ensure that the conditional variance is well defined in a GARCH(p,q) model, all the coefficients in the corresponding linear ARCH model of infinite order should be positive. Rewriting the GARCH(p,q) model as an ARCH(∞):

$$\begin{aligned}\sigma_t^2 &= \left(1 - \sum_{i=1}^{p} \beta_i L_i\right)^{-1} \left[\omega + \sum_{j=1}^{q} \alpha_j \varepsilon_{t-j}^2\right] \\ &= \omega^* + \sum_{k=0}^{\infty} \phi_k \varepsilon_{t-k-1}^2. \end{aligned} \tag{15.11}$$

[2]The GARCH model belongs to the class of deterministic conditional heteroscedasticity models in which the conditional variance is a function of variables that are in the information set available at time t.

$\sigma_t^2 \geq 0$ if $\omega^* \geq 0$ and all $\phi_k \geq 0$. The non-negativity of ω^* and ϕ_k is also a necessary condition for the non-negativity of σ_t^2. In order to make ω^* and $\{\phi_k\}_{k=0}^{\infty}$ well defined, let's assume that:

i. The roots of the polynomial $\beta(x) = 1$ lie outside the unit circle and $\omega \geq 0$. This is a condition for ω^* to be finite and positive.
ii. $\alpha(x)$ and $1 - \beta(x)$ have no common roots.

These conditions are establishing that neither $\sigma_t^2 \leq \infty$ nor $\{\sigma_t^2\}_{t=-\infty}^{\infty}$ is strictly stationary. For the simple GARCH(1,1) almost sure positivity of σ_t^2 requires (Nelson and Cao, 1992), along with conditions (i) and (ii), that

$$\omega \geq 0, \quad \beta_1 \geq 0, \quad \alpha_1 \geq 0. \tag{15.12}$$

For the GARCH(1,q) and GARCH(2,q) models these constraints can be relaxed, for example in the GARCH(1,2) model the necessary and sufficient conditions become

$$\begin{aligned} \omega &\geq 0, \\ 1 > \beta_1 &\geq 0, \\ \beta_1\alpha_1 + \alpha_2 &\geq 0, \\ \alpha_1 &\geq 0. \end{aligned} \tag{15.13}$$

For the GARCH(2,1) model the conditions are

$$\begin{aligned} \omega &\geq 0, \\ \alpha_1 &\geq 0, \\ \beta_1 &\geq 0, \\ \beta_1 + \beta_2 &< 1, \\ \beta_1^2 + 4\beta_2 &\geq 0. \end{aligned} \tag{15.14}$$

These constraints are less stringent than those proposed by Bollerslev (1986):

$$\omega \geq 0 \quad \beta_i \geq 0 \quad i = 1, \ldots, p \quad \alpha_j \geq 0 \quad j = 1, \ldots, q. \tag{15.15}$$

The conditions for GARCH(2,2) have been studied by He and Teräsvirta (1999). These results cannot be adopted in the multivariate case, where the requirement of positivity for $\{\sigma_t^2\}$ means the positive definiteness of the conditional variance–covariance matrix. In order for the GARCH parameters $\beta_1, \ldots, \beta_p$ to be identified, at least one of the ARCH coefficients α_i must be nonzero. In fact, if $\alpha_1 = \ldots = \alpha_q = 0$ the conditional and unconditional variances of ε_t are equal and $\beta_1, \ldots, \beta_p$ are unidentified nuisance parameters. From the point of view of the maximum likelihood estimation of a GARCH(p,q) model, we need to recursively calculate $\{\sigma_t^2\}_{t=0}^{\infty}$ starting from 0 applying equation (15.9), assuming arbitrary values for the pre-sample period $\{\sigma_{-1}^2, \ldots, \sigma_{-p}^2, \varepsilon_{-1}^2, \ldots, \varepsilon_{-q}^2\}$. The conditions (15.15) guarantee that $\{\sigma_t^2\}_{t=0}^{\infty}$ is not negative given arbitrary non-negative values for $\{\sigma_{-1}^2, \ldots, \sigma_{-p}^2, \varepsilon_{-1}^2, \ldots, \varepsilon_{-q}^2\}$. On the contrary, the conditions which guarantee that $\omega^* \geq 0$ and $\phi_k \geq 0$ (15.13) for the GARCH(1,2) model and (15.14) for the GARCH(2,1) model) do not. This problem can be solved by choosing the starting values that maintain non-negative $\{\sigma_t^2\}_{t=0}^{\infty}$ with probability 1, given non-negative

ω^* and $\{\phi_k\}_{k=0}^{\infty}$. Nelson and Cao (1992) suggest picking arbitrarily $\varepsilon^2 \geq 0$ and setting $\varepsilon_t^2 = \varepsilon^2$ for t from -1 to ∞ and $\sigma_t^2 = \sigma^2$ for $1 - p \leq t \leq 0$, where

$$\sigma^2 = \left(1 - \sum_{i=1}^{p} \beta_i\right)^{-1} \left[\omega + \varepsilon^2 \sum_{j=1}^{q} \alpha_j\right]$$
$$= \omega^* + \varepsilon^2 \sum_{k=0}^{\infty} \phi_k.$$

Doing so we have a sequence $\{\sigma_t^2\} \geq 0$ for all $t \geq 0$ with probability 1, as

$$\sigma_t^2 = \omega^* + \sum_{k=0}^{t-1} \phi_k \varepsilon_{t-k-1}^2 + \sum_{k=t}^{\infty} \phi_k \varepsilon^2.$$

Supposing that $\sum_{i=1}^{p} \beta_i + \sum_{j=1}^{q} \alpha_j < 1$, we can set σ^2 and ε^2 equal to their common unconditional mean:

$$\sigma^2 \equiv \varepsilon^2 \equiv \omega \Bigg/ \left(1 - \sum_{i=1}^{p} \beta_i - \sum_{j=1}^{q} \alpha_j\right).$$

In the stationary GARCH, Engle and Mezrich (1996) introduce *variance targeting*, namely they replace the intercept ω in equation (15.9) by $(1 - \sum_j \alpha_j - \sum_i \beta_i)\sigma^2$. The estimate of σ^2, that is $\widehat{\sigma}^2 = \sum_{t=1}^{T} \varepsilon_t^2$, is substituted for σ^2 before estimating the other parameters. The model contains one parameter less than the standard GARCH(p,q) model.

15.2.3 The Yule–Walker Equations for the Squared Process

The process $\{\varepsilon_t^2\}$ has an ARMA(m,p) representation

$$\varepsilon_t^2 = \omega + \sum_{j=1}^{m} (\alpha_j + \beta_j) \varepsilon_{t-j}^2 + \left(\upsilon_t - \sum_{i=1}^{p} \beta_i \upsilon_{t-i}\right)$$

where $m = \max(p, q)$, $E_{t-1}[\upsilon_t] = 0$, $\upsilon_t \in [-\sigma_t^2, \infty[$. Thus the classical results of ARMA models can be applied. In particular, we can study the autocovariance function (see Bollerslev, 1988), that is:

$$\gamma^2(k) = \mathrm{Cov}\left(\varepsilon_t^2, \varepsilon_{t-k}^2\right),$$
$$\gamma^2(k) = \mathrm{Cov}\left[\omega + \sum_{j=1}^{m} (\alpha_j + \beta_j) \varepsilon_{t-j}^2 + \left(\upsilon_t - \sum_{i=1}^{p} \beta_i \upsilon_{t-i}\right), \varepsilon_{t-k}^2\right],$$
$$\gamma^2(k) = \left[\sum_{j=1}^{m} (\alpha_j + \beta_j) \mathrm{Cov}\left(\varepsilon_{t-j}^2, \varepsilon_{t-k}^2\right)\right] + \mathrm{Cov}\left[\upsilon_t - \sum_{i=1}^{p} \beta_i \upsilon_{t-i}, \varepsilon_{t-k}^2\right]. \quad (15.16)$$

When k is big enough, the last term on the right of expression (15.16) is null. The sequence of autocovariances satisfies a linear difference equation of order $\max(p, q)$, for $k \geq p+1$:

$$\gamma^2(k) = \left[\sum_{j=1}^{m} (\alpha_j + \beta_j)\gamma^2(k-j) \right].$$

This system can be used to identify the lag order m and p, that is the p and q order if $q \geq p$ and the order p if $q < p$. The autocorrelation function of ε_t^2, if it exists, decays slowly, albeit still exponentially. For the ARCH model, the decay rate is too rapid compared with what is typically observed in financial time series, unless the maximum lag q is long.

15.2.4 Stationarity of the GARCH(p,q)

The process $\{\varepsilon_t\}$ which follows a GARCH(p,q) process is a martingale difference sequence. In order to study second order stationarity, it is sufficient to consider that

$$\mathrm{Var}[\varepsilon_t] = \mathrm{Var}[E_{t-1}(\varepsilon_t)] + E[\mathrm{Var}_{t-1}(\varepsilon_t)] = E\left[\sigma_t^2\right]$$

and show that it is asymptotically constant in time.

Proposition 15.2.1 *A process $\{\varepsilon_t\}$ which satisfies a GARCH(p,q) model with non-negative coefficients $\omega \geq 0$, $\alpha_i \geq 0\, i = 1, \ldots, q$, $\beta_i \geq 0\, i = 1, \ldots, p$ is covariance stationary if and only if*

$$\alpha(1) + \beta(1) < 1. \tag{15.17}$$

This is a sufficient but not necessary condition for strict stationarity. Every weakly stationary GARCH process is also strictly stationary. Since ARCH processes are thick tailed, the conditions for covariance stationarity are often more stringent than the conditions for strict stationarity. When $\alpha(1) + \beta(1) < 1$ the weakly stationary solution is unique and coincides with the unique stationary solution.

For the strictly stationary solution consider $\varepsilon_t^2 = z_t^2 \sigma_t^2$. The GARCH(1,1) can be written as

$$\sigma_t^2 = \omega + \sigma_{t-1}^2 \left(\alpha_1 z_{t-1}^2 + \beta_1\right). \tag{15.18}$$

Recursive substitution leads to the expression of the GARCH(1,1) model as

$$\sigma_t^2 = \omega \left[1 + \sum_{k=1}^{\infty} \prod_{i=1}^{k} \left(\beta_1 + \alpha_1 z_{t-i}^2\right) \right]. \tag{15.19}$$

Denoting

$$\begin{aligned} A_t &= \beta_1 + \alpha_1 z_t^2, \\ B_t &= \omega, \\ Y_t &= \sigma_{t+1}^2, \end{aligned}$$

it follows that $Y_t = \sigma_{t+1}^2$ is the solution of the random recurrence equation $Y_t = A_t Y_{t-1} + B_t$ where $\{A_t, B_t\}$ is i.i.d. Every strictly stationary solution $\{\sigma_t^2\}$ of equation (15.18) can be expressed as an appropriate function of the driving process $\{z_t\}$, so that the stationarity of $\{\sigma_t^2\}$ implies the stationarity of $\{\sigma_t^2, z_t\}$ and hence of $\{\varepsilon_t, \sigma_t\}$. In this way the existence of strictly stationary solutions of the GARCH(1,1) process can be reduced to the study of strictly stationary solutions of (15.18) (see Lindner, 2009). The solution $\{Y_t\}$ of the random recurrence equation (with i.i.d. coefficients) is a sequence of random variables. Every solution satisfies

$$\begin{aligned}Y_t &= A_t Y_{t-1} + B_t \\ &= A_t A_{t-1} Y_{t-2} + A_t B_{t-1} + B_t \\ &= \dots \\ &= \left(\prod_{j=0}^{k} A_{t-i}\right) Y_{t-k-1} + \sum_{i=0}^{k}\left(\prod_{j=0}^{i-1} A_{t-j}\right) B_{t-i}\end{aligned}$$

for all $k \in \mathbb{N} \cup \{0\}$, with $\prod_{j=0}^{-1} A_{t-j} = 1$ for the product over an empty index set. For the stationary solution to exist,

$$\lim_{k\to\infty}\left(\prod_{j=0}^{k} A_{t-i}\right) Y_{t-k-1} = 0 \quad \text{a.s.}$$

and $\sum_{i=0}^{k}(\prod_{j=0}^{i-1} A_{t-j})\, B_{t-i}$ converges almost surely as $k \to \infty$. In the GARCH(1,1) and ARCH(1) case,

$$\sigma_{t+1}^2 = Y_t = \left(\prod_{i=0}^{k} A_{t-i}\right)\sigma_{t-k}^2 + \omega \sum_{i=0}^{k}\left(\prod_{j=0}^{i-1} A_{t-j}\right). \tag{15.20}$$

Since this is a sum of non-negative components, it follows that $\sum_{i=0}^{\infty}\prod_{j=0}^{i-1} A_{t-j}$ converges almost surely for each t, and hence that $\prod_{i=0}^{k} A_{t-i}$ converges almost surely to 0 as $k \to \infty$. If $\{\sigma_{t+1}^2\}$ is strictly stationary, then $(\prod_{i=0}^{k} A_{t-i})\,\sigma_{t-k}^2$ converges, in distribution and probability, to 0 as $k \to \infty$. It follows that there is at most one strictly stationary solution $\sigma_t^2 = Y_{t-1}$, given by

$$Y_t = \omega \sum_{i=0}^{\infty}\left(\prod_{j=0}^{i-1} A_{t-j}\right). \tag{15.21}$$

Thus, the existence of a strictly stationary GARCH(1,1) or ARCH(1) process implies a.s. convergence of $\prod_{i=0}^{k} A_{-i}$ to 0 as $k \to \infty$. But also the converse holds, which implies that a strictly stationary solution of the GARCH(1,1)/ARCH(1) process exists if and only if $\prod_{i=0}^{k} A_{-i}$ converges a.s. to 0 as $k \to \infty$.

Nelson (1990) shows that when $\omega > 0$, $\sigma_t^2 < \infty$ a.s. and $\{\varepsilon_t, \sigma_t^2\}$ is strictly stationary if and only if $E[\ln(\beta_1 + \alpha_1 z_t^2)] < 0$. Given that

$$E\left[\ln\left(\beta_1 + \alpha_1 z_t^2\right)\right] \le \ln\left[E\left(\beta_1 + \alpha_1 z_t^2\right)\right] = \ln(\alpha_1 + \beta_1)$$

when $\alpha_1 + \beta_1 = 1$, the model is strictly stationary. Thus $E[\ln(\beta_1 + \alpha_1 z_t^2)] < 0$ is a weaker requirement than $\alpha_1 + \beta_1 < 1$. For the ARCH(1), with $\alpha_1 = 1$, $\beta_1 = 0$ and $z_t \sim$ i.i.d.(0, 1),

$$E\left[\ln\left(z_t^2\right)\right] \leq \ln\left[E\left(z_t^2\right)\right] = \ln(1).$$

Thus, the integrated ARCH(1) is strictly but not covariance stationary. In order to analyse the conditions for the existence of strictly stationary solutions of GARCH(p,q) we have to extend the random recurrence equation to the multidimensional case (see Bougerol and Picard, 1992a). Strict stationarity of multivariate random recurrence equations is studied in terms of the top Lyapunov exponent. Bougerol and Picard (1992b) have shown that irreducible recurrence equations with i.i.d. coefficients $\{A_t, B_t\}$, such that $E[\ln^+ \|A_0\|] < \infty$ and $E[\ln^+ \|B_0\|] < \infty$, admit a non-anticipative strictly stationary solution if and only if the top Lyapunov exponent associated with $\{A_t\}$ is strictly negative. Bougerol and Picard (1992a) showed that a GARCH(p,q) process admits a strictly stationary solution if and only if the top Lyapunov exponent associated with the sequence $\{A_t\}$ is strictly negative. This solution is unique.

15.2.5 Forecasting Volatility with GARCH

A GARCH(p,q) can be represented as an ARMA process, given that $\varepsilon_t^2 = \sigma_t^2 + \upsilon_t$, where $E_{t-1}[\upsilon_t] = 0$, $\upsilon_t \in [-\sigma_t^2, \infty]$:

$$\varepsilon_t^2 = \omega + \sum_{j=1}^{\max(p,q)} (\alpha_j + \beta_j)\varepsilon_{t-j}^2 + \left(\upsilon_t - \sum_{i=1}^{p} \beta_i \upsilon_{t-i}\right)$$

$\varepsilon_t^2 \sim$ARMA(m,p) with $m = \max(\mathrm{p}, \mathrm{q})$. Forecasting with a GARCH(p,q) (Engle and Bollerslev, 1986):

$$\sigma_{t+k}^2 = \omega + \sum_{i=1}^{n} \left[\alpha_i \varepsilon_{t+k-i}^2 + \beta_i \sigma_{t+k-i}^2\right] + \sum_{i=k}^{m} \left[\alpha_i \varepsilon_{t+k-i}^2 + \beta_i \sigma_{t+k-i}^2\right]$$

where $n = \min\{m, k-1\}$ and by definition summations from 1 to 0 and from $k > m$ to m are both equal to zero. Thus,

$$E_t\left[\sigma_{t+k}^2\right] = \omega + \sum_{i=1}^{n} \left[(\alpha_i + \beta_i) E_t\left(\sigma_{t+k-i}^2\right)\right] + \sum_{i=k}^{m} \left[\alpha_i \varepsilon_{t+k-i}^2 + \beta_i \sigma_{t+k-i}^2\right].$$

In particular, for GARCH(1,1) and $k > 2$:

$$\begin{aligned}
E_t\left[\sigma_{t+k}^2\right] &= \sum_{i=0}^{k-2} (\alpha_1 + \beta_1)^i \omega + (\alpha_1 + \beta_1)^{k-1} \sigma_{t+1}^2 \\
&= \omega \frac{[1 - (\alpha_1 + \beta_1)^{k-1}]}{[1 - (\alpha_1 + \beta_1)]} + (\alpha_1 + \beta_1)^{k-1} \sigma_{t+1}^2 \\
&= \sigma^2 [1 - (\alpha_1 + \beta_1)^{k-1}] + (\alpha_1 + \beta_1)^{k-1} \sigma_{t+1}^2 \\
&= \sigma^2 + (\alpha_1 + \beta_1)^{k-1} \left[\sigma_{t+1}^2 - \sigma^2\right].
\end{aligned}$$

When the process is covariance stationary, it follows that $E_t[\sigma_{t+k}^2]$ converges to σ^2 as $k \to \infty$.

15.3 THE IGARCH(*p*,*q*) MODEL

Definition 15.3.1 *The GARCH(p,q) process characterized by the first two conditional moments:*

$$E_{t-1}[\varepsilon_t] = 0,$$
$$\sigma_t^2 \equiv E_{t-1}\left[\varepsilon_t^2\right] = \omega + \sum_{i=1}^{q} \alpha_i \varepsilon_{t-i}^2 + \sum_{i=1}^{p} \beta_i \sigma_{t-i}^2$$

where $\omega \geq 0$, $\alpha_i \geq 0$ and $\beta_i \geq 0$ for all i and the polynomial

$$1 - \alpha(x) - \beta(x) = 0$$

has $d > 0$ unit root(s) and $\max\{p, q\} - d$ root(s) outside the unit circle is said to be:

i. Integrated in variance of order d if $\omega = 0$.
ii. Integrated in variance of order d with trend if $\omega > 0$.

The integrated GARCH(*p*,*q*) (IGARCH) models, both with and without trend, are therefore part of a wider class of models with a property called 'persistent variance' in which the current information remains important for the forecasts of the conditional variances for every horizon. So we have the GARCH(*p*,*q*) model when (necessary condition)

$$\alpha(1) + \beta(1) = 1.$$

To illustrate, consider the IGARCH(1,1) which is characterized by

$$\alpha_1 + \beta_1 = 1.$$

The process can be expressed as:

$$\sigma_t^2 = \omega + \alpha_1 \varepsilon_{t-1}^2 + (1 - \alpha_1)\sigma_{t-1}^2,$$
$$\sigma_t^2 = \omega + \sigma_{t-1}^2 + \alpha_1\left(\varepsilon_{t-1}^2 - \sigma_{t-1}^2\right) \qquad 0 < \alpha_1 \leq 1. \tag{15.22}$$

For this particular model the forecast of the conditional variance *k* steps ahead is:

$$E_t\left[\sigma_{t+k}^2\right] = (k-1)\,\omega + \sigma_{t+1}^2.$$

Nelson (1991) showed that when an IGARCH process is started at some finite time point, its behaviour depends on the intercept ω. If $\omega > 0$ then the unconditional variance of ε_t grows linearly with time. If $\omega = 0$ the realizations from the process collapse to zero almost surely. The parameter β_1 affects the pace of this convergence. It is important to notice that the unconditional variance of ε_t when the conditional variance follows the IGARCH model does not exist. In the case of GARCH(1,1) the possible explanation for the fact that the estimate of $\alpha_1 + \beta_1$ is close to one is that there is a switch in the intercept of a GARCH model during the estimation period (Diebold, 1986; Lamoureux and Lastrapes, 1990). This means that the underlying GARCH process is not stationary. The IGARCH(1,1) in expressions (15.22) can also be written in the ARIMA(0,1,1) form:

$$(1 - L)\varepsilon_t^2 = \omega + \upsilon_t - \beta_1 \upsilon_{t-1}, \tag{15.23}$$

where $\upsilon_t = \varepsilon_t^2 - \sigma_t^2$ is a martingale difference sequence with respect to σ_t^2.

15.4 A PERMANENT AND TRANSITORY COMPONENT MODEL OF VOLATILITY

Engle and Lee (1999) suggested that the high persistence and long memory in volatility may be due to a time-varying long-run volatility level. The finding of a unit root in the volatility process indicates that there is a stochastic trend as well as a transitory component in stock return volatility. The decomposition of the conditional variance of asset returns in a permanent and transitory component is a way to investigate the long-run and the short-run movement of volatility in the stock market (Engle and Lee, 1999). Using the variance targeting representation of the GARCH(1,1) model, we can write

$$\begin{aligned}\sigma_t^2 &= (1 - \alpha_1 - \beta_1)\sigma^2 + \alpha_1 \varepsilon_{t-1}^2 + \beta_1 \sigma_{t-1}^2 \\ &= \sigma^2 + \alpha_1 \left(\varepsilon_{t-1}^2 - \sigma^2\right) + \beta_1 \left(\sigma_{t-1}^2 - \sigma^2\right).\end{aligned}$$

The last two terms have expected value zero. This model is extended to allow the possibility that volatility is not constant in the long run. Let q_t be the *permanent component* of the conditional variance, the *component model* for the conditional variance is defined as

$$\sigma_t^2 = q_t + \alpha_1 \left(\varepsilon_{t-1}^2 - q_{t-1}\right) + \beta_1 \left(\sigma_{t-1}^2 - q_{t-1}\right). \tag{15.24}$$

The constant volatility σ^2 has been replaced by the time-varying trend q_t and its past value. Using the lag operator

$$(1 - \beta_1 L)\sigma_t^2 = [1 - (\alpha_1 + \beta_1)L]q_t + \alpha_1 \varepsilon_{t-1}^2$$

with

$$q_t = \omega + q_{t-1} + \phi \left(\varepsilon_{t-1}^2 - \sigma_{t-1}^2\right).$$

The forecasting error $\varepsilon_{t-1}^2 - \sigma_{t-1}^2$ serves as a driving force for the time-dependent movement of the trend. The difference between the conditional variance and its trend, $\sigma_{t-1}^2 - q_{t-1}$, is the *transitory component* of the conditional variance.

The multistep forecast of the trend is just the current trend plus a constant drift. In fact,

$$E_{t-1}[q_{t+k}] = \omega + E_{t-1}[q_{t+k-1}] + \phi E_{t-1}\left[\varepsilon_{t+k-1}^2 - \sigma_{t+k-1}^2\right]$$

but $E_{t-1}(\varepsilon^2_{t+k-1}) = E_{t-1}(\sigma^2_{t+k-1})$ such that $E_{t-1}[\varepsilon^2_{t+k-1} - \sigma^2_{t+k-1}] = 0$. Thus,

$$\begin{aligned} E_{t-1}[q_{t+k}] &= \omega + \omega + E_{t-1}[q_{t+k-2}] + \phi E_{t-1}\left[\varepsilon^2_{t+k-2} - \sigma^2_{t+k-2}\right] \\ &= k\omega + q_t. \end{aligned} \tag{15.25}$$

From equation (15.24), the forecast at time $t-1$ is

$$\begin{aligned} E_{t-1}\left(\sigma^2_{t+k}\right) - E_{t-1}(q_{t+k}) &= (\alpha_1 + \beta_1)\left(E_{t-1}\left(\sigma^2_{t+k-1}\right) - E_{t-1}(q_{t+k-1})\right) \\ &= (\alpha_1 + \beta_1)^k\left(\sigma^2_t - q_t\right). \end{aligned}$$

The forecast $E_{t-1}(\sigma^2_{t+k}) - E_{t-1}(q_{t+k})$, when $\alpha_1 + \beta_1 < 1$, will eventually converge to zero as the forecasting horizon extends into the remote future:

$$E_{t-1}\left(\sigma^2_{t+k}\right) - E_{t-1}(q_{t+k}) = 0 \text{ as } k \to \infty. \tag{15.26}$$

Therefore there will be no difference between the conditional variance and the trend in the long run. This is the motivation for q_t being called the permanent component of the conditional variance. Combining expressions (15.26) and (15.25), the long-run forecast of the conditional variance is just the current expectation of the trend plus a constant drift,

$$E_{t-1}\left(\sigma^2_{t+k}\right) = k\omega + q_t \text{ as } k \to \infty.$$

When the component model is extended to include non-unit-root processes, we have the general component model

$$\sigma^2_t = q_t + \alpha_1\left(\varepsilon^2_{t-1} - q_{t-1}\right) + \beta_1\left(\sigma^2_{t-1} - q_{t-1}\right), \tag{15.27}$$

$$q_t = \omega + \rho q_{t-1} + \phi\left(\varepsilon^2_{t-1} - \sigma^2_{t-1}\right), \tag{15.28}$$

where q_t still represents the persistent component of the conditional variance, as long as $\rho > (\alpha_1 + \beta_1)$. The multistep forecast of the conditional variance and the trend are

$$E_{t-1}\left(\sigma^2_{t+k}\right) - E_{t-1}(q_{t+k}) = (\alpha_1 + \beta_1)^k\left(\sigma^2_t - q_t\right) \tag{15.29}$$

and

$$E_{t-1}[q_{t+k}] = \frac{(1-\rho^k)}{(1-\rho)}\omega + \rho^k q_t, \tag{15.30}$$

for $\rho < 1$ and $(\alpha_1 + \beta_1) < 1$. If $\rho > (\alpha_1 + \beta_1)$, the transitory component in equation (15.29) decays faster than the trend in equation (15.30) so that the trend will dominate the forecast of the conditional variance as the forecasting horizon extends. The conditional variance will eventually converge to a constant since the trend itself is stationary,

$$E_{t-1}\left(\sigma^2_{t+k}\right) = E_{t-1}(q_{t+k}) = \frac{\omega}{1-\rho} \text{ as } k \to \infty.$$

By rewriting equation (15.24) as

$$\sigma_t^2 = (1 - \alpha_1 L - \beta_1 L)q_t + \alpha_1 \varepsilon_{t-1}^2 + \beta_1 \sigma_{t-1}^2$$

and equation (15.28) as

$$(1 - \rho L)\, q_t = \omega + \phi \left(\varepsilon_{t-1}^2 - \sigma_{t-1}^2\right) \tag{15.31}$$

and multiplying (15.27) by $(1 - \rho L)$, the general component model reduces to

$$(1 - \rho L)\, \sigma_t^2 = (1 - \rho L) \left[(1 - \alpha_1 L - \beta_1 L)q_t + \alpha_1 \varepsilon_{t-1}^2 + \beta_1 \sigma_{t-1}^2\right]. \tag{15.32}$$

Substituting (15.31) into (15.32),

$$\begin{aligned}(1 - \rho L)\, \sigma_t^2 = {} & (1 - \alpha_1 - \beta_1)\omega + (\phi + \alpha_1)\varepsilon_{t-1}^2 - (\rho\alpha_1 + (\alpha_1 + \beta_1)\phi)\varepsilon_{t-2}^2 \\ & + (\beta_1 - \phi)\sigma_{t-1}^2 + (\phi(\alpha_1 + \beta_1) - \beta_1 \rho)\sigma_{t-2}^2.\end{aligned}$$

A GARCH(2,2) process represents the underlying data-generating process for the conditional variance defined in the general component model. When $\rho = \phi = 0$, the general component model will reduce to the GARCH(1,1). In conclusion, the GARCH(1,1) only describes a single dynamic component of the conditional variance.

15.5 ASYMMETRIC MODELS

The GARCH model has been generalized and extended in various directions to increase the flexibility of the original model. The original GARCH specification assumes the response to a shock to be independent of the sign of the shock and just be a function of the size of the shock. However, a stylized fact of financial volatility is that bad news (negative shocks) tends to have a larger impact on volatility than good news (positive shocks). That is, volatility tends to be higher in a falling market than in a rising market. Black (1976) attributed this effect to the fact that bad news tends to drive down the stock price, thus increasing the leverage (i.e., the debt-to-equity ratio) of the stock and causing the stock to be more volatile. Based on this conjecture, the asymmetric news impact on volatility is commonly referred to as the leverage effect. Thus, the alternative parameterizations to the standard GARCH model aim at accommodating the asymmetry in the response. In this section we present the most popular asymmetric models in the literature.

15.5.1 The EGARCH(*p*,*q*) Model

The simple structure of equation (15.9) imposes important limitations on GARCH models (Nelson, 1991).

- The negative correlation between stock returns and changes in returns volatility; that is, the volatility tends to rise in response to 'bad news' (excess returns lower than expected) and to fall in response to 'good news' (excess returns higher than expected). GARCH models, however, assume that only the magnitude and not the positivity or negativity of unanticipated excess returns determines feature σ_t^2. If the distribution of z_t is symmetric, the change in variance tomorrow is conditionally uncorrelated with excess returns today (Nelson, 1991). If we write σ_t^2 as a function of lagged σ_t^2 and lagged z_t^2, where $\varepsilon_t^2 = z_t^2\sigma_t^2$:

$$\sigma_t^2 = \omega + \sum_{j=1}^{q} \alpha_j z_{t-j}^2 \sigma_{t-j}^2 + \sum_{i=1}^{p} \beta_i \sigma_{t-i}^2 \tag{15.33}$$

it is evident that the conditional variance is invariant to changes in sign of the z_t's. Moreover, the innovations $z_{t-j}^2\sigma_{t-j}^2$ are not i.i.d.

- Another limitation of GARCH models results from the non-negativity constraints on ω^* and ϕ_k in (15.11), which are imposed to ensure that σ_t^2 remains non-negative for all t with probability one. These constraints imply that increasing z_t^2 in any period increases σ_{t+m}^2 for all $m \geq 1$, ruling out random oscillatory behaviour in the σ_t^2 process.
- The GARCH models are not able to explain the observed covariance between ε_t^2 and ε_{t-j}. This is possible only if the conditional variance is expressed as an asymmetric function of ε_{t-j}.
- In the GARCH(1,1) model, shocks may persist in one norm and die out in another, so the conditional moments of GARCH(1,1) may explode even when the process is strictly stationary and ergodic.
- GARCH models essentially specify the behaviour of the square of the data. In this case a few large observations can dominate the sample.

The asymmetric models provide a mechanism that produces the so-called *leverage effect*, that is an unexpected price drop increases volatility more than an analogous unexpected price increase. The exponential GARCH(p,q) model (EGARCH(p,q)) put forward by Nelson (1991) provides a parameterization where σ_t^2 depends on both size and sign of lagged residuals. The model is defined as follows:

$$\ln\left(\sigma_t^2\right) = \omega + \sum_{i=1}^{q} \alpha_i[\phi z_{t-i} + \psi(|z_{t-i}| - E|z_{t-i}|)] + \sum_{i=1}^{p} \beta_i \ln\left(\sigma_{t-i}^2\right) \tag{15.34}$$

with $\alpha_1 \equiv 1$, $E|z_t| = (2/\pi)^{1/2}$ given that $z_t \sim$ i.i.d. $N(0,1)$, where the parameters ω, β_i, α_i are not restricted to be non-negative. Let us define

$$g(z_t) \equiv \phi z_t + \psi[|z_t| - E|z_t|]$$

by construction where $\{g(z_t)\}_{t=-\infty}^{\infty}$ is a zero-mean, i.i.d. random sequence. The components of $g(z_t)$ are ϕz_t and $\psi[|z_t| - E|z_t|]$, each with mean zero. If the distribution of z_t is symmetric, the components are orthogonal, though they are not independent. Over the range $0 < z_t < \infty$, $g(z_t)$ is linear in z_t with slope $\phi + \psi$ and over the range $-\infty < z_t \leq 0$, $g(z_t)$ is linear with slope $\phi - \psi$. Thus, $g(z_t)$ allows for the conditional variance process $\{\sigma_t^2\}$ to respond asymmetrically to rises and falls in stock price. The term $\psi[|z_t| - E|z_t|]$ represents a magnitude effect. If $\psi > 0$ and $\phi = 0$, the innovation in $\ln(\sigma_{t+1}^2)$ is positive (negative) when the magnitude of z_t is larger (smaller) than its expected value. If $\psi = 0$ and $\phi < 0$, the innovation in $\ln(\sigma_{t+1}^2)$ is now positive (negative) when returns innovations are negative (positive). A negative shock to the returns which would increase the debt-to-equity ratio and therefore increase uncertainty of future returns could be accounted for when $\alpha_i > 0$ and $\phi < 0$. As in the standard GARCH case, the first-order model is the most popular EGARCH in practice.

A number of authors, for example Nelson (1991), have found that standardized residuals from estimated GARCH models are leptokurtic relative to the normal, see also Engle and Gonzalez-Rivera (1991). Nelson (1991) assumes that z_t has a GED distribution (also called the exponential power family). The density of a GED random variable normalized to have mean zero and variance one is given by

$$f(z;\upsilon) = \frac{\upsilon \exp\left[-\left(\frac{1}{2}\right)|z/\lambda|^{\upsilon}\right]}{\lambda 2^{(1+1/\upsilon)}\Gamma(1/\upsilon)}, \qquad -\infty < z < \infty, \qquad 0 < \upsilon \leq \infty$$

where $\Gamma(\,)$ is the gamma function and

$$\lambda \equiv [2^{(-2/\upsilon)}\Gamma(1/\upsilon)/\Gamma(3/\upsilon)]^{1/2}$$

with υ a tail thickness parameter. When $\upsilon = 2$, z has a standard normal distribution. For $\upsilon < 2$, the distribution of z has thicker tails than the normal (e.g., when $\upsilon = 1$, z has a double exponential distribution) and for $\upsilon > 2$, the distribution of z has thinner tails than the normal (e.g., for $\upsilon = \infty$, z is uniformly distributed on the interval $[-3^{1/2}, 3^{1/2}]$). With this density, we obtain that $E|z_t| = \frac{\lambda 2^{1/\upsilon}\Gamma(2/\upsilon)}{\Gamma(1/\upsilon)}$ (Hamilton, 1994).

He *et al.* (2002) noted that the decay of autocorrelations of squared observations of the first-order EGARCH model is faster than exponential in the beginning, before it slows down towards an exponential rate. Moreover, Malmsten and Teräsvirta (2004) showed that the EGARCH(1,1) with normal errors is not sufficiently flexible for characterizing series with high kurtosis or slowly decaying autocorrelations. The choice of distribution of the standardized errors is particularly important in this case. Assuming normal errors means that the first-order autocorrelation of squared observations increases quite rapidly as a function of kurtosis for any fixed β_1 before the increase slows down. Nelson (1991) suggested using the GED for these errors, while the choice of t-distribution may imply infinite unconditional variance for $\{\varepsilon_t\}$. As in the case of GARCH(1,1), choosing an error distribution with fatter tails than the normal increases the kurtosis and, at the same time, lowers the autocorrelations of squared observations or absolute values.

15.5.2 Other Asymmetric Models

The asymmetric GARCH(p,q) (AGARCH) model (Engle, 1990):

$$\sigma_t^2 = \omega + \sum_{i=1}^{q} \alpha_i(\varepsilon_{t-i} + \gamma_i)^2 + \sum_{i=1}^{p} \beta_i \sigma_{t-i}^2 \qquad (15.35)$$

Here, negative values of γ imply that positive shocks will result in smaller increases in future volatility than negative shocks of the same absolute magnitude.

The nonlinear AGARCH(1,1) (NAGARCH) model by Engle and Ng (1993):

$$\sigma_t^2 = \omega + \alpha_1 \left(\frac{\varepsilon_{t-1}}{\sigma_{t-1}} + \gamma \right)^2 + \beta_1 \sigma_{t-1}^2. \tag{15.36}$$

The Glosten *et al.* (1993) model (GJR-GARCH):

$$\sigma_t^2 = \omega + \sum_{i=1}^{p} \beta_i \sigma_{t-i}^2 + \sum_{i=1}^{q} \left(\alpha_i \varepsilon_{t-1}^2 + \gamma_i S_{t-i}^- \varepsilon_{t-i}^2 \right), \tag{15.37}$$

where $S_t^- = \mathrm{I}(\varepsilon_t < 0)$, with $\mathrm{I}(\cdot)$ an indicator function obtaining value one when the argument is true and zero otherwise.

The QGARCH(p,q) by Sentana (1995):

$$\sigma_t^2 = \sigma^2 + \mathbf{\Psi}'\mathbf{x}_{t-q} + \mathbf{x}_{t-q}'\mathbf{A}\mathbf{x}_{t-q} + \sum_{i=1}^{p} \beta_i \sigma_{t-i}^2, \tag{15.38}$$

when $\mathbf{x}_{t-q} = (\varepsilon_{t-1}, \ldots, \varepsilon_{t-q})'$. The linear term ($\mathbf{\Psi}'\mathbf{x}_{t-q}$) allows for asymmetry. The off-diagonal elements of the symmetric parameter matrix $\mathbf{A}$ account for interaction effects of lagged values of x_t on the conditional variance. The conditional variance σ_t^2 is positive if and only if $\mathbf{A}$ in the quadratic form is positive definite. The QGARCH nests several asymmetric models. The generalized augmented ARCH (AARCH), which is an extension of the AARCH model by Bera *et al.* (1992), assumes $\mathbf{\Psi} = \mathbf{0}$. The ARCH($q$) model corresponds to $\mathbf{\Psi} = \mathbf{0}$, $\beta_i = 0, i = 1, \ldots, q$ and $\mathbf{A}$ diagonal. The asymmetric GARCH model assumes $\mathbf{A}$ to be diagonal. The linear standard deviation model corresponds to $\beta_i = 0$, $\sigma^2 = \rho^2$, $\mathbf{\Psi} = 2\rho\phi$ and $\mathbf{A} = \phi\phi'$:

$$\sigma_t^2 = (\rho + \phi'\mathbf{x}_{t-q})^2.$$

The threshold GARCH (TGARCH) introduces a threshold effect into the volatility:

$$\sigma_t = \omega + \sum_{i=1}^{q} (\alpha_{i,+}\varepsilon_{t-i}^+ - \alpha_{i,-}\varepsilon_{t-i}^-) + \sum_{i=1}^{p} \beta_i \sigma_{t-i}, \tag{15.39}$$

where

$$\varepsilon_{t-i}^+ = \max\{\varepsilon_{t-i}, 0\}$$

and

$$\varepsilon_{t-i}^- = \varepsilon_{t-i} - \varepsilon_{t-i}^+.$$

Under the constraints

$$\omega > 0, \quad \alpha_{i,+} \geq 0, \quad \alpha_{i,-} \geq 0, \quad \beta_i \geq 0$$

the variable σ_t is always strictly positive and represents the conditional standard deviation of ε_t. The GJR-GARCH model can be considered a variant of the TGARCH, obtained by squaring the variables in equation (15.39), see Franq and Zakoïan (2010). Through the coefficients $\alpha_{i,+}$ and $\alpha_{i,-}$, the current volatility depends on both the modulus and the sign of past returns.

15.5.3 The News Impact Curve

The news has an asymmetric effect on volatility. In the asymmetric volatility models, good news and bad news have different predictability for future volatility. The news impact curve (NIC), introduced by Pagan and Schwert (1990) and christened by Engle and Ng (1993), characterizes the impact of past return shocks on the return volatility which is implicit in a volatility model. Holding constant the information dated $t-2$ and earlier, we can examine the implied relation between ε_{t-1} and σ_t^2. All lagged conditional variances are evaluated at the level of the unconditional variance of the stock return. The NIC relates past return shocks (news) to current volatility. This curve measures how new information is incorporated into volatility estimates.

For the GARCH model the NIC is centred on $\varepsilon_{t-1} = 0$. In the case of EGARCH model the curve has its minimum at $\varepsilon_{t-1} = 0$ and is exponentially increasing in both directions but with different parameters.

GARCH(1,1):

$$\sigma_t^2 = \omega + \alpha\varepsilon_t^2 + \beta\sigma_{t-1}^2.$$

Given that $\sigma_{t-1}^2 = \sigma^2$, the NIC has the following expression:

$$\sigma_t^2 = A + \alpha\varepsilon_{t-1}^2,$$
$$A \equiv \omega + \beta\sigma^2.$$

EGARCH(1,1):

$$\ln\left(\sigma_t^2\right) = \omega + \beta\ln\left(\sigma_{t-1}^2\right) + \phi z_{t-1} + \psi(|z_{t-1}| - E|z_{t-1}|)$$

where $z_t = \varepsilon_t/\sigma_t$. The NIC is

$$\sigma_t^2 = \begin{cases} A\exp\left[\dfrac{\phi+\psi}{\sigma}\varepsilon_{t-1}\right], & \varepsilon_{t-1} > 0 \\ A & \varepsilon_{t-1} = 0 \\ A\exp\left[\dfrac{\phi-\psi}{\sigma}\varepsilon_{t-1}\right], & \varepsilon_{t-1} < 0 \end{cases}$$

$$A \equiv \sigma^{2\beta}\exp\left[\omega - \psi\sqrt{2/\pi}\right]$$

with $\phi < 0$, $\psi + \phi > 0$. Thus, it is evident from the NIC that the EGARCH allows good and bad news to have a different impact on the volatility, while the standard GARCH does not. Moreover, it allows big news to have a greater impact on the volatility than in the GARCH model. EGARCH would have higher variances in both directions because the exponential curve eventually dominates the quadrature.

For the AGARCH(1,1) model (Engle, 1990)

$$\sigma_t^2 = \omega + \alpha(\varepsilon_{t-1} + \gamma)^2 + \beta\sigma_{t-1}^2$$

the NIC is

$$\sigma_t^2 = A + \alpha(\varepsilon_{t-1} + \gamma)^2 \tag{15.40}$$
$$A \equiv \omega + \beta\sigma^2$$
$$\omega > 0, 0 \leq \beta < 1, \sigma > 0, 0 \leq \alpha < 1.$$

It is asymmetric and centred at $\varepsilon_{t-1} = -\gamma$.

Finally, for the GJR-GARCH model

$$\sigma_t^2 = \omega + \alpha\varepsilon_t^2 + \beta\sigma_{t-1}^2 + \gamma S_{t-1}^- \varepsilon_{t-1}^2$$

the NIC is

$$\sigma_t^2 = \begin{cases} A + \alpha\varepsilon_{t-1}^2, & \varepsilon_{t-1} > 0 \\ A + (\alpha + \gamma)\varepsilon_{t-1}^2, & \varepsilon_{t-1} < 0 \end{cases}$$
$$A \equiv \omega + \beta\sigma^2$$
$$\omega > 0, 0 \leq \beta < 1, \sigma > 0, 0 \leq \alpha < 1, \alpha + \beta < 1.$$

These differences between the NICs of the models have important implications for portfolio selection and asset pricing. Since predictable market volatility is related to market premium, the two models imply very different market risk premiums. Differences in predicted volatility after the arrival of some major news leads to a significant difference in the current option price and to different dynamic hedging strategies.

15.6 PERIODIC GARCH

One stylized fact that emerges from the analysis of commodity prices is that volatility is characterized by seasonal patterns. Periodic models for the volatility process constitute an alternative representation for the seasonal patterns observed in volatility. Periodic GARCH models have been introduced by Bollerslev and Ghysels (1996) and used for the analysis of periodicity in volatilities by Franses and Paap (2000) and Taylor (2004), among others, and in stochastic volatility models by Tsiakas (2006). Let y_t be the log-return observed S times intradaily, for a total number of observations which is T. The periodic GARCH P-GARCH(p,q) process (Bollerslev and Ghysels, 1996) $\{y_t\}$, defined on some probability space $(\Omega, \mathcal{A}, \mathcal{P})$, is a time-varying coefficient model for the conditional variance of the returns:

$$\sigma_t^2 = \text{Var}\left[y_t | \Phi_{t-1}^s\right] \qquad t = 1, \ldots, T \tag{15.41}$$

where Φ_{t-1}^s is a modified Borel σ-field filtration in which the Borel σ-field filtration, based on the realization of the $\{y_t\}$ process up to time $t-1$, is augmented by a process defining the stage of the periodic cycle at each point in time. The most straightforward P-GARCH model is obtained when the periodic cycle is purely repetitive. The conditional variance σ_t^2 is:

$$\sigma_t^2 = \omega_s + \sum_{i=1}^{p} \beta_{is}\sigma_{t-i}^2 + \sum_{j=1}^{q} \alpha_{js}\varepsilon_{t-j}^2 \qquad t = 1, \ldots, T;\ s = 1, \ldots, S \tag{15.42}$$

where S is the number of periods. In order to have σ_t^2 positive almost surely, restrictions have to be imposed on ω_s, β_{is} and α_{js}. These can easily be verified on a case-by-case basis following Nelson and Cao (1992). An example of such a repetitive cycle would be the intraday pattern observed in market activity associated with the regular opening and closing of financial markets.

15.6.1 Periodic EGARCH

In the periodic EGARCH (P-EGARCH) process, the logarithm of the conditional variance process is modelled as

$$\ln\left(\sigma_t^2\right) = \omega_s + \sum_{i=1}^{p} \beta_{is} \ln\left(\sigma_{t-i}^2\right) + \sum_{j=1}^{q} \alpha_{js} g_s(z_{t-j}) \quad t = 1, \ldots, T;\ s = 1, \ldots, S \tag{15.43}$$

or using the lag operator:

$$(1 - \beta_s(L)) \ln\left(\sigma_t^2\right) = \omega_s + \alpha_s(L) g_s(z_{t-1}) \tag{15.44}$$

where

$$g_s(z_t) = \psi_s[|z_t| - E(|z_t|)] + \gamma_s z_t$$

and

$$\alpha_s(L) = 1 + \alpha_{1s}L + \ldots + \alpha_{qs}L^q,$$
$$\beta_s(L) = \beta_{1s}L + \ldots + \beta_{ps}L^p.$$

The P-EGARCH(1,0) process

$$\ln\left(\sigma_t^2\right) = \omega_s + \beta_{1s} \ln\left(\sigma_{t-1}^2\right) + g_s(z_{t-1})$$

is weakly stationary if and only if

$$\left|\prod_{s=1}^{S} \beta_{1s}\right| < 1. \tag{15.45}$$

15.7 NESTING MODELS

The proliferation of GARCH models has inspired some authors to define families of GARCH models that would accommodate as many individual models as possible. The nesting shows the connection between models and permits standard nested tests to determine the relative quality of each of the model fits. In general, these nesting models are based on transformation of the conditional standard deviation. Taylor (1986) and Schwert (1989) first suggested ARCH models for the conditional standard deviation:

$$\sigma_t = \omega + \sum_{i=1}^{q} \alpha_i |\varepsilon_{t-i}| + \sum_{i=1}^{p} \beta_i \sigma_{t-i}. \tag{15.46}$$

Their argument follows Davidian and Carroll (1987) who show in a regression framework that variance estimators based on absolute residuals are robust to outliers. Because of Jensen's inequality, large shocks have a smaller effect on the conditional variance than in the standard GARCH model. Nelson and Foster (1994) show that a GARCH extension of the Taylor/Schwert model is a consistent estimator of the near diffusion processes; furthermore, they show that in the presence of leptokurtic distributions the absolute value GARCH is a more efficient filter of the conditional variance than standard GARCH.

The nonlinear GARCH by Higgins and Bera (1992), defined as

$$\sigma_t^\delta = \omega + \alpha_1 |\varepsilon_{t-1}|^\delta + \beta_1 \sigma_{t-1}^\delta, \tag{15.47}$$

can be thought of as an extension of the conditional standard deviation model; it parameterizes the conditional standard deviation raised to the power δ as a function of the lagged conditional standard deviations and the lagged absolute innovations raised to the same power. This formulation obviously reduces to the standard GARCH(p,q) model for $\delta = 2$.

The first nesting model that appeared in the literature was the asymmetric power APGARCH(p,q) by Ding *et al.* (1993); this model is defined as follows:

$$\sigma_t^\delta = \omega + \sum_{i=1}^{q} \alpha_i (|\varepsilon_{t-i}| - \gamma_i \varepsilon_{t-i})^\delta + \sum_{j=1}^{p} \beta_j \sigma_{t-j}^\delta \tag{15.48}$$

where

$$\begin{aligned} &\omega > 0, \quad \delta \geq 0 \\ &\alpha_i \geq 0, \quad -1 < \gamma_i < 1, \quad i = 1, \dots, q \\ &\beta_j \geq 0, \quad j = 1, \dots, p. \end{aligned}$$

This model imposes a Box–Cox transformation of the conditional standard deviation process and the asymmetric absolute residuals. The asymmetric response of volatility to positive and negative 'shocks' is the well-known leverage effect. If we assume the distribution of ε_t is conditionally normal, then the condition for existence of $E[\sigma_t^\delta]$ and $E|\varepsilon_t|^\delta$ is

$$\frac{1}{\sqrt{2\pi}} \sum_{i=1}^{q} \alpha_i \{(1+\gamma_i)^\delta + (1-\gamma_i)^\delta\} 2^{\frac{\delta-1}{2}} \Gamma\left(\frac{\delta+1}{2}\right) + \sum_{j=1}^{p} \beta_j < 1.$$

If this condition is satisfied, then when $\delta \geq 2$ we have ε_t covariance stationary. Karanasos and Kim (2006) study the autocorrelation structure of the general APGARCH(p,q) model. This generalized version of the GARCH model includes seven other models as special cases:

1. ARCH(q) model, just let $\delta = 2$ and $\gamma_i = 0, i = 1, \dots, q, \beta_j = 0, j = 1, \dots, p$.
2. GARCH(p,q) model, just let $\delta = 2$ and $\gamma_i = 0, i = 1, \dots, q$.
3. Taylor (1986), Schwert (1989) conditional standard deviation model, just let $\delta = 1$ and $\gamma_i = 0, i = 1, \dots, q$.
4. GJR-GARCH model, just let $\delta = 2$.

When $\delta = 2$ and $0 \le \gamma_i < 1$:

$$\begin{aligned}\sigma_t^2 &= \omega + \sum_{i=1}^{q} \alpha_i(|\varepsilon_{t-i}| - \gamma_i\varepsilon_{t-i})^2 + \sum_{j=1}^{p} \beta_j\sigma_{t-j}^2 \\ &= \omega + \sum_{i=1}^{q} \alpha_i(|\varepsilon_{t-i}|^2 + \gamma_i^2\varepsilon_{t-i}^2 - 2\gamma_i|\varepsilon_{t-i}|\varepsilon_{t-i}) + \sum_{j=1}^{p} \beta_j\sigma_{t-j}^2,\end{aligned}$$

$$\sigma_t^2 = \begin{cases} \omega + \sum_{i=1}^{q} \alpha_i^2(1+\gamma_i)^2\varepsilon_{t-i}^2 + \sum_{j=1}^{p} \beta_j\sigma_{t-j}^2, & \varepsilon_{t-i} < 0 \\ \omega + \sum_{i=1}^{q} \alpha_i(1-\gamma_i)^2\varepsilon_{t-i}^2 + \sum_{j=1}^{p} \beta_j\sigma_{t-j}^2, & \varepsilon_{t-i} > 0 \end{cases}$$

$$\sigma_t^2 = \omega + \sum_{i=1}^{q} \alpha_i(1-\gamma_i)^2\varepsilon_{t-i}^2 + \sum_{i=1}^{q} \alpha_i\{(1+\gamma_i)^2 - (1-\gamma_i)^2\}S_i^-\varepsilon_{t-i}^2 + \sum_{j=1}^{p} \beta_j\sigma_{t-j}^2,$$

$$\sigma_t^2 = \omega + \sum_{i=1}^{q} \alpha_i(1-\gamma_i)^2\varepsilon_{t-i}^2 + \sum_{j=1}^{p} \beta_j\sigma_{t-j}^2 + \sum_{i=1}^{q} 4\alpha_i\gamma_i S_i^-\varepsilon_{t-i}^2.$$

If we define

$$\begin{aligned}\alpha_i^* &= \alpha_i(1-\gamma_i)^2, \\ \gamma_i^* &= 4\alpha_i\gamma_i\end{aligned}$$

then we have

$$\sigma_t^2 = \omega + \sum_{i=1}^{p} \alpha_i^*\varepsilon_{t-i}^2 + \sum_{j=1}^{q} \beta_j\sigma_{t-j}^2 + \sum_{i=1}^{p} \gamma_i^* S_i^-\varepsilon_{t-i}^2$$

which is the GJR-GARCH model.

When $-1 \le \gamma_i < 0$ we have

$$\sigma_t^2 = \omega + \sum_{i=1}^{q} \alpha_i(|\varepsilon_{t-i}| - \gamma_i\varepsilon_{t-i})^2 + \sum_{j=1}^{p} \beta_j\sigma_{t-j}^2,$$

$$\sigma_t^2 = \begin{cases} \omega + \sum_{i=1}^{q} \alpha_i(1-\gamma_i)^2\varepsilon_{t-i}^2 + \sum_{j=1}^{p} \beta_j\sigma_{t-j}^2, & \varepsilon_{t-i} > 0 \\ \omega + \sum_{i=1}^{q} \alpha_i(1+\gamma_i)^2\varepsilon_{t-i}^2 + \sum_{j=1}^{p} \beta_j\sigma_{t-j}^2, & \varepsilon_{t-i} < 0 \end{cases}$$

$$\sigma_t^2 = \omega + \sum_{i=1}^{q} \alpha_i(1+\gamma_i)^2\varepsilon_{t-i}^2 + \sum_{j=1}^{p} \beta_j\sigma_{t-j}^2 + \sum_{i=1}^{q} \alpha_i\{(1-\gamma_i)^2 - (1+\gamma_i)^2\}S_i^+\varepsilon_{t-i}^2$$
$$= \omega + \sum_{i=1}^{q} \alpha_i(1+\gamma_i)^2\varepsilon_{t-i}^2 + \sum_{j=1}^{p} \beta_j\sigma_{t-j}^2 - \sum_{i=1}^{q} 4\alpha_i\gamma_i S_i^+\varepsilon_{t-i}^2$$

where $S_i^+ = 1 - S_i^-$. Let

$$\alpha_i^* = \alpha_i(1+\gamma_i)^2,$$
$$\gamma_i^* = -4\alpha_i\gamma_i$$

then we have

$$\sigma_t^2 = \omega + \sum_{i=1}^{q} \alpha_i^*\varepsilon_{t-i}^2 + \sum_{j=1}^{p} \beta_j\sigma_{t-j}^2 + \sum_{i=1}^{q} \gamma_i^* S_i^+\varepsilon_{t-i}^2$$

which allows positive shocks to have a stronger effect on volatility.

5. Zakoiän (1994) TARCH model, let $\delta = 1$ and $\beta_j = 0, j = 1, \ldots, p$. We have

$$\sigma_t = \omega + \sum_{i=1}^{q} \alpha_i(|\varepsilon_{t-i}| - \gamma_i\varepsilon_{t-i})$$
$$= \omega + \sum_{i=1}^{q} \alpha_i(1-\gamma_i)\varepsilon_{t-i}^+ - \sum_{i=1}^{q} \alpha_i(1+\gamma_i)\varepsilon_{t-i}^-.$$

Defining

$$\alpha_i^+ = \alpha_i(1-\gamma_i),$$
$$\gamma_i^- = \alpha_i(1+\gamma_i)$$

we have

$$\sigma_t = \omega + \sum_{i=1}^{q} \alpha_i^+\varepsilon_{t-i}^+ - \sum_{i=1}^{q} \gamma_i^-\varepsilon_{t-i}^-.$$

If we let $\beta_j \neq 0, j = 1, \ldots, q$ then we get a more general class of TARCH models.

6. Higgins and Bera (1992) NGARCH model, let $\gamma_i = 0, i = 1, \ldots, p$.

Hentschel (1995) defines the following model:

$$\frac{\sigma_t^\lambda - 1}{\lambda} = \omega + \alpha\sigma_{t-1}^\lambda f^\nu(z_{t-1}) + \beta\frac{\sigma_{t-1}^\lambda - 1}{\lambda} \tag{15.49}$$

where $\lambda > 0$ and

$$f^\nu(z_t) = |z_t - b| - c(z_t - b).$$

The parameter λ determines the shape of the transformations. For $\lambda > 1$ the transformation of σ_t is convex, while for $\lambda < 1$ it is concave. The parameter ν serves to transform the absolute value function $f(\cdot)$. The special cases are obtained by appropriately choosing the parameters λ, ν, b and c. The transformation $f^{\nu}(\cdot)$ controls the impact of shocks, ε_t, on the transformed conditional standard deviation, σ_t. The Box–Cox-type transformation of the σ_t makes it possible to nest a large number of GARCH models by allowing $\lambda \to 0$. In particular, when $\lambda = \nu = 1$ the model becomes

$$\sigma_t = \widetilde{\omega} + \alpha\sigma_{t-1}[|z_{t-1} - b| - c(z_{t-1} - b)] + \beta\sigma_{t-1}, \tag{15.50}$$

which is defined by Hentschel as the absolute value GARCH. A positive value of b causes a rightward shift of the NIC, and so one obtains asymmetry. But asymmetry can also be obtained by a rotation of the NIC. By allowing slopes of different magnitudes on either side of the origin, an NIC of this type also produces an asymmetric variance response. The rotation is governed by the parameter c: $c > 0$ corresponds to a clockwise rotation, which means that negative shocks increase the volatility more than positive shocks. The EGARCH model, the GJR-GARCH model and the threshold model by Zakoiän (1994) feature rotated NICs. When the shift and rotation are combined in one NIC, they can either reinforce or offset each other. The models (of order one) nested in Hentschel's model are:

1. EGARCH model with $\lambda = 0, \nu = 1$, b and c free, using $\lim_{\lambda\to 0}(\sigma_t^{\lambda} - 1)/\lambda = \log\sigma_t$.
2. GJR-GARCH model in (15.37) with $\lambda = \nu = 2$ and $b = 0$ with free c.
3. TGARCH model in (15.39) with $\lambda = \nu = 1, b = 0$.
4. GARCH model in (15.9) with $\lambda = \nu = 2$ and $b = c = 0$.
5. NAGARCH model in (15.36) with $\lambda = \nu = 2$ and $c = 0$. In this model the NIC is shifted to the right by the distance b.
6. APGARCH model in (15.48) with $\lambda = \nu, b = 0$.
7. Nonlinear GARCH in (15.47) with $\lambda = \nu, b = c = 0$.

The GARCH model, the NAGARCH model and the GJR-GARCH model differ only in their restrictions on b and c.

The augmented GARCH model by Duan (1997) is based on an auxiliary process, which can be loosely interpreted as a Box–Cox transformation of conditional variance. The auxiliary autoregressive process is defined in terms of some transformation of the error component of the observation system. The augmented GARCH(1,1) is defined as:

$$\varepsilon_t = z_t\sigma_t \quad z_t \sim D(0, 1), \tag{15.51}$$

$$\phi_t = \omega + \zeta_{1,t-1}\phi_{t-1} + \zeta_{2,t-1}, \tag{15.52}$$

$$\sigma_t^2 = \begin{cases} |\lambda\phi_t - \lambda - 1|^{1/\lambda} & \text{if } \lambda \neq 0 \\ \exp\{\phi_t - 1\} & \text{if } \lambda = 0 \end{cases} \tag{15.53}$$

where $(\zeta_{1,t}, \zeta_{2,t})$ is a strictly stationary sequence of random vectors with a continuous distribution, measurable with respect to the available information until t. The assumption of continuous distribution is important because it precludes the possibility of assigning a positive mass to the explosion point, that is $\lambda\phi_t - \lambda + 1 = 0$ when $\lambda < 0$. ε_t is an augmented GARCH(1,1) process if it satisfies equations (15.51)–(15.53) and

$$\zeta_{1,t} = \alpha_1 + \alpha_2|\varepsilon_t - c|^\delta + \alpha_3 \max(0, c - \varepsilon_t)^\delta, \tag{15.54}$$

$$\zeta_{2,t} = \alpha_4 \frac{|\varepsilon_t - c|^\delta - 1}{\delta} + \alpha_5 \frac{\max(0, c - \varepsilon_t)^\delta - 1}{\delta}. \tag{15.55}$$

The function $f(z;\delta) = (z^\delta - 1)/\delta$ for any $\delta \geq 0$ is the Box–Cox transformation so that $f(z;1) = (z-1)$ and $\lim_{\delta\to 0} f(z;\delta) = \ln\delta$. The augmented GARCH(1,1) nests as special cases several GARCH models, like the GARCH(1,1), EGARCH(1,1) and GJR-GARCH(1,1). This process is strictly stationary under a simple sufficiency condition.

He and Teräsvirta (1999) define another family of GARCH models:

$$\sigma_t^{2\delta} = \sum_{i=1}^{q} g(z_{t-i}) + \sum_{i=1}^{p} c_i(z_{t-i})\sigma_{t-i}^{2\delta} \quad \delta > 0, \tag{15.56}$$

where $\{g(z_{t-i})\}$ and $\{c_i(z_{t-i})\}$ are sequences of i.i.d. random variables. The standard GARCH(p,q) model is obtained by setting $g(z_t) = \omega/q$ and $c(z_{t-i}) = \alpha_i z_{t-i}^2 + \beta_i, i = 1, \ldots, q$ in equation (15.56). The GJR-GARCH, the absolute value GARCH, the quadratic GARCH and the power GARCH model belong to this family.

15.8 LONG-MEMORY GARCH MODELS

In applications it often occurs that the estimated sum of the parameters in the GARCH(1,1) model, $\widehat{\alpha}_1 + \widehat{\beta}_1$, is close to unity. In other words, it turns out that an IGARCH(1,1) model provides a reasonable approximation to the time data-generating process. A disturbing fact of IGARCH(1,1) is that this means assuming the unconditional variance of the process to be modelled does not exist. Furthermore, in the IGARCH model the implied effect of a shock for the optimal forecast of the future conditional variance will be to make the corresponding cumulative impulse response weights tend to a nonzero constant, so that the forecasts will increase linearly with the forecast horizon. This implies that the pricing of risky securities, including long-term options and futures contracts, may show extreme dependence on the initial conditions, or the current state of the economy. However, this extreme degree of dependence seems contrary to observed pricing behaviour. Taylor (1986), Dacorogna *et al.* (1993) and Ding *et al.* (1993) all report the presence of apparent long memory in the empirical autocorrelations for absolute and squared returns of various financial asset prices. These studies provide clear-cut evidence in favour of models with autocovariances decaying slowly with the lag as $k^{-\gamma}$, for some $0 < \gamma < 1$.

While the empirical analysis suggests that the long-range dependence is a feature of squared and absolute returns, there is no general agreement on the possible causes of this stylized fact. Granger and Ding (1996) have shown that contemporaneous aggregation of stable GARCH(1,1) processes can result in an aggregate process that exhibits hyperbolically decaying autocorrelations. While this property appears to be consistent with long memory, Zaffaroni (2007) has shown that the autocorrelation function is summable, which is inconsistent with it being classified as a long-memory process. A related argument of Andersen and Bollerslev (1997) shows how the contemporaneous aggregation of weakly dependent information flow processes can produce the property of long memory in volatility. A further justification is provided by Müller *et al.* (1997), who suggest that long memory in volatility can arise from the reaction of short-term dealers to the dynamics of a proxy for the expected volatility trend (coarse volatility), which causes persistence in the higher-frequency volatility (fine volatility) process.

While the above papers were concerned with the underlying causes of long-memory volatility, other studies have essentially been more sceptical about the validity of the finding of the long-memory property in volatility. In particular, it has been suggested that various types of structural change can explain the extreme persistence of volatility, and can also generate a series that appears to have long memory. In particular, Mikosch and Starica (1998) and Granger and Hyung (2004) have presented theoretical and simulation evidence that spurious long memory can be detected from a time series with breaks. Moreover, while Granger and Hyung (2004) have found that an occasional-breaks model provides an inferior forecasting performance compared with a long-memory model for S&P500 absolute returns, for the same series Starica and Granger (2005) have found that a nonstationary model allowing for breaks in the unconditional variance can outperform a long-memory model in forecasting, but not at short horizons. Furthermore, Diebold and Inoue (2001) have shown how Markov switching processes could generate long memory in the conditional mean, while Granger and Teräsvirta (1999) have shown that a process which switches in sign has the characteristics of long memory. The possible occurrence of structural breaks in conditional variance processes, generating extreme persistence of the IGARCH form, was originally suggested by Lamoureux and Lastrapes (1990) and Diebold (1986).

Long-range dependence or long memory (sometimes also referred to as strong dependence or persistence) denotes the property of time series to exhibit persistent behaviour. The concept of long memory was originally developed by Hurst (1951). Long memory can be defined in terms of decay rates of long-lag autocorrelations. In particular, a stationary process has long memory (or long-range dependence) if there exists a real number d and a constant $c_\rho > 0$ such that

$$\lim_{k\to\infty} \frac{\rho(k)}{c_\rho k^{2d-1}} = 1$$

where $\rho(k)$ is the autocorrelation at lag k and d is the long-memory parameter. The autocorrelations of a long-memory process are not summable. A stationary and invertible ARMA process has autocorrelations which are geometrically bounded, that is $|\rho(k)| \leq cm^{-k}$ where $0 < m < 1$ and hence a short memory process. An alternative, although not equivalent, definition of long-range dependence can be given by using the spectral density $f(\lambda)$ of the process:

$$\lim_{\lambda\to 0^+} \frac{f(\lambda)}{c_f|\lambda|^{-2d}} = 1 \quad 0 < c_f < \infty.$$

The spectral density $f(\lambda)$ has a pole and behaves like a constant c_f times λ^{-2d} at the origin. A popular approach to the modelling of long memory is represented by the ARFIMA class introduced by Granger and Joyeux (1980) and Hosking (1981). They generalize the class of ARIMA models by allowing a fractional degree of differencing. In the discrete-time long-memory fractionally integrated $I(d)$ class of processes, the propagation of shocks to the mean occurs at a slow hyperbolic rate of decay as opposed to the extremes of $I(0)$ exponential decay associated with the stationary and invertible ARMA class of processes, or the infinite persistence resulting from an $I(1)$ process. The ARFIMA(k,d,l) class of models for the discrete-time real-valued process $\{y_t\}$ is defined by (see Granger and Joyeux, 1980; Hosking, 1981):

$$a(L)(1-L)^d y_t = b(L)\varepsilon_t, \qquad (15.57)$$

where $a(L)$ and $b(L)$ are polynomials in L of orders k and l, respectively, and $\{\varepsilon_t\}$ is a mean-zero, serially uncorrelated process. All the roots of $a(L)$ and $b(L)$ lie outside the unit circle. The process is defined to be $I(d)$. The fractional differencing operator, $(1-L)^d$, has a binomial expansion. Using a Taylor–MacLaurin expansion in $z=0$:

$$\begin{aligned}(1-z)^d &= 1 - dz + \frac{d(d-1)}{2!}z^2 + \ldots \\ &= \sum_{j=0}^{\infty}\binom{d}{j}(-1)^j z^j\end{aligned}$$

where

$$\binom{d}{j} = \frac{d!}{(d-j)!j!}.$$

The coefficients of the powers of L^j decay slowly, being asymptotically proportional to $j^{-(1+d)}$. Given that

$$\Gamma(j+1) = j! = j\Gamma(j)$$

where $\Gamma(j)$ is the Gamma function:

$$\Gamma(j) = \int_0^{\infty} x^{j-1}\exp(-x)\mathrm{d}x \quad j > 0,$$

we can also write

$$\binom{d}{j} = \frac{d!}{(d-j)!j!} = \frac{\Gamma(j-d)}{\Gamma(-d)\Gamma(j+1)}$$

and it follows that

$$\begin{aligned}(1-L)^d &= \sum_{j=0}^{\infty}\binom{d}{j}(-1)^j z^j \\ &= \sum_{j=0}^{\infty}\frac{\Gamma(j-d)}{\Gamma(-d)\Gamma(j+1)}L^j \\ &= \sum_{j=0}^{\infty}\phi_j L^j \\ &= F(-d,1,1;L),\end{aligned}$$

where $F(-d,1,1;L)$ is the hypergeometric function defined as

$$F(m,n,s;x) = \Gamma(s)\Gamma(m)^{-1}\Gamma(n)^{-1}\sum_{j=0,\infty}\Gamma(m+j)\Gamma(n+j)\Gamma(s+j)^{-1}\Gamma(j+1)^{-1}x^j.$$

Provided that $\mathrm{Var}(\varepsilon_t) < \infty$ and $-0.5 < d < 0.5$, the $\{y_t\}$ process is weakly stationary and invertible and will possess unique infinite moving average and autoregressive representations. For $d < 1$ the process is mean reverting. While for $1/2 < d < 1$, y_t will not be covariance stationary it will nevertheless still be mean reverting. The ARFIMA model disentangles the short-run and the long-run dynamics, by modelling the short-run behaviour through the conventional ARMA lag polynomials $a(L)$ and $b(L)$ while the long-run characteristics are captured by the fractional differencing parameter d.

15.8.1 The FIGARCH Model

The FIGARCH process, proposed by Baillie *et al.* (1996), combines many of the features of the fractionally integrated process for the mean together with the regular GARCH process for the conditional variance. The FIGARCH model implies a slow hyperbolic rate of decay for the lagged squared innovations in the conditional variance function, although the cumulative impulse response weights associated with the influence of a volatility shock on the optimal forecasts of the future conditional variance eventually tend to zero, a property the model shares with weakly stationary GARCH processes. The FIGARCH model offers a competing view to the one according to which changes in parameters in a GARCH model are the main cause of the slow decay in the autocorrelations. However, the long-memory property (and even the existence of a stationary regime) of FIGARCH has not been established theoretically (see Giraitis *et al.*, 2000). The GARCH(p,q) process is ARMA(m,p) for ε_t^2, where $m = \max(p, q)$:

$$[1 - \alpha(L) - \beta(L)]\varepsilon_t^2 = \omega + [1 - \beta(L)]v_t \qquad (15.58)$$

where $v_t = \{\varepsilon_t - \sigma_t^2\}$ is a martingale difference sequence. In the covariance stationary GARCH model the effect of the past squared innovations on the current conditional variance decays exponentially with the lag length. When the autoregressive polynomial $1 - \alpha(x) - \beta(x)$ contains a unit root, we have the IGARCH(p,q) model which is defined as

$$\phi(L)(1 - L)\varepsilon_t^2 = \omega + [1 - \beta(L)]v_t \qquad (15.59)$$

where

$$\phi(L) \equiv [1 - \alpha(L) - \beta(L)](1 - L)^{-1}$$

is of order $m - 1$, $m = \max(p, q)$. The FIGARCH is simply obtained by replacing the $(1 - L)$ operator with the fractional differencing operator. Analogously to the ARFIMA(k,d,l) process for the mean, the FIGARCH(p,d,q) for $\{\varepsilon_t\}$ is naturally defined by

$$\phi(L)(1 - L)^d\varepsilon_t^2 = \omega + [1 - \beta(L)]v_t \qquad (15.60)$$

where $0 < d < 1$ and all the roots of $\phi(L)$ and $[1 - \beta(L)]$ lie outside the unit circle. This means that the process for $\{\varepsilon_t^2\}$ is an ARFIMA($m - 1$,d,p). Given that $v_t \equiv \varepsilon_t^2 - \sigma_t^2$, an alternative representation for the FIGARCH(p,d,q) model is

$$[1 - \beta(L)]\sigma_t^2 = \omega + [1 - \beta(L) - \phi(L)(1 - L)^d]\varepsilon_t^2, \qquad (15.61)$$

$$\sigma_t^2 = [1 - \beta(1)]^{-1}\omega + \lambda(L)\varepsilon_t^2 \qquad (15.62)$$

where

$$\lambda(L) \equiv 1 - [1 - \beta(L)]^{-1}\phi(L)(1 - L)^d \tag{15.63}$$

and $\lambda(L) = \lambda_1 L + \lambda_2 L^2 + \lambda_3 L^3 + \ldots$ The FIGARCH(p,d,q) is well defined and $\sigma_t^2 > 0$, a.s. $\forall t$, if all the coefficients in the infinite ARCH representation are non-negative, that is $\lambda_k > 0$ for $k = 0, 1, 2, \ldots$ For $0 < d \leq 1$ the $F(-d, 1, 1, ; L = 1) = 0$, so that $\lambda(1) = 1$. Consequently, the second moment of the unconditional distribution of ε_t is infinite and the FIGARCH process is not weakly stationary, a feature it shares with the IGARCH class of processes. Baillie *et al.* (1996) argue that since the higher-order lag coefficients in the infinite ARCH representation of any FIGARCH model may be dominated in absolute value sense by the corresponding IGARCH coefficients, it follows that the FIGARCH(p,d,q) class of processes is strictly stationary and ergodic for $0 \leq d \leq 1$.

However, the proof of existence of a stationary solution to (15.62) given in Baillie *et al.* (1996) does not seem to be correct (see Giraitis *et al.*, 2007). The question of the existence of a stationary solution to the FIGARCH equation (the 'FIGARCH problem') is open at present and seems very hard to solve. See Giraitis *et al.* (2000), Mikosch and Starica (2000, 2003) for discussion and controversies surrounding the FIGARCH case. The FIGARCH(p,d,q) model nests the covariance-stationary GARCH(p,q) model for $d = 0$ and the IGARCH(p,q) model for $d = 1$. Allowing for values of d in the interval between zero and unity gives an added flexibility that may be important when modelling long-term dependence in the conditional variance.

Considerable care should be exercised in interpreting persistence in nonlinear models. In this context, in which the conditional variance is parameterized as a linear function of past ε_t^2, the persistence is simply characterized in terms of the impulse response coefficients for the optimal forecast of the future conditional variance as a function of the time t innovation, v_t:

$$\gamma_k \equiv \frac{\partial E_t\left[\varepsilon_{t+k}^2\right]}{\partial v_t} - \frac{E_t\left[\varepsilon_{t+k-1}^2\right]}{\partial v_t}.$$

In more general conditional variance models the γ_i's will depend on the time t information set. For the FIGARCH models the impulse response coefficients are independent of t. The impulse response coefficients may be found from the coefficients in the $\gamma(L)$ lag polynomial:

$$\begin{aligned}(1 - L)\varepsilon_t^2 &= (1 - L)^{1-d}\phi(L)^{-1}\omega + (1 - L)^{1-d}\phi(L)^{-1}[1 - \beta(L)]v_t \\ &\equiv \zeta + \gamma(L)v_t.\end{aligned} \tag{15.64}$$

The long-run impact of past shocks for the volatility process may now be assessed in terms of the limit of the cumulative impulse response weights. In fact

$$\sum_{i=0}^{k} \gamma_i = \sum_{i=0}^{k} \left[\frac{\partial E_t\left(\varepsilon_{t+i}^2\right)}{\partial v_t} - \frac{E_t\left(\varepsilon_{t+i-1}^2\right)}{\partial v_t}\right] = \frac{\partial E_t\left(\varepsilon_{t+k}^2\right)}{\partial v_t}, \tag{15.65}$$

but

$$\lambda_k = \frac{\partial E_t\left(\varepsilon_{t+k}^2\right)}{\partial v_t}$$

then

$$\begin{aligned} \gamma(1) &= \lim_{k\to\infty} \sum_{i=0}^{k} \gamma_i = \lim_{k\to\infty} \lambda_k \\ &= F(d-1,1,1;1)\phi(1)^{-1}[1-\beta(1)]. \end{aligned} \tag{15.66}$$

For the covariance-stationary GARCH(p,q) model and the FIGARCH(p,d,q) model with $0 < d < 1$, shocks to the conditional variance will ultimately die out in a forecasting sense. Whereas shocks to the GARCH process die out at a fast exponential rate, for the FIGARCH model λ_k will eventually be dominated by a hyperbolic rate of decay. Thus, even though the cumulative impulse response function converges to zero for $0 \le d < 1$, the fractional differencing parameter provides important information regarding the pattern and speed with which shocks to the volatility process are propagated.

In contrast, for $d = 1$, $F(d-1,1,1;1) = 1$; the cumulative impulse response weights will converge to the nonzero constant $\gamma(1) = \phi(1)^{-1}[1-\beta(1)]$. Thus, from a forecasting perspective, shocks to σ_t^2 of the IGARCH model persist indefinitely. For $d > 1$, $F(d-1,1,1;1) = \infty$, resulting in an unrealistic explosive conditional variance process and $\gamma(1)$ being undefined.

As an example, consider the GARCH(1,1) model

$$\sigma_t^2 = \omega + \alpha_1\varepsilon_{t-1}^2 + \beta\sigma_{t-1}^2$$

in ARMA form

$$(1-\phi_1 L)\varepsilon_t^2 = \omega + (1-\beta_1 L)v_t$$

where $\phi_1 \equiv \alpha_1 + \beta_1$. The impulse response weights for this model are given by the coefficients in the polynomial

$$\gamma(L) = (1-L)(1-\phi_1 L)^{-1}(1-\beta_1 L)$$

where

$$\begin{aligned} \gamma_0 &= 1, \\ \gamma_1 &= \phi_1 - \beta_1 - 1, \\ \gamma_k &= (\phi_1 - \beta_1)(\phi_1 - 1)\phi^{k-2}, \quad k > 2. \end{aligned}$$

The cumulative impulse response weights equal

$$\lambda_k = (\phi_1 - \beta_1)\phi_1^{k-1}, \quad k > 1$$

and in the limit $\gamma(1) = 0$, provided that $0 < \phi_1 < 1$. Hence, the effect of a shock to the forecast of the future conditional variance tends to zero at a fast exponential rate. In the IGARCH(1,1) model, that is $\phi_1 = 1$,

$$(1-L)\varepsilon_t^2 = \omega + (1-\beta_1 L)v_t$$

the coefficients of $\lambda(L)$ are given by

$$\lambda_k = (1 - \beta_1), \quad \forall k > 1;$$

the cumulative impulse response weights equal the nonzero constant $\gamma(1) = 1 - \beta_1$. The FIGARCH(1,d,0) model is

$$(1 - \phi_1 L)^d \varepsilon_t^2 = \omega + (1 - \beta_1 L)v_t.$$

It is possible to show that the cumulative response coefficients in the infinite ARCH representation for the FIGARCH(1,d,0) model

$$\lambda(L) \equiv 1 - (1 - \beta_1 L)^{-1}(1 - L)^d$$

equal

$$\lambda_k = [1 - \beta_1 - (1 - d)k^{-1}]\Gamma(k + d - 1)\Gamma(k)^{-1}\Gamma(d)^{-1}$$

for $k > 1$ and $\lambda_0 = 1$. Thus, provided that $\omega > 0$, the condition $0 \leq \beta_1 < d \leq 1$ is both necessary and sufficient to ensure that the conditional variance in the FIGARCH(1,d,0) model is positive a.s. for all t. Furthermore it follows (by Sterling's formula) that for high lags k,

$$\lambda_k = [(1 - \beta_1)\Gamma(d)^{-1}]k^{d-1}.$$

In contrast to the covariance-stationary GARCH(1,1) model or the IGARCH(1,1) model, where shocks to the conditional variance either dissipate exponentially or persist indefinitely, for the FIGARCH(1,d,0) model the response of the conditional variance to past shocks decays at a slow hyperbolic rate.

15.8.2 The FIEGARCH Model

As the estimates of the standard GARCH(p,q) model often indicate an approximate unit root in the autoregressive polynomial, when estimating the EGARCH(p,q) model in (15.34) the largest root of the estimated polynomial $1 - \widehat{\beta}(x)$ is very close to unity. However, as noted by Nelson (1991), the EGARCH(p,q) model could be extended to allow for fractional orders of integration also. Bollerslev and Mikkelsen (1996) factorize the autoregressive polynomial $[1 - \beta(L)] = \phi(L)(1 - L)^d$ where all roots of $\phi(x) = 0$ lie outside the unit circle, so that the model may be written as

$$\ln(\sigma_t^2) = \omega + \phi(L)^{-1}(1 - L)^{-d}[1 + \alpha(L)]g(z_{t-1}) \qquad (15.67)$$

where $\alpha(L) = \alpha_1 L + \alpha_2 L^2 + \ldots + \alpha_q L^q$. The FIEGARCH($p$,$d$,$q$) formulation obviously nests the conventional EGARCH model for $d = 0$ and the integrated EGARCH model for $d = 1$. By analogy to the ARFIMA class of models for the conditional mean, $\{\ln(\sigma_t^2)\}$ is covariance stationary and invertible for d in the interval between -0.5 and 0.5. Shocks to the optimal forecasts for future values of $\ln(\sigma_t^2)$ will dissipate for all values of $d < 1$. Moreover, in contrast to the FIGARCH formulation, the parameters for the FIEGARCH do not have to satisfy any non-negativity constraints in order for the model to be well defined.

15.9 ESTIMATION

In comparison with other volatility models (e.g., standard stochastic volatility model) GARCH models are simpler to estimate, which has greatly contributed to their popularity. The volatility being a function of the past observations, the likelihood function has an explicit form which makes it easy to handle (see Francq and Zakoïan, 2009). Least-squares and quasi-maximum-likelihood estimations in ARCH models were considered in the seminal paper by Engle (1982). The asymptotic properties of the quasi-maximum-likelihood estimator (QMLE) has received broad interest in the last 20 years. The first papers limited their scope to ARCH (see Weiss, 1986) or GARCH(1,1) models (Lee and Hansen, 1994; Lumsdaine, 1996). The QMLE of the general GARCH(p,q) model is studied in Berkes and Horváth (2003, 2004), Berkes *et al.* (2003), Francq and Zakoïan (2004) and Hall and Yao (2003). Straumann (2005) presents a comprehensive monograph on the estimation of GARCH models.

15.9.1 Likelihood Computation

The procedure most often used in estimating $\theta_0 \in \Theta$ in ARCH models involves the maximization of a likelihood function constructed under the auxiliary assumption of an i.i.d. distribution for the standardized innovation $z_t(\theta)$. Let $f(z_t(\theta); \eta)$ denote the density function for $z_t(\theta) \equiv \varepsilon_t(\theta)/\sigma_t(\theta)$, with mean zero and variance one, where η is the nuisance parameter, $\eta \in H \subseteq R^k$. Let $(y_T, y_{T-1}, \ldots, y_1)$ be a sample realization from an ARCH model as defined by equations (15.1) to (15.5), and $\psi' \equiv (\theta', \eta')$ the combined $(m+k) \times 1$ parameter vector to be estimated for the conditional mean, variance and density functions. The log-likelihood function for the tth observation is then given by

$$l_t(y_t; \psi) = \ln\{f[z_t(\theta); \eta]\} - \frac{1}{2}\ln\left[\sigma_t^2(\theta)\right] \qquad t = 1, 2, \ldots \tag{15.68}$$

The term $-\frac{1}{2}\ln[\sigma_t^2(\theta)]$ on the right-hand side is the Jacobian that arises in the transformation from the standardized innovations, $z_t(\theta)$, to the observables y_t ($f(y_t; \psi) = f(z_t(\theta); \eta)|J|$, where $J = \frac{\partial z_t}{\partial y_t} = \frac{1}{\sigma_t(\theta)}$). The conditional log-likelihood function for the full sample equals the sum of the conditional log likelihoods in (15.68):

$$L_T(y_T, y_{T-1}, \ldots, y_1; \psi) = \sum_{t=1}^{T} l_t(y_t; \psi). \tag{15.69}$$

The maximum likelihood estimator for the true parameters $\psi_0' \equiv \left(\theta_0', \eta_0'\right)$, say $\widehat{\psi}_T$, is found by the maximization of equation (15.69). Assuming the conditional density and the $\mu_t(\theta)$ and $\sigma_t^2(\theta)$ functions to be differentiable for all $\psi \in \Theta \times H \equiv \Psi$, the maximum likelihood estimator is the solution to

$$S_T(y_T, y_{T-1}, \ldots, y_1; \widehat{\psi}) \equiv \sum_{t=1}^{T} s_t(y_t; \widehat{\psi}) = 0 \tag{15.70}$$

where $s_t \equiv \frac{\partial l_t(y_t,\psi)}{\partial \psi}$ is the score vector for the tth observation. In particular, for the conditional mean and variance parameters

$$\frac{\partial l_t(y_t,\psi)}{\partial \theta} = f[z_t(\theta);\eta]^{-1} f'[z_t(\theta);\eta]\frac{\partial z_t(\theta)}{\partial \theta} - \frac{1}{2}\left[\sigma_t^2(\theta)\right]^{-1}\frac{\partial \sigma_t^2}{\partial \theta} \tag{15.71}$$

where $f'[z_t(\theta);\eta] \equiv \frac{\partial f(z_t(\theta);\eta)}{\partial z_t}$ and

$$\frac{\partial z_t(\theta)}{\partial \theta} = \frac{\partial}{\partial \theta}\left(\frac{\varepsilon_t(\theta)}{\sqrt{\sigma_t^2}}\right) = \frac{-\frac{\partial \mu_t}{\partial \theta}\sqrt{\sigma_t^2} - \frac{1}{2}\left(\sigma_t^2\right)^{-1/2}\frac{\partial \sigma_t^2}{\partial \theta}\varepsilon_t(\theta)}{\sigma_t^2}$$

$$= -\frac{\partial \mu_t}{\partial \theta}\left(\sigma_t^2(\theta)\right)^{-1/2} - \frac{1}{2}\left(\sigma_t^2(\theta)\right)^{-3/2}\frac{\partial \sigma_t^2}{\partial \theta}\varepsilon_t(\theta)$$

where

$$\varepsilon_t(\theta) \equiv y_t - \mu_t(\theta).$$

In practice, the solution to the set of $m + k$ nonlinear equations in (15.70) is found by numerical optimization techniques.

In order to implement the maximum likelihood procedure, one needs to make an explicit assumption regarding the conditional density in equation (15.68). The most commonly employed distribution in the literature is the normal:

$$f[z_t(\theta);\eta] = (2\pi)^{-1/2}\exp\left\{-\frac{z_t(\theta)^2}{2}\right\}.$$

Since the normal distribution is uniquely determined by its first two moments, only the conditional mean and variance parameters enter the log-likelihood function in equation (15.69); that is, $\psi = \theta$. The log-likelihood for the tth observation is

$$l_t(\theta) = -\frac{1}{2}\ln(2\pi) - \frac{1}{2}z_t(\theta)^2 - \frac{1}{2}\ln\left(\sigma_t^2\right).$$

It follows that the score vector in (15.71) takes the form

$$s_t = -z_t\frac{\partial z_t}{\partial \theta} - \frac{1}{2}\left(\sigma_t^2(\theta)\right)^{-1}\frac{\partial\left(\sigma_t^2(\theta)\right)}{\partial \theta}$$

$$= \frac{\partial \mu_t(\theta)}{\partial \theta}\frac{\varepsilon_t(\theta)}{\sigma_t^2(\theta)} + \frac{1}{2}\left(\sigma_t^2(\theta)\right)^{-1}\frac{\partial \sigma_t^2(\theta)}{\partial \theta}\left[\frac{\varepsilon_t^2(\theta)}{\sigma_t^2(\theta)} - 1\right]. \tag{15.72}$$

As discussed in McCullough and Renfro (1999) and Brooks *et al.* (2001), there are several practical issues to consider in the maximization of the Gaussian log-likelihood:

$$L_T(y_T, y_{T-1}, \ldots, y_1; \theta) = \sum_{t=1}^{T} l_t(\theta)$$
$$= -\frac{T}{2}\ln(2\pi) - \frac{1}{2}\sum_{t=1}^{T}\frac{\varepsilon_t^2(\theta)}{\sigma_t^2(\theta)} - \frac{1}{2}\sum_{t=1}^{T}\ln\left(\sigma_t^2(\theta)\right). \qquad (15.73)$$

The conditional log-likelihood in (15.73) is used in practice since the unconditional distribution of the initial values is not known in closed form (Diebold and Schuermann, 1993 gave a computationally intensive numerical procedure for approximating the exact log-likelihood). When $\sigma_t^2(\theta)$ is modelled as a GARCH(p,q), starting values for the model parameters ω, α_i, $i = 1, \ldots, q$ and β_j, $j = 1, \ldots, p$ need to be chosen and an initialization of σ_t^2 and ε_t^2 must be supplied. If for simplicity $E_{t-1}[y_t] = \mu$, the sample mean of y_t is usually used as the starting value for μ, zero values are often given for the conditional variance parameters other than ω and α_1, and ω is set equal to the unconditional variance of y_t. For the initial values of σ_t^2 a possible choice is

$$\sigma_t^2 = \varepsilon_t^2 = \frac{1}{T}\sum_{t=1}^{T}\varepsilon_s^2 \quad t \leq 0,$$

where the initial values for ε_s are computed as the residuals from a regression of y_t on a constant. Once the log-likelihood is initialized, it can be maximized using numerical optimization techniques.

15.10 INFERENCE

15.10.1 Testing for ARCH Effects

Testing for the presence of ARCH effects has been considered extensively in the literature. A simple and frequently used test for the null hypothesis

$$H_0 : \alpha_1 = \alpha_2 = \ldots = \alpha_q = 0$$

against the alternative

$$H_1 : \alpha_1 \geq 0, \alpha_2 \geq 0, \ldots, \alpha_q \geq 0$$

with at least one strict inequality is the Lagrange multiplier (LM) test proposed by Engle (1982). The test is based upon the score and information matrix under the null computed assuming that the standardized innovation z_t is Gaussian distributed. When normality is assumed, an asymptotically equivalent statistic would be TR^2 where R^2 is the squared multiple correlation of the regression of $\widehat{\varepsilon}_t^2$ on an intercept and q lagged values of $\widehat{\varepsilon}_t^2$. The statistic will be asymptotically distributed as chi-square with q degrees of freedom when the null hypothesis is true. This will be an asymptotically locally most powerful test.

Lumsdaine and Ng (1999), however, argue that the LM test may reject if there is general misspecification in the conditional mean equation (15.10). They show that such misspecification causes the estimated residuals $\widehat{\varepsilon}_t$ to be serially correlated which, in turn, causes $\widehat{\varepsilon}_t^2$ to be serially correlated. Therefore, care should be exercised in specifying the conditional mean equation (15.10) prior to testing for ARCH effects.

Lee and King (1993) derive a locally most mean powerful (LMMP)-based score test for the presence of ARCH and GARCH disturbances. The test is based on the sum of the scores evaluated at the null hypothesis and nuisance parameters replaced by their ML estimates. In the absence of nuisance parameters, the test is LMMP. The sum of the scores is then standardized by dividing by its large sample standard error. The resulting test statistic has an asymptotic $N(0, 1)$ distribution. The test statistics used to test against an ARCH(q) process can also be used to test against a GARCH(p,q) process. In small samples, the test appears to have better power than the LM test and its asymptotic critical values were found to be at least as accurate.

Wald and likelihood ratio (LR) criteria could be used to test the hypothesis of conditional homoscedasticity, for example against a GARCH(1,1) alternative. The statistic associated with $H_0 : \alpha_1 = \beta_1 = 0$ against $H_1 : \alpha_1 \geq 0$ or $\beta_1 \geq 0$, with at least one strict inequality, does not have a χ^2 distribution with two degrees of freedom as the standard assumption that the true parameter value under H_0 does not lie on the border of the parameter space does not hold.

15.10.2 Test for Asymmetric Effects

If a negative return shock causes more volatility than a positive return shock of the same size, the GARCH model underpredicts the amount of volatility following bad news and overpredicts the amount of volatility following good news. Furthermore, if large return shocks cause more volatility than a quadratic function allows, then the standard GARCH model underpredicts volatility after a large return shock and overpredicts volatility after a small return shock.

Engle and Ng (1993) put forward three diagnostic tests for volatility models: the *sign bias test*, the *negative size bias test* and the *positive size bias test*. These tests examine whether we can predict the squared normalized residual by some variables observed in the past which are not included in the volatility model being used. If these variables can predict the squared normalized residual, then the variance model is misspecified. The sign bias test examines the impact of positive and negative return shocks on volatility not predicted by the model under consideration. The negative size bias test focuses on the different effects that large and small negative return shocks have on volatility which are not predicted by the volatility model. The positive size bias test focuses on the different impacts that large and small positive return shocks may have on volatility, which are not explained by the volatility model.

To derive the optimal form of these tests, we assume that the volatility model under the null hypothesis is a special case of a more general model of the following form:

$$\log\left(\sigma_t^2\right) = \log\left(\sigma_{0t}^2(\delta_0' z_{0t})\right) + \delta_a' z_{at} \tag{15.74}$$

where $\sigma_{0t}^2(\delta_0' z_{0t})$ is the volatility model hypothesized under the null, δ_0 is a $(k \times 1)$ vector of parameters under the null, z_{0t} is a $(k \times 1)$ vector of explanatory variables under the null, δ_a is an $(m \times 1)$ vector of additional parameters, z_{at} is an $(m \times 1)$ vector of missing explanatory variables.

This form encompasses both the GARCH and EGARCH models. For the GARCH(1,1) model

$$\sigma^2_{0t}(\delta_0' z_{0t}) = \delta_0' z_{0t},$$
$$z_{0t} \equiv \left[1, \sigma^2_{t-1}, \varepsilon^2_{t-1}\right]',$$
$$\delta_0 \equiv [\omega, \beta, \alpha]',$$
$$\delta_a = [\beta^*, \phi^*, \psi^*]',$$
$$z_{at} = \left[\log\left(\sigma^2_{t-1}\right), \frac{\varepsilon_{t-1}}{\sigma_{t-1}}, \left(\frac{|\varepsilon_{t-1}|}{\sigma_{t-1}} - \sqrt{2/\pi}\right)\right]'.$$

The encompassing model is

$$\log\left(\sigma_t^2\right) = \log\left[\omega + \beta\sigma^2_{t-1} + \alpha\varepsilon^2_{t-1}\right] + \beta^* \log\left(\sigma^2_{t-1}\right) + \phi^* \frac{\varepsilon_{t-1}}{\sigma_{t-1}} + \psi^* \left(\frac{|\varepsilon_{t-1}|}{\sigma_{t-1}} - \sqrt{2/\pi}\right)$$

when $\alpha = \beta = 0$ is an EGARCH(1,1) while with $\beta^* = \phi^* = \psi^* = 0$ it is a GARCH(1,1) model.

The null hypothesis is $\delta_a = 0$. Let z_t be the normalized residual corresponding to observation t under the volatility model hypothesized. That is, $z_t \equiv \frac{\varepsilon_t}{\sigma_t}$. The LM test statistic for $H_0 : \delta_a = 0$ in (15.74) is a test of $\delta_a = 0$ in the auxiliary regression

$$z_t^2 = z^{*\prime}_{0t}\delta_0 + z^{*\prime}_{at}\delta_a + u_t \tag{15.75}$$

where $z^*_{0t} \equiv \sigma^{-2}_{0t}(\frac{\partial\sigma^2_t}{\partial\delta_0})$, $z^*_{at} \equiv \sigma^{-2}_{0t}(\frac{\partial\sigma^2_t}{\partial\delta_a})$. Both $\frac{\partial\sigma^2_t}{\partial\delta_0}$ and $\frac{\partial\sigma^2_t}{\partial\delta_a}$ are evaluated at $\delta_a = 0$ and δ_0 (the maximum likelihood estimator of δ_0 under H_0). If the parameter restrictions are met, the right-hand-side variables in (15.75) should have no explanatory variables power at all.[3] Thus, the test is often computed as

$$\xi_{LM} = TR^2$$

where R^2 is the squared multiple correlation of (15.75) and T is the number of observations in the sample. The LM statistic is asymptotically distributed as a chi-square with m degrees of freedom when the null hypothesis is true, where m is the number of parameter restrictions. Under the encompassing model (15.74), $(\frac{\partial\sigma^2_t}{\partial\delta_a})$ evaluated under the null is equal to[4] $\sigma^2_{0t}z_{at}$, hence $z^*_{at} = z_{at}$ and $z^*_{0t} = z_{0t}/\sigma^2_t$. The regression actually involves regressing z_t^2 on a constant z^*_{0t} and z_{at}.

[3]However, for highly nonlinear models, the numerical optimization algorithm generally does not guarantee exact orthogonality of v_t^2 to z^*_{0t}. Engle and Ng (1993) propose regressing y_t^2 on z_{0t} alone, and use the residuals from this regression (which are now guaranteed to be orthogonal to z_{0t}) in place of v_t^2 in (15.75).

[4]In fact,

$$\sigma_t^2 = \sigma^2_{0t}(\delta_0' z_{0t})\exp(\delta_a' z_{at}),$$
$$\frac{\partial\sigma^2_t}{\partial\delta_a} = \sigma^2_{0t}z_{at}\exp(\delta_a' z_{at})$$

under the null, $\delta_a = 0$, $\frac{\partial\sigma^2_t}{\partial\delta_a} = \sigma^2_{0t}z_{at}$.

In practice, variables in z_{at} have to be chosen to test the presence of asymmetric effects. Engle and Ng (1993) propose a series of complementary tests based on the variables S_{t-1}, $S_{t-1}^{-}\varepsilon_{t-1}$ and $S_{t-1}^{+}\varepsilon_{t-1}$. The optimal form for conducting the *sign bias test* is

$$\hat{z}_t^2 = a + b_1 S_{t-1}^{-} + \gamma' z_{0t}^{*} + e_t$$

where $\hat{z}_t = \hat{\varepsilon}_t/\hat{\sigma}_t$ and $S_{t-1}^{-} = \mathrm{I}(\varepsilon_t < 0)$. The regression for the *negative size bias test* is

$$\hat{z}_t^2 = a + b_2 S_{t-1}^{-}\varepsilon_{t-1} + \gamma' z_{0t}^{*} + e_t$$

and for the *positive size bias test*

$$\hat{z}_t^2 = a + b_3 S_{t-1}^{+}\varepsilon_{t-1} + \gamma' z_{0t}^{*} + e_t$$

with $S_{t-1}^{+} = 1 - S_{t-1}^{-}$. The t-ratios for b_1, b_2 and b_3 are the sign bias, the negative size bias and the positive size bias test statistics, respectively. The joint test is obtained by adding the three variables in the variance equation (15.74) under the maintained specification:

$$\hat{z}_t^2 = a + b_1 S_{t-1}^{-} + b_2 S_{t-1}^{-}\varepsilon_{t-1} + b_3 S_{t-1}^{+}\varepsilon_{t-1} + \gamma' z_{0t}^{*} + e_t.$$

The test statistic is TR^2. If the volatility model is correct then $b_1 = b_2 = b_3 = 0$, $\gamma = 0$ and e_t is i.i.d. If z_{0t}^{*} is not included the test will be conservative; the size will be less than or equal to the nominal size and the power may be reduced.

15.11 MULTIVARIATE GARCH

Economics and finance present problems (e.g., the standard portfolio allocation problem, the risk management of a portfolio of assets, the pricing of derivative contracts based on more than one underlying asset, etc.) whose solutions need the specification and estimation of a multivariate distribution. In particular, the object of interest is often the conditional covariance matrix. The N-vector of asset returns r_t has a conditional distribution

$$r_t|\Phi_{t-1} \sim D(0, \Sigma_t) \quad t = 1, \ldots, T \tag{15.76}$$

where D is a continuous distribution. Σ_t is the conditional variance–covariance matrix assumed to be time-varying. Any multivariate volatility model has to ensure that the diagonal elements of Σ_t are strictly positive and that Σ_t is positive definite. The literature puts forward different parameterizations.

Firstly, one desirable feature of any parameterization is the feasibility of the estimation for increasing N, that is the number of assets. Unfortunately, this is not always the case. Secondly, any model specification should be general enough to allow for covariance spillovers and feedbacks. We can classify the existing multivariate GARCH models into three main strands:

1. direct generalizations of the univariate GARCH model of Bollerslev (1986) (VEC, BEKK and factor models);
2. linear combinations of univariate GARCH models ((generalized) orthogonal models and latent factor models);
3. nonlinear combinations of univariate GARCH models (constant and dynamic conditional correlation (DCC) models, copula-GARCH models).

Here we present only two alternative specifications, the BEKK and the DCC models, which can be considered benchmarks. The BEKK model specifies the conditional covariance matrix directly, whereas the DCC focuses on the conditional correlation matrix.

15.11.1 BEKK Parameterization of MGARCH

The BEKK (from 'Baba, Engle Kraft and Kroner'; see Engle and Kroner, 1995) representation of a multivariate GARCH(1,1) model is

$$\Sigma_t = CC' + Ar_{t-1}r'_{t-1}A' + B\Sigma_{t-1}B', \tag{15.77}$$

where C is a lower-triangular matrix. Given that Σ_0 is positive definite and either C or B are full rank, the parameterization guarantees the positive definiteness of the conditional variance matrix Σ_t; see Engle and Kroner (1995). Obvious restrictions are to assume that the matrices A and B are diagonal or scalar.

15.11.2 The Dynamic Conditional Correlation Model

In the *dynamic conditional correlation* GARCH, introduced by Engle (2002a), the conditional variance–covariance matrix is written as

$$\Sigma_t = H_t R_t H_t \quad t = 1, \ldots, T$$

where R_t is the conditional correlation matrix and the standardized returns are defined as

$$\varepsilon_t = H_t^{-1} r_t \quad t = 1, \ldots, T$$

where $H_t = \text{diag}\{\sigma_{1t}, \ldots, \sigma_{Nt}\}$ with

$$\sigma_{it} = \text{Var}_{t-1}[r_{it}]^{1/2} \quad i = 1, \ldots, N \quad t = 1, \ldots, T$$

with the σ_{it}^2 modelled as univariate GARCH processes. The conditional variance–covariance matrix of ε_t is the conditional correlation matrix of the asset returns:

$$\mathbb{E}_{t-1}(\varepsilon_t \varepsilon'_t) = H_t^{-1}\Sigma_t H_t^{-1} = R_t = \{\rho_{ij,t}\} \quad t = 1, \ldots, T$$

with

$$\rho_{ij,t} = \frac{q_{ij,t}}{\sqrt{q_{ii,t}q_{jj,t}}},$$

where the q_{ij} are modelled as

$$q_{ij,t} = \overline{\rho}_{ij} + \alpha(\varepsilon_{i,t-1}\varepsilon_{j,t-1} - \overline{\rho}_{ij}) + \beta(q_{ij,t-1} - \overline{\rho}_{ij}). \tag{15.78}$$

In matrix form:

$$Q_t = (1 - A - B)\overline{Q} + A(\varepsilon_{t-1}\varepsilon'_{t-1}) + B(Q_{t-1}), \tag{15.79}$$

where $\overline{Q}$ is estimated by $S = \frac{1}{T}\sum_t \widehat{\varepsilon}_t\widehat{\varepsilon}'_t$ and A and B are two scalars. The matrix $Q_t = \{q_{ij,t}\}$ is positive definite as long as it is a weighted average of positive definite and semidefinite matrices. However, Aielli (2011) suggests modifying the standard DCC in order to correct the asymptotic bias, which is due to the fact that $\frac{1}{T}\sum_t \hat{\varepsilon}_t\hat{\varepsilon}_t'$ does not converge to $\overline{Q}$.

Finally, the DCC model specification is:

$$\sigma_{it}^2 = \omega_i + \alpha_i r_{it-1}^2 + \beta_i \sigma_{it-1}^2, \tag{15.80}$$

$$Q_t = (1 - A - B)\overline{Q} + A(\varepsilon_{t-1}\varepsilon_{t-1}') + B(Q_{t-1}), \tag{15.81}$$

$$R_t = \mathrm{diag}\{Q_t\}^{-1/2} Q_t \,\mathrm{diag}\{Q_t\}^{-1/2}. \tag{15.82}$$

15.12 EMPIRICAL APPLICATIONS

15.12.1 Univariate Volatility Modelling

In this section, we illustrate how GARCH models can be employed in the analysis of volatility of commodity returns. The first example is based on the Northern Italy zonal day-ahead electricity prices (PZ Nord) between 2 January 2009 and 28 February, 2013, equalling 1520 daily observations. The Italian day-ahead power market is based on competitive auctions for every hour of delivery during the following day. The Italian market is separated into geographical zones according to the bottlenecks in the transmission grid. The auction algorithm solves a market coupling problem and different zonal prices are observed only in case of congestion in the relevant part of the transmission grid. The daily prices used in this analysis are therefore the arithmetic average of the 24-hourly prices for every calendar day, the so-called daily baseload price.

In Figure 15.4, percentage log-returns are shown. Volatility clustering is evident as long as the presence of extreme movements, in particular in the first part of the sample, is characterized by a tighter supply–demand balance. The descriptive statistics in Table 15.1 depict a series that features kurtosis larger than that of the standard normal density, moderate skewness and the presence of extreme movements.

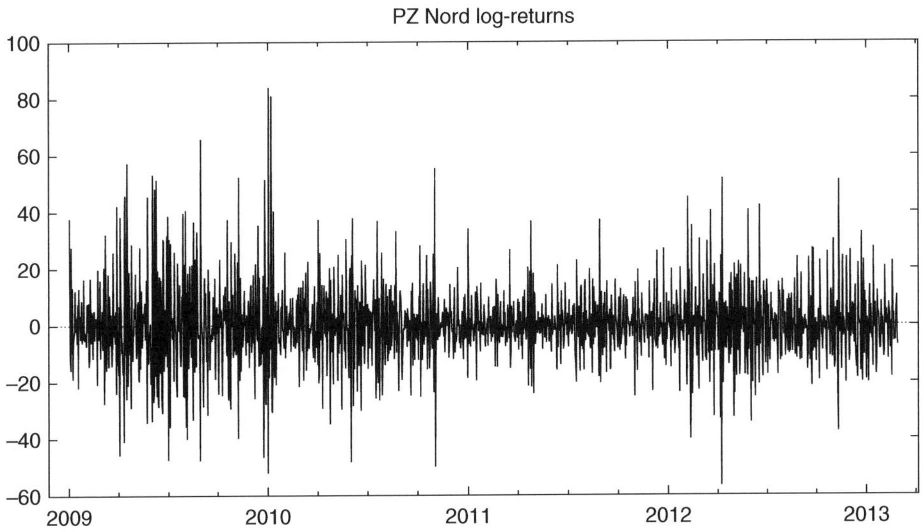

FIGURE 15.4 Daily returns: percentage changes in log-prices

TABLE 15.1 Descriptive statistics of daily percentage log-returns of PZ Nord

	Daily log-returns
Mean	−0.0032
Standard deviation	14.0337
Skewness	0.5959
Kurtosis	6.6182
Max	83.8663
Min	−56.7580

The spectrum estimate in Figure 15.5 illustrates the periodic behaviour of the log-returns. It is evident that three cycles are present with a period of 7, 3.5 and 2.33 days, respectively. This is consistent with the typical periodicity of daily electricity prices, which tend to be lower during weekends.

Thus, the conditional mean of the log-returns (y_t) is found to be well approximated by a multiplicative seasonal ARMA(1,1) × (3,1):

$$(1 - \phi_1 L)(1 - \Phi_1 L^7 - \Phi_2 L^{14} - \Phi_3 L^{21})r_t = c + (1 + \theta_1 L)(1 + \Theta_1 L^7)\varepsilon_t. \quad (15.83)$$

The distributional assumption behind the likelihood function is that the return innovations are conditionally normal. The Gaussian maximum likelihood estimates are reported in Table 15.2. The residuals, that is $\hat{\varepsilon}_t$, turn out to be leptokurtic, as shown by the Q–Q plot displayed in Figure 15.6.

The presence of time-varying conditional heteroscedasticity is also confirmed by the ARCH tests reported in Table 15.2 which clearly reject the null hypothesis of no ARCH effect.

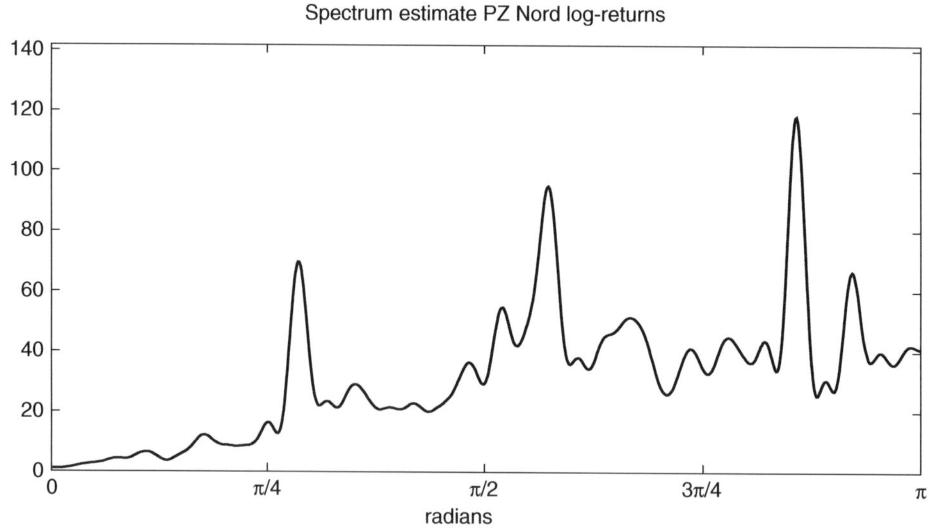

FIGURE 15.5 The estimated spectrum of the daily PZ Nord log-returns (Bartlett window is set to 80)

TABLE 15.2 Maximum likelihood estimates of multiplicative ARMA(1,1) × (3,1) and ARCH test computed with different number of lags (in parentheses)

	Coefficient	Std error	z	p-Value
c	0.002	0.003	0.856	0.392
ϕ_1	0.258	0.027	9.468	0.000
Φ_1	0.977	0.022	44.758	0.000
Φ_2	−0.064	0.026	−2.475	0.013
Φ_3	0.080	0.018	4.403	0.000
θ_1	−0.830	0.016	−50.644	0.000
Θ_1	−0.953	0.008	−124.924	0.000
ARCH(7)	153.513			0.000
ARCH(10)	175.397			0.000
ARCH(14)	191.743			0.000
ARCH(21)	197.538			0.000

The estimated spectrum of the multiplicative seasonal ARMA-squared residuals as specified in (15.83) is displayed in Figure 15.7. The peak in correspondence of frequency zero can be the outcome of long-range dependence. Further, there is also evidence of a seasonal component with a period of 7 days. Thus, we consider alternative specifications of the conditional variance in order to evaluate which model can capture the salient features of the data at hand.

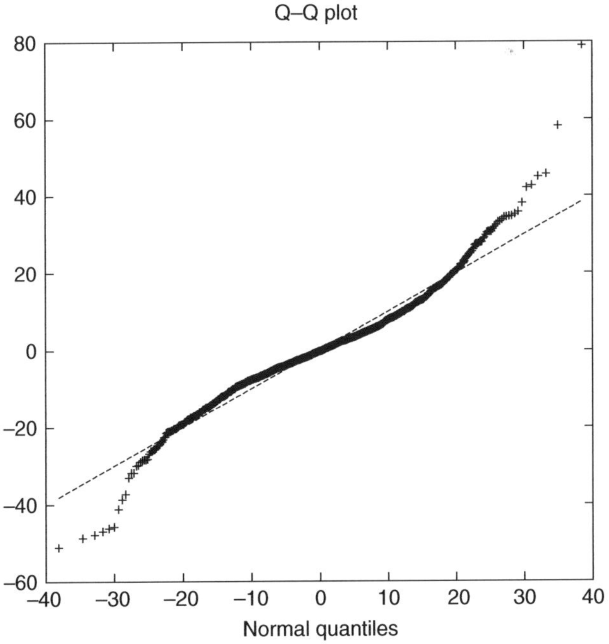

FIGURE 15.6 Q–Q plot of the residuals of the multiplicative seasonal ARMA(1,1) × (3,1)

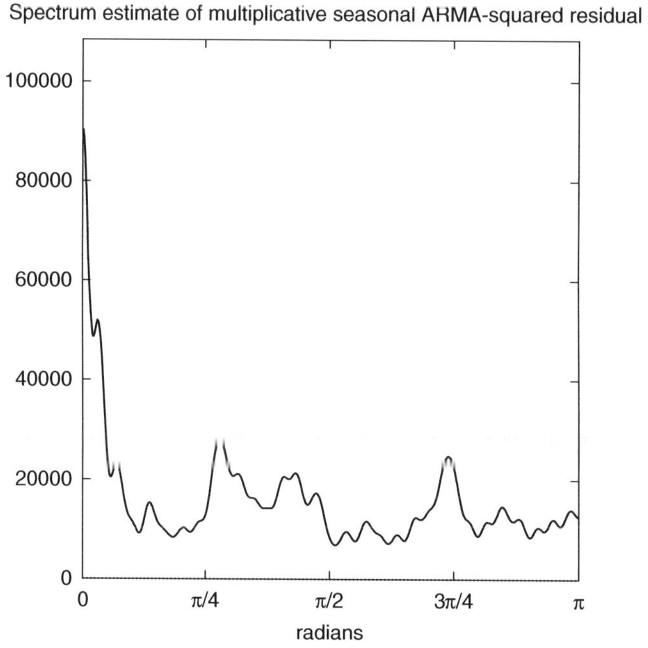

FIGURE 15.7 The estimated spectrum of multiplicative seasonal ARMA(1,1) × (3,1) squared residuals (Bartlett window is set to 80)

Estimation results for a number of alternative GARCH-type specifications are shown in Table 15.3. We consider the following models:

1. GARCH(1,1)

$$(1 - \beta L)\sigma_t^2 = \omega + \alpha\varepsilon_{t-1}^2.$$

2. GJR-GARCH(1,1)

$$(1 - \beta L)\sigma_t^2 = \omega + \left(\alpha\varepsilon_{t-1}^2 + \gamma S_{t-1}^- \varepsilon_{t-1}^2\right)$$

where $S_{t-1}^- = \mathrm{I}(\varepsilon_{t-1} < 0)$.

3. APGARCH(1,1)

$$\sigma_t^\delta = \omega + \alpha(|\varepsilon_{t-1}| - \gamma\varepsilon_{t-1})^\delta + \beta\sigma_{t-1}^\delta.$$

4. FIGARCH(1,d,1)

$$(1 - \beta L)\sigma_t^2 = \omega + [1 - \beta L - \phi L(1 - L)^d]\varepsilon_t^2.$$

5. PLM-EGARCH(1,d,0)

$$(1 - \beta L)(1 - L^7)^d \left(\ln\sigma_t^2 - \omega\right) = \psi(|z_{t-1}| - E|z_{t-1}|) + \gamma z_{t-1}. \qquad (15.84)$$

In Table 15.3, the Ljung–Box portmanteau statistics for serial correlation in the standardized return innovations $\hat{z}_t$ show that all models produce similar results for 10 and 50 lags while, when we consider 200 lags, the FIGARCH performs slightly better. The picture is completely

TABLE 15.3 Conditional variance model estimates. Robust standard errors in parentheses and p-values of the t ratio in square brackets. The values of the Ljung–Box portmanteau statistic for up to Kth-order serial dependence in the standardized residuals, $\hat{z}_t = \hat{\varepsilon}_t/\hat{\sigma}_t$ and squared standardized residuals, $\hat{z}_t^2$ are denoted $Q_K(\hat{z}_t)$ and $Q_K(\hat{z}_t^2)$, respectively. The table reports the p-value of the seasonality test, namely an F test of the regression of the standardized squared residual ($\hat{z}_t^2$) on a set of 23 dummies, one for each day of the week. The table reports the value of the maximized log-likelihood function and the Akaike and Schwarz (or Bayesian) information criteria

	GARCH(1,1)	GJR(1,1)	APGARCH(1,1)	FIGARCH(1,d,1)	PLM-EGARCH(1,d,0)
ω	5.233	5.244	5.221	10.881	4.375
	(2.003)	(2.033)	(2.149)	(4.473)	(0.126)
	[0.009]	[0.010]	[0.015]	[0.015]	[0.000]
α	0.170	0.170	0.174		
	(0.036)	(0.038)	(0.036)		
	[0.000]	[0.000]	[0.000]		
β	0.799	0.798	0.819	0.524	0.729
	(0.040)	(0.041)	(0.041)	(0.201)	(0.046)
	[0.000]		[0.000]	[0.009]	[0.000]
γ		0.010	0.010		−0.083
		(0.064)	(0.075)		(0.043)
		[0.882]	[0.899]		[0.056]
δ			1.416		
			(0.400)		
			[0.000]		
ϕ				0.251	
				(0.143)	
				1.750	
				[0.080]	
ψ					0.6598
					(0.102)
					[0.000]
d				0.499	0.214
				(0.172)	(0.039)
				[0.004]	[0.000]
T	1497	1497	1497	1497	1497
$Q_{10}(\hat{z}_t)$	9.423	13.342	13.241	9.508	12.278
	[0.492]	[0.205]	[0.211]	[0.485]	[0.267]
$Q_{50}(\hat{z}_t)$	66.070	65.880	65.614	70.836	72.097
	[0.063]	[0.065]	[0.068]	[0.028]	[0.022]
$Q_{200}(\hat{z}_t)$	269.709	269.590	269.235	252.500	254.352
	[0.001]	[0.001]	[0.001]	[0.007]	[0.006]
$Q_{10}(\hat{z}_t^2)$	12.245	12.441	13.422	5.493	6.457
	[0.269]	[0.257]	[0.201]	[0.886]	[0.775]
$Q_{50}(\hat{z}_t^2)$	68.886	69.696	69.934	60.036	42.113
	[0.039]	[0.034]	[0.033]	[0.080]	[0.778]
$Q_{200}(\hat{z}_t^2)$	246.370	250.205	244.756	219.180	174.778
	[0.014]	[0.009]	[0.017]	[0.123]	[0.900]
Seasonality test:	0.000	0.000	0.000	0.000	0.021
Log-likelihood	−5590.288	−5590.271	−5588.470	−5593.870	−4096.669
AIC	11188.575	11190.542	11188.939	11193.740	8205.338
BIC	11209.820	11217.098	11220.807	11209.674	8281.073

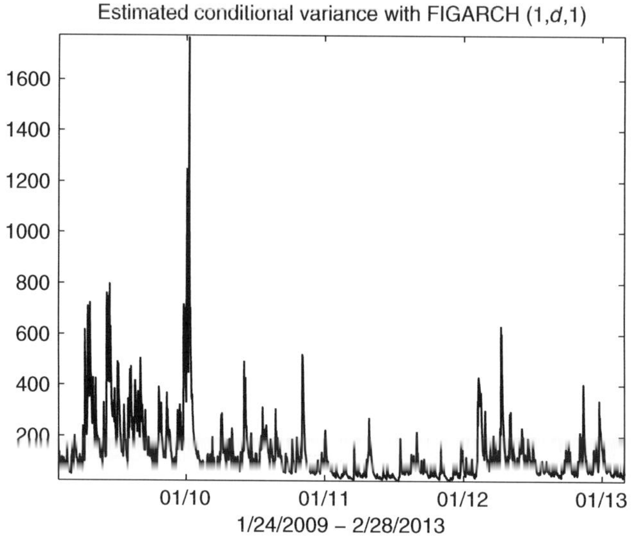

FIGURE 15.8 The estimated conditional variance with FIGARCH(1,d,1)

different if we look at the Ljung–Box test for the autocorrelation in the squared standardized residuals, that is $\hat{z}_t^2$, where for GARCH, GJR-GARCH, APGARCH models the null, when 50 and 200 lags are considered, is rejected. However, in GARCH-type models, p-values from standard χ^2 distributions are not reliable, but the statistics are still useful for model comparison. The table also shows the maximized log-likelihood, the Akaike and Schwarz (Bayesian) information criteria, reported as AIC and SIC, respectively. The models have similar values so it is difficult to distinguish among them on the basis of the reported information criteria. The point estimates suggest the absence of the leverage effect, as captured by the parameter γ, which is always not statistically significant. Instead, for what concerns the long memory, the fractional integration parameter in the FIGARCH model turns out to be highly significant (Figure 15.8 displays the conditional variance estimated with FIGARCH(1,d,1)). The first four models (i.e., GARCH, GJR-GARCH, APGARCH and FIGARCH) are clearly unable to catch the periodic patterns in volatility, as shown by the rejection of the null hypothesis of the seasonality test.

Finally, we consider the periodic long memory EGARCH (PLM-EGARCH) introduced by Bordignon *et al.* (2009), which is based on fractional seasonal filtering $(1 - L^S)$ of the log-conditional variance with $S = 7$. The parameter ψ of the news impact function is strongly significant, while the γ parameter, which takes a negative value corresponding to a leverage effect, is significant at the 10% level. The estimated fractional differencing parameter $\hat{d} = 0.214$ is strongly significant. The diagnostic tests in Table 15.3 show that the PLM-EGARCH provides an adequate fit of the long-memory component of the log-volatility as testified by the Ljung–Box statistics on $\hat{z}_t$ and $\hat{z}_t^2$. Moreover, even though it does not completely fit the periodic pattern in volatility it performs much better than the alternative models considered here.

15.12.2 A Simple Risk Measurement Application: A Bivariate Example with Copulas

The second illustration of the methodologies presented in the remainder of this chapter will be devoted to a simple risk managment application of GARCH models. We focus our attention on two futures products exchanged on the Intercontinental Exchange London, ICE Brent and ICE gasoil futures. This choice is driven not only by their paramount importance for the commodity industry, but also by the fact that the spread between crude oil and gasoil, the so-called gasoil crack, is one of the most liquid and traded spreads and this allows us to show the centrality of correctly modelling the dependence between different price series in a multivariate setting.

The prices of Brent, gasoil and gasoil crack are reported in Figure 15.9. A long position in the gasoil crack can be acquired by buying gasoil futures and selling the corresponding Brent futures. Since gasoil is traded in USD per metric ton while Brent in US$ per barrel, in order to compute the spread between the two commodities the conventional conversion factor of 7.45 barrel per metric ton is used. Moreover, gasoil trades in lots of 100 metric tons while Brent trades in lots of 1000 barrels, hence the minimum crack quantity is 4 lots (made up of 4 gasoil lots and 3 Brent lots).

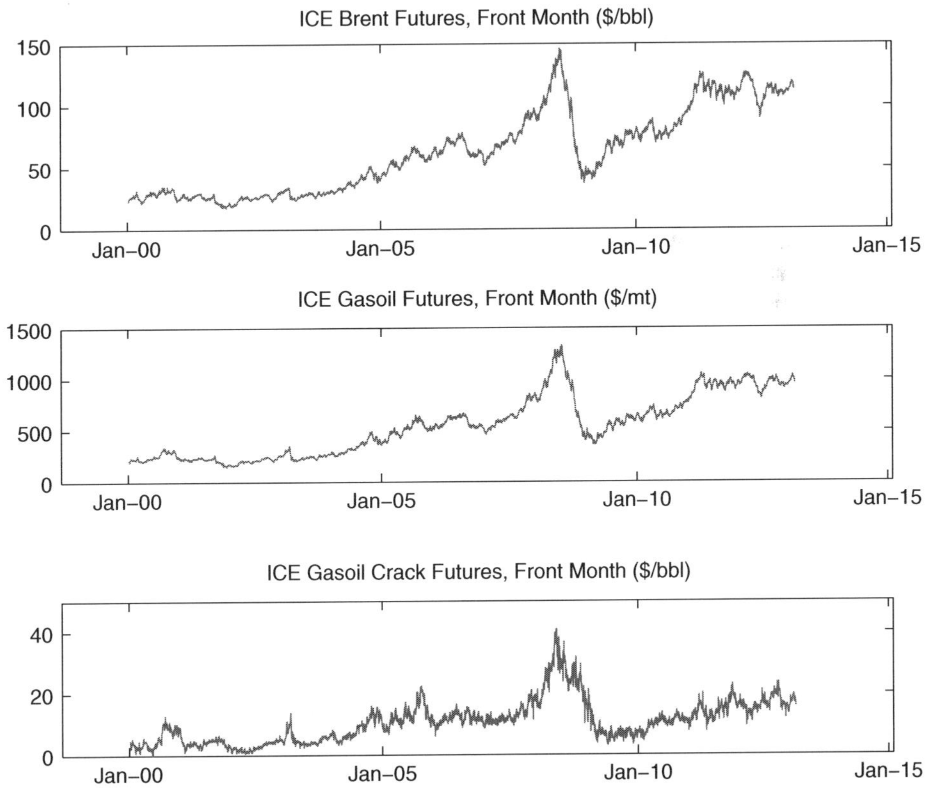

FIGURE 15.9 Prices of ICE Brent and gasoil front-month futures. Sample from January 2000 to February 2013

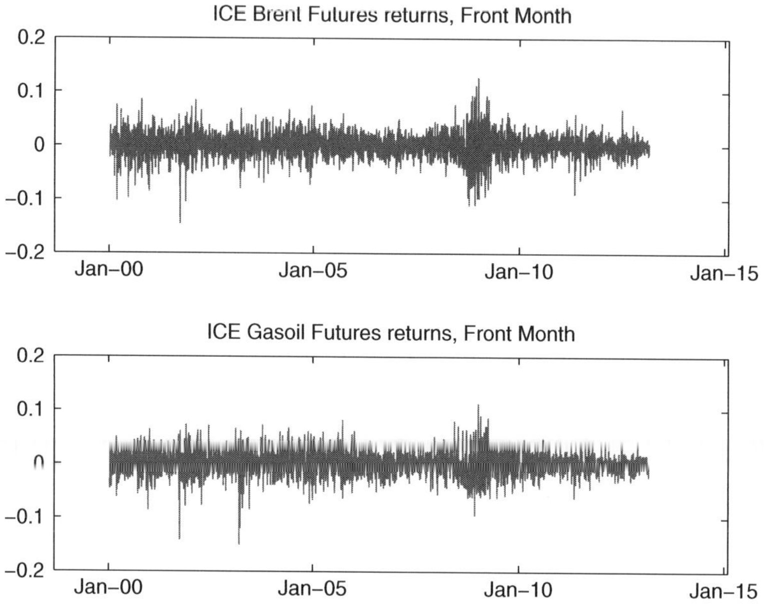

FIGURE 15.10 Daily log-returns of ICE Brent and gasoil front-month futures. Roll dates have been excluded. Sample from January 2000 to February 2013

Figure 15.10 shows the daily log returns of Brent and gasoil futures, whereas some descriptive statistics are reported in Table 15.4. In our analysis we use front-month futures and exclude roll dates (i.e., the dates on which the front-month futures go into delivery and are replaced as front-month products by the futures delivering in roughly a month). It is interesting to notice how these commodity series present some of the distinctive features of more traditional financial time series, such as heteroscedasticity, volatility clustering and excess kurtosis. Our sample runs from early 2000 to February 2013, for a total of 3200 trading days.

The first part of our application is a univariate exercise in which we use two mainstream GARCH models (the plain GARCH described in equation (15.9) and the asymmetric GJR

TABLE 15.4 Descriptive statistics of daily log-returns of Brent and gasoil front-month futures. Standard deviation is annualized

	Daily log-returns	
	Brent	**Gasoil**
Mean	0.0006	0.0006
Standard deviation	0.3547	0.3254
Skewness	−0.2617	−0.1622
Kurtosis	6.1353	5.5770
Max	0.1271	0.1126
Min	−0.1444	−0.1416

TABLE 15.5 Univariate GARCH VaR backtesting

	Brent futures 1-day 99% VaR	
	Unconditional coverage	***p*-Value Engle–Manganelli test**
GARCH *N*	0.0127	0.0003
GARCH *t*	0.0118	0.0114
GJR-GARCH *N*	0.0104	0.9859
GJR-GARCH *t*	0.0095	0.9721
	Gasoil futures 1-day 99% VaR	
	Unconditional coverage	***p*-Value Engle–Manganelli test**
Gaussian GARCH	0.0136	0.1840
GARCH *t*	0.0104	0.1775
Gaussian GJR-GARCH	0.0141	0.2071
GJR-GARCH *t*	0.0113	0.3532

described in equation (15.37)) in a VaR forecasting exercise. As the conditional mean specification we use an autoregressive model of order 1 which is enough to capture the slight autocorrelation present in our returns series. We estimate the models with a rolling estimation window of 1000 trading days and forecast the 99% VaR of a long position in Brent and gasoil futures for a holding period of one day. We then compare these daily VaR forecasts with the actual mark-to-market variations of our single asset portfolios to assess the ability of each model to adequately forecast the relevant quantile of the mark-to-market distribution. The VaR forecast properties are assessed by means of the simple unconditional coverage ratio (since a good 99% VaR forecasting model should allow roughly 1% of VaR violations) and the dynamic quantile test introduced by Engle and Manganelli (2004).

Since VaR forecasting boils down to a single quantile forecast, in order to distinguish the contribution of the volatility specification from the contribution of the distribution assumed for the innovations, we estimate our models considering both Gaussian and Student's *t* distributions.

The results of this univariate exercise are reported in Table 15.5 whereas Figures 15.11 and 15.12 show the 99% VaR. The VaR of the gasoil portfolio can be adequately predicted by each one of our model and distribution combinations, while the situation is more interesting in the Brent case. In fact, Brent futures volatilities present a marked asymmetry and the GJR-GARCH shows superior predictive ability with respect to its symmetric counterpart, being able to avoid the autocorrelation in VaR violations that triggers the rejection of the simple GARCH model as an adequate VaR forecasting model.

The same VaR forecasting exercise can of course be implemented in a bivariate setting. In this case our portfolio will be a long position in the gasoil crack, built up from a long position in gasoil futures and a short position in Brent futures. Figure 15.13 shows the conditional correlation obtained from a DCC-GARCH model, see equation (15.82): the correlation is clearly dynamic, with the lowest levels reached during the period of financial turmoil following the 2008 crisis.

However, analysing the scatterplots (Figure 15.14) of daily returns in the two subsamples 2000–2006 and 2007–2012 we notice how, in the second part of the sample, joint crashes tend

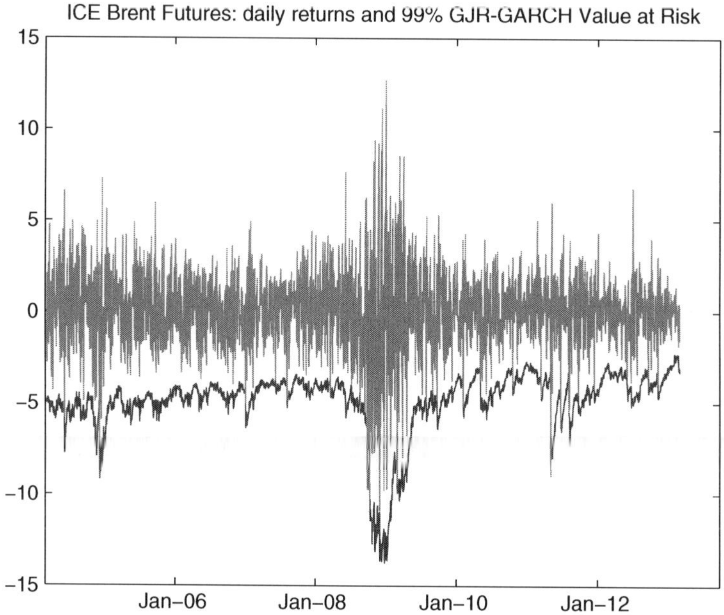

FIGURE 15.11 Daily percentage log-returns of ICE Brent and daily 99% VaR forecast (lower line) obtained from an AR(1)–GJR GARCH model

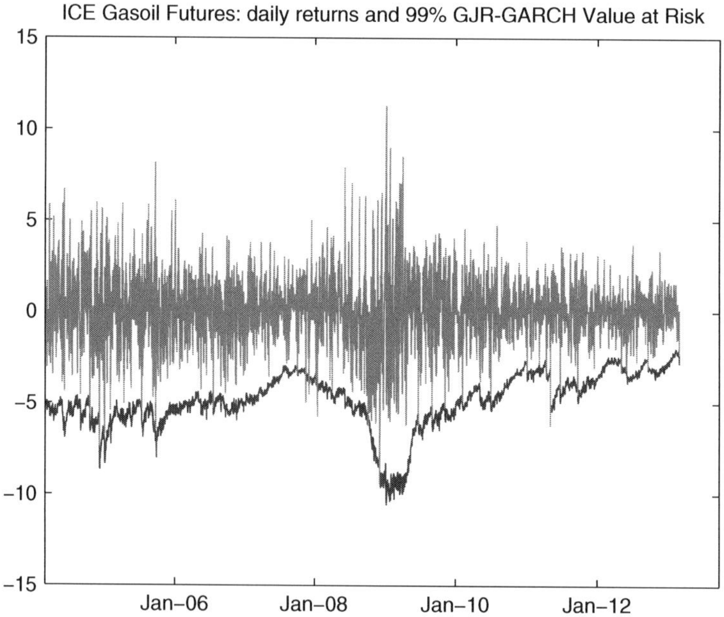

FIGURE 15.12 Daily percentage log-returns of ICE gasoil and daily 99% VaR forecast (lower line) obtained from an AR(1)–GJR GARCH model

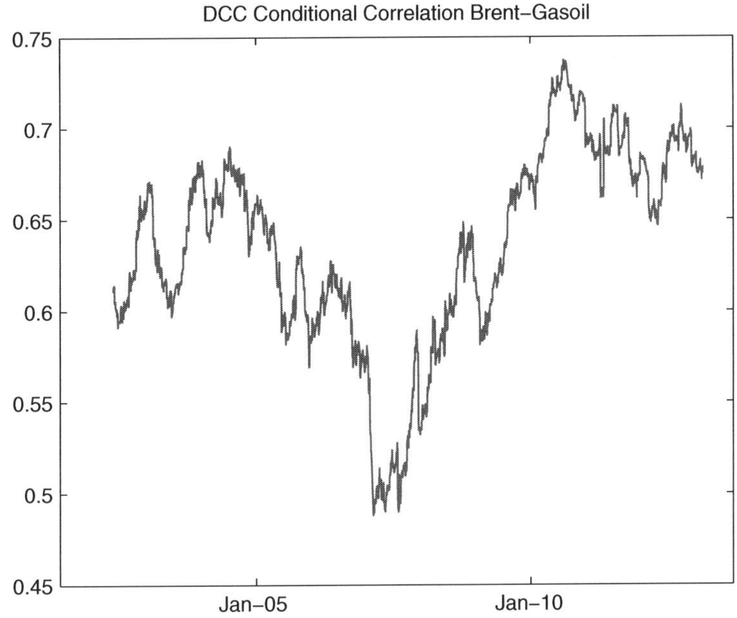

FIGURE 15.13 Gaussian DCC-GARCH(1,1) conditional correlation plot

to materialize with higher probability than that predicted by a bivariate Gaussian distribution, suggesting the possibility of tail dependence. As a further investigation of this hypothesis, Figure 15.15 reports the exceedence correlations between the two log-returns series, discussed in Ang and Chen (2002), and visually suggests the fact that Brent and gasoil returns have a stronger than Gaussian dependence away from the median. Moreover, this quantile dependence analysis shows a marked asymmetry in the tails of the multivariate distribution: there is a higher probability of joint crashes than under the multivariate Gaussian hypothesis. This

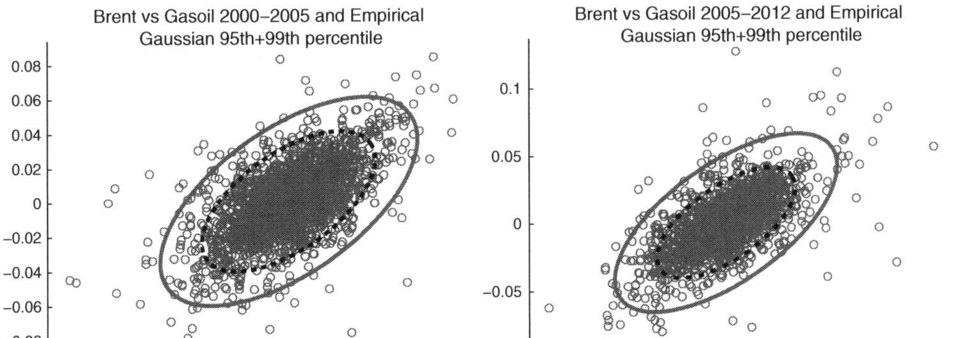

FIGURE 15.14 The daily return scatterplots of oil and gasoil. Left panel shows the 2000–2005 sample: the red dashed line is the empirical 95% quantile, the blue solid line is the 99% quantile. Right panel shows the 2006–2012 sample

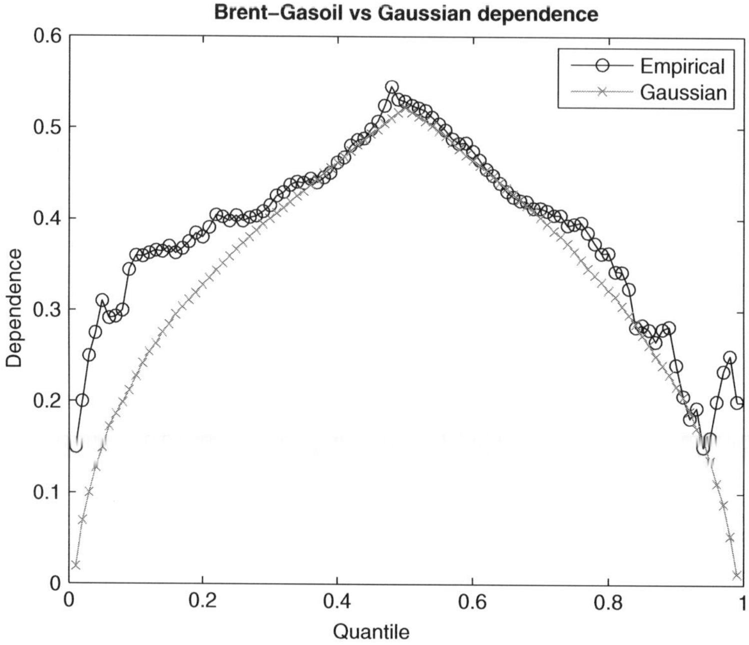

FIGURE 15.15 The quantile dependence analysis shows a marked asymmetry in the tails of the multivariate distribution: there is a higher probability of joint crashes than under the multivariate Gaussian hypothesis

implies that assuming a multivariate Gaussian distribution in our bivariate example will lead to a substantial underestimation of joint crashes probability. A viable strategy consists of specifying a conditional multivariate distribution using copula theory, which allows for a greater flexibility.

Let us assume that the vector of daily returns r_t is modelled as

$$r_t = \mu_t + u_t \quad t = 1, \ldots, T$$

where $E_{t-1}[r_t] = \mu_t$. The copula theory provides an easy way to deal with the (otherwise) complex multivariate modelling. The essential idea of the copula approach is that a joint distribution can be factorized into the marginals and a dependence function called a copula. Therefore, we assume that the vector of innovations u_t has a bivariate distribution $G(u_t; \psi)$, with continuous density function and parameter vector ψ. By the Sklar (1959) theorem, the joint distribution $G(u_{1,t}, u_{2,t}; \psi)$ can be expressed as follows:

$$G(u_{1,t}, u_{2,t}; \psi) = C(F_{1,t}(u_{1,t}; \delta_1), F_{2,t}(u_{2,t}; \delta_2); \gamma) \tag{15.85}$$

that is the joint distribution $G(.)$ is the copula $C(\cdot; \gamma)$ of the innovation marginal distributions, so $F_{1,t}(u_{1,t}; \delta_1)$ and $F_{2,t}(u_{2,t}; \delta_2)$, where γ, δ_1 and δ_2 are the copula and the marginal parameters, respectively. The copula *couples* the marginal distributions together in order to form a joint

TABLE 15.6 Bivariate portfolio VaR forecast results. The DCC model is estimated with marginal volatilities modelled as a GJR model. The Gaussian and SJC copulas are coupled with marginal volatilities estimated with Student's t densities

Gasoil crack 1-day 99% VaR		
	p-Value Engle–Manganelli test	
	2000–2006	2007–2013
Gaussian DCC-GJR	0.1440	0.0032
GJR t + Gaussian copula	0.4278	0.0675
GJR t + SJC copula	0.2188	0.4734

distribution. The dependence relationship is entirely determined by the copula, while scaling and shape (mean, standard deviation, skewness and kurtosis) are determined by the marginals (see Sklar, 1959; Joe, 1997; Nelsen, 1999). Copulae can therefore be used to obtain more realistic multivariate densities than the traditional joint normal one, which is simply the product of a normal copula and normal marginals. The marginal distributions do not need to be in any way similar to each other, nor is the choice of copula constrained by the choice of marginal distributions (see Patton, 2009).

To provide evidence that the dependence structure is indeed non-Gaussian, we performed a bivariate VaR forecasting using three different models. The first is the classic DCC-GARCH, which assumes multivariate Gaussian innovations. The second is a copula model in which the univariate GJR-GARCH with Student's t innovations is linked to a Gaussian copula. This second model has the advantage of far greater flexibility in the marginal models, since the univariate distributions need not be the same as in classical multivariate models. Finally, the third model shares the univariate specification of the second, but the dependence modelling is done with a symmetrized Joe Clayton copula (see Patton, 2006, eq. (15)), which is able to capture asymmetric tail dependence. One important computational drawback of copula models is that VaR is not available in closed form and needs to be computed through simulations.[5]

The results of the bivariate VaR backtest are reported in Table 15.6. The differences between the two subsamples are striking: in the first part of the sample, in fact, even the simplest Gaussian model can provide reliable VaR forecasts. After 2007, in contrast, the increase in tail dependence renders Gaussian models less precise in VaR forecasting since their underestimation of joint extreme events leads to a clustering of VaR violations during turbulent market periods (and conversely to unnecessarily higher VaR forecasts during calmer periods). The combination of these two facts implies an extremely inefficient capital allocation with potentially fatal consequences: our hypothetical trading firm in fact would end up with too little allocated capital when it was needed most and would allocate too much capital when the risk of its portfolio was lower.

[5]The interested reader can find an exhaustive presentation of VaR methods using copulas in Embrechts *et al.* (2003).

15.13 SOFTWARE

In this section we present some simple examples of the implementation of GARCH models with Eviews® and Matlab®. Eviews® allows a very fast implementation of several GARCH models through a simple graphical interface. Figure 15.16 shows the steps needed to import time series data from an Excel worksheet: the import section is available under the `File > Import > Import from file...` menu.

Once the data have been imported into an Eviews® workfile, it is possible to transform the price data (in this case front-month WTI prices spanning the 1986–2013 period) into log-returns issuing the command `series returns=dlog(value)`, where `value` is the name of the series containing the price time series. To obtain the descriptive statistics reported in Figure 15.17 it is necessary to open the relevant series from the workfile and then navigate through the `View > Descriptive Statistics & Tests > Histogram and Stats` menu.

As is evident from the descriptive statistics panel, WTI returns display the usual features of financial returns, namely negative skewness, excess kurtosis and a sharp rejection of the Gaussian distribution hypothesis. Moreover, an inspection of the returns chart in Figure 15.17 suggests the possibility of ARCH effects, given the evident volatility clustering. In order to further analyse the time series it is necessary to estimate an equation for the conditional mean. This can be performed from the `Quick > Estimate Equation...` menu as shown

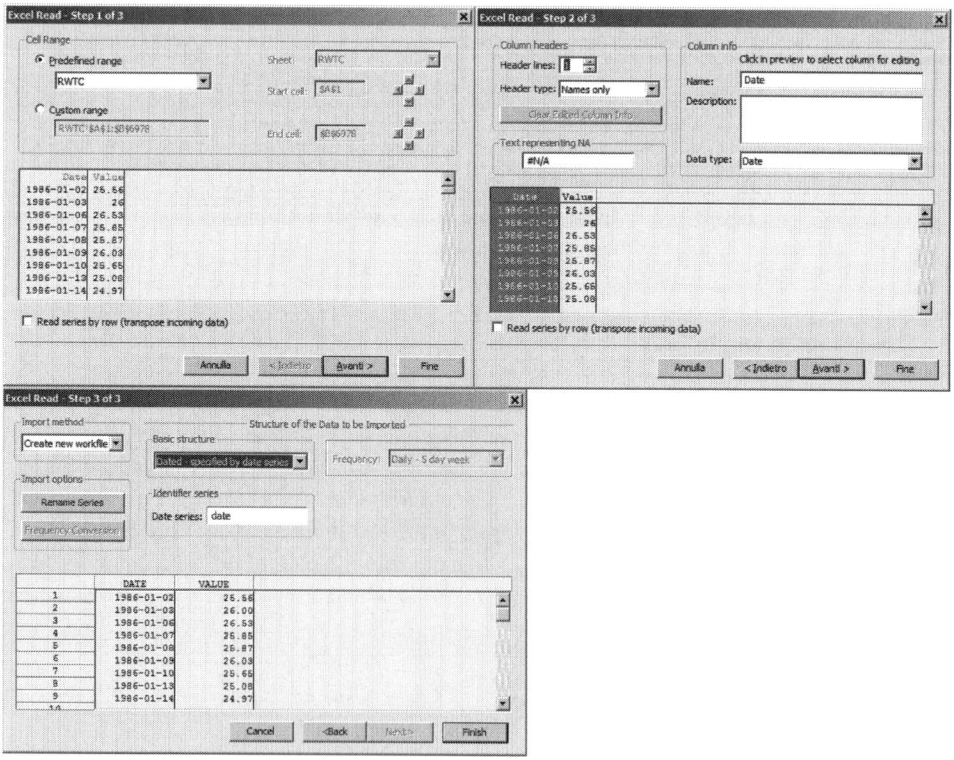

FIGURE 15.16 Excel import interface in Eviews®

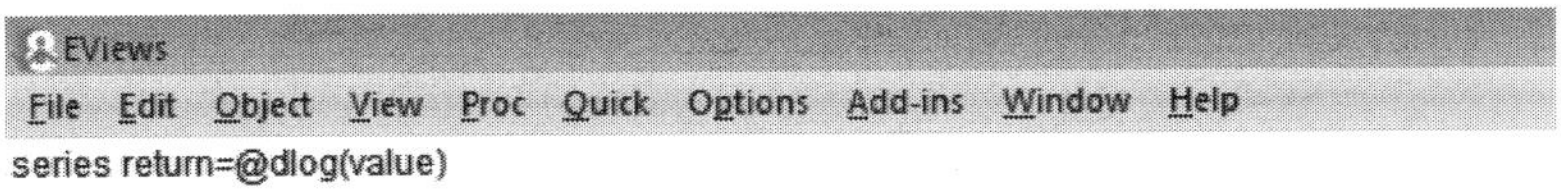

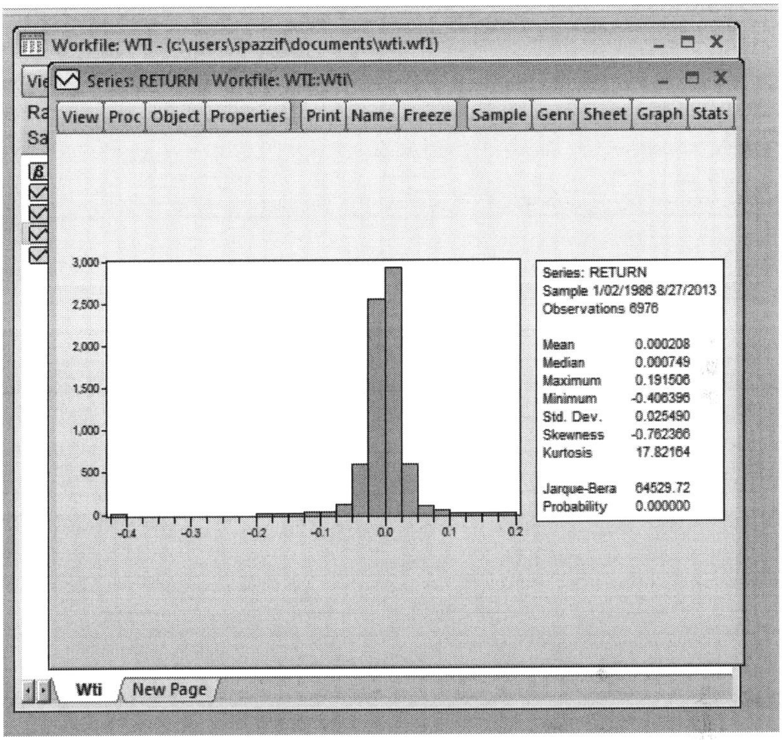

FIGURE 15.17 Descriptive statistics panel

in Figure 15.18, in which we issue the command to estimate a simple AR(1) model on the returns time series.

Figure 15.19 reports the estimation output, in which it appears evident that the returns do not possess any meaningful memory structure. In contrast, the correlogram of squared residuals shown in Figure 15.20 points to an underlying ARCH model, as confirmed by the battery of heteroscedasticity tests available under the `View > Residual Diagnostics > Heteroskedasticity Tests...` menu shown in Figure 15.21.

In order to estimate a GARCH model in Eviews® it is necessary to select the ARCH estimation method in the `Estimate Equation` panel shown in Figure 15.18. The GARCH menu is reported in Figure 15.22. It is possible to estimate GARCH, TARCH, EGARCH, PARCH and component ARCH models using Gaussian, Student's *t* and GED distributions for the innovations. After the estimation is complete, it is possible to retrieve the conditional volatility shown in Figure 15.23 under the menu `View > Garch Graph > Conditional Standard Deviation`. Finally, Figure 15.24 reports the correlogram of the standardized residuals squared, which confirms how an AR(1)–GARCH(1,1) model with Student's *t* innovations is able to completely characterize the data-generating process of our data set.

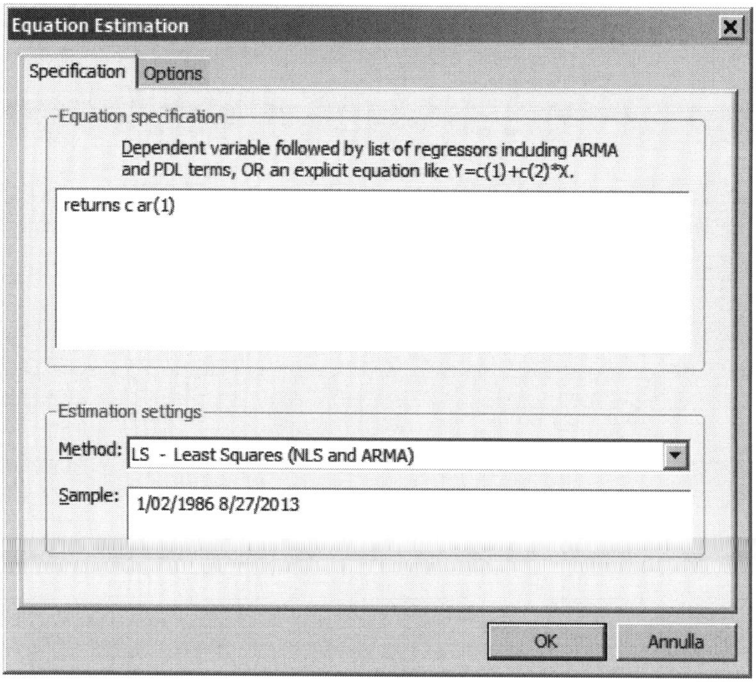

FIGURE 15.18 Interface to specify the conditional mean equation, in this case an AR(1) model

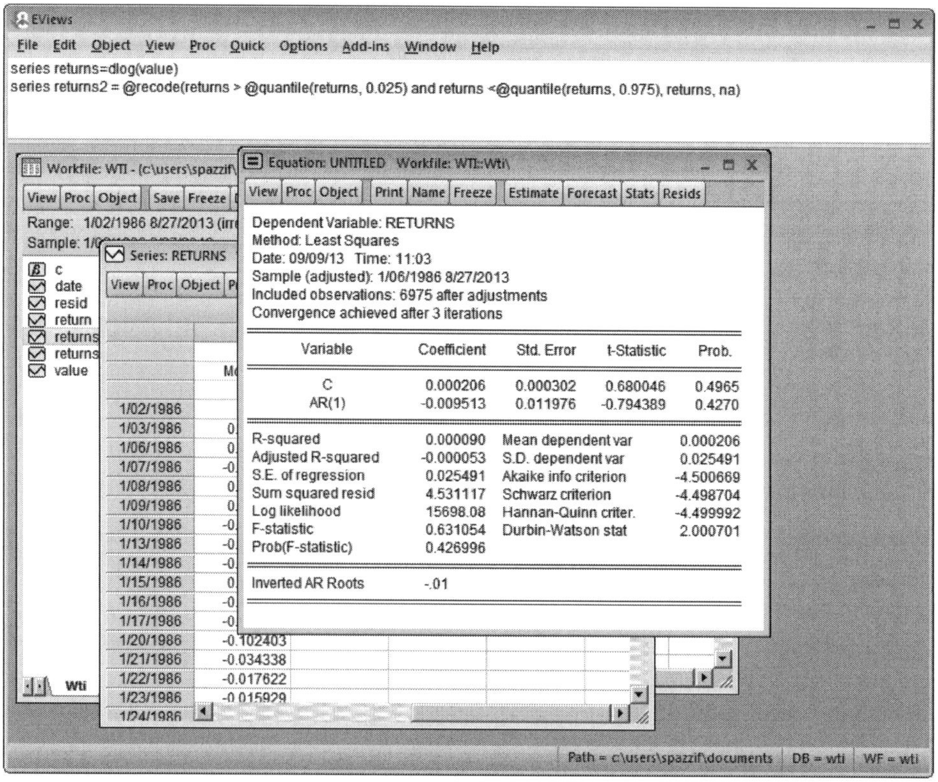

FIGURE 15.19 AR(1) model estimation output

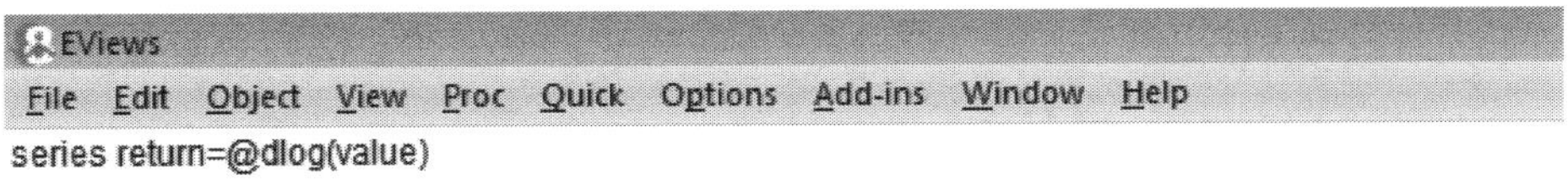

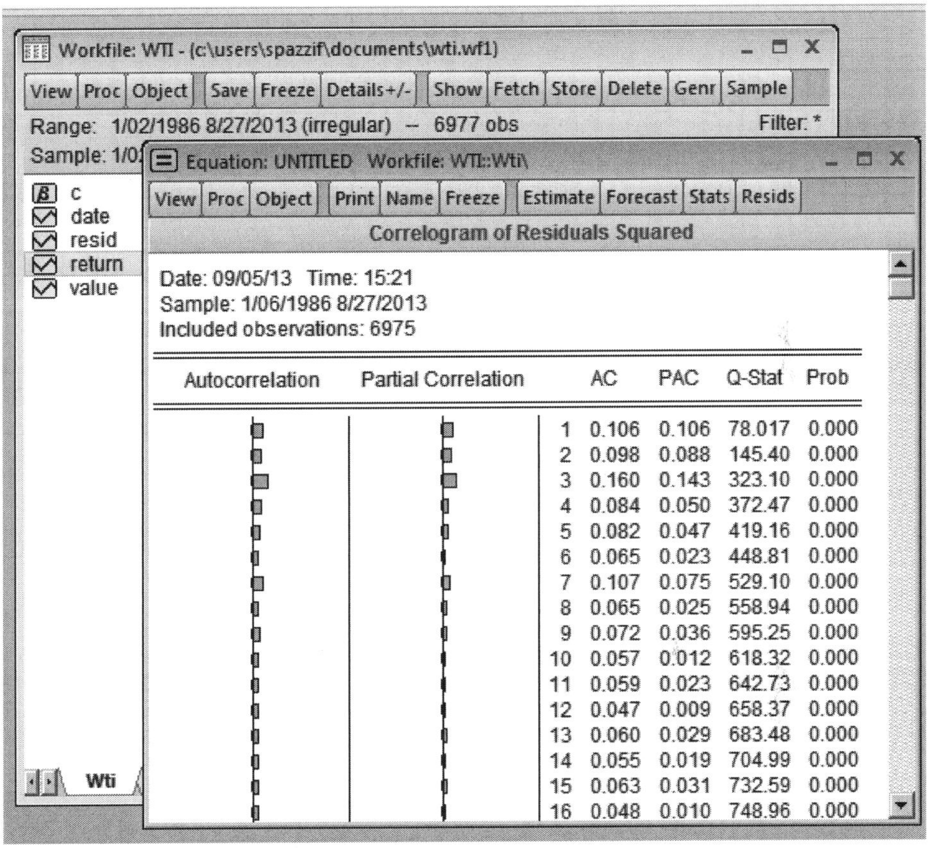

FIGURE 15.20 AR(1)-squared residual correlogram

In Matlab® there are several commands which allow the user to estimate ARMAX/GARCH models. The Econometric Toolbox™ has the following functions:

- `garchfit` estimates ARMAX/GARCH model parameters;
- `garchinfer` infers ARMAX/GARCH model innovations;
- `garchplot` plots ARMAX/GARCH model responses;
- `garchpred` forecasts ARMAX/GARCH model responses;
- `garchsim` simulates ARMAX/GARCH model responses.

For example, to define an AR(1)–GARCH(1,1) model specification we can use the following command:

```
   spec = garchset('VarianceModel', 'GARCH', 'R', 1, 'P', 1, 'Q',
1).
```

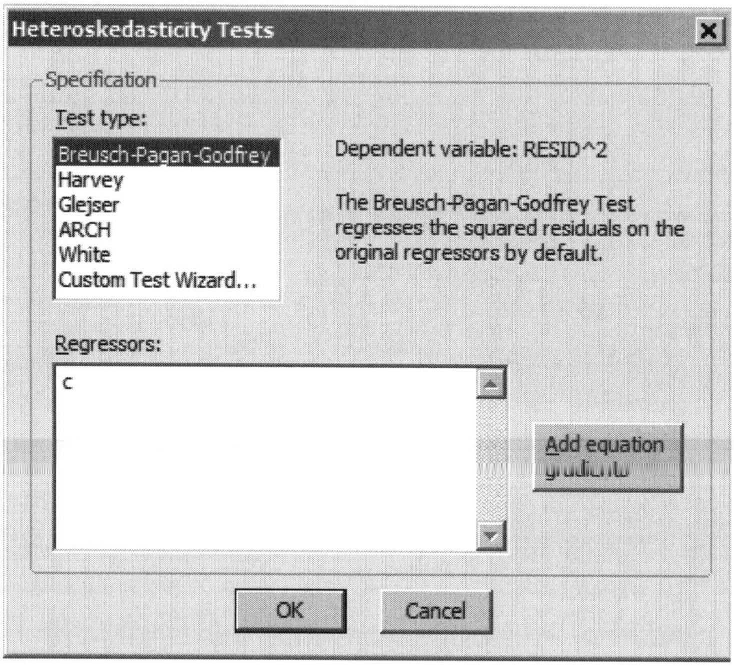

FIGURE 15.21 ARCH tests available in Eviews®

Then the following command:

```
[Coeff,Errors,LLF,Innovations,Sigmas,Summary] = garchfit(spec
                                                  ,Series)
```

estimates the model assuming the variable `Series` contains the time series of the returns used in the estimation. The outputs are:

- `Coeff` – GARCH specification structure containing the estimated coefficients.
- `Errors` – Structure containing the estimation errors (that is, the standard errors) of the coefficients.
- `LLF` – Optimized log-likelihood objective function value associated with the parameter estimates.
- `Innovations` – Innovations (that is, residuals) time series column vector.
- `Sigmas` – Conditional standard deviation vector corresponding to `Innovations`.
- `Summary` – Structure of summary information about the optimization process.

We refer the interested reader to the Matlab® online documentation.[6]

To calculate multiperiod forecasts from the estimated model, the following function can be used:

```
[SigmaForecast,MeanForecast,SigmaTotal] = garchpred(Spec,Series,
                                          NumPeriods).
```

[6]Available at `http://www.mathworks.it/it/help/matlab/index.html`.

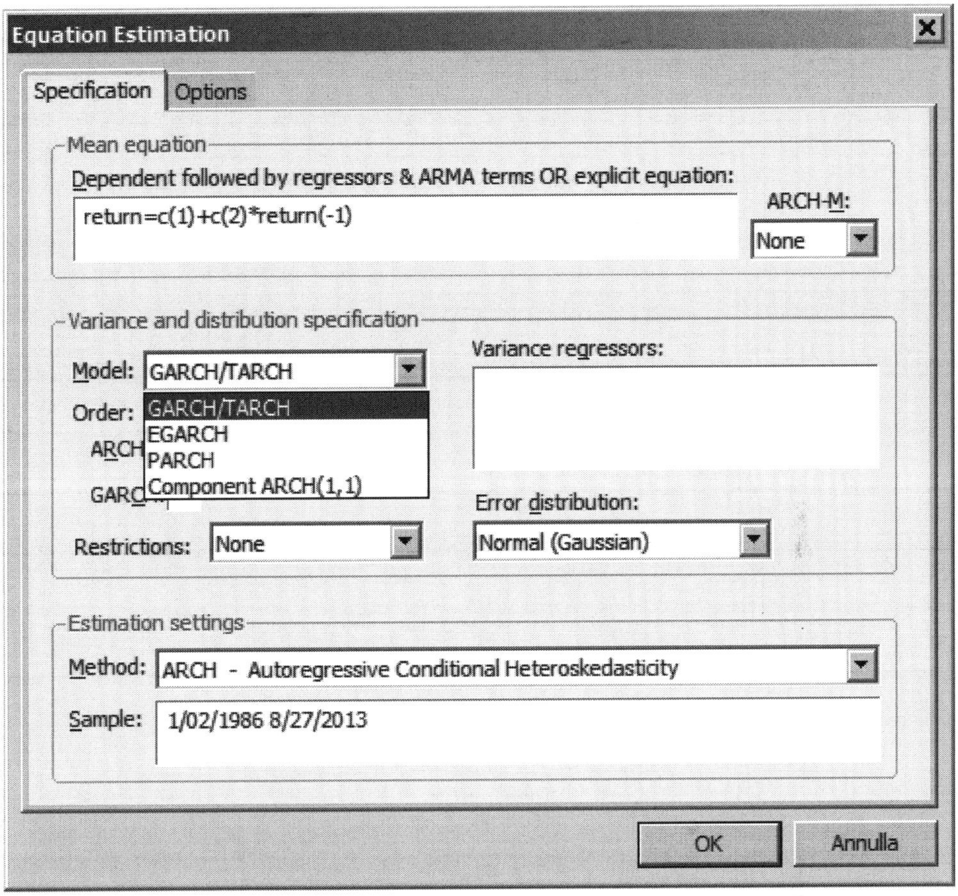

FIGURE 15.22 GARCH menu in Eviews®

The inputs of the `garchpred` function are:

- `Spec` – Specification structure for the conditional mean and variance models. See `garchset`.
- `Series` – Matrix of observations of the underlying univariate return series of interest for which `garchpred` generates forecasts. Each column of `Series` is an independent path. The last row of `Series` holds the most recent observation of each path.
- `NumPeriods` – Positive scalar integer representing the forecast horizon of interest, expressed in periods compatible with the sampling frequency of the input innovations column vector `Series`.

The outputs are:

- `SigmaForecast` – Matrix of conditional standard deviations of future innovations (model residuals) on a per-period basis. The standard deviations derive from the minimum mean square error (MMSE) forecasts associated with the recursive volatility model, for example `'GARCH'`, `'GJR'` or `'EGARCH'`, specified for the `'VarianceModel'` parameter in `Spec`.

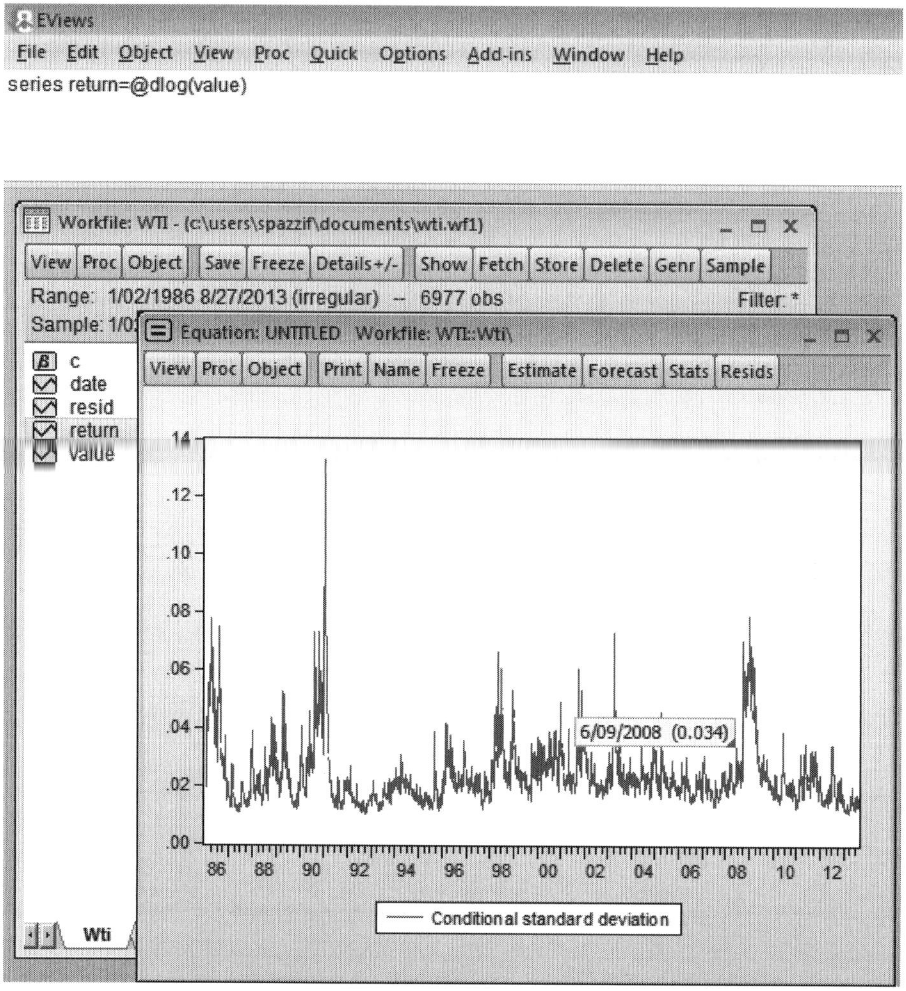

FIGURE 15.23 AR(1)–GARCH(1,1) conditional volatility

For GARCH(p,q) and GJR(p,q) models, `SigmaForecast` is the square root of the MMSE conditional variance forecasts. For EGARCH(p,q) models, `SigmaForecast` is the square root of the exponential of the MMSE forecasts of the logarithm of conditional variance.

- `MeanForecast` – Matrix of MMSE forecasts of the conditional mean of `Series` on a per-period basis. `MeanForecast` is the same size as `SigmaForecast`. The first row contains the forecast in the first period for each path of `Series`, the second row contains the forecast in the second period, and so on.
- `SigmaTotal` – Matrix of MMSE volatility forecasts of `Series` over multiperiod holding intervals. `SigmaTotal` is the same size as `SigmaForecast`. The first row contains the standard deviation of returns expected for assets held for one period for each path of `Series`, the second row contains the standard deviation of returns expected for assets held for two periods, and so on. The last row contains the standard deviations of the cumulative returns obtained if an asset was held for the entire `NumPeriods` forecast horizon.

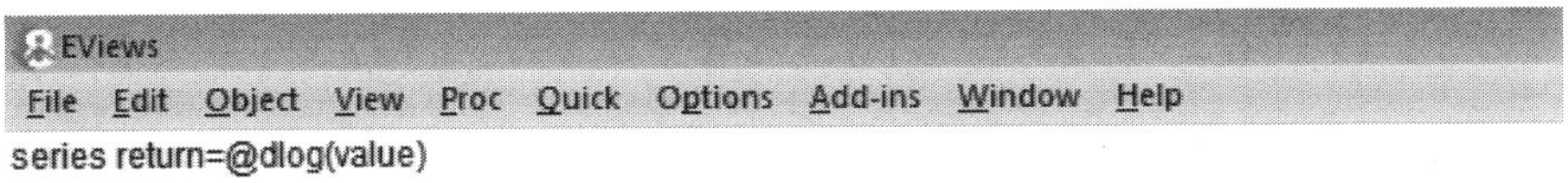

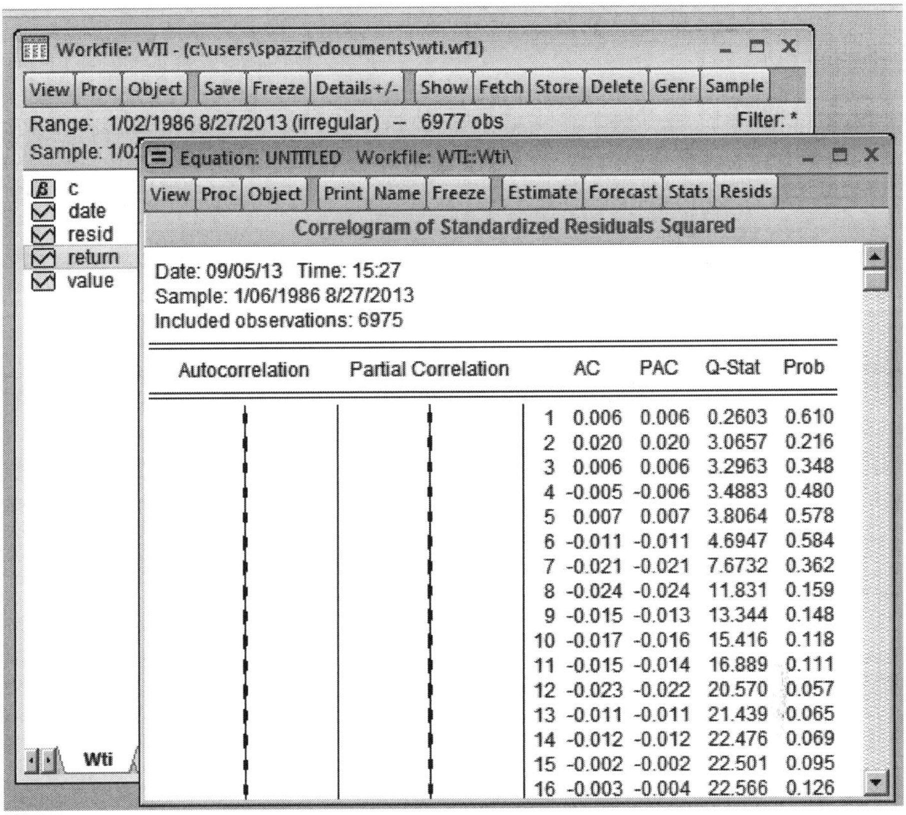

FIGURE 15.24 AR(1)–GARCH(1,1) standardized residual correlogram

The following code snippet shows a simple Matlab® script to estimate and forecast from an AR(1)–GARCH(1,1) model:

```
%Convert price vector to log-returns
wtiret = price2ret(wti);

%Compute ACF and PACF of returns series
autocorr(wtiret)
title('ACF with Bounds for Raw Return Series')

parcorr(wtiret)
title('PACF with Bounds for Raw Return Series')

```

```
%Compute ACF of squared returns
autocorr(wtiret.^2)
title('ACF of the Squared Returns')

%Use lbqtest to test the absence of serial correlation
[H,pValue,Stat,CriticalValue] = lbqtest(wtiret-mean(wtiret),
                                [10 15 20]',0.05)

%Use lbqtest on the squared returns series to test for ARCH effects
[H,pValue,Stat,CriticalValue] = lbqtest((wtiret-mean(wtiret)).^2,
                                [10 15 20]',0.05)

% Engle's ARCH test
[H,pValue,Stat,CriticalValue] = archtest(wtiret-mean(wtiret),
                                [10 15 20]',0.05)

%Specify an AR(1)-GARCH(1,1) model
spec = garchset('VarianceModel', 'GARCH', 'R', 1, 'P',1, 'Q', 1);

% Estimate the specified model
[estimatedspec,errors,LLF,innovations,sigmas,summary] = garchfit
                                                        (spec,wtiret);

%Display estimated parameters and associated standard errors
garchdisp(estimatedspec,errors)

%Plot residuals and estimated conditional volatilities
garchplot(innovations,sigmas,wtiret)

%Compute 10 step ahead forecasts
[sigmaForecast,meanForecast,sigmaTotal] = garchpred(estimatedspec,
                                          wtiret,10);
```

Moreover, the scripting capabilities of Matlab® allow the user to easily define the log-likelihood function for any kind of model specification, which can then be optimized using the functions contained in the Optimization Toolbox™.

REFERENCES

Aielli, G.P. (2011) Dynamic conditional correlation: On properties and estimation, Technical report, Dipartimento di scienze economiche e aziendali, Padua University.

Alom, F., Ward, B.D. and Hu, B. (2012) Modelling petroleum future price volatility: Analysing asymmetry and persistency of shocks, *OPEC Energy Review*, **36**(1), 1–24.

Andersen, T.G. and Bollerslev, T. (1997) Heterogeneous information arrivals and return volatility dynamics: Uncovering the long-run in high frequency returns, *Journal of Finance*, **52**, 975–1005.

Andersen, T.G. and Bollerslev, T. (1998) ARCH and GARCH models, in Kotz, S., Read, C. and Banks, D. (eds), *Encyclopedia of Statistical Sciences*, Vol. II, John Wiley & Sons, New York.

Andersen, T.G., Bollerslev, T., Christoffersen, P. and Diebold, F.X. (2006) Volatility and correlation forecasting, in Granger, C., Elliott, G. and Timmermann, A. (eds), *Handbook of Economic Forecasting*, North-Holland, Amsterdam, pp. 777–878.

Andersen, T.G., Bollerslev, T. and Diebold, F.X. (2009) Parametric and nonparametric volatility measurement, in Ait-Sahalia, Y. and Hansen, L. (eds), *Handbook of Financial Econometrics*, North-Holland, Amsterdam.

Ang, A. and Chen, J. (2002) Asymmetric correlations of equity portfolios, *Journal of Financial Economics*, **63**(3), 443–494.

Baillie, R.T., Bollerslev, T. and Mikkelsen, H. (1996) Fractionally integrated generalized autoregressive conditional heteroskedasticity, *Journal of Econometrics*, **74**, 3–30.

Baillie, R.T., Han, Y.-W., Myers, R.J. and Song, J. (2007) Long memory models for daily and high frequency commodity futures returns, *Journal of Futures Markets*, **27**(7), 643–668.

Bauwens, L., Laurent, S. and Rombouts, J. (2006) Multivariate GARCH models: A survey, *Journal of Applied Econometrics*, **21**, 79–110.

Bera, A. and Higgins, M. (1993) ARCH models: Properties, estimation and testing, *Journal of Economic Surveys*, **7**(4), 305–362.

Bera, A., Higgins, M. and Lee, S. (1992) Interaction between autocorrelation and conditional heteroskedasticity: A random-coefficient approach, *Journal of Business and Economic Statistics*, **10**, 133–142.

Berkes, I. and Horváth, L. (2003) The rate of consistency of the quasi-maximum likelihood estimator, *Statistics and Probability Letters*, **61**, 133–143.

Berkes, I. and Horváth, L. (2004) The efficiency of the estimators of the parameters in GARCH processes, *Annals of Statistics*, **32**, 633–655.

Berkes, I., Horváth, L. and Kokoszka, P. (2003) GARCH processes: Structure and estimation, *Bernoulli*, **9**, 201–227.

Black, F. (1976) Studies in stock price volatility changes, in Proceedings of the 1976 Business Meeting of the Business and Economics Statistics Section, American Statistical Association, pp. 177–181.

Bollerslev, T. (1986) Generalized autoregressive conditional heteroskedasticity, *Journal of Econometrics*, **31**, 307–327.

Bollerslev, T. (1988) On the correlation structure for the generalized autoregressive conditional heteroskedastic process, *Journal of Time Series Analysis*, **9**, 121–131.

Bollerslev, T. (2009) Glossary to ARCH (GARCH), in Bollerslev, T., Russell, J.R. and Watson, M. (eds), *Volatility and Time Series Econometrics: Essays in Honour of Robert F. Engle*, Oxford University Press, Oxford.

Bollerslev, T. and Ghysels, E. (1996) Periodic autoregressive conditional heteroscedasticity, *Journal of Business and Economic Statistics*, **14**, 139–151.

Bollerslev, T. and Mikkelsen, H.O. (1996) Modeling and pricing long memory in stock market volatility, *Journal of Econometrics*, **73**, 151–184.

Bollerslev, T., Chou, R. and Kroner, K. (1992) ARCH modeling in finance: A selective review of the theory and empirical evidence, *Journal of Econometrics*, **52**, 5–59.

Bollerslev, T., Engle, R.F. and Nelson, D.B. (1994) ARCH models, in Engle, R. and McFadden, D. (eds), *Handbook of Econometrics*, Vol. IV, Elsevier Science, Amsterdam.

Bordignon, S., Caporin, M. and Lisi, F. (2009) Periodic long-memory GARCH models, *Econometric Reviews*, **28**, 60–82.

Bougerol, P. and Picard, N. (1992a) Stationarity of GARCH processes and of some nonnegative time series, *Journal of Econometrics*, **52**, 115–127.

Bougerol, P. and Picard, N. (1992b) Strict stationarity of generalized autoregressive process, *The Annals of Probability*, **20**, 1714–1730.

Brooks, C., Burke, S. and Pesand, G. (2001) Benchmarks and the accuracy of GARCH model estimation, *International Journal of Forecasting*, **17**, 45–56.

Dacorogna, M., Muller, M., Nagler, U.A., Olsen, R.J. and Pictet, O.V. (1993) A geographical model for the daily and weekly seasonal volatility in the foreign exchange market, *Journal of International Money and Finance*, **12**, 413–438.

Davidian, M. and Carroll, R. (1987) Variance function estimation, *Journal of American Statistical Association*, **82**, 1079–1091.

Degiannakis, S. and Xekalaki, E. (2004) Autoregressive conditional heteroscedasticity (ARCH) models: A review, *Quality Technology and Quantitative Management*, **1**, 271–324.

Diebold, F. (1986) Modeling the persistence of conditional variances: A comment, *Econometric Reviews*, **5**, 51–56.

Diebold, F. (2004) The Nobel Memorial Prize for Robert F. Engle, *Scandinavian Journal of Economics*, **106**, 165–185.

Diebold, F. and Inoue, A. (2001) Long memory and regime switching, *Journal of Econometrics*, **105**, 131–159.

Diebold, F. and Lopez, J. (1995) Modeling volatility dynamics, in Hoover, K. (ed.), *Macroeconometrics: Developments, Tensions and Prospects*, Kluwer Academic Press, Dordrecht, pp. 427–472.

Diebold, F. and Schuermann, T. (1993) Exact maximum likelihood estimation of ARCH models, Technical report, Department of Economics, University of Pennsylvania.

Ding, Z., Granger, C. and Engle, R. (1993) A long memory property of stock market returns and a new model, *Journal of Empirical Finance*, **1**, 83–106.

Duan, J.-C. (1997) Augmented GARCH(p,q) process and its diffusion limit, *Journal of Econometrics*, **79**, 97–127.

Embrechts, P., Lindskog, F. and McNeil, A. (2003) Modelling dependence with copulas and applications to risk management, in Rachev, S.T. (ed.), *Handbook of Heavy Tailed Distributions in Finance*, North-Holland, Amsterdam, pp. 329–384.

Engle, R.F. (1982) Autoregressive conditional heteroskedasticity with estimates of the variance of UK inflation, *Econometrica*, **50**, 987–1008.

Engle, R.F. (1990) Discussion: Stock market volatility and the crash of 87, *Review of Financial Studies*, **3**, 103–106.

Engle, R.F. (2001) GARCH 101: The use of ARCH/GARCH models in applied econometrics, *Journal of Economic Perspectives*, **15**, 157–168.

Engle, R.F. (2002a) Dynamic conditional correlation: A simple class of multivariate GARCH models, *Journal of Business and Economic Statistics*, **20**, 339–350.

Engle, R.F. (2002b) New frontiers for ARCH models, *Journal of Applied Econometrics*, **17**, 425–446.

Engle, R.F. (2004) Nobel Lecture. Risk and volatility: Econometric models and financial practice, *American Economic Review*, **94**, 405–420.

Engle, R.F. and Bollerslev, T. (1986) Modeling the persistence of conditional variances, *Econometric Review*, **5**, 1–50.

Engle, R.F. and Gonzalez-Rivera, G. (1991) Semiparametric ARCH models, *Journal of Business and Economic Statistics*, **19**, 3–29.

Engle, R.F. and Kroner, K. (1995) Multivariate simultaneous generalized ARCH, *Econometric Theory*, **11**, 122–150.

Engle, R.F. and Lee, R.G. (1999) A permanent and transitory component model of stock return volatility, in Engle, R. and White, H. (eds), *Cointegration, Causality, and Forecasting: A Festschrift in Honor of Clive W.J. Granger*, Oxford University Press, Oxford, pp. 475–497.

Engle, R.F. and Manganelli, S. (2004) CAViaR: Conditional autoregressive value at risk by regression quantiles, *Journal of Business & Economic Statistics*, **22**(4), 367–381.

Engle, R.F. and Mezrich, J. (1996) GARCH for groups, *Risk*, **9**(8), 36–40.

Engle, R.F. and Ng, V.K. (1993) Measuring and testing the impact of news on volatility, *Journal of Finance*, **48**, 1749–1778.

Engle, R.F. and Patton, A.J. (2001) What good is a volatility model? *Quantitative Finance*, **1**, 237–245.

Francq, C. and Zakoïan, J.-M. (2004) Maximum likelihood estimation of pure GARCH and ARMAGARCH processes, *Bernoulli*, **10**, 605–637.
Francq, C. and Zakoïan, J.-M. (2009) A tour in the asymptotic theory of GARCH estimation, in Andersen, T., Davis, R.A., Kreiss, J.-P. and Mikosch, T. (eds), *Handbook of Financial Time Series*, Springer-Verlag, Berlin.
Franq, C. and Zakoïan, J.-M. (2010) *GARCH Models*, John Wiley & Sons, New York.
Franses, P. and Paap, R. (2000) Modelling day-of-the-week seasonality in the S&P-500 index, *Applied Financial Economics*, **10**, 483–488.
Giot, P. and Laurent, S. (2003) Market risk in commodity markets: A VaR approach, *Energy Economics*, **30**, 435–457.
Giraitis, L., Kokoszka, P. and Leipus, R. (2000) Stationary ARCH models: Dependence structure and central limit theorem, *Econometric Theory*, **16**, 3–22.
Giraitis, L., Leipus, R. and Surgailis, D. (2007) Recent advances in ARCH modelling, in Teyssière, G. and Kirman, A.P. (eds), *Long Memory in Economics*, Springer-Verlag, Berlin.
Glosten, L., Jagannathan, R. and Runkle, D. (1993) On the relationship between the expected value and the volatility of the nominal excess return on stocks, *Journal of Finance*, **48**, 1779–1801.
Granger, C. and Ding, Z. (1996) Modeling volatility persistence of speculative returns, *Journal of Econometrics*, **73**, 185–215.
Granger, C. and Hyung, N. (2004) Occasional structural breaks and long memory with an application to the S&P500 absolute returns, *Journal of Empirical Finance*, **11**, 399–421.
Granger, C.W.J. and Joyeux, R. (1980) An introduction to long-memory time series models and fractional differencing, *Journal of Time Series Analysis*, **4**, 221–238.
Granger, C. and Teräsvirta, T. (1999) A simple non linear time series model with misleading linear properties, *Economics Letters*, **62**, 161–165.
Hall, P. and Yao, Q. (2003) Inference in ARCH and GARCH models with heavy-tailed errors, *Econometrica*, **71**, 285–317.
Hamilton, J. (1994) *Time Series Analysis*, Princeton University Press, Princeton, NJ.
He, C. and Teräsvirta, T. (1999) Properties of moments of a family of GARCH processes, *Journal of Econometrics*, **92**, 173–192.
He, C., Teräsvirta, T. and Malmsten, H. (2002) Moment structure of a family of first-order exponential GARCH models, *Econometric Theory*, **18**, 868–885.
Hentschel, L. (1995) All in the family. Nesting symmetric and asymmetric GARCH models, *Journal of Financial Economics*, **39**, 71–104.
Higgins, M. and Bera, A. (1992) A class of nonlinear ARCH models, *International Economic Review*, **33**, 137–158.
Hosking, J. (1981) Fractional differencing, *Biometrika*, **68**, 165–176.
Hung, J.-C., Lee, M.-C. and Liu, H.-C. (2008) Estimation of value-at-risk for energy commodities via fat-tailed GARCH models, *Energy Economics*, **30**, 1173–1191.
Hurst, H. (1951) Long term storage capacity of reservoirs, *Transactions of the American Society of Civil Engineers*, **116**, 770–799.
Joe, H. (1997) *Multivariate Models and Dependence Concepts*, Chapman & Hall, New York.
Kang, S.H., Kang, S.-M. and Yoon, S.-M. (2009) Forecasting volatility of crude oil markets, *Energy Economics*, **31**(1), 119–125.
Karanasos, M. and Kim, J. (2006) A re-examination of the asymmetric power ARCH model, *Journal of Empirical Finance*, **13**, 113–128.
Kroner, K.F., Kneafsey, K.P. and Claessens, S. (1995) Forecasting volatility in commodity markets. *Journal of Forecasting* **14**(2), 77–95.
Lamoureux, C. and Lastrapes, W. (1990) Persistence in variance, structural change and the GARCH model, *Journal of Business and Economic Statistics*, **8**, 225–234.
Lee, J.H.H. and King, M.L. (1993) A locally most powerful based score test for GARCH and GARCH regression disturbances, *Journal of Business and Economic Statistics*, **11**, 17–27.

Lee, S.W. and Hansen, B.E. (1994) Asymptotic theory for the GARCH(1,1) quasimaximum likelihood estimator, *Econometric Theory*, **10**, 29–52.

Lindner, A. (2009) Stationarity, mixing, distributional properties and moments of GARCH(p,q)-processes, in Andersen, T., Davis, R.A. and Mikosch, T. (eds), *Handbook of Financial Time Series*, Springer-Verlag, Berlin.

Lumsdaine, R. (1996) Consistency and asymptotic normality of the quasi-maximum likelihood estimator in IGARCH(1,1) and covariance stationary GARCH(1,1) models, *Econometrica*, **64**, 575–596.

Lumsdaine, R.L. and Ng, S. (1999) Testing for ARCH in the presence of a possibly misspecified conditional mean, *Journal of Econometrics*, **93**, 257–279.

Malmsten, H. and Teräsvirta, T. (2004) Stylized facts of financial time series and three popular models of volatility, SSE/EFI Working Paper Series in Economics and Finance 563, Stockholm School of Economics.

McCullough, B. and Renfro, C. (1999) Benchmarks and software standards: A case study of GARCH procedures, *Journal of Economic and Social Measurement*, **25**, 59–71.

Mikosch, T. and Starica, C. (1998) Change of structure in financial time series, long range dependence and the GARCH model, Technical Report, University of Groningen.

Mikosch, T. and Starica, C. (2000) Is it really long memory we see in financial returns? in Embrechts, P. (ed.), *Extremes and Integrated Risk Management*, Risk Books, London.

Mikosch, T. and Starica, C. (2003) Long-range dependence effects and ARCH modelling, in Doukhan, P., Oppenheim, G. and Taqqu, M.S. (eds), *Theory and Applications of Long-Range Dependence*, Birkhäuser, Boston.

Müller, M., Dacorogna, M., Davé, M.M., Olsen, R.J., Pictet, O.V. and von Weizsacker, J. (1997) Volatilities of different time resolution – analyzing the dynamics of market components, *Journal of Empirical Finance*, **4**, 213–239.

Nelsen, R. (1999) *An Introduction to Copula*, Springer-Verlag, Berlin.

Nelson, D.B. (1990) Stationarity and persistence in the GARCH(1,1) model, *Econometric Theory*, **6**, 318–334.

Nelson, D.B. (1991) Conditional heteroskedasticity in asset returns: A new approach, *Econometrica*, **59**, 347–370.

Nelson, D.B. and Cao, C.Q. (1992) Inequality constraints in the univariate GARCH model, *Journal of Business and Economic Statistics*, **10**, 229–235.

Nelson, D.B. and Foster, D. (1994) Asymptotic filtering theory for univariate ARCH models, *Econometrica*, **62**, 561–573.

Pagan, A. (1996) The econometrics of financial markets, *Journal of Empirical Finance*, **3**, 15–102.

Pagan, A. and Schwert, G. (1990) Alternative models for conditional volatility, *Journal of Econometrics*, **45**, 267–290.

Palm, F. (1996) GARCH models of volatility, in Rao, C. and Maddala, G. (eds), *Handbook of Statistics*, Vol. 14, North-Holland, Amsterdam.

Patton, A.J. (2006) Modelling asymmetric exchange rate dependence, *International Economic Review*, **47**, 527–556.

Patton, A.J. (2009) Copula-based models for financial time series, in Andersen, T.G., Davis, R.A., Kreiss, J.-P. and Mikosch, T. (eds), *Handbook of Financial Time Series*, Springer-Verlag, Berlin.

Schwert, W. (1989) Why does stock market volatility change over time? *Journal of Finance*, **44**, 1115–1153.

Sentana, E. (1995) Quadratic ARCH models, *Review of Economic Studies*, **62**(4), 639–661.

Shephard, N. (1996) Statistical aspects of ARCH and stochastic volatility models, in Cox, D., Hinkley, D. and Barndorff-Nielsen, O. (eds), *Time Series Models in Econometrics, Finance and Other Fields*, Chapman & Hall, London, pp. 1–67.

Sklar, A. (1959) Fonctions de répartition à n dimensions et leurs marges, Technical Report, Publications de l'Institut de Statistique de L'Université de Paris 8, pp. 229–231.

Starica, C. and Granger, C. (2005) Non-stationarities in stock returns, *Review of Economics and Statistics*, **87**, 503–522.

Straumann, D. (2005) Estimation in conditionally heteroscedastic time series models, *Lecture Notes in Statistics*, Springer-Verlag, Berlin.

Taylor, N. (2004) Modeling discontinuous periodic conditional volatility: Evidence from the commodity futures market, *Journal of Futures Markets*, **24**, 805–834.

Taylor, S. (1986) *Modeling Financial Time Series*, John Wiley & Sons, New York.

Teräsvirta, T. (2009) An introduction to univariate GARCH models, in Andersen, T., Davis, R.A., Kreiss, J.-P. and Mikosch, T. (eds), *Handbook of Financial Time Series*, Springer-Verlag, Berlin.

Tsiakas, I. (2006) Periodic stochastic volatility and fat tails, *Journal of Financial Econometrics*, **4**, 90–135.

Weiss, A.A. (1986) Asymptotic theory for ARCH models: Estimation and testing, *Econometric Theory*, **2**, 107–131.

Zaffaroni, P. (2007) Contemporaneous aggregation of GARCH processes, *Journal of Time Series Analysis*, **28**, 521–544.

Zakoiän, J.-M. (1994) Threshold heteroskedastic models, *Journal of Economic Dynamics and Control*, **18**, 931–955.

CHAPTER 16

Pricing Commodity Swaps with Counterparty Credit Risk: The Case of Credit Value Adjustment

Marina Marena, Gianluca Fusai and Chiara Quaglini

16.1 INTRODUCTION

16.1.1 Energy Company Strategies in Derivative Instruments

The expansion of the liberalized physical commodity markets has led to the development of financial derivative instruments linked to energy commodities; this was followed by an increase in the number of energy companies acting as market operators both with hedging and trading purposes. It is acknowledged by energy companies that their activities expose them to relevant market and credit risks. For this reason the companies should measure, manage and limit these risks to maintain both the stability of cash flows, generated by the assets and contracts in the portfolio, and the company economic–financial balance. The most used derivative instrument for hedging purposes by oil, gas and power producers is the commodity swap. The floating leg of the commodity swap is usually indexed to oil products.

Since the commodity swap is an instrument traded over the counter (OTC), which is not managed by a central clearing house, it is necessary to estimate and quantify within the pricing activity the counterparty credit risk. This can be done by entering specific agreements such as the margining agreement, the exchange futures for physical, the additional collateralization or simply by adjusting the OTC derivative instrument risk-free value with a metric called credit value adjustment (CVA).

The purpose of this chapter is to illustrate the CVA computation with reference to an energy commodity swap contract. The analysis is performed using a popular commodity model introduced by Schwartz and Smith (2000). In addition, this paper also analyses the current

Handbook of Multi-Commodity Markets and Products: Structuring, Trading and Risk Management. Edited by Andrea Roncoroni, Gianluca Fusai and Mark Cummins.

international accounting framework for derivative instruments, focusing on the cash flow hedge included in IAS 39 and, for CVA, reporting the exposure draft on *Offsetting Financial Assets and Financial Liabilities* recently announced by the IASB and FASB, providing an example of how to assess the hedge effectiveness of a specific derivative instrument.

The rest of this chapter is organized as follows. In Section 16.2 we provide an accurate description of the company energy policy, which is a document written by energy firms on managing market and credit risks arising from trading and hedging activities. Section 16.3 analyses the main features of an energy commodity swap, which is the derivative instrument most used by energy firms for hedging purposes. Section 16.4 introduces the Schwartz and Smith commodity pricing model in order to describe the stochastic dynamics of the oil forward curve. Section 16.5 illustrates in detail how to calibrate, simulate and price a commodity swap resorting to this model. Section 16.6 takes a closer look at the counterparty credit risk, providing the definition and its quantitative estimation. Section 16.7 performs a sensitivity analysis to understand how changes in key model parameters affect the swap value and the CVA computation. Finally, Section 16.8 discusses the general international accounting framework for derivative instruments and CVA, providing an example of hedging effectiveness.

16.2 COMPANY ENERGY POLICY

Many energy companies develop a document called energy risk policy which defines the guidelines related to the governance, the managing risk strategy and the risk control on the commodity activities of the company. In particular, the risk policy commonly identifies as financial risks:

- the market risk (unexpected changes in commodity prices, exchange rates or interest rates);
- the liquidity risk (inability to fulfil the financial obligations in the short term);
- the credit risk (commercial/financial counterparty default or downgrading);
- the operational risk (fraud or equipment failure);
- the country risk (economic and political instability of the country where the company trades or invests).

For each unidentified financial risk, the policy provides a detailed definition, a list of risk management goals and a description of risk measurement methodologies. Here, we focus on how energy companies handle commodity risk (included in the market risk category) and credit risk.

16.2.1 Commodity Risk

16.2.1.1 Definition and Risk Management Goals Commodity risk is defined as the possibility of an economic margin fluctuation due to a commodity market price variation. Strong volatility of the economic margin can impact negatively on company earnings and cause the company to fail to reach its long-term goals defined in the business plan. The policy usually refers to the volatility of the commodities actively traded by the company or the commodities included in the pricing indexation formula. An energy company usually trades the following commodities:

- oil and refined oil products
- natural gas and liquefied natural gas
- coal
- power
- environmental certificates (e.g., carbon credit, green and white certificates).

The main goals of market risk management are to maintain stable the cash flows generated by the company's assets and contracts and to protect the asset fair value from depreciation. The policy also describes all the hedging activities that the company intends to undertake in order to pursue the aforementioned goals. The hedging activity is conducted by buying or selling authorized categories of energy derivatives. The most common ones are the following:

- commodity forwards
- commodity futures
- commodity swaps or contracts for differences
- commodity options (European, American and Asian)
- green and white certificates, carbon credit.

The abovementioned financial instruments must present a limited loss profile. Generally, short selling or any other anticipatory hedge activities are forbidden for hedging purposes.

16.2.1.2 Risk Measurement Methodology The commodity risk measurement methodology adopted by energy companies depends on the portfolio purpose. Regarding trading portfolios, the best practices are value at risk (VaR) and cash flow at risk (CFaR). The two methodologies are both characterized by a holding period of one day and a confidence level equal to 95%. Concerning the industrial portfolio, the most popular methodology is the profit at risk (PaR), with a holding period of one or more years and a confidence level equal to 95%.

16.2.2 Credit Risk

16.2.2.1 Definition and Risk Management Goals Credit risk is generally classified as counterparty risk related to both physical and financial contracts. Financial counterparty risk is defined as the possibility that the counterparty of an OTC financial contract will default prior to the expiration of the contract without fulfilling the contract's obligations, hence deteriorating the company's economic margin. The most important credit risk management tools aimed at the mitigation of credit risk are the following:

- Price adjustment (CVA or DVA). This is a value, positive or negative, which represents the market value of the credit risk of an instrument. This adjustment must be added to the risk-free market value of the contract.
- Margining agreement. This is a legally binding contract between the parties of a trade. It requires fixing a bilateral credit threshold – if the credit risk exceeds the limit, the counterparty must provide margin payments (subject to a minimum transfer amount) directly to or into a margining account.

- Exchange futures for physical (EFP). This is an off-market transaction in which one exchange, on the payment of a fee, offers to transfer an OTC physical transaction in a regular futures contracts position (shifting short futures contracts from one party's account to the other). In other words, one contracting party buys a commodity from the other counterparty at an agreed predetermined price, receiving short futures contracts in return.
- Additional collateralization. Here, one contracting party can demand additional protection against increased credit risk due to a downgrading of the counterparty.

16.2.2.2 Risk Measurement Methodology The two most widespread credit risk measurement metrics are the expected loss (the product of the credit exposure and the default probability) and the potential future exposure (the maximum credit exposure estimated to occur over a specified period of time with a given confidence level).

16.3 A FOCUS ON COMMODITY SWAP CONTRACTS

Energy companies usually buy forward commodities such as gas and oil directly from the producer at a variable price linked to an indexing pricing formula defined at the contract's inception. Following the liberalization of energy markets, the companies have to sell refined product or power to their client at the market price. The competition across companies pushes the market price down, narrowing the economic profit or even turning it to negative. So, in order to avoid economic losses and to keep margins stable, this category of contract is often used.

16.3.1 Definition and Main Features of a Commodity Swap

Commodity swaps are customizable and financially settled instruments traded OTC. Together with futures and forward contracts, swaps are instruments without optionality and, for this reason, they are easy to price. The standard fixed-for-floating swap agreement defines a sequence of settlement dates in the future and, on each of the settlement dates, it involves an exchange of cash flows: one counterparty (the so-called payer) pays the fixed price whereas the other counterparty (the so-called receiver) pays the floating price linked to a specified commodity indexation formula. When a swap contract involves net payments, that is only one payment will be made on each settlement date, it becomes a contract for difference. Hence, if the fixed price is above the floating price, the so-called payer pays the difference; vice versa, if the floating amount is above the fixed price, the payer receives the difference.

16.3.1.1 The Oil-Linked Indexation Formula Wholesalers make large capital investments which are required for exploring, producing and developing activities needed to satisfy the demand. The commodity gas is not sold as gas but its price is determined by an oil-linked formula that in the past guaranteed a competitive price compared with oil, the most liquid traded commodity. The formula is of the form

$$P_{gas} = \alpha X^{xyz} + \beta Y^{xyz},$$

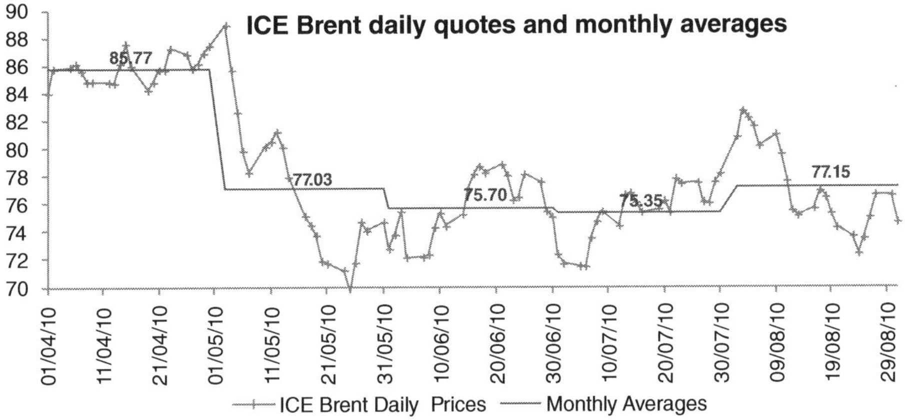

FIGURE 16.1 ICE Brent daily quotes and monthly averages.

where:

- α and β are constant coefficients;
- X and Y are the monthly oil prices (e.g., gas oil or fuel oil);
- x is the averaging period (e.g., 6/9 months);
- y is the time lag of the price fixing – for example, if we set it equal to 0, the price for month k is the averaging period that ends with month k–1;
- z is the recalculation frequency – for example, if we set it equal to 1, the formula is applied every month and we set a new price for the following month.

16.3.1.2 Example For a better understanding, let us consider a concrete example. Figure 16.1 illustrates the ICE Brent daily quotes in the period 1 April 2010 to 31 August 2010 and the corresponding monthly averages ranging from April to August. If we assume two settlement months, July and August, and an indexation formula of the form Brent^{301}, the floating payment exchanged in July will be the result of the averages of April ($85.77), May ($77.03) and June ($75.70). Hence, the variable leg would be equal to $79.5. To set a new price for the following settlement month, that is August, we repeat the procedure computing the average between the monthly averages of May ($77.03), June ($75.70) and July ($75.35), which gives as a result $76.03. The computations are illustrated in Figure 16.2.

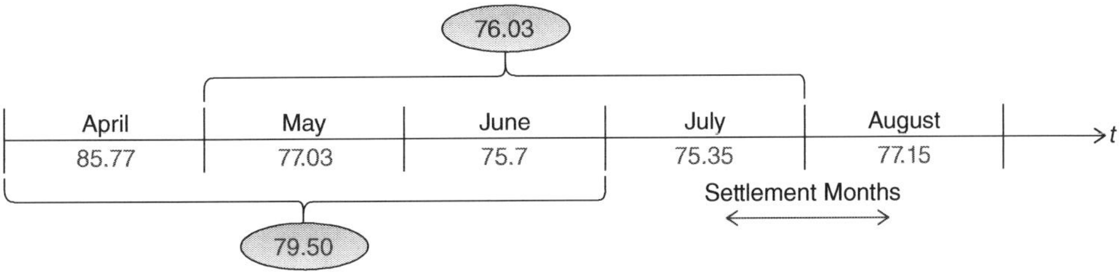

FIGURE 16.2 Calculation of the payoffs.

16.4 MODELLING THE DYNAMICS OF OIL SPOT PRICES AND THE FORWARD CURVE

Energy companies use current spot and forward oil prices to perform the marking to market of their financial and physical products. The market forward curve provides the market expectation (the so-called risk-neutral expectation) regarding future spot prices. However, for pricing and risk management, we not only need to know the expected future spot prices but their dispersion around their average values as well; much better if we could know the full probability distribution of futures spot prices. Clearly this is an impossible task, so we can use a model that is able to take into account the most important features we observe in oil spot prices and based on it, build a hypothetical probability distribution.

A reliable model should be able to fit typical features of oil prices, such as mean reversion, non-perfect correlation between futures contracts with different tenors and a decaying term structure of volatility (i.e., the volatility of percentage changes in futures prices having different time to maturity). With respect to the mean reversion pattern, it can be said that oil prices may temporarily rise or decline because of shocks caused by temporary supply/demand imbalances. However, in the long run, oil prices should revert to an equilibrium level which can be interpreted as the marginal cost of production. Non-perfect correlation refers to the fact that futures price changes do not have the same size and can even have opposite sign, generating in this way a change in the slope and curvature of the term structure. Finally, the term structure of volatility captures the fact that the volatility of a contract with different maturities can be different. In general, the longer the maturity, the lower the volatility.

Figure 16.3 illustrates the changes in term structure of oil prices over time. Figure 16.4 shows a typical shape of the term structure of volatility.

Finally, Table 16.1 provides the correlation matrix of changes in log-futures prices. We can appreciate, for example, that the correlation between changes in the 1-month futures prices and the 12-month ones turns out to be quite high (i.e., 94.04%) but not perfect. This suggests that more than one driving factor is necessary to describe the dynamics of the term structure and two factors may be enough. In addition, one factor should add more volatility to the short end of the term structure.

16.4.1 The Schwartz and Smith Pricing Model

This section introduces a popular dynamic stochastic model that can be used to price a commodity swap and compute the credit risk exposure of the two counterparties. The model we consider is the short-term/long-term model developed by Schwartz and Smith (2000). This model is parsimonious in its number of parameters but still able to capture the above-mentioned features of futures prices, such as mean reversion, non-perfect correlation in futures price changes with different tenors and the decaying shape of the volatility term structure.

Schwartz and Smith assume that the logarithm of spot price $S(t)$ is the sum of two components:

$$\ln S(t) = \chi(t) + \zeta(t).$$

Here, $\chi(t)$ represents short-term deviations in price due, for example, to supply disruption or unusual weather changes, whilst $\zeta(t)$ is the equilibrium price level, which reflects the

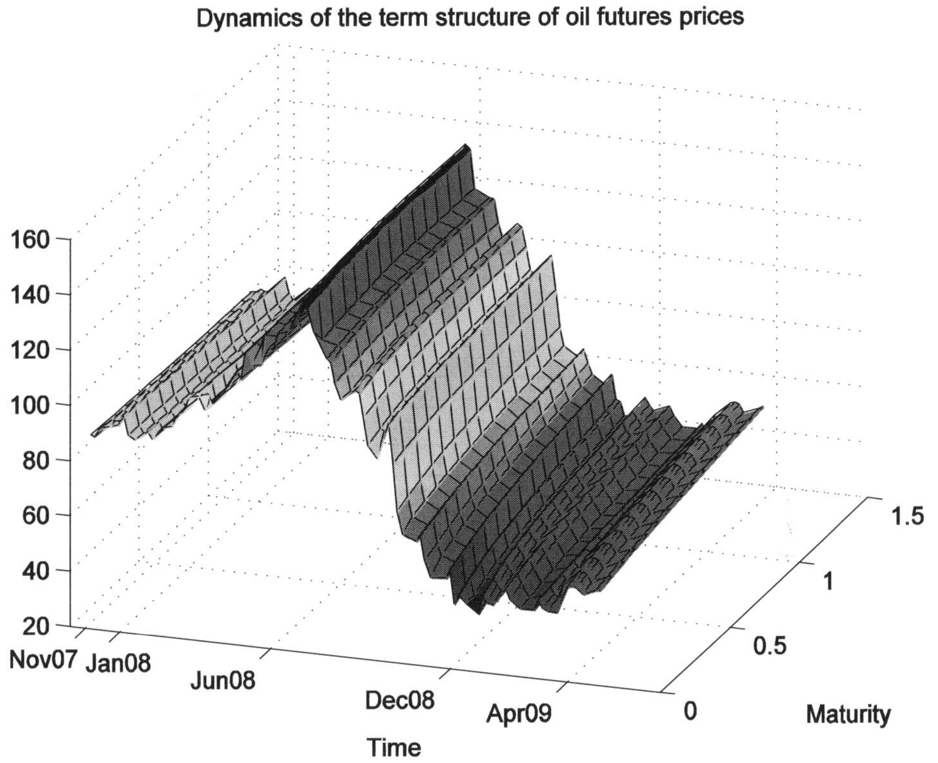

FIGURE 16.3 Movements of the term structures of oil futures prices from January 2008 to May 2009.

exhaustion of existing supply, the technology improvements for the exploration, production and discovery of the commodity, the inflation and political/regulatory effects as well.

In order to describe the short-term component dynamics, Schwartz and Smith use the well-known Vasicek model to describe the short-term interest rate evolution. The process is also called a mean-reverting Ornstein–Uhlenbeck process and postulates the following risk-neutral stochastic dynamics for $\chi(t)$:

$$d\chi(t) = (-\lambda_\chi - k_\chi \chi(t))dt + \sigma_\chi dW_\chi(t)$$

with initial condition $\chi(0) = \chi_0$. The equilibrium price level $\zeta(t)$, representing the long-term dynamics, is governed by an arithmetic Brownian motion process with drift $d\zeta(t) = \mu_\zeta dt + \sigma_\zeta dW_\zeta(t), \zeta(0) = \zeta_0$.

The two state variables are assumed to be jointly normally distributed. In particular, the conditional expectation of the two state variables at a future time T given their value at time t is given by

$$\begin{aligned} E_t(\chi(T)) &= \chi(t)e^{-k_\chi(T-t)} - \frac{\lambda_\chi}{k}(1 - e^{-k_\chi(T-t)}), \\ E_t(\zeta(T)) &= \zeta(t) + \mu_\zeta(T - t), \end{aligned}$$

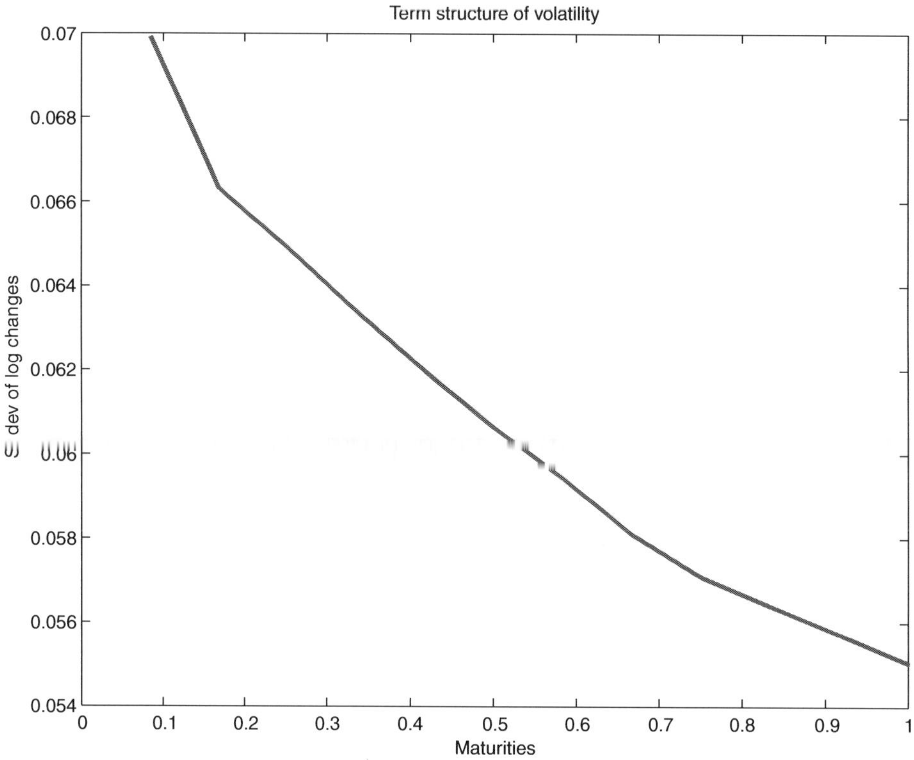

FIGURE 16.4 Term structure of volatility of oil futures prices. Here, volatility is defined as the standard deviation of the logarithmic changes of futures prices having different time to maturity.

and the covariance matrix is equal to:

$$\mathrm{Cov}_t\left(\chi(T),\zeta(T)\right) \equiv \Sigma(t,T) = \begin{bmatrix} \dfrac{\sigma_\chi^2}{2k_\chi}\left(1-e^{-2k_\chi(T-t)}\right) & \dfrac{\rho_{\chi,\zeta}\sigma_\chi\sigma_\zeta}{k_\chi}\left(1-e^{-k_\chi(T-t)}\right) \\ \dfrac{\rho_{\chi,\zeta}\sigma_\chi\sigma_\zeta}{k_\chi}\left(1-e^{-k_\chi(T-t)}\right) & \sigma_\zeta^2(T-t) \end{bmatrix}$$

TABLE 16.1 Correlation matrix of changes in log futures prices having different times to maturity (labels of rows and columns)

	1m	3m	6m	9m	12m
1m	100.00%	98.12%	96.60%	95.16%	94.04%
3m	98.12%	100.00%	99.34%	98.06%	97.01%
6m	96.60%	99.34%	100.00%	99.58%	98.96%
9m	95.16%	98.06%	99.58%	100.00%	99.83%
12m	94.04%	97.01%	98.96%	99.83%	100.00%

The parameter set $\theta = (k_\chi, \lambda_\chi, \sigma_\chi, \mu_\zeta, \sigma_\zeta, \rho_{\chi,\zeta})$ can be interpreted as follows:

- k_χ is a constant that determines the convergence speed of the process $\chi(t)$ to the (risk-neutral) long-run level $-\frac{\lambda_\chi}{k_\chi}$. Indeed, the long-run expected value of $\chi(T)$ is $\lim_{T\to\infty} E_t(\chi(T)) = -\frac{\lambda_\chi}{k_\chi}$.
- σ_χ and σ_ζ are the volatilities of the changes in the two state variables.
- $\rho_{\chi,\zeta}$ is the correlation between the two state variables.
- μ_ζ is the drift of the ABM process for equilibrium log-prices.

The log-forward curve at any given time t is given by:

$$\ln F(t, T; \chi(t), \zeta(t), \theta) \equiv \ln F(t, T) = e^{-k_\chi(T-t)}\chi(t) + \zeta(t) + \mu_\zeta(T-t)$$
$$-\frac{\lambda_\chi}{k_\chi}\left(1 - e^{k_\chi(T-t)}\right) + A(T-t),$$

where

$$A(t) = \frac{1}{2}\left(\left(1 - e^{-2k_\chi t}\right)\frac{\sigma_\chi^2}{2k_\chi} + \sigma_\zeta^2 t + 2\left(1 - e^{-k_\chi t}\right)\frac{\rho_{\chi,\zeta}\sigma_\zeta\sigma_\chi}{k_\chi}\right).$$

The most important implications of the above model are:

1. mean reversion of the futures price dynamics;
2. changes in futures prices of different tenors do not have perfect correlation;
3. the term structure of volatilities is, for long maturities, decaying.

16.4.1.1 Model Calibration The Schwartz and Smith two-factor model can be calibrated by collecting historical data and then using some filtering technique, such as the Kalman filter, to jointly estimate the model parameters and the unobservable factors.[1] The advantage of this procedure is that it allows us to fully identify the model either in the real world or under the risk-neutral measure. However, it is computationally intensive. A more practical approach is to perform, at the starting date $t = 0$, an implied calibration solving the following nonlinear least-squares problem:

$$\hat{\theta} = \arg\min \sum_{j=1}^{M} w_j(F^{mkt}(0, T_j) - F^{theo}(0, T_j; \theta))^2$$

where:

- $\theta = (k_\chi, \lambda_\chi, \sigma_\chi, \mu_\zeta, \sigma_\zeta, \rho_{\chi,\zeta})$ is the set of model parameters.
- $F^{mkt}(0, T)$ is the observed quoted market futures price to the observation date.

[1]Full details of the filtering approach can be found in the Schwartz and Smith original paper, pages 901–904, and Chapter 12 of this Handbook.

- $F^{theo}(0, T; \theta)$ is the theoretical forward price, given in the formula above, dependent on the parameter set θ and the current value of the two state variables.
- w_i are the weights attached at each maturity. This allows us, for example, to give more relevance to quotations we believe to be more liquid or representative of the market.
- M is the number of maturities considered.

Given that the two state variables are not directly observable we can include them in the calibration procedure, treating them as if they were additional unknown parameters to be estimated. This means that the parameter set to be estimated is augmented to $\theta^{AUG} = (\chi_0, \zeta_0, k_\chi, \lambda_\chi, \sigma_\chi, \mu_\zeta, \sigma_\zeta, \rho_{\chi,\zeta})$.

16.5 AN EMPIRICAL APPLICATION

In this section we detail the steps we followed for pricing and evaluating a commodity swap contract traded between an energy company and an investment bank. The tenor of the swap is approximately one year.

16.5.1 The Commodity Swap Features

The derivative instrument that we aim to price presents the following terms:

Transaction: Swap

Trade Date: 1 April 2010

Commodity: ICE Brent Component

Total Notional Quantity: 21,590 MWh

Effective Date: 1 January 2011

Termination Date: 31 March 2011

Settlement Date: 5th Business day following the end of each calculation period

Fixed Leg

Fixed Price Payer: Bank XYZ

Fixed Amount: Fixed price $*$ Notional quantity per calculation period

Floating Leg

Floating Price Payer: Energy Company ZYX

Floating Price: Power formula, $0.71 * \text{Brent}^{901}$ in EUR/MWh

Floating Amount: Floating price $*$ Notional quantity per calculation period

Pricing Dates: Each commodity business day during each relevant determination period

16.5.1.1 Commodity Reference Price

ICE Brent. The average of the monthly averages of the daily settlement prices per barrel of Brent crude oil on the ICE of the futures contract for

TABLE 16.2 Calculation and payment schedule of the swap

Notional quantity per application period (MWh)	Calculation period	Determination period	Settlement date
7440	Jan 2011	1 Apr 2010 to 31 Dec 2010	07 Feb 11
6720	Feb 2011	3 May 2010 to 31 Jan 2011	07 Mar 11
7430	Mar 2011	1 Jun 2010 to 28 Feb 2011	07 Apr 11

the first nearby month of the 9 months preceding the relevant calculation period. Each average is converted into euros using the FX conversion factor.

FX conversion factor. The monthly average of the daily foreign exchange rate USD/EUR during the relevant calculation period. The exchange rate is calculated by the ECB. The payment schedule is reported in Table 16.2.

16.5.2 Calibration of the Theoretical Schwartz and Smith Forward Curve

The data set we use for calibration is provided by the Bloomberg data service and consists of 12 values of monthly ICE Brent futures quotes (with monthly maturities from 1M to 12M). The expiry dates of all the monthly futures contracts can be downloaded from the Calendar section on the ICE website. Futures prices, expressed in dollars per barrel, are reported in Table 16.3.

We calibrate the Schwartz and Smith model at the trade date of the contract (1 April 2010), choosing the parameters that allow us to match the theoretical futures prices to the ICE Brent futures market curve observed in the market on the trade date. This procedure, also called the 'implied method', consists of a nonlinear least-squares minimization, as described previously. Figure 16.5 illustrates the market and the fitted theoretical curve (top panel) and the pricing errors in USD (lower panel).

Table 16.4 reports the calibrated parameter estimates of the Schwartz and Smith two-factor model, together with their 90% confidence interval, estimated by bootstrap resampling.

Both the speed of mean reversion, k_χ, and the coefficient of correlation, $\rho_{x\zeta}$, between the two state variables appear to be significantly different from 0. The drift of the long-term process, μ_ζ, and $-\lambda_\chi$turn out to be positive. This result is mainly due to the upward shape of the term structure of futures prices. It is also worth mentioning the long-term factor. This indicates that market oil prices deviate from their mean level more in the short term than in the long term. Finally, on the valuation date the state variables were estimated to be $\chi_0 = 1.044$ and $\zeta_0 = 3.3850$, respectively. These values correspond to a current spot price of \$83.8457 $(= \exp(1.0440 + 3.3850))$.

16.5.2.1 Pricing the Swap Contract A swap contract is fair if the present values of the two legs are equal, so that the net value of the contract is zero at inception. If $E_t(P_i)$ is the (risk-neutral) estimate at time t of the indexed floating payoff P_i exchanged against the

TABLE 16.3 Futures term structure on the inception date of the swap

ICE Brent Crude Oil

Trade date	Delivery month	Termination of trading	Settlement prices
01-apr-10	May10	15-apr-10	84.01
01-apr-10	Jun10	14-may-10	84.55
01-apr-10	Jul10	15-jun-10	84.99
01-apr-10	Aug10	15-jul-10	85.35
01-apr-10	Sep10	16-aug-10	85.59
01-apr-10	Oct10	15-sep-10	85.79
01-apr-10	Nov10	14-oct-10	85.96
01-apr-10	Dec10	15-nov-10	86.11
01-apr-10	Jan11	16-dec-10	86.26
01-apr-10	Feb11	14-jan-11	86.42
01-apr-10	Mar11	14-feb-11	86.58
01-apr-10	Apr11	16-mar-11	86.73
01-apr-10	May11	14-apr-11	86.87
01-apr-10	Jun11	16-may-11	86.98
01-apr-10	Jul11	15-jun-11	87.09
01-apr-10	Aug11	14-jul-11	87.19
01-apr-10	Sep11	16-aug-11	87.28
01-apr-10	Oct11	15-sep-11	87.37
01-apr-10	Nov11	14-oct-11	87.46
01-apr-10	Dec11	15-nov-11	87.55
01-apr-10	Jan12	15-dec-11	87.64
01-apr-10	Feb12	16-jan-12	87.73
01-apr-10	Mar12	14-feb-12	87.81
01-apr-10	Apr12	15-mar-12	87.89
01-apr-10	May12	13-apr-12	87.97
01-apr-10	Jun12	16-may-12	88.05
01-apr-10	Jul12	14-jun-12	88.10
01-apr-10	Aug12	16-jul-12	88.15
01-apr-10	Sep12	16-aug-12	88.20
01-apr-10	Oct12	13-sep-12	88.24
01-apr-10	Nov12	16-oct-12	88.28

swap fixed price at the settlement date T_i, then the present value of the floating leg (assuming deterministic interest rates, as we will do throughout this chapter) is given by

$$\sum_{i=1}^{n} E_t(P_i) \times df(t, T_i) \times V(T_i),$$

where $df(t, T)$ is the discount factor at time t of 1 euro due at time T (present value of 1 euro). The present value of the fixed payments is given by

$$F \times \sum_{i=1}^{n} df(t, T_i) \times V(T_i),$$

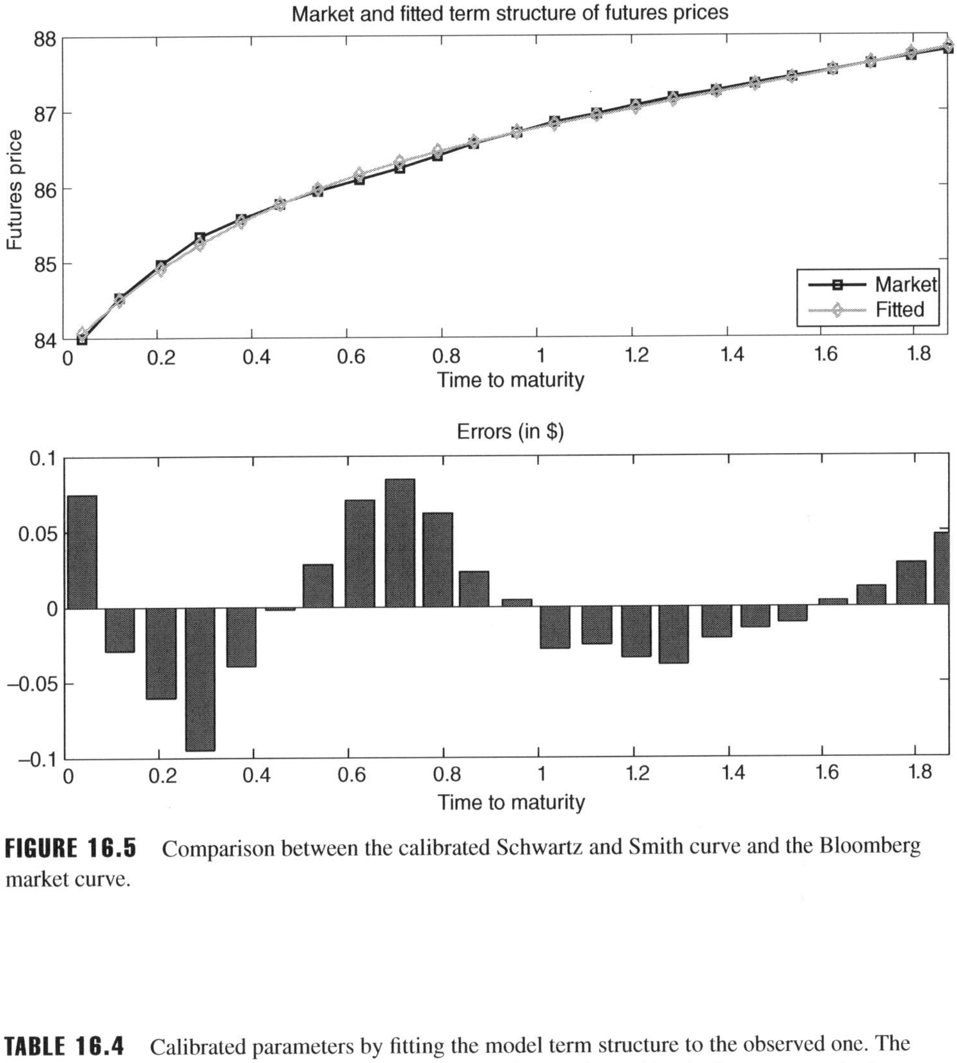

FIGURE 16.5 Comparison between the calibrated Schwartz and Smith curve and the Bloomberg market curve.

TABLE 16.4 Calibrated parameters by fitting the model term structure to the observed one. The lower and upper bounds of the 90% confidence interval are estimated by the bootstrap method

Parameters	NLS estimates	Lower bound	Upper bound
χ_0	1.0385	1.0342	1.0432
ζ_0	3.3906	3.3859	3.3947
μ_ζ	0.0208	0.0180	0.0238
k_χ	0.9333	0.9160	0.9494
λ_x	–0.9104	–0.9200	–0.8997
σ_x	0.4761	0.4519	0.5020
σ_ζ	0.0076	0.0003	0.0138
$\rho_{\chi,\zeta}$	0.2052	0.2040	0.2062

where $V(T_i)$ is equal to the total notional. The fair value of the swap at time t for the party that is receiving floating and paying fixed (the so-called payer swap) is given by

$$\sum_{i=1}^{n} E_t(P_i) \times df(t, T_i) \times V(T_i) - F \times \sum_{i=1}^{n} df(t, T_i) \times V(T_i).$$

This is zero if the fixed price $F = F(t; T_1, \ldots, T_n)$ satisfies

$$F \times \sum_{i=1}^{n} df(t, T_i) \times V(T_i) = \sum_{i=1}^{n} E_t(P_i) \times df(t, T_i) \times V(T_i).$$

The formula above states that the present value of the payments on the fixed leg must be equal to the present value of the expected payments on the floating leg. Solving this formula with respect to the fixed price F gives us the fair fixed price for a new swap starting in t:

$$F = F(t; T_1, \ldots T_n) = \frac{\sum_{i=1}^{n} E_t(P_i) \times df(t, T_i) \times V(T_i)}{\sum_{i=1}^{n} df(t, T_i) \times V(T_i)}.$$

In the contract under examination, we have $n = 3$. The computation of the expected value of the floating payments requires the expected discounted payoff. Let us introduce the quantity $Avg(m, y)$ that refers to the arithmetic average of oil spot prices observed in month m of year y. This arithmetic average is computed according to the contractual formula

$$Avg(m, y) = \frac{1}{n(m, y)} \sum_{l=1}^{n(m,y)} S(t_l(m, y)) \times FX(t_l(m, y)),$$

where $t_l(m, y)$ refers to the trading day l in month m of year y, $n(m, y)$ is the number of trading days in month m of year y, and $S(t)$ and $FX(t)$ are respectively the oil spot price and the spot currency rate observed in the market on trading day t. Assuming a deterministic evolution of the currency rate, or that we can hedge currency risk away in the forward market, we can replace, in the above expression, the spot currency rate by the forward currency rate we observe in the market on the inception date. Forward currency rates on the inception date are provided in Table 16.6 later. The market-based expected value can be computed by now replacing the oil spot price with the calibrated term structure of oil futures prices and the spot currency rate with the forward one. Therefore, at the inception date $t = 0$ we have

$$E_0(Avg(m, y)) = \frac{1}{n(m, y)} \sum_{l=1}^{n(m,y)} F(0, t_l(m, y); \chi_0, \zeta_0, \theta) \times FX(0, t_l(m, y)).$$

The determination of the fair value of the floating payments requires now the calculation of the following quantities:

$$E_0(P_1) = \frac{\sum_{m=4}^{12} E_0\,(Avg\,(m, 2010))}{9} \times 0.71,$$

$$E_0(P_2) = \frac{\sum_{m=5}^{12} E_0\,(Avg\,(m, 2010)) + E_0\,(Avg\,(1, 2011))}{9} \times 0.71,$$

$$E_0(P_3) = \frac{\sum_{m=6}^{12} E_0\,(Avg\,(m, 2010)) + \sum_{m=1}^{2} E_0\,(Avg\,(m, 2011))}{9} \times 0.71.$$

At inception, the market value of the swap to the payer of the fixed price is therefore

$$v(0) = \sum_{i=1}^{3} E_0(P_i)df(0, T_i)V(T_i) - F\sum_{i=1}^{3} df(0, T_i)V(T_i),$$

and it is zero if the fixed price is chosen according to

$$F = \frac{\sum_{i=1}^{3} E_0(P_i)df(0, T_i)V(T_i)}{\sum_{i=1}^{3} df(0, T_i)V(T_i)}.$$

The computation of the fixed price requires the model calibrated parameters, the term structure of the discount factors and the term structure of the currency forward rates. Discount factors have been obtained by a standard bootstrap procedure using euro LIBOR and EUR swap rates. The discount term structure is given in Table 16.5. The term structure of currency forward rates is given in Table 16.6. In both cases, data have been obtained from Bloomberg.

The fixed price that provides a zero value of the swap at inception turns out to be 44.76 EUR. The detailed computations are provided in Table 16.7.

Given the three expected payoffs (last column of Table 16.7), the fixed price is obtained by taking the ratio between:

a. The sum of the products of the values in columns 4-5-6-7-8 of Table 16.7; this sum is equal to 957,527.

b. The sum of the products of the values in columns 4 and 5 of Table 16.7; this sum is equal to 21,388.

The ratio between these two numbers gives the fixed price of 44.76 EUR. The correctness of the computations can be verified by referring to Table 16.8.

TABLE 16.5 Market (LIBOR and swap) rates, spot rates and discount factors

Term Structure of Discount Factors				
Market date	**Market rate**	**Spot rate**	**Discount factor**	**Source**
06-apr-10	0.325	0.325		Cash Rate
14-apr-10	0.344	0.344	0.999933	Cash Rate
07-may-10	0.400	0.400	0.999667	Cash Rate
07-jun-10	0.501	0.501	0.999152	Cash Rate
07-jul-10	0.635	0.635	0.998397	Cash Rate
09-aug-10	0.743	0.743	0.997447	Cash Rate
07-sep-10	0.838	0.838	0.996451	Cash Rate
07-oct-10	0.945	0.945	0.995219	Cash Rate
08-nov-10	0.987	0.987	0.994140	Cash Rate
07-dec-10	1.033	1.033	0.993047	Cash Rate
07-jan-11	1.088	1.088	0.991757	Cash Rate
07-feb-11	1.129	1.129	0.990495	Cash Rate
07-mar-11	1.170	1.170	0.989262	Cash Rate
07-apr-11	1.214	1.214	0.987841	Cash Rate
07-oct-11	1.280	1.282	0.981077	Swap Rate
10-apr-12	1.465	1.467	0.971182	Swap Rate
08-apr-13	1.804	1.812	0.947515	Swap Rate
07-apr-14	2.118	2.135	0.918951	Swap Rate
07-apr-15	2.392	2.421	0.887264	Swap Rate
07-apr-16	2.644	2.689	0.852838	Swap Rate
07-apr-17	2.841	2.900	0.818617	Swap Rate
09-apr-18	3.012	3.087	0.783955	Swap Rate
08-apr-19	3.153	3.244	0.750214	Swap Rate
07-apr-20	3.274	3.379	0.717251	Swap Rate
07-apr-21	3.370	3.488	0.685802	Swap Rate
07-apr-22	3.462	3.594	0.654610	Swap Rate
07-apr-25	3.654	3.819	0.570000	Swap Rate
08-apr-30	3.782	3.957	0.460145	Swap Rate
09-apr-35	3.758	3.881	0.385892	Swap Rate
09-apr-40	3.677	3.721	0.334101	Swap Rate
11-apr-45	3.604	3.581	0.291753	Swap Rate
07-apr-50	3.542	3.463	0.256178	Swap Rate
07-apr-55	3.516	3.418	0.220417	Swap Rate
07-apr-60	3.490	3.367	0.190898	Swap Rate

Column 1 of Table 16.8 gives the expected floating payoff, while column 2 gives the fixed payoff at the different settlement dates; these numbers have been obtained by multiplying the fixed price by the notional given in column 5 of Table 16.7. Then, in the third column of Table 16.8, we have the net payoff at each settlement date. Finally, the last column gives the present value and then in the last cell of Table 16.8 we sum the present value of the differences and obtain the confirmation of a zero value of the swap.

Away from inception, the swap contract can assume positive or negative values depending on the evolution of the term structure of futures prices as well as currency rates and interest

TABLE 16.6 Term structure of EUR/USD currency forward rates

Currency Forward Curve					
Term	**Dates**	**TTM**	**Bid**	**Ask**	**Mid**
Spot		0			0.7359000
ON	06/04/2010	0.0137	0.735803	0.736009	0.7359059
TN	07/04/2010	0.0164	0.735802	0.736002	0.7359019
SP	07/04/2010	0.0164	0.735800	0.736000	0.7359000
SN	08/04/2010	0.0192	0.735799	0.735999	0.7358989
1W	14/04/2010	0.0356	0.735792	0.735999	0.7358955
2W	21/04/2010	0.0548	0.735786	0.735995	0.7358905
3W	28/04/2010	0.0740	0.735788	0.735991	0.7358895
1M	07/05/2010	0.0986	0.735777	0.735982	0.7358795
2M	07/06/2010	0.1836	0.735768	0.735974	0.7358710
3M	07/07/2010	0.2658	0.735765	0.735977	0.7358710
4M	09/08/2010	0.3562	0.735804	0.736025	0.7359145
5M	07/09/2010	0.4356	0.735854	0.736081	0.7359675
6M	07/10/2010	0.5178	0.735882	0.736124	0.7360030
9M	07/01/2011	0.7699	0.735938	0.736219	0.7360785
1Y	07/04/2011	1.0164	0.735773	0.736082	0.7359275

TABLE 16.7 Computation of the fixed price of the swap

	Calculation Period						Expected average Brent
Settlement	Start	End	*df*(0,T)	Notional *V*(*T*)	Weighting	Average FX rate	price
07/02/2011	01/04/2010	31/12/2010	0.99177	7440	0.710	0.7359	85.4308
07/03/2011	03/05/2010	31/01/2011	0.99068	6720	0.710	0.7360	85.6950
07/04/2011	01/06/2010	28/02/2011	0.98942	7430	0.710	0.7360	85.9134
						Fixed Leg	**44.77**

rates. This fact opens up a problem of risk management of the contract. In addition, if the contract becomes too valuable, the risk that the counterparty that is losing will no longer be able to fulfil its obligations will increase. In order to fully appreciate how large this risk can be, we need to understand how big the fluctuations of the swap value can be. Monte Carlo simulation can help us in doing this. This is discussed in the next section.

TABLE 16.8 Computation of the fair value of the swap at inception

Floating	**Fixed**	**Expected payoff**	**PV(expected payoff)**
€332,319	€333,091	−€972	−€964
€300,914	€300,857	€57	€56
€333,561	€332,643	€918	€908
		Fair value €0.00	

16.5.3 The Monte Carlo Simulation of Oil Spot Prices

In this section we illustrate how to simulate the state variables and the futures term structure, given the calibrated parameters. This allows us to simulate as well the daily simulated net cash flows (profits or losses) on the swap contract and to find the time evolution of the fair value of the contract. This is important for measuring the potential loss due to counterparty default, as we will discuss shortly.

Before presenting the simulation scheme, we have to notice that the two counterparties – the bank and the energy company – both operate in the Eurozone and the swap payoff is paid in euros, whilst the oil price dynamics is in dollars. Therefore, all the simulated spot prices (in dollars) need to be converted into euros. We do this by using the term structure of forward exchange rates \$/€ listed on 1 April 2010, see Table 16.6. This amounts to assuming that the currency risk has been fully hedged in the forward market. If this is not the case, we should also postulate a stochastic process for the currency rate and simulate it jointly with the short term and long term components of the commodity process.

16.5.3.1 Simulating Forward Prices In order to estimate the value of the contract at a generic date, we can simulate step by step the two state variables through the following procedure. Let us define $K+1$ valuation dates $0 = t_0, t_1, \ldots, t_K$. With initial conditions given by the estimated values χ_0 and ζ_0, the two state variable dynamics can be simulated recursively, without any discretization error, by using the following bivariate stochastic difference equation:

$$\chi(t_k) = \chi(t_{k-1})e^{-k_\chi(t_k - t_{k-1})} - \left(1 - e^{-k_\chi(t_k - t_{k-1})}\right)\frac{\lambda_\chi}{k_\chi} + \eta_1(t_k),$$
$$\zeta(t_k) = \zeta(t_{k-1}) + \mu_\zeta(t_k - t_{k-1}) + \eta_2(t_k),$$

where η is a vector of Gaussian noises, distributed with zero mean and covariance matrix equal to $\Sigma(t_{k-1}, t_k)$.

The term structure of futures prices at time t_k with maturity T is then obtained by applying the futures price expression for $F(t_k, T)$, given previously. In particular, the simulated oil spot price at time t_k is

$$\ln S(t_k) = \chi(t_k) + \zeta(t_k).$$

Therefore, we proceed as follows:

1. Assign the initial values of the state variables.
2. At each time step, simulate the vector η from a bivariate Gaussian random variable[2] with zero mean and covariance matrix $\Sigma(t_{k-1}, t_k)$ and then update the values of the two state variables using the two stochastic difference equations.
3. At each time step, insert into the theoretical futures price formula the simulated values of the two state variables. Thus, we can obtain a simulated term structure of futures prices.

[2]The simulation of a bivariate normal random vector can be performed via the Cholesky decomposition of the covariance matrix, and by simulating independent Gaussian random variables. See Appendix of the present Handbook on A quick Review of Distributions Relevant in Finance.

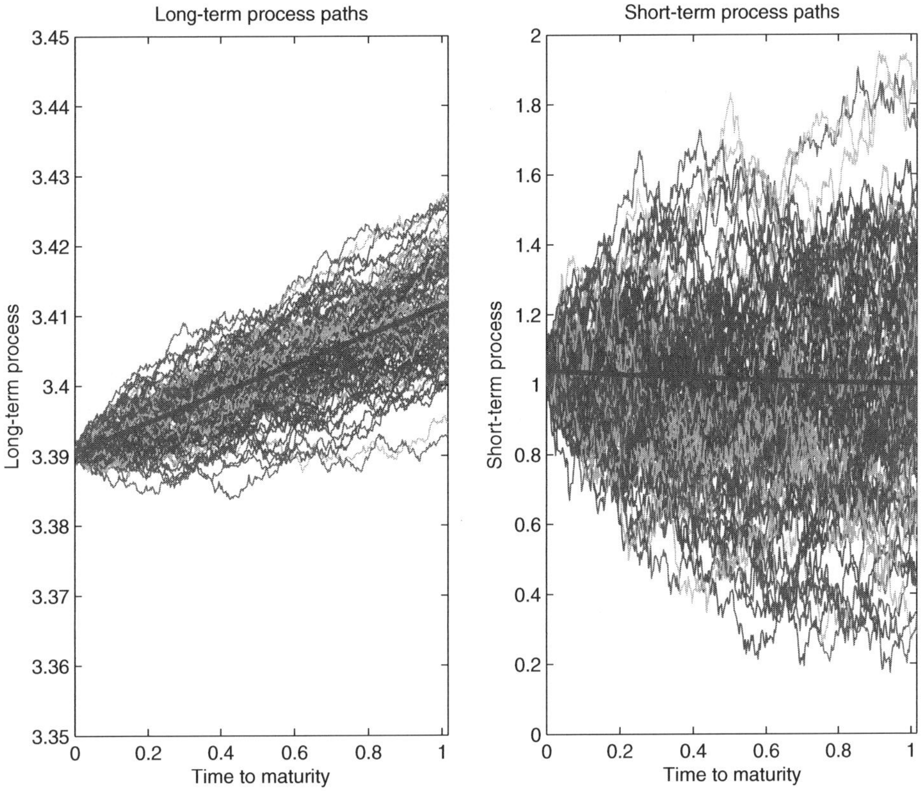

FIGURE 16.6 Monte Carlo paths of long-term (left panel) and short-term (right panel) processes. The thick line represents the mean value.

This curve is dollar denominated, so it needs to be converted into euros using the currency forward term structure.

4. Given the simulated term structure, price the swap contract by replacing the unknown amounts with their estimated values, according to the futures term structure. This step will be discussed in more detail later.
5. Repeat steps 2–3, up to the final settlement date of the contract.

The full procedure can be repeated a large number of times, 100,000 times say. Figure 16.6 shows some simulated paths of the short-term and long-term processes at any given date t. Figure 16.7 illustrates possible simulated trajectories of the oil spot prices at each date over the period 1 April 2010 to 28 February 2011. Figure 16.8 represents the evolution of a bunch of simulated front forward curves.

16.5.4 The Computation of Brent Forward Curves at Any Given Valuation Date

Pricing the swap under consideration requires computing the monthly averages that enter the contract's payoff. For instance, let us consider the first payoff of the commodity swap and let

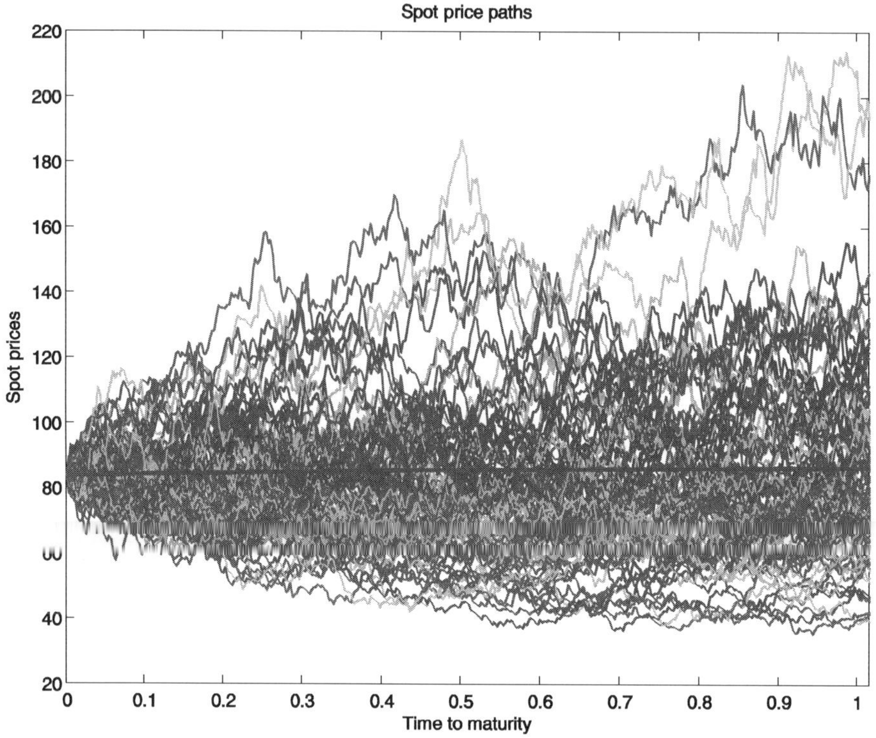

FIGURE 16.7 Monte Carlo paths of spot prices over the contract's life. The thick line represents the mean value

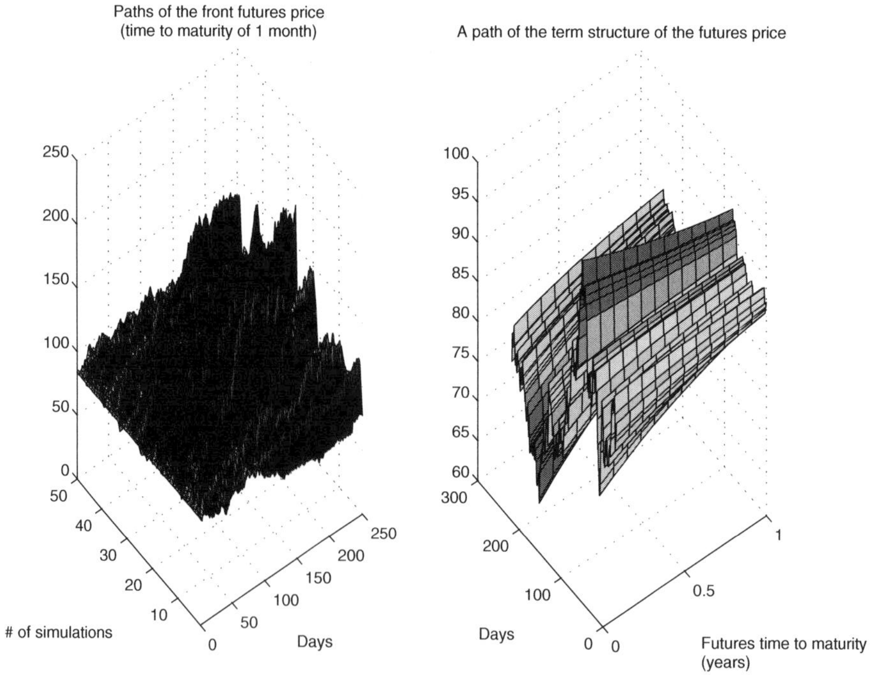

FIGURE 16.8 Simulated paths of the front futures price with time to maturity of 1 month (on the left); a simulated path of the term structure of the futures price (on the right)

TABLE 16.9 Computation of the payoff on 1 November 2010, considering both historical and simulated prices

April	May	June	July	Aug	Sept	Oct	Nov	Dec	Jan
historical							Sim n°1 Forecasting		Settlement Months
53.99	54.69	58.96	63.98	61.31	62.01	59.01	65.83	66.99	

Average (April–Dec): 60.66

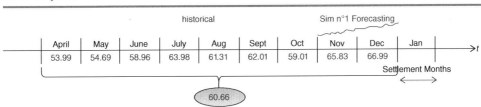

us suppose it is on 1 November 2010 (the 152nd day out of 264 trading days). The settlement date of the first payoff is 7 February 2011 and its value is given by the average of the oil monthly prices of April 2010, May 2010, June 2010, July 2010, August 2010, September 2010, October 2010, November 2010 and December 2010. Regarding the months preceding November, that is April 2010, May 2010, June 2010, July 2010, August 2010, September 2010 and October 2010, their monthly values are obtained by averaging the observed daily historical prices. Therefore, we have to simulate the daily prices from 1 November 2010 to 31 December 2010. Then, we have to compute the monthly averages of the forecasted daily prices for the months of November and December. Furthermore, each monthly average must be converted into euros; the monthly exchange rate is computed as the average of the currency forward rates observed at the inception date of the contract.

Table 16.9 illustrates how the first payoff is computed on 1 November 2010, considering a possible scenario of the monthly values for November and December given by the first simulation. In this case the value of the payoff is equal to €60.66.

The calculation of the fair value of the floating payments requires the computation of the expected discounted payoff at any given date t *and along each simulated path* j, that is we need to estimate

$$E_t\left(P_1^j\right) = \frac{\sum_{m=4}^{12} E_t(Avg^j(m,2010))}{9} \times 0.71,$$

$$E_t\left(P_2^j\right) = \frac{\sum_{m=5}^{12} E_t(Avg^j(m,2010)) + E_t(Avg^j(1,2011))}{9} \times 0.71,$$

$$E_t\left(P_3^j\right) = \frac{\sum_{m=6}^{12} E_t(Avg^j(m,2010)) + \sum_{m=1}^{2} E_t(Avg^j(m,2011))}{9} \times 0.71,$$

where:

- j refers to the different simulations, $j = 1, ..., M$;
- t are the daily trading dates ranging from 1 April 2010 to 28 February 2011 $(t = 1, \ldots, 264)$;
- 0.71 is the weighting coefficient of the Brent formula;

- $Avg^j(m, y)$ refers to the arithmetic average of oil spot prices observed in month m of year y in simulation j. This arithmetic average is computed according to the formula

$$Avg^j(m, y) = \frac{1}{n(m, y)} \sum_{l=1}^{n(m,y)} S^j(t_l(m, y)) \times FX(0, t_l(m, y)),$$

  where $t_j(m, y)$ refers to day l in month m of year y, $n(m, y)$ is the number of trading days in month m of year y and $FX(0, T)$ is the forward currency rate observed in the market at inception date for expiry T.

At time t, the expected value of the monthly average is computed using the prevailing term structure of futures prices. Therefore:

$$E_t(Avg^j(m, y)) = \frac{1}{n(m, y)} \sum_{l=1}^{n(m,y)} F(t, t_l(m, y); \chi^j(t), \zeta^j(t), \theta) \times FX(0, t_l(m, y)),$$

where $F(t, t_l(m, y); \chi^j(t), \zeta^j(t), \theta)$ is the model futures price in simulation j. The market value of the swap to the payer of the fixed price in simulation j at time t is given by

$$v^j(t) = \sum_{i=1}^{3} E_t\left(P_i^j\right) df(t, T_i)V(T_i) - F \sum_{i=1}^{3} df(t, T_i)V(T_i),$$

where F is the fixed price agreed on between the two counterparties at the inception date and T_i, $i = 1, \ldots, 3$ refer to the settlement dates of the different payoffs. The discount factor at time t for maturity T, $df(t, T)$, is computed as the forward discount factor using the market interest rate curve (euros) referred to 1 April 2010, available on Bloomberg at the trade date. In particular, if $df(0, T)$ is the discount curve at inception, then $df(t, T) = df(0, t)/df(0, T)$.

Notice that the above market value expression is valid provided $t \leq T_1$. If $T_1 < t \leq T_2$ then the simulated market value is

$$v^j(t) = \sum_{i=2}^{3} E_t\left(P_i^j\right) df(t, T_i)V(T_i) - F \sum_{i=2}^{3} df(t, T_i)V(T_i).$$

Finally, if $T_2 < t \leq T_3$, then

$$v^j(t) = E_t\left(P_3^j\right) df(t, T_3)V(T_3) - F df(t, T_3)V(T_3).$$

Figure 16.9 shows the time evolution of the fair value of the contract and for different simulations. It can be noticed that the fair value of the contract is zero at its inception. Thereafter, it can become positive or negative depending on the evolution of the futures prices term structure. As we approach the settlement dates, the uncertainty in the settlement amounts reduces. In particular, from 28 February 2011 onwards, all payoffs have already been set and the fair value becomes constant (apart from a discounting effect). Moving ahead in time, closer to the 'half life' of the contract, it is evident that the value of the net cash flows increases when

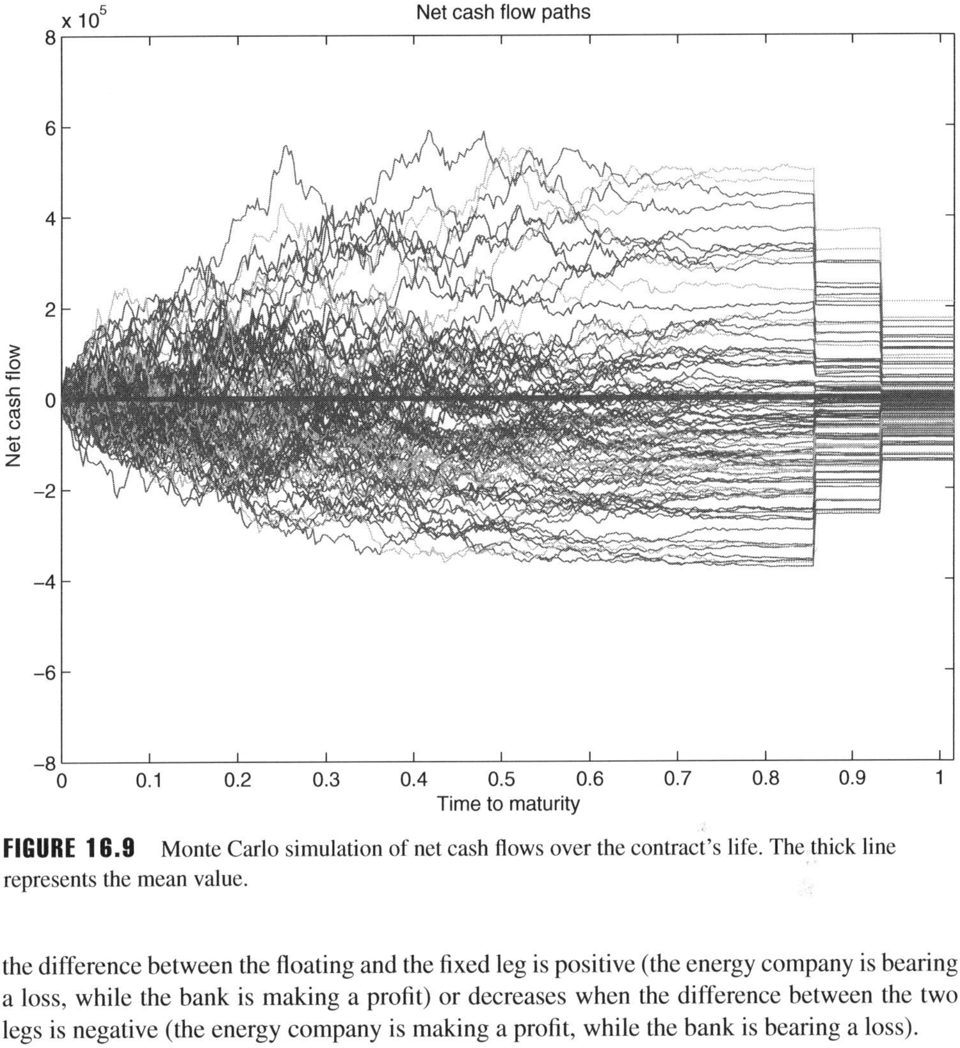

FIGURE 16.9 Monte Carlo simulation of net cash flows over the contract's life. The thick line represents the mean value.

the difference between the floating and the fixed leg is positive (the energy company is bearing a loss, while the bank is making a profit) or decreases when the difference between the two legs is negative (the energy company is making a profit, while the bank is bearing a loss).

16.6 MEASURING COUNTERPARTY RISK

If we operate with derivative contracts managed by a clearing house, the credit risk linked to a counterparty not fulfilling its obligations is negligible. On the contrary, the credit risk might increase for commodity derivative instruments traded OTC. The importance of assessing the counterparty credit risk in the OTC derivatives market has gained more interest after the financial crisis that began in 2007. For this reason, energy companies might take into consideration the counterparty credit risk (CCR) if they want to negotiate accurately the price of a commodity swap with another operator.

The most popular measure used by companies in order to adjust the default-free value of an instrument to incorporate the credit risk is the CVA. This is a metric which has the purpose of quantifying the exposure to default, commonly defined as the difference between the risk-free price of the derivative contract and the risky price. This value can also be considered as the cost of hedging the default risk. The exposure to a given counterparty on a swap position is the amount that would be lost by that counterparty in the event of default by the other counterparty. We follow the general method for computing credit risk adjustments when both counterparties are defaultable, as follows. One first calculates the market value at time T, X_T say, of default losses to counterparty A that are caused by any default of counterparty B that occurs before the default of A. (If the counterparty A defaults first then, under standard master agreements, there is no default loss to A caused by the default of B because all contracts are settled at the time of the default by A.) Similarly, one can calculate the market value Y_T of losses to the counterparty B through any default by the counterparty A that occurs before default by B. After accounting for the collateral, the difference, if positive, $X_T - Y_T$, multiplied by the percentage loss given default (LGD) is the net market value of the default losses to party A, as of time T. The risk-neutral expectation of this loss is then discounted, and this amount is summed over all potential default dates, T. We write

$$\text{CVA(A|B)} = E_0(\text{Present value of the loss to A, given default of B}).$$

The CVA can be calculated as unilateral or bilateral adjustment. As far as the former is concerned, the counterparty that performs the valuation considers itself as default free. Bilateral CVA takes into account the default by either counterparty and is interpreted as

$$\text{bCVA(A, B)} = \text{CVA (A|B)} - \text{CVA (B|A)}.$$

In order to enter into an uncollateralized transaction with a zero initial value, a counterparty A will receive from B its bilateral CVA, if it is positive, or will pay it if negative. On the contrary, if the transaction is collateralized, there is no need to compute the CVA.

The CVA of an OTC derivative contract with a given counterparty is therefore defined as the market value of the credit risk due to any failure to perform on agreements with that counterparty. Furthermore, it can be defined also as the difference between a risk-free contract (portfolio) and the contract (portfolio) that includes in its valuation the counterparty default risk.

The computation of the loss takes into account that, if counterparty B will default, A will have a loss if the value of the contract is positive to A. So, the loss to A given by the default of B at time t will be equal to

$$(1 - R_B)\max(V_A(t), 0),$$

where R_B is the so-called recovery rate of party B, that is the fraction of the loss that is recovered by A during the judicial procedure, and $V_A(t)$ is the value to A of the derivative contract. Similarly, the loss to B, given the default of A, will be equal to

$$(1 - R_A)\max(V_B(t), 0),$$

where R_A is the recovery rate of party A and $V_B(t)$ is the value to B of the swap contract at time t. Clearly, in a bilateral contract $V_B(t) = -V_A(t)$. Figure 16.10 shows BNP and Edison loss paths.

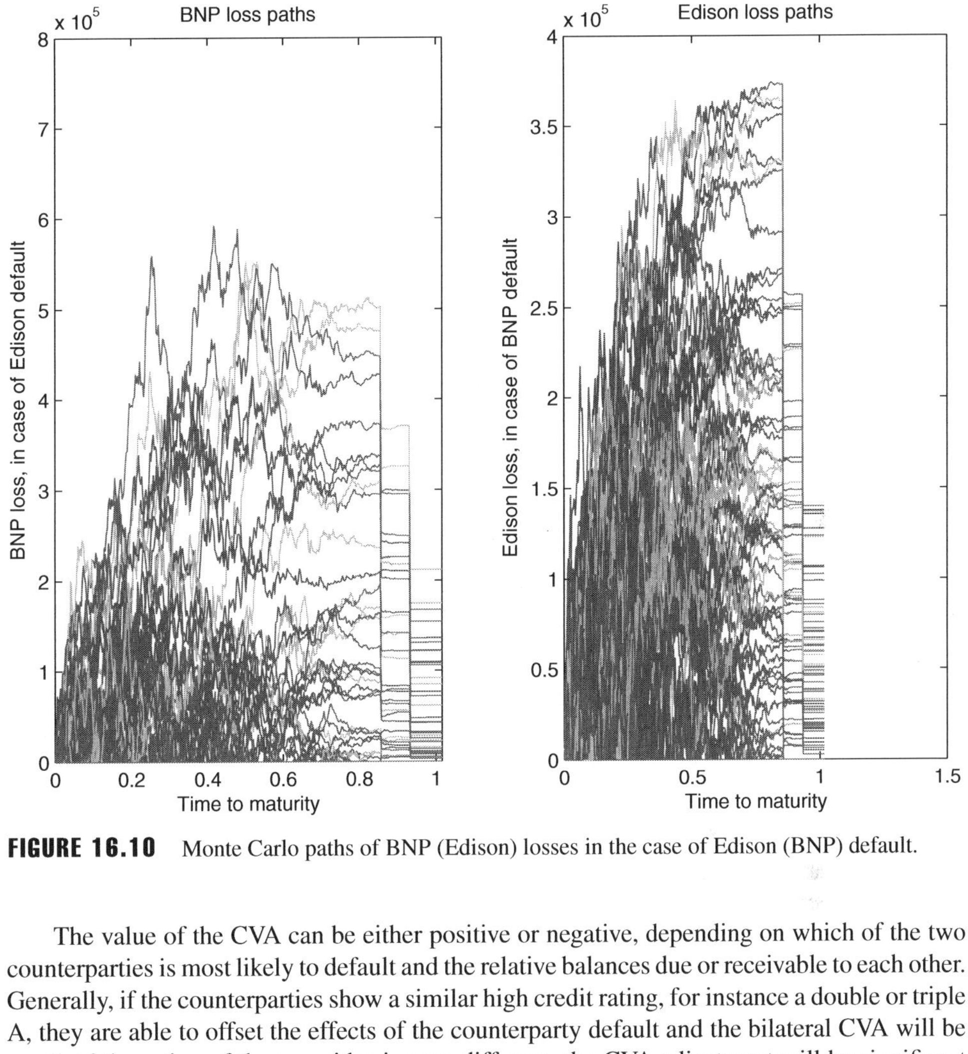

FIGURE 16.10 Monte Carlo paths of BNP (Edison) losses in the case of Edison (BNP) default.

The value of the CVA can be either positive or negative, depending on which of the two counterparties is most likely to default and the relative balances due or receivable to each other. Generally, if the counterparties show a similar high credit rating, for instance a double or triple A, they are able to offset the effects of the counterparty default and the bilateral CVA will be small. If the rating of the two sides is very different, the CVA adjustment will be significant and will be posted from the riskier party to the less risky party. This feature is analysed in more detail in Section 16.7. Another possibility consists of collateralizing the derivative transaction.

16.6.1 CVA Calculation

In order to compute the CVA of the commodity swap, we have to determine the market value of all future potential losses to the energy company due to the default by the bank (and vice versa) during the contract's life. For any given date t, $t \in \{t_0, t_1, \dots t_K\}$, we calculate the contract net exposure of all future potential losses to the energy company due to the default by the bank, $\max(V_A(t), 0)$. The unrecovered amount, that is the effective loss, will be $(1 - R_B)\max(V_A(t), 0)$. Similarly, the contract net exposure of all future potential losses to the bank caused by a default of the energy company is $\max(V_B(t), 0)$. Again, the unrecovered loss will be $(1 - R_A)\max(V_B(t), 0)$.

The above losses are nothing else but the payoff of a call option to purchase (sell) the contract of value $V(t)$ at time t. The expected discounted loss to A due to the default of B in the time interval (t_{k-1}, t_k) can be computed by the following (risk-neutral) expectation:

$$E_0\left((1 - R_B)\max(V_A(t_k), 0) 1_{\{\text{A survives up to } t_k\}} 1_{\{\text{B survives up to } t_{k-1} \text{ and defaults in } t_k\}} df(0, t_k)\right),$$

where $1_{\{x\}}$ is equal to 1 if the event x is true and 0 otherwise. If we assume independence between default event, contract value and deterministic recovery fraction and interest rates, then the expected loss can be computed as

$$(1 - R_B)E_0(\max(V_A(t_k), 0))E_0(1_{\{\text{A survives up to } t_k\}})E_0(1_{\{\text{B survives up to } t_{k-1} \text{ and defaults in } t_k\}})df(0, t_k).$$

If we let $Q(t, T)$ be the survival probability up to time T, upon survival at time t, we can write the expected loss due to the counterparty default on the time interval time $\left(t_{k-1}, t_k\right]$ as

$$(1 - R_B)E_0(\max(V_A(t_k), 0))\, Q_A(0, t_k)\, Q_B(0, t_{k-1})\, (1 - Q(0, t_{k-1}, t_k))\, df(0, t_k),$$

where $Q(0, t_{k-1}, t_k)$ is the forward survival probability at time t_k, conditional upon survival at time t_{k-1}, as of time 0, and is given by

$$Q(0, t_{k-1}, t_k) = \frac{Q(0, t_k)}{Q(0, t_{k-1})}.$$

The evaluation of the credit exposure requires a preliminary estimate of the underlying risk-neutral probabilities of default. These numbers are computed by using price data for credit derivatives (such as credit default swaps and bond prices) depending on the availability and quality of the data. The calibration procedure is described below. For this purpose we can use the market value of the two counterparties' credit default swap (CDS) spreads quoted on 1 April 2010 to extract implied default probabilities.

16.6.1.1 Extracting Implied Default Probabilities The CDS spread is the premium paid quarterly by the protection buyer (an operator that buys insurance in order to protect himself against the default of a loan he holds) to the protection seller and it is quoted in basis points per annum of the contract notional amount. To calibrate risk-neutral default probabilities using CDS data, we adopt the following standard approximation. Let CDS_A denote the CDS quoted spread for a given entity A and let LGD_A be the loss given default of entity A, both referring to a maturity as close as possible to the one under consideration. If we assume that default occurs on coupon payment dates[3] and that there are m coupon dates per year, then the per-coupon-period risk-neutral default probability $PD_A\left(0, \frac{1}{m}\right)$ satisfies[4]

$$\frac{CDS_A}{m} = LGD_A PD_A\left(0, \frac{1}{m}\right).$$

[3]For default between coupon dates, a more complicated formula can be used. See, for details, Duffie and Singleton (2003).

[4]More accurate estimations of the default probability are possible, similar to the bootstrapping procedure to extract spot rates from swap rates. See for example O'Kane and Turnbull (2003).

This formula states that the expected payment made by the protection buyer is equal to the CDS spread, while the product between the default probability and the loss given default represents his expected payoff.

The per-coupon-period risk-neutral survival probability can be computed as

$$Q_A\left(0, \frac{1}{m}\right) = 1 - PD_A\left(0, \frac{1}{m}\right).$$

A CDS spread typically provides the protection seller with quarterly payments, that is $m = 4$. Therefore, the quarterly risk-neutral default probability is computed according to the formula

$$PD_A\left(0, \frac{1}{4}\right) = \frac{CDS}{4\left(1 - R_A\right)}.$$

For example, if the CDS spread is 100 b.p. and we assume a recovery rate of 0.4, the quarterly default probability turns out to be

$$PD_A\left(0, \frac{1}{4}\right) = \frac{100/10000}{4(1-0.4)} = 4.16\%.$$

The quarterly survival probability will be $1 - 4.16\% = 95.83\%$, whilst the yearly survival probability turns out to be

$$Q_A(0, 1) = (1 - 0.0416)^4 = 84.35\%$$

and the one-year default probability is 15.65%. If we assume that the default event occurs with a constant intensity over time, we will have that

$$Q_A\,(0, t) = Q_A\,(0, 1)^t\,.$$

The formula above provides a quick and effective approach to extract the default probabilities from CDS quotations.

16.6.1.2 Calculating the Counterparties' Expected Losses We consider the case where both parties are exposed to default, so that we need to compute the bilateral adjustment bCVA. This involves some mandatory steps. First of all, we calculate the surviving probability of both the bank and the energy company at a future time t. In our analysis we considered, for example, the CDS spread of BNP Paribas (party A) and Edison SPA (party B) quoted on 1 April 2010. These have been obtained from Bloomberg and are equal to 38 and 52 basis points, respectively. The one-year survival probabilities of the two parties are 99.9983% and 99.9982%, respectively.

Afterwards, the expected loss to the bank at time t_k for the company defaulting in the time interval $(t_{k-1}, t_k]$ is

$$(1 - R_B)E_0(\max(V_A(t_k), 0))\,(0.999982)^{t_k}(0.999976)^{t_{k-1}}(1 - 0.999976)^{t_k - t_{k-1}}df(0, t_k).$$

TABLE 16.10 Monte Carlo estimates of market value exposures for both counterparties. Standard errors are reported in parentheses

Counterparties	Expected market value exposures
BPN	€321.263 (1.5)
Edison	€232.018 (0.86)

We can compute $E_0(\max(V_A(t_k), 0))$ by Monte Carlo simulation, that is

$$E_0(\max(V_A(t_k), 0)) = \frac{\sum_{s=1}^{M} \max(V_A^s(t_k), 0)}{M},$$

where M is the number of Monte Carlo simulations to compute the expected exposure at the grid time t_k. We set $M = 100{,}000$.

Summing over the different subperiods in the contract life, we get

$$\begin{aligned}\text{CVA(A|B)} = &\sum_{k=1}^{K}(1 - R_B)E_0(\max(V_A(t_k), 0))\,(0.999982)^{t_k}(0.999976)^{t_{k-1}}\\ &\times(1 - 0.999976)^{t_k - t_{k-1}} df(0, t_k).\end{aligned}$$

Similarly, we also have

$$\begin{aligned}\text{CVA(B|A)} = &\sum_{k=1}^{K}(1 - R_A)E_0(\max(V_B(t_k), 0))(0.999976)^{t_{k-1}}\\ &\times(1 - 0.999982)^{t_k - t_{k-1}}(0.999982)^{t_k} df(0, \mathrm{t_k}).\end{aligned}$$

The CVA estimates are reported in Table 16.10.

The expected bilateral credit cost to BNP is €89.244; the one-way CVA for BNP is €321.263.

16.6.2 Swap Fixed Price Adjustment for Counterparty Risk

The bCVA is often used for pre-deal contract pricing activity. Given the value of the CVA and the value of the contract on 1 April 2010, which were approximately equal to zero, we can compute the adjusted fixed price of the commodity swap at the contract's inception date. The credit risk adjusted value of the swap for the fixed payer A at the inception date is

$$AV(0) = \sum_{i=1}^{3} E_t(P_i)df(0, T_i)V(T_i) - F(0)\sum_{i=1}^{3} df(0, T_i)V(T_i) - \text{bCVA(A|B)}.$$

TABLE 16.11 bCVA(bank|energy) for different CDS spreads (columns refer to the bank and rows refer to the energy company)

	15	52	100	150
15	–0.048	229.314	523.245	828.210
38	–140.118	89.244	383.178	688.150
100	–523.616	–294.259	–0.324	304.658
150	–828.745	–599.398	–305.471	–0.489

We can obtain the adjusted fixed swap price AF by setting $AV(0) = 0$. This occurs if

$$AF(0; T_1, T_2, T_3) = \frac{\sum_{i=1}^{3} E_t(P_i)df(0, T_i)V(T_i) - \text{bCVA(A|B)}}{\sum_{i=1}^{3} df(0, T_i)V(T_i)}$$

$$= F(0; T_1, T_2, T_3) - \frac{\text{bCVA(A|B)}}{\sum_{i=1}^{3} df(0, T_i)V(T_i)}.$$

In our example, the adjusted fixed price equals €44.556. The difference between the adjusted and the unadjusted fixed price can be positive or negative depending on the sign of the bilateral CVA. In our example, $F = 44.7703, AF = 44.7661$, so the delta price is –€0.0042. The net credit loss adjustment is positive for A, therefore the adjusted fixed price paid by A will be lower than the unadjusted one. This difference appears to be small, mainly because the CDS spread we used as input to compute the survival probabilities was low and similar across counterparties.

Therefore, to better appreciate the credit risk exposure of the contract we recomputed the bilateral CVA under different values of the CDS spreads. The CDS spreads quoted by Bloomberg on 1 April 2010 were approximately 38 bps for the bank and 52 bps for the energy company, and they are reported in Tables 16.11 and 16.12, which show the bCVA and the delta price for different CDS spreads.

As can be appreciated from the tables, the higher the CDS spread difference between the two counterparties, the higher the bCVA (in absolute value) and the delta price. Figure 16.11 illustrates the counterparties' loss distributions over the contract's life. Not surprisingly, the distribution is not normal but heavily skewed.

TABLE 16.12 Delta price for different CDS spreads (columns refer to the bank and rows refer to the energy company)

	15	52	100	150
15	0.000	–0.011	–0.024	–0.039
38	0.007	–0.004	–0.018	–0.032
100	0.024	0.014	0.000	–0.014
150	0.039	0.028	0.014	0.000

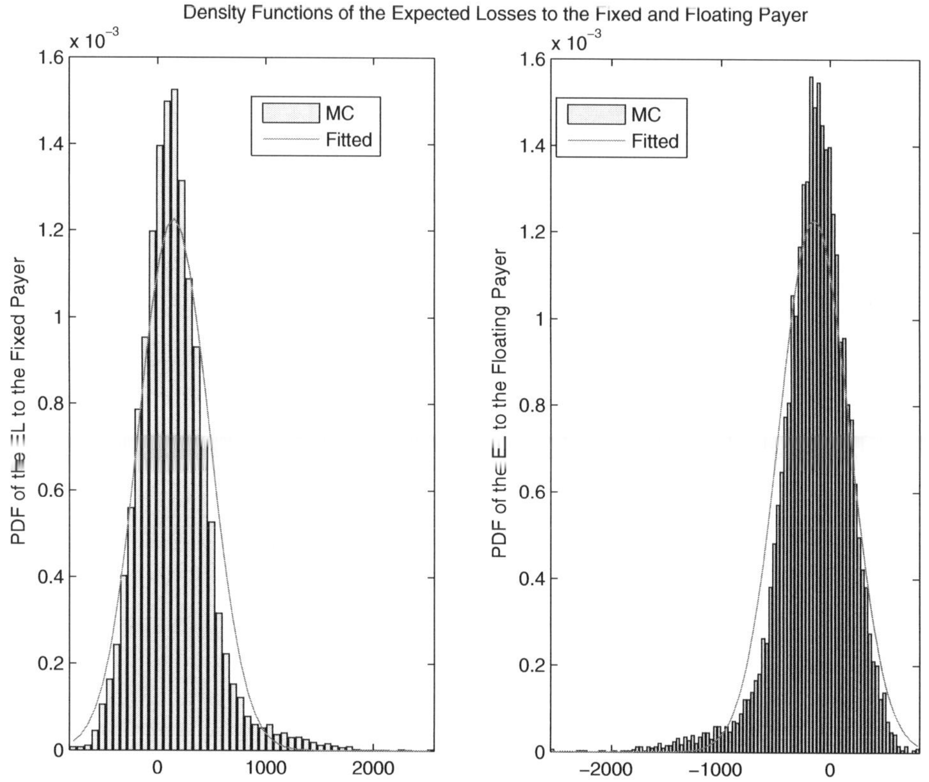

FIGURE 16.11 BNP Paribas (fixed payer) and Edison (floating payer) expected loss distributions.

16.6.3 Right- and Wrong-Way Risk

In the computation of the CVA, it is typical to assume independence between the default probability of the counterparty and the exposure at default. However, the default of the energy company is likely to be negatively correlated with the price of oil: the higher the oil price, the less likely the default of the oil company. Since the bank receives floating oil and pays fix, if oil prices are high, its exposure at default turns out to be high. On the contrary, the company default will be less likely. This phenomenon is called right-way risk and should reduce the CVA. In contrast, if the default of the energy company, for whatever reason, were more likely when the oil price rises, the bank would be exposed to so-called wrong-way risk, which increases the CVA value. This would be the case, for example, of an airline company. In order to quantify this effect, we recall that the expected loss to the bank can be computed as

$$\mathrm{CVA(A|B)}$$
$$= \sum_{k=1}^{K} E_0\left[(1 - R_B)\max(V_A(t_k), 0) 1_{\{\text{A survives up to } t_k\}} 1_{\{\text{B survives up to } t_{k-1} \text{ and defaults in } t_k\}} df(0, t_k)\right],$$

where A refers to the bank and B refers to the energy company.

If we assume that

- the recovery rate is deterministic,
- interest rates and default events are independent,
- the bank's default is independent of the exposure,

then we get

$$\text{CVA(A|B)} \\ = (1 - R_B) \sum_{k=1}^{K} E_0 \left[\max(V_A(t_k), 0)\, 1_{\{\text{B survives up to } t_{k-1} \text{ and defaults in } t_k\}} \right] Q_A(0, t_k)\, df(0, t_k).$$

In order to compute the expectations, we introduce a default intensity model. The default time is modelled as the first jump of an inhomogeneous Poisson process with stochastic default intensity following a Cox–Ingersoll–Ross process:[5]

$$d\lambda(t) = k_\lambda \left(\mu_\lambda - \lambda(t) \right) dt + \sigma_\lambda \sqrt{\lambda(t)} dW_\lambda(t),$$

with

$$k_\lambda, \mu_\lambda, \sigma_\lambda, \lambda(0) > 0.$$

The intensity turns out to be positive if the so-called Feller condition is satisfied:

$$k_\lambda \mu_\lambda \geq \sigma_\lambda^2.$$

The default probability can be computed (see Fang *et al.*, 2012) by

$$\Pr_t \left(\tau_B > s \right) = E \left(e^{\int_t^s \lambda(u) du} \right) = e^{a(t,s) + b(t,s)\lambda(t)}$$

where, setting $\gamma = \frac{1}{2}\sqrt{k_\lambda^2 + 2\sigma_\lambda}$, we have:

$$b(t, s) = \frac{-\sinh(\gamma(s-t))}{\gamma \cosh(\gamma(s-t)) + 0.5 k_\lambda \sinh(\gamma(s-t))},$$

$$a(t, s) = \frac{\gamma e^{0.5 k_\lambda (s-t)}}{\gamma \cosh(\gamma(s-t)) + 0.5 k_\lambda \sinh(\gamma(s-t))}.$$

We calibrate the parameters $\theta^{CIR} = \left(k_\lambda, \mu_\lambda, \sigma_\lambda, \lambda_0 \right)$, appearing in the default probability expression above, to that extracted from the CDS spreads as illustrated in O'Kane and Turnbull (2003). See Table 16.13.

[5] See the chapter on stochastic differential equations of the present Handbook.

TABLE 16.13 CIR calibrated parameters

Parameters	NLS estimates
k_λ	0.297
μ_λ	0.029
σ_λ	0.131
λ_0	0.004

Following Brigo *et al.* (2008), we correlate the default intensity to the commodity prices by correlating the corresponding Brownian shocks. We have:

$$corr\,(d\lambda(t), dS(t)) = \frac{\sigma_\chi \rho_{\chi\lambda} + \sigma_\zeta \rho_{\zeta\lambda}}{\sqrt{\sigma_\chi^2 + \sigma_\zeta^2 + 2\rho_{\chi\zeta}\sigma_\chi\sigma_\zeta}}.$$

If we assume:

$$\rho_{\chi\lambda} = \rho_{\zeta\lambda} = \rho_\lambda,$$

then the correlation parameter between the default intensity and the commodity factors is given by

$$\rho_\lambda = corr\,(d\lambda(t), dS(t)) \frac{\sqrt{\sigma_\chi^2 + \sigma_\zeta^2 + 2\rho_{\chi\zeta}\sigma_\chi\sigma_\zeta}}{\sigma_\chi \rho_{\chi\lambda} + \sigma_\zeta \rho_{\zeta\lambda}}.$$

To compute the expectations in the CVA formula, we jointly simulate the short-term commodity process, the long-term commodity process and the default intensity.

We use an Euler discretization scheme with daily time step:

$$\begin{aligned}
\chi(t_k) &= \chi(t_{k-1}) - (\lambda_\chi + k_\chi \chi(t_{k-1}))(t_k - t_{k-1}) + \sigma_\chi \sqrt{(t_k - t_{k-1})} Z_{t_k}^\chi, \\
\zeta(t_k) &= \zeta(t_{k-1}) + \mu_\zeta (t_k - t_{k-1}) + \sigma_\zeta \sqrt{(t_k - t_{k-1})} Z_{t_k}^\zeta, \\
\lambda(t_k) &= \lambda(t_{k-1}) + k_\lambda(\mu_\lambda - \lambda^+(t_{k-1}))(t_k - t_{k-1}) + \sigma_\lambda \sqrt{\lambda^+(t_{k-1})(t_k - t_{k-1})} Z_{t_k}^\lambda,
\end{aligned}$$

where

$$\lambda^+(t_k) = \max(\lambda(t_{k-1}), 0)$$

and $Z = (Z_{t_k}^\chi, Z_{t_k}^\zeta, Z_{t_k}^\lambda)$ is a vector of normal random variables with mean zero and instantaneous correlation matrix given by

$$Corr \equiv \begin{bmatrix} 1 & \rho_{\chi\zeta} & \rho_\lambda \\ \rho_{\chi\zeta} & 1 & \rho_\lambda \\ \rho_\lambda & \rho_\lambda & 1 \end{bmatrix}.$$

Let Γ denote the so-called hazard function:

$$\Gamma(t) = \int_0^t \lambda(u)\, du.$$

We can set

$$\Gamma(t_k) = \Gamma(t_{k-1}) + \lambda(t_{k-1})(t_k - t_{k-1}).$$

The simulation of the default time can be done by drawing a uniform random variable U on [0,1] and setting

$$\tau_B = \inf\{t > 0 : \exp(-\Gamma(t)) < U\}.$$

We investigate the impact of the correlation parameter between the default intensity and the commodity factors on the CVA. For different correlation coefficients, we re-price the swap and compute the CVA(A|B) using 200,000 Monte Carlo simulations. The results are reported in Figure 16.12. In our example, the relevant scenarios have negative correlation coefficients. More generally, Figure 16.12 shows that wrong- and right-way risk can have an important effect on the CVA.

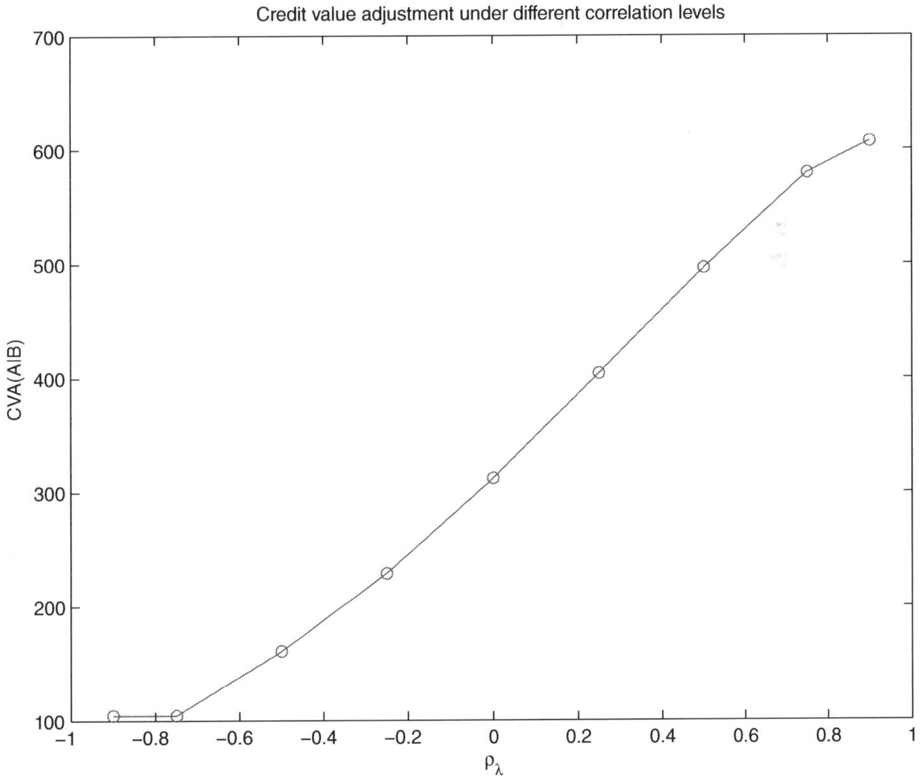

FIGURE 16.12 Credit value adjustments for different correlation parameters between the default intensity and the commodity factors.

The independence case corresponds to $\rho = 0$, the case previously examined. As ρ goes from negative to positive values, right-way risk becomes wrong-way risk and, as a consequence, the CVA increases. The change in the CVA can be very significant: if $\rho = -0.9$ we have a CVA approximately equal to 100, whilst if $\rho = 0.9$ the CVA can reach the value of 600. If ρ has a high negative value, it means that there is a strong negative correlation between the exposure on default and the energy default event: the higher the exposure for the bank, the less likely the default of the energy company, and vice versa. Therefore the CVA will be low. If ρ has a high positive value, it means that there is a strong positive correlation between the exposure on default and the energy default event: the higher the exposure for the bank, the more likely the default of the energy company, and vice versa. Therefore the CVA will be high.

16.7 SENSITIVITY ANALYSIS

In this section, we investigate the impact of changes of different model parameters on the current term structure of futures prices, bilateral CVA and delta price. Sensitivity analysis is a useful tool in order to ascertain which model variables account for most of the bilateral CVA variability. We shift each parameter, one at a time, while keeping all the others constant. Then we re-price the swap and re-compute the bilateral CVA.

Figure 16.13 shows the impact of each parameter on the term structure of futures prices. The most critical parameters are the short-term process parameters and the drift of the long-term process.

Table 16.14 reports the sensitivity results in euros. In particular, the scenarios for the shifts correspond to the upper and lower bound of the 90% confidence interval of the bootstrap distribution of each parameter. The CVA turns out to be particularly sensitive to the volatility parameters and to the long-run level of the short-term factor, the volatility of the short-term factor being the most influential parameter.

16.8 ACCOUNTING FOR DERIVATIVES AND CREDIT VALUE ADJUSTMENTS

(a) Framework Energy companies operate in markets both by entering into purchases (or sales) of energy physical contracts and by buying derivative contracts aimed at managing the commodity price volatility. Markets, commodity prices, interest and exchange rates expose energy companies to high risks relating to the assets' value change. For this reason, within the energy sector an increase of derivative contracts aimed at the mitigation of commodity price changes risk is expected.

The accounting identification rules used for recording on the balance sheet each different contract typology should take into consideration the qualification given by the accounting standards. The standards that have high impact on energy company activities and their economic results are the following:

- IAS 32
- IAS 39
- IFRS 7
- IFRS 9

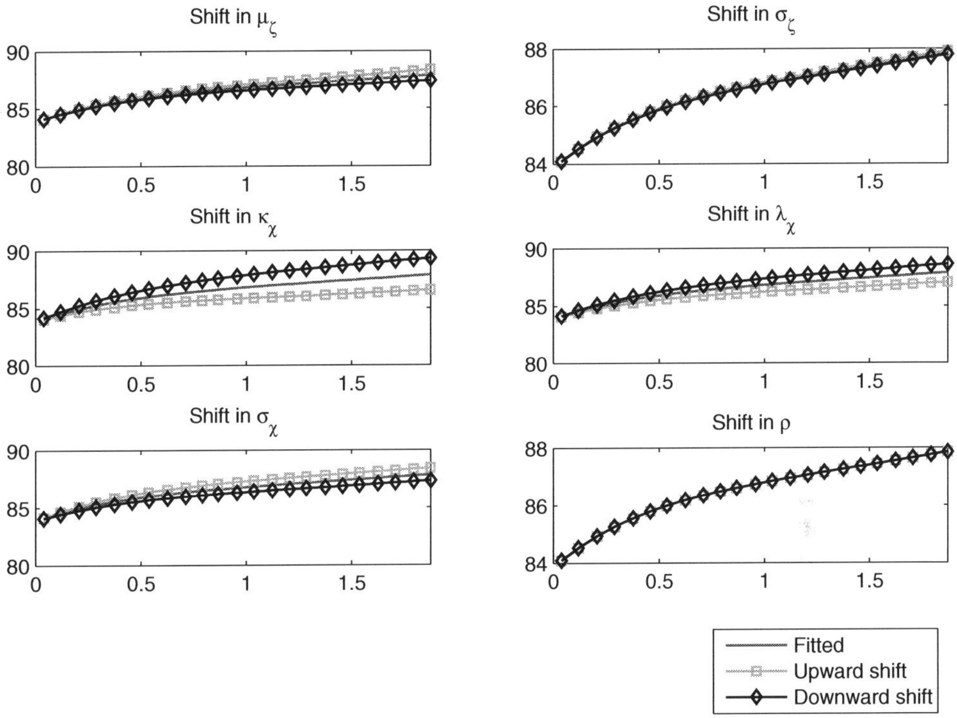

FIGURE 16.13 Sensitivity analysis for the term structure of futures prices. We consider the scenarios corresponding to the lower and upper bounds of the 90% confidence interval of each parameter, while keeping constant all other parameters.

In order to analyse the accounting framework for the financial instrument – the commodity swap – that we priced in previous chapters, hereafter we focus our attention on the accounting methodology called 'cash flow hedge' included in the IAS 39.

(b) IAS 39 The IAS 39, chapter 4, identifies four different categories of financial instruments. Each of the following categories applies different registration criteria:

- financial assets and liabilities at fair value
- held-to-maturity investments
- loans and receivables
- available for sales.

In particular, within the first of the categories must be registered both the held-for-trading assets and the hedging derivatives not designated for hedge accounting.

(c) Hedge accounting The hedge accounting departs from IAS 39. It can be used only if the derivative contract has a hedging purpose. The definition of a hedging purpose implies a match between the financial flows generated by the hedging instrument and those generated by the hedged item (efficiency test). However, in the utilities business, the complexity of hedge

TABLE 16.14 Sensitivity analysis for the bilateral CVA and the delta price (Δ). For each parameter, we consider the scenarios corresponding to the lower and upper bounds of the 90% confidence interval, estimated by bootstrap resampling, while keeping all other parameters constant. The middle row reports the calibrated parameter value, for comparison

Parameters	Scenario	bCVA	bCVA change (%)	Δ (BP)
μ_ζ	0.0180	89.06843	–0.20%	–42
	0.0208	89.24428	—	—
	0.0238	91.27499	2.28%	–43
κ_χ	0.9160	91.69712	2.75%	–43
	0.9333	89.24428	—	—
	0.9494	90.75802	1.70%	–42
λ_x	–0.9200	94.05655	5.39%	–44
	–0.9104	89.24428	—	—
	0.8997	88.80474	0.4[illegible]%	[illegible]
υ_x	0.4519	85.02756	–0.29%	–39
	0.4761	89.24428	—	—
	0.5020	95.84081	7.39%	–45
σ_ζ	0.0003	93.22639	4.46%	–44
	0.0076	89.24428	—	—
	0.0138	86.16046	–3.46%	–40
$\rho_{\chi,\zeta}$	0.2040	88.00408	–1.39%	–41
	0.2052	89.24428	—	—
	0.2062	90.31082	1.20%	–42

accounting rules together with their application burden might not always lead to classifying as a hedging the activities that are operationally defined as hedging. This issue is mainly due to either the complexity of the factors included in the price indexation formulas or to the demonstration of retrospective and prospective efficiency in high-volatility markets being subject to valuation elements (components).

Hedge accounting rules The IAS 39 distinguishes among three different accounting methodologies:

1. fair value hedge
2. cash flow hedge
3. hedges of a net investment in a foreign operation.

(d) Cash flow hedge (Cfh) The cash flow hedge is defined by IAS 39 as the hedging of an exposure to cash flow volatility due to a particular risk associated with a specific asset or liability. The purpose of the hedging activity is to stabilize future flows and the economic margins. The future cash flows deriving from different kinds of operations, such as long-term contracts, are defined as hedged items. Accordingly, within the IAS 39 framework, the future cash flows generated by the hedged item are not to be accounted for on the balance sheet at the inception of the hedge. On the contrary, the fair value of the hedging instrument is recognized in the balance sheet (equity). The fair value changes (gains and losses) of the hedging instrument that are proved to be effective in order to compensate the fluctuation of the future cash flows are registered directly in a separate component of equity, while the ineffective portion is accounted for immediately in the income statement. Finally, the fair value changes, previously accounted for in the equity, should be transferred to the P&L account in the same period in which the cash flows originating from the hedged item will influence the income statement. This is done to ensure that offsetting profits or losses generated by the derivative instrument and by the hedged item affect the profit in the same period.

If the hedging item is a derivative instrument, the ineffective value changes are registered in the income statement only if they represent an over-hedging. A hedging relation is qualified for cash flow hedge accounting only if it meets some specific restrictive conditions. The most important three conditions are the following:

- Documentation of the hedge at hedge initiation. This documentation identifies the hedging instrument, the hedged item, the nature of the hedged risk and the process followed by the energy company in assessing the efficiency of the hedging operation.
- Nature of the risk being hedged, defined in a specific section of the aforementioned formal documentation.
- Degree of hedging effectiveness. The hedging operation should continuously show a high level of efficiency in offsetting the cash flow changes related to the hedged risk. The effectiveness must be periodically monitored.

The level or degree of effectiveness that a hedging operation has in compensating the changes in the fair value or cash flow attributed to the hedge item is assessed by two tests, the prospective and the retrospective one. IAS 39 requires that test results are delimited in a range from 80% to 125%.

Regarding the retrospective effectiveness, the test is typically performed either on a period-by-period or a cumulative basis using the hypothetical derivative method. The most popular acceptable methodology for assessment of hedge efficiency is the dollar offset method. The valuation, according to the offset method, is done by an offset ratio that compares the fair value or cash flow modifications of the hedging instrument and the changes of the same values related to the underlying asset to hedge.

16.8.1 Example of Hedge Effectiveness

In this section we want to provide an example of how to assess hedge effectiveness. First of all we have to identify:

- The underlying asset – a long-term energy purchase contract.
- The hedging instrument – a commodity swap derivative.

Then, we evaluate our hedge operation at inception, 15 November 2010 and on a specific value date, 1 March 2011.

(a) Valuation at inception Table 16.15 shows the specifications of the hedged item for each reference month (January, February and March 2011): the calculation periods used for the determination of the Brent[901] prices, the volumes purchased by the energy company period by period, the amounts exchanged (computed as the product between prices and quantities) and the present value of those amounts. All the values in the table are expressed in dollars and

TABLE 16.15 Specifications and full fair value related to the hedged item

1. Underlying physical contract hedged item

Calc. Period – Start	Calc. Period – End	Month Ref.	Price Brent	Volume (MWh)	Settlement Figure (k $)	Present Value – Settlement Figure (k $)	df
01/04/2010	31/12/2010	gen-11	80.76	7.440	601	599	0,9976803
01/05/2010	31/01/2011	feb-11	80.91	6.720	544	542	0,9966977
01/06/2010	28/02/2011	mar-11	82.05	7.430	610	607	0,9954853
		Full Fair Value		**21.590**	**1.754**	**1.748**	

the cash flows are paid on these settlement dates: 7 February 2011 (ref. month, January 2011), 7 March 2011 (ref. month, February 2011), 7 April 2011 (ref. month, March 2011). The last row of the table shows the full fair value of the contract (in dollars) and the present value of the full fair value of the contract at inception, 15 November 2010. The full fair value (full FV), which is the present value (PV) of the full FV, is computed as the sum of all settlement figures (PV of settlement figures).

Within the dollar offset framework, we evaluate the hedge effectiveness by making a comparison between the fair value changes of the actual commodity swap (the hedging instrument) and the fair value changes of a hypothetical swap derivative that shares the same specifications with the long-term asset (that is, the same notional quantity and month references). Thus, the hypothetical derivative is expected to perfectly compensate the cash flows generated by the hedged item. The fixed price of the hypothetical swap is found by equating the PVs of the two full fair values (the hedged item's full FV and the hypothetical derivative full FV). The obtained fixed price turns out to be $81.25. See Table 16.16.

Table 16.17 provides the details for the hedging instrument (that is, the actual commodity swap):

- the commodity swap fixed price is $81.05;
- the differences between the fixed and the floating price for each reference month;
- the settlement figures (the products between the difference and the volumes at each reference month).

TABLE 16.16 The hypothetical derivative fixed leg

3. Hypothetical Derivative

Optimum Price-solver ($/MWh)	Volume (MWh)	Settlement Figure (k $)	Present Value – Settlement Figure (k $)
81.25	7.440	605	603
81.25	6.720	546	544
81.25	7.430	604	601
	21.590	1.754	1.748

TABLE 16.17 Specifications and full fair value related to the hedging item

2. Hedging Instrument (swap)									
Calc. Period – Start	**Calc. Period – End**	**Month Ref.**	**Price Brent**	**Fixed Price**	**Floating Price**	**Diff**	**Volume (MWh)**	**Settlement Figure (k $)**	**Present Value – Settlement Figure (k $)**
01/04/2010	31/12/2010	gen-11	80.76	81.05	80.76	0.29	7.440	2.1	2.1
01/05/2010	31/01/2011	feb-11	80.91	81.05	80.91	0.14	6.720	0.9	0.9
01/06/2010	28/02/2011	mar-11	82.05	81.05	82.05	−1.00	7.430	−7.4	−7.4
						Full Fair Value	**21.590**	**−4**	**−4**

TABLE 16.18 Valuation of the physical contract on 1 March 2011

1. Underlying physical contract-hedged item							
Calc. Period – Start	**Calc. Period – End**	**Month Ref.**	**Price Brent**	**Volume (MWh)**	**Settlement Figure (k $)**	**Present Value – Settlement Figure (K $)**	**df**
01/04/2010	31/12/2010	gen-11	–	–	–	–	–
01/05/2010	31/01/2011	feb-11	82.50	6.720	554	554	0.9998630
01/06/2010	28/02/2011	mar-11	85.29	7.430	634	633	0.9992300
				Full Fair Value	**14.150**	**1.188**	**1.188**

The sum of all the settlement figures (discounted settlement figures) gives as a result the total full fair value of the hedging instrument (PV of the full fair value of the hedging instrument).

(b) Valuation on 1 March 2011 Table 16.18 shows the valuation of the physical contract on 1 March 2011.

The floating payment referred to January 2011 has already been regulated on 7 February 2011. This is the reason why there is no price for that reference month. The fair value of the contract is now equal to $1,188,000. On this valuation date, it is noticeable that the 'hypothetical swap' value is no longer equal to zero. In fact, the full fair value of the fixed leg of the hypothetical derivative is lower than that of the physical floating leg (it stands at $1,150,000). See Table 16.19.

Also the full fair value of the actual swap has changed, as shown in Table 16.20. It has decreased dramatically from –$4000 registered on 15 November 2010 to –$41,000 on 1 March 2011.

At this point we have determined all the inputs to compute the offset ratio. The formula we apply is the following:

$$\text{Offset ratio (OR)} = \Delta FV_{\text{hedged item}}/\Delta FV_{\text{hedging instrument}}.$$

TABLE 16.19 Valuation of the hypothetical derivative on 1 March 2011

3. Hypothetical Derivative			
Optimum Price – solver ($/MWh)	**Volume (MWh)**	**Settlement Figure (K $)**	**Present Value – Settlement Figure (k $)**
–	–	–	–
81.25	6.720	546	546
81.25	7.430	604	603
	14.150	**1.150**	**1.149**

TABLE 16.20 Valuation of the hedging instrument on 1 March 2011

2. Hedging instrument (swap)									
Calc. Period – Start	**Calc. Period – End**	**Month Ref.**	**Price Brent**	**Fixed Price**	**Floating Price**	**Diff**	**Volume (MWh)**	**Settlement Figure (k $)**	**Present Value – Settlement Figure (k $)**
01/04/2010	31/12/2010	gen-11	-	-	-	-	-	-	
01/05/2010	31/01/2011	feb-11	82.50	81.0500	82.50	−1.45	6.720	−9.7	−9.7
01/06/2010	28/02/2011	mar-11	85.29	81.0500	85.29	−4.24	7.430	−31.5	−31.5
						Full Fair Value	**14.150**	**−41**	**−41**

TABLE 16.21 Representation of the inputs for the computation of the offset ratio

	Inception Date	01/03/2011	Δ	Offset Ratio%
Fair value hedged item ($/1000)	1.754	1.188.13	566.10	
Fair value fixed leg hypothetical ($/1000)	1.754	1.149.71	604.51	
Fair value differences ($/1000)	−0.00	38.41	−38.41	104%
Fair Value derivative instrument ($/1000)	−4.33	−41.24	36.91	

The hedge is effective if the absolute value of the above ratio falls in the range 80% to 125%.

Table 16.21 shows a few key values registered at inception (first column):

- the full fair values of both the legs of the hypothetical derivative (1,754k$ and 1,754k$);
- the difference between the fair values of the hypothetical derivative instrument legs (0.00);
- the fair value of the commodity swap (–4.33k$);

The same pivotal values are reported also for the value date (1 March 2011):

- the full fair values of both the legs of the hypothetical derivative (1.188,13k$ and 1.149,71k$);
- the difference between the fair values of the hypothetical derivative instrument legs (38.41k$);
- the fair value of the commodity swap (–41.24k$).

The third column of the table contains the differences of the fair values registered at inception and at the valuation date. The offset ratio is computed as $\frac{|-38.41\text{k}\$|}{|-36.91\text{k}\$|}$, so it is equal to 104% and therefore well inside the boundaries defining the hedge effectiveness. In conclusion, we can see that our hedging operation is effective.

16.8.2 Accounting for CVA

Accordingly with the exposure draft announced by both the IASB and the FASB on 28 January 2011 regarding the *Offsetting Financial Asset and Liabilities*, the CVA (and also the DVA) should be accounted for by following some steps. First of all, at contract inception the CVA need not be measured and registered on the balance sheet even if, generally, aggressive traders account for it in their pricing activity. Secondly, during every subsequent valuation date of the derivative instrument, the CVA should be determined as an adjustment against the gross fair value of a financial contract and aggregated to a separate account at portfolio level, for example for each counterparty.

Furthermore, the CVA should be considered on the hedging instrument while performing the effectiveness test. Before starting the test, the gross CVA should be allocated to the individual trades based on the gross exposure of each trade. Concerning the hedged item, the CVA should be considered only if any contractual cash flow is still collectible from such a hedged item and as soon as the hypothetical derivative simulates the hedged item, the CVA is not attributed to it.

As stated by the abovementioned exposure draft, paragraph 6: 'An entity shall offset a recognised financial asset and a recognised financial liability and shall present the net amount in the statement of financial position when the entity:

(a) *has an unconditional and legally enforceable right to set off the financial asset and financial liability; and*
(b) *intends either:*
  (i) *to settle the financial asset and financial liability on a net basis, or*
  (ii) *to realise the financial asset and settle the financial liability.'*

In order to meet the disclosure information regarding the rights of set-off and related arrangements, the 12th paragraph of the exposure draft states that: '... *an entity shall disclose, as the minimum, the following information separately for financial assets and financial liabilities recognised at the end of the reporting period by class of financial instruments:*

(a) *the gross amounts (before taking into account amounts offset in the statement of financial position and portfolio-level adjustments for the credit risk of each of the counterparties or the counterparties' net exposure to the credit risk of the entity);*
(b) *showing separately:*
  (i) *the amounts offset in accordance with the criteria in paragraph 6 to determine the net amounts presented in the statement of financial position;*
  (ii) *the portfolio-level adjustments made in the fair value measurement to reflect the effect of the entity's net exposure to the credit risk of counterparties or the counterparties' net exposure to the credit risk of the entity; and*
  (iii) *the net amount presented in the statement of financial position...'*

16.9 CONCLUSIONS

The expansion of the liberalized physical commodity markets has led to the development of OTC financial derivative instruments linked to energy commodities such as forwards and swaps; this was followed by an increase in the number of energy companies acting as market operators – both with hedging and trading purposes. The increasing use of OTC instruments not managed by a central clearing house has highlighted the importance of evaluating and quantifying the counterparty credit risk within pricing activity mainly by a metric defined as CVA, the credit value adjustment.

In this chapter we first detailed the main features of an energy commodity swap derivative instrument, outlining the determination of the floating leg. Then, we presented a two-factor pricing model developed by Schwartz and Smith and used it to price a real energy commodity swap. To fully consider all relevant aspects, we discussed how to use the model to assess the counterparty credit risk, via computation of the so-called credit value adjustment. We investigated the right-way risk impact on the CVA, that is the effect of the correlation parameter between the default intensity and the commodity factors on the credit adjustment. We performed a sensitivity analysis in order to assess the impact that a change of estimated Schwartz and Smith model parameters has on the CVA and on the adjusted fixed price. In the light of this analysis, we can state that the CVA and the change in the fixed price are both particularly sensitive to the volatility parameters and to the long-run level of the short-term factor, the volatility of the short-term factor being the most influential parameter.

Finally, we presented and discussed the international accounting framework for swap derivative instruments and for the CVA. First, we described the cash flow hedge – an accounting methodology embedded in IAS 39 – providing also an example of hedge effectiveness using the dollar offset method, and then we outlined the accounting methodology reported in the exposure draft issued by the IASB and FASB (2011).

REFERENCES

Brigo, D., Chourdakis, K. and Bakkar, I. (2008) Counterparty risk valuation for energy-commodities swaps: Impact of volatilities and correlation, available at SSRN: http://ssrn.com/abstract=1150818 or http://dx.doi.org/10.2139/ssrn.1150818.

Fang, W., Giuly, J. and Qiu, X. (2012) Credit risk modelling and CDS valuation, working paper.

O'Kane, D. and Turnbull, S. (2003) Valuation of credit default swaps, Fixed income quantitative credit research, Lehman Brothers.

Schwartz, E. and Smith, J.E. (2000) Short-term variations and long-term dynamics in commodity prices, *Management Science*, **46**, 893–911.

FURTHER READING

Bielecki, T., Brigo, D. and Patras, F. (2011) *Credit Risk Frontiers: Subprime Crisis, Pricing and Hedging, CVA, MBS, Ratings, and Liquidity*, Bloomberg Press, New York.

Burger, M., Graeber, B. and Schindlmayr, G. (2007) *Managing Energy Risk. An Integrated View on Power and Other Energy Markets (Wiley Finance Series)*, John Wiley & Sons, Chichester.

Duffie, D. and Singleton, K. (2003) *Credit Risk*, Princeton University Press, Princeton, NJ.

EIA. (2002) Derivatives and Risk Management in the Petroleum, Natural Gas, and Electricity Industries, Report no. SR/SMG/2002-01, Energy Information Administration, US Department of Energy.

Eydeland, A. and Wolyniec, K. (2003) *Energy and Power Risk Management, New Developments in Modeling, Pricing and Hedging (Wiley Finance Series)*, John Wiley & Sons, Hoboken, NJ.

Jarrow, R.A. and Yu, F. (2001) Counterparty risk and the pricing of defaultable securities, *Journal of Finance*, **50**(6), 106–117.

Kleinman, G. (2011) *Commodity Futures and Options: A Step-by-Step Guide to Successful Trading*, Prentice-Hall, Englewood Cliffs, NJ.

KPMG IFRG. (2012) Offsetting Financial Assets and Financial Liabilities.

Mauro, A. (1999) Price risk management in the energy industry: The value at risk approach, Working paper.

Polo, M. and Scarpa, C. (2003) The liberalisation of energy markets in Europe and Italy, IGIER working paper no. 230.

Pykhtin, M. and Rosen, D. (2010) Pricing counterparty risk at the trade level and CVA allocations, working paper.

Ramirez, J. (2007) *Accounting for Derivatives: Advanced Hedging under IFRS* (Wiley Finance Series), John Wiley & Sons, Chichester.

Resti, A. and Sironi, A. (2007) *Risk management and shareholders' value in banking, in Risk Measurement Models to Capital Allocation Policies* (Wiley Finance Series), John Wiley & Sons, Chichester.

Schubert, D. (2011) Fair-value accounting for CVA, www.risk.net/risk-magazine.

Subramani, V. (2001) Accounting for credit value adjustments, *e-Journal*, **60**(4), 565–567.

Tilman, L.M. (2003) *Asset Liability Management of Financial Institutions: Maximising Shareholder Value through Risk-Conscious Investing*, Euromoney Books, London.

Zhu, S.H. and Pykhtin, M. (2007) A guide to modeling counterparty credit risk, *GARP Risk Review*, Jul/Aug, pp. 16–22.

CHAPTER 17

Pricing Energy Spread Options

Fred Espen Benth and Hanna Zdanowicz

17.1 SPREAD OPTIONS IN ENERGY MARKETS

Consider a power producer operating a gas-fired power plant. The producer generates income from selling electricity in the market, at the expense of gas. Simply put, the producer generates electricity only at times when this is profitable, and switches off the plant otherwise. Hence, the producer earns the power price less production costs when this is positive, and nothing otherwise. The production costs will be proportional to the cost of purchasing gas, where the proportionality factor is referred to as the *heat rate*. The heat rate converts gas into the energy equivalents of power, taking into account also the efficiency of the power plant. In Figure 17.1 we plot the income on a given day for the producer, as a function of power and production costs.

Mathematically, the figure illustrates the function

$$\max(P(T) - hG(T), 0),$$

where $P(T)$ is the price of electricity, $G(T)$ the price of gas at time T and h is the heat rate. Traditionally, gas has been measured in terms of *British thermal units* (Btu), while power is measured in *megawatts* (MW). The heat rate converts the energy content of Btu into MW, and multiplies this by the efficiency rate of the power plant. The efficiency rate tells us how many units (measured in MW) of gas are required to produce a unit of power. If we fix the production cost $hG(T)$, then the profit as a function of the power price $P(T)$ will be the same as from a European call option on the power price with strike $hG(T)$.

The producer's income from power generation over a time period $[T_1, T_2]$ will be

$$\sum_{T=T_1}^{T_2} \max\left(P(T) - hG(T), 0\right).$$

Handbook of Multi-Commodity Markets and Products: Structuring, Trading and Risk Management. Edited by Andrea Roncoroni, Gianluca Fusai and Mark Cummins.

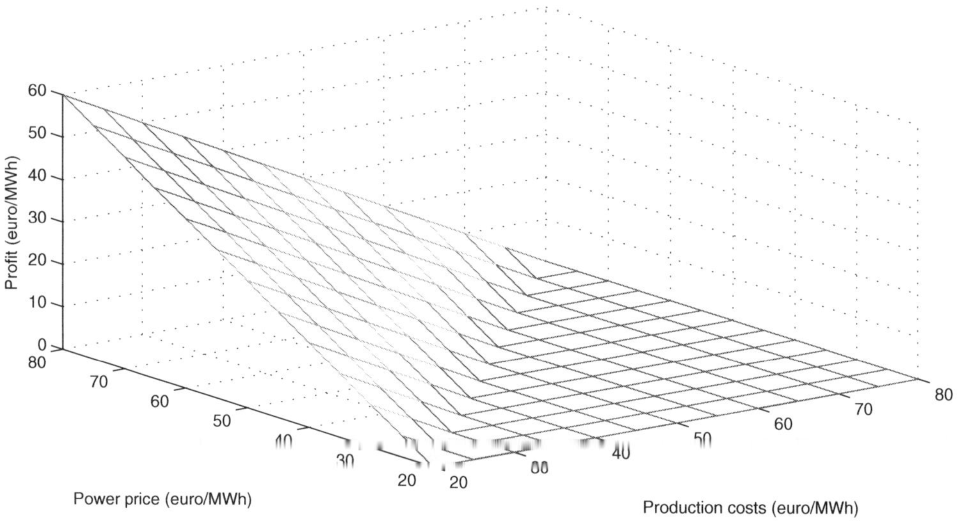

FIGURE 17.1 Profit function from running a gas-fired power plant.

This can be viewed as a strip of European call options written on the difference $P(T) - hG(T)$, or, on the *spread* between electricity and gas. In the marketplace, this difference is termed the *spark spread.*

Let us take power and gas prices in the German EEX market as a case. In Figure 17.2 we plot the daily power price $P(t)$ (light grey curve) along with the heat-rate-adjusted gas price $hG(t)$ (dark grey curve) for 2011. Weekends and public holidays are excluded, and prices on

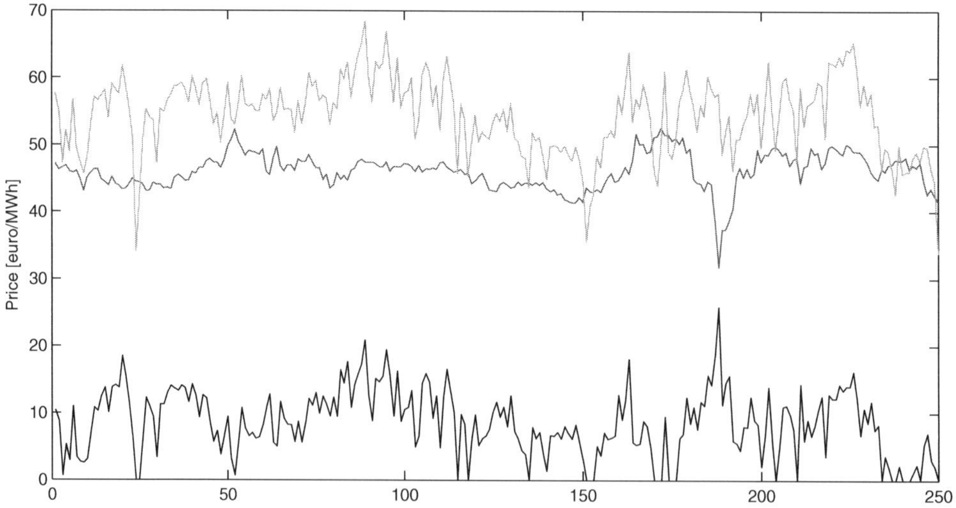

FIGURE 17.2 Daily spot prices for power (light grey) and natural gas (dark grey) traded at the German EEX market. Gas prices are converted into power with an efficiency factor (heat rate) of 49.13%. The spark spread truncated at zero is plotted in black.

'trading days' only are plotted. We show baseload power prices computed from averaging over the hourly spot prices, measured in euro/MWh. Further, the daily average spot price for natural gas traded on the same market is plotted, scaled by a heat rate of $h = 1/49.13\%$. As the natural gas prices are denominated in euro/MWh at the EEX, the heat rate will here contain only the efficiency factor of the gas-fired power plant. Our choice is to use an efficiency factor of 49.13%, which is in accordance with the number used in both UK and German spark spread tables.[1] The efficiency factor for a given gas-fired power plant ranges typically from 25% up to around 55% in Germany. As is evident from the plot, for most of the days in 2011 the gas-fired power plant yields a positive income since the power price is above the fuel costs $hG(t)$. However, on some days the production costs are above the power price, and the plant will lose money if it is not shut down. In black, we have plotted the spark spread truncated at zero, which is equal to the actual daily income per unit of power produced given that the power plant is not producing whenever it is not profitable. Summing up the black curve yields the total income per unit power produced by operation of the power plant. Thus, the payoff from owning the strip of European calls on the spark spread.

If the power plant has a very low rate of efficiency, the heat rate will become bigger and therefore the production costs much higher. This would be seen as an upscaling of the dark grey curve in Figure 17.2, resulting in more days of negative spark spread, or zero production.

The owner of a gas-fired power plant is in effect holding a strip of spark spread options. If the power plant is fueled by coal instead, the income can be viewed as holding a strip of *dark* spread options, being the difference between the power and coal price. Valuation of these derivatives provides us with a price for the power plant. This approach can be used in a real option valuation if one considers building a gas or coal-fired power plant (see Fusai and Roncoroni, 2008 for an extensive discussion and empirical study of spark spread option valuation).

In the market, power plants are also bought and sold virtually. *Tolling agreements* are financial derivatives which give the owner the right to operate a power plant virtually. For example, a tolling agreement on a gas-fired power plant yields an income stream proportional to that from a physically operated plant, as the holder of the tolling agreement will "produce" at maximum rate when this is profitable and not "produce" at all when the power price is below $hG(T)$.

In the European Union, a gas or coal-fired power plant must hold certificates to be allowed to emit carbon dioxide resulting from production. These certificates are traded on a market, the EU Emissions Trading Scheme, and induce an additional production cost. Indeed, the income from such a plant becomes

$$\sum_{T=T_1}^{T_2} \max(P(T) - hG(T) - C(T), 0),$$

where $C(T)$ is the carbon dioxide emission price. Thus, we have a spread option on three assets, which again we can view as a spread between power and the production cost, now being the sum of the gas and emission price.

[1]This is in accordance with figures presented at Wikipedia, article http://en.wikipedia.org/wiki/Spark_spread, visited in January 2013.

The power markets are gradually becoming more and more integrated. For example, new cables connecting the NordPool to the German EEX market are planned to be built. The value of such connection lines is given by the spread between Nordic and German power prices. Similarly, through LNG and pipelines, the gas markets worldwide are increasingly integrated, influencing the power markets as well.

From these examples, we can organize the various derivatives written on price differences into cross-commodity options and geographical spread options. The former class include options on the difference between two commodities related to the energy market, including power, gas, coal, oil and emissions. The latter are options on price differences within the same energy segment, but between different geographical marketplaces (e.g., EEX and NordPool power markets). Other, more classical financial options include calendar spreads, which we also find in the energy markets as options written on forwards with different delivery times. More recently, demand or volume-triggered spreads have emerged, where the payout from the option is dependent on specific weather events (such as lower-than-average wind speeds or warmer-than-average temperatures).[2] We encourage the reader to visit Carmona and Durrleman (2003) for an extensive survey of other spread options relevant to the energy markets, in particular the *crack* spread options traded at NYMEX, being options written on the difference between prices of refined oil qualities.

The remainder of this chapter is devoted to analysing the price of spread options in energy markets. Closely linked to pricing is the question of hedging the options, which we will also address. Our starting point will be a relatively general exponential price model for two energy commodities (power and gas, say), being a bivariate geometric Brownian motion with time-dependent drifts and volatilities. Such a model will include spot and forward price dynamics in many relevant situations occurring in the context of energy markets. The classical Margrabe formula for the price of an option to exchange one asset with another (or, in our context, a call option on the spread between the two assets) will be extended to our model. Furthermore, we extend the famous approximation formula of Kirk (1996) as well. In addition, we provide the reader with an introduction to another approximation formula suggested by Bjerksund and Stensland (2006), being a slight twist on Kirk's approach. Furthermore, a new approach based on Taylor expansion along the strike is suggested as an alternative approximation. In this procedure, the Margrabe formula appears as a zero-order approximation of a call spread option with non zero strike. The higher-order terms are analytically available, and conveniently, the error in this approximation can be quantified. Numerical examples illustrate the theory. We discuss spread options on spot and forwards, as both situations are easily accommodated in our general model.

The forthcoming analysis is organized as follows. In the next section we present the bivariate geometric Brownian motion model for the joint price dynamics of two energy commodities. We extend the Margrabe formula to price a call spread option with zero strike based on these dynamics. Different examples relevant for spread options in energy markets are presented. Then, in Section 17.3, hedging parameters for this option are derived, including the deltas and the gammas. The case of non zero strike spread options is analysed in Section 17.4, where we start off by introducing Kirk's approximation. The Bjerksund–Stensland approximation formula is discussed next. Finally, we introduce the approximation based on Taylor expansion of the option price as a function of the strike.

---

[2]We refer to Benth *et al.* (2012) for more on such options, also known as quanto options.

17.2 PRICING OF SPREAD OPTIONS WITH ZERO STRIKE

In 1976, Margrabe (see Margrabe, 1978) published his famous formula for the price of a so-called exchange option. He considers the value of the optionality to exchange one asset with another, which in our context is simply a call on the spread between two energy commodities with strike zero. Assuming that the prices of two assets follow a bivariate geometric Brownian motion, Margrabe derives a Black–Scholes-like formula for the price.

In energy markets, a slightly extended version of the Margrabe formula is required. We suppose that the energy commodity price dynamics (power and gas, say) follow a bivariate geometric Brownian motion with time-dependent expected return and volatility, formulated in the pricing measure Q directly. Mathematically, this is expressed as

$$\frac{dP(t)}{P(t)} = \mu_P(t)\,dt + \gamma_P(t)\,dW_P(t), \tag{17.1}$$

$$\frac{dG(t)}{G(t)} = \mu_G(t)\,dt + \gamma_G(t)\,dW_G(t), \tag{17.2}$$

where μ_P, μ_G, γ_P and γ_G are time-dependent functions and W_P, W_G are two correlated Brownian motions, that is $\mathbb{E}[dW_P(t)dW_G(t)] = \rho(t)\,dt$ for a time-dependent function $-1 < \rho(t) < 1$. We note that $\rho = 0$ corresponds to W_P and W_G being independent Brownian motions. Our dynamics model the returns of the two energy commodities, where the expected returns μ_k can vary with time as can the volatilities γ_k and correlation ρ, $k = P, G$.

We recover the classical framework of Margrabe by simply letting $\mu_k(t) = r > 0$, the risk-free interest rate, $\gamma_k(t) = \sigma_k > 0$, $k = P, G$, the volatilities, and a constant correlation $\rho(t) = \rho$. The stochastic dynamics of the two price variables will in this case be a classical two-dimensional geometric Brownian motion in the risk-neutral world.

In Figure 17.3 we show daily simulated values of the bivariate geometric Brownian motion dynamics for three different choices of correlation. For the sake of illustration, we have chosen constant parameters, with the drifts being equal to zero and both P and G having 30% annual volatility. Letting the starting values be 100, we see in the top plot the dynamics for a correlation being $\rho = -0.9$. Compared with the positively correlated case of $\rho = 0.9$ depicted at the bottom, the price dynamics are much more spread out. The independent case based on $\rho = 0$ is plotted in the middle.

The general bivariate geometric Brownian motion with time-dependent parameters will facilitate a number of relevant situations in energy. For example, if we are interested in the spread of forwards, a typical case in energy (and commodities in general) is the occurrence of the Samuelson effect in the volatility structure of the forward price, in the sense that the volatility decreases with time to maturity.[3] This requires a model with a time-dependent volatility function. Recall on the contrary that the drift will be zero for forward prices, as they trade at no cost. Further, if one has in mind the valuation of a power plant, it might be reasonable to assume that P and G are spot prices. Prices may show seasonal variations due to the impact of weather in demand (temperature) or supply (rain, wind and/or sun). As a power spot cannot in general be stored, the seasonality may appear in the expected return even under

[3]The 'Samuelson effect' was introduced by Samuelson (1965), and explained as a result of more information gradually becoming available about the underlying commodity as delivery approaches.

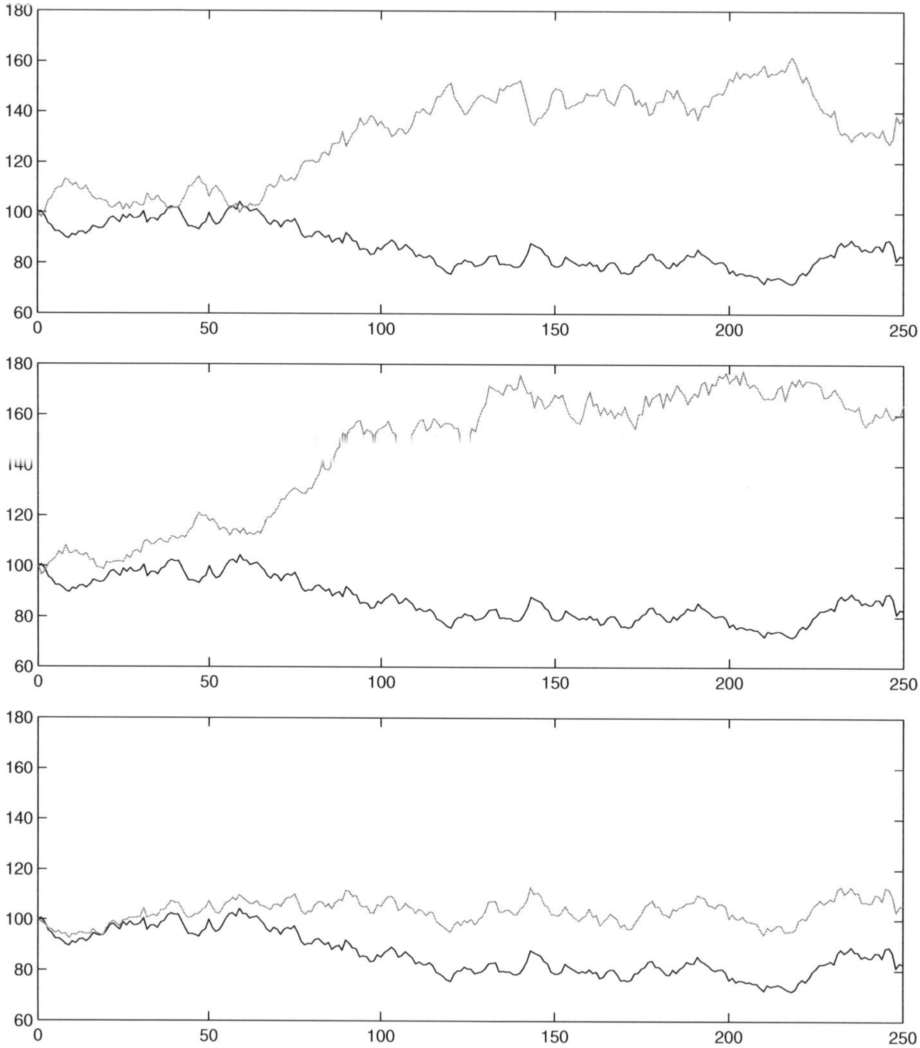

FIGURE 17.3 Two geometric Brownian motions being negatively correlated (top), independent (middle) and positively correlated (bottom).

the pricing measure Q. Also, market prices of risk may have seasonal patterns, which we can build into the drift when we model under Q. Spot volatilities may also be deterministically varying for the same reasons, of course. We will come back to this in a moment, with a more detailed discussion.

From the no-arbitrage theory of finance, we know that any option will have a price given by the present expected value of the payoff, where the expectation is taken under the pricing measure. For us, this means that the price $V(t)$ at time $t \geq 0$ of a spread option with zero strike and exercise at time $T \geq t$ is

$$V(t) = e^{-r(T-t)}\mathbb{E}_Q\left[\max(P(T) - hG(T), 0) \mid P(t), G(t)\right] . \tag{17.3}$$

Note that we condition on the current prices $P(t)$ and $G(t)$ of the two energy commodities. The heat rate h is naturally assumed to be positive.

We present the extended Margrabe formula in the next proposition:

Proposition 17.2.1 *The price of the spread option is*

$$V(t) = P(t)e^{\int_t^T (\mu_P(s)-r)\,ds}N(d_1) - hG(t)e^{\int_t^T (\mu_G(s)-r)\,ds}N(d_2),$$

with $d_2 = d_1 - \sqrt{\int_t^T \gamma^2(s)\,ds}$,

$$d_1 = \frac{\ln(P(t)/G(t)) - \ln h + \int_t^T (\mu_P(s) - \mu_G(s) + \frac{1}{2}\gamma^2(s))\,ds}{\sqrt{\int_t^T \gamma^2(s)\,ds}},$$

$$\gamma^2(s) = \gamma_P^2(s) - 2\rho(s)\gamma_P(s)\gamma_G(s) + \gamma_G^2(s),$$

and $N(\cdot)$ *being the cumulative standard normal distribution function.*

Recall that $N(x)$ is the probability that a normally distributed random variable with mean zero and variance one is less than x. It is implemented in most spreadsheets and software packages and can be computed directly. The term $\int_t^T \gamma^2(s)\,ds$ is the integrated (squared) volatility from current time up to time of exercise of the option. We can interpret $\gamma(s)$ as the volatility of the spread at time s.

Let us suppose for a moment that we are in the classical Margrabe case, with P and G being two assets that can be liquidly traded and a heat rate $h = 1$. Then, under the pricing measure Q, we will have that $\mu_P(s) = \mu_G(s) = r$. If we let $\rho(s) = \rho$, $\gamma_P(s) = \sigma_P$ and $\gamma_G(s) = \sigma_G$ be constants in addition, we recover the Margrabe formula

$$V(t) = P(t)N(d_1) - G(t)N(d_2), \tag{17.4}$$

with

$$d_1 = \frac{\ln(P(t)/G(t)) + \frac{1}{2}\sigma^2(T-t)}{\sigma\sqrt{T-t}}$$

and $d_2 = d_1 - \sigma\sqrt{T-t}$, for $\sigma^2 = \sigma_P^2 - 2\rho\sigma_P\sigma_G + \sigma_G^2$. We observe that the extended Margrabe formula in Proposition 17.2.1 has an explicit dependency in d_1 on the difference in drift $\mu_P(s) - \mu_G(s)$ between the two energies, a term which is naturally not occurring in the classical Margrabe formula.

In energy markets, like the markets for electricity in northern Europe, say, there is a seasonal pattern in prices. In the cold season, prices are generally higher than in the summer, due to demand for heating. In the Nordic electricity market NordPool, prices are very sensitive to temperature in the winter, while more stable in the summer season. This leads to spot price models (under the market probability) which can be modelled as

$$\frac{dP(t)}{P(t)} = \widetilde{\mu}_P(t)\,dt + \gamma_P(t)\,dB_P(t)\,.$$

Hence, the volatility γ_P and expected return $\widetilde{\mu}_P$ can vary with season. For example, one might think of a high volatility in winter compared with summer, and a strong positive drift in the autumn yielding increasing prices, while being negative in the late spring. We introduce a pricing measure Q which shifts the drift by a market price of risk $\theta_P(t)$, that is

$$\frac{dP(t)}{P(t)} = (\widetilde{\mu}_P(t) + \theta_P(t))\,dt + \gamma_P(t)\,dW_P(t)\,.$$

To model possible seasonal effects, we allow the market price of risk also to be time-dependent. Note that the 'risk-neutral' dynamics of the discounted power spot does not become a martingale[4] under Q, which is a distinctive feature of pricing measures in power markets.[5] We further remark that the drift and market price of risk in the Q dynamics may include storage costs and the convenience yield if we consider energy commodities like gas, coal and oil, say.

Suppose now that we would like to price the effect of having an interconnecting cable between the NordPool market and the German EEX market. We analyse the situation from the perspective of a Nordic producer with access to the cable. The producer has a possibility to sell power in the German market, whenever prices there are attractive. This is a call option on the spread between EEX and NordPool spot price, and if we suppose that the spot price in Germany is given by P and the NordPool price by G, having the dynamics under Q

$$\frac{dG(t)}{G(t)} = (\widetilde{\mu}_G(t) + \theta_G(t))\,dt + \gamma_G(t)\,dW_G(t)\,,$$

we can apply the Margrabe formula with $\mu_k(t) = \widetilde{\mu}_k(t) + \theta_k(t)$, $k = P, G$. In this case, we find that

$$d_1 = \frac{\ln(P(t)/G(t)) - \ln h + \int_t^T (\widetilde{\mu}_P(s) - \widetilde{\mu}_G(s) + \theta_P(s) - \theta_G(s) + \frac{1}{2}\gamma^2(s))\,ds}{\sqrt{\int_t^T \gamma^2(s)\,ds}}\,.$$

Thus, both the difference in drift and the difference in the market price of risk will play a role in the price determination.

[4]A martingale is a stochastic process for which future predictions are given by today's value. In particular, the discounted spot price is a martingale if its expected future value is constant.

[5]An extensive discussion about pricing measures in power and energy markets is provided by Benth *et al.* (2008).

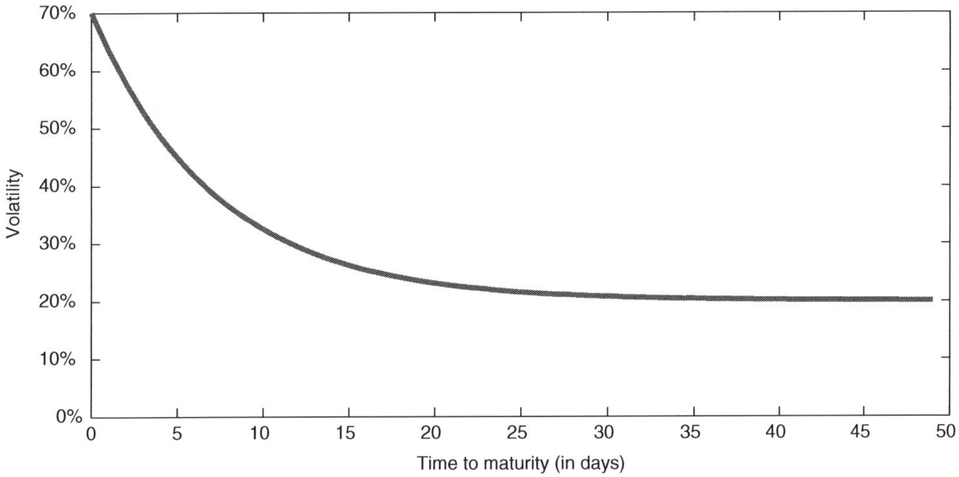

FIGURE 17.4 Volatility of the forward price dynamics in equation (17.5).

Consider next the case of a spread option written on two forwards. Let us suppose that a forward contract with delivery at time τ on the power P has forward price dynamics given by

$$\frac{dP(t,\tau)}{P(t,\tau)} = \left\{\sigma_{P1} + \sigma_{P2}\mathrm{e}^{-\alpha_P(\tau-t)}\right\}\, dW_P(t)\,, \tag{17.5}$$

for $t \leq \tau$ and positive constants σ_{ki}, α_k, $k = P, G$, $i = 1, 2$. These dynamics can be related to the two-factor Schwartz–Smith model[6] of spot price dynamics, where σ_{P1} is the volatility of the long-term factor of the spot, and $\sigma_{P2}\exp(-\alpha_P(\tau - t))$ accounts for the variations due to short-term fluctuations in the spot price. These short-term fluctuations are assumed to be mean-reverting at a speed α_P, with a volatility σ_{P2}, resulting in a Samuelson effect in the volatility of the forward. In Figure 17.4 we plot the volatility of the forward as a function of time to maturity $\tau - t$. In this example we have chosen σ_{P1} to be 20% (annually), whereas σ_{P2} is 50% annually. The mean-reversion speed α_P is chosen to be a reasonably fast one. We see that the volatility is exponentially increasing towards $\sigma_{P1} + \sigma_{P2} = 70\%$ as time to maturity goes to zero. In contrast, when we are far from maturity (that is, the time to maturity is large), the forward volatility is essentially equal to $\sigma_{P1} = 20\%$, the long-term volatility of the spot. We define the dynamics for $G(t, \tau)$ similarly. Hence, $\mu_P(s) = \mu_G(s) = 0$, $\gamma_k(t) = \sigma_{k1} + \sigma_{k2}\exp(-\alpha_k(T - t))$ for $k = P, G$. Finally, we suppose a constant correlation $\rho(t) = \rho$. Assume the spread option has exercise time $T \leq \tau$. To apply Margrabe's formula, we need to compute $\int_t^T \gamma^2(s)\, ds$. To this end, introduce the notation

$$\zeta_{P,G}(x, y) = \mathrm{e}^{-\frac{1}{2}(\alpha_P+\alpha_G)x}\left(1 - \mathrm{e}^{-\frac{1}{2}(\alpha_P+\alpha_G)y}\right). \tag{17.6}$$

[6]The Schwartz–Smith model appeared in Schwartz and Smith (2000), and has later been used extensively in many commodity markets, including energy and power.

We find from a direct (and admittedly tedious) computation that the "integrated volatility" becomes

$$\begin{aligned}\int_t^T \gamma^2(s)\,ds &= (\sigma_{P1}^2 - 2\rho\sigma_{P1}\sigma_{G1} + \sigma_{G1}^2)(T-t) \\ &+2\frac{\sigma_{P1}\sigma_{P2}}{\alpha_P}\zeta_{P,P}(\tau - T, T-t) - 2\rho\frac{\sigma_{P1}\sigma_{G2}}{\alpha_G}\zeta_{G,G}(\tau - T, T-t) \\ &-2\rho\frac{\sigma_{P2}\sigma_{G1}}{\alpha_P}\zeta_{P,P}(\tau - T, T-t) + \frac{\sigma_{G1}\sigma_{G2}}{\alpha_G}\zeta_{G,G}(\tau - T, T-t) \\ &+\frac{\sigma_P^2}{2\alpha_P}\zeta_{P,P}(2(\tau - T), 2(T-t)) - \frac{2\rho\sigma_P\sigma_G}{\alpha_P + \alpha_G}\zeta_{P,G}(2(\tau - T), 2(T-t)) \\ &+\frac{\sigma_G^2}{2\alpha_G}\zeta_{G,G}(2(\tau - T), 2(T-t)) \end{aligned} \tag{17.7}$$

Thus, we obtain a formula for the price of a spread call option on forwards:

$$V(t) = \mathrm{e}^{-r(T-t)}\left\{P(t)N(d_1) - hG(t)N(d_2)\right\}. \tag{17.8}$$

Here,

$$d_1 = \frac{\ln(P(t)/G(t)) - \ln h + \frac{1}{2}\int_t^T \gamma^2(s)\,ds}{\sqrt{\int_t^T \gamma^2(s)\,ds}},$$

and $d_2 = d_1 - \sqrt{\int_t^T \gamma^2(s)\,ds}$. We observe that this formula is analogous to the Black-76 formula[7] for call options written on forwards. We remark that $\tau - T$ is the time between the exercise of the spread option, T, and the time of delivery τ of the forward. In many cases $\tau = T$, and we simply find that

$$\zeta_{P,G}(0, y) = 1 - \mathrm{e}^{-\frac{1}{2}(\alpha_P + \alpha_G)y}.$$

The difference $T - t$ measures the time left until exercise of the option. If $\alpha_k(T-t)$ is large for $k = P, G$, we find that

$$\zeta_{P,G}(x, y) \sim \mathrm{e}^{-\frac{1}{2}(\alpha_P + \alpha_G)x}.$$

This may happen either if $T - t$ is large, or if the reversion rate α_k is big, $k = P, G$.

In markets for gas and electricity, the forward and futures contracts deliver over a given period of time. For example, in the EEX market one can enter forward contracts which deliver electricity over a specific month, January say. Rather than receiving the "spot" at a delivery

[7]The Black-76 formula is the famous Black–Scholes formula for call options on forwards. See Black (1976) for the precise statement.

time τ, a long position in the forward will result in delivery of 1 MW electricity over each hour in the month of January. The contracts are settled financially, so the total value of the delivery is (there are $31 \times 24 = 744$ hours in January)

$$\sum_{\tau=1}^{744} P(\tau).$$

The forward price is denoted in euro/MWh, which corresponds to a forward on the average spot price over the delivery period. In Benth and Koekebakker (2008), Heath–Jarrow–Morton dynamics for a power forward price for a contract with delivery over the period $[\tau_1, \tau_2]$ are proposed to be

$$\frac{dP(t, \tau_1, \tau_2)}{P(t, \tau_1, \tau_2)} = \left(\sigma_{P1} + \sigma_{P2} \mathrm{e}^{-\alpha_P(\tau_1 - t)}\right) dW_P(t), \tag{17.9}$$

stated under the pricing probability Q. We note that the dynamics are similar to the fixed delivery forward considered above. However, the interpretation of σ_{P2} is different. In fact, Benth and Koekebakker (2008) suggest modelling the volatility of $P(t, \tau_1, \tau_2)$ as the average over the delivery period of the volatility structure $\gamma_P(t, \tau) = \sigma_{P1} + \widetilde{\sigma}_{P2} \exp(-\alpha_P(\tau - t))$. We find this average to be

$$\frac{1}{\tau_2 - \tau_1} \int_{\tau_1}^{\tau_2} \gamma_P(t, \tau)\, d\tau = \sigma_{P1} + \frac{\widetilde{\sigma}_{P2}}{\alpha_P(\tau_2 - \tau_1)}(1 - \mathrm{e}^{-\alpha_P(\tau_2 - \tau_1)})\mathrm{e}^{-\alpha_P(\tau_1 - t)}.$$

By defining

$$\sigma_{P2} = \frac{\widetilde{\sigma}_{P2}}{\alpha_P(\tau_2 - \tau_1)}(1 - \mathrm{e}^{-\alpha_P(\tau_2 - \tau_1)})$$

we obtain the volatility structure of $P(t, \tau_1, \tau_2)$ stated in equation (17.9). We note in passing that Benth and Koekebakker (2008) found evidence of seasonality in the volatility term structure, which calls for additional time-dependent terms.

We continue with a discussion of the sensitivity of the option price with respect to the correlation ρ between the two energies. We analyse this in case the correlation is a constant, $\rho(t) = \rho$. To emphasize the dependency on ρ, we denote for the time being the spread call option price at time t by $V(t, \rho)$. We recall $V(t, \rho)$ from Proposition 17.2.1, and differentiating the integrated volatility function with respect to ρ gives

$$\frac{d}{d\rho} \int_t^T \gamma^2(s)\, ds = -2 \int_t^T \gamma_P(s)\gamma_G(s)\, ds,$$

which is negative as the volatilities γ_P and γ_G are naturally supposed to be positive. Hence, the total variance will decrease with an increasing correlation. A reasonable guess is thus that the spread option price decreases as well, and this is indeed true. A direct (but rather technical and cumbersome) differentiation yields

$$\frac{\partial V(t,\rho)}{\partial \rho} = -P(t)N'(d_1)\mathrm{e}^{\int_t^T (\mu_P(s)-r)\,ds} \frac{\int_t^T \gamma_P(s)\gamma_G(s)\,ds}{\sqrt{\int_t^T \gamma^2(s)\,ds}},$$

with d_1 and $\gamma(s)$ as in Proposition 17.2.1. Hence, we have for $\rho, \rho' \in (-1, 1)$ with $\rho < \rho'$,

$$V(t,-1) > V(t,\rho) > V(t,\rho') > V(t,1).$$

The more correlated the two energies are, the more the prices are collected together and the spread variation becomes smaller. This naturally leads to cheaper options. On the contrary, a strongly negative correlation will create a high variation in the spread, and thus more expensive option prices. Recall the simulated price series of two correlated geometric Brownian motions in Figure 17.3, where we clearly see how the prices are more collected together when they are positively correlated compared with negative correlation.

In Figure 17.5 we plot the spread option price as a function of correlation.

We have used constant volatilities of 30% annually in this example, with drifts being equal to the risk-free rate, which is set to zero. We have assumed one month until exercise of the option. A decreasing price for increasing correlation is clearly visible. The span of prices is

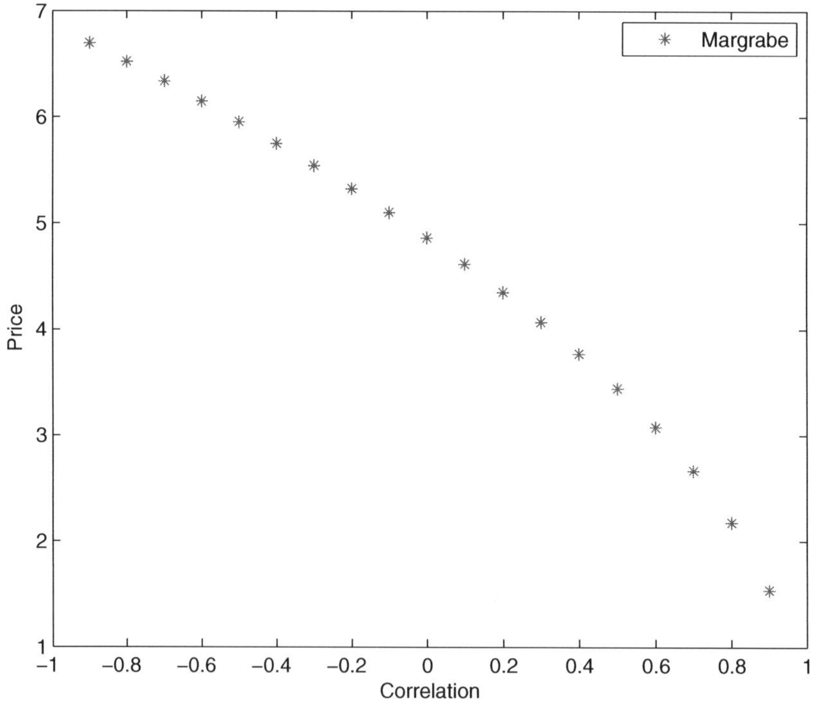

FIGURE 17.5 The spread option price as a function of correlation ρ between the Brownian motions.

rather big, ranging from around 7 for $\rho = -1$ down to 1 for $\rho = 1$. Interestingly, the price is concave in ρ, telling us that it has an increasing sensitivity to uncertainty in the correlation, the higher the correlation is.

We observe that in the boundary cases for $\rho = \pm 1$, the total variance becomes

$$\int_t^T (\gamma_P(s) \mp \gamma_G(s))^2 \, ds \, .$$

Obviously, in the degenerate case of $\gamma_P = \gamma_G$, the formula for $\partial V(t, \rho)/\partial \rho$ above does not hold for $\rho = 1$, as we divide by zero. But recalling Figure 17.5 we see that the limit $\rho \to 1$ gives a price.

17.3 ISSUES OF HEDGING

In this section we are concerned with the hedging of a spread call option. In the classical Margrabe context, it is assumed that the two assets P and G are liquidly tradeable, and we can find the hedging position in the two assets by the deltas of the price V with respect to P and G. The deltas provide information about the elasticity of the value of the option with respect to the underlying assets.

A direct differentiation of the price function V given in Proposition 17.2.1 yields the deltas

$$\frac{\partial V(t)}{\partial P(t)} = \mathrm{e}^{\int_t^T (\mu_P(s) - r)\, ds} N(d_1) \, ,$$
$$\frac{\partial V(t)}{\partial G(t)} = -h \mathrm{e}^{\int_t^T (\mu_G(s) - r)\, ds} N(d_2) \, .$$

Here, d_1 and d_2 are defined as in Proposition 17.2.1. In a perfectly liquid market, these deltas give the actual number of the two underlyings to hold in order to replicate a spread call option.

In energy markets, liquidity is typically a major issue and perfect hedging is not feasible. Approximative hedges must be found, taking the limitations of the market into account. For example, if P is the spot price of power, it is not at all possible to use delta hedging since electricity is not storable in general. One may also think of the situation where the spot is a physically traded commodity like gas and where storage facilities are required to construct a hedge. In these cases one can seek other tradeable instruments in order to build a hedge. A reasonable choice is to use forwards with a short time to delivery, which will be positively correlated with the spot price. We discuss this in more detail.

Conveniently, one may restate the spread option price in Margrabe's formula in terms of forwards. If P and G defined in equations (17.1) and (17.2) are the spot prices of two energy commodities under some pricing measure Q, we find the forward prices with a delivery time τ to be, respectively,

$$f_P(t, \tau) := \mathbb{E}_Q[P(\tau) \mid P(t)] = P(t) \exp\left(\int_t^\tau \mu_P(s)\, ds \right) , \tag{17.10}$$

$$f_G(t, \tau) := \mathbb{E}_Q[G(\tau) \mid G(t)] = G(t) \exp\left(\int_t^\tau \mu_G(s)\, ds \right) . \tag{17.11}$$

Recall that we can intepret μ_k as consisting of the interest rate r (cost of financing) and a convenience yield and/or cost of carry factor δ_k by

$$\mu_k(s) = r + \delta_k(s)\,, k = P, G\,.$$

This is in line with the theory of forward pricing in commodity markets.[8]

From Proposition 17.2.1 we see by direct insertion that the option price on the spread between the spot energy commodities can be rephrased as

$$V(t) = \mathrm{e}^{-r(T-t)}\left\{f_P(t,\tau)\mathrm{e}^{-\int_T^\tau \mu_P(s)\,ds}N(d_1) - hf_G(t,\tau)\mathrm{e}^{-\int_T^\tau \mu_G(s)\,ds}N(d_2)\right\} \tag{17.12}$$

for $\tau > T$. Here, $d_2 = d_1 - \sqrt{\int_t^T \gamma^2(s)\,ds}$ and

$$d_1 = \frac{\ln(f_P(t,\tau)/f_G(t,\tau)) - \ln h + \int_T^\tau (\mu_G(s) - \mu_P(s))\,ds + \frac{1}{2}\int_t^T \gamma^2(s)\,ds}{\sqrt{\int_t^T \gamma^2(s)\,ds}}\,.$$

Hence, we may use the forward contracts $f_P(t,\tau)$ and $f_G(t,\tau)$ with delivery τ *after* the exercise time T in a portfolio to hedge the spread option on $P(\tau)$ and $G(\tau)$.

We can similarly treat the situation where it is more convenient to use forwards with delivery τ prior to exercise of the spread T. For example, we could apply a roll-over strategy where we use contracts with delivery τ up until $t = \tau$, and then roll over to a new pair of forwards with later delivery. Also, we can easily accommodate the situation where we can choose different delivery times τ_P and τ_G for the two energy forwards f_P and f_G.

The representation of the spread option price in terms of forward prices is not surprising, since we can in fact consider the spread option on the spot prices as a spread option on the forwards. To this end, recall that for $\tau \geq T$, we have

$$P(T) = f_P(T,\tau)\mathrm{e}^{-\int_T^\tau \mu_P(s)\,ds}$$

and similarly for $G(T)$. Hence, the spread option has a payoff function that can be written as

$$\max\,(P(T) - hG(T), 0) = \max\left(f_P(T,\tau)\mathrm{e}^{-\int_T^\tau \mu_P(s)\,ds} - hf_G(T,\tau)\mathrm{e}^{-\int_T^\tau \mu_G(s)\,ds}, 0\right)\,.$$

Hence, we have a spread on the forwards, appropriately 'discounted' by μ_P and μ_G. Obviously, the price of this spread on forwards is equal to $V(t)$ as in equation (17.12).

[8]For an economical introduction to forward pricing in commodity markets, in particular energy, the reader is referred to Geman (2005). Here a treatment of storage and convenience yield, as well as the classical theory of contango and backwardation, is provided in the context of forward markets.

We end this section with explicit computations of the Greeks *gamma* and *cross gamma*. It holds that

$$\frac{\partial^2 V(t)}{\partial P(t)^2} = \frac{e^{\int_t^T (\mu_P(s)-r)\,ds}}{\sqrt{\int_t^T \gamma^2(s)\,ds}} \frac{\varphi(d_1)}{P(t)},$$

$$\frac{\partial^2 V(t)}{\partial G(t)^2} = h\frac{e^{\int_t^T (\mu_G(s)-r)\,ds}}{\sqrt{\int_t^T \gamma^2(s)\,ds}} \frac{\varphi(d_2)}{G(t)},$$

$$\frac{\partial^2 V(t)}{\partial P(t)\partial G(t)} = -\frac{e^{\int_t^T (\mu_P(s)-r)\,ds}}{\sqrt{\int_t^T \gamma^2(s)\,ds}} \frac{\varphi(d_1)}{G(t)},$$

where φ denotes the density function of a standard normal distribution. One may also derive other Greeks explicitly for the spread option.

17.4 PRICING OF SPREAD OPTIONS WITH NONZERO STRIKE

Margrabe's formula is not valid for spread call options where the strike is nonzero, that is, for options with payout at exercise

$$\max(P(T) - hG(T) - K, 0), \tag{17.13}$$

where the strike K is some real number. Note that as the difference between $P(T)$ and $hG(T)$ may become negative, it is relevant to consider strikes K being negative as well as positive.

Recall the introductory example of a coal/gas-fired power plant paying emission costs, which we argued could be valued as a strip of spread calls. Considering one such option, with exercise time T, it will have the payoff

$$\max(P(T) - hG(T) - C(T), 0)\,. \tag{17.14}$$

One can reduce the pricing of such a *trivariate* spread option to a spread option with payoff as in (17.13) where the strike is $K = 1$.

Let the carbon emission price be given as a geometric Brownian motion of the form

$$\frac{dC(t)}{C(t)} = \mu_C(t)\,dt + \gamma_C(t)\,dW_C(t) \tag{17.15}$$

under the pricing measure Q. Here, W_C is a Brownian motion which is correlated both to W_P and W_G. We introduce the notation $\rho_{PG}(t)$, $\rho_{CP}(t)$ and $\rho_{CG}(t)$ for the three different correlations (all being functions with values between -1 and 1), and remark that we must have

$$\rho_{CP}^2(t) + \rho_{CG}^2(t) + \rho_{PG}^2(t) \geq 1 + 2\rho_{CP}(t)\rho_{CG}(t)\rho_{PG}(t)$$

to ensure a well-defined trivariate correlated Brownian motion (W_P, W_G, W_C). If this condition is not satisfied, the covariance matrix for the three variables will not be positive-definite. We have the following result:

Proposition 17.4.1 *The price at time t of a trivariate spread with payoff as in (17.14) is*

$$V(t) = C(t)e^{\int_t^T(\mu_C(s)-r)\,ds}\mathbb{E}_{\widetilde{Q}}\left[\max\left(\widetilde{P}(T) - h\widetilde{G}(T) - 1, 0\right) \mid \widetilde{P}(t), \widetilde{G}(t)\right],$$

where $\widetilde{P}(t) = P(t)/C(t)$, $\widetilde{G}(t) = G(t)/C(t)$ *and the dynamics of* $\widetilde{P}$ *and* $\widetilde{G}$ *are, respectively,*

$$\frac{d\widetilde{P}(s)}{\widetilde{P}(s)} = \widetilde{\mu}_P(s)\,ds + \widetilde{\gamma}_P(s)\,d\widetilde{W}_P(s),$$

$$\frac{d\widetilde{G}(s)}{\widetilde{G}(s)} = \widetilde{\mu}_G(s)\,ds + \widetilde{\gamma}_G(s)\,d\widetilde{W}_G(s),$$

with $\widetilde{\mu}_i(s) = \mu_i(s) - \mu_C(s)$,

$$\widetilde{\gamma}_i^2(s) = \gamma_i^2(s) - 2\rho_{Ci}(s)\gamma_C(s)\gamma_i(s) + \gamma_C^2(s),$$

for $i = P, G$, *and two* $\widetilde{Q}$*-Brownian motions* $\widetilde{W}_P$ *and* $\widetilde{W}_G$ *being correlated by*

$$\widetilde{\rho}_{PG}(s) = \frac{\rho_{PG}(s)\gamma_P(s)\gamma_G(s) - \rho_{CP}(s)\gamma_P(s)\gamma_C(s) - \rho_{CG}(s)\gamma_G(s)\gamma_C(s) + \gamma_C^2(s)}{\sqrt{\widetilde{\gamma}_P(s)}\sqrt{\widetilde{\gamma}_G(s)}}.$$

The pricing formula above introduces two new energy price dynamics, $\widetilde{P}$ and $\widetilde{G}$, being bivariate geometric Brownian motions. In fact, these energies are simply the original price dynamics using the carbon emission price as numeraire. The expected return and volatility of the two energies are modified by the carbon return and volatility. In conclusion, by appropriately recasting the dynamics of the two energies, any trivariate spread option can be viewed as a spread option with nonzero strike.

Given the exponential models for the dynamics of P and G in equations (17.1) and (17.2), there exists no analytical pricing formula for spread call options when $K \neq 0$. Hence, one must resort to numerical pricing,[9] or deriving efficient approximation methods. In this section we will focus on the latter, and introduce and discuss some existing and some new ways to tackle the pricing problem of spread options with nonzero strikes. Our goal is to obtain formulas which are able to approximate the exact price

$$V(t, K) = e^{-r(T-t)}\mathbb{E}\left[\max\left(P(T) - G(T) - K, 0\right) \mid P(t), G(t)\right] \tag{17.16}$$

reasonably well in an efficient manner.

[9]For example, Monte Carlo simulations or numerical solution of partial differential equations, see Fusai and Roncoroni (2008) for these methods applied to spread options.

17.4.1 Kirk's Approximation Formula

The idea of Kirk (1996) is to suppose that $G(T) + K$ is log-normally distributed. In our context, we obtain the following approximative formula for the spread call option price generalizing Kirk's formula:

$$\widetilde{V}_{\text{Kirk}}(t, K) = \mathrm{e}^{\int_t^T (\mu_P(s)-r)ds} P(t)N(d_1) - \mathrm{e}^{\int_t^T (\mu_G(s)-r)ds} (hG(t) + K)N(d_2), \tag{17.17}$$

where $d_2 = d_1 - \sigma(t, T)$,

$$d_1 = \frac{\ln \frac{P(t)}{hG(t)+K} + \int_t^T (\mu_P(s) - \mu_G(s))\, ds + \frac{1}{2}\sigma^2(t, T)}{\sigma(t, T)}, \tag{17.18}$$

and

$$\sigma^2(t, T) = \int_t^T \gamma_P^2(s)ds - 2\frac{hG(t)}{hG(t) + K} \int_t^T \rho(s)\gamma_P(s)\gamma_G(s)ds + \left(\frac{hG(t)}{hG(t) + K}\right)^2 \int_t^T \gamma_G^2(s)ds. \tag{17.19}$$

Note that if we let $K = 0$, we recover Margrabe's formula in Proposition 17.2.1. Furthermore, letting $\mu_P(s) = \mu_G(s) = r$, constant correlation $\rho(t) = \rho$, and the volatilities being constants $\gamma_k(s) = \sigma_k > 0$ for $k = P, G$, we recover the original Kirk's approximation formula

$$\widetilde{V}_{\text{Kirk}}(t, K) = P(t)N(d_1) - (hG(t) + K)N(d_2)$$

with $d_2 = d_1 - \sigma\sqrt{T - t}$,

$$d_1 = \frac{\ln \frac{P(t)}{hG(t)+K} + \frac{1}{2}\sigma^2(T - t)}{\sigma\sqrt{T - t}},$$

and

$$\sigma^2 = \sigma_P^2 - 2\frac{hG(t)}{hG(t) + K}\rho\sigma_P\sigma_G + \left(\frac{hG(t)}{hG(t) + K}\right)^2 \sigma_G^2.$$

Bjerksund and Stensland (2006) suggest a modification of Kirk's approximation method. They allow for a different parameter attached to the strike K, namely, the spread call option value is approximated by the formula

$$\widetilde{V}_{\text{BS}}(t, K) = \mathrm{e}^{\int_t^T (\mu_P(s)-r)ds} P(t)N(d_1) - \mathrm{e}^{\int_t^T (\mu_G(s)-r)ds} hG(t)N(d_2) - e^{-r(T-t)}KN(d_3). \tag{17.20}$$

Here,

$$d_1 = \frac{\ln \frac{P(t)}{hG(t)+K} + \int_t^T (\mu_P(s) - \mu_G(s))ds + \frac{1}{2}\sigma_1^2(t,T)}{\sigma(t,T)},$$

$$d_2 = \frac{\ln \frac{P(t)}{hG(t)+K} + \int_t^T (\mu_P(s) - \mu_G(s))ds + \frac{1}{2}\sigma_2^2(t,T)}{\sigma(t,T)},$$

$$d_3 = \frac{\ln \frac{P(t)}{hG(t)+K} + \int_t^T (\mu_P(s) - \mu_G(s))ds + \frac{1}{2}\sigma_3^2(t,T)}{\sigma(t,T)},$$

and $\sigma(t,T)$ given in equation (17.19) as in Kirk's formula, and

$$\sigma_1^2(t,T) = \int_t^T \gamma_P^2(s)ds - 2\frac{hG(t)}{hG(t)+K}\int_t^T \rho(s)\gamma_P(s)\gamma_G(s)ds + \left(\frac{hG(t)}{hG(t)+K}\right)^2 \int_t^T \gamma_G^2(s)ds,$$

$$\sigma_2^2(t,T) = -\int_t^T \gamma_P^2(s)ds + 2\int_t^T \rho(s)\gamma_P(s)\gamma_G(s)ds + \frac{hG(t)}{hG(t)+K}\left(\frac{hG(t)}{hG(t)+K} - 2\right)\int_t^T \gamma_G^2(s)ds,$$

$$\sigma_3^2(t,T) = -\int_t^T \gamma_P^2(s)ds + \left(\frac{hG(t)}{hG(t)+K}\right)^2 \int_t^T \gamma_G^2(s)ds\,.$$

If we set $K = 0$, the Bjerksund–Stensland approximation coincides with the Margrabe formula in Proposition 17.2.1. We can also in this case recover the original Bjerksund–Stensland approximation introduced by assuming constant coefficients and $\mu_G = \mu_P = r$.

We consider some empirical examples to illustrate the performance of the two approximations. Suppose that we have two forwards, with price dynamics having volatilities given by $\gamma_k(t) = \sigma_{k1} + \sigma_{k2}\exp(-\alpha_k(\tau - t))$ for $t \leq \tau$, $k = P, G$ and τ being the delivery time of the forwards. The correlation $\rho(t)$ between the two Brownian motions W_P and W_G will be a constant. For simplicity, we let the parameter values in the specification of the forwards be the same, so that $\alpha_k = \alpha$ and $\sigma_{ki} = \sigma_i$, for $k = P, G$ and $i = 1, 2$. The 'long-term' level of the volatility is set to 20% annually, corresponding to $\sigma_1 = 0.0126$ on a daily scale. The 'short-term' volatility is assumed to be 50% annually, corresponding to $\sigma_2 = 0.0316$ on a daily scale. Here we let the number of trading days in a year be 250. The parameter α can be associated with a speed of mean reversion in the short-term variations factor of a Schwartz–Smith spot model, and we assume this to be $\alpha = 0.139$, which corresponds to a half-life of 5 days.[10] Finally, we let $t = 0$, and $P(0) = hG(0) = 100$ for simplicity. In the examples, we consider a call option on the spread

[10]Clewlow and Strickland (2000) introduce the concept of half-life for a mean-reverting process as a measure for how fast the process returns to its mean value. The half-life is defined as the average time it takes the process to return half-way back to its mean after a random shock. A high speed of mean reversion will imply that a shock is rapidly wiped out.

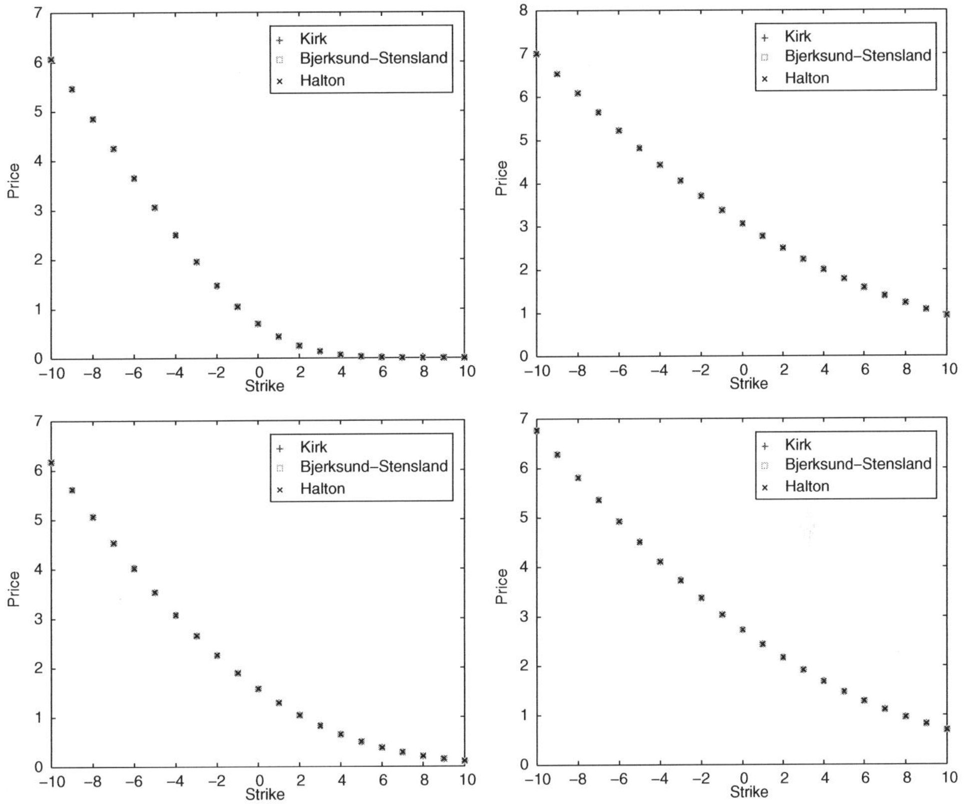

FIGURE 17.6 Plots of the approximative prices of Kirk and Bjerksund–Stensland as a function of the strike K along with the benchmark prices simulated by Halton quasi-Monte Carlo. The correlations are set to $\rho = 0.9, -0.9, -0.5$ and $\rho = 0.5$ going clockwise from the upper left-hand plot.

between the two forwards, with strike K ranging from -10 to 10. The delivery time τ of the forwards will be in the middle of a given month, while exercise of the options will take place at the beginning of the month so that $\tau - T = 10$ days (assuming five trading days in a week). We simulate benchmark prices for the various strikes based on quasi-Monte Carlo simulations using the Halton low-discrepancy sequence of numbers. We simulate until an accuracy in the first two decimal places is reached. In the panel of plots in Figure 17.6 we show the resulting benchmark prices along with the approximations of Kirk and Bjerksund–Stensland. The upper two plots show prices for correlations $\rho = 0.9$ (left) and $\rho = -0.9$ (right), whereas the lower two plots show the corresponding prices for $\rho = \pm 0.5$. The option prices are decreasing with the strike and concave. Since a negative correlation makes the difference $P(T) - hG(T)$ more spread out, the prices become more expensive than for positively correlated commodities. This is in line with our theoretical finding that the derivative of Margrabe's option price with respect to correlation is negative.

It is impossible on the graphs to distinguish the approximative prices from the benchmark. In the panel of plots presented in Figure 17.7 we show the relative errors (in percent) of the

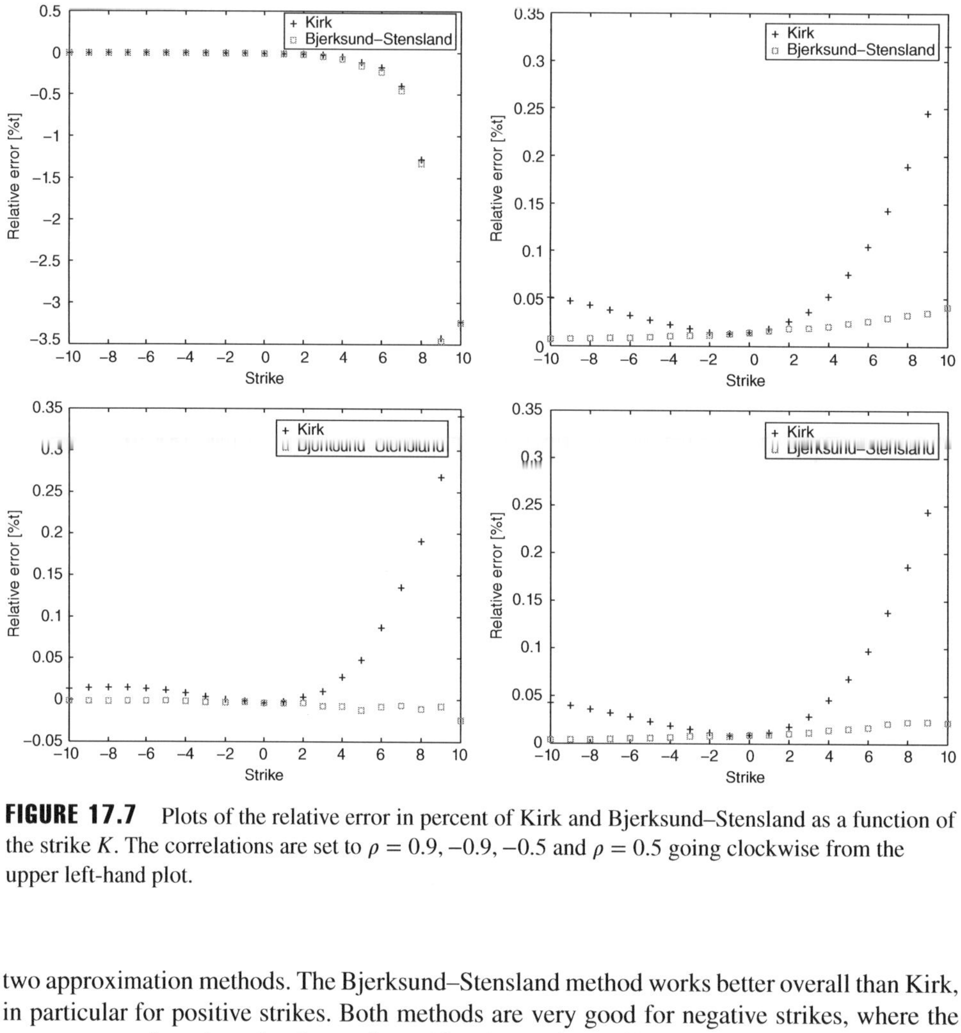

FIGURE 17.7 Plots of the relative error in percent of Kirk and Bjerksund–Stensland as a function of the strike K. The correlations are set to $\rho = 0.9, -0.9, -0.5$ and $\rho = 0.5$ going clockwise from the upper left-hand plot.

two approximation methods. The Bjerksund–Stensland method works better overall than Kirk, in particular for positive strikes. Both methods are very good for negative strikes, where the error seems to be minor (but increasing with a decreasing strike). However, for strikes bigger than 0 we observe an increase in the error with the strike, especially for the strongly positive correlated case where the two methods underprice around 2–3%. In the other cases, the error is around 0.3% at most, showing that the two approximations work well for smaller and/or negative correlations.

17.4.2 Approximation by Margrabe Based on Taylor Expansion

We want to investigate a new and alternative approximation of the spread option price for $K \neq 0$ based on Taylor expansion. The idea is to view the price $V(t, K)$ as a function of the strike, and Taylor expand this around $K = 0$. Such an approximation will involve the derivatives of the price with respect to the strike, and turns out to have the Margrabe formula as the zero-order approximation.

The Taylor representation of order N with remainder is given by

$$V(t,K) = \sum_{n=0}^{N} \frac{V^{(n)}(t,0)}{n!} K^n + \frac{V^{(N+1)}(t,\widetilde{K})}{(N+1)!} K^{N+1}. \tag{17.21}$$

Here, $V^{(n)}$ is the nth derivative of $V(t,K)$ with respect to K, using the convention that $V^{(0)} = V$. Moreover, in the error term we have $|\widetilde{K}| \leq |K|$.

Note that the zero order term is

$$V^{(0)}(t,0) = V(t,0) = \mathrm{e}^{-r(T-t)}\mathbb{E}[\max(P(T) - hG(T), 0) \mid P(t), G(t)],$$

which leads us back to the Margrabe formula in Proposition 17.2.1. The derivative of $V(t,K)$ at $K = 0$ is

$$V^{(1)}(t,0) = -\mathrm{e}^{-r(T-t)}N(d_3),$$

with

$$d_3 = \frac{\ln(P(t)/G(t)) - \ln h + \int_t^T (\mu_P(s) - \mu_G(s) - \frac{1}{2}(\gamma_P^2(s) + \gamma_G^2(s)))\, ds}{\sqrt{\int_t^T \gamma^2(s)\, ds}} \tag{17.22}$$

where $\gamma(s)$ is defined in Proposition 17.2.1. Hence, by appealing to the first-order Taylor approximation of $V(t,K)$ and again Proposition 17.2.1, we find

$$\widetilde{V}_1(t,K) = \mathrm{e}^{\int_t^T (\mu_P(s)-r)\, ds} P(t)N(d_1) - \mathrm{e}^{\int_t^T (\mu_G(s)-r)\, ds} hG(t)N(d_2) - \mathrm{e}^{-r(T-t)}KN(d_3). \tag{17.23}$$

Here, d_1 and d_2 are defined in Proposition 17.1, and d_3 in equation (17.22). This provides us with a first-order approximation of $V(t,K)$. The structure of $\widetilde{V}_1(t,K)$ is similar to that of Bjerksund–Stensland, however, it is important to note that in the latter approximation also d_1, d_2 and d_3 depend on K, which is not the case for $\widetilde{V}_1(t,K)$. Indeed, the first-order Taylor approximation is linear in K, while the approach of Bjerksund–Stensland is highly nonlinear.

Let us consider a numerical example based on the first-order Taylor approximation $\widetilde{V}_1(t,K)$ given in equation (17.23). We place ourselves in the same setting as described in the empirical example of the previous subsection, and apply the Halton quasi-Monte Carlo simulated prices as benchmarks. Note that from Figure 17.6 the price of a call spread decreases with the strike K and is concave. As the first-order Taylor price $\widetilde{V}_1(0,K)$ is based on approximating the price by following the gradient at $K = 0$, we are likely to have an increasing price error when moving away from the zero strike. This is indeed what we see in Figure 17.8. However, we find a very good approximation for strikes near zero. It is also important to note that the Taylor approximation is always below the true price as this is a concave function. The gradient at $K = 0$ naturally passes zero at a positive value of K, and giving

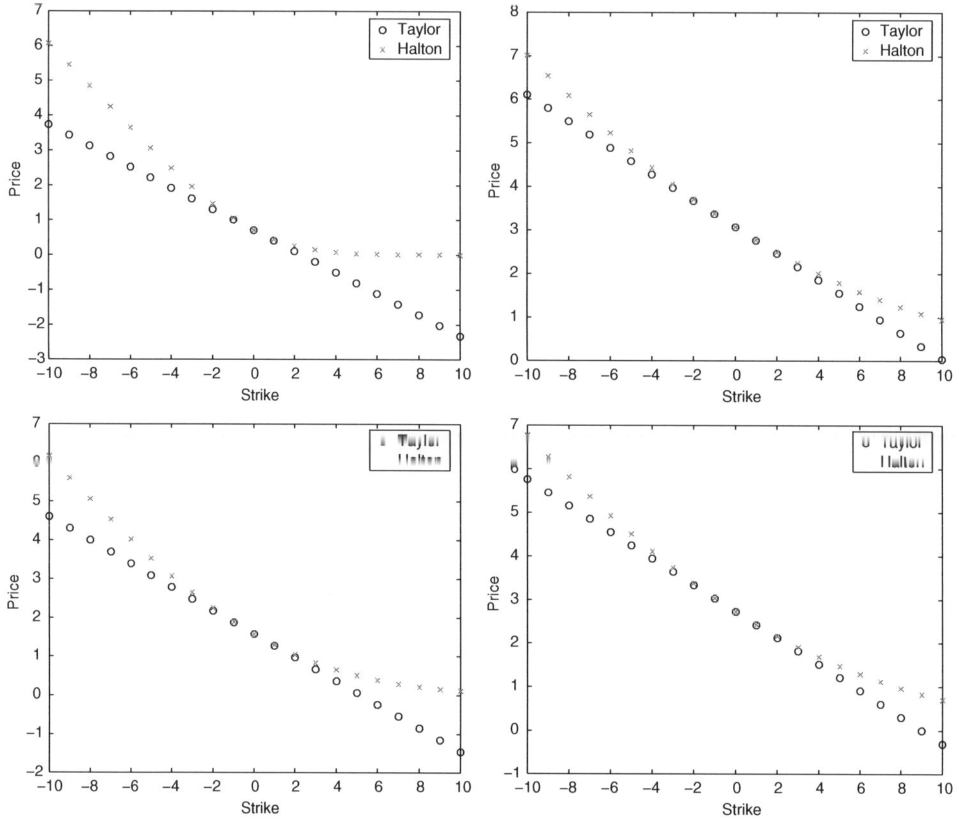

FIGURE 17.8 Plots of the first-order Taylor approximation $V_1(0, K)$ as a function of the strike K along with the benchmark prices simulated by Halton quasi-Monte Carlo. The correlations are set to $\rho = 0.9, -0.9, -0.5$ and $\rho = 0.5$ going clockwise from the upper left-hand plot.

negative prices for larger strikes. This is clearly unreasonable as the true prices must be positive.

As noted, the first-order Taylor approximation is linear in K, whereas both Kirk and Bjerksund–Stensland are nonlinear approximations. These seem to capture the curvature of the prices as a function of K much better, at least in the numerical examples we have considered. On the contrary, we can add a second-order term in the Taylor approximation to obtain a function being concave as well. This would require knowledge of $\widetilde{V}^{(2)}(t, 0)$, which is not as simple as $V^{(0)}(t, 0)$ and $\widetilde{V}^{(1)}(t, 0)$, unfortunately. It can be calculated as

$$\widetilde{V}^{(2)}(t, 0) = \mathrm{e}^{-r(T-t)} \int_{-\infty}^{\infty} \mathrm{e}^{-x} f_{P,G}(x, x)\, dx\,, \tag{17.24}$$

where $f_{P,G}$ is the bivariate normal probability density function of $\ln P(T)$ and $\ln G(T)$, given $P(t)$ and $G(t)$. We recall from probability theory that if (X, Y) are two bivariate normally distributed variables with mean μ_X and μ_Y and variances σ_X^2 and σ_Y^2, respectively, then their probability density function is

$$g_{X,Y}(x,y) = \frac{1}{2\pi\sigma_X\sigma_Y\sqrt{1-\rho^2}} \times \exp\left(-\frac{1}{2(1-\rho^2)}\left(\frac{(x-\mu_X)^2}{\sigma_X^2} - 2\rho\frac{(x-\mu_X)(y-\mu_Y)}{\sigma_X\sigma_Y} + \frac{(y-\mu_Y)^2}{\sigma_Y^2}\right)\right),$$

where the correlation between X and Y is ρ. From equations (17.1) and (17.2), we find that $\ln P(T)$ and $\ln G(T)$ given $P(t)$ and $G(t)$ have means

$$\mu_X = \ln P(t) + \int_t^T (\mu_P(s) - \frac{1}{2}\gamma_P^2(s))\, ds,$$

$$\mu_Y = \ln h + \ln G(t) + \int_t^T (\mu_G(s) - \frac{1}{2}\gamma_G^2(s))\, ds,$$

and variance–covariance matrix

$$\begin{pmatrix} \sigma_X^2 & \rho\sigma_X\sigma_Y \\ \rho\sigma_X\sigma_Y & \sigma_Y^2 \end{pmatrix} = \begin{pmatrix} \int_t^T \gamma_P^2(s)\, ds & \int_t^T \rho(s)\gamma_P(s)\gamma_G(s)\, ds \\ \int_t^T \rho(s)\gamma_P(s)\gamma_G(s)\, ds & \int_t^T \gamma_G^2(s)\, ds \end{pmatrix},$$

identifying σ_X^2, σ_Y^2 and the correlation ρ. The second-order Taylor approximation of $V(t,K)$ becomes

$$\widetilde{V}_2(t,K) = e^{\int_t^T (\mu_P(s)-r)\, ds} P(t)N(d_1) - e^{\int_t^T (\mu_G(s)-r)\, ds} hG(t)N(d_2) - e^{-r(T-t)}KN(d_3) + e^{-r(T-t)}K^2 \int_{-\infty}^{\infty} e^{-x} f_{P,G}(x,x)\, dx. \tag{17.25}$$

The last integral can be computed analytically, but the expression is too long and technical to be included here.

The advantage of the Taylor method is, as said earlier, that the error is accessible – which can be investigated from an analytical point of view. Such an analysis is lacking for the Kirk and Bjerksund–Stensland methods. Indeed, the error for the first-order Taylor price $\widetilde{V}_1(0,K)$ can be estimated from $\widetilde{V}^{(2)}(0,\widetilde{K})$ for $|\widetilde{K}| \leq |K|$, while the second-order approximation has an error which involves $\widetilde{V}^{(3)}(t,\widetilde{K})$. Error estimates provide precise statements about the domain of validity of the method. However, if such are lacking, as for Kirk and Bjerksund–Stensland, only empirical studies can provide confidence in the methodology.

17.4.3 Other Pricing Methods

We would like to briefly mention two other methods to approximate spread call options with strikes different from zero. The first method models the spread of the underlying commodities directly, while the other uses the Fourier transform.

Somewhat following the idea of Kirk, one may ask for distributional approximations of the spread $P(T) - hG(T)$. A simple idea would be to suppose that the spread is normally distributed, and compute the mean and variance from the specifications of $P(T)$ and $G(T)$. Defining $S(T)$ to be this normally distributed random variable, it is an easy exercise to compute the approximative spread call option price from the expression

$$\widetilde{V}(t, K) = \mathrm{e}^{-r(T-t)}\mathbb{E}\left[\max(S(T) - K, 0) \mid S(t)\right] ,$$

which is the same as computing Bachelier's price of a call option with strike K.[11] We remark that $S(t)$ will be given in terms of $P(t)$ and $G(t)$, while the mean and variance can be analytically computed in terms of the parameters of the two commodities.[12]

An empirical version of this way of approaching the valuation of spread call options is to model the spread *directly*. Based on statistical analysis of the spread data, one fits a suitable stochastic process and uses this to price a call option.[13] The disadvantage with this approach is that one loses the explicit connection with the marginal commodities P and G, which only enters implicitly in the statistical estimation of the spread.

Transform-based valuation of derivatives is popular in quantitative finance.[14] In our context, one can derive an integral representation of the spread option price based on the Fourier transform of the payoff function $\max(x - y - 1, 0)$ and the characteristic function of the logarithmic prices $\ln P(T)$ and $\ln G(T)$.[15] This paves the way for efficient numerical pricing using the fast Fourier transform. Even more, as the method is based on knowledge of the characteristic function of the logarithmic prices, one can go beyond Gaussian models as treated here. Price dynamics based on bivariate jump processes can be handled in many cases, a class of models which is relevant in energy markets.[16]

ACKNOWLEDGEMENT

Financial support from the project 'Managing Weather Risk in Electricity Markets (MAWREM)' funded by the Norwegian Research Council under the RENERGI programme is greatly acknowledged. We are grateful to Nina Lange and Steen Koekebakker for interesting discussions.

---

[11] In Davis and Etheridge (2006), the reader will find a translation of Louis Bachelier's PhD thesis from 1900, with historical accounts linking up his theory to today's modern approach to option pricing.

[12] This and more sophisticated distributional approximations have been studied in Borovkova *et al.*, (2007) and Carmona and Durrleman (2003).

[13] Benth and Šaltytė Benth (2006) fit a Vasicek mean-reversion model driven by a non-Gaussian process to the UK spark spread price data, and demonstrate how spread option prices can be computed efficiently using the Fourier transform.

[14] See, for example, Fusai and Roncoroni (2008).

[15] This method has been proposed and analysed for general financial markets by Hurd and Zhou (2010).

[16] See Caldana and Fusai (2013) for an extension of the Bjerksund–Stensland method to a non-Gaussian case based on the univariate Fourier transformation.

REFERENCES

Benth, F.E. and Koekebakker, S. (2008) Stochastic modeling of financial electricity contracts, *Energy Economics*, **30**(3), 1116–1157.

Benth, F.E. and Šaltytė Benth, J. (2006) Analytical approximation for the price dynamics of spark spread options, *Studies in Nonlinear Dynamics and Economics*, **10**(3), article 8 (electronic publication: http://www.bepress.com/snde/vol10/iss3/art8).

Benth, F.E., Šaltytė Benth, J. and Koekebakker, S. (2008) *Stochastic Modelling of Electricity and Related Markets*, World Scientific, in Singapore.

Benth, F.E., Lange, N. and Myklebust, T.Å. (2012) Pricing and hedging quanto options in energy markets, Available at SSRN: http://ssrn.com/abstract=2133935 or http://dx.doi.org/10.2139/ssrn.2133935.

Bjerksund, P. and Stensland, G. (2006) Closed form spread option valuation, NHH Department of Finance and Management Science, Discussion Paper No. 2006/20. Available at SSRN: http://ssrn.com/abstract=1145206 or http://dx.doi.org/10.2139/ssrn.1145206.

Black, F. (1976) The pricing of commodity contracts, *Journal of Financial Economics*, **3**, 169–179.

Borovkova, S., Permana, F.J. and van der Weide, J.A.M. (2007) A closed form approach to valuation and hedging of basket and spread option, *Journal of Derivatives*, **14**, 8–24.

Caldana, R. and Fusai, G. (2013) A general closed-form spread option pricing formula. Working paper, DISeI, Università del Piemonte Orientale.

Carmona, R. and Durrleman, V. (2003) Pricing and hedging spread options, *Siam Review*, **45**(4), 627–685.

Clewlow, L. and Strickland, C. (2000) *Energy Derivatives: Pricing and Risk Management*, Lacima Publications, London.

Davis, M. and Etheridge, A. (2006) *Louis Bachelier's Theory of Speculation. The Origins of Modern Finance*, Princeton University Press, Princeton, NJ.

Fusai, G. and Roncoroni, A. (2008) *Implementing Models in Quantitative Finance: Methods and Cases*, Springer-Verlag, Berlin.

Geman, H. (2005) *Commodities and Commodity Derivatives*, Wiley-Finance, Chichester.

Hurd, T. and Zhou, Z. (2010) A Fourier transform method for spread option pricing, *SIAM Journal of Financial Mathematics*, **1**, 142–157.

Kirk, E. (1996) Correlation in energy markets, In Kaminski, V. (ed.), *Managing Energy Price Risk*, Risk Publications and Enron, London, pp. 71–78.

Margrabe, W. (1978) The value of an option to exchange one asset for another, *Journal of Finance*, **33**(1), 177–186.

Samuelson, P. (1965) Proof that properly anticipated prices fluctuate randomly, *Industrial Management Review*, **6**, 41–44.

Schwartz, E. and Smith. J.E. (2000) Short-term variations and long-term dynamics in commodity prices *Management Science*, **46**(7), 893–911.

CHAPTER 18

Asian Options: Payoffs and Pricing Models

Gianluca Fusai, Marina Marena and Giovanni Longo

In this chapter, we describe and compare alternative procedures for pricing Asian options. Asian options are derivatives contracts written on an average price. More precisely, prices of an underlying security (or index) are recorded on a set of dates during the lifetime of the contract. At the option's maturity, a payoff is computed as a deterministic function of an average of these prices. As reported by Falloon and Turner (1999), the first contract linked to an average price was traded in 1987 by Bankers & Trust in Tokyo, hence the attribute 'Asian'.

Asian options are quite popular among commodity derivative traders and risk managers. This is due to several reasons.

Primarily, Asian options smooth possible market manipulations occurring near the expiry date. In general, the longer the averaging period, the smoother the path. This is shown in Figures 18.1 and 18.2. The first figure shows three simulated paths of the underlying and of its average: the strong oscillations in the underlying path disappear as we consider the time average. The second figure presents simulated paths of the two quantities and the simulated distributions one year in the future: the one that refers to the arithmetic average appears much less dispersed than the one referring to the underlying.

Secondly, Asian options provide a suitable hedge for firms facing a stream of cash flows. This is the case, for instance, with commodity end-users that are financially exposed to average prices. Asian-style options, and other options written on alternative definitions of average prices, are effective hedging devices in commodity markets. Eydeland and Wolyniec (2003) provide an example of how these derivatives play an important role in price risk management performed by local delivery companies in the gas market. Moreover, oil markets often use these securities to stabilize cash flows that stem from meeting obligations to clients.

A few examples of Asian options traded on organized markets are:

- The New York Mercantile Exchange (NYMEX) and Intercontinental Exchange (ICE) offer several average price products which are linked to energy products, e.g. Brent

Handbook of Multi-Commodity Markets and Products: Structuring, Trading and Risk Management. Edited by Andrea Roncoroni, Gianluca Fusai and Mark Cummins.

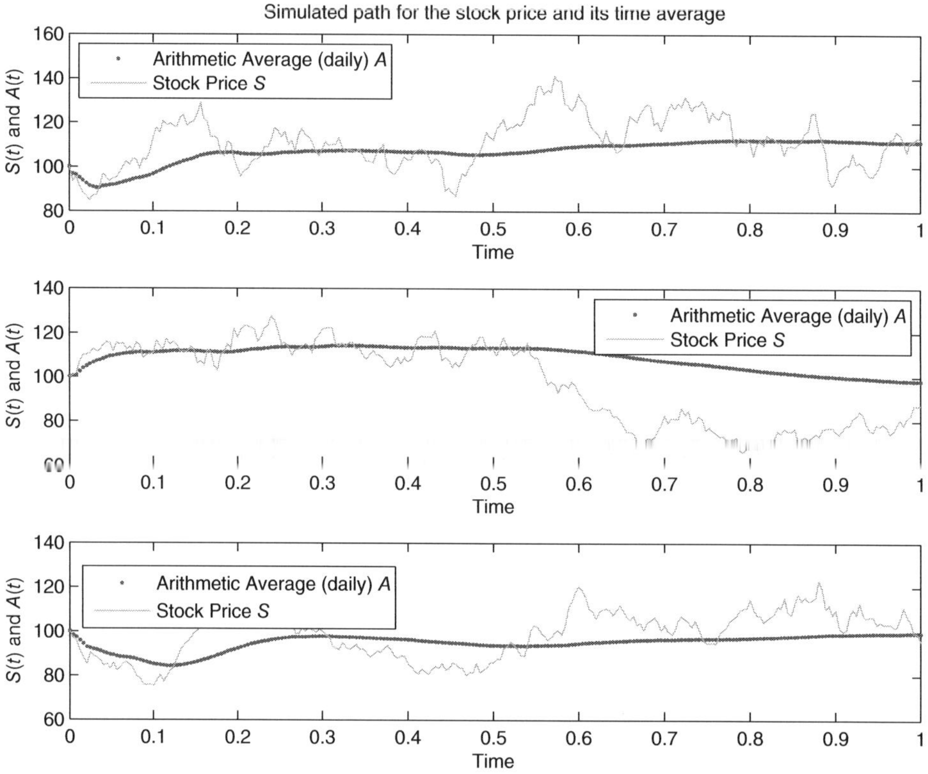

FIGURE 18.1 Simulated paths of spot price and its time (arithmetic) average

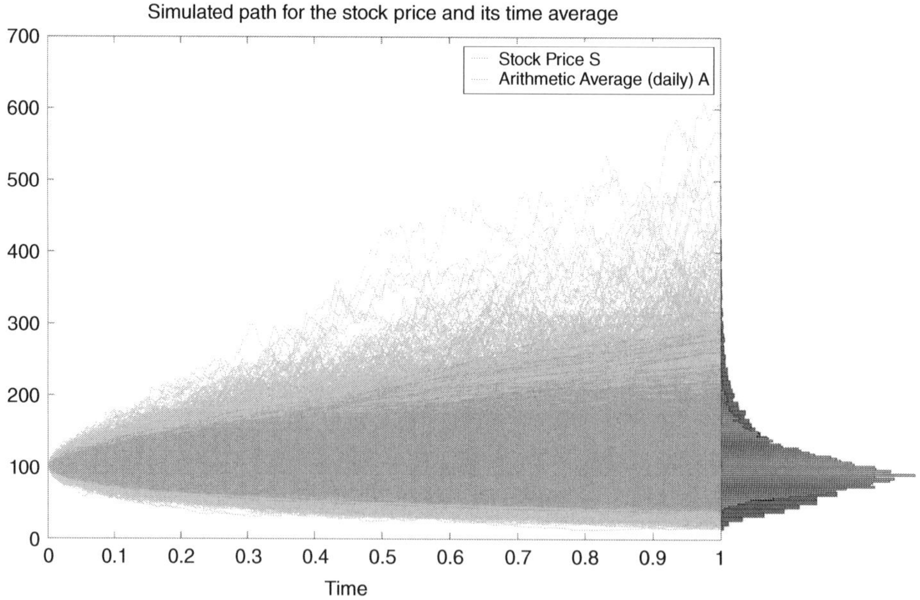

FIGURE 18.2 Simulated paths and terminal distribution of spot price and arithmetic average

TABLE 18.1 Average price options traded at NYMEX

WTI Average Price Option
Underlying Futures
Light Sweet Crude Oil Futures (CL)
Contract Unit
On expiration of a call option, the value will be the difference between the average daily settlement price during the calendar month of the first nearby underlying Light Sweet Crude Oil Futures and the strike price multiplied by 1000 barrels, or zero, whichever is greater. On expiration of a put option, the value will be the difference between the strike price and the average daily settlement price during the calendar month of the first nearby underlying Light Sweet Crude Oil Futures multiplied by 1000 barrels, or zero, whichever is greater.
Price Quotation
US dollars and cents per barrel
Option Style
Average Price non-early exercisable option
Minimum Fluctuation
$0.01 per barrel
Expiration of Trading
Trading ends the last business day of the calendar month
Listed Contracts CME ClearPort and Open Outcry: 72 consecutive months CME Globex: 1 consecutive month
Strike Prices
Twenty strike prices in increments of $0.50 (50) per barrel above and below the at-the-money strike price, and the next 10 strike prices in increments of $2.50 above the highest and below the lowest existing strike prices for a total of at least 61 strike prices. The at-the-money strike price is nearest to the previous day's close of the underlying futures contract. Strike price boundaries are adjusted according to the futures price movements. In addition, options trading can be conducted in strike price increments of $0.01.
Settlement Type
Financial
Exchange Rule
These contracts are listed with, and subject to, the rules and regulations of NYMEX

Source: http://www.cmegroup.com/trading/energy/crude-oil/light-sweet-crude_contractSpecs_options .html#prodType=AVP.

Average Price Options and WTI (West Texas Intermediate) Average Price Options. Details are provided in Tables 18.1 and 18.2.

- The London Metal Exchange (LME) offers Traded Average Price Options (TAPOs) based on the LME Monthly Average Settlement Price (MASP) for several metals, such as for copper grade A, high-grade primary aluminium, standard lead, primary nickel, special high-grade zinc, aluminium alloy and tin. Because many users in the industry price their physical material on the basis of the LME MASP, brokers developed off-exchange average price option products, known as Asians, which quickly became popular, particularly with large producers. To meet this growing demand, the LME developed the TAPO contracts. TAPO contracts complement existing LME futures and traded options contracts. Details for a copper TAPO contract are provided in Table 18.3.
- The Chicago Mercantile Exchange (CME) launched trading for three new cash-settled petroleum crack spread average price options contracts in July, 2009. These new average

TABLE 18.2 Average options on Brent traded at ICE

ICE Brent Average Price Option

Description

The Brent Average Price Option is based on the underlying ICE Brent 1st Line Future (I) and will automatically exercise into the settlement price of the 1st Line Future on the day of expiry of the options contract.

Contract Symbol I

Hedge Instrument: The delta hedge for the Brent Average Price Option is the ICE Brent 1st Line Swap Future (I)

Contract Size

1000 barrels

Unit of Trading

Any multiple of 1000 barrels

Currency

US dollars and cents

Trading Price Quotation

One cent ($0.01) per barrel

Settlement

Price Quotation: One tenth of one cent ($0.001) per barrel

Minimum Price Fluctuation

One tenth of one cent ($0.001) per barrel

Last trading day

Last trading day of the contract month

Option Type

Options are Asian-style and will be automatically exercised on the expiry day if they are in-the-money. The swap future resulting from exercise immediately goes to cash settlement, relieving market participants of the need to concern themselves with liquidation or exercise issues. If an option is out-of-the-money it will expire automatically. It is not permitted to exercise the option on any other day or in any other circumstances than the last trading day. No manual exercise is permitted.

Expiry

19:30 London Time (14:30 EST). Automatic exercise settings are pre-set to exercise contracts which are one minimum price fluctuation or more 'in-the-money' with reference to the relevant reference price. Members cannot override automatic exercise settings or manually enter exercise instructions for this contract. The reference price will be a price in USD and cents per barrel equal to the average of the settlement prices as made public by ICE for the Brent 1st Line Swap Future for the contract month. When exercised against, the Clearing House, at its discretion, selects sellers against which to exercise on a pro rata basis.

Option Premium / Daily Margin

The premium on the Brent Average Priced Option is paid/received on the business day following the day of trade. Net Liquidating Value (NLV) will be re-calculated each business day based on the relevant daily settlement prices. For buyers of options, the NLV credit will be used to off set their Original Margin (OM) requirement; for sellers of options, the NLV debit must be covered by cash or collateral in the same manner as the OM requirement. OM for all options contracts is based on the options delta.

Strike Price Intervals

Minimum $0.50 increment strike prices: $1.00 strikes from $20 to $240; $0.50 strikes, 20 strikes above and below ATM. The at-the-money strike price is the closed interval nearest to the previous business day's settlement price of the underlying contract.

Contract Series

Up to 72 consecutive months

Final Payment Date

Two Clearing House business days following the last trading day. Business Days: Publication days for ICE.

Source: https://www.theice.com/productguide/ProductSpec.shtml;jsessionid=2A767FBF878E8F31ADADC5ED9B70B639?specId=11523783.

TABLE 18.3 LME traded average price options (TAPO's) on copper specifications

TAPO CONTRACT SPECIFICATIONS

Contract Metals

Copper grade A, high-grade primary aluminium, standard lead, primary nickel, special high-grade zinc, aluminium alloy and tin.

Contract Date

The business day on which the contract is traded

Contract Period

Calendar months up to 27 months forward for copper grade A, high-grade primary aluminium, primary nickel, special high-grade zinc, and 15 months forward for standard lead, aluminium alloy and tin. Contracts can be traded daily up to and including the penultimate business day of the current month.

Option Type

Calls and puts based on the monthly average settlement price (MASP). No early exercise. Fixed period: The period between the first business day of the current month and the last business day of the month (inclusive).

Strike Price

$1 gradations

Currency

US dollars

Minimum Tick Size

0.01 USD (one cent)

Premium Payment

Next business day after the contract is traded.

Exercise

The exercise process is automatic once the LME monthly average settlement price is made official. A TAPO contract that is 'in-the-money' generates two futures trades per member which are equal and opposite in tonnage. One trade corresponds to the MASP and the other to the original strike price of the option.

Settlement Date

Settlement is two business days after exercise. The futures trades settle as per LME rules and regulations.

Margining

Like all existing LME contracts, TAPOs are margined using the SPAN methodology.

MASP

The arithmetic average of all settlement prices determined during the fixing period. This becomes an official LME price on the last day of the current month at 3.00 pm.

Source: http://www.lme.com/en-gb/trading/contract-types/tapos/.

options are the gasoil–Brent crude oil crack spread options, the heating oil–crude oil crack spread options, and the RBOB–crude oil crack spread options.

- The freight options currently traded are contracts to settle the difference between the average spot freight rate over a prespecified period of time and an agreed strike price. Freight options in the dry bulk market are traded on the Baltic Capesize Index (BCI), Baltic Panamax Index (BPI) and Baltic Supramax Index (BSI). The Baltic indices are calculated on a daily basis by the Baltic Exchange based on data supplied by a panel of independent international shipbrokers, and are reported in the market at 13:00 h London time. Freight

TABLE 18.4 Payoff structures of European and Asian options. $S(T)$ is the underlying price at option maturity T, whilst $A(T)$ stands for some form of averaging of the underlying asset price – see equations (18.1) and (18.2)

Type	Call	Put
European options	$(S(T) - K)^+$	$(K - S(T))^+$
Fixed-strike Asian options	$(A(T) - K)^+$	$(K - A(T))^+$
Floating strike Asian options	$(S(T) - A(T))^+$	$(A(T) - S(T))^+$

options on a Baltic index settle the difference between the arithmetic average of the spot Baltic assessments over the trading days of the settlement month and an agreed strike price. The options are executed between two counterparties through a broker primarily as an OTC contract, though the majority of the trades are subsequently cleared through a clearing house and quoted in terms of implied volatility.[1]

- Other examples include commodity-linked bonds on average bond prices and Asian-style catastrophe (CAT) insurance options with payoffs depending on the accumulated catastrophic losses, see Chang *et al.* (2010).

18.1 PAYOFF STRUCTURES

The payoff structure of plain vanilla European options, fixed and floating strike Asian options, is illustrated in Table 18.4. The quantity A in this table represents the (possibly weighted) arithmetic average of spot prices over a given time frame up to the option expiry. If we let $S(t)$ be the underlying spot price at time t, then A is given by

$$A(T) := A(0, T) = \sum_{i=0}^{N} w(t_i)S(t_i), \tag{18.1}$$

where $T = t_N$ refers to the option expiry and $t_i, i = 0, \ldots, N$, with $t_0 = 0$, refer to the so-called monitoring dates, that is, the dates at which the underlying price is taken for entering in the

[1]Implied volatilities of Baltic options assessments, i.e. implied volatility for an at-the-money option in the Dry Bulk Option market submitted by brokers at 17.30 (London), are published by the Baltic Exchange (see the website www.balticexchange.com). Options are at-the-money, i.e. strikes are set equal to the prevailing forward freight agreement rate. Market prices can be recovered, in line with market practice, by inserting the quoted volatility in the Asian option price formula of Turnbull and Wakeman and Levy, to be discussed later in this chapter. The market quotes are for forward start freight call options on the BCI, BPI and BSI for the next four quarters (+1Q, +2Q, +3Q, +4Q) and the next two calendar years (+1CAL and +2CAL). Each quarter contract consists of three options that expire at the end of each month in the quarter of interest, whereas a calendar contract is a strip of 12 monthly options. If on 4 January 2008 an investor holds the BCI+1Q, this contract comprises three freight options which settle at the end of April 2008, May and June 2008. The settlement prices of each of these options are given by the average of the BCI spot rates over the trading days of the respective settlement month. The main characteristics of freight market indexes are illustrated in Chapter 8. Additional information can be found in Nomikos *et al.* (2013).

computation of the average, w_i is the weight attributed to each observation (with the constraint that the sum of weights equals 1). The most common weighting scheme is equally, that is $w(t_i) = 1/(N+1)$. In general, the first monitoring date is the trade date.

It is common practice to price Asian options assuming that the average is recorded continuously over the option lifetime rather than at discrete dates. Therefore, the sum in formula (18.1) is replaced by an integral as follows:

$$A(T) = \int_0^T w(u)S(u)du. \tag{18.2}$$

Few variants to the above expression are possible, for example a partial average option for which the time interval taken into account for the average calculation is a subset of the full life of the option. In a forward starting option, the calculation of the average starts at a later instant with respect to the trade date, so that the time-to-maturity period is always larger than the time averaging periods. In the partial averaging case, (18.1) becomes

$$A(t_k, t_m) = \sum_{i=k}^{m} w(t_i)S(t_i)$$

where $0 < k < m < N$ and in the forward starting case, (18.1) becomes

$$A(t_k, t_N) = \sum_{i=k}^{N} w(t_i)S(t_i).$$

In the continuous monitoring case, the partial averaging and the forward starting options are respectively defined as $\int_{t_k}^{t_m} w(u)S(u)du$ and $\int_{t_k}^{T} w(u)S(u)du$.

Market practice assumes that the underlying asset price evolves according to Black–Scholes lognormal dynamics. Unfortunately, given this model setup, the average depends on a sum of correlated lognormal variates and the probability distribution of the average does not admit a simple analytical expression. Consequently, numerical approximations need to be developed for the purpose of pricing arithmetic Asian options. We review these in the next section.

18.2 PRICING ASIAN OPTIONS IN THE LOGNORMAL SETTING

This section illustrates the most common procedures for pricing Asian options in the Black–Scholes lognormal setting, that is assuming that the risk-neutral process for the underlying asset is a geometric Brownian motion satisfying

$$dS(t) = (r-q)\,S(t)\,dt + \sigma S(t)\,dW(t), S_0 = s_0, \tag{18.3}$$

where $W(t)$ is a standard Brownian motion, r is the continuously compounding rate of interest, q the continuous dividend yield and σ is the instantaneous percentage price volatility. It is convenient also to notice that (see Chapter 12)

$$S(t) = s_0 e^{\left(r-q-\frac{\sigma^2}{2}\right)t+\sigma W(t)}. \tag{18.4}$$

Given that the most common weighting is equally, we also have

$$A(T) = \frac{s_0}{T}\int_0^T e^{\left(r-q-\frac{\sigma^2}{2}\right)u+\sigma W(u)}du \quad \text{(continuous monitoring)},$$

or

$$A(T) = \frac{s_0}{N+1}\sum_{i=0}^{N} e^{\left(r-q-\frac{\sigma^2}{2}\right)t_i+\sigma W(t_i)} \quad \text{(discrete monitoring)}.$$

In both cases, continuous and discrete monitoring, the fixed strike Asian option fair price is given by

$$e^{-rT}\widetilde{E}_0\left(A(T)-K\right)^+, \tag{18.5}$$

where $\widetilde{E}_0$ denotes expectation under the risk-neutral probability measure. The pricing problem consists of finding the distribution function of $A(T)$.

If the option is into the averaging period, the above expectation can be computed by adjusting the strike price to take into account the average observed so far. In practice, if we let T_1 be the length of the averaging period so far, and $T-T_1$ the length of the remaining averaging period, the option price is given by

$$e^{-r(T-T_1)}\widetilde{E}_{T_1}\left(A\left(0,T\right)-K\right)^+. \tag{18.6}$$

The average price can be decomposed as

$$A(0,T) = \frac{T_1}{T}A(0,T_1) + \frac{T-T_1}{T}A(T_1,T).$$

Substituting this expression in (18.6), we obtain

$$e^{-r(T-T_1)}\frac{T-T_1}{T}\left(\bar{E}_{T_1}\left(A(T_1,T)-\hat{X}\right)^+\right),$$

where the modified strike price $\hat{X}$ is

$$\hat{X} = \frac{T}{T-T_1}\left(X - \frac{T_1}{T}A(0,T_1)\right)$$

and $A(0, T_1)$ is the average realized so far. In particular, if $\hat{X}$ is negative, that is

$$\frac{T_1}{T}A(0, T_1) > X,$$

it means that the call option at maturity will be exercised for sure: the average so far is so high that the remaining averaging period cannot make the option become out-of-the-money at maturity (vice versa, the put option will not be exercised for sure). Therefore, the call option value will be

$$e^{-r(T-T_1)}\frac{T-T_1}{T}\left(\tilde{E}_{T_1}\left(A(T_1, T) - \hat{X}\right)\right),$$

whilst the put option will be worthless. The computation of the expectation of the average is discussed in Boxes 18.1 and 18.2, depending on the monitoring convention. The extension to Asian options on futures prices is considered in Box 18.3.

Albeit there exist very accurate procedures to compute the expectation in (18.5) under a geometric Brownian motion, we restrict attention here to those that combine accuracy and implementation simplicity. To do this we briefly illustrate:

1. Approximation of the average distribution by fitting integer moments (Ju, 2002; Levy, 1992; Milevsky and Posner, 1998; Turnbull and Wakeman, 1991).
2. Computation of lower bound for the price (Rogers and Shi, 1992; Thompson, 1998).
3. Monte Carlo simulation (see, e.g., the discussion in Fu *et al.*, 1998).

The first method derives a probability distribution sharing a number of moments with the distribution of the price average. The second approach aims to calculate tight lower bounds for the exact option price. The third prices an Asian option resorting to simulation.

Other procedures, which are very accurate but whose implementation is not straightforward, such as the eigenfunction method in Lewis (1998), the numerical solution of the pricing partial differential equation (PDE) (Rogers and Shi, 1992; Vecer, 2001), the upper bound provided by Thompson (1998) and Rogers and Shi (1992), numerical inversion of a single Laplace transform (Geman and Yor, 1993; Lewis, 2002; Shaw, 1998) or of a double transform (Cai and Kou, 2012; Fusai, 2004) are not illustrated here. A detailed comparison among these procedures can be found in Fusai and Roncoroni (2008), chapter 15.

18.2.1 Moment Matching

Moment matching is the most popular approach for pricing Asian options. The average price is assigned an arbitrary probability density function constrained to match a number of moments of $A(T)$. Unfortunately, this method does not provide any assessment of the approximation error. This procedure consists of two steps:

1. Derive a closed-form expression for the moments of $A(T)$

$$\mu_n = \widetilde{E}_0\left[A_T^n\right].$$

Expressions for their computation are provided in Boxes 18.1 and 18.2, depending on the monitoring convention we adopt.

2. Choose and fit an arbitrary density function to a number of selected moments. Specifically, we consider lognormal and Edgeworth series approximations.

BOX 18.1 MOMENTS OF *A*(*T*) IN THE CONTINUOUSLY MONITORED CASE

If we consider the continuously monitored case, we have that (see Geman and Yor, 1993)

$$\mu_n := \frac{s_0^n}{T^n}\frac{n!}{\lambda^{2n}}\left\{\sum_{j=0}^{n} d_j^{(\gamma/\lambda)} \exp\left[\left(\frac{\lambda^2 j^2}{2} + \lambda j \gamma\right)T\right]\right\}, \qquad (18.7)$$

where

$$d_j^{(\beta)} = 2^n \prod_{\substack{0\leq i\leq n \\ i\neq j}} [(\beta+j)^2 - (\beta+i)^2]^{-1},$$

$$\lambda = \sigma, \qquad \gamma = \frac{r - q - \sigma^2/2}{\sigma}. \qquad (18.8)$$

Care has to be taken in computing moments when $r = q$. In particular, notice that if $r = q$, then $\mu_1 = s_0$ and

$$\mu_2 = \frac{2e^{\sigma^2 T} - 2(1 + \sigma^2 T)}{\sigma^4 T^2}.$$

For higher moments, a practical approach is to use the above expressions (18.7)–(18.8) setting $r = q + 0.000001$.

```
%%%%%%%%%%%%%%%%%%%%%%%%%%%%%%%%%%%%%%%%%%%%%%%%%%
%%%%COMPUTING MOMENTS OF THE ARITH AVERAGE%%%%
%%%%%%%%%%%%%%%%%%%%%%%%%%%%%%%%%%%%%%%%%%%%%%%%%%

function dj=djbeta(n, beta, j)
term = 1;
for i = 0:n
  if abs(i - j)>0
      term = term * (1 / ((beta + j) ^ 2 - (beta + i) ^ 2));
  end
end

  dj = term * (2 ^ n);

function mn=moment_n(n, v, lambda, t)
term = 0;
```

```
fac = 1;
for j = 0:n %Step -1
  term = term + ...
          djbeta(n, v / lambda, j) * ...
    exp((lambda * lambda * j * j / 2 + lambda * j * v) * t);
  if (j > 0)
      fac = fac * j;
  end
end
  mn = fac * term / (lambda ^ (2 * n));
```

By way of illustration, let us suppose that $r = 0.05$, $q = 0$, $\sigma = 0.2$, $\Delta = 1/12$ (i.e. 1 month) and $T = 1$, so that $m = 0.0025$. We have

n	1	2	3	4
μ_n	1.0254	2.1034	3.2367	4.4281

BOX 18.2 MOMENTS OF $A(T)$ IN THE DISCRETELY MONITORED CASE

In the following, we exploit a recursive formulation to compute the moments of $A(T)$. Given (18.4), let us define the log-price increment over a time step of length Δ

$$Z_k^\Delta \equiv m\Delta + \sigma X_k^\Delta, \quad k = 1, \ldots, N,$$

where $m = r - q - \frac{\sigma^2}{2}$, $\Delta = T/N$ and X_k^Δ is the increment of the Brownian motion, so that $X_k^\Delta \sim \mathcal{N}(0, \Delta)$. We are interested in the moments of

$$\begin{aligned}\sum_{k=0}^{N} S_{\Delta k} &= s_0 + s_0 e^{Z_1} + s_0 e^{Z_1+Z_2} + \cdots + s_0 e^{Z_1+\cdots+Z_N} \\ &= s_0\left(1 + e^{Z_1^\Delta}\left(1 + e^{Z_2^\Delta}\left(\cdots\left(1 + e^{Z_N^\Delta}\right)\right)\right)\right).\end{aligned}$$

Starting from $L_T^\Delta \equiv e^{Z_1^\Delta}$ and introducing recursively the quantities

$$L_k^\Delta \equiv e^{Z_k^\Delta}\left(1 + L_{k+1}^\Delta\right), \quad k = N-1, \ldots, 1, \tag{18.9}$$

we have $A(T) \equiv S_0\left(1 + L_1^{\Delta}\right)/(N+1)$. Recursion (18.9) translates into a formula for the moments of the arithmetic average. Indeed, from the independence of Z_k^{Δ} and L_{k+1}^{Δ} as well as from the definition of Z_k^{Δ}, we obtain

$$\widetilde{E}\{(L_k^{\Delta})^n\} = \widetilde{E}\{(e^{Z_k^{\Delta}}(1 + L_{k+1}^{\Delta}))^n\} \quad (18.10)$$

$$= \widetilde{E}\{e^{nZ_k^{\Delta}}\}\widetilde{E}\{(1 + L_{k+1}^{\Delta})^n\} \quad (18.11)$$

$$= \widetilde{E}\{e^{nZ_k^{\Delta}}\}\widetilde{E}\left\{\sum_{q=0}^{n} \frac{n}{q} (L_{k+1}^{\Delta})^q\right\} \quad (18.12)$$

$$= \phi_{\Delta}(n) \sum_{q=0}^{n} \frac{n}{q} E\{(L_{k+1}^{\Delta})^q\}, \quad (18.13)$$

where

$$\phi_{\Delta}(n) = \widetilde{E}\left(e^{nZ_k^{\Delta}}\right) = e^{(r-q-\frac{\sigma^2}{2})\Delta n + \frac{1}{2}\sigma^2 \Delta n^2}.$$

The recursion starts with

$$\widetilde{E}\{(L_N^{\Delta})^n\} \equiv \widetilde{E}\{e^{nZ_1^{\Delta}}\} = \phi_{\Delta}(n). \quad (18.14)$$

The moments of the arithmetic average can be computed as follows:

$$\widetilde{E}\left((A(T))^n\right) = \widetilde{E}\left(\frac{S_0^n\left(1 + L_1^{\Delta}\right)^n}{(N+1)^n}\right) = \frac{S_0^n}{(N+1)^n}\sum_{j=0}^{n}\binom{n}{j}\widetilde{E}\left\{(L_1^{\Delta})^j\right\}. \quad (18.15)$$

By way of illustration, let us suppose that $r = 0.05$, $q = 0$, $\sigma = 0.2$, $\Delta = 1/12$ (i.e. 1 month) and $T = 1$, so that $m = 0.0025$. In addition, we have

$$\phi(1) = 1.0042,\ \phi(2) = 1.0117,\ \phi(3) = 1.0228, \quad \phi(4) = 1.0373.$$

We can create the following table, which in each row provides the first four moments of $L_k^{\Delta}, k = 12, \ldots, 1$ at each time step.

Month	$n=0$	$n=1$	$n=2$	$n=3$	$n=4$
0	1	1	1	1	1
1	1	1.004175	1.011735	1.022755	1.037347
2	1	2.012544	4.067261	8.25413	16.82108
3	1	3.025122	9.199047	28.11916	86.40204
4	1	4.041928	16.43998	67.28876	277.1516
5	1	5.062980	25.82335	132.6866	686.8423
6	1	6.088295	37.38291	231.4961	1445.835
7	1	7.117891	51.15282	371.1677	2719.374
8	1	8.151787	67.16767	559.4264	4710.006
9	1	9.189999	85.46251	804.279	7660.109
10	1	10.23255	106.0728	1114.022	11854.55
11	1	11.27945	129.0346	1497.25	17623.5
12	1	12.33072	154.3842	1962.864	25345.33

For example, in the last row we can read the first four moments of L_1. They are computed from the moments in the previous row via

$$\begin{aligned}
\widetilde{E}\{(L_1)^1\} &= 1 \times 1 + 1 \times 11.2794 = 12.3307,\\
\widetilde{E}\{(L_1)^2\} &= 1 \times 1 + 2 \times 11.2794 + 1 \times 129.0346 = 154.3842,\\
\widetilde{E}\{(L_1)^3\} &= 1 \times 1 + 3 \times 11.2794 + 3 \times 129.0346 + 1 \times 1497.2503 = 1962.8637,\\
\widetilde{E}\{(L_1)^4\} &= 1 \times 1 + 4 \times 11.2794 + 6 \times 129.0346 + 4 \times 1497.2503 + 1\\
&\quad \times 17623.5018 = 25345.3255.
\end{aligned}$$

The first four moments of $A(1)$ can then be computed as follows (let us assume that $s_0 = 1$):

$$\begin{aligned}
\widetilde{E}\{(A(1))^1\} &= \frac{1 + 12.3307}{13} = \frac{13.3307}{13},\\
\widetilde{E}\{(A(1))^2\} &= \frac{11 \times 1 + 2 \times 12.3307 + 1 \times 154.3842}{13^2} = \frac{180.0456}{13^2},\\
\widetilde{E}\{(A(1))^3\} &= \frac{11 \times 1 + 3 \times 12.3307 + 3 \times 154.3842 + 1 \times 1962.8637}{13^3} = \frac{2464.0083}{13^3},\\
\widetilde{E}\{(A(1))^4\} &= \frac{11 \times 1 + 4 \times 12.3307 + 6 \times 154.3842 + 4 \times 1962.8637 + 1 \times 25345.3255}{13^4}\\
&= \frac{34173.4080}{13^4}.
\end{aligned}$$

18.2.1.1 Lognormal Approximation (Turnbull–Wakeman–Levy formula) In this approximation, see Levy (1992) and Turnbull and Wakeman (1991), we assume that the average $A(T)$ is lognormally distributed with mean m and variance v^2. The parameters m and v^2 are chosen to match exactly the mean and variance of the arithmetic average, given in

Boxes 18.1 and 18.2. Owing to its simplicity, this approximation has gained large popularity. The approximated Asian call option price turns out to be given by the modified Black–Scholes formula

$$c_{\log} = s_0 e^{m+v^2/2-rT}\mathcal{N}(d_1) - e^{-rT}\mathcal{N}(d_2), \tag{18.16}$$

where

$$\begin{aligned} m &= 2\log\mu_1 - \frac{1}{2}\log\mu_2, & v^2 &= \log\mu_2 - 2\log\mu_1, \\ d_1 &= \frac{\ln(s_0/K) + m + v^2}{v}, & d_2 &= d_1 - v. \end{aligned} \tag{18.17}$$

```
%%%%%%%%%%%%%%%%%%%%%%%%%%%%%%%%%%%%%%%%%%%%%%%%%%%%%%%
%%%%PRICING ASIAN OPTIONS VIA LOGNORMAL DISTRIBUTION%%%%
%%%%%%%%%%%%%%%%%%%%%%%%%%%%%%%%%%%%%%%%%%%%%%%%%%%%%%%
function res= AsianCalllog(Spot, strike, rf, sigma, t)

%Compute the first two moments of the Average
  m1 = moment_n(1, (rf - sigma * sigma / 2) / sigma, sigma, t) / t;
  m2 = moment_n(2, (rf - sigma * sigma / 2) / sigma, sigma, t) / t ^ 2;

%Fit the parameters of the lognormal density
  m = 2 * log(m1) - log(m2) / 2;
  v = sqrt(log(m2) - 2 * log(m1));

%Compute the Levy approximation
  d1 = (log(Spot / strike) + m + v * v) / v;
  d2 = d1 - v;
  esp = m + v * v / 2 - rf * t;
  nd1 = normcdf((log(Spot / strike) + m + v * v) / v,0,1);
  nd2 = normcdf((log(Spot / strike) + m + v * v) / v - v,0,1);

%The result
  res = Spot * exp(esp) * nd1 - exp(-rf * t) * strike * nd2;
```

18.2.1.2 Edgeworth Series Approximation The lognormal approximation only captures the mean and variance of the average. In order to fit the third and fourth moment as well, that is, skewness and kurtosis of the average, Turnbull and Wakeman (1991) proposed to adopt a fourth-order Edgeworth series expansion of the true (but unknown) distribution of $A(T)$ around the lognormal. This approximation works as follows.

Let k_n be the difference in the nth cumulant[2] between the exact distribution f and the approximate lognormal distribution l, namely $k_n = \chi_n(f) - \chi_n(l)$. We have:

$$\begin{aligned}
\chi_1(f) &= \mu_1, \\
\chi_2(f) &= \mu_2 - \mu_1^2, \\
\chi_3(f) &= \mu_3 - 3\mu_2\mu_1 + 2\mu_1^3, \\
\chi_4(f) &= \mu_4 - 4\mu_3\mu_1 - 3\mu_2^2 + 12\mu_2\mu_1^2 - 6\mu_1^4.
\end{aligned}$$

Parameters m and v^2 are set according to expression (18.17), so that $k_1 = k_2 = 0$, while the cumulants of the approximating lognormal distribution can be computed as

$$\chi_n(l) = \exp\left(nm + \frac{1}{2}n^2v^2\right), \qquad n = 1, 2, 3, 4.$$

The approximate Asian option price is given by

$$c_{\text{edg}} = c_{\log} + e^{-rT}\frac{s_0}{T}\left[-\frac{k_3}{6}\frac{\partial f_{\log}(y; m, v^2)}{\partial y} + \frac{k_4}{24}\frac{\partial^2 f_{\log}(y; m, v^2)}{\partial y^2}\right]_{y=TK/s_0}, \tag{18.18}$$

where $c_{\log}$ is defined in formula (18.16) and $f_{\log}(y; m, v^2)$ is the lognormal density with parameters m and v^2:

$$f_{\log}\left(y; m, v^2\right) = \frac{1}{\sqrt{2\pi v^2}y}\exp\left(-\frac{(\ln y - m)^2}{2v^2}\right), \quad y > 0.$$

The main problem of the Edgeworth series is that increasing the number of matched moments does not guarantee an improvement in the resulting approximation. Since the distribution of $A(T)$ is not univocally determined by its moments, the approximation (18.18) may even lead to a negative-valued density.[3]

To overcome this problem, Ju (2002) considers the Edgeworth series for approximating the distribution of $\ln A(T)$ with a normal distribution, and he obtains the following approximation:

$$c_{\text{Ju}} = c_{\log} + e^{-rT}K\left[z_1 n(y) + z_2\frac{\partial n(y)}{\partial y} + z_3\frac{\partial^2 n(y)}{\partial y^2}\right]_{y=\ln(K/s_0)}, \tag{18.19}$$

[2]Cumulants of a random variable are defined as coefficients in the Taylor expansion of the logarithm of the moment-generating function about the origin, and are related to moments.

[3]In the context of Asian options, a discussion of the conditions under which the Edgeworth expansion is positive and unimodal can be found in Ju (2002).

where $c_{\log}$ is given in (18.16), $n(y) = n(y; m, v^2)$ is the Gaussian density with mean m and variance v^2 given in (18.17):

$$n(y; m, v^2) = \frac{1}{\sqrt{2\pi v^2}} \exp\left(-\frac{(y-m)^2}{2v^2}\right),$$

and derivatives are computed as

$$\frac{\partial n(y; m, v^2)}{\partial y} = -\frac{(y-m)}{v^2} n(y; m, v^2),$$
$$\frac{\partial^2 n(y; m, v^2)}{\partial y^2} = \frac{(m^2 - v^2 - 2my + y^2)}{v^4} n\left(y; m, v^2\right).$$

The remaining coefficients are as follows:

$$z_1 = -\sigma^4 T^2 \left(\frac{1}{45} + \frac{x}{180} - \frac{11x^2}{15120} - \frac{x^3}{2520} + \frac{x^4}{113400}\right)$$
$$- \sigma^6 T^3 \left(\frac{1}{11340} - \frac{13x}{30240} - \frac{17x^2}{226800} + \frac{23x^3}{453600} + \frac{59x^4}{5987520}\right),$$
$$z_2 = -\sigma^4 T^2 \left(\frac{1}{90} + \frac{x}{360} - \frac{11x^2}{30240} - \frac{x^3}{5040} + \frac{x^4}{226800}\right)$$
$$+ \sigma^6 T^3 \left(\frac{31}{22680} + \frac{11x}{60480} - \frac{37x^2}{151200} - \frac{19x^3}{302400} + \frac{953x^4}{59875200}\right),$$
$$z_3 = \sigma^6 T^3 \left(\frac{2}{2835} - \frac{x}{60480} - \frac{2x^2}{14175} - \frac{17x^3}{907200} + \frac{13x^4}{124700}\right),$$
$$x = rT.$$

Other approximations based on the moments are given for example in Milevsky and Posner (1998), but they do not appear to be very accurate and therefore we do not consider them.

```
%%%%%%%%%%%%%%%%%%%%%%%%%%%%%%%%%%%%%%%%%%%%%%%%%%%%%%%%%
%%%%PRICING ASIAN OPTIONS USING THE JU APPROXIMATION%%%%
%%%%%%%%%%%%%%%%%%%%%%%%%%%%%%%%%%%%%%%%%%%%%%%%%%%%%%%%%
function res=AsianCallJu(Spot, strike, rf, sigma, t)
%parameters
rt = rf * t;
sgt = sigma * sqrt(t);
k = t* strike/ Spot;
y = log(strike / Spot);
%Compute the first two moments of the average
m1 = moment_n(1, (rt - sgt * sgt / 2) / sgt, sgt, 1);
m2 = moment_n(2, (rt - sgt * sgt / 2) / sgt, sgt, 1);
```

```
%compute m and v^2 (here just v)
meanlog = 2 * log(m1) - log(m2) / 2;
v = log(m2) - 2 * log(m1);
%additional terms
z1 = -(t ^ 2) * (sigma ^ 4) * (1 / 45 + rt / 180 - ...
   11 * rt * rt / 15120 - (rt ^ 3) / 2520 + (rt ^ 4) / 113400) - ...
    (t ^ 3) * (sigma ^ 6) * (1 / 11340 - 13 * rt / 30240 - ...
   17 * rt * rt / 226800 + 23 * (rt ^ 3) / 453600 + ...
   59 * (rt ^ 4) / 5987520);
z2 = -t * t * (sigma^ 4) * (1 / 90 + rt / 360 - ...
   11 * rt * rt / 30240 - (rt ^ 3) / 5040 + (rt ^ 4) / 226800) + ...
   (t ^ 3) * (sigma ^ 6) * (31 / 22680 + 11 * rt / 60480 - ...
   37 * rt * rt / 151200 - 19 * (rt ^ 3) / 302400 + ...
   953 * (rt ^ 4) / 59875200);

z3 = (t ^ 3) * (sigma ^ 6) * (2 / 2835 - rt / 60480 - ...
   2 * rt * rt / 14175 - 17 * (rt ^ 3) / 907200 + ...
   13 * (rt ^ 4) / 124700);

n = exp(-(y - meanlog) * (y - meanlog) / (2 * v)) / sqrt(2 * pi * v);
dn = -n * (y - meanlog) / v;
d2n = n * (meanlog ^ 2 - v - 2 * v * y + y ^ 2) / v ^ 2;
correction = z1 * n + z2 * dn + z3 * d2n;

%compute the price according to the lognormal approximation
calllog = AsianCalllog(Spot, strike, rf, sigma, t);

%Ju approximation
res= calllog + exp(-rt) * strike * correction;
```

BOX 18.3 ASIAN OPTIONS ON FUTURES PRICES

As illustrated in the introduction, in organized commodity and energy markets traded average options are based on futures or forward prices rather than on spot. This is equivalent to assuming that the cost-of-carry on the underlying asset is zero (i.e., the dynamics of the lognormal futures price is now $dF = \sigma F dW(t)$). If we use a moment-based formula for pricing the option, we observe that, the futures price being a martingale, the expected value of the average is equal to the current futures price and therefore we have to compute only the variance of the average. For example, Haug (2006) shows that the Turnbull and Wakeman formula becomes

$$e^{-rT}(FN(d_1) - KN(d_2)), \tag{18.20}$$

where

$$d_1 = \frac{\ln(F/X) + T\sigma_A^2/2}{\sqrt{T\sigma_A^2}}, \quad d_2 = d_1 - \sqrt{T\sigma_A^2},$$

and

$$T\sigma_A^2 = \ln\left(\frac{2e^{\sigma^2 T} - 2(1+\sigma^2 T)}{\sigma^4 T^2}\right).$$

18.2.2 Lower Price Bound

Rogers and Shi (1992), Thompson (1998) and Nielsen and Sandman (2003) obtain lower and upper bounds for the Asian option price. For a lower bound, the idea is simple and powerful. Consider the random variable

$$X = \frac{s_0}{T}\int_0^T e^{(r-\sigma^2/2)s+\sigma W_s}\,\mathrm{d}s - K.$$

The Asian option price is given by $\widetilde{E}_0(X^+)$. Using the iterated rule for conditional expectations, the fact that $X^+ \geq X$ and the positiveness of X^+, we have

$$\widetilde{E}_0(X^+) = \widetilde{E}_0[\widetilde{E}_0(X^+|Z)] \geq \widetilde{E}_0[\widetilde{E}_0(X|Z)^+] := c_{\text{low}},$$

for any conditioning variable Z. Rogers and Shi (1992) propose using $Z = \int_0^T W_s\,\mathrm{d}s$, and provide an analytical expression for the lower bound c_{low}.[4] Thompson (1998) obtained the same lower bound via a simpler expression

$$c \geq c_{\text{low}} = e^{-r}\left(\int_0^1 s_0 e^{\alpha t+\sigma^2 t/2}\mathcal{N}\left(\frac{-\gamma^* + \sigma t(1-t/2)}{1/\sqrt{3}}\right)\mathrm{d}t - K\mathcal{N}\left(\frac{-\gamma^*}{1/\sqrt{3}}\right)\right), \quad (18.21)$$

where $\alpha = r - \sigma^2/2$ and the option maturity T has been standardized to 1.[5] Here $\mathcal{N}(x)$ denotes the standard normal cumulative function and γ^* is the unique solution to the equation

$$\int_0^1 s_0 \exp\left(3\gamma^*\sigma t(1-t/2) + \alpha t + \frac{1}{2}\sigma^2(t - 3t^2(1-t/2)^2)\right)\mathrm{d}t = K. \quad (18.22)$$

[4]They also discuss how to measure the accuracy of the lower bound.

[5]For a general T, r and σ must be replaced by rT and $\sigma\sqrt{T}$, respectively.

Computation of γ^* can be done using standard root finder routines (e.g., the bisection method). A Matlab script providing the implementation of the above formula is given here.

```
%%%%%%%%%%%%%%%%%%%%%%%%%%%%%%%%%%%%%%%
%%%%%%%ASIAN PRICE LOWER BOUND%%%%%%%
%%%%%%%%%%%%%%%%%%%%%%%%%%%%%%%%%%%%%%%

function [asian_premium_lower]=...
get_AsianCall_Lower(spot, strike, t, sigma, rf)

%Scale parameters
rft=rf*t; sigmat=sigma*sqrt(t);
A = (rf - sigma * sigma / 2);

%find optimal value of gamma
gstar = get_gamma(spot,strike, rf, sigma);

arg2 = (-gstar) / (1 / (3 ^ 0.5));

%discount factor
df=exp(-rft);

%lower bound
asian_premium_lower = ...
    (quadgk(@(s) spot * exp(A * s + sigmat * ...
    sigmat * s / 2) .* ...
    normcdf((-gstar + sigmat * s .* (1 - s / 2)) ...
    / (1 / (3 ^ 0.5)),0,1),0,1) ...
    -strike*normcdf(arg2))*df;

%%Auxiliary function: Find optimal value of gamma
function res =get_gamma(spot, strike, rf , sigma)

sg2half=0.5*sigma*sigma;
A = (rf - sg2half);

res =fsolve(@(trialGamma) ...
 spot*quadgk(@(t) ...
 (exp(A * t + sg2half*t .*(1-3*t.*(1-t/2).*(1-t/2)) ...
 + 3*sigma*trialGamma*t.*(1-t/2))),0,1)-strike,0.0);
```

18.2.3 Monte Carlo Simulation

Monte Carlo simulation is a popular pricing technique due to its flexibility in dealing with complex payoffs and sophisticated dynamics. However, it is much slower with respect to alternative methods in achieving an acceptable precision. Indeed the accuracy can be ameliorated by increasing the number of simulations, but this also increases the computational cost. For this reason, it is often implemented by adopting reduction of variance techniques. This issue is indeed highly related to the pricing of Asian options and all Monte Carlo simulations proposed in the literature have been applying one of the variance reduction techniques. The basic crude Monte Carlo scheme is as follows:

1. Fix the number N of monitoring dates and the time step $\Delta = T/N$, so that the monitoring dates are $t_i = i \times \Delta$.
2. Starting from $S(0) = s_0$, simulate the spot prices at times $i\Delta$ along the jth path discretizing the solution (18.4):

$$S^{(j)}(i\Delta) = S^{(j)}((i-1)\Delta) \times e^{\left(r-\frac{\sigma^2}{2}\right)\Delta+\sigma\left(W^{(j)}(i\Delta)-W^{(j)}((i-1)\Delta)\right)}, i = 1, \ldots, N, \tag{18.23}$$

with $j = 1, \ldots, m$ where m is the number of simulations. The increment $W^{(j)}(i\Delta) - W^{(j)}((i-1)\Delta)$ is simulated according a $\mathcal{N}(0, \Delta)$. For example, we can set

$$W^{(j)}(i\Delta) - W^{(j)}((i-1)\Delta) = \sqrt{\Delta} \times \Phi^{-1}\left(u_i^{(j)}\right), \tag{18.24}$$

where u is a uniform(0,1) random variable and Φ^{-1} is the inverse cumulative distribution function of the standard normal distribution.
3. Update the average according to

$$A^{(j)}(i\Delta) = \frac{i-1}{i} \times A^{(j)}((i-1)\Delta) + \frac{S^{(j)}(i\Delta)}{i}, A^{(j)}(0) = s_0. \tag{18.25}$$

4. Compute the discounted Asian option payoff in the jth path:

$$\pi^{(j)} = e^{-r \times N \times \Delta}(A^{(j)}(n\Delta) - K)^+. \tag{18.26}$$

5. The option price is estimated by repeating steps 2 to 4 m times and discounting the payoff along each path and then averaging across simulations:

$$\hat{c} = \frac{1}{m}\sum_{j=1}^{m} \pi^{(j)}. \tag{18.27}$$

6. We can evaluate the accuracy of the estimate by computing the standard error:

$$se = \sqrt{\frac{\hat{\sigma}^2}{m}}, \tag{18.28}$$

where

$$\hat{\sigma}^2 = \frac{1}{m}\sum_{j=1}^{m}(\pi^{(j)} - \hat{c})^2.$$

7. The confidence interval at a given confidence level α, say $\alpha = 95\%$, is given by

$$\hat{c} \pm z_{1-\frac{\alpha}{2}} \times se,$$

where z_α is the quantile at the level α of the standard normal distribution.

A spreadsheet implementation of the above scheme is given in Figure 18.3. Cells B4:F13 refer to simulated standard normal random variables.[6] Cells G3:K13 refer to the simulation of $m = 5$ stock price paths over the next 10 days, according to equations (18.23) and (18.24). Cells L3:P13 refer to the simulation of the price average along time, see equation (18.25). In cells L18:P18 we compute the Asian option payoff for each simulated path, see equation (18.26). Finally, in cells L20 and L21 we average the payoffs across simulations, see equation (18.27), and then we discount it. Finally, we also compute the standard error of the estimate, see equation (18.28).

In Box 18.4, we illustrate how to modify the above Monte Carlo procedure in order to simulate the spot price consistently with the observed market forward curve.

```
%%%%%%%%%%%%%%%%%%%%%%%%%%%%%%%%%%%%
%%%%Asian Price by MC Simulation%%%%
%%%%%%%%%%%%%%%%%%%%%%%%%%%%%%%%%%%%

function [asian_mc, asian_mc_a, se, se_a]=...
get_AsianCall_MC(spot, strike, t, sigma, rate_cc, div_cc, ...
                 nsimul, ndates)

rf=rate_cc;
df=exp(-rf*t);

%Assigning Time step
dt=t/ndates;
timestep=[0:dt:t]';

%Simulate increments dW
dW=randn(ndates,nsimul)*dt^0.5;

%Simulate increments dlog-Price
dlogS=(rf-div_cc-sigma*sigma/2)*dt+sigma*dW;

%Simulate log-prices
logS=log(spot)+[zeros(1,nsimul);
        cumsum(dlogS)];

%Get spot price paths
prices=exp(logS);
```

[6]The generation of the Gaussian random variable can be done in Excel using the cell formula =NORM.S.INV(RAND()).

	A	B	C	D	E	F	G	H	I	J	K	L	M	N	O	P
1		Gaussian Random Number Simulations					Stock Price Simulations					Average Price Simulation				
2	Days	1	2	3	4	5	1	2	3	4	5	1	2	3	4	5
3	0	0	0	0	0	0	100	100	100	100	100	100	100	100	100	100
4	1	1.8221	-0.5164	0.6529	-0.2364	-1.7514	102.3214	99.3391	100.8193	99.6915	97.7992	101.1607	99.6695	100.4097	99.8458	98.8996
5	2	0.2093	0.0201	0.1253	2.5657	1.0475	102.5824	99.3544	100.9692	102.9697	99.0938	101.6346	99.5645	100.5962	100.8871	98.9644
6	3	0.8114	0.7554	0.6232	-1.6116	-0.1169	103.6304	100.2984	101.7582	100.8820	98.9376	102.1336	99.7480	100.8867	100.8858	98.9577
7	4	0.1104	1.0138	-1.1960	-0.3965	-0.9186	103.7649	101.5827	100.2205	100.3674	97.7849	102.4598	100.1149	100.7535	100.7821	98.7231
8	5	-0.2008	-1.5653	-0.6048	0.8771	-0.0415	103.4913	99.5813	99.4469	101.4770	97.7238	102.6317	100.0260	100.5357	100.8979	98.5566
9	6	-0.0189	1.3680	1.1475	-1.1853	1.5090	103.4563	101.3094	100.8909	99.9569	99.5972	102.7495	100.2093	100.5864	100.7635	98.7052
10	7	-1.5770	1.2193	-0.9852	-0.9897	-1.3226	101.4030	102.8738	99.6316	98.7036	97.9351	102.5812	100.5424	100.4671	100.5060	98.6089
11	8	1.5317	0.1025	0.6385	2.2352	-0.2277	103.3766	102.9971	100.4296	101.5239	97.6437	102.6696	100.8151	100.4629	100.6191	98.5017
12	9	0.0422	-0.2706	0.6627	-2.1106	0.9301	103.4216	102.6349	101.2650	98.8396	98.7895	102.7448	100.9971	100.5431	100.4412	98.5305
13	10	-0.2276	-1.0012	0.5876	-0.4821	0.7257	103.1140	101.3333	102.0103	98.2290	99.6905	102.7784	101.0277	100.6765	100.2401	98.6359
14																
15			=NORM.S.INV(RAND())					=H12*EXP((0.02-0.3*0.3/2)*(1/252)+0.2*C13* 1/ 50)^0.5)							=AVERAGE(J3:J13)	
16																
17											Simulation	1	2	3	4	5
18											Payoff	2.7784	1.0277	0.6765	0.2401	0.0000
19																
20											Price Estimate	0.94376	=AVERAGE(L17:P17)*EXP(-0.02*10/250)			
21											Std. Error	0.49143	=STDEV(L18:P18)/5^0.5			

FIGURE 18.3 Spreadsheet implementation of the Monte Carlo simulation for pricing an Asian option. Parameters: $r = 2\%$, $\sigma = 20\%$, $\Delta = 1/250$, 10 averaging points, 5 simulations, $s_0 = 100$, $K = 100$, $T - t = 10/250$

```
%Get time average
avg=sum(prices,1)./(ndates+1);

%Payoff
payoff =max(avg-strike,0)*df;

%Asian price
asian_mc=mean(payoff);

%Standard error of MC estimate
se=std(payoff)/sqrt(nsimul);
```

TABLE 18.5 Monte Carlo price estimates and standard errors for an arithmetic average option varying the number m of simulations. Parameters: $S(0) = 8.2$, $K = 8.5$, $r = 3\%$, $\sigma = 50\%$, $T = 0.5$, $N = 8$

m	10,000	20,000	40,000	80,000	160,000
MC	0.7776	0.7652	0.7553	0.7662	0.7661
s.e.	0.0117	0.0081	0.0057	0.0041	0.0029
ratio of s.e.		1.44	1.42	1.41	1.41

In Table 18.5 we report for different number m of simulations the MC estimate and the corresponding standard error. Notice that as we double the number of simulations the standard error reduces by a factor approximately equal to $\sqrt{2}$, as expected. Indeed, the standard error decreases as $1/\sqrt{m}$. So in order to reduce by a factor of 10 the standard error, we need to increase by a factor of 10^2 the number of simulations. This can be quite computationally intensive.

BOX 18.4 HOW TO INCLUDE FORWARD CURVES IN THE MONTE CARLO SIMULATION?

To simulate the spot price taking into account the information in the futures curve is particularly relevant in commodity markets where the futures term structure can show peculiar shapes, due to seasonality effects. An example is shown in Figure 18.4, where the evolution of the natural gas term structure in March 2007 is illustrated. For this reason, it would be important, if we decide to price Asian options via Monte Carlo, to take into account the futures term structure shape. This can be done according to the following procedure:

- Let $F(0, T)$ be the forward price quoted at time 0 for maturity T.
- It is well known that under the risk-neutral measure

$$\widetilde{E}_0 (S(T)) = F(0, T).$$

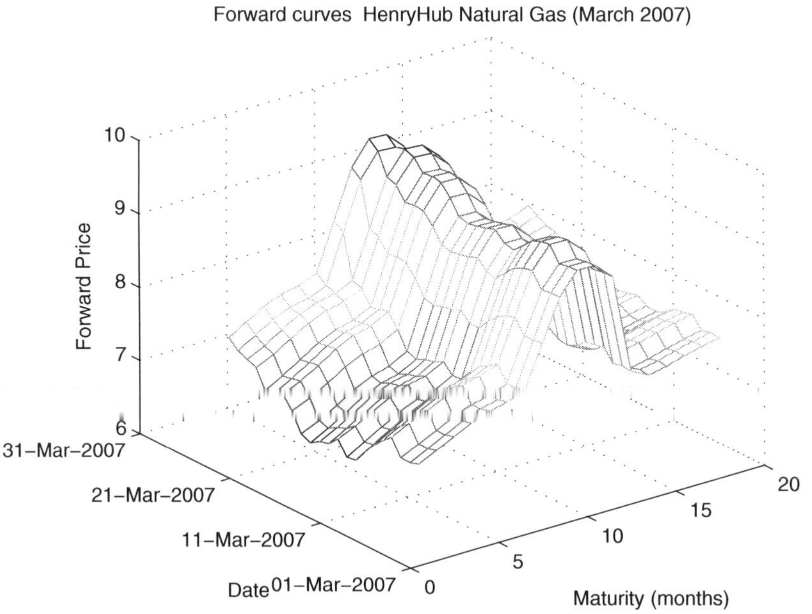

FIGURE 18.4 Natural gas forward curve evolution between 1 March and 31 March 2007

- If we assume a GBM process for the underlying with constant volatility, we have

$$S(T) = F(0,T) \times e^{-\frac{\sigma^2}{2}T+\sigma W(T)}.$$

- Given that we have forward quotations $F(0, T_i)$ for different maturities T_i, we can write

$$S(T_i) = F(0,T_i) \times e^{-\frac{\sigma^2}{2}T_i+\sigma W(T_i)},$$

$$S(T_{i+1}) = F(0,T_{i+1}) \times e^{-\frac{\sigma^2}{2}T_{i+1}+\sigma W(T_{i+1})},$$

and therefore

$$\frac{S(T_{i+1})}{S(T_i)} = \frac{F(0,T_{i+1}) \times e^{-\frac{\sigma^2}{2}T_{i+1}+\sigma W(T_{i+1})}}{F(0,T_i) \times e^{-\frac{\sigma^2}{2}T_i+\sigma W(T_i)}}.$$

In the presence of a forward curve $F(0, T)$, the simulation of the GBM process can be performed according to

$$S(T_{i+1}) = S(T_i) \times \frac{F(0,T_{i+1})}{F(0,T_i)} \times e^{-\frac{\sigma^2}{2}(T_{i+1}-T_i)+\sigma(W(T_{i+1})-W(T_i))},$$

starting from s_0 and using the fact that

$$W(T_{i+1}) - W(T_i) \sim \mathcal{N}(0, T_{i+1} - T_i).$$

The procedure:

1. Assign σ, and the forward curve.
2. Assign the monitoring dates and interpolate the forward curve at these dates; compute the ratios

$$f(i+1) = \frac{F(0, T_{i+1})}{F(0, T_i)}.$$

3. Simulate the increments

$$\epsilon(i+1) = -\frac{\sigma^2}{2}(T_{i+1} - T_i) + \sigma(W(T_{i+1}) - W(T_i)).$$

4. Starting from the initial date ($T_0 = 0$), $S\left(T_0\right) = F(0, 0)$, compute the simulated prices

$$S(T_{i+1}) = S(T_i) \times f(i+1) \times e^{\epsilon(i+1)}.$$

5. Update the computation of the average and at maturity compute the Asian option payoff.
6. Repeat the previous steps a large number of times and then average the discounted payoff.

18.2.3.1 Improving the Accuracy of Monte Carlo Simulation The accuracy of the above basic Monte Carlo simulation scheme can be improved by resorting to variance reduction techniques. The most common ones in the context of Asian option pricing are

- antithetic variate, and
- control variate.

`Antithetic variate` attempts to reduce the variance of the simulation error by introducing negative dependence between pairs of replications. In fact, this method works well if the covariance between the payoffs in the standard path and in the antithetic one is negative. Unfortunately, the preservation of negative correlation in the payoffs is not always guaranteed, so sometimes this procedure can be ineffective. `Control variate` exploits information about the errors in estimates of known quantities to reduce the error in an estimate of an unknown quantity. Both techniques are illustrated briefly in Boxes 18.5 and 18.6.

BOX 18.5 IMPROVING MONTE CARLO VIA VARIANCE REDUCTION: ANTITHETIC VARIATE

This procedure is based on the fact that if $u_i^{(j)} \sim U(0,1)$ (i.e., we do a random extraction from a standard uniform random variable), then

$$W^{(j)}(i) - W^{(j)}(i-1) = \sqrt{\Delta} \times \Phi^{-1}\left(u_i^{(j)}\right) \sim \mathcal{N}(0, \Delta).$$

It is also true that

$$-(W^{(j)}(i) - W^{(j)}(i-1)) = -\sqrt{\Delta} \times \Phi^{-1}\left(u_i^{(j)}\right) \sim \mathcal{N}(0, \Delta),$$

that is, dW and its opposite $-dW$ have the same Gaussian distribution (the mean is assumed to be zero). This observation can be exploited to better sample from the Gaussian distribution with respect to using two independent draws.

The idea of antithetic simulation consists of using both random numbers to get the so-called **antithetic path**

$$S^{(j)}(i\Delta) = S^{(j)}((i-1)\Delta) \times e^{\left(r-q-\frac{\sigma^2}{2}\right)\Delta + \sigma\left(W^{(j)}(i) - W^{(j)}(i-1)\right)}, i = 1, \ldots, N,$$
$$S_A^{(j)}(i\Delta) = S_A^{(j)}((i-1)\Delta) \times e^{\left(r-q-\frac{\sigma^2}{2}\right)\Delta + \sigma\left(W_A^{(j)}(i) - W_A^{(j)}(i-1)\right)}, i = 1, \ldots, N,$$

where

$$W_A^{(j)}(i) - W_A^{(j)}(i-1) = -(W^{(j)}(i) - W^{(j)}(i-1)).$$

The Asian option price is then computed using both paths

$$\frac{e^{-r \times N \times \Delta}}{m} \sum_{j=1}^{m} \frac{(A^{(j)}(n) - K)^+ + \left(A_A^{(j)}(n) - K\right)^+}{2},$$

where $A^{(j)}$ and $A_A^{(j)}$ are the time averages computed according to the standard path and to the antithetic one.

To grasp the benefit of this method, let us consider the following parameter set: $S(0) = 8.2$, $K = 8.5$, $r = 3\%$, $\sigma = 50\%$, $T = 0.5$, $N = 8$, with 100,000 and 200,000 simulations respectively. We have the results in the following table.

	100,000 MC runs			200,000 MC runs		
Method	**Price**	**s.e.**	**Seconds**	**Price**	**s.e.**	**Seconds**
Crude MC	0.76663	0.003671	0.7	0.76182	0.00257	3.6
Antithetic	0.76615	0.00194	1.3	0.762289	0.00136	6.5

We complete here the previous Matlab script including antithetic simulation.

```
%Antithetic Simulation
dlogS_a=(rf-q-sigma*sigma/2)*dt-dW;
logS_a=log(spot)+[zeros(1,nsimul);

cumsum(dlogS_a)];
prices_a=exp(logS_a);
avg_a=sum(prices_a,1)./(ndates+1);
payoff_a =max(avg_a-strike,0)*df;

asian_mc_a=(mean(payoff_a)+mean(payoff))/2;
se_a=std((payoff_a+payoff)/2)/sqrt(nsimul);
```

A simulated path and its antithetic path for the underlying and the average are illustrated in Figure 18.5.

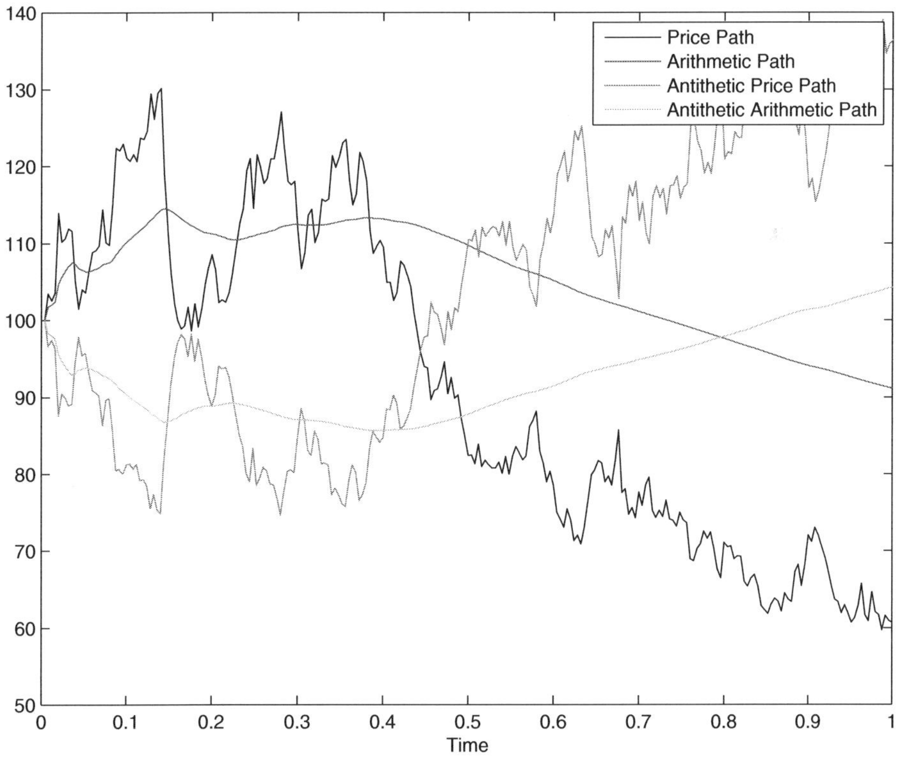

FIGURE 18.5 Simulated and antithetic path for the underlying and its time average

BOX 18.6 IMPROVING MONTE CARLO VIA VARIANCE REDUCTION: CONTROL VARIATES

Let us suppose that we need to estimate $\widetilde{E}(Y)$, where Y represents some payoff function. Using MC simulation we generate m i.i.d. replicas of Y, $Y^{(j)}$ say, and we estimate the above expected value by

$$\bar{Y} = \frac{1}{m}\sum_{j=1}^{m} Y^{(j)}.$$

The accuracy of this estimate can be measured by the variance of the estimator, that is σ^2/m (the square root of this quantity is called the standard error of the MC estimate). Let us now suppose that on each replication we can calculate another output, say $Z^{(j)}$ along $Y^{(j)}$. Moreover, let us suppose that $\widetilde{E}(Z)$ is known.

Then for any fixed number b we can calculate the additional quantity

$$Y^{(j)}(b) = Y^{(j)} - b(Z^{(j)} - \widetilde{E}(Z)),$$

which still provides an unbiased estimate of $\widetilde{E}(Y)$. Each $Y^{(j)}(b)$ has variance $\sigma_Y^2(b)$:

$$\begin{aligned}\sigma_Y^2(b) \equiv \widetilde{Var}(Y^{(j)}(b)) &= \widetilde{Var}(Y^{(j)} - b(Z^{(j)} - \widetilde{E}(Z))) \\ &= \sigma_Y^2 + b^2\sigma_Z^2 - 2b\sigma_{YZ}.\end{aligned}$$

The control variate estimator is given by

$$\bar{Y}(b) = \frac{1}{m}\sum_{j=1}^{m} Y^{(j)}(b),$$

and has variance

$$\frac{\sigma_Y^2(b)}{m}.$$

The optimal value of b that minimizes the variance of the control variate estimator is

$$b^* = \frac{\sigma_{YZ}}{\sigma_Z^2},$$

where σ_{YZ} is the covariance of the (simulated) values of Y and Z and σ_Z^2 is the variance of the control variate. The variance of $\bar{Y}(b^*)$ relative to the variance of $\bar{Y}$ is

$$\frac{\sigma_Y^2(b^*)}{\sigma_Y^2} = 1 - \rho_{ZY}^2.$$

We can make the following remarks:

- The higher the correlation ρ_{ZY} between Z and Y, the higher will be the reduction in the variance. Notice that very high negative correlations can be of some help.
- If the computational effort per replication is roughly the same with and without a control variate, then $1 - \rho^2_{ZY}$ measures the computational speed-up resulting from the use of a control; in other words, the number of simulations of $Y^{(j)}$ required to achieve the same variance as m replications of the control variate estimator is $N/(1 - \rho^2_{ZY})$.
- Given that the ratio $1/(1 - \rho^2_{ZY})$ approaches 1 very fast as $|\rho_{ZY}|$ decreases away from 1, in order to be effective the control variate must have a very high degree of correlation with Y.
- In practice, b^* must be estimated. We can run some preliminary simulation and estimate it using the sample counterparts.

The main issue in the implementation of the control variate technique is to find a convenient control variate. For arithmetic Asian options, it turns out that a good control variate is given by the geometric average G_T, defined as

$$G_T = e^{\frac{1}{T}\int_0^T \ln S(u)du} \tag{18.29}$$

in the continuous monitoring case, and

$$G_T = \left(\prod_{k=0}^{N} S_{\Delta k}\right)^{\frac{1}{N+1}}, \tag{18.30}$$

in the discrete one. The payoff of a geometric fixed strike call option is then $(G_T - K)^+$. For typical values of the volatility parameter, the correlation between geometric and arithmetic average is very high, as we can verify via Monte Carlo simulation, from the following table (here σ refers to the volatility of the underlying asset and ρ to the correlation between arithmetic and geometric average):

σ	$\rho\ (A(T), G(T))$
1%	1
10%	0.9998
50%	0.9960
100%	0.9820

The strong correlation between geometric and arithmetic average is shown via simulation in Table 18.6, for different volatility levels.

In order to make the CV procedure effective, we also need a closed-form formula for $\widetilde{E}(G_T - K)^+$. If the asset evolves according to a GBM process, geometric Asian options can be priced in closed form according to the formula

$$c_{geo} = s_0 e^{(m-r)T} \mathcal{N}(d_1) - K e^{-rT} \mathcal{N}(d_2), \tag{18.31}$$

with

$$d_1 = \frac{\ln\left(\frac{s_0}{K}\right) + \left(m + \frac{v^2}{2}\right)T}{v\sqrt{T}}, d_2 = d_1 - v\sqrt{T}.$$

Here, m depends on the monitoring frequency:

- discrete time monitoring

$$m = \frac{1}{2}\left(r - \frac{(N+2)}{6(N+1)}\sigma^2\right), \quad v = \sqrt{\frac{2N+1}{6(N+1)}}\sigma; \tag{18.32}$$

- continuous time monitoring

$$m = \frac{1}{2}\left(r - \frac{\sigma^2}{6}\right), \quad v = \frac{\sigma}{\sqrt{3}}. \tag{18.33}$$

Notice that in the above formula, the quantity v^2 refers to the variance of the log-geometric average and that the discrete monitoring version tends to the continuous one as we let the number of monitoring dates go to infinity, that is $N \to \infty$.

We therefore have the following algorithm:

1. Simulate the arithmetic and the geometric average.
2. Compute the Monte Carlo estimate of the two Asian options, MC^{Arit} and MC^{Geo} say.
3. Assuming $b = 1$, the control variate estimate is given by

$$CV^{Asia} = MC^{Arit} - MC^{Geo} + c_{geo}.$$

18.3 A COMPARISON

We discuss here the effectiveness of the alternative procedures described so far. A more detailed discussion and numerical examples can be found in Fusai and Roncoroni (2008). The experiment conducted here is under different sets of input parameters, as reported in Table 18.6. Numerical results are given in Table 18.7. In this table, we also add an upper bound, computed according to the procedure described in Fusai and Roncoroni (2008). The

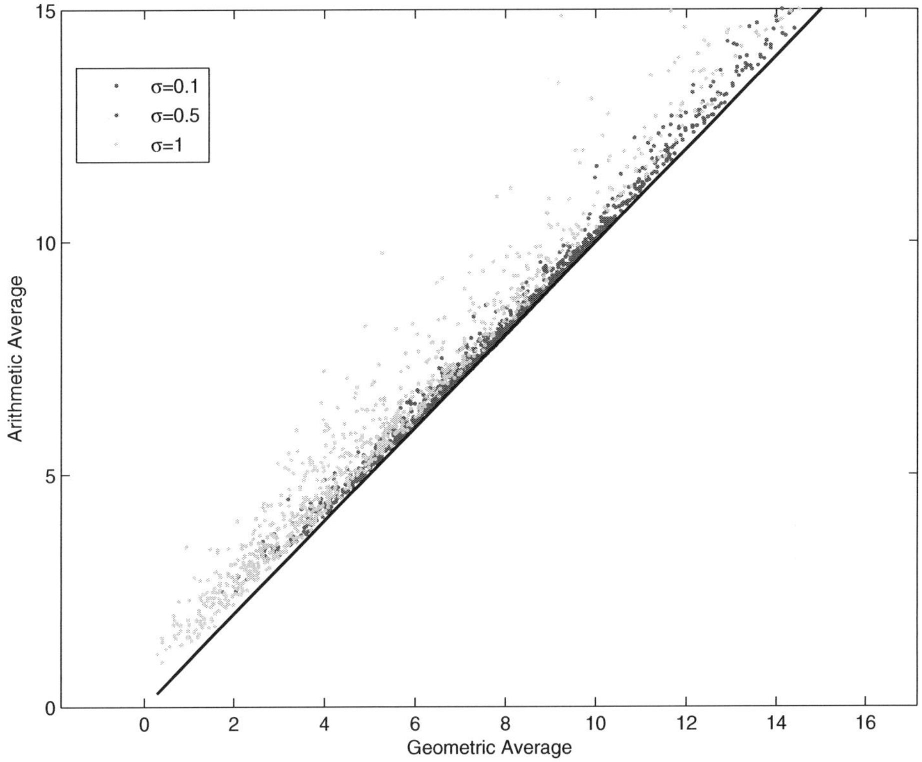

FIGURE 18.6 Simulated values of the geometric and arithmetic average for different volatility levels. The black line is the 45° line; notice that the arithmetic average is always higher than the geometric one, so this also provides a lower bound to the exact price

quantity $\sigma\sqrt{T}$ determines the accuracy of the method: in general, the lower its value, the more difficult it is to find an accurate numerical method (in some sense, this is curious because one is supposed to believe the contrary). However, the accuracy of the lower bound and of Monte Carlo simulation improves at smaller values of the parameter σ (or lower volatility or smaller time to maturity). Interestingly, the lower bound provides an exact approximation up to the third digit of Ju's method (and in Case 4 the two methods provide the same result up to the

TABLE 18.6 Parameter set

Example	s_0	K	r	σ	T	$\sigma\sqrt{T}$
1	1.9	2	0.05	0.5	1	0.5
2	2	2	0.05	0.5	1	0.5
3	2.1	2	0.05	0.5	1	0.5
4	2	2	0.02	0.1	1	0.1
5	2	2	0.18	0.3	1	0.3
6	2	2	0.0125	0.25	2	0.3535
7	2	2	0.05	0.5	2	0.7071

TABLE 18.7 Approximate prices for an Asian option under alternative numerical methods

Example	Lower	Levy	Edge	Ju	MC crude	SE crude	MC CV	SE CV	Upper
1	0.1931	0.1954	0.1948	0.1929	0.1951	0.0037	0.1938	0.0022	0.1938
2	0.2463	0.2498	0.2451	0.2462	0.2491	0.0043	0.2445	0.0024	0.2470
3	0.3061	0.3106	0.3014	0.3061	0.3097	0.0048	0.3095	0.0026	0.3069
4	0.0560	0.0561	0.0560	0.0560	0.0554	0.0008	0.0561	0.0004	0.0560
5	0.2184	0.2198	0.2175	0.2184	0.2138	0.0026	0.2182	0.0011	0.2185
6	0.1722	0.1735	0.1735	0.1722	0.1693	0.0028	0.1718	0.0016	0.1724
7	0.3498	0.3592	0.3639	0.3497	0.3445	0.0065	0.3446	0.0038	0.3526

MC = Monte Carlo, Lower = R–S–T lower bound, Levy = moment matching (lognormal approximation), edge = moment matching (Edgeworth series expansion), Ju = moment matching using normal series expansion, MC crude = plain Monte Carlo, SE crude = standard error plain Monte Carlo, MC CV = control variate Monte Carlo, SE CV = standard error control variate Monte Carlo, Upper = upper bound. We have run 1000000 MC simulations with 500 steps per year.

fourth digit). Edgeworth approximation sometimes returns a price estimate below the lower bound, showing that raising the number of fitted moments does not necessarily provide a better approximation. The Monte Carlo estimate, if the number of simulations is not large enough, can fall outside the lower–upper range.

18.4 THE FLEXIBLE SQUARE-ROOT MODEL

Commodity-linked derivatives should be priced consistently with all market price information available at the valuation time. In particular, traders need models which produce prices taking into account three sets of information:

1. The quoted forward/futures prices of the commodity, provided they are available.[7]
2. A time-varying volatility coefficient, a feature allowing our model to fit either the term structure of implied volatilities or a time-dependent, that is, seasonal, spot price historical volatility.
3. Spot price dynamics exhibiting mean reversion in their trend, a quality shown by some important classes of commodity prices, among which we cite agriculturals and energy-related products such as electricity and gas.

These features usually reflect properties related to the physical use of the commodity for industrial or consumption processes.

The specialized literature has examined these issues in great detail. Routledge *et al.* (2000) underline the impact of periodical components on the price dynamics of most commodities. Eydeland and Wolyniec (2003) show that the predictable component of electricity price dynamics is bound by weather and consumption-related features. Todorova (2004) notes

[7]For the purpose of our analysis, we assume interest rates are deterministic. This amounts to treating forward and futures prices as equivalent.

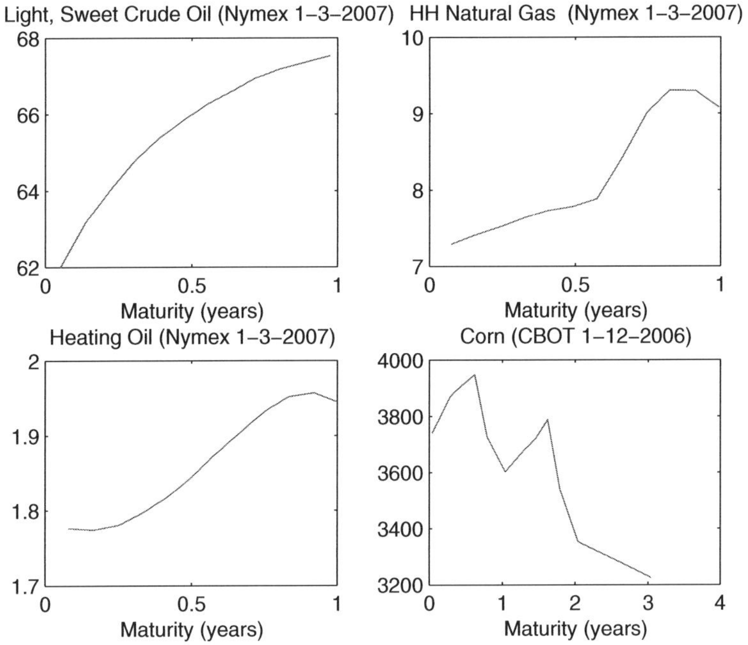

FIGURE 18.7 Futures curves for a sample of energy and agricultural commodities

that oil and gas markets show seasonal components affecting expected future spot prices, while Richter and Sorensen (2000) and Lien and Koekebakker (2004) find strong evidence of seasonality effects upon agricultural commodity prices. For most commodities, mean reversion is a stylized fact empirically accepted by several studies. In energy markets, the relevance of this property may vary across products and over time within the same commodity. For instance, Bessembinder *et al.* (1995) find clear evidence of mean reversion across 11 commodity markets, pointing out strong patterns for agriculturals and crude oil (see also Pindyck, 2001), and weak patterns for metals. Schwartz (1997) and Casassus and Collin-Dufresne (2005), among others, confirm the existence of a mean-reversion property in crude oil, copper, gold and silver. The case of electricity markets is rather peculiar. Geman and Roncoroni (2006) discover the existence of two competing mean-reversion effects in most US power markets: one is the traditional smooth reversion to average prices; the other stems from the spiky behaviour of electricity spot prices during periods of capacity congestion.

Figure 18.7 displays futures curves for light, sweet crude oil, natural gas and heating oil as quoted at NYMEX on 1 March 2007, and corn as reported by CBOT on 1 December 2006. The time-dependent component is plainly visible in the reported graphs. In particular, corn exhibits a clear seasonal pattern, which should be considered while pricing options on averages. Table 18.8 gives the implied volatility for different maturities for three different commodities and natural gas. Their periodical component is shown in Figure 18.8.

We now present a simple, yet effective method to make the spot dynamics include all price information implied by the quoted forward/futures curve, if any. This task can be achieved by letting the risk-neutral drift of spot price dynamics be time dependent. Moreover, the spot

TABLE 18.8 Term structures of implied volatilities for different commodities and maturities. Data from 4 October 2013

Month	1st	2nd	3rd	6th	12th	18th	24th	30th	60th
Crude	18.94	19.74	19.63	19.55	18.6	16.87	16.94	19.41	19.66
Heating oil	17.51	18.01	18.15	17.36	15.55	15.55	15.55	17.62	18.08
Natural gas	28.63	29.14	29.48	27.35	25.6	21.43	21.12	28.74	29.21

price volatility is allowed to reproduce any time pattern assigned by the user. We remark that the importance of assuming a time-varying drift goes beyond the ability to fit a quoted forward/future curve. For instance, Cartea and Williams (2008) point out that gas price dynamics exhibit a time-varying historical trend and market price of risk. Therefore, estimating these quantities may represent a viable alternative to directly fitting the risk neutral price drift to forward quotes. This option can be useful whenever forward/futures quotes are not available or their reliability is limited by, say, liquidity constraints.

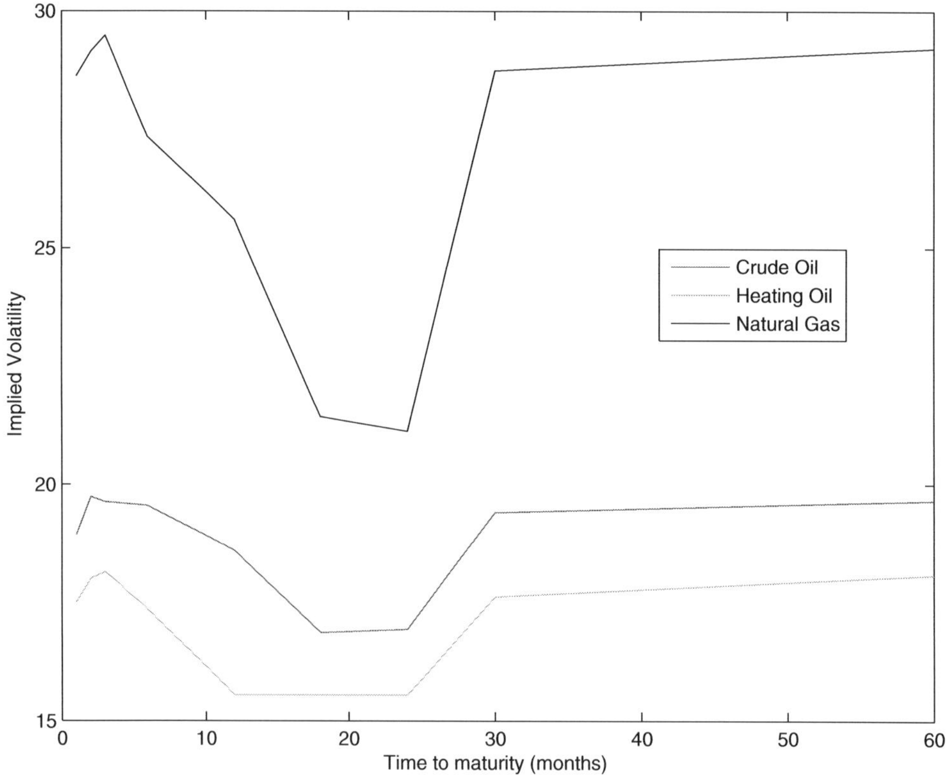

FIGURE 18.8 Periodical component affecting the volatility of three energy commodities. Data from 4 October 2013

18.4.1 General Setup

We adopt the same setup as before, so the time horizon $[0, T]$ is split into a number $N + 1$ of Δ-spaced monitoring dates $0, \Delta, \dots, N\Delta = T$ (the equally spaced assumption is made only for notational convenience, but it can easily be released). Our goal is to compute analytical formulae for fixed maturity options whose payoff structure depends on $\sum_{j=0}^{N} w_j S_{j\Delta}$ ($\sum_j w_j = 1$).

The option can be priced following a three-step algorithm devised by Fusai *et al.* (2008), which we now sketch here for the reader's convenience.

To this end, we start by assuming that the moment generating function (mgf) corresponding to the joint probability density of the pair consisting of the spot price $S_{N\Delta}$ and the cumulated spot price $\sum_{j=0}^{N} w_j S_{j\Delta}$ under the selected monitoring rule is known. This function is defined as

$$(\gamma, \mu) \to v_{0,x}(N, \Delta; \gamma, \mu) := \widetilde{E}_0\left(e^{-\gamma S_{n\Delta} - \mu \sum_{j=0}^{N} \alpha_j S_{j\Delta}}\right).$$

Table 18.9 illustrates instances of this function which correspond to traded options in the energy markets.

The fixed strike Asian-style option price can then be written as

$$C_{0,x}^{T}(k) = e^{-rT}\left(\frac{1}{2\pi\sqrt{-1}}\int_{a_l-\sqrt{-1}\infty}^{a_l+\sqrt{-1}\infty} e^{\mu k}\frac{v_{0,x}(\Delta, N; 0, \mu)}{\mu^2}d\mu + \sum_{j=0}^{N}\alpha_j F_{0,j\Delta} - K\right) \tag{18.34}$$

where x is the starting spot price ($x = s_0$) and a_l is a positive free parameter. If the analytical computation of the above integral in the complex plane is not possible, numerical evaluation is required. The use of the Fourier–Euler algorithm proposed by Abate and Whitt (1992) leads

TABLE 18.9 Moment generating functions relevant for a sample set of popular plain vanilla and Asian-style energy derivatives

Option	γ	μ	α_j	mgf $v_{0,x}$ $(N,\Delta;\gamma,\mu)$
Standard European	any	0	—	$\widetilde{E}_0[e^{-\gamma S_{N\Delta}}]$
Fixed strike std. Asian	0	any	$\frac{1}{N+1}$	$\widetilde{E}_0\left[e^{-\frac{\mu}{N+1}\sum_{j=0}^{N} S_{j\Delta}}\right]$
Fixed strike vol. weighted	0	any	$\frac{V_j}{\sum_i V_i}$	$\widetilde{E}_0\left[e^{-\frac{\mu}{\sum_i V_i}\sum_{j=0}^{N} V_j S_{j\Delta}}\right]$
Floating strike std. Asian	any	$-\gamma$	$\frac{1}{N+1}$ $\frac{1}{N+1}$	$\widetilde{E}_0\left[e^{-\gamma\left(S_{n\Delta}-\frac{1}{N+1}\sum_{j=0}^{N} S_{j\Delta}\right)}\right]$

to the following numerical inversion formula:

$$\mathcal{L}^{-1}\left[\frac{v_{0,s_0}^{N,\Delta}(0,\mu)}{\mu^2}\right](k) \approx \sum_{m=0}^{M}\binom{M}{m}2^{-m}d_{P+m}(k),$$

with

$$d_P(k) = \frac{e^{a_l/2}}{2k}Re\left(\frac{v_{0,s_0}^{N,\Delta}\left(0,\frac{a_l}{2k}\right)}{\mu^2}\right) + \frac{e^{a_l/2}}{k}\sum_{j=1}^{P}(-1)^j Re\left(\frac{v_{0,s_0}^{N,\Delta}\left(0,\frac{a_l+2j\pi i}{2k}\right)}{\mu^2}\right),$$

where $Re(x)$ is the real part of x, and P and M are suitable constants. We suggest adopting the following parametric setting: $a_l = 18.4$, $M = 25$, $N = 15$ (see Fusai and Roncoroni, 2008 for details).

The floating strike Asian-style option price can be priced by a similar formula, see Fusai *et al.* (2008). Option Greeks, such as Delta and Gamma, can be obtained by differentiating the Fourier transform of the option price with respect to the standing spot price x. Finally, we refer to the above-mentioned paper for the discussion of the continuous monitoring version.

The price dynamics that makes it possible to exploit the above procedure is the square-root process (see Chapter 12). We consider here the diffusion case, whilst the extension to allow for the inclusion of jumps is given in Marena *et al.* (2013).

In particular, the following two spot price dynamics make possible the explicit computation of the mgf.

- **Specification 1.** Square-root process with time-varying drift and volatility:

$$dS_t = \theta_t S_t dt + \sigma_t \sqrt{S_t} dW_t, \quad (18.35)$$
$$S_0 = x,$$

where

- the time-varying drift is chosen to fit the market observed term structure of forward prices $F(0,t)$ observed at time 0 for maturities t up to time $T = N\Delta$ by setting

$$\theta_T = \partial_T \ln \frac{F(0,T)}{x} = \partial_T \ln F(0,T); \quad (18.36)$$

- $(\sigma_t)_{t\geq 0}$ is a deterministic time-varying spot price volatility. σ_t^2 represents the time t variance of instantaneous price variations per unit of price value S_t and is expressed in $1/time$ units;
- $(W_t)_{t\geq 0}$ is a standard Brownian motion;
- x is the spot price, which can be estimated using $F(0,0)$.

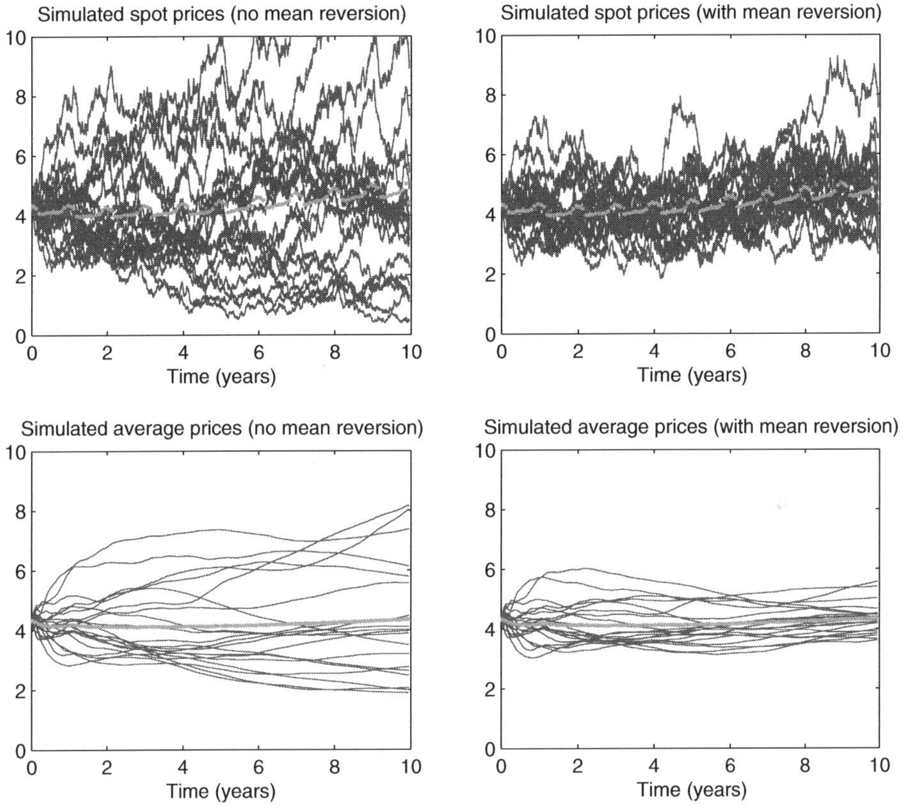

FIGURE 18.9 Simulated dynamics of the spot prices (top panels) and their time average (bottom panels). On the left, we simulate the dynamics according to model (18.35), whilst on the right dynamics (18.37) are simulated. The solid red curves refer to the market forward curve

- **Specification 2.** Square-root mean-reverting process with a time-varying trend:

$$dS_t = \beta(\eta_t - S_t)dt + \sigma_t\sqrt{S_t}dW_t, \tag{18.37}$$

where the additional parameters are

- β, the mean-reversion constant frequency expressed in $1/time$ units;
- $(\eta_t)_{t\geq 0}$, a deterministic time-varying price trend spot quotes revert to, that is selected such that the model fits the forward/futures price curve quoted in the market, by imposing

$$\eta(T) = F(0,T) + \frac{1}{\beta}\partial_T F(0,T). \tag{18.38}$$

Figure 18.9 shows simulated paths of the natural gas dynamics (18.35) and (18.37) and of their time-averaged prices. Both dynamics are fully consistent with the observed term structure of natural gas futures prices up to 5 years in the future (the futures curve refers to market quotes on 18 January 2014 at CME). However, the mean-reverting model does

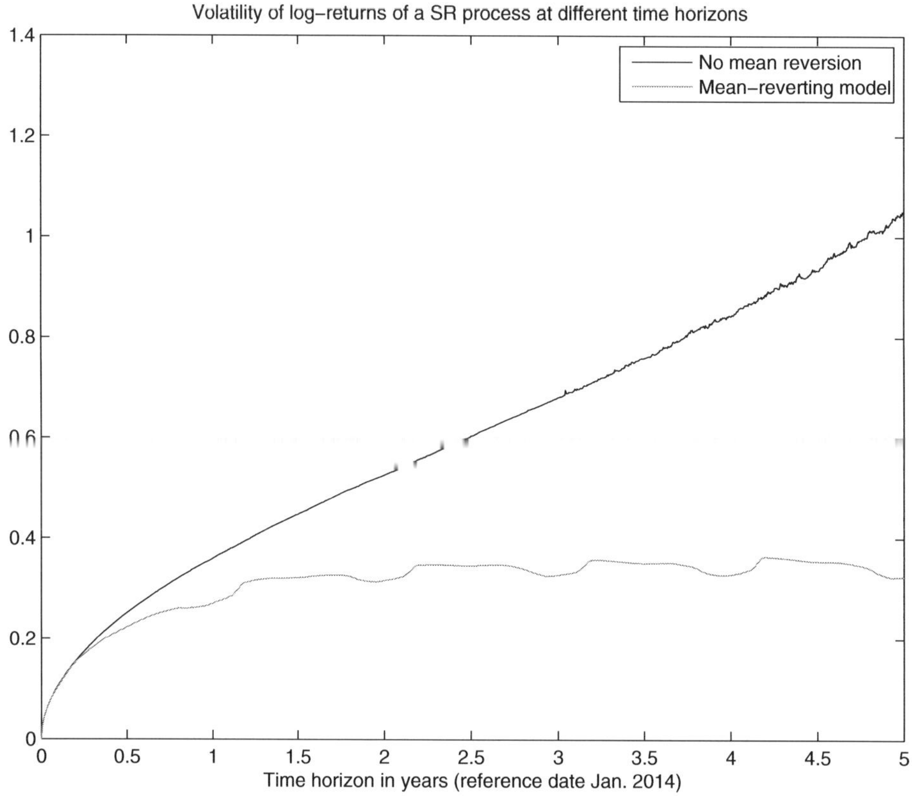

FIGURE 18.10 Volatility of log-returns in the SR models (18.35) and (18.37)

limit the probability of having future spot prices that deviate largely from the forward curve. Large deviations are instead possible in the model without mean reversion. In other words, the mean-reversion property generates a volatility of the log-return prices that tend to stabilize to a constant value as we consider longer and longer horizons, whilst without mean reversion the volatility increases with the time horizon. This is illustrated in Figure 18.10. Notice that in the mean-reverting model the seasonal shape of the forward curve affects the volatility of log-returns.

In both specifications, the drift terms are selected so that the dynamics is consistent with the market observed (or eventually the user's specified) forward price curve $(F_{0,T}, T \geq 0)$ quoted in the market, that is the restriction

$$\widetilde{E}_0(S_T) = F(0,T) \tag{18.39}$$

is satisfied. In addition, in both specifications, the drift restrictions that allow us to fit the market forward curve, that is the expressions (18.36) and (18.38), only apparently require a (numerical) differentiation with respect to the maturity. Indeed, see expressions (18.45) and (18.46) below, where this is not the case because the computation of the moment generating function turns out to require the values of the forward curve itself and not of its derivatives as well. Finally, we remark that the dynamics in (18.35) with constant parameters has been introduced by Dassios and Nagaradjasarma (2006), whilst (18.37) was introduced first by Cox *et al.* (1985) in order to model interest rate dynamics.

Proposition 18.4.1[8] provides the expression for the mgf in the case of time-dependent spot price drift and volatility.

Proposition 18.4.1 *Under commodity spot price dynamics* (18.35), *the moment generating function of the pair* $(S_{n\Delta}, \sum_{j=0}^{N} \alpha_j S_{j\Delta})$ *given the information available at time* 0 *is:*

$$v_{0,x}^{\theta}(N, \Delta; \gamma, \mu) = e^{-\Lambda_0^{\theta}(\Delta;\gamma,\mu)x}, \tag{18.40}$$

where the function $\Lambda_j^{\theta}(\Delta; \gamma, \mu)$ *satisfies the recursive equation*

$$\Lambda_j^{\theta}(\Delta; \gamma, \mu) = A_{j\Delta}^{\theta}\left(\Delta; \Lambda_{j+1}^{\theta}(\Delta; \gamma, \mu)\right) + \mu\alpha_j,$$

for $j = N-1, N-2, \ldots, 1, 0$, *with starting value*

$$\Lambda_N^{\theta}(\Delta, \gamma, \mu) = \gamma + \mu\alpha_N.$$

Here A^{θ} *is defined as*

$$A_t^{\theta}(\Delta; \gamma) = \frac{\gamma \frac{F_{0,t+\Delta}}{F_{0,t}}}{1 + \frac{\gamma}{2} F_{0,t+\Delta} \int_t^{t+\Delta} \frac{\sigma_s^2}{F_{0,s}} ds}, \tag{18.41}$$

and $y = S(t)$. *In addition, as byproduct, we obtain the moment generating function of the spot price*

$$\widetilde{E}_t(e^{-\gamma S_{t+\Delta}}) = v_{0,x}^{\theta}(1, \Delta; \gamma, 0) \tag{18.42}$$

and of the arithmetic average

$$\widetilde{E}_t\left(e^{-\mu \sum_{j=0}^{N} \alpha_j S_{j\Delta}}\right) = v_{0,x}^{\theta}(N, \Delta; 0, \mu). \tag{18.43}$$

If we replace in formula (18.34), the expression of the mgf in (18.42), we can price plain vanilla options according to the square-root process. If instead we use (18.43), we can price fixed strike Asian options. The expression of the joint mgf is relevant for pricing floating strike options, not considered here.

A practical illustration of the procedure is given in Box 18.7, where the pricing of an Asian option consistent with the market forward curve and the market term structure of implied volatility is considered. Notice that implied volatility usually refers to percentage

[8]The proof can be found in Fusai *et al.* (2008).

volatility of log-returns. In order to obtain the volatility to be used in the square-root model, we can use the following transformation:

$$\sigma_{GBM} S = \sigma_{SR} \sqrt{S},$$

so that

$$\sigma_{SR} = \sigma_{GBM} \sqrt{S}.$$

This transformation is implemented in the numerical example considered in Box 18.7.

BOX 18.7 PRICING ASIAN OPTIONS IN A FLEXIBLE FRAMEWORK

We provide here the Matlab code for the implementation of the pricing procedure. A numerical example is also presented.

```
%%%%%%%%%%%%%%%%%%%%%%%%%%%%%%%%%%%%%%%%%%%%%%%%%%%
%%%%Implement the Asian Price SQUARE Root Model%%%%
%%%%%%%%%%%%%%%%%%%%%%%%%%%%%%%%%%%%%%%%%%%%%%%%%%%
function res=...
Asian_SR(strike, FwdCurve, VolCurve, r, t, n, mAW, nAW, AAW )

%Computing the expected value of the arithmetic average
dt=t/n;
momasia=sum(int_FwdCurve(dt*[0:n], FwdCurve))/(n+1);

%Inversion of Laplace transform
eul=AW_LTinversion(@(mu)...
     SR_LT_Avg_dt(mu, FwdCurve, VolCurve, t, n), strike, ...
            mAW, nAW, AAW);

%Pricing Formula
res=exp(-r*t)*(eul + momasia - strike);

%Laplace transform wrt strike of the asian option in the
%discrete monitoring case CIR model
function res=SR_LT_Avg_dt(mu, FwdCurve, VolCurve, t, n)
    res=SR_DoubleLT_dt(0, mu, FwdCurve, VolCurve, t, n)/mu^2;

%%%Moment Generating Function of the SR Process
function res=SR_DoubleLT_dt(gam, mu, FwdCurve, VolCurve, t, n)
    res=exp(-int_FwdCurve(0, FwdCurve)*...
        Lambdafunction(t/n, gam, mu, FwdCurve, VolCurve,  n));
```

```
%%%Function Lambda in Proposition 1
function aDiscr=Lambdafunction(dt, gam, mu, FwdCurve, ...
                               VolCurve, n)
aDiscr = gam + mu/(n + 1);
for j = n - 1:-1:0
    aDiscr =Afunction(j*dt,(j+1)*dt, aDiscr, FwdCurve, ...
                      VolCurve) ...
                            + mu/(n + 1);
end

%%%Function A in Proposition 1
function  res=Afunction(t, T, gam, FwdCurve, VolCurve)
    den= 1 + 0.5*gam*int_FwdCurve(T,FwdCurve)*...
        quadgk(@(x) (int_VolCurve(x, VolCurve).^2)./...
              int_FwdCurve(x,FwdCurve), t, T);
    num=gam*int_FwdCurve(T,FwdCurve)/int_FwdCurve(t,FwdCurve);

    res=num./den;

%%%Interpolating the forward curve
function iFwdCurve = int_FwdCurve(t, FwdCurve)
pp=interp1(FwdCurve(:,1),FwdCurve(:,2),'pchip','pp');
f = @(x) ppval(pp,x);
iFwdCurve=f(t);

%%%Interpolating the volatility curve
function iVolCurve = int_VolCurve(t, VolCurve)
pp=interp1(VolCurve(:,1),VolCurve(:,2),'pchip','pp');
f = @(x) ppval(pp,x);
iVolCurve=f(t);

%%%Inversion of the Laplace transform
function euler1=AW_LTinversion(LTf_s, tvar, m, n, A)
%downloaded from
%http://www.columbia.edu/~ww2040/6711F12/tools.html
%and modified by Gianluca Fusai
a=zeros(m+n+1,1); S=zeros(n+m+1,1);

anot=exp(A/2)*arrayfun(LTf_s,A/(2*tvar))/(2*tvar);
anot=anot+exp(A/2)*real(arrayfun(LTf_s,(A/2+1i*pi)/tvar)...
                   *exp(1i*pi))/tvar;

k=[1:(m+n+1)];
a=exp(A/2)*real(arrayfun(LTf_s, (A/2+(1+k)*1i*pi)/tvar)...
```

```
                        *exp(1i*pi))/tvar;
S(1)=anot-a(1);

for k=2:n+m+1
   S(k)=S(k-1)+((-1)^k)*a(k);
end

euler1=S(n);
for k=1:m
   euler1=euler1+nchoosek(m,k)*S(n+k);
end
euler1=(2^(-m))*euler1;
```

Let us consider the following example:

```
%A Numerical Example
%Parameters: risk free rate and time to maturity
r=0.0525; ttm=1;
%Parameters LT inversion
mAW=12; nAW=20; AAW=18.4;
%Market Forward Curve
ng_fwd=[0 7.1409
0.074   7.288
0.1534  7.405
0.2438  7.52
0.3233  7.635
0.4055  7.73
0.4959  7.785
0.5726  7.88
0.663   8.45
0.7452  9.01
0.8247  9.3
0.9151  9.295
0.9945  9.075;



%Term Structure of Percentage Volatility
ng_vol=[0.  13.8
0.0833333   16.8
0.166667    14.1
0.25    16
0.333333    16.8
0.416667    20.4
0.5 22.7
0.583333    26.7
```

```
0.666667    22.5
0.75   18.7
0.833333    18.4
0.916667    16.1
1 13.8];

%Pricing for different monitoring dates and strike at 1
strike=mean(ng_fwd(:,2)); %fix strike approximately at-the-money

%Change GBM vol into SR vol
ng_vol(:,2)=(ng_vol(:,2)/100)*sqrt(max(ng_fwd(:,2)))

res(1)=Asian_SR(strike, ng_fwd, ng_vol, r, ttm, 12, mAW, nAW, AAW)
res(2)=Asian_SR(strike, ng_fwd, ng_vol, r, ttm, 24, mAW, nAW, AAW)
res(3)=Asian_SR(strike, ng_fwd, ng_vol, r, ttm, 36, mAW, nAW, AAW)
res(4)=Asian_SR(strike, ng_fwd, ng_vol, r, ttm, 48, mAW, nAW, AAW)
```

We have the results in the following table:

N	12	24	36	48
Premium	0.3602	0.3648	0.3661	0.3667
MC	0.3652	0.3628	0.3593	0.3564

An analytical expression for the mgf is available in the mean-reverting case as well and is given in the following proposition 18.4.2:[9]

Proposition 18.4.2 *Under spot price dynamics* (18.37)*, the moment generating function of the pair* $(S_{N\Delta}, \sum_{j=0}^{N} \alpha_j S_{j\Delta})$ *given the information available at time* 0 *is*

$$v_{0,x}^{\beta}(n, \Delta; \gamma, \mu) = e^{-\Lambda_0^{\beta}(\Delta;\gamma,\mu)x - \sum_{j=0}^{N-1} B_{j\Delta}^{\beta}\left(\Delta;\Lambda_{j+1}^{\beta}\left(\Delta;\gamma,\mu\right)\right)}, \tag{18.44}$$

where the function $\Lambda_j^{\beta}(\Delta; \gamma, \mu)$ *satisfies the recursive equation*

$$\Lambda_j^{\beta}(\Delta; \gamma, \mu) = A_{j\Delta}^{\beta}\left(\Delta; \Lambda_{j+1}^{\beta}(\Delta; \gamma, \mu)\right) + \mu\alpha_j,$$

[9]The proof can be found in Fusai *et al.* (2008).

for $j = N - 1, n - 2, \ldots, 0$, *with starting value*

$$\Lambda_N^\beta(\Delta, \gamma, \mu) = \gamma + \mu\alpha_N.$$

Here $A_{j\Delta}^\beta$ *and* B_t^β *are respectively given by*

$$A_t^\beta(\Delta; \gamma) = \frac{\gamma e^{-\beta\Delta}}{1 + \frac{\gamma}{2}\int_t^{t+\Delta} \sigma_s^2 e^{-\beta(t+\Delta-s)} ds}, \tag{18.45}$$

$$B_t^\beta(\Delta; \gamma) = \gamma F_{0,T} - F_{0,t} A_t^\beta(\Delta; \gamma) - \frac{1}{2}\int_t^{t+\Delta} F_{0,s}\sigma_s^2 A_s^\beta(\Delta; \gamma)^2 \, ds, \tag{18.46}$$

and $\gamma = S(t)$. *In addition, the moment generating function of* $S_{t+\Delta}$ *is* $v_{t,\eta}^\beta(1, \Delta; \gamma, 0)$, *whilst the moment generating function of the arithmetic average is* $v_{0,x}^\beta(N, \Delta; 0, \mu)$.

18.4.2 Numerical Results

In the original paper by Fusai *et al.* (2008) a few numerical tests have been conducted in order to examine:

- The discrepancy of prices stemming from the alternative assumptions of a discrete vs. continuous monitoring rule. For barrier options, Fusai *et al.* (2006) showed that price differences can be very large in spite of a relatively high monitoring frequency. For Asian options, the story is a bit different. As expected, price differences between discrete and continuous monitoring rules decrease as long as the number of monitoring dates increases. In addition, the convergence of the discretely monitored option price to the continuously monitored one is almost linear in the monitoring frequency, much faster than is known to occur for barrier options; that is, approximately like $1/\sqrt{N}$.
- The impact of including market information about the forward prices in the spot price dynamics for the purpose of pricing Asian-style options. This analysis is conducted using quotes taken from the Natural Gas Market at NYMEX. It turns out that a non-flat forward curve produces highly significant option price deviations from figures obtained in the case where such information is not accounted for by the underlying spot price model.
- The price differences between square-root and lognormal model. Option prices using the square-root model specification accurately approximate quotes stemming from the model assuming lognormal dynamics, provided the volatility coefficient is adequately chosen to reproduce prices of plain vanilla at-the-money options. This fact constitutes a major result since the new flexible method allows us to price Asian-style option prices in real time, with great accuracy and allowing for time-varying volatility, fitting a forward curve. Vice versa, numerical approximation for the geometric Brownian motion case requires intensive calculations and much greater computational time. This result is quite robust across the examined spectrum of parameters, the only case where significant discrepancies are observed related to deeply out-of-the-money options.

- Finally, the impact of including information about the time structure of historical volatility in the pricing device. A test on corn price data quoted at CBOT is performed. It turns out that using this information may result in significant price discrepancies compared with the quotes obtained using the market model represented by the geometric Brownian motion. These results suggest that when pricing Asian-style options in market contexts where a seasonal component strongly affects the evolution of spot price volatility, one should include this information as precisely as possible. This remark is particularly important for several commodity markets, such as energy and agriculturals, where the time variation of volatility is significantly pronounced.

18.4.3 A Case Study

In this final section we consider as a case study the computation of the fair value of Asian-style options taking into account market information. We consider the forward curve on Brent as quoted on 24 December 2013 at ICE. Values across all delivery months are reported in Table 18.10, where we indicate the exact day of trading termination and the time to maturity of the contract as expressed in year units.

Our final goal is to assess Asian-style option prices under a realistic market setting in the square-root model with mean reversion.

We begin by defining values for each of the input quantities indicated in step 0 of the pricing algorithm stated earlier. Our base case assumes that:

- Current time is 24 December 2013.
- Options expire on 14 March 2014 (the average is computed over 59 working days), 13 June 2014 (124 working days) and 13 November 2014 (233 working days).
- Averages are computed based on daily monitoring, that is, $\Delta = 1/250$ years.
- Strike index K is assumed to match the at-the-money level, defined as

$$\overline{Avg_{0,N}} := \frac{1}{N+1} \sum_{j=0}^{N} F(0, j\Delta),$$

  where $N = T/\Delta$.
- For each maturity, interest rate r is linearly interpolated from LIBOR quotes on value date. Quotes are given in Table 18.11. Interpolated values at option maturities are respectively 0.2096%, 0.2797% and 0.4071%. These values are converted to continuous compounding using the conversion formula $\ln(1 + \text{LIBOR})$.
- Mean-reversion frequency is set equal to $\beta = 0.1$ p.a.
- Current spot price is set equal to the shortest maturity futures price, i.e. 111.99 USD.
- Spot price volatility of log-returns under the GBM assumption is assumed equal to 0.20, a typical value for crude oil (see e.g., the implied volatility quotes in Table 18.8). This figure is transformed into spot price volatility in the square-root model according to

$$S \times 0.2 = \sqrt{S} \times \sigma_{SR},$$

TABLE 18.10 Crude Oil Futures prices quoted on 24 December 2013 at ICE

Delivery	Maturity (mm/dd/yy)	Days to expiry	Settlement	Volume
Feb14	1/16/14	23	111.99	26179
Mar14	2/13/14	51	111.65	7590
Apr14	3/14/14	80	111.33	2495
May14	4/15/14	112	110.95	936
Jun14	5/15/14	142	110.54	2538
Jul14	6/13/14	171	110.08	221
Aug14	7/16/14	204	109.55	125
Sep14	8/14/14	233	109.05	245
Oct14	9/15/14	265	108.55	47
Dec14	11/13/14	324	107.59	1862

Source: https://www.theice.com/productguide/ProductSpec.shtml?specId=219#data

so that

$$\sigma_{SR} = \sqrt{S} \times 0.2 = \sqrt{111.99} \times 0.2$$

and we set $\sigma_{SR} = 2$.

We price the Asian option using the analytical method described above. To benchmark our results we consider Monte Carlo simulation. In particular, given that with respect to the GBM dynamics no exact solution of the considered square-root stochastic equations is possible, we discretize the mean-reverting dynamics according to the Euler scheme using a time step Δ:

$$S(t+\Delta) = S(t) + \left(\int_t^{t+\Delta} \eta(s)ds - \beta S(t)\Delta \right) + F(0, t+\Delta) - F(0, t) + \sigma \sqrt{S(t)}\epsilon(t)\sqrt{\Delta},$$

where $\epsilon(t)$ is a sequence of i.i.d. standard Gaussian random variables. In particular, notice that the term $\int_t^{t+\Delta} \eta(s)ds$ can be approximated as follows:

$$\begin{aligned}\int_t^{t+\Delta} \eta(s)ds = & \int_t^{t+\Delta} \left(F(0,s) + \partial_s F(0,s)\right) ds \\ = & \frac{(F(0,t+\Delta)+F(0,t))\Delta}{2} + F(0, t+\Delta) - F(0,t).\end{aligned}$$

TABLE 18.11 US$ LIBOR rates across varying times-to-maturity. Quotes as of 24 December 2013

3m (93 days)	6m (185 days)	12m (370 days)
0.24585	0.34940	0.58360

TABLE 18.12 Asian-type option prices (exact and Monte Carlo estimate) for the mean-reverting model, varying the strike and the time horizon

Days	Strike	Exact	MC estimate	Confidence interval (3 std. errors)	
59	111.8683	1.9389	1.9403	1.9129	1.9676
124	111.5131	2.7947	2.8104	2.7706	2.8501
233	110.7821	3.7801	3.8022	3.748	3.8564

TABLE 18.13 Values of the forward curve at different horizons when it is set at a constant value. These values are used for pricing Asian options in Table 18.14

Days	59	124	233
min	111.56	110.793	109.05
avg	111.868	111.513	110.782
max	111.99	111.99	111.99

In conclusion, the Euler discretization allows us to simulate the spot price path according to

$$S(t+\Delta) = S(t) + \left(\frac{(F(0,t+\Delta)+F(0,t))}{2} - \beta S(t) \right) \Delta + F(0,t+\Delta) - F(0,t) + \sigma \epsilon(t) \sqrt{S(t)\Delta}.$$

Pricing results are given in Table 18.12. Exact and Monte Carlo estimates (100,000 simulations, time step $\Delta = 1/365$) agree quite well: exact prices always fall inside the three standard errors confidence interval.

The relevance of incorporating the market forward curve is examined in Tables 18.13 and 18.14 where different assumptions on the forward curve are examined. In particular, for each maturity, we price the Asian option using the market observed forward curve and we compare the price obtained assuming that the forward curve is flat at three different levels: the minimum forward price up to the option expiry, the average forward price up to the option expiry and the maximum forward price up to the option expiry. These values are reported in Table 18.13, whilst the corresponding Asian option prices are given in Table 18.14.

Finally, Table 18.15 shows that option prices decrease with an increase in the speed at which prices tend to revert back to their long-term trend. In fact, higher mean reversion reduces underlying price dispersions, so reducing the likelihood of ending up in-the-money.

TABLE 18.14 Asian option prices in the SR mean-reverting model at different horizons under different shapes of the forward curve: flat at the minimum (min)/average (avg)/maximum (max) level and the market observed one (market). Values are given in Table 18.13

Days	59	124	233
min	1.7868	2.4422	2.9551
avg	1.8506	2.6848	3.6281
market	1.9389	2.7947	3.7801
max	1.9998	3.0377	4.4083

TABLE 18.15 Asian option price vs. speed of mean reversion

β	0.1	0.2	0.3	0.4	0.5	0.6	0.7	0.8	0.9	1
Price	3.7801	3.6919	3.6068	3.5246	3.4452	3.3686	3.2945	3.2229	3.1536	3.0867

Further extensions might encompass pricing of Asian-style options written on a basket of prices and empirical examination of implied calibration of the model on plain vanilla quotes and comparison between model and market assessment of Asian options. Interesting results for basket options with possible applications to Asian options have been proposed in Caldana *et al.* (2014).

18.5 CONCLUSIONS

It is commonly held that pricing Asian-style options under the market model represented by a geometric Brownian motion is a difficult task. First, no closed-form expression exists for the fair option value. Second, information embedded within the standing market forward curve is neglected during the valuation process. Finally, prices are derived irrespective of the seasonal path exhibited by the spot price volatility or mean-reversion properties.

In this chapter, we have discussed standard models for pricing Asian options and more recent modelling achievements, particularly useful for pricing options in commodity markets where traders must quickly produce quotes compatible with the market view expressed in terms of forward prices, typically showing a seasonal behaviour and with a mean-reversion feature.

For the sake of completeness, we would like to mention more recent work by Cerny and Kyriakou (2011), Fusai and Meucci (2008), Fusai and Kyriakou (2014) and Marena *et al.* (2013). They consider the pricing of discrete monitoring Asian options in a more general framework allowing jumps and stochastic volatility. Finally, Ballotta *et al.* (2014) consider the hedging problem of Asian options in a non-Gaussian setting.

REFERENCES

Abate, J. and Whitt, W. (1992) The Fourier-series method for inverting transforms of probability distributions, *Queueing Systems Theory Applications*, **10**, 5–88.

Ballotta, L., Gerrard, J. and Kyriakou, I. (2014) Hedging of Asian options under exponential Levy models: Computation and performance, working Paper.

Bessembinder, H., Coughenour, J., Seguin, P. and Smoller, M. (1995) Mean reversion in equilibrium asset prices: Evidence from the futures term structure, *Journal of Finance*, **60**(1), 361–375.

Cai, N. and Kou, S.G. (2012) Pricing Asian options under a hyper-exponential jump diffusion model, *Operations Research*, **60**(1), 64–77.

Caldana, R., Fusai, G., Gnoatto, A. and Grasselli, M. (2014) General closed-form basket option pricing bounds, available at SSRN: http://ssrn.com/abstract=2376134 or http://dx.doi.org/10.2139/ssrn.2376134.

Cartea, Á. and Williams, T. (2008) UK gas markets: The market price of risk and applications to multiple interruptible supply contracts, *Energy Economics*, **30**(3), 829–846.

Casassus, J. and Collin-Dufresne, P. (2005) Stochastic convenience yield implied from commodity futures and interest rates, *Journal of Finance*, **60**(5), 2283–2331.

Cerny, A. and Kyriakou, I. (2011) An improved convolution algorithm for discretely sampled Asian options, *Quantitative Finance*, **11**(3), 381–389.

Chang, C.W., Chang, J.S.K. and Lu, W. (2010) Pricing catastrophe options with stochastic claim arrival intensity in claim time, *Journal of Banking and Finance*, **34**(1), 24–32.

Cox, J.C., Ingersoll, J.E. and Ross, S.A. (1985) A theory of the term structure of interest rates, *Econometrica*, **53**(2), 385–407.

Dassios, A. and Nagaradjasarma, J. (2006) The square root process and Asian options, *Quantitative Finance*, **6**(4), 337–347.

Eydeland, A. and Wolyniec, K. (2003) *Energy and Power Risk Management*, John Wiley & Sons, Hoboken, NJ.

Falloon, W. and Turner, D. (1999) The evolution of a market, in *Managing Energy Price Risk*, RiskBooks, London.

Fu, M.C., Madan, D. and Wang, T. (1998) Pricing continuous Asian options: A comparison of Monte Carlo and Laplace transform inversion methods, *Journal of Computational Finance*, **2**(1), 49–74.

Fusai, G. (2004) Pricing Asian options via Fourier and Laplace transforms, *Journal of Computational Finance*, **7**(3), 87–106.

Fusai, G. and Kyriakou, I. (2014) General optimized lower and upper bounds for discrete and continuous arithmetic Asian options, working Paper.

Fusai, G. and Meucci, A. (2008) Discretely monitored Asian options under Levy processes, *Journal of Banking and Finance*, **32**, 2076–2088.

Fusai, G. and Roncoroni, A. (2008) *Implementing Models in Quantitative Finance: Methods and Cases*, Springer-Verlag, Berlin.

Fusai, G., Abrahams, D. and Sgarra, C. (2006) An exact analytical solution of discrete barrier options, *Finance and Stochastics*, **10**, 1–26.

Fusai, G., Marena, M. and Roncoroni, A. (2008) A note on the analytical pricing of commodity Asian-style options under discrete monitoring, *Journal of Banking and Finance*, **32**(10), 2033–2045.

Geman, H. and Roncoroni, A. (2006) Understanding the fine structure of electricity prices, *The Journal of Business*, **79**(3), 1225–1261.

Geman, H. and Yor, M. (1993) Bessel processes, Asian options and perpetuities, *Mathematical Finance*, **3**(4), 349–375.

Haug, E. (2006) Asian options with cost of carry zero, working Paper.

Ju, N. (2002) Pricing Asian and basket options via Taylor expansion, *Journal of Computational Finance*, **5**, 79–103.

Levy, E. (1992) Pricing European average rate currency options, *Journal of International Money and Finance*, **11**, 474–491.

Lewis, A. (1998) Applications of eigenfunction expansions in continuous-time finance, *Mathematical Finance*, **8**, 349–383.

Lewis, A. (2002) Asian connections, *Wilmott Magazine*, July, pp. 57–63.

Lien, G. and Koekebakker, S. (2004) Volatility and price jumps in agricultural futures prices: Evidence from wheat options, *American Journal of Agricultural Economics*, **86**(4), 1018–1031.

Marena, M., Roncoroni, A. and Fusai, G. (2013) Asian options with jumps, Argo, *New Frontiers in Practical Risk Management*, **1**, 48–55.

Milevsky, M.A. and Posner, S.E. (1998) Asian options, the sum of lognormals and the reciprocal gamma distribution, *Journal of Financial and Quantitative Analysis*, **33**(3), 409–422.

Nielsen, J.A. and Sandmann, K. (2003) Pricing bounds on Asian options, *Journal of Financial and Quantitative Analysis*, **38**(2), 449–473.

Nomikos, N.K., Kyriakou, I., Papapostolou, N.C. and Pouliasis, P.K. (2013) Freight options: Price modeling and empirical analysis, *Transportation Research: E*, **51**, 82–94.

Pindyck, R. (2001) The dynamics of commodity spot and futures markets: A primer, *Energy Journal*, **22**(3), 1–29.

Richter, M.C. and Sorensen, C. (2000) Stochastic volatility and seasonality in commodity futures and options: The case of soybeans, working Paper, Department of Finance, Copenhagen Business School.

Rogers, L.C.G. and Shi, Z. (1992) The value of an Asian option, *Journal of Applied Probability*, **32**, 1077–1088.

Routledge, B.R., Seppi, D.J. and Spatt, C.S. (2000) Equilibrium forward curves for commodities, *Journal of Finance*, **55**(3), 1297–1338.

Schwartz, E.S. (1997) The stochastic behavior of commodity prices: Implications for valuation and hedging, *Journal of Finance*, **52**(3), 923–973.

Shaw, W.T. (1998) *Modeling Financial Derivatives with Mathematica*, Cambridge University Press, Cambridge.

Thompson, G.W.P. (1998) Fast narrow bounds on the value of Asian options, working Paper, University of Cambridge.

Todorova, M.I. (2004) Modeling energy commodity futures: Is seasonality part of it? *The Journal of Alternative Investments*, Fall.

Turnbull, S. and Wakeman, L. (1991) A quick algorithm for pricing European average options, *Journal of Financial and Quantitative Analysis*, **26**, 377–389.

Vecer, J. (2001) A new PDE approach for pricing arithmetic average Asian options, *Journal of Computational Finance*, **4**(4), 105–113.

CHAPTER 19

Natural Gas Storage Modelling

Álvaro Cartea, James Cheeseman and Sebastian Jaimungal

19.1 INTRODUCTION

When demand for a commodity is seasonal, whilst its production is relatively more stable and/or with a different seasonal pattern, being able to store it helps to reduce large price fluctuations as well as providing security of supply in unforeseen scenarios. Therefore, having access to storage is desirable but the costs to build the facility are very large and irreversible. The need of the market to smooth out price fluctuations, both between seasons as well as unexpected short-term deviations, and to ensure security of supply will determine the willingness to pay for such a facility.

The gas market is a good example of such a commodity and a key question is how much a gas storage facility is worth. The answer depends on many factors, some of which rely upon engineering specifications and others on financial characteristics of the commodity. For example, the rate of injection and withdrawal is a key determinant in the value of storage, but the higher these injection and withdrawal rates are, the more expensive it is to build and maintain. In contrast, the behaviour of gas prices over long- and short-term horizons is also decisive in the value of storage. Over long time scales, the value of storage is higher the more pronounced is the seasonality in gas prices and similarly, over short time scales, the higher the volatility of gas prices the more valuable is the storage facility.

In this chapter we show how to value a storage facility using least-squares Monte Carlo (LSMC). We present a toy model to understand how to employ the LSMC algorithm and then show how to incorporate realistic constraints into the valuation, including: the maximum capacity of the storage, injection and withdrawal rates and costs, and market constraints such as bid–ask spreads in the spot market and transaction costs.

Handbook of Multi-Commodity Markets and Products: Structuring, Trading and Risk Management. Edited by Andrea Roncoroni, Gianluca Fusai and Mark Cummins.

19.2 A SIMPLE MODEL OF STORAGE, FUTURES PRICES, SPOT PRICES AND CONVENIENCE YIELD

Storage costs and capacity have an immediate effect on spot and futures prices. Let us think of a simple example to illustrate the connection between storage and futures (in Section 19.3 we analyse in detail the valuation of a gas storage facility). Assume that there is enough storage capacity to cover demand over a long horizon, say for example one year, and storage costs are 1 pence per therm per year of storage. Assume further that today's spot price of gas is $S_t = 30$ pence/therm and that the risk-free rate is 0%. What is the 'reasonable price' for a futures contract that delivers one therm of gas in $T = 12$ months' time?

Any futures price different from 31 pence/therm would seem straightforward to arbitrage. If it costs 1 pence to store the commodity for 12 months, and the foregone interest rate is 0%, it is possible to replicate the futures by buying the gas today and storing it until time $T = 12$ months in the future. In this example we might want to make the extra assumption that storage capacity is large enough so that there is no 'fear' that spot supplies might unexpectedly dry up, triggering a shrinkage in supply and consequently making spot prices undergo an upward hike around time T.

In the example above, it is clear that storage costs and capacity have a bearing on futures prices (one can make the same claim the other way around, that futures prices affect the price of storage). In this section we explore, in a simple setting, the relationship between storage, spot prices, storage prices, expected spot prices, convenience yield and futures prices. Throughout this section we follow the discussion in Pindyck (2001).

The price of storage is equal to the marginal value of storage, which is calculated like the price of any other good: by demand and supply forces. In a competitive framework, the price that an investor is willing to pay for storage depends on the marginal profits he or she can obtain by holding an extra unit of gas in the storage. The flow of benefits to inventory holders from a marginal or extra unit of gas inventory is known in the literature as the **marginal convenience yield**. In this context we interpret **convenience yield** as the flow of benefits to the holder of a commodity inventory. These benefits arise from the use of inventories to reduce production and marketing costs, and to avoid stockouts, see Pindyck (2001) and Roncoroni (2010).

Denote by Ψ_t the price of storage (i.e., the marginal convenience yield) and by N_t the gas inventory levels at time t. We know that the demand for storage will depend on the price charged to investors to hold a unit of inventory. Therefore, the demand for storage can be written as $N_t(\Psi_t)$ and it is reasonable to assume that increases in the price of storage lead to a decrease in the inventory levels, that is $N_t'(\Psi_t) < 0$. Moreover, since the value of storage is expected to be low when the total stock of inventories is large, but can rise quickly when the stock becomes very small, it is also reasonable to assume $N_t''(\Psi_t) < 0$.

In Figure 19.1 we depict two plausible inverse demand functions for storage $\Psi(N_t)$. Another way to interpret the convexity shown by the demand function is the following. When storage levels are very low, for example N_t is close to 0, the economy places considerable value on these stocks and the value of an additional unit of gas in the storage capacity is deemed to be very valuable. Similarly, when the amount of gas in storage is very high, an additional unit of gas will be of very little value. Put differently, the value of storage is decreasing in the amount N_t held in the facility and the marginal benefits from storage are also decreasing in N_t; this is what gives us the convex shape of the demand curve shown in Figure 19.1.

There are many factors that can affect the demand for storage and in turn the price charged for it. Everything else being equal, in an economy with higher volatility of gas prices, storage is

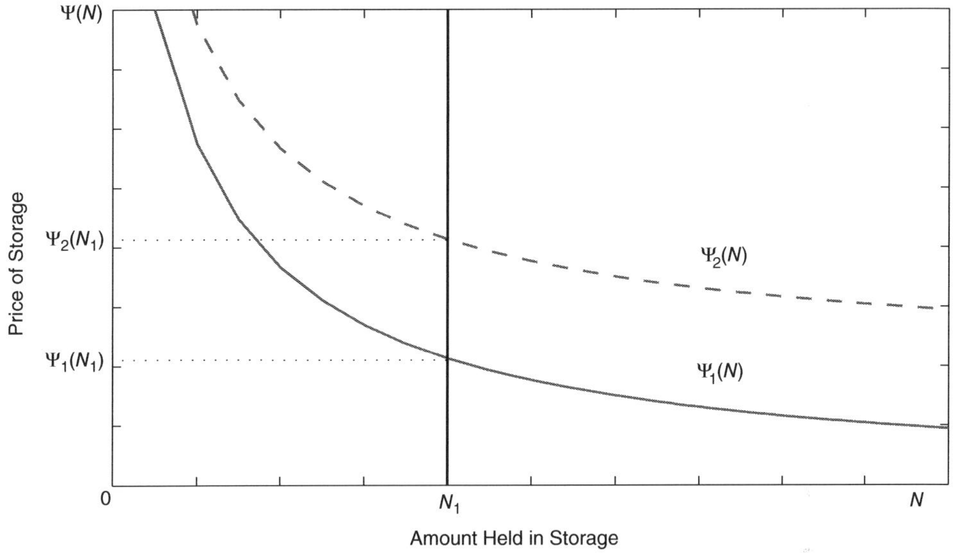

FIGURE 19.1 Demand for storage N at price Ψ.

more valuable or desirable than storage in an economy with low volatility of gas prices. After all, storage is used as a buffer to smooth out times of low and high demand (or equivalently low or high spot prices).

Thus, let us assume that the economy is at a steady state, where volatility of gas prices is σ_1 and demand for storage is $\Psi_1(N)$, as shown in Figure 19.1. Assume further that for this level of volatility the equilibrium price and quantity held in storage are $\Psi_1(N_1)$ and N_1, respectively. What happens if the gas market undergoes a permanent change and the volatility of prices jumps up to a new level $\sigma_2 > \sigma_1$?

We depict the new situation with the demand curve $\Psi_2(N)$ in the same figure. Comparing it to $\Psi_1(N)$, we see that with the increase in gas price volatility the price for storage has increased for all levels of N. We can explain this shift up in the demand curve in many different ways. For instance, investors know that in a more volatile market they would extract more value from gas inventories. Another intuitive explanation is to observe that because the economy uses storage as a buffer to smooth gas consumption, it will be willing to pay more for the ability to smooth gas consumption when volatility of prices is higher.

But what is the new equilibrium level for inventories in the steady state? So far we have established that when the economy learns that there has been a permanent increase in the volatility level of prices, demand for storage increases. We can also argue that the economy will require higher levels of inventories, say $N_2 > N_1$, to mitigate the extra volatility of prices. To see this we can see the intuition explaining the direction of the inventory adjustment by looking at an extreme case with very low volatility in gas prices. Imagine that price volatility drops to zero. This means that gas prices become a constant (not random), therefore one would expect that the economy places very little, or zero value, on storage.

Figure 19.2 depicts the price and inventory level adjustment as a consequence of the permanent increment in the volatility of gas prices. We must appreciate that the financial markets adjust quicker than the physical market. Although the market knows that the new

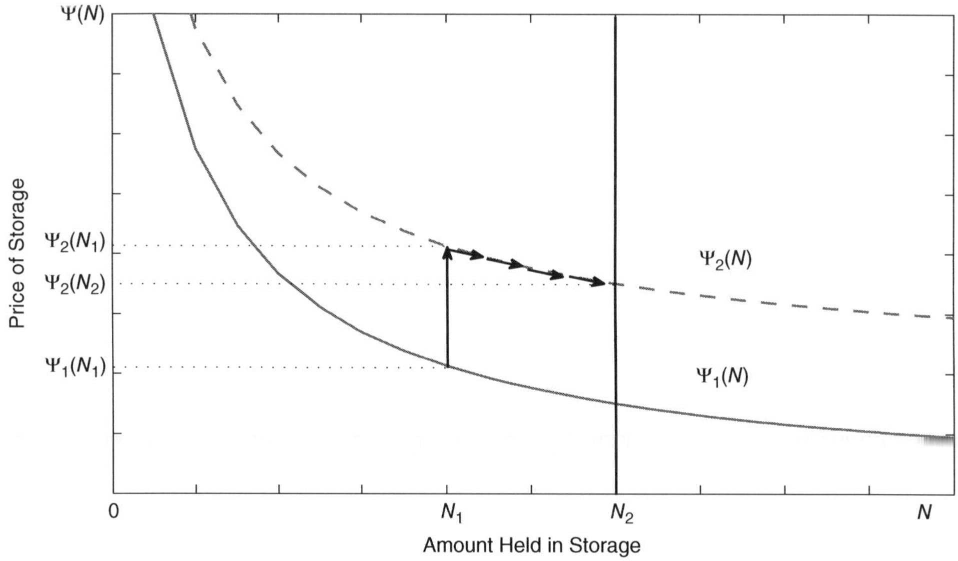

FIGURE 19.2 Price and inventory level adjustment after a permanent increase in gas price volatility.

level of inventories must be N_2, it will take time to build up the stocks. However, the marginal convenience yield does adapt immediately to the new market situation and the price for storage jumps from $\Psi_1(N_1)$ to $\Psi_2(N_1)$, and then it gradually falls to $\Psi_2(N_2)$.

19.3 VALUATION OF GAS STORAGE

Central to the problem of gas storage is its financial valuation, not only for investment decisions but also for operating strategies and hedging decisions for those wishing to trade around such assets. There are two approaches to the valuation of storage: intrinsic and extrinsic.

Intrinsic Valuation The value of a storage facility, like any option, is its premium, which is made up of two parts, intrinsic and extrinsic. Relating this to a standard American option, we have that the intrinsic value is the payoff from immediate exercise and the extrinsic value is the additional time value of the option, the possibility of increasing the payoff. The simplest approach to valuing storage is to compute the intrinsic value given the futures curve at the valuation date. This is the optimal combination of futures contracts which can be put in place, while respecting all the physical constraints of the storage facility, to extract value from the calendar spreads of the futures curve. This is somewhat equivalent to deciding when to exercise an American call option by looking at the current futures curve. That is, by picking the highest in-the-money value on the curve and entering into a futures contract to sell for $F(t, \tau)$ on date τ, in the knowledge that we can exercise our option on that date and buy the stock at the strike price making a profit of $F(t, \tau) - K$, where τ is our chosen exercise date and K the strike price. In this static valuation we ignore any possibility of the futures curve changing over time.

A rolling intrinsic valuation is similar to above, but we allow for stochastic changes in the futures curve throughout the duration of the contract. In practice we enter into the static futures position indicated by an intrinsic valuation, but if the futures curve changes such that we can adjust our positions to increase the intrinsic value then we do so. Again in terms of the American option example above, we proceed as for the intrinsic valuation but if the futures curve changes such that we can increase $F(t, \tau) - K$ by changing our planned exercise date and futures position then we do so.

Extrinsic Valuation The extrinsic value represents the optionality in the physical asset and together with the intrinsic value this makes up the premium. The extrinsic value is that of the flexibility of the storage, the ability to trade the daily volatility. An extrinsic valuation will give a value higher than both intrinsic methods, and can increase the value of storage from a few percent over the intrinsic to multiples of the intrinsic value depending upon the physical constraints of the facility and the dynamics of the underlying.

Two main methods of extrinsic valuation exist: trinomial tree forests, see for instance Manoliu (2004) and LSMC, see Longstaff and Schwartz (2001). Both are recursive, spot-based procedures and will fully value the storage premium based on creating an optimal strategy for the operation of the facility. While the tree method is undoubtedly the fastest, we are limited in as much as we can only practically use a geometric Brownian motion or single-factor mean-reverting model as the underlying. LSMC, however, is totally detached from the underlying price model and can be applied to any price path and can easily be extended to consider problems based around multiple commodity price simulations. For other methods and implementations, see Fusai and Roncoroni (2008), Jackson *et al.* (2007) and Jaimungal and Surkov (2011).

19.3.1 Least-Squares Monte Carlo

Longstaff and Schwartz (2001) originally applied the algorithm to valuing Bermudan options. Subsequently it has been extended and applied as a method for pricing swing options by Ibáñez (2004), and further to storage valuation by Carmona and Ludkovski (2007) and Boogert and de Jong (2008).

Reviewing the algorithm as presented in Longstaff and Schwartz (2001), we see that the intuition behind the least-squares approach is best appreciated through the original application, an American-style option. The holder of such an option may exercise at any time prior to maturity, and at every potential exercise time the decision whether to exercise or not depends upon assessing the value of continuing without exercising, the continuation value, against that of exercising immediately, the intrinsic value. Longstaff and Schwartz use a simple least-squares regression of the simulated future cashflows on the current simulated stock prices to obtain this continuation value as a conditional expectation and hence the optimal exercise time that maximizes the option value.

As in any Monte Carlo simulation of a path-dependent derivative, the time to maturity is discretized, into k discrete potential exercise times $0 < t_1 \leq t_2 \leq \ldots \leq t_k = T$ and the decision on whether to exercise or not is taken at every point by comparing the intrinsic value with the value of continuation. Using the notation from Longstaff and Schwartz (2001) we have that when $C(\omega, s; t, T)$ is the path of cashflows generated by the option, conditional on the option having not been exercised at or prior to time t and on the holder of the option following the optimal stopping strategy for all s $(t < s \leq T)$, and where ω is a sample path, the value of continuation at time t_i can be expressed as the risk-neutral expectation of the discounted future cashflows. We denote this continuation value as $Cont(\omega; t_i)$ and the above argument is represented formally as

$$Cont(\omega; t_i) = \mathbb{E}_{\mathbb{Q}} \left[\sum_{j=i+1}^{k} e^{-r(t_j - t_i)} C(\omega, s; t, T) \middle| \mathcal{F}_{t_i} \right],$$

where r is the risk-free rate and $\mathbb{Q}$ the risk-neutral pricing measure.

LSMC works recursively through the discretized times using least-squares regression to estimate the conditional expectation at $t_{k-1}, t_{k-2}, \ldots, t_1$. The LSMC is a recursive process since at each time the decision to exercise could change all subsequent cashflows and therefore $C(\omega, s; t_i, T)$ is not necessarily the same as $C(\omega, s; t_{i-1}, T)$. The initial step is always to define the cashflows at the final timestep t_k and for an American option this is the intrinsic value of the option at maturity.

Longstaff and Schwartz give an example using the set of Laguerre polynomials as the basis functions for the regression and with these polynomials, the estimate of $Cont(\omega; t_i)$ is represented as

$$Cont_M(\omega; t_i) = \sum_{j=0}^{M} a_j L_j(X),$$

where a_j and L_j are constant coefficients and the Laguerre polynomial terms respectively, M the number of basis functions and X the underlying spot prices. They report that if $M > 2$, the accuracy of the algorithm is not significantly dependent on the type or number of basis functions used, but more recent research shows that accuracy does depend on the choice of basis functions, see Stentoft (2004).

In Longstaff and Schwartz (2001), $Cont_M(\omega; t_i)$ is estimated by regressing the discounted values of $C(\omega, s; t_i, T)$ on the basis functions for the paths which are in-the-money, since the decision on whether to exercise or not is only required if the option has an intrinsic value greater than zero. Using only in-the-money paths reduces the number of basis functions required for an accurate estimation of the continuation values.[1] With the conditional expectation estimated we can decide if exercise is optimal at t_i for each in-the-money path by comparing the intrinsic value against $Cont_M(\omega; t_i)$. The algorithm continues recursively until we have the optimal decision for each point. We then discount the cashflow from each exercise point and take the average to find the value of the American put option, thus

$$C_t^A = \frac{1}{n} \sum_{p=0}^{p=n} -e^{-r(\tau_p - t)}(K - S_{\tau_p}),$$

where n is the number of paths.

It is important to note that when optimal exercise is indicated at t_i the subsequent cashflows are altered to zero, as if exercise has taken place at t_i then by definition it cannot take place

[1]In a storage problem we cannot make this simplifying assumption as all the cashflows which can be zero, positive or negative, must be considered.

at times $t_i < t \leq T$. It is these altered cashflows which feed into the next iteration where $Cont_M(\omega; t_{i-1})$ is estimated.

19.3.2 LSMC Greeks

In addition to the above algorithm for calculating the price of an American option we also have the opportunity to obtain the delta of the option at minimal additional computational expense. Instead of perturbing the underlying by a small amount, which would require re-running the algorithm, we make use of the following general theory. Writing the value of the American option, with strike K, optimal exercise time τ and maturity T, as the usual expected discounted payoff we have

$$C_t^A = e^{-r(\tau-t)}\mathbb{E}_{\mathbb{Q}}[C(S_\tau, \tau; K, T)|\mathcal{F}_t];$$

the delta is of course the differential of this expression with respect to the current spot S_t. For a call, differentiating inside the expectation and letting $\mathcal{H}$ denote the Heaviside function gives us the expression for the delta of the option as

$$\frac{\partial C_t^A}{\partial S_t} = e^{-r(\tau-t)}\mathbb{E}_{\mathbb{Q}}\left[-\frac{S_\tau}{S_t}\mathcal{H}(S_\tau - K)\right], \tag{19.1}$$

which in terms of an LSMC simulation works as follows. We create a new LSMC matrix in which, for every point that is indicated as an optimal exercise, we enter -1 and all other points are zero. If this is our 'stopping rule' matrix then the delta of the option is the average of the discounted ratio S_τ/S_t across all the simulated paths p, as below:

$$\frac{\partial C_t^A}{\partial S_t} = \frac{1}{n}\sum_{p=0}^{p=n} -e^{-r(\tau_p-t)}\frac{S_{\tau_p}}{S_t}.$$

Furthermore, differentiating (19.1) again with respect to S_t gives us the following expression:

$$\frac{\partial^2 C_t^A}{\partial S_t^2} = e^{-r(\tau-t)}\mathbb{E}_{\mathbb{Q}}\left[\left(\frac{S_\tau}{S_t}\right)^2 \delta(S_\tau - K)\right], \tag{19.2}$$

here $\delta(\cdot)$ is the dirac delta function (the derivative of the Heaviside function) for the gamma of the option, which can again be calculated from a single run of the LSMC algorithm; for other recent approaches see Piterbarg (2005) and Kaniel *et al.* (2008).

19.3.3 Extending the LSMC to Price Gas Storage

Here we discuss how to use the LSMC approach in the valuation of gas storage; for other extensions and the pricing of gas interruptible contracts, see Cartea and Williams (2008). If, for example, the LSMC is used to price American-style options, the algorithm would require a matrix of two dimensions, time and number of simulated paths, where on each path an estimate of the optimal exercise time, a stopping rule for the option, is obtained. In application to multiple exercise problems we must create a third dimension, for swing options this is the number of exercise rights. We then proceed as follows, say we have a swing option with N upswing rights then we create a standard two-dimensional LSMC matrix corresponding to each $N, N-1, \ldots, 1$ rights remaining and working recursively, our initial step is to set the final cashflow conditions. These are different from the American option as we have multiple exercise opportunities and therefore if we have N rights remaining, the final N timesteps in the Nth matrix must be assumed to be exercise points; intuitively, if the holder of a swing option is three days away from maturity and has three exercise rights left he will try to exercise on every day. The continuation values are estimated and then we must make the optimal exercise decision, but we must compare values from across the third dimension of our LSMC matrix.

Say we have N swing rights remaining, if we want to decide whether to exercise one of our N rights at time t_i, then we compare the value of not exercising and continuing with N rights with the value of exercising and continuing with $N-1$ rights. Introducing $Cont_M^N(\omega; t_i)$ as the continuation value with N rights remaining at time t_i, and recalling that ω is a sample path, we exercise a swing option with N rights remaining at time t_i if

$$Cont_M^N(\omega; t_i) < I(\omega; t_i) + Cont_M^{N-1}(\omega; t_i),$$

where $I(\omega; t_i)$ is the intrinsic value of exercising. That is, if the value of exercising one of our swing rights, $I(\omega; t_i)$, in addition to the value of continuing with one less right, $Cont_M^{N-1}(\omega; t_i)$, exceeds the value of not exercising and continuing with the current number of rights, then we exercise one right.

The many possible constraints of swing options, penalty functions, maximum number of upswings and downswings, all add complexity to the problem and change the way the algorithm proceeds. For instance, if a penalty is payable when the maximum number of swings is not reached then the final cashflow may be negative as it may be optimal to pay the penalty rather than suffer a loss from exercising.

19.3.4 Toy Storage Model

To simplify both the development of the LSMC code and the understanding of the theory, we present as an illustration a toy model before proceeding to a model with full physical constraints. Our model is as follows, we take eight simulated gas day-ahead price paths (recall that these are denoted by ω) discretized into four daily timesteps (shown in Table 19.1). Our LSMC matrix will then have three dimensions: simulation path, time and inventory level of the storage facility. The inventory level is discretized into three levels: full, half full and empty (100%, 50%, 0%). At any one time we can only inject or withdraw one unit (prices shown are per unit too) and the maximum capacity of the storage is two units. We assume that the storage contract commences with the facility empty and at the end of the contract we return the storage facility empty.

At each timestep for each volume level and simulated path our decision is whether to buy and inject one unit of gas, take no action or withdraw and sell one unit of gas from the inventory we are holding in the facility. Our rational decision is to take whichever action corresponds to maximizing our expected cashflow at the current timestep. It can be shown that the maximization problem is simply the comparison of three options: inject the maximum amount, do nothing or withdraw the maximum amount. Hence we have the following expressions to

TABLE 19.1 Toy price paths

t_0	t_1	t_2	t_3
25.0	150.2	83.7	42.5
25.0	27.5	40.4	9.4
25.0	52.9	72.3	42.9
25.0	26.0	39.0	76.2
25.0	58.8	100.6	99.1
25.0	116.8	104.3	18.9
25.0	12.6	73.6	32.4
25.0	63.3	17.0	68.8

evaluate:

$$\text{Cashflow}_{inj} = -S_t + Cont_t(V + v_{inj}), \tag{19.3}$$
$$\text{Cashflow}_{null} = Cont_t(V), \tag{19.4}$$
$$\text{Cashflow}_{wdraw} = S_t + Cont_t(V - v_{wdraw}), \tag{19.5}$$

where S_t are the simulated prices at timestep t, V the inventory level of the storage facility, v_{inj} and v_{wdraw} the maximum daily allowable amount of injection and withdrawal respectively and $Cont_t(v)$ the expected value at time t of continuing at volume level v.

In (19.3) we show the cashflow from buying (injecting) plus the expected value of continuing at the next volume level up, (19.4) represents neither injecting nor withdrawing and continuing at the current volume level and (19.5) is the cashflow from selling (withdrawing) then continuing at the next volume level down. Our operational decision will then be determined by the optimal volume action, v which maximizes:

$$\max_v \left[\text{Cashflow}_{inj}, \text{Cashflow}_{null}, \text{Cashflow}_{wdraw}\right]. \tag{19.6}$$

As the LSMC algorithm is a backwards induction the first step is to define the values in the cashflow matrix on the last days of trading. At the 100% level we withdraw and sell the maximum amount possible, one unit per day, at the current spot price on the two days prior to the end of the contract period in order to return the facility empty. At 50% we withdraw and sell on the final day and at 0% inventory we take no action. In Table 19.2 we show the LSMC matrix after this first step.

Starting at t_2, for volume levels of 50% and 0%[2] we discount the cashflows of the final timestep t_3 back one step and regress them on a second-order polynomial function of the spot price at t_2. On substitution of the spot prices back into the resulting polynomial we obtain our continuation values $Cont_t(V)$. Table 19.3 gives an example of the regression at the 50% inventory level, $Cont_{t_2}(50\%)$. Y are the discounted cashflows from t_3 and X are the t_2 spot prices (as in Longstaff and Schwartz (2001) we assume a discount factor of 0.94176). The regression yields $Y = 85.330 - 1.545X + 0.012X^2$ and the continuation values are $\mathbb{E}[Y|X]$.

[2]As the cashflow is already defined for the 100% volume level at t_2.

TABLE 19.2 Final cashflow conditions for discretized volume levels

100%				50%				0%			
t_0	t_1	t_2	t_3	t_0	t_1	t_2	t_3	t_0	t_1	t_2	t_3
—	—	83.7	42.5	—	—	—	42.5	—	—	—	0.0
—	—	40.4	9.4	—	—	—	9.4	—	—	—	0.0
—	—	72.3	42.9	—	—	—	42.9	—	—	—	0.0
—	—	39.0	76.2	—	—	—	76.2	—	—	—	0.0
—	—	100.6	99.1	—	—	—	99.1	—	—	—	0.0
—	—	104.3	18.9	—	—	—	18.9	—	—	—	0.0
—	—	73.6	32.4	—	—	—	32.4	—	—	—	0.0
—	—	17.0	68.8	—	—	—	68.8	—	—	—	0.0

At time t_2 and 50% volume level the maximization becomes (on substituting (19.3), (19.4) and (19.5) into (19.6)):

$$\max_{v} \left[-S_{t_2} + Cont_{t_2}(100\%), Cont_{t_2}(50\%) + S_{t_2}, Cont_{t_2}(0\%) \right]. \tag{19.7}$$

In (19.8), (19.9) and (19.10) we take a specific numerical example for the second price path, we have

$$-S_{t_2} + Cont_{t_2}(100\%) = -40.4 + 42.5, \tag{19.8}$$

$$Cont_{t_2}(50\%) = 42.5, \tag{19.9}$$

$$S_{t_2} + Cont_{t_2}(0\%) = 40.4 - 0.0. \tag{19.10}$$

Hence the optimal decision is to take no action and continue at the 50% level. As we see in Table 19.4, we enter zero in the cashflow matrix.

As above, we execute a regression for each volume level and then the maximizations for each level; this gives us the optimal action for each point in our matrix. Translating these actions into cashflow we obtain the amended cashflow matrix, shown in Table 19.4, where at

TABLE 19.3 Continuation value regression at t_2 for 50% volume level

Y	t_2 prices X	Continuation at t_2 $\mathbb{E}[Y\|X]$
40.0	83.7	40.1
8.9	40.4	42.5
40.4	72.3	36.3
71.7	39.0	43.3
93.3	100.6	51.3
17.8	104.3	54.7
30.5	73.6	36.6
64.8	17.0	62.5

TABLE 19.4 t_2 cashflow for discretized volume levels

100%				50%				0%			
t_0	t_1	t_2	t_3	t_0	t_1	t_2	t_3	t_0	t_1	t_2	t_3
—	—	83.7	42.5	—	—	83.7	0.0	—	—	0.0	0.0
—	—	40.4	9.4	—	—	0.0	9.4	—	—	−40.4	9.4
—	—	72.3	42.9	—	—	72.3	0.0	—	—	0.0	0.0
—	—	39.0	76.2	—	—	0.0	76.2	—	—	−39.0	76.2
—	—	100.6	99.1	—	—	100.6	0.0	—	—	0.0	0.0
—	—	104.3	18.9	—	—	104.3	0.0	—	—	0.0	0.0
—	—	73.6	32.4	—	—	73.6	0.0	—	—	0.0	0.0
—	—	17.0	68.8	—	—	0.0	68.8	—	—	−17.0	68.8

t_2 a positive cashflow indicates that withdrawing (selling) is optimal, a negative value indicates that injecting (buying) is optimal and obviously zero cashflow indicates no action is taken.

Note that at the subsequent timestep t_3 the cashflow is altered to reflect the values from the volume level we have jumped to at the previous iteration, for example in the first price path at the 50% volume level the optimal behaviour is to sell at 83.76 at t_2 and reduce our volume level to 0%. Therefore, the cashflow at t_3 is altered to 0.0, which is the t_3 value at 0% from the previous iteration (Table 19.2).

Before we move to the next iteration we must recalculate our continuation values with the amended cashflows at the current iteration. In our regression, in the next iteration Y will be the sum of the t_2 and t_3 values discounted back to t_1 and X the spot price at t_1. We repeat this process until we reach t_0 and arrive at the final cashflow matrices for all volume levels. The value of the storage, when the contract commences with the facility empty, is then the average of the sum of discounted cashflows from each row shown in Table 19.5. Table 19.6 shows the inventory levels corresponding to this cashflow and Table 19.7, the operating rule for the storage facility.

Figures 19.3 and 19.4 represent the data in Tables 19.5 and 19.6, respectively. In Tables 19.6 and 19.7 and Figure 19.4 we see that on every path we must inject (buy) at the first

TABLE 19.5 t_0 cashflow for 0% volume level

0%			
t_0	t_1	t_2	t_3
−25.0	150.2	0.0	0.0
−25.0	−27.5	40.4	9.4
−25.0	0.0	72.3	0.0
−25.0	−26.0	39.0	76.2
−25.0	0.0	100.6	0.0
−25.0	116.8	0.0	0.0
−25.0	−12.6	73.6	32.4
−25.0	63.3	−17.0	68.8

TABLE 19.6 t_0 inventory level for 0% volume level

0%			
t_0	t_1	t_2	t_3
50%	0%	0%	0%
50%	100%	50%	0%
50%	50%	0%	0%
50%	100%	50%	0%
50%	50%	0%	0%
50%	0%	0%	0%
50%	100%	50%	0%
50%	0%	50%	0%

timestep, increasing the inventory level to 50% and that all paths obey the final condition of zero inventory.

19.3.5 Storage LSMC

A storage facility is much like a swing option with an up and down swing option for every day of the contract, for instance, on any day we may buy gas and inject it into storage or withdraw gas and sell it to the market. The injection and withdrawal limits are governed by 'ratchets', see Figure 19.5, which are volume dependent and unique to each type of storage facility. These occur as the inventory level increases and it becomes harder to inject more gas and as the inventory level decreases and it becomes harder to withdraw more gas.

Our action is also governed by minimum and maximum inventory levels that apply across the duration of the storage contract, and initial and final conditions which stipulate the inventory state in which the facility is obtained and must be returned. There may also be a penalty, dependent on the volume level and spot price for breaking any of these constraints. The type of facility may also dictate fixed injection and withdrawal costs which pay for the additional energy required to operate in injection or withdrawal mode. In addition to the

TABLE 19.7 t_0 operation rule for 0% volume level

0%			
t_0	t_1	t_2	t_3
inj	wdraw	—	—
inj	inj	wdraw	wdraw
inj	—	wdraw	—
inj	inj	wdraw	wdraw
inj	—	wdraw	—
inj	wdraw	—	—
inj	inj	wdraw	wdraw
inj	wdraw	inj	wdraw

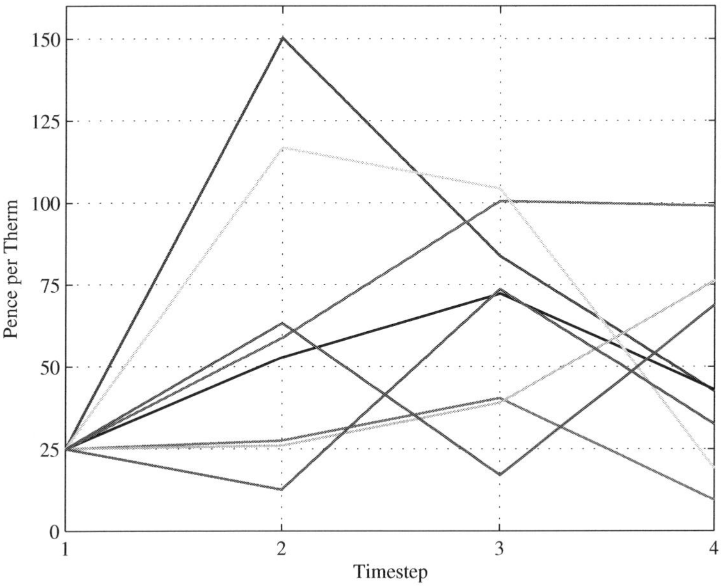

FIGURE 19.3 Toy model price paths. The eight simulated spot price paths on which we base the storage operation.

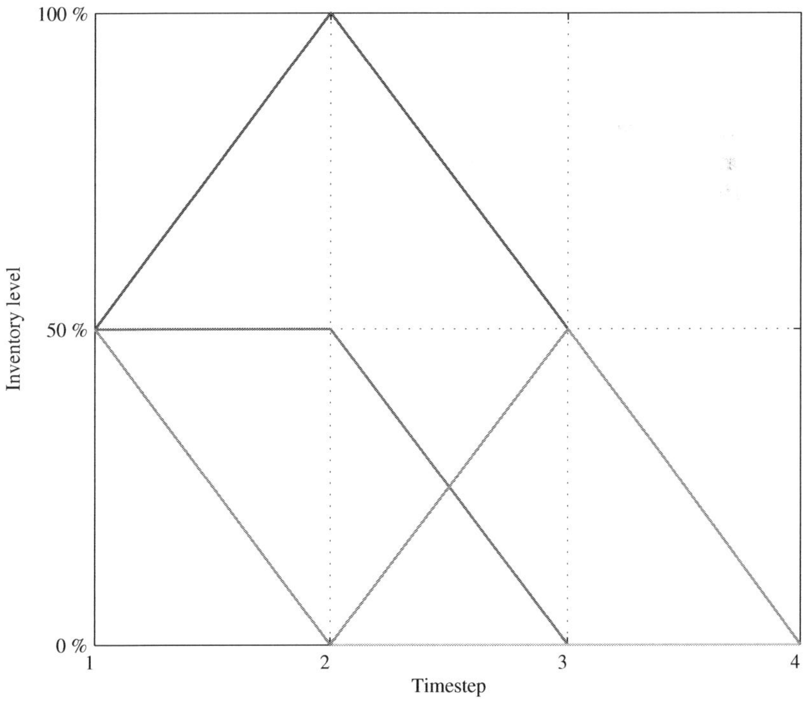

FIGURE 19.4 Toy model optimal inventory levels. Each colour corresponds to the spot price paths in Figure 19.3. Multiple paths follow the same trajectory and therefore are not visible.

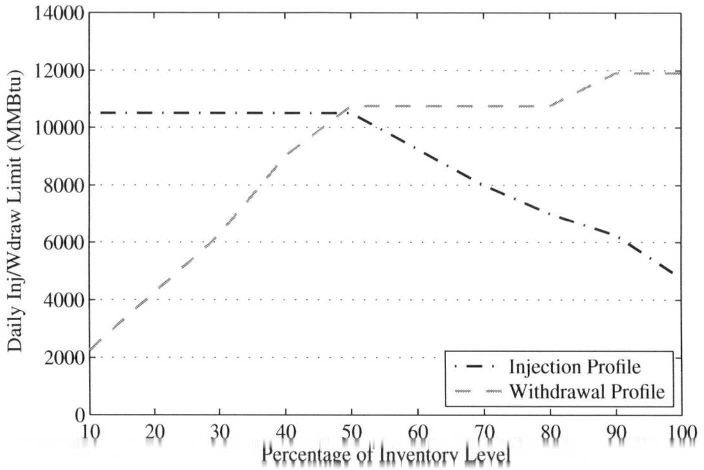

FIGURE 19.5 Example of physical ratchets, from Gray and Khandelwal (2004).

physical constraints we are also governed by market constraints such as a bid–ask spread, transaction costs and of course the discount rate.

To value a storage facility we again set up a three-dimensional LSMC matrix, with the third dimension being the volume of gas in the storage facility. In this way we can accommodate the above constraints by making the appropriate comparisons with continuation values across the different volume levels.

So, working recursively from maturity back to time zero, at inventory level V, we compare three possible actions: inject volume v_i and continue at inventory level $V + v_i$, take no action and continue at inventory level V, or withdraw volume v_w and continue at inventory level $V - v_w$. Obviously the physical constraints above – ratchets, maximum and minimum inventory levels and the initial and terminal constraints – define the allowed sets of v_i and v_w from which we can choose.

To summarize we value a storage facility subject to the following constraints:

- V_{max}, the maximum capacity of the storage facility.
- V_i, the inventory level at which the storage contract is initiated.
- V_f, the inventory level at which the storage contract must be returned at the end of the contract.
- $v_{inj}(V)$ and $v_{wdraw}(V)$, the ratchets (i.e., the inventory-level-dependent injection and withdrawal rates); simulated as represented in Figure 19.6.
- C_{inj} and C_{wdraw}, fixed injection and withdrawal costs in pence per therm.
- BA, C_{trans} and r, the market constraints, bid–ask spread, transaction costs and the discount rate respectively.

19.3.6 Swing Options

If we allow N withdrawals which in total are equal to the full volume of the facility, and no injections, then we simulate a swing option with N downswing rights (put rights). Specific

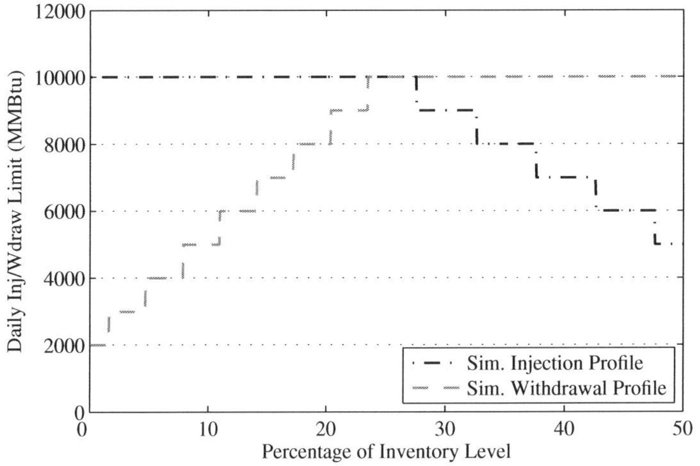

FIGURE 19.6 Simulated ratchets, volume-dependent injection and withdrawal profiles.

numerical comparison with the results from table 3.1 in Ibáñez (2004) are given in Table 19.8, where we have a strike price of 40 and a risk-free rate of 0.0488, again under a standard log-normal process. We see a close match to the swing values for in- and at-the-money values of S but some divergence in the results for out-of-the-money values of S and higher numbers of swing rights. This could be a result of only simulating at 12 exercise points.

19.3.7 Closed-Form Storage Solution

When the underlying spot price process is the following single-factor model from Weston (2004).

$$\frac{\mathrm{d}S_t}{S_t} = \ln\left(\frac{\bar{S}}{S}\right)\mathrm{d}t + \sigma \mathrm{d}W_t,$$

TABLE 19.8 Percentage difference between LSMC (12 exercise points and 100,000 simulations, 50,000 antithetic) values and those from Ibáñez (2004) for a swing put option with N rights

S	σ	T	$N=1$	$N=2$	$N=3$	$N=4$	$N=5$	$N=6$
35	0.25	0.25	0.215	0.385	0.334	0.249	0.287	0.270
35	0.50	0.25	0.142	0.006	0.200	0.310	0.401	0.505
40	0.25	0.25	−0.660	−0.428	0.501	0.464	0.543	0.918
40	0.50	0.25	−0.287	0.055	−0.104	0.408	0.648	0.855
45	0.25	0.25	−1.314	0.518	1.267	1.627	2.598	3.417
45	0.50	0.25	−0.605	1.105	2.070	1.175	0.770	2.651

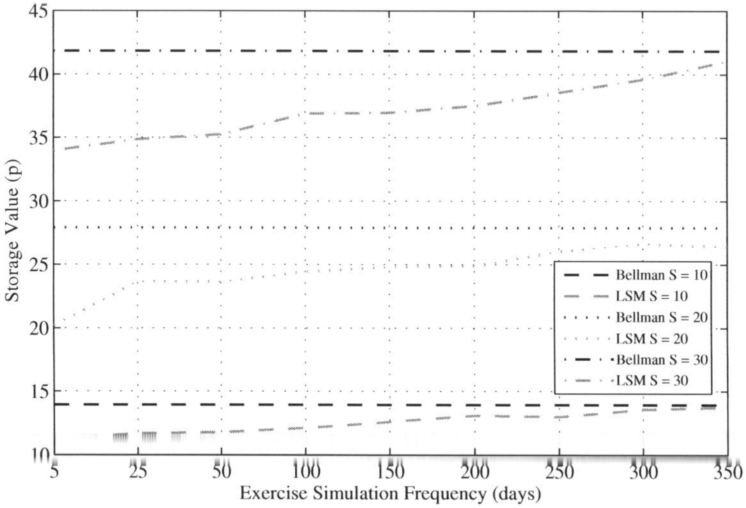

FIGURE 19.7 LSMC calculation of storage value with 1000 simulated paths compared with closed-form Bellman equation for a range of simulated exercise frequencies and spot prices.

we have the following closed-form Bellman equation for a storage problem defined at three timesteps:

$$V_1(x, S) = \max_{a_1} \left[\left(\beta\bar{S} - S \right) a_1 \right] + \beta\bar{S} \left(x - x_{min} \right) \\ + \beta\bar{S}(x_{max} - x_{min}) \left(\beta N\left(\frac{\ln \beta}{\sigma} + \frac{\sigma}{2} \right) - N\left(\frac{\ln \beta}{\sigma} - \frac{\sigma}{2} \right) \right), \qquad (19.11)$$

where $\bar{S}$ and σ are the mean and volatility of the underlying respectively, S is the initial underlying value, β is a discount factor suitable for the system being modelled and N the number of timesteps. x_{max} and x_{min} are the maximum and minimum storage limits and a_1 is the amount we may add or subtract from the initial amount in storage, x. A simplifying assumption in the derivation of this closed-form solution is that $x_{min} - x > a_{min}$ and $x_{max} - x < a_{max}$; this in effect allows us to sell all the gas in storage on the last timestep or indeed to fill the storage facility completely in any one single timestep.

We set the underlying of our LSMC algorithm to (19.11) and, taking $\beta = 1$ (equivalent to a risk-free discount rate of zero), we present a comparison of the values from (19.11), the Bellman equation against those from the LSMC algorithm with a range of exercise frequencies and values of S and $\bar{S}$. In Figure 19.7 we see convergence towards the closed-form value for increased exercise frequency.

19.3.8 Monte Carlo Convergence

In Figure 19.8 we show that as we increase the number of sample paths simulated in the LSMC algorithm, from 10 to 10^5, the calculated value of an American put option converges to the value calculated by finite difference from Longstaff and Schwartz (2001). The upper

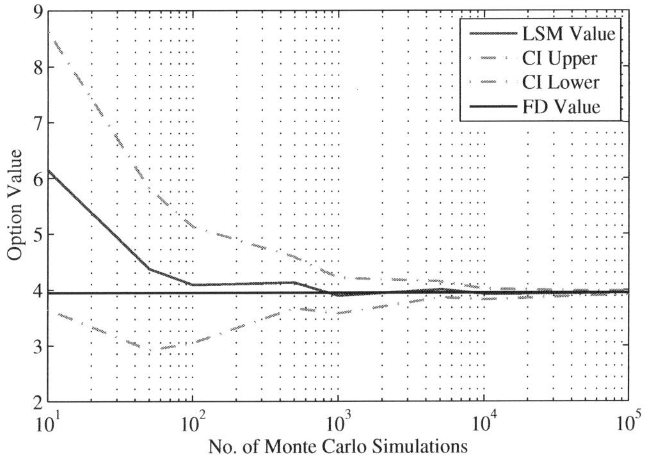

FIGURE 19.8 LSMC calculation of American put option with finite difference calculated value of 3.948.

and lower bounds are a 95% confidence interval, which is 1.6% of the option value with 10^5 sample paths.

Early exercise options can be exercised on any day prior to maturity and as such it would be intuitive to think that we must discretize the time dimension in our LSMC matrix to at least represent this daily frequency. In the case of storage it is physically possible to exercise the right to inject or withdraw every day of the contract and therefore it would seem necessary to simulate every day to achieve the correct valuation.

In Figure 19.9 we show the LSMC calculated value of an American option for a range of simulated exercise opportunity frequencies, from monthly to daily, and in Figure 19.10 a

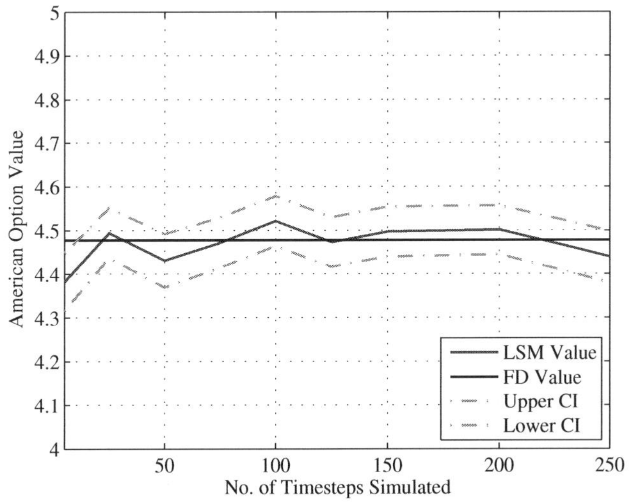

FIGURE 19.9 LSMC calculation of American put option, maturity 1 year, with FD value 4.478.

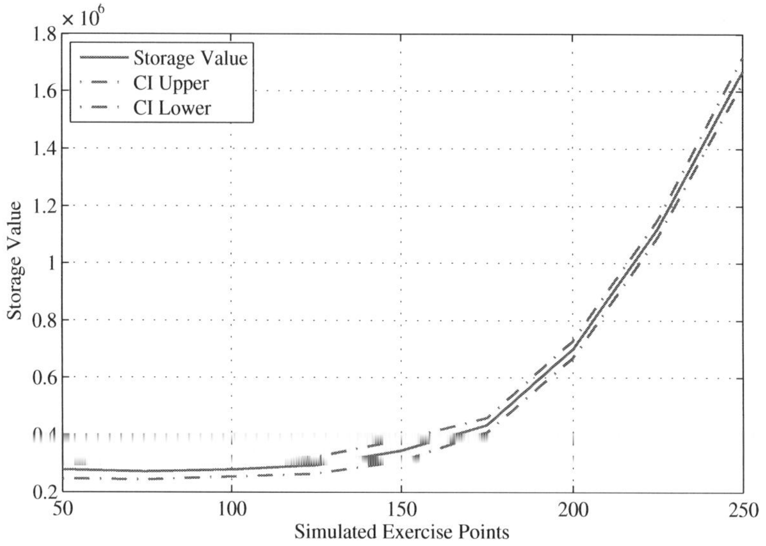

FIGURE 19.10 LSMC value of 1 Bcf of storage for a range of simulated exercise frequencies and contract maturity 1 year.

similar comparison for a storage value simulation. For the American case we see that the value converges to the finite difference value at a weekly frequency (the frequency used in Longstaff and Schwartz (2001)), and moreover further increases in frequency do not reduce the size of the confidence interval or improve the convergence. This is due to the fact that the American option has only one exercise opportunity.

In the case of storage this convergence does not emerge and the value increases with the frequency; we note that the size of the confidence interval, with only 100 simulated paths, is less than 5% of the storage value, and does not alter with increased frequencies. Both these results are to be expected as we require a simulation of every day to fully value the flexibility of the facility and the strong mean reversion of the simulated underlying reduces the variance across multiple simulations.

19.3.9 Simulated Storage Operations

In this section we present some basic tests of the performance of the LSMC algorithm in determining the optimal operation of a storage facility with various simplistic underlying price paths. Our storage facility has a total capacity of 1 Bcf, approximately equivalent to 1×10^6 MMBtu, with fixed maximum daily injection and withdrawal rates of 10,000 MMBtu. The facility is received empty and must be returned empty. The contract duration is 1 year and the risk-free rate is 6%.

In Figures 19.11, 19.12 and 19.13 we represent the gas price as a stepped function and see that the algorithm replicates a bang-bang operation policy, maximizing the value of the storage, under the volumetric constraints and the initial and terminal conditions. In Figure 19.11 we also show the inventory path under simulated ratchets and we see that they require us to start injecting earlier and to withdraw for longer, decreasing the amount

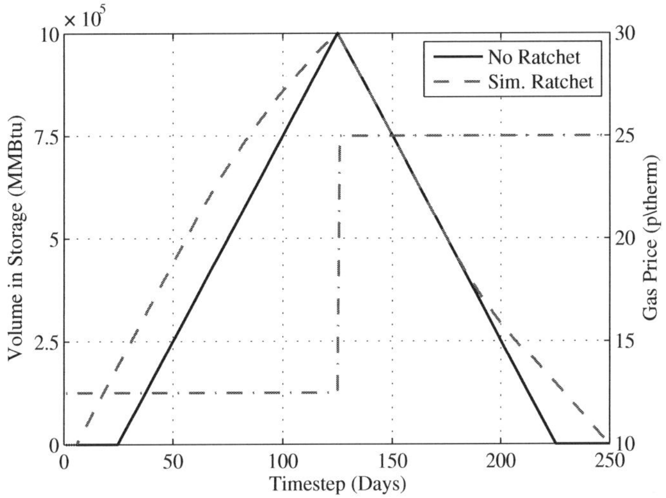

FIGURE 19.11 Storage operation with and without ratchets and with step function gas price (dashed line).

by which negative cashflows from the injection phase are discounted and increasing the discount on the positive cashflows from the withdrawal phase, hence lowering the value of the storage.

If we now simulate the price path as mean reversion to a constant drift then we obtain the results in Figures 19.14 and 19.15 respectively for positive and negative drifts. In the case of a positive drift the storage operation is similar to the bang-bang policies but further refinement is seen in small adjustments in the volume level to take advantage of the volatility of the underlying. With negative drift we see a rapid cycling of the gas in storage as we

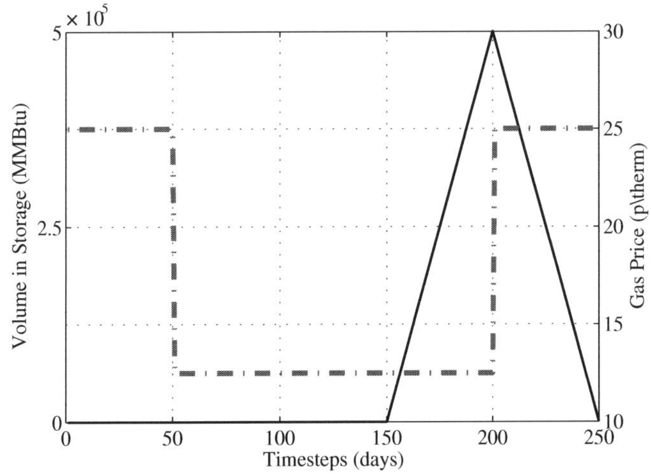

FIGURE 19.12 Storage operation with double step function gas price (dashed line).

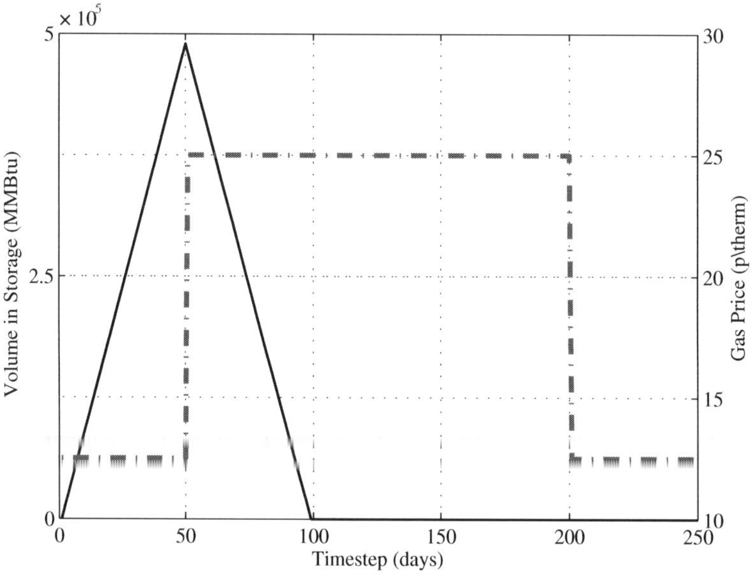

FIGURE 19.13 Storage operation with double step function gas price (dashed line).

cannot benefit from the negative drift by selling first as we commence at zero inventory level.

Finally, in Figure 19.16 we introduce a seasonal element to the underlying, and observe that the optimal policy is as an overall calendar spread (buy summer, sell winter) with smaller daily adjustments to trade the volatility.

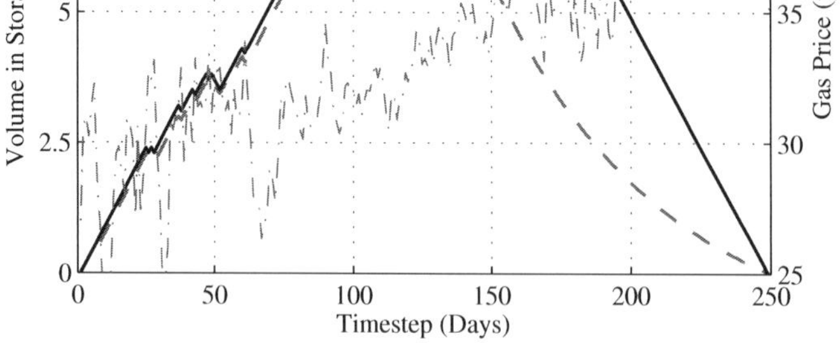

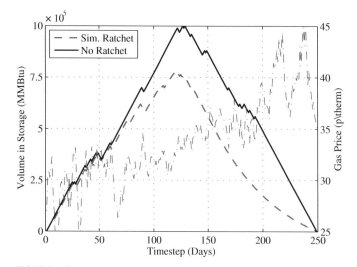

FIGURE 19.14 Storage operation with and without ratchets with gas price mean reverting to a positive drift (dashed line).

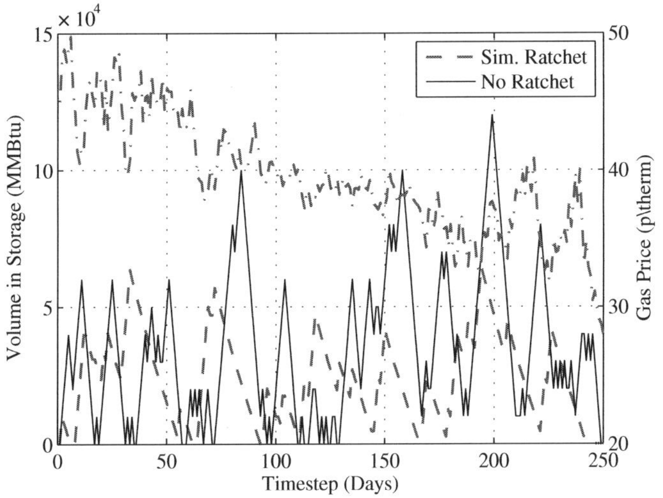

FIGURE 19.15 Storage operation with and without ratchets with gas price mean reverting to a negative drift (dashed line).

19.3.10 Storage Value

19.3.10.1 Typical Storage Contract We value a contract on a storage capacity of 1 million therms with daily injection and withdrawal rates of 100,000 therms, we receive and must return the facility empty. We value a contract duration of 1 year, with a daily trading frequency and zero interest rates, across a range of contract start dates from 1 January to 30 June 2008. In Figure 19.17 we show the intrinsic value and the premium with and without

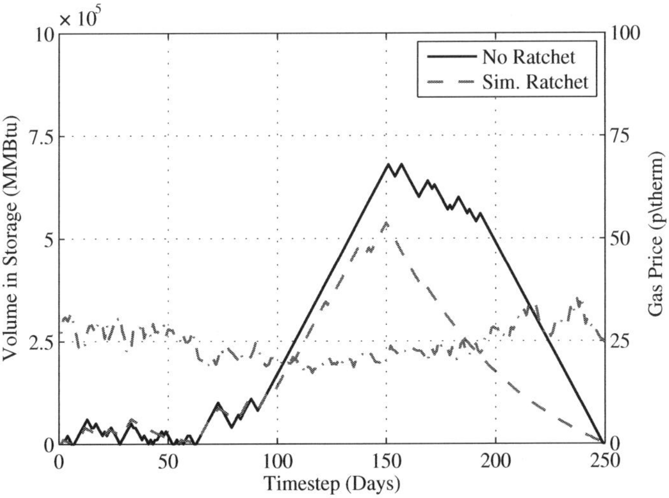

FIGURE 19.16 Storage operation with and without ratchets with gas price mean reverting to a deterministic seasonality (dashed line).

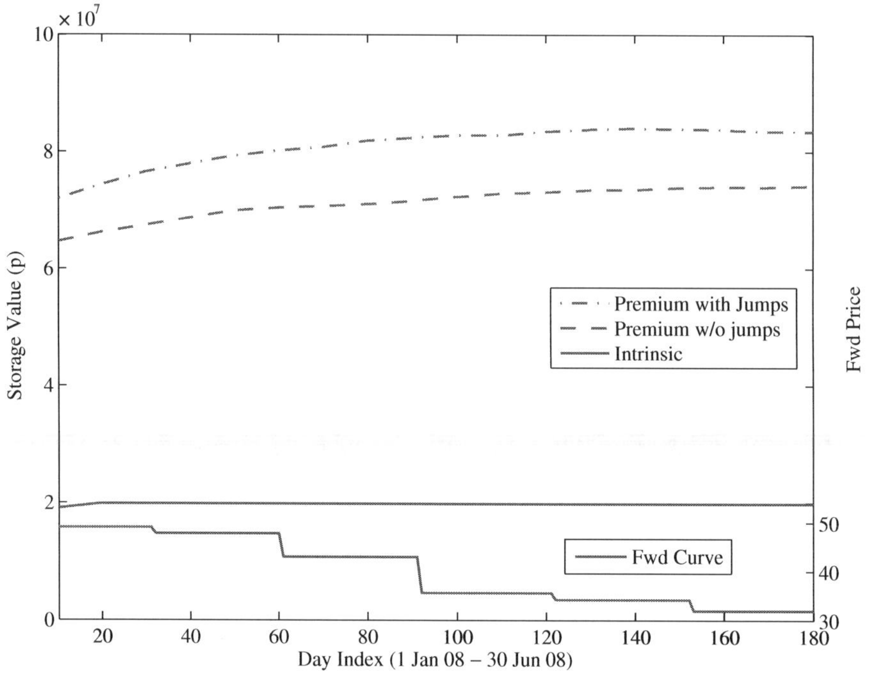

FIGURE 19.17 Storage valuation in pence, intrinsic and extrinsic with and without jumps, LSMC valuation with 1000 paths.

jumps added to the price process; we also show the futures curve to which the spot price was calibrated.

In Figure 19.17 we see that the most basic indicator of the storage value, the intrinsic value, is constant across the contract start dates. The intrinsic value is the optimal combination of futures contracts given a static view of the futures curve on a particular date, and subject to the physical constraints of the storage facility. As the gas futures curve is dominated by a repeating seasonal pattern, the relative difference in prices across the year is constant as we change the start date of our storage contract. This results in a constant intrinsic value regardless of any contango or backwardation inherent in the market.

In the range of winter start dates, where we see a higher spot price, the premia (with and without jumps) are lower than spring and summer start dates. When we start a storage contract with zero inventory our first action can only be to inject gas. If we start the contract in winter we wait until the low summer prices to fully fill our facility, then selling the following winter. If, in contrast, we start a contract in the summer then the situation is reversed and we immediately fill our storage and sell the following winter. Throughout the duration of both these cases we trade not only the overall calendar spread but the daily volatility as well. The calendar spread is constant regardless of when the contract starts as it depends only on the relative difference of summer and winter prices. This implies that the difference in storage premia across the year must arise from the way in which the daily volatility is traded, specifically from the increased flexibility of having more gas at an earlier date in the case of a summer start contract.

In respect of the jumps, our path simulation with jumps gives spot prices in the range of 150–200 pence per therm, and approximately 7 jumps per year. This is in comparison with normal prices in the range of 7–100 pence per therm. With this comparison in mind we see that the majority of the extrinsic value comes from the volatility of the price process rather than the jumps, as the extrinsic value shows an increase of 2.5×10^7 over the intrinsic value, whereas the extrinsic value with jumps shows only a further 1×10^7 increase.

REFERENCES

Boogert, A. and de Jong, C. (2008) Gas storage valuation using a Monte Carlo method, *The Journal of Derivatives*, **15**(3), 81–98.

Carmona, R. and Ludkovski, M. (2007) Gas storage and supply guarantees: An optimal switching approach, working Paper.

Cartea, Á. and Williams, T. (2008) UK gas markets: The market price of risk and applications to multiple interruptible supply contracts, *Energy Economics*, **30**(3), 829–846.

Fusai, G. and Roncoroni, A. (2008) *Implementing Models in Quantitative Finance: Methods and Cases*, Springer-Verlag, Berlin.

Gray, J. and Khandelwal, P. (2004) Towards a realistic gas storage model, *Commodities Now*, pp. 1–5.

Ibáñez, A. (2004) Valuation by simulation of contingent claims with multiple early exercise opportunities, *Mathematical Finance*, **14**(2), 223–248.

Jackson, K.R., Jaimungal, S. and Surkov, V. (2007) Fourier space timestepping for option pricing with Levy models, *Journal of Computational Finance*, **12**(2), 1–29.

Jaimungal, S. and Surkov, V. (2011) Lévy-based cross-commodity models and derivative valuation, *SIAM Journal on Financial Mathematics*, **2**(1), 464–487.

Kaniel, R., Tompaidis, S. and Zemlianov, A. (2008) Efficient computation of hedging parameters for discretely exercisable options, *Operations Research*, **56**(4), 811–826.

Longstaff, F.A. and Schwartz, E.S. (2001) Valuing American options by simulation: A simple least-squares approach, *The Review of Financial Studies*, **14**(1), 113–147.

Manoliu, M. (2004) Storage options valuation using multilevel trees and calendar spreads, *International Journal of Theoretical and Applied Finance*, **7**(4), 425–464.

Pindyck, R. (2001) The dynamics of commodity spot and futures markets: A primer, *Energy Journal*, **22**(3), 1–29.

Piterbarg, V.V. (2005) Pricing and hedging callable LIBOR exotics in forward LIBOR models, *The Journal of Computational Finance*, **8**(2), 65–117.

Roncoroni, A. (2010) Commodity price models, *Encyclopedia of Quantitative Finance*, pp. 298–303.

Stentoft, L. (2004) Assessing the least squares Monte-Carlo approach to American option valuation, *Review of Derivatives Research*, **7**(2), 129–168.

Weston, T. (2004) *Real Options and Energy Management: Using Options Methodology to Enhance Capital Budgeting Decisions*, Risk Books, London.

CHAPTER 20

Commodity-Linked Arbitrage Strategies and Portfolio Management

Viviana Fanelli

The aim of an investor or a speculator who operates in the markets is to select and apply successful investment strategies that enable profit to be made, more or less in line with his risk profile. An individual could trade in specific assets, for example when physical assets for industrial processes are needed or for hedging or simply for speculation, or he could select and manage a portfolio of assets again for hedging or simply for broad-based, diversified investing. Recently there has been growing interest in commodity markets; on the one hand because they offer arbitrage opportunities that can be exploited using appropriate trading rules, while on the other hand because, given their intrinsic risk–return characteristics, commodities provide diversification of risk for traditional portfolios.

This chapter is divided into two parts. In the first part, a detailed discussion of commodity-linked arbitrage strategy is carried out. First, the efficient market hypothesis theory is illustrated, as formulated by Fama (1970) and according to later reinterpretations. Some of the assumptions underlying the efficient market hypothesis do not hold in commodity markets that reveal temporary inefficiencies. These inefficiencies give rise to arbitrage opportunities that can be identified through statistical methods, some of which are presented in this chapter. Several trading techniques are reviewed, from the most basic and classic strategies defined within the *technical analysis* class, to the more modern strategies defined within the *statistical arbitrage* class. Finally, using commodity market data empirical analyses have been carried out to implement trading strategies and verify their reliability.

The second part of the chapter deals with the description of commodity characteristics and with portfolio optimization. First, commodities are classified by asset type and the main commodity investment classes are presented. Then, the characteristics of commodity futures returns and risk premiums are discussed. Finally, through a portfolio risk–return analysis it is shown how commodities represent a good diversifier of portfolio risk and possible risk measures are described that can be used in portfolio optimization with commodities.

Handbook of Multi-Commodity Markets and Products: Structuring, Trading and Risk Management. Edited by Andrea Roncoroni, Gianluca Fusai and Mark Cummins.

20.1 COMMODITY-LINKED ARBITRAGE STRATEGIES

20.1.1 The Efficient Market Hypothesis

Extensive literature is devoted to the study of the so-called efficient market hypothesis, with results that sometimes support the hypothesis, while others reject it. According to a formulation of Fama (1970), a market is efficient if prices always fully reflect all available information. His study focuses on the capital market role and market mechanisms and his conclusions are based on extensive analysis and discussion of the theoretical and empirical literature of the previous 25 years regarding the efficiency of the market. Fama distinguishes three distinct categories of market efficiency, which are verified on the basis of empirical tests concerning the adjustment of stock prices to information available on the market: weak form efficiency, semi-strong form efficiency and strong form efficiency. There is weak form efficiency if the set of information available to investors contains only historical prices. Efficiency is in semi-strong form if the set also includes all information publicly available. Efficiency is in strong form if the set also includes private information to which only certain types of investors have access. Fama himself acknowledges that this latest version of efficiency is definitely false because it assumes that information costs and trading costs are zero, so it is regarded as a benchmark in determining the level of costs. He also argues that the hypothesis of market efficiency is tested jointly as equilibrium model and model of asset pricing. That is, the pricing model defines the appropriate way in which information is reflected in the price, so any anomalies in the behaviour of returns may be due either to a market failure or to a bad market equilibrium model. In particular, Fama (1970) defines the random walk model for the determination of expected returns as an extension of the fair game efficient markets model. In this way, he establishes the price process characteristics and the equilibrium conditions that must be tested for market efficiency.

LeRoy (1989) makes a clear analysis on the definition of efficient markets and supports the concept that market efficiency can be deduced from the mechanisms of equilibrium price formation in competitive markets in which agents are rational individuals. In particular, operators have access to all available information and the process of equilibrium price formation does not give rise to any possible applications of profitable trading strategies. In mathematical terms, prices follow martingales. Some empirical evidence, however, reveals that investors do not always behave rationally, reacting in the same manner to new information. They overreact at times, pushing prices away from their fair market value, so that only by taking opposite positions to the previous negotiations can equilibrium be restored. This phenomenon gives rise to the so-called reversals, possible market inefficiencies, investigated by Niederhoffer and Osborne (1966).

Fama (1970) defends the validity of the efficient market hypothesis and suggests that even when price changes are not serially independent, but there is a convincing economic explanation of this dependence, then the market is still efficient. Fama (1976) then proposes a new definition of capital market efficiency. The conditions that must be verified for efficiency are twofold: all information relevant to the determination of prices is known and there are rational expectations, namely agents know the structure of the model and the values of the parameters.

A critical review of the efficient market hypothesis is made by Fama (1991). He changes the categories in which he had classified the tests for market efficiency in 1970. Instead of weak form tests, he defines tests for return predictability, which include not only tests about the ability to forecast the past return, taking into account the dividend yield and interest rates, but also about the cross-sectional predictability of returns, consisting of the analysis of the asset pricing model used and its anomalies. He substitutes the semi-strong form tests with event studies and the strong form tests with tests for private information.

20.1.2 Risk Arbitrage Opportunities in Commodity Markets

As pointed out in the previous section, according to the efficient market hypothesis, a market is efficient if prices incorporate all currently available information. The assumptions underlying the efficient market hypothesis are no transaction costs, costless information, all market participants as rational individuals, and all implications for both current prices and distributions of future prices generally accepted by all market participants, that is rational expectations of the ex-post rational prices exist. In a perfectly efficient market no profitable trading strategies can be applied because traders could never earn abnormal returns.

Obviously the assumptions that transaction and information costs are equal to zero are unrealistic in actual markets and in order to preserve market efficiency these costs should be absorbed by possible extra returns so that equilibrium prices would always be guaranteed. Regarding commodity markets, some empirical evidence from the literature of temporary market inefficiency is discussed and results from profitable trading rule implementations are shown to offer arbitrageurs and hedgers useful and practical investment tools.

In the following, some examples from the literature of historical market inefficiencies are shown: two in the agricultural sector, two in the metal sector, three in the energy sector and the last example refers to an arbitrage opportunity existing between the oil futures market and the shipping freight market.

Regarding the agricultural sector, possible arbitrage opportunities exist between the soybean futures market and related futures markets. Johnson *et al.* (1991) test market inefficiency of the soy complex futures price spread, that is a processing (crushing) spread of soybean, soyoil and soymeal, using a combination of profit margin rules. In particular, if positive profit margins, that is gross crushing margins exceed processing costs, are implied by soy complex futures prices, then a trader takes a normal soybean crush position, that is long soybean, short soymeal and short soyoil. This strategy is consistent with market mechanisms. In fact, positive profit margins are an incentive for the crusher to crush soybean so that supplies of meal and oil and their prices increase in relation to soybean supply and price, resulting in a corresponding change in the soy complex spread. Furthermore, the gross crushing margin moves towards crushing costs, alternatively long-run arbitrage occurs. The authors find that only nearby soy complex futures spreads trading guarantees an efficient market, because at trade lengths longer than 5.5 months, arbitrage opportunities and profitable trading exist. Liu (2005) examines the relations among the hog, corn and soybean futures markets in order to find any market inefficiency. He considers the so-called hog spread obtained by taking a short position on hog futures and long positions on corn and soybean futures. He studies the cointegration relation among the three futures prices by applying the Johansen (1988, 1991) methodologies and accounting for seasonality and time trends and he finds that the three series are cointegrated, indicating the presence of a mean-reverting tendency to a long-run equilibrium for the hog spread. Then the author applies trading simulations that generate significant profits net of transaction costs, suggesting that some inefficiencies exist in the three futures markets because prices, that should reflect all available information and expectations, do not capture the mean-reverting tendency, therefore providing arbitrage opportunities.

With regard to the metal sector, in the 1980s Ma and Soenen (1988) find arbitrage opportunities existing between gold and silver futures markets. In fact they analyse the parity relationship between silver and gold spot prices and verify that it persists also on futures markets. Profitable trading opportunities derive from temporary disparities and they are more favourable in future markets than spot markets as the transaction costs are more moderate. Kenourgios and Samitas (2004) investigate the hypothesis of market efficiency for the copper futures market and the hypothesis that futures prices are unbiased estimators of future spot prices using cointegration and error correction models. They find that for the period considered, January 1989–April 2000, the copper futures market is not efficient in both the short and long run and futures prices are not unbiased estimates of future spot prices.

Regarding the energy sector, the historical empirical evidence of arbitrage opportunities in petroleum futures markets is considered. Girma and Paulson (1999) use cointegration theory to investigate the economic and statistical relationship among crude oil, unleaded gasoline and heating oil futures prices. They find that price time series are cointegrated and so the crack spreads 3:2:1, 1:1:0 and 1:0:1 converge to a long run equilibrium. Arbitrage opportunities derive from temporary mispricing between crude oil and its refined products and they are identified and exploited to profit by applying the trading rule 5-day and 10-day moving averages. Poitras and Teoh (2003) design a filter-based day trading strategy to individuate trading signals for the crack spread. In particular, they suggest that because the opening price for the crude oil futures market is five minutes earlier than the opening time for the end-product futures markets, the opening price of crude oil is driven by factors specific to that individual oil complex component. So, crack spread values can exhibit significant overnight price reversal and then the open-to-close reversal is exploited during the day to profit. Asche *et al.* (2003) study the relationships between crude oil and its refined products, applying the multivariate cointegration methodology according to Johansen (1988). They also find that there exists a long-run relationship between the prices of crude oil and end products, except between prices of crude oil and heavy oil. Consequently, a long-run relationship exists among refined products themselves. Furthermore, they point out that crude oil is a weak exogenous variable, meaning that the price of crude oil determines the price of its refined products, but it is not true the other way round. Even from this study it can be deduced that some market inefficiencies in relative pricing can be exploited to realize arbitrage profits.

Finally, the relationship among tanker freight rates, physical crude oil (UK Brent and Nigerian Bonny) and crude oil futures (WTI) is explored by Alizadeh and Nomikos (2004). The cost-of-carry relation links the physical (spot) price with the WTI futures price through the cost of transportation, the tanker freight rate, that, if the market is efficient, should explain the physical crude and WTI futures price differentials. Actually they use a vector error correction model and find that there exists a long-run relationship only between freight rates and oil prices, and not between freight rates and physical–financial differentials. This results in the existence of arbitrage opportunities often due to regional supply, demand imbalance, regulatory changes and some market distortions. They simulate profitable trading strategies to exploit these arbitrage opportunities.

According to the literature, the most common methodology used to investigate the existence of arbitrage opportunities on commodity markets is based on cointegration techniques. Cointegration is used to analyse the long-run equilibrium among futures prices. If price time series are cointegrated and have stationary cointegrating regression residuals, the relative prices are stationary as well and revert to a 'normal' level. The deviations from the long-run equilibrium or normal level or average can be considered as mispricings and they can be exploited as arbitrage opportunities. In fact, an arbitrageur at a favourable point of time can invest in the mispricing and reverse his position when, according to the mispricing property of stationarity, its dynamics mean-revert. Two or more price time series that are individually integrated to the same order of integration and are nonstationary at the price level are cointegrated if there exists a linear combination of a lower order. The most popular method of testing cointegration is the cointegration regression introduced by Granger (1983). The regression coefficients are estimated by the ordinary least-squares method, but in order for the time series to be cointegrated, the regression residual must be stationary. Assume that P_t^0 is the target time series that is regressed upon a set of time series, called the cointegrating series, $P_t^1, P_t^2, \ldots, P_t^n$, such that

$$P_t^0 = \beta_0 + \beta_1 P_t^1 + \beta_2 P_t^2 + \ldots + \beta_n P_t^n + \epsilon_t$$

where ϵ_t are the regression residuals and β_i with $i = 0, 1, \ldots, n$ are the regression coefficients. The stationarity of the time series can be checked by the Dickey–Fuller test (DF) and the augmented Dickey–Fuller test (ADF) that look for unit roots in the price time series. In order to define an arbitrage strategy with the mispricing time series, investors have to know if the time series is stationary, namely if it deviates from the particular nonstationary dynamics of the random walk. A theoretical problem about the low power of classical statistical tests like DF and ADF to clearly identify the behaviour of the time series dynamics is well known in the econometrics field. There is a more robust test of the *variance ratio* to verify if the dynamics of the time series deviate from the random walk behaviour. This is used by Burgess (1999) in his study investigating the statistical arbitrage opportunities in stock markets. The strength of the variance ratio test is that its application to time series over time gives the possibility of finding out if the dynamics of the time series is trending or mean-reverting. The variance ratio statistic is defined as the normalized ratio of the long-term variance calculated over a period τ to single-period variance. If the variance ratio statistic is calculated over the price time series, the variance ratio function is automatically obtained. Values of variance ratio bigger than one for any τ suggest that the price series is positively serially correlated and has a trending behaviour; meanwhile, values of variance ratio less than one for any τ suggest that the price series is negatively serially correlated and has a mean-reverting behaviour.

The variance ratio test is applied here to study the relationship existing between the Brent futures first month traded at the Intercontinental Exchange (ICE – formerly the International Petroleum Exchange (IPE)) in London and the prices of some related distillates:[1] the 'Rotterdam Premium Gasoline unleaded Fob Cargoes' (PUR) quote by Platt's as a light distillate, the gas oil future first month traded on ICE as a middle distillate product and finally the North West Europe (NWE) 'Low Sulphur Fuel Oil cargoes'(LSFO), the NWE 'High Sulphur Fuel Oil Barger' (HSFO) and the NWE 'Cts180 Bunker Fuel Oil' as heavy distillate products. A portfolio is considered that is characterized by the virtual refinery model, based on the production relation between the crude, that is the input for the refinery and the products that represent the output. The considered data set is formed by the time series that span from 25/10/2000 to 19/10/2009, all prices quoted weekly in US dollars per barrel (bbl).[2] The Brent futures price is regressed on the refined product prices and the resulting cointegration

[1]This analysis is carried out with the collaboration of Andrea Bucca, Manager, Corporate Risk Management, Glencore International Ltd, London.

[2]Gretl and Excel software were used for the analysis.

TABLE 20.1 Cointegration regression for Brent and distillates

Variable	Coefficient	Std Error	*t*-Statistic	Probability
Coefficient	−0.000995663	0.15801813	−0.006300942	0.994975371
LSFO	−0.143760525	0.035937055	−4.000342461	7.38121E-05
HSFO	1.109299632	0.08714746	12.72899557	5.80452E-32
Cst180	−0.673658848	0.073211454	−9.201549972	1.28414E-18
PUR	0.204821928	0.011393414	17.97722201	5.48275E-55
Gas Oil	0.477137322	0.011549116	41.31375233	4.463E-156

regression coefficients are presented in Table 20.1. Figure 20.1 displays the variance ratio (VR) profile obtained for the residuals, which are called mispricings. It can be observed that all VR values are less than one and the VR function is decreasing. Therefore, the deviation of the mispricing process from a random walk is strong and the mispricing clearly follows a mean-reverting process, evidencing the presence of predictability that can be used to define profitable trading strategies.

20.1.3 Basic Quantitative Trading Strategies

The arbitrage opportunities that arise on commodity markets are of notable interest to investors and speculators that study and develop quantitative methods and trading strategies. The basic quantitative trading strategies referred to here come from the field of technical analysis. Technical analysis is a discipline that aims to interpret the movements of the market in order to profit from trading assets. It emerged more than 100 years ago to meet the demand for an analytical tool for trading, which set aside the fundamental aspects of the quoted assets.

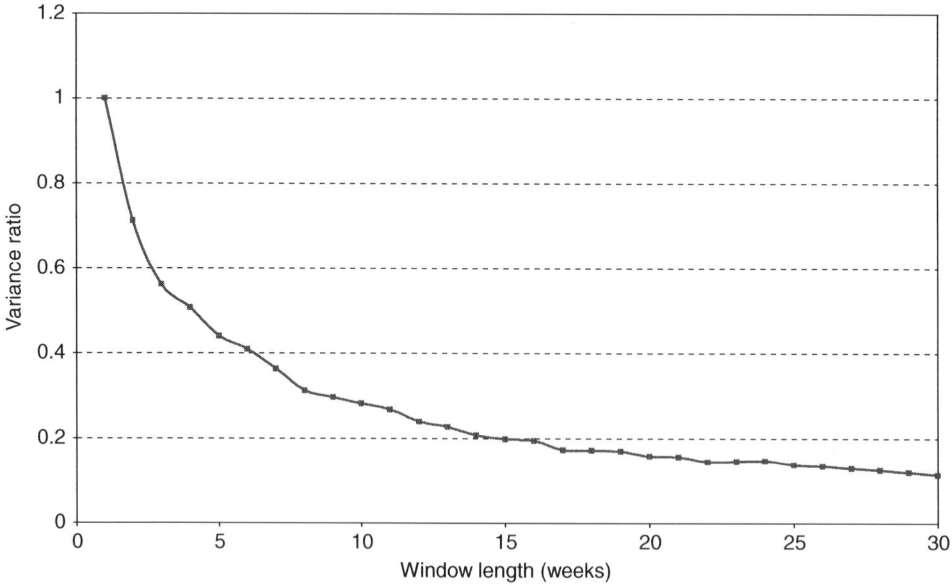

FIGURE 20.1 Variance ratio function

The major base assumption is that all relevant information is not publicly available in time to operate successfully on the market. Prices are observed systematically to understand the dynamics of the market, and increases and decreases in prices are no longer analysed on the basis of the cause and effect relation, as is done in fundamental analysis, but only for effect. Prices reflect all fundamental, political and psychological elements known to the market, in short they reflect the demand and supply equilibrium in any moment. Technical analysts seek to identify some typical situations and financial behaviour on the market that affect asset quotations and that systematically repeat themselves over time. This means analysts assume the existence of trends that are a lagged response of the market prices to the underlying factors governing those prices. Analysts in such a way exploit their expectation on prices to buy or sell assets and make profits.

Technical analysis techniques adapt well to commodity futures markets (Alexander, 2008) where transaction costs are low and do not erode profitability. These costs have been estimated in the study of Locke and Venkatesh (1997) to vary in a range between 0.0004% and 0.033%.

It is suggested here that the basic trading rules used to formulate more advanced trading strategies are: filter rules, support and resistance rules, moving averages and channel break outs. In order to show how these strategies work if applied to commodity markets, reference is made to the analysis carried out by Brandoni and Roncoroni (2008).[3] They consider seven daily time series from 2002 to 2008, comprising closing prices of some commodity futures: crude oil (CO), copper (HG), gold (GD), unleaded gasoline (XB), natural gas (NG), silver (SI) – most traded on NYMEX – and the time series of the peakload calendar futures of the European Energy Exchange (EEX). The buy-and-hold strategy is applied to these data and its results are compared with those obtained by applying the other strategies mentioned above. In order to evaluate the profitability of the trading rules, the following performance indicators defined in Fusai and Roncoroni (2008) are calculated. The first indicator is the total net profit (TNP), given by the difference between the total gross profit and the total gross loss obtained from applying the strategy. The second indicator is the profit factor (PF), calculated as the ratio of the winning trade gross profit over the losing trade gross loss. This measure calculates how many dollars are gained for each dollar lost, namely it measures the risk of the single strategy. Long-term operators generally use the strategy only if the profit factor is greater than 2. Also, the total number of trades has to be considered and it should be between 10 and 20 trades per year. Furthermore, it is useful to calculate the average trade (AT), that is the average net profit across all trades, the average winning/losing trade (AWT/ALT), that is the average profit/loss across all winning/losing trades, and also the ratio between the average winning trade and the average losing trade as an additional measure of the trading rule risk. In order to evaluate the risk of the trading strategy, the maximum losing trade (MLT) and the maximum winning trade (MWT) are determined. In general, if the total profit is linked to only one win that exceeds 25% of the total profit, then the strategy is risky. The same consideration can be made about the maximum loss. Finally, a significant historical performance measure is the maximum drawdown (MADD), which represents the top cumulative loss an investor would have incurred if he had gone long a moment before reaching the maximum peak. The maximum drawdown therefore represents the largest margin necessary to cover the highest possible loss produced by the strategy. Other indicators, which are not but could be considered, are the maximum number of consecutive losses or the one-way break-even trading measure.

---

[3]The numerical results were obtained using Matlab software.

TABLE 20.2 Buy-and-hold strategy over the period 1/2002–10/2008

Commodity	Total net profit	Maximum drawdown	Profit factor	Average winning trade	Average losing trade
CO	43.68	0.58	1.058	0.8685	−0.92
EEX	51.72	0.306	1.152	0.49	−0.51
HG	106.75	0.586	1.041	3.09	−3.23
GC	471.3	0.288	1.117	4.95	−5.09
XB	106.473	0.614	1.020	6.21	−6.64
NG	4.61	0.727	1.031	0.17	−0.17
SI	5520.577		1.046	12.99	−15.69

TABLE 20.3 Buy-and-hold strategy over the period 1/2002–12/2005

Commodity	Total net profit	Maximum drawdown	Profit factor	Average winning trade	Average losing trade
CO	37.98	0.318	1.135	0.60	−0.60
EEX	36.92	0.198	1.378	0.32	−0.30
HG	150.35	0.182	1.257	1.42	−1.27
GC	239.7	0.152	1.191	2.80	−2.79
XB	311.81	0.333	1.122	5.50	−5.33
NG	8.76	0.537	1.116	0.17	−0.15
SI	435.5	0.328	1.136	6.57	−7.31

The data are analysed on two subperiods, [2002, 2005] and [2006, 2008], with the scope to verify an eventual change of the trading rule performance over the subperiods. Tables 20.2 to 20.4 contain the results of the performance indicators obtained by applying the buy-and-hold strategy to the time series over the entire period and over the two subperiods.

The filter technique was used for the first time by Alexander (1961, 1964). It is a mechanical rule which attempts to identify movements in stock trends by applying some criteria for trading. In particular, an $x\%$ filter defines the following rule. If the market moves up $x\%$ or more, meaning that the price of the observed asset rises above this percentage, there is a signal to buy and the long position is maintained until it moves down $x\%$ or more, that is the asset price decreases at least $x\%$ from a subsequent high. Analogously, the signal to sell is when

TABLE 20.4 Buy-and-hold strategy over the period 1/2006–10/2008

Commodity	Total net profit	Maximum drawdown	Profit factor	Average winning trade	Average losing trade
CO	3.33	0.587	1.007	1.25	−1.36
EEX	18.33	0.306	1.077	0.68	−0.71
HG	−44.25	0.586	0.978	5.48	−5.76
GC	218	0.288	1.079	7.99	−8.13
XB	−214.4	0.614	0.926	7.18	−8.49
NG	−3.6	0.605	0.949	0.19	−0.20
SI	89.5	0.577	1.010	21.80	−27.19

TABLE 20.5 Filter strategy over the period 1/2002–10/2008

Commodity	Total net profit	Maximum drawdown	Profit factor	Average winning trade	Average losing trade
CO	49.160	0.405	1.291	4.744	−2.641
EEX	81.67	0.150	1.645	2.22	−0.92
HG	92.65	0.710	1.127	24.86	−9.97
GC	616.6	0.333	1.367	16.07	−8.28
XB	−6.099	0.552	0.994	41.04	−24.78
NG	−7.385	0.870	0.869	0.66	−0.39
SI	385.1	0.484	1.062	37.07	−20.73

the closing price of the asset moves down $x\%$ or more and the short position is maintained until the price rises $x\%$ above the subsequent low, at which time the position is closed out to go long. Alexander (1961, 1964) studies stock and commodity price movements and argues, using empirical tests, the idea that in speculative markets price changes appear to follow a random walk over time, according to the perfect market hypothesis, but, indeed, once a trend is initiated it tends to persist so that filters produce profits. Fama and Blume (1966) analyse the dynamics of 30 securities belonging to the Dow Jones Industrial Average, applying filters to the time series of data from 1950 to 1960. They conclude that even though some filters generate extra profits compared with the buy-and-hold strategy, the consideration of transaction costs denies any profitable results for an active management of the positions. The empirical results for a 5% strategy applied on the above data are shown in Tables 20.5, 20.6 and 20.7. From the performance of the filter rule reported in the tables, the profit for crude oil, electricity and gold is greater than the profit obtained by applying the buy-and-hold strategy, but the profit factor lower than 2 indicates a strategy that is too risky for all commodities. Furthermore, the number of trades is so much higher that it eliminates the advantage deriving from profits once transaction costs have been considered. From the analysis over the single subperiods, the 5% filter rule seems interesting for the unleaded gasoline due to its high profit factor, but actually this result depends on the fact that there is only one trade that affects the gross profit by more than 75%.

The channel break-out rule is based on the fact that price moves according to a trend, and it is possible to delimit its movement, tracing out a trendline that connects lows in a rising market or highs in a declining market with the channel line parallel to the trendline. Then the price zigzags back and forth between the two lines of the channel. The rule developed

TABLE 20.6 Filter strategy over the period 1/2002–12/2005

Commodity	Total net profit	Maximum drawdown	Profit factor	Average winning trade	Average losing trade
CO	3.680	0.380	1.051	2.636	−1.775
EEX	26.350	0.150	1.652	1.452	−0.663
HG	2	0.377	1.007	3.11	−1.79
GC	73.4	0.333	1.136	8.76	−4.77
XB	158.36	0.130	7.252	45.92	−8.44
NG	−1.753	0.717	0.939	0.62	−0.37
SI	93	0.299	1.055	19.668	−10.474

TABLE 20.7 Filter strategy over the period 1/2006–10/2008

Commodity	Total net profit	Maximum drawdown	Profit factor	Average winning trade	Average losing trade
CO	−5.04	0.594	0.980	3.015	−1.626
EEX	58.03	0.120	1.688	2.906	−1.110
HG	−99.60	0.559	0.915	13.862	−7.832
GC	547.70	0.193	1.486	22.955	0.193
XB	−236.87	0.668	0.855	16.829	−9.230
NG	−7.36	0.796	0.731	0.647	−0.428
SI	294	0.484	1.066	55.505	−32.938

by Sullivan *et al.* (1999) says to buy when the closing price exceeds the upper limit of the channel given by the maximum price over an established time interval without taking into consideration the actual closing price, and to sell when the price moves below the lower limit obtained as a percentage of the indicated maximum. The long and short positions are kept for a fixed number of days, during which every other signal is ignored. This means that the financial operator does not have an active position on the market. Tables 20.8, 20.9 and 20.10 display the values of the performance indicators for the channel break-out rule. Interesting results for crude oil, unleaded gasoline and electricity can be found by referring to Table 20.10, but they are linked to few winning trades that affect the gross profit with a percentage greater than 25%.

The support and resistance can be seen as the lines of a channel in correspondence to which prices react. In particular, a support represents a level at which the concentration of the asset demand is so high that it pulls the prices up. On the contrary, at the resistance level the high concentration of supply pulls the prices down. A simple trading rule is to buy when the closing price exceeds the maximum occurring in a fixed period, and to sell if the closing price is below the minimum realized in the fixed period. Some percentage filter could be introduced for this rule in order to limit the influence of false signals from the market. The empirical results regarding the performance indicators are given in Tables 20.11, 20.12 and 20.13. Comparing these values with those of Tables 20.2, 20.3 and 20.4, it can be deduced that the support-and-resistance strategy is more profitable than the buy-and-hold strategy.

The last rule analysed is the moving average. Moving averages are the most commonly used trading rules in technical analysis. They are trend-following indicators and consist of the average of the closing prices for the designated number of preceding periods. The adopted

TABLE 20.8 Channel break-out rule over the period 1/2002–10/2008

Commodity	Total net profit	Maximum drawdown	Profit factor	Average winning trade	Average losing trade
CO	60.840	0.579	2.007	5.051	−3.020
EEX	59.83	0.153	4.086	3.77	−2.42
HG	98.4	0.347	1.369	21.49	−12.13
GC	208.5	0.206	1.550	32.63	−19.94
XB	115.639	0.584	1.205	28.27	−24.47
NG	6.646	0.883	1.632	0.75	−0.42
SI	206.8	0.589	1.247	54.93	−44.05

TABLE 20.9 Channel break-out rule over the period 1/2002–12/2005

Commodity	Total net profit	Maximum drawdown	Profit factor	Average winning trade	Average losing trade
CO	27.820	0.579	0.835	2.318	−2.775
EEX	32.850	0.072	19.352	2.665	−0.90
HG	52.65	0.224	2.266	7.85	−2.97
GC	15.8	0.206	1.099	16.01	−14.57
XB	0.52	0.497	1.002	21.52	−18.61
NG	1.145	0.742	1.139	0.72	−0.64
SI	158	0.383	1.653	36.455	−22.05

TABLE 20.10 Channel break-out rule over the period 1/2006–10/2008

Commodity	Total net profit	Maximum drawdown	Profit factor	Average winning trade	Average losing trade
CO	61.08	0.159	3.255	8.015	−3.386
EEX	25.42	0.142	2.471	6.100	−2.88
HG	56.05	0.347	1.261	54.200	−30.71
GC	162.60	0.172	1.773	62.167	−30.06
XB	154.15	0.242	1.630	36.251	−34.94
NG	0.70	0.698	1.129	0.679	−0.49
SI	217	0.372	1.365	115.929	−84.90

TABLE 20.11 Support and resistance rule over the period 1/2002–10/2008

Commodity	Total net profit	Maximum drawdown	Profit factor	Average winning trade	Average losing trade
CO	53.820	0.557	1.798	13.477	−4.498
EEX	68.9	0.288	4.492	8.00	−3.29
HG	146.6	0.593	1.480	50.24	−27.78
GC	42.1	0.376	1.093	70.84	−34.91
XB	76.233	0.647	1.129	83.27	−36.87
NG	−6.707	0.960	0.692	2.51	−1.09
SI	−187.5	0.615	0.883	236.53	−89.26

TABLE 20.12 Support and resistance rule over the period 1/2002–12/2005

Commodity	Total net profit	Maximum drawdown	Profit factor	Average winning trade	Average losing trade
CO	−16.440	0.557	0.447	4.423	−2.701
EEX	40.460	0.141	/	8.092	/
HG	56	0.383	2.018	22.20	−9.17
GC	−62.5	0.376	0.682	33.45	−21.81
XB	−49.73	0.522	0.776	43.15	−27.79
NG	−3.621	0.867	0.579	2.49	−0.61
SI	−173	0.498	0.602	65.375	−39.482

TABLE 20.13 Support and resistance rule over the period 1/2006–10/2008

Commodity	Total net profit	Maximum drawdown	Profit factor	Average winning trade	Average losing trade
CO	67.14	0.329	2.897	17.088	−8.848
EEX	21.77	0.288	1.917	15.173	−3.393
HG	69.85	0.593	1.279	64.080	−50.110
GC	36.80	0.357	1.133	104.733	−55.480
XB	298.76	0.360	2.438	101.319	−41.566
NG	−6.12	0.857	0.542	2.416	−1.909
SI	−162	0.615	0.862	336.733	−167.486

rule is known as double crossover. A buy signal occurs when the short-term moving average crosses over the long-term moving average. A short selling signal is when the short-term moving average crosses under the long-term moving average. In implementing this rule an arithmetic moving average is used or alternatively an exponential moving average. The rule can be modified by introducing two different types of filters to avoid false trading signals. A percentage filter requires that the difference between the short-term and long-term moving averages is higher than a fixed value. A temporal filter that provides buying and selling signals remains valid for a minimum number of days. The moving average strategy (5, 20) is applied to the data, meaning that the short-term moving average is calculated over 5 days, the long-term one over 20 days. As can be seen from Tables 20.14, 20.15 and 20.16, the profit factors of crude oil, unleaded gasoline and electricity are higher compared with the corresponding values for the buy-and-hold strategy, in particular if one refers to the results of Table 20.16.

In order to verify the reliability of the analysed trading rules, a bootstrapping technique is used. Bootstrapping is a statistical method of resampling to approximate the sample distribution of a statistic. It allows us to build a confidence interval and calculate the p-values test when the statistical distribution is known. According to bootstrapping, 500 time series have been simulated on the basis of the GARCH(1,1) model and then the different profitable trading rules have been applied. The simulated returns of the strategy are calculated and the percentage of simulated strategies that have a mean return greater than those obtainable with the empirical series is estimated. This percentage represents the p-value, that is the probability that the chosen GARCH(1,1) model gives a mean return analogous to the empirical ones. The results of bootstrapping are given in Table 20.17. The p-values demonstrate that the extra profit obtained

TABLE 20.14 Moving average (5,20) rule over the period 1/2002–10/2008

Commodity	Total net profit	Maximum drawdown	Profit factor	Average winning trade	Average losing trade
CO	95.210	0.427	1.806	5.335	−2.273
EEX	106.58	0.137	4.040	4.29	−1.17
HG	243.35	0.601	1.460	22.72	−7.45
GC	−16.6	0.378	0.980	24.65	−14.07
XB	522.433	0.475	1.593	36.93	−17.62
NG	7.095	0.656	1.275	0.94	−0.44
SI	−427.4	0.603	0.827	61.71	−41.76

TABLE 20.15 Moving average (5,20) rule over the period 1/2002–12/2005

Commodity	Total net profit	Maximum drawdown	Profit factor	Average winning trade	Average losing trade
CO	10.630	0.427	1.225	2.760	−1.434
EEX	34.300	0.137	3.539	2.988	−0.844
HG	−80.45	0.601	0.604	6.82	−4.06
GC	42.2	0.165	1.195	14.36	−6.76
XB	−106.08	0.475	0.806	20.93	−17.60
NG	1.803	0.656	1.141	0.77	−0.39
SI	−204	0.542	0.744	29.675	−23.447

TABLE 20.16 Moving average (5,20) rule over the period 1/2006–10/2008

Commodity	Total net profit	Maximum drawdown	Profit factor	Average winning trade	Average losing trade
CO	86.74	0.218	2.267	8.623	−3.604
EEX	70.08	0.132	4.506	5.629	−1.538
HG	341.25	0.390	2.098	40.756	−16.361
GC	−54.80	0.356	0.909	38.950	−22.226
XB	548.25	0.378	2.681	58.290	−17.163
NG	1.12	0.520	1.085	0.955	−0.508
SI	−267	0.518	0.840	116.642	−66.668

TABLE 20.17 Bootstrapping statistic results

	Moving average rule	
Commodity	***N****	**Mean**
CO (I per)	48	9.60%
CO (II per)	98	19.60%
EEX (I per)	26	5%
EEX (II per)	15	3%
XB (I per)	57	11%
XB (II per)	25	5%
	Support and resistance rule	
Commodity	***N****	**Mean**
CO (I per)	251	50%
CO (II per)	143	29%
EEX (I per)	82	16%
EEX (II per)	169	34%
XB (I per)	247	49%
XB (II per)	138	28%

*Number of series with returns greater than those calculated on the historical data.

from the application of the moving average rule cannot be generated by a GARCH(1,1) model, whereas they are more significant for the support-and-resistance rule.

It is important to stress that in the studies developed in this chapter, the problem of data snooping is not considered. According to White (2000), data snooping occurs when a data set is used more than once for purposes of inference or model selection. Using the same data more times in the same analysis group can lead to obtaining satisfactory results that are simply due to chance rather than to the accuracy of the adopted method. This problem is difficult to address in practice because typically only a single time series is available for analysis.

20.1.4 A General Statistical Arbitrage Trading Methodology

The first practice of statistical arbitrage pairs trading dates back to the 1980s, when a group of mathematicians, physicists and computer scientists, led by the Wall Street quant Nunzio Tartaglia, used statistical techniques to develop quantitative arbitrage strategies for trading securities in pairs. Their methodology consists of selecting two securities that have similar characteristics and whose prices tend to move together. These assets are often selected on the basis of intuition, economic fundamentals, long-term correlations or simply past experience. When a short-term mispricing in the pairs emerges, this is interpreted as an arbitrage opportunity that is exploited by selling the higher-priced security and buying the lower-priced security with the expectation that the mispricing vanishes. This trading strategy was called 'Pairs Trading'.

In the 1990s the growing requirement of models that could properly describe sophisticated trading strategies was satisfied with the emergence of the so-called statistical arbitrage models. For years the interest of professionals and academics had been focused on the development of new statistical arbitrage strategies, until 2002 when the weak performance of the models, principally due to the consequences of the dramatic changes in market dynamics after the crisis of 2000, caused a loss of confidence in statistical arbitrage methods. Pole (2007) suggests that a new interest in statistical arbitrage models came about in 2006, when the use of more accurate and advanced algorithms spread.

Statistical arbitrage, indicated as StatArb, can be described as the attempt to profit from pricing inefficiencies, which are identified using mathematical and statistical tools. According to Burgess (1999), a statistical arbitrage is a generalization of the traditional zero-risk or pure arbitrage. In the latter case, fair-price relationships between asset pairs with identical cash flows are constructed and pure arbitrage opportunities are identified when prices deviate from these relationships. Burgess (1999) suggests that on markets, zero-risk opportunities do not exist, due to several uncertain factors such as uncertain future dividend rates, market volatility during the short time required to carry out the lock-in trades, failure to 'fill' all legs of the trade, causing a residual 'unhedged risk' and the 'basis risk'. Basis risk is due to fluctuations in the differences between spot and futures prices prior to the expiry date. It is, on the one hand, a source of uncertainty when positions on securities have to be marked to market at current prices by operators due to exchange regulations and companies' internal requirements. On the other hand, it is a source of opportunity because an arbitrageur can assume positions on some securities and revert the trades before the expiry date, when profits are realized. So the so-called statistical arbitrage opportunities rely on the statistical properties of the security mispricings whose dynamics fluctuate around a stable level.

For Bondarenko (2003), the definition of statistical arbitrage opportunity derives from the concept of pure arbitrage opportunity. A pure arbitrage opportunity is a zero-cost trading strategy by which gains are received with no possibility of losses. Instead, a statistical arbitrage opportunity is a zero-cost trading strategy for which the expected payoff is positive and the conditional expected payoff in each state of the economy is non-negative, meaning that the strategy payoff can be negative in some elementary states, as long as the average payoff in each final state is non-negative.

A statistical arbitrage methodology based on quantitative methods is proposed by many authors, like Burgess (1999), Vidyamurthy (2004), Elliott *et al.* (2005), Do *et al.* (2006) and Bertram (2010). Their studies aim to exploit the rising arbitrage opportunities on stock markets. Generally, a statistical arbitrage methodology consists of three steps.

1. Statistical mispricing dynamics investigation: assets are selected so that their prices are in long-run equilibrium and the deviations from this equilibrium, called statistical mispricings, have potentially predictable components in their dynamics. Tests are implemented for evaluating the potentially predictable components.
2. Predictive models development: statistical and quantitative methods are used to formulate models that identify arbitrage opportunities forecasting changes in mispricing dynamics.
3. Statistical trading strategies implementation: appropriate trading rules are implemented to profit and performance indicators are calculated to evaluate the reliability of the adopted strategy.

20.1.4.1 Statistical Mispricing Dynamics Investigation The first step of the methodology consists of constructing the so-called statistical mispricing time series that contain some predictable components. A target commodity or a target set of commodities is identified and its value is replicated with a portfolio of other selected commodities. The composition of the portfolio is determined by the use of cointegration regression. By means of cointegration the time series are selected in such a way that their combinations are stationary, and therefore a relationship of long-run equilibrium, the so-called fair-price relationship among commodities, is defined. The deviations from this fair-price relationship represent the statistical mispricings. The use of a price combination, that is relative prices, instead of the absolute price has a financial meaning that comes from the theory of asset pricing models, such as CAPM (Capital Asset Pricing Model) and APT (Arbitrage Pricing Theory). According to this theory, changes in asset prices are due both to a systematic component, common to each asset and representing the exposure to market-wide risk, and to a residual or idiosyncratic component that depends on the specific characteristics of the asset. The cointegration linear composition of the relative mispricings acts to nullify the nonstationary systematic components, leaving only the stationary-specific components. Namely, because the prices of the selected commodities share a common long-term equilibrium, a weighted sum of their time series forms a long–short portfolio which has the common component return equal to zero. This means that the mispricing, considered as a portfolio of commodities, is statistically independent of and then immunized against market-wide risks. Consequently, the mispricing portfolio dynamics are affected only by specific component dynamics of commodity that are potentially predictable.

The trading of only one target commodity is considered here, along with the replication portfolio of its value. All the commodities are chosen in the set of all possible commodities.

At a generic time t, the value of the target commodity is indicated by $T(t)$ and the value of the replication portfolio, which is a synthetic asset, is denoted by $X(t)$. For any time $t \geq 0$, the following fair-price relationship holds:

$$X(t) = E[T(t)|\mathbf{C}(t)] = T(t), \tag{20.1}$$

representing a long-term relationship among variables, where $E[\cdot|\mathbf{C}(t)]$ denotes the expectation conditional on the price vector of commodities, $\mathbf{C}(t)$, at time t. It follows from equation (20.1) that the statistical mispricing at time t is given by the deviation from the fair-price relationship

$$M(t) = T(t) - X(t). \tag{20.2}$$

The methodology most commonly adopted to construct the series of the statistical mispricings is based on cointegration techniques. The synthetic asset $X(t)$ is obtained as a linear combination of n commodities, whose prices are $C^i(t)$ with $i = 0, 1, \ldots, n$, that is

$$X(t) = \sum_i \beta_i C^i(t), \qquad i = 0, 1, \ldots, n \tag{20.3}$$

where β_i with $i = 0, 1, \ldots, n$ are the respective weights and, in particular, β_0 is the constant. Bearing in mind the relation (20.1), the coefficients β_i are estimated by a cointegration regression of the time series of the target price $T(t)$ against the historical prices of the commodities comprising the replication portfolio. Finally, the value of the corresponding statistical mispricing portfolio, for each t, is obtained by substituting (20.3) back into (20.2):

$$M(t) = T(t) - \sum_i \beta_i C^i(t), \qquad i = 0, 1, \ldots, n, \tag{20.4}$$

consisting of the commodities $\{T, C^1, C^2, \ldots, C^n\}$ according to the weights $\{1, -\beta_1, -\beta_2, \ldots, -\beta_n\}$, meaning that the mispricing portfolio assumes a long position on the target commodity and short positions on the commodities comprising the replication portfolio.

It can be concluded that at a generic time t, $M(t)$ represents the excess value of the target price compared with the value of the replication portfolio and it can be seen as a 'stochastically de-trended' version of the original target price with respect to the observed time series. Hence, $M(t)$ behaves as a proxy of nondirectly observed risk factors, which determine a stochastic trend that is common to many market prices.

Then, statistical and quantitative tools are used to individuate arbitrage opportunities which can be exploited to profit. In particular, one has to verify that the mispricing dynamics contain predictable components that allow us to predict a mean-reverting behaviour so that using appropriate trading strategies, an operator can focus on getting the investment timing right, relying on the fact that in the long run the mispricing corrects. There exist several statistical methods to test the existence of predictability in the mispricing dynamics.

One method is to analyse the autocorrelation function of the mispricing time series in order to study its short-term effects and find out whether the future value of the time series is related to the past value and hence the presence of a predictable component; in particular, mean-reverting behaviour is sought. The stationarity of the time series may be verified through the ADF test, but because of its very low power in identifying the deviation of time series from random walk behaviour, the variance ration test, described in Section 20.1.2, can be used to demonstrate that mispricing dynamics follow mean reversion, such as that described by the following Ornstein–Uhlenbeck process:

$$dM(t) = -\rho(M(t) - \mu)dt + \sigma dW(t). \tag{20.5}$$

In (20.5) all the parameters are positive and μ represents the equilibrium or mean value supported by fundamentals, σ is the degree of volatility around it caused by shocks, and ρ is the rate by which these shocks dissipate and the variable reverts towards the mean. This model allows us to make predictions for the mispricing and consequently trading strategies can be developed on the simulated mispricing, so that the strategy performance can be evaluated.

A different methodology to study the existence of predictability conditions fulfilled by the spread dynamics of cross combinations of petroleum futures contracts, crude oils and related products is used by Alizadeh and Nomikos (2008). The stationarity of the relationship between different pairs of futures prices is investigated by using a vector error correction model (VECM) (Johansen, 1988). The error correction term represents the spread between the log-futures prices, with the short-run price dynamics expressed by the lagged cross-market terms, while the long-run price processes are reflected in the cointegration vector. For the cointegrated pairs, the Granger causality test is implemented to determine whether one time series is useful in forecasting another one (Granger, 1969). Their results reveal that the relationship between petroleum futures prices can be used to develop trading strategies and determine the timing of profitable investing.

20.1.4.2 Predictive Models Development In the first step of the statistical arbitrage methodology, possible arbitrage opportunities on commodity markets are investigated through the construction of mispricing time series that hold some predictable components. In the second step, models for forecasting the mispricing dynamics are formulated. Building such models involves tackling problems such as high noise, low degree of prior knowledge, small sample sizes and potential time variation, that is nonstationarity, in the underlying data-generating processes. So it becomes important to develop a model that captures most features of the mispricing dynamics contained in the deterministic mispricing components themselves. In particular, predictive models aim to model mispricing dynamics as a function of the information contained in the level of the mispricing itself, in past mispricing changes and in other external variables which can either directly influence mispricing evolution or serve to modulate the information contained in other variables. According to Burgess (1999), in general, the steps to follow for developing a predictive/forecasting model are:

1. selection of the information set;
2. model specification – variable selection and specification of parameterized functional form;
3. parameter estimation;
4. backtesting – eventual model reformulation and returning to step two;
5. model application.

The best model minimizes the bias of the model caused by the assumptions and restrictions made at each step and the variance of the model due to data sample selection in the phase of parameter estimation. The two approaches mostly used are the stochastic approach, whereby the dynamics of mispricing are described by stochastic processes, and the artificial neural network approach, whereby mathematical algorithms learn about market predictions and forecast the future mispricing dynamics. In both cases, statistical trading rules generate trading signals conditioned upon the output of forecasting models.

Regarding the models based on stochastic modelling, as described in the previous paragraph, mispricing dynamics are usually represented as mean-reverting processes (i.e., equation (20.5)). Concerning this, Elliott *et al.* (2005) model the spread between two stocks belonging to the same financial sector by a mean-reverting Gaussian Markov chain model. In particular, the spread is observed in Gaussian noise. The parameters of the processes are estimated by filter methods and calibrated to market data. A trading strategy is formulated considering the state process of the model and the observation process, which is a noisy observation of some state processes and represents the observed spread.

An example of predictable models that can be used in statistical arbitrage trading and based on artificial neural networks (ANN) is described by Kulkarni and Haidar (2009). Using an ANN model, no assumptions on mispricing dynamics are made and so general deterministic components of dynamics are captured. For this reason, ANN model both direct nonlinearities and also interaction effects without having to know them in advance. One can describe the ANN model as a mapping model, that is it maps the information available in the market to the desirable target, an output that represents the forecast with a certain grade of accuracy. Basically the model imitates the market: historical and current information is the input that market participants react to, according to their understanding, positions, speculations, analysis, etc. All the market participant activities are aggregated to form the output, usually represented by the closing price. A well-formulated ANN model should guarantee in-sample accuracy, the ability to perform with new market data and consistency of the network output. Kulkarni and Haidar (2009) use a three-layer feedforward network with a backpropagation algorithm to forecast crude oil prices for the short term. Furthermore, they find that futures prices of crude oil contain new information about the oil spot price direction.

20.1.4.3 Statistical Trading Strategies Implementation The third step of the methodology consists of defining some trading rules based on the predictive model developed at the second step. Either basic trading rules can be used, like those described in Section 20.1.3, or combinations of them in creative strategies tailored to suit specific markets. Trading rules provide signals for buying or selling the spread/mispricing and furthermore they determine the timing of the transactions.

Alizadeh and Nomikos (2008) use the moving average as a basic quantitative rule for their trading strategy. They consider the spread between log futures prices of petroleum products and calculate four moving averages on the time series obtained. One moving average is fast, that is it is calculated on the short term (MA(1)) while the other three moving averages are slow, that is calculated on the long term (MA(4), MA(8), MA(12)). The difference between one slow moving average and the fast moving average represents the indicator of buying or selling in the petroleum futures spread. If this difference is positive, there is a buy signal, otherwise if negative, there is a sell signal. As for every trading strategy, the evaluation of transaction costs has particular importance, so the authors assume, according to the past literature, a transaction cost of 0.2% for every trip of initiating and reversing the trade. They evaluate the performance of the strategies, related to different combinations of moving averages, on the basis of the annualized mean return, the standard deviation and the Sharpe ratio, that is the ratio of average return and standard deviation. The values of the moving average (MA) strategy performance indicators are compared with the indicator values of the benchmark buy-and-hold strategy. In general, the mean returns of the MA strategies are higher than those of the benchmark strategy, while the standard deviations are lower, meaning that the Sharpe ratios indicate that most of the MA strategies outperform the buy-and-hold strategy. In addition, another indicator of performance is given by the historical cumulative returns, allowing one to decide which strategy is advantageous to adopt in terms of benefits obtained.

The study developed in Section 20.1.2 around a portfolio characterized by the virtual refinery model is reconsidered. Using a large sample of data spanning 25/10/2000 to 19/10/2009, the data is split into two parts: data from 25/10/2000 to 26/12/2005 are used for developing the model through an in-sample analysis; data from 02/01/2006 to 19/10/2009 are used for testing the model and evaluating its out-of-sample performance. The mispricing portfolio, whose value at time t is indicated by $M(t)$, is obtained by applying the cointegration technique described in Section 20.1.2 to in-sample analysis data. As in Burgess (1999), a statistical arbitrage trading strategy (SATS) is defined that not only states the sign of the mispricing portfolio transaction, but also defines the transaction magnitude depending on the size of the mispricing as follows:

$$\text{SATS} = -M(t)\begin{cases} \text{if } M(t) < 0, & \text{the mispricing portfolio must be bought} \\ \text{if } M(t) > 0, & \text{the mispricing portfolio must be sold.} \end{cases}$$

The strategy described above is applied both to the in-sample and to the out-of-sample data and the performance compared to assess the functioning of the model from a forecasting perspective. The strategy is implemented using Excel and Matlab software. Each week t the return of the strategy SATR is calculated by the following formula:

$$\text{SATR}(t) = \text{SATS}(t)\frac{\Delta M(t)}{\text{Abs}[M(t)]} - c|\Delta M(t)|, \tag{20.6}$$

where $\Delta M(t)$ represents the variation of the mispricing value between two successive periods, $\text{Abs}[M(t)]$ is the sum of all the mispricing portfolio components taking in absolute values and c is the percentage transaction cost. For the measurement of the trading performance for each year, the following three performance indicators are used:

- Total return, given by the cumulative profit of the strategy over the past time period.
- Sharpe ratio, which indicates the amount of profitability per unit of risk and is calculated as the ratio of the annualized mean profitability of the strategy to its annualized standard deviation of the profit.
- Percentage profitable weeks, obtained as the percentage of periods corresponding to positive $\text{SATR}(t)$ values.

The results for the in-sample data are illustrated in Table 20.18, while those for the out-of-sample data are in Table 20.19.

From this simple analysis, it can be seen that the forecasting model performs well for the out-of-sample years, in line with the results obtained in-sample. This statement is confirmed by Figure 20.2, which shows the paths over the reference period 2005–2009 of the actual Brent futures prices and the forecasted prices calculated using the estimated regression parameters. Furthermore, one can assert that the fair-price relationship built from the in-sample analysis holds over time.

TABLE 20.18 In-sample performance of the SATS

Year	2001	2002	2003	2004	2005
Total return	12.79%	6.43%	6.52%	10.63%	21.94%
Sharpe ratio	2.01	2.03	1.95	1.90	0.03
Profitable weeks	58.33%	57.69%	59.62%	61.54%	57.69%

TABLE 20.19 Out-of-sample performance of the SATS

Year	2006	2007	2008	2009
Total return	19.94%	27.13%	162.17%	13.53%
Sharpe ratio	1.85	1.11	0.81	1.12
Profitable weeks	52.17%	50.94%	52.94%	42.86%

In Figure 20.3 it is shown how the trading strategy works, in particular the SATS curve gives the signal for buying or selling the mispricing according to the rule defined above.

In order to illustrate the effectiveness of the implemented strategy, consider the results for years 2008 and 2009 displayed in Table 20.19. One expects a total return of 162.17% for year 2008, much greater than that of 13.53% expected for year 2009. This profitability scenario is confirmed by the presence of a higher percentage of profitable days for 2008 with respect to 2009. The opposite conclusion is drawn if one considers the index of the Sharpe

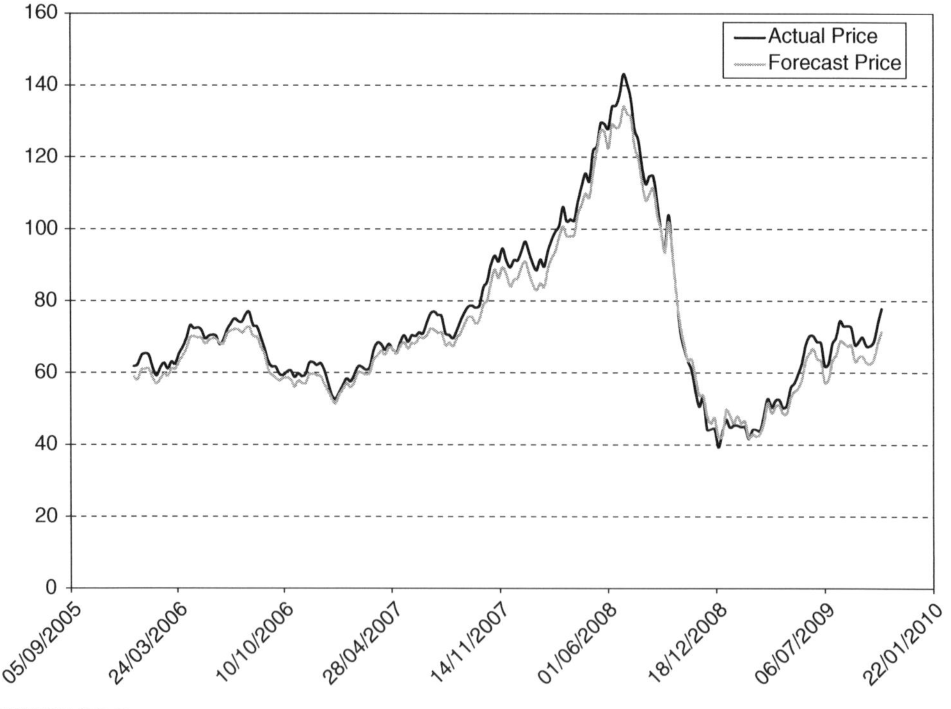

FIGURE 20.2 Brent futures actual prices vs. forecast prices

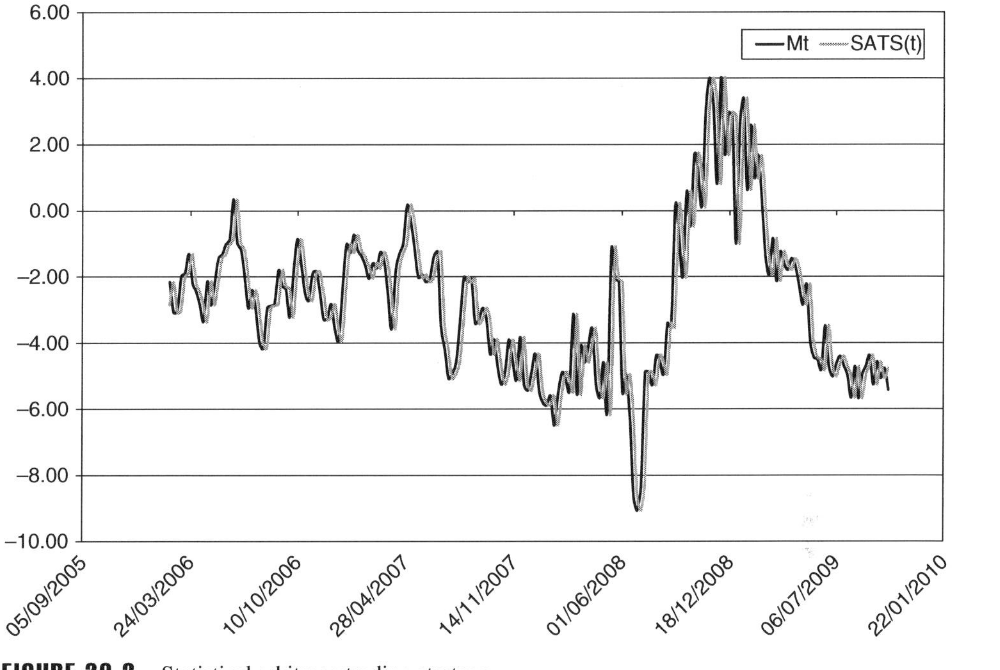

FIGURE 20.3 Statistical arbitrage trading strategy

ratio as an indicator of performance, because it is lower for 2008 than 2009. In fact, the amplitude and oscillation frequency of the graph of the strategy (Figure 20.3) reflect a higher variability of profits due to the volatility of the Brent future price being greater in 2008 than in 2009. Consequently, an optimal strategy can be developed and updated daily, taking into consideration the model forecasts and the expected values of the three indices of performance (total return, Sharpe ratio and profitable periods), so that any trading decision will be taken in line with the specific risk profile.

20.2 PORTFOLIO OPTIMIZATION WITH COMMODITIES

20.2.1 Commodities as an Asset Class

Academics and practitioners currently treat commodities as a particular asset class in a portfolio context. According to the definition of asset class, commodities are characterized by a homogeneous risk–return profile, that is high internal correlation, and a heterogeneous risk–return profile towards other asset classes, that is low external correlation (as will be seen in the next paragraphs). However, the particular characteristic of this asset class is that commodities like energy, livestock or grain do not generate continuous cash flows, so that it is not possible to assess the reward received and the risk assumed from the purchase of a commodity. Consequently, commodity prices cannot be determined by the net present value method or discounting future cash flows, but may be derived from the intersection of supply and demand on specific markets and by considering inventories.

One can distinguish different ways of investing in this asset class and they can be classified according to Geman (2005) as follows:

Purchasing the physical commodity in the spot market. The transaction can be either direct or through an intermediary but in either case it is not easy to implement. The purchase of precious metals is the sole exception due to their low current costs and the fact that they do not require storage capacity, but with the drawback that a portfolio consisting of precious metals does not guarantee an efficient diversification.

Purchasing stocks of commodity-related companies. Through this kind of investment one obtains indirect exposure to commodities, which introduces a noise component to the investment due to the characteristics of specific natural resource companies, to the inherent risks and to other external factors that influence share prices.

Purchasing commodity futures. One makes a direct investment in a specific commodity taking a long or short position in futures contracts written on it. Futures contracts are traded on exchanges through the intermediation of a clearing house that manages the margin system. Only investors that have built an account with a broker can execute transactions on the exchange.

Purchasing commodity options. The underlying of the options can be a spot price or futures price and the investor can develop a buy-and-hold strategy or an active strategy trading the option before its maturity when this is convenient.

Investing in commodity futures indexes and commodity-related notes. Index investment is an easy and passive investment in commodities that gets exposure to a specific sector. Commodity-related notes are linked to major commodity indexes, such as the DJ-AIG or GSCI, and are issued by investment banks, financial institutions or individual commodity producers that raise capital and invest it in indexes or commodity index derivatives.

Different kinds of investors operate on commodity markets. There are physical traders or commercial investors that use futures markets to manage position exposure related to actual flows of goods and seek to hedge their production and consumption. For example, in soft commodity markets commercial producers and users of agricultural products trade with the aim of earning returns from an under-explored asset class in times of high inflation and low interest rates. On the one hand, investment in soft commodities provides liquidity in derivatives markets and makes price discovery more efficient. On the other hand, it increases commodity price volatility.

Domanski and Heath (2007) identify some kinds of financial investors. There are financial traders that focus on exploiting arbitrage opportunities using traditional arbitrage strategies. Arbitrage opportunities can, for example, arise as a consequence of commercial investors acting on futures markets. In fact, the futures price can deviate from the relevant spot price plus the cost of carry, that is the cost of financing a position in the spot market, causing arbitrage opportunities.

Then there are financial investors that apply long-term strategies to passively manage portfolios. Often, long-only futures strategies are put in place in order to allow diversification into a commodity portfolio at a relatively low cost. Another reason that pushes investors to assume a long position in commodity futures is the possibility of earning positive roll returns when the market is in backwardation. The profitability of these strategies depends on the persistence of factors that cause backwardated markets.

Other investors are instead interested in short-term investments, such as hedge funds. Hedge funds are highly leveraged portfolios of investments that are actively managed using various trading strategies. They trade commodities, but also stocks, futures, derivatives or structured products, and take long or short positions in global and domestic markets. Fusaro and Vasey (2006) discuss the existence and the growing importance of energy and environmental hedge funds. The environmental hedge funds, also called green hedge funds, represent investment opportunities in emerging environmental financial markets. In recent years, the entrance of the energy hedge funds, stuffed with expert traders from other markets, in commodity markets produced relevant returns. As a result, many ex-traders and investment banks created new hedge funds. Furthermore, existing funds, especially larger macro funds, introduced new exposure to energy markets. In the face of high risk-adjusted returns, Till and Gunzberg (2006) suggest that a commodity investor supports an idiosyncratic risk related to the specific commodity and macro risks that include those risks that create unplanned correlations. In particular, Fusaro and Vasey (2006) believe that in addition to the price risk (typical hedge fund risk), an energy hedge fund supports volumetric risk, operational risk, geopolitical risk, event risk, regulatory risk, weather risk, tax risk, and the like.

Finally, there are speculators that make a profit when prices either rise or fall rapidly, taking advantage of the divergence between futures and expected future spot prices. But speculators also have the important role of taking offsetting positions to companies that trade in commodities futures or hold physical commodities to hedge against rapid rises and falls in price. However, many market participants operate for both speculation and commercial trading, so that no robust and well-founded definition of speculation allows us to separate speculative activity from hedging and other commercial trading activities.

20.2.2 Commodity Futures Return Characteristics

Commodity markets are regularly affected by supply–demand imbalance. The only way to equilibrate supply and demand is via changes to either the inventory level or the price. When the short-run excess demand for most commodities cannot be satisfied by immediate new supplies, inventories are sold up to capacity to buyers. In this situation the price will possibly increase or might remain constant until sufficient inventories are rebuilt. If inventories are lacking, prices will suddenly rise within a few days. The market reacts in the opposite way to an ample supply of stored inventories or to a price decrease. This asymmetrical pattern is the reason behind one of the return characteristics: positive skewness.

In order to deal with the risk of spot prices and the lack of physical commodities, investment in commodities is typically done through futures markets. A futures price represents a bet on the future spot price. In fact, by entering into a futures contract an investor assumes the risk of unexpected movements in the future spot price, in exchange for receiving a risk premium, given by the difference between the current futures price and the expected future price. In mathematical terms, we can state that at date t the risk premium $rp(t)$ for an investor that observes the futures price $F(t,T)$ for delivery at date $T > t$ is

$$rp(t) = F(t,T) - E[S(T)|\mathcal{F}_t],$$

where $S(T)$ is the spot price at time T and $E[\cdot|\mathcal{F}_t]$ denotes the expected value under the real probability measure conditional on the information available at time t, $\mathcal{F}_t$.

The first theory that supported investment in commodity futures was the theory of *normal backwardation* (Keynes, 1930). Commodity futures are in some ways analogous to insurance contracts. The theory posits a world where producers of commodities would seek to hedge the price risk of their output. Speculators would be long futures in order to provide insurance against the risk of futures price fluctuations in exchange for a risk premium. In particular, long speculators would fix a futures price which is below the spot price expected at maturity of the futures contract. The risk premium is calculated by 'backwardating' the futures price relative to the expected future spot price.

The value of a futures contract at origination is zero, whereas long and short investors post collateral that will be used for the daily settlement of profits and losses. The collateral is typically calculated as a fraction of the notional value of the future position. One can assume a fully collateralized commodity futures investment and according to the literature (Booth and Fama, 1992; Erb and Harvey, 2006; Kat and Oomen, 2006a), the total return received by investors at a generic date $t \geq 0$ can be decomposed into three components:

- collateral return, CR_t;
- spot return, SR_t;
- roll return, RR_t;

so that we can state

$$\text{Total return received} = CR_t + SR_t + RR_t.$$

The collateral return is also called the cash return because typically the whole futures position is collateralized by cash and the investor receives the return at the spot interest rate. Other times, collateralization is obtained by purchasing risk-free investments.

The spot return is a relative change in commodity spot prices. Spot prices are volatile and are driven by the supply and demand characteristics of the particular commodity market. If $S(t)$ is the spot price at time t, the spot return is

$$SR_t = \frac{S(t) - S(t-1)}{S(t-1)}.$$

The roll return stems from the procedure of rolling over the market exposure in commodity futures when an investor decides to maintain his futures position after the maturity date of the contract. In this case, the expiring futures is sold and a yet-to-expire contract is bought. If the futures price curve is in backwardation, that is futures prices decline with time to maturity, the roll return, calculated as the relative difference between the futures price and the spot price, is positive. When the curve is in contango, that is futures prices rise with time to maturity, the roll return is negative and a loss is incurred. Given the futures price at time t with delivery at date $T > t$, $F(t, T)$, the roll return is

$$RR_t = \frac{F(t,T) - S(t)}{S(t)}.$$

The sum of the spot return and the roll return represents the excess return.

Finally, if a portfolio combines different commodities, another return component should be considered: diversification or rebalancing return. The behaviour of the constituents' prices over time determines the weights of the constituents within the portfolio. The weights are positive if the performance is good, negative if bad. So, the return of the equally weighted portfolio exceeds the average returns for its constituents. The diversification return is defined as the difference between the rebalanced portfolio geometric return and the weighted average geometric return of the portfolio constituents.

The characteristics of commodity returns are now analysed using historical data.[4] Seven time series of commodity futures logarithm returns have been analysed; namely, the time series of crude oil (CO), copper (HG), gold (GD), unleaded gasoline (XB), natural gas (NG), silver (SI) traded on the NYMEX and the time series of the peakload calendar futures of the European Energy Exchange (EEX). The daily time series span from 2002 to 2008 and consist of the closing prices of the futures contracts more actively traded in the market. Time series of futures logarithmic returns are constructed by rolling contracts over on the first day of the expiry month of the nearby contract. Table 20.20 displays the results of the statistical analysis carried out on the time series considered. Annualized average returns, μ, are positive for all the commodities and crude oil and natural gas exhibit the maximum daily returns. The values of the annualized standard deviation, σ, confirm the results obtained by Kat and Oomen (2006a) regarding the variability of commodity prices. Kat and Oomen (2006a) carry out an exhaustive and interesting univariate analysis of futures returns of 42 commodities. They find that energy commodities are more volatile than other commodities, such as gold. Additionally, comparing the behaviour of the commodity prices during the different phases of the business cycle, they suggest that energy commodities have the highest volatility during recessions. However, they argue that the volatility of commodity futures is not excessive and comparable with that of US large cap stocks.

It is known that commodities have positive exposure to supply shocks, so it can be commonly thought that futures returns are positively skewed. In contrast, all the considered time series are negatively skewed with the exception of natural gas. Kat and Oomen (2006a) also find that 24 out of 42 commodities are negatively skewed. Commodities belonging to the agricultural sector mostly present distributions that are positively skewed. Furthermore, the skewness in commodity futures returns might be considered minimal and insignificant.

Regarding the kurtosis of the returns distribution, values in Table 20.20 show that five of the seven time series analysed are leptokurtic, except those of crude oil and unleaded gasoline that are platykurtic. These results are in line with those of Kat and Oomen (2006a). The Jarque–Bera test checks the deviation of the distribution from a normal distribution. The results suggest each time series has a normal distribution.

Finally, looking at the data concerning the autocorrelation, that is the coefficient $\rho(i)$ with lags of days $i = 1, \ldots, 5$, it can be deduced that, for one day lag, five out of the seven time series show a negative autocorrelation p(1). A negative coefficient of one day lag means that the futures return of one day is connected with the return of the next day in the sense that a rise in one day is more likely to be followed by a fall in the next day and vice versa. The mechanism that works when the autocorrelation coefficient is positive is exactly the opposite. A rise (fall) is more likely followed by a rise (fall) the next day. Extending the lag time, a link between more distant returns can be obtained. Kat and Oomen (2006a) find positive autocorrelation for most commodity futures returns and they suggest it might be symptomatic of behavioural biases, prolonged impact of shocks, contagion in events, etc.

20.2.3 Risk Premiums in Commodity Markets

One of the main reasons for investing in an asset and holding it passively in a portfolio is the possibility of earning risk premiums. At least, this works for stocks and bonds, and in the

[4]Reference is made to statistical results obtained in Brandoni and Roncoroni (2008).

TABLE 20.20 Statistics of the commodity returns

	CO	EEX	HG	GC	XB	NG	SI
N	1739	1479	1724	1720	[illegible]	1719	1733
Time interval	1/02–10/08	1/02–11/08	1/02–6/08	1/02–11/08	[illegible]	1/02–11/08	1/02–11/08
Average	0.00064688	0.0005921	0.0005592	0.00057489	[illegible]	0.00061337	0.00045946
μ	0.163014	0.1492092	0.1409184	0.14487228	[illegible]	0.15456924	0.11578392
σ	0.020896	0.0007621	0.019762	0.012016	[illegible]	0.035667	0.02087
Skewness	−0.17373	−0.22049	−0.43146	−0.35878	[illegible]	0.73253	−1.3111
Kurtosis	1.421	4.1728	4.3525	3.9704	[illegible]	6.8825	8.9779
Jarque–Bera	189	97	185	104	[illegible]	1233	3077
$\rho(1)$	−0.0690	0.1318	−0.0807	0.0033	[illegible]	−0.009	−0.009
$\rho(2)$	0.0314	−0.0232	0.011	−0.0031	[illegible]	0.0088	0.0063
$\rho(3)$	0.0302	0.0024	−0.0143	0.0356	[illegible]	−0.0285	0.0282
$\rho(4)$	0.0540	0.0952	0.0218	−0.0052	[illegible]	0.0124	−0.0098
$\rho(5)$	−0.0337	0.0628	0.006	0.002	[illegible]	−0.0444	0.0049

literature many authors have examined and investigated the existence of risk premiums for commodities.

As discussed in the previous section, commodity total return is equal to the sum of three components: collateral return, spot return and roll return. Assuming that the investor uses T-bills or high-grade floating rate notes as collateral, the collateral return will be equal to the short rate. Thus, if the sum of the spot return and the roll return represents the futures return, the excess return over the short rate on a fully collateralized commodity investment equals the futures return (Kat and Oomen, 2006a), that is

$$\text{Excess return} = \text{spot return} + \text{roll return} = \text{futures return}.$$

Therefore, the risk premium on a collateralized futures investment is equal to the expected futures return. Clearly, only when futures prices do not correctly reflect expected future spot prices do risk premiums exist, because the deviation of the futures price from the expected future spot price causes the expected roll return and the expected spot return does not offset to zero.

While stocks and bonds almost surely offer a risk premium, for commodity futures investments it is necessary to hedge demand in order to pull the futures price away from the expected future spot price. In this way, futures volatility is likely to increase and, consequently, the expected return will be positive or negative depending on the hedging pressure direction. According to different commodities and to different years, hedging pressure varies and can impact mostly on supply or demand, generating respectively a positive or negative expected futures return. Sometimes zero or even negative risk premiums can characterize commodity futures, and reasonably they should not be attractive assets for any portfolio allocation. Despite this though, they will be considered as long as the lack of expected return is compensated by significant positive skewness and low or even negative correlation with other asset classes.

In the literature, empirical studies have been carried out to investigate the existence and nature of commodity risk premiums. Dusak (1987) analyses the existence of risk premiums for wheat, corn and soybean futures over the period 1952–1967 and within the CAPM framework. She finds that both risk premium and beta measuring systematic risk are close to zero, but she uses a database that is limited in scope.

Bodie and Rosansky (1980) provide an analysis of the return rates of commodity futures traded in the United States from 1950 to 1976 and find evidence of positive excess return for 22 of the 23 individual commodities evaluated, but with marginal statistical significance.

Gorton and Rouwenhorst (2006) use 36 commodity futures to construct an equally weighted index and investigate its monthly returns over the period between July 1959 and December 2004 in order to study commodity futures proprieties as an asset class. The risk premium of the index when the commodity futures are fully collateralized is about 5% per annum, whereas for individual commodities the presence of positive risk premium varies.

Doran (2005) estimates the risk premium of natural gas through a new methodology. He uses a parametric model with stochastic volatility, which has separate arrivals and volatility jumps, to describe the evolution of forward prices in natural gas. The instantaneous parameter estimates and quasi-Monte Carlo simulations are used to combine the risk-neutral and real-world distributions in order to find estimated ex-post realized volatilities and option prices. Minimizing the differences between the estimated and actual ex-post volatilities and option prices, he solves for the market price of risk. He finds a negative risk premium for natural gas contracts.

Kat and Oomen (2006a) consider 142 different commodity futures trading on 26 different exchanges in eight different countries, covering the period January 1965–February 2005. They report only the results of the study developed on 42 out of 142 daily settlement prices. They find the majority of commodities do not offer a risk premium, 13 out of 42 have negative futures returns, especially agricultural commodities. On the contrary, energy commodities exhibit positive excess returns. They also analyse the behaviour of commodity prices according to different phases of the business cycle. They find that, for example, during the start of a recession phase, energy, meat and livestock perform well, whereas agricultural commodities and metals exhibit their worst returns. Energy and soybean complexes perform badly during the end of a recession. Furthermore, as an economy grows strongly, inflation and interest rates push up and consequently, commodity returns are likely to be different in different monetary and inflationary environments. They argue that energy and industrial metals tend to perform particularly well in a restrictive monetary environment and particularly badly in an expansive monetary environment. Meat and livestock give bad results in a restrictive environment. Oats, cocoa, orange juice and Azuki beans perform worst during the start of a recession and best at the end. Others, like energy, behave in exactly the opposite way.

20.2.4 Commodities as a Portfolio Diversifier

An exercise of portfolio management mainly consists of two phases, the first concerns the selection of assets that will be included in the portfolio, while the second is characterized by the portfolio management strategy (active or passive). The following will only deal with the first phase. During this phase, the assets are selected in order that the performance of the portfolio meets certain criteria of optimality, maximizing return and minimizing risk. In particular, in this first stage the fundamental goal is to analyse the relationship between returns on the asset classes considered and within each asset class so as to construct a well-diversified portfolio.

Many authors in the literature, such as Gorton and Rouwenhorst (2006), Erb and Harvey (2006), Kat and Oomen (2006b), have analysed and studied the properties and characteristics of commodities, in particular commodity futures, and they have deduced that commodities are a good candidate to diversify a portfolio in which there are traditional assets, such as stocks and bonds.

In general, comparing the commodity index S&P GSCI and a market stock index, commodity futures contracts are highly volatile. Gorton and Rouwenhorst (2006) construct an equally weighted index of commodity futures considering various commodities and compare its performance with those of the S&P 500 total return index for stocks and the Ibbotson corporate bond total return index for bonds during the period from July 1959 to December 2004. The authors observe that stocks and commodity futures have approximately the same average annualized return that outperforms that of bonds, but, on the contrary, their returns are more volatile than those of bonds.

One can classify commodities into five main categories (Kat and Oomen, 2006b): grain and oil seeds, softs, meat and livestock, energy and metals. Commodity futures tend to exhibit high correlation between different types of commodities that belong to the same category and low correlation between commodities of different category groups. An exception is softs, characterized by low internal dependency. Consequently, portfolio diversification is promoted by investing across different category groups.

A very significant characteristic is that commodity futures are negatively correlated with stocks and bonds. Kat and Oomen (2006b) attribute this feature to two reasons: contrary to stocks and bonds, commodities generate positive returns to shock events and they perform in the opposite way with respect to stocks and bonds through the different phases of the business cycle (expansion and recession). The correlation between stocks and commodity futures varies over the different phases of the business cycle and according to the commodity category. In general, it is weakly positive or negative. The correlation for energy increases towards the end of periods of expansion and decreases, even becoming negative, towards the end of recessions, with the exact opposite phenomenon occurring for metals. The correlation between commodity futures and bond returns is also very weak and tends to be relatively low towards the end of expansion periods and relatively high during recession.

Finally, commodities provide a hedge against inflation due to the differing relationship that exists between commodities and inflation relative to that between stocks or bonds and inflation. In fact, for example, when there is strong economic growth, there is an upward pressure on commodities, producer and consumer prices and interest rates leading to a reduction in the growth potential of company profits. In addition, the value of stock and bond returns diminishes, being calculated through the discounted cash flows method, whereas commodities maintain their high value. This means that high inflation impacts negatively on stock and bond returns, but positively on commodities. This is also due to the fact that commodity prices (food, energy) are one of the components of the price index used for measuring inflation. Furthermore, it is important to stress that commodities are a reliable hedge against unexpected inflation (change in inflation rate). If one considers the subdivision of commodity return into spot return and roll return, the unexpected inflation is positively correlated with the spot return, while the dependence between inflation and roll return is insignificant. Greer (2000) argues that unexpected general inflation, which affects market movements, causes a drop in bond and stock prices but an increase in futures prices, such that commodity futures indexes go up in value. This means that stock and bond returns are positively correlated with unexpected inflation, whereas commodity futures indexes are negatively correlated.

Jensen and Mercer (2002) study the performance of a typical portfolio, consisting of US equities, foreign equities, corporate bonds and treasury bills, upon adding commodity futures and according to different monetary policies of the Federal Reserve. They show that the benefits of an allocation strategy with commodity futures accrue during periods of restrictive monetary policy. They highlight that benefits vary across different types of futures contracts; one can earn large returns from metals, energy and agricultural futures during periods of restrictive monetary policy, whereas one can profit from livestock contracts when the Federal Reserve follows an expansive monetary policy.

In conclusion, given all the features of commodity futures described above, an allocation in commodities yields diversification benefits for a portfolio, whether consisting of commodities belonging to different category groups and/or consisting of traditional assets (stocks, bonds, cash). But in the phase of portfolio selection, an investor should consider not only the fact that the risk of the portfolio decreases with the addition of commodities, but also that the risk premium offered by commodities is poor or negative, with the exception of energy, so that low gains are likely. In this context, portfolio optimization is used to find the proper portfolio composition according to a return/risk analysis.

20.2.5 Risk–Return Optimization in Commodity Portfolios

In the previous section, reference was made to the portfolio selection problem and the potentially important role commodities can play in diversifying risk, with the aim being to select investment assets that collectively have lower risk than any individual asset. The concept of diversification as a means of increasing the expected return of the portfolio, while reducing volatility, is the foundation of Modern Portfolio Theory (MPT), founded more than 50 years ago. The pioneer of MPT is Markowitz (1952), who theorized the mean–variance approach to solve the problem of optimal portfolio allocation. Mean–variance optimization requires three sets of input for the asset classes that belong to a given opportunity set: returns, standard deviations and correlations. The result of the mean–variance optimization is a set of efficient asset allocations whose coordinates form the efficient frontier in the mean–variance plane. Efficient allocations maximize expected return for a given level of risk, or equivalently, minimize risk for a given level of return. One can describe a mean–variance problem in the following way. Consider n assets with the expected value and the variance of the ith asset return being respectively μ_i and $\sigma_{ii} = \sigma_i^2$, and with the covariance between the ith asset and the jth asset being σ_{ij}, with $i, j = 1, 2, \ldots, n$ (i not equal to j). The vector $\mathbf{w}^\top = [w_1, \ldots, w_i, \ldots, w_n]$ indicates the portfolio allocation, that is the composition of the portfolio such that the amount w_i is proportional to the wealth allocated to the ith asset and $\sum_{i=1}^{n} w_i = 1$. The optimization problem can equivalently take one of the two following formulations:

$$\begin{array}{ll} \min\limits_{\mathbf{w}\in C} \sigma_p^2(\mathbf{w}) \Leftrightarrow & \max\limits_{\mathbf{w}\in C} \mu_p(\mathbf{w}) \\ \mu_p(\mathbf{w}) = \overline{\mu} & \sigma_p^2(\mathbf{w}) = \overline{\sigma_p^2} \\ \sum\limits_{i=1}^{n} w_i = 1 & \sum\limits_{i=1}^{n} w_i = 1 \end{array} \tag{20.7}$$

where μ_p and σ_p^2 are respectively the expected return and the variance of the portfolio return and C is the opportunity set of the allocations that fulfil the condition $\sum_{i=1}^{n} w_i = 1$. More precisely in problem (20.7), given a level of return $\overline{\mu}$, the investor aims to find the allocation $\mathbf{w}$ that minimizes the portfolio risk, or conversely, given a level of risk $\overline{\sigma_p^2}$, the investor maximizes the portfolio return. The expected return μ_p and the variance σ_p^2 can be expressed as $\mu_p = \sum_{i=1}^{n} w_i \mu_i$ and $\sigma_p^2 = \sum_{i=1}^{n} \sum_{j=1}^{n} w_i w_j \sigma_{ij}$. If the weight w_i assumes a negative value, the ith asset is short-sold. The allocations that solve problem (20.7) are efficient allocations. Markowitz's mean–variance optimization is the primary tool utilized by investors for investing in assets and finding efficient allocations. MPT is used here to demonstrate that by including commodities in a portfolio of traditional assets (bonds, stocks), the efficient frontier obtained by solving problem (20.7) dominates, in that it is always above, the efficient frontier of the traditional portfolio itself. Comparison is made between the efficient frontiers with and without the commodities asset class and the allocations that are historically optimal are found. Once two efficient portfolios are found, then to draw the efficient frontiers the two fund theorem is applied, which states that all the portfolios on the Markowitz efficient frontier can be obtained as a one-parameter family of linear combinations of any two of them. Thus, varying the parameter, that is the weights of the two portfolios, one calculates different pairings of mean and variance. Market proxies are considered in order to create exposure to stock markets and bond markets. The proxies for asset classes are market indexes: S&P 500 for US stocks, MSCI EAFE for international stocks, Lehman Bond Composite-U.S. for US bonds, Lehman Bond Composite-Global for international bonds and Dow Jones-AIG Commodity Index (DJ-AIGCI) for commodities. DJ-AIGCI is an index composed of futures contracts on commodities over

19 raw materials and designed to provide a benchmark-diversified commodity futures market. It is conceivable that the following analysis can be conducted taking into account specific commodities, perhaps using benchmark indexes as proxies. Furthermore, cross-commodity portfolios can be studied. The considered time series are monthly and about 10 years long, from January 2001 to August 2010. Table 20.21 shows the values of the mean returns and the matrix of variance–covariance.

Figure 20.4 plots the efficient frontiers of portfolios with and without the commodities asset class in the plane (σ_p, μ_p). The frontier with the commodities asset class dominates the frontier without it. This means that commodities are effectively a good diversifier as, for a given level of risk, including commodities in a traditional portfolio of bonds and stocks allows one to reach a higher level of return.

An analogous but more detailed analysis is carried out by Idzorek (2006). He studies the role of commodities in a strategic asset allocation. He creates an exposure to stocks and bonds and to inflation through market proxies, such as market indexes. The mean–variance approach is used to investigate and compare, using historical data, the efficient frontiers with and without the commodities asset class. Furthermore, Idzorek (2006) uses three other approaches to demonstrate the advantage achieved by combining investments in commodities and traditional assets. The first approach developed is the CAPM, which is commonly not considered applicable to the commodities asset class due to the lack of market capitalization. In fact, the CAPM is a general equilibrium model that considers the investment in a portfolio given by a combination of a risk-free asset and a market portfolio. The market portfolio contains all the assets existing in the market according to their capitalization. In the CAPM theory, the return of any asset is decomposed into two components: the portion correlated with the market and associated with nondiversifiable risk, and the portion uncorrelated with the market and associated with idiosyncratic and diversifiable risk. If we represent the CAPM as a univariate factor model, the return of the kth asset at time t, r_t^k, is obtained using the following formula:

$$r_t^k = x_t^k + \beta_t^k r_t^M,$$

where x_t^k is the component associated with idiosyncratic risk and $\beta_t^k r_t^M$ represents the component associated with nondiversifiable risk, β_t^k being a measure of the sensitivity of r_t^k to variations of the market return r_t^M. After having developed a technique to estimate the commodity market capitalization, Idzorek (2006) creates forward-looking efficient frontiers with and without commodities. Then, using the building block methodology and the Black–Litterman model (Black and Litterman, 1992) he obtains similar results.

The mean–variance approach of Markowitz is also used by Yu (2003) to develop a model for evaluating the risk of profit-making arising in deregulated multi-pooled electricity markets. In fact, in these markets fringe producers and bigger producers have to face short-term, spatial market risk and in the paper no oligopolistic strategies can be adopted. The Markowitz model is extended as a mixed-integer programming model to include constraints that take into account transaction costs and other practical constraints (for example physical plant constraints). Through the estimation of the correlation of geographically separated markets and the consideration of wheeling administration, the author captures the spatial dynamic. He studies the cases of New York Power Pool and Pennsylvania–Maryland Power Pool and finds an efficient frontier that is neither smooth nor concave due to the additional constraints.

TABLE 20.21 Portfolio optimization input

Variance–covariance matrix	Stocks	Inter. stocks	Bonds	Inter. bonds	Commodities	Annual return
Stock	0.000739537	0.000985831	4.51266E-06	8.59857E-06	0.000709619	0.013702063
Inter. stocks	0.000985831	0.001402361	1.06724E-06	2.3627E-05	0.000993395	0.042065815
Bonds	4.51266E-06	1.06724E-06	7.9515E-06	1.07317E-05	2.03513E-06	0.026163929
Inter. bonds	8.59857E-06	2.3627E-05	1.07317E-05	2.04264E-05	8.48137E-06	0.028749019
Commodities	0.000709619	0.000993395	2.03513E-06	8.48137E-06	0.000791465	0.017416709

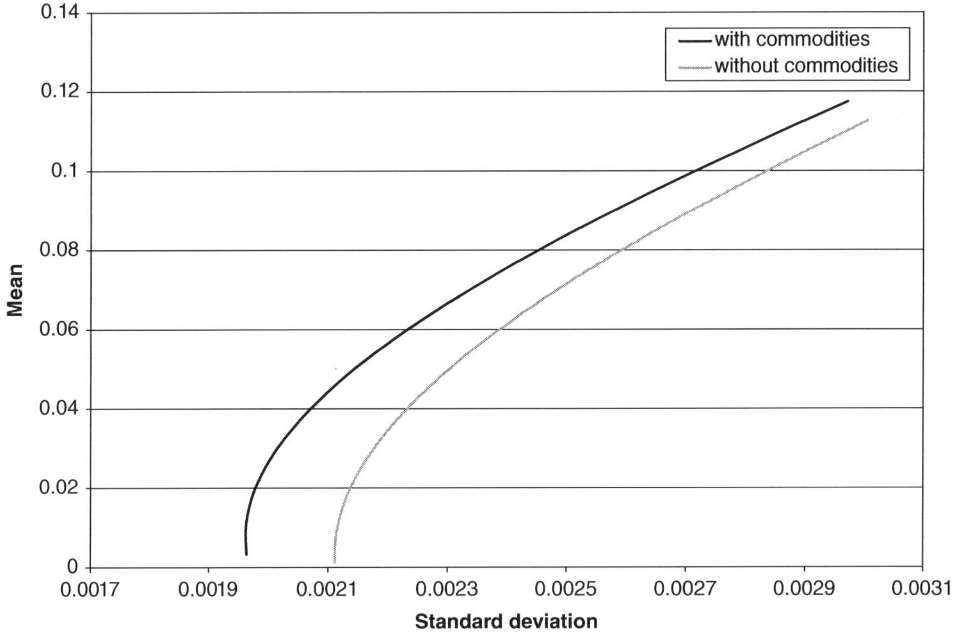

FIGURE 20.4 Efficient frontiers comparison

MPT is widely used in the literature to solve problems of allocation in different physical or financial contracts for electricity generators or purchasers, and in order to manage price risk, delivery risk and volumetric risk, or simply to minimize costs or maximize profits.

Liu and Wu (2007) consider the case of the generation companies (Gencos) that in deregulated electricity markets have to manage the risks of price and delivery in order to guarantee their profits. The risk management takes place through portfolio diversification; trading energy through both different physical trading approaches (spot markets, contract markets) and financial trading approaches (futures contracts, swaps, options, etc.). So, basically, the two kinds of risks faced are the risk of price fluctuations on spot markets and the delivery risk due to transmission congestion. The authors analyse an energy system based on locational marginal pricing. One way suggested by Liu and Wu (2007) to solve the problems for a Genco of maximizing the expected return and simultaneously minimizing the variance of the return of a portfolio that allocates energy between spot and bilateral contract markets is via the following quadratic programming exercise:

$$\max_{w_i} U = E[r_C] - \frac{1}{2}A\sigma^2(r_C) \tag{20.8}$$

$$\text{s.t.} \quad \sum_{i=1}^{n+1} w_i = 1$$

$$w_i \geq 0.$$

In (20.8), U is the utility function of the Genco, $E[r_C]$ is the expected return of the portfolio, given by the combination of the expected energy contract returns, $\sigma^2(r_C)$ is the variance of the portfolio return, w_i, $i = 1, \dots, n+1$, is the weight of the ith contract in the portfolio, and A is the weighting factor that reflects the decision maker's preference for or aversion to risk. If A is positive the decision maker is risk averse, a negative A indicates risk loving and if A is equal to zero, he/she is risk neutral. It should be highlighted that trading approaches for the Genco include risk-free contracts that refer to a local counterparty, risky contracts between Genco and a nonlocal counterparty and risky spot deals. Furthermore, if a congestion in the transmission system happens, the Genco has to pay all or part of the congestion charge, which is given by the product of the spot price difference between the two locations involved and the transmitted energy (MWh), all according to specific market rules. The congestion rate is included as a factor in nonlocal bilateral contract return–variance evaluation. Then, PJM market data are used to illustrate the presented approach of allocating energy between markets.

Huisman *et al.* (2009) study the problem of electricity purchasers in deregulated markets, which must provide electricity to a company or a pool of clients according to their future expected electricity consumption. So electricity purchasers aim to manage a portfolio of contracts (day-ahead contracts, forwards, futures, swaps, etc.) and direct or indirect investments in energy production facilities in order to minimize expected costs, while trying to limit the variance of these contracts. In particular, Huisman *et al.* (2009) consider a purchaser that has the opportunity to enter, at time t, either in a peak contract or in an off-peak contract. A peak contract delivers 1 MW of electricity in all the peak hours of day T at a price fixed at time $t < T$, whereas an off-peak contract delivers 1 MW in all the off-peak hours of day T at a fixed price. The authors propose the following mean–variance optimization problem to find the optimal allocations in peak and off-peak forward contracts:

$$\begin{aligned} &\min_{\theta_o, \theta_p} E_t\{C(T)\} \\ s.t. \quad &var_t\{C(T)\} \leq \sigma^2_{max}. \end{aligned} \tag{20.9}$$

In (20.9), the number of off-peak contracts θ_o and the number of peak contracts θ_p that minimize the total costs $C(T)$ for a generic purchaser are found. Total costs consist of the costs of off-peak and peak forward contracts and the costs of the purchase in the day-ahead market for the requested electricity that is left and not provided by futures contracts. Then, total costs are uncertain because they depend on the volumes and day-ahead prices. The constraint of problem (20.9) is that the costs variance $var_t\{C(T)\}$ must be below a maximum level of variance established by the purchaser, σ^2_{max}. The optimal allocation for the purchaser is found in two steps. In the first step, the set of optimal allocations that satisfy all producers is obtained and based on the difference in risk premiums per unit of day-ahead risk as a measure of relative costs of hedging risk in the day-ahead markets. In the second step, the purchaser chooses among the optimal allocations those that are in accordance with his risk profile. Finally, the authors discuss the managerial uses and implications of their model.

It is important to stress that there are problems that can be more properly tackled by choosing a risk measure different from portfolio variance. In such cases, Value at Risk (VaR) or Conditional Value at Risk (CVaR) should be used. VaR measures the maximum expected portfolio loss over a holding period and according to a confidence level c. VaR is the absolute value of the quantile of the left tail of the portfolio return (r_p) distribution corresponding to the confidence level c:

$$VaR_c(r_p) \equiv |Q_{r_p}(1-c)|,$$

where Q_{r_p} is the quantile of the return distribution.

A VaR constraint is included in the problem formulated by Oum and Oren (2009) in order to maximize the hedged profit of load serving entities (LSEs). An LSE has the obligation to serve load to consumers. The LSE is exposed to two types of risk: the price risk deriving from trading electricity on the wholesale spot market and so from the uncertainty of its prices, and the volumetric risk due to the required load variation. The authors build a self-financing hedging portfolio consisting of a risk-free bond, a forward contract and a spectrum of call and put options with different strike prices. The proposed problem is the following:

$$\begin{aligned} &\max_{x(p)} E[Y(x)] \\ s.t. \quad & E^Q[x(p)] = 0 \\ & VaR_c(Y(x)) \leq V_0, \end{aligned} \tag{20.10}$$

where $Y(x)$ is the hedged profit, $E[\cdot]$ and $E^Q[\cdot]$ denote the expectation under the objective/real probability measure and risk-neutral measure, respectively, $x(p)$ is the payoff function of an exotic option used for hedging the LSE revenue and that is replicated using standard derivatives, such as forwards, calls and puts, p is the electricity price and V_0 is a fixed level of risk that is not exceeded. The profit of the LSE depends on two correlated variables, price and demand, so solving analytically problem (20.10) becomes difficult. Oum and Oren (2009) propose an approximation method that restricts the search for the optimal VaR constrained portfolio on the mean–variance efficient frontier.

A robust portfolio optimization technique using liquidity-adjusted VaR (L-VaR) as risk measure is proposed by AlJanabi (2012). The author analyses, from a portfolio manager's perspective, the optimal commodity portfolio selection problem under normal and adverse distributional assumptions. He implements different long trading scenarios or a combination of long/short commodity trading strategies. The suggested technique is used for minimizing L-VaR under budget constraints that are formulated considering a realistic and meaningful financial situation and applications.

One main drawback of the VaR is that it does not promote diversification. Furthermore, optimizing an allocation by minimizing the VaR does not consider the distributional properties beyond the c-quantile. So, regardless of the distribution at the left of the VaR the optimization result does not change. Finally, the VaR is easily determined if the return distribution is normal, whereas it becomes difficult if it is not clearly identifiable, especially if it is discrete, nonconvex, nonsmooth and with multiple local extremes. As an alternative to VaR, the risk measure used is CVaR.

CVaR is a coherent measure of risk (Artzner *et al.*, 1999). It can be defined as the expected value of the portfolio return conditional that the return is less than the quantile corresponding to the confidence level c, that is

$$CVaR_c(r_p) \equiv E[r_p | r_p \leq Q_{r_p}(1-c)]. \tag{20.11}$$

A return–risk optimization portfolio problem can be formulated in the following way:

$$\begin{aligned} &\min_{w_i} CVaR_c(r_p) \\ s.t. \quad & r_p \geq \overline{\mu}, \\ & \sum_i w_i = 1 \\ w_i \geq 0, \quad & \forall i = 1, \ldots, n, \end{aligned} \tag{20.12}$$

where w_i, $i = 1, \dots, n$, are the portfolio weights and r_p is the portfolio return. The parameter $\overline{\mu}$ represents a boundary for portfolio returns, so that all allocations that fulfil the constraints of problem (20.12) are feasible portfolios and among these portfolios, the efficient portfolios can be identified by minimizing the CVaR. So problem (20.12) is a generalization of the Markowitz mean–variance optimization problem. An example of mean–risk optimization of electricity portfolios minimizing CVaR is the model developed by Eichhorn *et al.* (2004). They maximize the mean book value of a portfolio consisting of physical components and energy derivatives at the end of the optimization horizon, and simultaneously minimize the risk measured by CVaR. They apply their methodology to solve the problem for a municipal power utility.

SYMBOLS

$T(t)$	the price of a target commodity at time t
$X(t)$	the price of a synthetic asset at time t
$M(t)$	the value of the statistical mispricing at time t
$\mathbf{C}(t)$	the price vector of commodities at time t
$E[\cdot]$	the expectation
SATS	statistical arbitrage trading strategy
$rp(t)$	the risk premium at time t
$F(t, T)$	the futures price at time t for delivery at date $T > t$
$S(t)$	the spot price at time t
r_t^k	the return of the kth asset at time t
VaR_c	value at risk at the confidence level c
$CVaR_c$	conditional value at risk at the confidence level c
w_i	the weight of the ith asset in the portfolio

REFERENCES

Alexander, C. (2008) *Timing Techniques for Commodity Futures Markets: Effective Strategy and Tactics for Short-term and Long-term Traders*, McGraw-Hill, New York.

Alexander, S.S. (1961) Price movements in speculative markets: Trends or random walks, *Industrial Management Review*, **2**, 7–26.

Alexander, S.S. (1964) Price movements in speculative markets: Trends or random walks, no. 2, *Industrial Management Review*, **5**, 25–46.

Alizadeh, A.H. and Nomikos, N.K. (2004) Cost of carry, causality and arbitrage between oil futures and tanker freight markets, *Transportation Research Part E*, **40**(4), 297–316.

Alizadeh, A.H. and Nomikos, N.K. (2008) Performance of statistical arbitrage in petroleum futures markets, *The Journal of Energy Markets*, **1**(2), 3–33.

AlJanabi, M.A. (2012) Optimal commodity asset allocation with a coherent market risk modelling, *Review of Financial Economics*, **21**, 131–140.

Artzner, P., Delbaen, F., Eber, J.-M. and Heath, D. (1999) Coherent measures of risk, *Mathematical Finance*, **9**(3), 203–228.

Asche, F., Gjølberg, O. and Völker, T. (2003) Price relationships in the petroleum market: An analysis of crude oil and refined product prices, *Energy Economics*, **25**(3), 289–301.

Bertram, W. (2010) Analytic solutions for optimal statistical arbitrage trading, *Physica A*, **389**(11), 2234–2243.

Black, F. and Litterman, R. (1992) Global portfolio optimization, *Financial Analysts Journal*, **48**(5), 28–43.

Bodie, Z. and Rosansky, V.I. (1980) Risk and returns in commodity futures, *Financial Analysts Journal*, **36**(3), 27–39.

Bondarenko, O. (2003) Statistical arbitrage and securities prices, *Review of Financial Studies*, **16**(3), 875–919.

Booth, D.G. and Fama, E.F. (1992) Diversification returns and asset contributions, *Financial Analysts Journal*, **48**(3), 26–32.

Brandoni, C. and Roncoroni, A. (2008) Analisi di modelli di statistical arbitrage e applicazioni ai mercati delle commodity, Progect work: corso di Alta formazione in Energy Finance e Commodity Trading, MIPPolitecnico di Milano.

Burgess, A.N. (1999) A computational methodology for modelling the dynamics of statistical arbitrage, Ph.D. Thesis, London Business School.

Do, B., Faff, R. and Hamza, K. (2006) A new approach to modeling and estimation for pairs trading, working Paper, Monash University.

Domanski, D. and Heath, A. (2007) Financial investors and commodity markets, *BIS Quarterly Review*.

Doran, J.S. (2005) Estimation of the risk premiums in energy markets, *The ICFAI Journal of Derivatives Markets*, **II**(4), 23–54.

Dusak, K. (1987) Futures trading and investor returns: An investigation of commodity market risk premiums, *Journal of Political Economy*, **81**(6), 1387–1406.

Eichhorn, A., Gröwe-Kuska, N., Liebscher, A., Römisch, W., Spangardt, G. and Wergner, I. (2004) Mean-risk optimization of electricity portfolios, *Proceedings in Applied Mathematics and Mechanics*, **4**, 3–6.

Elliott, R., van der Hoek, J. and Malcolm, W. (2005) Pairs trading, *Quantitative Finance*, **5**(3), 271–276.

Erb, C.B. and Harvey, C.B. (2006) The tactical and strategic value of commodity futures, available at SSRN: http://ssrn.com/abstract=650923.

Fama, E. (1970) Efficient capital markets: A review of theory and empirical work, *The Journal of Finance*, **25**(2), 383–417.

Fama, E. (1976) *Foundation of Finance*, Basic Books, New York.

Fama, E. (1991) Efficient capital markets: II, *The Journal of Finance*, **46**(5), 1575–1617.

Fama, E.F. and Blume, M.E. (1966) Filter rules and stock-market trading, *The Journal of Business*, **39**(1), 226–241.

Fusai, G. and Roncoroni, A. (2008) *Implementing Models in Quantitative Finance: Methods and Cases*, Springer-Verlag, Berlin.

Fusaro, P. and Vasey, G. (2006) *Energy and Environmental Hedge Funds – The New Investment Paradigm*, John Wiley & Sons, Chichester.

Geman, H. (2005) *Commodities and Commodity Derivatives: Modeling and Pricing for Agriculturals, Metal and Energy*, John Wiley & Sons, Chichester.

Girma, P. and Paulson, A.S. (1999) Risk arbitrage opportunities in petroleum futures spreads, *The Journal of Futures Markets*, **19**(8), 931–955.

Gorton, G. and Rouwenhorst, K.G. (2006) Facts and fantasies about commodity futures, *Financial Analysts Journal*, **62**(2), 47–68.

Granger, C. (1969) Investigating casual relations by econometric models and cross-spectral methods, *Econometrica*, **37**(3), 424–438.

Granger, C.W.J. (1983) Cointegrated variables and error-correcting models, UCSD Discussion Paper.

Greer, R.J. (2000) The nature of commodity index returns, *The Journal of Alternative Investments*, **3**(1), 45–53.

Huisman, R., Mahieu, R. and Schlichter, F. (2009) Electricity portfolio management: Optimal peak/off-peak allocations, *Energy Economics*, **31**(1), 169–174.

Idzorek, T.M. (2006) Strategic asset allocation and commodities Technical Report, Ibbotson Associates.

Jensen, G.R. and Mercer, J.M. (2002) Tactical asset allocation and commodity futures, *The Journal of Portfolio Management*, **28**(4), 100–111.

Johansen, S. (1988) Statistical analysis of cointegration vectors, *Journal of Economic Dynamics and Control*, **12**(2&3), 231–254.

Johansen, S. (1991) Examination and hypothesis testing of cointegration vectors in Gaussian vector autoregressive models, *Econometrica*, **59**(6), 1551–1581.

Johnson, R., Zulauf, C.R., Irwin, S.H. and Gerlow, M.E. (1991) The soybean complex spread: An examination of market efficiency from the viewpoint of a production process, *Journal of Futures Markets*, **11**(1), 25–37.

Kat, M.H. and Oomen, R.C.A. (2006a) What every investor should know about commodities, Part I: Univariate return analysis, Cass Business School Research Paper, available at SSRN: http://ssrn.com/abstract=878361.

Kat, M.H. and Oomen, R.C.A. (2006b) What every investor should know about commodities, Part II: Multivariate return analysis, Cass Business School Research Paper, available at SSRN: http://ssrn.com/abstract=908609.

Kenourgios, D.F. and Samitas, A.G. (2004) Testing the efficiency of the copper futures market: New evidence from London Metal Exchange, *Global Business and Economics Review*, pp. 261–271.

Keynes, J.M. (1930) *A Treatise on Money*, Vol. **2**, Macmillan, London.

Kulkarni, S. and Haidar, I. (2009) Forecasting model for crude oil price using artificial neural networks and commodity futures, *Journal of Computer Science and Information Security*, **2**(1), 81–88.

LeRoy, S.F. (1989) Efficient capital markets and martingales, *Journal of Economic Literature*, **27**(4), 1583–1621.

Liu, M. and Wu, F. (2007) Portfolio optimization in electricity markets, *Electric Power Systems Research*, **77**(8), 1000–1009.

Liu, Q.W. (2005) Price relations among hog, corn and soybean meal futures, *Journal of Futures Markets*, **25**(5), 491–514.

Locke, P.R. and Venkatesh, P.C. (1997) Futures market transaction costs, *Journal of Futures Markets*, **17**(2), 229–245.

Ma, C.K. and Soenen, L.A. (1988) Arbitrage opportunities in metal futures markets, *Journal of Futures Markets*, **8**(2), 199–209.

Markowitz, H.M. (1952) Portfolio selection, *The Journal of Finance*, **7**(1), 77–91.

Niederhoffer, V. and Osborne, M.F.M. (1966) Market making and reversal of the stock exchange, *Journal of the American Statistical Association*, **61**(316), 897–916.

Oum, Y. and Oren, S. (2009) VaR constrained hedging of fixed price load following obligations in competitive electricity markets, *Risk and Decision Analysis*, **1**(1), 43–56.

Poitras, G. and Teoh, A. (2003) The crack spread: Day trading the oil futures complex, *Derivatives Use, Trading, & Regulation*, **9**(2), 102–116.

Pole, A. (2007) *Statistical Arbitrage*, John Wiley & Sons, Chichester.

Sullivan, R., Timmermann, A. and White, H. (1999) Data-snooping, technical trading rule performance, and the bootstrap, *Journal of Finance*, **54**(5), 1647–1691.

Till, H. and Gunzberg, J. (2006) Absolute Returns in Commodity (Natural Resource) Futures Investments.

Vidyamurthy, G. (2004) *Pairs Trading: Quantitative Methods and Analysis*, John Wiley & Sons, New York.

White, H. (2000) A reality check for data snooping, *Econometrica*, **68**(5), 1097–1126.

Yu, Z. (2003) A spatial mean-variance MIP model for energy market risk analysis, *Energy Economics*, **25**(3), 255–268.

CHAPTER 21

Econometric Analysis of Energy and Commodity Markets: Multiple Hypothesis Testing Techniques

Mark Cummins

21.1 INTRODUCTION

As with other areas of empirical finance, the econometric analysis of energy and commodity markets involves applying a suite of appropriate econometric tests to a range of appropriate time series, cross-sectional or panel data. Such empirical studies, by their very nature, suffer from the well-established problem of data snooping bias, whereby there is a non-negligible likelihood that statistically significant results may be identified by random chance alone rather than as a result of any underlying statistical relationships. White (2000) describes data snooping bias as resulting from a given set of data being used more than once for purposes of inference or model selection, whereby any statistically significant results are due to chance rather than to any merit inherent in the methodology. In the statistical and econometric literature, this phenomenon is more commonly referred to as the multiple comparisons problem that results from multiple hypothesis testing. Although the problem is well established in the literature, much of the empirical finance work to date (across all market classes, including energy and commodities) either ignores or is unaware of the problem.

Rather than present a comprehensive literature review, the interested reader is instead directed to the work of Romano *et al.* (2010), who provide a detailed exposition of the issues pertaining to multiple hypothesis testing, outlining the recent key literature in the area. However, relevant literature will be referenced throughout the following sections, which showcase the application of multiple hypothesis-testing techniques to control for the multiple comparisons problem within a range of energy and commodity applications. Multiple hypothesis testing procedures can broadly be categorized as *p-value-based* approaches that assume the existence of and work on a set of available p-values and *resampling-based* approaches that utilize bootstrapping (often as part of a recursive methodology) to identify statistical significance

Handbook of Multi-Commodity Markets and Products: Structuring, Trading and Risk Management. Edited by Andrea Roncoroni, Gianluca Fusai and Mark Cummins.

on the basis of some defined criterion for the hypothesis testing (e.g., mean daily log returns, mean Sharpe ratio outperformance, etc.). Full details of these concepts, along with specific control procedures from the literature, are presented in this chapter. Specifically, three studies are presented that serve to showcase the issue of multiple hypothesis testing from a practical perspective for both academics and industry participants alike. The studies may be described as follows:

- **Energy–Emissions Market Interactions.** The first study is the work of Cummins (2013a) analysing the interactions between the energy (i.e., oil, gas, coal and power) and emissions markets that serves in part to establish how integrated the markets have become in recent years. In theory, the energy markets should serve as a driver of emissions prices. However, there is conflicting evidence of this in the literature, which is fuelled in no small part by the issues surrounding Phase I and Phase II of the European Union Emissions Trading Scheme (EU ETS), such as the oversupply of allowances, the global recession, uncertainty (at the time) over the structure of Phase III, etc. This study investigates such energy and emissions market interactions, applying vector autoregression and Granger-causality testing to a large system of energy and emissions data. In so doing, the multiple comparisons problem described above presents itself. A suite of *p*-value class procedures are applied to control for the multiple comparisons problem in this case, giving greater statistical confidence around the conclusions drawn.
- **Emissions Market Interactions.** The second study is the work of Cummins (2013b), which looks specifically at market interactions within the EU ETS. In particular, the study focuses on European Union Allowance (EUA) and Certified Emissions Reduction (CER) units, both of which are allowable instruments (although CERs only to a limited extent) for compliance purposes under the EU ETS. EUA and CER forward curves are constructed from a comprehensive set of emissions data and vector autoregression and Granger-causality testing employed to analyse the statistical relationships. The multiple comparisons problem again surfaces as a result of this testing framework. As with the previous study, a suite of *p*-value class procedures is applied to control for the multiple comparisons problem in this context.
- **Quantitative Spread Trading in Oil Markets.** The third study is the recent work of Cummins and Bucca (2012), which looks at quantitative spread trading in the crude oil and refined products markets. Specifically, the authors apply an innovative statistical arbitrage trading model to a large range of common-commodity and cross-commodity spreads, including calendar, locational and crack spreads. The multiple comparisons problem presents itself again here as the overall objective is to identify, with statistical confidence, profitable trading strategies from the range of trading strategies implemented. However, unlike the two previous studies, a suite of resampling class procedures is applied in order to control for the multiple comparisons problem in this instance, where the criterion used for the hypothesis testing is the mean daily log return.

21.2 MULTIPLE HYPOTHESIS TESTING

As outlined previously, multiple hypothesis testing (MHT) procedures can broadly be categorized as *p-value-based* approaches that assume the existence of and work on a set of available

p-values and *resampling-based* approaches that utilize bootstrapping (often as part of a recursive methodology) to identify statistical significance on the basis of some defined criterion (see, e.g., White, 2000; Hansen, 2005; Romano and Wolf, 2007, 2010; and, for empirical applications, Sullivan *et al.*, 1999; Hsu and Kuan, 2005; Qui and Wu, 2006; Park and Irwin, 2007; Marshall *et al.*, 2008; Cummins and Bucca, 2012). Within both classifications of MHT procedure, specific procedures are developed around one of four key criteria for controlling the multiple comparisons problem. These key criteria are: (i) the generalized familywise error rate, (ii) the per-familywise error rate, (iii) the false discovery proportion and (iv) the false discovery rate. The literature has evolved over recent decades, and in particular over recent years, towards more generalized procedures that offer the advantage of greater *power* over earlier procedures, where power is loosely defined, as in Romano *et al.* (2010), as the ability to reject a null hypothesis when it is false, as should be done. Earlier procedures in the literature suffer from excessive conservativeness, in the sense that in attempting to control for *false discoveries* (i.e., rejection of *true* null hypotheses) such procedures make it very difficult to identify *true discoveries* (i.e., rejection of *false* null hypotheses). Recent generalized procedures seek to relax this constraint and so increase the power of the testing.

Before proceeding to discuss the three empirical studies outlined in Section 21.1, the following subsections present a formal definition for each of the generalized familywise error rate, per-familywise error rate, false discovery proportion and false discovery rate criteria in turn. In preparation for the generalized procedures to be described later, a brief discussion is also given on the difference between single-step and stepwise procedures, the latter forming the basis of more recent and superior generalized techniques.

21.2.1 Generalized Familywise Error Rate

Before introducing the generalized concept, first note that the familywise error rate (FWER) is defined as the probability that at least *one or more* false discoveries occur. Consistent with the notation of Romano *et al.* (2010), the following definition is made:

$$\text{FWER} \equiv P\{\text{reject at least one null hypothesis } H_{0,i} : i \in I\},$$

where $H_{0,i}$, $i = 1, \ldots, s$, is a set of null hypotheses ($s \geq 1$) and I is the set of true null hypotheses. So the FWER describes the probability of making at least one false discovery. Controlling the FWER involves setting a significance level α and requiring that FWER $\leq \alpha$. So, for example, if the significance is set at 1% then controlling the FWER means ensuring that the probability of making one or more false discoveries from the family of multiple hypothesis tests is less than or equal to 1%. However, this approach is particularly conservative given that it does not allow even for one false discovery and so as a result is criticized for lacking *power*. The greater the total number of hypotheses s, the more difficult it is to make true discoveries.

To deal with these weaknesses, the concept of the generalized FWER has been considered in the literature. The generalized FWER seeks to control for k (where $k \geq 1$) or more false discoveries and, in so doing, allows for greater power in MHT applications. The generalized k-FWER is defined as follows:

$$k\text{-FWER} \equiv P\{\text{reject at least } k \text{ null hypothesis } H_{0,i} : i \in I\}.$$

Controlling the k-FWER involves setting a significance level α and requiring that k-FWER $\leq \alpha$. The choice of k is set by the user and the greater this choice then the greater the power in identifying true discoveries, at the expense of potentially making some false discoveries. So, for example, consider a problem that implements 1000 hypothesis tests simultaneously. If k is chosen to be 10 (representing 1% of the tests considered) and the significance level is set at 1% then controlling the k-FWER means ensuring that the probability of making 10 or more false discoveries from the family of multiple hypothesis tests is less than or equal to 1%. See Romano *et al.* (2010) for a full discussion.

21.2.2 Per-Familywise Error Rate

The per-familywise error rate (PFER) is a measure that is directly related to the familywise error rate and is defined as follows:

$$\text{PFER} \equiv E(F),$$

where F denotes the number of false rejections identified by an MHT procedure and $E(\cdot)$ is the expectations operator, such that $E(F)$ is the expected value of F. So the PFER describes the expected number of false discoveries from the application of an MHT procedure. Controlling the PFER involves setting a rejection threshold level $\lambda \in [0, \infty)$ and requiring that PFER $\leq \lambda$. The choice of λ is set by the user and the greater this choice then the greater the power in identifying true discoveries, although at the expense of potentially making some false discoveries.

An issue with the PFER is that controlling for the multiple comparisons problem in this way allows for little to be concluded about the realized value of F. This is because the PFER focuses on the expected number of rejections. In contrast, the k-FWER allows one to be confident at the $(1-\alpha)$ level that there are at most $(k-1)$ false discoveries among the rejected hypotheses. See Romano *et al.* (2010) for a full discussion.

21.2.3 False Discovery Proportion

The false discovery proportion (FDP) is formally defined as follows:

$$\text{FDP} \equiv \begin{cases} \frac{FR}{TR}, & TR > 0 \\ 0, & TR = 0 \end{cases},$$

where FR denotes the number of false rejections and TR denotes the total number of rejections under an MHT procedure. Controlling the FDP involves setting a proportion level γ and a significance level α and requiring that

$$P\{\text{FDP} > \gamma\} \leq \alpha.$$

So the FDP describes the ratio of false rejections to the total number of rejections achieved, which can naturally run from 0% to 100%. The choice of proportion γ is made by the user depending on the level of power required. See Romano *et al.* (2010) for a full discussion.

21.2.4 False Discovery Rate

The false discovery rate is defined as follows:

$$\text{FDR} \equiv E(\text{FDP}).$$

So the FDR represents the expected false discovery proportion and controlling the FDR involves setting a proportion level $\gamma \in [0, 1)$ and requiring that FDR $\leq \gamma$. Similar to the issue raised with the PFER, the FDR is such that it allows for little to be concluded about the realized FDP. This is because the FDR focuses on the expected false discovery proportion. In contrast, the FDP allows one to be confident at the $(1 - \alpha)$ level that the proportion of false discoveries among all rejected hypotheses is at most γ. See Romano *et al.* (2010) for a full discussion.

21.2.5 Single-Step and Stepwise Procedures

The generalized MHT procedures presented in the forthcoming sections will be based on either the generalized familywise error rate or the false discovery proportion. As outlined in the previous sections, the generalized nature of the procedures means that they have the attractive property of greater power compared to earlier, more conservative procedures in the literature. The majority of the MHT procedures employed have an additional property that makes them even more attractive. This is the stepwise property of the procedures, whereby the process of rejecting hypotheses involves a sequence of steps that allow for the recursive rejection of hypothesis tests. The steps involve the adjustment of the critical values against which hypothesis tests are rejected, which contrasts to the earlier single-step procedures that apply a single critical value across all hypotheses in determining those to be rejected. The stepwise adjustment procedure involves decreasing the critical values to be applied to the remaining hypotheses at a given step based on information from those hypotheses already rejected in previous steps. The stepwise procedures stop when no more hypotheses are rejected.

Of the stepwise procedures, there are two classifications: stepdown and stepup. The former classification involves procedures that work down from the most significant hypothesis to the least significant hypothesis. The latter classification involves procedures that work up from the least significant hypothesis to the most significant hypothesis. The procedures used in the sections to come are exclusively stepdown. See Romano *et al.* (2010) for a full discussion.

21.3 ENERGY–EMISSIONS MARKET INTERACTIONS

This section provides a brief synopsis of the recent work of Cummins (2013a), who examines the interaction between the EUA emissions market and some of the main European and global energy markets. Such interactions have been studied in the literature by a number of authors and the next subsection provides a brief review.

21.3.1 Literature Review

Since the launch of the EU ETS, there has been an exponential increase in the number of papers on emissions markets. The majority of these papers focus on the performance and/or the structural features of the EU ETS, such as Zetterberg *et al.* (2004), Betz and Sato

(2006), Grubb and Neuhoff (2006), Hepburn *et al.* (2006), Neuhoff *et al.* (2006), Convery and Redmond (2007) and Ellerman and Buchner (2008). Other papers have focused on the factors affecting the price of CO_2, such as Mansanet-Bataller *et al.* (2007), Alberola *et al.* (2008) and Mansanet-Bataller and Pardo (2009), while a further body of literature has focused on the modelling of emission prices, such as Benz and Truck (2009).

Boutaba (2008) investigated interactions among the European carbon markets that trade EUAs and CERs, using data from the following markets: European Climate Exchange, Nordic Power Exchange, Powernext, European Energy Exchange, Energy Exchange Austria and SendeCO2. The results of the cointegration testing indicate that a number of cointegrating relationships exist between the different markets and, hence, a high degree of price transmission. Powernext, Nordic Power Exchange and Energy Exchange Austria are shown to have leading roles as short-term channels of causality from changes in the carbon markets.

An analysis of the relationship between the EU ETS and the Clean Development Mechanism is given by Nazifi (2010), in particular, the dynamic interaction between EUA and CER prices. Cointegration tests conclude that EUA and CER prices did not appear to be cointegrated. Granger-causality tests conclude that CER prices do not have a statistically significant effect on EUA prices. However, a Granger-causality relationship was found from EUA prices to CER prices. Chevallier (2010) also investigated the inter-relationship between EUA and CER price series, using a much longer data set than Nazifi (2010). It was found that EUA and CER affect each other significantly through a vector autoregression (VAR) model, extending the results of Nazifi (2010).

Bunn and Fezzi (2007) examine the interactions between emissions markets and a range of energy markets. The authors show evidence of statistically significant interactions between emissions, gas and electricity prices. Chemarin *et al.* (2008) and Fell (2008) study French and Nordic electricity markets respectively, examining the interplay with emissions markets. Keppler and Mansanet-Bataller (2010) analyse the relationship in a similar style study using daily carbon, energy and weather data spanning the Phase I and Phase II periods of the EU ETS. Based on Phase I, carbon futures prices Granger-cause spot prices. Furthermore, the clean spark spread (CSS), clean dark spread (CDS) and unexpected temperature changes are shown to Granger-cause carbon future prices. For Phase II, evidence is provided that both the CSS and CDS have bidirectional causality with carbon futures. Carbon futures prices are found to Granger-cause gas prices. Nazifi and Milunovich (2010) provide evidence that the Dec 2008 EUA futures contract exerts a causal effect on gas prices and that electricity prices exert a causal effect on spot carbon.

21.3.2 Data Description

For the analysis to follow, EUA price data were acquired from the ICE European Climate Exchange (ECX), which is the leading marketplace for trading emissions in Europe. All of the energy price series were obtained through the Reuters Xtra 3000 trading platform. Daily data are used over the sample period 8th Apr 2008 to 4th Jun 2010. For the EUA price data, the futures contracts with annual settlement dates ranging from Dec 2010 to Dec 2014 are used. All prices are quoted in euros per ton of CO_2e.

The most widely recognized and relevant prices to Europe for oil, natural gas, coal and electricity are used. Brent and West Texas Intermediate (WTI) front-month prices are considered for oil. For natural gas, front-month prices for the National Balancing Point (NBP)

TABLE 21.1 List of energy markets

Brent Oil	European Power Exchange (EPEX) – France
West Texas Intermediate (WTI) Oil	European Energy Exchange (EEX) – Germany
National Balancing Point (NBP) Natural Gas – UK	Anglo-Dutch Energy Exchange (APX) – UK/Netherlands
Henry Hub (HH) Natural Gas – USA	Italian Power Exchange (GME) – Italy
API 2 (Northwest Europe) Coal	Polish Power Exchange (POX) – Poland
API 4 (South Africa's Richards Bay) Coal	OMEL – Spain
	Energy Exchange (EXAA) – Austria

in the UK and, as a global benchmark, Henry Hub in the USA are considered. For coal, front-month prices for the API 2 Northwest Europe index and the API 4 South Africa Richards Bay index are used in the analysis. For electricity, there are seven different regional markets taken into account; namely, Austria, France, Germany, Italy, Poland, Spain and the Netherlands. In these cases base, peak and off-peak electricity prices are used. The regional focus and the segmentation of prices into base, peak and off-peak are central to the analysis. Table 21.1 provides a summary list of the energy markets. Descriptive statistics are presented in Tables 21.2 and 21.3.

21.3.3 Testing Framework

For the empirical analysis in this section, vector autoregression modelling and Granger-causality testing is implemented, with multiple hypothesis testing procedures employed to control for the multiple comparisons problem that exists in this setup. The following subsections provide the specific details of each.

21.3.3.1 Vector Autoregression To describe the dynamic relationship between the energy and emissions market, a VAR model is used. In general terms, consider a system of N variables of interest and let $Y_t \equiv \{y_{1,t}, \ldots, y_{N,t}\}$ be a set of observations of this system at time t. The VAR(p) model describes the relation between Y_t and its lags up to order p. Formally, the VAR(p) model is defined as follows:

$$Y_t = \Upsilon + \Gamma_1 Y_{t-1} + \cdots + \Gamma_p Y_{t-p} + \varepsilon_t,$$

where Υ is an $(N \times 1)$ vector of constants, $\Gamma_j, j = 1, \ldots, p$, are $(N \times N)$ matrices of constant coefficients and ε_t is an $(N \times 1)$ vector of independent random variables following a multivariate normal distribution $N(0, \Sigma)$.

From the description of the energy and emissions data in Section 21.3.2, there are 32 variables in total for the VAR specification. To determine the optimal lag order for this VAR model, information criterion tests are used. Specifically, the Akaike information criterion (AIC), Bayesian information criterion (BIC) and Hanna–Quinn criterion (HQC) tests are implemented and the lag order is chosen where there is consistency between at least two of these tests. The information criterion tests show that the optimal lag is one in this case, with consistency between all three tests. So the system variable Y_t is described by a VAR(1) model. Given that the VAR model requires stationarity in the system variable, the log returns associated with the energy and emissions time series are used as inputs.

TABLE 21.2 Descriptive statistics I

Variable	Mean	Median	Minimum	Maximum
WTI ($/bbl)	78.2795	73.5000	33.8700	145.290
Brent ($/bbl)	78.1286	73.5250	36.6100	146.080
HH ($/mmBtu)	5.88509	4.79900	2.50800	13.5770
NBP (Sterling pence/therm)	43.6531	34.8100	18.2500	85.2600
API4 ($/tonne)	89.5875	80.7500	53.5000	189.500
API2 ($/tonne)	99.4685	77.8250	54.6500	224.000
EPEX B (euro/MWh)	54.7200	48.5710	15.1310	118.162
EPEX P (euro/MWh)	65.5564	57.2430	14.8670	152.265
EPEX OP (euro/MWh)	41.2901	37.7790	10.1910	85.7550
EEX B (euro/MWh)	51.8948	45.0350	7.21000	117.350
EEX P (euro/MWh)	61.8950	52.7800	9.47000	151.150
EEX OP (euro/MWh)	[illegible]	[illegible]	1.19000	[illegible]
APX B (euro/MWh)	53.1934	46.5900	21.0400	118.590
APX P (euro/MWh)	62.7674	55.2900	20.5300	152.340
APX OP (euro/MWh)	38.8819	37.6200	7.40000	119.970
GME B (euro/MWh)	73.5086	69.3550	28.9100	119.390
GME P (euro/MWh)	90.0288	85.3250	30.9100	159.220
GME OP (euro/MWh)	57.0971	55.5000	21.4600	90.4200
POX B (euro/MWh)	47.7881	45.5400	24.3100	81.2900
POX P (euro/MWh)	53.9054	48.9250	24.6600	101.280
POX OP (euro/MWh)	40.5588	39.1550	19.1600	64.5100
OMEL B (euro/MWh)	44.7249	37.9350	2.47000	79.6500
OMEL P (euro/MWh)	47.8839	40.4550	2.07000	86.4300
OMEL OP (euro/MWh)	41.6104	36.7150	3.40000	73.8100
EXAA B (euro/MWh)	52.6487	46.0400	13.1500	119.000
EXAA P (euro/MWh)	63.9116	55.0350	22.9000	153.000
EXAA OP (euro/MWh)	41.5963	38.1500	11.0300	84.9900
EUA Dec-10 (euro/MWh)	17.3320	14.8800	8.43000	31.7100
EUA Dec-11 (euro/MWh)	18.0062	15.4950	8.90000	32.9000
EUA Dec-12 (euro/MWh)	18.9361	16.3850	9.43000	34.3800
EUA Dec-13 (euro/MWh)	20.2992	17.6000	11.3000	36.4300
EUA Dec-14 (euro/MWh)	21.3764	18.7800	12.3000	37.7800

21.3.3.2 Granger Causality Granger causality seeks to establish if there is a causal link between variables under consideration. In its most general form, it asks the question whether $y_{j,t}$ is explained by lags of the variable $y_{i,t}$ up to order p, that is, $y_{i,t-1}, y_{i,t-2}, \dots, y_{i,t-p}$. Within the VAR framework, this is said to be the case if any one of the regression coefficients of the lagged terms is deemed statistically significant for a chosen confidence level. The null hypothesis is that the regression coefficients of the lagged terms are simultaneously zero. Table 21.4 summarizes the null hypotheses and associated implied restrictions on the VAR system.

21.3.3.3 *p*-Value-Based MHT Procedures In Section 21.3.4, it will be shown that the VAR and Granger-causality testing lead to 2080 hypothesis tests being performed simultaneously. This is a clear case of the multiple comparisons problem. Given the availability of

TABLE 21.3 Descriptive statistics II

Variable	Std. deviation	C.V.	Skewness	Ex. kurtosis
WTI	27.3161	0.348957	0.674559	−0.284088
Brent	26.5431	0.339736	0.779906	−0.166577
HH	2.69462	0.457873	1.33988	0.762525
NBP	17.6216	0.403673	0.521157	−1.18824
API4	32.5672	0.363524	1.20133	0.446173
API2	44.4216	0.446590	1.31149	0.318713
EPEX B	20.1879	0.368931	0.806209	−0.212018
EPEX P	25.8479	0.394285	0.916241	0.101776
EPEX OP	15.3542	0.371861	0.712083	−0.246221
EEX B	19.2285	0.370529	0.957099	0.226878
EEX P	24.8369	0.401275	1.09006	0.637668
EEX OP	14.5246	0.346413	0.718419	0.0427895
APX B	20.2066	0.379871	0.926595	0.0346629
APX P	23.9158	0.381023	0.994198	0.452386
APX OP	13.2402	0.340522	1.06959	3.20861
GME B	17.6960	0.240733	0.457865	−0.515635
GME P	23.7680	0.264004	0.640601	0.0478782
GME OP	14.0402	0.245900	0.317852	−0.623075
POX B	11.5225	0.241116	0.699953	−0.242605
POX P	15.4163	0.285988	0.846362	−0.242476
POX OP	8.27625	0.204055	0.506744	−0.0670837
OMEL B	16.0982	0.359939	0.293987	−0.627397
OMEL P	17.5388	0.366278	0.345009	−0.567726
OMEL OP	15.0230	0.361040	0.222147	−0.620893
EXAA B	19.4318	0.369083	1.02864	0.353212
EXAA P	25.0036	0.391222	1.19774	0.819074
EXAA OP	14.2937	0.343629	0.799118	−0.0220681
EUA Dec-10	5.63185	0.324940	0.966338	−0.548518
EUA Dec-11	5.78585	0.321326	0.967768	−0.554651
EUA Dec-12	5.95077	0.314255	0.959457	−0.553310
EUA Dec-13	6.11639	0.301313	0.967888	−0.516939
EUA Dec-14	6.14750	0.287584	0.974413	−0.465382

p-values from the hypothesis testing, p-value-based MHT procedures are used to control for the multiple comparisons problem. Two classes of generalized procedure will be used in particular; the first class seeks to control the generalized familywise error rate, while the second class seeks to control the false discovery proportion. Two specific procedures from each class of generalized procedures will be described below and used for the empirical analysis. The study allows for a direct comparison of the alternative k-FWER and FDP procedures.

TABLE 21.4 Granger causality: hypotheses and implied restrictions

Null hypotheses	Implied restrictions
Lags of $y_{i,t}$ do not explain current $y_{j,t}$, $i, j = 1, \dots, N$	$\Gamma_1(j,i) = \cdots = \Gamma_p(j,i) = 0$

Before discussing the generalized k-FWER procedures, two common techniques for controlling the more conservative FWER are presented; namely, that of Bonferroni (see Romano *et al.*, 2010) and that of Holm (1979). Assume that for the set of hypothesis tests $H_{0,i}, i = 1, \ldots, s$, there are available p-values $\hat{p}_i, i = 1, \ldots, s$. The Bonferroni method controls for the FWER by adjusting the significance level such that hypothesis $H_{0,i}$ is deemed rejected if and only if (iff)

$$\hat{p}_i \leq \alpha/s.$$

Criticisms against the Bonferroni method include its conservativeness and that it represents a single-step procedure. Holm (1979) proposes an improved stepdown procedure, whereby for the ordered p-values that run from the most significant down to the least significant, that is, where $\hat{p}_{(1)} \leq \hat{p}_{(2)} \cdots \leq \hat{p}_{(s)}$, the ordered hypothesis $H_{0,(i)}$ is rejected iff

$$\hat{p}_{(i)} \leq \alpha_{(i)} \equiv \alpha/(s - i + 1).$$

It is important to emphasize the subtle difference in notation introduced here. $H_{0,i}$ is the ith hypothesis test considered and $\hat{p}_i$ is the associated p-value. In contrast, $H_{0,(i)}$ is used to denote the ith hypothesis when all hypotheses are ordered in terms of significance from the most significant up to the least significant, with $\hat{p}_{(i)}$ denoting the associated ordered p-value. Although the Holm (1979) procedure is a stepwise procedure that offers greater power over the single-step Bonferroni procedure, the approach is still conservative in its control of the FWER.

As described in Section 21.2, these weaknesses are dealt with using generalized approaches. Generalized k-FWER versions of the Bonferroni and Holm methods are introduced next for this purpose. The generalized Bonferroni method is defined by Romano *et al.* (2010) whereby the significance level is adjusted such that hypothesis $H_{0,(i)}$ is deemed rejected iff

$$\hat{p}_{(i)} \leq \alpha_{(i)} \equiv k \cdot \alpha/s.$$

This procedure has the advantage of being much less conservative than the Bonferroni method and also being robust to the dependence structure of the hypothesis tests. This procedure will herein be referred to as the GB (for 'generalized Bonferroni') procedure.

A limitation of the GB methodology is that it is still a single-step method. Lehmann and Romano (2005) therefore propose a stepdown method that generalizes the method of Holm (1979) by means of defining the following set of cut-off values for comparison against the ordered p-values $\hat{p}_{(i)}, i = 1, \ldots, s$:

$$\alpha_{(i)} \equiv \begin{cases} \frac{k\alpha}{s}, & i \leq k \\ \frac{k\alpha}{s+k-i}, & i > k \end{cases}.$$

This procedure also has the advantage of being robust to the dependence structure of the hypothesis tests, with the additional advantage of being a superior stepwise procedure. The procedure will herein be referred to as the GH (for 'generalized Holm') procedure and represents the second k-FWER procedure to be used in this study.

Turning next to the FDP, recall that it is formally defined as follows:

$$\text{FDP} \equiv \begin{cases} \frac{FR}{TR}, & TR > 0 \\ 0, & TR = 0 \end{cases},$$

where *FR* denotes the number of false rejections and *TR* denotes the total number of rejections. Lehmann and Romano (2005) develop a stepdown procedure that controls the FDP, whereby for a given proportion γ and significance level α,

$$P\{\text{FDP} > \gamma\} \leq \alpha.$$

The procedure is again recursive and rejects in this case the null hypothesis $H_{0,(i)}$ iff $\hat{p}_{(i)} \leq \alpha'_{(i)}$, where the cut-off values are defined as follows:

$$\alpha'_{(i)} \equiv \alpha_{(i)}/C,$$

where

$$\alpha_{(i)} = \frac{(\lfloor \gamma i \rfloor + 1)\,\alpha}{s + \lfloor \gamma i \rfloor + 1 - i}$$

and

$$C \equiv C_{(\lfloor \gamma s \rfloor + 1)} = \sum_{j=1}^{\lfloor \gamma s \rfloor + 1} (1/j).$$

In the above, the notation $\lfloor x \rfloor$ is used to denote the largest integer lower than x. This procedure is specifically designed by the authors to be robust to the dependence structure of the p-values and is seen as an extension of a special-case version of the procedure with $C = 1$. This methodology will herein be referred to as the LR (for 'Lehmann–Romano') procedure.

One issue with the LR procedure described above is that it is quite conservative in its normalization by the factor C; an issue which Romano *et al.* (2010) admit may deter researchers from its use. To address this conservativeness, Romano and Shaikh (2006) propose an improved stepdown procedure, whereby higher cut-off values are defined as follows:

$$\alpha''_i \equiv \alpha_i/D,$$

where α_i is the same as for the LR procedure, and

$$D \equiv D(\gamma, \alpha, s) = \max_{|I|} S(\gamma, \alpha, |I|),$$

$$S(\gamma, \alpha, |I|) \equiv |I| \sum_{j=1}^{N} \frac{\beta_j - \beta_{j-1}}{j},$$

$$N \equiv N(\gamma, \alpha, |I|) = \min\left\{ \lfloor \gamma s \rfloor + 1, |I|, \left\lfloor \gamma \left(\frac{s - |I|}{1 - \gamma} + 1 \right) \right\rfloor + 1 \right\},$$

and where

$$\beta_0 \equiv 0,$$
$$\beta_m \equiv \frac{m}{\max\left\{s + m - \left\lceil \frac{m}{\gamma} \right\rceil + 1, |I|\right\}}, m = 1, \ldots, \lfloor \gamma s \rfloor,$$

and

$$\beta_{\lfloor \gamma s \rfloor + 1} \equiv \frac{\lfloor \gamma s \rfloor + 1}{|I|}.$$

The term $|I|$ is the number of elements in I, where as per Section 21.2, I denotes the set of true null hypotheses. $|I|$ is naturally bounded between zero and the total number of hypothesis tests, s under consideration. In practice, the above procedure involves circulating through all the possible values for $|I|$ within these bounds, from which the maximum value of $S(\gamma, \alpha, |I|)$ may be determined. This procedure is again robust to the dependence structure of the p-values and offers a greater possibility of rejecting hypotheses in the search for true discoveries compared with the LR procedure. The procedure is herein referred to as the RS (for 'Romano–Shaikh') procedure.

So, in summary, this section outlines two MHT procedures within the class of generalized familywise error rate procedures, that is the GB and GH procedures, and two MHT procedures within the class of false discovery proportion procedures, that is the LR and RS procedures. Applying this suite of MHT procedures allows for an empirical comparison of the alternative approaches.

21.3.4 Empirical Results

The specific choices for the GB and GH procedures used are $k = 20$, such that no more than 2.5% of the tests represent false discoveries, and $\alpha = 5\%$ as the significance level. The specific choices for the LR and RS procedures used are $\gamma = 5\%$ for the proportion parameter and $\alpha = 5\%$, such that the FDP ensures $P\{\gamma > 5\%\} \leq \alpha = 5\%$. The results from applying the four MHT procedures to the VAR and Granger-causality testing are presented in Tables 21.5 and 21.6. Each tick symbolizes that a given hypothesis test is significant under a given MHT procedure.

The GB and GH procedures both identify 76 VAR coefficients and 76 Granger-causality relationships as being statistically significant from the 2080 simultaneous hypothesis tests conducted. Given that the lag order of the VAR model is one, that is a VAR(1) model is used, the Granger-causality results coincide as expected with the VAR regression coefficient results exactly, with the former allowing for easy interpretation of the direction of causality. Some very interesting relationships are identified, with all bar one being within the power markets; the one exception is a link between the Henry Hub and NBP gas markets. Most interestingly, over the sample period Apr 2008–Jun 2010, covering approximately the first half of Phase II of the EU ETS, no statistically significant relationship is established between emissions 'markets' and any of the energy markets. This is contradictory to the theory that energy prices should act as drivers of emissions prices and is also counter to much of the reported literature. However, it is emphasized again that this study explicitly accounts for the multiple comparisons problem

TABLE 21.5 VAR results post-MHT

VAR relationship	Coefficient	*p*-Value	GB	GH	LR	RS
NBP–HH(−1)	0.194	7.263E-05	✓	✓		
EPEX B–EPEX OP(−1)	−0.116	5.188E-04	✓	✓		
EPEX B–OMEL OP(−1)	0.270	1.852E-03	✓	✓		
EPEX P–EPEX P(−1)	−0.939	4.807E-05	✓	✓		
EPEX P–EPEX OP(−1)	−0.141	7.324E-04	✓	✓		
EPEX P–OMEL OP(−1)	0.333	2.087E-03	✓	✓		
EPEX OP–EPEX OP(−1)	−0.178	3.313E-05	✓	✓		
EEX P–EPEX OP(−1)	−0.135	2.210E-03	✓	✓		
EEX OP–EEX B(−1)	1.489	1.124E-05	✓	✓		✓
EEX OP–EEX P(−1)	−1.187	1.544E-09	✓	✓	✓	✓
EEX OP–EEX OP(−1)	−1.059	2.220E-16	✓	✓	✓	✓
EEX OP–POX P(−1)	8.137	2.197E-03	✓	✓		
EEX OP–POX OP(−1)	5.124	1.505E-03	✓	✓		
APX B–EPEX OP(−1)	−0.107	8.175E-04	✓	✓		
APX B–APX B(−1)	−0.554	1.503E-05	✓	✓		
APX OP–APX OP(−1)	−0.301	3.992E-06	✓	✓	✓	✓
GME P–GME P(−1)	−2.564	3.161E-04	✓	✓		
POX B–EPEX OP(−1)	−0.068	7.774E-05	✓	✓		
POX P–EPEX OP(−1)	−0.090	1.645E-05	✓	✓		
OMEL B–APX B(−1)	−0.475	1.316E-03	✓	✓		
OMEL B–APX P(−1)	0.411	1.673E-04	✓	✓		
OMEL B–OMEL B(−1)	−0.484	5.181E-05	✓	✓		
OMEL B–OMEL P(−1)	0.457	6.573E-14	✓	✓	✓	✓
OMEL B–EXAA B(−1)	−0.935	4.848E-07	✓	✓	✓	✓
OMEL B–EXAA P(−1)	0.654	1.954E-08	✓	✓	✓	✓
OMEL B–EXAA OP(−1)	0.317	1.504E-03	✓	✓		
OMEL OP–OMEL P(−1)	0.267	1.122E-06	✓	✓	✓	✓
OMEL OP–OMEL OP(−1)	−0.544	1.083E-09	✓	✓	✓	✓
OMEL OP–EXAA B(−1)	−0.882	2.213E-07	✓	✓	✓	✓
OMEL OP–EXAA P(−1)	0.548	2.533E-07	✓	✓	✓	✓
OMEL OP–EXAA OP(−1)	0.366	6.391E-05	✓	✓		
EXAA B–EPEX B(−1)	0.659	7.425E-04	✓	✓		
EXAA B–EPEX P(−1)	−0.618	3.394E-04	✓	✓		
EXAA B–EPEX OP(−1)	−0.136	1.487E-05	✓	✓		
EXAA P–EPEX OP(−1)	−0.161	1.667E-05	✓	✓		
EXAA OP–EPEX P(−1)	−0.522	1.110E-03	✓	✓		
EXAA OP–EPEX OP(−1)	−0.113	1.054E-04	✓	✓		
EXAA OP–EXAA OP(−1)	−0.491	5.310E-10	✓	✓	✓	✓

*Source: Cummins (2013a).

in its application of the MHT procedures. Within each of the regional power markets, with the exception of Poland, several relationships and causal effects are shown to exist between and amongst base, peak and off-peak prices. Moreover, there appear to be several cross-regional relationships and causal effects in the European power markets. In particular, French power prices are shown to have a causal effect on the German, Polish and Austrian power markets, whereas Spanish power prices are shown to have a causal effect on the French power market.

TABLE 21.6 Granger causality results post-MHT*

Granger causality	*p*-Value	GB	GH	LR	RS
HH ⇒ NBP	7.263E-05	✓	✓		
EPEX OP ⇒ EPEX B	5.188E-04	✓	✓		
OMEL OP ⇒ EPEX B	1.852E-03	✓	✓		
EPEX P ⇒ EPEX P	4.807E-05	✓	✓		
EPEX OP ⇒ EPEX P	7.324E-04	✓	✓		
OMEL OP ⇒ EPEX P	2.087E-03	✓	✓		
EPEX OP ⇒ EPEX OP	3.313E-05	✓	✓		
EPEX OP ⇒ EEX P	2.210E-03	✓	✓		
EEX B ⇒ EEX OP	1.124E-05	✓	✓		✓
EEX P ⇒ EEX OP	1.544E-09	✓	✓	✓	✓
EEX OP ⇒ EEX OP	2.220E-16	✓	✓	✓	✓
POX P ⇒ EEX OP	2.197E-03	✓	✓		
POX OP ⇒ EEX OP	1.505E-03	✓	✓		
EPEX OP ⇒ APX B	8.175E-04	✓	✓		
APX B ⇒ APX B	1.503E-05	✓	✓		
APX OP ⇒ APX OP	3.992E-06	✓	✓	✓	✓
GME P ⇒ GME P	3.161E-04	✓	✓		
EPEX OP ⇒ POX B	7.774E-05	✓	✓		
EPEX OP ⇒ POX P	1.645E-05	✓	✓		
APX B ⇒ OMEL B	1.316E-03	✓	✓		
APX P ⇒ OMEL B	1.673E-04	✓	✓		
OMEL B ⇒ OMEL B	5.181E-05	✓	✓		
OMEL P ⇒ OMEL B	6.573E-14	✓	✓	✓	✓
EXAA B ⇒ OMEL B	4.848E-07	✓	✓	✓	✓
EXAA P ⇒ OMEL B	1.954E-08	✓	✓	✓	✓
EXAA OP ⇒ OMEL B	1.504E-03	✓	✓		
OMEL P ⇒ OMEL OP	1.122E-06	✓	✓	✓	✓
OMEL OP ⇒ OMEL OP	1.083E-09	✓	✓	✓	✓
EXAA B ⇒ OMEL OP	2.213E-07	✓	✓	✓	✓
EXAA P ⇒ OMEL OP	2.533E-07	✓	✓	✓	✓
EXAA OP ⇒ OMEL OP	6.391E-05	✓	✓		
EPEX B ⇒ EXAA B	7.425E-04	✓	✓		
EPEX P ⇒ EXAA B	3.394E-04	✓	✓		
EPEX OP ⇒ EXAA B	1.487E-05	✓	✓		
EPEX OP ⇒ EXAA P	1.667E-05	✓	✓		
EPEX P ⇒ EXAA OP	1.110E-03	✓	✓		
EPEX OP ⇒ EXAA OP	1.054E-04	✓	✓		
EXAA OP ⇒ EXAA OP	5.310E-10	✓	✓	✓	✓

*Source: Cummins (2013a).

The Spanish power market appears to be influenced by power prices on the Anglo-Dutch and Austrian power exchanges. The Polish power markets are shown to have a causal effect on German power prices.

In contrast to the results of the GB and GH procedures, the LR and RS procedures identify far fewer statistically significant relationships; the LR procedure identifying 22 VAR coefficients and 22 Granger-causality relationships and the RS procedure identifying 24 VAR coefficients and 24 Granger-causality relationships. Despite the generalized and stepwise nature of the LR and RS procedures, they are significantly more conservative than the GB and GH procedures. This can be seen by plotting the cut-off values under each of the four MHT procedures against the sequence of ordered (from least significant to most significant) p-values (Figure 21.1). Interestingly, under the LR and RS procedures many of the regional and cross-regional relationships and causal effects drop away. Indeed, on a regional basis, it is only really in the case of the German and Spanish power markets that statistical relations are established between and amongst base, peak and off-peak prices. On a cross-regional basis, only the Austrian power market is shown to have a causal effect on Spanish power prices.

21.4 EMISSIONS MARKET INTERACTIONS

To again showcase the application of MHT procedures, this section references the recent work of Cummins (2013b), who looks specifically at market interactions within the EU ETS. In particular, the study focuses on EUA and CER units, both of which are allowable instruments (although CERs only to a limited extent) for compliance purposes under the EU ETS. EUA and CER forward curves are constructed from a comprehensive set of emissions data and VAR and Granger-causality testing employed to analyse the statistical relationships. The multiple comparisons problem again surfaces as a result of this testing framework. The same suite of p-value class procedures as described in the previous section are applied here to control for the multiple comparisons problem in this context. A full literature review is available in Cummins (2013b), and so the discussion in the section will focus on the testing framework and the empirical results.

21.4.1 Testing Framework and Data

The testing framework is exactly the same as that described in Section 21.3.3 in its use of VAR modelling, Granger-causality testing and p-value MHT procedures to control for the multiple comparisons problem. To get a sense of the scale of the multiple comparisons problem it is first necessary to discuss the data set used by Cummins (2013b).

A comprehensive data set of EUA and CER emissions prices is considered in the study. This data spans the period 14th May 2008–31st May 2012. It incorporates the December maturity futures contracts that span the Phase II period and that extend into the Phase III period. Specifically, for the EUA and CER data the futures contracts range from the December 2008 expiry up to the December 2020 expiry. Rather than analyse the calendar maturity contracts, the approach taken in the study is to create fixed-maturity EUA and CER forward curves by means of rolling the futures contracts at expiry.[1] So the front end of the forward curve represents the rolled prompt December contract, the second point on the forward curve represents the second December contract, and so on. The issues pertaining to rolling EUA and CER futures contracts are considered by Carchano *et al.* (2012). Last-day rolling is deemed sufficient for the price discovery focus of this study and aligns with the previous studies of Mansanet-Bataller *et al.* (2011), Chevallier (2010, 2011) and Mansanet-Bataller and Pardo (2011).

[1]The term 'forward curve' is used here and throughout the chapter on the understanding that futures contracts are used for its construction.

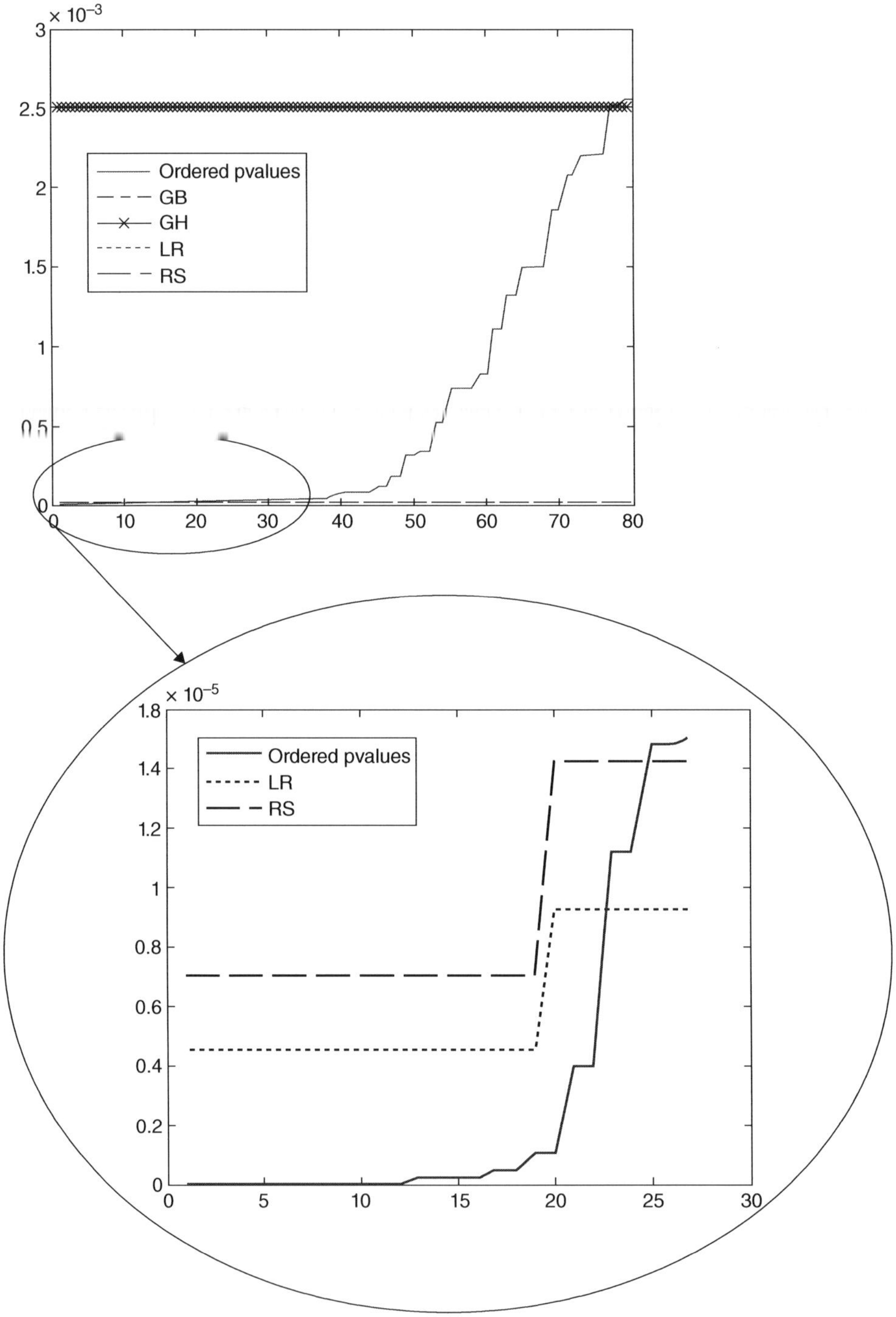

FIGURE 21.1 Cut-off values for the LR, RS, GB and GH procedures.

Two subperiods are considered for the analysis. The first subperiod spans the period 14th May 2008–20th Jan 2011, within which the available futures contracts allow for the construction of an EUA forward that runs from the prompt December contract to the fifth December contract (denoted EUA-D1, … , EUA-D5) and a CER forward curve that runs from prompt December contract to the second December contract (denoted CER-D1, CER-D2). The second subperiod spans the period 21st Jan 2011–31st May 2012. Over this period, the increased availability of EUA and CER futures contracts allows for the construction of respective forward curves that run from the prompt December contract to the ninth December contract (EUA-D1, … , EUA-D9 and CER-D1, … , CER-D9). It is on these constructed EUA and CER forward curves that the VAR and Granger causality testing is performed. Given that the VAR model requires stationarity in the system variable, the log returns from the constructed forward curves are used as inputs.

The VAR and Granger-causality testing is to be performed on the EUA and CER forward curves constructed for the two Phase II subperiods. So, for the first subperiod, the system variable $Y_t = \{\text{EUA-D1}_t, \ldots, \text{EUA-D5}_t, \text{ CER-D1}_t, \text{ CER-D2}_t\}$ and therefore is of dimension seven. On this basis, implementation of the VAR model involves 56 regression coefficient tests, including the constant terms. The Granger-causality testing involves 49 tests covering all of the pairwise relationships. For the second subperiod, the system variable $Y_t = \{\text{EUA-D1}_t, \ldots, \text{EUA-D9}_t, \text{ CER-D1}_t, \ldots, \text{CER-D9}_t\}$, which leads to 342 regression coefficient tests and 324 Granger-causality tests. So a total of 771 hypothesis tests are examined simultaneously within this framework, justifying the need to apply the MHT procedures. The specific choices for the GB and GH procedures used are $k = 20$, such that no more than 2.5% of the tests represent false discoveries, and $\alpha = 5\%$ as the significance level. The specific choices for the LR and RS procedures used are $\gamma = 5\%$ for the proportion parameter and $\alpha = 5\%$, such that the FDP ensures $P\{\gamma > 5\%\} \leq \alpha = 5\%$.

21.4.2 Empirical Results

The results reported by Cummins (2013b) show interesting results between the two Phase II subperiods considered for the analysis. For the first subperiod, none of the MHT procedures show statistical significance for any of the tests performed. So there is no evidence of term structure interactions in either the EUA forward curve or the CER forward curve. Additionally, there is no evidence of any cross-interaction between the EUA and CER forward curves. In contrast, for the second subperiod, the class of generalized familywise error rate procedures shows evidence that the second December EUA contract (and not the prompt December contract) returns have a causal effect on the entire EUA forward curve, suggesting markets are working to a two-year time horizon. The second December EUA contract returns are also shown to have a causal effect on CER returns, particularly at the long end of the CER forward curve. The evidence further suggests that term structure causal effects exist within the CER forward curve. Specifically, lags in the seventh and eighth December contract returns are shown to have a causal effect on the long end of the CER forward curve. In contrast to the above evidence, the class of false discovery proportion procedures shows no evidence at all to support term structure, or indeed cross-market, EUA and CER interactions, meaning the conclusions drawn need to be taken with a degree of caution. However, the false discovery proportion procedures are much more conservative than the generalized familywise error rate procedures and so the researcher needs to be conscious of these differences. For further details of the analysis and for further discussion, the interested reader is directed to Cummins (2013b).

21.5 QUANTITATIVE SPREAD TRADING IN OIL MARKETS

The study discussed in this section is quite different from the previous two studies from the point of view of the MHT methodology in particular. It references the recent work of Cummins and Bucca (2012), who look at quantitative spread trading in the crude oil and refined products markets. Specifically, the authors apply the innovative statistical arbitrage trading model of Bertram (2010) to a large range of common-commodity and cross-commodity spreads, including calendar, locational and crack spreads. The multiple comparisons problem presents here given that the overall objective is to identify, with statistical confidence, profitable trading strategies from the range of trading strategies implemented. However, unlike the two previous studies, a suite of resampling class procedures is applied in order to control for the multiple comparisons problem in this instance. In so doing, a defined criterion needs to be set out for the hypothesis testing and in this case this is chosen to be the mean daily log return.

21.5.1 Testing Framework and Data

For the empirical analysis in this study, a comprehensive data set of crude oil and refined product futures contracts is used, comprising WTI and Brent on the crude oil side and gasoil (GO) and heating oil (HO) on the refined products side. These commodities are chosen on the basis of size, importance and liquidity. WTI and HO are both traded on the New York Mercentile Exchange (NYMEX), while Brent and GO are both traded on the Intercontinental Exchange (ICE). The data set covers the 11-year period from 3rd Jan 2000 to 31st Dec 2010. Most notably, this period covers the record high crude oil prices recorded in 2008 and the subsequent collapse in the latter part of the same year resulting from the global economic crisis, in addition to the gradual recovery in crude oil prices over 2009–2010. All relevant conversions were done to ensure the time series are quoted consistently in dollars per barrel.

The data set includes futures curves for WTI, Brent and HO running from the prompt month up to month 12, with the GO futures curve running from the prompt month up to month six. These choices are made to ensure sufficient liquidity from a trading perspective, with the construction of the individual time series explicitly taking into account the rolling of futures contracts. Transaction costs and contract liquidity are discussed in more detail in the study. For the quantitative spread trading analysis, the full range of common and cross-commodity spreads (including calendar, crack and locational spreads) is considered. With 42 different maturity contracts across the four commodity groups, a total of 861 individual spreads are available for analysis. Finally, nonsynchronicity bias is avoided with all time series being observed at the same time of 5.15pm EDT, coinciding with the close of the WTI crude oil market.

The statistical arbitrage trading model of Bertram (2010) that is used for the analysis is described in detail in the following section. Although the associated mathematics is quite complicated, underlying the model is a very simple mean-reverting Ornstein–Uhlenbeck (OU) process that is used to describe the dynamics of a given spread. The innovation over existing literature is that the statistical arbitrage trading model of Bertram (2010) determines optimal trade execution signals (i.e., entry and exit levels), albeit this optimality is model based within the context of the OU spread price dynamics rather than empirically optimal. Analytical expressions are derived by Bertram (2010) for the optimal entry and exit levels, which may be solved easily. So, the application of the trading model in practice is relatively straightforward, in that the underlying OU process is first estimated against an historical time series for the given spread. The estimated parameters are then used in determining the optimal entry and exit levels from the analytic expressions and then, with the trade execution signals in place, the model may be tested and evaluated out-of-sample.

A number of alternative in-sample and out-of-sample periods are considered for estimation and evaluation of the spread trading strategies. Specifically, eight separate one-year out-of-sample periods are considered for evaluation of trading strategy performance; namely, each year over the period 2003–2010. These choices allow for a wider testing of the optimal statistical arbitrage trading model and an examination of trading profitability over time. Three separate in-sample periods are then considered for the estimation of the trading models and the generation of trading signals to be applied out-of-sample. One-year, two-year and three-year periods are considered for estimation, where for convenience of construction 252 trade days are assumed in each year. So, for example, the two-year in-sample period includes the 2×252 trade dates prior to the start of the out-of-sample period. Given the daily frequency of the data, these choices are seen as reasonable to capture consistent mean-reversion effects, while at the same time examining the impact of alternative estimation periods. Hence, for each out-of-sample period, a total of 2583 (i.e., 3×861) individual trading strategies are tested simultaneously. Hence, it is quite clear that the multiple comparisons problem exists in this case. However, as already outlined, resampling-based MHT techniques are required for control purposes here and the detail of these is presented in Section 20.5.3.

21.5.2 Optimal Statistical Arbitrage Model

This section provides a detailed mathematical exposition of the novel optimal statistical arbitrage trading model of Bertram (2010). The issue of optimal statistical arbitrage trading is approached by first assuming that the spread between two asset log-price series, denoted s_t, is given by the following zero-mean OU process:[2]

$$ds_t = -\alpha s_t dt + \sigma dW_t, \tag{21.1}$$

with $\alpha, \sigma > 0$ and W_t denoting a Wiener process. Defining the entry and exit levels of the trading strategy by a and m respectively, a complete trade cycle is the time taken for the spread process to transition from a to m and then return back to a. Formally, the trade cycle time is defined as follows:

$$\mathcal{T} \equiv \mathcal{T}_{a\to m} + \mathcal{T}_{m\to a},$$

where $\mathcal{T}_{a\to m}$ is the time to transition from a to m and $\mathcal{T}_{m\to a}$ is the time to transition from m to a, and the independence of the two times follows from the Markovian property of the OU process. Given relative transaction costs c, the total log return from one trade cycle of the statistical arbitrage trading strategy is given by $r(a, m, c) \equiv m - a - c$, which is deterministic but for which the associated trading cycle time is stochastic. In this context, Bertram (2010)

[2]The zero-mean assumption does not present any issue in practice. The optimal entry and exit levels obtained can easily be translated to account for a non-zero mean in empirical data.

proposes the following expected return per unit time and variance of return per unit time measures:

$$\xi(a,m,c) \equiv \frac{r(a,m,c)}{E(\mathcal{T})},$$
$$\varsigma(a,m,c) \equiv \frac{r^2(a,m,c)\,V(\mathcal{T})}{E^3(\mathcal{T})},$$

where $E(\mathcal{T}) = E(\mathcal{T}_{a\to m}) + E(\mathcal{T}_{m\to a})$ is the expected trade cycle time and $V(\mathcal{T}) = V(\mathcal{T}_{a\to m}) + V(\mathcal{T}_{m\to a})$ is the variance of the trade cycle time. Following a transformation of the OU process to a dimensionless system, and drawing on the first-passage time theory of Thomas (1975), Sato (1977) and Ricciardi and Sato (1988), Bertram (2010) derives the following analytic expressions for $E(\mathcal{T})$, $V(\mathcal{T})$, $\xi(a,m,c)$ and $\varsigma(a,m,c)$:

$$E(\mathcal{T}) = \frac{\pi}{\alpha}\left(\mathrm{Erfi}\left(\frac{m\sqrt{\alpha}}{\sigma}\right) - \mathrm{Erfi}\left(\frac{a\sqrt{\alpha}}{\sigma}\right)\right),$$

$$V(\mathcal{T}) = \frac{w_1\left(\frac{m\sqrt{2\alpha}}{\sigma}\right) - w_1\left(\frac{a\sqrt{2\alpha}}{\sigma}\right) - w_2\left(\frac{m\sqrt{2\alpha}}{\sigma}\right) + w_2\left(\frac{a\sqrt{2\alpha}}{\sigma}\right)}{\alpha^2},$$

$$\xi(a,m,c) = \frac{\alpha(m-a-c)}{\pi\left(\mathrm{Erfi}\left(\frac{m\sqrt{\alpha}}{\sigma}\right) - \mathrm{Erfi}\left(\frac{a\sqrt{\alpha}}{\sigma}\right)\right)},$$

$$\varsigma(a,m,c) = \alpha(m-a-c)^2\,\frac{w_1\left(\frac{m\sqrt{2\alpha}}{\sigma}\right) - w_1\left(\frac{a\sqrt{2\alpha}}{\sigma}\right) - w_2\left(\frac{m\sqrt{2\alpha}}{\sigma}\right) + w_2\left(\frac{a\sqrt{2\alpha}}{\sigma}\right)}{\pi^3\left(\mathrm{Erfi}\left(\frac{m\sqrt{\alpha}}{\sigma}\right) - \mathrm{Erfi}\left(\frac{a\sqrt{\alpha}}{\sigma}\right)\right)^3},$$

where Erfi (z) is the imaginary error function,

$$w_1(z) \equiv \left(\frac{1}{2}\sum_{g=1}^{\infty}\Gamma\left(\frac{g}{2}\right)\left(\sqrt{2}z\right)^g/g!\right)^2 - \left(\frac{1}{2}\sum_{g=1}^{\infty}(-1)^g\,\Gamma\left(\frac{g}{2}\right)\left(\sqrt{2}z\right)^g/g!\right)^2,$$

$$w_2(z) \equiv \sum_{g=1}^{\infty}\Gamma\left(\frac{(2g-1)}{2}\right)\Psi\left(\frac{(2g-1)}{2}\right)\left(\sqrt{2}z\right)^{(2g-1)}/(2g-1)!,$$

and $\Psi(z) \equiv \psi(z) - \psi(1)$, with $\Gamma(z)$ and $\psi(z)$ the gamma and digamma functions respectively.

With these analytical results in place, it is shown that the optimal entry and exit levels a^* and m^* may be derived by maximizing the expected return per unit time $\xi(a,m,c)$. It is established that $m^* = -a^*$, $a^* < 0$, and it is shown that a^* is the root of the equation

$$\exp\left(\frac{\alpha a^2}{\sigma^2}\right)(2a+c) - \sigma\sqrt{\frac{\pi}{\alpha}}\,\mathrm{Erfi}\left(\frac{a\sqrt{\alpha}}{\sigma}\right) = 0.$$

21.5.3 Resampling-Based MHT Procedures

Towards building a framework to identify profitable trading strategies, with statistical significance, on the set of calendar and crack spreads in the study, the associated hypothesis tests need to be established. The approach taken in the study is to formally identify those spread trading strategies that, with statistical significance, outperform a given benchmark in terms of mean daily log return. The benchmark is defined as in Hsu and Kuan (2005) as equivalent to taking no position in the spread, and so the hypothesis tests look to identify departures from the zero-mean daily log return. Letting ζ_i denote the daily log return of trading strategy i and $\theta_i \equiv E(\zeta_i)$, then the hypothesis tests may be formalized as follows:

$$H_{0,i} : \theta_i \leq 0 \quad \text{vs.} \quad H_{1,i} : \theta_i > 0,$$

for a full set of hypothesis tests $\{1, \ldots, s\}$, where s is as before set equal to the number of tests considered. The appropriate estimate of θ_i is the mean daily log return observed on trading strategy i over a given historical period with n daily observations. Letting $\zeta_{t,i}, t = 1, \ldots, n$, denote the daily log return of trading strategy i at time t, the estimate $\hat{\theta}_{n,i} = \sum_{t=1}^{n} \zeta_{t,i}/n$. Given that θ_i is unknown, implementing the stepdown and balanced stepdown procedures requires use of appropriate bootstrapping techniques. This involves replacing the true specification $(\hat{\theta}_{n,i} - \theta_i)$ with the estimates $\left(\hat{\theta}^*_{n,i}(b) - \hat{\theta}_{n,i}\right)$, where $\hat{\theta}^*_{n,i}(b)$ are bootstrap estimates of θ_i and $b = 1, \ldots, B$, are the indices for the bootstrap samples.

The objective is to control for the multiple comparisons in this scenario through the generalized familywise error rate, which as discussed offers greater power whilst also implicitly accounting for the dependence structure that exists between the tests. This section continues as follows: Section 21.5.3.1 presents a single-step procedure as described by Romano *et al.* (2010); Section 21.5.3.2 presents the stepwise procedure of Romano and Wolf (2007), which serves as an improvement on the single-step approach by allowing for subsequent iterative steps to identify additional hypothesis rejections; and Section 21.5.3.3 presents the balanced stepwise procedure of Romano and Wolf (2010), which is a marked improvement again that allows for balance amongst the hypothesis tests in the sense that each is treated equally in terms of power, that is in the identification of true discoveries.

21.5.3.1 Single-Step Procedure Assume a set of test statistics $T_{n,i} = \hat{\theta}_{n,i}$ associated with the hypothesis tests, where n is introduced to denote the sample size of the data used for estimation. Letting $A \equiv \{1, \ldots, s\}$, the single-step procedure proceeds by rejecting all hypotheses where $T_{n,i} \geq c_{n,A}(1-\alpha, k)$, and where $c_{n,A}(1-\alpha, k)$ represents the $(1-\alpha)$-quantile of the distribution of k-max$(\hat{\theta}_{n,i} - \theta_i)$ under the probability measure P_θ. With P_θ unknown, the critical value $c_{n,A}(1-\alpha, k)$ is also unknown. However, an estimated critical value may be determined using appropriate bootstrapping techniques. That is, the critical value $\hat{c}_{n,A}(1-\alpha, k)$ is estimated as the $(1-\alpha)$-quantile of the distribution of k-max $\left(\hat{\theta}^*_{n,i} - \hat{\theta}_{n,i}\right)$ for $\hat{P}_\theta$ an unrestricted estimate of P_θ. See Romano and Wolf (2007) for further technical details.

21.5.3.2 Stepdown Procedure The stepwise procedure of Romano and Wolf (2007) improves on the single-step procedure described in the previous section by allowing for subsequent iterative steps to identify additional hypothesis rejections. The stepdown procedure is constructed such that at each stage, information on the rejected hypotheses to date is used in retesting for significance on the remaining hypotheses. Romano and Wolf (2007) describe the following steps to the algorithm:

- **Step 1.** Let A_1 denote the full set of hypothesis indices, that is $A_1 \equiv \{1, \ldots, s\}$. If the maximum test statistic observed, that is max $\left(T_{n,i}\right)$, is less than or equal to the estimated critical value $\hat{c}_{n,A_1}(1 - \alpha, k)$ then fail to reject all null hypotheses and stop the algorithm. Otherwise, proceed to reject all null hypotheses $H_{0,i}$ for which the associated test statistics exceed the critical value level, that is, where $T_{n,i} > \hat{c}_{n,A_1}(1 - \alpha, k)$.
- **Step 2.** Let R_2 denote the set of indices for the hypotheses rejected in Step 1 and let A_2 denote the indices for those hypotheses not rejected. If the number of elements in R_2 is less than k, that is $\left|R_2\right| < k$, then stop the algorithm as the probability of k or more false discoveries is zero in this case. Otherwise, the appropriate critical value to be applied at this stage is calculated as follows:

$$\hat{d}_{n,A_2}(1 - \alpha, k) = \max_{I \subseteq R_2, |I| = k-1} \{\hat{c}_{n,K}(1 - \alpha, k) : K \equiv A_2 \cup I\}.$$

  Hence, additional hypotheses from A_2 are rejected if $T_{n,i} > \hat{d}_{n,A_2}(1 - \alpha, k), i \in A_2$. If no further rejections are made then stop the algorithm.

  ⋮

- **Step *j*.** Let R_j denote the set of indices for the hypotheses rejected up to Step $(j - 1)$ and let A_j denote the indices for those hypotheses not rejected. The critical value to be applied at this stage is calculated as follows:

$$\hat{d}_{n,A_j}(1 - \alpha, k) = \max_{I \subseteq R_j, |I| = k-1} \{\hat{c}_{n,K}(1 - \alpha, k) : K \equiv A_j \cup I\}.$$

  Hence, additional hypotheses from A_j are rejected if $T_{n,i} > \hat{d}_{n,A_j}(1 - \alpha, k), i \in A_j$. If no further rejections are made then stop the algorithm.

  ⋮

From the description of the algorithm above, at each stage j in the stepwise procedure the hypotheses that are not rejected thus far are retested over a smaller population of hypothesis tests than previously. The size of this smaller population is given by $(|A_j| + k - 1)$, which includes all the hypotheses within A_j in addition to $(k - 1)$ hypotheses drawn from those already rejected, that is drawn from R_j. Given that control of the generalized k-FWER is the premise of the procedure, it is expected that there are at most $(k - 1)$ false discoveries amongst the set of hypotheses rejected R_j. However, it is not known which of the rejected hypotheses may represent false discoveries. Hence, it is necessary to circulate through all combinations of R_j, of size $(k - 1)$, in order to obtain the maximum critical value $\hat{d}_{n,A_j}(1 - \alpha, k)$ against which to test the hypotheses within A_j. See Romano and Wolf (2007) for further technical details.

Operative Method In requiring to circulate through all subsets of R_j, of size $(k - 1)$, in order to obtain the maximum critical value to apply at each stage of the stepdown procedure, the algorithm can become highly, if not excessively, computationally burdensome. Depending on the $|R_j|$ and the value of k, the number of combinations ${}^{|R_j|}C_{k-1}$ can become very large. Romano and Wolf (2007) therefore suggest an operative method that reduces this computational burden, while at the same time maintaining many of the attractive properties of the algorithm.[3]

For this, first consider the hypothesis tests rejected up to step $(j-1)$ and place these in descending order of test statistic, that is

$$T_{n,r_1} \geq T_{n,r_2} \geq \ldots \geq T_{n,r_{|R_j|}},$$

where $\{r_1, r_2, \ldots, r_{|R_j|}\}$ is the appropriate permutation of associated hypothesis test indices that gives this ordering. Now consider a user-defined maximum number of combinations, N_{max}, at each step of the algorithm. Then choose an integer value such that ${}^{M}C_{k-1} \leq N_{max}$ and replace the critical value calculation at each step j of the algorithm with the following:

$$\hat{d}_{n,A_j}(1-\alpha,k) = \max_{I \subseteq \left\{r_{\max(1,|R_j|-M+1)},\ldots,r_{|R_j|}\right\}, |I|=k-1} \{\hat{c}_{n,K}(1-\alpha,k) : K \equiv A_j \cup I\}.$$

What this serves to do is replace circulating through all the hypothesis tests rejected to date with circulating through only the M least significant hypothesis tests rejected. Of course, in the case where $M \geq |R_j|$ this amounts to circulating through all the hypotheses rejected. Although this approach is premised on the assumption that the (up to $k-1$) false discoveries lie within the least significant hypotheses rejected so far, it does offer significant computational efficiencies for the algorithm. It is this operative method that is used for the empirical analysis in the final section.

21.5.3.3 Balanced Stepdown Procedure Whereas the stepwise procedure of the previous section is an improvement on the single-step procedure of Section 21.5.3.1, it does not offer by construction balance in the sense that each hypothesis test is treated equally in terms of power. The balanced stepwise procedure of Romano and Wolf (2010) addresses this issue.

Introducing some notation, let $H_{n,i}(\cdot, P_\theta)$ denote the distribution function of $(\hat{\theta}_{n,i} - \theta_i)$ and let $c_{n,i}(\gamma)$ denote the γ-quantile of this distribution. The confidence interval

$$\{\theta_i : \hat{\theta}_{n,i} - \theta_i \leq c_{n,i}(\gamma)\}$$

then has coverage probability γ. Balance is the property that the marginal confidence intervals for a population of s simultaneous hypothesis tests have the same probability coverage. Within the context of controlling the generalized k-FWER, the overall objective is to ensure that the simultaneous confidence interval covers all parameters $\theta_i, i = 1, \ldots, s$, except for at most

[3]The generic algorithm offers a number of attractive features. Firstly, the generic algorithm is conservative in its rejection of hypotheses. Secondly, the generic algorithm also allows for finite-sample control of the k-FWER under P_θ. Thirdly, the bootstrap construction is such that the generic algorithm provides asymptotic control in the case of contiguous alternatives. Romano and Wolf (2007) provide a more detailed discussion.

$(k-1)$ of them, for a given limiting probability $(1-\alpha)$, while at the same time ensuring balance (at least asymptotically). So, what is sought is that

$$P_\theta\{\hat{\theta}_{n,i}-\theta_i \le c_{n,i}(\gamma) \quad \text{for all but at most } (k-1) \text{ of the hypotheses}\}$$

$$\equiv P_\theta\{H_{n,i}(\hat{\theta}_{n,i}-\theta_i, P_\theta) \le \gamma \quad \text{for all but at most } (k-1) \text{ of the hypotheses}\}$$

$$\equiv P_\theta\{k\text{-max}(H_{n,i}(\hat{\theta}_{n,i}-\theta_i, P_\theta)) \le \gamma\} = 1-\alpha.$$

Letting $L_{n,\{1,\ldots,s\}}(k, P_\theta)$ denote the distribution of k-max$(H_{n,i}(\hat{\theta}_{n,i}-\theta_i, P_\theta))$, the appropriate choice of the coverage probability γ is then $L^{-1}_{n,\{1,\ldots,s\}}(1-\alpha, k, P_\theta)$.

As before, given that P_θ is unknown, it is necessary to use appropriate bootstrapping techniques to generate an estimate of the coverage probability $L^{-1}_{n,\{1,\ldots,s\}}(1-\alpha, k, P_\theta)$, under $\hat{P}_\theta$. Therefore, from this development it is possible to define the simultaneous confidence interval

$$\left\{\theta_i : \hat{\theta}_{n,i}-\theta_i \le H^{-1}_{n,i}\left(L^{-1}_{n,\{1,\ldots,s\}}(1-\alpha, k, \hat{P}_\theta), \hat{P}_\theta\right)\right\}.$$

The right-hand side of the above inequality will form the basis of the critical value definitions used within the stepdown procedure. See Romano and Wolf (2010) for further technical details. Note that although the above development was made assuming the full set of hypothesis tests, it equally applies to any subset $K \subseteq \{1,\ldots,S\}$. Hence, the balanced stepwise algorithm may now be described as follows.

- **Step 1.** Let A_1 denote the full set of hypothesis indices, that is $A_1 \equiv \{1,\ldots,s\}$. If, for each hypothesis test, the associated test statistic $T_{n,i}$ is less than or equal to the corresponding critical value estimate $\hat{c}_{n,A_1,i}(1-\alpha,k) \equiv H^{-1}_{n,i}\left(L^{-1}_{n,A_1}(1-\alpha,k,\hat{P}_\theta), \hat{P}_\theta\right)$ then fail to reject all null hypotheses and stop the algorithm. Otherwise, proceed to reject all null hypotheses $H_{0,i}$ for which the associated test statistics exceed the critical value level, that is, where $T_{n,i} > \hat{c}_{n,A_1,i}(1-\alpha,k)$.
- **Step 2.** Let R_2 denote the set of indices for the hypotheses rejected in Step 1 and let A_2 denote the indices for those hypotheses not rejected. If the number of elements in R_2 is less than k, that is, $|R_2| < k$, then stop the algorithm as the probability of k or more false discoveries is zero in this case. Otherwise, the appropriate critical value to be applied for each hypothesis test s at this stage is calculated as follows:

$$\hat{d}_{n,A_2,i}(1-\alpha,k) = \max_{I\subseteq R_2, |I|=k-1}\{\hat{c}_{n,K,i}(1-\alpha,k) : K \equiv A_2 \cup I\}.$$

Hence, additional hypotheses from A_2 are rejected if $T_{n,i} > \hat{d}_{n,A_2,i}(1-\alpha,k)$, $i \in A_2$. If no further rejections are made then stop the algorithm.

⋮

- **Step *j*.** Let R_j denote the set of indices for the hypotheses rejected up to Step $(j-1)$ and let A_j denote the indices for those hypotheses not rejected. The appropriate critical value to be applied for each hypothesis test s at this stage is calculated as follows:

$$\hat{d}_{n,A_j,i}(1-\alpha,k) = \max_{I \subseteq R_j, |I|=k-1} \{\hat{c}_{n,K,i}(1-\alpha,k) : K \equiv A_j \cup I\}.$$

Hence, additional hypotheses from A_j are rejected if $T_{n,i} > \hat{d}_{n,A_j,i}(1-\alpha,k), i \in A_j$. If no further rejections are made then stop the algorithm.

⋮

Similar to the stepwise algorithm of the previous section, at each stage j in the stepwise procedure the hypotheses that are not rejected thus far are retested over a smaller population of hypothesis tests than previously. The size of this smaller population is given by $(|A_j| + k - 1)$, which includes all the hypotheses within A_j, in addition to $(k-1)$ hypotheses drawn from those hypotheses already rejected, that is drawn from R_j. Given that control of the generalized k-FWER is the premise of the procedure, it is expected that there are at most $(k-1)$ false discoveries amongst the set of hypotheses rejected R_j. However, it is not known which of the rejected hypotheses may represent false discoveries. Hence, it is necessary to circulate through all combinations of R_j, of size $(k-1)$, in order to obtain the appropriate critical values. Where the algorithm departs significantly from the previous section is that a maximum critical value $\hat{d}_{n,A_j,i}(1-\alpha,k)$ must be determined for each hypothesis test s. This adds an additional layer of computational burden on the algorithm.

Operative Method Similar to the stepdown procedure of Section 21.5.3.2, the need to circulate through all subsets of R_j, of size $(k-1)$, in order to obtain, in this case, a set of maximum critical values to apply at each stage of the stepdown procedure means the algorithm can become excessively computationally burdensome. Romano and Wolf (2010) therefore suggest an operative method that reduces this computational burden in the spirit of that proposed by the authors for the stepdown procedure (Romano and Wolf, 2007).

It is first necessary to be able to order the hypothesis tests rejected up to step $(j-1)$ in terms of significance. To this end, it is noted that marginal p-values can be obtained as follows:

$$\hat{p}_{n,i} \equiv 1 - H_{n,i}(\hat{\theta}_{n,i}, \hat{P}_\theta).$$

This gives the following ascending order for the significance of the hypothesis tests:

$$\hat{p}_{n,r_1} \le \hat{p}_{n,r_2} \le \dots \le \hat{p}_{n,r_{|R_j|}},$$

where $\{r_1, r_2, \dots, r_{|R_j|}\}$ is the appropriate permutation of associated hypothesis test indices that gives this ordering. As before, a maximum number of combinations, N_{max}, at each step of the algorithm is defined. Then an integer value M is chosen such that ${}^{M}C_{k-1} \le N_{max}$, leading to the calculation of the critical values as follows:

$$\hat{d}_{n,A_j,i}(1-\alpha,k) = \max_{I \subseteq \left\{ r_{\max(1,|R_j|-M+1)}, \dots, r_{|R_j|} \right\}, |I|=k-1} \{\hat{c}_{n,K,i}(1-\alpha,k) : K \equiv A_j \cup I\}.$$

The rationale for this approach is the exact same as that described in Section 21.5.3.2, with the same effect being the introduction of significant computational efficiencies to the algorithm. It is this operative method that is used for the empirical analysis in the final section.

21.5.4 Empirical Results

This study examines the quantitative trading of spreads in the crude oil (WTI and Brent) and refined products (heating oil and gasoil) markets, making a number of important conclusions. Firstly, it is shown that the novel statistical arbitrage trading model of Bertram (2010), when applied to a wide range of spreads (including calendar, crack and locational spreads), leads to profitable spread trading. It is further shown that the performance is quite robust to varying transaction costs. Secondly, it is shown that generalized stepwise procedures are essential in controlling for data snooping bias within such quantitative trading applications. The stepdown procedure of Romano and Wolf (2007) and the balanced stepdown procedure of Romano and Wolf (2010) offer greater power to reject false null hypotheses, with the balanced stepdown procedure offering equal treatment in the identification of profitable strategies. Profitable trading strategies are identified, after applying these MHT procedures, with results reflecting the aggregation of dynamically taking long and short positions in the spreads. This rigorous application of the MHT procedures allows for greater statistical confidence in the results reported and the conclusions drawn. For the top 10 and top 20 categories of trading strategy, average daily returns fall within the approximate range 0.07%–0.55%, with trade lengths of 9–55 days and Sharpe ratios of between 2 and 4 in many cases. Thirdly, the study provides some interesting insights for both academics and practitioners in its practical comparison of the stepwise and the balanced stepwise procedures in the context of this trading application. The balanced stepdown procedure, being unbiased in its approach, is shown to identify many more profitable trading strategies compared with the nonbalanced stepdown procedure. For instance, a collapse in the number of profitable trading strategies is seen in 2008, reflecting the impact of the credit crisis and the distortion of spreads relative to previous years. Whereas the stepdown procedure fails to identify any profitable strategies, the balanced procedure is successful in identifying a limited number of profitable strategies. For further details of the analysis and for further discussion, the interested reader is directed to Cummins and Bucca (2012).

REFERENCES

Alberola, E., Chevallier, J. and Cheze, B. (2008) Price drivers and structural breaks in European carbon prices 2005–2007, *Energy Policy*, **36**, 787–797.

Benz, E. and Truck, S. (2009) Modeling the price dynamics of CO_2 emission allowances, *Energy Economics*, **31**, 4-15.

Bertram, W.K. (2010) Analytic solutions for optimal statistical arbitrage trading, *Physica A*, **389**, 2234–2243.

Betz, R. and Sato, M. (2006) Emissions trading: Lessons learnt from the 1st phase of the EU ETS and prospects for the 2nd phase, *Climate Policy*, **6**, 351–359.

Boutaba, M. (2008) Dynamic linkages among European carbon markets: Insights on price transmission, Working Paper.

Bunn, D.W. and Fezzi, C. (2007) Interaction of European carbon trading and energy prices, The Fondazione Eni Enrico Mattei Note di Lavoro Series, Fondazione Eni Enrico Mattei, Working Paper No. 63.

Carchano, O., Medina, V. and Pardo, A. (2012) Rolling over EUAs and CERs, Working Paper.

Chemarin, S., Heinen, A. and Strobl, E. (2008) Electricity, carbon and weather in France: Where do we stand? Working Paper, Ecole Polytechnique.

Chevallier, J. (2010) EUAs and CERs: Vector autoregression, impulse response function and cointegration analysis, *Economics Bulletin*, **30**, 558–576.

Chevallier, J. (2011) A model of carbon price interactions with macroeconomic and energy dynamics, *Energy Economics*, **33**(6), 1295–1312.

Convery, F. and Redmond, L. (2007) Market and price developments in the European Union emissions trading scheme, *Review of Environmental Economics and Policy*, **1**, 88–111.

Cummins, M. (2013a) Multiple comparisons problem: Recent advances applied to energy and emissions, *Applied Economics Letters*, **20**, 903–909.

Cummins, M. (2013b) EU ETS market interactions: A multiple hypothesis testing approach, *Applied Energy*, **111**, 701–709.

Cummins, M. and Bucca, A. (2012) Quantitative spread trading in the crude oil and products markets, *Quantitative Finance*, **12**, 1857–1875.

Ellerman, A. and Buchner, B. (2008) Over-allocation or abatement? A preliminary analysis of the EU ETS based on the 2005–06 emissions data, *Environmental and Resource Economics*, **41**, 267–287.

Fell, H. (2008) EU ETS and Nordic electricity, Discussion Paper, Resources for the Future.

Grubb, M. and Neuhoff, K. (2006) Allocation and competitiveness in the EU emissions trading scheme: Policy overview, *Climate Policy*, **6**(1), 7–30.

Hansen, P.R. (2005) A test for superior predictive ability, *Journal of Business and Economics Statistics*, **23**, 365–380.

Hepburn, C., Grubb, M., Neuhoff, K., Matthes, F. and Tse, M. (2006) Auctioning of EU ETS phase II allowances: How and why, *Climate Policy*, **6**(1), 137–160.

Holm, S. (1979) A simple sequentially rejective multiple test procedure, *Scandinavian Journal of Statistics*, **6**, 65–70.

Hsu, P.H. and Kuan, C.M. (2005) Re-examining the profitability of technical analysis with White's reality check, Working Paper.

Keppler, J. and Mansanet-Bataller, M. (2010) Causalities between CO_2, electricity, and other energy variables during phase I and phase II of the EU ETS, *Energy Policy*, **38**, 3329–3341.

Lehmann, E.L. and Romano, J.P. (2005) Generalizations of the familywise error rate, *Annals of Statistics*, **33**(3), 1138–1154.

Mansanet-Bataller, M. and Pardo, A. (2009) Impacts of regulatory announcements on CO_2 prices, *The Journal of Energy Markets*, **2**, 1–33.

Mansanet-Bataller, M. and Pardo, A. (2011) CO_2 prices and portfolio management, *International Journal of Global Energy Issues*, **35**, 154–177.

Mansanet-Bataller, M., Chevallier, J., Hervé, M. and Alberola, E. (2011) EUA and sCER Phase II price drivers: Unveiling the reasons for the existence of the EUA–sCER spread, *Energy Policy*, **39**, 1056–1069.

Mansanet-Bataller, M., Pardo, A. and Valor, E. (2007) CO_2 prices, energy and weather, *The Energy Journal*, **28**, 73–92.

Marshall, B.R., Cahan, R.H. and Cahan, J.M. (2008) Can commodity futures be profitably traded with quantitative market timing strategies? Working Paper.

Nazifi, F. (2010) Modeling the price spread between the EUA and the CER carbon prices, Working Paper.

Nazifi, F. and Milunovich, G. (2010) Measuring the impact of carbon allowance trading on energy prices, *Energy and Environment*, **21**, 367–383.

Neuhoff, K., Keats, K. and Sato, M. (2006) Allocation, incentives and distortions: The impact of EU ETS emissions allowance allocations to the electricity sector, *Climate Policy*, **6**, 73–92.

Park, C.H. and Irwin, S.H. (2007) What do we know about the profitability of technical analysis? *Journal of Economic Surveys*, **21**, 786–826.

Qui, M. and Wu, Y. (2006) Technical trading-rule profitability, data snooping, and reality check: Evidence from the foreign exchange market, *Journal of Money, Credit, and Banking*, **38**, 2135–2158.

Ricciardi, L.M. and Sato, S. (1988) First-passage-time density and moments of the Ornstein–Uhlenbeck process, *Journal of Applied Probability*, **25**, 43–57.

Romano, J.P. and Shaikh, A.M. (2006) On stepdown control of the false discovery proportion. In Rojo, J. (ed.), *2nd Lehmann Symposium – Optimality*, IMS Lecture Notes – Monograph Series, pp. 33–50.

Romano, J.P. and Wolf, M. (2007) Control of generalized error rates in multiple testing, *Annals of Statistics*, **35**, 1378–1408.

Romano, J.P. and Wolf, M. (2010) Balanced control of generalized error rates, *Annals of Statistics*, **38**, 598–633.

Romano, J.P., Shaikh, A.M. and Wolf, M. (2010) Hypothesis testing in econometrics, *Annual Review of Economics*, **2**, 75–104.

Sato, S. (1977) Evaluation of the first-passage time probability to a square root boundary for the Wiener process, *Journal of Applied Probability*, **14**, 850–856.

Sullivan, R., Timmermann, A. and White, H. (1999) Data-snooping, technical trading rule performance, and the bootstrap, *Journal of Finance*, **54**, 1647–1691.

Thomas, M.U. (1975) Some mean first-passage time approximations for the Ornstein–Uhlenbeck process, *Journal of Applied Probability*, **12**, 600–604.

White, H. (2000) A reality check for data snooping, *Econometrica*, **68**, 1097–1126.

Zetterberg, L., Nilsson, K., Ahman, M., Kumlin, A. and Birgersdotter, L. (2004) Analysis of National Allocation Plans for the EU ETS, IVL Swedish Environmental Research Institute Report.

APPENDIX

A Quick Review of Distributions Relevant in Finance with Matlab® Examples*

Laura Ballotta and Gianluca Fusai

In this Appendix, we quickly review the properties of distributions relevant in finance, like the

- normal distribution
- lognormal distribution
- chi-square distribution
- non-central chi-square distribution
- Poisson distribution
- exponential distribution
- Gamma distribution
- multivariate Gaussian distribution.

We also present a standard procedure to simulate random variables via the so-called inverse method.

A.1 THE NORMAL DISTRIBUTION

Fact A.1.1 (Normal Distribution) *A normal (Gaussian) random variable on $\Re$ with expected value $\mu \in \Re$ and standard deviation $\sigma \in \Re^+$ has density function (pdf) $\phi_{\mu,\sigma}(x)$ and cumulative distribution (cdf) $\Phi_{\mu,\sigma}(x)$ given by:*

$$\phi_{\mu,\sigma}(x) = f_X(x; \mu, \sigma) = \frac{1}{\sqrt{2\pi\sigma^2}} \exp\left(-\frac{1}{2}\left(\frac{x-\mu}{\sigma}\right)^2\right), x \in \Re$$

*The figures in this Appendix have been produced in The MathWorks, Inc. MATLAB® R2009a.

Handbook of Multi-Commodity Markets and Products: Structuring, Trading and Risk Management. Edited by Andrea Roncoroni, Gianluca Fusai and Mark Cummins.

TABLE A.1 Probability intervals of the Gaussian distribution

k	$\mu - k\sigma$	$\mu + k\sigma$	$\Pr(\mu - k\sigma < X < \mu + k\sigma)$
1	−0.3542	0.2742	0.6827
2	−0.6684	0.5884	0.9545
3	−0.9826	0.9026	0.9973
4	−1.2968	1.2168	0.9999
5	−1.611	1.531	1.0000

TABLE A.2 Moments of the Gaussian distribution

Support	$x \in (-\infty; +\infty)$
Mean	$\mathbb{E}(X) = \mu$
Variance	$\mathbb{V}ar(X) = \sigma^2$
Skewness	$\frac{\mathbb{E}((X-\mu)^3)}{\sigma^3} = 0$
Kurtosis	$\frac{\mathbb{E}((X-\mu)^4)}{\sigma^4} = 3$
Central odd moments	$\mathbb{E}((X-\mu)^{2n+1}) = 0$
Central even moments	$\mathbb{E}((X-\mu)^{2n}) = \frac{(2n)!}{n!}\frac{\sigma^{2n}}{2^n}$

and

$$\Phi_{\mu,\sigma}(x) = F_X(x; \mu, \sigma) = \int_{-\infty}^{x} \phi_{\mu,\sigma}(s)\, ds.$$

We write $X \sim \mathcal{N}(\mu, \sigma^2)$*. If* $\mu = 0$ *and* $\sigma = 1$ *we have the so-called unit standard Gaussian random variable. In particular, if* $Z \sim \mathcal{N}(0, 1)$*, then*

$$X = \mu + \sigma Z \sim \mathcal{N}(\mu, \sigma^2).$$

Given the cdf, we can compute the probability that X falls in a given interval:

$$\Pr(a < X < b) = \Phi_{0,1}\left(\frac{b-\mu}{\sigma}\right) - \Phi_{0,1}\left(\frac{a-\mu}{\sigma}\right).$$

We produce Table A.1. Table A.2 illustrates the main properties of the Gaussian distribution. The resulting pdf and cdf are shown in Figure A.1.

Matlab Code

```
%%%%%%%%%%%%%%%%%%%%%%%%%%%%%%%%%%%%%%%%
%%%%PLOT OF THE GAUSSIAN DISTRIBUTION%%%%
%%%%%%%%%%%%%%%%%%%%%%%%%%%%%%%%%%%%%%%%
%assign parameters
mu=0.2;
```

```
sg=0.1;
%assign x-range
x=linspace(-0.4,0.8,100);
%compute pdf and cdf
pdfg=pdf('norm',x,mu,sg);
cdfg=cdf('norm',x,mu,sg);
%make the plot
plot(x,pdfg,'r',x,cdfg,'b');
%define the limits in the x-axis
xlim([-0.4 0.8])
%insert the legend
legend('Gaussian pdf','Gaussian cdf')
%print the figure
print(h,'-djpeg','FigGaussianpdf.jpg')
```

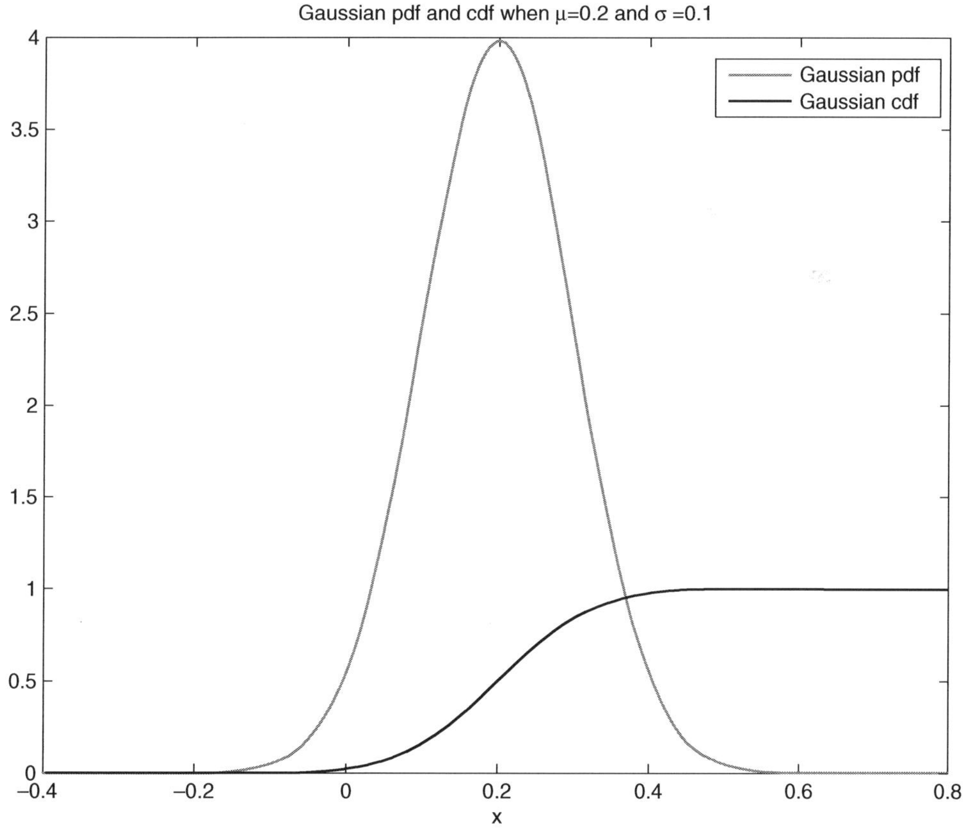

FIGURE A.1 Density and cumulative distribution of the Gaussian random variable

A.2 THE LOGNORMAL DISTRIBUTION

Fact A.2.1 (Lognormal Distribution) *Let X be a normal r.v. with mean μ and standard deviation σ. Then the r.v.*

$$Y = \exp(X)$$

is said to have a `lognormal distribution` *with parameters μ and σ and density $f_Y(y; \mu, \sigma)$ given by*

$$f_Y(y; \mu, \sigma) = \frac{1}{y\sqrt{2\pi\sigma^2}} \exp\left(-\frac{1}{2}\left(\frac{\ln y - \mu}{\sigma}\right)^2\right), y \in \Re^+.$$

Moreover:

$$\mathbb{E}(Y) = e^{\mu + \frac{1}{2}\sigma^2}$$

and

$$\mathbb{V}ar(Y) = e^{2\mu+\sigma^2}(e^{\sigma^2} - 1).$$

We write $X \sim \mathcal{LN}(\mu, \sigma^2)$.

The relationship between densities of the Gaussian and lognormal distribution is depicted in Figure A.2.

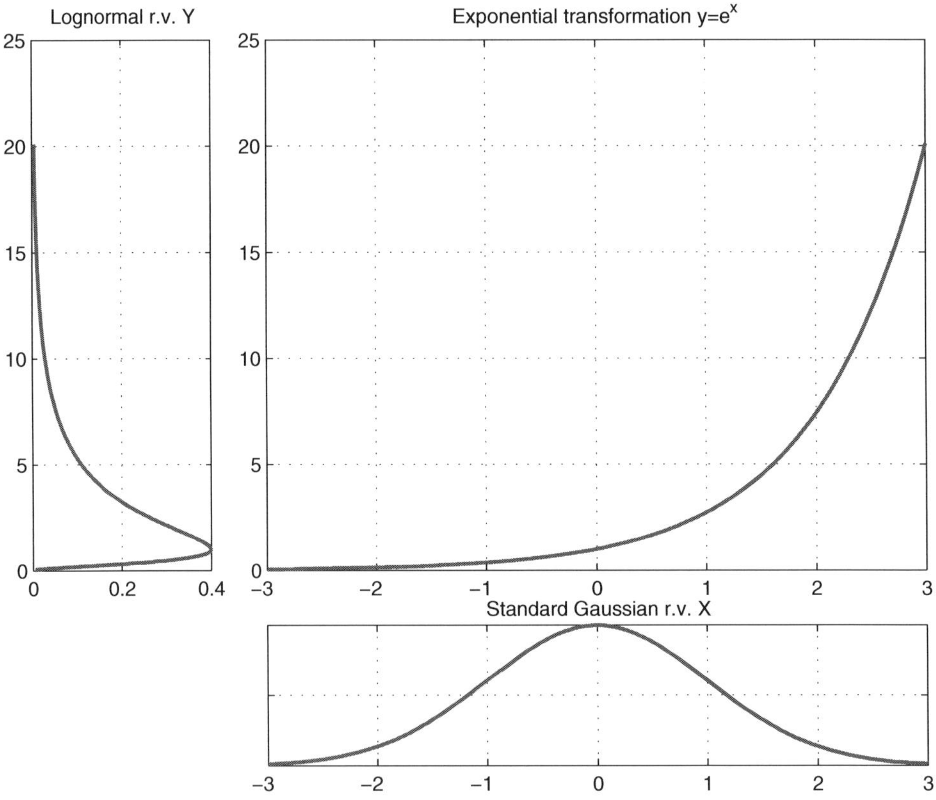

FIGURE A.2 Densities of the Gaussian and lognormal random variables

TABLE A.3 Moments of the lognormal distribution

Support	$y \in [0; +\infty)$
Mean	$\mathbb{E}(Y) = e^{\mu+\frac{1}{2}\sigma^2}$
Variance	$\mathbb{V}ar(Y) = e^{2\mu+\sigma^2}(e^{\sigma^2} - 1)$
Skewness	$\frac{\mathbb{E}((Y-\mathbb{E}(Y))^3)}{(\mathbb{V}ar(Y))^{\frac{3}{2}}} = (e^{\sigma^2} + 2)\sqrt{e^{\sigma^2} - 1}$
Kurtosis	$\frac{\mathbb{E}((Y-\mathbb{E}(Y))^4)}{(\mathbb{V}ar(Y))^2} = e^{4\sigma^2} + 2e^{3\sigma^2} + 3e^{2\sigma^2} - 3$
Moments	$\mathbb{E}(Y^n) = e^{n\mu+\frac{1}{2}n^2\sigma^2}$

The cumulative density function of a lognormal r.v. is given by:

$$
\begin{aligned}
F_Y(y) &= \Pr(Y \leq y) \\
&= \Pr(e^X \leq y), \ \textit{where } X \sim \mathcal{N}(\mu, \sigma^2) \\
&= \Pr(X \leq \ln(y)) \\
&= \Phi_{\mu,\sigma^2}(\ln(y)) \\
&= \Phi_{0,1}\left(\frac{\ln(y) - \mu}{\sigma}\right).
\end{aligned}
$$

Given the cdf, we can compute the probability that X falls in a given interval:

$$
\Pr(a < Y < b) = \Phi_{\mu,\sigma^2}(\ln(b)) - \Phi_{\mu,\sigma^2}(\ln(a)) = \Phi_{0,1}\left(\frac{\ln(b) - \mu}{\sigma}\right) - \Phi_{0,1}\left(\frac{\ln(a) - \mu}{\sigma}\right).
$$

The main properties of the lognormal distribution are summarized in Table A.3. The resulting pdf and cdf are shown in Figure A.3.

Matlab Code

```
%%%%%%%%%%%%%%%%%%%%%%%%%%%%%%%%%%%%%%%%%%%%%
%%%%PLOT OF THE LOGNORMAL DISTRIBUTION%%%%
%%%%%%%%%%%%%%%%%%%%%%%%%%%%%%%%%%%%%%%%%%%%%
%assign parameters
mu=0.2; sg=0.1;
%assign x-range
x=linspace(0.0,2,100);
%compute pdf and cdf
pdflg=pdf('lognorm',x,mu,sg);
cdflg=cdf('lognorm',x,mu,sg);
%make the plot
h=figure('Color', [ 1 1 1])
plot(x,pdflg,'r',x,cdflg,'b');
%define the limits in the x-axis
```

```
xlim([0 2]); xlabel('x');
%insert title
title('Lognormal pdf and cdf when \mu=0.2 and \sigma =0.1')
%insert the legend
legend('Log-normal pdf','Log-normal cdf')
%print the figure
%print(h,'-dpng','FigLogGaussianpdf.jpg')
```

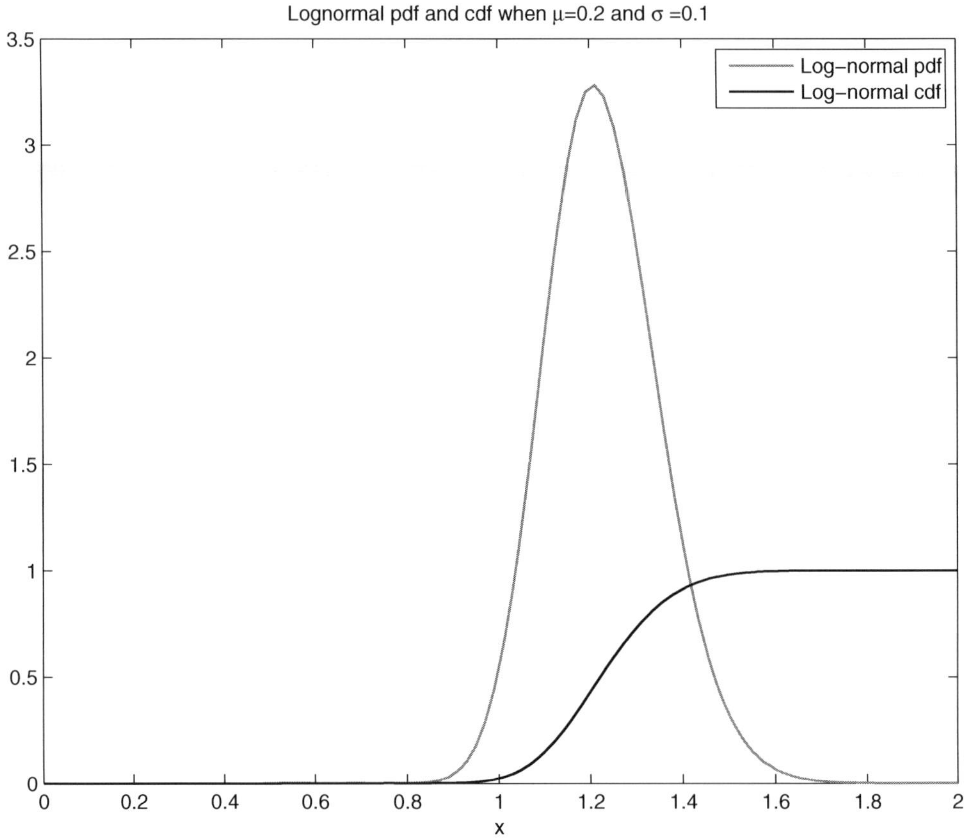

FIGURE A.3 Density and cumulative distribution of the lognormal random variable

A.3 THE CHI-SQUARE DISTRIBUTION

Fact A.3.1 (Chi-Square Distribution) *Let X_i, $i = 1, \dots, n$, be n independent normal random variables with zero mean and unit standard deviation. Then the r.v.*

$$Y = \sum_{i=1}^{n} X_i^2$$

TABLE A.4 Moments of the chi-square distribution

Support	$y \in [0; +\infty)$
Mean	$\mathbb{E}(Y) = n$
Variance	$\mathbb{V}ar(Y) = 2n$
Skewness	$\frac{\mathbb{E}((Y-n)^3)}{(2n)^{\frac{3}{2}}} = \sqrt{\frac{8}{n}}$
Excess kurtosis	$\frac{\mathbb{E}((Y-n)^4)}{(2n)^2} - 3 = \frac{12}{n}$
Moments	$\mathbb{E}(Y^m) = 2^m \frac{\Gamma\left(m + \frac{n}{2}\right)}{\Gamma\left(\frac{n}{2}\right)}$

is said to have a `chi-square distribution` *with n degrees of freedom and density* $f_Y(y; n)$ *given by*

$$f_Y(y; n) = \frac{e^{-y/2} y^{n/2-1}}{2^{n/2}\Gamma(n/2)}, y \in \Re^+,$$

where $\Gamma(n)$ *is the Gamma function*

$$\Gamma(n) = \int_0^\infty t^{n-1} e^{-t} dt,$$

and if n is an integer $\Gamma(n) = (n-1)!$. *Moreover:*

$$\mathbb{E}(X) = n$$

and

$$\mathbb{V}ar(X) = 2n.$$

We write $Y \sim \chi_n^2$.

The main properties of the chi-square distribution are summarized in Table A.4. The resulting pdf and cdf are shown in Figure A.4. Figure A.5 illustrates the different shape of the chi-square distribution for increasing number of degrees of freedom.

Matlab Code

```
%%%%%%%%%%%%%%%%%%%%%%%%%%%%%%%%%%%%%%
%%%%PLOT OF THE Chi-2 DISTRIBUTION%%%%
%%%%%%%%%%%%%%%%%%%%%%%%%%%%%%%%%%%%%%
clear all;
%assign parameters
n=5; %degrees of freedom
%assign x-range
x=linspace(0,20,100);
%compute pdf and cdf
pdfchi2=pdf('chi2',x,n);
```

```
cdfchi2=cdf('chi2',x,n);
%make the plot
h=figure('Color', [ 1 1 1])
plot(x,pdfchi2,'r',x,cdfchi2,'b')
xlabel('x')
title('Chi−Square pdf and cdf when \mu=0.2 and \sigma =0.1')
legend('Chi−Square pdf','Chi−Square cdf')
print(h,'−djpeg','FigChiSquarepdf.jpg')
```

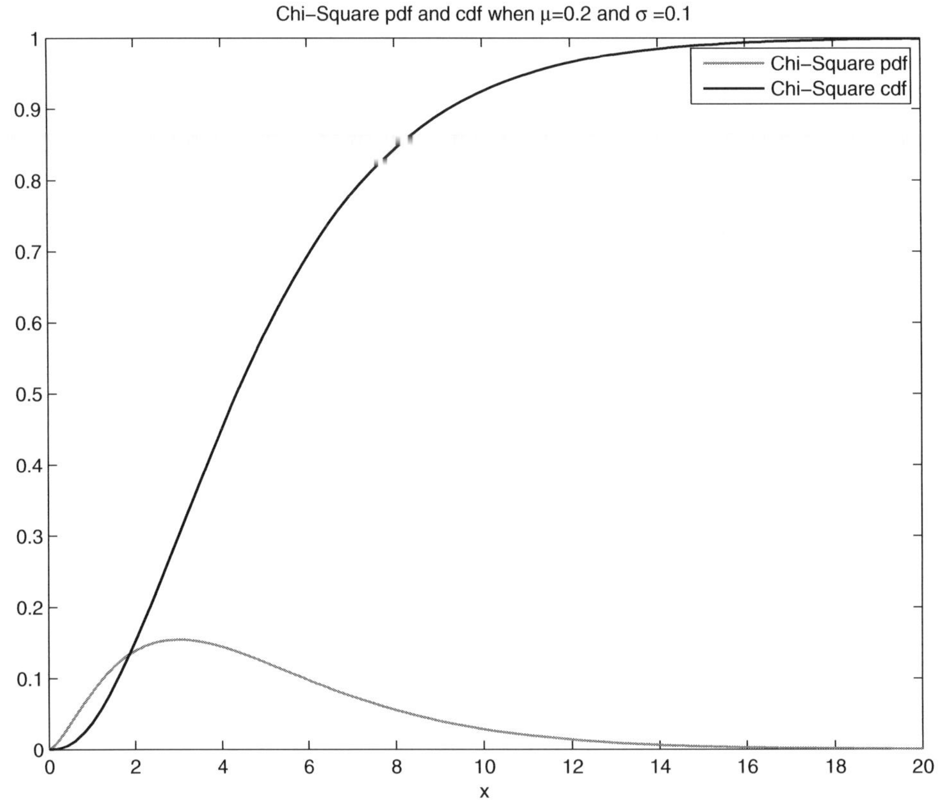

FIGURE A.4 Density and cumulative distribution of the chi-square random variable with dof ($n = 20$)

Matlab Code

```
%%%%%%%%%%%%%%%%%%%%%%%%%%%%%%%%%%%%%%%%%%%%%%%%%%%%%%%%
%%%%THE Chi−2 DISTRIBUTION AND THE DEGREES OF FREEDOM%%%%
%%%%%%%%%%%%%%%%%%%%%%%%%%%%%%%%%%%%%%%%%%%%%%%%%%%%%%%%
clear all;
%assign parameters
n=[5 10 20 50]; %degrees of freedom
%assign x−range
```

```
x=linspace(0,100,300);
%compute pdf and cdf
for i=1:length(n)
  pdfchi2(i,:)=pdf('chi2',x,n,n(i));
end
h=figure('Color', [ 1 1 1])
plot(x,pdfchi2,'.')
xlabel('x')
legend('n=5','n=10','n=20','n=50')
title('The Chi-Square pdf varying ...
the number n of degrees of freedom')
```

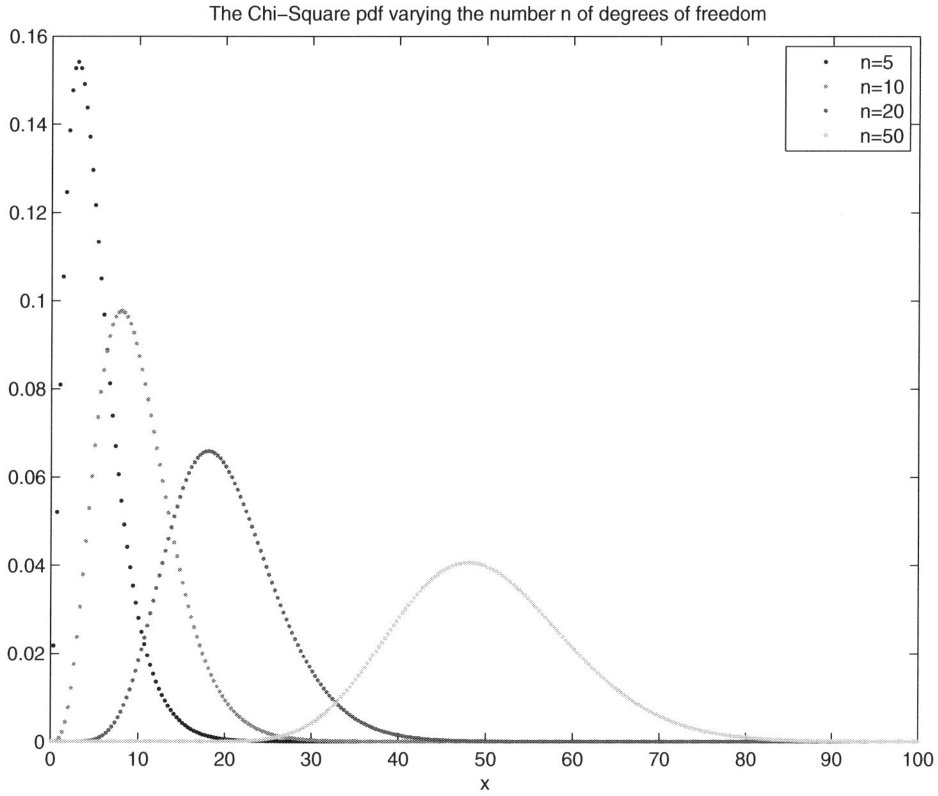

FIGURE A.5 Density of the chi-square random variable varying n

A.4 THE NON-CENTRAL CHI-SQUARE DISTRIBUTION

Fact A.4.1 (Non-Central Chi-Square Distribution) *Let X_i, $i = 1, \ldots, n$, be n independent normal random variables with zero mean and unit standard deviation. Then the r.v.*

$$Y = \sum_{i=1}^{n} (X_i + \delta_i)^2$$

TABLE A.5 Moments of the non-central chi-square distribution

Support	$y \in [0; +\infty)$
Mean	$\mathbb{E}(Y) = n + d$
Variance	$\mathbb{V}ar(Y) = 2 \times (n + 2d)$
Skewness	$\frac{\mathbb{E}((Y - \mathbb{E}(Y))^3)}{(\mathbb{V}ar(Y))^{\frac{3}{2}}} = \frac{2^{3/2}(n + 3d)}{(k + 2d)^{3/2}}$
Excess kurtosis	$\frac{\mathbb{E}((Y - \mathbb{E}(Y))^4)}{(\mathbb{V}ar(Y))^2} - 3 = \frac{12(n + 4d)}{(k + 2d)^2}$

is said to have a `non-central chi-square distribution` *with n degrees of freedom and non-centrality parameter d:*

$$d = \sum_i^n \delta_i^2$$

and density $f_Y(y; \mu, \sigma)$ *given by*

$$f_Y(y; n) = e^{-(y+d)/2} \frac{x^{n/2-1}}{2^{n/2}} \sum_{k=0}^{\infty} \frac{d^k}{2^{2k} k! \Gamma(k + 1/2n)}, y \in \Re^+.$$

Moreover:

$$\mathbb{E}(Y) = n + d$$

and

$$\mathbb{V}ar(Y) = 2(n + 2d).$$

We write $Y \sim \chi^2_{n,d}$.

Remark A.4.1 *We can make the following observations:*

- *The non-centrality parameter depends on the sum* $d = \sum_i^n \delta_i^2$, *not on the individual values of the parameters* δ_i.
- *If* $d = 0$, *the non-central chi-square distribution collapses to the chi-square distribution.*
- *Here we are assuming that n is an integer parameter; this is not necessary.*

Table A.5 illustrates the main properties of the non-central chi-square distribution. The resulting pdf and cdf are shown in Figure A.6. Figure A.7 illustrates the different shape of the density for different values of the parameter of non-centrality d.

Matlab Code

```
%%%%%%%%%%%%%%%%%%%%%%%%%%%%%%%%%%%%%%%%%%%%%%%%%%%%%%%%%%%%%%%
%%%%PLOT OF THE Non Central Chi-2 DISTRIBUTION%%%%
%%%%%%%%%%%%%%%%%%%%%%%%%%%%%%%%%%%%%%%%%%%%%%%%%%%%%%%%%%%%%%%
clear all;
%assign parameters
n=5; %degrees of freedom
noncentralpar=2;%non centrality parameter
%assign x-range
```

```
x=linspace(0,20,100);
%compute pdf and cdf
pdfncchi2=pdf('ncx2',x,n,noncentralpar);
cdfncchi2=cdf('ncx2',x,n,noncentralpar);
%make the plot
h=figure('Color', [ 1 1 1])
plot(x,pdfncchi2,'r',x,cdfncchi2,'b')
xlabel('x')
title('Non central Chi—Square pdf and cdf when n=5 and d =2')
legend('Non Central Chi—Square pdf',...
'Non Central Chi—Square cdf')
print(h,'—djpeg','FigNCChiSquarepdf.jpg')
```

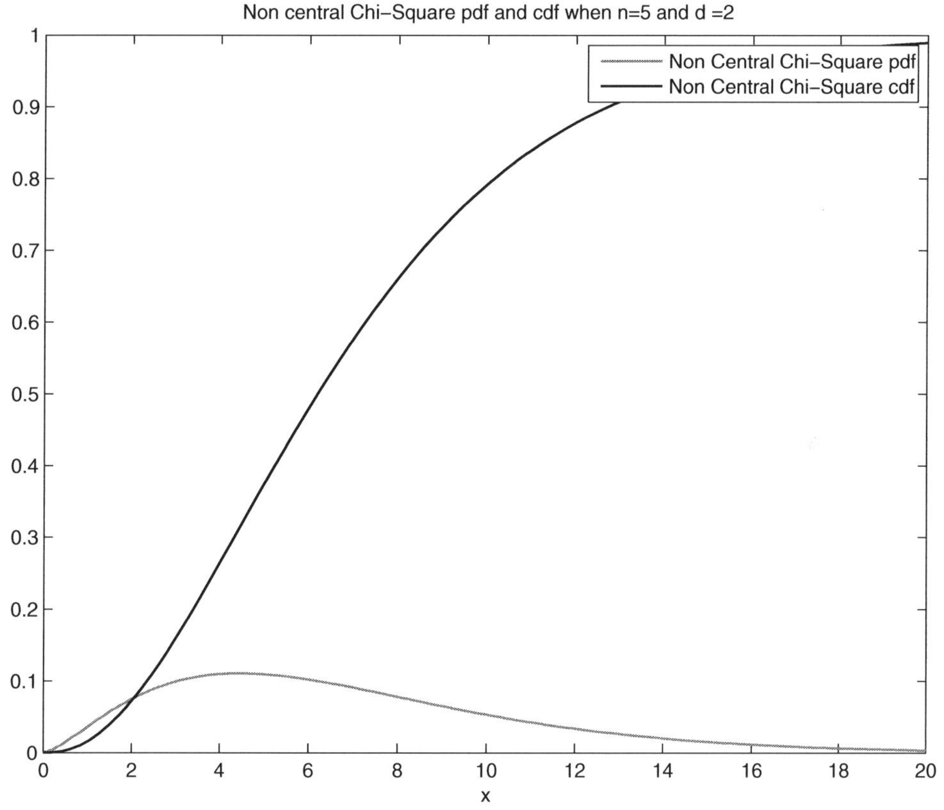

FIGURE A.6 Density and cdf of the non-central chi-square distribution with $n = 5$ and $d = 2$

Matlab Code

```
%%%%%%%%%%%%%%%%%%%%%%%%%%%%%%%%%%%
%%%%THE NCChi—2 DISTRIBUTION AND%%%%
%%%%THE PARAMETER OF NON CENTRALITY
%%%%%%%%%%%%%%%%%%%%%%%%%%%%%%%%%%%
```

```
clear all;
%assign parameters
n=15; %degrees of freedom
ncp=[0.5 1.5 3 5 10];%non centrality parameter
%assign x-range
x=linspace(0,20,300);
%compute pdf and cdf
for i=1:length(ncp)
  pdfncchi2(i,:)=pdf('ncx2',x,ncp(i));
end
h=figure('Color', [ 1 1 1])
plot(x,pdfncchi2,'.')
xlabel('x')
legend('d=0.5','d=1.5','d=3','d=5','d=10')
title('The Non-Central Chi-Square pdf varying the non ...
centrality parameter and with n=15 of degrees of freedom')
print(h,'-djpeg','FigNCChiParSquarepdf.jpg')
```

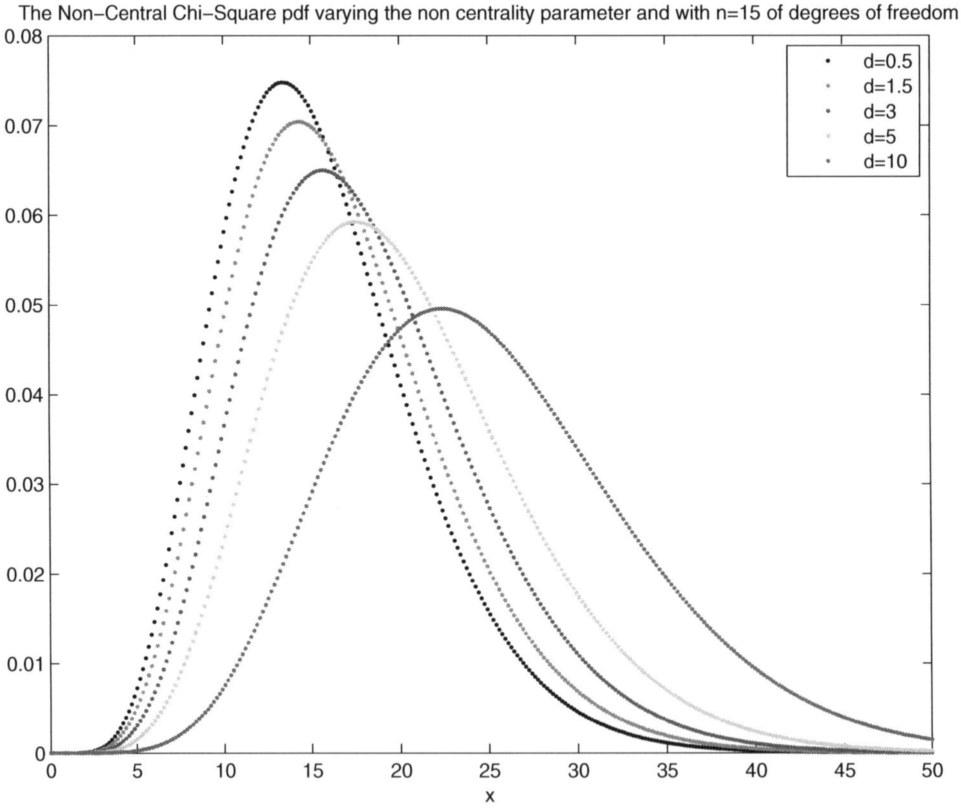

FIGURE A.7 Density of the non-central chi-square distribution varying the parameter of non-centrality *d*

A.5 THE POISSON DISTRIBUTION

Fact A.5.1 (Poisson Distribution) *A Poisson random variable N with rate λ has probability mass*

$$p_N(n) = \frac{e^{-\lambda}\lambda^n}{n!}.$$

Moreover:

$$\mathbb{E}(N) = \lambda$$

and

$$\mathbb{V}ar(N) = \lambda.$$

We write $N \sim Poi(\lambda)$.

Table A.6 illustrates the main properties of the Poisson distribution. The resulting probability mass function and cdf are shown in Figure A.8. The impact of the rate of arrival λ is represented in Figure A.9.

TABLE A.6 Moments of the Poisson distribution

Support	$n \in 0, 1, 2, \cdots$
Mean	$\mathbb{E}(N) = \lambda$
Variance	$\mathbb{V}ar(N) = \lambda$
Skewness	$\frac{\mathbb{E}((N-\lambda)^3)}{\lambda^{\frac{3}{2}}} = \frac{1}{\sqrt{\lambda}}$
Excess kurtosis	$\frac{\mathbb{E}((N-\lambda)^4)}{\lambda^2} - 3 = \frac{1}{\lambda}$

Matlab Code

```
%%%%%%%%%%%%%%%%%%%%%%%%%%%%%%%%%%%%%%%
%%%%PLOT OF THE Poisson DISTRIBUTION%%%%
%%%%%%%%%%%%%%%%%%%%%%%%%%%%%%%%%%%%%%%
clear all;
%assign parameters
lambda=5; %rate of arrival
%assign x-range
x=(0:1:20);
%compute pdf and cdf
pdfpoil=poisspdf(x,lambda);
cdfpoil=poisscdf(x,lambda);
%make the plot
h=figure('Color', [ 1 1 1])
plot(x,pdfpoil,'--o r',x,cdfpoil,'-o b')
```

```
xlabel('x')
title('Poisson pdf and cdf when \lambda = 5')
legend('Poisson pdf',...
'Poisson cdf')
print(h,'djpeg','FigPoisson1pdf.jpg')
```

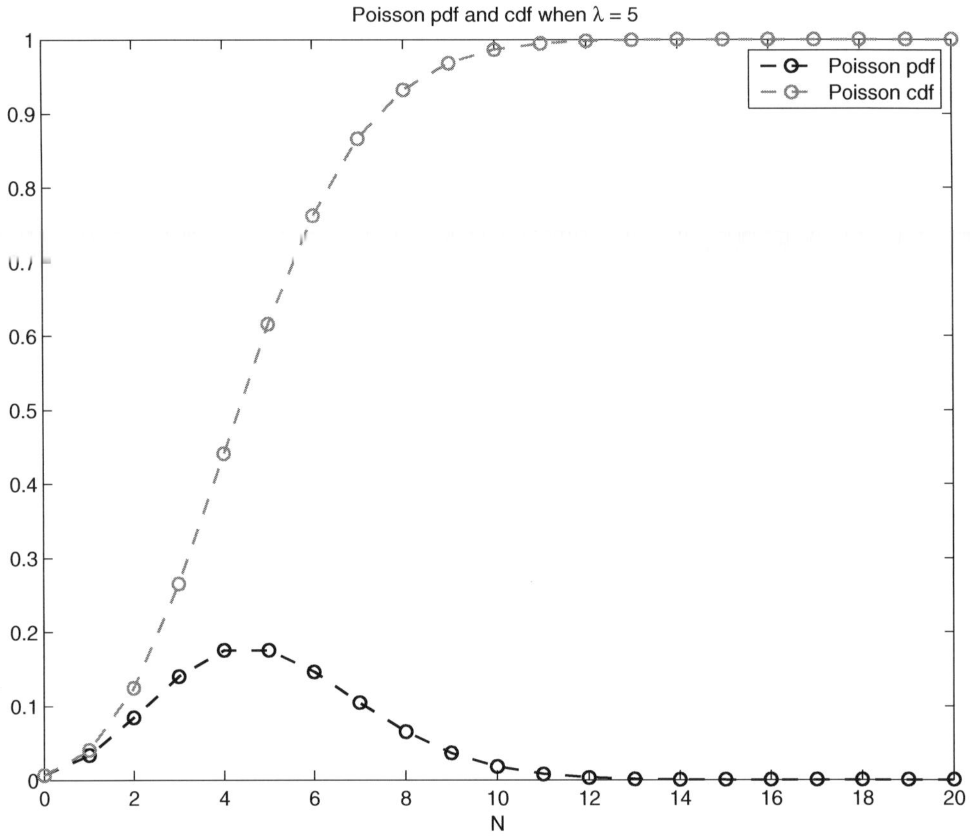

FIGURE A.8 Density and cdf of the Poisson distribution with $\lambda = 5$. The functions are only defined at integer values of x. The connecting lines are only guides for the eye

Matlab Code

```
%%%%%%%%%%%%%%%%%%%%%%%%%%%%%%%%%%%%%%%%%%%%%%%%%%%%%%%%%%%%
%%%%The Poisson DISTRIBUTION and the rate of arrival%%%%
%%%%%%%%%%%%%%%%%%%%%%%%%%%%%%%%%%%%%%%%%%%%%%%%%%%%%%%%%%%%
clear all;
%assign parameters
lambda=[0.5 1 5 10]; %rate of arrival
%assign x-range
x=(0:1:20);
```

```
%compute pdf and cdf
for i=1:length(lambda)
  pdfpoil(i,:)=poisspdf(x,lambda(i));
  cdfpoil(i,:)=poisscdf(x,lambda(i));
end
%make the plot
h=figure('Color', [ 1 1 1])
subplot(2,1,1)
plot(x,pdfpoil,'--o')
xlabel('x')
title('Poisson pdf varying the rate of arrival \lambda')
legend('\lambda = 0.5','\lambda = 1',...
'\lambda = 5','\lambda = 10')
subplot(2,1,2)
plot(x,cdfpoil,'o')
xlabel('x')
title('Poisson cdf varying the rate of arrival \lambda')
print(h,'-djpeg','FigPoisson2pdf.jpg')
```

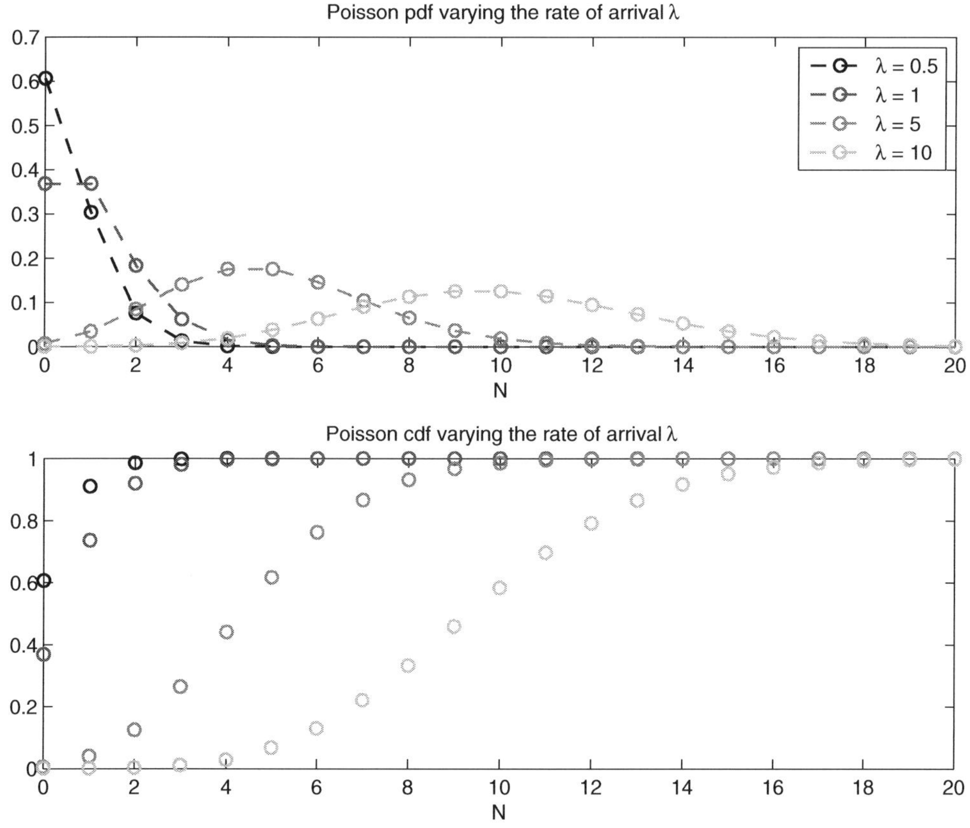

FIGURE A.9 Density and cdf of the Poisson distribution varying the rate of arrival λ

A.6 THE EXPONENTIAL DISTRIBUTION

Fact A.6.1 (Exponential Distribution) *A non-negative random variable X is said to have an* `exponential distribution` *with parameter λ when its density is given by*

$$f_X(x;\lambda) = \begin{cases} \lambda e^{-\lambda x}, & x \geq 0, \\ 0, & x < 0, \end{cases}$$

and its cdf is given by

$$F_X(x;\lambda) = \begin{cases} 1 - e^{-\lambda x}, & x \geq 0, \\ 0, & x < 0. \end{cases}$$

Moreover:

$$\mathbb{E}(X) = \lambda^{-1}$$

and

$$\mathbb{V}ar(X) = \lambda^{-2}.$$

We write $X \sim Exp(\lambda)$.

Table A.7 illustrates the main properties of the exponential distribution, whilst pdf and cdf are shown in Figure A.10.

TABLE A.7 Moments of the exponential distribution

Support	$x \in [0; +\infty)$
Mean	$\mathbb{E}(X) = \frac{1}{\lambda}$
Variance	$\mathbb{V}ar(X) = \frac{1}{\lambda^2}$
Skewness	$\frac{\mathbb{E}((X-\mathbb{E}(X))^3)}{(\mathbb{V}ar(X))^{\frac{3}{2}}} = 2$
Kurtosis	$\frac{\mathbb{E}((X-\mathbb{E}(X))^4)}{(\mathbb{V}ar(X))^2} = 9$

Matlab Code

```
%%%%%%%%%%%%%%%%%%%%%%%%%%%%%%%%%%%%%%%%%%%%
%%%%PLOT OF THE Exponential DISTRIBUTION%%%%
%%%%%%%%%%%%%%%%%%%%%%%%%%%%%%%%%%%%%%%%%%%%
clear all;
%assign parameters
lambda=1.5; %rate of arrival
%assign x-range
x=linspace(0,5,100);
%compute pdf and cdf
pdfexpl=exppdf(x,lambda^(-1));
cdfexpl=expcdf(x,lambda^(-1));
%make the plot
h=figure('Color', [ 1 1 1])
```

```
plot(x,pdfexpl,'- r',x,cdfexpl,'- b')
xlabel('x')
title('Exponential pdf and cdf when \lambda = 1.5')
legend('Exponential pdf',...
'Exponential cdf')
print(h,'-djpeg','Figexpopdf.jpg')
```

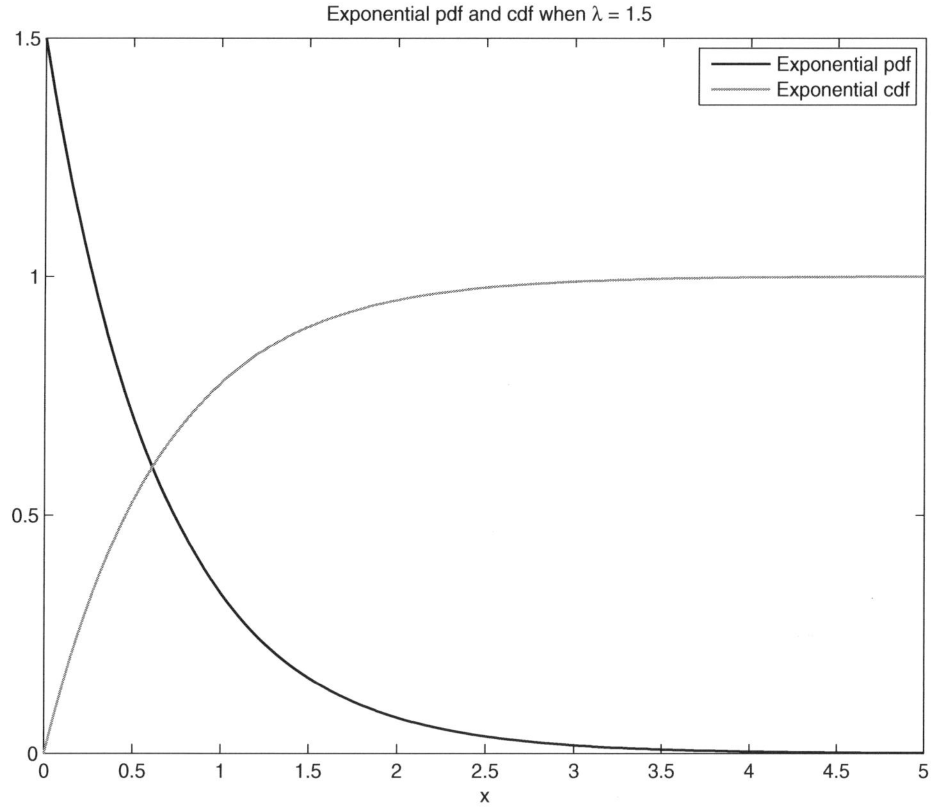

FIGURE A.10 Density and cdf of the exponential distribution with $\lambda = 1.5$

A.7 THE GAMMA DISTRIBUTION

Fact A.7.1 (Gamma Distribution) *A non-negative random variable X is said to have a* `Gamma distribution` *with shape parameter* α *and rate parameter* λ *when its density is given by*

$$f_X(x; \alpha, \lambda) = \frac{1}{\Gamma(\alpha)} \lambda^{\alpha} x^{\alpha-1} e^{-\lambda x},$$

where $\Gamma(\alpha)$ *is the Gamma function, which is defined as*

$$\Gamma(\alpha) = \int_0^{\infty} x^{\alpha-1} e^{-x} dx.$$

TABLE A.8 Moments of the Gamma distribution

Support	$x \in [0; +\infty)$
Mean	$\mathbb{E}(X) = \frac{\alpha}{\lambda}$
Variance	$\mathbb{V}ar(X) = \frac{\alpha}{\lambda^2}$
Skewness	$\frac{\mathbb{E}((X - \mathbb{E}(X))^3)}{(\mathbb{V}ar(X))^{\frac{3}{2}}} = \frac{2}{\sqrt{\alpha}}$
Kurtosis	$\frac{\mathbb{E}((X - \mathbb{E}(X))^4)}{(\mathbb{V}ar(X))^2} = 3 + \frac{6}{\alpha}$

Moreover:

$$\mathbb{E}(X) = \frac{\alpha}{\lambda}$$

and

$$\mathbb{V}ar(X) = \frac{\alpha}{\lambda^2}.$$

We write $X \sim \Gamma(\alpha, \lambda)$.

Remark A.7.1

- *A Gamma random variable with parameter* $\lambda = \frac{1}{2}$, *that is* $X \sim \Gamma(\alpha, \frac{1}{2})$, *is distributed according to a chi-square distribution with* 2α *degrees of freedom.*
- *A Gamma random variable with* $\alpha = 1$, *that is* $X \sim \Gamma(1, \lambda)$, *is distributed according to an exponential distribution of parameter* λ.

Table A.8 illustrates the main properties of the Gamma distribution. Figures A.11 and A.12 show the Gamma pdf and cdf for different values of the parameters α and λ.

Matlab Code

```
%%%%%%%%%%%%%%%%%%%%%%%%%%%%%%%%%%%%%%
%%%%PLOT OF THE Gamma DISTRIBUTION%%%%
%%%%%%%%%%%%%%%%%%%%%%%%%%%%%%%%%%%%%%
clear all;
%assign parameters
alpha=5; %shape parameter
lambda=0.5; %rate parameter
%assign x-range
x=linspace(0,30,200);
%compute pdf and cdf
pdfgamma=gampdf(x,alpha,lambda^(-1));
cdfgamma=gamcdf(x,alpha,lambda^(-1));
%make the plot
h=figure('Color', [ 1 1 1])
```

```
plot(x,pdfgamma,'- r',x,cdfgamma,'- b')
xlabel('x')
title('Gamma pdf and cdf when\alpha =5 \lambda = 0.5')
legend('Gamma pdf',...
'Gamma cdf')
print(h,'-djpeg','FigGamma1pdf.jpg')
```

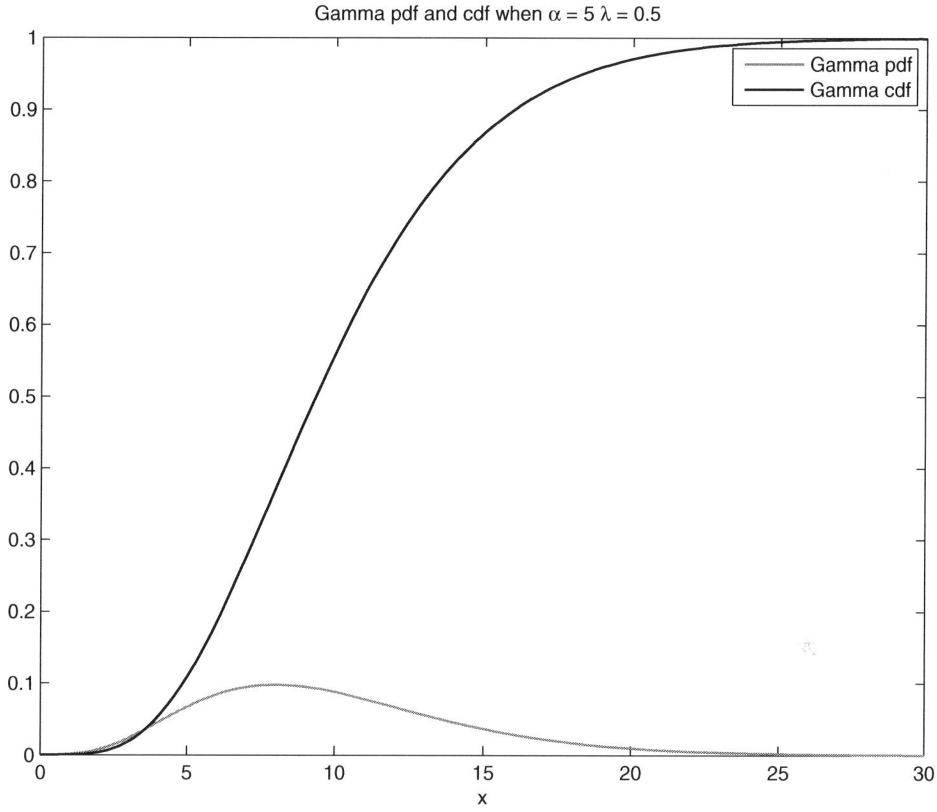

FIGURE A.11 Density and cdf of the Gamma distribution with $\alpha = 5, \lambda = 0.5$

Matlab Code

```
%%%%%%%%%%%%%%%%%%%%%%%%%%%%%%%%%%%%%%%%%%%%%%%%%%%%%%%%%
%%The Gamma DISTRIBUTION and the shape/rate parameters%%
%%%%%%%%%%%%%%%%%%%%%%%%%%%%%%%%%%%%%%%%%%%%%%%%%%%%%%%%%
alpha=[1 2 5 10];
lambda=[0.5 0.5 0.5 2]; %rate parameter
%assign x-range
x=linspace(0,30,200);
%compute pdf and cdf
for i=1:length(alpha)
```

```
  pdfgamma(i,:)=gampdf(x,alpha(i),lambda(i)^(−1));
  cdfgamma(i,:)=gamcdf(x,alpha(i),lambda(i)^(−1));
end
%make the plot
h=figure('Color', [ 1 1 1])
subplot(2,1,1)
plot(x,pdfgamma,'−')
xlabel('x')
title('Gamma pdf varying \alpha and \lambda')
legend('\alpha = 1, \lambda = 0.5','\alpha = 2, \lambda = 0.5',...
'\alpha = 5, \lambda = 0.5','\alpha = 10, \lambda = 2')
subplot(2,1,2)
plot(x,cdfgamma,'−')
xlabel('x')
title('Gamma cdf varying \alpha and \lambda')
legend('\alpha = 1, \lambda = 0.5','\alpha = 2, \lambda = 0.5',...
'\alpha = 5, \lambda = 0.5','\alpha = 10, \lambda = 2')
print(h,'−djpeg','FigGamma2pdf.jpg')
```

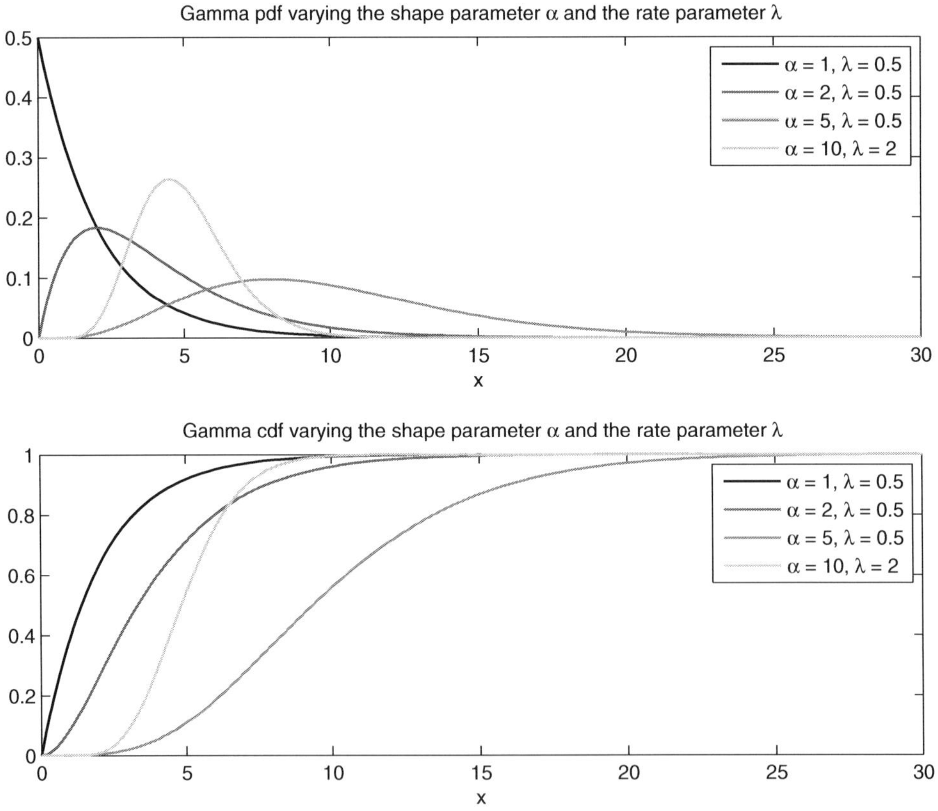

FIGURE A.12 Density and cdf of the Gamma distribution varying the shape parameter α and the rate parameter λ

A.8 THE MULTIVARIATE NORMAL DISTRIBUTION

Fact A.8.1 (Multivariate Gaussian Distribution) *Let μ be an $(N \times 1)$ vector and Σ an $(N \times N)$ matrix, symmetric and positive definite. A random vector $\mathbf{X} = (X_1, \ldots, X_N)$ is distributed according to a multivariate normal distribution with parameters μ and Σ, and we write*

$$\mathbf{X} \sim \mathcal{N}(\mu, \Sigma),$$

if its density function $f_{\mathbf{X}}(\mathbf{x})$ is given by

$$f_{\mathbf{X}}(\mathbf{x}) = \frac{1}{\sqrt{(2\pi)^N \det(\Sigma)}} \exp\left(-\frac{1}{2}(\mathbf{x} - \mu)'\Sigma^{-1}(\mathbf{x} - \mu)\right),$$

where $\det(\Sigma)$ is the determinant of the matrix Σ and Σ^{-1} is the inverse of the matrix Σ.

If $\mathbf{X} \sim \mathcal{N}(\mu, \Sigma)$, then

$$\mathbb{E}(\mathbf{X}) = \mu, \mathbb{V}(\mathbf{X}) = \Sigma,$$

and we call μ the expected value (or mean) vector and Σ the covariance matrix. In particular, this means that a multivariate Gaussian distribution is determined by its mean vector and covariance matrix.

The mean vector is a vector with N components. The ith component is denoted by μ_i and it represents the expected value of X_i:

$$\mu = \begin{bmatrix} \mu_1 \\ \vdots \\ \mu_i \\ \vdots \\ \mu_N \end{bmatrix} = \begin{bmatrix} \mathbb{E}(X_1) \\ \mathbb{E}(X_i) \\ \mathbb{E}(X_N) \end{bmatrix}.$$

The covariance matrix $\Sigma_{N\times N}$:

- *is a squared and symmetric matrix;*
- *is positive definite, that is*

$$\mathbf{x}'\Sigma\mathbf{x} > 0 \, \forall \mathbf{x} \in R^N, \mathbf{x} \neq \mathbf{0};$$

- *is made up of N variances (on the diagonal and denoted by σ_i^2) and $N \times (N-1)/2$ covariances (denoted by σ_{ij} with $\sigma_{ij} = \sigma_{ji}$).*

$$\Sigma_{N\times N} = \begin{bmatrix} \sigma_1^2 & & \cdots & & \sigma_{1,N} \\ & \sigma_2^2 & & & \\ \vdots & & \ddots & & \vdots \\ & & & \sigma_{N-1}^2 & \\ \sigma_{N,1} & & \cdots & & \sigma_N^2 \end{bmatrix}$$

where

$$\sigma_i^2 = \mathbb{V}(X_i); \sigma_{ij} = \mathbb{C}ov(X_i, X_j) = \mathbb{E}((X_i - \mu_i)(X_j - \mu_j)).$$

Definition A.8.1 *We say that the random vector $\mathbf{Z} = (Z_1, \ldots, Z_N)$ has a multivariate standard normal distribution if*

$$\mu = \mathbf{0}_N \text{ and } \Sigma = \mathbf{I}_N,$$

where $\mathbf{0}_N$ is a vector of zeros and $\mathbf{I}_N$ is the identity matrix of order N. It follows that Z_i and Z_j are uncorrelated and (being normal) also independent. The density function is simply

$$f_Z(\mathbf{z}) = \frac{1}{\sqrt{(2\pi)^N}} \exp\left(-\frac{1}{2}\mathbf{z}'\mathbf{z}\right) = \frac{1}{\sqrt{(2\pi)^N}} \exp\left(-\frac{1}{2}\sum_{i=1}^{N} z_i^2\right).$$

A.8.1 The Bivariate Normal Distribution

If $N = 2$, the mean vector and the covariance matrix can be written as

$$\mu = \begin{bmatrix}\mu_1\\ \mu_2\end{bmatrix}; \Sigma_{2\times 2} = \begin{bmatrix}\sigma_1^2 & \rho\sigma_1\sigma_2\\ \rho\sigma_1\sigma_2 & \sigma_2^2\end{bmatrix}; \Sigma_{2\times 2}^{-1} = \frac{1}{1-\rho^2}\begin{bmatrix}\frac{1}{\sigma_1^2} & -\frac{\rho}{\sigma_1\sigma_2}\\ -\frac{\rho}{\sigma_1\sigma_2} & \frac{1}{\sigma_2^2}\end{bmatrix}$$

where $\rho = \mathrm{Corr}(Y_1, Y_2)$ and the density function becomes

$$f_X(\mathbf{x}) = \frac{\exp\left(-\frac{1}{2(1-\rho^2)}\left(\frac{(x_1-\mu_1)^2}{\sigma_1^2} - 2\rho\frac{(x_1-\mu_1)(x_2-\mu_2)}{\sigma_1\sigma_2} + \frac{(x_2-\mu_2)^2}{\sigma_2^2}\right)\right)}{2\pi\sigma_1\sigma_2\sqrt{1-\rho^2}}.$$

The corresponding density is bell-shaped with maximum in (μ_1,μ_2).

The contour lines, that is the combinations of x_1 and x_2 such that the density is constant, are described by the equation

$$-\frac{1}{2(1-\rho^2)}\left(\frac{(x_1-\mu_1)^2}{\sigma_1^2} - 2\rho\frac{(x_1-\mu_1)(x_2-\mu_2)}{\sigma_1\sigma_2} + \frac{(x_2-\mu_2)^2}{\sigma_2^2}\right) = k,$$

which is the equation of an ellipse. Figures A.13–A.15 show the bivariate Normal density (left panel) and the corresponding contour plot (right panel) for different levels of the correlations, ρ.

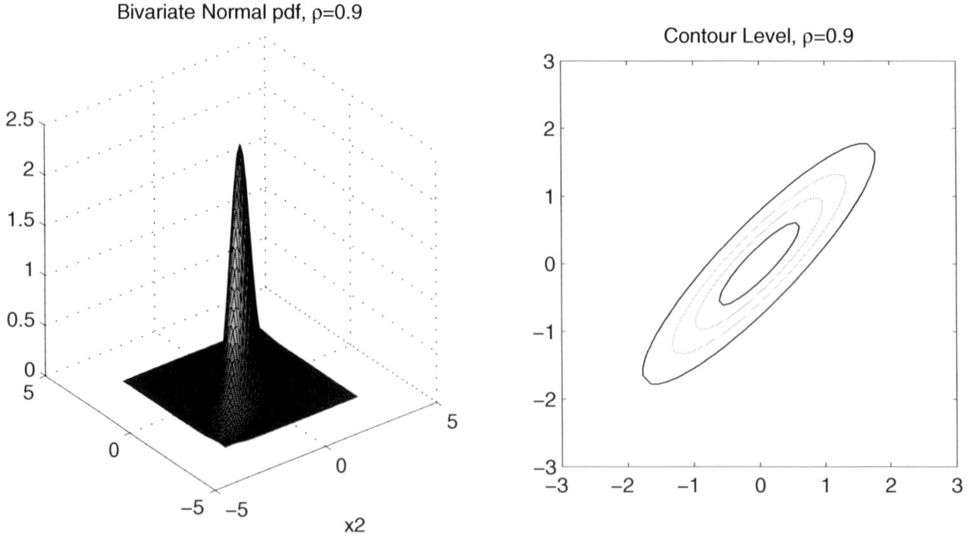

FIGURE A.13 Bivariate Gaussian distribution ($\rho = 0.9$)

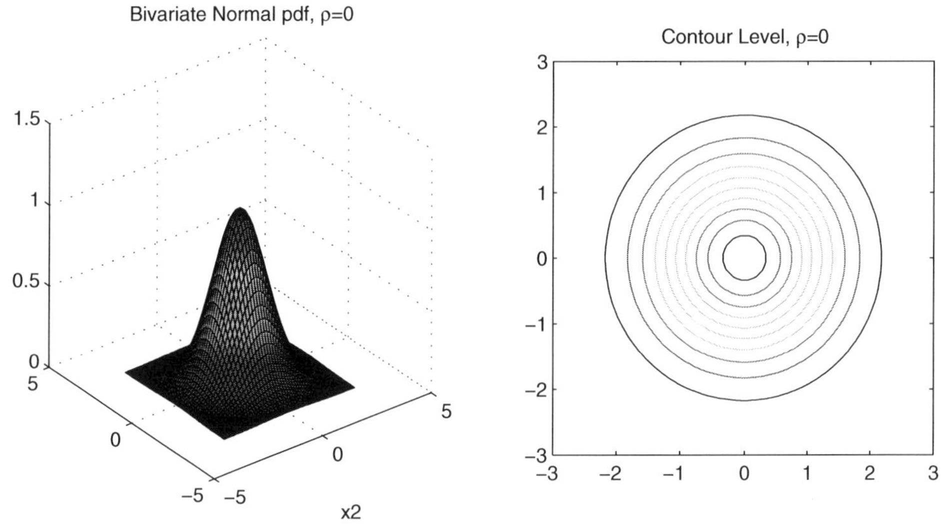

FIGURE A.14 Bivariate Gaussian distribution ($\rho = 0$)

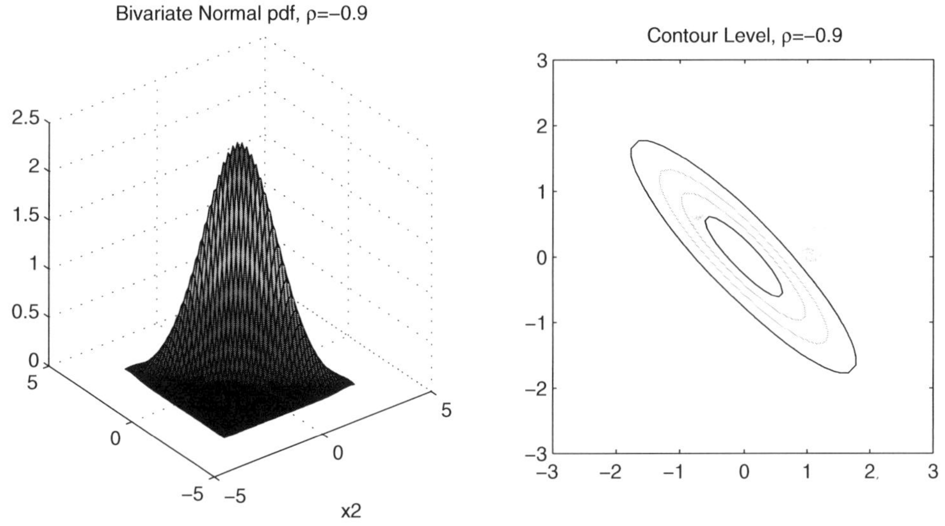

FIGURE A.15 Bivariate Gaussian distribution ($\rho = -0.9$)

A.8.2 An Important Fact About Sum of Gaussian Random Variables

Matlab Code

```
%%%%%%%%%%%%%%%%%%%%%%%%%%%%%%%%%%%%%%%%%%%%%%
%%%%%%%%PLOT OF THE BIVARIATE GAUSSIAN%%%%%%%%
%%%%%%%%POSITIVE CORRELATION%%%%%%%%%%%%%%%%%%
%%%%%%%%%%%%%%%%%%%%%%%%%%%%%%%%%%%%%%%%%%%%%%
```

```
%correlation
rho=0.9;
%variances and covariances
s1=0.3^2; s2=0.5^2; s12=rho*(s1*s2)^0.5;
factor=2*pi*(s1*s2)^0.5;
m=zeros(2,1); %mean vector
npoints1=50;
npoints2=50;
x1=linspace(m(1)-3*s1^0.5,m(1)+3*s1^0.5,npoints1);
x2=linspace(m(2)-3*s2^0.5,m(2)+3*s2^0.5,npoints2);
[x1mesh, x2mesh]=...
meshgrid((x1-m(1))/s1^0.5,(x2-m(2))/s2^0.5);
x1x2mesh=-2*rho*x1mesh.*x2mesh;
pdfbiv=exp(-(x1mesh.^2+x1x2mesh+x2mesh.^2)...
/((2*(1-rho^2))))/(factor*(1-rho^2)^0.5);
figure1=figure('PaperSize',[20.98 29.68],'Color',[1 1 1]);
subplot(1,2,1); surf(x1mesh,x2mesh,pdfbiv)
axis square
title('Bivariate Normal pdf, \rho=0.9')
xlabel('x1'),xlabel('x2')
subplot(1,2,2); contour(x1mesh,x2mesh,pdfbiv)
title('Contour Level, \rho=0.9')
axis square
```

Fact A.8.2 *The marginal distributions of a vector X can all be Gaussian without the joint being multivariate Gaussian.*

Example A.8.1 *Let* $X_1 \sim \mathcal{N}(0, 1)$ *and*

$$X_2 = \begin{cases} X_1 & \text{if} \quad -c < X_1 < c \\ -X_1 & \text{elsewhere.} \end{cases}$$

We have

$$\Pr(X_2 < x) = \begin{cases} \Pr(X_1 < x) & \text{if} \quad -c < X_1 < c \\ \Pr(X_1 > -x) & \text{elsewhere} \end{cases}$$

and the density is

$$f_{X_2}(x) = \begin{cases} f_{X_1}(x) & \text{if} \quad -c < X_1 < c \\ f_{X_1}(x) & \text{elsewhere} \end{cases} = f_{X_1}(x)$$

and therefore it is Gaussian as well. This is illustrated in Figure A.16.

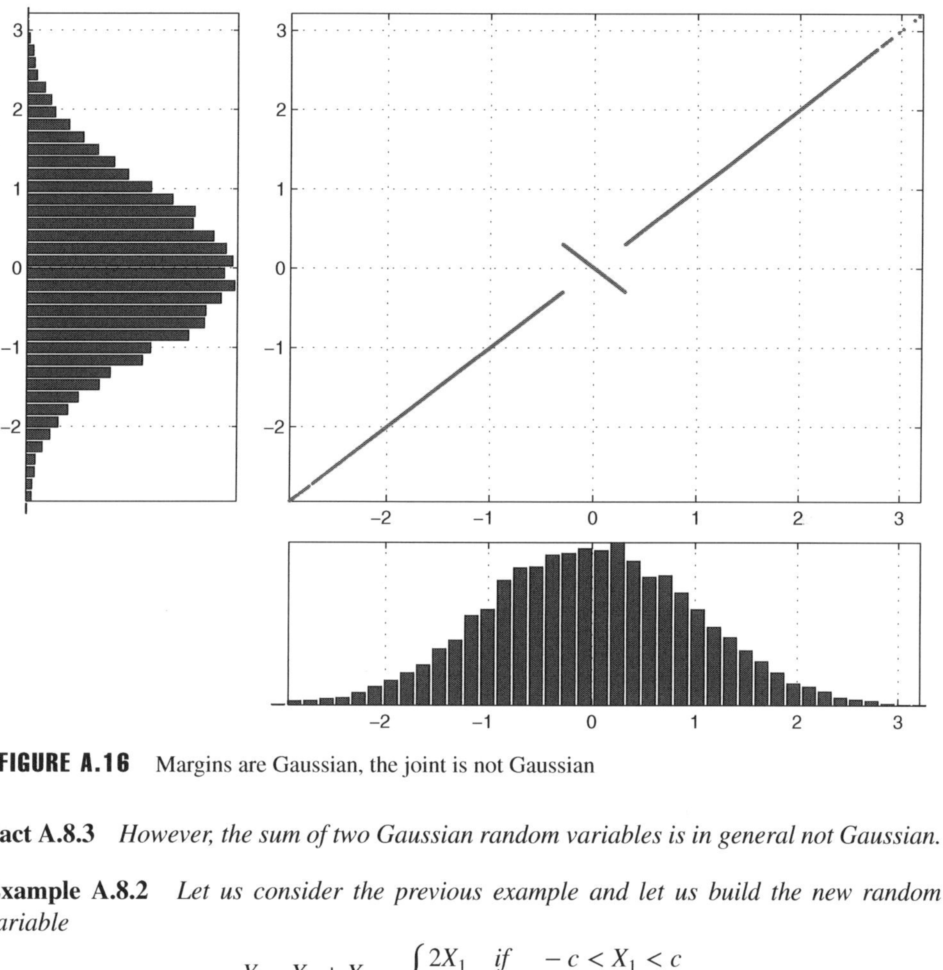

FIGURE A.16 Margins are Gaussian, the joint is not Gaussian

Fact A.8.3 *However, the sum of two Gaussian random variables is in general not Gaussian.*

Example A.8.2 *Let us consider the previous example and let us build the new random variable*

$$Y = X_1 + X_2 = \begin{cases} 2X_1 & \text{if} \quad -c < X_1 < c \\ 0 & \text{elsewhere} \end{cases}$$

that is clearly not Gaussian, as shown in Figure A.17.

A.9 SIMULATING RANDOM VARIABLES

Many applications entail sampling random variables from prespecified distributions. A very popular general technique to achieve this is the inverse transform method. This method is implementable if the cumulative density function and its inverse can be computed without difficulty. The idea is formalized in Fact A.9.1 and illustrated in Figure A.18.

Fact A.9.1 *Suppose we need to simulate a random variable X with cumulative distribution function F_X, that is such that $\mathbb{P}(X \leq x) = F_X(x)$. Then, the inverse transform method sets*

$$X = F_X^{-1}(U), \quad U \sim Unif[0, 1],$$

where F_X^{-1} is the inverse of F_X and $Unif[0, 1]$ denotes the uniform distribution on $[0, 1]$.

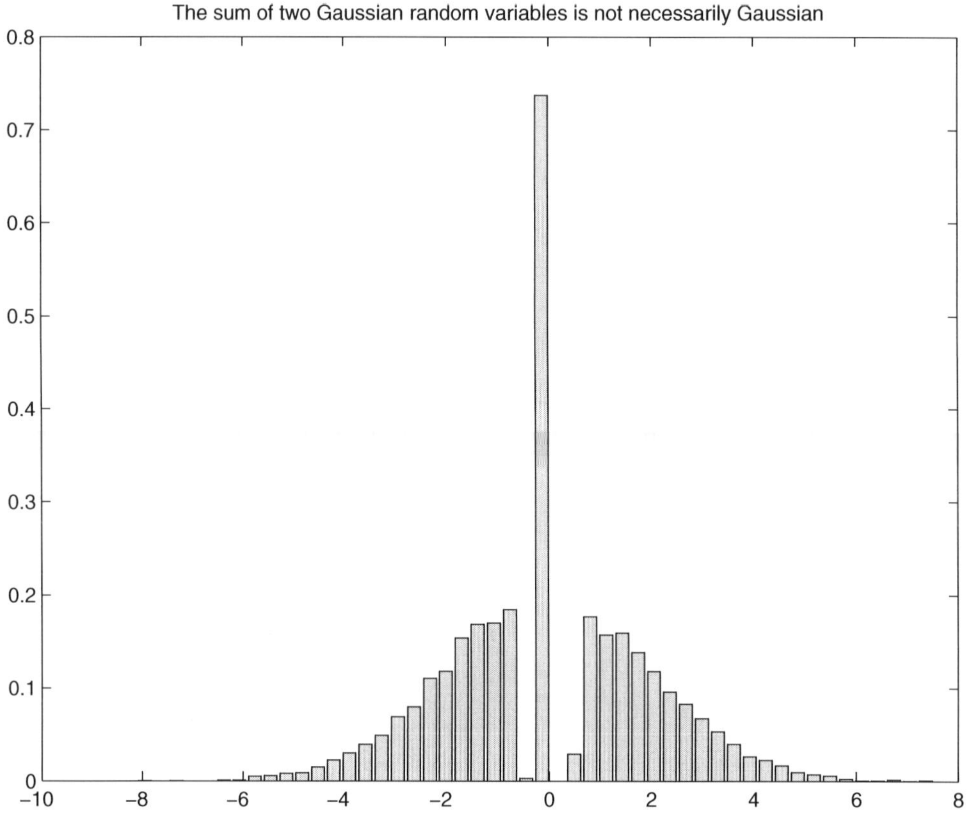

FIGURE A.17 Sum of Gaussian random variables is not necessarily Gaussian

A.9.1 Example: Sampling from the Normal Distribution

We refer to the properties presented in Section A.1.

- In Excel, simulation of Gaussian r.v.s can be performed by inputting in a cell the command =NORMSINV(RAND()).
- In Matlab, we can simulate Gaussian random numbers by simulating uniform random numbers through the command

```
>U=rand(1,1)
```

  and then applying to it the inverse Gaussian cdf

```
>Z=norminv(U,0,1);
```

- If we are interested in generating Gaussian random variables with assigned mean μ and standard deviation σ we can use

```
>X=norminv(U,mu,sigma);
```

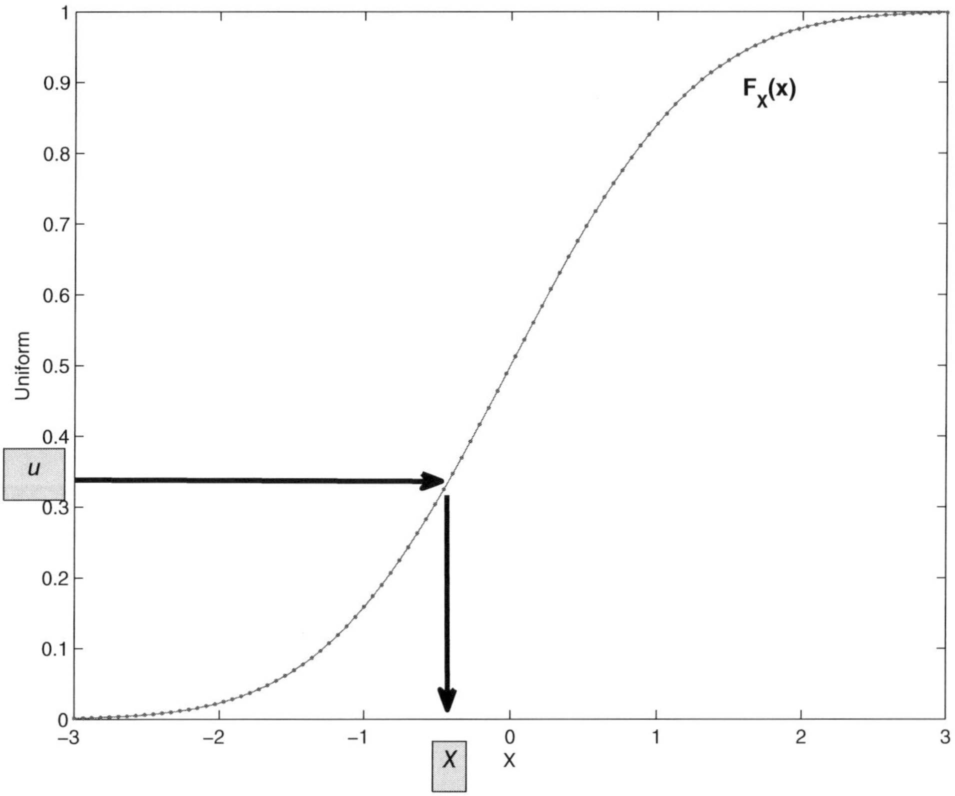

FIGURE A.18 Inverse transform method for a hypothetical cdf F_X

This is illustrated in detail below.

Matlab Code

```
%%%%%%%%%%%%%%%%%%%%%%%%%%%%%%%%%%%%%%%%%%%%%%%%%%%%%%%%%%%%
% SIMULATION OF STD GAUSSIAN RANDOM VARIABLES BY INVERSION %
%%%%%%%%%%%%%%%%%%%%%%%%%%%%%%%%%%%%%%%%%%%%%%%%%%%%%%%%%%%%
clear all; close all
%assign parameters
NSim=10^6;
%simulate a sample of Uniform(0,1) random variables
R=rand(1,NSim);
%simulate the sample of standard Gaussian r.v. by inversion
X = norminv(R,0,1);
%make the plot
h=figure('Color', [ 1 1 1]);
subplot(4,4,[1 5 9]);
u=linspace(0,1,50);
```

```
hist(R,u); view(90,-90)
title('Uniform r.v.')
set(gca,'XTick',[0:0.1:1])
set(gca,'YTickLabel',''); grid on
subplot(4,4,[2:4 6:8 10:12]);
x=linspace(-4,4,100);
f = ksdensity(X,x,'function','cdf');
plot(x,f);
title('Inversion of the cdf')
set(gca,'XTick',[-4:1:4])
set(gca,'YTick',[0:0.1:1]); grid on
subplot(4,4,[14:16]);
histfit(X,100)
title('Standard Gaussian r.v.')
set(gca,'XTick',[-4:1:4])
set(gca,'YTickLabel',''); grid on
```

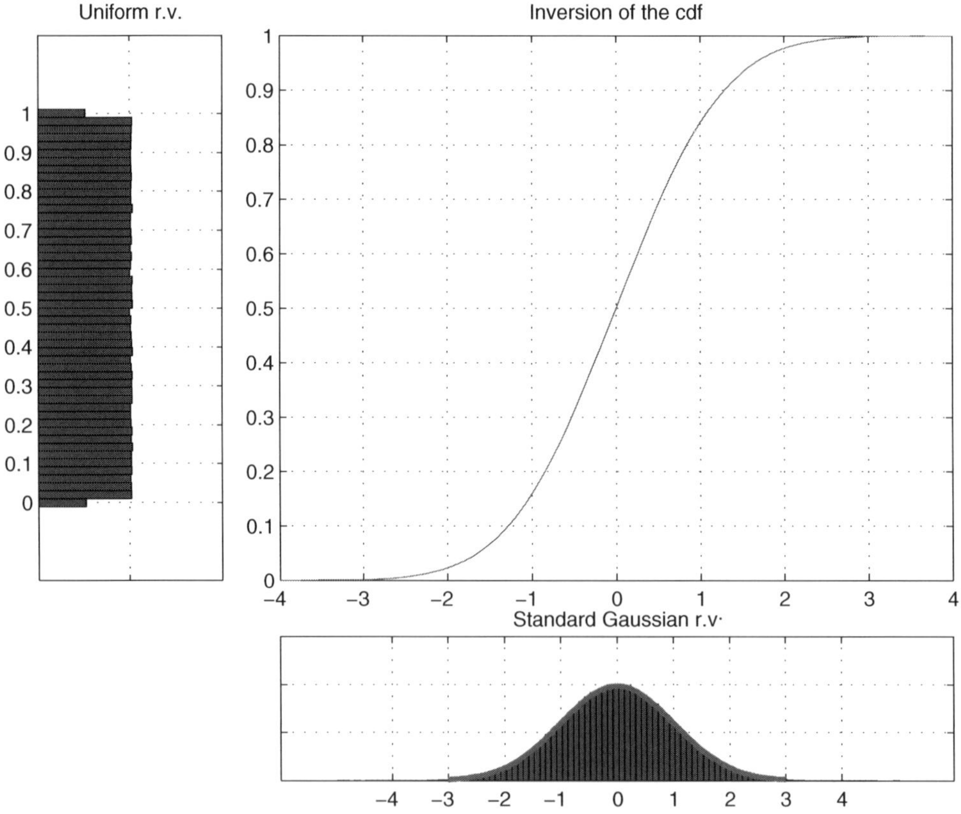

FIGURE A.19 Sampling from the standard Gaussian distribution

- A more direct approach in Matlab is through the command

```
>Z=randn(1,1);
```

- If we are interested in generating Gaussian random variables with assigned mean μ and standard deviation σ we just do

```
>X=mu+Z*sigma;
```

This is illustrated in detail below.

Matlab Code

```
%%%%%%%%%%%%%%%%%%%%%%%%%%%%%%%%%%%%%%%%%%%%%%%%%%%%%%%
% SIMULATION OF GAUSSIAN RANDOM VARIABLE BY INVERSION %
%%%%%%%%%%%%%%%%%%%%%%%%%%%%%%%%%%%%%%%%%%%%%%%%%%%%%%%
clear all; close all
%assign parameters
NSim=10^6; mu=0.2; sg=0.1;
%simulate a sample of Uniform(0,1) random variables
R=rand(1,NSim);
%simulate the sample of non standard Gaussian r.v. by inversion
X = norminv(R,mu,sg);
h=figure('Color', [ 1 1 1]);
subplot(4,4,[1 5 9]);
u=linspace(0,1,50);
hist(R,u); view(90,-90)
title('Uniform r.v.')
set(gca,'XTick',[0:0.1:1])
set(gca,'YTickLabel',''); grid on
subplot(4,4,[2:4 6:8 10:12]);
x=linspace(-0.3,0.5,100);
f = ksdensity(X,x,'function','cdf');
plot(x,f);
title('Inversion of the cdf')
set(gca,'XTick',[-0.3:0.1:0.5])
set(gca,'YTick',[0:0.1:1]); grid on
subplot(4,4,[14:16]);
histfit(X,100)
title('Gaussian r.v.'); xlim([-0.3 0.5]);
set(gca,'XTick',[-0.3:0.1:0.5])
set(gca,'YTickLabel',''); grid on
```

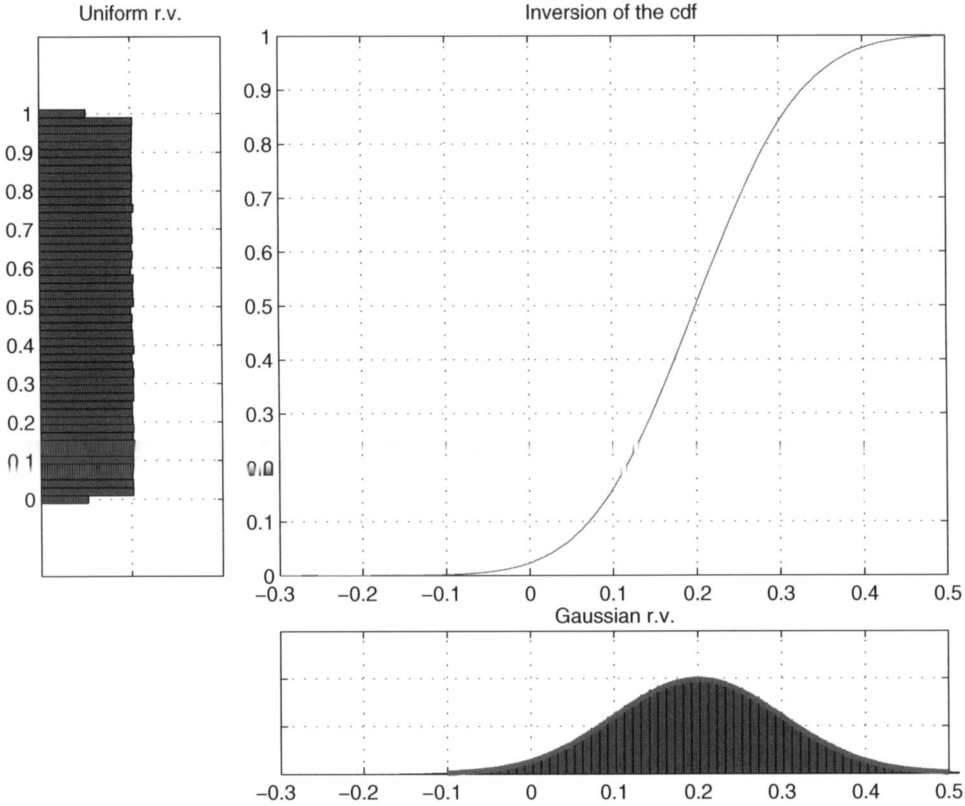

FIGURE A.20 Sampling from the Gaussian distribution with $\mu = 0.2$ and $\sigma = 0.1$

A.9.2 Example: Sampling from the Lognormal Distribution

We can exploit the relationship between the Gaussian and lognormal distribution. In the following lines we simulate 10,000 lognormal variables with parameters $\mu = 0.05$ and $\sigma = 0.2$.

```
>mu=0.05;
>sigma=0.2
>X=mu+Z*randn(10000,1);
>Y=exp(X);
```

Matlab Code

```
%%%%%%%%%%%%%%%%%%%%%%%%%%%%%%%%%%%%%%%%%%
% SIMULATION OF LOGNORMAL RANDOM VARIABLES %
%%%%%%%%%%%%%%%%%%%%%%%%%%%%%%%%%%%%%%%%%%
clear all;
close all
```

```
%assign parameters
NSim=10^6;
mu=0.05;
sigma=0.2;
%simulate the sample of Gaussian r.v.
X = mu+sigma*randn(NSim,1);
%simulate the Lognormal
%by exponential transformation
Y=exp(X);
h=figure('Color', [ 1 1 1]);
histfit(Y,100,'lognormal');
title('Simulated Lognormal Random Variables')
```

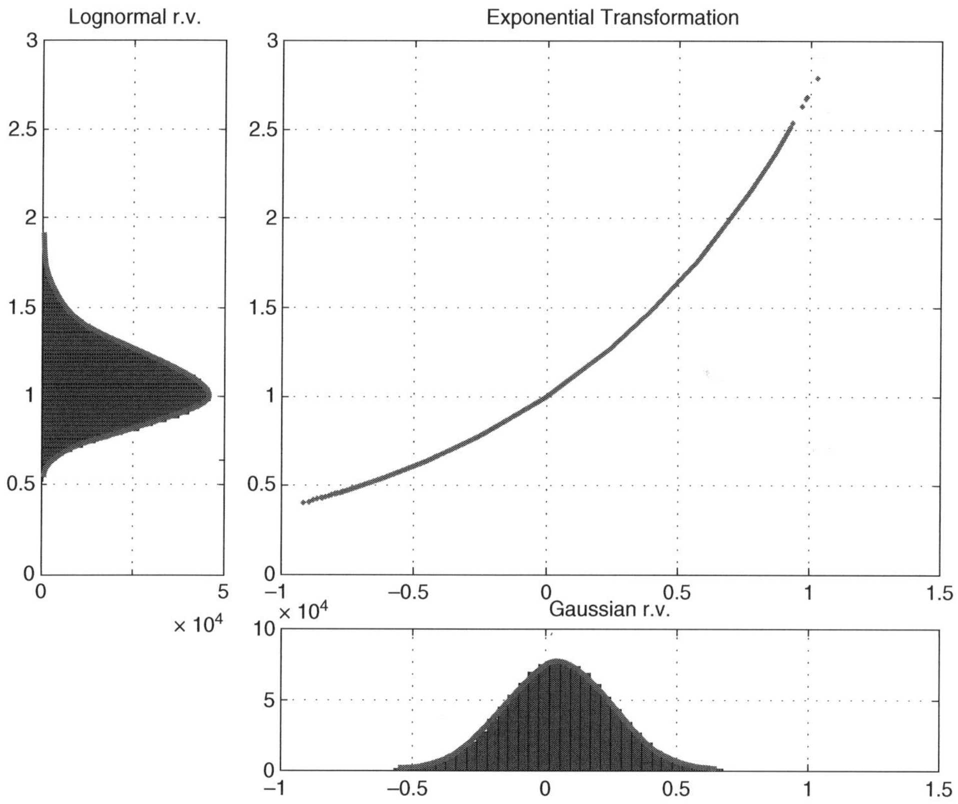

FIGURE A.21 Sampling from the lognormal distribution with parameters $\mu = 0.05$ and $\sigma = 0.2$

A.9.3 Example: Sampling from the Poisson Distribution

We refer to the properties presented in Section A.5. This is illustrated in detail below.

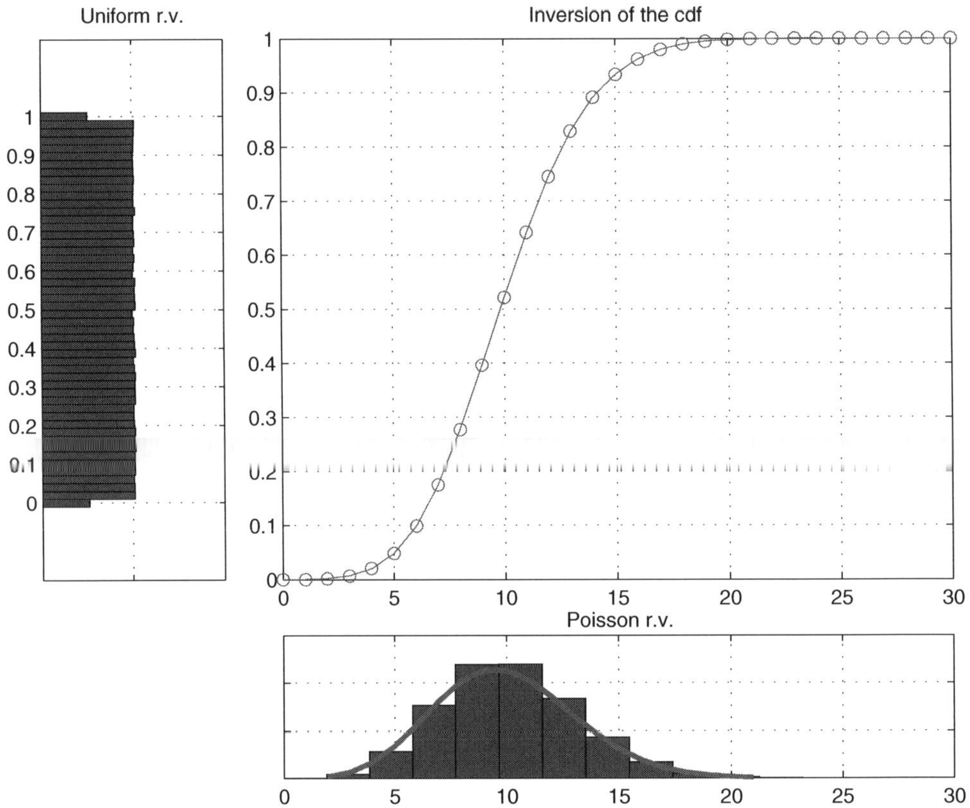

FIGURE A.22 Sampling from the Poisson distribution with $\lambda = 10$

Matlab Code

```
%%%%%%%%%%%%%%%%%%%%%%%%%%%%%%%%%%%%%%%%%%%%%%%%%%%%%%%
% SIMULATION OF POISSON RANDOM VARIABLE BY INVERSION %
%%%%%%%%%%%%%%%%%%%%%%%%%%%%%%%%%%%%%%%%%%%%%%%%%%%%%%%
clear all; close all
%assign parameters
NSim=10^6; lambdaP=10;
%simulate a sample of Uniform(0,1) random variables
R=rand(1,NSim);
%simulate the sample of Poisson r.v. by inversion
X = poissinv(R,lambdaP);
h=figure('Color', [ 1 1 1]);
subplot(4,4,[1 5 9]);
u=linspace(0,1,50);
hist(R,u); view(90,-90)
title('Uniform r.v.')
set(gca,'XTick',[0:0.1:1])
```

```
set(gca,'YTickLabel','')
grid on
subplot(4,4,[2:4 6:8 10:12]);
x=(0:1:30);
f = ksdensity(X,x,'function','cdf');
plot(x,f,'-o');
title('Inversion of the cdf')
set(gca,'XTick',[0:5:30])
set(gca,'YTick',[0:0.1:1]); grid on
subplot(4,4,[14:16]);
histfit(X,15,'poisson')
title('Poisson r.v.')
set(gca,'XTick',[0:5:30])
set(gca,'YTickLabel',''); grid on
```

A.9.4 Example: Sampling from the Gamma Distribution

We refer to the properties presented in Section A.7. This is illustrated in detail below.

Matlab Code

```
%%%%%%%%%%%%%%%%%%%%%%%%%%%%%%%%%%%%%%%%%%%%%%%%%%%%
% SIMULATION OF GAMMA RANDOM VARIABLE BY INVERSION %
%%%%%%%%%%%%%%%%%%%%%%%%%%%%%%%%%%%%%%%%%%%%%%%%%%%%
clear all; close all
%assign parameters
NSim=10^6; alpha=2; lambdaG=0.5;
%simulate the corresponding sample of Gamma r.v. by inversion
X = gaminv(R,alpha,lambdaG^(-1));
h=figure('Color', [ 1 1 1]); subplot(4,4,[1 5 9]);
u=linspace(0,1,50); hist(R,u); view(90,-90);
title('Uniform r.v.')
set(gca,'XTick',[0:0.1:1])
set(gca,'YTickLabel',''); grid on
subplot(4,4,[2:4 6:8 10:12]);
x=linspace(0,20,200);
f = ksdensity(X,x,'function','cdf');
plot(x,f);
title('Inversion of the cdf')
set(gca,'XTick',[0:2:20])
set(gca,'YTick',[0:0.1:1]); grid on
subplot(4,4,[14:16]); histfit(X,100,'gamma')
title('Gamma r.v.'); xlim([0 20]);
set(gca,'XTick',[0:2:20])
set(gca,'YTickLabel',''); grid on
```

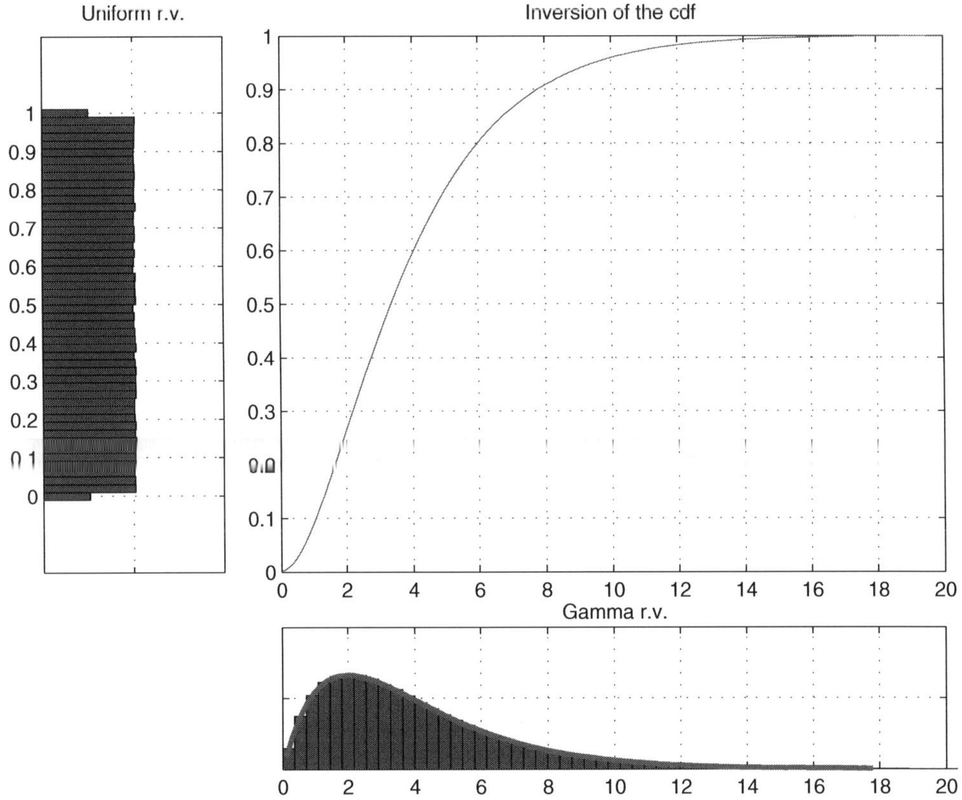

FIGURE A.23 Sampling from the Gamma distribution with $\alpha = 2$, $\lambda = 0.5$

A.9.5 Example: Sampling from the Chi-Square Distribution

A chi-square distribution is a special case of the Gamma distribution with shape parameter α. Therefore, the simulation turns out to be a special case of the Gamma. However, notice that Matlab has a built-in function to sample directly from the chi-square distribution. In the following lines we simulate 10,000 chi-square random variables with dof 5.

```
>df=5;
>chi2=chi2rnd(df,10000,1);
```

A.9.6 Example: Sampling from the Non-Central Chi-Square Distribution

Matlab provides a routine that allows us to compute the inverse cdf of this distribution, (ncx2inv(p,df,nc), where p is the probability level, df is the number of degrees of freedom and nc is the parameter of non-centrality). Matlab also provides a random number generator for this distribution. The function ncx2rnd(df,nc, m,n) returns a matrix mxn of random numbers chosen from the non-central chi-square distribution with degrees of freedom df and positive non-centrality parameter nc. In the following lines we simulate 10,000 chi-square random variables with dof 5.9 and parameter of non-centrality equal to 4.5.

```
>df=5.9;
>nc=4.5
>chi2nc=ncx2rnd(df,nc, 10000,1);
```

A.9.7 Example: Sampling from the Multivariate Normal Distribution

We refer to the properties presented in Section A.8. Further, we note the following:

Fact A.9.2 $\mathbf{X} \sim \mathcal{N}(\mu, \Sigma)$ *if and only if it admits the representation*

$$\mathbf{X} = \mu + \mathbf{AZ}, \tag{A.1}$$

where $\mathbf{Z} = (Z_1, \ldots, Z_N)$ *is a a multivariate standard normal distribution and* $\mathbf{A}$ *is an* $(N \times N)$ *lower triangular matrix with strictly positive diagonal entries.*

Fact A.9.3 *It follows that:*

$$\Sigma = \mathbb{V}ar(\mathbf{X}) = \mathbb{V}ar(\mathbf{AZ}) = \mathbf{A}\mathbb{V}ar(\mathbf{Z})\mathbf{A}' = \mathbf{A}\mathbb{I}\mathbf{A}' = \mathbf{AA}',$$

and we have the so-called Cholesky decomposition of Σ*:*

$$\Sigma = \mathbf{AA}';$$

this guarantees that Σ *is semidefinite positive. If* $rank(\mathbf{A}) = N$, Σ *is definite positive. This is known as Cholesky decomposition.*

Example A.9.1 *Let*

$$\Sigma = \begin{bmatrix} 0.04 & 0.024 \\ 0.024 & 0.09 \end{bmatrix}.$$

In order to find its Cholesky decomposition, we need to look for a 2×2 *lower triangular matrix* $\mathbf{A}$ *such that*

$$\begin{bmatrix} 0.04 & 0.024 \\ 0.024 & 0.09 \end{bmatrix} = \begin{bmatrix} a_{11} & 0 \\ a_{21} & a_{22} \end{bmatrix} \begin{bmatrix} a_{11} & a_{21} \\ 0 & a_{22} \end{bmatrix} = \begin{bmatrix} a_{11}^2 & a_{11}a_{21} \\ a_{11}a_{21} & a_{21}^2 + a_{22}^2 \end{bmatrix},$$

that is we have to set

$$\begin{cases} a_{11}^2 = 0.04 \\ a_{11}a_{21} = 0.024 \\ a_{21}^2 + a_{22}^2 = 0.09 \end{cases} \Longrightarrow \begin{cases} a_{11} = \sqrt{0.04} = 0.2 \\ a_{21} = \frac{0.024}{0.2} = 0.12 \\ a_{22} = \sqrt{0.09 - (0.12)^2} = \sqrt{0.0756} = 0.27495 \end{cases}$$

and therefore

$$\mathbf{A} = \begin{bmatrix} 0.2 & 0 \\ 0.12 & 0.2749545 \end{bmatrix}.$$

- The Cholesky decomposition forms the basis of simulation methods for multivariate Gaussian random variables.
- It can be verified that if

$$\Sigma = \begin{bmatrix} \sigma_1^2 & \rho\sigma_1\sigma_2 \\ \rho\sigma_1\sigma_2 & \sigma_2^2 \end{bmatrix},$$

then

$$\mathbf{A} = \begin{bmatrix} \sigma_1 & 0 \\ \rho\sigma_2 & \sigma_2\sqrt{1-\rho^2} \end{bmatrix}.$$

- This means that in order to perform Monte Carlo simulation we need to simulate Z_1 and Z_2 independently and according to a standard normal random variable and then to set

$$X_1 = \mu_1 + \sigma_1 Z_1,$$
$$X_2 = \mu_2 + \rho\sigma_2 Z_1 + \sigma_2\sqrt{1-\rho^2}Z_2.$$

Example A.9.2 *In the bivariate case, we can apply the Cholesky decomposition of the previous example and obtain*

$$\Sigma = \begin{bmatrix} 0.04 & 0.024 \\ 0.024 & 0.09 \end{bmatrix} \Longrightarrow \mathbf{A} = \begin{bmatrix} 0.2 & 0 \\ 0.4 \times 0.3 & 0.3 \times \sqrt{1-0.4^2} \end{bmatrix}$$

so that correlated Gaussian r.v.s are simulated according to

$$X_1 = \mu_1 + 0.2 \times Z_1,$$
$$X_2 = \mu_2 + 0.4 \times 0.3 \times Z_1 + 0.3 \times \sqrt{1-0.4^2} \times Z_2.$$

In Matlab we can simulate a multivariate Gaussian distribution using the command mvnrnd that takes as parameters the mean vector, the covariance matrix and the number of simulations. This is illustrated in details in the following Matlab script.

Matlab Code

```
%%%%%%%%%%%%%%%%%%%%%%%%%%%%%%%%%%%%%%%%%%%%%%%%%%%%%%%%%%%%
%%%% SIMULATION OF BIVARIATE NORMAL RANDOM VARIABLE %%%%
%%%%%%%%%%%%%%%%%%%%%%%%%%%%%%%%%%%%%%%%%%%%%%%%%%%%%%%%%%%%
clear all
close all
%assign parameters
```

```
NSim=10^6;
rho=0.9; mu1=0; mu2=0; s1=0.3^2; s2=0.5^2; s12=rho*(s1*s2)^0.5;
%simulate the corresponding sample of bivariate Gaussian r.v.
Mu=[mu1 mu2]; VC=[s1 s12; s12 s2];
X = mvnrnd(Mu,VC,10000);
X1=X(:,1); X2=X(:,2);
h=figure('Color', [ 1 1 1]);
subplot(4,4,[1 5 9]);
histfit(X1,100)
set(gca,'YTickLabel','')
view(90,-90)
grid on
subplot(4,4,[2:4 6:8 10:12]);
plot(X2,X1,'+')
grid on
subplot(4,4,[14:16]);
histfit(X2,100)
set(gca,'YTickLabel','')
grid on
```

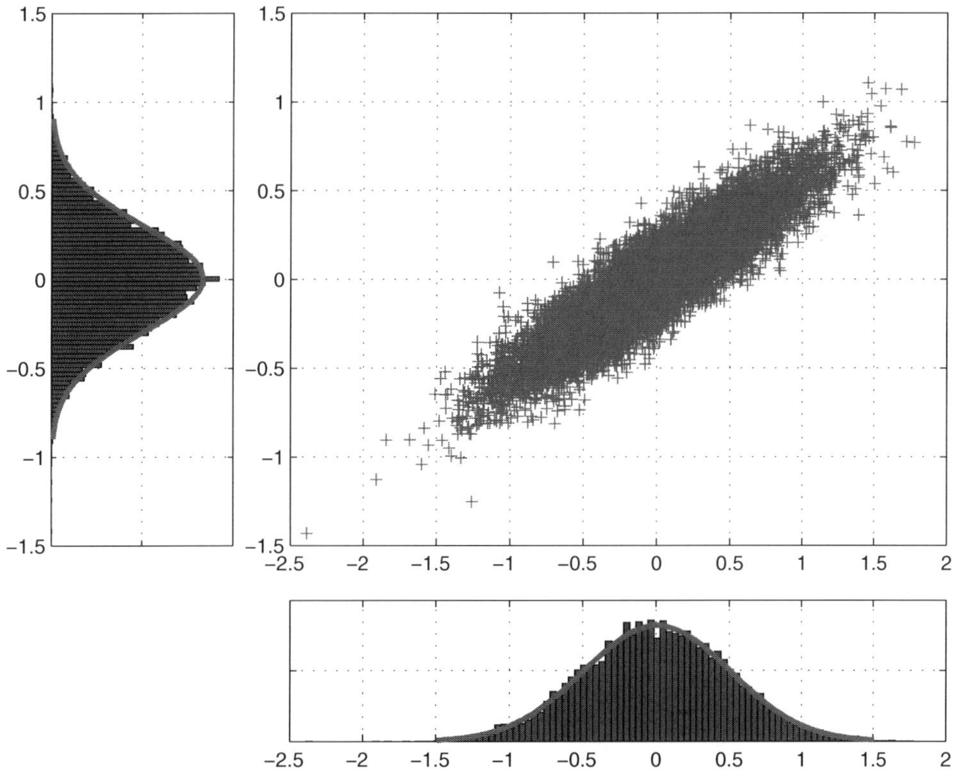

FIGURE A.24 Sampling from the bivariate Gaussian distribution (positive correlation)

Index

Handbook of Multi-Commodity Markets and Products: Structuring, Trading and Risk Management. Edited by Andrea Roncoroni, Gianluca Fusai and Mark Cummins.

Index compiled by Terry Halliday